# THE OXFORD HANDBOOK OF
# HAPPINESS

# THE OXFORD HANDBOOK OF
# HAPPINESS

*Edited by*
SUSAN A. DAVID, ILONA BONIWELL,
*and*
AMANDA CONLEY AYERS

UNIVERSITY PRESS

Great Clarendon Street, Oxford OX2 6DP
United Kingdom

Oxford University Press is a department of the University of Oxford.
It furthers the University's objective of excellence in research, scholarship,
and education by publishing worldwide. Oxford is a registered trade mark of
Oxford University Press in the UK and in certain other countries

© Chapter 1–17 and 19–79 Oxford University Press, 2013
© Chapter 18 Rowman and Littlefield, 2004

The moral rights of the authors have been asserted

First Published in 2013
Impression: 1

All rights reserved. No part of this publication may be reproduced, stored in
a retrieval system, or transmitted, in any form or by any means, without the
prior permission in writing of Oxford University Press, or as expressly permitted
by law, by licence or under terms agreed with the appropriate reprographics
rights organization. Enquiries concerning reproduction outside the scope of the
above should be sent to the Rights Department, Oxford University Press, at the
address above

You must not circulate this work in any other form
and you must impose this same condition on any acquirer

British Library Cataloguing in Publication Data
Data available

ISBN 978–0–19–955725–7

Printed and bound in Great Britain by
CPI Group (UK) Ltd, Croydon, CR0 4YY

Whilst every effort has been made to ensure that the contents of this work
are as complete, accurate and-up-to-date as possible at the date of writing,
Oxford University Press is not able to give any guarantee or assurance that
such is the case. Readers are urged to take appropriately qualified medical
advice in all cases. The information in this work is intended to be useful to the
general reader, but should not be used as a means of self-diagnosis or for the
prescription of medication.

Links to third party websites are provided by Oxford in good faith and
for information only. Oxford disclaims any responsibility for the materials
contained in any third party website referenced in this work.

# Dedications

To Anthony and Noah: the source of my abiding happiness.

Susan David

To my children, Thomas and Sophie, you fill each day with the most unexpected delights. Thank you.

Amanda Conley Ayers

TASHICHHODZONG
THIMPHU, BHUTAN

# Foreword

It is humbling and deeply gratifying to be asked to write the foreword to the *Handbook of Happiness*. The invitation from the editors must be inspired by my country's philosophy of Gross National Happiness, and not any expertise on my part. Nonetheless, I thank you for the opportunity to share my personal thoughts on some aspects of the subject.

It was my father who said, "Gross National Happiness (GNH) is more important than Gross National Product (GNP)" in 1974. Since then, GNH has come to mean so many things. To me it signifies simply—Development with Values—where we strive for the benefits of economic growth and modernization while ensuring that in our drive for economic progress we do not forget to nurture that which makes us united, harmonious, and secure as Bhutanese. Whether it is our strong community structure or our culture and heritage, our traditional respect for the environment or the desire for a peaceful coexistence with other nations, the duty of the Bhutanese State is to ensure that these invaluable elements contributing to the happiness and well-being of our people are protected and strengthened. Our government must be human.

Thus, for Bhutan, Gross National Happiness is the bridge between the fundamental values of Kindness, Equality, and Humanity and the necessary pursuit of economic growth.

So for me, as for all Bhutanese, building a modern literature on Happiness is important. Not because we might be able to better experience happiness as we know it, but because the Happiness in Gross National Happiness means much more. It is easy to measure wealth or even the power and influence of nations. Too often, these figures are accepted so easily that the truth of the millions affected by inequality, poverty, neglect, apathy, and despair remain hidden and unaddressed. In identifying Happiness as a development goal, it is not being implied that Happiness can or should become another variable to be measured. We are simply trying to bring a more profound, humane, and deeper meaning and purpose to the measuring of economic growth.

For individuals, pursuing true happiness implies striving towards a certain purity, a nobility of goal—some sort of perfection. It cannot arise from wrongful, harmful, or contrived circumstances. It is not something to be achieved in solitude or for the moment. Thus, in a nation seeking growth while creating the conditions for promoting "happiness," it is more likely that we will see such qualities as rule of law, good governance, technology, robust economies, and good education combine with values of equality, equity, justice, compassion, and commitment to the welfare of fellow citizens and future generations—and with respect for other peoples and nations and all sentient beings.

Modernization and political change have nurtured the individual's freedom, but it has also led to a less desirable and unconscious freeing of the individual from his obligations to society and the greater good. As a result, certain inherent values have gone missing. The wonderful thing about placing Happiness in development conversation is that Happiness feeds on community and fraternity. Happiness reminds us that ultimately this is a world of people, of families, of communities all alike—of human beings seeking the same thing. When we grasp this universal simplicity—this sense of a shared planet and a shared fate for those who walk on it in a common quest for happiness, well-being, and contentment—the answer to national and global problems will come closer at hand.

Inserting Happiness into Bhutan's pursuit of growth gives us a National Conscience guiding us towards making wise decisions for a better future. It reminds us that as we strive for success as individuals or as a nation, we also have a responsibility to the greater good, to future generations, to the world, and to other living beings.

I feel blessed to be born in a country that, though small and faced with great challenges, has found in its own humanity the inspiration to think differently about growth or progress. We do not seek to preach Gross National Happiness, but to share our thoughts, and more importantly, to gain the wisdom of others' experiences. So I thank you all on behalf of the people of Bhutan, for your dedication and for the hard work that has been invested in this book, from which we will seek to learn.

Jigme Khesar
King of Bhutan

# Foreword

THERE is a growing recognition that the goals governments have typically focused on, such as GDP, are only a means to an end, and that end is happiness. The great economist John Maynard Keynes said this in the 1930's, and more recently the UK's prime minister, David Cameron, and former French President Sarkozy's Commission on the measurement of economic and social progress have come to the same conclusion. It is no longer sufficient to measure economic progress; we must also consider social and environmental progress, and we must measure subjective well-being.

Among the individual governments that have begun to consider well-being as the most fundamental goal of human progress, Bhutan has shown extraordinary initiative. In 2011 the country's prime minister, Jigmi Thinley, played a key role in persuading the United Nations to adopt a "happiness resolution", and in April of 2012, Bhutan hosted a United Nations "High Level Meeting on Happiness and Well-being". I was honored to be among the participants. This meeting of fellow scholars and governmental, business, and spiritual leaders was so well attended that it exceeded the capacity of the General Assembly room of the UN. The entire group united around the idea of a new economic paradigm, and at the heart of this paradigm is human happiness. It is not the ephemeral happiness that some talk about, but rather what is described as "the deep abiding happiness that comes from living life in full harmony with the natural world, with our communities and fellow beings" (Royal Government of Bhutan, 2012, p. 89).

As those of us at the High Level Meeting worked to take this agenda forward, a host of exciting conclusions emerged. The main recommendations from the final report included the statement that "constructive and positive education [is] perhaps the most important facilitator of the mindset necessary to support an economic paradigm based on happiness and well-being" (Royal Government of Bhutan, 2012, p. 59).

An impressive body of research is helping us to understand the determinants of happiness and well-being. For example, we now know that genes play a certain role in well-being, but we also know that the early environment, which includes both parenting and education, is profoundly important. Happiness is a skill that we can learn, and while there is evidence that it can be learned at any stage in the life course, there is no better time to learn it than in those early years.

There are many positive psychological interventions, and many skills related to well-being which have been used to develop abiding happiness. One approach that has been shown to have lasting benefits across a wide range of well-being outcomes is mindfulness training. Mindfulness training is a secular program with roots in ancient philosophical traditions, which focuses on awareness of moment-to-moment experiences, in the mind, in the body, and in our immediate physical and social surroundings. Mindfulness is not just another positive psychology or well-being intervention—it is foundational to all other approaches, and augments their impacts. A sub-group at the UN meeting advised that we need to: "Teach mindfulness widely to counteract the psychic hunger that causes materialism as the primary spirituality of our time" (Royal Government of Bhutan, 2012, p. 150). This recommendation is well supported by contemporary research, which not only shows that mindfulness has substantial and wide-ranging benefits for well-being, but also demonstrates that training in mindfulness enhances the effects of other interventions, such as coaching and cognitive behavioral therapy (e.g., Spence, Cavanagh & Grant, 2008).

My own interest in well-being came from decades of research on aging. Originally I studied Alzheimer's disease and disability in old age, gathering data from tens of thousands of elderly people across the United Kingdom, and internationally. Because we were studying these phenomena at the population level, we had information from people right across the board—those who were doing badly, and those who remained in good health. I was repeatedly drawn to the large number of people who were aging well, and wondered what we might learn from them. An important clue came from one of the truly great minds in the field of population studies or epidemiology, Geoffrey Rose (Rose, 1992, 2008). He demonstrated that a tiny shift in the average symptoms of a disease at the population level would lead to major changes in both illness and exceptional health. For example, if you look at heart disease, the prevalence in the population is related to the average blood pressure in the population, or the average level of cholesterol. If you can reduce these symptoms for the average person, there will be far fewer people who actually develop the disease, and far more people who flourish.

This tells us that the risk of a disorder is not just an individual matter, based solely on genes, experiences, or coping styles. The risk of a disorder is related to what is happening to the population in which we live. A strategy that looks only at individuals will never succeed; what we need is a strategy that shifts the average for a whole population towards flourishing. We need to identify the underlying determinants of health and disorder, and change them for everyone. In the context of happiness, we therefore need to identify the major determinants of well-being, and shift the population toward mental flourishing (Huppert, 2009; Huppert & So, 2011)

The *Oxford Handbook of Happiness* is an important resource to help us move in this direction. The breadth of topics in the handbook surpasses what has traditionally been done in positive psychology. Furthermore, the cross-national perspectives found in this book will challenge our assumptions. Well-being is not the same for all people or all nations. This is important because when developing interventions, we need to think about the particular group for whom the interventions are being developed. The Handbook offers a nuanced approach to what well-being is all about, how we need to measure it, and what changes we are looking for. The scholar or practitioner dipping into this book is fortunate in gaining access to a marvelous wealth of knowledge and perspective in this field. He or she will have the opportunity to further the agenda that more and more people recognize as underpinning this endeavor: the achievement of deep, abiding happiness.

Felicia Huppert  
Cambridge, England  
2012

## REFERENCES

Huppert, F. A. (2009). A new approach to reducing disorder and improving well-being. *Perspectives on Psychological Science, 4*, 108–111.

Huppert, F. A. & So, T.T.C (2011). Flourishing across Europe: application of a new conceptual framework for defining well-being. *Social Indicators Research*, (Published online 15 December 2011, DOI: 10.1007/s11205-011-9966-7).

Rose, G. (1992). *The strategy of preventive medicine*. Oxford, England: Oxford University Press.

Rose, G. (2008). *Rose's strategy of preventive medicine* (2nd ed., rev.). Oxford, England: Oxford University Press.

Royal Government of Bhutan (2012). *The Report of the High-Level Meeting on Wellbeing and Happiness: Defining a New Economic Paradigm*. New York: The Permanent Mission of the Kingdom of Bhutan to the United Nations. Thimphu: Office of the Prime Minister.

Spence, G.B., Cavanagh, M.J. & Grant, A.M. (2008). The integration of mindfulness training and health coaching: An exploratory study. *Coaching: An International Journal of Theory, Research and Practice, 1*(2), 1–19.

# Acknowledgements

This text is a testament to the efforts of many people. For each of these 79 chapters, numerous steps were required to generate the knowledge presented: ideas were fostered; grants were written; research was painstakingly conducted and replicated; and scientific papers were written, revised, and published. Much of this work was accomplished over many years by our expert chapter contributors, each an authority in his or her respective field. It is to these exemplary individuals that I extend my greatest thanks and appreciation. Without your hard work, the science of human happiness would not exist.

From beginning to end, the team of professionals at Oxford University Press was an outstanding partner in taking this project from proposal to reality. Martin Baum's idea of creating an end-to-end, cross-disciplinary volume on human happiness was both timely and insightful. Charlotte Green, Abigail Stanley, and the book team graciously facilitated every aspect of the volume with the highest level of attention to detail. Thank you to all of you.

This book would not have been published were it not for the rare combination of outstanding editing skills, organization, and social nous shown by Christina Congleton. A very special thank you is also due to the other Evidence Based Psychology team members: Jennifer Lee, Kimbette Fenol, Karen Monteiro, and Anthony Samir: your stellar support for this complex project made all the difference. A strong vote of thanks is also due to our many clients: your understanding that happiness research impacts on many facets of your own work provided the inspiration and impetus for this book.

The thought leaders at the Institute of Coaching—Carol Kauffman, Margaret Moore, Ruth Ann Harnisch, Laurel Doggett, and the rest of the team—are dedicated to using evidence to positively impact human experience. Thank you for the inspiration, foresight, and insight that you continue to provide, and for your tremendous contribution to our field of study.

My mother, Veronica, my late father, Sidney, and Christopher, Madeleine, Liezel, Alex, Sam, Charlotte, Moshe, Robyn, and Richard have taught me much about joy, gratitude, perseverance, and acceptance. Anthony Samir, my husband and life partner for almost two decades: my deep happiness has its roots in you. Thank you. Noah David: you were born during the editing of this book. Your joy, sense of wonder, and unfolding understanding of the world redoubled my commitment to this work. You affirmed my conviction that happiness research is relevant to our daily lives. Its lessons teach us how to meaningfully enrich life for ourselves, our children, and their children to follow

Susan David, Ph.D.

# Contents

*List of Contributors*     xxiii
*List of Abbreviations*     xxix

1. Introduction     1
   Susan A. David, Ilona Boniwell, and Amanda Conley Ayers

## SECTION I PSYCHOLOGICAL APPROACHES TO HAPPINESS

Section Editor: Joar Vittersø

2. Introduction to Psychological Approaches to Happiness     11
   Joar Vittersø

3. The Broaden-and-Build Theory of Positive Emotions: Form, Function, and Mechanisms     17
   Anne M. Conway, Michele M. Tugade, Lahnna I. Catalino, and Barbara L. Fredrickson

4. The Endowment–Contrast Model: A Lens for Happiness Research     35
   Dale Griffin and Richard Gonzalez

5. Past, Present, and Future of Flow     60
   Antonella Delle Fave

6. Emotionally Intelligent Happiness     73
   Alia J. Crum and Peter Salovey

7. Religious Engagement and Well-being     88
   David G. Myers

8. Positive Psychological Experiences and Psychopathology: A Self-Regulatory Perspective     101
   Patty Ferssizidis, Todd B. Kashdan, Rachel A. Marquart, and Michael F. Steger

9. The Rewards of Happiness     119
   Katherine Jacobs Bao and Sonja Lyubomirsky

10. Happiness Experienced: The Science of Subjective Well-being  134
    William Pavot and Ed Diener

# SECTION II PSYCHOLOGICAL DEFINITIONS OF HAPPINESS

Section Editor: Joar Vitterso

11. Introduction to Psychological Definitions of Happiness  155
    Joar Vitterso

12. Notions of the Good Life  161
    Ruut Veenhoven

13. Subjective Well-being  174
    Felicity F. Miao, Minkyung Koo, and Shigehiro Oishi

14. Measuring Happiness and Subjective Well-being  185
    Robert A. Cummins

15. Eudaimonia  201
    Veronika Huta

16. What Makes for a Life Well Lived? Autonomy and its Relation to Full Functioning and Organismic Wellness  214
    Christopher P. Niemiec and Richard M. Ryan

17. Functional Well-being: Happiness as Feelings, Evaluations, and Functioning  227
    Joar Vitterso

# SECTION III PHILOSOPHICAL APPROACHES TO HAPPINESS

Section Editor: James O. Pawelski

18. Introduction to Philosophical Approaches to Happiness  247
    James O. Pawelski

19. The Pursuit of Happiness in History  252
    Darrin M. McMahon

20. Happiness in Early Chinese Thought  263
    Philip J. Ivanhoe

21. Continental Contributions to our Understanding of Happiness
    and Suffering   279
    EMMY VAN DEURZEN

22. The Seductions of Happiness   291
    RAYMOND ANGELO BELLIOTTI

23. The Nature and Significance of Happiness   303
    DANIEL M. HAYBRON

24. Philosophical Methods in Happiness Research   315
    VALERIE TIBERIUS

25. Happiness and Its Opposites   326
    JAMES O. PAWELSKI

# SECTION IV SPIRITUAL APPROACHES TO HAPPINESS

SECTION EDITOR: JANE HENRY

26. Introduction to Spiritual Approaches to Happiness   339
    JANE HENRY

27. A Buddhist View of Happiness   344
    MATTHIEU RICARD

28. Relational Buddhism: An Integrative Psychology of Happiness
    amidst Existential Suffering   357
    G. T. MAURITS KWEE

29. Well-being from the Hindu/Sanātana Dharma Perspective   371
    KIRAN KUMAR K. SALAGAME

30. Flourishing through Meditation and Mindfulness   384
    PETER MALINOWSKI

31. Heaven on Earth: Beneficial Effects of Sanctification for Individual
    and Interpersonal Well-being   397
    ANNETTE MAHONEY, KENNETH I. PARGAMENT, AND
    KRYSTAL M. HERNANDEZ

32. Quieting the Mind and Low Arousal Routes to Happiness   411
    JANE HENRY

# SECTION V  HAPPINESS AND SOCIETY

SECTION EDITOR: SAM THOMPSON

33. Introduction to Happiness and Society  427
    SAM THOMPSON

34. Economics and the Study of Individual Happiness  431
    BRUNO S. FREY AND ALOIS STUTZER

35. Comparing Well-being Across Nations: Conceptual and
    Empirical Issues  448
    WILLIAM TOV AND EVELYN W. M. AU

36. The Geography of Happiness  465
    DIMITRIS BALLAS AND DANNY DORLING

37. Well-being in Consumer Societies  482
    AARON AHUVIA AND ELIF IZBERK-BILGIN

38. Well-being and Sustainable Development  498
    SAM THOMPSON, NIC MARKS, AND TIM JACKSON

39. Well-being and Public Policy  517
    GEOFF MULGAN

# SECTION VI  POSITIVE EDUCATION

SECTION EDITORS: ILONA BONIWELL AND NASH POPOVIC

40. Introduction to Positive Education  535
    ILONA BONIWELL

41. Education and Well-being  540
    JOHN WHITE

42. Should Education Have Happiness Lessons?  551
    NASH POPOVIC

43. Well-being and Resilience in Education  563
    TONI NOBLE AND HELEN MCGRATH

44. Happiness in the Classroom  579
    JENNIFER M. FOX EADES, CARMEL PROCTOR, AND MARTIN ASHLEY

45. Applying Happiness and Well-being Research to the Teaching
    and Learning Process  592
    LAURA MCINERNEY

46. Resilience Education 609
    JANE E. GILLHAM, RACHEL M. ABENAVOLI, STEVEN M. BRUNWASSER,
    MARK LINKINS, KAREN J. REIVICH, AND MARTIN E. P. SELIGMAN

47. Teaching for Wisdom 631
    ROBERT J. STERNBERG

48. Going Beyond the Accidental: Happiness, Education, and the
    Wellington College Experience 644
    IAN MORRIS

49. Positive Education at Geelong Grammar School 657
    MATHEW A. WHITE

# SECTION VII HAPPINESS AND ORGANIZATIONS

SECTION EDITORS: ARRAN CAZA AND KIM S. CAMERON

50. An Introduction to Happiness and Organizations 671
    ARRAN CAZA AND KIM S. CAMERON

51. Virtuousness as a Source of Happiness in Organizations 676
    KIM S. CAMERON AND ARRAN CAZA

52. How Work Shapes Well-being 693
    BRIANNA BARKER CAZA AND AMY WRZESNIEWSKI

53. Work Design and Happiness: An Active, Reciprocal Perspective 711
    BEN J. SEARLE AND SHARON K. PARKER

54. Jobs and Job-Holders: Two Sources of Happiness and Unhappiness 733
    PETER WARR

55. Managing Psychological Capital in Organizations: Cognitive,
    Affective, Conative, and Social Mechanisms of Happiness 751
    CAROLYN M. YOUSSEF AND FRED LUTHANS

56. Reflected Best Self Engagement at Work: Positive Identity,
    Alignment, and the Pursuit of Vitality and Value Creation 767
    LAURA MORGAN ROBERTS

57. Encouraging Employee Happiness 783
    THOMAS A. WRIGHT

58. Executive Well-being 798
    JAMES CAMPBELL QUICK AND JONATHAN D. QUICK

## SECTION VIII RELATIONSHIPS AND HAPPINESS

Section Editor: Melikşah Demir

59. Introduction to Relationships and Happiness — 817
Melikşah Demir

60. Close Relationships and Happiness — 821
Shimon Saphire-Bernstein and Shelley E. Taylor

61. Adult Attachment and Happiness: Individual Differences in the Experience and Consequences of Positive Emotions — 834
Mario Mikulincer and Phillip R. Shaver

62. Perceived Social Support and Happiness: The Role of Personality and Relational Processes — 847
Brian Lakey

63. Friendship and Happiness — 860
Melikşah Demir, Haley Orthel, and Adrian Keith Andelin

## SECTION IX DEVELOPMENT, STABILITY, AND CHANGE OF HAPPINESS

Section Editor: Kate Hefferon

64. Introduction to Development, Stability, and Change of Happiness — 873
Kate Hefferon

65. An Evolutionary Psychological Perspective on Happiness — 875
Sarah E. Hill, Danielle J. DelPriore, and Brett Major

66. Set-Point Theory May Now Need Replacing: Death of a Paradigm? — 887
Bruce Headey

67. Variety is the Spice of Happiness: The Hedonic Adaptation Prevention Model — 901
Kennon M. Sheldon, Julia Boehm, and Sonja Lyubomirsky

68. Promotion and Protection of Positive Mental Health: Towards Complete Mental Health in Human Development — 915
Corey L. M. Keyes

69. Post-traumatic Growth: Eudaimonic Happiness in the Aftermath of Adversity — 926
Stephen Joseph and Kate Hefferon

70. Creating a Stable Architectural Framework of Existence: Proposing a Model of Lifelong Meaning  941
   MICHAEL F. STEGER, ANNA BEEBY, SAMANTHA GARRETT, AND TODD B. KASHDAN

# SECTION X   HAPPINESS INTERVENTIONS

SECTION EDITORS: GORDON B. SPENCE AND SUZY GREEN

71. Introduction to Happiness Interventions  957
   GORDON B. SPENCE AND SUZY GREEN

72. Increasing Happiness in the General Population: Empirically Supported Self-help?  962
   ACACIA C. PARKS, STEPHEN M. SCHUELLER, AND ARBER TASIMI

73. Positive Psychology in Practice: Positive Psychotherapy  978
   TAYYAB RASHID

74. Happiness in Valued Living: Acceptance and Commitment Therapy as a Model for Change  994
   LOUISE HAYES

75. Coaching and Well-being: A Brief Review of Existing Evidence, Relevant Theory, and Implications for Practitioners  1009
   GORDON B. SPENCE AND ANTHONY M. GRANT

76. Mindfulness and Cultivating Well-being in Older Adults  1026
   LAURA M. HSU AND ELLEN J. LANGER

77. Well-being Therapy: Theoretical Background, Clinical Implications, and Future Directions  1037
   GIOVANNI A. FAVA AND CHIARA RUINI

78. The Collaborative Recovery Model: Developing Positive Institutions to Facilitate Recovery in Enduring Mental Illness  1050
   LINDSAY G. OADES, TREVOR P. CROWE, AND FRANK P. DEANE

79. Conclusion: The Future of Happiness  1067
   SUSAN A. DAVID, ILONA BONIWELL, AND AMANDA CONLEY AYERS

Contributor Index  1071
Author Index  1073
Subject Index  1077

# List of Contributors

**Aaron Ahuvia** Department of Management Studies, University of Michigan–Dearborn, Dearborn, MI, USA

**Rachel M. Abenavoli** Human Development & Family Studies, Pennsylvania State University, University Park, PA, USA

**Adrian Keith Andelin** Department of Psychology, Northern Arizona University, Flagstaff, AZ, USA

**Martin Ashley** Faculty of Education, Edge Hill University, Ormskirk, UK

**Evelyn W. M. Au** School of Social Sciences, Singapore Management University, Singapore

**Dimitris Ballas** Department of Geography, University of Sheffield, Sheffield, UK

**Anna Beeby** Department of Psychology, Colorado State University, Fort Collins, CO, USA

**Raymond Angelo Belliotti** SUNY Fredonia, New York, NY, USA

**Julia Boehm** Department of Society, Human Development, and Health, Harvard School of Public Health, Boston, MA, USA

**Ilona Boniwell** School of Psychology, The University of East London, London, UK; and Positran, Paris, France

**Steven M. Brunwasser** Department of Psychology, University of Michigan, Ann Arbor, MI, USA

**Kim S. Cameron** Ross School of Business, University of Michigan, and School of Education, Ann Arbor, MI, USA

**Lahnna I. Catalino** Department of Psychology, University of North Carolina, Chapel Hill, NC, USA

**Arran Caza** Department of International Business and Asian Studies, Griffith University, QLD, Australia

**Brianna Barker Caza** Wake Forest University, Winston-Salem, NC, USA

**Amanda Conley Ayers** Evidence Based Psychology, Cambridge, MA, USA

**Anne M. Conway** School of Social Work, Columbia University, New York, NY, USA

**Trevor P. Crowe** Illawarra Institute for Mental Health, University of Wollongong, NSW, Australia

**Alia J. Crum** Department of Psychology, Yale University, New Haven, CT, USA

**Robert A. Cummins** School of Psychology, Faculty of Health, Deakin University, Burwood, VIC, Australia

**Susan A. David** Institute of Coaching, McLean Hospital, Belmont, MA; Department of Psychiatry, Harvard Medical School, Cambridge, MA; and Evidence Based Psychology, Cambridge, MA, USA

**Frank P. Deane** Illawarra Institute for Mental Health and School of Psychology, University of Wollongong, NSW, Australia

**Antonella Delle Fave** Dipartimento di Scienze Biomediche e Cliniche "Luigi Sacco", Università degli Studi di Milano, Milano, Italy

**Danielle J. DelPriore** Department of Psychology, Texas Christian University, Fort Worth, TX, USA

**Melikşah Demir** Department of Psychology, Northern Arizona University, Flagstaff, AZ, USA

**Ed Diener** Department of Psychology, University of Illinois at Urbana-Champaign, Champaign, IL; and The Gallup Organization, NE, USA

**Danny Dorling** Department of Geography, University of Sheffield, Sheffield, UK

**Jennifer M. Fox Eades** Department of Education, Edge Hill University, Macclesfield, UK

**Giovanni A. Fava** Department of Psychology, University of Bologna, Italy

**Patty Ferssizidis** George Mason University, Fairfax, VA, USA

**Barbara L. Fredrickson** University of North Carolina, Chapel Hill, NC, USA

**Bruno S. Frey** Department of Economics, University of Zurich, Switzerland

**Samantha Garrett** Department of Psychology, Colorado State University, Fort Collins, CO, USA

**Jane E. Gillham** Psychology Department, Swarthmore College, Swarthmore, PA, USA; and Psychology Department and Positive Psychology Center, University of Pennsylvania, Philadelphia, PA, USA

**Richard Gonzalez** Department of Psychology, University of Michigan, Ann Arbor, MI, USA

**Anthony M. Grant** Coaching Psychology Unit, School of Psychology, University of Sydney, NSW, Australia

**Suzy Green** The Positivity Institute, Sydney, Australia

**Dale Griffin** Sauder School of Business, University of British Columbia, Vancouver, BC, Canada

**Louise Hayes** Orygen Youth Health Research Centre, The University of Melbourne, Australia

**Daniel M. Haybron** Saint Louis University, St Louis, MO, USA

**Bruce Headey** Faculty of Business and Economics, Melbourne Institute, Melbourne, VIC, Australia

**Kate Hefferon** School of Psychology, University of East London, London, UK

**Jane Henry** Applied Psychology, Open University, Milton Keynes, UK

**Krystal M. Hernandez** Department of Psychology, Bowling Green State University, Bowling Green, OH, USA

**Sarah E. Hill** Texas Christian University, Fort Worth, TX, USA

**Laura M. Hsu** School of Education, Merrimack College, North Andover, MA, USA

**Veronika Huta** School of Psychology, University of Ottawa, Ottawa, ON, Canada

**Philip J. Ivanhoe** City University of Hong Kong, Kowloon, Hong Kong

**Elif Izberk-Bilgin** Department of Management Studies, University of Michigan-Dearborn, Dearborn, MI, USA

**Tim Jackson** Centre for Environmental Strategy, University of Surrey, Guilford, UK

**Katherine Jacobs Bao** Department of Psychology, University of California, Riverside, CA, USA

**Stephen Joseph** Psychology, Health & Social Care, Faculty of Social Sciences, School of Sociology and Social Policy, University of Nottingham, Nottingham, UK

**Todd B. Kashdan** Department of Psychology, George Mason University, Fairfax, VA, USA

**Corey L. M. Keyes** Department of Sociology, Emory University, Atlanta, GA, USA

**Minkyung Koo** Department of Business Administration, University of Illinois at Urbana-Champaign, Champaign, IL, USA

**G.T. Maurits Kwee** University of Flores, Buenos Aires, Argentina; Institute for Relational Buddhism, Amsterdam, The Netherlands; and Taos Institute, USA

**Brian Lakey** Psychology Department, Grand Valley State University, Allendale, MI, USA

**Ellen J. Langer** Department of Psychology, Harvard University, Cambridge, MA, USA

**Mark Linkins** VIA Institute on Character, Cincinnati, OH, USA

**Fred Luthans** Department of Management, University of Nebraska–Lincoln, Lincoln, NE, USA

**Sonja Lyubomirsky** Department of Psychology, University of California, Riverside, CA, USA

**Helen McGrath** Faculty of Arts and Education, School of Education, Deakin University, Australia

**Darrin M. McMahon** Florida State University, Tallahassee, FL, USA

**Laura McInerney**  Positive Psychology, London, UK

**Annette Mahoney**  Department of Psychology, Bowling Green State University, Bowling Green, OH, USA

**Brett Major**  Texas Christian University, Fort Worth, TX, USA

**Peter Malinowski**  Liverpool John Moores University, Liverpool, UK

**Nic Marks**  nef (the new economics foundation), London, UK

**Rachel A. Marquart**  Department of Psychology, George Mason University, Fairfax, VA, USA

**Felicity F. Miao**  Department of Psychology, University of Virginia, Charlottesville, VA, USA

**Mario Mikulincer**  School of Psychology, Interdisciplinary Center, Herzliya, Israel

**Ian Morris**  Wellington College, Berkshire, UK

**Geoff Mulgan**  The National Endowment for Science, Technology and the Arts (NESTA), London, UK

**David G. Myers**  Department of Psychology, Hope College, Holland, MI, USA

**Christopher P. Niemiec**  Department of Clinical and Social Sciences in Psychology, University of Rochester, Rochester, NY, USA

**Toni Noble**  School of Educational Leadership, Faculty of Education, Australian Catholic University, Australia

**Lindsay G. Oades**  Australian Institute of Business Wellbeing, Sydney Business School, University of Wollongong, NSW, Australia

**Shigehiro Oishi**  Department of Psychology, University of Virginia, Charlottesville, VA, USA

**Haley Orthel**  Department of Psychology, Northern Arizona University, Flagstaff, AZ, USA

**Kenneth I. Pargament**  Department of Psychology Bowling Green State University, Bowling Green, OH, USA

**Sharon K. Parker**  UWA Business School, The University of Western Australia, Crawley, WA, Australia

**Acacia C. Parks**  Department of Psychology, Hiram College, Hiram, OH, USA

**William Pavot**  Department of Social Science, Southwest Minnesota State University, Marshall, MN, USA

**James O. Pawelski**  Positive Psychology Center, University of Pennsylvania, Philadelphia, PA, USA

**Nash Popovic**  University of East London, London, UK

**Carmel Proctor**  Positive Psychology Research Centre, Channel Islands

**James Campbell Quick**  Goolsby Leadership Academy, The University of Texas at Arlington, Arlington, TX, USA; and Lancaster University Management School, Lancashire, UK

**Jonathan D. Quick**  Management Sciences for Health, Cambridge, MA; and Harvard Medical School, Cambridge, MA, USA

**Tayyab Rashid**  University of Toronto Scarborough, ON, Canada

**Karen J. Reivich**  Psychology Department and Positive Psychology Center, University of Pennsylvania, Philadelphia, PA USA

**Matthieu Ricard**  Shechen Tennyi Dargyeling, Kathmandu, Nepal

**Laura Morgan Roberts**  Antioch University, Yellow Springs, OH, USA

**Chiara Ruini**  University of Bologna, Bologna, Italy

**Richard M. Ryan**  Department of Clinical and Social Sciences in Psychology, University of Rochester, Rochester, NY, USA

**Kiran Kumar K. Salagame**  Department of Studies in Psychology, University of Mysore, Karnataka, India.

**Peter Salovey**  Department of Psychology, Yale University, New Haven, CT, USA

**Shimon Saphire-Bernstein**  Department of Psychology, University of California at Los Angeles, Los Angeles, CA, USA

**Stephen M. Schueller**  Department of Psychiatry, University of California, San Francisco, CA, USA

**Ben J. Searle**  Department of Psychology, Macquarie University, North Ryde, NSW, Australia

**Martin E. P. Seligman**  Psychology Department and Positive Psychology Center, University of Pennsylvania, Philadelphia, PA, USA

**Phillip R. Shaver**  Department of Psychology, University of California, Davis, Davis, CA, USA

**Kennon M. Sheldon**  Department of Psychology, University of Missouri–Columbia, Columbia, MO, USA

**Gordon B. Spence**  Australian Institute of Business Wellbeing, Sydney Business School, University of Wollongong, NSW, Australia

**Michael F. Steger**  Department of Psychology, Colorado State University, Fort Collins, CO, USA; School of Behavioural Sciences, North-West University, Vanderbijlpark, South Africa

**Robert J. Sternberg**  Oklahoma State University, Stillwater, OK, USA

**Alois Stutzer**  Faculty of Business and Economics, University of Basel, Basel, Switzerland

**Arber Tasimi**  Department of Psychology, Yale University, New Haven, CT, USA

**Shelley E. Taylor**  Department of Psychology, University of California at Los Angeles, Los Angeles, USA

**Valerie Tiberius**  Department of Philosophy, University of Minnesota, Minneapolis, MN, USA

**Sam Thompson**  Institute for Psychology, Health and Society, University of Liverpool, Liverpool, UK

**William Tov**  School of Social Sciences, Singapore Management University, Singapore

**Michele M. Tugade**  Department of Psychology, Vassar College, Poughkeepsie, NY, USA

**Emmy van Deurzen**  Middlesex University and the New School of Psychotherapy and Counselling, UK

**Ruut Veenhoven**  Erasmus University, Rotterdam, The Netherlands; North-West University, South Africa

**Joar Vittersø**  Department of Psychology, University of Tromsø, Tromsø, Norway

**Carolyn M. Youssef**  College of Business, Bellevue University, Bellevue, NE, USA

**Peter Warr**  Institute of Work Psychology, University of Sheffield, Sheffield, UK

**John White**  Institute of Education, London, UK

**Mathew A. White**  Melbourne Graduate School of Education, The University of Melbourne, Carlton, VIC, Australia

**Thomas A. Wright**  Fordham University, New York, NY, USA

**Amy Wrzesniewski**  Yale University, New Haven, CT, USA

# List of Abbreviations

| | |
|---|---|
| ACT | Acceptance and Commitment Therapy |
| AM | anxiety management |
| AR | assimilation resistance |
| BDI | Beck Depression Inventory |
| CASEL | Collaborative on Academic Social and Emotional Learning |
| CBR | community-based resources |
| CBT | cognitive behavioral therapy |
| CCT | consumer culture theory |
| CGT | Collaborative Goal Technology |
| CID | Clinical Interview for Depression |
| $CO_2$ | carbon dioxide |
| CRM | Collaborative Recovery Model |
| DALY | disability life-adjusted year |
| DBP | diastolic blood pressure |
| DRM | Day Reconstruction Method |
| DSM-IV | *Diagnostic and Statistical Manual of Mental Disorders, Fourth Edition* |
| E–C | Endowment–Contrast [model] |
| EI | emotional intelligence |
| ES | emotional state |
| ESM | Experience Sampling Method |
| ESS-H | empirically supported self-help |
| FC | functional contextualism |
| FQ | Flow Questionnaire |
| FWBA | functional well-being approach |
| G | generalizability |
| GAD | generalized anxiety disorder |
| GDP | gross domestic product |
| GNH | gross national happiness |
| GNP | gross national product |
| GWP | Gallup World Poll |
| HADS | Hospital Anxiety and Depression Scale |
| HAP | hedonic adaptation prevention |
| HPA | hypothalamic–pituitary–adrenal |
| HPMood | homeostatically protected mood |
| IMO | intrinsically motivated orientation |
| LifeJET | Life Journey Enhancement Tools |
| LKM | loving-kindness meditation |
| LS | life satisfaction |

| | |
|---|---|
| LSA | Life Satisfaction Approach |
| MB | mindfulness-based |
| MBCT | mindfulness-based cognitive therapy |
| MBSR | mindfulness-based stress reduction |
| MDD | major depressive disorder |
| MDE | major depression episode |
| MHPP | mental health promotion and protection |
| MIDUS | National Study of Midlife Development in the United States |
| NA | negative affect |
| nef | new economics foundation |
| OFC | orbitofrontal cortex |
| Ofsted | Office for Standards in Education, Children's Services and Skills |
| ONS | Office of National Statistics |
| OR | odds ratio |
| PA | positive affect |
| PANAS | Positive and Negative Affect Schedule |
| PD | panic disorder |
| PDE | Personal Development Education |
| POB | positive organizational behavior |
| POS | positive organizational scholarship |
| PPT | positive psychotherapy |
| PRP | Penn Resiliency Program |
| PSE | Personal and Social Education |
| PsyCap | psychological capital |
| PTG | post-traumatic growth |
| PTGI | Post-traumatic Growth Inventory |
| PTSD | post-traumatic stress disorder |
| PWB | psychological well-being |
| PWI | Personal Well-being Index |
| RBS | reflected best self |
| RFT | relational frame theory |
| RRT | relational regulation theory |
| SAD | social anxiety disorder |
| SBP | systolic blood pressure |
| SD | standard deviation |
| SDT | self-determination theory |
| SEAL | Social and Emotional Aspects of Learning |
| SEL | social and emotional learning |
| SHM | sustainable happiness model |
| SRM | Social Relations Model |
| SSSM | standard social science model |
| SWB | subjective well-being |
| SWLS | Satisfaction With Life Scale |
| VIA | Values In Action |
| WBT | well-being therapy |
| WDH | World Database of Happiness |

# CHAPTER 1

# INTRODUCTION

## SUSAN A. DAVID[1,3], ILONA BONIWELL[2,4], AND AMANDA CONLEY AYERS[3]

[1] Harvard Medical School, USA; [2]The University of East London, UK; [3]Evidence Based Psychology, USA; [4]Positran, Paris, France

## THE RATIONALE FOR *The Oxford Handbook of Happiness*

In front of you is a product of more than 3 years of work, decades of research, and many centuries of thinking. In the opening speech to the first World Congress of Positive Psychology held in Philadelphia, USA, in 2009, the founder of the positive psychology field Professor Martin Seligman called for the discipline to expand its boundaries and transform into "positive social science," uniting psychologists, economists, sociologists, policymakers, philosophers, educators, health and business researchers and practitioners, and thinkers in the fields of religion and spirituality. *The Oxford Handbook of Happiness* is one of the first publications worldwide to follow this call. It is intended as the definitive text for scholars, researchers, teachers, and practitioners interested and invested in the study and practice of human happiness.

We propose that the study of happiness is at the nexus of four major scientific developments:

1. The growing field of positive psychology, which researches the conditions that make people flourish.
2. Advances in the biological and affective sciences which have contributed to the understanding of positive emotions.
3. Positive organizational scholarship (POS), an emerging discipline aimed at investigating and fostering excellence in organizations.
4. Findings from across research domains indicating that gross domestic product (GDP) and similar traditional markers of economic and societal well-being are insufficient.

Let us consider these in turn.

1. While much research had occurred prior, 1998 brought with it the establishment of the field of positive psychology or the science of positive aspects of human life, such as

happiness, well-being, and flourishing. It is often summarized in the words of its founders, Martin Seligman and Mihaly Csikszentmihalyi, as the "scientific study of optimal human functioning [that] aims to discover and promote the factors that allow individuals and communities to thrive" (2000, p. 5).

Positive psychologists claim that psychology as a whole has more often than not focused on the shortcomings of individuals as compared with their potentials. Whilst this claim may or may not be true for all areas of psychology (for example, cognitive psychology studies the internal mental processes of often perfectly well-functioning individuals), the positive psychology approach places an explicit emphasis on the potential of individuals and on researching factors that make life worth living. Nowadays, positive psychology is a rapidly developing field that has helped to dramatically reshape our understanding of happiness as its central phenomenon of interest through the development of a number of reliable measures and an overall increase in associated research outputs.

2. It is hard to dispute the point that a truly objective measure of happiness would probably avoid subjective accounts, and rely instead on independent biological or neuropsychological assessments. Whilst it is not yet possible to study our cognitive evaluations of well-being (life satisfaction) using imaging technologies, considerable advances have been made in our understanding of brain mechanisms that underlie affective style. For example, using magnetic resonance imaging technologies in a series of studies, Davidson (2005) investigated which areas of the brain are active at the time of processing different types of stimuli. These studies have demonstrated that positive affect is processed in the left prefrontal cortex and amygdala, areas stipulated to be both rich in dopamine receptors and essential to cognitive processing and flexibility, whilst negative affect is processed in the right prefrontal cortex. Neuropsychological studies have further demonstrated that mindfulness meditation produces changes in brain activation associated with reductions in negative affect and increases in positive affect. These and similar advances signal considerable hope for future developments in the field.

3. POS is a sister field to positive psychology with its focus on rigorous organizational research and careful studies of organization-based interventions. Concerned broadly with organizational flourishing, it addresses human excellence, resilience, and healing, organizational welfare, potentialities, possibilities, and affirmative bias. In a way POS is an umbrella term, bringing together a wide variety of topics, methods of research, and organizational processes, originating in the fields of psychology, sociology, and organizational behavior. The unifying focus is the enablement of extraordinary effectiveness and exceptional performance in organizations through the application of research-based principles, such as the identification of strengths, fostering virtuousness, and facilitation of elevating factors.

4. GDP is a limited measure of societal progress, not only because it does not capture the emotional aspects of individual lives, but also because it is an imperfect measure of economic well-being (due to omissions of the value of home productions, the value-added impact of public services, and the distribution of income). For several years, since the introduction of the Gross National Happiness Index by the government of Bhutan, many countries around the world have begun to develop happiness indicators.

In the UK, from 2010 onwards the Office for National Statistics was charged with developing a new measure of national well-being, bringing together a set of indicators that reflect the social and environmental/sustainability aspects of society, including subjective happiness. In order to understand what it is that matters most to people in the UK, the first step in the measure development was to open the question to a national debate that generated 175 events involving 7250 people and a total of 34,000 responses (some of which were from groups and national organizations, such as the British Psychological Society, thus representing tens of thousands more responders). The next step is the development of a national framework, informed by responses to the national debate, expert opinion, researchers and academics working in the area, international initiatives around happiness, and an advisory forum (Matheson, 2011).

The international trend towards considering the social and economic dimensions of well-being shows that UK is not the only country to take steps in this direction. On the initiative of President Sarkozy of France, a commission was recently created to report on the measurement of economic performance and social progress, looking explicitly to the assessment of well-being (Stiglitz, Sen, & Fitoussi, 2009). In Italy, the Statistical Institute in collaboration with the National Council of Economy and Labour are jointly taking forward the question of measurement of "sustainable progress." Both Canada and Australia are making steps in the same direction. The government of Bhutan, however, can still be considered the world leader through its pioneering work with the United Nations to develop a reference framework for a new happiness-based economic paradigm aimed at sustainability.

## The Multiple Definitions of Happiness

For the purposes of this volume we chose to consider happiness in its broadest sense, treating it as an umbrella concept for notions such as well-being, subjective well-being, psychological well-being, hedonism, eudaimonia, health, flourishing, and so on. In doing this, we hope to achieve a broad conceptualization that is theoretically sound and practically useful.

Although these terms overlap to some extent and are often used interchangeably, we can also identify some differences between them. Within the psychological literature the term *happiness* is seen as a common-sense, lay representation of well-being. The second meaning of this term refers to a so-called *hedonic* or pleasure-centered aspect of well-being. *Flourishing*, on the other hand, refers to an aspect of well-being concerned with growth and self-transcendence (going beyond oneself in pursuit of a meaningful action). *Well-being* itself is an umbrella term for a number of concepts related to human wellness. It encompasses a range of specific psychological definitions, such as *subjective well-being* (SWB).

The notion of SWB is currently the dominant conception of well-being in psychological literature. SWB is considered a multidimensional construct, with several distinct but related aspects treated as a single theoretical construct. SWB encompasses how people evaluate their own lives in terms of both affective (how we feel) and cognitive (how we think) components (Diener, Suh, Lucas, & Smith, 1999). The affective component refers to both moods and emotions associated with the experiencing of momentary events. The cognitive component, represented by life satisfaction, relates to the way individuals perceive their lives and refers to a discrepancy between the present situation and what is thought to be the ideal or deserved standard. Life satisfaction is conceptually similar to the way Veenhoven (1996) defines *happiness* as the degree to which individuals judge their lives favorably.

Most current research places happiness/well-being within one of two traditions: the hedonic and the eudaimonic. The *hedonic approach* (mentioned earlier) defines it as the pursuit of positive emotion, seeking maximum pleasure and a pleasant life overall with instant gratification. The *eudaimonic approach* looks beyond this, and is concerned with change, growth, and breaking homeostasis. Waterman (1993) defines eudaimonia as "an ethical theory that calls people to recognize and to live in accordance with the daimon or true self" (p. 678). Peterson, Park, and Seligman (2005, p. 26) suggest that "uniting eudaimonic emphases is the premise that people should develop what is best within themselves and then use these skills and talents in the service of greater goods." Ryff's eudaimonic model of *psychological well-being* is arguably the best known in the eudaimonic tradition. It contains six factors: self-acceptance, positive relations with others, autonomy, environmental mastery, purpose in life, and personal growth (Ryff & Keyes, 1995).

Amongst other related terms, *health*, according to the World Health Organization (1946, p. 100), is a state of complete physical, mental, and social (subjective) well-being and not merely the absence of disease or infirmity. *Quality of life* is proposed as the degree to which a person enjoys the important possibilities of his or her life, including aspects of "being," "belonging," and "becoming" (Renwick & Brown, 1996), whilst engagement can be defined as an involvement with and enthusiasm for work (Kahn, 1990).

While a consensus is emerging in some areas of happiness scholarship, in others there is robust debate and a divergence of opinion. The breadth of this volume is representative of the range of influential scholarship in the field and is therefore inclusive of conceptualizations that are given serious consideration in the academic literature.

## The Scope and Structure of the Volume

*The Oxford Handbook of Happiness* addresses a need for a coherent, multidisciplinary, accessible text on the current state-of-the-art in happiness research and evidence-based practice. The distinguishing features of this handbook are:

- Up-to-date information incorporating recent developments in the emerging field of happiness.
- A comprehensive volume on happiness including the different components of subjective well-being, life satisfaction, and eudaimonic well-being.
- A multidisciplinary perspective drawing from leading contributors in the areas of psychology, evolution, education, health, philosophy, spirituality, business, coaching, counseling, social policy, and economics.
- An inclusive scope of theoretical underpinnings, measurement, and development.
- A strong applied element integrated into many chapters of the book.

The volume is divided into ten sections that focus on psychological, philosophical, spiritual, and developmental approaches to happiness; happiness in society, education, organizations, and relationships; and definitions of and interventions for happiness. Each section is edited by a section editor who is a specialist in the relevant field of study. However, some of the topics cross several sections. For example, spirituality is present not only in Section IV, but also in Sections I and III. Philosophy is prominent in Sections III and IV. Despite not having an explicitly associated section, history runs through many parts of the volume, including Sections II, III, IV, V, and VI.

The handbook is comprised of 79 chapters including the introductory and concluding pieces. The number of chapters is reflective of the breath and depth of happiness as a field of scholarship. We have aimed for a gold standard in our choice of contributors, both in terms of a strong empirical basis, wherever relevant, and/or robust intellectual scholarship. Ed Diener, Joar Vitterso, Peter Salovey, Sonja Lyubomirsky, Richard Ryan, Matthieu Ricard, Robert Sternberg, and Martin Seligman, are amongst many distinguished section editors and chapter contributors.

Importantly, despite the multidisciplinary nature of the volume, there is an obvious preponderance of contributions by people with training in psychology. We believe that since happiness at its core is an internal human phenomenon, and psychology is the study of such phenomena, the relatively larger weighting of contributions by psychologists is not disproportionate. Included also is the scholarship that extends the discussion of happiness beyond the intrapersonal emotional and behavioral context and interfaces with relationships, society, systems, education, organizations, and philosophical approaches, providing what we believe is true and appropriately weighted multidisciplinary coverage of the area.

Renowned Norwegian scholar Joar Vitterso plays a pivotal role in the handbook as editor of two sections. The first of these, "Psychological Approaches to Happiness," is concerned with the impact of sophisticated methodology and advances in conceptual understanding on the science of happiness as approached from the psychological perspective. It provides an in-depth overview of happiness theories, measures, and correlates. From positive emotions and the impact of emotional intelligence on functional behavior and subsequently happiness, it also considers happiness from the point of view of cognition and decision-making. It further explores happiness as flow, and contradictions in the impact of religiosity on well-being as well as in the outcomes of happiness.

In Professor Vitterso's second section—"Psychological Definitions of Happiness"—the focus is on definitions of happiness. This starts with an excursion into the domain of philosophy and discusses how the Ancient Greek and Utilitarian notions of happiness underlie the definitions studied by psychologists today. The first chapter unites the multiple happiness definitions under a broad umbrella of quality of life, arranging them into a fourfold scheme that is also mapped with biological taxonomies. The following two chapters explore the concept of subjective well-being, the major scientific representation of a common sense happiness concept. From then on, the section explores further definitions of happiness, ranging from eudaimonic well-being and the concept of a fully-functioning person, through to an integrative functional well-being model developed by Vitterso himself.

The "Philosophical Approaches to Happiness" section offers multiple perspectives on happiness, escaping a common bias towards Aristotelian and Utilitarian viewpoints. The two first historical overviews of happiness in early Western and Chinese traditions demonstrate, amongst other points, that these perspectives have changed dramatically throughout history and depending on cultural contexts. An analysis of more recent continental philosophical thought coming from the existential tradition is complemented by modern philosophical reflections on the subject. Another important contribution to this section concerns philosophical methods in happiness research. The editor of this section, James Pawelski, who is also the director of education at the Positive Psychology Center at the University of Pennsylvania, contributes a chapter on the opposites of different conceptions of happiness, keeping in line with the critical approach of the whole section.

A section on "Spiritual Approaches to Happiness" is a rare find in the academic well-being literature and is a valuable and worthwhile addition to the volume. The editor, Jane Henry, an applied and academic psychologist working in the area of adult development, has selected chapters that draw on the Eastern religious and philosophical conceptions of happiness, with their emphasis on contentment and being at one with the universe. Two chapters explore the Buddhist understanding of happiness as a state of mind, interpersonal positive emotions, and the place of the individual in the world. Two chapters examine similarities and differences between psychological and spiritual approaches to the subject matter. Other chapters focus on different strategies derived from spiritual traditions (mindfulness, meditation, relaxation, silence, acceptance, and commitment therapy), their implementation, and limitations of this implementation in the Western world.

The next section, "Happiness and Society," is edited by one of the leading scientists in the area of public policy, Sam Thompson, a co-author of the Happy Planet Index (Abdallah, Thompson, Michaelson, Marks, & Steuer, 2009). It takes us another step away from the world of psychology into the domain of economics and policy-making, tackling the subject of happiness at a societal level. It traverses the Easterlin paradox, cross-cultural comparisons in happiness levels and the extent to which these follow the GDP trends, a deconstruction of happiness of the Danes, geographical influences on happiness, the impact of consumerism, and using happiness findings to build a sustainable society. This section is a call to governments across the world to introduce and critically test policies aimed at increasing well-being.

Happiness and education are brought together by the second editor of this handbook, Ilona Boniwell in the "Positive Education" section. This presents the subject from historical, philosophical, educational, and psychological perspectives. Raising questions about the purpose of education and whether education may need happiness lessons at all, the section considers how happiness and other contributing variables (e.g., resilience, wisdom, flow) can be fostered in the classroom. In addition, one fundamental issue is raised and addressed throughout the section—whether so-called happiness lessons should be timetabled, offered through cross-curricula means or developed through an overall school ethos. The section is somewhat unusual is that it offers two extended case studies, that of Wellington College in the UK and Geelong Grammar School in Australia. Both are pioneers in introducing happiness education, albeit based on different approaches.

The seventh section, "Happiness and Organizations," discusses happiness from the perspective of POS. Section editors—distinguished organizational psychologists Arran Caza and Kim Cameron—point out in their introduction that although organizational studies have largely been oriented to positive outcomes, happiness per se is a relatively new area of focus in organizational research and practice. However, rather than naively celebrating these new happiness lenses, they note the importance of achieving a flexible balance between positivity and negativity in organizational interventions identifying, for example, the benefits of negative feedback on performance. The section reviews the wealth of work in this area, ranging from chapters on virtues, job design, psychological capital, best self, and health in organizations through to sources of happiness amongst executives and the complexity of evaluating the impact of work on happiness from various perspectives.

Whilst much of happiness research has focused on intrapersonal factors, the section on "Relationships and Happiness" addresses the interpersonal nature of happiness. Grounded in the controversial debate on the centrality of relationships to human happiness, with the opinions and research findings ranging from essential (Diener & Seligman, 2002) to overstated (Lucas & Dyrenforth, 2006), section editor Melikşah Demir navigates us through current issues to future research questions. The picture is far from straightforward: marital quality is a stronger correlate of happiness than marital status, the quality of friendships is more important than their number, and psychological consequences of positive emotions are moderated by attachment orientation.

The subsequent section edited by Kate Hefferon takes a life-course perspective on the "Development, Stability, and Change of Happiness." The first chapter after the introduction evaluates barriers to happiness imposed by evolution and offers possible clues as to how these can be overcome. Returning once again to the acclaimed Easterlin paradox, this time from a critical perspective, the next chapter challenges the proposed unchangeability of happiness over one's lifetime. The following piece discusses psychological strategies to prevent hedonic adaptation. The section goes on to consider the concepts of positive mental health, post-traumatic growth, and lifelong meaning from the perspective of eudaimonic happiness.

Applying research to practice is the explicit focus of the final section, "Happiness Interventions." Coaching researchers and practitioners Gordon Spence and Suzy Green bring together a fascinating selection of chapters that consider how happiness and well-being can be increased, carefully examining the complex effects of targeted interventions, most of which have been revealed through randomized controlled trials. Chapters range from those addressing happiness interventions in the general population and mental health patients (through positive psychotherapy, acceptance and commitment therapy, well-being therapy, mindfulness, and a collaborative recovery framework) to empirical evidence for coaching to enhance happiness.

Whilst many similar topics have already been touched upon in existing edited volumes, many of the chapters in the handbook can be considered truly unique, including, but not limited to, those on psychopathology and happiness, philosophical methods in happiness research, interpersonal positive emotions, exploration of Chinese philosophical thought on the subject, evolutionary approaches to happiness, and multiple chapters on eudaimonic well-being.

## Conclusion

There are times when happiness appears overrated—when evaluating multiple reincarnations of smilies, glancing through yet another magazine article on ten steps to happiness, reading a thoughtful critique of the concept, or even in conducting yet another—after midnight—edit of this volume. Sometimes though, we wake up in the morning with the yearning for happiness. This usually happens in the absence of the corresponding affect, when the awakening does not bring with it the expected freshness of joy. Then happiness becomes important, due to the very absence of it. And then it becomes crystal clear that we can suffocate the yearning under the pillow, we can ignore it if we wish, and minimize the importance all we like, but when the happiness is not there, we miss it dearly. When asked what we would most like for our children, we respond instinctively "to be happy," or when a person we are with tells us "I am not happy with you," we know where the relationship is heading. Whether we choose it or not, happiness is a fundamental part of our existence, central to the way we view ourselves in the world, and, as this volume will confirm, causal for many life outcomes. As editors, we resign ourselves fully to agreement with the "pursuit of happiness" being an essential human right. Importantly, however, according to Benjamin Franklin, "The Constitution only guarantees you the right to pursue happiness. You have to catch it yourself." This is where the handbook can be most useful, by offering us some keys to the essence of happiness and the means for its lifelong pursuit.

## References

Abdallah, S., Thompson, S., Michaelson, J., Marks, N., & Steuer, N. (2009). *The (un)happy planet index 2.0: Why good lives don't have to cost the Earth*. London, UK: nef.

Davidson, R. J. (2005). Well-being and affective style: neural substrates and biobehavioural correlates. In F. A. Huppert, N. Baylis, & B. Keverne. (Eds.) *The science of well-being* (pp. 107–139). Oxford, UK: Oxford University Press.

Diener, E., & Seligman, M. E. P. (2002). Very happy people. *Psychological Science*, 13, 81–84.

Diener, E., Suh, E., Lucas, R., & Smith, H. (1999). Subjective well-being: Three decades of progress. *Psychological Bulletin*, 125, 276–302.

Kahn, W. A. (1990). Psychological conditions of personal engagement and disengagement at work. *The Academy of Management Journal*, 33, 692–724.

Lucas, R. E., & Dyrenforth, P. S. (2006). Does the existence of social relationships matter for subjective well-being? In K. D. Vohs & E. J. Finkel (Eds.), *Self and relationships: connecting intrapersonal and interpersonal processes* (pp. 254–273). New York: Guilford.

Matheson, K. (2011). Foreword. In *National statistician's reflections on the national debate on measuring national well-being* (p. 2). London: Office for National Statistics.

Peterson, C., Park, N., & Seligman, M. E. P. (2005). Orientations to happiness and life satisfaction: The full life versus the empty life. *Journal of Happiness Studies*, 6, 25–41.

Renwick, R., & Brown, I. (1996). The Centre for Health Promotion's conceptual approach to quality of life. In R. Renwick, I. Brown, & M. Nager (Eds.), *Quality of life in health promotion and rehabilitation: Conceptual approaches, issues and applications* (pp. 75–86). Thousand Oaks, CA: Sage.

Ryff, C. D., & Keyes, C. L. M. (1995). The structure of psychological well-being revisited. *Journal of Personality and Social Psychology*, 69, 719–727.

Seligman, M. E. P., & Csikszentmihalyi, M. (2000). Positive psychology: An introduction. *American Psychologist*, 55, 5–14.

Stiglitz, J. E., Sen, A., & Fitoussi, J.-P. (2009). *Report by the commission on the measurement of economic performance and social progress*. Paris, France: The Commission.

Veenhoven, R. (1996). Developments in satisfaction research. *Social Indicators Research*, 37, 1–47.

Waterman, A. S. (1993). Two conceptions of happiness: Contrasts of personal expressiveness (eudaimonia) and hedonic enjoyment. *Journal of Personality and Social Psychology*, 64, 678–691.

World Health Organization (1946). *Preamble to the Constitution as adopted by the International Health Conference*. Geneva: Official Records of the World Health Organization, no. 2.

# SECTION I

# PSYCHOLOGICAL APPROACHES TO HAPPINESS

CHAPTER 2

# INTRODUCTION TO PSYCHOLOGICAL APPROACHES TO HAPPINESS

JOAR VITTERSØ

University of Tromsø, Norway

In his book *Novum Organum* (1620), Sir Francis Bacon proposed that scientific knowledge should be collected and organized to help civilizations learn how to develop a better world (see Rees & Wakely, 2004). This message still speaks to the ultimate goals of academic endeavors, and I can think of no domain better suited to fulfill this call from the Enlightenment than the scientific study of happiness.

But even if philosophers of past centuries understood the importance of scientific knowledge, they might have been naive in understanding how such knowledge translates into political wisdom. Advancement in cognitive psychology illustrates, for example, that wishful thinking and forceful metaphors often are more effective than facts and logical reasoning when it comes to political decisions (Lakoff, 2008). For instance, 90% of the population in the USA prefers a more equal distribution of wealth than today's historic high inequality level—some estimates suggest that the top 1% of Americans hold nearly 50% of the wealth (Norton & Ariely, 2011). A stronger focus on the basic ingredients of a good life, on psychological rather than economic growth, might thus support democratic processes in creating better societies.

Secondly, since emotions and satisfaction are fundamental mechanisms in the process of turning objective facts into subjective beliefs (e.g., Westen, 2007), happiness research may also help push Bacon's vision forward. In struggling to understand the qualities of a good life, the science of well-being produces general knowledge on beliefs and decision-making.

On the surface, the idea of studying happiness scientifically may look naive. Hence, it is quite understandable that it took time for the field to gain academic credibility. For example, in Headley Cantril's (1965) seminal work on life satisfaction, the term happiness does not even appear in the index. And when Norman Bradburn intended to publish a book on happiness in the 1960s, he was advised against using the term "happiness" in the title—it was deemed as too unscientific (Bradburn, 1969). But as the present handbook testifies, the professional view on happiness has changed dramatically since Bradburn published his book, and so has the attitude in public discourse and among policy-makers.

For example, in February 2008 President Sarkozy of France created a commission to report on the measurement of economic performance and social progress. The commission was chaired by economist Joseph E. Stiglitz, and its report aimed to identify the limits of gross domestic product (GDP) as an indicator of economic performance and social progress (Stiglitz, Sen, & Fitoussi, 2009). The report emphasizes three areas which require further attention by statistical offices and policy-makers: better measurement of the domestic production of goods and services, the incorporation of sustainability considerations, and the measurement of quality of life.

*The Oxford Handbook of Happiness* is written in the spirit of Francis Bacon and reflects scientific approaches to several of the issues addressed in the Stiglitz report. The handbook also documents the amazing development of methods and research designs in happiness research. The field is no longer driven forward by surveys alone; a myriad of supplementary techniques and empirical perspectives has emerged. Grounded in methodological and conceptual developments, the current section of the handbook paints a portrait of the most up-to-date knowledge and insights of modern happiness research, while also giving glimpses into its future.

The first section of the book opens with a spearheading idea about positive emotions. The broaden-and-build theory is a successful integration of emotion theory in a well-being framework, and it is presented by Anne Conway, Michele Tugade, Lahnna Catalino, and Barbara Fredrickson in Chapter 3. Challenging the idea that positive emotions basically serve the function of aimless activation or inactivity, Conway and coauthors review a domain that has grown considerably over the last decade. A huge body of research now exists to support the hypothesis that positive emotions broaden people's momentary thought–action repertoires and lead to actions that build enduring personal resources. As for the broadening effect, the chapter shows how positive emotions stimulate expansive attention and increased openness to experience. For instance, in one of the studies reviewed in this chapter, it was shown that participants induced to experience positive mood demonstrated greater attention breadth as measured by an eye-tracking technology. As for the build effect, the reasoning suggests that the benefits of broadened attention will add up over time to build psychological, physical, and social resources. Again, evidence suggests that positive emotions build intellectual resources, secure attachment, and cognition. For instance, one experiment revealed how a skill-based meditation intervention, teaching participants to self-generate positive emotions, was associated with improvements in self-acceptance, physical health, competence, improved relations with others, and sense of purpose in life. The chapter concludes by anticipating the need for a better understanding of the nuances between different positive emotions, and for improved modeling of the trajectories of human development.

Chapter 4 deals with happiness from the point of view of cognition and decision-making. In it, Dale Griffin and Richard Gonzales present the Endowment–Contrast (E–C) model for measuring well-being. The framework was developed to account for observations that run counter to rational decision theory, which simply assumes that individuals choose the alternative that makes them most happy. Borrowing Tversky's formal models for turning a complex problem into a testable analysis, the E–C model has been able to point out how the "rational man" and other simplistic approaches to well-being are misleading guides to better lives. The way people think about their lives can fundamentally change their preferences in various situations. In other words, happiness is not just about the choices we make, but also about how these choices are consumed. In order to understand subjective experiences and how they are represented symbolically, we must realize that life satisfaction comes from a combination of both the hedonic valence of events (endowments), and the standards against which we evaluate the events (contrasts). The contrasts serve to counterbalance the endowment, or valence, of the experience. For example, the impact of a positive event in the past may reduce current life satisfaction because of contrast effects. The positive past sets up a high standard against which the current state of affairs is evaluated. For similar reasons, a negative event in the past may increase current life satisfaction because the negativity operates as a contrast. But the contrast effect is only active when the events they are referring to are relevant for the evaluation. For instance, given that the current situation is dominated by a positive mood, the evaluation of one's life satisfaction is left untouched by contrast effects. Hence, when an ongoing positive experience dominates the judgment, one's life satisfaction is a result of endowment effects only. These principles make the E–C model different from the more widespread adaptations models of well-being, and they also separate it from the "mood as information" approach. A series of examples are offered to illustrate these differences, and to clarify the model's ability to explain why so many individual choices do not increase life satisfaction.

In Chapter 5, Antonella Delle Fave presents a concept with an amazing history. Introduced by Mihaly Csikszentmihalyi more than 30 years ago as a term unheard of by readers of scientific literature, "flow" is now a familiar term to a surprisingly high number of lay people and scholars from all over the world. The flow phenomenon is hard to pin down conceptually, but basically it refers to an optimal experience that reflects a complex and highly structured state of consciousness. Under the right circumstances the flow state contributes to personal development, social integration, and cultural change. Delle Fave reviews the historical roots and cultural consistency of the concept, which comprises a mixture of changeable and continuous feelings associated with concentrated action. She focuses on flow as a dynamic and intrinsic mental state associated with challenging tasks that are perceived to be in balance with perceived skills, and how this description seems to be recognized across age, gender, and various cultural groups across the globe. Delle Fave further clarifies the diversity of assessment strategies that have been developed to capture this elusive phenomenon, and she brings up the intriguing issue of cross-cultural validity of central concepts in flow theory. For example, the English term "challenge" does not always translate easily to other languages and cultural traditions. The chapter ends with suggestions concerning the possibility of developing flow-based interventions in various areas of our societies, and points out promising future research agendas.

Chapter 6, by Alia Crum and Peter Salovey, explains the basic principles of emotional intelligence and how it may assist in the pursuit of happiness. The premise of their message is that emotions have functions. Emotions communicate, motivate, and facilitate, hence they cannot be understood in the hedonic terminology of a subjective experience that merely accounts for the balance between positive and negative affects. Emotions are not just responses to circumstances, they also cause functional behavior. Crum and Salovey argue that better lives can be cultivated first and foremost by a change in mindset. By learning about emotions—by becoming more emotionally intelligent—the full spectrum of our feelings may be utilized to facilitate happier lives and more functional lifestyles. The metaphors people adopt, and the myths they perpetuate, shape emotional life and happiness levels. If emotions are perceived, used, understood, and managed more functionally, we will be able to navigate our lives in more successful ways.

Will religious engagement lead to human flourishing? Or is it perhaps toxic? These questions give momentum to Chapter 7, by David Myers. It turns out that even if pretty good data exist to throw light on the topic, the effect of religion on well-being is rather complicated. For example, the happiest countries in the world, like Denmark, Norway, Sweden, Australia, Canada, and the Netherlands, are relatively irreligious. On the other hand, there are several irreligious nations represented at the low end of the list of healthy and flourishing nations, exemplified by North Korea, China, Vietnam, and the former Soviet states. Similarly, if one looks at differences between states within the USA, the most religious ones often reveal an unfavorable well-being record. At the state level, religious engagement correlates with high rates of crime and smoking, and with lower education and income. However, if the data are analyzed at the level of individuals, the picture is reversed. People with high religious engagement smoke less and commit fewer acts of crime than their less religious counterparts. Religious individuals also stand out as better citizens, since religious attendance correlates positively with involvement in community service, jury duty, voting, charity participation, and the frequency of talking with neighbors. Last but not least, self-reported happiness correlates positively with religiousness. The associations found between religiosity and well-being illustrates the perils of the so-called ecological fallacy, which is to (mistakenly) draw conclusions about individuals from data analyzed at an aggregated level. Several of the examples provided in Myers's chapter nicely illustrate this dilemma. However, Myers carefully avoids the perils of the ecological fallacy in his analyses, and he concludes that even if religion has had a mixed association with bigotry and tolerance, and also with misery and well-being, it appears that on balance, religion tends to foster human virtues, altruism, and happiness.

Unlike the other authors in this book, Patty Ferssizidis, Todd Kashdan, Rachel Marquart, and Michael Steger take the experience of psychopathology as their point of departure. Chapter 8 starts by looking at the harsh emotions in life—and then it looks back into the positive ones. This is a creative approach to well-being research and their chapter, which is entitled "Positive Psychological Experiences and Psychopathology: A Self-Regulatory Perspective," gives an overview of how people with various psychological disorders experience positive events and emotional states. The chapter examines the effect of psychopathology on functioning and finding meaning, and the authors review literature on how people suffering from depression and anxiety actually do experience their lives. Basically, the impaired psychological functioning that follows from psychopathological problems hampers emotional well-being. Although there might be examples of positive growth in the pathological populations it is, on balance, far better to be symptom free than suffering from anxieties and depression. Interestingly, the drawbacks of pathology also turn out to reduce the quality of life for people with too much positive emotion, such as mania and hypomania. For example, these groups are frequently reported to be more irritable and more maladaptive in their striving after achievement. The lack of meaning and positive emotion experienced among people with various psychological disorders is interpreted as dysfunctional self-regulating processes. The chapter concludes that, in order to improve our understanding of how daily experiences facilitate positive functioning and well-being, better strategies for investigating the depth and breadth of meaningful and rewarding experiences should be developed in future research.

Happiness is typically considered to be the ultimate dependent variable of social sciences. But some researchers have turned this idea upside down and started to ask if being a happy person also raises the likelihood of accruing rewards in important domains of life. The ninth chapter of the book, by Katherine Jacobs Bao and Sonja Lyubomirsky, provides a closer look at this promising perspective. The authors define happiness as the frequent experience of positive emotions, and they use terms such as positive affect, pleasant mood, and high well-being when referring to individuals who often experience positive emotions. With this stance, Jacobs Bao and Lyubomirsky show how happiness promotes a series of benefits and values for individuals who are fortunate to have a lot of it. For example, a good mood strengthens people's immune system, and this finding is replicated in both longitudinal and experimental research. The chapter further argues that the frequent experience of positive affect plays a causal role in the attainment of success. The reason is that positive affect helps build skill and motivates people to approach people and situations. For example, happy people are more likely to get married and to stay so, and happy people seem better able to obtain a job and feel more financially independent. Positive emotions also signal that things are going well, which allows people to feel more safe and secure as they approach novel situations. For instance, studies show that happy people are better at so-called "active coping" which helps build "upward spirals" toward health and well-being. The chapter also points to some of the benefits of negative emotions, but concludes that for the long-term effects, a stable positive disposition outweighs a negative one.

William Pavot and Ed Diener have written the last chapter of the section (Chapter 10). It presents the most recent findings regarding the experience of happiness and it looks to future research opportunities. The authors provide an overview of well-being theories and measurement traditions in happiness research, and pay particular interest to the issue of top-down versus bottom-up theories. The former refers to the view that happiness can be attributed to long-lasting propensities that predispose an individual to have certain experiences. Bottom-up theories, on the other hand, claim that an individual's overall happiness represents a summation of the ongoing negative and positive experiences over a lifetime. Based on this framework, the chapter presents updated studies on the correlates of happiness, such as the relationship between subjective well-being and gender, age, and material status. Pavot and Diener give a thorough review of the association between personality and subjective well-being, as well as the latest studies on happiness and heritability. The growing interest in cultural aspects of happiness research is well covered in the chapter, which ends with an interesting discussion of the life outcomes of happy individuals and happy societies. Better social relationships, better health, and better psychological functioning, the chapter argues, are among the benefits of happiness. As for future directions, Pavot and Diener point to the need for a better understanding of the relation between subjective well-being and psychological well-being.

A good society is populated by happy people. And even if there is not one correct answer to the question of what it means for a person to be happy, the following chapters offer a unique step towards a fuller understanding of this fascinating, persistent and gigantic issue. This section clearly contributes valuable knowledge for the gradual development of a better world.

## References

Bradburn, N. M. (1969). *The structure of psychological well-being*. Chicago, IL: Aldine.

Cantril, H. (1965). *The pattern of human concerns*. New Brunswick, NJ: Rutgers University Press.

Lakoff, G. (2008). *The political mind. Why you can't understand 21st-century politics with an 18th-century brain*. New York, NY: Viking.

Norton, M. I., & Ariely, D. (2011). Building a better America—One wealth quintile at a time. *Perspectives on Psychological Science, 6*, 9–12.

Rees, G., & Wakely, M. (Eds.). (2004). *The instauratio magna. Part II: Novum organum and associated texts*. Oxford, UK: Clarendon Press.

Stiglitz, J. E., Sen, A., & Fitoussi, J.-P. (2009). *Report by the commission on the measurement of economic performance and social progress*. Paris, France: Commission.

Westen, D. (2007). *The political brain*. New York, NY: PublicAffairs.

CHAPTER 3

# THE BROADEN-AND-BUILD THEORY OF POSITIVE EMOTIONS: FORM, FUNCTION, AND MECHANISMS

ANNE M. CONWAY[1], MICHELE M. TUGADE[2], LAHNNA I. CATALINO[3], AND BARBARA L. FREDRICKSON[3]

[1]Columbia University, USA; [2]Vasar College, USA; [3]University of North Carolina, USA

MANY of the most wonderful moments in life are infused with positive emotions. We may feel joy playing with children; love sharing with family members; and awe in the presence of natural beauty. During these moments, we feel a subjective sense of pleasure. Positive emotions feel good. But, beyond just feeling good, do positive emotions serve any function for us in either the short or long term?

Across the past decade, questions such as these have led to an explosion of research and significant advances in our understanding of positive emotions. In this chapter, we present the broaden-and-build theory of positive emotions (Fredrickson, 1998, 2001, 2004) as a framework for addressing these questions and understanding the nature, origins, and consequences of positive emotions. Next, we review evidence supporting the first part of the theory—the broaden effect—with a particular focus on attention and cognitive flexibility. Then we review evidence supporting the second part of the theory—the build effect—which has implications for lifespan development. Taken together, this work underscores the role of positive emotions in generating long-term resources such as well-being and resilience. We consider possible mechanisms underlying the broaden and build effects and provide evidence for the undo effect of positive emotions. Finally, we conclude with directions for future research.

# Broaden-and-Build Theory of Positive Emotions

The broaden-and-build theory of positive emotions was proposed to account for the unique effects of positive versus negative emotions that could not be explained by existing theories of emotions. For example, according to numerous theories (Frijda, 1986; Lazarus, 1991; Levenson, 1994), emotions were viewed as engendering specific behavioral action tendencies. Fear fueled the urge to escape, whereas anger sparked attack, and so on. From an evolutionary perspective, the specific action tendencies paired with discrete emotions functioned to ensure human ancestors' survival. Each discrete emotion had a specific action tendency, and consequently, served an adaptive function. Yet, unlike negative emotions such as fear and anger, the specific action tendencies of positive emotions were less specified. Compared to the action urges generated by negative emotions, those generated by positive emotions are considerably less clear and specific and in some cases, may call forth the action of "not acting." For example, joy and contentment appear to generate aimless activation and inactivity, respectively (Frijda, 1986). Such vagueness and lack of specificity led to the proposal that positive emotions may, in fact, serve functions quite distinct from negative emotions. But if not to act to enhance immediate survival, what, if any, function do positive emotions serve?

According to the broaden-and-build theory, rather than fueling specific action tendencies, positive emotions appear to spark broadened and expansive thought–action tendencies. They affect our thoughts and attention, and by leading to broadened and expansive attention, positive emotions fuel flexible and creative thinking and problem-solving approaches, which accumulate and build long-term psychological, physical, and social resources (Fredrickson, 1998, 2001, 2004). These new resources, in turn, would have increased the odds that human ancestors survived subsequent threats to life and limb.

In the following sections, we describe these two central effects of the broaden-and-build theory—the broaden effect and the build effect—and provide supporting evidence across a variety of domains. Toward that end, we first address the following questions: (1) What is a broadened thought–action repertoire? and (2) What evidence exists to support the claim that positive emotions broaden thought–action repertoires?

## The broaden effect

The broaden effect is a primary claim in the broaden-and-build theory. Rather than directly fueling specific physical actions, positive emotions appear to generate non-specific, broadened cognitive changes, which may lead to behavioral changes (Fredrickson, 1998). Positive emotions spark broad alterations in "thought–action" tendencies. One form in which positive emotions impact cognitive change is a broadened and expansive scope of attention.

### Attention

Within this widened scope of attention, individuals experience and attend to a larger distribution that includes more features of the surround that may have otherwise been excluded.

This broaden effect is in direct contrast to the well-known narrowing effect of negative emotions on attention.

For example, a considerable body of research has documented that under conditions of negative affect and threat, individuals engage in significantly more narrowed and focused attention and selectively attend to negative information. Fear and anxiety have been reported to narrow an individual's attentional focus (Derryberry & Tucker, 1994; Mogg, Millar, & Bradley, 2000; Mogg et al., 2000). Likewise, significant attention to threat has been demonstrated for anxious versus non-anxious individuals (for review see Bar-Haim, Lamy, Pergamin, Bakermans-Kranenburg, & IJzendoorn, 2007). Anxious individuals show faster attention and automatic engagement with threat-related versus neutral stimuli and slower time to disengage (Fox, Russo, Bowles, & Dutton, 2001), reflecting effects at multiple stages of information processing.

Like negative emotions, positive emotions also impact our attention and thought–action repertoires, only they broaden rather than narrow them. Whereas negative emotions may occur in threatening situations and constrict our attention to facilitate a quick response, positive emotions generally occur in safe contexts and stimulate expansive attention, and increase openness and receptivity to a range of experiences. To illustrate the unique effect of positive emotions and broadened attention, we present a series of studies showing the broadened attention effect. These include studies of visual attention utilizing global–local processing, executive attention, and emotional information processing tasks.

Global–local processing tasks assess the extent to which participants attend to global and holistic versus local and detailed features of a stimulus. One example includes an image with two geometric figures: (1) a large letter "T" composed of five smaller letter "Ls," and (2) a large letter "L" composed of five smaller letter "Ts." Participants are asked to find the letter "T" as quickly as possible requiring them to make a decision about a figure based on holistic (global) or elemental (local) features.

Utilizing a measure like this, research supports the effect of positive emotions widening attentional scope. In one experiment, participants were induced to feel positive, negative, or neutral states by watching film clips (Fredrickson & Branigan, 2005). Participants who viewed the positive emotion films were more likely to show a global preference compared to the other conditions. In another experiment, participants who frequently smiled were faster at recognizing global targets relative to local targets (Johnson, Waugh, & Fredrickson, 2010). Frequent smiling improved the ability to process information holistically.

Positive emotions have also been found to impact attention on traditional executive attention tasks. In a study conducted by Rowe, Hirsh, and Anderson (2007), broadened attention following positive emotion was assessed with the Eriksen flanker task (Eriksen & Eriksen, 1974). Participants were presented with a screen with a central target flanked by congruent (e.g., "NNNNN") or incongruent (e.g., "EENEE") adjacent stimuli. Response slowing is typically observed when the central target is flanked by incompatible stimuli. Target/distractor distance was also manipulated ("E E N E E") and results revealed a significant effect of positive affect on attentional breadth. Compared to sad and neutral conditions, the positive affect condition showed significantly greater reaction time to incongruent versus congruent stimuli. This response slowing was also demonstrated for trials with the greatest target/distractor distance providing evidence for increased attentional scope, facilitating inclusion of peripheral information.

Additional evidence supporting the broadened attentional effect of positive emotions derives from studies of affective picture processing. Utilizing eye-tracking technology, participants' eye movements (in response to affective pictures) were assessed following positive mood induction (Wadlinger & Isaacowitz, 2006). Results revealed that those who were induced to experience positive mood demonstrated greater attention breadth while viewing pictures. This included longer fixation to peripheral aspects of images. Interestingly, fixation and broadened attention were longer for positive versus negative and neutral images. This evidence for attentional expansion following positive affect, coupled with elaborate processing of positive stimuli, suggests potentially important directions for future studies of mechanisms underlying thought–action tendencies, such as a possible motivation or incentive to maintain an even greater expansion of attention. We elaborate on this proposal in later sections. Next, however, we describe the broaden effects on cognition.

## Cognition

Another form that positive emotions take involves the broadened influence on cognition, or more specifically, increased cognitive flexibility and creativity. As with expanding attention, positive emotions also broaden and expand one's thinking to allow for greater flexibility, creativity, and the generation of unusual and innovative problem solving. Positive emotions motivate individuals to pursue novel, creative, and unscripted paths of thought and action (Fredrickson, 1998) and "give[s] rise to an enlarged cognitive context" (Isen, 1987, p. 222).

Classic research by Isen and colleagues provides striking evidence for positive emotions' effects on flexible and innovative thinking. Those experiencing positive affect have named more unusual associations to neutral words, used more inclusive categories, and generated novel problem solving strategies (Ashby, Isen, & Turken, 1999). In one experiment, participants were induced to feel positive or neutral emotions and then completed Mednicks' Remote Associates Test, which requires individuals to generate a word that relates to three other words (Isen, Daubman, & Nowicki, 1987). In this experiment, participants induced to feel positive emotions generated more correct answers than those induced to feel neutral emotions, demonstrating a broadened scope of cognitive flexibility.

Positive emotions also broaden cognition as demonstrated by generating creative and novel uses for everyday objects. When given a problem to solve using a candle, a box of thumbtacks, and a book of matches, Isen and colleagues (1987) found that 75% of the participants who were induced to feel positive emotions were able to solve the problem, compared to 20% of the neutral and 13% of the negative groups. Likewise, positive emotions broadened cognition by facilitating problem solving in studies in which participants were asked to generate unusual uses for everyday objects (Ziv, 1976).

Positive emotions also appear to influence participants' thoughts about actions in which they would like to engage. Specifically, Fredrickson and Branigan (2005) reported that compared to those in negative and neutral conditions, participants induced to experience positive emotions generated a large and varied list of behaviors in which they wanted to engage. This study provides intriguing findings on the effect of positive emotions on broadened cognition and desired behavior and possible influences on thought–action repertoires. Could an additional feature of positive emotions be to spark reward-seeking behavior following broadened cognition? We address this question later. Next, however, we address another important effect of positive emotions—how we view and understand others.

## Social cognition

The broadened effect on social cognition refers to an expansion of how we view ourselves in relation to others. As with attention and cognition, positive emotions widen and expand our interpersonal scope and promote flexible and creative ways of processing social information. One of these areas includes how one views the self and the broadened effect of self-expansion.

Self-expansion refers to incorporating aspects of another person's character as one's own (Aron, Aron, & Smollen, 1992). It represents the degree of perceived similarity, overlap, and interconnectedness between the self and another. Findings reveal that positive emotions are key predictors of changes in social cognition and spark self-expansive views in relationships. Indeed, individuals who report frequent experiences of positive emotions were more likely to report significant overlap between self and other (Waugh & Fredrickson, 2006). This has been demonstrated in first-year university students reporting on new roommate relations within the first week of the semester and again at 1 month.

Results also indicate that positive emotions broaden our perception of self and other with respect to racial categories. Specifically, in a series of experiments conducted by Johnson and Fredrickson (2005), participants induced to experience positive emotions, compared to those in negative or neutral conditions, showed significant improvement in their ability to recognize people of a different race reducing an effect called the "own-race bias" in face recognition. Positive emotions appeared to eliminate the robust "own-race bias" in facial recognition through broadened and expanded views of self and others such that perceived similarities across social categories were broadened and perceived differences between social groups became diminished.

Overall, the form positive emotions take in the short term is one of broadened attention and cognition. We experience increased breadth and expansion of our attentional scope, thoughts, and problem-solving approaches, and views of self in relation to others. These broadened effects, in turn, spark decision-making (and possibly action), that over time lead to the second effect of the broaden-and-build theory—the build effect.

# Evidence for the build effect

According to the broaden-and-build theory, positive emotions spark broadened and expansive cognitive changes that lead to altered patterns of decision-making and actions that reflect investment in intellectual, personal, and social domains (Fredrickson, 1998). Over time, these consequential patterns of thoughts and actions accumulate, and build long-term psychological, physical, and social resources (Fredrickson, 1998, 2001, 2004). These may "add up" over time, leading to quantitative changes across development (e.g., increased levels of well-being), yet they may also lead to qualitatively new changes, such as when a child begins to think abstractly. Perhaps it was Piaget (1962) who illustrated this best when he described how children's play and engagement with the environment afforded the opportunity to develop qualitatively new knowledge and stages of cognitive thought.

Evidence suggesting that positive emotions build intellectual resources can be found in studies such as anticipatory smiling, joint attention, secure attachment, and cognition. For example, studies have assessed relations between infant positive affect and joint attention, which reflects a form of broadened attention involving the triadic coordination of attention between self, others, and a third object (Tomasello, 1995). Infants high on positive affect demonstrate significantly higher levels of initiating joint attention with another, presumably because engaging in shared attention is rewarding (Nichols, Martin, & Fox, 2005). Likewise, 6-month-old infants who engage in more smiling behavior demonstrated more anticipatory smiling (smiling at a toy object and then at an adult) during a joint attention task at 9 months (Parlade et al., 2008), and higher levels of social competence at 30 months (Parlade et al., 2008). Higher levels of joint attention at 12 months were also associated with higher levels of: (1) expressive language and cognitive ability at 24 months, and (2) social competence at 30 months.

More direct evidence can also be found in a recent intervention designed to enhance the developmental outcomes of socially deprived children from Romanian orphanages. Young children from the institution were randomly assigned to a foster care intervention or to remain in the institution at approximately 21 months of age. Compared to children who remained in the institution and a community-based comparison group, children in the foster care intervention demonstrated significantly higher levels of positive affect and attention at 42 months (Ghera et al., 2009). These children also evidenced significant growth in cognitive abilities from 30 and 42 months to 54 months as assessed by the Baley Scales of Infant Development (BSID-II; Bayley, 1993) and the Wechsler Preschool Primary Scale of Intelligence—Revised (WPPSI-R; Weschler, 1989) compared to the institutionalized group (Nelson et al., 2007). Interestingly, caregiver quality, as assessed by increased positive affect and sensitive responding, was enhanced in the intervention group, providing support that early environmental experiences infused with positive affect build long-term resources.

Significant effects of maternal positive affect on additional long-term outcomes have also been demonstrated. Maternal positive expressions during mother–infant free play have been found to be associated with: (1) a reduction in infant crying across the first year of life (Conway, McDonough, Clark, & Smith, 2001), and (2) attentional flexibility and behavioral competence at 33 months (Conway, 2002; Conway, McDonough, & Sameroff, 2002). Likewise, parent–infant interactions characterized by shared positive affect predict secure attachment, compliance, the internalization of values and goals, the development of conscience, and positive emotional expression with peers (Ainsworth, Behlar, Waters, & Wall, 1978; Denham, Mitchell-Copeland, Strandberg, Auerbach, & Blair, 1997; Kochanska, 1997; Kochanska & Aksan, 1995; Kochanska & Murray, 2000; Kochanska, Murray, & Coy, 1997). Links between parental positive emotional expression and children's emotion regulation and social competence have also been reported with school-age children (Boyum & Parke, 1995; Eisenberg et al., 2001).

These findings suggest that cumulative exposure to maternal positive affect and individual and relational experiences of positive affect may, over time, build long-term attentional, cognitive, and social resources in childhood. Yet, these effects are also evident during adulthood. Next, we review emerging findings demonstrating the powerful build effects of positive emotions on adults' well-being and resilience.

## *Well-being*

One of the central tenets of the broaden-and-build theory is the importance of positive emotions for individuals' trajectories towards growth and well-being (Fredrickson, 1998). In the last few years, research has begun to show how positive emotions may be key ingredients on the path towards a satisfying and fulfilling life. In a direct test of the build effect, adults were randomized to a skills based intervention or wait list control. The purpose of the 7-week skills-based intervention was to teach participants to self-generate positive emotions through a practice of loving-kindness meditation (LKM). LKM involved thinking of a person for whom they already felt warm and tender feelings (e.g., a close loved one), and then extending these warm feeling to themselves and then to an ever-widening circle of others. Findings indicated that compared to wait-list controls, participants who learned LKM reported more positive emotion throughout the 7-week intervention, which was associated with improvements in self-acceptance, physical health, competence, improved relations with others, and sense of purpose in life (Fredrickson, Cohn, Coffey, Pek, & Finkel, 2008). Growth in these resources also predicted increases in life satisfaction and fewer depressive symptoms among LKM participants. This field experiment provides striking evidence for the build effect and specifically the role of frequent positive emotion in the cultivation of well-being.

In addition to frequency, the *strength* of positive emotional responses may build optimal mental health or flourishing. Flourishing refers to being satisfied with life, being free of mental health concerns, and functioning significantly better than others (Fredrickson & Losada, 2005; Keyes, 2007). It has been found to be associated with higher levels of education, more positive versus negative emotions, and physical health (Keyes, 2007).

To assess build effects related to flourishing, adults were classified into three groups based on their mental health. Flourishers were individuals high in mental health (positive affect, psychological/social functioning) with an absence of mental health problems (e.g., depression, anxiety, substance abuse); non-flourishers included individuals without mental health problems but also without signs of flourishing; and the depressed group included individuals who endorsed mild-to-moderate symptoms of depression. Compared to non-flourishers and depressed groups, flourishers generally reported more positive emotions when engaging in pleasant activities including helping, playing, learning, and engaging in spiritual activity (Catalino & Fredrickson, 2011). Moreover, this greater positive emotional reactivity predicted higher levels of two facets of the cognitive resource mindfulness—*observing* and *non-reactivity to inner experience*—which, in turn, predicted changes in signs of flourishing over time, confirming the build effect and importance of positive emotions in the maintenance of optimal mental health and flourishing.

To assess the underlying processes that contribute to well-being, Cohn, Fredrickson, Brown, Mikels, and Conway (2009) tracked daily emotional experiences of young adults for 1 month. Findings indicated that those who experienced more positive emotions throughout the month showed increases in resilience and life satisfaction. Interestingly, the link between positive emotions and increased life satisfaction was mediated by increases in resilience. These results reveal that experiences of positive emotions help people improve life quality by building resilience, a key psychological resource.

## Resilience

Resilience is characterized by effective coping despite significant loss, hardship, or adversity in one's life (Block & Kremen, 1996; Cicchetti & Tucker, 1994; Luthar, 2003; Masten, 2001) and it is an important consequence of positive emotions. Research shows that resilience is comprised of both state and trait characteristics. When faced with adversity, "low-resilient individuals" are more easily thwarted and are less efficient in returning to normative levels of functioning in their daily lives. In contrast, when either mildly disrupted or faced with significant adversity, "high-resilient individuals" have an ability to change course efficiently, allowing them the flexibility needed to adapt to stress-inducing disturbances in their lives.

To examine trait differences in resilience, Tugade and Fredrickson (2004) examined patterns of cardiovascular recovery from negative emotional arousal among low- and high-resilient individuals. Participants were asked to prepare a self-relevant speech, which they believed would be videotaped for evaluation; this task reliably and robustly induced subjective reports of anxiety. In addition to increasing self-reports of anxiety, the speech preparation task induced cardiovascular arousal for all participants. Two important differences in trait resilience emerged. First, high-resilient (versus low-resilient) individuals were more likely to report experiencing positive emotions, such as interest, alongside their self-reported anxiety. Second, when informed that they would not have to give their speech, high-resilient participants evidenced faster cardiovascular recovery from the arousal, reflecting the ability to physiologically "bounce back" from stress. Mediation analyses revealed that the experience of positive emotions contributed to high-resilient participants' abilities to achieve accelerated cardiovascular recovery from negative emotional arousal (Tugade & Fredrickson, 2004). These findings suggest that high-resilient individuals make use of positive emotions to cope with stress (Tugade & Fredrickson, 2004, 2007; Tugade, Fredrickson, & Barrett, 2004).

Trait resilient individuals also benefit from the ability to self-generate positive emotions in the midst of a national catastrophe, such as the September 11, 2001 attacks on the United States (Fredrickson et al., 2003). Compared to low-resilient individuals, high-resilient individuals evidenced: (1) lower levels of self-reported depressive symptoms, and (2) greater post-crisis growth (more self-reported optimism, life satisfaction, and tranquility) in the aftermath of the September 11 attacks. Notably, more frequent experiences of positive emotions in the midst of tragedy mediated the relations between trait resilience and these outcomes of lesser depression and more post-crisis growth. These findings indicate that positive emotions are the active ingredients that predict the healthy responses of resilient individuals in the face of threat and adversity (Tugade et al., 2004). Other longitudinal studies have also shown that the ability to generate positive emotions can be beneficial for coping with adverse experiences such as the death of a loved one, illness, violence, national disaster, or caregiving for a loved one with chronic illness (e.g., Bonanno, 2004, 2005; Bonanno, Papa, & O'Neill, 2001; Bonanno et al., 2002). For example, there is growing evidence for the salutary nature of positive emotions in the bereavement process. Behavioral markers of positive emotional experience, such as smiling and laughing while discussing a recent loss of a loved one, are associated with better adjustment over time and stronger social relationships (Bonanno & Keltner, 1997; Keltner & Bonanno, 1997). Experiences of positive emotions have long-lasting consequences for individuals, helping them to build resilience in the face of daily and ongoing stressors and have important implications for future research and practice.

Consistent with the observation that high-resilient individuals benefit from cultivating positive emotions to cope with stress and adversity, laboratory experiments document that positive emotions serve to rapidly downregulate, or "undo" negative emotional experiences. Specifically, when participants induced to feel anxiety (e.g., using the speech-preparation task described earlier) were randomly assigned to turn their attention to a film that elicited one of two positive emotions (contentment, mild joy), a negative emotion, or a neutral state, those experiencing either of the positive emotions showed significantly faster cardiovascular recovery from negative emotional arousal (Fredrickson, Mancuso, Branigan, & Tugade 2000; see also Fredrickson & Levenson, 1998).

Evidence that positive emotions undo the physiological arousal generated by negative emotions also suggests that they may restore depleted ego resources important for self-regulation. Ego depletion refers to the idea that self-regulation is a limited resource that can be diminished when engaging in activities that require self-control or willpower impairing one's self-control in subsequent situations (Muraven, Tice, & Baumeister, 1998). Across four studies, researchers found that positive (vs. neutral or sad) emotion improved self-regulation (e.g., task persistence, physical stamina) following ego depletion (Tice, Baumeister, Shmeuli, & Muraven, 2007).

In sum, a considerable amount of research has been conducted demonstrating that, in the short term, positive emotions broaden multiple forms of attention and cognitive processes. Likewise, from infancy through adulthood, positive emotions also build long-term resources ranging from infant attention to resilience. From the proliferation of studies, our understanding of the functions of positive emotions has considerably broadened and expanded. Yet, to build even greater knowledge about these effects of positive emotions—the broaden effect and the build effect—a number of questions still remain, particularly those related to underlying mechanisms.

# FUTURE DIRECTIONS

Here we outline promising future directions, starting with questions related to the underlying mechanisms of broaden and build effects. Specifically, to the extent that positive emotions broaden attention and spark cognitive changes, how does such expanded awareness lead to decision-making or action? Likewise, how do positive emotional experiences lead to the development of long-term resources?

## Neural mechanisms and correlates of broaden and build effects

Affective neuroscience represents a key approach to investigating how emotion is represented and embodied in the brain and provides a promising framework with which to probe questions about underlying mechanisms. Specifically, if positive emotions broaden attention and spark cognitive flexibility, what processes are involved and are they associated with decision-making or action? Likewise, how do positive emotional experiences lead to the development of long-term resources? If positive emotions fuel broadened effects on cognition and stimulate enduring mental shifts, how does this build new, long-term resources?

We propose that mechanisms underlying the link between broaden and build effects, in part, include the generation of new learning and response-outcome contingencies, or more precisely, thought-outcome contingencies. Specifically, positive emotions broaden thought–action repertoires, stimulating novel and innovative thought-outcomes, and potentially, response-outcome contingencies. Momentary experiences of positive emotions may strengthen associations such that individuals accumulate an increase in the quantity and variety of positively conditioned associations. This may result in more engagement in the environment, affording greater contact with sources of potential and actualized rewards. In contrast to an accumulated learning history in which the actions of depressed individuals do not result in positive reinforcement, and do not accumulate and build over time (Ferster, 1973, 1981; Lewinsohn, Biglan, & Zeiss, 1976), we propose that positive emotions fuel an accumulated learning history in which broadened thoughts and actions lead to highly reinforcing contingencies. This accumulated history of positively reinforced contingencies may be a critical mechanism linking broadened thinking to decision-making, and ultimately to the build effect of long-term resources. In sum, the link between momentary broaden effects of positive emotions and the build effect on long-term resources may be partially mediated by reward-associated learning contingencies and related neural circuitry.

Moreover, novel outcomes generated by broaden effects may prime individuals to accumulate more rewarding outcomes. As previously described, Wadlinger and Isaacowitz (2006) reported that, compared to controls, participants in positive moods demonstrated greater broadened effects of attention as evidenced by longer gaze fixations and eye movements toward the periphery of pictoral stimuli. Similarly, these participants demonstrated greater broaden effects to positive versus negative and neutral images, suggesting that positive moods may have sensitized them to rewarding stimuli. Therefore, under conditions of positive mood, thresholds to experience broaden effects on attention may be reduced, facilitating more elaborate processing of information. This may also reflect incentives to maintain and create even greater degrees of expansion and broadened attention.

Activation of critical neurotransmitter systems such as dopamine may also account for and mediate relations between broaden and build effects. For example, an increase in dopamine production may be a key mechanism linking the enhancing effect of positive affect on cognitive flexibility (Ashby et al., 1999). Dopamine activity appears to have reward functions and varies in levels of magnitude and probability. Based on reinforcement learning principles, Schultz (1998, 2010) states that the specific reward delivery (e.g., magnitude, probability) is coded in the dopamine response as a prediction error. A reward that is better than predicted elicits activation (positive prediction error), whereas one that is fully predicted elicits no activation (no response), and one worse than predicted induces a reduction (negative prediction) (Schultz, 2010). Therefore, dopamine neurons only respond when the rewards are better than predicted. Consequently, only increasing rewards will provide continued reinforcement via dopaminergic mechanisms. This may impact our need for rewards fueling cumulative experiences of positive emotions and accumulated histories of thought-contingent and response-contingent behavior, which over time may build long-term resources.

This raises intriguing questions with respect to the broaden effect: Is it possible that the experience of positive affect broadens attention and cognitive flexibility only when the experience and reward is better than predicted? Is dopamine activation and, specifically, a positive prediction error, a necessary correlate of the broaden effect? We propose that rewards that are better than expected and corresponding dopamine activation may be associated with novelty and creativity. Consequently, if dopamine activation only occurs under conditions when the reward is better than expected, this may be an important correlate of the broaden effect.

To further probe neural mechanisms and regions correlated with broadened thinking and decision-making or action, regions of interest may include the nucleus accumbens, which may modulate subsequent behavior in terms of gain seeking behavior, and the orbitofrontal cortex (OFC) which computes reward magnitude and expected reward value and can represent outcomes and expected outcomes (Rolls & Grabenhorst, 2008). However, the OFC does not represent actions such as motor responses or movements (Rolls & Grabenhorst, 2008), but information from the OFC can contribute to action-outcome learning implemented in the anterior cingulate cortex (Rushworth, Behrens, Rudebeck, & Walton 2007). Thus, with respect to reward processing, cortical-basal ganglia circuitry is critical (Haber & Knutson, 2010). Further research is needed to examine the role of the cortical-basal ganglia loops in reward-related goal-directed behavior as it may be a promising avenue for probing underlying mechanisms of thought–action repertoires.

Likewise, investigating processes at the interface of cognition and reward may help elucidate potential neural correlates and targets of build effects, particularly during sensitive periods of development such as adolescence. Indeed, prior research has demonstrated increased proliferation of synapses in the prefrontal cortex during adolescence along with significant reductions in gray matter, which are associated with significant improvement in cognitive control and flexibility (Giedd et al., 1996). In early adolescence, participants show increased activation in the prefrontal cortex suggesting greater effort and recruitment of this region for cognitive control, yet demonstrate less efficiency in performance (Luna, Thulborn, & Munoz, 2001). Conversely, reward systems are highly activated as evidenced by greater reward seeking, and difficulties delaying reward obtainment, along with differences in regions recruited during reward processing (Dahl, 2004; Geir & Luna, 2009). This protracted development of the cognitive control system coupled with heightened reward seeking renders adolescents vulnerable to significant risk-taking and mortality (Dahl, 2004). Therefore, is it possible that positive emotional experiences may yield build effects by facilitating the development and interconnectivity of these systems during this heightened period of neural plasticity (e.g., reorganization of neural pathways based on experience)? If so, would positive affect interventions designed to promote cognitive control at the interface of cognition and reward demonstrate build effects? Investigations of internal and externally driven influences utilizing affective neuroscience methods to probe potential neural mediators and moderators of build effects are urgently needed.

## Distinct positive emotions, social transmission, and embodied cognition

With advancements in the field of positive emotions, emerging theory and research point to the need to examine differentiation amongst distinct positive emotions. Current emotion theories indicate that positive emotions can be uniquely classified based on form and function (e.g., Ellsworth & Smith, 1988; Fredrickson, 1998, 2001; Keltner & Shiota, 2003; Smith, 1991), unique patterns of behavioral displays (e.g., posture, voice, touch, and gaze; Keltner & Shiota, 2003), and distinct motivational functions (e.g., Smith, 1991; Izard, 1977; Keltner & Haidt, 2003). For instance, elevation predicts altruistic behavior, above and beyond feelings of happiness or amusement (Schnall, Roper, & Fesler, 2009). A nuanced examination of distinct positive emotions may reveal how positive emotions broaden and build in different ways (Fredrickson, 1998, 2001), and provide important information about these specific affective experiences.

Other research may investigate novel ways that positive emotions can "broaden" and "build" by investigating whether and how positive emotions contribute to different forms of psychological expansion, such as social transmission. The concept of social transmission or "virality" indicates that ideas, behavior, and phenomena may spread over time from one person to another via immediate or more distant social connections (Berger & Milkman, 2012). Research on emotional contagion, for instance, shows that positive emotions can transfer across people's social networks, having a "ripple effect" of positive emotions. As demonstrated in a 20-year longitudinal study, positive emotions (e.g., happiness) can spread between individuals, thereby forming clusters of such people within a social network. According to this research, one possible explanation is that positive emotions depend on the positive emotions of others with whom people interact (Fowler & Christakis, 2008). Understanding the mechanisms that explain this "ripple effect" will require additional empirical investigation.

The study of positive emotions may also add to growing area of research that focuses on embodied cognition (e.g., Barsalou, 2008; Niedenthal, 2007). Theories of embodied cognition posit that sensory and motor re-experiencing (i.e., "embodiment") occurs when one perceives emotion via processes such as reading affective words, recalling affective memories, or observing affective facial expressions. Research has shown that people express slight (imperceptible) smiles and frowns (e.g., activity in the zygomaticus major and corrugator supercilii muscles, assessed via facial electromyography) when presented with subliminal happy or angry faces (Dimberg, Thunberg, & Elmehed, 2000), suggesting that emotions can be embodied even outside of one's awareness.

Related theories of embodied cognition focus on the sensory-rich experiences reflected in common emotion metaphors. For instance, a study showed that those experiencing social inclusion (e.g., recalling a time when they felt included by others) estimated higher room temperatures, thereby embodying the "warm reception" of social acceptance. In contrast, those experiencing social exclusion (e.g., recalling a time when others left them out) estimated lower temperatures in the same room, thereby embodying the "cold chill" of social rejection (Zhong & Leonardelli, 2008). When considering the embodiment of positive emotions, several new questions may be tested. Metaphorically, positive emotions help individuals to "look on the bright side." In line with theories of embodied cognition, does activating positive emotion produce sensory experiences of brightness or clarity? This might help explain why people who report greater positive emotional experiences show selective attentional patterns toward positive images (Isaacowitz, 2005), which has been shown to promote adaptive outcomes in emotion regulation (Wadlinger & Isaacowitz, 2006).

Similarly, a common metaphor—"the burden has been lifted"—describes the experience of relief once a stressful experience has passed. Might experiencing positive emotions influence perceptions of lightness in heavy objects? If an important problem has been successfully managed, then positive emotions may be useful for easing efforts and re-energizing an individual once a stressor has passed. Theories of embodied cognition reveal how representations of emotional states may be grounded in sensory-motor processes (Barsalou, 2008; Niedenthal, 2007). Research endeavors that investigate positive emotions and embodied cognition may have important implications for understanding how positive emotions and the broaden and build effects are represented in one's body, mind, and brain. Individual differences in these effects will be important to explore as they have the potential to enhance our understanding of personally salient aspects of positive emotions and ways to personally tailor interventions and practices designed to enhance positive emotions and promote long-term resources.

# Summary

Evidence regarding the form and function of positive emotions has grown substantially in the last decade, with data accumulating to support key tenets of the broaden-and-build theory. Specifically, positive emotions have been shown to broaden and expand our attention, fueling novel approaches to thought and action. Over time, positive emotions "add up" leading to the long-term build effect on consequential personal resources. In addition, positive emotions likely build resources through non-linear and indirect trajectories. Investigating these trajectories will be critical to furthering our understanding of how experiences of positive emotion reverberate and multiply, leading to growth and adaption within a dynamic system with effects that span well beyond initial conditions (VanderVen, 2008). Applications to enhance positive emotions could spur the development of resources with far-reaching effects. Indeed, the empirical foundation has been laid for further and more nuanced investigations of positive emotional experiences and the numerous functions they may serve.

# References

Ainsworth, M. S., Blehar, M. C., Waters, E., & Wall, S. (1978). *Patterns of attachment: A psychological study of the strange situation.* Potomac, MD.: Lawrence Erlbaum.

Aron, A., Aron, E. N., & Smollan, D. (1992). Inclusion of others in the self sale and the structure of interpersonal closeness. *Journal of Personality and Social Psychology, 63,* 596–612.

Ashby, F. G., Isen, A., & Turken, A. (1999). A neuropsychological theory of positive affect and its influence on cognition. *Psychological Review, 106,* 529–550.

Bayley, N. (1993). *Bayley scales of infant development—Second edition.* San Antonio, TX: The Psychological Corporation.

Bar-Haim, Y., Lamy, D., Pergamin, L., Bakermans-Kranenburg, M. J., & IJzendoorn, M. H. (2007). Threat-related attentional bias in anxious and nonanxious individuals: A meta-analytic study. *Psychological Bulletin, 133,* 1–24.

Barsalou, L. W. (2008). Grounded cognition. *Annual Review of Psychology, 59,* 617–645.

Berger, J., & Milkman, K. A. (2012). What makes online content viral? *Journal of Marketing Research, 49*(2), 192–205.

Block, J., & Kremen, A. M. (1996). IQ and ego-resiliency: Conceptual and empirical connections and separateness. *Journal of Personality and Social Psychology, 70,* 349–361.

Bonanno, G. A. (2004). Loss, trauma, and human resilience: Have we underestimated the human capacity to thrive after extremely aversive events? *American Psychologist, 59*(1), 20–28.

Bonanno, G. A. (2005). Resilience in the face of potential trauma. *Current Directions in Psychological Science, 14,* 135–138.

Bonanno, G. A., & Keltner, D. (1997). Facial expressions of emotion and the course of conjugal bereavement. *Journal of Abnormal Psychology, 106*(1), 126–137.

Bonanno, G. A., Papa, A., & O'Neill, K. (2001). Loss and human resilience. *Applied and Preventive Psychology, 10*, 193–206.

Bonanno, G. A., Wortman, C. B., Lehman, D. R., Tweed, R. G., Haring, M., Sonnega, J., ... Nesse RM. (2002). Resilience to loss and chronic grief: A prospective study from pre-loss to 18 months post- loss. *Journal of Personality and Social Psychology, 83*, 1150–1164.

Boyum, L. A., & Parke, R. D. (1995). The role of family emotional expressiveness in the development of children's social competence. *Journal of Marriage and Family, 57*, 593–608.

Catalino, L. I., & Fredrickson, B. L. (2011). A Tuesday in the life of a flourisher: The role of positive emotional reactivity in optimal mental health. A Tuesday in the life of a flourisher: the role of positive emotional reactivity in optimal mental health. *Emotion, 11*(4), 938–950.

Cicchetti, D., & Tucker, D. (1994). Development and self-regulatory structures of the mind. *Development and Psychopathology. Special Issue: Neural Plasticity, Sensitive Periods, and Psychopathology, 6*(4), 533–549.

Cohn, M.A., Fredrickson, B.L., Brown, S.L., Mikels, J.A., & Conway, A.M. (2009). Happiness unpacked: Positive emotions increase life satisfaction by building resilience. *Emotion, 9*, 361–368.

Conway, A. (2002, August). *Does maternal positive affect in infant play promote early strengths?* Paper presented at the Positive Psychology Summer Institute, Wilmington, DE.

Conway, A., McDonough, S., Clark, J., & Smith, A. (2001, April). *Predictors of long-term cry reduction in infancy: The role of maternal positive affect.* Poster presented at the biennial meeting for the Society for Research in Child Development. Minneapolis, MN.

Conway, A., McDonough, S., & Sameroff, A. (2002, April). *Maternal positive affect promotes the development of emotion regulation and child competence.* Poster presented at the International Conference on Infant Studies. Toronto, Canada.

Dahl, R. E. (2004). Adolescent brain development: Periods of vulnerabilities and opportunities. *Annals of the New York Academy of Sciences, 1021*, 1–22.

Denham, S., Mitchell-Copeland, J., Strandberg, K., Auerbach, S., & Blair, K. (1997). Parental contributions to preschoolers' emotional competence: Direct and indirect effects. *Motivation and Emotion, 21*(1), 65–86.

Derryberry, D., & Tucker, D. M. (1994). Motivating the focus of attention. In P. M. Neidethnal & S. Kitayama (Eds.), *The heart's eye: Emotional influences in perception and attention* (pp. 167–196). San Diego, CA: Academic Press.

Dimberg, U., Thunberg, M., & Elmehed, K. (2000). Unconscious facial reactions to emotional facial expressions. *Psychological Science, 11*, 86–89.

Eisenberg, N., Gershoff, E. T., Fabes, R. A., Shepard, S. A., Cumberland, A. J., Losoya, S. H., ... Murphy, B. C. (2001). Mothers' emotional expressivity and children's behavioral problems and social competence: Mediation through children's regulation. *Developmental Psychology, 37*(4), 473–490.

Ellsworth, P. C., & Smith, C. A. (1988). Shades of joy: Patterns of appraisal differentiating pleasant emotions. *Cognition and Emotion, 2*, 301–331.

Eriksen, B. A., & Eriksen, C. W. (1974). Effects of noise letters upon the identification of a target letter in a nonsearch task. *Perception and Psychophysics, 16*, 143–149.

Ferster, C. B. (1973). A functional analysis of depression. *American Psychologist, 28*, 857–870.

Ferster, C. B. (1981). A functional analysis of behavior therapy. In L. P. Rehm (Ed.), *Behavior therapy for depression: Present status and future directions* (pp. 181–196). New York, NY: Academic Press.

Fowler, J. H., & Christakis, N. A. (2008). Dynamic spread of happiness in a large social network: Longitudinal analysis over 20 years in the Framingham Heart Study. *British Medical Journal, 338*, 2338.

Fox, E., Russo, R., Bowles, R., & Dutton, K. (2001). Do threatening stimuli draw or hold visual attention in subclinical anxiety? *Journal of Experimental Psychology: General, 130*, 681–700.

Fredrickson, B. L. (1998). What good are positive emotions? *Review of General Psychology. Special Issue: New Directions in Research on Emotion, 2*(3), 300–319.

Fredrickson, B. L. (2001). The role of positive emotions in positive psychology: The broaden-and-build theory of positive emotions. *American Psychologist, 56*, 218–226.

Fredrickson, B. L. (2004). Gratitude, like other positive emotions, broadens and builds. In R. A. Emmons & M. E. McCullough (Eds.), *The psychology of gratitude* (pp. 145–166). New York, NY: Oxford University Press.

Fredrickson, B. L., & Branigan, C. (2005). Positive emotions broaden the scope of attention and thought-action repertoires. *Cognition and Emotion, 19*, 313–332.

Fredrickson, B. L., Cohn, M. A., Coffey, K. A., Pek, J., & Finkel, S. M. (2008). Open hearts build lives: Positive emotions, induced through loving-kindness meditation, build consequential personal resources. *Journal of Personality and Social Psychology, 95*, 1045–1062.

Fredrickson, B. L., & Levenson, R. W. (1998). Positive emotions speed recovery from the cardiovascular sequelae of negative emotions. *Cognition and Emotion, 12*, 191–220.

Fredrickson, B. L., & Losada, M. F. (2005). Positive affect and complex dynamics of human flourishing. *American Psychology, 60*, 678–686.

Fredrickson, B. L., Mancuso, R. A., Branigan, C., & Tugade, M. M. (2000). The undoing effect of positive emotions. *Motivation and Emotion, 24*(4), 237–258.

Fredrickson, B. L., Tugade, M. M., Waugh, C. E., & Larkin, G. (2003). What good are positive emotions in crises?: A prospective study of resilience and emotions following the terrorist attacks on the United States on September 11th, 2001. *Journal of Personality and Social Psychology, 84*, 365–376.

Frijda, N. H. (1986). *The emotions.* Cambridge, UK: Cambridge University Press.

Geier, C., & Luna, B. (2009). The maturation of incentive processing and cognitive control. *Pharmacology, Biochemistry and Behavior, 93*, 212–221.

Ghera, M. M., Marshall, P. J., Fox, N. A., Zeanah, C. H., Nelson, C. A., Smyke, A. T., & Guthrie, D. (2009). The effects of foster care intervention on socially deprived institutionalized children's attention and positive affect: Results from the BEIP study. *Journal of Child Psychology and Psychiatry, 50*, 246–253.

Giedd, J., Vaituzis, C.A., Hamburger, S.D., Lange, N., Rajapakse, J.C., Kaysen, D., ... Rapoport, J. (1996). Quantitative MRI of the temporal lobe, amygdala, and hippocampus in normal human development: Ages 4–18 years. *The Journal of Comparative Neurology, 366*, 223–230.

Haber, S. N., & Knutson, B. (2010). The reward circuit: Linking primate anatomy and human imaging. *Neuropsychopharmacology Reviews, 35*, 4–26.

Isaacowitz, D. M. (2005). The gaze of the optimist. *Personality and Social Psychology Bulletin, 31*, 407–415.

Isen, A. M. (1987). Positive affect, cognitive processes, and social behavior. *Advances in Experimental Social Psychology, 20*, 203–253.

Isen, A. M., Daubman, K. A., & Nowicki, G. P. (1987). Positive affect facilitates creative problem solving. *Journal of Personality and Social Psychology, 52*, 1122–1131.

Izard, C. E. (1977). *Human emotions*. New York, NY: Plenum.

Johnson, K. J., Waugh, C. E., & Fredrickson, B. L. (2010). Smile to see the forest: Facially expressed positive emotions broaden cognition. *Cognition and Emotion*, 24(2), 299–321.

Keltner, D., & Bonanno, G. A. (1997). A study of laughter and dissociation: Distinct correlates of laughter and smiling during bereavement. *Journal of Personality and Social Psychology*, 73(4), 687–702.

Keltner, D., & Haidt, J. (2003). Approaching awe, a moral, spiritual, and aesthetic emotion. *Cognition and Emotion*, 17, 297–314.

Keltner, D., & Shiota, M. N. (2003). New displays and new emotions: A commentary on Rozin and Cohen. *Emotion*, 3, 86–91.

Keyes, C. L. M. (2007). Promoting and protecting mental health as flourishing: A complementary strategy for improving national mental health. *American Psychologist*, 62, 95–108.

Kochanska, G. (1997). Multiple pathways to conscience for children with different temperaments: From toddlerhood to age 5. *Developmental Psychology*, 33, 228–240.

Kochanska, G., & Askan, N. (1995). Mother-child mutually positive affect, the quality of child compliance to requests and prohibitions and maternal control as correlates of early internalization. *Child Development*, 66, 236–254.

Kochanska, G., & Murray, K. (2000). Mother-child mutually responsive orientation and conscience development: From toddler to early school age. *Child Development*, 71(2), 417–431.

Kochanska, G., Murray, K., & Coy, K. C. (1997). Inhibitory control as a contributor to conscience in childhood: From toddler to early school age. *Child Development*, 68, 263–277.

Lazarus, R. S. (1991). *Emotion and adaptation*. New York, NY: Oxford University Press.

Levenson, R. W. (1994). Human emotions: A functional view. In P. Ekman & R. Davidson (Eds.), *The nature of emotion: Fundamental questions* (pp. 123–126). New York, NY: Oxford University Press.

Lewinsohn, P. M., Biglan, A., & Zeiss, A. S. (1976). Behavioral treatment of depression. In P. O. Davidson (Ed.), *The behavioral management of anxiety, depression and pain* (pp. 91–146). New York, NY: Brunner/Mazel.

Luna, B., Thulborn, K. R., & Munoz, D. P. (2001). Maturation of widely distributed brain function subserves cognitive development. *NeuroImage*, 13, 786–793.

Luthar, S. S. (Ed.). (2003). *Resilience and vulnerability: Adaptation in the context of childhood adversities*. New York, NY: Cambridge University Press.

Masten, A. S. (2001). Ordinary magic: Resilience processes in development. *American Psychologist*, 56(3), 227–238.

Masten, A. S., Best, K. M., & Garmezy, N. (1990). Resilience and development: Contributions from the study of children who overcome adversity. *Development and Psychopathology*, 2, 425–444.

Mogg, K., McNamara, J., Powys, M., Rawlinson, H., Seiffer, A., & Bradley, B. P. (2000). Selective attention to threat: A test of two cognitive models of anxiety. *Cognition and Emotion*, 14, 375–399.

Mogg, K., Millar, N., & Bradley, B. P. (2002). Biases in eye movements to threatening facial expressions in generalized anxiety disorder and depressive disorder. *Journal of Abnormal Psychology*, 109, 695–704.

Muraven, M., Tice, D. M., & Baumeister, R. F. (1998). Self-control as a limited resource: Regulatory depletion patterns. *Journal of Personality and Social Psychology*, 74, 774–789.

Nelson, C. A., Zeanah, C. H., Fox, N. A., Marshall, P. J., Smyke, A. T., & Guthrie, D. (2007). Cognitive recovery in socially deprived young children: The Bucharest Early Intervention Project. *Science, 318*, 1937–1940.

Nichols, K. E., Martin, J. N., & Fox, N. A. (2005). Individual differences in the development of social communication: Joint attention and temperament. *Cognition, Brain, Behavior, 9*, 317–328.

Niedenthal, P. M. (2007). Embodying emotion. *Science, 316*, 1002–1005.

Parlade, M. V., Messinger, D. S., Delgado, C. E. F., Kaiser, M. Y., Van Hecke, A. V., & Mundy, P. C. (2008). Anticipatory smiling: Linking early affective communication and social outcome. *Infant Behavior and Development, 32*, 33–43.

Piaget, J. (1962). *Play, dreams and imitation in childhood.* New York, NY: Norton.

Revenson, T. A. (2003). Scenes from a marriage: Examining support, coping and gender within the context of chronic illness. In J. Suls & K. Wallston (Eds.). *Social psychological foundations in health* (pp. 531–559). Malden, MA: Blackwell Publishing.

Rolls, E. T., & Grabenhorst, F. (2008). The orbitofrontal cortex and beyond: From affect to decision-making. *Progress in Neurobiology, 86*, 216–244.

Rowe, G., Hirsh, J. B., & Anderson, A. K. (2007). Positive affect increases the breadth of attentional selection. *Proceedings of the National Academy of Sciences of the United States of America, 104*, 383–388.

Rushworth, M. F., Behrens, T. E., Rudebeck, P. H., Walton, M. E. (2007). Contrasting roles for cingulate and orbitofrontal cortex in decisions and social behaviour. *Trends in Cognitive Science, 11*, 168–176.

Schnall, S., Roper, J., & Fesler, D. (2009). Elevation leads to altruistic behavior. *Psychological Science, 21*, 315–320.

Schultz, W. (1998). Predictive reward signal of dopamine neurons. *Journal of Neurophysiology, 80*, 1–27.

Schultz, W. (2010). Dopamine signals for reward value and risk: Basic and recent data. *Behavioral and Brain Functions, 6*, 24.

Smith, C. A. (1991). The self, appraisal, and coping. In C. R. Snyder & D. R. Forsyth (Eds.), *Handbook of social and clinical psychology: The health perspective* (pp. 116–137). New York, NY: Pergamon Press.

Tice, D. M., Baumeister, R. F., Shmeuli, D., & Muraven, M. (2007). Restoring the self: Positive affect helps improve self-regulation following ego depletion. *Journal of Experimental Social Psychology, 43*, 379–384.

Tomasello, M. (1995). Joint attention as social cognition. In C. Moore & P. Dunham (Eds.), *Joint attention: Its origins and role in development* (pp. 103–130). Hillsdale, NJ: Lawrence Erlbaum.

Tugade, M. M., & Fredrickson, B. L. (2004). Resilient individuals use positive emotions to bounce back from negative emotional experiences. *Journal of Personality and Social Psychology, 86*(2), 320–333.

Tugade, M. M., & Fredrickson, B. L. (2007). Regulation of positive emotions: Emotion regulation strategies that promote resilience. *Journal of Happiness Studies, 8*(3), 311–333.

Tugade, M. M., Fredrickson, B. L., & Barrett, L. F. (2004). Psychological resilience and positive emotional granularity: Examining the benefits of positive emotions on coping and health. *Journal of Personality. Special Issue: Emotions, Personality, and Health, 72*(6), 1161–1190.

VanderVen, K. (2008). *Promoting positive development in early childhood: Building blocks for a successful start.* New York, NY: Springer.

Wadlinger, H. A., & Isaacowitz, D. M. (2006). Positive mood broadens visual attention to positive stimuli. *Motivation and Emotion, 30*, 87–99.

Waugh, C. E., & Fredrickson, B. L. (2006). Nice to know you: Positive emotions, self-other overlap, and complex understanding in the formation of a new relationship. *Journal of Positive Psychology, 1*, 93–106.

Wechsler, D. (1989). *The Wechsler preschool and primary scale of intelligence-revised.* San Antonio, TX. The Psychological Corporation.

Zhong, C. B. & Leonardelli, G. J. (2008). Cold and lonely: Does social exclusion literally feel cold? *Psychological Science, 19*, 838–842.

Ziv, A. (1976). Facilitating effects of humor on creativity. *Journal of Educational Psychology, 68*, 318–322.

CHAPTER 4

# THE ENDOWMENT–CONTRAST MODEL: A LENS FOR HAPPINESS RESEARCH

DALE GRIFFIN[1] AND RICHARD GONZALEZ[2]

[1]University of British Columbia, Canada; [2]University of Michigan, USA

In this chapter we review the Endowment–Contrast (E–C) framework for assessing well-being (Tversky & Griffin, 1991), examine extensions and applications, and apply it to new empirical approaches to well-being research. The E–C model is a set of tools to use in thinking about—and measuring—happiness and well-being. The framework fits firmly in the "social constructionist" perspective on well-being, focusing as it does on the cognitive aggregation of hedonic impact over time and the distinction between objective circumstances and subjective value. We first review the historical context in which the framework was developed, describe the fundamental building blocks of the theory, and illustrate selected developments and applications. We then describe the generalization of the original framework and its application to the choice–judgment discrepancy, and close with a discussion of the relevance of the framework to new distinctions in the measurement of well-being.

## THE HISTORICAL CONTEXT: HEDONIC PSYCHOLOGY IN THE 1980S

The development of the E–C framework was motivated primarily by a reaction against some of the prevailing ideas of the time. One influential idea was the notion, associated with the work of Parducci (1984) on range-frequency theory, that intense pleasures should be restricted or avoided to prevent a contrast effect such that small daily pleasures become experienced as neutral or even disappointing. In the Parduccian view, intense but rare pleasures provide full value in the experience and do not chip away at the value of small pleasures. Thus, a fabulous honeymoon trip might add to life satisfaction because of the one-time pleasure without serving as a daily standard of comparison that reduces the pleasure of neighborhood walks with one's spouse. However, a regular round of cruises and luxury vacations might become both dull and leave daily life feeling especially flat. A second widely shared viewpoint was that the deliberate pursuit of happiness is doomed to failure because of the "hedonic treadmill" (Brickman & Campbell, 1971) caused by changing adaptation levels (Helson, 1964). Why strive for a life of peak pleasures when lottery winners seemed to revert back to average levels of satisfaction and citizens of rich nations seemed hardly happier than those of poor nations? Related to this was the everyday observation that the same economic or social stimulus that led to despair in one person left another person's well-being untouched. How could a prescriptive approach to maximizing well-being have any currency given the observed variability in response to bad and good life events?

A third contributor to the zeitgeist of well-being research in the late 1980s and early 1990s was the frustration with the uncertain epistemological status of verbal reports of well-being, happiness, and life satisfaction. What if the lottery winner was truly happier, but used different language—language responsive to adaptation effects—to express those feelings? Perhaps neuroscience would come to the rescue and provide a gold standard measure of true happiness; or perhaps asking people for willingness to pay for different states of life or health would overcome such a deep and apparently unsolvable problem.

A fourth important element of this intellectual period was that happiness and well-being were entering the mainstream of social science, in the sense that researchers from public policy, law, health, and economics were all joining psychologists and sociologists in searching for what made people less miserable, and in some cases, for what made people happy. Even at that time, a minority of economists (in particular, Easterlin, 1974) were sufficiently convinced by survey evidence on self-reported well-being to propose relativistic theories adapted from psychology that focused on adaptation and satisfaction. However, mainstream economics brought with it two fundamental canons of belief: more money was preferable to less money (in happiness, health, and marital partners), and the proper measure of utility was choice. Who knew what people meant by reports of happiness, satisfaction, or well-being? Who knew if people had the insight to reflect on what was good for them? What mattered was action, behavior, and observed commitment to one state of the world over another.

The E–C model was developed as a counter-argument to these prevailing ideas, but its own brand of constructionism was also powerfully shaped by three more immediate methodological influences. The first of these was Amos Tversky's trademark use of simple formal models to turn a complex and messy problem into a sharp, testable analysis. We develop this further through detailed examination later in this chapter.

A second immediate influence was the work Tversky was carrying out at that time with Kahneman, Slovic, and others on contingent models of judgment (Slovic, Griffin, & Tversky, 1990; Tversky, Sattath, & Slovic, 1988; Tversky, Slovic, & Kahneman, 1990). These models explained the causes and implications of preference reversals, where people would choose A over B, but be willing to pay more money for B than A. These were "contingent" models of judgment and choice because the specific information that the decision-maker noticed and used was contingent or conditional on the method of elicitation of preferences (e.g., rating or pricing or choice or elimination of alternatives). In particular, different methods of elicitation focused the decision-maker on different aspects of the options under consideration, or on different ways to justify choice, or made different aspects of the options easier to compute and therefore weighted more heavily in the revealed preference.

A third major influence that shaped the E–C model was the contemporary work of Fritz Strack and Nobert Schwarz on experiential versus cognitive effects on reported well-being, which was to some extent a social psychological analogue to the contingent judgment perspective. This line of work demonstrated that seemingly trivial manipulations such as spending time in an unpleasant room, or even answering a question about the frequency of recent dating experiences, could change the frame of reference by which life satisfaction was judged. Like models of contingent judgments, the work by Strack, Schwarz, and colleagues implied that answers to well-being questions in survey format were inextricably constructionist in that answers were sensitive to the way that target and surrounding questions were asked, the moods they aroused, and the memories they brought to mind (e.g., Strack, Schwarz, & Gschneidinger, 1985). In other words, there seemed to be no single right answer to the question of how happy a person was: their true happiness—as measured by their response to a specific question at a specific time—"truly" did depend on the accessibility of memories and emotions, and the integration and interpretation of those accessible building blocks.

## Endowment and Contrast: A Personal History

The fundamental insight underlying the endowment and contrast model emerged after many hours of talking about happiness and satisfaction; in particular about whether peak experiences today necessarily led to reduced pleasure in the future. What of that great dinner in New York at a conference? What of reading a fantastic book or seeing a great movie? What of a honeymoon trip to southern Spain? The insight, presented on Tversky's small whiteboard in his office, was simply represented as $Sat_2 = E_2 + E_1 - C_1$. Satisfaction at the time of Event 2 (a French dinner in one's home town) is a function of the (positive) Endowment yielded by the second dinner plus the Endowment yielded (through memory) of the positive experience of the first dinner minus the contrast effect capturing the (negative) discrepancy between the French dining experience in New York and the local French dinner. Over time, the insight would have been represented as

$$Sat_2 = aE_2 + w_e E_1 - w_c C_1 \qquad (1)$$

to emphasize that all events are weighted contributors to well-being and that the key shifts in weights are those between $w_e$ and $w_c$, the relative impact of the first dinner's endowment and contrast effects. Then, for some weeks afterward, Tversky would bring up real-life examples and see how well the simple representation held up—what of the aging professor whose greatest lifetime contribution was his dissertation, or the young comedian whose greatest exposure was as a break-through act on late-night television? Did their experiences fit? And what about the stories from Stouffer's sociological classic *The American Soldier*, where African-American soldiers stationed in the south of the USA were simultaneously poorer, less free, and more satisfied than African-American soldiers stationed in the north (Stouffer, Suchman, DeVinney, Star, & Williams, 1949)? And while the academic literature from Easterlin to Parducci to

Schwarz would shape the content of the model, it was the test of the anecdote that determined whether the model would survive on the whiteboard or suffer erasure.

The conceptual building blocks of the model are similarity and the role of memory as carriers of (subjectively processed) event quality across time. Tversky and Griffin (1991) asserted that without memory, the concept of life satisfaction or overall well-being would not exist. They pointed to the example of an amnesiac patient who could not decide how happy he was. "The stronger the memory of the past, the greater its impact on present well-being. With no memory, there can be no endowment and no contrast, just immediate pleasures and pains" (p. 102). The memory of event quality in the past thus affects the future both through a direct effect, the endowment (the core effect that keeps giving), and an indirect effect, the contrast (the comparative effect that keeps taking away). An important condition of the model is that it focuses on the symbolic effect of past experiences. Thus, the E–C model is about the dual direct and indirect effects from recalling the evaluation of the event, not from reliving or re-experiencing the event. This distinction was important initially to separate the model from the "mood as information" model of Strack and Schwarz, which implicated mood generated by experience and re-experience as the carrier of contrast and assimilation effects. The distinction is also important as we look at the extensions to the E–C model that tend to merge it with an experiential processing model.

As Tversky and Griffin noted:

> There is little novelty in suggesting that well-being depends both on the nature of the experience that is being evaluated and on the standard of evaluation … Many authors have observed that satisfaction is directly related to the quality of the experience, or its endowment, and inversely related to the evaluation standard, which serves as a contrast. What is perhaps less obvious is the observation that the same (past) event makes a dual contribution to well-being (Tversky & Griffin, 1991, p. 102).

Furthermore, every past hedonic event has this dual capability, but the weight of endowment varies with features of the prior event (e.g., its quality, salience, and intensity), whereas the weight of the contrast varies with features of the relationship between the prior and current event (e.g., the similarity or relevance of the past event to the current event). A honeymoon trip to Spain will contribute to future well-being through the endowment effect to the extent that the original trip was intensely pleasurable and highly memorable. The same Segovian honeymoon may, by the contrast effect, cast a pall on future vacations as a couple (high relevance), but is unlikely to diminish the pleasures of a conference-related trip (low relevance). This implies that the weight or magnitude of the endowment effect could be manipulated by cues that make a specific past event more salient, and that the weight or magnitude of the contrast effect could be manipulated by focusing manipulations that make a past event more or less relevant to setting a standard for a given current event. The final model on the whiteboard was thus:

$$\begin{aligned}\text{Satisfaction} &= \text{Endowment} + \text{Contrast} \\ &= E_{12} + C_{12} \\ &= E_1 + E_2 + r_{12}d_{12}.\end{aligned} \quad (2)$$

Here $r_{12}$ indicates the relatedness of the two events, and $d_{12}$ represents the signed hedonic discrepancy between the two events (again, where the hedonic value refers to the symbolic evaluation stored in memory, not to the actual subjective experience or objective of the event itself.) In retrospect, we can recognize one hidden parameter in the model, reflecting that endowment effects from the past will fade with reduced salience, yielding:

$$\text{Satisfaction} = s_1 E_1 + E_2 + r_{12} d_{12}. \tag{3}$$

This model raises the important question of whether individual differences in happiness are at least partly determined by these weights: happy individuals may have the predisposition to look to the past for happy events that reflect endowment and unhappy events that generate contrast, and happy people may be able to convince themselves that contrasting negative events are more relevant as standards of comparison than contrasting positive events. This key question was raised in the statement of the original model, but as we shall see, it has only recently been addressed.

## Applying the Endowment–Contrast Decomposition

Tversky and Griffin provided two "definitional" empirical studies to demonstrate the simultaneous operation of endowment and contrast effects. The two studies examined the effects of the past on the present by holding constant the value of present effects, and varying the relevance or similarity of the past to the current event. We provide here a more detailed account of the logic of the identification of endowment and contrast effects in an empirical design than was presented in the original chapter, and we present a revised symbolic vocabulary in the hope of simplifying the presentation. In the scenario study, participants first read a positive or negative story set in the past (1 week ago) from one of four domains (dating, academic achievement, social interaction, or movie-going) and then read a neutral story set in the present about the same or a different domain. This combination yields a 2 × 2 crossed design (positive/negative past story that is related/unrelated to current neutral story) fully within-subject. For each pair of past/present stories, participants rated the protagonist's level of happiness with life overall.

The results of this study are presented in Fig. 4.1 in the form of a bar graph with the negative past event conditions presented first, broken down by unrelated and related past events. The E–C model predicts a significant interaction between positivity of the past event and relatedness between the two events, because the endowment effects (positive versus negative across the two conditions) are the only effects operating in the unrelated past conditions but are opposed by countervailing contrast effects in the related past conditions. Both the graph and the 2 × 2 analysis of variance analysis confirm this. However, the total endowment and contrast effects can also be derived from the individual cell-level comparisons,[1] under the assumption that for the time 2 neutral event $E_2 = 0$ and thus can be ignored, that for unrelated events $r_{12} = 0$ and hence $C_{12} = 0$ for unrelated events, and that the salience of the

---

[1] Although analysis of well-being surveys is increasingly conducted using only ordinal assumptions for scales of well-being, we treat the decomposition of satisfaction using interval scaling assumptions, consistent with the original statement of the theory.

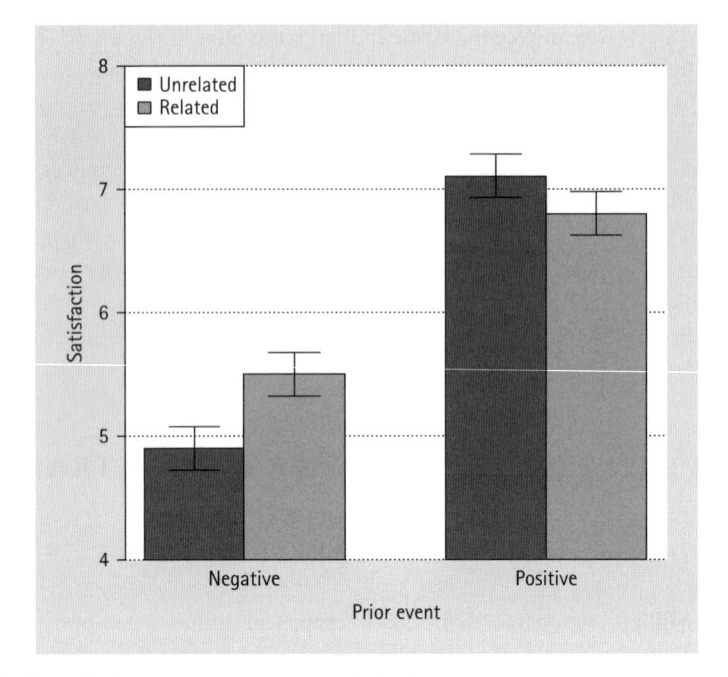

**FIG. 4.1** Effect of prior event on current satisfaction.

past events was very high, $s = 1$, as the stories from the past were read immediately before the stories from the present.

As the cell mean (7.1; Table 4.1) for the positive unrelated past event condition consists of the overall grand mean (6.1) plus ($E_1^+$), the positive endowment effect is simply $E_1^+ = 7.1 - 6.1 = 1.0$. By the same logic, the cell mean for the negative unrelated past event condition (4.9) consists of the overall grand mean (6.1) plus ($E_1^-$), yielding a negative endowment effect of $E_1^- = 4.9 - 6.1 = -1.2$. The overall endowment effect from the past is the sum of these absolute values, or 2.2. The isolation of the contrast effects is somewhat complicated by the fact that the two related conditions involve the counteracting forces of endowment and contrast.

### Table 4.1 Story condition

| | Effect | |
|---|---|---|
| | E | C |
| Positive Unrelated (M = 7.1) | + | |
| Positive Related (M = 6.8) | + | − |
| Negative Unrelated (M = 4.9) | − | |
| Negative Related (M = 5.5) | − | + |

However, if we take the difference between the positive related and positive unrelated conditions, we see that the positive endowment effect cancels out, isolating the negative effect of contrast. Thus, the negative contrast effect associated with a past positive event is simply 6.8 − 7.1 = −0.3; a reduction of 0.3 scale points of satisfaction. Taking the difference between the negative related and negative unrelated conditions, the negative endowment effect cancels out, isolating the positive effect of contrast: the positive contrast effect associated with a past negative event is simply 5.5 − 4.9 = 0.6. The sum of these absolute values is 0.9, indicating that the total contrast effect was somewhat less than half the size of the total endowment effect, not surprising given the high salience of the past stories.

The second study illustrating the E–C decomposition used actual money as a reward, which provides a standard scale on which we can compare the relative power of positive and negative contrast effects. In this study, participants rated their satisfaction with the experience of playing two investment games, different types of computer-controlled stock markets. Like the first study, the two games played in sequence could be similar or dissimilar. The games were manipulated so that all participants won a payoff of $4 in the second game, but either $2 or $6 in the first game. Thus, in a conceptually equivalent design to the first study, after completing the second game, participants could look back to the past at either a better or worse experience that was more or less related. However, in this case participants took part in only one cell of the design. As in the scenario study, the E–C model predicts a greater difference in satisfaction between the large and small past payoff conditions when the games are unrelated, because those participants will experience relatively pure negative and positive endowment effects. However, for those experiencing related games, the past also has a contrasting effect on current satisfaction. The same set of contrast weights can be used as presented earlier for study 1, but note the stronger assumption here: the relatedness coefficient $r_{12}$ is again assumed to be 0 when the games are different—this allows the same decomposition—but whereas stories of dating and schooling success are clearly unrelated, it is less clear that the results of two different investment games would be seen as completely unrelated. This simplifying assumption, when it does not hold, will understate the magnitude of the endowment effect, as we shall see shortly.

As can be seen in Fig. 4.2, there is a substantial difference in satisfaction between the small and large unrelated past reward conditions, whereas participants in the two related conditions are almost equally satisfied, implying that the contrast effects almost perfectly offset the endowments. As the second payoff of $4 is constant across all 4 cells, it is "absorbed" into the grand mean of 7.5. Again, assuming that the less similar experiences were completely unrelated, the difference between the positive unrelated mean and the grand mean reflects the positive endowment (8.7 − 7.5 = 1.2), and the comparable deviation from the negative unrelated mean reflects the negative endowment (6.4 − 7.5 = −1.1); the total endowment from the prior payoff is thus 2.3. Again, subtracting the positive unrelated mean from the positive related mean isolates the negative contrast effect (7.5 − 8.7 = −1.2), and subtracting the negative unrelated mean from the negative related mean isolates the positive contrast effect from a negative experience (7.3 − 6.4 = 0.9). Consistent with the key tenet of loss aversion (Kahneman & Tversky, 1979), that losses from a reference point loom larger than gains, the negative contrast is larger than the positive contrast. The total contrast, 2.1, is almost equal to the total endowment, as implied by the shape of the bar graph.

These two studies clarify how the cognitive or symbolic nature of the E–C processes differ from more perceptual models of adaptation effects, such as hedonic treadmill (Brickman &

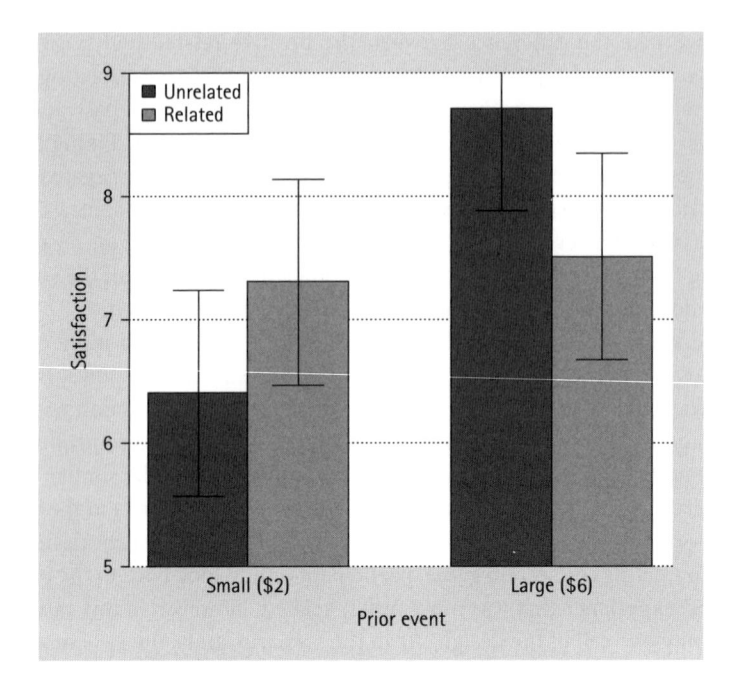

FIG. 4.2 Effect of prior game winnings on current satisfaction.

Campbell, 1971) or range-frequency theory (Parducci, 1984). The key primitive in the E–C framework is the hedonic value of events: events contribute to happiness or satisfaction directly and inversely depending on the closeness and salience of the relation between the target and background events. The key primitive in the adaptation models is the setting of the hedonic scale of experience or measurement: with repetition, the extraordinary becomes ordinary, the exquisite becomes mundane. The adaptation of lottery winners and paraplegics is sometimes described as a contrast effect, such that the accident victim comes to value his or her remaining powers and pleasures all the more due to lowered expectations ("It could be worse") while the lottery winner finds his or her expectations continually dashed through high expectations ("Everything should be wonderful"). The key diagnostic test between contrast and adaptation is whether the momentary hedonic experience is diminished or enhanced because it is made in comparison to a reference state or event (contrast) or whether the hedonic experience itself is intrinsically more or less positive (see Kahneman (1999) for a more general and detailed discussion of the nature of adaptation effects in perception and in judgment).

Just as contrast is fundamentally different from adaptation, so endowment effects in these studies are fundamentally distinct from the class of phenomena known as assimilation effects. Traditionally, assimilation effects refer to the biased interpretation of a new stimulus driven by prior expectations, beliefs, or cognitive schemas, so that the new stimulus is perceived or interpreted to match the prior expectation or belief more than it really does. Simultaneous assimilation is also possible, as when a neutral stimulus appears to be part of a category when other prototypical members of that category surround it. The endowment process is clearly different: the background event or information is not used to change the construal of some target event, but in fact adds its endowment to the experience independent of any categorization or construal effects on the target event. Thus, endowment does not compete with assimilation but adds another explanatory concept.

Tversky and Griffin offered alternative explanations of two studies from the mood as information paradigm, applying the E–C decomposition to varying time between experiences and varying relatedness across experiences. The two applications are informative as to the nature of the assumptions necessary to isolate these effects in the E–C framework. Take, for example, the study first presented in Strack et al. (1985) where participants were asked to report their current well-being on a 10-point scale after reporting (a) either a positive or negative life event that actually occurred to them, (b) either recently or in the past. The cell means for the four relevant conditions are presented in Fig. 4.3 in the form of a bar graph, ordered so that conditions defined by events in the present come first, and within that, ordered by positive and negative events. This allows us to use the decomposition table presented for the first study (Table 4.1), with past/present replacing related/unrelated. Like an unrelated event in the past, the positive event in the present provides no contrast, only endowment, so its contribution to satisfaction comes entirely from its positive endowment effect; the same logic holds for those thinking about a negative event in the present; their satisfaction comes only from the negative endowment, and all other effects are zero. This assumption (that the present contributes only endowment) seems reasonable, and provides estimates of the positive endowment (the positive present cell mean – grand mean = 8.9 – 8 = 0.9), and negative endowment (7.1 – 8 = –0.9), and provides an estimate of the total endowment of 1.8 units.

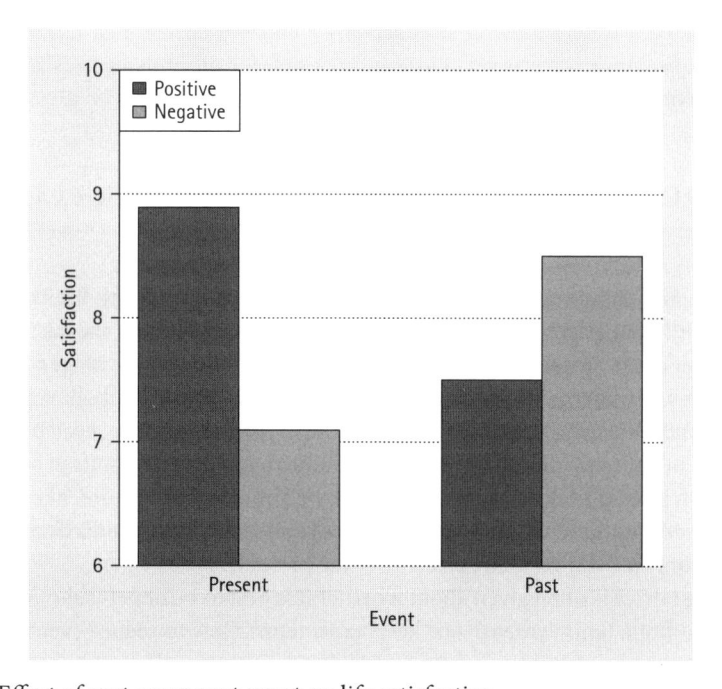

FIG. 4.3 Effect of past or present event on life satisfaction.

The isolation of the contrast effect relies on a substantially stronger assumption, which is that the amount of the endowment effect is the same for past events and present events. If so, then the same paired-cell subtractions as used in the first two studies are appropriate. On one hand, the degree of salience may be roughly equal because participants are asked to think about both events in the same way and immediately before making the satisfaction judgment; on the other hand, the thoughts about the current event may carry a greater experiential weight and, due to temporal construal (Liberman & Trope, 1998), may be thought of in a more concrete fashion. The resolution of this issue depends on how closely we follow Tversky and Griffin's original distinction between symbolic and experiential effects on well-being: if endowment depends only on salience and not on the degree of re-experienced mood, then this decomposition is appropriate. Following this assumption, we find that the negative contrast associated with the positive past event is −1.4 (7.5 − 8.9) and the positive contrast associated with the negative past event is 1.4 (8.5 − 7.1), yielding a total contrast of 2.8, substantially larger than the total endowment. Note that if the assumption of equal endowment (equal salience) of past and present events is violated, the contrast effect will be overstated.

Another application of the E–C framework to the mood as information paradigm examined the effect of putting participants in a pleasant or unpleasant room for an hour before measuring their general life satisfaction and satisfaction with their housing. This application involves another assumption, which is that environmental quality is related to one's current housing but largely unrelated (not at all similar) to one's general life. In other words, "a specific event … is likely to have a significant contrast effect in the domain to which it belongs, and little or no contrast effect in others." (Tversky & Griffin, 1991, p. 111). Thus, our application of the weighting matrix from study 1 proceeds by replacing "unrelated versus related" with "general life satisfaction versus satisfaction with housing". In brief, the resulting decomposition revealed a total endowment effect of 1.3 and a total contrast effect of 2.5. Here the standard of comparison was very close and relevant for the housing satisfaction, and led to the strong contrast effect.

## Endowment and Contrast Generalized

Although the first half of the original statement of the E–C framework limited its application fairly tightly to temporally ordered events using memory to link the past and present, the second half of the chapter provided a substantial broadening of the range of applications beyond events and memories of events. The authors noted that the symbolic representations of both past and future can be consumed, resulting in pain or pleasure. Fearfully imagining the results of an upcoming medical test or hopefully imagining the results of an admissions interview both give and take away well-being. Expectations of the future, like memories of the past, can serve as both direct sources of pleasure and pain, and standards of comparison that enhance or take away from the pleasure of the present time.

Conflicting advice is often given about whether it is best to be hopeful about the future—and enjoy that hope (endowment)—or keep expectations low to reduce eventual, and perhaps inevitable, contrast. But less recognized is that consuming pleasant hope for the future may also reduce the pleasure of present experiences through a contrast effect on the present.

Probability seems to play a key role in determining the relative balance of endowment and contrast from expectations about the future. Very low probability events still provide some endowment through hope and fear, but no contrast. Long-shot bets, whether in lotteries or on horses, produce pleasurable hope and day-dreams, but are so improbable that they do not lead to great disappointment (future contrast) or reduce current pleasures (simultaneous contrast). Likewise, unlikely but tragic health diagnoses provide anxiety or terror during the experience of expectation but little elation after they are ruled out, because a better outcome was always so likely. Thus, it seems that probability moderates the balance of endowment and contrast from expectations about the future much as relatedness or relevance does for memories from the past.

Schwarz and Strack (1999) present data collected by Schwarz and Hippler that allow us to apply the E–C decomposition to data from the inclusion/exclusion paradigm. In this study, university students were asked to recall a positive or negative event from 2 years before; half of the students were reminded that such events took place before university, when they were still high school students. The salience and perceived magnitude of this role transition should thus signal that the past events were not informative about one's current life satisfaction. The E–C decomposition for this paradigm is presented in Table 4.2, on the assumption that past irrelevant events (signaled by the high-school/university divide) provide only contrast, whereas past relevant events provide both contrast and endowment.

The grand mean across all cells is 7.6. Thus the negative contrast effect from recalling a positive event (and being reminded of the distance from high school) is substantial (6.2 − 7.6 = −1.4); the positive contrast effect is moderate (8.2 − 7.6 = 0.6), and the total contrast effect is large: 2 units. The positive endowment is isolated by subtracting the positive irrelevant mean (6.2) from the positive relevant mean (8.7), which yields 2.5, and the negative endowment is isolated by subtracting the negative irrelevant mean (8.2) from the negative relevant mean (7.4), yielding 0.8. The total endowment is thus 3.3, substantially larger than the contrast effect.

A shared implication of the E–C framework, the inclusion/exclusion model, and the Empathy–Contrast model (Brandstatter, 2000) is that the existence of two countervailing psychological forces in the aggregation of hedonic events over time makes it difficult to find strong relations between objective life circumstances and general life satisfaction. A very positive event may have a net negative or positive contribution to later well-being depending on the way it is represented and processed at the later time.

### Table 4.2 Past memory condition

| | Effect | |
|---|---|---|
| | E | C |
| Positive Irrelevant (M = 6.2) | | − |
| Positive Relevant (M = 8.7) | + | − |
| Negative Irrelevant (M = 8.2) | | + |
| Negative Relevant (M = 7.4) | − | + |

# Extensions of the Endowment–Contrast Model

## A preference for happy endings

Ross and Simonson (1991) noted that the E–C model and the operation of loss aversion together predict a general preference for happy endings. In the case of an unhappy ending, a good prior event will take away from the pleasure of a later less-good event; because losses loom larger than gains, the negative contrast effect will be stronger than the comparable positive contrast from reversing the order. In the case of a happy ending, the positive contrast adds to the pleasure of the later good event, consistent with the E–C framework. Ross and Simonson added two novel contributions. First, they used a willingness-to-pay measure for a video game, showing that when a good video game was evaluated after a poor game, participants were willing to pay an additional $3 on average for the same good game compared to when the poor game was evaluated last. Second, they linked the happy ending effect to the preference for segregating rather than integrating hedonic outcomes. Consider one relevant example,

> Mr. A received $120 from the electric company for overpayments he had made during the year. Later that day, he lost a $20 bill.
>
> Mr. B received $100 from the electric company for overpayments.

Who was happier? A or B?

As predicted, for both mixed gains and mixed losses, people thought that integrating the outcomes (as in case B here) would make people happier when the happier event came first. This implies that the negative contrast effect from experiencing the good event first reduces the overall pleasure below that created from the one-shot payment. On the other hand, people thought that segregating the outcomes (as in case A here) would make people happier when the happier event came last, implying that the positive contrast effect from experiencing the good event last enhances the overall pleasure beyond that created by the one shot payment.

This analysis is important because it provides the basis for deliberate strategies that people can use to maximize their welfare from a combination of events.

## The relation between wage rates and job satisfaction

Groot and van den Brink (1999) examined the empirical phenomenon that wage level is virtually unrelated to job satisfaction and proposed an explanation that closely overlaps with the E–C framework. According to their model, "Higher wages increase job satisfaction, but as … aspirations and preferences are changed as well by the higher wage level part or most of this wage effect disappears" (p. 363). Their notion of "preference drift" can be interpreted as either a true adaptation effect to higher wages or a negative effect of contrast working through expectations. Using a standard probit regression model, Groot and van den Brink find a negative, but insignificant, effect of wages on job satisfaction. However, adding a term representing an expectations-based contrast or preference drift, so that higher wages require a higher threshold for satisfaction, changes the coefficient for wage on job satisfaction to a more sensible positive and significant value.

## The Contrast–Empathy model of social comparison

In motivating the Contrast–Empathy model, Brandstatter pointed out that the effects of social comparison have been interpreted in terms of contrast: feeling good if one performs better than another (especially a relevant other, Tesser, 1988), or feeling worse and motivated to do better if one performs more poorly than another. Festinger's (1954) classic social comparison theory can be seen as a contrast theory (self–other) of comparative satisfaction. Contrast can also be seen as a central mechanism in equity theories of satisfaction, which postulate that people weigh the relative value of inputs and outputs to determine the fairness of outcomes. However, according to Brandstatter, this traditional focus on contrast and the informational role of social comparison neglects the emotional impact of another person's outcomes on the perceiver. If the comparison target is liked or otherwise close to us, we feel good for them if they succeed; if the target person is disliked, we feel good at them if they fail. Brandstatter argues that the pleasure or pain felt upon the good or bad experience of a close target is due to the emotion of empathy (empathic joy or empathic distress) whereas the pleasure or pain felt upon the bad or good experience of a disliked target is due to the emotion of malicious joy or envy.

Brandstatter motivated his model with a little-known comment from Brickman, Coates, and Janoff-Bulman's (1978) classic study of paraplegics, where they reported that interviewers were often depressed by their feelings of empathy with the victim—rather than cheered up by contrast. Later, Tesser (1988, 1991) proposed that people gain from reflecting the high performance or standing of others when the relationship is close and the comparison dimension is of low personal relevance, but suffer from dissatisfaction when a distant other or high-relevance dimension invokes a comparison.

The novel aspect of Bransdstatter's Contrast–Empathy model is that a given social comparison can yield both contrast and empathic emotion effects, which can have additive or offsetting effects on one's own satisfaction. The tendency to compare in a competitive sense is heightened for a self-relevant dimension, enhancing the contrast effect. The tendency to feel empathy is heightened for a close positive relationship, enhancing the endowment-like effect (the tendency to feel malicious pleasure is heightened for a distant negative relationship, which introduces a kind of reverse endowment effect). Thus, pure contrast (competitive comparison) will occur for a self-relevant dimension with a target for which one feels neutral. Empathy will dominate for a non-relevant dimension with a target with which one has an extremely close warm relationship. Other combinations of relevance and closeness will lead to mixtures of contrast and empathy. Looking only at positive and negative relationships, positive (better than) and negative (worse than) comparisons, and low and high relevance dimensions yields eight cells, as shown in Table 4.3.

Using a generalization of the linear decomposition from the E–C model (displayed in contrast form in Table 4.3), we can see that the greatest satisfaction comes from a downward comparison on an irrelevant dimension towards someone whom one feels cold or negative. Greatest dissatisfaction comes from an upwards comparison on a self-relevant dimension towards someone whom one feels cold or negative.

Table 4.3 Relationship, comparison level, and relevance condition

|  | Effect | |
|---|---|---|
|  | E | C |
| Warm, Upward, High Relevance (M = −3.3) | + | − |
| Warm, Upward, Low Relevance (M = −2.5) | + | − |
| Warm, Downward, High Relevance (M = 1.3) | − | ++ |
| Warm, Downward, Low Relevance (M = 0.3) | − | + |
| Cold, Upward, High Relevance (M = −4.0) | − | − |
| Cold, Upward, Low Relevance (M = −2.5) | − | − |
| Cold, Downward, High Relevance (M = 3.5) | + | ++ |
| Cold, Downward, Low Relevance (M = 2.3) | + | + |

The empathy effects in the four "warm relationship" rows refer to empathic joy and pity, and are analogous to endowment effects created by another person's successes or failures; in the four "cold relationship" rows they refer to malicious pleasure and envy/disappointment, which are essentially reverse endowment effects. The warmth–cold or positive–negative relationship is a continuous variable, with intensity of the effect controlled by the intensity of the relationship, analogous to the salience parameter implicit in the original E–C framework.

The cell means presented are derived from a study (Brandstatter, 2000, study 2) where participants were presented with a set of salary comparisons between two individuals who varied in the warmth of their relationship and how self-relevant salary was to them both. Participants rated the satisfaction of three target individuals 21 times to indicate satisfaction with salary comparisons that ranged from −30% to +30%. We provide the approximate cell means for satisfaction at the 20% and +20% salary comparison level (estimated from aggregated regression lines, rescaled to a −5 to +5 range of dissatisfaction–satisfaction).

The close, warm relationships used were still relatively distant (friends from school years), so we would expect a relatively weak effect of empathy compared to contrast. Looking at the cell means, we can see that all downward comparisons led to satisfaction and all upward comparisons led to dissatisfaction, consistent with the dominance of contrast. The highest level of satisfaction was, as predicted by the Contrast–Empathy theory, in the negative relationship, relevant dimension, downward comparison cell. The highest level of dissatisfaction, again consistent with Brandstatter's predictions, was in the negative relationship, relevant dimension, upward comparison cell. The overall grand mean is −0.6, which is consistent with losses looming larger than gains. The empathy effects cannot be isolated, but the relative contrast effects between low and high relevance can be computed for every matched pairs of cells. The largest relative contrast effect is for comparing the high and low relevance version of the cold relationship upward comparison (difference = 1.5), and smallest for the warm relationship upward comparison (difference = 0.08) implying that the power of the contrast effect is also somewhat sensitive to the quality of the interpersonal relationship.

An interesting application of the Contrast–Empathy model is to intergroup or international comparisons of well-being. It is often assumed that a relatively wealthy individual in a poor country would feel highly satisfied because of the dominance of local comparisons. However, the Contrast–Empathy model implies that individuals who identify with their own region might experience off-setting feelings of empathy and contrast relative to the worse-off majority around them. Helliwell, Barrington-Leigh, Harris, and Huang (2010) examined direct and contextual effects of income and social resources on life satisfaction across 50 nations. They found that having good friends had substantial positive effects both at an individual level and a contextual level. The individual-level coefficient represents the comparison of individuals within a country who have friends versus those who do not—a standard social support finding. The contextual effect is more intriguing, as it represents the comparison of individuals who come from countries where people, on average, are more or less likely to have friends. This, then, is a societal empathetic endowment effect à la Brandstatter.

## The affective Endowment–Contrast model

Brandstatter's model of social comparison was developed by integrating several approaches in the social comparison literature. Despite this, the resulting model is a close analogue to the E–C model with additional emotional processing. Cheng (2004) directly applied the E–C framework to emotion and mood, using emotional experience rather than symbolic consumption as the building blocks of satisfaction. Cheng's approach builds upon Bradburn's (1969) affect balance model, which posits that overall well-being is a function of the difference between positive affect (PA) and negative affect (NA). However, Cheng notes that this linear discrepancy model ignores context or interaction effects that may arise through adaptation: positive affect may have a greater impact when negative affect is predominant. "When life is smooth, the effect of adding more positive experiences may be marginal." Thus, the affective approach predicts that overall life satisfaction can be modeled by a linear additive term and an interactive term, so that affective well-being = (PA − NA) + (PA × NA). According to Cheng's definition, the main effects of PA and NA are equivalent to endowment effects, and the interaction is equivalent to contrast effects. Following Tversky and Griffin's original approach, the affect model examines the effect of the past on the present; unlike the original model, it looks at the aggregated balance of positive and negative emotions, not on the effect of a specific past experience. Thus, the focus is no longer on the direct and indirect effects of a given event on well-being, but on how a given emotional experience will have a different effect on well-being depending on the makeup of the rest of the set of experiences. To test this model, Cheng collected diary data twice daily for 4 weeks using a set of adjectives representing current positive and negative affect. The average levels of PA and NA (and their interaction) were then related to the reported general life satisfaction a week after the conclusion of the 4 weeks. Significant regression coefficients were found for PA, NA, and their interaction, although the effect size for PA dwarfed the other terms. A plot of the relevant interaction (slopes for PA on satisfaction broken down by high NA, + 1 SD, and low NA, −1 SD) showed that the effect of PA was stronger for those high in NA. This is consistent with the view that PA has a greater impact against a background of regular NA (or conversely that PA has a reduced impact—perhaps because of adaptation—against a background of more positive than negative affect).

## Applications of the Endowment–Contrast Model to Real-Life Experiences

Partly motivated by the capacity of some Holocaust survivors to find meaning and satisfaction in comparing the present to the worst times of life (and of others to reflect long and painfully on those terrible times), Liberman, Boehm, Lyubomirsky, and Ross (2009) examined the dispositional tendency to use contrast and endowment strategically to enhance happiness. Their central tool was a measure of propensity to dwell on negative or positive endowments from the past (thereby contributing negatively or positively to well-being) versus negative or positive contrasts from the past (thereby contributing positively or negatively to well-being). Notably, endowment self-report items measured both the tendency to re-experience past events ("When I think about happy events in the past, I often smile or laugh"; "I sometimes dwell on unhappy past events and even relive them in a way that makes me feel sad and depressed") and the tendency to strategically use such memories to boost happiness or to reflect on how the past continues to poison the present ("When I recall happy events in the past, I realize how much they enrich my life"; "When I recall unhappy events in the past, I realize what a negative effect they had on my life"). Recall that endowment effects are assumed to be greatest for events that are highly salient, easy to recall, and informative about the present.

Contrast items measured the self-reported tendency to use the past as a standard of comparison ("The comparison of the present with unhappy past events makes me feel content and grateful"; "When I recall particular happy events in the past, the contrast with the present makes me a little sad and depressed"), but for negative contrast, also implicated a belief in a generally declining quality of life ("I often think about ways in which things have gotten worse for me than they used to be").

The authors related these propensity measures to a general measure of dispositional affective happiness ("Some people are generally very happy. They enjoy life regardless of what is going on..."). Across three samples in Israel and the USA, the authors find consistent moderate correlations (with the appropriate signs) between dispositional happiness and self-reported tendencies to use positive endowment, negative endowment, and negative contrast as inputs to present happiness. Support for the positive contrast strategy was found only in the American sample. These results were found whether the E–C propensity items referred to the past in general or to memories of a specific past happy or unhappy event.

As the authors note, the findings are consistent with the claim that happy and unhappy people think about the past differently, but cannot distinguish between an account where happiness drives the use of memories and one where the use of memories drives happiness. Like each of the application studies, the Liberman et al. investigation highlights the difference between the original conception of endowment as a symbolic, cognitive effect and the broader, more experiential conception that includes savoring, rumination, and emotional reliving of the event.

The complexities of interpreting natural experiences in the E–C framework explains why so few naturalistic studies have followed this model. The general statement of the theory—beginning with the narrow account of the dual functions of past hedonic experiences on current life satisfaction and broadening to an account that included "memories and expectations; successes and failures of the past, hopes and fears of the future"—is a conceptual framework for thinking about the role of endowment and contrast in measurements of well-being. The extensions of the model to social comparisons and emotional experiences serve to further broaden the toolbox of applications.

## Utility versus Well-Being, Choice versus Judgment

Psychologists and sociologists talk of well-being, happiness, and satisfaction whereas economists traditionally restrict their vocabulary of motivation to the concept of utility. However, even utility can be used in two different senses (Kahneman & Tversky, 1984): experience utility, the pleasure or pain from the actual experience of an event or outcome, and decision utility, the anticipated gain in pleasure at the time of choosing (or *predicted utility*; Kahneman & Varey, 1992). Experience utility, like well-being, is generally assessed by judgmental methods such as ratings, pricing, or satisfaction thermometers. Decision value is generally inferred from choices, typically binary in nature. Most naturally, judgments take place after the event is experienced; choices take place in advance and require an assessment of predicted utility.

However, even when choice and judgment are both made prospectively and broadly measure decision utility, they differ in how they are affected by contrast and endowment. Given the prominence of choice in economic measurement, we first explore the choice–judgment discrepancy and review relevant research before following up the more general issue of how well-being measures differ in their sensitivity to endowment and contrast.

There are two key methodological differences between choice and judgment, both of which have implications for the role of contrast and endowment. First, choice requires a binary outcome whereas judgment requires a continuous measurement scale. The forced-choice methodology favors the option that is highest on the most important dimension (the "prominence effect"; Tversky, Sattath, & Slovic, 1988) because it leads to a search for a single dominating reason to choose. A continuous scale of judgment leads to a broader focus on combining multiple inputs to form the final judgment (Slovic et al., 1990). In general, endowment (the actual amount of money or pleasure or pain) is a more prominent or justifiable reason to choose than contrast, and hence dominates choice, whereas judgment is based on a combination of both contrast and endowment.

Second, choice is fundamentally comparative whereas judgment is largely absolute. The focus in choice is what is different between options. This leads salient qualitative differences across conditions to loom larger in choice than in judgment. Consider two job scenarios that are comparable in every way but differ by $50 in annual salary. If all else is equal, everyone will choose the job with the higher salary, a huge effect size. Yet the difference in judged attractiveness of each job taken alone will surely be vanishingly small.

Consider the related versus unrelated stock market games described earlier to make this point: Clearly, everyone would choose the negative contrast condition (where total earnings were $10 based on an initial reward of $6 and a final reward of $4) rather than the positive contrast condition (where total earnings were $6 based on an initial reward of $2 and a final reward of $4) if they compared the two outcomes. In this case, the chooser thinks not about happiness or satisfaction, or the processes that would lead to either, but simply about the dominating argument that $10 is better than $6. Yet, the satisfaction judgments were indistinguishable across conditions because they reflected the joint (countervailing) effects of contrast and endowment.

Tversky and Griffin tested this intuition in a job choice scenario experiment that equated endowment with total annual salary and contrast with the standard of comparison salary. The results have been widely cited by economists, although, as we later describe, its implied methodological critique of using choice as the sole or privileged measure of utility has not affected economic practice. Student participants were asked to imagine they had a job offer as a junior editor at two magazines: one position paid $35,000 as an annual salary, but most other similar workers received $38,000 per year; the second position paid $33,000, with most similar workers receiving $30,000. Participants were asked either to choose the job they would take, or to indicate which job would make them happier. The reversal in observed "preference" between conditions was dramatic: 84% of participants chose the job with the higher salary (endowment) and higher comparison level (negative contrast), but 62% expected to be more satisfied with the job that was defined by a lower comparison level (positive contrast) and lower salary (endowment).

To examine whether these results generalized to actual experiences, Tversky and Griffin (1991) assessed satisfaction versus choice with rewards from a pair of two-part competitive games. The design placed particularly strong pressures on participants to be consistent across measures as it assessed satisfaction and choice within subjects, with the choice coming *after* the measure of satisfaction with the two outcomes. Any participant who showed a "reversal" from satisfaction to choice was thus fully aware of his or her own inconsistency. Contrast was created by providing feedback on both practice and reward trials—improvement created a positive contrast and declining performance created a negative contrast. Each participant improved in one game, but received a higher reward for the other game ($3 versus $1). After each game, participants rated their satisfaction with their performance; after completing both tasks and both satisfaction ratings, participants were asked to choose which task they would choose to do. For those participants who gave non-identical ratings of satisfaction across the two tasks, a little more than half (54%) expressed greater satisfaction with the positive contrast, low-payoff task. However, 75% of those also chose the negative contrast, high-payoff task, again consistent with the notion that the payoff, representing endowment, loomed larger in choice than in judgment, presumably because it provided a more compelling reason to choose.

It is noteworthy that econometric analyses of the relation between well-being and whether one's neighbors are richer or poorer than oneself support the notion that relative income can drive happiness (Luttmer, 2005): controlling for one's own salary, having higher earning neighbors is associated with lower levels of happiness, consistent with a contrast effect, and having a higher standard of comparison income within a job category is associated with lower levels of job satisfaction (Clark & Oswald, 1996).

The implications of the choice–judgment discrepancy for the economic study of well-being can be seen by its application to Pareto optimality. This simple economic principle defines an acceptable (or Pareto optimal) allocation of resources as one that improves everyone's lot: the change entails no losers, only winners. As a choice criterion, this has considerable force; one should prefer a world where one's lot is improved, even if other people's lots are improved more. However, judged (and experienced) satisfaction may go down, not up, under Pareto optimality. Consider an organization that provides 100% salary increases to a few executives, and 5% salary increases to everyone else. Surely, everyone in the organization would choose this state of affairs over the previous state. All the same, the negative effects of the contrast and comparison would make most of the individuals less satisfied with their lot.

Another dramatic example of the choice–judgment discrepancy comes from a study of Olympic athletes (Medvec, Madey, & Gilovich, 1995): silver medalists feel worse than lower-performing athletes, presumably because of the pain of comparison. Yet, it is absurd to believe that an athlete would choose to come in fourth or sixth and give up the endowment value of a second-place finish in order to avoid the painful contrast effect. This colorful example also highlights the subtle variety of comparison processes that can create contrast: the silver medalists did not use the gold medalists as the standard, but instead were haunted by the ease of imagining themselves on the gold podium.[2] This example invites the question of what choice measures measure, and what is utility, if people systematically make choices that do not maximize their experienced pleasure.

In a series of survey studies, Solnick and Hemenway (1998, 2005; see also Alpizar, Carlsson, & Johansson-Stenman, 2005; Carlsson, Johansson-Stenman, & Martinsson, 2007) examined the role of comparison/interpersonal contrast (which they term "positional concerns") across a range of goods, including salary, attractiveness, and vacation time. For example participants were asked to choose between a world in which they earn $50,000 and others earn $25,000, and a world in which they earn $100,000 and others earn $200,000; and between a world in which they have 2 weeks of vacation time and others have 1 week, and a world in which they have 4 weeks of vacation time and others have 8 weeks. Respondents preferred being relatively more attractive than others, were indifferent about relative versus absolute education and relative versus absolute salary, and strongly preferred a longer absolute vacation than a comparatively longer (but absolutely shorter) vacation. The authors argue that positional concerns (i.e., contrast and comparison) need to be incorporated into public policy. "Benefits to the rich will hurt the poor if the poor, like everyone else, care about their relative standing. The majority of respondents to our survey rejected the prospect of everyone becoming richer if it was accompanied by a fall in their own relative standing" (Solnick and Hemenway, 1998).

A more general explanatory account that characterizes domains where choice may deviate from judgment, and contrast will be more important is the evaluability model (Hsee, 1996; Hsee, Loewenstein, Blount, & Bazerman, 1999). According to this framework, choice is a paradigmatic example of a "joint" or comparative evaluation mode whereas judgment is a paradigmatic example of a "single" or non-comparative evaluation mode. The tendency for joint evaluations such as choice to deviate from single evaluations such as satisfaction judgment is accentuated when the stimulus dimensions are low in "evaluability", that is, when it is difficult to determine what is a high and low level of the stimulus without a guiding comparison or norm. For example, temperature is inherently evaluable—it is clear that

---

[2] Van Dijk and Zeelenberg (2005) show that counterfactual regret is controlled by the similarity between the obtained and the foregone object, consistent with the E–C account.

life in a city with a mean temperature of 4°C will be dominated by feeling cold, while life in a city with a mean temperature of 30°C will be dominated by feeling hot. It is possible to make an informed judgment of the impact of temperature on one's quality of life just by considering the temperature in a single city. On the other hand, money is not intrinsically evaluable and hence is difficult to weigh without a norm or comparative option.

This joint-separate evaluation framework was motivated by an early example of Bazerman, Loewenstein, and White (1992), where respondents were asked to choose (joint evaluation: comparative) or rate (single evaluation: absolute) which settlement option was more acceptable: $600 to the self and $800 to a neighbor, or $500 to the self and $500 to the neighbor. Given that money is not intrinsically evaluable, participants who *rated* the acceptability of one option at a time focused mostly on the relative information (the negative contrast); thus the equal payoff was rated as more acceptable by 71% of respondents. However, when participants were asked to indicate (in a comparative mode) which option was more acceptable, 75% selected the unequal, higher payoff (better endowment, less contrast). Money—not intrinsically evaluable when evaluated singly—loomed large when comparison made the differences in one's own payoffs prominent. Another example brings the evaluability concept into the domain of well-being: Hsee (1993) presented participants with two hypothetical salary options, a higher absolute amount with a decreasing trend over 4 years, and one with a lower absolute amount but an increasing trend over time. In joint evaluation mode (choice), participants slightly preferred the higher overall salary because the mean difference was highly salient; however, in the separate evaluation mode (judgment) participants clearly preferred the option with the increasing salary trajectory. Again, this analysis using evaluability coincides with the endowment-contrast account of the choice–judgment discrepancy.

The evaluability and E–C approaches to the choice–judgment discrepancy converge in these examples, but they are based on related but distinct explanatory frameworks. For example, the job choice salary reversal example from Tversky and Griffin (1991) compared choice and satisfaction measures that are both in a joint evaluation mode, and so cannot be explained by evaluability. The evaluability framework adds to the E–C framework two important guiding principles. The first is that joint evaluation (choice) will tend to systematically overpredict the impact of non-evaluable dimensions relative to single evaluation judgment—or to experience—and tend to systematically underpredict the impact of highly evaluable dimensions (Hsee, Hastie, & Chen, 2008). Second, the evaluability framework provides an explanation for which types of resources will be preferred for absolute magnitude versus positional advantage: resources such as intelligence and attractiveness, which are inherently non-evaluable without a standard of comparison, will be chosen for positional advantage; resources such as days of vacation or hours of sleep, which are inherently evaluable even without a standard, will be chosen for absolute advantage. Putting the two principles together, and realizing that endowment will generally be less evaluable than contrast, which carries with it a standard of comparison, should help provide a roadmap to those areas of life where contrast versus endowment will dominate people's choices, and whether such choices will be reflected in experience.

The purpose of the E–C analysis of the choice–judgment discrepancy was to highlight the possibility that there may be no single gold standard of well-being or utility. However, John Stuart Mill (1863) was clear in his mind that choice—and the comparative stance—is superior, and that the associated focus on the most prominent dimension was justified, especially when that dimension referred to a more cultured outlook.

Now it is an unquestionable fact that those who are equally acquainted with, and equally capable of appreciating and enjoying both, do give a most marked preference to the manner of existence which employs their higher faculties .... It is better to be a human being dissatisfied than a pig satisfied; better to be a Socrates dissatisfied than a fool satisfied. *And if the fool, or the pig, is of a different opinion, it is because they know only their own side of the question.* The other party to the comparison knows both sides. (p. 14, italics added)

## On the assessment of well-being: the role of endowment and contrast

One of the major areas of progress in the study of well-being over the 20 years since the publication of the E–C framework has been the clarification of the status of different measures of well-being. The vast number of well-being measures can be roughly classified into four clusters: affective measures, happiness measures, life satisfaction measures, and comparative life satisfaction measures. The measurement clusters move from the most affective and tied to immediate experience (based on immediate feelings and described as measuring hedonic well-being (Stone, Schwartz, Broderick, & Deaton, 2010) or objective happiness (Kahneman, 1999)) to the most cognitive and summative (based on systematic thought and reflection, described as global well-being).

What lessons does the E–C framework have for understanding the role of different measures? The key question, as always, is the contribution to expressed well-being from the direct immediate experience, the direct contextual endowment, and the indirect contextual contrast. At first thought, one might imagine that the more affectively immediate measures would be more responsive to endowment whereas the more reflective measures would be relatively more responsive to contrast and comparison. However, the evidence is mixed. Consider immediate experience sampling measures, a family of measures ranging from asking respondents about their contemporaneous experience of positive and negative emotions to asking respondents to keep diaries of emotions experienced during specific events, either at specific times of the day or at randomly indicated times. Kahneman, Krueger, and colleagues (e.g., Kahneman & Krueger, 2006) have suggested a U-index to summarize such measures (an index assessing the relative time spent in unpleasant emotions).

In a cross-country analysis, Kahneman and Krueger (2006) found that French women report spending more time in a pleasurable state than American women, but nonetheless report lower life satisfaction—in other words, a contradiction between measures of "objective" and "subjective" well-being. The authors interpret this as a possible extremity bias for Americans, and conclude that caution is warranted for cross-national comparisons of global satisfaction. In addition, it seems possible that the cultural reversal arises due to different standards of comparison, which weigh more heavily in satisfaction than in immediate pleasure. Momentary experiences show only a small impact of life circumstances, whereas satisfaction reflects income and material wealth, as described as follows.

Diener, Kahneman, and colleagues have contrasted the relation between income and immediate affective responses and that of income and global measures of satisfaction (Diener, Kahneman, Tov, & Arora, 2010). The measure of satisfaction that is least directly influenced by affect is the Cantril ladder (Cantril, 1965), which asks respondents to report (on a visual ladder) where their life falls from the worst possible to the best possible life imaginable.

The Cantril ladder is a particularly interesting measure from the viewpoint of the E-C framework because it contradicts the usual rule that more cognitive and less experiential measures are more reflective of contrast. By asking for a comparative judgment with truly global anchors (the worst versus best possible life brings to mind the extremes that the world has to offer) the ladder minimizes the effect of contrast, at least in the judgment process. Thus, to the extent that individuals face different contexts—whether national, neighborhood, or notional comparisons—these should have minimal effects on the ladder, as long as people can imagine roughly similar best and worst possible worlds. This is consistent with the finding that the ladder is most responsive to objective circumstances in international comparisons of well-being.

## Concluding Remarks

The focus of research on happiness has changed dramatically in the 20 years since the E-C framework was first presented. In particular, the field has a much clearer understanding of the complexities of different measurement procedures. Nonetheless, a cautionary note about accepting well-being measures at face value is still valuable. Consider the recent announcement about the introduction of a "well-being index" to the UK (as well as to many other European countries).

> One government source said: "If you want to know things – Should I live in Exeter rather than London? What will it do to my quality of life? – you need a large enough sample size and if you have a big sample, and have more than one a year, then people can make a proper analysis on what to do with their life." (Stratton, *The Guardian*, November 14 2010)

The notion of a "well-being index" presupposes that a single number, or at most a vector of numbers, will be sufficient to indicate whether people in London or Exeter are happier or more satisfied. However, the E-C framework implies that the way that people think about their lives, as well as the questions they are asked, can fundamentally shift—even reverse—their preferences across situations. Thus, the E-C framework can still play a useful role in preventing a simplistic—and hence misleading—approach to measuring well-being.

## References

Alpizar, F., Carlsson, F., & Johansson-Stenman, O. (2005). How much do we care about absolute versus relative income and consumption? *Journal of Economic Behavior and Organization*, 56, 405–421.

Bazerman, M. H., Loewenstein, G. F., & White, S. B. (1992). Reversals of preference in allocation decisions: Judging an alternative versus choosing among alternatives. *Administrative Science Quarterly*, 37, 220–240.

Bradburn, N. M. (1969). *The structure of psychological well-being*. Chicago, IL: Aldine.

Brandstatter, E. (2000). Comparison based satisfaction: Contrast and empathy. *European Journal of Social Psychology*, 30, 673–703.

Brickman, P., & Campbell, D. T. (1971). Hedonic relativism and planning the good society. In M. H. Appley (Ed.), *Adaptation-level theory: A symposium* (pp. 287–302). New York, NY: Academic Press.

Brickman, P., Coates, D., & Janoff-Bulman, R. (1978). Lottery winners and accident victims: Is happiness relative? *Journal of Personality and Social Psychology, 36*, 917–927.

Cantril, H. (1965). *The pattern of human concerns*. New Brunswick, NJ: Rutgers University Press.

Carlsson, F., Johansson-Stenman, O., Martinsson, P., (2007). Do you enjoy having more than others? Survey evidence of positional goods. *Economica, 74*, 586–598.

Cheng, S. T. (2004). Endowment and contrast: The role of positive and negative emotions on well-being appraisal. *Personality and Individual Differences, 37*, 905–915; 28, 195–223.

Clark, A. E., & Oswald, A. J. (1996). Satisfaction and comparison income. *Journal of Public Economics, 61*, 359–381.

Diener, E., Kahneman, D., Tov, W. & Arora, R. (2010). Income's association with judgments of life versus feelings. In E. Diener, J. F. Helliwell, & D. Kahneman, (Eds.), *International differences in well-being* (pp. 3–15). Oxford, UK: Oxford University Press.

Easterlin, R. A. (1974). Does economic growth improve the human lot? In P. A. David, & M. W. Reder (Eds.), *Nations and households in economic growth: Essays in honor of Moses Abramovitz* (pp. 89–125). New York, NY: Academic Press.

Festinger, L. (1954). A theory of social comparison processes. *Human Relations, 7*, 117–140.

Groot, W., & van den Brink, H. M. (1999). Job satisfaction and preference drift. *Economics Letters, 33*, 363–367.

Helliwell, J. F., Barrington-Leigh, C., Harris, A., & Huang, H. (2010). International evidence on the social context of well-being. *International Differences in Well-Being, 38*, 291–328.

Helson, H. (1964). *Adaptation-level theory*. New York, NY: Harper and Row.

Hsee, C. K. (1993). *When trend of monetary outcomes matters: Separate versus joint evaluation and judgment of feelings versus choice*. Unpublished manuscript, The University of Chicago, Chicago, IL.

Hsee, C. K. (1996). The evaluability hypothesis: An explanation for preference reversals between joint and separate evaluations of alternatives. *Organizational Behavior and Human Decision Processes, 67*, 247–257.

Hsee, C. K., Hastie, R., & Chen, J. (2008). Hedonomics: bridging decision research with happiness research. *Perspectives on Psychological Sciences, 3*, 224–243.

Hsee, C. K., Loewenstein, G. F., Blount, S., & Bazerman, M. H. (1999). Preference reversals between joint and separate evaluations of options: A review and theoretical analysis. *Psychological Bulletin, 125*, 576–590.

Kahneman, D. (1999). Objective happiness. In D. Kahneman, E. Diener, & N. Schwarz (Eds.), *Well-being: The foundations of hedonic psychology* (pp. 3–25). New York, NY: Russell Sage Foundation.

Kahneman, D., & Krueger, A. B. (2006). Developments in the measurement of subjective well-being. *Journal of Economic Perspectives, 20*, 3–24.

Kahneman, D., & Tversky, A. (1979). Prospect theory: An analysis of decision under risk. *Econometrica, 47*, 263–292.

Kahneman, D., & Tversky, A. (1984). Choices, values and frames. *American Psychologist, 39*, 341–350.

Kahneman, D., & Varey, C. (1992). Experiences extended across time: Evaluation of moments and episodes. *Journal of Behavioral Decision Making, 5*, 169–185.

Liberman, N., & Trope, Y. (1998). The role of feasibility and desirability consideration in near and distant future decisions: A test of temporal construal theory. *Journal of Personality and Social Psychology, 75*, 5–18.

Liberman, V., Boehm, J. K., Lyubomirsky, S., & Ross, L. D. (2009). Happiness and memory: Affective significance of endowment and contrast. *Emotion, 9*, 666–680.

Luttmer, E. F. P. (2005). Neighbors as negatives: Relative earnings and well-being. *Quarterly Journal of Economics, 120*, 963–1002.

Medvec, V. H., Madey, S. F., & Gilovich, T. (1995). When less is more: Counterfactual thinking and satisfaction among Olympic medalists. *Journal of Personality and Social Psychology, 69*, 603–610.

Mill, J. S. (1863). *Utilitarianism*. London, UK: Parker, Son, and Bourn.

Parducci, A. (1984). Value judgment: Toward a relational theory of happiness. In J. B. Eiser (Ed.), *Attitudinal judgment* (pp. 3–22). New York, NY: Springer Verlag.

Ross, Jr., W. T., & Simonson, I. (1991). Evaluations of pairs of experiences: A preference for happy endings. *Journal of Behavioral Decision Making, 4*, 155–161.

Rota, L. M., & Zellner, D. A. (2007). The categorization effect in hedonic contrast: Experts differ from novices. *Psychonomic Bulletin & Review, 14*, 179–183.

Schwarz, N., & Bless, H. (1992). Constructing reality and its alternatives: An inclusion/exclusion model of assimilation and contrast effects in social judgment. In L. L. Martin, & A. Tesser (Eds.), *The construction of social judgments* (pp. 217–245). Hillsdale, NJ: Erlbaum.

Schwarz, N., & Strack, F. (1999). Reports of subjective well-being: Judgmental processes and their methodological implications. In D. Kahneman, E. Diener & N. Schwarz (Eds.), *Well-being: The foundations of hedonic psychology* (pp. 61–84). New York. NY: Russell Sage Foundation.

Slovic, P., Griffin, D., & Tversky, A. (1990). Compatibility effects in judgment and choice. In R. M. Hogarth (Ed.), *Insights in decision making* (pp. 5–27). Chicago, IL: University of Chicago Press.

Solnick, S. J., & Hemenway, D. (1998). Is more always better? A survey of positional concerns. *Journal of Economic Behavior & Organization, 37*, 373–83.

Solnick, S. J., & Hemenway, D. (2005). Are positional concerns stronger in some domains than in others? *American Economic Review, 95*, 147–151.

Stone, A. A., Schwartz, J. E., Broderick, J. E., & Deaton, A. (2010). A snapshot of the age distribution of psychological well-being in the United States. *Proceedings of the National Academy of Sciences of the United States of America, 107*, 9985–9990.

Stouffer, S. A., Suchman, E. A., DeVinney, L. C., Star, S. A., & Williams, R. M., Jr. (1949). *The American soldier*. Princeton, NJ: Princeton University Press.

Strack, F., Schwarz, N., & Gschneidinger, E. (1985). Happiness and reminiscing: The role of time perspective, affect, and mode of thinking. *Journal of Personality and Social Psychology, 47*, 1460–1469.

Stratton, A. (2010, November 14). Happiness index to gauge Britain's national mood. *The Guardian*. Retrieved from http://www.guardian.co.uk/

Tesser, A. (1988). Toward a self-evaluation maintenance model of social behavior. In L. Berkowitz (Ed.), *Advances in experimental social psychology* (pp. 181–227). New York, NY: Academic Press.

Tesser, A. (1991). Emotion in social comparison and reflection processes. In J. Suls & T. A. Wills (Eds.), *Social comparison: Contemporary theory and research* (pp. 115–145). Hillsdale, NJ: Erlbaum.

Tversky, A., & Griffin, D. (1991). Endowment and contrast in judgments of well-being. In F. Strack, M. Argyle, & N. Schwarz (Eds.), *Subjective well-being: An interdisciplinary perspective* (pp. 101–118). Oxford, UK: Pergamon.

Tversky, A., Sattath, S., & Slovic, P. (1988). Contingent weighting in judgment and choice. *Psychological Review, 95*, 371–384.

Tversky, A., Slovic, P., & Kahneman, D. (1990). The causes of preference reversal. *American Economic Review, 80*, 204–217.

Van Dijk, E., & Zeelenberg, M. (2005). On the psychology of 'if only': Regret and the comparison of factual and counterfactual outcomes. *Organizational Behavior and Human Decision Processes, 97*, 152–160.

CHAPTER 5

# PAST, PRESENT, AND FUTURE OF FLOW

ANTONELLA DELLE FAVE

Università degli Studi di Milano, Italy

FLOW, or optimal experience, is a complex and highly structured state of consciousness, which contributes to shaping individuals' developmental pathways. This chapter will provide an overview of the theoretical foundations of flow and of its potential as an intervention tool to promote well-being in various domains. The historical context of flow conceptualization, as well as future research directions, will be outlined.

## FLOW EXPERIENCE: ITS FEATURES AND ITS DEVELOPMENTAL ROLE

Mihaly Csikszentmihalyi first described flow experience in a book titled *Beyond Boredom and Anxiety* (1975). He had identified this peculiarly positive and complex state of mind through interviews with people whose work or leisure life involved engaging and challenging tasks, such as performing surgery, creating art, climbing mountains, or playing chess. These people unanimously reported experiences of deep involvement in performing such tasks; more specifically, they described the perception of high challenges, deep concentration, absorption, enjoyment, control of the situation, clear goals, and intrinsic gratification.

Csikszentmihalyi labeled this experience as flow to synthetically express the feeling of fluidity and continuity in concentration and action described by most participants. He summarized the factors related to flow experiences into nine dimensions (1975): clear goals; immediate feedback; high challenges matched with adequate personal skills; merging of action and awareness; concentration on the task at hand; perceived control of the situation; loss of self-consciousness; altered sense of time; and intrinsic motivation. These nine dimensions were confirmed by a great number of studies. Due to its pervasive positivity, flow was also defined as optimal experience, and the two terms are often used interchangeably (Csikszentmihalyi & Csikszentmihalyi, 1988).

Studies conducted on samples widely differing in culture, age, health conditions, educational level, and occupation show that flow can occur during very different activities or contexts of daily life, such as work, study, sports, arts and crafts, and social interactions (Csikszentmihalyi & Csikszentmihalyi, 1988; Csikszentmihalyi & Lefevre, 1989; Haworth & Evans, 1995; Jackson & Csikszentmihalyi, 1999; Massimini & Delle Fave, 2000; Persson, Eklund, & Isacsson, 1999). The role of contextual dimensions in fostering flow has been investigated, especially as concerns family (Hektner, 2001; Rathunde, 2001) and school (Shernoff & Csikszentmihalyi, 2009). However, regardless of the ongoing task, the onset of flow is associated to a specific condition: the task has to be challenging enough to require the mobilization of personal skills, promoting concentration and engagement. Repetitive and low-information activities are very rarely associated with flow, while complex activities requiring specific capabilities, autonomous initiative, and focused attention are widely reported. These studies also shed light on the psychological structure of flow. It comprises a cognitive and stable core, including high concentration and control of the situation. These components do not show remarkable variations across samples and activities (Delle Fave & Massimini, 2005a). On the contrary, affective and motivational variables widely vary across activities, according to their compulsory or voluntary nature.

Optimal experience shows an intrinsically dynamic aspect, which is embedded in the perceived match between high challenges and adequate personal skills. This match is dynamic in that the perception of high challenges promotes the increase in the related skills; increased competence, in its turn, encourages the individual to search for more complex challenges that will require higher capabilities in order to be faced. This virtuous cycle fosters development through both the ceaseless acquisition of increasingly complex information and the refinement of skills in specific activities and domains. This process, defined as *psychological selection* (Csikszentmihalyi & Massimini, 1985), fosters growth and identity building, in that it orients individuals' preferential cultivation of a specific set of interests, relations, values, and goals throughout life. Optimal experience can be considered the "psychic compass" orienting psychological selection and supporting the developmental trajectory each individual autonomously builds and follows throughout life (Massimini & Delle Fave, 2000).

Given the interdependence of individuals and culture, the growth of complexity at the individual level involves a constructive information exchange with the environment. Through the harmonization of individual pursuits and achievements with environmental opportunities for action, human beings can actively promote changes which enhance the complexity of their cultural system. From this perspective, the role of flow is twofold: It supports the preferential replication of the associated activities within one's own life span, at the same time promoting the survival and spreading of such activities, or any other kind of information, within the culture (Csikszentmihalyi & Massimini, 1985). Moreover, individuals are evolving systems; they constantly revise their world representations and interpretations through new configurations of information and new attributions of meaning that can be used to solve new problems, develop new skills, and shape new ideas. With the support of optimal experience, the human ability to select and to create challenges that enhance psychic complexity can be considered the basis of cultural change (Delle Fave, 2007).

## The Assessment of Flow

Several instruments have been developed to study optimal experience. The Flow Questionnaire (FQ, Csikszentmihalyi, 1975; Delle Fave & Massimini, 1988) investigates its occurrence and its psychological features. Participants are asked to read three quotations that describe flow, to report whether they have ever had similar experiences in their life, and—if yes—to list the associated activities. Participants are then asked to select from their list the activity promoting the most intense and pervasive states of flow, and to describe the associated experience through 0–8 point scales, investigating the nine flow dimensions listed earlier. FQ also explores the individual and environmental conditions which contribute to the onset and maintenance of flow (Massimini, Csikszentmihalyi, & Delle Fave, 1988).

The Flow State Scale (FSS) and the Dispositional Flow Scale (DFS) were developed and first validated in physical activity settings, and have since been used in other domains as well (Jackson & Eklund 2002; Jackson & Marsh, 1996). Both the DFS and FSS assess the nine dimensions of flow through 36 items on a scale ranging from 1 (strongly disagree) to 5 (strongly agree). More recently, two brief measures were developed: Short Flow, an aggregate measure drawn from the FSS, and Core Flow, focusing on the phenomenology of the flow experience itself (Martin & Jackson, 2008).

The Flow Short Scale (Engeser & Rheinberg, 2008) measures the components of flow through ten seven-point items. The WOrk-reLated Flow inventory (WOLF; Bakker, 2008) measures flow at work, however focusing on only three basic dimensions of the experience: absorption, enjoyment, and intrinsic motivation. Participants are asked to assess the frequency of these feelings during the preceding week (0 = never, 6 = every day).

The Experience Sampling Method (ESM; Csikszentmihalyi, Larson, and Prescott, 1977; Hektner, Schmidt, & Csikszentmihalyi, 2007) was not explicitly designed to study flow; rather, it has the more general aim of investigating contextual and experiential aspects of daily life through repeated self-reports filled out during the real-time unfolding of events and situations. During a standard ESM session, participants carry an electronic device for 1 week sending random signals six to eight times a day. At each signal reception, they are asked to fill out a form, investigating contextual aspects (such as ongoing activity, location, and companionship), and the perceived level of affective, cognitive, and motivational variables; satisfaction; short- and long-term importance of the activity; perceived challenges and skills. The raw values of each variable can be transformed into z-scores before analysis.

The information gathered through ESM allowed for the development of models to analyze the changes in the quality of experience according to the challenges/skills relationship. The first model (Massimini, Csikszentmihalyi, & Carli, 1987) identified eight different experiences, each of them characterized by a specific ratio between challenge and skill z-scores. As expected, flow proved to be associated with the above-average challenge/above-average skill condition. A subsequent more conservative model distinguished among four different experiences (Csikszentmihalyi & LeFevre, 1989), while another approach took the absolute value of the difference between challenge and skill as the basis for interpreting findings (Moneta & Csikszentmihalyi, 1996). All these models substantially confirmed the theoretical expectations.

## Flow and Cultures

Studies conducted in individualistic and collectivistic cultures showed consistencies in both the phenomenology and the contextual aspects of optimal experience (Delle Fave, 2007;

Delle Fave & Massimini, 2004, 2005a, 2005b). The psychological features of flow, and their variations according to the associated activities, were confirmed across cultures. However, these studies raised a crucial methodological and conceptual issue concerning the translation and interpretation of the English term "challenge". The problem originally emerged during the preparation of the first Italian version of FQ (Massimini, Csikszentmihalyi, & Delle Fave, 1986). Pilot studies showed that the literal translation of the term challenge was well suited for situations characterized by competition, external evaluation, and high social expectations, such as sport games, work, and study. However, it did not fit situations such as reading, painting, contemplating a landscape, or talking to a friend. In another study conducted with English-speaking Indian participants the same problem arose (Swarup & Delle Fave, 1999). Therefore, a new item was added to the FQ: "How much was the activity an opportunity for action and self-expression?" The differences observed in most participants' ratings of the two items confirmed the usefulness of this solution. Subsequent studies conducted in various non-Western cultures with the FQ and ESM included the double wording of the term challenge. Findings showed that the item emphasizing opportunities for action and self-expression better fit the theoretical expectations (Delle Fave & Massimini, 2004). Further investigations are needed to disentangle this topic, which seems to be related to differences in cultural emphasis on competition/achievement versus personal growth/self-expression. This aspect is particularly important when studying flow in collectivistic cultures and in societies valuing sharing and interconnectedness more than individual achievements.

Taking into account the cautions just described, cross-cultural studies confirmed that flow can foster optimal functioning, skill enhancement, and a fruitful information exchange with the environment through the creative engagement in self-selected tasks, independent of performance outcomes or social expectations. These aspects should be taken into account in interventions aimed at promoting individual and social empowerment, especially in situations of cultural change, in multicultural settings, and in international cooperation programs.

As concerns cultural change, the transition from rural life to industrialization often creates severe imbalances in the life of people and communities. At the individual level, complex and creative opportunities for optimal experience, such as traditional jobs, collective rituals, and handicrafts, are substituted by repetitive and mechanical tasks, passive leisure, and social isolation. The spreading of technology produces an increasing dependence on artifacts, more and more numerous and expensive, thus emphasizing socioeconomic differences. In developing countries only elite groups benefit from modernization facilities, whereas the majority, especially in the outskirts of urban areas, are forced to abandon the traditional lifestyle, without finding meaningful opportunities for action—and survival—in the new environment. Data collected in different cultural contexts have shown some of the negative effects of this phenomenon on the quality of experience (Delle Fave, Massimini & Bassi, 2011). On the other hand, these findings have also highlighted the positive role of the bicultural strategy, that is, the ability to preserve original traditions and, at the same time, to introduce new information in a cultural system, preserving its flexibility and stability (LaFromboise, Coleman, & Gerton, 1993). In particular, a study exploring the opportunities for optimal experiences reported by Navajo adolescents and young adults highlighted a balanced distribution of flow-related activities between traditional and modernized domains (Delle Fave, 1999). This bicultural strategy helps Navajo youth maintain the sense of belonging to their own tradition, while at the same time developing the skills and behaviors necessary to successfully integrate into American life. Similar findings were obtained among village girls studying in a boarding school in Uganda (Stokart, Cavallo, Fianco, & Lombardi, 2007) and among adolescents from Nepal (Delle Fave & Massimini, 2005a).

As concerns multicultural settings, immigrants and minorities often face integration difficulties. Investigating immigrants' perceived sources for optimal experience in the new environment and the quality of experience reported in daily life before and after migration can provide suggestions about their real opportunities for action and degree of acculturative stress. Psychosocial adjustment to a new culture can be related to several factors: the cultural distance between the homeland and the hosting country; immigrant status; job opportunities; and the availability of a social and family network in the hosting country. A study conducted among first-generation immigrants settled in Italy from four different cultures (Delle Fave & Bassi, 2009) showed that the individual and group level of psychosocial adjustment was related to the retrieval of flow in daily life, to the variety of activity domains associated with it, and to the positive evaluation of daily life challenges. Similarly, data gathered among Rom and Sinti communities settled in Italy suggested that the problems created by an often difficult intercultural relationship can be at least clarified through the evaluation of the quality of daily experience, life goals, and priorities perceived by the individuals (Delle Fave, Bassi, & Massimini, 2003). This information could help promote interaction and provide suggestions for the development of multicultural policies.

Finally, international cooperation programs are essential for well-being promotion in developing countries. However, intervention strategies are often based on Western models, unrelated to local traditions, and sometimes even culturally disruptive (Delle Fave & Massimini, 2004). A growing awareness of these problems led to the diffusion of CBR (community-based resources) centers in Asia, Africa, and South America. Their intervention directly relies on the competence and know-how of community members. The main inspiring principle of CBR is that a sustainable cultural development has to start from the efforts of the community, from the local awareness of priorities and from the choice of intervention strategies coherent and suited to the local culture. The effectiveness of CBR strategies in promoting individual well-being and social integration was investigated among young people with disabilities in Nepal and among adolescents who were rescued from street life in Brazil and Kenya (Delle Fave & Massimini, 2005b). Most participants in these studies reported flow in their daily life activities. Moreover, they often stressed the developmental role of facing daily challenges related to the lack of facilities typical of a developing country.

These results suggest that the positive impact of optimal experience on individual development can be included in the guidelines for designing interventions aimed at promoting individual and community empowerment, thus deserving specific attention as concerns social policies.

## The Misuse of Flow

The pursuit and attainment of positive experiences does not necessarily guarantee well-being and development in the long run. Some activities can be perceived as sources of optimal experience; they can be actively cultivated but eventually turn out to be inadequate means towards personal growth, self-actualization, and harmonious integration of the individual in the social context. This is true, for example, of drug addiction (Delle Fave & Massimini, 2003). A flow-like experience is often reported in the first period of drug intake. Besides substance-related variations, drugs induce the perception of merging with the environment, deep involvement, isolation from the surrounding world, and psychophysical well-being. However, the experience is chemically induced, and the individual becomes progressively disengaged from reality, dependent on drugs, unable to pursue other daily challenges, and physically weak and marginalized from the social context. Similar findings were detected in studies conducted among recreational and pathological gamblers (Wanner, Ladouceur, Auclair, & Vitaro, 2006). Participants reported each dimension of flow. However, pathological gamblers had lower mean levels with respect to the majority of flow dimensions, and higher levels of self-consciousness.

Negative outcomes also arise from antisocial activities, such as stealing, which have sometimes been quoted as sources of flow by homeless people and street youth. These activities are often articulated enough to offer high challenge and opportunities for engagement, and for the mobilization of a considerable amount of knowledge and technical abilities. Participants also underline the enjoyment in performing the activity for its own sake, regardless of material rewards (Delle Fave & Massimini, 2005b). But again, this behavior causes marginalization and psychosocial maladjustment. Similarly, flow-like absorption is often reported in combat situations, in which it contributes both to the subjective well-being and to the efficiency of soldiers (Harari, 2008).

These findings partly explain the difficulties usually arising in treatment programs addressed to addicts and maladjusted individuals (Downey, Rosengren & Donovan, 2001). Professionals and social workers often neglect the dramatic fact that drug intake and antisocial behaviors provide positive feelings and exciting experiences, even though transitory and substantially disruptive in the long run. Intervention should aim at the reconstruction of a new personal identity, through the engagement in activities complex enough to provide the individual with challenges and involvement, but also with opportunities for integration and participation (Downey et al., 2001).

## A Historical Perspective: Scientific Convergences and the Emergence of Flow

The emergence of Csikszentmihalyi's approach from previous research trends, as well as its singularity among other contemporary conceptualizations, can be better understood taking into account the cultural and scientific zeitgeist surrounding the development of flow theory. Particular attention will be paid to two core aspects of flow: the relationship between perceived challenges and personal skills, and intrinsic motivation.

Researchers started to study the effects of perceived challenges on behavior early on. Yerkes and Dodson (1908) pioneered this trend by investigating the modifiability of behavior in the dancing mouse. In particular, they were interested in identifying the intensity of a stimulus which most effectively promoted learning. Their findings highlighted an inverted U-shaped function between arousal and performance. More specifically, a certain amount of arousal (a disagreeable electric shock, in that case) facilitated learning or performance in mice. The optimal level of arousal, however, differed according to the difficulty of the task to be performed. If the task was complex, a low intensity of the electric stimulus was most effective in fostering learning; the opposite was true of relatively simple tasks, which required high levels of arousal.

Yerkes and Dodson's studies opened the way to the broader investigation of the impact of environmental demands on individual behavior, as well as to the exploration of individual resources that could be mobilized or acquired. Studies in the domain of education showed that engagement in optimally challenging situations captures attention and maximizes learning (Dewey, 1934; Piaget, 1950; Vygotsky, 1978). In the late 1950s, researchers focused on the pervasive human tendency to relate life events and situations to specific causes (Heider, 1958). Through the constructs of locus of causality (Weiner, 1972) and locus of control (Rotter, 1966) scholars attempted to investigate the beliefs people hold regarding the role and effectiveness of their abilities, skills and efforts in coping with life demands and events.

In the 1960s and 1970s the relationship between perceived *demands* and *resources* was investigated, moving from the assumption that environmental demands can be appraised as challenges and opportunities for action or—on the contrary—as threats and obstacles. The investigation of stress and coping provided an important contribution to this field. According to the cognitive-transactional theory developed by Lazarus (1966), stress results from an imbalance between perceived demands and resources. Stress arises when individuals perceive that they cannot adequately cope with demands or threats to their well-being (Lazarus, 1966). Antonovsky (1979) used the term salutogenesis to describe the processes and coping strategies that promote a good quality of life in adverse situations. He related this positive adaptation to the sense of coherence (SOC), a general orientation towards reality comprising three dimensions: comprehensibility, manageability, and meaningfulness. People with high SOC perceive adverse conditions as opportunities for development, and they feel confident to cope with them through the mobilization of personal and environmental resources. In 1977, Bandura formalized the construct of self-efficacy, which has found wide application in a great variety of domains, from occupational psychology to education. Self-efficacious people pursue high achievements and are relatively unaffected by failures, they show perseverance and an internal locus of control, and they primarily perceive challenges as opportunities for action and engagement (Bandura, 1997). In the same period Kobasa and her colleagues (Kobasa, 1979; Kobasa, Maddi, & Kahn, 1982) focused on personality traits that could mitigate the illness-provoking effects of stressful life events. They found that high-stress/low-illness individuals showed, by comparison with high-stress/high-illness individuals, higher control, commitment, and interest in change perceived as a challenge and not as a threat. These studies led to the formalization of the construct of *hardiness*.

In the field of motivation studies, incentive-based models were gradually supplanted by putting greater emphasis on the active and creative role of the individual. Maslow (1971) introduced the concept of self-actualization, a need which stems from the person's subjective perception of her own potentials and meanings. Maslow stressed the human capability to set goals that foster the implementation of complexity at the psychological and behavioral levels. In 1975, Edward Deci brought to the attention of researchers the concept of *intrinsic motivation*. Later on, this concept was included in the framework of Self-Determination Theory (SDT, Ryan & Deci, 2000). Research on SDT has shown that individuals tend to preferentially pursue self-determined goals, and this tendency is related to the three basic psychological needs for autonomy, competence, and relatedness. These needs do not necessarily provide individuals with extrinsic or material rewards. Rather, they promote the refinement of skills and competence in specific domains, the expansion of the interpersonal network, a creative and autonomous interaction with the environment, and well-being (Ryan & Deci, 2000).

Csikszentmihalyi's contribution emerged from this research context, with some characteristics that made it unique and innovative. First of all, it focused on the phenomenology of a conscious experience. Flow is a complex psychic event emerging from the integration of motivations, emotions, and cognitive evaluations. Secondly, flow experience is embodied in a living organism interacting moment-by-moment with the environment. To analyze it here and now, during its occurrence in the stream of daily life, scales and questionnaires are not sufficient. The development of ESM was crucial for understanding flow; moreover, it also shed light on the broader phenomenology of daily fluctuation of experience in relation to the interplay between perceived demand and resources. Thirdly, the study of flow revealed the growth mechanism embedded in the dynamic relationship between perceived challenges and skills, and its potential for promoting well-being and complexity in individuals. Finally, Csikszentmihalyi was a true pioneer in focusing on the positive side of experience and behavior. He brought to the attention of colleagues and practitioners the existence of a positive and complex state of mind, shared by all human beings as a part of normal psychological functioning, and acting as a powerful engine of development and self-actualization.

## Current Advancements and Future Directions

A promising field of exploration for researchers interested in flow is the identification of personality factors that can mediate the perceived balance between challenges and skills. Few studies have been conducted in this field till now. Abuhamdeh and Csikszentmihalyi (2009) focused on intrinsically motivated orientation (IMO) as a trait-level moderator of the relationship between level of difficulty and enjoyment among chess players. Findings showed that individuals high in IMO enjoyed more difficult games than individuals low in IMO. Moreover, the relationship between difficulty and enjoyment was curvilinear, thus confirming the key role of "optimal challenges" in promoting well-being and performance. Eisenberger, Jones, Stinglhamber, Shanock, and Randall (2005) detected that the combination of high skill and high challenge resulted in an enhanced experience at work for achievement-oriented employees, whereas employees low in need for achievement failed to experience high skill and challenge more favorably than other skill–challenge combinations. Engeser and Rheinberg (2008), through a longitudinal study with college students, showed that the challenge/skill relationship was moderated by the perceived importance of the activity and by the achievement motive. Keller and Blomann (2008) found that individuals characterized by a strong internal locus of control were more sensitive to the challenge/skill balance and experienced flow more often than individuals with a weak internal locus of control. Personality characteristics such as optimism, self-esteem, and extraversion have been associated with optimal experience in learning (Schmidt, Shernoff, & Csikszentmihalyi, 2007).

Another important topic deserving further exploration concerns the role of the challenge/skill relationship in promoting flow in different life domains. This would open the way to flow-based intervention in various areas of society. Some recent examples highlight the potentials of this approach. The Job Demands–Resources (JD–R) model (Demerouti, Bakker, Nachreiner, & Schaufeli, 2000; Schaufeli & Bakker, 2004) was designed for application in the work setting. Its use in various occupational contexts showed that resources such as opportunities for self-development and performance feedback enable employees to better cope with work demands (Bakker, Demerouti, & Euwema, 2005). Flow appears when there is a balance between job demands and resources (Bakker & Demerouti, 2007). Work-related flow has a positive impact on personal and organizational resources (Salanova, Bakker, & Llorens, 2006). Bassi, Steca, Delle Fave, and Caprara (2007) investigated learning activities and the subjective experience of students with different levels of perceived self-efficacy. Findings showed that high self-efficacy students mostly associated class work and homework with optimal experience, while low self-efficacy students prominently associated learning tasks with low challenges. Flow has been increasingly investigated also in the domain of new technologies. The highly interactive structure of these devices facilitates users' involvement and absorption, promoting a unique experience-defined presence (Heeter, 1992; Lessiter et al., 2001). This mechanism does not depend upon the quality of the information; it is rather a feature of the medium itself (Gaggioli, Bassi, & Delle Fave, 2003). However, a study on internet activities showed that the perception of challenge was not related to hardware or software features, but to individuals' interests and intellectual sources such as tracking or retrieving information (Chen, Wigand, & Nilan, 1999). Further studies suggest that flow mediates the relationship between presence and enjoyment during on-line games (Weibel, Wissmath, Habegger, Steiner, & Groner, 2008). Considering the enormous interest virtual reality devices are raising thanks to their applications in various domains, Web and virtual reality designers should take these findings into account, focusing more on internal concerns of users and less on the external nature of the environment.

A wide range of topics are still in their infancy within basic and applied research on flow: the study of its neurophysiological underpinnings; as well as the applications in the domains of psychotherapy, health psychology, physical rehabilitation, and community empowerment. The preliminary findings obtained so far in these domains nevertheless show the potential of this approach.

# References

Abuhamdeh, S., & Csikszentmihalyi, M. (2009). Intrinsic and extrinsic motivational orientations in the competitive context: An examination of person–situation interactions. *Journal of Personality, 77*, 1615–1635.

Antonovsky, A. (1979). *Health, stress and coping*. San Francisco, CA: Jossey Bass.

Bakker, A. B. (2008). The work-related flow inventory: Construction and initial validation of the WOLF. *Journal of Vocational Behavior, 72*, 400–414.

Bakker, A. B., & Demerouti, E. (2007). The job demands-resources model: State of the art. *Journal of Managerial Psychology, 22*, 309–328.

Bakker, A. B., Demerouti, E., & Euwema, M. C. (2005). Job resources buffer the impact of job demands on burnout. *Journal of Occupational Health Psychology, 10*, 170–180.

Bandura, A. (1977). Self-efficacy: Toward a unifying theory of behavioural change. *Psychological review, 84*, 191–215.

Bandura, A. (1997). *Self-efficacy: The exercise of control*. New York, NY: Freeman.

Bassi, M., Steca, P., Delle Fave, A., & Caprara, G. V. (2007). Academic self-efficacy beliefs and quality of experience in learning. *Journal of Youth and Adolescence, 36*, 301–312.

Chen, H., Wigand R. T., & Nilan, M. S. (1999). Optimal experience of Web activities. *Computers in Human Behavior, 15*, 585–608.

Csikszentmihalyi, M. (1975). *Beyond boredom and anxiety*. San Francisco, CA: Jossey Bass.

Csikszentmihalyi, M., & Csikszentmihalyi, I. (Eds.). (1988). *Optimal experience. Psychological studies of flow in consciousness*. New York, NY: Cambridge University Press.

Csikszentmihalyi, M., Larson, R. W., & Prescott, S. (1977). The ecology of adolescent activity and experience. *Journal of Youth and Adolescence, 6*, 281–294.

Csikszentmihalyi, M., & LeFevre, J. (1989). Optimal experience in work and leisure. *Journal of Personality and Social Psychology, 56*, 815–822.

Csikszentmihalyi, M., & Massimini, F. (1985). On the psychological selection of biocultural information. *New Ideas in Psychology, 3*, 115–138.

Deci, E. L. (1975). *Intrinsic motivation*. New York, NY: Plenum.

Delle Fave, A. (1999). Individual development and bicultural identity: the Navajo way. In A. Delle Fave & F. Meli (Eds.) *Modernization and cultural identity* (pp. 49–68). Milano, Italy: Edizioni Dell'Arco.

Delle Fave, A. (2007). Individual development and community empowerment: Suggestions from studies on optimal experience. In J. Haworth & G. Hart (Eds.), *Well-being: Individual, community, and societal perspectives* (pp. 41–56). London: Palgrave Macmillan.

Delle Fave, A., & Bassi, M. (2009). Sharing optimal experiences and promoting good community life in a multicultural society. *Journal of Positive Psychology, 4*, 280–289.

Delle Fave, A., Bassi, M., & Massimini, F. (2003). Coping with boundaries: The quality of daily experience of Rom Nomads in Europe. *Psychology and Developing Societies, 15*, 87–102.

Delle Fave, A., & Massimini F. (1988). Modernization and the changing contexts of flow in work and leisure. In M. Csikszentmihalyi & I. Csikszentmihalyi (Eds.), *Optimal experience. Psychological studies of flow in consciousness* (pp. 193–213). New York, NY: Cambridge University Press.

Delle Fave, A., & Massimini, F. (2003). Drug addiction: The paradox of mimetic optimal experience. In J. Henry (Ed.), *European positive psychology proceedings*, 31–38. Leicester, UK: British Psychological Society.

Delle Fave, A., & Massimini, F. (2004). The cross-cultural investigation of optimal experience. *Ricerche di Psicologia, 27*, 79–102.

Delle Fave, A., & Massimini, F. (2005a). The investigation of optimal experience and apathy: Developmental and psychosocial implications. *European Psychologist, 10*, 264–274.

Delle Fave, A., & Massimini, F. (2005b). The relevance of subjective wellbeing to social policies: optimal experience and tailored intervention. In F. Huppert, B. Keverne, & N. Baylis (Eds.), *The science of wellbeing* (pp. 379–404). Oxford: Oxford University Press.

Delle Fave, A., Massimini, F., & Bassi, M. (2011). *Psychological selection and optimal experience across cultures*. Dordrecht, NL: Springer.

Demerouti, E., Bakker, A. B., Nachreiner, F., & Schaufeli, W. B. (2000). A model of burnout and life satisfaction among nurses. *Journal of Advanced Nursing, 32*, 454–464.

Dewey, J. (1934). *Art as experience*. New York, NY: Capricorn Books.

Downey, L., Rosengren, D. B., & Donovan, D. M. (2001). Sources of motivation for abstinence. A replication analysis of the Reasons for Quitting Questionnaire. *Addictive Behaviors, 26*, 79–89.

Eisenberger, R., Jones, J. R., Stinglhamber, F., Shanock, L., & Randall, A. T. (2005). Flow experiences at work: For high need achievers alone? *Journal of Organizational Behavior, 26*, 755–775.

Engeser, S., & Rheinberg, F. (2008). Flow, performance and moderators of challenge-skill balance. *Motivation and Emotion, 32*, 158–172.

Gaggioli, A., Bassi, M., & Delle Fave, A. (2003). Quality of experience in virtual environments. In G. Riva, F. Davide, & W. Ijsselsteijn (Eds.), *Being there: Concepts, effects and measurement of user presence in synthetic environments* (pp. 121–135). Amsterdam, The Netherlands: IOS Press.

Harari, Y. N. (2008). Combat flow: Military, political, and ethical dimensions of subjective well-being in war. *Review of General Psychology, 12*, 253–264.

Haworth, J. J., & Evans, S. (1995). Challenge, skill and positive subjective states in the daily life of a sample of YTS students. *Journal of Occupational and Organizational Psychology, 68*, 109–121.

Heeter, C. (1992). Being there: The subjective experience of presence. *Presence: Teleoperators and virtual environments, 1*, 262–271.

Heider, F. (1958). *The psychology of interpersonal relations*. New York, NY: Wiley.

Hektner, J. M. (2001). Family, school, and community predictors of adolescent growth conducive experiences: Global and specific approaches. *Applied Developmental Science, 5*, 172–183.

Hektner, J. M., Schmidt, J., & Csikszentmihalyi, M. (2007). *Experience sampling method. Measuring the quality of everyday life*. Thousand Oaks, CA: Sage.

Jackson, S. A., & Csikszentmihalyi, M. (1999). *Flow in sports: The keys to optimal experiences and performances*. Champaign, IL: Human Kinetics.

Jackson, S. A., & Eklund, R. C. (2002). Assessing flow in physical activity: The flow state scale-2 and dispositional flow scale-2. *Journal of Sport & Exercise Psychology, 24*, 133–150.

Jackson, S. A., & Marsh, H. W. (1996). Development and validation of a scale to measure optimal experience: The flow state scale. *Journal of Sport & Exercise Psychology, 18*, 17–35.

Keller, J., & Blomann, F. (2008). Locus of control and the flow experience: An experimental analysis. *European Journal of Personality, 22*, 1–19.

Kobasa, S. C. (1979). Personality and resistance to illness. *American Journal of Community Psychology, 7*, 413–423.

Kobasa, S. C, Maddi, S. R, & Kahn, S. (1982). Hardiness and health: A prospective study. *Journal of Personality and Social Psychology, 42*, 168–177.

LaFromboise, T., Coleman, H. L. K., & Gerton, J. (1993). Psychological impact of biculturalism: Evidence and theory. *Psychological Bulletin, 114*, 395–412.

Lazarus, R. (1966). *Psychological stress and the coping process*. New York, NY: McGraw-Hill.

Lessiter, J., Freeman, J., Keogh, E., & Davidoff, J. D. (2001). A cross-media presence questionnaire: The ITC Sense of Presence Inventory, *Presence: Teleoperators and Virtual Environments, 10*, 282–297.

Martin, J., & Jackson, S. A. (2008). Brief approaches to assessing task absorption and enhanced subjective experience: Examining "short" and "core" flow in diverse performance domains. *Motivation and Emotion, 32*, 141–157.

Maslow, A. (1971). *The farther reaches of human nature*. New York, NY: Viking Press.

Massimini, F., Csikszentmihalyi, M., & Carli, M. (1987). Optimal experience: A tool for psychiatric rehabilitation. *Journal of Nervous and Mental Disease*, 175, 545–549.

Massimini, F., Csikszentmihalyi, M., & Delle Fave, A. (1986). Selezione psicologica e flusso di coscienza. In F. Massimini & P. Inghilleri (Eds.), *L'esperienza quotidiana: Teoria e metodo d'analisi* (pp. 133–180). Milano, Italy: Franco Angeli.

Massimini, F., Csikszentmihalyi, M., & Delle Fave, A. (1988). Flow and biocultural evolution. In M. Csikszentmihalyi, & I. Csikszentmihalyi (Eds.), *Optimal experience* (pp. 60–81). New York, NY: Cambridge University Press.

Massimini, F., & Delle Fave, A. (2000). Individual development in a bio-cultural perspective. *American Psychologist*, 55, 24–33.

Moneta, G. B., & Csikszentmihalyi, M. (1996). The effect of perceived challenges and skills on the quality of subjective experience. *Journal of Personality*, 64, 275–310.

Persson, D., Eklund, M., & Isacsson, Å. (1999). The experience of everyday occupations and its relation to sense of coherence – a methodological study. *Journal of Occupational Science*, 6, 13–26.

Piaget, J. (1950). *Introduction à l'épistémologie génétique* (3 volumes). Paris, France: PUF.

Rathunde, K. (2001). Family context and the development of undivided interest: A longitudinal study of family support and challenge and adolescents' quality of experience. *Applied Developmental Science*, 5, 158–171.

Rotter, J. B. (1966). Generalized expectancies for internal versus external control of reinforcement. *Psychological Monographs*, 80, 609.

Ryan, R. M., & Deci, E. L. (2000). Self-determination theory and the facilitation of intrinsic motivation, social development, and well-being. *American Psychologist*, 55, 68–78.

Salanova, M., Bakker, A. B., & Llorens, S. (2006). Flow at work: Evidence for an upward spiral of personal and organizational resources. *Journal of Happiness Studies*, 7, 1–22.

Schaufeli, W. B., & Bakker, A. B. (2004). Job demands, job resources, and their relationship with burnout and engagement: A multisample study. *Journal of Organizational Behavior*, 25, 293–315.

Schmidt, J., Shernoff, D., & Csikszentmihalyi, M. (2007). Individual and situational factors related to the experience of flow in adolescence: A multilevel approach. In A. D. Ong & M. van Dulmen (Eds.), *The handbook of methods in positive psychology* (pp. 542–558). Oxford, UK: Oxford University Press.

Shernoff, D., & Csikszentmihalyi, M. (2009). Flow in schools. Cultivating engaged learners and optimal learning environments. In R. Gilman, E. Huebner, & M. Furlong (Eds.), *Handbook of positive psychology in schools* (pp. 131–145). New York, NY: Taylor & Francis.

Stokart, Z., Cavallo, M., Fianco, A., & Lombardi M. (2007). Esperienza ottimale e identità femminile: Uno studio transculturale su tre gruppi di adolescenti. In A. Delle Fave (Ed.), *La condivisione del benessere. Il contributo della psicologia positiva* (pp. 313–331). Milano, Italy: Franco Angeli.

Swarup, S., & Delle Fave, A. (1999). From India to Europe: Cultural change and the quality of experience. In A. Delle Fave & F. Meli (Eds.), *Modernization and cultural identity* (pp. 103–120). Milano, Italy: Edizioni Dell'Arco.

Vygotsky, L. (1978). *Mind in society*. Cambridge, MA: Harvard University Press.

Wanner, B., Ladouceur, R., Auclair, A.V., & Vitaro, F. (2006). Flow and dissociation: Examination of mean levels, cross-links, and links to emotional well-being across sports and recreational and pathological gambling. *Journal of Gambling Studies*, 22, 289–304.

Weibel, D., Wissmath, B., Habegger, S., Steiner, Y., & Groner, R. (2008). Playing online games against computer- vs. human-controlled opponents: Effects on presence, flow, and enjoyment. *Computers in Human Behavior, 24,* 2274–2291.

Weiner, B. (1972). *Theories of motivation.* Chicago, IL: Markham.

Yerkes, R. M., & Dodson, J. D. (1908). The relation of strength of stimulus to rapidity of habit-formation. *Journal of Comparative Neurology and Psychology, 18,* 459–482.

# CHAPTER 6

# EMOTIONALLY INTELLIGENT HAPPINESS

## ALIA J. CRUM AND PETER SALOVEY
Yale University, USA

The focus on psychological and philosophical thinking about the pursuit of happiness has been sharp and swift, with over 4000 books on the topic published in the last year alone. Although reflection on happiness dates back more than 2500 years to the ideas of Confucius, Buddha, and Aristotle, the recent rise in attention has been notably more systematic and scientific. With antiquity, academia, and popular media on its side, it would seem as though happiness would be a safe pursuit. But the truth is, the mere idea of happiness still seems to produce a subtle twinge of unease.

Why is it that we are uncomfortable being happy? Superficially, the pursuit of happiness can seem cliché, even trite. But the discomfort reaches far beneath the skin. There is a lack of clarity surrounding the definition of what real happiness means. We have felt first hand the fleeting nature of happiness and that it often abandons us when we most expect it and somehow appears in moments we do not expect it at all. And despite our strongest wishes to view all things through a rosy lens, in our quietest moments we confront with tentative resolution that there is something noble, even valuable, in the inevitability of challenging times and the inescapability of negative emotions (e.g., Parrott, 1991). Perhaps most discomforting of all is the thought: Do I really deserve to be happy when there is so much suffering around me?

Just as the positive psychology movement has flourished in the past several years, so too has the scientific understanding of the emotional experience. Whereas emotions historically have been considered aspects of the human condition that prohibit us from living a reasoned, rational, and successful life and therefore something to learn to overcome, master, and avoid, recent research has focused primarily on the value of emotions in achieving these goals. Our work on *emotional intelligence* (EI) began with the assumption that emotions are psychological resources to help us think clearly and behave appropriately (Salovey & Mayer, 1990).

In an attempt to address the hesitation and fragility surrounding happiness, we propose uniting the pursuit of happiness with EI. We define EI happiness as *having the ability to experience emotion in the service of living vitally, meaningfully, socially, and successfully.* In this chapter, we offer theoretical and scientific support for this hypothesis in the pursuit of a "happiness" that is more proactive, integrated, grounded, and sustainable.

## WHERE IS HAPPINESS ON THE ROLLER COASTER OF EMOTIONS?

The emotional experience is often likened to a roller-coaster ride: moments of joy, pleasure, and pride can be followed by the experience of anger, pain, and shame. The ride might look something like Fig. 6.1.

Of course, the height of the peaks, the depth of the falls, and the length of time spent within and between them differ among individuals (e.g., Larsen & Diener, 1987). Such baseline differences in emotional tendencies are often referred to as *affective style* (e.g., Davidson, 1992). Happiness, often construed as the tendency to experience more positive than negative emotions, may be seen as the time one spends at the top of the emotional ride. If the goal is to increase happiness, it seems logical to work to increase and sustain the peaks of the ride and to somehow avoid the inevitable falls. The problem is that, much to our chagrin, even in peak moments of bliss, time cannot be suspended, and the emotional ride must run its course. At best it feels like an exhilarating experience. At worst we feel uncontrollably strapped in, subjected to a random ride of emotional highs and lows. Over time such a ride can be exhausting. Cynical of the emotional experience, afraid or unwilling to experience emotion at all, we seek only one option: to get off the roller coaster.

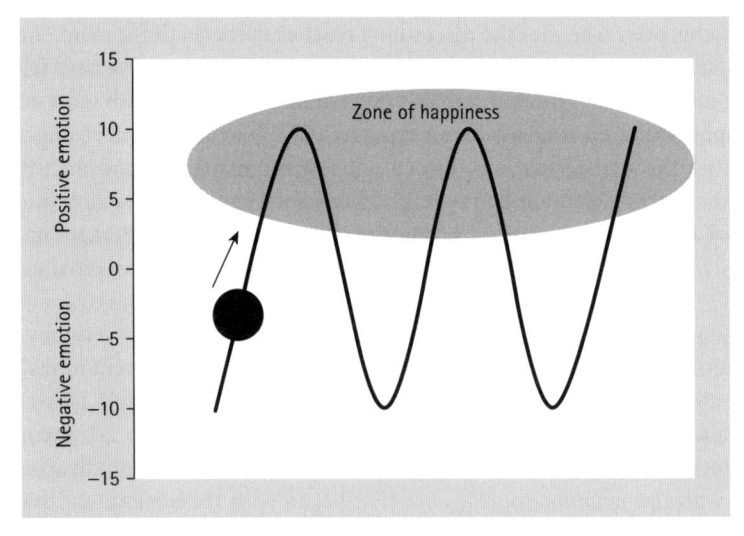

**FIG. 6.1** Emotions experienced as a roller-coaster ride: happiness is experienced passively and unsustainably.

# It's not Just a Ride: The Functionality of Emotions

The roller-coaster metaphor, while perhaps experientially accurate, is limited. It assumes that emotions are merely feelings and that people are by and large hedonistic seeking only to increase positive emotions and to avoid or eliminate negative emotions. This assumption is both wrong and misleading: There is more to emotions than subjective feelings, and there is more to human motivation than hedonism (e.g., Higgins, 1997; Parrott, 1993).

Emotions—both positive and negative—are essential for optimal human functioning (Darwin, 1872/1965; e.g., Mayer, Salovey, & Caruso, 2004). Emotions can be thought of as "short-lived, biologically based reactions that reflect our appraisals of ongoing events and manifest themselves in subjective experience, expressive behavior, and physiological responding" (Richards, 2002, p. 308). Specifically, emotions serve three essential roles: First, emotions serve the function of *messengers*, reflecting and relaying information about how one's body is functioning and the extent to which one is making progress toward goals (e.g., Higgins, 1997). Second, emotions serve as *motivators*, energizing one's cognitive and behavioral resources to the goals and projects that most need our attention (e.g., Frijda, 1986). Lastly, emotions are key *facilitators*, stimulating the acquisition of additional resources (social, physical, and mental) that may be necessary to achieve those goals.

## Emotions as messengers

Emotional reactions are at their essence a form of evaluation: People's feelings inform them about what they like, want, and value and the extent to which they are achieving their goals (Clore & Parrott, 1991; Lazarus, 1991; Scheier & Carver, 1992). The emotional message consists of two components. Emotional *valence* relays information about how good or bad something is. Positive emotions such as happiness, gratitude, pride, love, and hope relay the message that one is meeting one's goals, that a bad event has passed, or that one's relationship with another is secure. Negative emotions such as fear, sadness, shame, anger, guilt, disgust, anxiety, disappointment, embarrassment, envy, and hatred relay the message that something is wrong or that no progress toward a goal has been made. The second component of the emotional messenger is *arousal*, which relays information about the importance or urgency of a particular situation. To survive, the human system is forced to process an incredible amount of information: The complexity of evaluating this information is often too great to be held in conscious awareness and thus, we must rely on our emotional feelings which serve as a synthetic analysis of this information.

## Emotions as motivators

Beyond relaying important information regarding the valence and urgency of a particular situation, emotions also serve as motivators, literally generating the energy to think and act in ways that correspond to the emotional message (e.g., Frijda, 1986). In general, negative emotions motivate avoidance behavior and a more conservative, methodical, and analytical approach to problem solving, whereas positive emotions motivate approach behavior and are associated with a more holistic, creative, and flexible style of thinking (Fazio, Eiser & Shook, 2004; Isen, 2000). This emotional motivation system, however, is extremely fine-tuned and specific. For example, the emotion of anger, having relayed the information that one is being blocked from a particular goal, also provides the energy and readiness to oppose or attack whatever is getting in the way. Similarly, the emotion of sadness, in providing the information that one has lost something of value, is also associated with reduced energy thereby motivating an individual to give up opposition to a disliked circumstance or abandoning a goal. Anxiety involves a tendency to be vigilant for threats, jealousy involves the tendency to monitor relationships that may have been taken for granted, and shame motivates the tendency to monitor others' opinions in the service of reestablishing reputation. Positive emotions broaden people's ideas about possible actions, opening their awareness to a wider range of thoughts and actions. All of these aspects are specific and functional to each emotion and, fascinatingly, tend to operate with little conscious awareness or intention (Fredrickson & Losada, 2005).

## Emotions as facilitators

Often a particular goal cannot be achieved without the acquisition of resources outside those at the immediate disposal of the individual. Emotions serve to facilitate this process. First, the experience of emotion actually builds mental resources by facilitating the process of learning and growth: The contemplative mindset associated with serenity is associated with reflective and integrative thinking from which humans are able to assimilate and learn from their experiences (e.g., Fredrickson, 2003), and negative emotions focus one's attention to an important or salient problem, helping them methodically and logically to generate accurate solutions. Secondly, the experience of emotions actually builds physical resources. Positive emotions can facilitate a buffering system for the autonomic nervous system which improves health and builds immunity (e.g., Cohen, Doyle, Turner, Alper, & Skoner, 2003), and negative emotions, while often associated with compromised health status (Salovey, Rothman, Detweiler, & Steward, 2000), can serve as catalysts for positive physical change in both hormone balance and functional health status (Epel, McEwen, & Ickovics, 1998). Lastly, emotions build social resources via their signaling response to others: One person's anger can induce another's fear, one person's fear can induce calmness and care in another (Dimberg & Öhman, 1996), and the highly attractive and contagious nature of positive emotions builds social resources through forging social alliances which can facilitate helping behavior (Hatfield, Cacioppo, & Rapson, 1994).

# EMOTIONAL INTELLIGENCE: FACILITATING FUNCTION

Emotions are intended to help facilitate the achievement of a successful and flourishing life. Yet, our hardwired emotional system is not perfect. The utility of emotional experience in achieving one's highest goals needs to be fine-tuned, guided, and supplemented by higher order awareness, skills, and intentions. Although EI has been conceptualized in many ways (e.g., specific ability approach, cohesive global ability, and a mixed-model approach; Matthews, Zeidner, & Roberts, 2007; Mayer, Salovey, & Caruso, 2004, 2008; McCrae, 2000) at its most fundamental level, EI is a set of abilities including the ability to perceive, use, understand, and manage emotions. As two decades of research suggest, these abilities can help consciously and skillfully exploit the inherent functionality of emotions thereby achieving a more successful and fulfilling life (reviewed by Mayer, Roberts, & Barsade, 2008).

Take the following case into consideration. When Annie started working at her new job over a year ago she was happy and often worked in a joyful and enthusiastic manner. Over the past several weeks, however, Annie's mood has become considerably more negative. Most people would assume that this negative mood should be cause for concern and, if the response is prolonged, Annie might conclude that she is no longer happy with work. This judgment may spur a host of behaviors including seeking another job, complaining to colleagues, or buying one of the 4000 books on happiness to improve her sense of happiness at work. But before jumping to conclusions, it is useful to consider a more emotionally intelligent response.

The first step of this process, long before Annie makes the summary judgment that she is unhappy with her job, is for Annie to *perceive* her emotions accurately. Fortunately, Annie's emotional perception ability is highly tuned and, rather then just feeling a diffuse feeling of negativity or frustration, she recognizes at the most basic level, a feeling of anger. Once Annie accurately perceives herself to be angry she can implement her ability to *understand* emotion. Whereas most people would understand anger to signify the fact that, say, her boss and the people around her are incompetent, Annie is more emotionally intelligent. She realizes that the purpose of anger is really quite simple: It is indicating to her that she is being impeded from achieving a valuable goal.

Because Annie is able to recognize and understand the more basic motivational message of the emotion of anger, she can begin to consider possible goals that she has construed—either consciously or unconsciously—in the domain of work. She realizes that there are several goals that are currently being impeded, including her goal to make money (she just learned that bonuses would be cut back to 70% this year), and her goal to perform optimally so that she can make a positive impact in the company (the project is delayed, her colleague has been out sick for a week, and she has been unable to schedule a meeting with corporate headquarters). Annie understands that her negative emotion of anger is actually signaling to her that she cares about doing well at her job, not that she dislikes it, and that she is upset with her colleague because the project is not getting done as quickly as she would like making her feel as though she is not performing up to her capability, not because her colleague is inordinately lazy. Emotional knowledge can range from the very basic to the very complex, and fortunately for Annie, her knowledge is strong. Annie not only understands the basic function of anger but she also understands that if she does not do something about it, her anger is likely to progress into sadness and frustration, eventually leading her to give up on her goal of performing well at work.

Annie also knows that beyond the informational message is the motivational one, and because she is aware of this she can *use* her emotion in the most adaptive manner possible. Annie does so by taking advantage of the endorphin release from the emotion of anger to fuel her work, and she uses her narrowed attention to help her think more critically about potential problems and possible solutions.

Of course, the more hardwired response to anger might not be the most adaptive approach in the modern workforce and thus, the most emotionally intelligent response also requires Annie to *manage* her emotions. For this, Annie employs several strategies. First, Annie reassesses her goals. She decides that her goal of being a positive influence at work is indeed something she values, and that she does not want to change or give up this goal. She also realizes that her financial goals might not be feasible and, because this is out of her control, she chooses to release her strong hold on those intentions for the time being. Annie also chooses to reappraise (e.g., Gross, 1998; Lazarus, 1994) her experience not as a threat to her professional career but as a challenge. Because she views it as a challenge, Annie is motivated to improve her ability to work in less than optimal situations and to find creative ways to do well despite the challenging situation, and become a role model in the process. Furthermore, Annie honors the fact that she will still feel frustrated and even angry at times because she does indeed care about the situation, so she works to manage her emotions behaviorally, by employing deep breathing or mindfulness techniques to calm her sympathetic nervous system response (Benson & Klipper, 2000; Davidson et al., 2003) so that she can feel her emotions, but still operate out of purpose and get the job done.

## THE FRUITS OF EMOTIONAL INTELLIGENCE

As the example of Annie illustrates, emotions are inherently designed to help us achieve our goals and EI is a set of abilities which can help facilitate this. Not surprisingly, EI is linked with a variety of positive outcomes that can facilitate the process of living socially, successfully, and vitally.

### Living socially

The ability to perceive, use, understand, and manage emotions has obvious associations with living socially and connecting meaningfully with others (e.g., Casey, Garrett, Brackett, & Rivers, 2007; Lopes, Salovey, Côté, Beers, & Petty, 2005). EI consistently predicts positive social outcomes in both children and adults: Emotional knowledge among five-year-olds positively predicted their social skills in the third grade (Izard et al., 2001). Individuals with higher EI scores tend to have more friends and better relationships with those friends and family members (Lopes et al., 2005). People have more positive perceptions of emotionally intelligent individuals than individuals who lack these skills (Brackett, Rivers, Shiffman, Lerner, & Salovey, 2006). Furthermore, EI relates to the ability to be sensitive to and willing to help others, encouraging mutually fulfilling relationships: Couples with high levels of EI experience less conflict, fewer destructive responses to conflict, and better relationship quality overall (Brackett et al., 2006; Brackett, Warner, & Bosco, 2005).

### Living successfully

EI plays a significant role in increasing performance and achievement in both academics and at work. EI influences the ability to interact and communicate effectively with others as well as the ability to manage conflict, handle stress, and perform under pressure. Emotional perception is associated with successful problem analyses (Matsumoto, 2006) and better negotiation skills (Elfenbein, Foo, White, Tan, & Aik, 2007; Mueller & Curhan, 2006). Lopes, Grewal, Kadis, Gall, and Salovey (2006) found that, in a population of 44 financial workers, total EI correlated with higher company rank, merit increases, peer- and supervisor-rated sociability and leadership potential. Other studies have found that the ability to perceive emotions related to enhanced performance and workplace effectiveness of physicians, human service workers, school teachers and principals, and business managers (Elfenbein et al., 2007). With few exceptions, these associations remain significant after controlling for other predictors such as age, gender, education, IQ, and personality traits.

## Living vitally

An inherent component of emotions is their physiological manifestation in both the cardiovascular and immune systems. Whereas in general, positive emotions are said to produce positive physiological outcomes and negative emotions are said to be associated with compromised health status, greater EI can produce a more vital state of being, regardless of the emotions one experiences. Emotions have both a direct effect on health (via cardiovascular and immune systems) as well as a negative effect on health (via health behaviors such as drinking, eating, smoking, and exercise) (Ng & Jeffery, 2003; Trinidad & Johnson, 2002). Thus, EI can buffer the effect of stress and negative emotion on the hypothalamic–pituitary–adrenal axis and sympathetic nervous system and indirectly by decreasing the likelihood of unhealthy behaviors, which are more likely during times of stress or negative emotion (e.g., Mikolajczak, Roy, Luminet, Fillée, & de Timary, 2007; Salovey & Grewal, 2005). A meta-analytic investigation looking at the relationship between EI and health found that this is indeed the case. Specifically, EI correlates with physical health to a moderate degree, and EI has been associated with better physical health in a variety of contexts, including fewer self-reported physiological symptoms and illnesses, better recovery following surgery, and increased longevity (e.g., Peterson, Seligman & Vaillant, 1988; Salovey et al., 2000; Scheier & Carver, 1985; Scheier et al., 1989).

## A Change in Metaphors: Emotionally Intelligent Happiness

It is logical to assume that because EI is highly associated with improved social, occupational, and physiological functioning, the achievement of these states will, in turn, bring about happiness and satisfaction. The research supports this reasoning at least to some degree and suggests that EI correlates with psychological well-being and life satisfaction (Brackett & Mayer, 2003; Brackett et al., 2006; Ciarrochi, Chan, & Caputi, 2000).

Fascinatingly, however, the causal direction in these studies is ambiguous. One of the most important findings in the literature on happiness and positive affect in the last decade has been the consistent conclusion that positive emotions are not merely a consequence of achievement of success, physical health, and meaningful relationships, but are also a cause

(Fredrickson & Losada, 2005). People assume that a particular relationship will bring them happiness and fail to see that being happy in the first place is one of the most attractive qualities. People assume that the promotion they receive at work will bring positive emotion and neglect the fact that positive emotion is essential for productivity. And they believe that achieving good health will help them feel good, when simply deciding to feel good is one of the best things you can do for your health. In one study, Diener and colleagues found that people who are happier at one point in time are more likely to achieve a positive outcome at a later time—such as a call-back for a job, a healthy marriage, and fewer illnesses (Diener, Nickerson, Lucas, & Sandvik, 2002). Furthermore, college freshmen who reported higher levels of cheerfulness also reported higher income and job-satisfaction and less frequent unemployment than their less cheerful peers 19 years later (Diener et al., 2002).

Unfortunately, the self-perpetuating spiral of positive emotions and positive outcomes does not always operate in this ideal form. First, positive emotion does not invariably produce positive outcomes. In experimental research, induced positive affect decreases accuracy when engaging highly detailed tasks that require more thorough analytic cognitions, which may in turn lead to poor decision-making (Parrott, 1993). Extremely high levels of positive affect can decrease the motivation to change or improve life circumstances, evidenced by the finding that those at the highest levels of happiness are less financially successful than those at moderate levels (Oishi, Diener, & Lucas, 2007). Perhaps more problematically, positive outcomes do not invariably produce positive emotion and happiness. Achievement and wealth are not always associated with happiness. Above a certain threshold income level (enough to meet the basic needs of food, shelter, and security), the correlation between wealth and happiness is surprisingly weak (Csikszentmihalyi, 2000). Other studies on the relative happiness of lottery winners and on 49 of the wealthiest people of the USA (according to the list published annually in *Forbes* magazine) confirm that wealth does not guarantee happiness (Brickman, Coates, & Janoff-Bulman, 1978; Diener, Horwitz, & Emmons, 1985).

One potential confound with this understanding is the fact that happiness and positive affect are often used interchangeably and that they are often intertwined with more functional assessments of living such as well-being and life satisfaction. For example, well-being may consist of four components: life satisfaction (global judgments of one's life), satisfaction with important domains (e.g., work satisfaction), positive affect (experiencing many pleasant emotions and moods), and low levels of negative affect (experiencing few unpleasant emotions and moods) (Diener, Napa-Scollon, Oishi, Dzokoto, & Suh, 2000). In this light, positive emotions are assumed to promote well-being and negative emotions are assumed to reverse it. This view may be problematic. Negative emotions and difficult situations can be both functional and useful in propelling an individual to higher levels of well-being. Furthermore, life is tough. On a small scale there are the everyday pressures, disappointments, conflicts, and stressors. Then there are the larger ones: there is injustice, sickness, even death. Things happen which are too egregious to think about, not to mention discuss in a book on happiness. Unfortunately, the occurrences are a fact of life and denying them is futile if not also detrimental. It is only when we can have the strength to face them that we have the power to transform their significance into something more meaningful.

In recognition of this, researchers in the field of positive psychology have proposed several different types of happiness and well-being. For example, Ryan and Deci (2001) proposed a distinction between eudaimonic and hedonic well-being. The hedonic perspective views well-being in terms of pleasure attainment and pain avoidance. Hedonic well-being is most commonly assessed by measurements of subjective well-being, a person's cognitive and affective evaluation of their life. The eudaimonic perspective goes beyond the assessment of simple pleasure and pain and views well-being as the extent to which a person is fully functioning, living a life of meaning and self-realization. From the eudaimonic perspective, feeling a complete range of emotional experiences is seen as a positive characteristic of a fully functioning individual. More recently, the term *flourishing* has been proposed to mean both feeling well and functioning well. And, as research on this topic suggests, functioning well requires a certain degree of struggle (e.g., Keyes, 2007; Vittersø, Søholt, Hetland, Thoresen & Røysamb, 2010). Traditional Eastern thought takes a similar perspective. Rather than viewing happiness as a momentary or fleeting emotion aroused by sensory or conceptual stimuli, Buddhists view happiness, or *suhka*, as an "enduring trait that arises from a mind in a state of equilibrium and entails a conceptually unstructured and unfiltered awareness of the true nature of reality" (Ekman, Davidson, Ricard, & Wallace, 2005, p. 60). Buddhists view its opposite, *duhkha*, as not simply an unpleasant feeling, but more generally, a "basic vulnerability to suffering and pain due to misapprehending the nature of reality" (Ekman et al., 2005 p. 60). To achieve *suhka*, Buddhists and other Eastern philosophies believe that the radical transformation of consciousness is necessary.

EI, too, can add greater clarity and specificity to the definition and understanding of happiness and well-being. In order to more accurately reflect the emotional experience in this relationship however, a more constructive metaphor is needed. Rather than viewing the emotional experience as a roller-coaster ride, the emotional experience might be better likened to a weather pattern. This metaphorical representation is distinct in several ways. First, it more accurately reflects the functionality of the emotional experience: days of rain are not only inevitable, but are necessary. Second, it underscores a fundamental point of distinction between emotional experience and the functioning lifestyle: It invites us to experience our emotions fully, but still operate out of purpose and intention. Rather than having to exit the ride to accomplish a set of goals, living vitally, socially, and successfully can occur in the midst, in spite of, or even because of the weather. If the wind picks up, we just zip up our jackets. Finally, in this metaphor, happiness is no longer a static point or line of positive emotion but the entirety of the emotional experience, with its seasonal and diurnal—even hourly—changes in weather.

Emotionally intelligent individuals in this metaphorical representation are highly in tune with the weather pattern of their own dispositions. They more accurately perceive subtle changes in temperature, and they understand the causes and consequences of those changes. They also acknowledge how the weather of their emotions influences their thinking and behaving (Fig. 6.2). While they are aware of the general tendency to be cautious and stay inside when the weather is gloomy and to explore and be creative when the clouds are clear, they also recognize that they need not be victimized by these motivational pulls and that they can show up for work even if it means driving through the sleet and snow. When the leaves change or the clouds come, they can appreciate the colors rather than cursing them, understanding that there is a time and reason for these changes. They know that that the sun is always there behind the clouds and that sometimes it is okay to dance in the rain. Emotionally intelligent happiness is the peace of mind that comes from knowing that one is capable of handling any situation that arises—no matter how painful or how challenging it can be—and having the ability to experience emotion in the service of living vitally, meaningfully, socially and successfully.

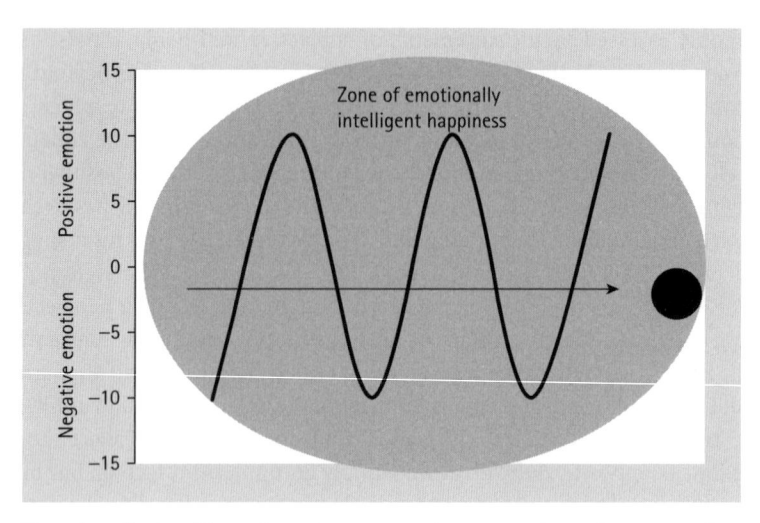

FIG. 6.2 Emotionally intelligent happiness: emotions experienced as a weather pattern in the service of living vitally, meaningfully, socially, and successfully.

## Cultivating Emotionally Intelligent Happiness

People are highly motivated to achieve happiness, yet their efforts are often futile. Despite the fact that the USA has seen huge increases in national wealth, income, and affluence over the past half century (from 1957 to the late 1990s, after-tax income, in constant 1995 dollars, has more than doubled), Myers (2000) reports that the percentage of Americans who describe themselves as happy has remained remarkably constant at about 30%. Research on affective forecasting further substantiates the fact that the pursuit of happiness via material or circumstantial gain is illusive at best and counteractive at worst (Gilbert & Ebert, 2002). In the search for a more sustainable happiness, the EI perspective suggests that a fundamental shift must be made away from a focus on achieving a particular circumstance to a focus on cultivating a higher state of awareness regarding one's emotions and their relationship to one's desired values and goals. This shift can be accomplished by a subtle change in mindset and a gradual accumulation of emotionally intelligent skills.

The cultivation of sustainable happiness first requires a change in mindset. The typical approach to happiness often leaves people on a "hedonic treadmill," in which they undergo momentary phases of increased positive affect (e.g., winning the lottery, attaining tenure, etc.), but quickly return to baseline levels of happiness (Bar-Anan, Wilson, & Gilbert, 2009). The EI perspective offers a simple solution to this unsatisfying pattern: Make a conscious mindset change that focuses upon experiencing all emotions in the service of valued actions, rather than focusing on increasing positive emotion and reducing negative emotion through the achievement of particular outcomes. This distinction may be subtle, but it is fundamental. Take Annie's case for example. When Annie's moods take a sudden downturn, instead of focusing her attention and resources on how to change her circumstances so that she can feel happier, the emotionally intelligent approach would be for Annie to focus her attention first on feeling, identifying, and learning from her emotions. In this mindset, Annie will not become subjected to acting reactively out of her emotions (as in the case of the emotional roller coaster) but will instead be able to proactively utilize the full spectrum (or weather pattern) of her emotions in a way that best facilitates the achievement of her goals while maintaining her health and social relationships.

An important caveat in the emotionally intelligent approach to sustainable happiness is that in order to feel, identify, and learn from their emotions, people may have to endure a period of frustration or negative emotion. One potential barrier in achieving this shift in mindset is that people mistakenly believe that "bad" emotions should be suppressed, managed, and avoided. Interestingly, research on such emotion regulation has demonstrated that while emotion regulation may be an important aspect of human functioning, an unwillingness to experience emotions (i.e., experiential avoidance) can actually be a major cause of psychopathology (e.g., Blackledge & Hayes, 2001). One reason for this is that conscious attempts to suppress or regulate emotions sometimes backfire and are associated with increased physiological activity and corresponding health issues (e.g., Gross, 2002). Furthermore, the act of regulating emotions depletes mental resources needed to perform successfully on other tasks (e.g., Baumeister, Bratslavsky, Muraven, & Tice, 1998) and the tendency to make emotion regulation a priority often results in the sacrifice of long-term pursuits (e.g., weight loss) for short-term hedonic behavior (e.g., eating cake) (e.g., Vohs & Heatherton, 2000). In this light, if one tries to regulate one's emotions by altering one's perception or experience of them, one runs the risk of missing out on the greater possibility or significance of them. If one can increase acceptance of and openness to the experience of emotion, one will likely be better able to perceive and understand the actual significance of that emotion in the context of "what is" (i.e., emotional clarity). Furthermore, if individuals can orient themselves to the possibility of their emotions without having to avoid them, they can more effectively use their energy typically given over to resignation, avoidance, or control of these emotions and choose to act in a way that is congruent with their highest values and goals (e.g., Hayes, Strosahl, & Wilson, 1999).

The development and application of emotional skills can help facilitate the shift in mindset necessary for enduring negative emotions and achieving sustainable happiness. Felicitously, the research suggests that EI is a set of labile skills that can be improved through training—similar to music, mathematics, or sports. In-depth and comprehensive programs have been developed to increase EI abilities and can be found in the workplace and in school systems, and recent longitudinal studies support efficacy and impact of these programs (e.g., Brackett et al., 2008). And both laboratory and applied studies suggest that training in skills such as meditation might actually be able to neurologically remove us from the roller coaster of emotions and into a more spacious and aware field of consciousness in which one's dispositional response to emotions is more naturally adaptive.

# Conclusion

Although the pursuit of happiness may be an inalienable right, it seems as though the achievement of happiness is not so fundamental. The mindsets we adopt, the myths we perpetuate, and the metaphors we hold can keep us stuck in a perilous place. As with any valuable goal, the achievement of happiness takes design and work: It requires the application of a finely cultivated set of skills toward a carefully constructed intention. In this view, happiness is a dynamic state marked by a set of attainable abilities as opposed to a static state of random ups and downs. Not only are negative emotions and challenging emotions embraced, but they are honored and put to work in the fulfillment of reaching valued goals. Although the care and cultivation of the weather pattern of emotions may require donning a raincoat from time to time, there is beauty in the storm, sustainability in the acceptance, and strength in the confidence that we can live fully with or without perpetual warmth and sunshine.

# References

Bar-Anan, Y., Wilson, T. D., & Gilbert, D. T. (2009). The feeling of uncertainty intensifies affective reactions. *Emotion, 9*(1), 123–127.

Baumeister, R. F., Bratslavsky, E., Muraven, M., & Tice, D. M. (1998). Ego depletion: Is the active self a limited resource? *Journal of Personality and Social Psychology, 74*(5), 1252–1265.

Benson, H., & Klipper, M. Z. (2000). *The relaxation response.* New York, NY: Harper Paperbacks.

Blackledge, J. T., & Hayes, S. C. (2001). Emotion regulation in acceptance and commitment therapy. *Journal of Clinical Psychology, 57*(2), 243–255.

Brackett, M. A., & Mayer, J. D. (2003). Convergent, discriminant, and incremental validity of competing measures of emotional intelligence. *Personality and Social Psychology Bulletin, 29*(9), 1147–1158.

Brackett, M. A., Patti, J., Stern, R., Rivers, S. E., Elbertson, N. A., Chisholm, C., & Salovey, P. (2008). A sustainable, skill-based approach to building emotionally literate schools. In M. Hughes, H. L. Thompson, & J. B. Terrell (Eds.), *Handbook for developing emotional and social intelligence* (pp. 329–58). San Francisco, CA: Pfeiffer.

Brackett, M. A., Rivers, S. E., Shiffman, S., Lerner, N., & Salovey, P. (2006). Relating emotional abilities to social functioning: A comparison of self-report and performance measures of emotional intelligence. *Journal of Personality and Social Psychology, 91*(4), 780–795.

Brackett, M. A., Warner, R. M., & Bosco, J. S. (2005). Emotional intelligence and relationship quality among couples. *Personal Relationships, 12*(2), 197–212.

Brickman, P., Coates, D., & Janoff-Bulman, R. (1978). Lottery winners and accident victims: Is happiness relative? *Journal of Personality and Social Psychology, 36*(8), 917–927.

Casey, J. J., Garrett, J., Brackett, M. A., & Rivers, S. (2007). Emotional intelligence, relationship quality, and partner selection. In G. Geher, & G. Miller (Eds.), *Mating intelligence: Sex, relationships, and the mind's reproductive system* (pp. 263–82). New York, NY: Lawrence Erlbaum.

Ciarrochi, J. V., Chan, A. Y. C., & Caputi, P. (2000). A critical evaluation of the emotional intelligence construct. *Personality and Individual Differences, 28*(3), 539–561.

Clore, G. L., & Parrott, W. G. (1991). Moods and their vicissitudes: Thoughts and feelings as information. In J. P. Forgas (Ed.), *Emotion and social judgments* (pp. 107–23). Oxford, UK: Pergamon Press.

Cohen, S., Doyle, W. J., Turner, R. B., Alper, C. M., & Skoner, D. P. (2003). Emotional style and susceptibility to the common cold. *Psychosomatic Medicine, 65*(4), 652–657.

Csikszentmihalyi, M. (2000). Happiness, flow, and economic equality. *American Psychologist*, 55(10), 1163–1163.

Darwin, C. (1965). *The expression of emotions in man and animals*. Chicago, IL: University of Chicago Press. (Original work published 1872).

Davidson, R. J. (1992). Emotion and affective style: Hemispheric substrates. *Psychological Science*, 3(1), 39–43.

Davidson, R. J., Kabat-Zinn, J., Schumacher, J., Rosenkranz, M., Muller, D., Santorelli, S. F., ... Sheridan, J. F. (2003). Alterations in brain and immune function produced by mindfulness mediation. *Psychosomatic Medicine*, 65, 564–570.

Diener, E., Horwitz, J., & Emmons, R. A. (1985). Happiness of the very wealthy. *Social Indicators Research*, 16(3), 263–274.

Diener, E., Napa-Scollon, C. K., Oishi, S., Dzokoto, V., & Suh, E. M. (2000). Positivity and the construction of life satisfaction judgments: Global happiness is not the sum of its parts. *Journal of Happiness Studies*, 1(2), 159–176.

Diener, E., Nickerson, C., Lucas, R. E., & Sandvik, E. (2002). Dispositional affect and job outcomes. *Social Indicators Research*, 59(3), 229–259.

Dimberg, U., & Öhman, A. (1996). Behold the wrath: Psychophysiological responses to facial stimuli. *Motivation and Emotion*, 20(2), 149–182.

Ekman, P., Davidson, R. J., Ricard, M., Wallace, B. A. (2005). Buddhist and psychological perspectives on emotions and well-being. *Current Directions in Psychological Science*, 14(2), 59–63.

Elfenbein, H. A., Foo, M. D., White, J., Tan, H. H., & Aik, V. C. (2007). Reading your counterpart: The benefit of emotion recognition accuracy for effectiveness in negotiation. *Journal of Nonverbal Behavior*, 31(4), 205–223.

Epel, E. S., McEwen, B. S., & Ickovics, J. R. (1998). Embodying psychological thriving: Physical thriving in response to stress. *Journal of Social Issues*, 54(2), 301–322.

Fazio, R. H., Eiser, J. R., & Shook, N. J. (2004). Attitude formation through exploration: Valence asymmetries. *Journal of Personality and Social Psychology*, 87(3), 293–311.

Fredrickson, B. L. (2003). The value of positive emotions: The emerging science of positive psychology is coming to understand why it's good to feel good. *American Scientist*, 91(4), 330–335.

Fredrickson, B. L., & Losada, M. F. (2005). Positive affect and the complex dynamics of human flourishing. *American Psychologist*, 60(7), 678–686.

Frijda, N. H. (1986). *The emotions*. Cambridge, UK: Cambridge University Press.

Gilbert, D. T., & Ebert, J. E. J. (2002). Decisions and revisions: The affective forecasting of changeable outcomes. *Journal of Personality and Social Psychology*, 82(4), 503–514.

Gross, J. J. (1998). The emerging field of emotion regulation: An integrative review. *Review of General Psychology*, 2(3), 271–299.

Gross, J. J. (2002). Emotion regulation: Affective, cognitive, and social consequences. *Psychophysiology*, 39, 281–291.

Hatfield, E., Cacioppo, J. T., & Rapson, R. L. (1994). *Emotional contagion: Studies in emotion and social interaction*. Cambridge, UK: Cambridge University Press.

Hayes, S. C., Strosahl, K., & Wilson, K. G. (1999). *Acceptance and commitment therapy*. New York, NY: Guilford Press.

Higgins, E. T. (1997). Beyond pleasure and pain. *American Psychologist*, 52(12), 1280–1300.

Isen, A. M. (2000). Positive affect and decision making. In M. Lewis, & J. M. Haviland-Jones (Eds.), *Handbook of emotions* (2nd ed.). (pp. 417–35). New York, NY: Guilford Press.

Izard, C., Fine, S., Schultz, D., Mostow, A., Ackerman, B., & Youngstrom, E. (2001). Emotion knowledge as a predictor of social behavior and academic competence in children at risk. *Psychological Science, 12*(1), 18–23.

Keyes, C. L. M. (2007). Promoting and protecting mental health as flourishing. *American Psychologist, 62*(2), 95–108.

Larsen, R. J., & Diener, E. (1987). Affect intensity as an individual difference characteristic: A review. *Journal of Research in Personality, 21*(1), 1–39.

Lazarus, R. S. (1991). Cognition and motivation in emotion. *American Psychologist, 46*(4), 352–67.

Lazarus, R. S. (1994). Appraisal: The long and the short of it. In P. Ekman, & R. Davidson (Eds.), *The nature of emotion: Fundamental questions.* (pp. 208–215). Oxford, UK: Oxford University Press.

Lopes, P. N., Grewal, D., Kadis, J., Gall, M., & Salovey, P. (2006). Evidence that emotional intelligence is related to job performance and affect and attitudes at work. *Psicothema, 18*, 132–138.

Lopes, P. N., Salovey, P., Côté, S., Beers, M., & Petty, R. E. (2005). Emotion regulation abilities and the quality of social interaction. *Emotion, 5*(1), 113–118.

Matsumoto, D. (2006). Culture and nonverbal behavior. In *The Sage handbook of nonverbal communication* (pp. 219–35). Thousand Oaks, CA: Sage Publications.

Matthews, G., Zeidner, M., & Roberts, R.D. (Eds.). (2007). *The science of emotional intelligence: Knowns and unknowns.* New York, NY: Oxford University Press.

Mayer, J. D., Roberts, R. D., & Barsade, S. G. (2008). Human abilities: Emotional intelligence. *Annual Review of Psychology, 59*, 507–536.

Mayer, J. D., Salovey, P., & Caruso, D. R. (2004). Emotional intelligence: Theory, findings, and implications. *Psychological Inquiry, 15*(3), 197–215.

Mayer, J. D., Salovey, P., & Caruso, D. R. (2008). Emotional intelligence: New ability or eclectic traits? *American Psychologist, 63*(6), 503–517.

McCrae, R. R. (2000). Emotional intelligence from the perspective of the five-factor model of personality. In R. Bar-On & J. D. A. Parker (Eds.), *The handbook of emotional intelligence: Theory, development, assessment, and application at home, school, and in the workplace* (pp. 263–276). San Francisco, CA: Jossey-Bass.

Mikolajczak, M., Roy, E., Luminet, O., Fillee, C., & Timary, P. (2007). The moderating impact of emotional intelligence on free cortisol responses to stress. *Psychoneuroendocrinology, 32*(8–10), 1000–1012.

Mueller, J. S., & Curhan, J. R. (2006). Emotional intelligence and counterpart mood induction in a negotiation. *International Journal of Conflict Management, 17*(2), 110–128.

Myers, D. G. (2000). The funds, friends, and faith of happy people. *American Psychologist, 55*(1), 56–67.

Ng, D. M., & Jeffery, R. W. (2003). Relationships between perceived stress and health behaviors in a sample of working adults. *Health Psychology, 22*(6), 638–642.

Oishi, S., Diener, E., & Lucas, R. E. (2007). The optimum level of well-being: Can people be too happy? *Perspectives on Psychological Science, 2*(4), 346–360.

Parrott, W. G. (1991). The emotional experiences of envy and jealousy. In P. Salovey (Ed.), *The psychology of jealousy and envy* (pp. 3–30). New York, NY: Guilford Press.

Parrott, W. G. (1993). Beyond hedonism: Motives for inhibiting good moods and for maintaining bad moods. In D. M. Wegner, & J. W. Pennebaker (Eds.), *Handbook of mental control* (pp. 278–305). Englewood Cliffs, NJ: Prentice Hall.

Peterson, C., Seligman, M. E. P., & Vaillant, G. E. (1988). Pessimistic explanatory style is a risk factor for physical illness: A thirty-five-year longitudinal study. *Journal of Personality and Social Psychology, 55*(1), 23–27.

Richards, J. M. (2002). Emotion, emotion regulation, and hopeful thinking. *Psychological Inquiry*, *13*(4), 308–311.

Ryan, R. M., & Deci, E. L. (2001). On happiness and human potentials: A review of research on hedonic and eudaimonic well-being. *Annual Review of Psychology*, *52*, 141–166.

Salovey, P., & Grewal, D. (2005). The science of emotional intelligence. *Current Directions in Psychological Science*, *14*(6), 281–285.

Salovey, P., & Mayer, J. D. (1990). Emotional intelligence. *Imagination, Cognition and Personality*, *9*(3), 185–222.

Salovey, P., Rothman, A. J., Detweiler, J. B., & Steward, W. T. (2000). Emotional states and physical health. *The American Psychologist*, *55*(1), 110–121.

Scheier, M. F., & Carver, C. S. (1985). Optimism, coping, and health: Assessment and implications of generalized outcome expectancies. *Health Psychology*, *4*(3), 219–247.

Scheier, M. F., & Carver, C. S. (1992). Effects of optimism on psychological and physical well-being: Theoretical overview and empirical update. *Cognitive Therapy and Research*, *16*(2), 201–228.

Scheier, M. F., Matthews, K. A., Owens, J. F., Magovern, G. J., Lefebvre, R. C., Abbott, R. A., & Carver, C. S. (1989). Dispositional optimism and recovery from coronary artery bypass surgery: The beneficial effects on physical and psychological well-being. *Journal of Personality and Social Psychology*, *57*(6), 1024–1040.

Trinidad, D. R., & Johnson, C. A. (2002). The association between emotional intelligence and early adolescent tobacco and alcohol use. *Personality and Individual Differences*, *32*(1), 95–105.

Vittersø, J., Søholt, Y., Hetland, A., Thoresen, I. A., Røysamb, E. (2010). Was Hercules happy? Some answers from a functional model of human well-being. *Social Indicators Research*, *95*(1), 1–18.

Vohs, K. D., & Heatherton, T. F. (2000). Self-regulatory failure: A resource-depletion approach. *Psychological Science*, *11*(3), 249–254.

CHAPTER 7

# RELIGIOUS ENGAGEMENT AND WELL-BEING

DAVID G. MYERS

Hope College, USA

## Introduction

Is religion, on balance, toxic? Or is religious engagement more often linked with human flourishing? Religion, observed Freud (1928/1964, p. 126), is a kind of sickness—an "obsessional neurosis" that leads people to live sexually repressed, uptight, unhappy lives. Recent "new atheist" bestsellers go further. Religion is "the root of all evil," declared a British television series derived from Richard Dawkins' *The God Delusion*. Ergo, argued Dawkins, indoctrinating children into religion is a form of child abuse. "Religion is violent, irrational, intolerant, allied to racism and tribalism and bigotry, invested in ignorance and hostile to free inquiry, contemptuous of women and coercive toward children," wrote Christopher Hitchens (2007) in *God is Not Great*. In his *Letter to a Christian Nation*, Sam Harris (2006) offered a crisp synopsis of the new atheism: Religion is "both false and dangerous."

Or are religion's defenders right to believe that an engaged religious faith supports "joy" and "abundant life"—civility, happiness, health, and helpfulness? Religion is nearly universal—68% of all humans say that religion is an important part of their daily lives (Diener, Tay, & Myers, 2011)—because it serves adaptive purposes, say evolutionary analyses. Religion has fostered morality, social cohesion, and group survival (Wade, 2010; Wilson, 2003; Wright, 2009).

Without making any presumptions of the truth or falsity of theism, this chapter summarizes social science evidence concerning associations between religiosity and well-being.

## COMPARING RELIGIOUS AND IRRELIGIOUS POPULATIONS VERSUS INDIVIDUALS

"The Judeo-Christian worldview [is] the basis for a just, free and stable society," one conservative religious organization (the Family Research Council) proclaims in its mission statement. Cultures that reject God will suffer increased crime, poverty, divorce, and disease, assert faith's defenders.

If that is true, then highly religious places should be peaceful, healthy, and flourishing. But as sociologist Philip Zuckerman (2006, 2009) and others have documented, such places often are not. Countries with the highest rates of happiness, life expectancy, literacy, gender equality, income, and education—and with the lowest rates of homicide, AIDS, infant mortality, and teen pregnancy—tend to be relatively secular. If you must relocate to another country, and wish for a civil, healthy, flourishing place, seek out relatively irreligious Norway, Sweden, Australia, Canada, or the Netherlands.

Such analyses of secularity's association with civility have been faulted for cherry-picking their social health measures and their countries. For example, they exclude suicide rates, which, as Fig. 7.1 illustrates, are higher in less religious countries. And they generally omit irreligious North Korea, China, Vietnam, and the former Soviet states, where life has not

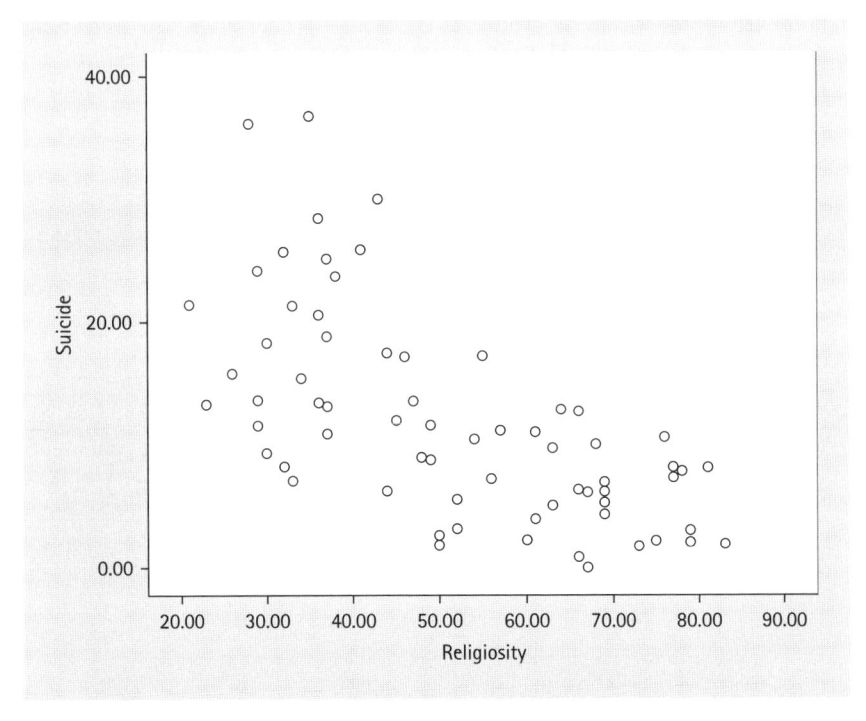

FIG. 7.1 Religiosity (as assessed by Gallup Index) and suicide rates across 67 countries. (Data provided courtesy of Brett Pelham, Gallup Organization, 2008.)

been so grand. Instead, they focus on secular countries whose values were fed by a Judeo-Christian heritage.

Still, Zuckerman has a point, as I confirmed in new Gallup survey data from 152 countries (Fig. 7.2). In countries where most people say that religion is *not* an important part of their daily life and where most people have *not* attended religious services in the last week, people tend to report high quality of life. Folks in highly religious countries (Pakistan, Uganda, the Philippines) mostly rate their lives well below the best possible life.

Moreover, the correlation between secularity and civility also occurs in US state-by-state comparisons. The Southern states all have higher religious adherence rates than do the West Coast states. They also have much higher crime and smoking rates, as shown in Figs 7.3 and 7.4.

But countries and states differ in many ways that covary with religiosity, including education, income, and race. Secular places tend to have educated, higher-income populations, for example. Thus comparing places compares populations that differ in countless ways.

Moreover, it is individuals (not populations) who experience more or less faith, health, and crime. And, ironically, the correlations across individuals run the other direction. Compared with never-attenders, the most religiously engaged Americans are about one-fourth as likely to be smokers or to have been arrested (see Figs 7.5 and 7.6).

Simple correlations of smoking and crime with religious attendance leave many factors uncontrolled. (Perhaps religious engagement rides along with some other causal factor. Or perhaps non-smoking, law-abiding, married folks seek out faith communities.) But these associations also appear within subgroups, as in the negative correlation between religiosity and arrest rates among those with lots of education and those with little education.

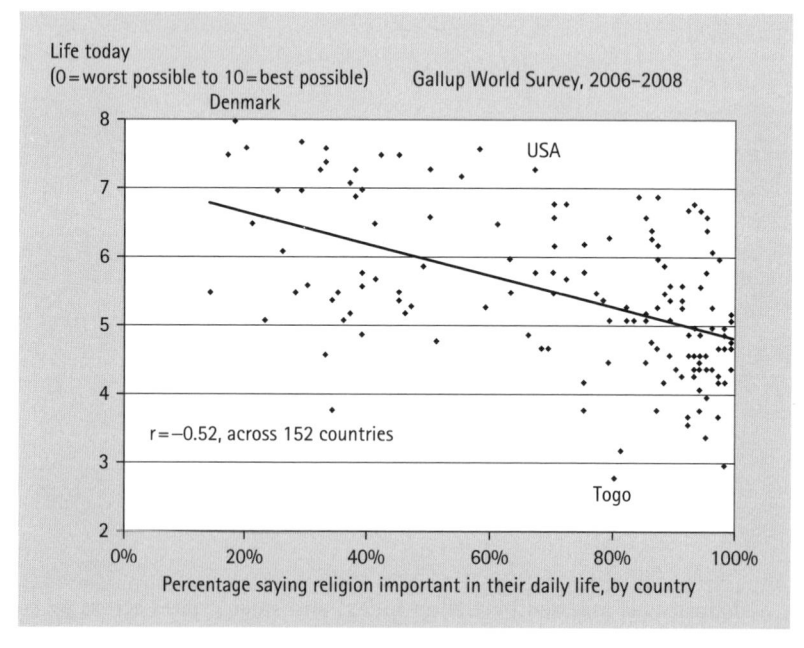

**FIG. 7.2** Religiosity and life satisfaction of 152 countries (data harvested from www.worldview.gallup.com).

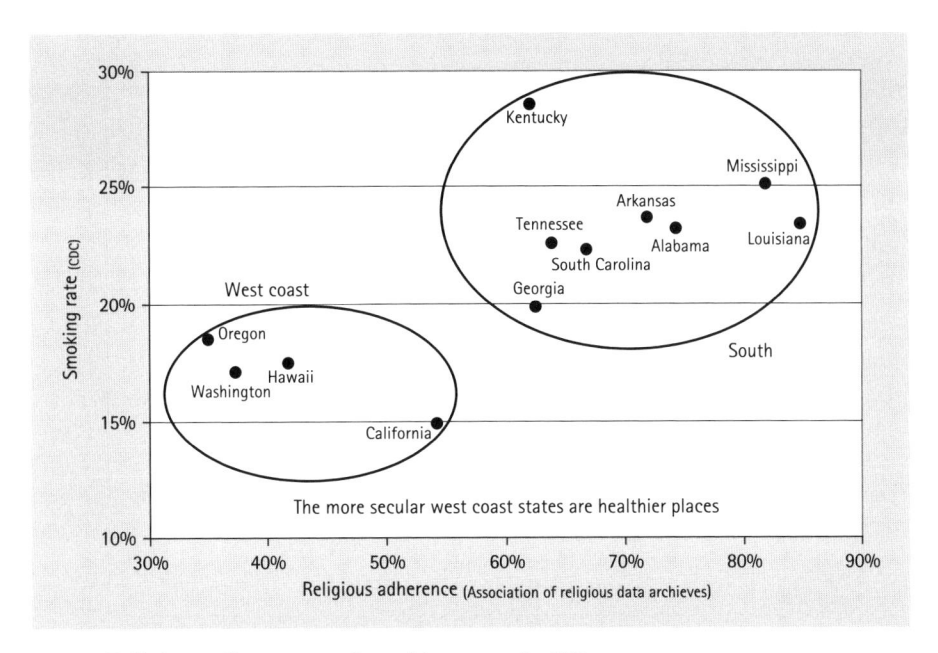

FIG. 7.3 Religious adherence and smoking rates, by US states.

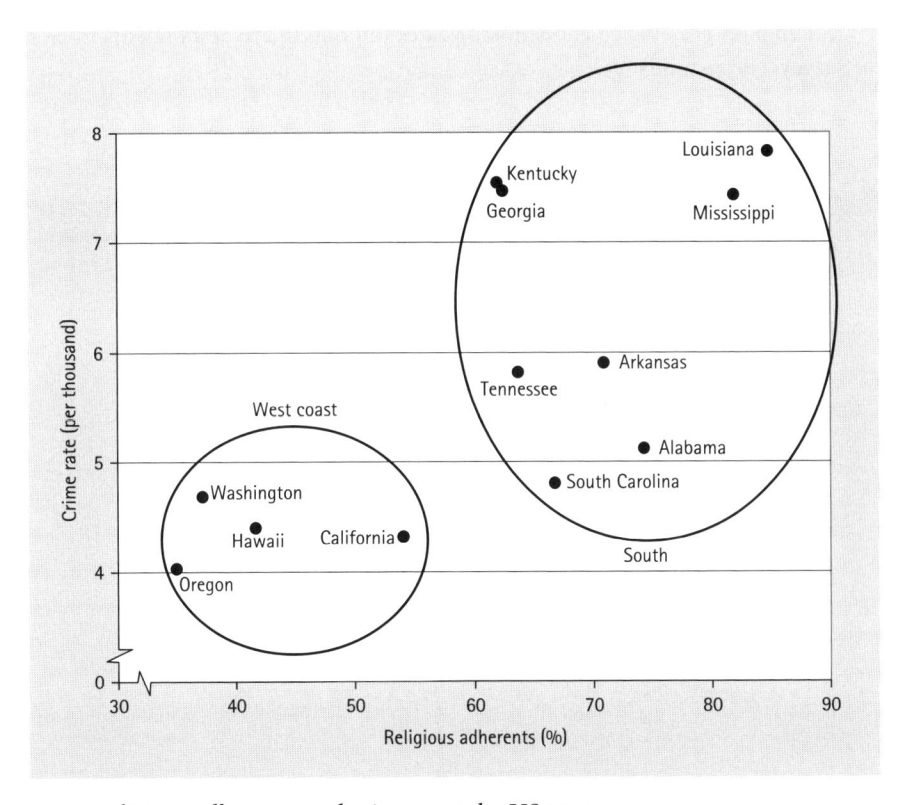

FIG. 7.4 Religious adherence and crime rates, by US states.

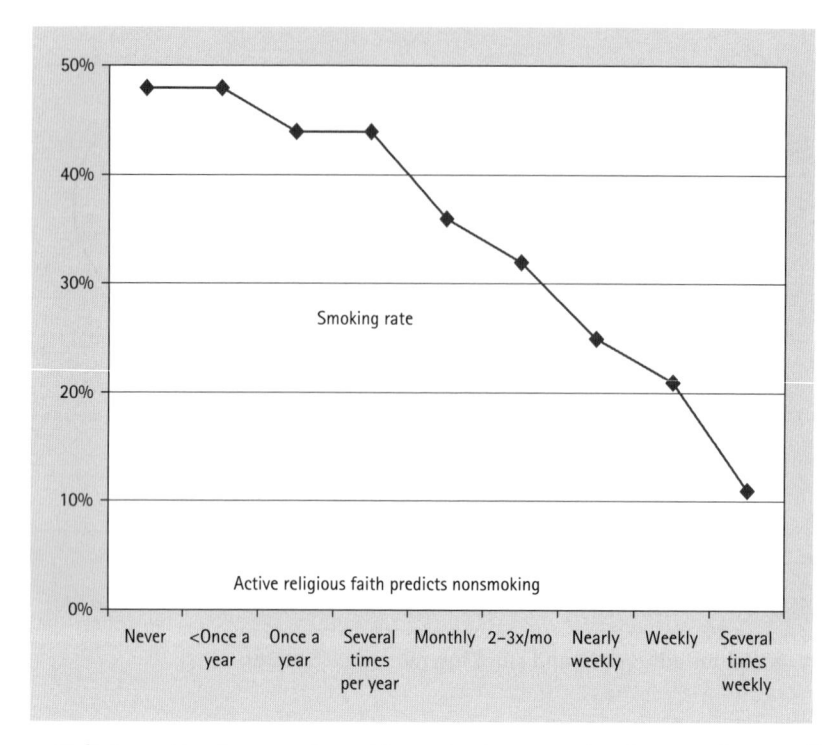

FIG. 7.5 Religious attendance and smoking rates (among 16,276 respondents to General Social Surveys, 1972–2008).

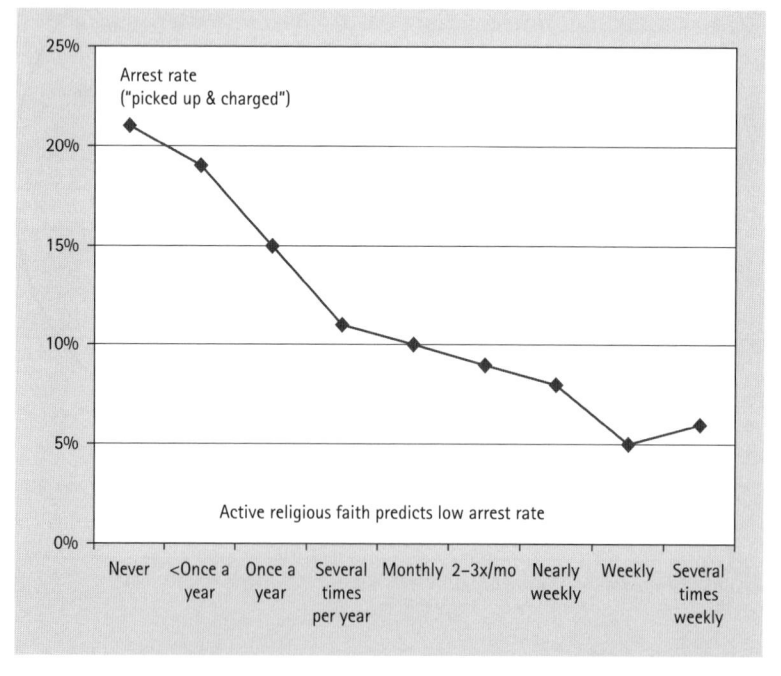

FIG. 7.6 Religious attendance and arrest rate (among 10,535 respondents to General Social Surveys, 1972–2008).

Thus, my first observation is that comparing *places* and comparing *people* reveals a "religious engagement paradox": Religious engagement correlates *negatively* with well-being across aggregate levels (nations, states) and *positively* across individuals. Answers sometimes depend on how we ask questions. There is, as Zuckerman has noted, a "great socio-religious irony" in that traditionally religious behaviors and values (such as non-smoking and obeying the law) are sometimes most practiced in irreligious countries and states, which suggests what he calls "the virtues of Godlessness." Nevertheless, it remains for future scholarship to plumb another irony: Within nations, the same religion-affirmed behaviors are most practiced by the most religious *individuals*. The virtues of Godliness?

Elsewhere, my colleagues and I have shown the religious engagement paradox to be similarly true for other measures of human flourishing (Diener, Tay, & Myers, 2010):

- Across *states*, religious engagement predicts shorter life expectancy. Across *individuals*, religious engagement predicts longer life expectancy.
- Across *states*, religious engagement predicts nominally higher divorce rates. Across *individuals*, religious engagement predicts lower divorce rate.
- Across *states*, religious engagement predicts higher teen pregnancy and birth rates. Across *individuals*, religious engagement predicts more support for "waiting 'til married," less teen sexual activity, and modestly fewer teen births.

## GODLESSNESS, GODLINESS, AND GOODNESS

The public debate over whether godliness fosters goodness has largely been waged as a battle of historical anecdotes. We have religion partly to thank for the horrors of the Crusades and Inquisition, for the Bible-banging KKK, and for the gay-bashing religious right. But we also have religion to thank for much of the antislavery, civil rights, and antiapartheid movements, and for the faith-based founding of hospitals, hospices, and universities.

But, say religion's skeptics, remember the 9/11 terrorists whose dastardly acts were bolstered by the confidence that their martyrdom would send them through a wormhole to an afterlife of bliss? "To fill a world with religion, or religions of the Abrahamic kind, is like littering the streets with loaded guns," wrote Richard Dawkins after 9/11. And do any of us believe that the hyper-religious Taliban and science-scorning fundamentalists are making the world a better place? Indeed not, acknowledge many religious advocates, agreeing that religion at its worst can be toxic and superstitious. But, they say, the genocidal Stalin and Mao, and more recently the brutal Pol Pot, Nicolae Ceaușescu, and Kim Jong-il, demonstrate the destructive power of an inhumane atheism that places no inherent value on human life.

The extremes—the best and the worst acts associated with religion and irreligion—capture our attention but rhetorically cancel each other. Thus we are left to wonder: On balance, is religion in everyday life more malevolent or benevolent?

## Prejudice

Fundamentalist faith feeds favoritism. In mid-twentieth century American correlational studies, conservative religiosity predicted racial prejudice. The tightly drawn circle that defined "us" excluded "them."

Nevertheless, noted Gordon Allport (1954/1979, p. 444), religion's links with prejudice have been paradoxical. Religion "makes prejudice and it unmakes prejudice." Church members were more prejudiced than non-members. But in study after study, faithful attenders, and those "intrinsically religious," were *less* prejudiced than nominally religious occasional attenders. Similarly, reports Northern Ireland social psychologist Ed Cairns from his studies of Catholic–Protestant hostilities, "the more people believed or went to church, the less prejudice they showed" (personal communication, May 16, 2007). "Catholic" and "Protestant" is, for some, a social identity marked by little spiritual engagement.

## Virtues

"Religiousness . . . has been empirically linked to a range of human virtues," report Christopher Peterson and Martin Seligman (2004, p. 609), "including forgiveness, kindness, and compassion."

*Forgiveness*, or something akin to it, is a shared feature of Islam, Judaism, Christianity, Buddhism, and Hinduism. In both laboratory and clinical intervention studies, forgiveness (letting go of hurtful and bitter thoughts and emotions without denying or excusing wrongdoing) has predicted improved emotional and physical well-being.

*Gratitude*—"a felt sense of wonder, thankfulness, and appreciation for life" (Emmons & Shelton, 2002, p. 460)—is another faith-promoted virtue. And it, too, fosters well-being. Students who keep a weekly journal of things for which they are grateful "feel better about their lives as a whole," report Emmons and Shelton. Ditto for those keeping daily gratitude logs.

*Compassion*, and its related virtues—kindness, nurturance, care, altruistic love—are likewise shared across faiths. Shalom Schwartz and Sipke Huismans (1995) found highly religious people expressed less hedonism and self-focus. This was true of Jews in Israel, Calvinists in the Netherlands, Catholics in Spain, the Orthodox in Greece, and Lutherans and Catholics in western Germany. Religions "exhort people to pursue causes greater than their personal desires," surmised Schwartz and Huismans. "The opposed orientation, self-indulgent materialism, seeks happiness in the pursuit and consumption of material goods."

## Volunteerism

Do the compassionate values of actively religious people predispose action? In National Opinion Research Center surveys of Americans "Volunteering some time to community service" has been deemed a "very important obligation" by 19% of those attending religious services less than once a year and by 40% of those attending weekly or more.

Does the walk match the talk? In studies of collegians and the general public, religiously engaged individuals (compared with those uncommitted) have reported volunteering more hours as relief workers, tutors, and campaigners for social justice. Among the 12% of Americans whom Gallup classified as "highly spiritually committed," 45% reported currently working among the infirm, the poor, or the elderly—double the 22% among those "highly uncommitted." In an ensuing Gallup survey, charitable and social service volunteering was reported by 50% of those who rated religion as "very important" and by 28% of those who rated it "not very important."

Public policy researcher Robert Putnam wondered if these religious links with volunteerism extend to non-religious communal organizations—to hobby clubs, professional associations, service clubs, and self-help groups. He reports in *Bowling Alone* (2000, p. 67) that "It was membership in religious groups that was most closely associated with other forms of civic involvement, like voting, jury service, community projects, talking with neighbors, and giving to charity." In follow-up research (personal communication, April 23, 2007), he finds that, even after controlling for other factors, religiously engaged people are more involved in community, in giving to secular organizations, and in volunteering.

Is this seeming effect of what Putnam calls "social involvement in a moral community" a peculiarly American phenomenon? In their analysis of 117,007 responses to European Values Surveys and World Values Surveys in 53 countries, Stijn Ruiter and Nan Dirk De Graaf (2006) found that "People who attend church twice a week are more than 5 times more likely to volunteer than people who never visit church."

In perhaps the most comprehensive aggregation of survey data from the planet earth, Gallup interviewed more than a quarter of a million people from 140 countries between 2006 and 2008 (Pelham & Crabtree, 2008). People were asked, "Have you done any of the following in the last month?" Fig. 7.7 indicates that, across the world, highly religious people reported volunteering about one and a half times as often as those less religious.

## Charitable giving

The quip, "when it comes to giving, some people stop at nothing" appears seldom true of those religiously engaged. In one late 1980s Gallup survey, Americans who never attended religious services reported giving away 1.1% of their incomes. Weekly attenders were two and a half times as generous. Judging from their self-reports, this 24% of the population reporting gave 48% of all individual charitable contributions. Ensuing 1990 and 1992 Gallup

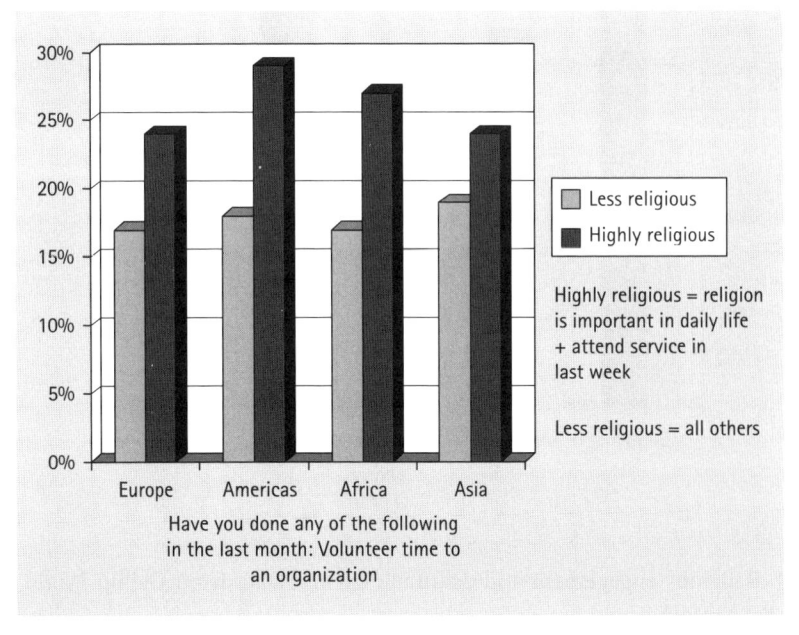

FIG. 7.7 Religious engagement and volunteerism. Data from Gallup World Surveys (Pelham & Crabtree, 2008).

surveys, and a 2001 Independent Sector survey, replicated the religiosity–philanthropy correlation. And so did the 2006 to 2008 Gallup world surveys, as shown in Fig. 7.8.

Does the higher rate of giving among religiously engaged people reflect a higher giving capacity? To the contrary, report the Gallup researchers. The annual income, in dollars, of those highly religious was significantly less ($10,000) than among the less religious comparison group ($17,500). "Seen in this light, the data presented here offer compelling evidence of the role of religious dedication in helping to encourage supportive community-oriented behaviors in areas where they may be most needed" (Pelham & Crabtree, 2008).

But is the generosity targeted primarily to people's own faith communities? (That could still be self-giving, but more ingroup focused.) The *Index of Global Philanthropy, 2007* reports—similarly to Robert Putnam's analyses of volunteering—that "Religious people are more charitable than the non-religious not only in giving to their congregations, but also—regardless of income, region, social class, and other demographic variables—significantly more charitable in their secular donations and informal giving" (Center for Global Prosperity, 2007, p. 22).

Researchers have also experimented with the religion factor by investigating whether subtly priming religious concepts affects generosity. Participants in one experiment by University of British Columbia researchers Azim Shariff and Ara Norenzayan (2007) first unscrambled sentences, which for some included the words *spirit, divine, God,* and *prophet*. When then given a choice of how many $1 coins to keep versus give to an unseen stranger, those primed with the religious concepts were more than doubly generous ($4.22 on average, versus $1.84). Follow-up experiments in the USA and Belgium have replicated the

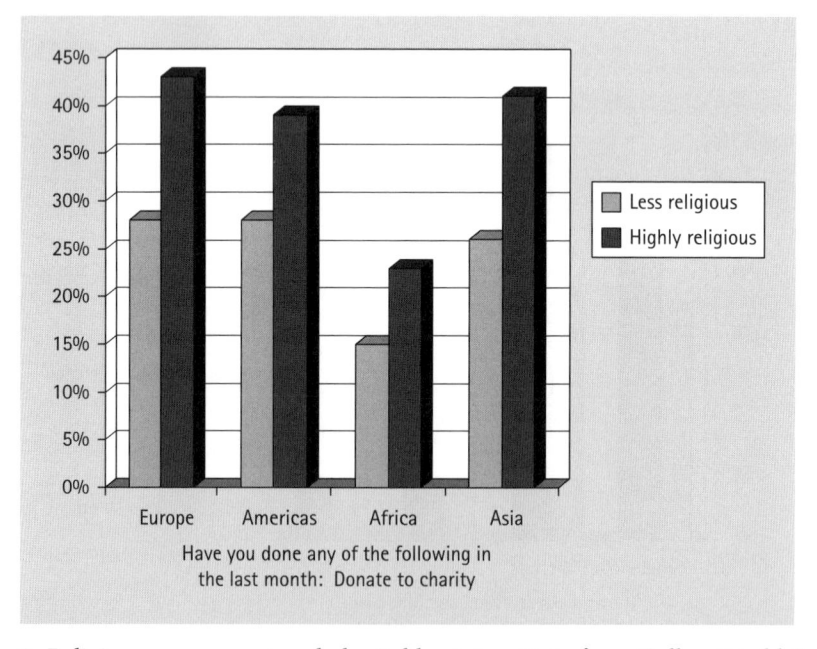

FIG. 7.8 Religious engagement and charitable giving. Data from Gallup World Surveys (Pelham & Crabtree, 2008).

phenomenon: priming religious cognition increases prosocial behavior (Pichon, Boccato, & Saroglou, 2007; Randolph-Seng & Nielsen, 2007).

## Religious Engagement and Happiness

We do not need research to know that people of all faiths and none exhibit both mirth and misery, mischief and morality. But we do need research to assess whether religion predicts joy or whether Christopher Hitchens is right that religion does "not make its adherents happy" (2007, p. 16).

The weight of the evidence suggests that religious engagement correlates with happiness. This is dramatically evident in the rate of self-reported "very happy" Americans, which ranges from 27% of those never attending religious services up to 48% of those attending more than weekly (Fig. 7.9).

Other surveys have found much the same. The Gallup Organization's 1984 "Religion in America" survey revealed that individuals highest in "spiritual commitment" (those consistently agreeing with statements such as "My religious faith is the most important influence in my life") were twice as likely as those least spiritually committed to report being "very happy." A more recent Pew study (2006) found 43% "very happy" among frequent (weekly or more) religious attenders, but only 26% among those seldom or never attending.

Other studies have focused on special populations. One meta-analysis of life satisfaction among older adults found that the best predictors were health and religiosity (Okun & Stock,

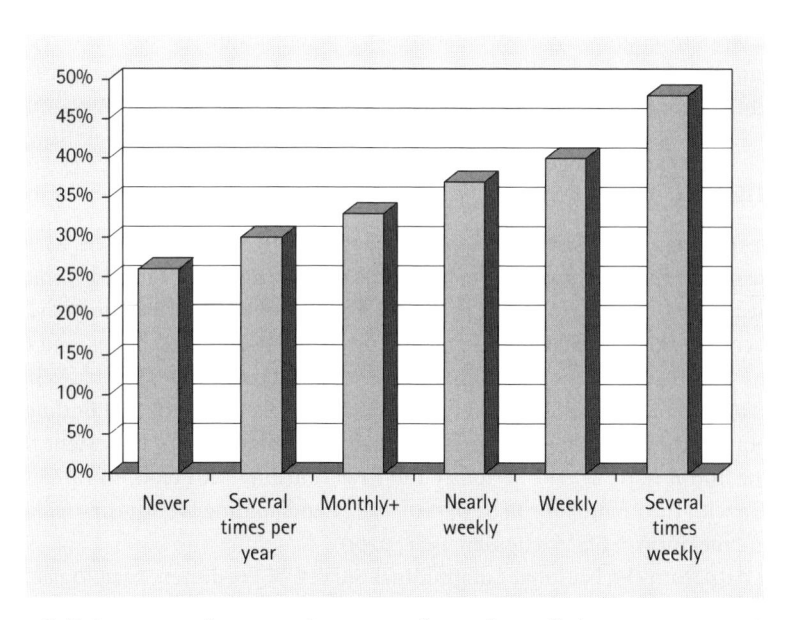

FIG. 7.9 Religious attendance and percent "very happy" (among 47,909 Americans responding in the General Social Surveys, 1972–2008).

1987). Elderly people tended to be happier and more satisfied if religiously committed and engaged. Those coping with crisis and loss—people recently widowed, mothers of developmentally challenged children, and those recovering from divorce, unemployment, illness, or bereavement—also have been observed to cope more successfully when such stresses are "buffered" by religious faith.

Seeking to explain the widely recognized correlation between religious engagement and well-being, researchers have entertained various possibilities.

## Social support

If humans have a basic "need to belong"—to connect with one another in close, supportive, enduring relationships—then might the millions of faith communities worldwide provide a source for such social support? Religion implies community ("religio" derives from the Latin *religare*, which means to bind together). People in faith communities talk of "the fellowship of kindred spirits," "the ties of love that bind," "the bearing of one another's burdens." Especially when bad things happen, religious engagement entails social support.

## Self-control

The social benefit of religious engagement matters. Yet after controlling for social support, some correlation between religion and well-being remains. In their *Psychological Bulletin* review, Michael McCullough and Brian Willoughby (2009) note that religiosity predicts diminished risk of crime, teen pregnancy, drug abuse, and smoking—and increased likelihood of longevity, marital satisfaction, and school success. Self-control also predicts all these things and may, McCullough and Willoughby theorize, mediate religion's beneficial associations. It makes sense, they argue, given evidence that agriculture (which requires a delay of gratification) and organized religion appeared at about the same time and place. Religious engagement enhances self-regulation, they surmise, which pays multiple dividends.

## Meaning and purpose

The nineteenth-century Polish poet Cyprian Norwid observed that "To be what is called happy; one should have 1) something to live on, 2) something to live for, and 3) something to die for. The lack of one of these results in drama. The lack of two results in tragedy."

Studies confirm that a sense of life purpose predicts positive well-being, and that many people find such through religious faith. Loss of meaning contributes to today's historically high depression rate, Martin Seligman (1988) has concluded. He adds that finding meaning requires "an attachment to something larger than the lonely self. To the extent that young people now find it hard to take seriously their relationship with God, to care about their relationship with the country, or to be part of a large and abiding family, they will find it difficult to find meaning in life" (Seligman, 1988, p. 55).

Mining data from the National Longitudinal Survey of Freshmen, sociologist Margarita Mooney (2008) observed that religiously active students studied more, got better grades, and were more satisfied with college (even after controlling for other factors that predict achievement). Religion, she concluded, "provides a work ethic or sense of meaning in college."

## Terror management

Many religions offer support, motivate self-control, suggest purposes for living, and also propose an ultimate hope, especially for those confronting what psychologists Jeff Greenberg, Mark Landau, Sheldon Solomon, and Tom Pyszczynski call "the terror resulting from our awareness of vulnerability and death" (in press).

Different faiths offer different paths. But most offer their adherents a sense that they—or something they are part of—will not ultimately be defeated by death. Aware of "the great enemy" death, they offer a hope that in the end (as the fourteenth-century mystic Julian of Norwich famously said), "all shall be well, and all shall be well, and all manner of things shall be well." Such hope may help people cope with threats. And it may explain why, in a recent national study, "belief in life after death was consistently and directly related to better mental health after controlling for other variables" (Flannelly et al., 2006).

For reasons such as these, evolutionary biologist David Sloan Wilson (2007), a self-described atheist, sees group-survival-promoting wisdom underlying religion. "Religious believers," he reports, "are more prosocial than non-believers, feel better about themselves, use their time more constructively, and engage in long-term planning rather than gratifying their impulsive desires. On a moment-by-moment basis, they report being more happy, active, sociable, involved, and excited."

So, religion has had mixed associations with bigotry and tolerance, and also with misery and well-being. On balance, however, it appears that faith fosters flourishing.

## REFERENCES

Allport, G. (1954/1979). *The nature of prejudice*. Boston, MA: Addison-Wesley.

Center for Global Prosperity (2007). *The index of global philanthropy*. Washington, DC: Center for Global Prosperity.

Colasanto, D. (1989, November). Americans show commitment to helping those in need. *Gallup Report*, 290.

Dawkins, R. (2001, September 15). Religion's misguided missiles. *The Guardian*. Retrieved from http://www.guardian.co.uk.

Dawkins, R. (2006). *The God delusion*. Boston, MA: Houghton Mifflin.

Diener, E., Tay, L., & Myers, D. (2010). Supporting online material for religiosity and happiness across the world. Unpublished manuscript.

Diener, E., Tay, L., & Myers, D. (2011). The religion paradox: If religion makes people happy, why are so many dropping out? *Journal of Personality and Social Psychology*, 101(6), 1278–1290.

Emmons, R., & Shelton, C. (2002). Gratitude and the science of positive psychology. In C. R. Snyder and S. J. Lopez (Eds.), *Handbook of positive psychology* (pp. 459–471). New York, NY: Oxford University Press.

Flannelly, K. J., Koenig, H. G., Ellison, C. G., Galek, K., & Krause, N. (2006). Belief in life after death and mental health—Findings from a national survey. *Journal of Nervous and Mental Disease*, 194, 524–529.

Freud, S. (1928/1964). *The standard edition of the complete psychological works of Sigmund Freud, Vol. IX*. J. Strachey (Ed. and Trans.), in collaboration with A. Freud, assisted by A. Strachey & A. Tyson. London: Hogarth Press and Institute of Psycho-Analysis.

Gallup, G., Jr. (1984, March). Religion in America. *Gallup Report*, 222.

Greenberg, J., Landau, M., Solomon, S., & Pyszczynski, T. (in press). What is the primary psychological function of religion? In D. Wulff (Ed.), *Handbook of the psychology of religion.* Oxford, UK: Oxford University Press.

Harris, S. (2006). *Letter to a Christian nation.* New York, NY: Alfred A. Knopf.

Hitchens, C. (2007). *God is not great: How religion poisons everything.* New York, NY: Twelve.

McCullough, M. E., & Willoughby, B. L. B. (2009). Religion, self-control, and self-regulation: Associations, explanations, and implications. *Psychological Bulletin, 135,* 69–93.

Mooney, M. (2008). Religion, college grades, and satisfaction among students at elite colleges and universities. Unpublished manuscript. Department of Sociology, University of North Carolina.

Norwid, C. (1976). Quoted in Tatarkiewicz, W., *Analysis of happiness.* The Hague: Martinus Nijhoff.

Okun, M. A., & Stock. W. A. (1987). Correlates and components of subjective well-being among the elderly. *Journal of Applied Gerontology, 6,* 95–112.

Pelham, B., & Crabtree, S. (2008, October). Worldwide, highly religious more likely to help others. Gallup Inc. Retrieved from http://www.gallup.com.

Peterson, C., & Seligman, M. E. P. (2004). *Character strengths and virtues: A handbook and classification.* New York, NY: Oxford University Press.

Pew (2006, February 13). Are we happy yet? *Pew Research Center.* Retrieved from http://www.pewresearch.org.

Pichon, I., Boccato, G., & Saroglou, V. (2007). Nonconscious influences of religion on prosociality: A priming study. *European Journal of Social Psychology, 37,* 1032–1045.

Putnam, R. (2000). *Bowling alone.* New York, NY: Simon & Schuster.

Randolph-Seng, B., & Nielsen, M. E. (2007). Honesty: One effect of primed religious representations. *International Journal for the Psychology of Religion, 17,* 303–315.

Ruiter, S., & De Graaf, N. D. (2006). National context, religiosity, and volunteering: Results from 53 countries. *American Sociological Review, 71,* 191–210.

Schwartz, S., & Huismans, S. (1995). Value priorities and religiosity in four Western religions. *Social Psychology Quarterly, 58,* 88–107.

Seligman, M. E. P. (1988, October). Boomer blues. *Psychology Today,* 50–55.

Shariff, A. F., & Norenzayan, A. (2007). God is watching you: Priming God concepts increases prosocial behavior in an anonymous economic game. *Psychological Science, 18,* 803–809.

Wade, N. (2010). *The faith instinct: How religion evolved and why it endures.* New York, NY: Penguin.

Wilson, D. S. (2003). *Darwin's cathedral: Evolution, religion, and the nature of society.* Chicago, IL: University of Chicago Press.

Wilson, D. S. (2007, July 4). Beyond demonic memes: Why Richard Dawkins is wrong about religion. *eSkeptic.* Retrieved from http://www.skeptic.com/skeptic/07-07-04.html.

Wright, R. (2009). *The evolution of God.* New York, NY: Little, Brown.

Zuckerman, P. (2006, August–Sept.). Is faith good for us? *Free Inquiry, 35*–38.

Zuckerman, P. (2009, January 30). The virtues of godlessness: The least religious nations are also the most healthy and successful. *Chronicle of Higher Education,* B4.

# CHAPTER 8

# POSITIVE PSYCHOLOGICAL EXPERIENCES AND PSYCHOPATHOLOGY: A SELF-REGULATORY PERSPECTIVE

PATTY FERSSIZIDIS[1], TODD B. KASHDAN[1], RACHEL A. MARQUART[1], AND MICHAEL F. STEGER[2]

[1]George Mason University, USA; [2]Colorado State University, USA

HAPPY people, by definition, tend to be psychologically healthy. They experience a high frequency of positive emotions, few symptoms of psychopathology (Diener & Seligman, 2002), and a high quality of life in work, relationship, and health domains (Lyubomirsky, King, & Diener 2005). People who are happy also report a number of adaptive characteristics that are often lacking in people suffering from psychopathology, including effective coping and problem-solving strategies, greater self-esteem, optimism, and social and physical activity (Lyubomirsky et al., 2005). While the pursuit for achieving psychological health and happiness may be challenging for the average person, it is often futile when psychological disorders are present. After all, mental disorder is defined by excessive distress and/or impaired functioning in life domains.

The psychopathology literature is replete with a focus on negative emotions and impairment. It is often assumed that people with psychological problems are less successful at recognizing and responding to environmental reward cues. Yet only a select number of disorders are characterized by a diminished capacity for rewarding experiences, and some people endure profound distress with little disruption to the positive experiences in their life. It is our goal in this chapter to focus on discussing elements of happiness across psychological disorders and along the way to propose future directions for research in this area. We also aim to highlight certain disorders characterized by a diminished capacity for positive experiences and quality of life in particular areas.

Emotional experiences influence how we think and act. When people feel good, they are more likely to approach goals and work toward building resources which, in turn, contribute to greater happiness (Elliot & Thrash, 2002; Fredrickson, 2001; Lyubomirsky, 2001). Feeling bad, on the other hand, leads to greater avoidance which in turn, stunts goal attainment and resource building. For decades, scientists assumed that positive emotions and approach behaviors comprised one end of a continuum opposite negative emotions and avoidance behaviors. However recent advances in personality, motivation, and social neuroscience suggest that while approach and avoidance systems are related, they represent relatively independent aspects of functioning (Cacioppo & Bernston, 1994; Carver, 2001).

The weak inverse relation between positive and negative affect and underlying temperaments supports the notion of relatively independent approach and avoidance systems (Clark, Watson, & Mineka, 1994). This means that as a general rule, knowing that someone is experiencing significant distress offers little insight into how that person experiences positive events. However, there are important caveats. Disorders such as social anxiety disorder, depression, and schizophrenia show strong links to an underactive approach system, resulting in attenuated positive emotions and lost opportunities for enriching and meaningful life experiences (Blanchard, Mueser, & Belalck, 1998; Kashdan, 2007; Rottenberg, 2005; Steger, 2012).

In this chapter, we discuss the nuances of how people with various psychological conditions experience positive emotions and events. Due to space constraints, we have narrowed our focus to discussing the most prevalent psychological disorders: anxiety and mood disorders.

# Anxiety Disorders

Approximately 20% of people in the world will suffer from an anxiety disorder during their lifetime (Kessler, Chiu, Demler, & Walters, 2005). The personal burden of an anxiety disorder often extends beyond emotional pain to include infrequent rewarding moments, diminished satisfaction and meaning in life, and impaired relationships (Olatunji, Cisler, & Tolin, 2007). So what is it about chronic anxiety that leads to diminished positive experiences and fewer positive relationships? Recent work on emotion and self-regulation suggest that a person's approach for managing anxiety influences positive experiences.

People suffering from anxiety disorders characteristically devote substantial time and energy on attempts to control and escape contact with anxious thoughts, feelings, and bodily sensations. Controlling and avoiding unpleasant internal experiences can be an adaptive short-term strategy for coping with stress in certain situations. For instance, a nervous job applicant might try to restrain anxious thoughts and behaviors during an interview. However, when avoiding contact with negative emotions becomes a default strategy to deal with daily hassles and momentary distress, fewer resources are available for constructing a satisfying and engaging life (Vohs, Baumeister, & Ciarocco, 2005). This is because self-control is an exhaustible resource. At any given point in time, we have a limited supply of self-regulatory resources (e.g., attention, willpower, energy) to manage ongoing events (Muraven & Baumeister, 2000). When self-control resources are depleted, people become less effective in subsequent tasks requiring them. This resource drain is proposed to diminish contact with present experiences and interfere with progress toward valued goals (Hayes, Luoma, Bond, Masuda, & Lillis, 2006).

For people with anxiety disorders, excessive attempts to manage anxiety deplete the resources needed to extract rewards from present experiences, pursue aspirational goals, and develop relationships. Self-regulatory resource drain can also exacerbate distress and functional impairment. We regard present-moment awareness and curiosity as key means for people to derive positive experiences from life, with maladaptive self-regulation strategies—such as those described earlier—serving to erode people's ability to be in the moment. In the next section, we apply this self-regulatory framework to each of the anxiety disorders below to elucidate how maladaptive attempts to cope with anxiety can cripple rewarding experiences.

## Trauma responses

Most people will experience at least one potentially traumatic event during their lifetime. There is extensive variability in how people respond to these events. While some people go on to experience chronic disruption in their lives, others are able to recover from impairments over time, and a final group of people are able to cope and continue functioning with little disruption (Bonanno, 2004). Despite these diverse responses to potentially traumatic events, positive experiences in trauma survivors have received scant attention.

Within this small body of research, there is a growing literature on the idea that people may come through trauma with positive changes in their functioning. Some people emerge from trauma with a new perspective on what matters in life. This ability to find meaning in trauma has led some researchers to conclude that people "grow" or develop psychologically as a result of adversity. While this may be the case for certain people, far too much of the work linking enhanced functioning to trauma exposure is limited by a failure to attend to pre-trauma functioning (Westphal & Bonanno, 2007). While this discussion extends beyond the scope of this chapter, we want to emphasize that some people adapt well to adverse events and can, at times, find benefit in these experiences.

Research focusing on the ability to maintain healthy, symptom-free functioning has shown that resilient people have a greater capacity for generative experiences (e.g., developing hobbies, new relationships) and positive emotions after trauma (Keltner & Bonanno, 1997). Resilient people are better able to express positive emotions with behaviors such as humor, smiling, and laughter, while simultaneously experiencing perturbations following adverse events. Expressing positive emotions in certain contexts can be adaptive as positive expressions can evoke beneficial responses in others during a time when support is needed. For instance, the expression of genuine positive emotion (e.g., smiles and laughter) while discussing certain negative life events, such as the death of a spouse, elicited a favorable response from others and was related to improved adjustment (Papa & Bonanno, 2008). But positive emotional expressiveness may not always be helpful. Papa and Bonanno (2008) explored how displaying positive emotions in contexts generally viewed as inappropriate (e.g., laughing at another's misfortune) would be perceived by others. The findings revealed that genuinely smiling or laughing while speaking about more socially inappropriate topics (e.g., death of a child, child abuse) elicited a negative response from others and was not linked to any mental health benefits.

Much of the trauma literature focuses on subclinical trauma impairments and post-traumatic stress disorder (PTSD). The few studies examining how people with PTSD experience positive events are isolated to studies of PTSD in combat veterans. Findings show that veterans suffering from PTSD report fewer rewarding social interactions and relationships and less altruistic behavior and leisure activities compared to veterans without disorder (Frueh, Turner, Beidel, & Cahill, 2001; Riggs, Bryne, Weathers, & Litz, 1998). PTSD in veterans has also been linked to fewer positive emotions and intrinsically motivating activities in daily life and fewer character strengths—including hope, optimism, gratitude, and forgiveness—as measured by self-report and informant ratings (Kashdan, Julian, Merritt, & Uswatte, 2006; Kashdan, Uswatte, & Julian, 2006).

The shortage of meaningful and rewarding experiences in veterans with PTSD may be a function of self-regulatory resource drain. Embedded in the constellation of symptoms that comprise PTSD is an impaired capacity for self-regulation. While adaptive coping necessitates a willingness to confront and work with distressing stimuli, people with PTSD engage in excessive attempts to avoid or escape them. This avoidance can stunt the coping process and contribute to distress (Plumb, Orsillo, & Luterek, 2004), poorer quality of life (Kashdan, Morina, & Priebe, 2009), and the maintenance of PTSD (Marx & Sloan, 2005). Avoidance of unpleasant experiences can also leave a person unresponsive to environmental cues. People with PTSD who report emotional numbness show attenuated reactions to positive, rewarding stimuli (Litz, Orsillo, Kaloupek, & Weathers, 2000; Orsillo, Batten, Plumb, Luterek, & Roessner, 2004). Further, organizing one's life around attempts to regulate unwanted emotions can limit personal growth opportunities and diminish well-being. For instance, when asked what they think about, plan for, and try to accomplish in their daily lives, combat veterans with PTSD endorse more strivings related to controlling and avoiding emotions than anything else (Kashdan, Breen, & Julian, 2010). Importantly, these efforts fail to translate into any discernible benefits in terms of well-being (such as joy or meaning). Conversely, veterans without PTSD endorse more strivings such as being a good father and kind person that are unrelated to regulating emotions, and subsequently receive greater benefit from their pursuits. These findings shed light on how actions made with the intention to protect the self may not only fail to protect, but stunt a person's ability to thrive.

We are just beginning to understand how people's responses in the aftermath of trauma influence their enduring abilities to live a good life. Future work can expand on this in several ways. We need a better understanding of the factors that contribute to how people prioritize and pursue life goals following trauma. It is also imperative to understand how these processes are influenced by personality and situational characteristics during pre-trauma periods. By studying people prior to and following trauma exposure, we can better identify the conditions that lead to resilience, recovery, or disorder. Finally, greater efforts are needed to extend this line of research beyond combat trauma to include other traumatic events.

## Social anxiety disorder

The advantages of close relationships are extensive, including greater self-esteem, better physical health, and an increased sense of well-being and life satisfaction (Diener & Seligman, 2002; Leary, 2004; Sedikides, Oliver, & Campbell, 1994). Thus, it makes sense that a disorder that impairs a person's ability to form and maintain relationships might be especially relevant to reductions in positive experiences and happiness.

Socially anxiety is characterized by a fear of being scrutinized by other people because this is liable to lead to negative evaluation and/or rejection (Rapee & Heimberg, 1997). Thus, people with social anxiety disorder (SAD) tend to be hyperfocused on making a good impression on others. Yet, they often doubt their ability to do so as they believe their anxiety will disrupt their social performance (Rapee & Heimberg, 1997). As a result, people with SAD frequently go into "prevention mode" where they devote substantial time and effort to controlling or escaping anxious thoughts and feelings. This prevention focus includes excessive attempts to avoid anxiety-provoking stimuli and engaging in "safety" behaviors (e.g., limited eye contact, talking very little) in hopes of deflecting attention and minimizing the possibility of rejection (Clark & Wells, 1995). While these efforts may reduce the likelihood of rejection, they also leave the socially anxious person less responsive to the outside world. As a result, people who are socially anxious are less likely to pursue activities that could generate positive outcomes.

Social anxiety disorder has commonly been associated with elevated negative affect. However there is substantial evidence that, at least for some people, social anxiety has a stable, moderate, inverse relation with both positive affect and curiosity and exploratory tendencies (for reviews, see Kashdan (2007) and Kashdan, Weeks, and Savostyanova (2011)). However, much of this research has relied on global questionnaires to measure the presence and frequency of positive emotions—a retrospective approach that cannot disentangle information processing and reporting biases from actual experiences. Further, emotional experiences are dynamic processes that change over the course of the day. To best understand how anxiety influences the way people structure their day and pursue potentially rewarding opportunities, these experiences need to be assessed as they arise in ecologically valid settings.

There have been several attempts to capture positive emotions in everyday life for people with varying levels of social anxiety. In one particular study, participants reported on their current situation and positive emotions during four random prompts per day for 2 weeks (Kashdan & Collins, 2010). Overall, people who were more socially anxious reported fewer positive emotions compared to their less anxious peers. Importantly, this effect remained regardless of whether socially anxious people happened to be spending time alone or with others when prompted. This finding is consistent with other work showing socially anxious people report attenuated positive experiences when interacting with others, whether with someone they know or a stranger (Brown, Silvia, Myin-Germeys, & Kwapil, 2007).

Given the self-regulation difficulties of people with SAD, the occurrence of pleasurable experiences in socially anxious people can be expected to vary as a function of the amount of self-regulatory resources deployed to manage anxiety. Kashdan and Steger (2006) examined how social anxiety and emotion regulation attempts on a given day influenced subsequent positive experiences over the course of 21 days. Of people with greater trait social anxiety, those who reported heightened social anxiety and greater attempts to suppress their emotions on a given day reported 24% fewer positive events than other socially anxious people. In this same study, endorsing low social anxiety alone was not enough to yield positive outcomes. The highest frequency of positive events and emotions in a given day were reported by people with low social anxiety and greater tendencies to accept, work with, and express their emotions on a given day. These findings highlight the importance of studying how self regulation impacts emotional experiences in the context of daily life (instead of relying solely on global questionnaires and interviews).

Recent research examining the sexual relationships of socially anxious people adds further support to the notion that social anxiety is characterized by a diminished capacity for positive experiences. Using a 3-week daily diary methodology, Kashdan et al. (2011) found that women with high social anxiety (but not men) engaged in less sexual activity compared to less anxious women. Compared to their less anxious peers, socially anxious men and women were more likely to rate their sexual episodes as less pleasurable and to feel less emotionally connected to their sex partners. Importantly, despite being in romantic relationships perceived as close and intimate, people with high social anxiety reported feelings of connectedness during sex that were as low as ratings by non-anxious people in unsatisfying romantic relationships. In other words, having a close romantic partner did not contribute to an improved quality of sex life in socially anxious people. Of note, none of these social anxiety effects could be accounted for by shared variance with depressive symptoms.

Findings from studies on cognitive processing and the neural networks of people with social anxiety further support the notion of an underactive approach system. One cognitive bias that is particularly relevant to social anxiety is the processing of facial expressions. Facial expressions convey important information, such as like and dislike, that can signal either approach or avoidance behaviors. For a socially anxious person, being able to quickly and accurately interpret a person's expressions can be advantageous as they navigate the social world. Recent laboratory work has examined how quickly people with varying levels of social anxiety can recognize positive and negative facial expressions (Silvia, Allan, Beauchamp, Maschauer, & Workman, 2006). While level of social anxiety did not influence how quickly people recognized sad and angry faces, people with elevated social anxiety were slower at detecting happy faces.

Beyond subjective and behavioral reports of attenuated positive experiences in social anxiety, people with SAD show deficient dopaminergic activity in the brain, with dopamine being associated with reward sensitivity and approach behavior (Sareen et al., 2007; Schneier et al., 2000). To capture the neurobiological changes associated with social anxiety in a more dynamic situation, Davidson and colleagues (2000) measured an electroencephalogram while a person anticipated making a speech in front of strangers. Compared to healthy controls, people with SAD displayed greater reactivity in the right anterior and lateral prefrontal cortex. This pattern of activation suggests decreased approach-related motivation. Together, these findings imply that the neural circuitry of people with SAD may be wired in a way that makes them less responsive to rewarding stimuli. It will be important for future research to replicate these findings and broaden this work to more ecologically valid situations.

With the exception of a few studies, the extant research assumes socially anxious people are a homogenous group. However people with social anxiety differ in the type and amount of social situations which cause them to feel anxious and to date, several subgroups have been identified within the disorder. People with generalized SAD become anxious in a variety of social situations whereas people with non-generalized SAD report concerns specific to performance situations (e.g., public speaking). The evidence suggests that while attenuated positive experiences and approach-related behaviors are associated with the generalized subtype, the non-generalized subtype is only weakly related to diminished positive emotions and exploratory tendencies (Hughes et al., 2006; Kashdan, 2002). Further, recent evidence suggests that at least 20% of people with elevated social anxiety fit an atypical profile characterized by risk-prone, approach-oriented behavior (Kashdan & McKnight, 2010). These people might act aggressively to maintain dominance over others in order to reduce the likelihood of being rejected, and engage in impulsive and risky behaviors to obtain immediate gratification (e.g., having sex with a stranger). Despite this atypical presentation, risk-prone behaviors appear to serve the same function as the shy and inhibited behaviors of more prototypical socially anxious people—to control anxiety and reduce the risk of rejection.

Recent research on social anxiety has greatly enhanced our understanding of positive psychological experiences within the disorder. Future work can examine the temporal sequence of the onset of SAD and presence and reactions to positive events. For instance, are people with an underactive approach system more likely to develop SAD or do the features of the disorder make appetitive activity too costly? Does social anxiety inhibit mindfulness and curiosity or do people with SAD have pre-existing lower levels? Also, we need to know more about how the daily activities of people with social anxiety problems influence their capacity to generate positive events and experiences. Do they organize their lives in a way that disrupts their own ability to obtain meaning and health? Finally, we need to develop a more thorough understanding of how positive experiences are cultivated and how people respond to rewards across different subgroups of SAD, particularly in the atypical risk-prone SAD group of which we know little.

## Generalized anxiety disorder

Generalized anxiety disorder (GAD) was once used as a default diagnosis for people presenting with anxiety problems who did not fit into another, well-defined diagnostic category. However over a decade of research has linked GAD to a unique profile characterized by catastrophic "what if" thinking and persistent, uncontrollable worry. These cognitive processes not only obstruct opportunities for positive experiences, but contribute to significant life disruptions including problematic relationships with others, poor work performance, and substantial reductions in quality of life (Henning, Turk, Mennin, Fresco, & Heimberg, 2007).

Several theoretical models emerged to explain the mechanisms that contribute to and maintain catastrophic thinking and chronic worry. Where these theories and the data converge is that people with GAD use worry as a tool to achieve their goal of avoiding contact with unpleasant thoughts, feelings, and sensations. For most people, worry can be an adaptive short-term response for dealing with anxiety as it activates solutions for managing potentially stressful situations. For people with GAD, worry becomes maladaptive because it is used excessively (even when there is little or no reason to worry) and it fails to mobilize action or relieve concerns that something bad may happen. In addition to worrying about everyday life events (e.g., conflict at work), people with GAD worry about future events that have a low probability of occurring (e.g., developing an illness, being in an accident). The paradox is that many people with GAD overvalue the benefit of worry (e.g., "Worry keeps me safe") but also fear its prolonged use (e.g., "All this worry is going to make me go crazy"). In a vicious cycle, concerns over the potential negative effects of worry can magnify anxiety and stimulate an even greater reliance on worry in an attempt to cope with these beliefs (Wells & Carter, 1999).

From a self-regulatory perspective, excessive attempts to control unwanted thoughts and feelings via worry can lead to a resource drain that leaves a person less open and responsive to opportunities for positive experiences. Being focused on the future is incompatible with present-moment awareness and curiosity. Thus it would be expected that people with GAD would experience a subsequent reduction in pleasurable experiences. To date, no one has systematically studied how regular attempts to manage unwanted thoughts and feelings in daily life impacts the occurrence of positive outcomes in people suffering from GAD. However, findings from correlational studies support a link between GAD and attenuated positive experiences. For instance, people with GAD are more likely than healthy controls to show impairments in their ability to savor positive events (Roemer, Salters, Raffa, & Orsillo, 2005).

The dysregulated emotional experiences associated with GAD appear to stem from a deficit in the ability to understand and regulate emotions. People with GAD experience negative emotions easily, intensely, and frequently (Brown, Chorpita, & Barlow, 1998) and this is proposed to result from a relative lack of knowledge about emotions and how to cope with them (Roemer & Orsillo, 2002). People with GAD have difficulty identifying and differentiating basic emotions such as anger, fear, disgust, and joy (Salters-Pedneault et al., 2006). When a person cannot identify how they are feeling, they are less able to use emotions as a source of information and are more likely to dwell on, misinterpret, and amplify the physiological sensations that accompany negative emotional arousal (Taylor, Bagby, & Parker, 1997). Consequently, people who struggle to identify their emotional experience are less successful in their efforts to manage their emotions (Barrett, Gross, Christensen, & Benvenuto, 2001; Kashdan, Ferssizidis, Collins, & Muraven, 2010). As a result, people with GAD have difficulty coping with negative emotions and fail to capitalize on positive events.

As is the case with all psychological disorders, there is variability in how people within a given diagnostic category experience both life disruptions and positive outcomes. Using a sample of older adults (ages 60–80) diagnosed with GAD, Bourland et al. (2000) found that older adults with GAD who were more optimistic and had a higher income reported greater life satisfaction. In addition, being optimistic was associated with fewer depressive symptoms and a decreased tendency to worry. Of note, these participants were part of a larger treatment intervention study and as such, optimism scores in this sample may have been influenced by the context in which the study was conducted. Further, the correlational nature of this study cannot answer whether optimism works as a buffer against elevated depression symptoms and worry, or if simply being less impaired allows for greater optimism. However these findings reinforce the need for additional work to assess the therapeutic benefits of building strengths.

The study of positive psychological functioning in GAD is underdeveloped and only beginning to be understood. The evidence thus far suggests that people with GAD experience few rewarding events, perhaps as a result of an impaired capacity for self-regulation. One avenue for future research is to observe how people identify and work with emotional experiences in daily life and how these processes influence approach-related behavior and reward responsiveness. How do strengths and the capacity for mindfulness influence these processes? Can teaching people greater clarity of emotions stimulate more successful emotion regulation?

# Depressive Disorders

The depressive disorders are among the most prevalent and burdensome psychological conditions. It is estimated that one out of seven people will suffer from a depressive disorder during their lifetime (Kessler, 2005). These emotional disturbances have a high rate of relapse and adversely affect functioning across numerous life domains. Additionally, people with depressive disorders are at substantially higher risk for substance abuse problems and suicide as compared to people with other psychological conditions (Demyttenaere, 2006; McKnight & Kashdan, 2009). Because of their high prevalence, chronic nature, and pervasive impact, these disorders represent one of the most costly health care problems.

Of all the psychological disorders, the most profound variations in the capacity for positive psychological experiences are found in the depressive disorders. The core feature associated with disrupted positive experiences in people suffering from depressive conditions appears to be a dysfunctional approach system. Whereas diminished approach-related behaviors and positive emotions are characteristic of depression, the bipolar spectrum disorders are associated with increased appetitive activity and abnormally elevated mood (Clark et al., 1994). Despite how it manifests, a dysfunctional approach system in the context of a depressive disorder contributes to significant life disruption.

The following sections elucidate how impairments in the approach system that leave a person unresponsive to positive stimuli or overly sensitive to rewarding experiences obstruct opportunities for enriching and meaningful life experiences.

## Depression

Depression is the number one cause of disability in developing nations (Murray & Lopez, 1996), accounting for an estimated 20% of all economic costs related to mental illness (Greenberg, Stiglin, Finkelstein, & Berndt, 1993). Theories that have been developed to explain depression highlight a multitude of factors that contribute to its development and maintenance. Because we cannot adequately review all of these factors, we focus on several core aspects of depression that are particularly relevant to positive psychological functioning—social, motivational, and affective deficits.

Similar to SAD, depression is associated with impoverished social experiences. Depressed people report an underdeveloped social support system, fewer close relationships, and greater interpersonal conflict. They are also less likely to derive benefits from their social lives. Depressed people report less intimacy and enjoyment in social interactions, even in the context of close relationships (Nezlek, Hampton, & Shean, 2000). Further, other people report that depressed people are less pleasurable to be around and in turn, elicit fewer favorable and caring responses from others (Joiner & Coyne, 1999).

These interpersonal difficulties might stem from how depressed people respond to environmental cues. Researchers have found that depressed people are less attuned to stimuli that promote social connection and fulfillment. People who are clinically depressed show preferential attention to sad over happy stimuli (Gotlib, et al., 2004). They also have a tendency to interpret neutral and ambiguous facial expressions and situations as being less positive and more negative (Joiner & Coyne, 1999). This negativity bias limits awareness of positive environmental cues thereby limiting opportunities for rewards to be realized.

Depressed people also exhibit motivational and affective disturbances that interfere with positive psychological functioning. Indeed, a hallmark feature of major depressive disorder is the diminished capacity to experience pleasure (i.e., anhedonia). Rather than savor positive emotional experiences, depressed people engage in attempts to dampen or suppress them (Eisner, Johnson, & Carver, 2009). Clinically depressed people also exhibit signs of deficient appetitive motivation (e.g., fatigue, psychomotor retardation, and apathy). In everyday life, this translates into less engagement in activities associated with enhancing well-being. For instance, people who are depressed report less commitment and progress towards personal goals and are more likely to hold on to unattainable goals compared to non-depressed peers (Schultheiss, Jones, Davis, & Kley, 2008). When personal goals are unmet, the rewarding outcomes associated with goal attainment are lost. Further, failure to reach goals often increases frustration and feelings of depression which leaves less energy to pursue other potentially gratifying activities.

Recent scientific research suggests that people who are depressed are not only less responsive to positive experiences, but less responsive to all emotion cues, regardless of valence (Rottenberg, 2005). Laboratory work has shown that people who are clinically depressed show less reactivity to both reward and punishment cues (e.g., winning/losing money in a gambling task; Henriques & Davidson, 2000) as well as to other positively and negatively valenced stimuli (e.g., words, images and film clips; Berenbaum & Oltmanns, 1992; Rottenberg, Kasch, Gross, & Gotlib, 2002; Sloan, Strauss, Quirk, & Sajatovic, 1997; Thomas et al., 2001). These findings support a conceptualization of depression as a disorder characterized by constricted emotional reactivity. Nonetheless, others have found that depressed people show greater reactivity to reward cues when they perceive the reward as being attributable to global and stable causes (Must et al., 2006; Needles & Abramson, 1990).

Because the controlled measurement of emotional reactivity in laboratory settings cannot capture the nuances of how depressed people respond to positive and negative events in their natural environment, two studies have examined emotional responsiveness using a daily diary methodology. One study found that people with clinically elevated depression were more reactive to positive and negative events compared to their less depressed peers (Nezlek & Gable, 2001). People who were more depressed experienced greater increases in well-being on days when positive events occurred and greater depressive thinking on days when negative events occurred. Similarly, Steger and Kashdan (2009) found that people with elevated depression experienced greater emotional reactivity to positive and negative social interactions. Depressed people experienced less well-being on days when they had negative social interactions. And despite having fewer positive interactions overall, depressed people incurred greater benefit from their positive interactions compared to their less depressed peers.

Findings on emotional reactivity in depression diverge across laboratory and naturalistic observations. This may be a result of methodological differences. First, real-life situations may be associated with greater threat and reward than laboratory tasks, thus leading to greater emotional reactivity to everyday events. Second, most of the lab-based studies included participants who met the diagnostic criteria for major depressive disorder whereas the daily diary studies modeled depressive symptoms on a continuum. By definition, people who meet diagnostic criteria for depression experience significant life impairment across multiple areas. This is not necessarily the case for people who score high on a measure of depression. Together, these findings suggest that focusing on level of self-reported distress and negative symptoms may be less relevant than assessing functional capacity when attempting to understand the difference between normal depressive experiences and disorder.

A different set of researchers have explored whether cultivating character strengths can enhance well-being and reduce depressive symptoms. Using a non-clinical sample, people who practiced being thankful for three good things in their life on a daily basis reported fewer depressive symptoms and greater happiness over time (Seligman, Steen, Park, & Peterson, 2005). Similarly, people instructed to identify their signature strengths and then to use one of those strengths in a new way each day demonstrated fewer depressive symptoms and greater happiness and over time. Intervention efforts aimed at building character strengths have yielded short-term positive results in reducing depressive symptoms, building positive emotions, and enhancing engagement and meaning in life (Duckworth, Steen, & Seligman, 2005). Despite these gains, after a few months no differences were found with a placebo–control condition. However, building character strengths may boost resilience to depression. One program found that cultivating optimism in school-aged children helped offset the risk of developing depression (Gillham, Reivich, Jaycox, & Seligman, 1995). Children who were identified as at risk for depression prior to the intervention were half as likely (22%) to report moderate to severe symptoms of depression 2 years following the intervention as compared to children in the control group (44%). Similarly, children receiving the intervention who were not at risk for depression reported significantly fewer depression symptoms at the 2-year follow-up compared to their peers in the control group.

Future work can expand upon what we know by assessing the temporal sequence of how attenuated positive functioning develops in relation to depression. Does being depressed make a person less responsive to the world around them or does an unresponsive approach system place a person at risk for depression? Additional research is also needed to fully examine how cultivating character strengths in clinically depressed samples can increase rewarding experiences in daily life and help prevent relapse.

## Bipolar spectrum disorders

For people experiencing mania and its milder variant hypomania, approach behavior and engagement in pleasurable activities come naturally. The benefits of these experiences, however, are short-lived. An overly sensitive reaction to positive events coupled with a persistently elevated or irritable mood can lead to disturbances in behavior and thinking that result in significant life problems. Also, periods of mania/hypomania rarely exist in isolation; they typically alternate with depressive episodes in what is known as bipolar spectrum disorders. When mania and hypomania occur in the context of bipolar disorder, the positive outcomes associated with these mood states (e.g., creativity) suffer.

In contrast to the motivational and affective deficits present in depression, mania and hypomania are associated with an overly sensitive approach system. This includes a faster, more exaggerated, and persistent pattern of responding to reward opportunities (Urosevic, Abramson, Harmon-Jones, & Alloy, 2008). People at risk and diagnosed with bipolar disorder endorse more excitement and enthusiasm in response to rewarding stimuli (see Johnson (2005) for a review). People with bipolar disorder also display greater physiological arousal and neural activity in the brain regions associated with positive affect and approach motivation when exposed to rewards cues (Elliott et al., 2004; Lawrence et al., 2004).

Given this sensitivity to reward cues, a large body of research has focused on goal attainment in the bipolar spectrum disorders. Compared to healthy controls, people with bipolar disorder exhibit greater achievement efforts. They are more likely to set high goals and devote substantial efforts to attain these goals (Lam, Wright, & Smith, 2004). While ambition is not inherently good or bad, high achievement striving can become maladaptive when it leads to potentially negative consequences (as is often the case during periods of mania). For example, people in a manic episode tend to endorse greater approach motivation to potentially rewarding events even when the pursuit contains an element of threat or punishment (Meyer, Beevers, Johnson, & Simmons, 2007). There is also evidence to suggest that goal pursuit can contribute to manic symptoms. Following initial positive successes in goal attainment, people with bipolar disorder report increased confidence and approach motivation (Eisner et al., 2009). This leads to more intense goal pursuit and subsequent increases in manic symptoms (Lozano & Johnson, 2001). Because life goals are perceived as more attainable following initial success, people with bipolar disorders are more likely to tackle increasingly difficult tasks and to be less perceptive of danger and punishment cues.

Certain positive emotional experiences may also contribute to symptoms of mania in the context of bipolar disorders. Using a sample of recovered bipolar patients, Gruber and colleagues (2009) found that people who reported greater self-compassion experienced fewer manic symptoms whereas greater joy and amusement were associated with elevated manic symptoms. While future studies are needed to replicate these results, initial findings suggest that certain positive emotions (joy and amusement) may represent a vulnerability to the onset of a manic episode and that monitoring the intensity of these emotions might aid relapse prevention. These findings also highlight the potential therapeutic role of building certain strengths, such as compassion, to offset manic episodes.

Taken together, there is substantial support for a dysregulated approach system in bipolar disorder. However we need a better understanding of how people with bipolar disorders experience and regulate manic and hypomanic symptoms in daily life and how these processes impact subsequent functioning. Future work can assess if and when people with bipolar spectrum disorders use their heightened reactivity to positive events to generate meaningful experiences. An important link in this relationship may be a person's capacity to self-regulate. People who can effectively regulate their responses to positive events may be at less risk for going into a manic episode.

## Conclusions and Future Directions

Happiness derives from a variety of sources. Because humans are social creatures, a considerable amount of rewarding and meaningful experiences arise from interacting and developing relationships with others. Yet some variants of psychopathology are characterized by pervasive interpersonal difficulties that interfere with the capacity to develop and maintain significant, lasting relationships. Both social anxiety and depression are among the few disorders characterized by a deficient ability to generate pleasurable and meaningful experiences. While this chapter focused on positive functioning in relation to anxiety and mood disorders, it should be noted that other forms of psychopathology have links to deficient positive experiences. For instance, people with schizophrenic-spectrum disorders also present with emotional deficits (especially in positive affect) in social contexts. In fact, social anhedonia, or the inability to obtain pleasure from social exchanges, has been linked to the development of schizophrenia-spectrum conditions (Kwapil, 1998).

It has long been assumed that if the frequency of positive experiences increases, there will be a subsequent reduction in negative experiences. Implicit in this assumption is that negative experiences are "bad" and that we should get rid of them. However there is evidence suggesting that negative experiences can be adaptive and lead to enhanced psychological and social functioning (e.g., guilt motivating prosocial behavior; enhanced intimacy following conflict). In addition, excessive or socially unacceptable positive experiences can be maladaptive (e.g., mania, paraphilias). Recent research on mindfulness, curiosity, and psychological flexibility emphasize that emotions are sources of information that help us navigate our complex social worlds and improve quality of life (Hayes et al., 2006; Kashdan & Rottenberg, 2010). When a person exerts significant time and energy on attempts to avoid or minimize unwanted emotional experiences, there is less "space" to devote to meaningful and positive life experiences.

It is clear from the present review that the study of how elements of happiness relate to psychopathology is in its infancy. Although intriguing, much of the research is limited by a reliance on analogue samples, retrospective global reports, cross-sectional methods, and little attempt to address causal mechanisms. Asking people to describe past events and to make global evaluations is inherently flawed and there is evidence to support the notion that retrospective evaluations of thought processes and emotions differ substantially from how these phenomena are experienced in the moment (Stone, Shiffman, Atienza, & Nebeling, 2007). In addition, extant research has neglected to explore how actual behavior relates to positive functioning across various contexts. Where, when, and with whom do people with disorders have the most pleasurable experiences? What are the antecedents and consequences of positive events and experiences? Can the benefits of extremely intense positive events spill over into upcoming days, leading to prolonged positive experiences? These and other dynamic, contextually driven questions can be examined with experience sampling and other methodologies that explicitly address multiple time points and situational parameters (this includes how emotional disturbances unfold during meaningful life transitions).

This chapter was meant to provide an overview of how people with various psychological disorders experience positive events and emotion states. As work in this area continues, researchers need to continue developing strategies for capturing the depth and breadth of meaningful and rewarding experiences in daily life, and how these events facilitate positive functioning and well-being.

# References

Barrett, L. F., Gross, J., Christensen, T. C., & Benvenuto, M. (2001). Knowing what you're feeling and knowing what to do about it: Mapping the relation between emotion differentiation and emotion regulation. *Cognition and Emotion, 15*, 713–724.

Berenbaum, H., & Oltmanns, T. F. (1992). Emotional experience and expression in schizophrenia and depression. *Journal of Abnormal Psychology, 101*, 37–44.

Blanchard, J. J., Mueser, K. T., & Bellack, A. S. (1998). Anhedonia, positive and negative affect, and social functioning in schizophrenia. *Schizophrenia Bulletin, 24*, 413–424.

Bonanno, G. (2004). Loss, trauma, and human resilience: Have we underestimated the human capacity to thrive after extremely aversive events? *American Psychologist, 59*(1), 20–28.

Borkovec, T. D. (2002). Life in the future versus life in the present. *Clinical Psychology: Science and Practice, 9*, 76–80.

Bourland, S. L., Stanley, M. A., Snyder, A. G., Novy, D. M., Beck, J. G., Averill, P. M., & Swann, A. C. (2000). Quality of life in older adults with generalized anxiety disorder. *Aging and Mental Health, 4*, 315–323.

Brown, T. A., Chorpita, B. F., & Barlow, D. H. (1998). Structural relationships among dimensions of the *DSM? IV* anxiety and mood disorders and dimensions of negative affect, positive affect, and autonomic arousal. *Journal of Abnormal Psychology, 107*, 179–192.

Brown, L. H., Silvia, P. J., Myin-Germeys, I., & Kwapil, T. R. (2007). When the need to belong goes wrong: The expression of social anhedonia and social anxiety in daily life. *Psychological Science, 18*, 778–782.

Cacioppo, J. T., & Berntson, G. G. (1994). Relationship between attitudes and evaluative space: A critical review, with emphasis on the separability of positive and negative substrates. *Psychological Bulletin, 115*, 401–423.

Carver, C. S. (2001). Affect and the functional bases of behavior: On the dimensional structure of affective experience. *Personality and Social Psychology Review, 5*, 345–356.

Clark, D. M., & Wells, A. (1995). A cognitive model of social phobia. In R. G. Heimberg, M. R. Liebowitz, D. A. Hope, & F. R. Schneier (Eds.), *Social phobia: Diagnosis, assessment, and treatment* (pp. 69–94). New York, NY: The Guilford Press.

Clark, L. A., Watson, D., & Mineka, S. (1994). Temperament, personality, and the mood and anxiety disorders. *Journal of Abnormal Psychology, 103*, 103–116.

Davidson, R. J., Marshall, J. R., Tomarken, A. J., & Henriques, J. B. (2000). While a phobic waits: Regional brain electrical and autonomic activity in social phobics during anticipation of public speaking. *Biological Psychiatry, 47*, 85–95.

Demyttenaere, K. (2006). Quality of life in depression and anxiety: Does it matter? *International Journal of Psychiatry in Clinical Practice, 10*, 27–30.

Diener, E., & Seligman, M. E. P. (2002). Very happy people. *Psychological Science, 13*, 81–84.

Duckworth, A. L., Steen, T. A., & Seligman, M. E. P. (2005). Positive psychology in clinical practice. *Annual Review of Clinical Psychology, 1*, 629–651.

Eisner, L., Johnson, S. L., & Carver, C. S. (2009). Cognitive responses to failure and success relate uniquely to bipolar depression versus mania. *Journal of Abnormal Psychology, 117*, 154–163.

Elliot, A. J., & Thrash, T. M. (2002). Approach–avoidance motivation in personality: Approach and avoidance temperaments and goals. *Journal of Personality and Social Psychology, 82*, 804–818.

Elliott, R., Ogilvie, A., Rubinsztein, J. S., Calderon, G., Dolan, R., & Sahakian, B. J. (2004). Abnormal ventral frontal response during performance of an affective go/no go task in patients with mania. *Biological Psychiatry, 55*, 1163–1170.

Fredrickson, B. L. (2001). The role of positive emotions in positive psychology: The broaden-and-build theory of positive emotions. *American Psychologist, 56*, 218–226.

Frueh, B. C., Turner, S. M., Beidel, D. C., & Cahill, S. P. (2001). Assessment of social functioning in combat veterans with PTSD. *Aggression and Violent Behavior, 6*, 79–90.

Gillham, J. E., Reivich, K. J., Jaycox, L. H., & Seligman, M. E. P. (1995). Preventing depressive symptoms in schoolchildren: Two year follow-up. *Psychological Science, 6*, 343–351.

Gotlib, I. H., Kasch, K. L., Traill, S. K., Joormann, J., Arnow, B. A., & Johnson, S. L. (2004). Coherence and specificity of information processing biases in depression and social phobia. *Journal of Abnormal Psychology, 113*, 386–398.

Greenberg, P. E., Stiglin, L. E., Finkelstein, S. N, & Berndt, E. R. (1993). The economic burden of depression in 1990. *Journal of Clinical Psychiatry, 54*, 405–418.

Gruber, J., Culver, J. L., Johnson, S. L., Nam, J., Keller, K. L., & Ketter, T. K. (2009). Do positive emotions predict symptomatic change in bipolar disorder? *Bipolar Disorders, 11*, 330–336.

Hayes, S. C., Luoma, J., Bond, F., Masuda, A., & Lillis, J. (2006). Acceptance and commitment therapy: Model, processes, and outcomes. *Behaviour Research and Therapy, 1*, 1–25.

Henning, E. R., Turk, C. L., Mennin, D. S., Fresco, D. M., & Heimberg, R. G. (2007). Impairment and quality of life in individuals with generalized anxiety disorder. *Depression and Anxiety, 24*, 342–349.

Henriques, J. B., & Davidson, R. J. (2000). Decreased responsiveness to reward in depression. *Cognition and Emotion, 14*, 711–724.

Hughes, A. A., Heimberg, R. G., Coles, M. E., Gibb, B. E., Liebowitz, M. R., & Schneier, F. R. (2006). Relations of the factors of the tripartite model of anxiety and depression to types of social anxiety. *Behaviour Research and Therapy, 44*, 1629–1641.

Johnson, S. L. (2005). Life events in bipolar disorder: Towards more specific models. *Clinical Psychology Review, 25*, 1008–1027.

Joiner, T. E., Jr., & Coyne, J. C. (1999). *The interactional nature of depression.* Washington, DC: American Psychological Association.

Kashdan, T. B. (2002). Social anxiety dimensions, neuroticism, and the contours of positive psychological functioning. *Cognitive Therapy and Research, 26*, 789–810.

Kashdan, T. B. (2007). Social anxiety spectrum and diminished positive experiences: Theoretical synthesis and meta-analysis. *Clinical Psychology Review, 27*, 348–365.

Kashdan, T. B., Adams, L., Savostyanova, A. A., Ferssizidis, P., McKnight, P. E., & Nezlek, J. B. (2011). Effects of social anxiety and depressive symptoms on the frequency and quality of sexual activity: A daily process approach. *Behaviour Research and Therapy, 49*, 352–360.

Kashdan, T. B., Breen, W. E., & Julian, T. (2010). Everyday strivings in combat veterans with posttraumatic stress disorder: Problems arise when avoidance and emotion regulation dominate. *Behavior Therapy, 41*, 350–363.

Kashdan, T. B., & Collins, R. L. (2010). Social anxiety and the experience of positive emotions and anger in everyday life: An ecological momentary assessment approach. *Anxiety, Stress, & Coping, 23*, 259–272.

Kashdan, T. B., Julian, T., Merritt, K., & Uswatte, G. (2006). Social anxiety and posttraumatic stress in combat veterans: Relations to well-being and character strengths. *Behaviour Research and Therapy, 44*, 561–583.

Kashdan, T. B., & McKnight, P. E. (2010). The darker side of social anxiety: When aggressive impulsivity prevails over shy inhibition. *Current Directions in Psychological Science, 19*, 47–50.

Kashdan, T. B., Morina, N., & Priebe, S. (2009). Post-traumatic stress disorder, social anxiety disorder, and depression in survivors of the Kosovo War: Experiential avoidance as a contributor to distress and quality of life. *Journal of Anxiety Disorders, 23*, 185–196.

Kashdan, T. B., & Rottenberg, J. (2010). Psychological flexibility as a fundamental aspect of health. *Clinical Psychology Review, 30*, 865–878.

Kashdan, T. B., & Steger, M. (2006). Expanding the topography of social anxiety: An experience sampling assessment of positive emotions and events, and emotion suppression. *Psychological Science, 17*, 120–128.

Kashdan, T. B., Uswatte, G., & Julian, T. (2006). Gratitude and hedonic and eudaimonic well-being in Vietnam War veterans. *Behaviour Research and Therapy, 44,* 177–199.

Kashdan, T. B., Weeks, J. W., & Savostyanova, A. A. (2011). Whether, how, and when social anxiety shapes positive experiences and events: A self-regulatory framework and treatment implications. *Clinical Psychology Review,* 31, 786–799.

Kashdan, T. B., Ferssizidis, P., Collins, R. L., & Muraven, M. (2010). Emotion differentiation as resilience to excessive alcohol use: An ecological momentary assessment in underage social drinkers. *Psychological Science, 21,* 1341–1347.

Keltner, D., & Bonanno, G. A. (1997). A study of laughter and dissociation: Distinct correlates of laughter and smiling during bereavement. *Journal of Personality and Social Psychology, 73,* 687–702.

Kessler R. C., Chiu, W. T., Demler, O., & Walters, E. E. (2005). Prevalence, severity, and comorbidity of twelve-month DSM-IV disorders in the National Comorbidity Survey Replication (NCS-R). *Archives of General Psychiatry, 62*(6), 617–627.

Kwapil, T. R. (1998). Social anhedonia as a predictor of the development of schizophrenia-spectrum disorders. *Journal of Abnormal Psychology, 107,* 558–565.

Lam, D., Wright, K., & Smith, N. (2004). Dysfunctional assumptions in bipolar disorder. *Journal of Affective Disorders, 79*(1–3), 193–199.

Lawrence, N. S., Williams, A. M., Surguladze, S., Giampietro, V., Brammer, M., Andrew, C., & Phillips, M. L. (2004). Subcortical and ventral prefrontal cortical neural responses to facial expressions distinguish patients with bipolar disorder and major depression. *Biological Psychiatry, 55,* 578–587.

Leary, M. R. (2004). The sociometer, self-esteem, and the regulation of interpersonal behavior. In R. F. Baumeister & K. D. Vohs (Eds.), *Handbook of self-regulation: Research theory, and applications* (pp. 373–391). New York, NY: Guildford Press.

Litz, B. T., Orsillo, S. M., Kaloupek, D., & Weathers, F. (2000). Emotional processing in post-traumatic stress disorder. *Journal of Abnormal Psychology, 109,* 26–39.

Lozano, B. L., & Johnson, S. L. (2001). Can personality traits predict increases in manic and depressive symptoms? *Journal of Affective Disorders, 63,* 103–111.

Lyubomirsky, S. (2001). Why are some people happier than others?: The role of cognitive and motivational processes in well-being. *American Psychologist, 56,* 239–249.

Lyubomirsky, S., King, L. A., & Diener, E. (2005). The benefits of frequent positive affect. *Psychological Bulletin, 131,* 803–855.

Marx, B. P., & Sloan, D. M. (2005). Experiential avoidance, peritraumatic dissociation, and post-traumatic stress disorder. *Behaviour Research and Therapy, 43,* 569–583.

McKnight, P. E., & Kashdan, T. B. (2009). The importance of functional impairment to mental health outcomes: A case for reassessing our goals in depression treatment research. *Clinical Psychology Review, 29,* 243–259.

Meyer, B., Beevers, C. G., Johnson, S. L., & Simmons, E. (2007). Unique association of approach motivation and mania vulnerability. *Cognition and Emotion, 21,* 1647–1668.

Muraven, M. R., & Baumeister, R. F. (2000). Self-regulation and depletion of limited resources: Does self-control resemble a muscle? *Psychological Bulletin, 126,* 247–259.

Murray, C. J. L., & Lopez, A. D. (1996). *The global burden of disease.* Cambridge, MA: Harvard University Press.

Must, A., Juha, A., Rimanoczy, A., Szabo, Z., Janka, Z., & Keri, S. (2006). Major depressive disorder, serotonin transporter, and personality traits: Why patients use suboptimal decision-making strategies? *Journal of Affective Disorders, 103,* 273–276.

Needles, D. J., & Abramson, L. Y. (1990). Positive life events, attributional style, and hopefulness: Testing a model of recovery from depression. *Journal of Abnormal Psychology, 99*, 156–165.

Nezlek, J. B., Hampton, C. P., & Shean, G. D. (2000). Clinical depression and day-to-day social interaction in a community sample. *Journal of Abnormal Psychology, 109*, 11–19.

Nezlek, J. B., & Gable, S. L. (2001). Depression as a moderator of relationships between positive daily events and day-to-day psychological adjustment. *Personality and Social Psychology Bulletin, 27*, 1692–1704.

Olatunji, B. O., Cisler, J. M., & Tolin, D. F. (2007). Quality of life in the anxiety disorders: A meta-analytic review. *Clinical Psychology Review, 27*, 572–581.

Orsillo, S. M., Batten, S. V., Plumb, J. C., Luterek, J. A., & Roessner, B. M. (2004). An experimental study of emotional responding in women with posttraumatic stress disorder related to interpersonal violence. *Journal of Traumatic Stress, 17*, 241–248.

Papa, A., & Bonanno, G. A. (2008). Smiling in the face of adversity: Interpersonal and intrapersonal functions of smiling. *Emotion, 8*, 1–12.

Plumb, J. C., Orsillo, S. M., & Luterek, J. A. (2004). A preliminary test of the role of experiential avoidance in post-event functioning. *Journal of Behavior Therapy and Experimental Psychiatry, 35*, 245–257.

Rapee, R. M., & Heimberg, R. G. (1997). A cognitive-behavioral model of anxiety in social phobia. *Behaviour Research and Therapy, 35*, 741–756.

Riggs, D. S., Byrne, C. A., Weathers, F. W., & Litz, B. T. (1998). The quality of the intimate relationships of male Vietnam war veterans: Problems associated with posttraumatic stress disorder. *Journal of Traumatic Stress, 11*, 87–101.

Roemer, L., & Orsillo, S. M. (2002). Expanding our conceptualization of and treatment for generalized anxiety disorder: Integrating mindfulness/acceptance-based approaches with existing cognitive-behavioral models. *Clinical Psychology: Science and Practice, 9*, 54–68.

Roemer, L., Salters, K., Raffa, S., & Orsillo, S. M. (2005). Fear and avoidance of internal experiences in GAD: Preliminary tests of a conceptual model. *Cognitive Therapy and Research, 29*, 71–88.

Rottenberg, J. (2005). Mood and emotion in major depression. *Current Directions in Psychological Science, 14*, 167–170.

Rottenberg, J., Kasch, K. L., Gross, J. J., & Gotlib, I. H. (2002). Sadness and amusement reactivity differentially predict concurrent and prospective functioning in major depressive disorder. *Emotion, 2*, 135–146.

Salters-Pedneault, K., Roemer, L., Tull, M. T., Rucker, L., & Mennin, D. S. (2006). Evidence of broad deficits in emotion regulation associated with chronic worry and generalized anxiety disorder. *Cognitive Therapy and Research, 30*, 469–480.

Sareen, J., Campbell, D., Leslie, W., Malisza, K., Stein, M., Paulus, M., & Reiss, J. (2007). Striatal function in generalized social phobia: A functional magnetic resonance imaging study. *Biological Psychiatry, 61*(3), 396–404.

Schneier, F. R., Liebowitz, M. R., Abi-Dargham, A., Zea-Ponce, Y., Shu-Hsing, L., & Laruelle, M. (2000). Low dopamine D2 receptor binding potential in social phobia. *American Journal of Psychiatry, 157*, 457–459.

Schultheiss, O. C., Jones, N. M., Davis, A. Q., & Kley, C. (2008). The role of implicit motivation in hot and cold goal pursuit: Effects on goal progress, goal rumination, and depressive symptoms. *Journal of Research in Personality, 42*, 971–987.

Sedikides, C., Oliver, M. B., & Campbell, K. (1994). Perceived benefits and costs of romantic relationships for women and men: Implications for exchange theory. *Personal Relationships, 1*, 5–21.

Seligman, M. E. P., Steen, T., Park, N., & Peterson, C. (2005). Positive psychology progress: Empirical validation of interventions. *American Psychologist, 60,* 410–421.

Silvia, P. J., Allan, W. D., Beauchamp, D. L., Maschauer, E. L., & Workman, J. O. (2006). Biased recognition of happy facial expressions in social anxiety. *Journal of Social and Clinical Psychology, 25,* 585–602.

Sloan, D. M., Strauss, M. E., Quirk, S. W., & Sajatovic, M. (1997). Subjective and expressive emotional responses in depression. *Journal of Affective Disorders, 46,* 135–141.

Steger, M. F. (2012). Experiencing meaning in life: Optimal functioning at the nexus of well-being psychopathology, and spirituality. In P. T. P. Wong (Ed.), *The human quest for meaning: Theories, research, and applications* (2nd Ed). Mahwah, NJ: Lawrence Erlbaum Associates.

Steger, M. F., & Kashdan, T. B. (2009). Depression and everyday social activity, belonging, and well-being. *Journal of Counseling Psychology, 56,* 289–300.

Stone, A. A., Shiffman, S., Atienza, A. & Nebeling, L. (2007). *The science of real-time data capture.* New York, NY: Oxford University Press.

Taylor, G. J., Bagby, R. M., & Parker, J. D. A. (1997). *Disorders of affect regulation: Alexithymia in medical and psychiatric illness.* Cambridge, UK: Cambridge University Press.

Thomas, K. M., Drevets, W. C., Dahl, R. E., Ryan, N. D., Birmaher, B., Eccard, C. H., ... Casey, B. J. (2001). Amygdala response to fearful faces in anxious and depressed children. *Archives of General Psychiatry, 58,* 1057–1063.

Urosevic, S., Abramson, L. Y., Harmon-Jones, E., & Alloy, L. B. (2008). Dysregulation of the behavioral approach system (BAS) in bipolar spectrum disorders: Review of theory and evidence. *Clinical Psychology Review, 28,* 1188–1205.

Vohs, K. D., Baumeister, R. F., & Ciarocco, N. J. (2005). Self-regulation and self-presentation: Regulatory resource depletion impairs impression management and effortful self-presentation depletes regulatory resources. *Journal of Personality and Social Psychology, 88,* 632–657.

Wells, A., & Carter, K. (1999). Preliminary tests of a cognitive model of generalized anxiety disorder. *Behavior Research and Therapy, 37,* 585–594.

Westphal, M., & Bonanno, G. A. (2007). Posttraumatic growth and resilience to trauma: Different sides of the same coin or different coins? *Applied Psychology: An International Review, 56,* 416–426.

# CHAPTER 9

# THE REWARDS OF HAPPINESS

### KATHERINE JACOBS BAO AND SONJA LYUBOMIRSKY

University of California, Riverside, USA

SUCCESS—OR the attainment of rewards valued in one's culture—is assumed to foster happiness. Many people believe that securing a promotion, getting married, or recovering from a chronic illness will make them happier, and they are right to think so. Happiness is indeed correlated with numerous positive characteristics, resources, and outcomes (Diener, Suh, Lucas, & Smith, 1999), and enjoying them undoubtedly contributes to overall well-being. However, the finding that happiness and success are correlated means that the opposite causal direction may also hold. Being happy in the first place could cause people to be more successful in a variety of domains. In other words, happiness may lead people to accrue a great many rewards in life. In this chapter, we argue on behalf of this causal pathway, and present evidence in its support (see Lyubomirsky, King, and Diener (2005) for a more in-depth review).

## EARLY RESEARCH AND THEORETICAL BACKGROUND

The study of happiness is a relatively new research area. Its roots can be traced back to humanistic psychology, which arose as an alternative to behaviorist and clinical approaches (e.g., Rogers, 1961). Humanistic psychology shone a light on the positive aspects of human beings and their behavior, focusing on constructs such as health (as opposed to illness), self-actualization (the realization of one's true potential), and creativity (Aanstoos, Serlin, & Greening, 2000). More recently, psychologists have begun to emphasize the study of people's strengths (as opposed to their weaknesses and pathologies) and the prevention of mental disorders, rather than only their treatment (Seligman & Csikszentmihalyi, 2000). This new focus has encouraged the growth of research on happiness and positive emotions, which characterizes present-day positive psychology.

What, then, is happiness? For the purposes of this chapter, we define happiness as the frequent experience of positive emotions (Diener, Sandvick, & Pavot, 1991). Accordingly, we use terms such as positive affect, pleasant mood, and high well-being to refer to individuals who often experience positive emotions. Happiness is generally measured using self-report questionnaires, such as the Subjective Happiness Scale (Lyubomirsky & Lepper, 1999), the Positive and Negative Affect Schedule (Watson, Clark, & Tellegen, 1988), and the Satisfaction With Life Scale (Diener, Emmons, Larsen, & Griffin, 1985). Although these scales are not tapping into the exact same construct, they do distinguish between people who frequently experience positive emotions and those who do not.

Our central thesis is that being a happy person raises the likelihood of accruing rewards in all the important life domains, such as relationships, work, and health. How does happiness engender success? We argue that the key underlying mechanism, or ingredient, is *positive affect*. Happy people frequently experience positive emotions (Diener et al., 1991), and positive emotions are associated with active, approach-oriented behavior. Accordingly, those who experience positive emotions are more likely to go out and meet new people, enter novel situations, and pursue important goals (Carver, 2003; Elliot & Thrash, 2002; Lyubomirsky, 2001). According to the broaden-and-build theory (Fredrickson, 2001), positive emotions also broaden people's "thought–action repertoires" (e.g., prompting them to generate more ideas and instigate new actions) and allow them to build physical, social, intellectual, and psychological resources. Thus, people who experience frequent positive moods can presumably develop skills and relationships that help them to succeed in a variety of domains.

Furthermore, positive affect acts as a signal that things are going well—a situation that grants individuals the opportunity and freedom to be active and sociable, to help others, to be flexible and productive, and to engage in healthy behaviors and effective coping (Hill & Buss, 2008; Lyubomirsky et al., 2005). We argue that these very characteristics help people to succeed at culturally-valued goals. This is in part because people are more likely to actively work toward new goals while experiencing positive moods (Lyubomirsky et al., 2005). Equally important is that those who habitually experience positive emotions are likely to have accumulated skills and resources during their positive experiences. Consequently, such individuals are both more likely to take steps in order to pursue their goals and to succeed in attaining them.

In this chapter, our aim is to provide a brief review, with some key examples, of the literature on the relationship between happiness and success, as well as to update the most recent published comprehensive review (Lyubomirsky et al., 2005). Readers are additionally advised to consult analyses of more specific literatures, including those regarding health (Pressman & Cohen, 2005), mortality (Chida & Steptoe, 2008), creativity (Amabile, Barsade, Mueller, & Staw, 2005; Baas, De Dreu, & Nijstad, 2008), and job performance (Kaplan, Bradley, Luchman, & Haynes, 2009).

# Research Methods

A variety of research methods have been used to study the relationship between happiness and success. Cross-sectional studies allow us to observe whether an association exists between two variables (e.g., happiness and health), but cannot tell us the direction of the relationship (e.g., whether happiness leads to good health or good health leads to happiness). Thus, from these studies, we can determine that happiness is related to success, but we do not know if happiness causes success or if success causes happiness or if some third factor altogether causes both success and happiness. Accordingly, correlational studies can only answer questions like "Are happy people successful people?" and "Are long-term happiness and short-term positive affect associated with adaptive skills and characteristics?" Because cross-sectional studies are the least informative as to the causal nature of the relationship, we will not review such studies in this chapter (however, see Lyubomirsky et al. (2005) for a comprehensive review of cross-sectional research in this area).

Longitudinal studies are more informative than cross-sectional ones because they examine whether happiness precedes success during the course of time (e.g., happiness assessed at age 40 and health assessed at age 50). Thus, longitudinal studies can answer questions such as, "Does happiness precede success?" and "Do happiness and positive affect pave the way for behaviors paralleling success?" (Lyubomirsky et al., 2005). However, longitudinal studies still cannot establish a causal relationship between happiness and success, because, like cross-sectional studies, longitudinal investigations are subject to the "third-variable" problem. In other words, because such studies do not take place in a controlled environment, where only positive affect is manipulated, there may be other variables (e.g., personality, biological, or family characteristics) that account for the relationship between happiness and success. Thus, we cannot conclude that happiness causes success from longitudinal studies.

Fortunately, experimental studies, which typically induce people to experience positive emotions and then assess the consequences, do allow us to establish the direction of causality. Although experiments are not perfect either—for example, the laboratory typically lacks what researchers call "ecological validity" and is sometimes problematic to generalize to real-word naturalistic settings—they can answer questions like "Does positive affect lead to behaviors paralleling success?" (Lyubomirsky et al., 2005). For example, if we make someone happy temporarily, will he or she show signs of a momentarily strengthened immune system?

The ideal method, however, for answering our causal question involves an "experimental longitudinal" design. These types of studies—also called randomized controlled interventions—aim to increase long-term happiness and follow people over time in the "real world" to measure how they and their lives have changed as a result. Accordingly, such investigations are able to test for a long-term causal relationship, answering questions like, "Does induced happiness lead to behaviors paralleling success several weeks, months, or years from now?"

The small but growing area of happiness intervention research provides indirect evidence for a link between happiness and success. If such interventions increase happiness, then it is reasonable to conclude that they should also bolster the rewards of happiness—for example, stronger interpersonal relationships, superior physical health, or more helping behavior. As just one example, studies have shown that practicing gratitude boosts happiness (e.g., Emmons & McCullough, 2003; Lyubomirsky, Sheldon, & Schkade, 2005). At the same time, gratitude predicts more prosocial behavior (McCullough, Kilpatrick, Emmons, & Larsen, 2001), lower depression (Woodward, Moua, & Watkins, 1998), fewer post-traumatic stress disorder symptoms (Masingale et al., 2001), and stronger social bonds (Emmons & Shelton,

2002; McCullough et al., 2001; McCullough & Tsang, 2004; see Lambert, Graham, and Fincham (2009) for a review). However, it is important to show that gratitude has these benefits via its effects on happiness. In one study with suggestive findings in this respect, life satisfaction was found to mediate—or underlie—the relationship between gratitude and materialism (Lambert, Fincham, Stillman, & Dean, 2009). Thus, expressing gratitude both increased people's life satisfaction and lowered their materialism, and life satisfaction was found to be responsible for the gratitude-materialism link.

Another long-term intervention found that people randomly assigned to practice loving-kindness meditation for 9 weeks experienced more positive emotions over time (Cohn, Fredrickson, Brown, Mikels, & Conway, 2009). These positive emotions further produced increases in personal resources, such as greater social support and diminished illness symptoms, which predicted increased life satisfaction. In other words, individuals who were experimentally induced to be happier were able to "build" their psychological and social resources, which in turn led to increases in life satisfaction. Although still largely indirect, such research is beginning to suggest that boosting long-term happiness may have positive effects on other important aspects of people's lives.

In the following sections, we review some of the more direct longitudinal and experimental studies that provide support for the hypothesis that happiness causes successful outcomes and behaviors.

## Longitudinal Research

### Social relationships

To begin, happiness has been found to predict success in a variety of social settings. As one important example shows, how happy a person is raises the probability that he or she will eventually marry. In a 15-year Australian study, unmarried participants whose happiness levels were one standard deviation above the mean were 1.5 times more likely to be married at a later point in time than those whose happiness levels were at the mean (Marks & Fleming, 1999). Those who were two standard deviations above the mean were twice as likely to be married later. In a 16-year German study, people who reported high life satisfaction were more likely to be married 4 or more years later than those who reported lower life satisfaction (Lucas, Clark, Georgellis, & Diener, 2003). Another study with a similar design measured subjective well-being in young single individuals. Those who eventually married had higher subjective well-being as young adults than those who remained single (Stutzer & Frey, 2006). Taken together, the evidence suggests that happy single people are more likely to eventually find marriage partners than their less happy single peers.

Being happy apparently predicts not only the likelihood of getting married but having a strong marriage. A 6-year-long Australian investigation found that respondents' happiness early in the study was associated with higher marital satisfaction later (Headey & Veenhoven, 1989). In an intriguing study with a US sample, Harker and Keltner (2001) examined displays of positive affect in female college senior yearbook photos. They found that women who expressed sincere positive affect (i.e., "Duchenne" smiles) at age 21 were more likely to be married 6 years later and less likely to be single 22 years later. The expression of genuine positive affect in the photos also predicted marital satisfaction 31 years later. However, a recent study that used high school yearbook photos with respondents in their 50s was unable to replicate these results (Freese, Meland, & Irwin, 2007).

Happiness is also related to higher levels of activity and social interaction. In a sample of older adults, those who were happier at one point in time were more likely to participate in activities 18 months later (Kozma & Stones, 1983; Stones & Kozma, 1986). Similarly, in another study, positive affect measured at the start predicted the amount of time people participated in recreational and social activities later in the study, even after taking into account their initial activity levels (Lucas, 2001). And, in a 4-week study of nursing home residents, positive affect (specifically, interest rather than pleasure) was related to activity levels (Meeks, Young, & Looney, 2007). So, people who are happy and experience frequent good moods tend to be more active in social and recreational activities, even when the activities are assessed much later.

## Work life

A number of studies have also longitudinally examined the relationships between happiness, positive emotions, and employment outcomes. Roberts, Caspi, and Moffitt (2003) found that positive affect measured at age 18 predicted several work-related outcomes, such as obtaining a job, having high job satisfaction, and feeling financially independent, at age 26. These positive job outcomes also triggered increases in positive affect, so the relationship was apparently bidirectional. High positive affect has also been shown to predict less absenteeism from the job 5 months later (Pelled & Xin, 1999) and better supervisor evaluations 1.5 years later (Staw, Sutton, & Pelled, 1995). Furthermore, a study that tracked participants over the course of 2 months found that positive affect predicted self-rated work productivity over this period (Zelenski, Murphy, & Jenkins, 2008). Taken together, this research shows that workers who are high in positive affect experience more success in the workplace and display more behaviors that promote success.

One such success-promoting behavior is creative thinking. Good moods have been found to prospectively predict creativity, especially in the workplace. In one study, positive affect expressed by employees at work predicted their creativity levels, as rated by their supervisors, 1.5 years later (Staw et al., 1995). In another investigation of employee creativity, Amabile and colleagues (2005) followed employees from seven companies for an average of 19 weeks. Self-reported positive affect preceded creative thought by up to 2 days, but creative thought did not predict later positive affect. So it appears that positive moods lead to creativity, but creativity may not lead to positive moods.

A similar relationship has been established between happiness and income. In a 15-year Australian panel study, self-reported happiness predicted increases in income during later periods (Marks & Fleming, 1999). Replicating and extending this finding, a Russian panel study found that people's happiness in the first year of the study was associated with higher income and lower unemployment 5 years later (Graham, Eggers, & Sukhtankar, 2004). Researchers have also found that higher levels of cheerfulness, measured during the first year of college, predict greater income 16 years later, even after controlling for parental income (Diener, Nickerson, Lucas, & Sandvik, 2002). This evidence leads us to conclude that being a happy person is associated with earning a higher income many years later.

## Health

Happiness has also been shown to predict people's physical health; in other words, people who are happier at a particular point in time have been found to be healthier months or years down the road. For instance, in a Finnish twin study, higher life satisfaction predicted a lower risk of suicide 20 years later, even after controlling for other risk factors, (Koivumaa-Honkanen, Honkanen, Koskenvuo, Viinamaeki, & Kaprio, 2001). Also, happier people have been found to have better self-reported health, to miss fewer days at work due to sickness, and to have fewer hospital visits 5 years later than their less happy peers (Graham et al., 2004). Positive mood has been shown to predict a lower incidence of stroke 6 years later (especially for men; Ostir, Markides, Peek, & Goodwin, 2000), and, in another study, individuals with higher life satisfaction and more positive perceptions of future happiness (and no mobility limitations) reported relatively fewer mobility limitations 8 years later (Collins, Goldman, & Rodriguez, 2008). In a diabetic sample, higher levels of positive affect were found to predict lower levels of glycosylated hemoglobin, an indicator of how well one's diabetes is under control (Tsenkova, Love, Singer, & Ryff, 2008). In addition, positive affect in this study was found to be the key ingredient responsible for the relationship between effective coping and chemical indicators of well-controlled diabetes. As a final example of research in this area, in a diary investigation of patients with sickle cell disease, positive affect during Day 1 was associated with lower self-reported pain during Day 3 (Gil et al., 2004). All of these studies support the idea that happiness at Time 1 is associated with superior physical health outcomes at Time 2.

Perhaps most impressive is research showing that we can predict how long a person will live from how happy he or she currently is. Unhappiness has been found to be associated with higher mortality rates in studies of healthy individuals, those who suffer from medical conditions, and even those who have experienced sudden accidents. For example, low subjective well-being was revealed to be associated with more automobile fatalities (Kirkcaldy & Furnham, 2000), and low satisfaction with life predicted both unintentional and intentional injuries over a 19-year period (Koivumaa-Honkanen, Honkanen, Koskenvuo, Viinamaeki, & Kaprio, 2002). In an oft-cited study of nuns, those who expressed more positive affect in autobiographies written as young adults had a 2.5 times lower risk of mortality when they were in their 80s and 90s (Danner, Snowdon, & Friesen, 2001). So relative happiness in one's youth is related to longevity.

Happiness has also been found to be associated with reduced mortality in people suffering from various illnesses, such as end-stage renal disease (Devins, Mann, Mandin, & Leonard, 1990), breast cancer (Levy, Lee, Bagley, & Lippman, 1988), spinal cord injuries (Krause, Sternberg, Lottes, & Maides, 1997), diabetes (Moskowitz, Epel, & Acree, 2008), and HIV (Ickovics et al., 2006). A recent meta-analytic review found that happiness was associated with reduced mortality in both sick and healthy populations (Chida & Steptoe, 2008).

One of the likely reasons—or "mechanisms"—that happiness fosters longevity and health is by bolstering an individual's immune function. For example, an oft-cited study found that healthy volunteers with a positive emotional style were relatively less likely to develop a cold after exposure to a cold virus—an effect that interestingly was independent of negative emotional style, or other health-related variables like age, sex, and body mass (Cohen, Doyle, Turner, Alper, & Skoner, 2003). Other research showed that positive affect and other psychological resources were negatively related to declines in T-cell counts, indicating stronger immunity, in people with HIV (Ickovics et al., 2006). Thus, happiness appears to predict stronger immune function, which is associated with a lower risk of becoming ill.

Another relevant line of research addresses the question of whether happiness measured at one point in time is related to how well a person copes with problems in his or her life at a later point. In this way, superior coping skills could also explain why happier people are healthier. For example, in women who were getting a biopsy for potential breast cancer, positive mood predicted so-called "engaged" coping (Chen et al., 1996). In another longitudinal investigation, positive affect, measured weekly, was associated with an effective type of coping called "active" coping in a sample of women with rheumatoid arthritis (Hamilton, Zautra, & Reich, 2005). Several studies have even found evidence for an "upward spiral" effect involving positive emotion and coping. Fredrickson and Joiner (2002) found that positive affect assessed at the outset of the study predicted effective coping and even more positive experiences later in the study. Corroborating these results, positive affect and positive coping were found to build on each other over the course of 2 months (Burns et al., 2008). Another study measured people's resilience over a 1-month period (Cohn et al., 2009). Positive emotions were found to predict increases in resilience and to mediate (i.e., explain) the relationship between initial and final resilience. Such studies provide evidence for an upward spiral, in which positive affect leads to effective coping, and coping helps bring about later positive experiences.

# Experimental Research

## Social relationships

Corroborating and extending the longitudinal data, experimental studies provide evidence for a causal relationship between happy mood and a variety of positive resources and outcomes. For example, in the domain of interpersonal relationships, people induced to feel happy tend to recall positive information about another person and are more apt to report having positive feelings toward a stranger than those induced to feel sad (Baron, 1987, 1993; Griffitt, 1970). People made to feel happy are also more outgoing and active. Participants induced into a positive mood have been found to be more sociable and to self-disclose more to strangers (Cunningham, 1988b; Isen, 1970). Also, when people are induced to feel happy, they report more interest in leisure activities (Cunningham, 1988a), and are more likely to acknowledge enjoying a boring task (Hirt, Melton, McDonald, Harackiewicz, 1996). Overall, people put in a good mood have more positive perceptions of others, are more sociable and active, and are more likely to enjoy their activities than those not in a good mood.

Positive mood also appears to be beneficial for negotiation and conflict resolution—behaviors that are critical for the maintenance of interpersonal relationships. Studies have shown that people who are induced to experience positive affect prefer to resolve conflicts through collaboration rather than avoidance (Baron, Fortin, Frei, Hauver, & Shack, 1990), to make relatively more concessions during negotiations (Baron, 1990), and to be relatively more cooperative and less competitive in bargaining tasks (Forgas, 1998). Furthermore, when put in a positive mood, both individuals and groups have been found to be relatively more likely to reach the most optimal agreements and less likely to stop negotiation and use more aggressive strategies (Carnevale & Isen, 1986; Carnevale, 2008). Thus, research suggests that the experience of positive affect stimulates people to be relatively better able to resolve problems and to cooperate with their peers.

## Prosocial behavior

People who are induced into positive moods are more likely to contribute to charity (Cunningham, Steinberg, & Grev, 1980; Isen, 1970) and to needy children (Rosenhan, Underwood, & Moore, 1974), and to give significantly more money when they do contribute, than those induced into negative moods (Isen, 1970). In general, a wealth of experimental research shows that those put in a happy mood are relatively more likely to engage in all kinds of helpful behaviors, such as donating blood (O'Malley & Andrews, 1983) and helping an experimenter with a boring task (Berkowitz, 1987). Indeed, an event as trivial as finding a dime can boost people's moods and stimulate them to assist a stranger who has dropped some papers (Cunningham et al., 1980). For example, in one study, researchers found that individuals induced into a positive mood were not only more likely to help, but also to help for a longer period of time, than a control group (Baron & Bronfen, 1994). Thus, good moods galvanize people to engage in relatively more prosocial behavior.

## Creativity

Although longitudinal evidence is lacking in this area, experiments show that happy people tend to be relatively more creative. When laboratory participants are induced into a happy mood, they receive relatively higher scores on originality and flexibility (see Isen (1993) for a review). For example, people put in a good mood scored relatively higher on a creativity measure (Estrada, Isen, & Young, 1994) and showed relatively more variety-seeking behavior (Kahn & Isen, 1993). This may be because positive affect leads people to feel secure and thus to seek novel experiences and variety (Isen, 1993; cf. Hill & Buss, 2008). Dreisbach and Goschke (2004) found that participants put in a positive mood, rather than a negative or neutral mood, had greater cognitive flexibility, but also had increased distractibility. A review of creativity experiments concluded that induced positive affect produces more creativity than neutral affect, but, interestingly, not more than negative affect (Baas, De Dreu, & Nijstad, 2008).

## Health

Experimental studies also reveal that being in a positive mood—even temporarily—has health benefits. For example, individuals induced into a happy mood have relatively higher pain thresholds (Alden, Dale, & DeGood, 2001; Cogan, Cogan, Waltz, & McCue, 1987) and lower blood pressure reactivity in response to stress (Smith, Ruiz, & Uchino, 2004). In another study, participants were asked to imagine that they had kidney cancer and then were induced into a positive or negative mood. Relative to those in negative moods, those in positive moods reported greater optimism about their prognosis and ability to deal with the disease, as well as a stronger intent to overcome the illness and follow the treatment protocol

(Schuettler & Kiviniemi, 2006). Another study found that, among participants low in trait seriousness, those induced into a positive mood felt less stressed, reported better physical health, and had lower blood pressure than those who had not received the intervention (Papousek & Schulter, 2008). Thus, being happy appears not only to make people feel healthier, but prompts them to react to stress in more adaptive ways.

Positive mood is also related to healthy behavior, although few studies have been conducted to examine this relationship. Tice and colleagues, for example, have discovered the role of positive emotion in counteracting so-called ego depletion, which occurs when people experience a loss of cognitive (i.e., thinking) capacity when trying to control their behavior (Tice, Baumeister, Schmueli, & Muraven, 2007). For example, turning down an appetizing snack becomes more difficult the longer one is exposed to it and the more one is distracted by a demanding task. However, when participants are induced into a positive mood after an ego depletion task, they perform as well as non-depleted participants and significantly better than those who do not receive the positive mood induction (Tice et al., 2007; Tice & Wallace, 2000). So, positive affect may boost our cognitive resources after they have been depleted, which increases our capacity to resist behaviors that hold immediate gratification but long-term health costs, like excessive eating, drinking, and smoking.

Finally, research shows that immune functioning can be improved by positive mood. For example, a small sample of actors was instructed to reflect on certain scenarios, in order to induce different emotions. Those put in a good mood showed stronger immune function than those in a neutral mood (Futterman, Kemeny, Shapiro, & Fahey, 1994). Also, participants who watched an amusing video had increased immune function afterward (Dillon, Minchoff, & Baker, 1985; Lefcourt, Davidson-Katz, & Kueneman, 1990; McClelland & Cheriff, 1997; however, see Martin (2002) for a critique of these data). In other words, a good mood strengthens people's immune systems—at least temporarily—which is associated with better health.

## Conclusions

Taken together, the empirical evidence suggests that happiness plays a causal role in the attainment of success, as well as in the practice of behaviors related to success. This occurs, we argue, through the frequent experience of positive affect, which makes happy individuals more likely to approach people and situations, and helps build their intellectual, social, physical, and psychological resources and skills (Carver, 2003; Elliot & Thrash, 2002; Fredrickson, 2001; Lyubomirsky, 2001). Positive emotions also signal that things are going well, which allows people to feel more safe and secure as they approach others and novel situations, thus affording them the opportunity to be more creative, productive, sociable, and active, as well as to engage in prosocial and healthful behaviors.

The evidence reviewed in this chapter may easily give rise to the conclusion that the happier a person is, the better. However, we would caution readers not to draw such a broad generalization. Indeed, Oishi, Diener, and Lucas (2007) suggest that the optimal level of well-being depends on the domain. Their findings reveal that it is moderately happy people—not extremely happy ones—who have the highest levels of income, education, and political participation. A possible explanation is that the happiest individuals have less motivation than moderately happy ones to improve their current standing in those domains. However, Oishi and colleagues also find that when it comes to relationships, it is best to be in the happiest group (i.e., a 9 or 10 on a 10-point scale). If a person is not completely satisfied with a relationship, he or she might try to change something, perhaps by seeking other partners or ending the relationship, which would obviously harm it. If a person is very highly satisfied, in contrast, he or she might idealize their partner in ways that could trigger self-fulfilling prophecies and upward spirals (Murray, Holmes, & Griffin, 1996). Thus, happiness, in general, appears to be valuable for achieving a range of successful outcomes, but the optimal level of happiness may depend on the particular domain.

Our analysis further calls into question whether there exist any situations in which it might be beneficial to be unhappy or to experience particular negative emotions. For example, the experience of mild discontent may serve a critical function for activists who are protesting against the status quo. When it comes to short-term outcomes, negative emotions may also be valuable for specific circumstances. In certain social situations, such as a funeral or a vigil, or when a colleague has received news of loss or failure, displays of positive affect may be judged negatively by others. Thus, we are certainly not suggesting that only happy people can be successful. In fact, we would argue that chronic, or inflexible, happiness is not ideal. There is value to negative emotions (Clore, 1994), and happy, well-adjusted people tend to experience a mix of both positive and negative affect (Diener & Seligman, 2002). In sum, any particular emotion may be beneficial in a narrow set of circumstances, but, as we have shown here, positive emotions appear to be beneficial in a wide variety of circumstances and life domains.

## References

Aanstoos, C. Serlin, I., & Greening, T. (2000). History of Division 32 (Humanistic Psychology) of the American Psychological Association. In D. Dewsbury (Ed.), *Unification through division: Histories of the divisions of the American Psychological Association* (Vol. V., pp. 85–112). Washington, DC: American Psychological Association.

Alden, A. L., Dale, J. A., & DeGood, D. E. (2001). Interactive effects of the affect quality and directional focus of mental imagery on pain analgesia. *Applied Psychophysiology and Biofeedback, 26*, 117–126.

Amabile, T. M., Barsade, S. G., Mueller, J. S. & Staw, B. M. (2005). Affect and creativity at work. *Administrative Science Quarterly, 50*, 367–403.

Baas, M., De Dreu, C. K. W., & Nijstad, B. A. (2008). A meta-analysis of 25 years of mood-creativity research: Hedonic tone, activation, or regulatory focus? *Psychological Bulletin, 134*, 779–806.

Baron, R. A. (1987). Interviewer's moods and reactions to job applicants: The influence of affective states on applied social judgments. *Journal of Applied Social Psychology, 17*, 911–926.

Baron, R. A. (1990). Environmentally induced positive affect: Its impact on self-efficacy, task performance, negotiation, and conflict. *Journal of Applied Social Psychology, 20*, 368–384.

Baron, R. A. (1993). Interviewer's moods and evaluations of job applicants: The role of applicant qualifications. *Journal of Applied Social Psychology, 23*, 253–271.

Baron, R. A., & Bronfen, M. I. (1994). A whiff of reality: Empirical evidence concerning the effects of pleasant fragrances on work-related behavior. *Journal of Applied Social Psychology, 24*, 1179–1203.

Baron, R. A., Fortin, S. P., Frei, R. L., Hauver, L. A., & Shack, M. L. (1990). Reducing organizational conflict: The role of socially-induced positive affect. *International Journal of Conflict Management, 1,* 133–152.

Berkowitz, L. (1987). Mood, self-awareness, and willingness to help. *Journal of Personality and Social Psychology, 52,* 721–729.

Burns, A. B., Brown, J. S., Sachs-Ericsson, N., Plant, E. A., Curtis, J. T., Fredrickson, B. L., & Joiner, T. E. (2008). Upward spirals of positive emotion and coping: Replication, extension, and initial exploration of neurochemical substrates. *Personality and Individual Differences, 44,* 360–370.

Carnevale, P. J. (2008). Positive affect and decision frame in negotiation. *Group Decision and Negotiation, 17,* 51–63.

Carnevale, P. J. D., & Isen, A. M. (1986). The influence of positive affect and visual access on the discovery of integrative solutions in bilateral negotiation. *Organizational Behavior and Human Decision Processes, 37,* 1–13.

Carver, C. S. (2003). Pleasure as a sign you can attend to something else: Placing positive feelings within a general model of affect. *Cognition and Emotion, 17,* 241–261.

Chen, C. C., David, A., Thompson, K., Smith, C., Lea, S., & Fahy, T. (1996). Coping strategies and psychiatric morbidity in women attending breast assessment clinics. *Journal of Psychosomatic Research, 40,* 265–270.

Chida, Y., & Steptoe, A. (2008). Positive psychological well-being and mortality: A quantitative review of prospective observational studies. *Psychosomatic Medicine, 70,* 741–756.

Clore, G. L. (1994). Why emotions are felt. In P. Ekman & R. J. Davidson (Eds.), *The nature of emotion: Fundamental questions* (pp. 103–111). New York, NY: Oxford University Press.

Cogan, R., Cogan, D., Waltz, W., & McCue, M. (1987). Effects of laughter and relaxation on discomfort thresholds. *Journal of Behavioral Medicine, 10,* 139–144.

Cohen, S., Doyle, W. J., Turner, R. B., Alper, C. M. & Skoner, D. P. (2003). Emotional style and susceptibility to the common cold. *Psychosomatic Medicine, 65,* 652–657.

Cohn, M. A., Fredrickson, B. L., Brown, S. L., Mikels, J. A., & Conway, A. M. (2009). Happiness unpacked: Positive emotions increase life satisfaction by building resilience. *Emotion, 9,* 361–368.

Collins, A. L., Goldman, N., & Rodriguez, G. (2008). Is positive well-being protective of mobility limitations among older adults? *Journal of Gerontology: Psychological Sciences, 63,* 321–327.

Cunningham, M. R. (1988a). Does happiness mean friendliness? Induced mood and heterosexual self-disclosure. *Personality and Social Psychology Bulletin, 14,* 283–297.

Cunningham, M. R. (1988b). What do you do when you're happy or blue? Mood, expectancies, and behavioral interest. *Motivation and Emotion, 12,* 309–331.

Cunningham, M. R., Steinberg, J., & Grev, R. (1980). Wanting to and having to help: Separate motivations for positive mood and guilt-induced helping. *Journal of Personality and Social Psychology, 38,* 181–192.

Danner, D. D., Snowdon, D. A., & Friesen, W. V. (2001). Positive emotions in early life and longevity: Findings from the nun study. *Journal of Personality and Social Psychology, 80,* 804–813.

Devins, G. M., Mann, J., Mandin, H. P., & Leonard, C. (1990). Psychosocial predictors of survival in end-stage renal disease. *Journal of Nervous and Mental Disease, 178,* 127–133.

Diener, E., Emmons, R. A., Larsen, R. J., & Griffin, S. (1985). The satisfaction with life scale. *Journal of Personality Assessment, 49,* 71–75.

Diener, E., Nickerson, C., Lucas, R. E., & Sandvik, E. (2002). Dispositional affect and job outcomes. *Social Indicators Research*, *59*, 229–259.

Diener, E., Sandvik, E., & Pavot, W. (1991). Happiness is the frequency, not the intensity, of positive versus negative affect. In F. Strack, M. Argyle, & N. Schwartz (Eds.), *Subjective well-being: An interdisciplinary perspective* (pp. 119–139). Oxford, UK: Pergamon Press.

Diener, E., & Seligman, M. E. P. (2002). Very happy people. *Psychological Science*, *13*, 81–84.

Diener, E., Suh, E. M., Lucas, R. E., & Smith, H. L. (1999). Subjective well-being: Three decades of progress. *Psychological Bulletin*, *125*, 276–302.

Dillon, K. M., Minchoff, B., & Baker, K. H. (1985). Positive emotional states and enhancement of the immune system. *International Journal of Psychiatry in Medicine*, *15*, 13–18.

Dreisbach, G., & Goschke, T. (2004). How positive affect modulates cognitive control: Reduced perseveration at the cost of increased distractibility. *Journal of Experimental Psychology: Learning, Memory, and Cognition*, *30*, 343–53.

Elliot, A. J., & Thrash, T. M. (2002). Approach-avoidance motivation in personality: Approach and avoidance temperaments and goals. *Journal of Personality and Social Psychology*, *82*, 804–818.

Emmons, R. A., & McCullough, M. E. (2003). Counting blessings versus burdens: An experimental investigation of gratitude and subjective well-being in daily life. *Journal of Personality and Social Psychology*, *84*(2), 377–389.

Emmons, R. A., & Shelton, C. S. (2002). Gratitude and the science of positive psychology. In C. R. Snyder and S. J. Lopez (Eds.), *Handbook of positive psychology* (pp. 459–471). New York, NY: Oxford University Press.

Estrada, C., Isen, A. M., & Young, M. J. (1994). Positive affect influences creative problem solving and reported source of practice satisfaction in physicians. *Motivation and Emotion*, *18*, 285–299.

Forgas, J. P. (1998). On feeling good and getting your way: Mood effects on negotiating strategies and outcomes. *Journal of Personality and Social Psychology*, *74*, 565–577.

Fredrickson, B. L. (2001). The role of positive emotions in positive psychology: The broaden-and-build theory of positive emotions. *American Psychologist*, *56*, 218–226.

Fredrickson, B. L., Cohn, M. A., Coffey, K. A., Pek, J., & Finkel, S. M. (2008). Open hearts build lives: Positive emotions, induced through loving-kindness meditation, build consequential personal resources. *Journal of Personality and Social Psychology*, *95*, 1045–1062.

Fredrickson, B. L., & Joiner, T. (2002). Positive emotions trigger upward spirals toward emotional well-being. *Psychological Science*, *13*, 172–175.

Freese, J., Meland, S., & Irwin, W. (2007). Expressions of positive emotion in photographs, personality, and later-life marital and health outcomes. *Journal of Research on Personality*, *41*, 488–97.

Futterman, A. D., Kemeny, M. E., Shapiro, D., & Fahey, J. L. (1994). Immunological and physiological changes associated with induced positive and negative mood. *Psychosomatic Medicine*, *56*, 499–511.

Gil, K. M., Carson, J. W., Porter, L. S., Scipio, C., Bediako, S. M., & Orringer, E. (2004). Daily mood and stress predict pain, health care use, and work activity in African American adults with sickle cell disease. *Health Psychology*, *23*, 267–274.

Graham, C., Eggers, A., & Sukhtankar, S. (2004). Does happiness pay? An exploration based on panel data from Russia. *Journal of Economic Behavior and Organization*, *55*, 319–342.

Griffitt, W. (1970). Environmental effects on interpersonal affective behavior: Ambient effective temperature and attraction. *Journal of Personality & Social Psychology*, *15*, 240–244.

Hamilton, N. A., Zautra, A. J., & Reich, J. W. (2005). Affect and pain in rheumatoid arthritis: Do individual differences in affective regulation and affect intensity predict emotional recovery from pain? *Annals of Behavioral Medicine, 29*, 216–224.

Harker, L., & Keltner, D. (2001). Expressions of positive emotions in women's college yearbook pictures and their relationship to personality and life outcomes across adulthood. *Journal of Personality and Social Psychology, 80*, 112–124.

Headey, B., & Veenhoven, R. (1989). Does happiness induce a rosy outlook? In R. Veenhoven (Ed.), *How harmful is happiness? Consequences of enjoying life or not* (pp. 106–127). Rotterdam, the Netherlands: Universitaire Pers Rotterdam.

Hill, S. E., & Buss, D. M. (2008). Evolution and subjective well-being. In M. Eid & R. J. Larsen (Eds.), *The science of subjective well-being* (pp. 62–79). New York, NY: Guilford Press.

Hirt, E. R., Melton, R. J., McDonald, H. E., & Harackiewicz, J. M. (1996). Processing goals, task interest, and the mood-performance relationship: A mediational analysis. *Journal of Personality and Social Psychology, 71*, 245–261.

Ickovics, J. R., Milan, S., Boland, R., Schoenbaum, E., Schuman, P., & Vlahov, D. (2006). Psychological resources protect health: 5-year survival and immune function among HIV-infected women from four US cities. *Journal of Acquired Immune Deficiency Syndromes, 20*, 1851–1860.

Isen, A. M. (1970). Success, failure, attention and reaction to others: The warm glow of success. *Journal of Personality and Social Psychology, 15*, 294–301.

Isen, A. M. (1993). Positive affect and decision making. In M. Lewis & J. Haviland (Eds.), *Handbook of emotions* (pp. 261–277). New York, NY: The Guilford Press.

Kahn, B. E., & Isen, A. M. (1993). The influence of positive affect on variety-seeking among safe, enjoyable products. *Journal of Consumer Research, 20*, 257–270.

Kaplan, S., Bradley, J. C., Luchman, J. N., & Haynes, D. (2009). On the role of positive and negative affectivity in job performance: A meta-analytic investigation. *Journal of Applied Psychology, 94*, 162–176.

Kirkcaldy, B. D., & Furnham, A. (2000). Positive affectivity, psychological well-being, accident- and traffic-deaths, and suicide: An international comparison. *Studia Psychologica, 42*, 97–104.

Koivumaa-Honkanen, H., Honkanen, R., Koskenvuo, M., Viinamaeki, H., & Kaprio, J. (2002). Life satisfaction as a predictor of fatal injury in a 20-year follow-up. *Acta Psychiatrica Scandinavica, 105*, 444–450.

Koivumaa-Honkanen, H., Honkanen, R., Viinamaeki, H., Heikkilae, K., Kaprio, J., & Koskenvuo, M. (2001). Life satisfaction and suicide: A 20-year follow-up study. *American Journal of Psychiatry, 158*, 433–439.

Kozma, A., & Stones, M. J. (1983). Predictors of happiness. *Journal of Gerontology, 38*, 626–628.

Krause, J. S., Sternberg, M., Lottes, S., & Maides, J. (1997). Mortality after spinal cord injury: An 11-year prospective study. *Archives of Physical Medicine and Rehabilitation, 78*, 815–821.

Lambert, N., Fincham, F. D., Stillman, T. L., & Dean, L. R. (2009). More gratitude, less materialism: The mediating role of life satisfaction. *Journal of Positive Psychology, 4*, 32–42.

Lambert, N., Graham, & Fincham, F. D. (2009). A prototype analysis of gratitude: Varieties of gratitude experiences. *Personality and Social Psychology Bulletin, 35*, 1193–1207.

Lefcourt, H., Davidson-Katz, K., & Kueneman, K. (1990). Humor and immune system functioning. *International Journal of Humor Research, 3*, 305–321.

Levy, S. M., Lee, J., Bagley, C., & Lippman, M. (1988). Survival hazards analysis in first recurrent breast cancer patients: Seven-year follow-up. *Psychosomatic Medicine, 50*, 520–528.

Lucas, R. E. (2001). Pleasant affect and sociability: Towards a comprehensive model of extraverted feelings and behaviors. *Dissertation Abstracts International, 61* (10-B), 5610. (UMI No. AAI9990068).

Lucas, R. E., Clark, A. E., Georgellis, Y., & Diener, E. (2003). Re-examining adaptation and the set point model of happiness: Reactions to changes in marital status. *Journal of Personality and Social Psychology, 84,* 527–539.

Lyubomirsky, S. (2001). Why are some people happier than others?: The role of cognitive and motivational processes in well-being. *American Psychologist, 56,* 239–249.

Lyubomirsky, S., King, L., & Diener, E. (2005). The benefits of frequent positive affect: Does happiness lead to success? *Psychological Bulletin, 131,* 803–855.

Lyubomirsky, S., Sheldon, K. M., & Schkade, D. (2005). Pursuing happiness: The architecture of sustainable change. *Review of General Psychology, 9,* 111–131.

Lyubomirsky, S., & Lepper, H. (1999). A measure of subjective happiness: Preliminary reliability and construct validation. *Social Indicators Research, 46,* 137–155.

Marks, G. N., & Fleming, N. (1999). Influences and consequences of well-being among Australian young people: 1980–1995. *Social Indicators Research, 46,* 301–323.

Martin, R. A. (2002). Is laughter the best medicine? Humor, laughter, and physical health. *Current Directions in Psychological Science, 11,* 216–220.

Masingale, A. M., Schoonover, S., Kraft, S., Burton, R., Waring, S., Fouad, B., ... Watkins, P. (2001). *Gratitude and post-traumatic symptomatology in a college sample.* Paper submitted for presentation at the convention of the International Society for Traumatic Stress Studies, New Orleans, LA.

McClelland, D. C., & Cheriff, A. D. (1997). The immunoenhancing effects of humor on secretory IgA and resistance to respiratory infection. *Psychology and Health, 12,* 329–344.

McCullough, M. E., Kilpatrick, S. D., Emmons, R. A., & Larson, D. B. (2001). Is gratitude a moral affect? *Psychological Bulletin, 127,* 249–266.

McCullough, M. E., & Tsang, J. (2004). Parent of the virtues? The prosocial contours of gratitude. In R. A. Emmons & M. E. McCullough (Eds.), *The psychology of gratitude* (pp. 123–141). New York, NY: Oxford University Press.

Meeks, S., Young, C. M., & Looney, S. W. (2007). Intra- versus inter-individual correlations between affect and activities among depressed and non-depressed nursing home residents. *Aging and Mental Health, 11,* 751–760.

Moskowitz, J. T., Epel, E. S., & Acree, M. (2008). Positive affect uniquely predicts lower risk of mortality in people with diabetes. *Health Psychology, 27,* S73-S82.

Murray, S. L., Holmes, J. G., & Griffin, D. W. (1996). The self-fulfilling nature of positive illusions in romantic relationships: Love is not blind, but prescient. *Journal of Personality and Social Psychology, 71,* 1155–1180.

Oishi, S., Diener, E., & Lucas, R. E. (2007). The optimal level of well-being: Can we be too happy? *Perspectives on Psychological Science, 2,* 346–360.

O'Malley, M. N. & Andrews, L. (1983). The effect of mood and incentives on helping: Are there some things money can't buy? *Motivation and Emotion, 7,* 179–189.

Ostir, G. V., Markides, K. S., Black, S. A., & Goodwin, J. S. (2000). Emotional well-being predicts subsequent functional independence and survival. *Journal of the American Geriatrics Society, 48,* 473–478.

Papousek, I., & Schulter, G. (2008). Effects of a mood enhancing intervention on subjective well-being and cardiovascular parameters. *International Journal of Behavioral Medicine, 15,* 293–302.

Pelled, L. H., & Xin, K. R. (1999). Down and out: An investigation of the relationship between mood and employee withdrawal behavior. *Journal of Management, 25,* 875–895.

Pressman, S. D., & Cohen, S. (2005). Does positive affect influence health? *Psychological Bulletin, 131,* 925–971.

Roberts, B. W., Caspi, A., & Moffitt, T. E. (2003). Work experiences and personality development in young adulthood. *Journal of Personality and Social Psychology, 84,* 582–593.

Rogers, C. (1961). *On becoming a person.* Boston, MA: Houghton Mifflin.

Rosenhan, D. L., Underwood, B. & Moore, B. (1974). Affect moderates self-gratification and altruism. *Journal of Personality and Social Psychology, 30,* 546–552.

Seligman, M. E. P., & Csikszentmihalyi, M. (2000). Positive psychology: An introduction. *American Psychologist, 55,* 5–14.

Schuettler, D., & Kiviniemi, M. T. (2006). The effect of positive and negative affect when considering chronic illness diagnoses. *Journal of Applied Social Psychology, 36,* 2599–2618.

Sheldon, K. M., & Lyubomirsky, S. (2006). How to increase and sustain positive emotion: The effects of expressing gratitude and visualizing best possible selves. *The Journal of Positive Psychology, 1,* 73–82.

Smith, T. W., Ruiz, J. M., & Uchino, B. N. (2004). Mental activation of supportive ties, hostility, and cardiovascular reactivity to laboratory stress in young men and women. *Health Psychology, 23,* 476–485.

Staw, B. M., Sutton, R. I., & Pelled, L. H. (1995). Employee positive emotion and favorable outcomes at the workplace. *Organization Science, 5,* 51–71.

Stones, M. J., & Kozma, A. (1986). "Happy are they who are happy . . ." A test between two causal models of relationships between happiness and its correlates. *Experimental Aging Research, 12,* 23–29.

Stutzer, A., & Frey, B. S. (2006). Does marriage make people happy, or do happy people get married? *Journal of Socio-Economics, 35,* 326–347.

Tice, D. M., Baumeister, R. F., Shmueli, D., & Muraven, M. (2007). Restoring the self: Positive affect helps improve self-regulation following ego depletion. *Journal of Experimental Social Psychology, 43,* 379–384.

Tice, D. M. & Wallace, H. (2000). Mood and emotion control: Some thoughts on the state of the field. *Psychological Inquiry, 11,* 214–217.

Tsenkova, V. K., Love, G. D., Singer, B., & Ryff, C. D. (2008). Coping and positive affect predict longitudinal change in glycosylated hemoglobin. *Health Psychology, 27,* S163–71.

Watson, D., Clark, L. A., & Tellegen, A. (1988). Development and validation of brief measures of positive and negative affect: The PANAS scales. *Journal of Personality and Social Psychology, 54,* 1063–1070.

Woodward, K. M., Moua, G. K., & Watkins, P. C. (1998). *Depressed individuals show less gratitude.* Presentation at the 1998 joint convention of the Western Psychological Association and the Rocky Mountain Psychological Association, Albuquerque, NM.

Zelenski, J. M., Murphy, S. A., & Jenkins, D. A. (2008). The happy-productive worker thesis revisited. *Journal of Happiness Studies, 9,* 521–537.

# CHAPTER 10

# HAPPINESS EXPERIENCED: THE SCIENCE OF SUBJECTIVE WELL-BEING

WILLIAM PAVOT[1] AND ED DIENER[2]

[1]Southwest Minnesota State University, USA; [2]University of Illinois at Urbana-Champaign and The Gallup Organization, USA

## Happiness Experienced: The Science of Subjective Well-Being

In this chapter, we will present an overview of some of the major findings from research on subjective well-being (SWB). In the opening sections we will offer a definition of SWB along with some discussion of its philosophical lineage, and a brief review of some alternative theoretical approaches. Sections on the assessment of SWB, correlates of SWB, personality and SWB, cultural factors, and life outcomes that appear to be related to SWB follow. Concluding sections focus on ongoing issues, and offer suggestions for further research.

## Defining Subjective Well-Being

A number of definitions of SWB have been proposed; although varying somewhat in detail, commonalities are evident. For example, several of the early investigators (Andrews & Withey, 1976; Campbell, Converse, & Rodgers, 1976; Veenhoven, 1984) noted that SWB includes both affective and cognitive aspects. The affective component involves the experienced feelings of the individual, both positive and negative. The relative balance of positive and negative feelings (e.g., Bradburn, 1969) determines the overall hedonic level that a person experiences. The cognitive component, often referred to as satisfaction, involves an evaluation or judgment of the "... discrepancy between aspiration and achievement" (Campbell, Converse, & Rodgers, 1976, p. 8) as perceived by the individual. When this evaluation process is directed toward an overall judgment of life as a whole, the term "life satisfaction" or "satisfaction with life" is applied (e.g., Pavot & Diener, 1993a).

As empirical evidence began to accumulate, it became clear that positive affect (PA) and negative affect (NA) often are experienced relatively independently of each other (Bradburn, 1969; Diener & Emmons, 1984; Emmons & Diener, 1985; Watson, Clark, & Tellegen, 1988), particularly when measured over time. This in turn led many to regard SWB as having three components: PA, NA, and life satisfaction. The hedonic or affective components of SWB often are partially correlated with the life satisfaction component, as ongoing emotional experiences tend to influence the appraisal of life events and circumstances, and such appraisals in turn tend to evoke emotional reactions. But when treated (and assessed) as separate components, the affective and life satisfaction components often make unique contributions to the overall understanding of the experience of SWB. While this "tripartite theory" structure (Arthaud-Day, Rode, Mooney, & Near, 2005, p. 449) has not been universally embraced, it has gained wide acceptance by many researchers as a good working model for SWB.

Based on recent empirical findings, a movement toward a four-component structural model for SWB has been proposed (Diener, Scollon, & Lucas, 2004). Essentially this model divides the satisfaction component of SWB into two parts: life satisfaction and domain satisfaction. Assessing specific life domains (e.g., marital relations, work, housing, or health) can provide a more specific and detailed view of the experience of SWB for each individual or for particular groups of individuals. The weight assigned to various life domains by each person will likely show at least some variation, and that variation may have important empirical implications. For example, Diener, Lucas, Oishi, and Suh (2002) found that happy individuals tend to attach heavy weight to the most positive domains in their lives; unhappy individuals weigh the worst domains in their life heavily. These distinct processes have clear implications for the way individuals construct global judgments of SWB. The assessment of domain satisfaction might be especially important for researchers investigating particular areas such as those previously noted. The choice of the number and nature of specific domains to be assessed may vary depending on the goals of the individual research program; for some purposes, the assessment of satisfaction with specific domains might not be appropriate. But the consideration of domain satisfaction, independently from global satisfaction or satisfaction with life, represents an additional component of overall SWB.

Regardless of the particular model considered, the three "hallmarks" of SWB still serve to delineate the general concept (Diener, 1984, p. 543). First, SWB is subjective in nature; it is an expression of the experience of the individual. External, objective factors or conditions such as health, wealth, and virtue (Kammann, 1983) generally are not included in the definition of SWB. These factors may well influence an individual's SWB, but they are not inherent or necessary components (Diener, 1984). Second, SWB does not only represent the absence of negative factors, but also includes positive experiences as well. Third, it includes a global assessment, not just a focused evaluation of only a single life domain (Diener, 1984, 1994).

In sum, the construct of SWB is broadly based and multifaceted, encompassing both affective and cognitive processes, and subject to the individual's perceptual interpretation of ongoing events and experiences. As such, it cannot be inferred directly from objective circumstances, but rather must be understood from the individual's perspective. As will be discussed in a later section, SWB tends to be moderately stable over time, yet also tends to show sensitivity to ongoing experience and changing circumstances.

# Theoretical Approaches to Subjective Well-Being

A diverse array of theoretical models or approaches to SWB has been developed. Many of these models can be categorized based on their emphasis of a bottom-up versus top-down approach to SWB (Diener, 1984; Schimmack, 2008). Theories based on a bottom-up perspective assume that an individual's overall experience of SWB represents a summation of the ongoing positive and negative events and emotions that the individual experiences on a moment-to-moment and day-to-day basis. If these ongoing experiences are predominantly positive, the person will experience SWB. This perspective implies that SWB should be relatively labile, as specific positive and negative experiences would change on a day-to-day basis.

Top-down theories make the assumption that some underlying process (or processes) tend(s) to predispose an individual to experiencing an overall affective tone that exerts a ubiquitous effect on the evaluation of life as a whole. Some researchers have proposed that this overall affective tone stems from personality traits (Costa & McCrae, 1980; Headey & Wearing, 1992), whereas others have proposed that it is the product of chronic cognitive processes (Diener & Biswas-Diener, 2008; Robinson & Compton, 2008). Overall, these models view SWB as somewhat more stable in nature. Day-to-day experiences may exert a transitory effect, but, according to these models, people tend to return to their previous "set-point" (e.g., Headey, 2008). Further, it appears that personality can influence the life events that an individual experiences (Magnus, Diener, Fujita, & Pavot, 1993). Thus, personality potentially has both a direct effect on SWB by setting a person's emotional tone (e.g., temperament) and an indirect effect by partially determining the life events that a person experiences.

The debate between top-down theory advocates and those who prefer a bottom-up perspective has many aspects, but two central issues have become salient (Diener & Ryan, 2009). First, should SWB be understood as a stable personality trait, or as a more transient and changeable state? The second issue involves the influence of pleasant events in determining SWB. Is low SWB simply the result of a lack of pleasant events? Or do people with low SWB derive less pleasure from the same events that others find positive and enjoyable (Diener & Ryan, 2009)?

Several research efforts have focused on the question of top-down versus bottom-up influences on SWB. Using meta-analytic methodology, Heller, Watson, and Ilies (2004) found evidence that was not supportive of an overall top-down model for SWB; however, path analyses were supportive of a temperament-based top-down model of life satisfaction, and an integrative model which included the influence of domain satisfaction on life satisfaction. In a review of pertinent studies, Schimmack (2008) found evidence that changes in specific domains can exert an influence on overall life satisfaction whereas a top-down influence on life satisfaction was not as clearly supported by the data. But for the affective components of SWB, the influence of personality traits (e.g., extraversion and neuroticism) was stronger (Schimmack, 2008).

Considering this evidence, it appears that SWB, as experienced by the individual, involves an interplay of both top-down factors, such as personality traits, and bottom-up factors such as life experiences. The influence of personality on the affective components of PA and NA is somewhat better established than it is for life satisfaction; the effect of satisfaction with specific domains can be detected at the life satisfaction level. But judgments of life satisfaction are also influenced by the affective components of SWB (Suh, Diener, Oishi, & Triandis, 1998).

Despite some evidence for the bottom-up influence of life events and changes in domain satisfaction on overall SWB, several longitudinal studies have shown levels of SWB to be relatively stable for many people over time (e.g., Lucas, Diener, & Suh, 1996; Magnus, Diener, Fujita, & Pavot, 1993). Such findings are more favorable to top-down explanations as they indicate that, despite ongoing life events and changing life circumstances, levels of SWB appear to be fairly constant. A well-established and frequently evoked explanation for these findings of stability is the principle of the "hedonic treadmill" (Brickman and Campbell, 1971). Essentially, the hedonic treadmill principle asserts that the impact of life events and life changes, whether positive or negative, may initially be powerful, but rather quickly dissipates due to habituation or adaptation to the new circumstances. The hedonic treadmill implies that people tend to return to an affective neutral point after experiencing life changes; therefore life events and experiences have no lasting impact on SWB.

One difficulty with the original concept of the hedonic treadmill is that it fails to account for long-term individual differences in SWB, yet these differences have been consistently observed (Diener, Lucas, & Scollon, 2006). Large differences have been observed at the societal level; nations show considerable variation between each other in both affective and cognitive levels of SWB, indicating less than complete adaptation to varying societal conditions (Diener, Kahneman, & Helliwell, 2010). It also appears that most people report a level of SWB that is at least modestly above the neutral point (Diener & C. Diener, 1996). Gradually the assumption that people return to affective neutrality was replaced by the concept of a set-point for SWB (Headey, 2008). This set-point represents an individual's stable, chronic level of SWB. Several research lines (Costa & McCrae, 1980; Pavot, Diener, & Fujita, 1990; Headey & Wearing, 1992) have linked the SWB set-point to personality, particularly to the temperament-level traits of extraversion and neuroticism.

Many individuals do show considerable stability in SWB over long periods of time, but the effects of adaptation or a personality-based set-point have been shown to have limitations (Diener, Lucas, & Scollon, 2006). Some life events, such as unemployment or the death of a spouse (Lucas, Clark, Georgellis, & Diener, 2004) produce long-term changes in SWB. Additionally, it appears that there are individual differences in the degree to which people adapt to life events, with some individuals showing adaptation or set-point stability while others do not (Lucas, Clark, Georgellis, & Diener, 2003; Headey, 2008).

The preponderance of current evidence suggests that most people tend to have relatively stable levels of SWB, and that this stability appears to be related to personality or chronic cognitive processes. This does not suggest, however, that an individual's level of SWB is rigidly fixed or impervious to life events or changing circumstances. SWB levels can and do change in response to events, and in some cases the changes are enduring.

Proponents of a number of other theoretical approaches have also contributed to the understanding of SWB. Telic theories of SWB, for example, have a focus on the attainment of a goal, the fulfillment of a need, or the achievement of some desired end state as a source of happiness (Diener, 1984). Several theories of well-being (Cantor & Sanderson, 1999; Emmons, 1986; Ryan & Deci, 2000) emphasize need fulfillment or goal attainment as central to the experience of SWB. Some of these needs are inborn in nature (Ryan & Deci, 2000; Ryff & Singer, 1996), but additional goals may be acquired or learned (Emmons, 1986). There has been some debate as to whether it is the pursuit of goals or their attainment that is important (Carver, Lawrence, & Scheier, 1996; Csikszentimihalyi, 1990); others have pointed out that some goals might produce pleasure in the short term but could have long-term negative consequences (Diener, 1984). Having numerous important goals can contribute to life satisfaction and self-esteem, but the pressure to achieve those goals can also increase anxiety and stress (Pomerantz, Saxon, & Oishi, 2000).

Other researchers have focused on the importance of social comparison or the perceived discrepancy between one's current state and some desired or ideal state. Multiple Discrepancy Theory (Michalos, 1985), for example, proposes that people compare their present state or situation to multiple standards, such as past experiences, aspirations, other people, or some other benchmark. Judgments of satisfaction are determined by the degree of discrepancy between one's present state and these standards. If the comparison standard is higher than the individuals present state, decreased satisfaction will be experienced; if the individual's present state is perceived as higher than the standard, the result will be an increased level of satisfaction. Often a salient standard of comparison is the relative standing of proximate others on the relevant dimension. Social comparison can exert at least a transient influence on SWB judgments (Diener & Fujita, 1997), but this effect does not appear to be a lasting one.

## Measurement Issues

As already noted, a hallmark of the SWB construct is that it reflects the subjective experience of the individual. In order to assess this subjective experience, most research efforts have relied heavily on some form of self-report methodology. Early on, many of these measures were brief, often consisting of a single item embedded in a larger survey (see Diener (1984) for a review of these early measures). These brief assessments were a popular choice, presumably because of the convenience and flexibility that they offered. But the convenience of single-item assessments also involved some potential drawbacks. With a single item, for example, it is not possible to separately assess the affective and cognitive components of SWB. Perhaps more importantly, when single-item measures of SWB are embedded in a larger survey, it is possible that the survey questions placed before the SWB item might influence how the individual interprets and responds to the SWB item (Strack, Martin, and Schwarz, 1988). It has also been demonstrated that relatively subtle contextual factors, such as the momentary mood state of the respondent, can influence global reports of SWB (Schwarz & Strack, 1999). Under some circumstances, the influence of these contextual factors can be large; single-item measures appear to be particularly vulnerable to these effects (Pavot & Diener, 1993b). The results of a meta-analysis (Schimmack and Oishi, 2005), however, indicated that these effects were generally small, relative to chronically accessible information, particularly for judgments of life satisfaction. Nevertheless, it remains important to be aware of these potential confounding factors, and to create research designs that minimize their effects. One strategy involves making multiple assessments of SWB across several occasions, and then averaging the results, thus reducing the effects of any specific contextual factors present during one measurement occasion. Using multiple measures of SWB, preferably measures that are dedicated to the assessment of both the affective and cognitive components of SWB, will serve to both reduce these contextual effects and to produce a more complete assessment.

Many self-report instruments for the assessment of SWB are available. They range from relatively simple omnibus assessments, such as the Fordyce Happiness Measures (Fordyce, 1977) to more complex measures, for example, the 29-item Oxford Happiness Inventory (Argyle, Martin, & Lu, 1995). Some measures are focused on the affective components of SWB, including the Scale of Positive and Negative Experience (SPANE; Diener et al., 2010) and the Positive and Negative Affect Schedule (PANAS; Watson, Clark, & Tellegen, 1988). Other measures are dedicated to the assessment of the life satisfaction component, such as the Satisfaction With Life Scale (SWLS; Diener, Emmons, Larsen, & Griffin, 1985; Pavot & Diener, 2008). These and additional self-report measures of SWB are reviewed and discussed elsewhere (Diener, 1984, 2009a; Pavot, 2008; Pavot & Diener, 2003).

The theme of repeated assessments is reflected in two innovative research methodologies: Experience-Sampling Methodology (ESM) and the Day Reconstruction Method (DRM; Kahneman, Krueger, Schkade, Schwarz, and Stone, 2004). ESM methodology involves gathering reports of ongoing affective experiences from people as they go about their daily lives. Using some form of a cue/response device (e.g., Palm Pilot), the individual receives prompts at random moments throughout the day, and is asked to respond with a brief report of their affective state. The assessments usually are obtained over a period of days or weeks (e.g., Sandvik, Diener, & Seidlitz, 1993). The result of an ESM assessment is a read-out of the respondent's affective state, obtained in "real time," with reduced risk from contamination from memory biases compared to a retrospective report. For some researchers, such ESM data represents the best assessment of "objective happiness" (Kahneman, 1999, p. 3). But ESM methodology does pose some challenges, in terms of data management and analysis (Scollon, Kim-Prieto, & Diener, 2003). ESM also tends to reduce the respondents ability to apply their own unique criteria and individual calculus to the process of creating a summary judgment of their own SWB.

The DRM (Kahneman et al., 2004) offers something of a compromise between traditional self-report assessments and ESM. With DRM, respondents recall memories from the previous day, and then record these recalled memories in a diary format, which is later evaluated for affective content. The DRM approach allows for a more holistic view of the respondents experience, but it moves away from the direct on-line assessment feature of ESM.

Probably the most common type of indirect assessment is the informant report. Most often, informant reports are obtained from other family members, college roommates, teachers, or others who have extended interaction with the target individual. Informant reports have been shown to correlate with self-reports of SWB (Pavot, Diener, Colvin, & Sandvik, 1991; Sandvik, Diener, & Seidlitz, 1993). Informant reports are an important supplement to self-reports; they provide cross-method validation for self-reports, and they also represent evidence of the stable nature of the SWB construct. A detailed analysis of studies using both self-reports and informant ratings of SWB is available in Schneider and Schimmack (2009).

In addition to informant reports, other indirect techniques have been demonstrated to have some utility in the assessment of SWB. The analysis of the content of clinical-style interviews, memory bias techniques (Sandvik, Diener, & Seidlitz, 1993), and the content analysis of writing samples (Danner, Snowdon, & Friesen, 2001) have all been employed in the indirect assessment of SWB.

## CORRELATES OF SUBJECTIVE WELL-BEING

A great many variables have been examined with regard to their relation to SWB. One fundamental demographic categorization is gender, and many researchers have examined their data for gender-related differences in SWB (e.g., Andrews & Withey, 1976; Campbell et al., 1976; Fujita, Diener & Sandvik, 1991). When average levels of SWB are considered, no substantial differences between women and men have been consistently demonstrated. It does appear, however, that women are more likely to report very high or very low levels of SWB (Fujita et al., 1991), indicating that women are more likely to experience emotion, both positive and negative, more intensely than men.

Age is also considered an important demographic characteristic; as such, it has been examined for a relation to SWB in many studies. Although some early research appeared to confirm a commonly held stereotype of older adults as unhappy (Bradburn & Caplovitz, 1965; Wilson, 1967), recent studies have revealed a more positive outlook. Several research efforts have indicated that the life satisfaction component of SWB tends to remain steady or even increase over time for many individuals (Horley & Lavery, 1995), declining only near the end of life (Mroczek & Spiro, 2005). The affective components of SWB, PA and NA, both tend to show some modest decrease in late adulthood (Charles, Reynolds, & Gatz, 2001). This would suggest that, while the intensity of emotional experience diminishes, the balance of PA and NA is relatively constant.

Taken as a whole, current evidence indicates that there is no overall decline in SWB in late adulthood for most individuals, up to the end stage of life; most of the available data suggests an overall increase in SWB as adulthood progresses.

Another significant demographic characteristic is marital status. A large percentage of people eventually choose to marry; but does married life contribute to happiness? And what effect does divorce have on SWB? Married people tend to report higher levels of SWB than people who are not married (Lucas, Clark, Georgellis, & Diener, 2003). Potential explanations for the association between marriage and SWB have been examined. One involves evidence that happier people are more likely to marry and successfully maintain their marriage (Mastekaasa, 1992). This explanation suggests that SWB is a cause, rather than an effect, of marriage. It also appears likely that marriage provides a measure of both social and material support (Argyle & Martin, 1991); in other words, the effects of marriage contribute to greater SWB. A large longitudinal study conducted by Lucas (2005) indicates that both of these factors may be responsible for the SWB-marriage link. Lucas found evidence for both selection effects (married individuals were more satisfied with life long before they married) and additional positive benefits beyond selection, especially immediately around the time of marriage. Furthermore, Lucas et al. (2003) found that some people were more satisfied with life after marriage than before marriage, and others were less satisfied.

In examining the end of relationships, the negative impact on SWB is clear, and this negative impact is generally long-term in nature. Lucas (2005) found that long-term levels of satisfaction after divorce were lower than long-term satisfaction levels before divorce. In his study, there was evidence for some adaptation, but not a complete restoration of SWB. In the case of widowhood, Lucas's (2005) longitudinal data indicate that adaptation involves an extended period of time (8 years), and even then is incomplete.

The relation between SWB and money or income is intricate. At the simplest level, there is a positive correlation between income and SWB. The impact of money on SWB is strongest for individuals living at levels of poverty or near-poverty, but tends to decrease as the level of income increases (Diener, Ng, & Tov, 2009), although income still has some positive effects on SWB above the poverty level (Oishi, Diener, Lucas, & Suh, 1999). Americans at the highest income brackets report a level of SWB that is slightly higher than average; however, a large fraction (more than one-third) of these wealthy individuals report below average SWB (Diener, Horowitz, & Emmons, 1985). Recently, Diener, Ng, Harter and Arora (2010) found that income is much more strongly related to satisfaction than it is to PA and NA. Another finding of the Diener et al. (2010) study is that the effects of income on life satisfaction are in part due to the benefits of income on need fulfillment, and in part due to desires that are not dependent on needs.

Other aspects of culture will be discussed in a later section, but it appears that culture can mediate the effects of income on SWB. Biswas-Diener and Diener (2006) assessed the life satisfaction of pavement dwellers in the slums of Calcutta, and found a surprisingly robust level of satisfaction, relative to groups of homeless individuals in the USA. This despite the fact that the homeless in the USA had access to more resources, such as food, clean water, and medical care, relative to their counterparts in India.

For a number of years, researchers examining the relation between income and SWB were confronted with paradoxical findings in their data. Most often identified as the "Easterlin paradox," after it was highlighted in an article by Richard Easterlin (1974), this problem has generated much debate in the field. The essence of the paradox is the finding that, while income differences between individuals are usually positively correlated with SWB, when national incomes increase, there is often little or no corresponding increase in SWB. This assertion was challenged by others (e.g., Hagerty & Veenhoven, 2003), but a clear resolution was lacking. A recent study by Diener, Kahneman, Tov, and Arora (2010) has moved the field toward resolution of the paradox. In his original demonstration, Easterlin focused on "happiness" as the variable of interest. In their more recent study, Diener et al. (2010) presented evidence that material variables were more closely related to the life satisfaction component of SWB, whereas measures of affect were less associated with material variables. "Happiness" reports fall between life satisfaction and the affective components of SWB, but closer to the affective end than life satisfaction (Diener et al., 2010). When life satisfaction judgments were considered, there was a strong association between those judgments and income level. While these findings do not represent a complete resolution of the paradox, they do suggest an explanation for a portion of the issue. The also suggest that, in the case of income and SWB, it is important to distinguish between the affective and judgmental components of SWB, rather than to rely on measures of "happiness" (Diener et al., 2010). In the case of money, the relation with life satisfaction judgments is clear. But social and psychological factors, which are more strongly related to the emotional components of SWB, also contribute to the overall well-being of people (Diener & Ryan, 2011).

For many people, religious beliefs and practices are a central part of life, and it does appear that, for many, religion enhances the quality of life (e.g., Ferriss, 2002). Religiosity, when assessed at a national level, has been linked to greater life satisfaction and reduced suicide rates (Diener & Seligman, 2004; Helliwell, 2007). Yet ongoing research involving international comparisons indicate that some nations with high levels of well-being are not highly religious, whereas some highly religious nations report low levels of well-being. These findings suggest a more complex relation between religion and SWB.

Many other demographic variables have been examined for their relation to SWB. Most have been shown to have modest impact on long-term well-being. Standing in some contrast, research has identified a number of personality dispositions that have been consistently shown to predict SWB over the long term.

## Personality and Subjective Well-Being

Although the connection between personality and SWB had been noted earlier (Wilson, 1967), an influential article by Costa and McCrae (1980) highlighted the correlation of two temperament-level personality traits, extraversion and neuroticism, with the affective components of SWB. Specifically, Costa and McCrae (1980) found that extraversion was consistently correlated with PA, but not NA, and neuroticism was reliably correlated with NA, but not PA. Their findings indicated these two personality traits act as independent influences on SWB, and that personality was predictive of PA and NA over time (a 10-year interval) (Costa & McCrae, 1980). Since that time, many additional studies (e.g., Larsen & Ketelaar, 1991; Rusting & Larsen, 1997; Lucas & Baird, 2004) have replicated these correlations. Still more recently, a meta-analysis (Steel, Schmidt, & Shultz, 2008) has confirmed that the relations between extraversion/PA and neuroticism/NA are robust.

The relation between personality and SWB is consistent and substantial, but it has yet to be fully explained. Two general theoretical orientations are prominent (McCrae & Costa, 1991). Temperament theories propose a direct, unmediated influence of temperament level personality traits on a person's affective experience. As an alternative, instrumental theories posit an indirect pathway of influence; personality predisposes an individual toward particular activities and life events, and it is the experience of these events that generates an emotional response, and this in turn influences the individual's SWB (Costa & McCrae, 1991).

Although some evidence for the instrumental effects of personality on life events has been presented (e.g., Magnus, Diener, Fujita, & Pavot, 1993), by comparison, explanations focused on temperament abound. The work of Jeoffery Gray (1981, 1991), for example, has clear implications regarding the personality/SWB connection. Gray has proposed a model of motivation based on three systems: the behavioral activation system (BAS), the behavioral inhibition system (BIS), and the fight–flight system (FFS). The BAS is identified as a regulatory system which governs reactions to environmental signals of reward and nonpunishment; the BIS is hypothesized to regulate reactions to signals of punishment and nonreward. These two systems appear to map onto temperament-level personality, with the BAS corresponding to extraversion, and the BIS relating to neuroticism. Individuals higher in extraversion possess a stronger BAS system, which in turn predisposes them to react more strongly to signals of reward from the environment, and to experience more positive emotion. People with higher levels of neuroticism have a stronger BIS, which has the effect of orienting them more toward signals of punishment, and consequently intensifies their experience of negative emotion.

One approach to understanding the mechanism(s) that may underlie both personality and SWB involves research on heritability, which has been the focus of a number of behavior-genetic studies. Most commonly, participants in these studies are members of monozygotic (MZ; identical) or dizygotic (DZ; fraternal) twin pairs. Assessments of personality and/or SWB are completed by individual participants, and then the results are compared with those of their twin on the same measures. Ideally, the additive effects of genetics would be expected to be observed in cross-twin correlations approximately twice as large for MZ twins as those observed for DZ twins. It is also possible to separate the relative effects of genes versus environment by including twin pairs who were separated shortly after birth by adoption, and subsequently raised in separate family environments. Using techniques similar to these, Tellegen et al. (1988) found strong evidence for a powerful genetic influence on personality characteristics associated with the affective components of SWB; subsequent research (Roysamb, Harris, Magnus, Vitterso, & Tambs, 2002; Stubbe, Posthuma, Boomsma, & De Geus, 2005) has found comparable effects to those of Tellegen et al. (1988).

In sum, the evidence from heritability studies indicates that a substantial proportion (40–50%) of the variance in SWB can be accounted for by genetics. Despite the gaps in understanding of the precise mechanisms of expression, a significant biological influence on SWB is apparent.

## Culture and Subjective Well-Being

As is true of many other psychological constructs, international research of SWB has revealed that an individual's society and culture exert a substantial and complex influence on her or his happiness. The picture of SWB that has emerged from cross-cultural research indicates that some elements of SWB are common across cultures, but other aspects are unique to specific societies and cultural groups (Diener, 2009b).

A good demonstration of both commonality and uniqueness involves the emotional facets of SWB. On one hand, when emotions are examined at a broad or aggregate level, there is good evidence for commonality (Tov & Diener, 2007). Similar structures for PA and NA have been identified in comparisons of individuals from Japan and USA (Watson, Clark, & Tellegen, 1984); Kuppens, Ceulemans, Timmerman, Diener, and Kim-Prieto (2006) found PA and NA to be strong universal dimensions, and found some nation-level dimensions of PA and NA as well. On the other hand, however, specific emotions may be experienced as positive or negative, depending on cultural norms. In individualist cultures, for example, pride is generally a positive, enjoyable emotion that highlights individual achievement or accomplishment. In contrast, in many collectivist cultures, pride is not valued as it tends to bring focus on the self, and separates the individual from the group (Kitayama & Marcus, 2000; Scollon, Diener, Oishi, & Biswas-Diener, 2004). Thus, while it is reasonable to compare emotion across cultures at an aggregate level, it is also imperative that specific emotions be examined for their meaning, valance, and impact on SWB within a given culture.

Beyond structural comparisons such as these, it is also important to examine the causes of SWB in different cultures. Are the causes of SWB culture-specific, or are there universal factors involved?

The available evidence suggests that there are several universal causes of happiness, such as fulfilling basic needs (Diener & Tay, 2011). On the other hand, some correlates of SWB seem to differ substantially across cultures. For instance, Diener and M. Diener (1995) found that self-esteem is more strongly associated with life satisfaction in individualistic compared to collectivistic nations.

# LIFE OUTCOMES/BENEFITS OF SUBJECTIVE WELL-BEING

One of the curious aspects of happiness research has been the relative lack of interest in what happiness does (or does not) do for us. What benefits does happiness bring? What, if any, are the costs to happiness? Even when attention has been focused on these questions (Veenhoven, 1988), response to them has been limited.

In a major review, Lyubomirsky, King, and Diener (2005) presented extensive evidence for the substantial benefits of SWB. The benefits of high SWB are evident across a wide range of domains, grouped by Diener and Ryan (2009) into four categories: social relationships, health and longevity, work and income, and benefits at the societal level.

Good social relationships appear to be a necessary condition for high SWB (Diener & Seligman, 2002). Further, it may be the case that the causal arrow points both ways: experiencing positive social interactions enhances well-being, but initial high SWB also appears to enhance and increase social interaction (e.g., Fredrickson, 2001). High SWB individuals tend to generate their own social support systems (Cunningham, 1988).

A number of studies have linked SWB to better health, fewer physical symptoms, and even longevity. Roysamb, Tambs, Reichborn-Kjennerud, Neale, and Harris (2003), for example, found that respondents who reported higher SWB also reported better health, and that both genetic and environmental factors contributed to the relation. Danner, Snowdon, and Friesen (2001) found that subjective well-being expressed as positive emotionality in young adulthood was predictive of the longevity of a group of Catholic nuns living in a shared environment. Summarizing the evidence from their review of studies related to the role of SWB in health and longevity, Diener and Chan (2011) conclude that the evidence for a causal influence of SWB is clear.

The benefits of high SWB also appear in the domains of work and income. In the workplace such benefits are expressed in the form of higher productivity, dependability, and overall work quality (Staw, Sutton, & Pelled, 1994). And high SWB individuals are likely to earn more money, and this advantage appears to be consistent across a wide range of occupations (Diener, Nickerson, Lucas, & Sandvik, 2002)

## FUTURE DIRECTIONS

A number of issues and questions remain for future research efforts to address. At the theoretical level, it would be useful to further explore the commonalities and differences between the various well-being constructs, such as SWB and PWB (psychological well-being) (Kashdan, Biswas-Diener, & King, 2008; Ryff, 1989; Ryff & Singer, 1996). It will also be important to further explore the effects and limitations of adaptation (e.g., Diener, Lucas, & Scollon, 2006; Oishi, Diener, Choi, Kim-Prieto, & Choi, 2007).

Another important future direction involves the application of measures of SWB as social indicators of national well-being. Most of the indicators currently in use are based on objective assessments, such as economic trends, crime rates and educational attainment. These indicators, while important, are not able to capture the subjective aspects of the quality of life within nations. Economic indicators, for instance, can often diverge from subjective reports of quality of life (Diener & Seligman, 2004). Subjective indicators, such as reports of SWB, could provide an additional evaluative dimension to inform policy decisions within a given nation. More detailed discussions of the potential role of national accounts of well-being are available in Diener and Seligman (2004) and Diener, Lucas, Schimmack, and Helliwell (2009).

At the level of assessment, both new measures of well-being and a higher level of methodological rigor are desirable goals. The current norm of cross-sectional studies using simple survey assessments needs to be replaced by longitudinal research with multiple-item assessments that measure both the affective and the cognitive/judgmental aspects of SWB. A more sophisticated level of assessment will be particularly important as measures of SWB take their place alongside economic and other objective indicators of national well-being (Diener & Seligman, 2004).

Much more research is needed with respect to cultural differences in SWB, going beyond comparing levels of SWB and moving into more understanding of the meaning of SWB in unique cultures. Questions involving both the structure of SWB and the causes of SWB will be important to examine cross-culturally.

## REFERENCES

Andrews, F. M., & Withey, S. B. (1976). *Social indicators of well-being: America's perception of life quality*. New York, NY: Plenum Press.

Argyle, M., & Martin, M. (1991). The psychological causes of happiness. In F. Strack, M. Argyle, & N. Schwarz (Eds.), *Subjective Well-Being: An Interdisciplinary Perspective* (pp. 77–100). Elmsford, NY: Pergamon Press.

Argyle, M., Martin, M., & Lu, L. (1995). Testing for stress and happiness: The role of social and cognitive factors. In C. D. Spielberger & I. G. Sarason (Eds.), *Stress and Emotion* (Vol. 15, pp. 173–187). Washington, DC: Taylor & Francis.

Arthaud-Day, M. L., Rode, J. C., Mooney, C. H., & Near, J. P. (2005). The subjective well-being construct: A test of its convergent, discriminant, and factorial validity. *Social Indicators Research, 74*, 445–476.

Biswas-Diener, R., & Diener, E. (2006). The subjective well-being of the homeless, and lessons for happiness. *Social Indicators Research, 76*, 185–205.

Bradburn, N. M. (1969). *The structure of psychological well-being*. Chicago, IL: Aldine.

Bradburn, N. M., & Caplovitz, D. (1965). *Reports of happiness*. Chicago, IL: Aldine.

Brickman, P., & Campbell, D. T. (1971). Hedonic relativism and planning the good society. In M. H. Appley (Ed.), *Adaptation-level Theory: A Symposium*. (pp. 287–305). New York, NY: Academic Press.

Campbell, A., Converse, P.E., & Rodgers, W. L. (1976). *The quality of American life*. New York, NY: Russell Sage Foundation.

Cantor, N., & Sanderson, C. A. (1999). Life task participation and well-being: The importance of taking part in daily life. In D. Kahneman, E. Diener, & N. Schwarz (Eds.), *Well-being: The Foundations of Hedonic Psychology*. New York, NY: Russell Sage Foundation.

Carver, C. S., Lawrence, J. W., & Scheier, M. F. (1996). A control-process perspective on the origins of affect. In L. L. Martin & A. Tesser (Eds.), *Striving and Feeling: Interactions Among Goals, Affect, and Regulation* (pp. 12–52). Mahwah, NJ: Lawrence Erlbaum Associates.

Charles, S. T., Reynolds, C. A., & Gatz, M. (2001). Age-related differences and change in positive and negative affect over 23 years. *Journal of Personality and Social Psychology, 80*, 136–151.

Costa, P. T., Jr., & McCrae, R. R. (1980). Influence of extraversion and neuroticism on subjective well-being: Happy and unhappy people. *Journal of Personality and Social Psychology, 38*, 668–678.

Costa, P. T., & McCrae, R. R. (1991). *Revised NEO Personality Inventory (NEO PI-R) and NEO Five Factor Inventory (NEO-FFI)*. Odessa, FL: Psychological Assessment Resources, Inc.

Csikszentmihalyi, M. (1990). *Flow: The Psychology of Optimal Experience*. New York, NY: Harper Perennial.

Cunningham, M. R. (1988). Does happiness mean friendliness? Induced mood and heterosexual disclosure. *Personality and Social Psychology Bulletin, 14*, 283–97

Danner, D. D., Snowdon, D. A., & Friesen, W. V. (2001). Positive emotions in early life and longevity: Findings from the nun study. *Journal of Personality and Social Psychology, 80*, 804–813.

Diener, E. (1984). Subjective well-being. *Psychological Bulletin, 95*, 542–575.

Diener, E. (1994). Assessing subjective well-being: Progress and opportunities. *Social Indicators Research, 31*, p. 103–157.

Diener, E. (2000). Subjective well-being: The science of happiness and a proposal for a national index. *American Psychologist, 55*, 34–43.

Diener, E. (2009a). *Assessing well-being: The collected works of Ed Diener*. Social Indicators Research Series, Volume 39. The Netherlands: Springer.

Diener, E. (2009b). *Culture and well-being: The collected works of Ed Diener*. Social Indicators Research Series, Volume 38. The Netherlands: Springer.

Diener, E., & Biswas-Diener, R. (2008). *Happiness: Unlocking the mysteries of psychological wealth*. Oxford, UK: Blackwell.

Diener, E., & Chan, M. (2011). Happy people live longer: Subjective well-being contributes to health and longevity. *Applied Psychology: Health and Well-Being, 3*, 1–43.

Diener, E., & Diener, C. (1996). Most people are happy. *Psychological Science, 7*, 181–185.

Diener, E., & Diener, M. (1995). Cross-cultural correlates of life satisfaction and self-esteem. *Journal of Personality and Social Psychology, 68*, 653–663.

Diener, E., & Emmons, R. A. (1984). The independence of positive and negative affect. *Journal of Personality and Social Psychology, 47*, 1105–1117.

Diener, E., Emmons, R. A., Larsen, R. J., & Griffin, S. (1985). The Satisfaction With Life Scale. *Journal of Personality Assessment, 49*, 71–75.

Diener, E., & Fujita, F. (1997). Social comparisons and subjective well-being. In B. Buunk & R. Gibbons (Eds.), *Health, Coping and Social Comparison*. Mahwah, NJ: Erlbaum.

Diener, E., Horowitz, J., & Emmons, R. A. (1985). Happiness of the very wealthy. *Social Indicators Research, 16*, 263–274.

Diener, E., Kahneman, D., & Helliwell, J. (Eds.) (2010). Introduction. *International Differences in Well-Being*. Oxford, UK: Oxford University Press.

Diener, E., Kahneman, D., Tov, W., & Arora, R. (2010). Income's association with judgments of life versus feelings. In E. Diener, D. Kahneman, & J. Helliwell, (Eds.), *International Differences in Well-Being* (pp. 1–15). Oxford, UK: Oxford University Press.

Diener, E., Lucas, R. E., Oishi, S., & Suh, E. M. (2002). Looking up and down: Weighting good and bad information in life satisfaction judgments. *Personality and Social Psychology Bulletin, 28*, 437–445.

Diener, E., Lucas, R. E., Schimmack, U., & Helliwell, J. (2009). *Well-being for public policy*. Oxford, UK: Oxford University Press.

Diener, E., Lucas, R. E., and Scollon, C. N. (2006). Beyond the hedonic treadmill: Revising the adaptation theory of well-being. *American Psychologist, 61*, 305–314.

Diener, E., Ng, W., Harter, J., & Arora, R. (2010). Wealth and happiness across the world: Material prosperity predicts life evaluation, whereas psychosocial prosperity predicts positive feeling. *Journal of Personality and Social Psychology, 99*, 52–61.

Diener, E., Ng, W., & Tov, W. (2009). Balance in life and declining marginal utility of diverse resources. *Applied Research in Quality of Life, 3*, 277–291.

Diener, E., Nickerson, C., Lucas, R. E., & Sandvik, E. (2002). Dispositional affect and job outcomes. *Social Indicators Research, 59*, 229–259.

Diener, E., & Ryan, K. (2009). Subjective well-being: A general overview. *South African Journal of Psychology, 39*, 391–406.

Diener, E., & Ryan, K. (2011). National accounts of well-being for public policy. In S. I. Donaldson, M. Csikszentmihalyi, & J. Nakamura (Eds.), *Applied Positive Psychology: Improving Everyday Life, Health, Schools, Work, and Society* (pp. 15–34). New York, NY: Routledge.

Diener, E., & Seligman, M. E. P. (2002). Very happy people. *Psychological Science, 13*, 81–84.

Diener, E., & Seligman, M. E. P. (2004). Beyond money: Toward an economy of well-being. *Psychological Science in the Public Interest, 5*, 1–31.

Diener, E., Scollon, C. N., & Lucas, R E. (2004). The evolving concept of subjective well-being: The multifaceted nature of happiness. *Advances in Cell Aging and Gerontology, 15*, 187–219.

Diener, E., & Tay, L. (2011). Needs and subjective well-being around the world. *Journal of Personality and Social Psychology, 101*, 354–365.

Diener, E., Wirtz, D., Tov, W., Kim-Prieto, C., Choi, D., Oishi, S., & Biswas-Diener, R. (2010). New well-being measures: Short scales to assess flourishing and positive and negative feelings. *Social Indicators Research, 97*, 143–156.

Easterlin, R. A. (1974). Does economic growth improve the human lot? Some empirical evidence. In P. A. David & M. W. Reder (Eds.), *Nations and Households in Economic Growth*. New York, NY: Academic Press.

Emmons, R. A. (1986). Personal strivings: An approach to personality and subjective well-being. *Journal of Personality and Social Psychology, 51*, 1058–1068.

Emmons, R. A., & Diener, E. (1985). Personality correlates of subjective well-being. *Journal of Personality and Social Psychology, 11*, 89–97.

Ferriss, A. L. (2002). Religion and quality of life. *Journal of Happiness Studies, 3*, 199–215.

Fordyce, M. W. (1977). *The Happiness Measures: A sixty-second index of emotional well-being and mental health*. Unpublished manuscript. Edison Community College, Ft. Myers, FL.

Fredrickson, B. L. (2001). The role of positive emotions in positive psychology: The broaden-and-build theory of positive emotions. *American Psychologist, 56*, 218–226.

Fujita, F., Diener, E., & Sandvik, E. (1991). Gender differences in negative affect and well-being: The case for emotional intensity. *Journal of Personality and Social Psychology, 61*, 427–424.

Gray, J. A. (1981). A critique of Eysenck's theory of personality. In H. J. Eysenck (Ed.), *A Model for Personality* (pp. 246–276). New York, NY: Springer-Verlag.

Gray, J. A. (1991). Neural systems, emotion, and personality. In J. Madden (Ed.), *Neurobiology of Learning, Emotion, and Affect* (pp. 273–306). New York, NY: Raven Press.

Hagerty, M., & Veenhoven, R. (2003). Wealth and happiness revisited—growing national income does go with greater happiness. *Social Indicators Research, 64*, 1–27.

Headey, B. (2008). The Set-point theory of well-being: Negative results and consequent revisions. *Social Indicators Research, 86*, 389–403.

Headey, B., & Wearing, A. (1992). *Understanding happiness: A theory of subjective well-being*. Melbourne, Australia: Longman Cheshire.

Helliwell, J. F. (2007). Well-being and social capital: Does suicide pose a puzzle? *Social Indicators Research, 81*, 455–496.

Heller, D., Watson, D., & Ilies, R. (2004). The role of person versus situation in life satisfaction: A critical examination. *Psychological Bulletin, 130*, 574–600.

Horley, J., & Lavery, J. J. (1995). Subjective well-being and age. *Social Indicators Research, 34*, 275–282.

Kahneman, D. (1999). Objective happiness. In D. Kahneman, E. Diener & N. Schwarz (Eds.), *Well-being: The Foundations of Hedonic Psychology*. (pp. 3–25). New York, NY: Russell Sage Foundation.

Kahneman, D., Krueger, A. B., Schkade, D. A., Schwarz, N., & Stone, A. A. (2004). A survey method for characterizing daily life experience: The day reconstruction method. *Science, 306*, 1776–1780.

Kammann, R. (1983). Objective circumstances, life satisfactions and sense of well-being: Consistencies across time and place. *New Zealand Psychologist, 12*, 14–22.

Kashdan, T. B., Biswas-Diener, R., & King, L. A. (2008). Reconsidering happiness: The costs of distinguishing between hedonics and eudaimonia. *The Journal of Positive Psychology, 3*, 219–233.

Kitayama, S., & Marcus, H. R. (2000). The pursuit of happiness and the realization of sympathy: Cultural patterns of self, social relations, and well-being. In E. Diener & E. M. Suh (Eds.), *Culture and Subjective Well-Being* (pp. 113–161). Cambridge, MA: MIT Press.

Kuppens, P., Ceulemans, E., Timmerman, M E., Diener, E., & Kim-Prieto, C. (2006). Universal intracultural and intercultural dimensions of the recalled frequency of emotional experience. *Journal of Cross-Cultural Psychology, 37*, 491–515.

Larsen, R. J., & Ketelaar, T. (1991). Personality and susceptibility to positive and negative emotional states. *Journal of Personality and Social Psychology, 61*, 132–140.

Lucas, R. E. (2005). Time does not heal all wounds: A longitudinal study of reaction and adaptation to divorce. *Psychological Science, 16*, 945–950.

Lucas, R. E., & Baird, B. M. (2004). Extraversion and emotional reactivity. *Journal of Personality and Social Psychology, 86*, 473–485.

Lucas, R. E., Clark, A. E., Georgellis, Y., & Diener, E. (2003). Reexamining adaptation and the set-point model of happiness: Reactions to changes in marital status. *Journal of Personality and Social Psychology, 84*, 527–539.

Lucas, R. E., Clark, A. E., Georgellis, Y., & Diener, E. (2004). Unemployment alters the set-point for life satisfaction. *Psychological Science, 15*, 8–13.

Lucas, R. E., Diener, E., & Suh, E. (1996). Discriminant validity of well-being measures. *Journal of Personality and Social Psychology, 71*, 616–628.

Lyubomirsky, S., King, L., & Diener, E. (2005). The benefits of frequent positive affect: Does happiness lead to success? *Psychological Bulletin, 131*, 803–855.

Magnus, K., Diener, E., Fujita, F., & Pavot, W. (1993). Personality and events: A longitudinal analysis. *Journal of Personality and Social Psychology, 65*, 1046–1053.

Mastekaasa, A. (1992). Marriage and psychological well-being: Some evidence on selection into marriage. *Journal of Marriage and the Family, 54*, 901–911.

McCrae, R. R., & Costa, P. T. Jr. (1991). Adding liebe und arbeit: The full five-factor model and well-being. *Personality and Social Psychology Bulletin, 17*, 227–232.

Michalos, A. C. (1985). Multiple discrepancies theory (MDT). *Social Indicators Research, 16*, 347–413.

Mroczek, D. K., & Spiro, A., III. (2005). Change in life satisfaction during adulthood: Findings from the Veterans Affairs Normative Aging Study. *Journal of Personality and Social Psychology, 88*, 189–202.

Oishi, S., Diener, E., Choi, D. W., Kim-Prieto, C., & Choi, I. (2007). The dynamics of daily events and well-being across cultures: When less is more. *Journal of Personality and Social Psychology, 93*, 685–698.

Oishi, S., Diener, E., Lucas, R. E., & Suh, E. M. (1999). Cross-cultural variations in predictors of life satisfaction: Perspectives from needs and values. *Personality and Social Psychology Bulletin, 25*, 980–990.

Pavot, W. (2008). The assessment of subjective well-being: Successes and shortfalls. In M. Eid & R. J. Larsen (Eds.), *The Science of Subjective Well-Being* (pp. 124–140). New York, NY: Guilford Press.

Pavot, W. & Diener, E. (1993a). Review of the Satisfaction With Life Scale. *Psychological Assessment, 5*, 164–172.

Pavot, W., & Diener, E. (1993b). The affective and cognitive context of self-reported measures of subjective well-being. *Social Indicators Research, 28*, 1–20.

Pavot, W., & Diener, E. (2003). Well-being (including life satisfaction). In R. F. Ballesteros (Ed.), *Encyclopedia of Psychological Assessment* (Vol. 2, pp. 1097–1101). London, UK: Sage.

Pavot, W., & Diener, E. (2008). The Satisfaction With Life Scale and the emerging construct of life satisfaction. *The Journal of Positive Psychology, 3*, 137–152.

Pavot, W., Diener, E., Colvin, C. R., & Sandvik, E. (1991). Further validation of the Satisfaction With Life Scale: Evidence for the cross-method convergence of well-being measures. *Journal of Personality Assessment, 57*, 149–161.

Pavot, W., Diener, E., & Fujita, F. (1990). Extraversion and happiness. *Personality and Individual Differences, 11*, 1299–1306.

Pomerantz, E. M., Saxon, J. L., & Oishi S. (2000). The psychological trade-offs of goal investment. *Journal of Personality and Social Psychology, 79*, 617–630.

Robinson, M. D., & Compton, R J. (2008). The happy mind in action: The cognitive basis of subjective well-being. In M. Eid & R. J. Larsen, (Eds.), *The Science of Subjective Well-Being* (pp. 220–238). New York, NY: Guilford Press.

Roysamb, E., Harris, J. R., Magnus, P., Vitterso, J., & Tambs, K. (2002). Subjective well-being: Sex-specific effects of genetic and environmental factors. *Personality and Individual Differences*, 32, 211–223.

Roysamb, E., Tambs, K., Reichborn-Kjennerud, E., Neale, M.C., and Harris, J. R. (2003). Happiness and health: Environmental and genetic contributions to the relationships between subjective well-being, perceived health, and somatic illness. *Journal of Personality and Social Psychology*, 85, 1136–1146.

Rusting, C. L., & Larsen, R. J. (1997). Extraversion, neuroticism, and susceptibility to positive and negative affect: A test of two theoretical models. *Personality and Individual Differences*, 22, 607–612.

Ryan, R. M., & Deci, E. L. (2000). Self-determination theory and the facilitation of intrinsic motivation, social development, and well-being. *American Psychologist*, 55, 68–78.

Ryan, R. M., & Deci, E. L. (2001). On happiness and human potentials: A review of research on hedonic and eudaimonic well-being. *Annual Review of Psychology*, 52, 141–166.

Ryff, C. (1989). Happiness is everything, or is it? Explorations on the meaning of psychological well-being. *Journal of Personality and Social Psychology*, 57, 1069–1081.

Ryff, C. D., & Singer, B. (1996). Psychological well-being: Meaning, measurement, and implications for psychotherapy research. *Psychotherapy and Psychosomatics*, 65, 14–23.

Sandvik, E., Diener, E., & Seidlitz, L. (1993). Subjective well-being: The convergence and stability of self-report and nonself-report measures. *Journal of Personality*, 61, 317–342.

Schimmack, U. (2008). The structure of subjective well-being. In M. Eid & R. J. Larsen (Eds.), *The Science of Subjective Well-Being* (pp. 97–123). New York, NY: Guilford.

Schimmack, U., & Oishi, S. (2005). The influence of chronically and temporarily accessible information on life satisfaction judgments. *Journal of Personality and Social Psychology*, 89, 395–406.

Schneider, L., & Schimmack, U. (2009). Self-informant agreement in well-being ratings: A meta-analysis. *Social Indicators Research*, 94, 363–376.

Schwarz, N., & Strack, F. (1999). Reports of subjective well-being: Judgmental processes and their methodological implications. In Kahneman, D., Diener, E., & Schwarz, N. (Eds.), *Well-Being: The Foundations of Hedonic Psychology* (pp. 61–84). New York, NY: Russell Sage Foundation.

Scollon, C. N., Diener, E., Oishi, S., & Biswas-Diener, R. (2004). Emotions across cultures and methods. *Journal of Cross-Cultural Psychology*, 35, 304–326.

Scollon, C. N., Kim-Prieto, C., & Diener, E. (2003). Experience sampling: Promises and pitfalls, strengths and weaknesses. *Journal of Happiness Studies*, 4, 5–34.

Staw, B. M., Sutton, R. I., & Pelled, L. H. (1994). Employee positive emotion and favorable outcomes at the workplace. *Organization Science*, 5, 51–71.

Steel, P., Schmidt, J., & Shultz J. (2008). Refining the relationship between personality and subjective well-being. *Psychological Bulletin*, 134, 138–161.

Strack, F., Martin, L. L., & Schwarz, N. (1988). Priming and communications: Social determinants of information use in judgments of life satisfaction. *European Journal of Social Psychology*, 18, 429–442.

Stubbe, J. H., Posthuma, D., Boomsma, D. I., & De Geus, E. J. C. (2005). Heritability of life satisfaction in adults: A twin-family study. *Psychological Medicine*, 35, 1–8.

Suh, E., Diener, E., Oishi, S. & Triandis, H C. (1998). The shifting basis of life satisfaction judgments across cultures: Emotions versus norms. *Journal of Personality and Social Psychology*, 74, 482–493.

Tellegen, A., Lykken, D. T., Bouchard, T. J., Wilcox, K. J., Segal N. L., & Rich, S. (1988). Personality similarity in twins reared apart and together. *Journal of Personality and Social Psychology*, 54, 1031–1039.

Tov, W., & Diener, E. (2007). Culture and subjective well-being. In S. Kitayama & D. Cohen (Eds.), *Handbook of Cultural Psychology*. New York, NY: Guilford Press.

Veenhoven, R. (1984). *Conditions of happiness*. Dordrecht, the Netherlands: D. Reidel.

Veenhoven, R. (1988). The utility of happiness. *Social Indicators Research*, 20, 333–354.

Watson, D., Clark, L. A., & Tellegen, A. (1984). Cross-cultural convergence in the structure of mood: A Japanese replication and a comparison with U. S. findings. *Journal of Personality and Social Psychology*, 47, 127–144.

Watson, D., Clark, L.A., & Tellegen, A. (1988). Development and validation of brief measures of positive and negative affect: The PANAS scales. *Journal of Personality and Social Psychology*, 54, 1063–1070.

Wilson, W. (1967). Correlates of avowed happiness. *Psychological Bulletin*, 67, 294–306.

# SECTION II

# PSYCHOLOGICAL DEFINITIONS OF HAPPINESS

# CHAPTER 11

# INTRODUCTION TO PSYCHOLOGICAL DEFINITIONS OF HAPPINESS

JOAR VITTERSØ

University of Tromsø, Norway

THREE decades ago Ernst Mayr, a highly esteemed biologist, published an outstanding review on the growth of scientific thinking in general, and of biological thinking in particular (Mayr, 1982). His analysis revealed that science seems to make progress, not so much by individual discoveries, experimental procedures, or the proposal of new theories, but rather by the gradual but decisive development of new concepts and the abandonment of those that had previously been dominant. "Those are not far wrong who insist that the progress of science consists principally in the progress of scientific concepts," Mayr argued (1982, p. 24). For example, nothing seemed to have strengthened the theory of natural selection as much as the continuing refutation of old concepts and competing theories.

Related to Mayr's criteria for progress, the scientific thinking on happiness is dominated more by developing new concepts than by abandoning old ones and some trends are clearer than others. For instance, before modern psychology, the concept of happiness was dominated by the thinking of two periods (Fellows, 1966). The first period was that of the ancient Greek philosophers, and the second took off with the utilitarianism of the nineteenth century.

In the Greek period, four conceptualizations of the good life competed for attention (McMahon, 2008). From the pure hedonism of Aristippus we got the idea that happiness is the sum of momentary pleasures (J. Watson, 1895), a position that was partly reborn with Bentham's utilitarianism (Bentham, 1789/1948) and more recently with Kahneman's theory of objective happiness (Kahneman, 1999; Kahneman, Wakker, & Sarin, 1997). A softer hedonistic position was defended by Epicurus who argued that life should not be lived to maximize momentary pleasures, but to maximize pleasures with life as a whole. Today we recognize Epicurus' ideas in the concept of life satisfaction (Diener, 2006) and in Kahneman's revised theory of hedonic happiness (e.g., Kahneman, Schkade, Fischler, Krueger, & Krilla, 2010). A third position from the high days of Greek philosophy was Stoicism, coming from Zeno and his argument that happiness is secured by detachment from emotional life.

Finally, the fourth approach to happiness sprang from Aristotle and the claim that the good life follows from the exercise of virtuous activities. Elements of Stoicism and Aristotelian happiness have been reborn in what currently is referred to as eudaimonic well-being. In it one will find both tendencies to reduce the role of feelings in well-being (e.g., Ryan & Deci, 2001; Ryff, 1989), and tendencies to reintroduce the Aristotelian idea of activity-based "higher pleasures" and the development of one's potential as the core constructs in a theory of happiness (e.g., Huta & Ryan, 2010; Waterman, 2008).

To the Greek philosophers, true happiness could not be achieved outside the circle of privileged, wealthy men. With the Enlightenment, by contrast, an egalitarian notion of the concept emerged for the first time. All people had a right to happiness. So, even if Adam Smith argued that greed is good, he also believed that it was a deception that the rich owned more means to happiness than the poor (Kenny & Kenny, 2006). And Bentham's version of hedonism is well known for the support it gave to "the greatest amount of happiness for the greatest number of people." Another leading utilitarian, John Stuart Mill, observed a conflict between the reductionism of Bentham and the moralism of Aristotle. Thus Mill attempted to follow Aristotle in separating higher pleasures from lower pleasures, and he thought of happiness as depending on doing the right activities and on the realization of potentials (Nussbaum, 2007). But he also picked up the idea of a subjective and one-dimensional concept of happiness from Bentham, which forced Mill to believe that pleasures of different kinds could be summoned into a single dimension by a judgmental process, quite similar to the idea of life satisfaction in current literature. But whereas Bentham believed in pleasure as a one-dimensional feeling state, Mill believed in pleasure as a one-dimensional evaluation, or, in philosophical jargon, a one-dimensional rank of attitude (Sumner, 1996).

This brief history points out how modern conceptions of happiness stand on the shoulders of philosophical thinking. But as a scientific discipline, happiness research was not born until the end of the 1950s. Scattered attempts of empirical investigations had taken place earlier (e.g., Beckham, 1929; Hartmann, 1934; Ilsager, 1948; Ruckmick, 1925; Sailor, 1931; G. Watson, 1930), but it seems fair to say that a milestone was reached when Gurin and his colleagues set out to ask a representative sample of the population of the USA explicitly about their overall happiness in life (Gurin, Veroff, & Feld, 1960). Shortly after, Cantril surveyed a broader sample of nations. His concepts were those of human concerns and life satisfaction, thus introducing the evaluative dimension to happiness studies (Cantril, 1965). The combination of good feelings and favorable evaluations gave birth to the concept of subjective well-being as we know it today, and the duality of experiences and evaluations has dominated modern happiness research, thanks to researchers such as Andrews and Withey (1976), Campbell, Converse, and Rodgers (1976), Michalos (1980), Veenhoven (1984), and Diener (1984).

The current section testifies to this development, and takes it further. The following chapters explore the many understandings of happiness that exist today and illustrate that without conceptual clarifications, the study of happiness hardly make sense.

This section opens with a chapter by Ruut Veenhoven, a true old-timer in happiness research. Veenhoven is highly aware of the many meanings of happiness, and has limited the scope of his review to the concept as referring to quality of life as a whole. To help classify the relevant themes of this perspective, Veenhoven suggests that the qualities of a life can be summarized in a fourfold matrix. The first domain in this table accounts for the distinction between life chances and life results, or outcomes. In the second dimension a distinction is made between the external and internal qualities of life. By this route, Veenhoven is able to pin down many concepts relevant for a proper understanding of the good life. For example, the livability of the environment (the standard of living) is an external life chance, whereas the utility of life (the significance of life) is an external life result. Life-ability (how well we are equipped to cope with the problems of life) is an inner life chance, and appreciation of life (self-reported life satisfaction) is an inner life result. Veenhoven shows how his scheme has analogies to taxonomies in biology, and clarifies how central concepts in quality of life literature fit into the quadrants. The author also provides an opinion as to how the central meaning from of the other chapters in this section fit into the fourfold matrix of life qualities.

Two conceptual presentations of hedonic or subjective well-being (SWB) follow Veenhoven's contribution. In Chapter 13, Felicity Miao, Minkyung Koo, and Shigehiro Oishi provide an updated review of the SWB perspective. The authors declare SWB to be the sum of two affective and two cognitive components, and encourage well-being researchers to measure all four components of the concept: positive emotions, negative emotions, life satisfaction, and domain satisfaction. After a clear synopsis of the history of happiness research and after debating the issues of measurement, Miao and coauthors highlight important findings from SWB research. They point to the modest impact from demographic variability and to the puzzling relation between material wealth and well-being and the importance of positive social relationships. Newer insights on adaptation and cultural variation are then presented, as are the relatively recent concerns for the effects of happiness and intervention strategies for the enhancement of higher well-being. When it comes to future research needs, the authors are clear in their advice: Better theoretical models that make sense of the dynamic influences of subjective well-being brought forth by sophisticated research techniques are needed.

Robert A. Cummins (Chapter 14) provides another articulation of happiness research. Acknowledging how the lack of a proper understanding of the concept is a barrier for progress in the field, Cummins clarifies his own position before the chapter proceeds to the issue of how happiness can be measured. Like most researchers, Cummins regards subjective well-being to involve both affective and cognitive processes. However, Cummins also adds a cybernetic element to his SWB construct, entitled homeostatically protected mood, which he describes as a positive sense of well-being. This stable mood component is the driving force of both the affective and the cognitive elements of SWB. By analogy to the homeostatic regulation of body temperature, he suggests that individuals are genetically determined to maintain a level of well-being in the area between 60 and 90 on a scale running from 0 to 100. In other words, for an individual with a SWB set-point of 70, some regulatory mechanisms will be activated in order to reduce the level of well-being for that individual if the level temporarily increases to, say, 75. If the SWB level is reduced to 65, other kinds of mechanisms will kick in to push SWB back to its normal level. Based on this architecture, and after briefly having discussed qualitative methods, Cummins presents his thinking on how happiness should be measured. Issues such as item weighting, proxy data, and data cleaning are nicely summarized, as is the special case of how happiness may be measured in low-functioning populations. The chapter concludes with a presentation of scales that Cummins suggests not be used, and a handful of scales recommended for use in happiness research.

In Chapter 15, Veronika Huta asks how humans can increase their fulfillment in life. This is a pointed question that encircles the homeland of eudaimonic inquiries.

Conceptually, the academic playground of eudaimonia has fussy boarders, but is roughly associated with developing the best in oneself in accordance with one's true self and deeper principles. Huta reviews ancient and current perspectives on the relation between fulfillment and happiness, and shows how eudaimonic well-being is a multifaceted concept by presenting a handful of eudaimonic oriented theories. For example, self-determination theory is related to eudaimonia in its view of autonomy, which includes the idea of being true to oneself. In flow theory, self-fulfillment occurs for individuals who skillfully engage in challenging activities that stretch their abilities. The notion of psychological well-being is eudaimonic in proposing that well-being is not about good feelings, but rather about objectively realizing one's potentials. Personal expressiveness is another member of the eudaimonic family, one that stresses the subjective experiences that follow from the development of potentials. When developing the best in oneself one also feels fully alive, is the main argument of personal expressiveness theory. In the authentic happiness approach, eudaimonia is seen as activities in the service of something grander than the actor's own self. The functional model of well-being emphasizes how fulfillment in life depends on a variety of emotions with different functions: engagement and interest prepare us to make plans and assist when acting on important life goals, pleasure and satisfaction reward us when the goals are accomplished or are about to be accomplished. In Huta's own work, the motives for different categories of activities are taken as the eudaimonic markers. Some goals seek to develop the best in oneself, and these have a eudaimonic nature, others aim for pleasure and comfort and these goals are hedonic.

Christopher Niemiec and Richard Ryan provide a broad analysis of the fully functioning person (Chapter 16). A good life depends on psychological functioning and optimal experiences, because these elements are associated with autonomous self-regulation, pursuit and attainment of intrinsic values, and a mindful awareness of present experience. The authors embrace the eudaimonic perspective on well-being, but do not dismiss important elements of subjective well-being, such as the role played by satisfaction when it comes to rewarding the fulfillment of important needs. The chapter provides a clear description of self-determination theory and how recent years have witnessed an impressive accumulation of evidence suggesting its importance for well-being. The continuous, rather than dichotomous, difference between intrinsic and extrinsic motivation is presented, with a description of how it relates to the pursuit and attainment of important life goals. The authors are also concerned with mindfulness and how a receptive attention to present experience seems important to a life well lived. The authors conclude that happiness seems to accompany a harmony between thoughts, feelings, and actions, which in turn seem to benefit from well-functioning autonomy, competence, and social relatedness.

In the last chapter of the section, Vitterso reviews emotional, evaluative, and functional approaches to the study of human well-being. The author worries about the valuable information that gets lost when the study of happiness is reduced to simply asking people if they are happy or satisfied with their lives overall. A life is valuable in many different ways—not all of them are reflected as pleasure or in a statement of good versus bad. Happiness research may have been led astray in its eagerness to reduce the fullness of human emotions into a polarization of positive versus negative affects. For example, what we appreciate by way of experiencing novelty, engagement, and commitment to important life goals tends to slip away when the good life is operationalized as self-reported happiness or life satisfaction. As an alternative to such a one-dimensional approach, Chapter 17 proposes that theories of well-being should be attached to detailed observations of the diversity and dynamics between subjective experiences, evaluations, and life goals. Feelings and evaluations make little sense if they are isolated from the goals and plans held by those who experience the feelings and make the evaluations. To account for these themes, a functional well-being model is presented in order to explain, not only pleasant feelings and evaluations, but also a unifying representation of goals and plans. The concept of optimal functioning is offered to account for the process of creating plans and acting upon them to reach idiosyncratic goals and to fulfill basic needs in a manner that appears as meaningful. In other words, the functional well-being approach presents a taxonomy of happiness that incorporates good feelings and positive evaluations, but that in addition includes the idea of good functioning.

Pasteur famously stated that only the prepared mind makes discoveries. It is the editors' hope that readers of the present chapters will be better prepared to making new discoveries that will turn out to be important for future happiness research.

## REFERENCES

Andrews, F. M., & Withey, S. B. (1976). *Social indicators of well-being*. New York, NY: Plenum Press.

Beckham, A. S. (1929). Is the negro happy? *Journal of Abnormal and Social Psychology, 24*, 186–190.

Bentham, J. (1948). *An introduction to the principles of moral and legislation*. New York, NY: Hafner. (Original work published 1789). (Available from http://www.econlib.org/library/Bentham/bnthPML1.html).

Campbell, A., Converse, P. E., & Rodgers, W. L. (1976). *The quality of American life*. New York, NY: Sage.

Cantril, H. (1965). *The pattern of human concerns*. New Brunswick, NJ: Rutgers University Press.

Diener, E. (1984). Subjective well-being. *Psychological Bulletin, 95*, 542–575.

Diener, E. (2006). Guidelines for national indicators of subjective well-being and ill-being. *Journal of Happiness Studies, 7*, 397–404.

Fellows, E. W. (1966). Happiness: A survey of research. *Journal of Humanistic Psychology, 6*, 17–30.

Gurin, G., Veroff, J., & Feld, S. (1960). *Americans view their mental health*. New York, NY: Basic Books.

Hartmann, G. W. (1934). Personality traits associated with variations in happiness. *Journal of Abnormal and Social Psychology, 29*, 202–212.

Huta, V., & Ryan, R. (2010). Pursuing pleasure or virtue: The differential and overlapping well-being benefits of hedonic and eudaimonic motives. *Journal of Happiness Studies, 11*, 735–762.

Ilsager, H. (1948). Factors contributing to happiness among Danish college students. *The Journal of Social Psychology, 28*, 217–246.

Kahneman, D. (1999). Objective happiness. In D. Kahneman, E. Diener & N. Schwarz (Eds.), *Well-being: The Foundations of Hedonic Psychology* (pp. 3–25). New York, NY: Russell Sage Foundation.

Kahneman, D., Schkade, D. A., Fischler, C., Krueger, A. B., & Krilla, A. (2010). The structure of well-being in two cities: Life satisfaction and experienced happiness in Columbus, Ohio; and Rennes, France. In E. Diener, J. F. Helliwell, & D. Kahneman (Eds.), *International differences in well-being* (pp. 16–33). Oxford, UK: Oxford University Press.

Kahneman, D., Wakker, P. P., & Sarin, R. (1997). Back to Bentham? Explorations of experienced utility. *Quarterly Journal of Economics, 112*, 375–405.

Kenny, A., & Kenny, C. (2006). *Life, liberty, and the pursuit of utility. Happiness in philosophical and economic thought.* Exeter, UK: Imprint Academic.

Mayr, E. (1982). *The growth of biological thought. Diversity, evolution, and inheritance.* Cambridge, MA: Harvard University Press.

McMahon, D. M. (2008). The pursuit of happiness in history. In M. Eid & R. J. Larsen (Eds.), *The science of subjective well-being* (pp. 80–93). New York, NY: Guilford Press.

Michalos, A. C. (1980). Satisfaction and happiness. *Social Indicators Research, 8*, 385–422.

Nussbaum, M. C. (2007). Mill between Aristotle and Bentham. In L. Bruni & P. L. Porta (Eds.), *Economics and happiness. Framing the analysis* (pp. 170–183). Oxford, UK: Oxford University Press.

Ruckmick, C. A. (1925). The psychology of pleasantness. *Psychological Review, 32*, 362–383.

Ryan, R. M., & Deci, E. D. (2001). On happiness and human potentials: A review of research on hedonic and eudaimonic well-being. *Annual Review of Psychology, 52*, 141–166.

Ryff, C. D. (1989). Happiness is everything, or is it? Explorations on the meaning of psychological well-being. *Journal of Personality and Social Psychology, 57*, 1069–1081.

Sailor, R. C. (1931). *Happiness self-estimates of young men.* New York, NY: Columbia University.

Sumner, L. W. (1996). *Welfare, happiness, and ethics.* Oxford, UK: Clarendon Press.

Veenhoven, R. (1984). *Conditions of happiness.* Dordrecht, the Netherlands: Kluwer Academic.

Waterman, A. S. (2008). Reconsidering happiness: A eudaimonist's perspective. *Journal of Positive Psychology, 3*, 234–252.

Watson, G. (1930). Happiness among adult students of education. *Journal of Educational Psychology, 21*, 79–109.

Watson, J. (1895). *Hedonistic theories. From Aristippus to Spencer.* London, UK: Macmillan.

# CHAPTER 12

# NOTIONS OF THE GOOD LIFE

### RUUT VEENHOVEN

Erasmus University Rotterdam, The Netherlands
North-West University, South Africa

The word "happiness" has many different meanings. In the broadest sense it denotes the quality of life as a whole and in the most limited sense it refers to a moment of bliss. This "Handbook of Happiness" is about happiness in a broad sense and could as well have been entitled "Handbook of Quality of Life" or "Handbook of Well-being." Given the breadth of the topic, it is useful to start this section with an inspection of the more specific meanings of the word happiness and explain which of these meanings are used in the following chapters.

## Four Qualities of Life

Let us start with the term with the broadest connotation, that is, "quality of life." This term suggests that there is such a thing as a single quality of life, but we have never agreed on what that quality is. The term *quality* is easily used in rhetoric but the concept crumbles when analyzed scientifically, and it appears to be "multidimensional". After ages of fruitless discussion, it is time to acknowledge that we cannot meaningfully put all the good in one hat. So we ought to think of different *qualities* of life. In this context it is useful to distinguish between chances for a good life and outcomes of life, and between external and internal qualities of life.

### Chances and outcomes

Much of the literature on the good life is about chances, the preconditions that act upon an individual's life, for example having loving parents or, conversely, losing one's parents in a car accident. These "chances" are not the same as "outcomes", or life results. Chances can fail to be cultivated, as in the cases of gifted people who squander their talents. Conversely, people sometimes make much of their life in spite of poor chances, as in the case of migrants who start with nothing and work hard to build successful lives.

Table 12.1 Four qualities of life

|  | External qualities | Internal qualities |
|---|---|---|
| Life chances | Livability of environment | Life-ability of the person |
| Life outcomes | Utility of life | Appreciation of life |

This distinction between chances and outcomes is quite common in the field of public health research. Preconditions for good health, such as adequate nutrition and professional care, are seldom mixed in with health itself. Much health research is aimed at assessing the relationships between chances and outcomes; for instance by checking whether common nutritional advice really yields extra years lived in good health. However, chances and outcomes are less well distinguished in other fields.

## External and internal qualities

A second difference is between "external" and "internal" qualities of life. In the first case the quality is in the environment, in the latter it is in the individual. Lane (1994) made this distinction clear by extricating "quality of society" from "quality of persons." This distinction is also quite commonly made in public health. External pathogens are distinguished from internal disorders, and researchers try to identify the mechanisms by which the former produce the latter and the conditions in which this is more and less likely. Yet again this basic insight is often lacking in discussions in other fields.

The combination of these two dichotomies yields a fourfold matrix. This classification is presented in Table 12.1. The distinction between chances and outcomes is presented vertically, the difference between external and internal qualities is shown horizontally.

## Two kinds of life chances

In the upper half of the scheme in Table 12.1 we see two variants of potential quality of life: the external opportunities in one's environment and the internal capacities to exploit these. The external chances are denoted by the term *livability*, while the internal chances are identified by the term *life-ability*. This distinction is not new, however, the language used to describe these conditions is; in the literature on the psychology of stress these conditions often bear negative connotations, for example outer "burden" and inner "bearing power."

### Livability of the environment

The top left quadrant represents the meaning of good living conditions. These can be physical conditions such as clean air or social conditions such as mutual trust. Often the terms "quality of life" and "well-being" are used in this particular meaning, especially in the writings of ecologists and sociologists. Economists (e.g. Allardt, 1976) sometimes use the term "welfare" while another term used by sociologists is "level of living." "Livability" is a better word, because it does not have the limited connotation of material conditions. It also refers explicitly to a characteristic of the environment, for example, physical aspects of livability are moderate temperature and fresh air, while some social aspects are rule of law and freedom. Elsewhere I have explored the concept of livability in more detail (Veenhoven, 1996, pp. 7–9).

### Life-ability of the person

The top right quadrant in Table 12.1 denotes inner life chances, that is, how well we are equipped to cope with the problems of life. This involves physical abilities such as good sight, as well as mental abilities such as social intelligence. This aspect of the good life is also known by different names. The words "quality of life" and "well-being" are also used to denote this specific meaning, especially by doctors and psychologists. There are more names, however. In biology the phenomenon is referred to as "adaptive potential." On other occasions it is denoted by the medical term "health," in the medium variant of the word,[1] or by psychological terms such as "efficacy" or "potency." I prefer the simple term "life-ability," which contrasts elegantly with "livability."

## Two kinds of life outcomes

The lower half of the scheme in Table 12.1 is about the quality of life with respect to its outcomes. These outcomes can be judged by the value they provide to one's environment as well as the value they provide to the self. The worth of a life for the external environment is denoted by the term "utility of life." The inner valuation is called "appreciation of life." These matters are, of course, related. Knowing that one's life is useful will typically add to the appreciation of it. Yet, not all useful lives are happy lives, and neither are all "useless" lives unhappy.

### Utility of life

The bottom left quadrant represents the external outcomes of life, that is, the product or result of one's life endeavors. There is no current generic term for these effects of a persons life on his or her environment. Gerson (1976, p. 795) referred to "transcendental" conceptions of quality of life. Another appellation is "meaning of life," which denotes a universal sense of significance or purpose and is beyond a subjective sense of meaning (Frankl, 1946). I prefer the more simple "utility of life," admitting that this label may also give rise to misunderstanding.[2] Be aware that this external outcome does not require inner awareness. A person's life may be useful from some viewpoints, without them knowing, as demonstrated by Victor Frankl's logo-therapy, that aims to help people recognize and believe in the meanings of their life that they are not able to see for themselves.

### Appreciation of life

Finally, the bottom right quadrant represents the internal outcomes of life. That is, how the individual judges or perceives the quality of their own life. This is commonly referred to by terms such as "subjective well-being," "life-satisfaction," and "happiness" in a limited sense of the word. Life has more of this quality, the more and the longer it is enjoyed. In fairy tales this combination of intensity and duration is denoted with the phrase "they lived long and happily ever after."

[1] There are three main meanings for health: The maxi variant is all the good (World Health Organization (WHO) definition), the medium variant is life-ability, and the mini variant is absence of physical defect.
[2] A problem with this term is that the utilitarians used the word "utility" for subjective appreciation of life, the sum of pleasures and pains.

Table 12.2 Comparable concepts in biology

|  | External qualities | Internal qualities |
|---|---|---|
| Life chances | Biotope | Fitness |
| Life outcomes | Adaptation: continuation of species | Adaptation: long and happy life |

## Similar distinctions in biology

In evolutionary biology, external living conditions are referred to as the "biotope" or "habitat." A biotope can be more or less suitable (livable) for a species, depending on, for example, availability of food, shelter, and competition. Inner capabilities to survive in that environment are called "fitness." This latter term acknowledges that capabilities must meet (fit) environmental demand. Unlike moral philosophers, biologists see no quality in a capacity that is not functional.

This chance-constellation is seen to result in "adaptation," and good adaptation is seen to manifest in "survival," that is, a relatively long life. An organism that perishes prematurely has adapted less well than the one that completed its expected lifetime. In humans, good adaptation also reflects in increased hedonic experience. Continuous stress and pain are indicative of poor adaptation, while positive experiences, like pleasure and joy, denote good adaptation. As humans are capable of reflecting on their experiences, their feelings of pleasure and pain condense into overall appraisals of life satisfaction. So, human adaptation manifests in long *and* happy living. Though inner experience is no great issue in biology, this idea is implied in its logic. These biological concepts are summarized in Table 12.2.

## MEANINGS WITHIN QUALITY QUADRANTS

Most discussions of the good life deal with more specific values than the four qualities of life discerned here. Within each of the quadrants there is a myriad of submeanings, most of which are known under different names. It would require a voluminous book to record all the terms and meanings used in the literature. I present some of the main variants next. The main points are summarized in Table 12.3.

## Aspects of livability

Livability is an umbrella term for the various qualities of the environment that seem relevant for meeting human needs. In rhetorical use, the word refers mostly to specific kinds of qualities which typically root in some broader perception of a good society. The circumstantial qualities that are emphasized differ widely across contexts and disciplines.

For example, ecologists see livability in the natural environment and describe it in terms of pollution, global warming, and degradation of nature. Currently, they associate livability typically with environmental preservation. City planners see livability in the built environment and associate it with such things as sewer systems, traffic jams, and ghetto formation. Here the good life is seen as a fruit of human intervention.

Table 12.3 Some submeanings within quality-quadrants

|  | Outer qualities | Inner qualities |
|---|---|---|
| Life chances | **Livability of environment:**<br>• Ecological:<br>  e.g., moderate climate, clean air, spacious housing<br>• Social:<br>  e.g., freedom, equality, and brotherhood<br>• Economical:<br>  e.g., wealthy nation, generous social security, smooth economic development<br>• Cultural:<br>  e.g., flourishing of arts and sciences, mass education<br>• Etc… | **Life-ability of the person:**<br>• Physical health:<br>  negative: free of disease<br>  positive: energetic, resilient<br>• Mental health:<br>  negative: free of mental defects<br>  positive: autonomous, creative<br>• Knowledge:<br>  e.g., literacy, schooling<br>• Skills:<br>  e.g., intelligence, manners<br>• Art of living:<br>  e.g., varied lifestyle, differentiated taste<br>• Etc… |
| Life outcomes | **Objective utility of life:**<br>• External utility<br>  e.g., for intimates: rearing children, care for friends,<br>  e.g., for society: being a good citizen,<br>  e.g., for mankind: leaving an invention<br>• Moral perfection<br>  e.g., authenticity, compassion, originality<br>• Etc… | **Subjective appreciation of life:**<br>• Appraisal of life-aspects:<br>  e.g., satisfaction with job<br>  e.g., satisfaction with variety<br>• Prevailing moods:<br>  e.g., depression, ennui,<br>  e.g., zest<br>• Overall appraisals:<br>  Affective: general mood-level<br>  Cognitive: contentment with life |

In the sociological view, society is central. Firstly, livability is associated with the quality of society as a whole. Classic concepts of a good society stress material welfare and social equality, sometimes equating the concept more or less with the welfare state (Bellah et al., 1992). Current notions emphasize close networks, strong norms, and active voluntary associations. The reverse of this livability concept is social fragmentation. Secondly, livability is seen in one's position in society and equated with one's position on the social ladder. For a long time the emphasis was on the "under-class," people at the bottom of the social ladder seen to be "deprived." Currently attentions have shifted form the "underclass" to what I call the "outer-class" where poor livability is seen as a matter of "social exclusion."

# Kinds of life-ability

The most common depiction of this life-ability is the absence of functional defects. This is "health" in the limited sense, sometimes referred to as "negative health." In this context doctors focus on unimpaired functioning of the body, while psychologists stress the absence of mental defects. In their language, quality of life and well-being are often synonymous with mental health. This use of words presupposes a "normal" level of functioning. Good quality of life is the body and mind working as designed. This is the common meaning used in curative care.

Next to absence of disease one can consider excellence of function. This is referred to as "positive health" and associated with energy and resilience. Psychological concepts of positive mental health also involve autonomy, reality control, creativity, and inner synergy of traits and strivings. A new term in this context is "emotional intelligence" (Goleman, 1998). Though originally meant for specific mental skills, this term has come to denote a broad range of mental capabilities. This broader definition is the favorite in training professions.

A further step is to evaluate capability in a developmental perspective and to include acquisition of new skills for living. This is commonly denoted by the term "self-actualization" (Maslow, 1970). From this point of view, a middle-aged man is not "well" if he behaves like an adolescent, even if he functions without problems at this level. Since abilities do not develop in idleness, this quality of life is close to the "activity" which is close to Aristotle's concept of eudaimonia that he defined as "virtuous activity in accordance with reason" (Ostenfelt, 1994). This quality concept is also currently used in the training professions.

Lastly, the term "art of living" denotes special life-abilities; in most contexts this quality is distinguished from mental health and sometimes even attributed to slightly disturbed persons. Art of living is associated with refined tastes, an ability to enjoy life, and an original style of life.

## Criteria for utility of life

When evaluating the external effects of a life, one can consider its functionality for the environment. In this context, doctors stress how essential a patient's life is to their intimates. The life of a mother with young children is valued more highly than the life of a woman of the same age without children.

At a higher level, quality of life is seen in contributions to society. Historians see quality in the addition an individual can make to human culture, and rate, for example, the lives of great inventors higher than those of anonymous peasants. Moralists see quality in the preservation of the moral order, and would deem the life of a saint to be better than that of a sinner.

In this vein the quality of a life is also linked to effects on the ecosystem. Ecologists see more quality in a life lived in a "sustainable" manner than in the life of a polluter. In a broader view, the utility of life can be seen in its consequences for long-term evolution. As an individual's life can have many environmental effects, the number of such utilities is almost infinite.

Apart from its functional utility, life is also judged on its moral or esthetic value. Most of us would attribute more quality to the life of Florence Nightingale than to that of a criminal, even if it appeared that her good works had a negative result in the end (for example, medical care for soldiers lowered the threshold for warfare). In classic moral philosophy this is called virtuous living, and is often presented as the essence of true happiness. This concept of exemplaric utility sometimes merges with notions of inner life-ability, in particular in the case of self-actualization. Self-development is deemed good, even if it might complicate life (VonWright, 1963).

This quality criterion is external, that is, individuals need not be aware of their usefulness or may actually despise it. It is an outsider that appraises the quality of the individual's life on the basis of an external criterion. In religious thinking, such a judgment is made by God on the basis of eternal truth, in postmodern thought it is narrated by self-proclaimed experts on the basis of local conviction.

Clearly, the utility of life is not easy to grasp; both the criteria and those who would judge it, are multifarious and this prohibits comprehensive measurement of this quality of life.

# Appreciations of life

Humans are capable of evaluating their life in different ways. As already noted, we can appraise our situation affectively. We feel good or bad about particular things and our mood level signals overall adaptation. As in animals, these affective appraisals are automatic, but unlike other animals, humans can reflect on that experience. We have an idea of how we have felt over the last year, while a cat does not. Humans can also judge life cognitively by comparing life as it is with notions of how it should be.

## *Cognition and affect*

Most human evaluations are based on two sources of information, that is, intuitive affective appraisal and cognitively guided evaluation. The mix depends mainly on the object. Tangible things such as our income are typically evaluated by cognitive comparison; intangible matters such as sexual attractiveness are evaluated by how they feel, that is, intuitive affective appraisal. This dual evaluation system probably makes the human experiential repertoire richer than that of our fellow-creatures.

In evaluating our life we typically summarize this rich experience in overall appraisals. For instance we appreciate particular domains of life. When asked how we feel about our "work" or our "marriage," we will mostly have an opinion. Likewise, most people form ideas about separate qualities of their life, for instance, how "challenging" their life is and whether there is any "meaning" in it. Next to these appraisals of particular parts of our life, we also evaluate the quality of our life as a whole. Such judgments are made in different time-perspectives, in the past, the present, and the future. As the future is less palpable than the past and the present, hopes and fears depend more on affective inclination than on cognitive calculation.

Mostly such judgments are not very salient in our consciousness. Now and then they come to mind spontaneously, and they can be recalled and refreshed when needed. Sometimes, however, life-appraisals develop into pervasive mental syndromes such as depression.

## *Dominance of affect*

Many scholars think of happiness as the result of a cognitive operation. For instance, utilitarian philosopher Jeremy Bentham (1789/1983) spoke of a "mental calculus." More recently, Andrews and Withey (1976) suggest that individuals compute a weighed average of earlier life-aspect evaluations, while Michalos's (1985) multiple discrepancy theory presumes that individuals compare life as it is with various standards of how it should be. Many philosophers see happiness as an estimate of success in realizing one's life-plan (e.g., Nordenfelt, 1989).

Yet there are good reasons to assume that overall life-satisfaction is mostly inferred from affective experience (Veenhoven, 2009). One reason is that life as a whole is not a suitable object for calculative evaluation. Life has many aspects and there is usually not one clear-cut ideal model to compare it with. Another reason seems to be that affective signals tend to dominate;

seemingly cognitive appraisals are often instigated by affective cues (Zajonc, 1980). This fits the theory that the affective system is the older in evolutionary terms, and that cognition works as an addition to that navigation system rather than as a replacement (Veenhoven, 2009).

This issue has important consequences for the significance of subjective appreciation as a criterion for quality of life. If appreciation is a matter of mere comparison with arbitrary standards, there is little of value in a positive evaluation; dissatisfaction is then an indication of high demands. If, however, life satisfaction signals the degree to which innate needs are met, it denotes how well we thrive.

Whatever the method of assessment, the fact that we are able to come to an overall evaluation of life is quite important. Later on in this chapter we will see that this is the only basis for encompassing judgments of the quality of life.

## Meanings Denoted by Related Terms

With the help of the taxonomy given earlier, we can now clarify the substantive meaning of several terms that are commonly used for denoting qualities of life. This enumeration is not exhaustive; the goal is to illustrate this approach. The following diagrams refer to Table 12.1 and indicate which of the four qualities of life are at stake. The darker the shade of a quadrant, the more that particular quality of life is addressed.

## Adjustment

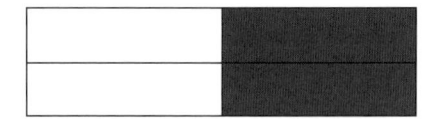

This term came into use in the 1940s (see Cavan et al., 1949), particularly in gerontological studies of "adjustment to old age," and was used interchangeably with "adaptation." These words were soon ousted by phrases like "morale," "psychological well-being," and "life-satisfaction." Adjustment refers to personal qualities; hence it belongs on the right side of our matrix. Adjustment denotes how well a person deals with life, and refers to both equipment and success. Hence the concept does not fit one quadrant, but covers both life-abilities and life-appraisals. In the diagram this is indicated by two equally dark quadrants.

## Art of living

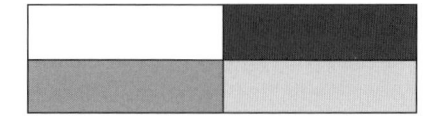

The expression "art of living" refers, first of all, to a person's life-ability and therefore belongs in the top right quadrant. As noted earlier, the term depicts mostly the quality of a lifestyle, typically refined Epicurianism, but sometimes the wisdom of simple living is also valued as artistry. This main meaning is reflected in the dark colored quadrant. Yet the term bears other connotations, capacity is often associated with its intended results, hence art of living tends to be equated with happiness, or at least with sensory gratification. Further, the life of an artist is sometimes valued as a piece of art in itself, which has some external utility. For instance, we see quality in the life of Casanova, renowned for his love of life and refined enjoyments, even though the man himself seems not to have been particularly happy. The adjunct connotations of the word are indicated in gray.

## Capability

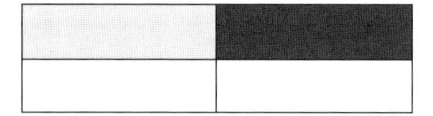

In Sen's (1985) work, the word "capability" denotes the abilities required to improve one's situation, typically in the context of developing countries. Nussbaum rather refers to capability as "being able to live a truly human life" in the context of affluent society. "Being able" requires both freedom from external restraints and personal skills. Freedom from external restraints belongs in the top left quadrant of the matrix, while the personal competency to use environmental chances belongs in the top right quadrant. In Sen's work, the emphasis is in the top left quadrant, in particular where he argues against discrimination. Yet he also highlights education, which is an individual quality. In Nussbaum and Sen's (1993) work the emphasis is in the top right quadrant. Most of the capabilities on her list are inner aptitudes, e.g., practical reason and imagination. Yet she also mentions protection against violent assault, which is an environmental factor.[3]

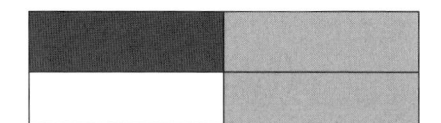

## Deprivation

The word "deprivation" refers to a shortfall of something. When used in an absolute sense it means failure to meet basic human needs, when used in a relative sense it means being less well off than others. The word is typically used in the latter meaning, while suggesting the former. Current specifications of this notion are "poverty" and "social exclusion."

In most contexts the lack is in external conditions of life, and concerns access to income, power, and prestige. In social policy this kind of deprivation is typically met with redistribution of these scarce resources. This main meaning belongs in the livability quadrant.

---

[3] These concepts are discussed in more detail in Veenhoven (2010b).

Sometimes the word also refers to deficiency in the capacity to stand up for oneself. The political cure for this problem is "empowerment," common ingredients of which are general education, political training, and boosting of self-esteem. The latter adjunct definition belongs in the life-ability quadrant.

Usually these conditions are associated with individual happiness. Hence measures of deprivation often include items on dissatisfaction, depression, and suicidal ideation. Enjoyment of life in spite of objective deprivation is seen as an anomaly and referred to as "resignation" (Zapf, 1984).

## Happiness

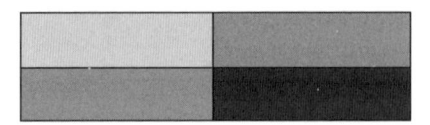

As noted in the introduction to this chapter, the word "happiness" has often been used as a generic for all worth and is, in this sense, synonymous with comprehensive quality of life or "well-being." I distinguished four qualities of life (Table 12.1), one of which "appreciation of life" (bottom right quadrant), typically indicates satisfaction with life as a whole. The latter use of the word is most common in present day "happiness studies" and is the conceptual focus of the World Database of Happiness (Veenhoven, 2010a).

Beyond this main denotation of the word, there are still further adjunctive uses of the term. This appears for example in the well known definition of happiness given by Tatarkiewicz (1975, p. 16) as "... *justified* satisfaction with life." The adjective "justified" means that mere enjoyment of life does not constitute (true) happiness if it occurs in objective situations, for example a prisoner cannot be really happy. Similarly, Tatarkiewicz would not call someone happy when the evaluation is based on misperception, such as when the enjoyment is derived from a "useless" life.

## NOTIONS OF HAPPINESS ADDRESSED IN THIS VOLUME

What kinds of happiness are addressed in this section on "Definitions of Happiness"? Using the conceptual matrix we can place the meanings addressed in each of the chapters.

## Eudaimonic happiness: Chapters 15 and 16

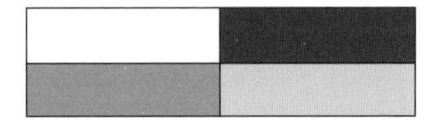

The term *eudaimonic* happiness is commonly used in contrast with *hedonic* happiness, and denotes that simply feeling good is not everything. The essence of a good life is seen in "living good" rather than in "enjoying life" and living good is seen as "psychological development." In the words of Niemiec and Ryan in this volume (Chapter 16): "Eudaimonia . . . describes a process of living based on contemplation, virtue, and realization of potentials." In this context, philosophers emphasize intellectual development, while psychologist associate it with "full functioning" and "living in accord with one's true nature" (cf. Huta).

In this view of the good life, the emphasis is on life-ability in the top right quadrant of our conceptual matrix. Still, subjective enjoyment of life is commonly seen as an inseparable by-product of psychological thriving and for that reason the bottom right quadrant is colored gray. Likewise, individual thriving is often associated with living a useful life and for that reason the bottom left quadrant is colored gray as well.

## Subjective well-being: Chapter 13

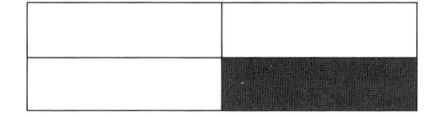

The term *subjective well-being* (SWB) is often used in one breath with "life-satisfaction" and "happiness" and denotes "appreciation of life" in the bottom right quadrant. Following Diener (1984), Miao, Koo, and Oishi use the term for the subjective appreciation of life of one's life as a whole. "Appreciation" is seen to involve both affective enjoyment and cognitive contentment. "A person who scores high on subjective well-being should experience many positive and few negative emotions, while also reporting high life and specific domain evaluations."

## Happiness: Chapter 14

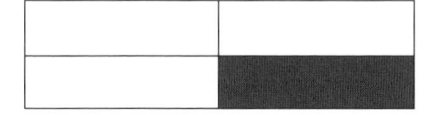

In Chapter 14, Cummins uses the term happiness in a wider meaning and incorporates both affective and cognitive appraisals of life. In that use of the word, happiness is synonymous with subjective well-being (SWB) as defined by Diener, discussed in Chapters 13 and 15.

## Functional well-being: Chapter 17

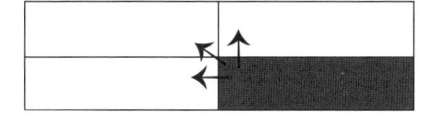

In the last chapter of this section, Vitterso introduces the notion of "functional well-being." He considers not only how well we feel, but also the effects of that experience on other qualities of life. In this view, well-being as such belongs in the bottom right quadrant. The functional effects are depicted with arrows pointing to the other quadrants.

# Conclusion

The term happiness is used for four different notions of the good life. In this section on "Definitions of Happiness" the emphasis is on two of these: "life ability" and "life satisfaction." In other words: this section is about psychological well-being, both in the objective sense of thriving well and in the subjective sense of enjoying life.

## References

Allardt, A. (1976). Dimensions of welfare in a comparative Scandinavian study. *Acta Sociologica*, 19, 227-239.

Andrews, F., & Withey, S. (1976). *Social indicators of wellbeing: American perceptions of quality of life.* New York, NY: Plenum Press.

Bellah, R. N., Madsen, R., Sullivan, W. R., Swidler, A., & Tipton, S. M. (1992). *The good society.* New York, NY: Vintage books.

Bentham, J. (1983). An introduction into the principles of morals and legislation. In: *The collected works of Jeremy Bentham.* Oxford, UK: Clarendon Press. (Original work published 1789).

Cavan, R.S., Burgess, E.W., Goldhamer, H., & Havighurst, R.J. (1949). *Personal adjustment in old age.* Chicago, IL: Science Research Associates.

Diener, E. (1984). Subjective wellbeing. *Psychological Bulletin*, 95, 542–575.

Frankl, V. (1946). *Man's search for meaning, an introduction to logo-therapy.* Boston, MA: Beacon Press.

Gerson, E. M. (1976). On quality of life. *American Sociological Review*, 41, 793–806.

Goleman, D. (1998). *Working with emotional intelligence.* New York, NY: Bantam Books.

Jahoda, M. (1958). *Current concepts of positive mental health.* New York, NY: Basic Books.

Lane, R. E. (1994).Quality of life and quality of persons. A new role for government. *Political theory*, 22, 219–252.

Maslow, A. H. (1970). *Motivation and personality.* New York, NY: Harper & Row.

Michalos, A. (1985). Multiple Discrepancy Theory (MDT). *Social Indicators Research*, 16, 347–413.

Nordenfelt, L. (1989). Quality of life and happiness. In S. Bjork & J. Vang, J. (Eds.), *Assessing quality of life. Health service studies nr 1* (pp. 17–26). Klintland, Sweden: Samhall.

Nussbaum, M. C., & Sen, A. (Eds.). (1993). *The quality of life.* Oxford, UK: Clarendon Press

Ostenfelt, E. (1994). Aristotle on the good life and quality of life. In: Nordenfelt, L. (Ed.), *Concepts and measurement of quality of life in healthcare* (pp. 19–34). Dordrecht, the Netherlands: Kluwer Academic.

Sen, A. (1985). *Commodities and capabilities.* Oxford, UK: Oxford University Press.

Tatarkiewicz, W. (1975). *Analysis of happiness.* The Hague, Netherlands: Martinus Nijhoff.

Veenhoven, R. (1984). *Conditions of happiness.* Dordrecht, the Netherlands: Kluwer Academic.

Veenhoven, R. (1996). Happy life-expectancy. *Social Indicators Research*, 39, 1–58

Veenhoven, R. (2009). How do we assess how happy we are? In A. K. Dutt & B. Radcliff (Eds.), *Happiness, economics and politics: Towards a multi-disciplinary approach* (pp. 45–69). Cheltenham UK: Edward Elgar Publishers.

Veenhoven, R. (2010a). *World Database of Happiness: Continuous register of scientific research on subjective enjoyment of life*. Rotterdam, the Netherlands: Erasmus University Rotterdam. (Available at: http://worlddatabaseofhappiness.eur.nl).

Veenhoven, R. (2010b). Capability and happiness: Conceptual difference and reality links. *Journal of Socio-Economics*, 39, 44–50.

VonWright, G. H. (1963). *The varieties of goodness*. London, UK: Routledge & Kegan.

Zajonc, R. B. (1980). Feeling and thinking: preference needs no inference. *American Psychologist*, 35, 151–175

Zapf, W. (1984). Individuelle Wohlfahrt: Lebensbedingungen und wahrgenommene Lebensqualität. In W. Glatzer & W. Zapf (Eds.), *Lebensqualität in der Bundesrepublik. Objective Lebensbedingungen und subjectives Wohlbefinden* (pp. 13–26). Frankfurt am Main, Germany: Campus Verlag.

# CHAPTER 13

# SUBJECTIVE WELL-BEING

## FELICITY F. MIAO[1], MINKYUNG KOO[2], AND SHIGEHIRO OISHI[1]

[1]University of Virginia, USA; [2]University of Illinois at Urbana-Champaign, USA

SUBJECTIVE well-being (SWB) is typically defined as the sum of affective and cognitive components (Diener, 1984; Diener, Suh, Lucas, & Smith, 1999). The balance of positive and negative emotions constitutes affective well-being, while an individual's evaluation of her life constitutes cognitive well-being. A person who scores high on SWB should experience many positive and few negative emotions and moods, while also reporting high life and domain-specific evaluations.

## BRIEF HISTORY OF SUBJECTIVE WELL-BEING

Only in the last 200 years or so have individuals viewed happiness as something that can be attained. Indeed, Thomas Jefferson famously claimed the "pursuit of happiness" as an "unalienable right" in the Declaration of Independence. The ancient Greeks certainly did not consider happiness something that could be actively pursued; in fact, they believed it could only be judged upon one's death (see McMahon, 2006, for a comprehensive history of happiness). The ancient Greek's term for happiness was "eudaimonia." Aristotle used the term eudaimonia (good spirit) interchangeably with the Greek term "makario" (blessed). Thus, happiness for ancient Greeks was vulnerable to external conditions and luck (Nussbaum, 2000). McMahon believes the shift from a happiness of fortune to a happiness of pleasure began during the seventeenth and eighteenth centuries. During this time, some individuals began believing that happiness could be attained in the present life, and not just in the afterlife.

The birth of psychological science was accompanied by the scientific study of well-being. For instance, the psychologist George Van Ness Dearborn published *The Emotion of Joy* in 1899, a book summarizing the literature on the psychophysiology and psychobiology of positive emotions. In 1925, Flugel already used a daily diary method to chart the type and intensity of emotions. Since the 1940s, large-scale national surveys have been conducted. Many of these surveys have included a single-item life satisfaction scale (e.g., self-anchoring ladder scale; Cantril, 1965). Bradburn (1969) introduced a multi-item affect balance scale in a large national survey and expanded the measurement tool of SWB. He also found that positive and negative affect are not polar opposites, but instead somewhat independent constructs. This finding highlights the importance of assessing positive and negative emotions separately.

The earliest review of work on SWB was authored by Wilson (1967) on "avowed happiness." By the early 1980s, SWB had become its own field. Since then, many important reviews have been published (Diener, 1984; Diener, Oishi, & Lucas, 2003; Diener et al., 1999; Kesebir & Diener, 2008; Lyubomirsky, King, & Diener, 2005). Furthermore, multiple edited volumes (Diener & Suh, 2000; Eid & Larsen, 2008; Kahneman, Diener, & Schwarz, 1999; Strack, Argyle, & Schwarz, 1991) are also devoted to the science of SWB.

# Measurement of Subjective Well-being

Many scales exist to measure different components of well-being. For the cognitive component, the most commonly used life satisfaction scale is the five-item Satisfaction with Life Scale (Diener, Emmons, Larsen, & Griffin, 1985). Although many researchers use the Positive and Negative Affect Schedule (PANAS; Watson, Clark, & Tellegen, 1988), the PANAS focuses exclusively on high arousal affect items. It may be useful to consider scales such as the Affect Valuation Index (Tsai, Knutson, & Fung, 2006) if researchers are interested in measuring both high and low arousal positive and negative emotions. Furthermore, the PANAS requires researchers to infer subjective feelings of well-being from affect ratings. The Subjective Happiness Scale (Lyubomirsky & Lepper, 1999) attempts to capture global, subjective feelings of happiness from the participant that may be distinct from actual affect experienced in the previous week.

Self-report measures of SWB demonstrate convergent and discriminant validity. Sandvik, Diener, and Seidlitz (1993), for instance, found that informant reports of well-being (from family and friends), online judgments of affect from experience sampling, as well as judgments of well-being from independent raters all converge with self-report measures of SWB. Using a multitrait multimethod approach, Lucas, Diener, and Suh (1996) also found that the components of SWB are distinct from one other and also from related constructs such as self-esteem and optimism.

Self-reported SWB measures also exhibit predictive validity. Participants' memories for recent positive and negative events correspond to measures of SWB (Sandvik et al., 1993) and are a reliable predictor of future behavior (Wirtz, Krueger, Scollon, & Diener, 2003). However, global self-reports of SWB are far from perfect. For instance, global self-reports are influenced by moods at the time of judgments (Schwarz & Strack, 1999; see, however, Eid & Diener, 2004, for a relatively small current mood effect). Global reports are also prone to memory bias (see Kahneman, 1999). They are also influenced by temporarily accessible constructs such as preceding questions (Schwarz & Strack, 1999; see, however, a meta-analysis by Schimmack & Oishi, 2005, that shows a small effect size for item-order effects).

Researchers have employed various online measures of well-being such as the experience sampling method (Schimmack, 2003; Scollon, Kim-Prieto, & Diener, 2003). Recently, the Daily Reconstruction Method (Kahneman, Krueger, Schkade, Schwarz, & Stone, 2004) has been developed to ease the respondent burden from traditional experience sampling studies and to also allow for weighted analyses of experiences by capturing the duration of various affective experiences.

## Current Subjective Well-being Findings

### Demographic correlates of subjective well-being

Age is associated with more positive affect and less negative affect (Mroczek & Kolarz, 1998). However, this effect is often small and complex. For instance, the relation between age and positive affect is linear among men, but curvilinear among women. Similarly, marital status is associated with life satisfaction and happiness, but the effect is small (Diener et al., 1999). A large-scale longitudinal study has shown that the positive effect of marriage on life satisfaction is also short-lived (Lucas, Clark, Georgellis, & Diener, 2003). Religiosity is also positively associated with life satisfaction. However, its effect size is very small (0.06 in the USA; Diener & Clifton, 2002). Overall, demographic variables are not strongly associated with SWB.

### Material wealth and subjective well-being

There are significant positive correlations of the relationship between income and SWB at the level of individuals and nations (see Diener & Biswas-Diener, 2002; Diener & Oishi, 2000; Stevenson & Wolfers, 2008). The correlation between income and SWB is small to moderate at the level of individuals, ranging from 0.10–0.30 (Diener & Biswas-Diener, 2002). In contrast, the correlation between nations is large, often exceeding 0.50. The most controversial is the relation between income and SWB over time within a nation. Whereas real income has grown enormously since the Second World War in the USA and Japan, the mean level of life satisfaction and happiness has not changed much in these nations. Diener and Oishi (2000) analyzed data from 15 nations and found significant positive correlations in some nations (e.g., Portugal, Italy), but negative correlations in others (e.g., Belgium, UK). Stevenson and Wolfers (2008) analyzed more nations and found that in many nations economic growth was associated with an increase in life satisfaction. However, they also found that in the USA and Belgium, economic growth did not result in an increase in the mean level of life satisfaction over time. Thus, it is still unclear whether economic growth gives rise to higher levels of SWB of nations.

The relation between economic growth and SWB of the nation is complex in part because an increase in material wealth might also entail an increase in materialism (Diener & Biswas-Diener, 2002; Diener & Oishi, 2000). Indeed, spending money on or even pondering a material purchase (e.g., a piece of jewelry) makes one less happy than spending money on or pondering an experiential purchase (e.g., concert tickets; Van Boven & Gilovich, 2003). Furthermore, the target of a monetary purchase also seems to influence SWB.

Spending money on others makes individuals happier than when the same amount is spent on themselves (Dunn, Aknin, & Norton, 2008).

## Interpersonal relationships and subjective well-being

Diener and Seligman (2002) found that good social relationships are a necessary component of very happy individuals' lives. These individuals spent less time alone and more time with others, and rated their relationships with others more favorably than unhappy individuals. Furthermore, informant ratings of these happy individuals agreed that they had better social relationships. Recently, several researchers advocated that felt understanding (the feeling that others understand the core aspects of the self) might be a critical link between social relationships and SWB (see Oishi, Krochik, & Akimoto, 2010, for a review).

Having strong social relationships is also a way to ensure that one benefits from the spread of happiness. In a longitudinal social network analysis of 5000 individuals from the Framingham Heart Study, Fowler and Christakis (2008) found that interacting with other happy individuals is likely to increase an individual's own happiness, especially if the individual is more central in the social network. Most notably, friends and neighbors who are geographically close exert more influence on one's own happiness (increasing the probability of happiness by 34% and 25% respectively), compared to coresident spouses and geographically close siblings (8% and 14% respectively).

## Personality, heritability, and individual differences

Extraversion and neuroticism are some of the most consistent predictors of SWB (see Lucas, 2008; Steel, Schmidt, & Shultz, 2008 for review). According to the meta-analysis by Steel et al. (2008), the correlation between extraversion and SWB ranged from 0.35 to 0.57, after correcting for measurement errors. The correlation between neuroticism and SWB ranged from −0.35 to −0.72, after correcting for measurement errors. At the more specific facet level, cheerfulness and depression were the strongest predictors (Schimmack, Oishi, Furr, & Funder, 2004). The correlation between cheerfulness and life satisfaction, for instance, was around 0.51 without correcting for measurement errors, whereas the correlation between depression and life satisfaction was between −0.52 and −0.57, without correcting for measurement errors. Indeed, these facets alone explained SWB better than broad traits of extraversion and neuroticism. Several researchers have shown heritability of SWB. For instance, Lykken and Tellengen (1996) famously argued that about 80% of stable individual differences in SWB are determined by genetic factors.

In addition, there are many individual differences associated with mean levels of SWB. Self-esteem is strongly associated with SWB, particularly in individualistic nations such as the USA and Australia (Diener, Diener, & Diener, 1995). Optimism is another trait strongly associated with SWB (Lucas et al., 1996). Likewise, individuals who are making steady progress toward personally important goals are shown to be high in SWB (Brunstein, 1993; Emmons, 1986), although the type of goals that they are pursuing moderates the positive effect of goal progress (Oishi & Diener, 2001; Sheldon & Kasser, 1998). Other interesting individual differences include satisficers versus maximizers (Schwartz et al., 2002), attention to abstract versus specific information (Updegraff & Suh, 2007), and categorization speed of positive versus negative words (Robinson, Vargas, Tamir, & Solberg, 2004). Finally, the source of happiness (what makes people happy) differs across individuals, depending on their values (Oishi, Diener, Suh, & Lucas, 1999).

## Hedonic adaptation

According to the hedonic treadmill model (Brickman & Campbell, 1971), an event that was once intensely pleasant or distressing soon becomes part of one's daily life, and then exerts little influence on one's well-being. More recently, Wilson and Gilbert (2008) proposed that explanation is a critical factor in hedonic adaptation processes. When one explains why some events happened to them, the events stop exerting any impact on one's well-being. This is because an explanation gives a closure to the events. Although most existing models of hedonic adaptation implicitly assume that the adaptation process is universal and inevitable, recent research suggests that the magnitude, speed, and direction of the adaptation differ significantly across individuals (Diener, Lucas, & Scollon, 2006). For example, some individuals went back to the baseline level of life satisfaction within 1 year of marriage while others stayed at a higher level than before marriage (Lucas et al., 2003). In addition, individuals do not adapt to certain major life events such as divorce, unemployment, or being disabled (see Lucas (2007) for reviews).

## Culture and subjective well-being

Cross-cultural research has identified large cultural differences in the mean levels and predictors of SWB (reviewed by Diener et al., 2003). For example, wealthy, individualistic nations tend to be higher in SWB than poor, collectivistic nations (Diener et al., 1995). Likewise, the frequency of positive emotion is a stronger predictor of life satisfaction in individualistic nations than in collectivistic nations (e.g., Schimmack, Radhakrishnan, Oishi, Dzokoto, & Ahadi, 2002; Suh, Diener, Oishi, & Triandis, 1998). Also, satisfaction with self-esteem predicts global life satisfaction more strongly in individualistic nations than those in collectivistic nations (e.g., Diener & Diener, 1995). In addition, research has shown that European Americans feel happier when their independent selfhood is affirmed, while East Asians feel happier when their interdependent selfhood is affirmed (Kitayama & Markus, 2000). For example, Japanese experienced happiness when they felt socially engaging emotions (e.g., friendly), whereas Americans experienced happiness when they felt socially disengaging emotions (e.g., pride; Kitayama, Mesquita, & Karasawa, 2006). Likewise, European Americans experienced increased happiness when they achieved independent goals (e.g., having fun), whereas Asian Americans experienced increased happiness when they attained interdependent goals (e.g., approval from significant others; Oishi & Diener, 2001).

## Interventions

As early as the 1960s, researchers found that older adults become happier when they reflect on their life (Butler, 1963; Coleman, 1974). Researchers created various intervention programs such as guiding people to adopt the characteristics of happy people (Fordyce, 1977, 1983), engaging in group discussions, or practicing positive-feeling statements (Lichter, Haye, & Kammann, 1980). Recently, as research in SWB flourishes, a great number of studies have revealed more diverse activities that can increase happiness. These interventions include writing a journal in which people describe life events for which they feel grateful (Emmons & McCullough, 2003), practicing forgiveness (McCullough, Pargament, & Thoresen, 2000), thinking about intensely positive experiences (Burton & King, 2004), performing random acts of kindness (Lyubomirsky, Sheldon, & Schkade, 2005), writing a letter of gratitude to someone (Seligman, Steen, Park, & Peterson, 2005), receiving happiness training (Goldwurm, Baruffi, & Colombo, 2003), engaging in productive activities (Baker, Cahalin, Gerst, & Burr, 2005), and setting and planning for goals (MacLeod, Coates, & Hetherton, 2008). Recent research on interventions also revealed various moderating factors. These include the types of processing positive events (e.g., thinking versus talking; Bryant, Smart, & King, 2005; Lyubomirsky, Sousa, & Dickerhoof, 2006) and the focus of positive events (Koo, Algoe, Wilson, & Gilbert, 2008).

## Consequences of subjective well-being

Lyubomirsky, King, et al. (2005) conducted a comprehensive meta-analysis of 225 papers on the outcomes of happiness. Happy people are more likely to earn higher incomes, have more satisfying romantic relationships or marriages, and receive more support from colleagues at work compared to less happy people. In addition, happy people are more likely to live longer and be healthier (see Pressman & Cohen, 2005, for a comprehensive review on this issue).

Although these studies support a general account for positive benefits of happiness, the relation between happiness and its outcomes is not always linear. Oishi, Diener, and Lucas (2007) divided the outcomes of happiness into two classes: achievement domains (e.g., income, education) and relationship domains. They showed that the relationship between happiness and its outcome is linear in romantic relationships but not in achievement domains. For example, the optimal level of happiness was moderate in terms of income and education. The main reason is that there are two different motivations that serve well in each of the two domains: improvement motivation and self-enhancement motivation. Improvement motivation (e.g., self-criticism, self-improvement) is beneficial in the achievement domains because this mindset makes clear what needs to be done to improve one's skills and performance. In contrast, positive illusion and self-enhancement motives serve well in romantic relationships, in which one might not want to pay too much attention to one's partner's weaknesses.

# FUTURE RESEARCH

As we strive to better understand the sources and consequences of SWB, future research should place greater emphasis on the measurement of SWB and the methodological approach to SWB (e.g., Eid & Diener, 2004; Oishi, 2006; Vittersø, Biswas-Diener, & Diener, 2005). Currently, researchers do not always pay full attention to all four components of SWB: positive affect, negative affect, global life satisfaction, and domain-specific satisfaction.

While these four components define the study of SWB, a richer understanding of how all components interrelate is needed. For example, Diener, Scollon, Oishi, Dzokoto, and Suh (2000) found that global life satisfaction is not the sum of domain-specific satisfactions, and Kitayama, Markus, and Kurokawa (2000) found that while American culture emphasizes the primacy of positive affect over negative affect, the relationship between the two types of affect is much more balanced in Japanese culture. Therefore, future research should first aim to identify the unique contribution of each component to the study of subjective well-being. Second, the study of SWB would benefit from increasing its multimethod approach. In order to advance science, we also need to simultaneously upgrade the SWB toolbox. The longitudinal social network analysis approach (Fowler & Christakis, 2008) mentioned earlier is an excellent example of a sophisticated method that captures the dynamics of everyday social interaction across time. The ease with which biological methods are now available to SWB scientists should also prompt us to examine questions of gene–environment interaction (e.g., Caspi et al., 2003) in order to determine which individuals are more vulnerable to specific life conditions.

The science of SWB has blossomed over the past 25 years. In the future, we should expect to see new theoretical models that make sense of the dynamic influences of SWB, brought forth by sophisticated research techniques.

## REFERENCES

Baker, L.A., Cahalin, L. P., Gerst, K., & Burr, J. A. (2005). Productive activities and subjective well-being among older adults: The influence of number of activities and time commitment. *Social Indicators Research, 73*, 431–458.

Bradburn, N. M. (1969). *The structure of psychological well-being.* Chicago, IL: Aldine.

Brickman, P. & Campbell, D. T. (1971). Hedonic relativism and planning the good society. In M. H. Apley (Ed.), *Adaptation-level theory: A symposium* (pp. 287–302). New York, NY: Academic.

Brunstein, J. (1993). Personal goals and subjective well-being: A longitudinal study. *Journal of Personality and Social Psychology, 65*, 1061–1070.

Bryant, F. B., Smart, C. M., & King, S.P. (2005). Using the past to enhance the present: Boosting happiness through positive reminiscence. *Journal of Happiness Studies, 6*, 227–260.

Burton, C. M., & King, L. A. (2004). The health benefits of writing about intensely positive experiences. *Journal of Research in Personality, 38*, 150–163.

Butler, R.N. (1963). The life review: An interpretation of reminiscence in the aged. *Psychiatry, 26*, 65–76.

Cantril, H. (1965). *The pattern of human concern.* New Brunswick, NJ: Rutgers University.

Caspi, A., Sugden, K., Moffitt, T. E., Taylor, A., Craig, I. W., Harrington, H., … Poulton, R. (2003). Influence of life stress on depression: Moderation by a polymorphism in the 5-HTT gene. *Science, 301*, 386–389.

Coleman, P.G. (1974). Measuring reminiscence characteristics from conversation as adaptive features of old age. *International Journal of Aging and Human Development, 5*, 281–294.

Dearborn, G. V. N. (1899). *The emotion of joy.* New York, NY: Macmillan.

Diener, E. (1984). Subjective well-being. *Psychological Bulletin, 93*, 542–575.

Diener, E., & Biswas-Diener, R. (2002). Will money increase subjective well-being? A literature review and guide to needed research. *Social Indicators Research, 57*, 119–169.

Diener, E., & Clifton, D. (2002). Life satisfaction and religiosity in broad probability samples. *Psychological Inquiry, 13,* 206–209.

Diener, E., & Diener, M. (1995). Cross-cultural correlates of life satisfaction and self-esteem. *Journal of Personality and Social Psychology, 68,* 653–663.

Diener, E., Diener, M., & Diener, C. (1995). Factors predicting the subjective well-being of nations. *Journal of Personality and Social Psychology, 69,* 851–864.

Diener, E., Emmons, R. A., Larsen, R. L., & Griffin, S. (1985). The Satisfaction with Life Scale. *Journal of Personality Assessment, 49,* 71–75.

Diener, E., Lucas, R. E., & Scollon, C. N. (2006). Beyond the hedonic treadmill: Revising the adaptation theory of well-being. *American Psychologist, 61,* 305–314.

Diener, E., & Oishi, S. (2000). Money and happiness: Income and subjective well-being across nations. In E. Diener & E. M. Suh (Eds.), *Culture and subjective well-being* (pp. 185–218). Cambridge, MA: MIT.

Diener, E., Oishi, S., & Lucas, R. E. (2003). Personality, culture, and subjective well-being: Emotional and cognitive evaluations of life. *Annual Review of Psychology, 54,* 403–425.

Diener, E., Scollon, C. N., Oishi, S., Dzokoto, V., & Suh, E. (2000). Positivity and the construction of life satisfaction judgments: Global happiness is not the sum of its parts. *Journal of Happiness Studies, 1,* 159–176.

Diener, E. & Seligman, M. E. P. (2002). Very happy people. *Psychological Science, 13,* 80–83.

Diener, E. & Suh, E. M. (Eds.). (2000). *Culture and subjective well-being.* Cambridge, MA: MIT.

Diener, E., Suh, E. M., Lucas, R. E., & Smith, H. (1999). Subjective well-being: Three decades of progress. *Psychological Bulletin, 125,* 276–302.

Dunn, E. W., Aknin, L. B., & Norton, M. I. (2008). Spending money on others promotes happiness. *Science, 319,* 1687–1688.

Eid, M., & Diener, E. (2004). Global judgments of subjective well-being: Situational variability and long-term stability. *Social Indicators Research, 65,* 245–277.

Eid, M., & Larsen, R. J. (Eds.). (2008). *The science of subjective well-being.* New York, NY: Guilford.

Emmons, R. A. (1986). Personal strivings: An approach to personality and subjective well-being. *Journal of Personality and Social Psychology, 51,* 1058–1068.

Emmons, R. A., & McCullough, M. E. (2003). Counting blessings versus burdens: Experimental studies of gratitude and subjective well-being in daily life. *Journal of Personality and Social Psychology, 84,* 377–389.

Flugel, J. C. (1925). A quantitative study of feeling and emotion in everyday life. *British Journal of Psychology, 15,* 318–355.

Fordyce, M. W. (1977). Development of a program to increase personal happiness. *Journal of Counseling Psychology, 24,* 511–520.

Fordyce, M. W. (1983). A program to increase happiness: Further studies. *Journal of Counseling Psychology, 30,* 483–498.

Fowler, J. H., & Christakis, N. A. (2008). Dynamic spread of happiness in a large social network: longitudinal analysis over 20 years in the Framingham Heart Study. *British Medical Journal, 337,* 23–28.

Goldwurm, G. F., Baruffi, M., & Colombo, F. (2003). Improving subjective well being for the promotion of health: The Milan project. *Homeostasis in Health and Disease, 42,* 157–162.

Kahneman, D. (1999). Objective happiness. In D. Kahneman, E. Diener, & N. Schwarz (Eds.), *Well-being: The foundations of hedonic psychology* (pp. 3–25). New York, NY: Russell Sage Foundation.

Kahneman, D., Diener, E., & Schwarz, N. (Eds.). (1999). *Well-being: The foundations of hedonic psychology*. New York, NY: Russell Sage Foundation.

Kahneman, D., Krueger, A. B., Schkade, D. A., Schwarz, N., & Stone, A. A. (2004). A survey method for characterizing daily life experience: The Day Reconstruction Method. *Science, 306*, 1776–1780.

Kesebir, P., & Diener, E. (2008). In pursuit of happiness: Empirical answers to philosophical questions. *Perspectives on Psychological Science, 3*, 117–125.

Kitayama, S., & Markus, H. R. (2000). The pursuit of happiness and the realization of sympathy: Cultural patterns of self, social relations, and well-being. In E. Diener & Suh, E. (Eds.), *Subjective well-being across cultures* (pp. 113–161). Cambridge, MA: MIT.

Kitayama, S., Markus, H. R., & Kurokawa, M. (2000). Culture, emotion, and well-being: Good feelings in Japan and the United States. *Cognition & Emotion, 14*, 93–124.

Kitayama, S., Mesquita, B., & Karasawa, M. (2006). The emotional basis of independent and interdependent selves: Socially disengaging and engaging emotions in the US and Japan. *Journal of Personality and Social Psychology, 91*, 890–903.

Koo, M., Algoe, S., Wilson, T. D., & Gilbert, D. T. (2008). It's a wonderful life: Mentally subtracting positive events improves people's affective states, contrary to their affective forecasts. *Journal of Personality and Social Psychology, 95*, 1217–1224.

Lichter, S., Haye, K., & Kammann, R. (1980). Increasing happiness through cognitive retraining. *New Zealand Psychologist, 9*, 57–64.

Lucas, R. E. (2007). Adaptation and the set-point model of subjective well-being: Does happiness change after major life events? *Current Directions in Psychological Science, 16*, 75–79.

Lucas, R. E. (2008). Personality and subjective well-being. In M. Eid & R. J. Larsen (Eds.), *The science of subjective well-being* (pp. 171–194). New York, NY: Guilford.

Lucas, R. E., Clark, A. E., Georgellis, Y., & Diener, E. (2003). Reexamining adaptation and the set point model of happiness: Reactions to changes in marital status. *Journal of Personality and Social Psychology, 84*, 527–539.

Lucas, R. E., Diener, E., & Suh, E. (1996). Discriminant validity of well-being measures. *Journal of Personality and Social Psychology, 71*, 616–628.

Lykken, D. & Tellegen, A. (1996). Happiness is a stochastic phenomenon. *Psychological Science, 7*, 186–189.

Lyubomirsky, S., King, L., & Diener, E. (2005). The benefits of frequent positive affect: Does happiness lead to success? *Psychological Bulletin, 131*, 803–855.

Lyubomirsky, S., & Lepper, H. (1999). A measure of subjective happiness: Preliminary reliability and construct validation. *Social Indicators Research, 46*, 137–155.

Lyubomirsky, S., Sheldon, K. M., & Schkade, D. (2005). Pursuing happiness: The architecture of sustainable change. *Review of General Psychology, 9*, 111–131.

Lyubomirsky, S., Sousa, L., Dickerhoof, R. (2006). The costs and benefits of writing, talking, and thinking about life's triumphs and defeats. *Journal of Personality and Social Psychology, 90*, 692–708.

MacLeod, A. K., Coates, E., & Hetherton, J. (2008). Increasing well-being through teaching goal-setting and planning skills: Results of a brief intervention. *Journal of Happiness Studies, 9*, 185–196.

McCullough, M. E., Pargament, K. I., & Thoresen, C. E. (Eds.). (2000). *Forgiveness: Theory, research, and practice*. New York, NY: Guilford.

McMahon, D. M. (2006). *Happiness: A history*. New York, NY: Atlantic Monthly.

Mroczek, D. K., & Kolarz, C. M. (1998). The effect of age on positive and negative affect: A developmental perspective on happiness. *Journal of Personality and Social Psychology, 75,* 1333–1349.

Nussbaum, M. C. (2000). *The fragility of goodness: Luck and ethics in Greek tragedy and philosophy.* Cambridge, UK: Cambridge University.

Oishi, S. (2006). The concept of life satisfaction across cultures: An IRT analysis. *Journal of Research in Personality, 41,* 411–423.

Oishi, S., & Diener, E. (2001). Goals, culture, and subjective well-being. *Personality and Social Psychology Bulletin, 27,* 1674–1682.

Oishi, S., Diener, E., & Lucas, R. E. (2007). The optimal levels of happiness: Can we be too happy? *Perspectives on Psychological Science, 2,* 346–360.

Oishi, S., Diener, E., Suh, E., & Lucas, R. E. (1999). Value as a moderator in subjective well-being. *Journal of Personality, 67,* 157–184.

Oishi, S., Krochik, M., & Akimoto, S. (2010). Felt understanding as a bridge between close relationships and subjective well-being: Antecedents and consequences across individuals and cultures. *Social and Personality Psychology Compass, 4,* 403–416.

Pressman, S. D., & Cohen, S. (2005). Does positive affect influence health? *Psychological Bulletin, 131,* 925–971.

Robinson, M. D., Vargas, P. T., Tamir, M., & Solberg, M. C. (2004). Using and being used by categories: The case of negative evaluations and daily well-being. *Psychological Science, 15,* 521–526.

Sandvik, E., Diener, E., & Seidlitz, L. (1993). Subjective well-being: The convergence and stability of self-report and non-self-report measures. *Journal of Personality, 61,* 317–342.

Schimmack, U. (2003). Affect measurement in experience sampling research. *Journal of Happiness Studies, 4,* 79–106.

Schimmack U., & Oishi, S. (2005). Chronically accessible versus temporarily accessible sources of life satisfaction judgments. *Journal of Personality and Social Psychology, 89,* 395–406.

Schimmack, U., Oishi, S., Furr, F. M., & Funder, D. C. (2004). Personality and life satisfaction: A facet level analysis. *Personality and Social Psychology Bulletin, 30,* 1062–1075.

Schimmack, U., Radhakrishnan, P., Oishi, S., Dzokoto, V., & Ahadi, S. (2002). Culture, personality, and subjective well-being: Integrating process models of life satisfaction. *Journal of Personality and Social Psychology, 82,* 582–593.

Schwartz, B., Ward, A., Monterosso, J., Lyubomirsky, S., White, K., & Lehman, D. R. (2002). Maximizing versus satisficing: Happiness is matter of choice. *Journal of Personality and Social Psychology, 83,* 1178–1197.

Schwarz, N., & Strack, F. (1999). Reports of subjective well-being: Judgmental processes and their methodological implications. In D. Kahneman, E. Diener, & N. Schwarz (Eds.), *Well-being: The foundations of hedonic psychology* (pp. 61–84). New York, NY: Russell Sage Foundation.

Scollon, C. N., Kim-Prieto, C., & Diener, E. (2003). Experience sampling: Promises and pitfalls, strengths and weaknesses. *Journal of Happiness Studies: An Interdisciplinary Periodical on Subjective Well-Being, 4,* 5–34.

Seligman, M. E. P., Steen, T. A., Park, N., & Peterson, C. (2005). Positive psychology progress: Empirical validation of interventions. *American Psychologist, 60,* 410–421.

Sheldon, K. M., & Kasser, T. (1998). Pursuing personal goals: Skills enable progress, but not all progress is beneficial. *Personality and Social Psychology Bulletin, 24,* 1319–1331.

Steel, P., Schmidt, J., & Shultz, J. (2008). Refining the relationship between personality and subjective well-being. *Psychological Bulletin, 134*, 138–161.

Stevenson, B., & Wolfers, J. (2008). Economic growth and subjective well-being: Reassessing the Easterlin paradox, *Brookings Papers on Economic Activity, 1*, 1–87.

Strack, F., Argyle, M., & Schwarz, N. (Eds.). (1991). *Subjective well-being: An interdisciplinary perspective*. Oxford, UK: Pergamon.

Suh, E., Diener, E., Oishi, S., & Triandis, H. C. (1998). The shifting basis of life satisfaction judgments across cultures: Emotions versus norms. *Journal of Personality and Social Psychology, 74*, 482–493.

Tsai, J. L., Knutson, B., & Fung, H. H. (2006). Cultural variation in affect valuation. *Journal of Personality and Social Psychology, 90*, 288–307.

Updegraff, J. A., & Suh, E. M. (2007). Happiness is a warm abstract thought: Self-construal abstractness and subjective well-being. *Journal of Positive Psychology, 2*, 18–28.

Van Boven, L., & Gilovich, T. (2003). To do or to have? That is the question. *Journal of Personality and Social Psychology, 85*, 1193–1202.

Vittersø, J., Biswas-Diener, R., & Diener, E (2005). The divergent meanings of life satisfaction: Item response modeling of the Satisfaction with Life Scale in Greenland and Norway. *Social Indicators Research, 74*, 327–348.

Watson, D., Clark, L. A., & Tellegen, A. (1988). Development and validation of brief measures of positive and negative affect: The PANAS scales. *Journal of Personality and Social Psychology, 54*, 1063–1070.

Wilson, T. D., & Gilbert, D. T. (2008). Explaining away: A model of affective adaptation. *Perspectives on Psychological Science, 5*, 370–386.

Wilson, W. (1967). Correlates of avowed happiness. *Psychological Bulletin, 67*, 294–306.

Wirtz, D., Kruger, J., Scollon, C. N., & Diener, E. (2003). What to do on spring break? The role of predicted, on-line, and remembered experience in future choice. *Psychological Science, 14*, 520–524.

CHAPTER 14

# MEASURING HAPPINESS AND SUBJECTIVE WELL-BEING

ROBERT A. CUMMINS

Deakin University, Australia

This chapter begins by defining the constructs of happiness and subjective well-being in terms of taxonomy and conceptual frameworks. Issues of measurement are addressed separately for qualitative and quantitative methodology. Two special areas of measurement difficulty are then discussed: the validity of data derived from low-functioning populations and cross-cultural measurement equivalence. Finally, specific scales are considered in terms of their consistency with the foregoing analysis.

## THE CONSTRUCT OF HAPPINESS

### Definitions

One of the persistent barriers to understanding happiness is the meaning of the term itself (see Diener (2006) for a review). Indeed, the diversity of constructs referred to as "happiness" is nothing short of extraordinary. It may be used as a blanket term to include all positive feelings about the self (Veenhoven, 2010), as a synonym for subjective well-being (SWB; e.g., Chang & Nayga, 2010), as referring to average levels of positive and negative affect (Seidlitz & Diener, 1993), and as a single affect within the classification system described by the circumplex model of affect (Russell, 2003). "Happiness" is also used to imply different temporal durations, as a long-duration positive mood trait (Seidlitz & Diener, 1993), or as a short-duration positive emotion. The latter is consistent with the term "happy" in common English usage, which refers to a transient, positive state of mind that has been caused by a specific experience, such as a pleasant social interaction (Diener, Scollon, & Lucas, 2004).

These meanings are all so different from one another that simply assembling literature on measurement under the term "happiness" would be uninformative.

In order to bring some cohesion to the definition of happiness for this review, the following rules will be applied.

1. The term will not be used as a blanket term for positive feelings. This is insufficiently precise given the multiple positive constructs that are subsumed. Such broad usage is better represented by a term such as "subjective quality of life" (see, e.g., Alvarez, Bados, & Pero, 2010).

2. The term will be used to describe a single affect within the circumplex model of affect (see, e.g., Yik, Russell, & Feldman Barrett, 1999).

3. The term "happiness" will be separated into its two temporal meanings. "Emotional happiness" refers to a short-term affect generated in response to some novel event or transitory internal state. "Mood happiness" refers to a genetically-based, long-term, dispositional affect that is an important component of both SWB and homeostatically protected mood (HPMood; see later).

4. The context of the happiness experience follows the logic of Diener, Sandvik, and Pavot (1991), who consider happiness as "relatively frequent positive affect and infrequent negative affect" (p. 123).

5. While "happiness" will be regarded as an important part of SWB, it will not be used as a synonym. SWB is conventionally measured by questions of "satisfaction" rather than "happiness" (see the Personal Well-being Index (PWI); International Wellbeing Group, 2006). It is, moreover, generally agreed that SWB comprises both affective and cognitive elements (Diener, 2006), and that happiness is one of the main affective components (Blore, Stokes, Mellor, Firth, & Cummins, 2011; Davern, Cummins, & Stokes, 2007).

# Happiness as part of subjective well-being

The systematic study of SWB is now over 35 years old. While there had been some prior research, two extraordinary publications (see Andrews & Withey, 1976; Campbell, Converse, & Rodgers, 1976) launched the idea that SWB could be reliably measured. Both reports also found such measures to be remarkably stable, and it is this stability and reliability of measurement that has made SWB such an attractive area for study.

So, how should we measure SWB? This has been, and remains, a highly contentious issue. While the construction of various measurement scales will be presented in the final section of this chapter, it is appropriate to first ask what SWB is thought to be. The answer to this question will drive what is measured, and there are three main views.

## *Discrepancy theories*

A detailed account of discrepancy theories can be found in Cummins (2009). The first proponents of the idea that SWB arises from cognitive discrepancies were published independently of one another in 1976 (Campbell et al., 1976; Michalos, 1976). Campbell et al. (1976) argue that satisfaction with any aspect of life reflects the gap between one's current perceived reality and the level to which one aspires. Michalos (1976), on the other hand, states the discrepancy as "What is your life worth to you now—in terms of the good and bad things that might be expected?" According to these authors, small discrepancies equate to high satisfaction.

While discrepancy theory has generated much interesting research, the measurement of discrepancies is problematic (see Cummins, 2009) and the measurement scales seem rather too complex to gain popularity. Moreover, two predictions of discrepancy theories, regarding the nature of SWB, are contestable. The first prediction is that, because SWB is generated from a comparison between one's present perceived state and some other imagined state, SWB is a product of cognitive processing.

The second prediction, foreseen by both Campbell et al. (1976) and Michalos (1976), is a dark side to SWB interpretation caused by adaptation. For example, because people adapt to poor living conditions, a discrepancy between their perceived current conditions and the conditions to which they aspire will be contaminated by adaptation to their actual circumstances of living. Because of this, high levels of SWB (assumed by a small discrepancy) may not indicate a life of high quality. High SWB, in these terms, may simply indicate successful adaptation and reduced levels of aspiration.

Both of these predictions rest on the assumption that SWB is a product of cognitive discrepancies. It is argued within the later section on HPMood that this assumption is false.

## *The tripartite model*

Also publishing in 1976, Andrews and Withey proposed that, while evaluations of life satisfaction comprise both cognitive and affective components, affective evaluations dominate. This may have been the result of using the affect-dominated "Delighted–Terrible" response scale for their measurements. However, building on this conception of SWB as comprising both affect and cognition, Diener, Emmons, Larsen, and Griffin (1985) proposed their tripartite model.

In this model, SWB comprises three "separable" components: positive affect, negative affect, and life satisfaction (see also Arthaud-Day, Rode, Mooney, & Near, 2005; Pavot & Diener, 1993). Thus, high SWB can be defined by frequent positive affect, infrequent negative affect, and a global sense of satisfaction with life (Myers & Diener, 1995), where the latter refers to cognitive judgmental processes (Diener & Diener, 1996)

Two decades later, their model was expanded to four components (Diener et al., 2004), with life satisfaction split into "satisfaction with life as a whole" and "satisfaction with individual life domains." They regard each of these components as a distinct way of evaluating one's life. They also regard the affective components in state terms, reflecting the "immediate, on-line reactions to the good and bad conditions of one's life" (p. 198). Both of these notions are contentious.

Taking first the satisfaction split, it is true that satisfaction with life as a whole and domain satisfaction are assessed by different questions, but it is an empirical issue as to the extent that they represent different forms of evaluation. Both forms of satisfaction share much of their variance and, indeed, this is the basis for the construction of the PWI (International Wellbeing Group, 2006). The eight domains of the PWI, which each measure satisfaction, together explain some 50–60% of the variance in life as a whole. Moreover, of this, only some 15% is unique variance contributed by the domains independently of one another. The remainder comprises shared variance between the domains.

The picture that emerges from such analysis is that, while each domain shares much of its variance with life as a whole and the other domains, each also contributes a small amount of unique information. It has been proposed (Cummins, 2010; Davern et al., 2007) that the shared variance is positive mood, while the unique variance represents the cognitive evaluation of each domain (e.g., satisfaction with health). Thus, in this light, it rather overstates the case to say these two forms of satisfaction are "distinct" ways of evaluating one's life. Rather, they seem to be similar forms of evaluation with a slight difference in the extent of their cognitive content.

Moving now to the affect in SWB, the contention (Diener et al., 2004) that this is dominantly state affect is inconsistent with much research. Certainly any question of satisfaction will have some state content, reflecting the moment-to-moment influence of life experience. However, it is generally considered that normally dominating this momentary experience is the much stronger trait affect. This represents the long-term, dispositional form of affect which is traditionally thought to be derived from personality (see Costa & McCrae, 1980; Lykken & Tellegen, 1996).

In summary, the tripartite model has clearly introduced happiness (positive affect) into the definition of SWB, along with a cognitive evaluation component generated by questions of satisfaction. However, the extent to which either cognition or affect dominates, and whether the happiness is state or trait, are in contention. These issues appear to be clarified by the most recent approach to defining the nature of SWB, which is through HPMood.

## *Homeostatically protected mood*

The theory of SWB homeostasis proposes that SWB is actively controlled and maintained for each person in a manner analogous to the homeostatic maintenance of body temperature (see Cummins, 2010; Cummins & Nistico, 2002). It proposes that a genetically hard-wired homeostatic system attempts to maintain a normal positive sense of well-being, and that this well-being is normally manifested as a generalized, and rather abstract, positive view of the self, which is the essence of SWB.

This generalized positive view may be measured through asking "How satisfied are you with your life as a whole?," and this question has been used in population surveys for over 35 years (Andrews & Withey, 1976). Not surprisingly, given the extraordinary generality of this question, the response that people give does not represent a cognitive evaluation of their life. Rather it reflects a deep and stable positive mood state that we initially called "core affect" (Davern et al., 2007), but which we now refer to as HPMood (Cummins, 2010).

HPMood seems to comprise three main affects. They are dominated by a sense of contentment, flavored with a touch of happiness and arousal. We propose that this general, abstract, positive view of the self is generated genetically as a level of positivity which is an individual difference between people. The level of HPMood represents the SWB "set-point" for each person; it is this "set-point" that the homeostatic system seeks to defend. As one consequence, the SWB that people experience has the following characteristics:

1. The experienced level of SWB is normally very stable. Certainly, unusually pleasant or unpleasant events may cause experienced SWB to change. Such events generate affect-as-emotion, which can dominate HPMood and cause the person to experience a level of affect that lies outside their set-point range of HPMood. However, over a period of

time, homeostasis will normally return SWB to its previous level (see, e.g., Hanestad & Albrektsen, 1992; Headey & Wearing, 1989)

2. The normal genetic set-point for HPMood lies in the "satisfied" sector of the dissatisfied–satisfied continuum. More precisely, on a scale where 0 represents complete dissatisfaction with life and 100 represents complete satisfaction, individual set-points are proposed to lie within the range of about 60–90 points (Cummins, Gullone, & Lau, 2002).

3. While we initially hypothesized that the origin of this trait positive mood was from personality, as has been suggested by numerous prior researchers (e.g., Oishi & Diener, 2001) this now appears to be incorrect. As initially demonstrated by Davern et al. (2007) and confirmed by Blore et al. (2011) and Tomyn and Cummins (2011), structural modeling has revealed that the positive affect in HPMood drives both personality and SWB. In other words, personality correlates with SWB only because both variables are being influenced by HPMood.

A more complete description of how homeostasis is proposed to operate may be found in Cummins (2010). The point to be made here, however, is that the affect of mood happiness is a central component of SWB.

## Principles of Measurement

There are two broad approaches to the measurement of happiness and SWB. Each of these will now be considered.

## Qualitative approaches

Researchers collect qualitative data for various reasons—sometimes the wrong ones. Qualitative methods may be used in investigations of happiness because the researchers think either no similar study precedes them or there are no adequate quantitative scales. Both assumptions are frequently wrong (see Morse & Richards, 2002). If "qualitative" is entered as a search-word into the Bibliography of the Australian Centre on Quality of Life (ACQOL, 2010) the search produces a list of over 75 publications with this word in the title. While this is far from the complete set of relevant literature, it is indicative of the many, many studies on happiness and SWB reporting qualitative data.

Importantly, when seeking to discover the experience of well-being, such studies tend to report much the same findings. The researchers are usually looking for themes in the interviews they conduct, and the following two themes, at least, are almost guaranteed to be found (see, e.g., Bowling et al., 2003; Choe, Padilla, Chae, & Kim, 2001; Lu & Shih, 1997). One is relationships, particularly with partner, family, and friends. The other is money, in terms of earned income, material goods, or the worry attached to income uncertainty.

Other "themes" discovered from the use of focus groups or in-depth interviews are likely to have been influenced by the interviewer. Focus groups are a major hazard in this regard. The initial introduction and first exploration of ideas will inevitably take the group's thoughts in some general direction and social norms then act to restrict the scope of the discussion.

Participants then start to operate within a limited conceptual framework in searching for further contributions.

Even one-on-one interviews concerning happiness are not immune from bias. The interviewer is almost certain to provide cues for the direction of the conversation, even by showing differential positive feedback in relation to some topics rather than others. Largely because of such biases, interviews with people who have an intellectual disability, for example, will come up with "rights" and "community integration" (e.g., Schalock & Keith, 1993) as a big issues for their well-being. However, it cannot be assumed that such emergent themes are actually important to personal happiness. There can also be no assurance that major themes have not been missed, particularly in relation to taboo topics.

Despite these problems, there is an important place for a qualitative approach under certain conditions, such as when the group under investigation is very different from mainstream Western culture. Some new theme or culturally relevant insight may then be discovered in addition to those already known. Qualitative methods can also usefully explore facets of SWB such as meaning, culture, and process. However, in order to capitalize on this potential, it is vital that the interviewer be expert in the extant literature concerning happiness and SWB. Only with such knowledge can they avoid information already known and seek new possibilities. This is the precise opposite of a "grounded theory" approach (Glaser & Strauss, 1967) to understanding the meaning of SWB which, in relation to this research area, is way past its use-by date.

In summary, while a qualitative approach to data gathering may provide new insights into happiness, the chances of this happening are quite slim unless two conditions are met. One is that the population or mechanism under investigation is unusual, and the other is that the interviewer is well-versed in the current literature, both qualitative and quantitative.

## Quantitative approaches

While quantitative research is fairly immune to the issues raised for qualitative approaches, it has other problems of its own. Perhaps the most unfortunate is that so few researchers appear to be aware of the vast array of scales available. Worse, they tend to use particular scales on the rationale that some previous researcher has done so, instead of making a selection based on applicability to theory and strong psychometric criteria. As a sad consequence, many reported results have been generated by such poor scales that they cannot be simply interpreted. To assist the quantitative researcher to avoid this pitfall, the ACQOL site has been created. Here, the search word "happiness" identifies over 40 scales.

Four issues will be addressed relating to the use of quantitative happiness and SWB data: item weightings, proxy data, data cleaning, and factorial structure.

### *Item weighting*

It seems intuitive that the responses to questions of happiness or satisfaction with particular life areas should be weighted in relation to one another. After all, if someone responds that they are very satisfied with their wealth, and yet ascribes no importance to wealth, surely their level of wealth satisfaction should be discounted in relation to other life areas they regard as important? Surprisingly, the answer to this question is—no. All such weighting schemes are psychometrically flawed.

As an example of the psychometric problems, Trauer and Mackinnon (2001) have demonstrated that weighting satisfaction by importance is an invalid procedure. Such multiplicative composites (importance × satisfaction) are actually interaction terms, and their generation violates several important statistical requirements for such combinations, such as equality of variance of each component. As has been cogently argued by Hagerty and Land (2007), the best form of weighting is simply to assume an equal weighting for all variables in a scale; that is, to use a weighting of 1 for all items.

## Proxy data

The technique of proxy responding involves asking someone to report on the happiness of another person. It is quite commonly used in situations where people cannot provide self-reports. This may be because they have a severe intellectual or cognitive disability, or because they are too young to have the cognitive maturity to answer for themselves. Unfortunately, however, proxy data are neither valid nor reliable (Cummins, 2002).

There are a number of reasons for this. The most obvious is that, no matter how well the proxy thinks they know the other person, they lack direct access to the person's feelings. This means that their judgments, based on observable behaviors, are often wrong. The second reason is vested interest. Take teachers, for example. They will report that the children in their care feel safer than the children feel themselves to be (Ben-Arieh, McDonell, & Attar-Schwartz, 2009). The third reason is the inherent bias caused by HPMood. If a proxy rates the happiness of someone for whom they have no direct responsibility, they will rate that person's happiness as lower than their own. This is due to the positively enhanced perception of self induced by HPMood, and the absence of that positivity bias in the evaluation of another person.

## Data cleaning

It is quite disturbing to observe how few empirical papers report the systematic use of data cleaning techniques prior to data analysis. In the absence of such a procedure, data sets will inevitably contain random errors of data recording or transcription that will compromise the results. But SWB data often contain a more sinister form of systematic error.

Happiness data, most particularly when derived from people who have limited understanding, will contain some consistently high scores representing an acquiescent response style. Unless these data are removed from the data set prior to analysis, they will form a subset of high scores that will systematically distort results. One defense against this problem is to check for response sets. These are most evident when the respondent scores at the top of the scale in a consistent manner. Such responding may indicate either an acquiescent response style or a lack of understanding. No matter the cause, the lack of variation and the high values will distort the data analysis.

## Factor analysis

It is very common in the literature for authors to simply assume that the subscales they use to generate results have factored as the scale originators intended. This is an unrealistic assumption, most particularly when the sample being analyzed differs in some major way from the sample originally used to develop the scale (see, e.g., Rivera-Medina, Caraballo,

Rodriguez-Cordero, Bernal, & Davila-Marrero, 2010). Clearly, if the subscales are not working as intended, this will compromise the interpretation of results.

In summary, there is more to data analysis than simply using a statistical package to generate results. Both the nature of the data and the performance of the scales must be carefully checked for reliability prior to further data processing.

## MEASURING HAPPINESS IN LOW-FUNCTIONING POPULATIONS

Measuring the happiness of young children or people who have a cognitive impairment by self-report is fraught with difficulty. For such groups, it cannot be assumed that their response reflects a valid measurement of happiness. When people do not understand the question they are being asked, or how they should use the response scale, they are likely to still provide a response fueled by social acquiescence. So, there are various safeguards that should be undertaken when measuring the happiness of such groups, such as:

1. Pre-testing, to establish respondent competence, is essential. Whenever there is doubt as to whether the respondent is competent to make a valid response, it is necessary to conduct a competence pre-test. This allows the exclusion of people who cannot understand the task they are being asked to perform. For an example of such a protocol see Cummins and Lau (2006).

2. Questions must be kept simple and unambiguous. Questions must refer to just one unambiguous topic, be phrased in the positive, and contain no words that lie outside common usage of the respondent group.

3. The response options must be understood before questioning commences. The response choice must be simple and the respondent must be familiar with the response options before questioning commences.

4. Verbal presentations must be tightly controlled. The interviewer must *not* attempt to re-interpret questions or responses. Any such attempts will result in a different question being asked from the one intended. A question can be repeated if it is not heard in the first instance but, if no response or an indeterminate response is provided, the interviewer should proceed to the next item.

5. All of the issues raised under the earlier "Quantitive Approaches" section are especially relevant here. Young children, or people who have a severe or profound level of intellectual disability, or advanced dementia, cannot provide a reliable self-report. Moreover, as has been discussed, they cannot have their level of happiness measured by proxy. So their general levels of happiness can only be estimated by indirect means.

One such method is to measure happiness through behavior. For this purpose, Green and Reid (1996) define happiness as "any facial expression or vocalization typically considered to be an indicator of happiness among people without disabilities including smiling, laughing, and yelling while smiling" (p. 69).

While some measure of success has been reported using this technique (e.g., Green & Reid, 1999), care needs to be taken. As noted by these authors there are three major methodological issues as follows:

1. The extent to which such behaviors reflect an inner state of happiness cannot be known with certainty. However, as long as the indicative behaviors are restricted to the most obvious forms of such behaviors, the technique has strong face validity.
2. Reliability of measurement can be enhanced by limiting observations to overt behavior displays.
3. One major concern is whether the manifest behavior represents happiness or is intended to serve some other purpose. For example, the act of smiling may occur for social or operant reasons that have nothing to do with felt happiness. Smiling may represent an attempt to avoid displeasing someone who is providing a service or attempting to be humorous.

The extent to which these issues threaten valid happiness measurement depends, to some extent, on the level of cognition the respondent brings to the situation. While people who are profoundly intellectually disabled are unlikely to exhibit socially manipulative behaviors, the probability increases for people with higher levels of cognitive functioning. As an example, Yu et al. (2002) found no difference in the levels of observed happiness between people with profound or severe levels of intellectual disability when the measures were taken at work. However, when the two groups were compared during leisure activities "provided by staff for the participants' enjoyment" (p. 423), the happiness ratings of those with severe disability were four times those of respondents with profound levels. Of course, it is not possible to know whether the cognitive advantage of the former group allowed them to experience greater happiness at leisure. It does seem prudent, however, to regard the observational measurement technique as potentially less valid for people with higher levels of cognitive functioning.

The final approach to be mentioned is not a way of measuring happiness, but rather a way of adjusting environments to increase happiness. It involves the determination of preferences between options. A detailed and thoughtful description of this methodology is provided by Green et al. (1988). Parenthetically, it is notable that authors found no correlation between such preferences displayed by respondents and those based on caregiver opinion. This is consistent with the caveats on proxy-generated data discussed earlier.

In summary, measuring the happiness of immature or low-functioning people is difficult to get right and may, indeed, not be possible. If there is any doubt concerning responder competence, then pre-testing is essential. And importantly, the act of responding to a question of happiness cannot be taken as evidence of response validity.

# Cross-cultural Equivalence of Measured Happiness

It is common to find lists where countries are being compared on their levels of SWB or happiness (e. g., Happy Planet Index, 2010; Kekic, 2004), and for the authors to assume that such differences represent valid international comparisons. Unfortunately, however, the assumption of response equivalence is incorrect and such comparisons are invalid. There are two reasons. The first is a problem of translation—that there is often no simple equivalence between the terms used to describe emotions in different languages. The second reason is cultural response bias. This phenomenon has been well documented, most particularly between Asian (East/South-East) and North American/Australian cultures (e.g., Iwata, Roberts, & Kawakami, 1995; Lee, Jones, Mineyama, & Zhang, 2002; Stening & Everett, 1984). When self-report data are compared between equivalent demographic groups, people from Asian cultures show a higher tendency to avoid the upper end of self-evaluative, positive response scales, when compared to Westerners.

Several reasons for this difference have been proposed. In a study comparing respondents from Hong Kong and Australia, Lau, Cummins, and McPherson (2005) found the bias to be linked to modesty, concern at tempting the fates by rating oneself too high, and having a different view of what the maximum scale score represents. An additional explanation (Kim, Peng, & Chiu, 2008) calls on the common Eastern belief in the dialectical self (the idea that one can have both a positive and negative self) compared to the Western belief in an internally consistent self (the notion that having a positive self implies not having a negative self). It has also been suggested that people from Asian and Western cultures differ in terms of their valuing of various personal attributes (see Brown, 2008; Tsai, Miao, Seppala, Fung, & Yeung, 2007).

By whatever means it arises, this tendency by indigenous Asians to avoid the positive end of the response scale results in lower overall scores. This, then, gives the appearance that people from these countries have lower levels of happiness than do people from Western countries. As is now clear, such an interpretation is false because the differences are contaminated by cultural response bias. Interestingly, such biases are not confined to ratings of happiness, and have also been shown for other self-evaluative constructs (Brown, 2008; Chen, Lee, & Stevenson, 1995).

## Scales that are not Recommended

The most fundamental psychometric characteristic of a scale is its construct validity—that is, the scale measures the construct for which it was devised. So if a scale is called a "happiness scale," then it is a reasonable assumption that it should measure happiness. But what kind of happiness does it measure? Due to the variety of meanings listed in this section of the handbook, happiness scales show great variation in content. So it is incumbent on the researcher to be clear about what, exactly, any scale under consideration is intended to measure.

For many scales, understanding construct validity is not easy. Few such scales have a theoretical basis for their construction and they commonly include items tapping other constructs such as perceived control, self-esteem, optimism, positive affect, extraversion, and others. Such "composite" scales are not recommended for research use. To allow precise interpretation, scales should measure single constructs. Two scales which are not recommended to measure happiness are as follows.

The Oxford Happiness Inventory (Hills & Argyle, 2002)–despite its explicit title, this scale is a good example of an eclectic mix that contains a little bit of everything. It contains items on control, self-esteem, optimism, positive and negative affect, and personality. As a consequence it tends to correlate quite highly with almost any other well-being scale. But how such correlations are to be interpreted is most uncertain. The composite score has no simple conceptual structure. Because of this it cannot be recommended (for a detailed critique see Kashdan, (2004)).

The Scales of Psychological Well-being (Ryff, 1989)—due to its title, many researchers assume that this popular scale can be used as a measure of SWB. It cannot. The instrument has six subscales: self-acceptance, positive relations with others, autonomy, environmental mastery, purpose of life, and personal growth. These subscale names are what it purports to measure, not SWB (Clarke, Marshall, Ryff, & Wheaton, 2001; Kafka & Kozma, 2002).

## Recommended Measurement Scales

The oldest form of measurement scale for happiness was devised by Gurin, Veroff, and Feld (1960) using the single question, "Taking all things together, how would you say things are these days – would you say that you are very happy, pretty happy, or not too happy?" In 1976, Andrews and Withey adopted a similar format to measure SWB, asking "How satisfied are you with your life as a whole?"

Both of these questions are clear, simple, parsimonious measures of global happiness or life satisfaction, and both have been very widely used. They also have a statistical limitation. Since they are single items, they are psychometrically inferior to multi-item scales because they generate more error variance. Because of this, Andrews and Withey proposed that "life as a whole" could also be measured by asking about the satisfaction of its component parts (domains). Many subsequent scales have been devised along these lines and an extensive listing of such instruments is found at ACQOL (2010).

From all of the scales available to measure happiness and SWB, just five are recommended as being both psychometrically sound and consistent with the framework that has been outlined. The first two are the single questions of happiness or life satisfaction listed earlier. Both measure SWB as a personal, abstract, and global construct. No one can compute the answer to either question in terms of cognition. So they are answered by reference to the ongoing mood state, which normally approximates the set-point of HPMood. The statistical issue with single items has been discussed. However, since "happiness" is a single affect on the circumplex, by definition it cannot be measured by a multi-item scale. What can be measured in this way, however, is HPMood.

So the first multi-item scale to be recommended measures HPMood (Davern et al., 2007). This scale comprises just three items, these are content, happy, and excited (or alert). The instructions are "Please indicate how each of the following describes your feelings when you think about your life in general". The respondent uses an 11-point unipolar response scale ranging from (0) "not at all" to (10) "extremely."

Two other scales are recommended to measure SWB, and the first of these is the most widely used scale for this purpose. The Satisfaction with Life Scale (Diener et al., 1985) is designed to measure global life satisfaction through five items, each of which involves an overall judgment of life in general. The scores from these items are then summed to create a measure of SWB. For a copy of the scale and its psychometric properties go to http://internal.psychology.illinois.edu/~ediener/SWLS.html.

The importance of the SWLS is that it represents an expanded version of "life as a whole." The items are not designed to give individual insights into the structure of SWB. This differs from the second SWB scale to be recommended. The PWI (International Wellbeing Group, 2006) has a quite different design. It is intended as the "first-level deconstruction" of life as a whole. Until very recently the PWI contained seven items, referred to as "domains," where each represents a broad, semi-abstract area of life. The theoretical basis for the PWI is that the domains together describe the experience of overall life satisfaction. The manual is available from International Wellbeing Group (2006).

The PWI is designed to be a "work in progress," with the scale evolving as new data show ways for it to be successfully modified. The International Wellbeing Group oversees this evolution and in 2006 an eighth domain of Spiritual/Religious satisfaction was added to the scale.

The disadvantage of the PWI over the SWLS is that, because the domains are slightly more specific in their focus, they are further away from HPMood. The advantage of the PWI is that each of the domains carries its own unique information concerning a broad aspect of life. Because of this, the scale can be analyzed at either the level of individual domains or by combining the domains to form a single SWB score. There are also parallel versions of the PWI for adults who have a cognitive or intellectual disability and school-children (International Wellbeing Group, 2006).

# Conclusions

The understanding of happiness and subjective well-being has developed substantially during the past 30 years. However, the literature is confusing, caused in large part by the lack of agreement concerning what measurement scales to use, and why. Future researchers can assist the process of conceptual consolidation by clearly stating why they have selected their scale of choice from the vast array available. The continued development of a systematic, scientific literature on happiness will be greatly facilitated by the adoption of standard forms of measurement.

## Acknowledgments

I thank Ann-Marie James for her assistance in producing this manuscript. I also gratefully acknowledge comments made by the following people on an earlier draft: Christine Baxter, Kay Cook, Wendy Kennedy, Markus Lorburgs, and Amy Warden.

## References

ACQOL. (2010). *Australian Centre on Quality of Life—Bibliography*. Retrieved October 25, 2010, from http://www.deakin.edu.au/research/acqol/bibliography/biblio_list_by_letter.php

Alvarez, I., Bados, A., & Pero, M. (2010). Factorial structure and validity of the multicultural Quality of Life Index. *Quality of Life Research, 19*, 225–229.

Andrews, F. M., & Withey, S. B. (1976). *Social indicators of well-being: Americans' perceptions of life quality*. New York, NY: Plenum Press.

Arthaud-Day, M. L., Rode, J. C., Mooney, C. H., & Near, J. P. (2005). The subjective well-being construct: A test of its convergent, discriminant, and factorial validity. *Social Indicators Research, 74*, 445–476.

Ben-Arieh, A., McDonell, J., & Attar-Schwartz, S. (2009). Safety and home-school relations as indicators of children well being: Whose perspective counts? *Social Indicators Research, 90*, 339–350.

Blore, J., Stokes, M. A., Mellor, D., Firth, L., & Cummins, R. A. (2011). Comparing multiple discrepancies theory to affective models of subjective wellbeing. *Social Indicators Research, 100*, 1–16.

Bowling, A., Gabriel, Z., Dykes, J., Dowding, L. M., Evans, O., Fleissig, A., … Sutton, S. (2003). Let's ask them: A national survey of definitions of quality of life and its enhancement among people aged 65 and over. *International Journal of Aging & Human Development, 56*, 269–306.

Brown, R. A. (2008). American and Japanese beliefs about self-esteem. *Asian Journal of Social Psychology, 11*, 293–299.

Campbell, A., Converse, P. E., & Rodgers, W. L. (1976). *The quality of American life: Perceptions, evaluations, and satisfactions*. New York, NY: Russell Sage Foundation.

Chang, H. H., & Nayga, R. M. (2010). Childhood obesity and unhappiness: The influence of soft drinks and fast food consumption. *Journal of Happiness Studies, 11*, 261–276.

Chen, C., Lee, S.-Y., & Stevenson, H. W. (1995). Response style and cross-cultural comparisons of rating scales among east Asian and North American students. *Psychological Science, 6*, 170–175.

Choe, M. A., Padilla, G. V., Chae, Y. R., & Kim, S. (2001). Quality of life for patients with diabetes in Korea- I: The meaning of health-related quality of life. *International Journal of Nursing Studies, 38*, 673–682.

Clarke, P. J., Marshall, V. W., Ryff, C. D., & Wheaton, B. (2001). Measuring psychological well-being in the Canadian Study of Health and Aging. *International Psychogeriatrics, 33*, 79–90.

Costa, P. T., & McCrae, R. R. (1980). Influence of extraversion and neuroticism on subjective well-being: Happy and unhappy people. *Journal of Personality and Social Psychology, 38*, 668–678.

Cummins, R. A. (2002). Proxy responding for subjective well-being: A review. *International Review of Research in Mental Retardation, 25*, 183–207.

Cummins, R. A. (2009). Measuring life balance through discrepancy theories and subjective well-being. In K. Matuska & C. Christiansen (Eds.), *Life balance: Multidisciplinary theories and research* (pp. 73–93). New York, NY: Slack Incorporated.

Cummins, R. A. (2010). Subjective wellbeing, homeostatically protected mood and depression: A synthesis. *Journal of Happiness Studies, 11*, 1–17.

Cummins, R. A., Gullone, E., & Lau, A. L. D. (2002). A model of subjective well being homeostasis: The role of personality. In E. Gullone & R. A. Cummins (Eds.), *The universality of subjective wellbeing indicators: Social Indicators Research Series* (pp. 7–46). Dordrecht, the Netherlands: Kluwer.

Cummins, R. A., & Lau, A. L. D. (2006). *Personal Wellbeing Index—Intellectual Disability*. Melbourne, Australia: Australian Centre on Quality of Life, Deakin University. Retrieved October 25, 2010, from http://www.deakin.edu.au/research/acqol/instruments/index.htm

Cummins, R. A., & Nistico, H. (2002). Maintaining life satisfaction: The role of positive cognitive bias. *Journal of Happiness Studies, 3*, 37–69.

Davern, M., Cummins, R. A., & Stokes, M. (2007). Subjective wellbeing as an affective/cognitive construct. *Journal of Happiness Studies, 8,* 429–449.

Diener, E. (2006). Guidelines for national indicators of subjective well-being and ill-being. *Applied Research in Quality of Life, 1,* 151–157.

Diener, E., & Diener, C. (1996). Most people are happy. *Psychological Science, 7,* 181–185.

Diener, E., Emmons, R. A., Larsen, R. J., & Griffin, S. (1985). The satisfaction with life scale. *Journal of Personality and Social Psychology, 49,* 71–75.

Diener, E., Sandvik, E., & Pavot, W. (1991). Happiness is the frequency, not the intensity, of positive versus negative affect. In F. Strack, M. Argyle & N. Schwarz (Eds.), *Subjective well-being: An interdisciplinary perspective* (pp. 119–137). New York, NY: Plenum Press.

Diener, E., Scollon, C. N., & Lucas, R. E. (2004). The evolving concept of subjective well-being: The multifaceted nature of happiness. In P. T. Costa & I. C. Siegler (Eds.), *Recent Advances in Psychology and Aging* (pp. 188–219). Amsterdam, the Netherlands: Elsevier Science BV.

Glaser, B. J., & Strauss, A. (1967). *The discovery of grounded theory: Strategies for qualitative research.* Chicago, IL: Aldine Publishing.

Green, C. W., & Reid, D. H. (1996). Defining, validating, and increasing indices of happiness among people with profound multiple disabilities. *Journal of Applied Behavior Analysis, 29,* 67–78.

Green, C. W., & Reid, D. H. (1999). A behavioral approach to identifying sources of happiness and unhappiness among individuals with profound multiple disabilities. *Behavior Modification, 23,* 280–294.

Green, C. W., Reid, D. H., White, L. K., Halford, R. C., Brittain, D. P., & Gardner, S. M. (1988). Identifying reinforcers for persons with profound handicaps: Staff opinion versus systematic assessment of preferences. *Journal of Applied Behavior Analysis, 21,* 31–43.

Gurin, G., Veroff, J., & Feld, S. (1960). *Americans view their mental health: A nationwide interview survey. Joint Commission on Mental Illness and Health.* Monograph Series, No. 4. New York, NY: Basic Books.

Hagerty, M. R., & Land, K. C. (2007). Contructing summary indices of quality of life—A model for the effect of heterogeneous importance weights. *Sociological Methods & Research, 35,* 455–496.

Hanestad, B. R., & Albrektsen, G. (1992). The stability of quality of life experience in people with Type 1 diabetes over a period of a year. *Journal of Advanced Nursing, 17,* 777–784.

Happy Planet Index. (2010). *Happy Planet Index.* London: New Economics Foundation. Retrieved October 28, 2010 from http://www.happyplanetindex.org/public-data/files/happy-planet-index-2-0.pdf.

Headey, B., & Wearing, A. (1989). Personality, life events, and subjective well-being: Toward a dynamic equilibrium model. *Journal of Personality and Social Psychology, 57,* 731–739.

Hills, P., & Argyle, M. (2002). The Oxford Happiness Questionnaire: A compact scale for the measurement of psychological well-being. *Personality and Individual Differences, 33,* 1073–1082.

International Wellbeing Group. (2006). *Personal Wellbeing Index Manual.* Melbourne, Australia: Deain University. Retrieved October 25, 2010 from http://www.deakin.edu.au/research/acqol/instruments/wellbeing_index.htm

Iwata, N., Roberts, C. R., & Kawakami, N. (1995). Japan-USA comparison of responses to depression scale items among adult workers. *Psychiatry Research, 58,* 237–245.

Kafka, G. J., & Kozma, A. (2002). The construct validity of Ryff's scales of psychological well-being (SPWB) and their relationship to measures of subjective well-being. *Social Indicators Research, 57,* 171–190.

Kashdan, T. B. (2004). The assessment of subjective well-being (issues raised by the Oxford Happiness Questionnaire). *Personality and Individual Differences, 36*, 1225.

Kekic, L. (2004, November 17). The World's Best Country. *The Economist*. Retrieved October 25, 2010 from http://www.economist.com/theworldin/international/displayStory.cfm?story_id=3372495&d=2005.

Kim, Y. H., Peng, S. Q., & Chiu, C. Y. (2008). Explaining self-esteem differences between Chinese and North Americans: Dialectical self (vs. self-consistency) or lack of positive self-regard. *Self and Identity, 7*, 113–128.

Lau, A. L. D., Cummins, R. A., & McPherson, W. (2005). An investigation into the cross-cultural equivalence of the personal wellbeing index. *Social Indicators Research, 72*, 403–430.

Lee, J. W., Jones, P. S., Mineyama, Y., & Zhang, X. E. (2002). Cultural differences in responses to a Likert scale. *Research in Nursing & Health, 25*, 295–306.

Lu, L., & Shih, J. B. (1997). Sources of happiness: A qualitative approach. *Journal of Social Psychology, 137*, 181–187.

Lykken, D., & Tellegen, A. (1996). Happiness in a stochastic phenomenon. *Psychological Science, 7*, 186–189.

Michalos, A. C. (1976). Measuring the quality of life. In W. R. Shea & J. King-Farlow (Eds.), *Values and the Quality of life* (pp. 24–37). New York, NY: Science History Publications.

Morse, J. M., & Richards, L. (2002). *Readme first for a users guide to qualitative methods*. Thousand Oaks, CA: Sage.

Myers, D. G., & Diener, E. (1995). Who is happy? *Psychological Science, 6*, 10–19.

Oishi, S., & Diener, E. (2001). Re-examining the general positivity model of subjective well-being: The discrepancy between specific and global domain satisfaction. *Journal of Personality and Social Psychology, 69*, 641–666.

Pavot, W., & Diener, E. (1993). The affective and cognitive context of self-reported measures of subjective well-being. *Social Indicators Research, 28*, 1–20.

Rivera-Medina, C. L., Caraballo, J. N., Rodriguez-Cordero, E. R., Bernal, G., & Davila-Marrero, E. (2010). Factor structure of the CES-D and measurement invariance across gender for low-income Puerto Ricans in a probability sample. *Journal of Consulting and Clinical Psychology, 78*, 398–408.

Russell, J. A. (2003). Core affect and the psychological construction of emotion. *Psychological Review, 110*, 145–172.

Ryff, C. D. (1989). Happiness is everything, or is it? Explorations on the meaning of psychological well-being. *Journal of Personality and Social Psychology, 57*, 1069–1081.

Schalock, R. L., & Keith, K. D. (1993). *Quality of Life Questionnaire Manual*. Worthington, OH: IDS Publishing Corporation.

Seidlitz, L., & Diener, E. (1993). Memory for positive versus negative life events: Theories for the differences between happy and unhappy persons. *Journal of Personality and Social Psychology, 64*, 654–664.

Stening, B. W., & Everett, J. E. (1984). Response styles in a cross-cultural managerial study. *Journal of Social Psychology, 122*, 151–156.

Tomyn, A. J., & Cummins, R. A. (2011). Subjective wellbeing as an affective construct: Theory validation with adolescents. *Journal of Happiness Studies, 12*, 897–914.

Trauer, T., & Mackinnon, A. (2001). Why are we weighting? The role of importance ratings in quality of life measurement. *Quality of Life Research, 10*, 579–585.

Tsai, J. L., Miao, F. F., Seppala, E., Fung, H. H., & Yeung, D. Y. (2007). Influence and adjustment goals: Sources of cultural differences in ideal affect. *Journal of Personality and Social Psychology, 92*, 1102–1117.

Veenhoven, R. (2010). *World database of happiness.* Retrieved October 25, 2010, from http://worlddatabaseofhappiness.eur.nl

Yik, M. S. M., Russell, J. A., & Feldman Barrett, L. (1999). Structure of self-reported current affect: integration and beyond. *Journal of Personality and Social Psychology, 77,* 600–619.

Yu, D. C. T., Spevack, S., Hiebert, R., Martin, T. L., Goodman, R., Martin, T. G., … Martin, G. L. (2002). Happiness indices among persons with profound and severe disabilities during leisure and work activities: A comparison. *Education and Training in Mental Retardation and Developmental Disabilities, 37,* 421–426.

# CHAPTER 15

# EUDAIMONIA

## VERONIKA HUTA

University of Ottawa, Canada

## THE DIFFERENCE BETWEEN EUDAIMONIA AND HEDONIA

This chapter provides an overview of eudaimonia. The topic is often better understood in terms of what it is not, however. Eudaimonia will therefore be contrasted with hedonia, which is usually the first topic that people think of when considering well-being. Much of the chapter will focus on pulling together an understanding of the meaning of eudaimonia, since the literature is still largely at the stage of attempting to define the concept, and there is relatively little research on eudaimonia's correlates.

## THE TERMS EUDAIMONIA AND HEDONIA

Roughly speaking, eudaimonia includes states and/or pursuits associated with using and developing the best in oneself, in accordance with one's true self and one's deeper principles. Hedonia includes states and/or pursuits associated with pleasure and enjoyment, and the absence of pain and discomfort.[1] Thus, we have the age-old distinction between virtue and pleasure.

As will be clear from the review of the literature, however, eudaimonia is a multifaceted concept, and different authors have focused on different facets. Furthermore, as discussed by Ryan, Huta, and Deci (2008), eudaimonia is sometimes conceptualized as a form of well-being, sometimes as a way of acting/thinking, and sometimes as both, which has made it difficult to arrive at a single definition. Nevertheless, after a review of the literature, I will provide a summary of common themes that cut across the different views.

---

[1] I avoid the terms "hedonism" and "hedonistic," and instead use "hedonia" and "hedonic." The former terms have accumulated too many negative connotations, and I do not view hedonia as maladaptive (unless taken to extremes).

## Conceptions of Eudaimonia by Various Individuals and Schools of Thought

### Historical philosophers

The term *eudaimonia* was used in ancient Greece and popularized by Aristotle in the fourth century BCE in his essay *Nicomachean Ethics* (see Arisotle, 2001). Eudaimonia is often translated as "happiness," and thus might be mistaken for enjoyment or pleasure; however, it is better translated as flourishing or excellence. More precisely, Aristotle defined eudaimonia as active behavior that exhibits excellence and virtue in accordance with reason and contemplation—those faculties which differentiate us from other species—and is performed for its own sake. His conception included moral virtues like justice, kindness, courage, and honesty, as well as intellectual activity and high performance at any activity, such as one's profession.

Other ancient philosophers who advocated eudaimonia include Plato (in the fourth century BCE), as well as Zeno of Citium, the originator of Stoic philosophy (beginning in the third century BCE). These had a somewhat narrower conception, including only moral virtues and reason.

Around the same time, another philosopher was advocating hedonia. In the fourth century BCE, Aristippus (who was initially a pupil of Socrates but then founded the Cyrenaic school of thought) argued that pleasure is the only good and pain is the only evil, regardless of their sources, and he especially emphasized immediate physical gratification.

Various philosophers since have sided with either the hedonic or eudaimonic camp. For example, Marcus Aurelius (in the second century), who is considered a Stoic philosopher, believed that happiness is achieved through noble and reasonable thought, and developed a series of aphorisms for acting in accordance with virtue and justice rather than selfishness or vain extrinsic rewards, and for making good use of one's time. Kant (in the eighteenth century) advocated living in accordance with moral obligation or duty that is universally valid and that is grasped through reason, genuinely intended, and pursued as an end in itself.

On the hedonic end, Hobbes's (seventeenth-century) egoistical hedonism asserted that the good life involves maximizing personal pleasure and minimizing personal pain. And Bentham's (nineteenth-century) utilitarianism, which was more statistically and socially defined, asserted that the greatest good was determined by the greatest frequency, intensity, and duration of pleasure and happiness for the greatest number of people, and similarly the smallest amount of pain.

The eudaimonic–hedonic distinction, therefore, has a long philosophical history.

### Religion

In addition to philosophical teachings, some religions have been an equally ancient source of eudaimonic thought. Though we will not discuss religions in detail, a review of eudaimonia would be incomplete without at least a mention of these. Religions including Christianity in the West and Confucianism in the East include ethical philosophies that direct people towards some conception of what it means to be a better person. They include principles such as virtue, humaneness, and delay of gratification. Though religions are sometimes criticized as being dogmatic and prejudicial, they have also been the world's most widespread, systematic, and enduring advocates of such eudaimonic principles.

## Theoretical work by modern psychologists and psychiatrists

In modern psychology and psychiatry, the distinction between eudaimonic and hedonic views of well-being is also apparent. First, eudaimonia has played a central role in the theoretical writings of several influential authors.

Maslow (1970) believed that humans have a natural need to *self-actualize*, i.e., strive for something greater in life and be all that they can be. This tendency is at the top of his hierarchy of basic human needs, and is expected to arise once the more basic biological, safety, belonging, and esteem needs are met. Maslow conducted biographical analyses of historical figures whom he considered self-actualized (e.g., Albert Einstein, William James), and described them as rising to challenges; realistic and able to differentiate between the genuine and inauthentic; focused more on means than ends; autonomous, natural, and nonconformist; accepting of self and others; guided by a strong personal ethic; and having an ongoing freshness in appreciating life's experiences. Maslow also reported that more self-actualized individuals have more peak experiences—moments of great emotion or understanding, when one feels particularly aware, alive, and connected with oneself and the surrounding world.

Various other theorists have similarly defined the good life as developing one's potential to the fullest. Jung (1933) spoke of *individuation* as the process of becoming fully oneself, autonomous, aware, and well integrated. Allport (1955) defined psychological well-being as *maturity*, which includes expressing one's true self, seeing things realistically, relating constructively to others, and having a personalized conscience. And Rogers (1961) advocated being *fully functioning*, and thus using all of one's capacities when appropriate, including joy and suffering.

By comparison, Freud's (1920) theory placed more emphasis on hedonic satisfaction. According to his *pleasure principle*, tension-reduction and pleasure are the ultimate goals of life, though this is somewhat balanced by his *reality principle*, which states that we must learn to accept pain and postpone gratification because of the exigencies of reality.

## Empirical work by modern psychologists

In addition to theoretical authors, researchers are also debating the two views of well-being—see Ryff and Singer (1998) versus Diener, Sapyta, and Suh (1998); Kashdan, Biswas-Diener, and King (2008) versus Waterman (2008) and Ryan and Huta (2009); and Kahneman (1999) versus Seligman (2002).

Let us review a number of research programs, as they have appeared in chronological order.

Beginning in the early 1970s and researched widely today, self-determination theory is related to eudaimonia in its view of *autonomy* as a central cause of well-being (Ryan & Deci, 2000). Autonomy includes being true to oneself, having different aspects of oneself well integrated, and endorsing one's activities rather than being controlled by external or internal pressures. Autonomy can be assessed with a variety of scales, from trait-level measures (including the General Causality Orientation Scale; Deci & Ryan, 1985), to state-level measures (e.g., Reis, Sheldon, Gable, Roscoe, & Ryan, 2000), to domain-specific measures (e.g., learning, prosocial, healthcare, exercise, religion, and friendship domains—see http://www.psych.rochester.edu/SDT/). Research has shown that autonomy relates to persistence, cognitive flexibility, conceptual learning, creativity, self-actualization, vitality, and a wide-range of other well-being indices; it relates negatively to interest in extrinsic matters such as money, material possessions, image, and status. Recently, Ryan and colleagues (2008; Niemiec and Ryan, Chapter 16, this volume) proposed that eudaimonia includes three additional characteristics: acting with awareness; acting in line with objectively valid and enduring psychological needs rather than momentary impulses; and pursuing goals that are ends in themselves (e.g., personal growth, community contribution) rather than means to an end (e.g., money, image, power).

Also in the 1970s, Csíkszentmihályi (1990) introduced the concept of *flow*, an optimal state experienced when one skillfully engages in a challenging activity. It is the state achieved by rock climbers when they feel at one with the rock, by musicians when their playing seems to flow of its own accord, and by any of us when we are so engaged in an activity that nothing else seems to matter, we no longer see ourselves from the outside, and even time seems to stop. Csíkszentmihályi and colleagues have studied flow using experience-sampling, where each participant reports their momentary state at multiple time points (Csíkszentmihályi & Larson, 1987)—this provides state-level assessments of flow, which can also be aggregated into trait-level assessments. During flow, one does not view oneself as happy—to step into an evaluative mindset would be to break out of the immersion. Only afterward does one view the flow experience as wonderful. Csíkszentmihályi describes flow as *autotelic*, i.e., an end in itself rather than a means to an end. He argues that flow fosters personal evolution because the challenging activity stretches a person's abilities; he also reports findings that flow promotes positive affect, creativity, concentration, learning, meaning and purpose in life, and a sense of transcendence or connection with a greater whole.

Some years later, Ryff (1989) introduced her conception of eudaimonia. She argued that well-being is better defined by objectively realizing one's potential and flourishing in the face of life's existential challenges, than by subjectively feeling good. More specifically, Ryff proposed that eudaimonia consists of what she called *psychological well-being*: personal growth, purpose in life, autonomy, environmental mastery, positive relations with others, and self-acceptance. These characteristics are assessed at the trait level using the Psychological Well-Being scale (Ryff & Keyes, 1995), the most frequently employed measure of eudaimonia to date. Confirmatory factor analyses show a better fit when treating psychological well-being and hedonic well-being (indexed by positive affect, negative affect, life satisfaction, and happiness) as two factors rather than part of one factor, though the factors correlated around $r = 0.80$ (Gallagher, Lopez, & Preacher, 2009; Keyes, Shmotkin, & Ryff, 2002). Studies have related the Psychological Well-Being scale to many variables, including lower mental illness, successful aging, physical health, and positive cardiovascular, neuroendocrine, and immune functioning (Keyes & Annas, 2009; Ryff et al., 2006). Furthermore, the scale is associated with greater left than right superior frontal brain activation, providing biological evidence for its link with well-being and goal-directed behavior (Urry et al., 2004).

In the early 1990s, Waterman proposed a description of eudaimonia that he called *personal expressiveness* (Waterman et al., 2003). It is characterized by six feelings about one's most representative activities, assessed at the trait level using the Personally Expressive Activities Questionnaire (Waterman, Schwartz, & Conti, 2008): that these activities make one feel alive, that they express who one really is, that one is intensely involved in them, that they are what one was meant to do, that they make one particularly complete or fulfilled, and that one has a special fit or meshing with them. Waterman contrasted personal expressiveness with a measure of hedonic enjoyment (including enjoyment, pleasure, satisfaction, feeling good, feeling a warm glow, and feeling happy). The distinction was subtle, with the scales correlating around $r = 0.80$. Nevertheless, relative to hedonic enjoyment, personal expressiveness related more to activities that allowed one to develop one's best potentials, as well as activities that involved high challenge and high skill (i.e., flow activities). Further, personal expressiveness tended to be accompanied by hedonic enjoyment, while hedonic enjoyment was not necessarily accompanied by personal expressiveness. Waterman (1981) also reviewed literature showing that a eudaimonic concern with personal excellence and development is positively (not negatively, as is sometimes believed) related to prosocial behavior.

Vittersø has written a number of papers delineating differences between eudaimonia and hedonia (e.g., Vittersø, 2003; Vittersø, Oelmann, & Wang, 2009; Vittersø, Søholt, Hetland, Thoresen, & Røysamb, 2010). At the trait level, he has operationalized eudaimonia using personal growth and openness to experience, while he has operationalized hedonia as life satisfaction. At the state level, he has operationalized eudaimonia using interest, engagement, and challenge, while operationalizing hedonia as pleasure, positive affect, low negative affect, pleasantness, and easiness. Vittersø provides evidence that eudaimonia is related to but distinct from hedonia, and that trait-level eudaimonia predicts state-level eudaimonia, while trait-level hedonia predicts state-level hedonia. Furthermore, Vittersø and colleagues have proposed a model where eudaimonia signals and promotes change, growth, and accommodation, while hedonia signals and regulates stability, assimilation, and return to homeostasis. These authors also discuss possible neurological mechanisms: the dopamine systems that underlie interest and novelty-seeking may support eudaimonia, while the endogenous opioid systems that underlie pleasure and regulation of homeostatic processes may support hedonia.

In 2002, Seligman discussed eudaimonia as a *life of meaning*, i.e., a life where one considers the broader implications of one's actions and serves the greater good. He differentiated the pursuit of meaning from the pursuit of pleasure as well as the pursuit of engagement (the latter concept relates to flow, but focuses largely on the absorption component and less on personal evolution and excellence). Seligman's theory has been operationalized using the trait-level Orientations to Happiness scale (Peterson, Park, & Seligman, 2005; Vella-Brodrick, Park, & Peterson, 2009), where the eudaimonia items separate cleanly into their own factor and have high internal consistency, thereby supporting the distinctness and coherence of the eudaimonia concept. The eudaimonia and hedonia scales correlate around $r = 0.20$, showing a weak positive relationship. The studies showed that each pursuit related to life satisfaction, positive affect, and negative affect, though eudaimonia and engagement related more strongly than did pleasure. Also, a combination of these pursuits related to greater life satisfaction than any one pursuit on its own. This supported the hypothesis that the greatest well-being is found in *the full life*, which combines the different paths to well-being.

In our own work (Huta & Ryan, 2010), we have defined eudaimonia and hedonia as motives for activities, i.e., as seeking to use and develop the best in oneself, and seeking to experience pleasure and comfort. The items in our *Hedonic and Eudaimonic Motives for Activities* scale separate cleanly into eudaimonic and hedonic factors, and each subscale has high internal consistency. We have used the scale in several correlational and experience-sampling studies as well as an experimental intervention, to conduct both trait-level and state-level assessments. With this measure, eudaimonia and hedonia correlate positively at the trait level as others have found, around $r = 0.30$, indicating that people who frequently pursue eudaimonia also frequently pursue hedonia; but interestingly, they correlate negatively around $r = -0.30$ at the state level, indicating that a momentary activity tends to be eudaimonic or hedonic but not often both. We have found that eudaimonia relates more than hedonia to *elevating experience* (including awe, inspiration, and transcendence), a sense of meaning, feeling connected with oneself, and a sense of competence; hedonia relates more to positive affect and carefreeness, and to lower negative affect; both pursuits relate similarly to vitality and life satisfaction. Paralleling the findings of Peterson et al. (2005), we found that people with both eudaimonic and hedonic pursuits scored higher on most well-being outcomes than people with only one pursuit or the other. In the intervention study, which lasted 10 days, people in the hedonia condition had more well-being benefits immediately after the 10 days, while people in the eudaimonia condition had more benefits 3 months later.

## Factor analytic studies

Taking a more statistical approach, several factor analytic studies have examined evidence for a eudaimonic–hedonic distinction. Compton, Smith, Cornish, and Qualls (1996) performed exploratory factor analysis of various measures of well-being and ways of behaving, and found a factor reflecting eudaimonic concepts (including self-actualization, maturity, and openness to experience), and a factor reflecting subjective well-being (including affect balance, life satisfaction, happiness, and self-esteem); these factors correlated $r = 0.36$. McGregor and Little (1998) factor analyzed various aspects of peoples' personal projects, and found that the degree to which these represented integrity (e.g., were congruent with one's values and identity), and the degree to which they were fun, formed separate factors. Furthermore, the fun of projects correlated with happiness, while the integrity of projects correlated with meaning.

# COMMON THEMES IN CONCEPTIONS OF EUDAIMONIA

The conceptions of eudaimonia reviewed in the previous section differ considerably. Yet a general overview can be obtained by extracting common themes that appear in at least some of the conceptions. The themes can be organized into two groups: eudaimonia as a way of behaving, and eudaimonia as a form of well-being.

Eudaimonia as a way of behaving includes the following themes:

- *Excellence*. The concept that one is striving for something good/better or high/higher. However, whether the goodness of one's actions is to be judged subjectively or objectively and consensually is a matter of debate.
- *Authenticity/autonomy*. Acting in line with one's true self and deep values, and striving to integrate the different aspects of oneself.
- *Development*. Following a purpose that promotes personal evolution and realization of one's potential.
- *Full functioning*. Using the full range of what one is, as appropriate, including unpleasant emotions.
- *Broad scope of concern*. Striving to serve a greater good, whether it be the welfare of entities beyond oneself, or some long-term goal for the self or others that transcends the immediate moment.
- *Engagement*. Actively applying oneself, rising to the challenge, and being deeply immersed.
- *Autotelism*. Focusing on the quality of the means to an end, or seeing the means or process as an end in itself.
- *Contemplation*. Thinking about the meaning of one's actions, and being guided by abstract principles.
- *Acceptance*. While striving for excellence, simultaneously embracing and working with reality, oneself, and others as they are.

Eudaimonia as a form of well-being includes the following themes:

- *Meaning*. Feeling that one's activities and experiences are meaningful and valuable.
- *Elevation*. A sense of being inspired, enriched, and raised to a higher or broader level of functioning.
- *Awe*. Feelings of awe, wonder, and being deeply moved, i.e., experiencing life's events on a deeper level.
- *Connection*. Feelings of connection with, awareness of, and harmony with oneself, one's activities, or a broader or longer-term context.
- *Aliveness*. Feeling alive and present.
- *Fulfillment*. Feeling fulfilled and complete, and that one does not wish anything more.
- *Competence*. Competence and mastery in life's important domains. While some researchers define this more as a subjective feeling (e.g., Ryan & Deci, 2000), others define it more as a quality that could be judged objectively (e.g., Ryff, 1989).

## Causes of Eudaimonia

While there has been some research on the consequences of eudaimonia, little is known about its predictors. I have thus far conducted two retrospective correlational studies on the question (Huta, 2012). The first study showed that participants engaged in eudaimonic pursuits if their parents had been high on responsiveness and/or demandingness, the two dimensions that define positive parenting; hedonic pursuits did not relate to either parenting dimension. The second study showed that people engaged in eudaimonic pursuits if their parents had either verbally endorsed eudaimonia or actually role modeled it by pursuing eudaimonia themselves. However, people derived well-being from eudaimonic pursuits only if their parents had role modeled eudaimonia, not if their parents had merely verbally endorsed it.

## Why has Eudaimonia been slow to Receive Empirical Attention?

Though eudaimonia is central to the question of human well-being, researchers have been slow, even reluctant, to address it. There are a number of reasons for this (see also Biswas-Diener, Kashdan, & King, 2009; Kashdan, Biswas-Diener, & King, 2008).

### Scope of the concept

First, a bewildering array of topics has fallen under the umbrella term "eudaimonia," and the topics have hailed not only from psychology but also from philosophy, ethics, and spirituality. Thus, eudaimonia is not easy to define, operationalize, or manipulate in research. Suggestions for addressing the definition of eudaimonia appear in the "Future Directions" section.

### Abstractness, subtlety, and subjectivity

Eudaimonia is also abstract and subtle. In my view, eudaimonic pursuits arise from a dialogue between seeking one's true self and striving towards ideals (in the language of nineteenth-century romantic poets, the ideals of truth, beauty, sacredness, or love). Such guiding forces are less pre-wired than hedonia—they need to first be identified and developed, and then must be kept in mind to some degree if they are to be pursued. This makes eudaimonia easily overlooked, somewhat difficult to achieve, and easily disrupted (Vitterso, Oelmann, & Wang, 2009). It is more elusive than hedonia for all of us, researchers included. Furthermore, the profession of psychology has deep roots in behaviorism, and thus finds it difficult to encompass such a subjectively experienced phenomenon. Despite its subtlety, eudaimonia is no less real. And while biological, cognitive, and behavioral analyses of eudaimonia are certainly informative, eudaimonia is most directly understood at the phenomenological level of analysis (Ryan & Deci, 2006).

### The centrality of values

Moreover, eudaimonia is inextricably tied to values. Eudaimonic pursuits are guided by beliefs of what it means to do something right or authentically. Eudaimonia has been called a _higher pleasure_ (Seligman, 2002). And some authors have delineated specific positive characteristics of a eudaimonic person, such as mastery of life's tasks, positive relations with others, self-acceptance, and autonomy (Maslow, 1970; Ryff, 1989). Yet a growing number of psychologists are becoming comfortable with terms like *virtue* and *character*, and interest in eudaimonia research has increased considerably in recent years. This is largely thanks to the work and ceaseless efforts of Martin Seligman, Christopher Peterson, and their colleagues. There is increasing recognition that values are an integral part of human experience, and that they guide (and sometimes misguide) much of what we do. Furthermore, higher pleasures do not mean *better* pleasures—a higher pleasure is one that employs and stimulates capacities that differentiate us from other animals, including the ability to be guided by values and vision.

## FUTURE DIRECTIONS

Research on eudaimonia is in its infancy. The definition of eudaimonia remains diffuse, and many empirical questions have yet to be tested. Some key future directions are as follows.

### Defining eudaimonia

The challenge of defining eudaimonia actually needs to be addressed in two ways: by reaching a better consensus on the definition, but also by broadening the comfort zone of researchers.

In moving toward a consensual definition, we need to address one basic question before we even begin discussing the characteristics that should be included: Is eudaimonia a way of behaving, a form of well-being, or both? I personally see it (and hedonia) as one's way of behaving (which includes one's way of thinking), which can be assessed at either the trait level or the state level.

Clearly defining eudaimonia as a way of behaving addresses several key criticisms of the related literature (Biswas-Diener et al., 2009; Kashdan et al., 2008; Ryan et al., 2008), and would go a long way toward resolving the debates that have bogged this area down: (1) the blurring, in some cases, of the boundary between pursuits and outcomes—defining eudaimonia as a way of behaving clearly differentiates it from feelings of well-being, and thus it can be studied as a predictor, while various forms of well-being can be studied as its outcomes; (2) the asymmetrical treatment of eudaimonia and hedonia in other cases, such that eudaimonia is discussed as a way of behaving, while hedonia is discussed in terms of well-being—defining both eudaimonia and hedonia as ways of behaving makes it possible to compare them in equal terms; and (3) the a priori assumption that certain forms of well-being, such as vitality and feelings of meaning, should be labeled as "eudaimonic well-being," while other forms of well-being including life satisfaction, positive affect, and negative affect should be called "hedonic well-being," before much empirical support is accumulated for these two groupings—defining eudaimonia and hedonia as pursuits makes it possible to study both of them as predictors of the same well-being outcomes, including those originally labeled as "eudaimonic" and "hedonic," and permits an empirical test of whether certain outcomes relate more to eudaimonia or hedonia.

There is also a practical benefit to treating eudaimonia and hedonia as ways of behaving. As reviewed earlier, the studies which treated them as ways of behaving showed only weak to moderate correlations between them, and thus good distinctness, while studies which treated them as forms of well-being or mixtures of pursuits and well-being showed very high correlations.

As for core features of eudaimonia, I see striving for excellence and authenticity as the primary features. I suspect, however, that as much debate remains about this point as about whether eudaimonia is a pursuit or a type of well-being.

At the same time as we aim to better define eudaimonia, we also need to stretch our comfort zone. At this early stage in developing the research, the rich diversity of perspectives is beneficial. If we rush into a foreclosed identity for eudaimonia, we may end up with an incomplete or biased definition. Eventually, however, eudaimonic researchers will need to reach a better consensus, or at least organize the different perspectives and understand how they relate to each other.

In addition, we need not be apologetic about the fact that eudaimonia is a broad concept. It is certainly one of the broader concepts in psychology, but if we consider, for example, the incredible scope of descriptors that Costa and McCrae (1992) represented with each Big Five personality label, eudaimonia is in good company.

We also need to be a little more experience-driven and a little less logistics-driven—just because a broad concept is difficult (but not impossible) to operationalize does not make it invalid. The long history of the topic, the growing interest in the topic, and the accumulating research evidence, all indicate that the eudaimonia concept corresponds to a true phenomenon in human experience.

## Outcomes of eudaimonia

If we (tentatively) treat eudaimonia as a way of behaving, there are many important outcomes that we have yet to study. These include forms of psychological well-being (e.g., serenity has received little attention), other psychological benefits (e.g., insight, maturity, stages of moral development, creativity, sustained attention, increased skill, progress toward goals, healthy behaviors), and mental illness. Physical outcomes, such as those already studied in relation to Ryff's eudaimonia scale, could be studied in relation to other eudaimonia conceptions as well. And it would be valuable to investigate whether eudaimonia is especially beneficial under certain circumstances. For example, eudaimonic individuals may find greater fulfillment in working than do hedonic individuals. Eudaimonia may also help people to cope with trauma, and buffer them against despair, because of its link with meaning and purpose.

In addition to promoting personal benefits, eudaimonia is likely to foster the well-being of one's surrounding world. The broad scope of concern of a eudaimonic individual is likely to benefit close others, the broader social community, and even the environment.

For all of these outcomes, it will be important to show that the benefits of eudaimonia somehow differ from those of hedonia—otherwise we may be reinventing the wheel.

## Predictors of eudaimonia

If eudaimonia plays a role in well-being, then it is essential that we determine what leads people to be eudaimonic in the first place. Potential distal and ongoing predictors include cultural background, religious background, the values and guidance provided by one's parents and role models, life experiences such as fulfillment of psychological needs and past challenges, and opportunities permitted by life circumstances such as basic security and daily responsibilities; personality and genetics may also play a role. Potential proximal predictors include a person's recent physical well-being—one may be motivated to invest in eudaimonia if one feels rested and well; and recent psychological well-being—Fredrickson's (2001) broaden-and-build theory suggests that positive emotions in general should foster eudaimonia, because they broaden awareness and promote novel behavior and development, and Haidt's (2000) work suggests that elevating experience should be a particularly strong motivator of virtuous behavior.

## Concluding Remarks

The concept of eudaimonia is based on a fundamental human question: What choices can a person make to increase their fulfillment in life? Research in this area has much potential to help people lead more fulfilling, inspiring, and meaningful lives. As we move forward in developing this literature, let us treat the topic with the respect it is due. It is important that we continually be open to learning from our findings and observations, and growing in our understanding—that is, let us be eudaimonic in our own approach to the subject.

## References

Allport, G. (1955). *Becoming: Basic considerations for a psychology of personality*. New Haven, CT: Yale University Press.

Aristotle. (2001). Nichomachean ethics. In R. McKeon (Ed.), *The basic works of Aristotle* (pp. 928–1112). New York, NY: The Modern Library.

Biswas-Diener, R., Kashdan, T.B., & King, L.A. (2009). Two traditions of happiness research, not two distinct types of happiness. *Journal of Positive Psychology, 4*, 208–211.

Compton, W. C., Smith, M. L., Cornish, K. A., & Qualls, D. L. (1996). Factor structure of mental health measures. *Journal of Personality and Social Psychology, 71*, 406–413.

Costa, P. T., Jr., & McCrae, R. R. (1992). *Revised NEO Personality Inventory (NEO-PI-R) and NEO Five-Factor Inventory (NEO-FFI) manual*. Odessa, FL: Psychological Assessment Resources.

Csíkszentmihályi, M. (1990). *Flow: The psychology of optimal experience*. New York, NY: Harper and Row.

Csíkszentmihályi, M., & Larson, R. (1987). Validity and reliability of the experience sampling method. *Journal of Nervous and Mental Disease, 175*, 526–536.

Deci, E. L., & Ryan, R. M. (1985). The general causality orientations scale: Self-determination in personality. *Journal of Research in Personality, 19*, 109–134.

Diener, E., Sapyta, J. J., & Suh, E. (1998). Subjective well-being is essential to well-being. *Psychological Inquiry, 9*, 33–37.

Fredrickson, B. L. (2001). The role of positive emotions in positive psychology: The broaden-and-build theory of positive emotions. *American Psychologist, 56*, 218–226.

Freud, S. (1920). *A general introduction to psychoanalysis*. New York, NY: Boni and Liveright.

Fromm, E. (1981). Primary and secondary process in waking and in altered states of consciousness. *Academic Psychology Bulletin, 3*, 29–45.

Gallagher, M. W., Lopez, S. J., & Preacher, K. J. (2009). The hierarchical structure of well-being. *Journal of Personality, 77*, 1025–1050.

Haidt, J. (2000). The positive emotion of elevation. *Prevention and Treatment, 3*, Article 3.

Huta, V., & Ryan, R. M. (2010). Pursuing pleasure or virtue: The differential and overlapping well-being benefits of hedonic and eudaimonic motives. *Journal of Happiness Studies, 11*, 735–762.

Huta, V. (2012). Linking peoples' pursuit of eudaimonia and hedonia with characteristics of their parents: Parenting styles, verbally endorsed values, and role modeling. *Journal of Happiness Studies, 13*, 47–61.

Jung, C. G. (1933). *Modern man in search of a soul*. New York, NY: Harcourt, Brace, & World.

Kahneman, D. (1999). Objective happiness. In D. Kahneman, E. Diener, and N. Schwartz (Eds.), *Well-being: The foundations of hedonic psychology* (pp. 3–25). New York, NY: Russell Sage.

Kashdan, T. B., Biswas-Diener, R., & King, L. A. (2008). Reconsidering happiness: The costs of distinguishing between hedonics and eudaimonia. *Journal of Positive Psychology, 3*, 219–233.

Keyes, C. L. M., & Annas, J. (2009). Feeling good and functioning well: Distinctive concepts in ancient philosophy and contemporary science. *Journal of Positive Psychology, 4*, 197–201.

Keyes, C. L. M., Shmotkin, D., & Ryff, C. D. (2002). Optimizing well-being: The empirical encounter of two traditions. *Journal of Personality and Social Psychology, 82*, 1007–1022.

Maslow, A. (1970). *Motivation and personality* (2nd ed.). New York, NY: Harper and Row.

McGregor, I., & Little, B. R. (1998). Personal projects, happiness, and meaning: On doing well and being yourself. *Journal of Personality and Social Psychology, 74*, 494–512.

Peterson, C., Park, N., & Seligman, M. E. P. (2005). Orientations to happiness and life satisfaction: The full life versus the empty life. *Journal of Happiness Studies, 6*, 25–41.

Reis, H. T., Sheldon, K. M., Gable, S. L., Roscoe, J., & Ryan, R. M. (2000). Daily well-being: The role of autonomy, competence, and relatedness. *Personality and Social Psychology Bulletin, 26*, 419–435.

Rogers, C. R. (1961). *On becoming a person*. Boston, MA: Houghton Mifflin.

Ryan, R. M., & Deci, E. L. (2000). Self-determination theory and the facilitation of intrinsic motivation, social development, and well-being. *American Psychologist, 55*, 68–78.

Ryan, R. M., & Deci, E. L. (2006). Self-regulation and the problem of human autonomy: Does psychology need choice, self-determination, and will? *Journal of Personality, 74*, 1557–1585.

Ryan, R. M., & Huta, V. (2009). Wellness as healthy functioning or wellness as happiness: The importance of eudaimonic thinking. *Journal of Positive Psychology, 4*, 202–204.

Ryan, R. M., Huta, V., & Deci, E. L. (2008). Living well: A self-determination theory perspective on eudaimonia. *Journal of Happiness Studies, 9*, 139–170.

Ryff, C. D. (1989). Happiness is everything, or is it? Explorations on the meaning of psychological well-being. *Journal of Personality and Social Psychology, 57*, 1069–1081.

Ryff, C. D., Love, G. D., Urry, H. L., Muller, D., Rosenkranz, M. A., Friedman, E. M., ... Singer, B. (2006). Psychological well-being and ill-being: Do they have distinct or mirrored biological correlates? *Psychotherapy and Psychosomatics, 75*, 85–95.

Ryff, C. D, & Keyes, C. L. M. (1995). The structure of psychological well-being revisited. *Journal of Personality and Social Psychology, 69*, 719–27.

Seligman, M. (2002). *Authentic happiness*. New York, NY: Free Press.

Urry, H. L., Nitschke, J. B., Dolski, I., Jackson, D. C., Dalton, K. M., Mueller, C. J., ... Davidson, R. J. (2004). Making a life worth living: Neural correlates of well-being. *Psychological Science, 15*, 367–372.

Vella-Brodrick, D. A., Park, N., & Peterson, C. (2009). Three ways to be happy: Pleasure, engagement, and meaning – findings from Australian and US Samples. *Social Indicators Research*, *90*, 165–179.

Vittersø, J. (2003). Flow versus life satisfaction: A projective use of cartoons to illustrate the difference between the evaluation approach and the intrinsic motivation approach to subjective quality of life. *Journal of Happiness Studies*, *4*, 141–167.

Vittersø, J., Oelmann, H. I., & Wang, A. W. (2009). Life satisfaction is not a balanced estimator of the good life: Evidence from reaction time measures and self-reported emotions. *Journal of Happiness Studies*, *10*, 1–17.

Vittersø, J., Søholt, Y., Hetland, A., Thoresen, I. A., & Røysamb, E. (2010). Was Hercules happy? Some answers from a functional model of human well-being. *Social Indicators Research*, *95*, 1–18.

Waterman, A. S. (1981). Individualism and interdependence. *American Psychologist*, *36*, 762–773.

Waterman, A. S. (2008). Reconsidering happiness: A eudaimonist's perspective. *Journal of Positive Psychology*, *3*, 234–252.

Waterman, A. S., Schwartz, S. J., Goldbacher, E., Green, H., Miller, C., & Philip, S. (2003). Predicting the subjective experience of intrinsic motivation: The roles of self-determination, the balance of challenges and skills, and self-realization values. *Personality and Social Psychology Bulletin 29*, 1447–1458.

Waterman, A. S., Schwartz, S. J., & Conti, R. (2008). The implications of two conceptions of happiness (hedonic enjoyment and eudaimonia) for the understanding of intrinsic motivation. *Journal of Happiness Studies*, *9*, 41–79.

CHAPTER 16

# WHAT MAKES FOR A LIFE WELL LIVED? AUTONOMY AND ITS RELATION TO FULL FUNCTIONING AND ORGANISMIC WELLNESS

## CHRISTOPHER P. NIEMIEC AND RICHARD M. RYAN

University of Rochester, USA

> But what is happiness except the simple harmony between a man and the life he leads?
>
> (Albert Camus)
>
> Happiness is when what you think, what you say, and what you do are in harmony.
>
> (Mohandas K. Gandhi)

THINKERS from a wide range of academic disciplines recognize the tendencies toward full functioning and organismic wellness as inherent to the human condition. For instance, some developmental theorists, most notably Gottlieb (2003), consider all living entities to be self-organizing systems and view the capacity for reorganization as essential to the promotion of adaptive experience. Such views are echoed by organismic biologists, who speculate that the emergent properties of agency and organization may be defining features of life itself (Kauffman & Clayton, 2006). Thus, at a biological level the behaviors of living things can be thought of as oriented toward maintenance and enhancement of the organism (Goldstein, 1963).

This general view of the proactive organism oriented toward growth and integration can also be found in several psychological theories of personality and development. For instance, psychoanalytic theorists view the ego as a synthetic process that develops toward autonomy and integration (Loevinger, 1976) and serves the critical function of managing intrapsychic and interpersonal conflict (Freud, 1923/1960). Within the humanistic tradition, Rogers (1963) posited an actualizing tendency that orients individuals toward realizing their full potential. Finally, developmental psychologists maintain that the process of development occurs through differentiation of information and integration of novel experiences with pre-existing aspects of the self to form a coherent, hierarchically organized whole (Piaget, 1971).

Although diverse in their focus, such organismic perspectives from the biological, personality, and developmental sciences converge to suggest a natural inclination toward psychological synthesis and integration, from which a unified sense of self derives. This sense of self, in turn, provides the basis for healthy cognitive, affective, behavioral, and social functioning—in short, the basis for organismic wellness (Ryan & Deci, 2002).

## Two Distinct Philosophical Views of "The Good Life"

Well-being can be defined as optimal human experience and psychological functioning (Ryan & Deci, 2001). Theory and research on well-being has burgeoned over the last decade with the advent of the positive psychology movement (Seligman & Csikszentmihalyi, 2000). This paradigm shift (Kuhn, 1962) stresses the importance of examining both the darker (psychopathology) and brighter (flourishing) sides of experience to obtain a more complete understanding of psychological functioning. The field of positive psychology acknowledges that wellness does not simply reflect the absence of physical disease and/or psychological distress, and thus calls for empirical examinations of the factors that produce optimal experience.

Interestingly, whereas the capacity for well-being is widely acknowledged in current psychological theory, there is less agreement on what constitutes "the good life" and, indeed, considerable debate has centered on how such a life may be achieved. The origins of two distinct philosophical views of "the good life"—namely, hedonism and eudaimonism—can be traced to the beginnings of intellectual history, yet such opposing views continue to have a profound impact on theory and research in psychology (for a spirited discussion on this topic, see Kashdan, Biswas-Diener, & King, 2008; Ryan & Huta, 2009; Waterman, 2008). In what follows, we provide an overview of the distinction between hedonic and eudaimonic approaches to the conception and promotion of well-being, which will offer a theoretical context into which a discussion of research from self-determination theory on the antecedents of full functioning and organismic wellness—that is, "the good life"—can be provided.

## The hedonic approach

An ethical philosophy, hedonism focuses on maximizing pleasure and minimizing pain as the path to happiness. The roots of this approach to "the good life" can be found in the writings of the Greek philosopher Aristippus of Cyrene, who argued that the experience of pleasure, irrespective of its source or cause, is the only good. Within psychology, those who espouse the hedonic view (Kahneman, Diener, & Schwarz, 1999) endorse a broad conception of wellness based on pleasure attainment and pain avoidance. Operationally, well-being is typically defined subjectively as the presence of pleasant emotions, the absence of unpleasant emotions, and the belief that life is satisfying in general. The sum of these affective and cognitive variables is termed subjective well-being (Diener, 1984).

With its definition of happiness based in subjective appraisals of current life experiences, the hedonic approach makes no a priori assumptions about what types of activities are expected to produce well-being, nor does this view posit any universal factors that would typically contribute to or detract from wellness. Indeed, the hedonic approach is largely atheoretical, as hedonic psychologists want people to identify what makes them happy (Kashdan et al., 2008). Although not logically necessary, hedonic psychologists tend to endorse a culturally relativistic perspective on happiness and frequently align with the *standard social science model* (SSSM; Barkow, Cosmides, & Tooby, 1992), which depicts humans as malleable and able to be shaped by predominant social factors. According to the SSSM, individuals are born *tabula rasa* and acquire important cultural values, beliefs, and norms for appropriate behavior through socialization. In line with this view, well-being results from attainment of culturally valued goals, no matter what those are. Hedonic psychologists thus typically maintain that multiple, idiosyncratic paths may be taken to achieve "the good life."

## The eudaimonic approach

Traditionally viewed in juxtaposition and, indeed, in contrast to the hedonic approach to happiness, eudaimonism is an ethical philosophy that stresses the importance of living in a way that represents human excellence. The roots of this perspective on "the good life" can be found in the *Nicomachean Ethics* (Aristotle, 4th century BCE/2002), in which Aristotle presented a practical, rather than theoretical, guide to achieving wellness. Eudaimonia, which was Aristotle's notion of well-being, is etymologically rooted in the Greek words *eu* (good) and *daimon* (spirit) and describes a process of living based on contemplation, virtue, and realization of potentials. Within psychology, those who espouse the eudaimonic view (Ryan, Huta, & Deci, 2008; Ryff & Singer, 2008; Waterman, 2008) posit that full functioning is an objective condition that involves living in accord with one's true nature, or daimon, and is experienced subjectively as personal expressiveness (Waterman, 1993) and vitality (Ryan & Frederick, 1997).

In contrast to the SSSM perspective in which humans' views of and routes to happiness are molded by cultural factors, eudaimonic theorists ascribe universal contents to human nature. Based on their compatibility with this nature, particular "ways of being" are theorized either to enhance or undermine the well-being of all individuals, regardless of their gender, age, culture, social class, or any other delimiting factor. In line with Aristotle's intent in outlining his theory of "the good life," eudaimonic theorists take a functional approach to examining the specific values and practices that promote or hinder full functioning and organismic wellness.

# Self-Determination Theory: Meta-Theoretical and Theoretical Underpinnings

Self-determination theory (SDT; Deci & Ryan, 2000; Niemiec, Ryan, & Deci, 2010; Ryan & Deci, 2000b; Vansteenkiste, Niemiec, & Soenens, 2010) is an approach to human motivation, emotion, and personality in social contexts that is interested in spontaneous hedonic processes, such as interest and enjoyment, and eudaimonic perspectives on well-being and integrity. With its philosophical roots grounded in organismic theory (Ryan & Deci, 2002), SDT posits that humans are proactive organisms who seek out opportunities to feel choiceful, effective, and close to important others, as such experiences support their natural tendencies toward psychological (autonomy) and interpersonal (homonomy) integration (Angyal, 1965). Yet people remain vulnerable to passivity, control, incompetence, and isolation, particularly when social conditions are not supportive of their inherent psychological growth tendencies. Thus, SDT assumes a dialectical perspective in which humans' natural propensities toward intrapersonal and social integration are met either by supportive or thwarting social contexts.

At the core of SDT is the postulate that all people require certain key nutriments to function in a healthy, integrated way. Specifically, SDT posits the existence of three basic psychological needs for autonomy, competence, and relatedness that, when satisfied, support the organismic tendencies toward psychological growth and internalization of ambient values, beliefs, and practices into the self. The *need for autonomy* (de Charms, 1968) refers to the experience that behavior is enacted with a sense of choicefulness, volition, and self-endorsement. The *need for competence* (White, 1959) refers to the experiences of effectance and mastery in interacting with the social and physical surroundings. The *need for relatedness* (Baumeister & Leary, 1995) refers to the experience of deep, meaningful, and mutually supportive connections with important others.

Together, the needs for autonomy, competence, and relatedness specify the *psychological content* of human nature. Simply stated, all individuals require satisfaction of these needs for optimal psychological and social functioning. As a unifying principle in SDT, the concept of basic psychological needs is used to categorize aspects of the environment, as well as specific values and practices, as either supportive of or detrimental to full functioning and organismic wellness. Social and personal factors that foster satisfaction of these needs are theorized to facilitate optimal experience and wellness, whereas those factors that thwart need satisfaction are expected to undermine healthy functioning. Thus, by examining their association with the basic psychological needs, it is possible to develop a more complete understanding of the compatibility of different "ways of being" with one's underlying nature.

It is worthwhile to note that SDT's specification of the basic psychological needs as *universal* requirements for optimal functioning and wellness is not without critics. Indeed, some theorists have questioned the importance of autonomy for individuals from Eastern cultures (Markus & Kitayama, 2003), for women (Jordan, 1997), and for working-class persons (Stephens, Markus, & Townsend, 2007), suggesting that they do not need autonomy (for a more thorough discussion, see Vansteenkiste et al., 2010). However, SDT asserts that when people are deprived of autonomy—regardless of whether they value it—they will experience lower wellness, and data support this claim. Autonomy, which reflects the inner endorsement of what one does in life, is thus a component of integrity and wellness across cultures, and is at the very heart of what it means to live in accord with one's nature.

# Self-determination Theory: The Antecedents of "The Good Life"

SDT is deeply interested in how people live. Researchers in this tradition have examined various aspects of motivated behavior, including the values around which individuals organize their lives and the motives that direct their behavior. Rather than taking a descriptive approach (cf. Schwartz, 1992), SDT is unabashedly prescriptive and proscriptive in suggesting that certain types of values and practices are more likely than others to promote full functioning and organismic wellness. Only those pursuits that facilitate satisfaction of the basic psychological needs for autonomy, competence, and relatedness are theorized to promote well-being. In what follows, we present findings from three areas of research in SDT on the antecedents of "the good life." Specifically, we examine the correlates of: (1) behavior that is regulated with an experience of autonomy, rather than heteronomy; (2) the pursuit and attainment of intrinsic (relative to extrinsic) aspirations; and (3) being mindfully aware of internal and external experiences as they occur.

## Motives that underlie behavior

Research in SDT began with investigations into the factors that either support or diminish *intrinsic motivation*, which refers to doing an activity for its own sake and is accompanied by feelings of interest, enjoyment, satisfaction, and fun (Ryan & Deci, 2000a). Intrinsic motivation is considered to be the embodiment of the proactive organism and is a natural wellspring of psychological, physical, and social health. When intrinsically motivated, people engage their physical and social surroundings with an experience of volition so as to expand their capacities and develop new ways of interfacing with the world. In line with SDT, research has shown that intrinsic motivation is supported by meaningful choice (Patall, Cooper, & Robinson, 2008) and competence (Vallerand & Reid, 1984), but is also readily undermined by controlling rewards and other pressures and inducements (Deci, Koestner, & Ryan, 1999). Thus, intrinsic motivation is a source of both positive development and experiences of interest and enjoyment (Huta & Ryan, 2010), and is inherently tied to satisfaction of the basic psychological needs.

Despite the importance of intrinsic motivation to the promotion of growth and well-being, with age people typically spend less time engaged in exploration and play and more time fulfilling responsibilities and obligations. *Extrinsic motivation* refers to doing an activity to accomplish an outcome separate from the behavior itself (Ryan & Deci, 2000a). Originally, some theorists (Harter, 1981) viewed extrinsic motivation in opposition to intrinsic motivation and, thus, extrinsic motivation was thought to lack self-determination. In contrast, SDT posits that extrinsic motivations can vary in the degree to which they are volitional (Ryan & Connell, 1989), and specifies four types of extrinsic motivation that exist along an underlying continuum of autonomy.

## Types of extrinsic motivation

The least autonomous type of extrinsic motivation is labeled *external regulation*, in which the behavior is performed solely to comply with external demands, typically to obtain a reward or to avoid punishment. For example, a smoker may make a quit attempt because of pressure from a spouse or physician. Such behaviors are perceived as originating outside the self and are experienced as relatively controlling. The next type of extrinsic motivation is labeled *introjected regulation*, in which the reason for the behavior has been partially internalized, but the behavior is enacted to satisfy internal (rather than external) contingencies, typically to enhance feelings of pride and self-esteem or to avoid feelings of guilt and shame. For example, a student may study to avoid feeling guilty for not having done so. Although such behaviors emanate from dynamic forces inside the person (rather than the social environment), these forces are nonetheless perceived as acting on the self and, as with external regulation, are experienced as relatively controlling.

With fuller internalization, the regulation of behavior is experienced as more autonomous. The next type of extrinsic motivation is labeled *identified regulation*, in which the reason for the behavior is understood, valued, and personally endorsed. For example, a patient with diabetes may enact lifestyle changes because of the personal importance of healthy living. Such behaviors are perceived as originating inside the self and are experienced as relatively autonomous. The final type of extrinsic motivation is labeled *integrated regulation*, in which the reason for the behavior has been brought into harmony and coherence with other identifications and aspects of the self. For example, a student may pursue a medical degree so as to help those in need, a goal that aligns with other personally endorsed values such as altruism and benevolence. Such behaviors are fully internalized and, as with identified regulation, are experienced as relatively autonomous. In line with SDT, the natural, active process of coming to endorse the value of extrinsically motivated behaviors (internalization; Ryan, 1993) has been shown to be facilitated by need satisfaction in such domains as parenting (Niemiec et al., 2006), education (Jang, Reeve, Ryan, & Kim, 2009), and work (Baard, Deci, & Ryan, 2004).

## Correlates of relative autonomy

One of the central aspects of Aristotle's conception of eudaimonia is that actions are actively chosen, reflectively endorsed, and in accord with deeply held values and beliefs. If so, then it follows that the relative autonomy with which extrinsic motivation is regulated would be differentially associated with full functioning and organismic wellness. The empirical evidence supporting this claim is extensive and has been presented elsewhere (Deci & Ryan, 2000), so herein we cite several illustrative examples.

In the education domain, elementary students' autonomous self-regulation has been shown to promote greater conceptual learning (Grolnick & Ryan, 1987) and teacher-rated adjustment (Grolnick, Ryan, & Deci, 1991). Interestingly, Ryan and Connell (1989) found that introjected regulation predicted anxiety amplification following perceived academic failures while identified regulation predicted positive coping with failures, although both regulatory styles were associated with parent-ratings of students' being "motivated." Among college students, autonomous reasons for learning organic chemistry have been related to greater interest and perceived competence, lower anxiety, and higher performance in the course (Black & Deci, 2000). Notably, the benefits of autonomy extend beyond classroom experiences, as autonomous self-regulation has been associated with lower dropout (Vallerand & Bissonnette, 1992) and higher global evaluations of psychological health (Niemiec et al., 2006).

Autonomy yields functional benefits in other life domains as well. In the realm of healthcare, autonomous self-regulation for smoking cessation has been shown to promote enhanced vitality (Niemiec, Ryan, et al. 2010) and smokers' likelihood of maintaining long-term tobacco abstinence (Williams, Niemiec, et al. 2009). Among patients with diabetes, Williams, Patrick, et al. (2009) found that autonomous self-regulation for medication use predicted higher perceived competence and quality of life, greater medication adherence, and improved physiological outcomes. In the work domain, autonomous self-regulation among unemployed individuals has been associated with higher well-being and job-search intensity (Vansteenkiste, Lens, De Witte, De Witte, & Deci, 2004).

Autonomy is critical to full functioning and organismic wellness in multiple contexts, including sport, relationships, work, and religion. The findings from studies across these domains have shown that autonomous self-regulation is associated with increased behavioral persistence; improved task performance; and greater psychological, physical, and social wellness. Thus, the relative autonomy with which behavior is regulated appears to be an important antecedent of "the good life."

## Pursuit and attainment of life goals

Other research has examined the aspirations around which individuals organize and direct their behavior over extended periods of time. Some theorists outside SDT (Locke & Latham, 1990) have argued that people are most likely to experience wellness when they attain valued goals, regardless of their content. According to Aristotle's conception of eudaimonia, however, living well entails pursuing ends that are of inherent worth. If so, then it follows that the pursuit and attainment of certain types of values are more likely than others to contribute to well-being.

Within SDT, different types of aspirations have been distinguished according to their association with satisfaction of the basic psychological needs (Ryan, Sheldon, Kasser, & Deci, 1996). Using factor analysis, Kasser and Ryan (1996) found evidence for two categories of life goals. One factor was labeled *extrinsic aspirations* and included values for wealth, fame, and an appealing image. Such goals are unlikely to be associated with need satisfaction. The second factor was labeled *intrinsic aspirations* and included values for personal growth, close relationships, community contribution, and physical health. Such goals are likely to facilitate need satisfaction. The structural distinction between the intrinsic and extrinsic aspirations has been observed across 15 cultures throughout the world (Grouzet et al., 2005). Therefore, an important question concerns whether the pursuit and attainment of intrinsic (relative to extrinsic) aspirations differentially predict full functioning and organismic wellness.

## Pursuit of life goals

Research in SDT on life goals began with examinations of the correlates of *pursuing* intrinsic (relative to extrinsic) aspirations. Kasser and Ryan (1996) found that those who placed strong importance on intrinsic (relative to extrinsic) aspirations reported higher well-being and lower ill-being. Similar results have been obtained across diverse countries (Ryan et al., 1999) and contexts (Niemiec, Ryan, Deci, & Williams, 2009). Vansteenkiste et al. (2007) reported that adult employees who held an extrinsic (relative to intrinsic) work value orientation evidenced less work-related satisfaction, dedication, and vitality, and more work-family conflict, emotional exhaustion, and turn-over intention. The deleterious consequences of holding an extrinsic (relative to intrinsic) work value orientation were mediated by need satisfaction experienced at work. In the exercise domain, Sebire, Standage, and Vansteenkiste (2009) showed that intrinsic (relative to extrinsic) goals predicted cognitive, affective, and behavioral outcomes through their associations with autonomy, competence, and relatedness.

## Attainment of life goals

Other research in SDT on life goals has examined the correlates of *attaining* intrinsic (relative to extrinsic) aspirations. In line with expectancy-value theories, most contemporary goal theorists suggest that attainment of valued goals is beneficial to well-being (Locke & Latham, 1990). In contrast, because of their differential associations with the basic psychological needs, SDT asserts that attainment of intrinsic aspirations is likely to promote wellness, whereas attainment of extrinsic aspirations is unlikely to benefit well-being, and may contribute to ill-being. Studies have provided evidence to support these claims. Kasser and Ryan (2001) found those who attained intrinsic (relative to extrinsic) aspirations reported higher psychological health and quality of interpersonal relationships. Similar results have been obtained in Russia (Ryan et al., 1999). In a sample of senior citizens, Van Hiel and Vansteenkiste (2009) reported that attainment of intrinsic aspirations was associated with higher ego-integrity and death acceptance, whereas attainment of extrinsic aspirations was associated with more despair. Niemiec, Ryan, and Deci (2009) examined young adults' aspiration attainment from 1–2 years post-college, an important period marked by transition into adult identities and lifestyles. Results showed that attainment of intrinsic aspirations promoted psychological health, whereas attainment of extrinsic aspirations was unassociated with well-being and actually contributed to ill-being. In line with SDT, the benefits of attaining intrinsic aspirations for psychological health were mediated by satisfaction of the basic psychological needs.

To summarize, research from SDT has shown that pursuit and attainment of intrinsic (relative to extrinsic) aspirations are associated with enhancement of psychological, physical, and social health. Importantly, such associations have been observed in numerous life contexts and across diverse cultures, lending credibility to the postulate that need satisfaction, which accrues from pursuit and attainment of intrinsic aspirations, is a universal component of optimal functioning and wellness. Thus, the values around which individuals organize their lives appear to be important antecedents of "the good life."

## Mindful awareness and attention

Recent research in SDT has examined the role of awareness in fostering a reflective stance toward experience. According to Aristotle's conception of eudaimonia, contemplation is essential to the development of virtue and realization of potentials, and indeed reflectivity is an important component of autonomy within various philosophical traditions (Dworkin, 1988; Ricoeur, 1966). If so, then it follows that relaxed, non-judgmental awareness of ongoing experience would promote volition, pursuit of outcomes that are of inherent value, and less defensive responding to threat.

Brown and Ryan (2003) initiated a program of research focused on *mindfulness*, or receptive attention to present experience. When mindful, people perceive internal and external experiences without distortion or automatic reactions, and thus remain open to responding in reflective, self-endorsed ways. In line with SDT, mindfulness has been shown to promote autonomy and well-being (Brown & Ryan, 2003), adoption of intrinsic (relative to extrinsic) aspirations and engagement in ecologically responsible behavior (Brown & Kasser, 2005), and constructive responding to romantic relationship conflict (Barnes, Brown, Krusemark, Campbell, & Rogge, 2007) and life stressors (Weinstein, Brown, & Ryan, 2009). Niemiec, Brown, et al. (2010) examined the role of mindfulness in ameliorating defensive responding to existential threat. Results demonstrated that less mindful individuals responded to mortality salience with higher worldview defense and self-esteem striving, whereas those more mindful showed no such defense. To summarize, research from SDT on mindfulness has shown that this mode of conscious processing yields benefits for personal, interpersonal, and societal well-being. Thus, the receptive, non-judgmental attention to ongoing experience that characterizes mindful awareness appears to be an important antecedent of "the good life."

## Concluding Comments

What makes for a life well lived? Using SDT, we sketched an approach to "the good life" and presented research showing that full functioning and organismic wellness are associated with autonomous self-regulation, pursuit and attainment of intrinsic values, and mindful awareness of present experience. Although SDT embraces the eudaimonic perspective, we do not dismiss the importance of subjective well-being, which has been associated with satisfaction of the basic psychological needs (Sheldon & Niemiec, 2006). Rather, we stress the importance of autonomy to the experience of harmony among thoughts, feelings, and actions, which the quotes by Camus and Gandhi that opened this chapter suggest is *sine qua non* for happiness.

## References

Angyal, A. (1965). *Neurosis and treatment: A holistic theory.* New York, NY: Wiley.
Aristotle (2002). *Nicomachean ethics.* (S. Broadie & C. Rowe, Trans.). Oxford, UK: Oxford University Press. (Original work published fourth century BCE).

Baard, P. P., Deci, E. L., & Ryan, R. M. (2004). Intrinsic need satisfaction: A motivational basis of performance and well-being in two work settings. *Journal of Applied Social Psychology, 34*, 2045–2068.

Barkow, J. H., Cosmides, L., & Tooby, J. (1992). *The adapted mind: Evolutionary psychology and the generation of culture.* New York, NY: Oxford University Press.

Barnes, S., Brown, K. W., Krusemark, E., Campbell, W. K., & Rogge, R. D. (2007). The role of mindfulness in romantic relationship satisfaction and responses to relationship stress. *Journal of Marital and Family Therapy, 33*, 482–500.

Baumeister, R. F., & Leary, M. R. (1995). The need to belong: Desire for interpersonal attachments as a fundamental human motivation. *Psychological Bulletin, 117*, 497–529.

Black, A. E., & Deci, E. L. (2000). The effects of instructors' autonomy support and students' autonomous motivation on learning organic chemistry: A self-determination theory perspective. *Science Education, 84*, 740–756.

Brown, K. W., & Kasser, T. (2005). Are psychological and ecological well-being compatible? The role of values, mindfulness, and lifestyle. *Social Indicators Research, 74*, 349–368.

Brown, K. W., & Ryan, R. M. (2003). The benefits of being present: Mindfulness and its role in psychological well-being. *Journal of Personality and Social Psychology, 84*, 822–848.

de Charms, R. (1968). *Personal causation.* New York, NY: Academic Press.

Deci, E. L., Koestner, R., & Ryan, R. M. (1999). A meta-analytic review of experiments examining the effects of extrinsic rewards on intrinsic motivation. *Psychological Bulletin, 125*, 627–668.

Deci, E. L., & Ryan, R. M. (2000). The "what" and "why" of goal pursuits: Human needs and the self-determination of behavior. *Psychological Inquiry, 11*, 227–268.

Diener, E. (1984). Subjective well-being. *Psychological Bulletin, 95*, 542–575.

Dworkin, G. (1988). *The theory and practice of autonomy.* New York, NY: Cambridge.

Freud, S. (1960). *The ego and the id.* New York, NY: Norton. (Original work published 1923.)

Goldstein, K. (1963). *The organism.* Boston, MA: Beacon Press.

Gottlieb, G. (2003). Probabilistic epigenesis of development. In J. Valsiner & K. J. Connolly (Eds.), *Handbook of developmental psychology* (pp. 3–17). London, UK: Sage.

Grolnick, W. S., & Ryan, R. M. (1987). Autonomy in children's learning: An experimental and individual difference investigation. *Journal of Personality and Social Psychology, 52*, 890–898.

Grolnick, W. S., Ryan, R. M., & Deci, E. L. (1991). Inner resources for school achievement: Motivational mediators of children's perceptions of their parents. *Journal of Educational Psychology, 83*, 508–517.

Grouzet, F. M. E., Kasser, T., Ahuvia, A., Dols, J. M. F., Kim, Y., Lau, S., ... Sheldon, K.M. (2005). The structure of goal contents across 15 cultures. *Journal of Personality and Social Psychology, 89*, 800–816.

Harter, S. (1981). A new self-report scale of intrinsic versus extrinsic orientation in the classroom: Motivational and informational components. *Developmental Psychology, 17*, 300–312.

Huta, V., & Ryan, R. M. (2010). Pursuing pleasure or virtue: The differential and overlapping well-being benefits of hedonic and eudaimonic motives. *Journal of Happiness Studies, 11*, 735–766.

Jang, H., Reeve, J., Ryan, R. M., & Kim, A. (2009). Can self-determination theory explain what underlies the productive, satisfying learning experiences of collectivistically oriented Korean students? *Journal of Educational Psychology, 101*, 644–661.

Jordan, J. V. (1997). Do you believe that the concepts of self and autonomy are useful in understanding women? In J. V. Jordan (Ed.), *Women's growth in diversity: More writings from the Stone Center* (pp. 29–32). New York, NY: The Guilford Press.

Kahneman, D., Diener, E., & Schwarz, N. (Eds.) (1999). *Well-being: The foundations of hedonic psychology*. New York, NY: Russell Sage Foundation.

Kashdan, T. B., Biswas-Diener, R., & King, L. A. (2008). Reconsidering happiness: The costs of distinguishing between hedonics and eudaimonia. *The Journal of Positive Psychology*, 3, 219–233.

Kasser, T., & Ryan, R. M. (1996). Further examining the American dream: Differential correlates of intrinsic and extrinsic goals. *Personality and Social Psychology Bulletin*, 22, 280–287.

Kasser, T., & Ryan, R. M. (2001). Be careful what you wish for: Optimal functioning and the relative attainment of intrinsic and extrinsic goals. In P. Schmuck & K. M. Sheldon (Eds.), *Life goals and well-being: Towards a positive psychology of human striving* (pp. 116–131). Seattle, WA: Hogrefe & Huber Publishers.

Kauffman, S., & Clayton, P. (2006). On emergence, agency, and organization. *Biology and Philosophy*, 21, 501–521.

Kuhn, T. S. (1962). *The structure of scientific revolutions*. Chicago, IL: University of Chicago Press.

Locke, E. A., & Latham, G. P. (1990). *A theory of goal setting and task performance*. Englewood Cliffs, NJ: Prentice Hall.

Loevinger, J. (1976). *Ego development*. San Francisco, CA: Jossey-Bass.

Markus, H. R., & Kitayama, S. K. (2003). Models of agency: Sociocultural diversity in the construction of action. In V. Murphy-Berman & J. J. Berman (Eds.), *Nebraska symposium on motivation: Cross-cultural differences in perspectives on self* (Vol. 49, pp. 1–57). Lincoln, NE: University of Nebraska Press.

Niemiec, C. P., Brown, K. W., Kashdan, T. B., Cozzolino, P. J., Breen, W. E., Levesque-Bristol, C., Ryan R. M. (2010). Being present in the face of existential threat: The role of trait mindfulness in reducing defensive responses to mortality salience. *Journal of Personality and Social Psychology*, 99, 344–65.

Niemiec, C. P., Lynch, M. F., Vansteenkiste, M., Bernstein, J., Deci, E. L., & Ryan, R. M. (2006). The antecedents and consequences of autonomous self-regulation for college: A self-determination theory perspective on socialization. *Journal of Adolescence*, 29, 761–775.

Niemiec, C. P., Ryan, R. M., & Deci, E. L. (2009). The path taken: Consequences of attaining intrinsic and extrinsic aspirations in post-college life. *Journal of Research in Personality*, 43, 291–306.

Niemiec, C. P., Ryan, R. M., & Deci, E. L. (2010). Self-determination theory and the relation of autonomy to self-regulatory processes and personality development. In R. H. Hoyle (Ed.), *Handbook of personality and self-regulation* (pp. 169–191). Malden, MA: Blackwell Publishing.

Niemiec, C. P., Ryan, R. M., Deci, E. L., & Williams, G. C. (2009). Aspiring to physical health: The role of aspirations for physical health in facilitating long-term tobacco abstinence. *Patient Education and Counseling*, 74, 250–257.

Niemiec, C. P., Ryan, R. M., Patrick, H., Deci, E. L., & Williams, G. C. (2010). The energization of health-behavior change: Examining the associations among autonomous self-regulation, subjective vitality, depressive symptoms, and tobacco abstinence. *The Journal of Positive Psychology*, 5, 122–138.

Patall, E. A., Cooper, H., & Robinson, C. (2008). The effects of choice on intrinsic motivation and related outcomes: A meta-analysis of research findings. *Psychological Bulletin*, 134, 270–300.

Piaget, J. (1971). *Biology and knowledge*. Chicago, IL: University of Chicago Press.

Ricoeur, P. (1966). *Freedom and nature: The voluntary and the involuntary* (E. V. Kohak, Trans.). Chicago, IL: Northwestern University Press.

Rogers, C. R. (1963). The actualizing tendency in relation to "motives" and to consciousness. In M. R. Jones (Ed.), *Nebraska symposium on motivation* (Vol. 11, pp. 1–24). Lincoln, NE: University of Nebraska Press.

Ryan, R. M. (1993). Agency and organization: Intrinsic motivation, autonomy and the self in psychological development. In J. Jacobs (Ed.), *Nebraska symposium on motivation: Developmental perspectives on motivation* (Vol. 40, pp. 1–56). Lincoln, NE: University of Nebraska Press.

Ryan, R. M., Chirkov, V. I., Little, T. D., Sheldon, K. M., Timoshina, E., & Deci, E. L. (1999). The American dream in Russia: Extrinsic aspirations and well-being in two cultures. *Personality and Social Psychology Bulletin, 25*, 1509–1524.

Ryan, R. M., & Connell, J. P. (1989). Perceived locus of causality and internalization: Examining reasons for acting in two domains. *Journal of Personality and Social Psychology, 57*, 749–761.

Ryan, R. M., & Deci, E. L. (2000a). Intrinsic and extrinsic motivations: Classic definitions and new directions. *Contemporary Educational Psychology, 25*, 54–67.

Ryan, R. M., & Deci, E. L. (2000b). Self-determination theory and the facilitation of intrinsic motivation, social development, and well-being. *American Psychologist, 55*, 68–78.

Ryan, R. M., & Deci, E. L. (2001). On happiness and human potentials: A review of research on hedonic and eudaimonic well-being. In S. T. Fiske, D. L. Schacter, & C. Zahn-Waxler (Eds.), *Annual review of psychology* (Vol. 52, pp. 141–166). Palo Alto, CA: Annual Reviews, Inc.

Ryan, R. M., & Deci, E. L. (2002). Overview of self-determination theory: An organismic dialectical perspective. In E. L. Deci & R. M. Ryan (Eds.), *Handbook of self-determination research* (pp. 3–33). Rochester, NY: University of Rochester Press.

Ryan, R. M., & Frederick, C. (1997). On energy, personality, and health: Subjective vitality as a dynamic reflection of well-being. *Journal of Personality, 65*, 529–565.

Ryan, R. M., & Huta, V. (2009). Wellness as healthy functioning or wellness as happiness: The importance of eudaimonic thinking (response to Kashdan et al. and Waterman discussion). *The Journal of Positive Psychology, 4*, 202–204.

Ryan, R. M., Huta, V., & Deci, E. L. (2008). Living well: A self-determination theory perspective on eudaimonia. *Journal of Happiness Studies, 9*, 139–170.

Ryan, R. M., Sheldon, K. M., Kasser, T., & Deci, E. L. (1996). All goals are not created equal: An organismic perspective on the nature of goals and their regulation. In P. M. Gollwitzer & J. A. Bargh (Eds.), *The psychology of action: Linking cognition and motivation to behavior* (pp. 7–26). New York, NY: Guilford Press.

Ryff, C. D., & Singer, B. H. (2008). Know thyself and become what you are: A eudaimonic approach to psychological well-being. *Journal of Happiness Studies, 9*, 13–39.

Schwartz, S. H. (1992). Universals in the content and structure of values: Theoretical advances and empirical tests in 20 countries. In M. Zanna (Ed.), *Advances in experimental social psychology* (Vol. 25, pp. 1–65). New York, NY: Academic Press.

Sebire, S. J., Standage, M., & Vansteenkiste, M. (2009). Examining intrinsic versus extrinsic exercise goals: Cognitive, affective, and behavioral outcomes. *Journal of Sport and Exercise Psychology, 31*, 189–210.

Seligman, M. E. P., & Csikszentmihalyi, M. (2000). Positive psychology: An introduction. *American Psychologist, 55*, 5–14.

Sheldon, K. M., & Niemiec, C. P. (2006). It's not just the amount that counts: Balanced need satisfaction also affects well-being. *Journal of Personality and Social Psychology, 91*, 331–341.

Stephens, N. M., Markus, H. R., & Townsend, S. S. M. (2007). Choice as an act of meaning: The case of social class. *Journal of Personality and Social Psychology, 93*, 814–830.

Vallerand, R. J., & Bissonnette, R. (1992). Intrinsic, extrinsic, and amotivational styles as predictors of behavior: A prospective study. *Journal of Personality, 60,* 599–620.

Vallerand, R. J., & Reid, G. (1984). On the causal effects of perceived competence on intrinsic motivation: A test of cognitive evaluation theory. *Journal of Sport Psychology, 6,* 94–102.

Van Hiel, A., & Vansteenkiste, M. (2009). Ambitions fulfilled? The effects of intrinsic and extrinsic goal attainment on older adults' ego-integrity and death attitudes. *International Journal of Aging and Human Development, 68,* 27–51.

Vansteenkiste, M., Lens, W., De Witte, S., De Witte, H., & Deci, E. L. (2004). The "why" and "why not" of job search behaviour: Their relation to searching, unemployment experience, and well-being. *European Journal of Social Psychology, 34,* 345–363.

Vansteenkiste, M., Neyrinck, B., Niemiec, C. P., Soenens, B., De Witte, H., & Van den Broeck, A. (2007). On the relations among work value orientations, psychological need satisfaction and job outcomes: A self-determination theory approach. *Journal of Occupational and Organizational Psychology, 80,* 251–277.

Vansteenkiste, M., Niemiec, C. P., & Soenens, B. (2010). The development of the five mini-theories of self-determination theory: An historical overview, emerging trends, and future directions. In T. Urdan & S. Karabenick (Eds.), *Advances in motivation and achievement, vol. 16: The decade ahead* (pp. 105–166). London, UK: Emerald.

Waterman, A. S. (1993). Two conceptions of happiness: Contrasts of personal expressiveness (eudaimonia) and hedonic enjoyment. *Journal of Personality and Social Psychology, 64,* 678–691.

Waterman, A. S. (2008). Reconsidering happiness: A eudaimonist's perspective. *The Journal of Positive Psychology, 3,* 234–252.

Weinstein, N., Brown, K. W., & Ryan, R. M. (2009). A multi-method examination of the effects of mindfulness on stress attribution, coping, and emotional well-being. *Journal of Research in Personality, 43,* 374–385.

White, R. W. (1959). Motivation reconsidered: The concept of competence. *Psychological Review, 66,* 297–333.

Williams, G. C., Niemiec, C. P., Patrick, H., Ryan, R. M., & Deci, E. L. (2009). The importance of supporting autonomy and perceived competence in facilitating long-term tobacco abstinence. *Annals of Behavioral Medicine, 37,* 315–324.

Williams, G. C., Patrick, H., Niemiec, C. P., Williams, L. K., Divine, G., Lafata, J. E., ... Pladevall, M. (2009). Reducing the health risks of diabetes: How self-determination theory may help improve medication adherence and quality of life. *The Diabetes Educator, 35,* 484–492.

# CHAPTER 17

# FUNCTIONAL WELL-BEING: HAPPINESS AS FEELINGS, EVALUATIONS, AND FUNCTIONING

JOAR VITTERSØ

University of Tromsø, Norway

TOWARDS the end of his life, ill and in pain, Sigmund Freud is said to have refused any drugs except aspirin. Rather than not being able to reason clearly, the old thinker preferred to work in torment (Griffin, 1986). Freud's choice is a red herring to hedonists, who believe that the quality of a person's life can be expressed as a single hedonic value: the balance between pleasure and pain (e.g., Vitterso, 2009). The less constrained perspective of subjective well-being (SWB) trusts that an adequate representation of human well-being is secured if evaluations of life are added to the hedonic value. People do not only feel, they also think about their lives (Kahneman & Riis, 2005), and SWB researchers claim that evaluations in terms of goodness and badness account for the "thinking about" element of a happy life. But the present chapter asks if the essence of well-being really is captured by analyses of hedonic balances and life satisfaction. The goal is to show that it is not very likely.

This chapter begins with a review of the literature on emotions and feelings. By this route it will be shown that feelings and emotions have many dimensions and that they all must be investigated in order to understand the good life. Hence, happiness research may have been led astray in its eagerness to reduce the fullness of human emotions into a polarization of positivity and negativity.

Next, the concept of evaluation is analyzed under the assumption that a subjective judgment of a life's degree of favorability is a necessary, but not sufficient ingredient for a theory of well-being. A life is valuable in different ways—not all of them are reflected in a statement of good versus bad. For example, the good–bad dimension is biased towards familiarity and comfort. As a result, what we value by way of experiencing novelty, engagement, and commitment to important life goals tends to slip away when happiness is measured as life satisfaction (Vitterso, Oelmann, & Wang, 2009).

Feelings and evaluations make little sense if they are isolated from the goals and plans held by those who experience the feelings and make the evaluations. To account for these themes, the functional well-being approach (FWBA) proposes that the idea of "thinking about life" should include not only evaluations, but also a concept that takes care of a unifying representation of goals and plans.

The concept of optimal functioning (or good functioning) is offered to account for the process of creating plans and acting upon them to reach idiosyncratic goals and to fulfill basic needs in a manner that appears as meaningful. Hence, in developing a model of functional well-being the chapter takes a step toward a taxonomy of happiness that incorporates good feelings and positive evaluations. These concepts include the idea of good functioning, even when, and this is the crux of the FWBA, the functional element is not experienced as pleasant or does not contribute to elevated evaluations of life satisfaction. The "boxology" of this message is laid out in Fig. 17.1.

The FWBA uses the term "functional" in two ways. First, the concept has something to say about the functions that are attributed to emotions, feelings, and evaluations, and this perspective is reviewed in the first two parts of the chapter. Second, functional also refers to the idea of optimal functioning, which is the topic of the last section.

## Feelings

Feelings had no central place in Aristotle's idea of the good life (Solomon, 2008), and ethical rather than emotional concerns have typically dominated historical and philosophical

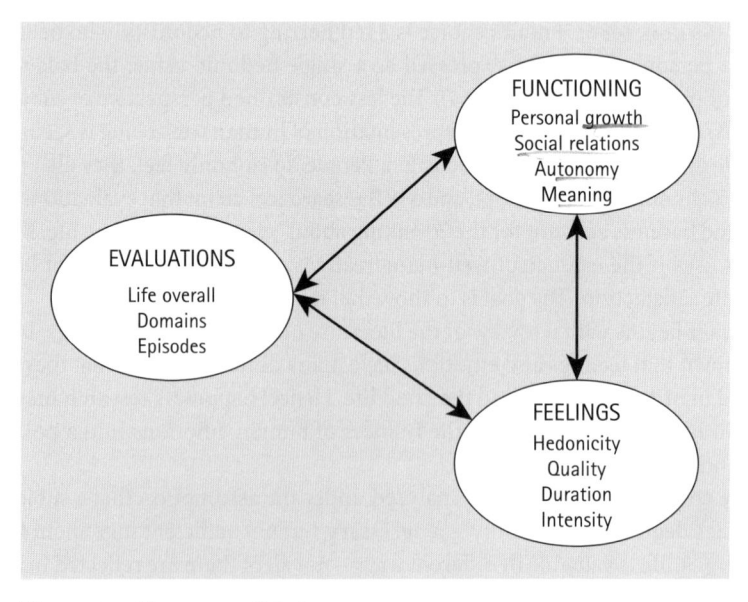

FIG. 17.1 Elements of human well-being.

accounts of happiness (von Wright, 1963). By contrast, feelings have been a core element in much psychological thinking about the good life, and Sully (1886) argued more than 100 years ago that feelings were the true elements of happiness. Early users of the term "psychological well-being" defined the concept as affective (e.g., Bradburn, 1969), although, and perhaps somewhat surprisingly, the emphasis put on feelings in current psychological theories of happiness varies. For instance, in Ryff's (1989) conceptualization of psychological well-being, feelings are stripped away by the argument that no sophisticated theories connect good feelings to human well-being. Affects are important in SWB research (Larsen & Eid, 2008), but life satisfaction is still the most dominant variable in this tradition. Self-determination theory (Deci & Ryan, 2000; Ryan & Deci, 2001) does not pay much attention to theories of emotions, and in his theory of authentic happiness, Seligman (2002, p. 35) claims that "a person can be happy even if he or she does not have much in the way of positive emotion."

## Emotions, feelings, and functions

Feelings are not the same as emotions (Ellsworth, 1994), they are both broader and narrower. They are broader in the sense that as long as we are conscious we always feel something, but these feelings are not necessarily emotional. A general feeling state reflects what it is like to have subjective experiences such as eating a banana, seeing a red tomato, feeling happy or "being me" (Damasio, 1999; Humphrey, 2006; Lambie & Marcel, 2002; Nagel, 1974). Feelings are also narrower than emotions in the sense that a feeling is one among several components of an emotion. Emotions comprise physiological processes, bodily expressions, and action readiness in addition to feeling quality (Oatley & Jenkins, 1996).

Emotions and feelings have functions. Emotions are considered functional because they assist in the management of human action, by guiding our attention and prompting action in relation to events that have implications for our concerns (Oatley, 1998). The feeling of bodily sensations is functional because they inform us about the state of our immediate environment: the *quality* of a sensation describes the nature of the stimulus, the *intensity* has to do with the magnitude of the stimulus, time identifies the *duration* of the exposure to the stimulus, whereas *hedonicity* (i.e., the feeling of pleasantness or unpleasantness) defines the usefulness of the stimulus (Cabanac, 2010). Feelings of bodily processes in the service of regulating homeostatic processes are also important for human well-being.

When feelings and emotions are considered to be functional in the FWBA it means, among other things, that both positive and negative emotions are important for a good life. The idea of an "affect balance" is thus considered misleading, particularly when analyzed at the level of moments or episodes. Negative emotions such as anger and sadness are important in maintaining healthy social relations and in reorganizing plans and goals after a severe loss, which are the major functions of anger and sadness respectively (Oatley, 1992). There is value in other negative emotions as well: people seek out fear if it is safely contained (Hetland & Vittersø, 2012) and without painful feelings humans would die prematurely (Melzack & Wall, 1996). But as SWB researchers point out (e.g., Miao, Koo, & Oishi, Chapter 13, this volume), too many negative feelings are inconsistent with a happy life, and when analyzed at the level of emotional dispositions (trait emotions), negative emotionality is indicative of reduced well-being.

On the other hand, too much positive emotion may not be optimal for a good life either (Oishi, Diener, & Lucas, 2007; Oishi & Koo, 2008; Ferssizidis, Kashdan, Marquart, & Steger, Chapter 8, this volume) and the challenge for a science of well-being is to specify the functional balance of a variety of feeling states. Towards this end the FWBA suggests that we study emotions thoroughly by analyzing quality, hedonicity, intensity, and duration, rather than limiting the scope to broad clusters of positive and negative emotions. If happiness hides in the details of our emotional lives, we lose its essence by staring at overall statements about positivity (see Field, 1934, 1981, for a telling case).

## The functions of positive feelings

Some scholars suggest that it is hard to pin down the function of positive emotions (e.g., Lazarus, 1991). There is, of course, a general agreement that we feel satisfied when things go our way, and emotion researchers generally subscribe to the notion that pleasure reflects well-functioning (note that satisfaction is not only a judgment, one may also feel satisfied or contented). On the other hand, it has been argued that pleasure has a rather specific role, namely to signal to our mental system that a goal has been reached. In this view, the function of pleasure is to provide respite from effortful behavior and to prepare us for the pursuit of alternative goals (Carver, 2003).

From a physiological point if view, the function of pleasure is to communicate that the return to a homeostatic set-point has been successful (Leyton, 2010; Panksepp, 1998). Another evolutionary advantage is simply that the ability to feel pleasure saves our mental system from creating and storing an enormously large database of potential benefits and dangers. Because we feel pleasure and displeasure the survival of our ancestors did not depend on detailed knowledge, for example, about the relation between a foul odor and bacterial contamination, between sweet tastes and nutrient-rich food, or between sex and the reproductive mechanisms of DNA (Johnston, 2003).

Fredrickson has proposed a model in which the positive emotions are grouped together for other purposes. The "broaden-and-build" theory (Cohn & Fredrickson, 2009) is basically concerned with the functional distinction between positive and negative emotions, and not with the distinctions among the different positive emotions. This is what the theory suggests in terms of functionality: Positive emotions broaden people's momentary thought–action repertoires and lead to actions that build enduring personal resources. Fredrickson and her colleagues have established an impressive body of evidence in support of the theory and the empirical backing keeps growing (see Conway, Tugade, Catalino & Fredrickson, Chapter 3, this volume). Although Fredrickson is aware that positive emotions might have different phenomenologies and perhaps distinct thought–action repertoires (e.g., Conway et al., Chapter 3, this volume; Fredrickson, 2000), thus far it seems that the broaden-and-build theory treats all positive emotions more or less the same when it comes to functions.

By contrast, a growing number of studies in affective neuroscience suggest that emotions are better conceived of as reflecting at least two different categories of positive emotions, each with distinct functions. This thinking is elegantly summed up in the title of a recent article by Barbano and Cador (2007): "Opioids for hedonic experience and dopamine to get ready for it." In explaining, Barbano and Cador claim that dopamine appears to be much more involved in the approach, anticipation, and "wanting" aspects of behavior, whereas the pleasantness of hedonicity seems to be regulated by other brain systems, such as endogenous opioids. This point has earlier been made by Berridge (1995, 2003) and it is well summarized in a literature review by Burgdorf and Panksepp (2006). Recently Litt, Khan, and Shiv (2010) even demonstrated that by manipulating the accessibility of a desired outcome, people can come to both want something more and like it less.

Leyton (2010) defends the view that three different classes of positive emotions exists. The first is desire, which reflects the focused interest in a goal object and the drive to obtain it. The second class is happiness, which Leyton considers to be an affective state linked to the appraisal that progress is being made. The third category of positive emotions is pleasure; the response to obtaining a goal.

Early thinkers of happiness, from Aristotle to Bentham, were not equipped with sufficient knowledge to understand the functional role of feeling momentary pleasure, satisfaction, or happiness. Neither did they understand that these functions differed from those of feeling engaged and interested. Such knowledge is available today and in the FWBA attempts are made to include it as an explicit element of happiness modeling. For example, a successful life can only be sustained by organisms that manage to maintain a balance between stability and change (Caspi & Roberts, 2001; Fraley & Roberts, 2005; Magnusson & Mahoney, 2003). But if pleasure, satisfaction, and happiness are markers of the stability elements of life, and not the change elements, the well-being literature is biased. It is biased towards the comfort of homeostatic balance (Vittersø, Søholt, Hetland, Thorsen, & Røysamb, 2010). For instance, in one paper Straume and Vittersø (2012) showed that difficult work tasks increased the mean level of inspiration among 465 Norwegian job-holders, while they reduced the mean level of momentary happiness. A measure of personal growth predicted both state happiness and inspirations in this study, whereas a measure of life satisfaction did not. If inspiration is regarded as valuable for well-being, these results demonstrate that self-reports of momentary happiness cannot fully account for ongoing emotional well-being. Our study further illustrates that compared with measures of life satisfaction, a personal growth variable may be a better predictor of good feelings if the goal being pursued is difficult to accomplish.

## Is pleasure a feeling, an evaluation—or both?

The term pleasure has a multitude of meanings. It is a common translation for the ancient Greek *hêdonê*, which implies that hedonic well-being is about pleasure. For example, hedonism is the doctrine that pleasure is the only moral good and that everyone aims only at pleasure. This idea is famously articulated by Bentham (1789/1948): "Nature has placed mankind under the governance of two sovereign masters, pain and pleasure. It is for them alone to point out what we ought to do, as well as to determine what we shall do."

Early psychologists were also concerned about pleasure, like Thorndike in his law of effect, Freud in his pleasure principle, and William James in his theorizing about the important role of pleasure in subjective experiences. For the old introspective psychologists, like Wundt, the dimension of pleasure-displeasure was an irreducible "qualia" that could not be accounted for by other kinds of mental content (e.g., Beebe-Center, 1965).

Frijda (2010) argues strongly against the view that pleasure is a psychological primitive, or qualia. To him, pleasure does not even have a characteristic phenomenology. Frijda claims that pleasure never stands alone, but always operates as a "gloss of niceness" added to some other experience. In other words, pleasure can be categorized as an evaluation of a feeling state (see Schimmack and Crites (2005) for a different view). James Mill viewed pleasure as an evaluation when he proposed that feeling states are of three different kinds: "The first is of such a kind, that I care not whether it is long or short; the second is of such a kind that I would put an end to it instantly if I could; the third is of such a kind that I like it prolonged. To distinguish these feelings I give them names. I call the first Indifferent; the second, Painful; the third, Pleasurable; very often, for shortness, I call the second, Pain, the third, Pleasure." (Mill as cited in Sumner (1996, p. 90)). The idea of pleasure as an evaluation is further demonstrated in the example of eating chocolate. Chocolate is typically both sweet and pleasant—until one has eaten enough. After having had more than one's fill, a new mouthful is distasteful and unpleasant, but the chocolate still tastes sweet. Thus sweetness and pleasure are separable dimensions of a feeling state (Small, Zatorre, Dagher, Evans, & Jones-Gotman, 2001).

A view more in line with Wundt's approach is taken in the theory of core affect (Russell, 2003, 2009). The theory proposes that any conscious feeling is a single integral blend of valence (i.e., hedonicity) and activation. Much like the taste of strong coffee—being the result of (relatively) little water and a lot of ground coffee beans—the feeling of interest is the result of some pleasantness and much activation. In the core affect approach then, pleasure cannot be separated from the feeling quality of a mental state. A somewhat similar, but far more sophisticated, perspective is found in appraisal theories (Clore & Ortony, 2008; Smith & Ellsworth, 1985).

The FWBA pays respect both to Frijda's "pleasure as an evaluation" position and to the view that pleasure is a distinct feeling state, which is typically articulated in affective neuroscience. However, and following common criticism against the theory of core affect (e.g., Scherer, 2009), the FWBA rejects the idea that pleasure and activation constitute the quality of every possible feeling state that we may have. Hence, in the FWBA the term "pleasure" is given two different meanings. When people talk about pleasure, they *sometimes* use the term as an evaluation, as a description of the "gloss" of a feeling state. But under other circumstances pleasure refers to the quality of a mental feeling state in itself. Enjoying the first pint of beer on a warm and sunny day in the spring is pleasant (at least if you live in Norway), and in such a case the beer has produced a mental state of pleasantness, which is a genuine phenomenological state and not just an additional gloss on top of the sensations involved (see Lambie and Marcel (2002) for an elaboration of this view).

# Evaluations

The mind continuously evaluates whether perceptions from the outside and interceptions from the inside appear favorable or not (Kagan, 2002; Kahneman, 1999; Lazarus, 1991; Shizgal, 1999). To many well-being researchers these evaluative processes make up the essence of human happiness. For instance, a recent consensus document (Diener, 2006, pp. 399–400), defines subjective well-being as:

> all the various types of evaluations, both positive and negative, that people make of their lives. It includes reflective cognitive evaluations, such as life satisfaction and work satisfaction, interest and engagement, and affective reactions to life events, such as joy and sadness. Thus, subjective well-being is an umbrella term for the different valuations people make regarding

their lives, the events happening to them, their bodies and minds, and the circumstances in which they live.

The stance adopted by this definition is formidable. It aspires to cover *every possible* good–bad judgment (i.e., both affective and cognitive) that can be made by an individual regarding *every aspect* of his or her *entire life*. It is hard to imagine how the mind can keep track of all this information. The continuous stream of different evaluations must obviously be chunked into broad units of some kind, but there is no easy way of determining the number of categories to which these valuations should be assigned. Strict hedonism suggests that they should all be carved into the single category of pleasure (net of pain). Kahneman seems to argue that evaluations can be summarized in the two categories of experienced evaluations and remembered evaluations.[1] In his early writings, Diener (1984) advised that the proper number of categories in subjective well-being research is three (life satisfaction, positive affect, and negative affect) whereas more recently he has recommended adding domain satisfaction as a fourth category (e.g., Diener, Suh, Lucas, & Smith, 1999).

Other conceptualizations of evaluative information are of course possible. In their highly influential book on well-being, Andrews and Withey (1976) presented a model of happiness with three levels of evaluative specificity. At the first level, distinct evaluative "criteria" are combined with a series of applicable life domains. The criteria are located along the columns in a matrix of evaluations, and the domains to be evaluated are located along the rows. Each cell mean reflects a particular evaluation (for example, about achieved success, about safety, about joy, or any other relevant evaluation a person may make) related to a particular domain (such as house, job, family life, or any other relevant domain in a person's life).

At the second level of the evaluative model, each row mean reflects the sum of all possible evaluations that can be made for a particular domain, and each column mean reflects the sum of a particular evaluation across all the possible domains. Resembling statistical analyses of variance, the rightmost bottom cell in Andrews and Withey's matrix summarizes the "grand mean", which they refer to as "perceived quality of life". The grand mean is the third level of evaluative well-being, but in contrast to the mathematical preciseness of an ANOVA table, empirical evidence suggests that the cell means of well-being evaluations do not add up to an overall "grand mean".

The lack of coherence between kinds of, and levels of, evaluative information is a nightmare for happiness researchers. The reason is that science does not provide a procedure for deciding which level or which kind should count as happiness. For instance, in a recent comparison of working women in France and the USA, Krueger and colleagues (2009) found that the French reported more happy moments whereas the US women reported higher overall happiness. But which are most important for well-being, the episodes of everyday life or the overall judgment we make in retrospect?

It has also been demonstrated that low-arousal activities such as relaxing or watching TV typically generate very happy moments (Kahneman, Krueger, Schkade, Schwarz, & Stone, 2004, 2006). In contrast, studies focusing on overall happiness show that individuals who

---

[1] It seems that Kahneman's account of experienced well-being is evaluative rather than phenomenological (see Kahneman & Riis, 2005; Kahneman, Schkade, Fischler, Krueger, & Krilla, 2010). The SWB literature is not always clear about whether the affective components are restricted to the evaluative attributes of emotions and feelings, or if the phenomenological—the non-evaluative—qualities of affects are included in the analysis.

watch a lot of television, or lead sedate lives, in general are less happy than people who rarely watch TV or are physically active (Frey, Benesch, & Stutzer, 2007; Hellevik, 2008). In other words, collecting activities that in themselves generate high momentary happiness does not necessarily provide high life satisfaction.

## Life satisfaction

The dominant evaluative concept in happiness research is life satisfaction. Traditionally this term was considered to be a rational comparison of what people have, to what they think they deserve, expect, or may reasonably aspire to (Campbell, Converse, & Rodgers, 1976). According to this view satisfaction can be precisely defined as the perceived discrepancy between aspiration and achievement, ranging from the perception of fulfillment to that of deprivation. However, no finite set of aspirations (what many psychologists today would call goals) seem to exist in our minds, which is quite obvious from a functional point of view. In a complex and changing world a permanent set of goals would not be efficient, given the mind's limited capacity for information processing. In order to be functional, our goals must be somewhat malleable.

Besides being dysfunctional, the idea that satisfaction is a calculation of gaps between goals and reality runs into more trouble when confronted with empirical observations of survey responses. Participants only need about 3 seconds to answer questions such as "How satisfied are you with you life overall?" or "Taking all things together, how happy are you with your life?"—and that includes reading the item (Vitterrsø, Oelmann, et al., 2009).

These results suggest that if "thinking about life" is the question, life satisfaction is not the answer. Human lives are complex, and thinking about them certainly takes more than a few seconds. To complicate the matter even more, consider the responses often given in qualitative interviews about happiness. In my experience, most informants have a hard time figuring out what the concept of happiness really means to them (you can easily try this exercise yourself). Hence, while people respond quickly when asked *how much* happiness they have in their lives, they don't necessarily have an articulated idea about *what* happiness is. This oddity should be of some concern for happiness researchers.

Rather than considering life satisfaction as the result of a calculation of all possible discrepancies between aspirations and reality, or alternatively as an overall good–bad evaluation about every conceivable aspect of a whole life, it may be more useful to think about life satisfaction as an attitude towards one's own life. Attitudes are conventionally considered to be evaluative judgments of an object in terms of goodness or badness, or "a psychological tendency that is expressed by evaluating a particular entity with some degree of favor or disfavor" (Eagly & Chaiken, 1993, p. 1).

To use the term "attitude" rather than overall happiness as a description of life satisfaction will have consequences for how we interpret research results. For example, situational factors such as income, education, gender, and age typically explain 5–20% of the variance in measures of life satisfaction (Andrews & Withey, 1976; Campbell et al., 1976; Diener, Helliwell, & Kahneman, 2010). These results change meaning if spelled out as attitudes: claiming that circumstances account for about 10% of our attitudes toward life reads differently than claiming that circumstances account for about 10% of the happiness in our lives.

# Functioning

In the philosophy of happiness, optimal functioning is frequently considered to be a human ideal. Aristotle envisioned that the ultimate function of our actions and goal pursuits is to provide happiness (McGill, 1967) and some thinkers even considered optimal functioning to be as natural for human beings as producing silk is for a silkworm (Gewirth, 1998). Humanistic psychology has nourished the idea that good functioning is the essential feature of a good life as well. Rogers (1961) spent much time developing his concept of the fully functioning person, and he proposed that individuals are naturally oriented toward realizing their full potential and that this tendency is the only true human motive (Rogers, 1963). Health psychologists have been concerned with human functioning, particularly when health breaks down so that individuals no longer can keep their jobs, avoid lifestyle illnesses, or sustain their social relationships. Ryff (1989) adopted the term "positive psychological functioning" from early versions of health sciences, arguing that this perspective provided a firm theoretical basis for the study of well-being.

A third view on optimal functioning comes from Amartya Sen, who has fought for a functioning perspective of well-being for decades (Nussbaum & Sen, 1993; Sen, 2000). In Sen's terminology, a "functioning" is a lifestyle: what a person manages to do or to be, while a capability reflects a person's ability to achieve a given functioning. In other words, capabilities reflect a person's freedom of choice between possible lifestyles (e.g., Clark, 2006).

## What does it mean to function well?

The term optimal functioning is vague, but borrowing Nussbaum's (1992) motto, "it is better to be vaguely right than precisely wrong," four candidates are presented in order to suggest a rudimentary taxonomy of good functioning. They are autonomy, social relations, meaning, and personal growth. This quartet speaks to the issue of an optimally functioning self, about "bringing oneself to flourishing completion" (Gewirth, 1998) or realizing one's full potential (Rogers, 1961). Now, the optimally functioning self is a difficult idea and many factors can cause us to misinterpret our "true selves" (Wilson, 2002; Wilson & Dunn, 2004). We often pursue more than one self (Markus & Nurius, 1986), and from the extreme position of postmodernism, it has even been argued that the self merely acts like a chameleon in continuous change (Gergen, 1991). On the other hand, the notion of a "true self" is widespread in folk wisdom (Schneider, 1999) and there is a growing literature showing that elements of a "true self" can be empirically operationalized and analyzed in relation to life meaning and other indicators of a good life (Johnson, Robinson, & Mitchell, 2004; Schlegel, Hicks, Arndt, & King, 2009; Sheldon, Ryan, & Rawsthorne, 1997).

To steer away from some of the conceptual confusion, one might anchor the term in the theoretical texture of current social cognition and say that an optimally functioning self is one that strives to create and execute plans that lead to fulfillment of needs and important life goals. These processes can be conceptualized within the framework of self-regulating systems (Lewis & Granic, 2002; Valsiner, 1997), within recent approaches to consciousness (Zelazo, Moscovitch, & Thompson, 2007), or within a Piagetian terminology of functioning as an inborn tendency to strive toward an expansion of mental and physical capacities, and to integrate and understand surroundings (Piaget, 1971).

The four selected candidates of good functioning are an attempt to make the imprecise idea of an optimally functioning self rather more concrete. The list could be made very much longer and alternative taxonomies do indeed exist (e.g., Keyes, 1998; Ryan & Deci, 2001; Ryff, 1989; Sheldon, 2007). It should also be realized that the literature on authenticity, social relations, meaning, and personal growth is huge, and that only a cursory review can be provided of the research relevant to these concepts. Interested readers are encouraged to consult the original publications for details.

Autonomy reflects the inner endorsement of what one does in life. The concept is well articulated in the self-determination theory (Deci & Ryan, 2000; Niemiec & Ryan, Chapter 16, this volume; Ryan & Deci, 2001), which claims that humans have an innate tendency to actively learn, grow and integrate their surroundings. The self-determined nature of the self, which is referred to as autonomy in the present chapter, is associated with, but not reducible, to happiness (Ryan & Huta, 2009).

Without social relations, humans do not function (Baumeister & Leary, 1995). Over the course of human evolution, those who cooperated successfully with others were more likely to survive and pass on their genes. As reviewed by Jacobs Bao and Lyubomirsky (Chapter 9, this volume), there are many connections between a high-quality social life and happiness. However, social relations contribute to human well-being over and above their impact on feelings and evaluations. It is simply hard to conceive of a good life that is not also functioning well socially (e.g., Baumeister, 2005; Bowlby, 1969; Haidt, 2006; Harlow & Suomi, 1979; Helliwell & Putnam, 2005).

Meaning is a third element of optimal functioning. Perceptions of meaning are tightly connected with a unified self, but not always with self-reported happiness. This point has been elegantly demonstrated in an article by McGregor and Little (1998). These authors observed that research often fails to find a relation between integrity and happiness, and the fundamental difference between the two concepts is proposed as an explanation for why they do not covary. McGregor and Little were able to show that individuals who emphasized efficiency in life also scored high on subjective well-being, whereas individuals who emphasized integrity reported much meaning in life. SWB and meaning were not highly correlated. Based on their results and theoretical insights, McGregor and Little suggested that important goals ("personal projects" in their terminology) sustain two different functions: the instrumental function relates to efficiency and corresponds to feelings of happiness; the symbolic function relates to integrity and produces experience of meaning.

Humans must change continuously in order to function effectively (Aspinwall & Staudinger, 2003; Kagan, 2002; Piaget, 1950; Valsiner, 1998). In the FWBA, these change processes are the fourth pillar of optimal functioning and they are referred to as "personal growth". The central theme in personal growth is the issue of how a mental structure adapts to the unknown. The adaptation process is accounted for in the FWBA by a terminology borrowed from scheme theory (Eckblad, 1981). Scheme theory is concerned with cognitive, emotional, and motivational systems and how they change their structure and content. Eckblad has developed the concept of assimilation resistance (AR) to explain how various subjective experiences are produced when cognitive structures interact with environments of different degrees of familiarity. For example, pleasure is taken as a typical response to the processing of familiar information (low AR), whereas interest dominates a mental system that is in the process of spontaneous expansion (which means medium AR and undisturbed attention). The causal direction between cognitive processes and subjective experiences is bidirectional. The level of AR primes certain feeling states, but the feelings feed back to the cognitive operations as well. For example, in learning to perceive a new object, the unfamiliarity of the object may arouse a feeling of interest. In return, the state of interest excites attention to be focused long enough for the perceiver to achieve the essential features of the object. Hence, feelings such as interest and engagement maintain focused attention over longer time spans, which are needed for a mental structure to grow.

A sustained attention is also necessary for commitment to difficult life goals, and this point is important in the FWBA. Whereas a pleasant mind is easily distracted (Carver, 2003), an engaged mind keeps attending to the current goal (Higgins, 2006). Sustained attention is needed for personal growth, and feelings such as pleasure, satisfaction and happiness stimulate rapid attention shifts (Damasio, 2004). Thus, the hedonic bias inherent in much well-being research prevents it from capturing the essentials of personal growth. A more detailed review of these arguments is provided in Vittersø et al. (2010) and in Vittersø, Overwien, and Martinsen (2009).

## Does it feel good to function well?

Despite its conceptual disputes, the happiness literature converges on the idea that "functioning good means feeling good." For instance, Aristotle considered pleasure to be a token of "unimpeded functioning," and Spinoza talked about "pleasure as a man's transition from a less state of perfection to a greater" (cited in Frijda, 2007, p. 69). Waterman (Waterman, 2008; Waterman, Schwartz, & Conti, 2008) has proposed that people typically feel good when their true potentials are realized. He refers to these experiences as personal expressiveness, which is typically described as "feeling really alive" or "feeling fulfilled."

The flow theory (Csikszentmihalyi, 1975; Delle Fave, Chapter 5, this volume) also suggests that a companionship exists between optimal experiences (flow) and optimal functioning. Flow occurs when challenges and skills are high and in balance (but see Løvoll and Vittersø (submitted) for a different perspective). Flow theory is hedonic in suggesting that an imbalance of perceived skills and/or challenges will reduce the quality of the current feeling state, and the drop in enjoyment will motivate the individual to re-enter the flow state. Due to the inherent enjoyment (or hedonic feeling) of maintaining a balance between challenges and skills, optimal functioning becomes intrinsically rewarding (Csikszentmihalyi, 2009). Hence, flow theory expects that skill development should be highly enjoyable and that optimal functioning is a hedonically driven activity.

In contrast to the "functioning good means feeling good" assumption of happiness theories, observations made possible by methodological improvements in the study of expert performance suggest that the connection between pleasure and functioning is more complex (Ericsson, 2009). For example, Ericsson and his colleagues (Ericsson, Krampe, & Tesch-Römer, 1993) claim that flow is almost antithetical to optimal performance, because skills do not develop from enjoyment but from commitment to an activity. It is engagement combined with a well-defined task with an appropriate difficulty level, informative feedback, and opportunities for repetition and corrections of errors that stimulate the growth of potential. The label Ericsson contrives to this process is *deliberate practice* (Ericsson et al., 1993). A huge literature now documents how the parts and parcels of deliberate practice enable people to become better at doing things, and the evidence suggests that enjoyment contributes little to the process. For instance, studies of extraordinary musicians, chess-players, and other groups of experts show that the most relevant activities to improve performance are rated as the least enjoyable (Ericsson et al., 1993).

The lack of pleasure during skill development was recently demonstrated by Warholm and Vittersø (submitted). During a week, daily self-reports on emotions, satisfaction, and skill improvement were collected from a sample of Norwegian employees. In order to enhance proficiency, participants agreed that once a day they would devote extra effort to a particular work task. At the end of each day they also reported their experiences while working on the task they wanted to become better at. Warholm and Vittersø found that events described as pleasant also were evaluated as satisfactory. But pleasure and satisfaction were unrelated to skill improvement. Interest, on the other hand, significantly predicted skill improvement, but was unrelated to satisfaction with the event. These results corroborate an important idea in the functional approach to well-being, which is that pleasure predicts satisfaction, but is basically unrelated to the development of skills and potentials (Vittersø, et al., 2010).

## Not all functioning is optimal functioning

The "no pain, no gain" approach of deliberate practice does not necessarily apply to all optimal functioning. The kind of expertise studied by Ericsson and his colleagues may, at least sometimes, fall outside the range of the autonomic and meaningful competence that are "built" in the service of a fully functioning person. For example, in a study comparing professional and amateur singers, Grape, Sandgren, Hansson, Ericson, and Theorell (2003) found that the professionals were more concentrated and less satisfied during a singing lesson, as compared with amateurs. The amateurs seemed to put less effort into the practice, but they reported more enjoyment, release of tension, and overall well-being than did the professionals. If singing joyfully together with friends is a major goal for the amateurs, could it then be argued that these singers were closer to optimal functioning than the professionals?

Despite these objections, it is hard to reconcile how the concept of optimal functioning can survive without backing from theories of skill development. The most promising accounts of excellent performance suggest that if potentials are to be fulfilled, the tedious steps of deliberate practice cannot be replaced by playful enjoyment or a pleasant coast down the hill.

## Concluding Remarks

This chapter is a long argument against reductionism in well-being research. Although all sciences need to condense complexity into comprehensible models, "reductio ad absurdum" leads us nowhere. Economists are often criticized for transforming the variety of human goodness to a flat metric of money. Well-being research may fall prey to a similar criticism by trading one shaky reduction for another. If the richness of human feelings is reduced to a hedonic balance (a "hedon" metric), or the subtle wonders of human lives to an evaluation of goodness (a "goodon" metric), we risk throwing out the baby with the bathwater. If our well-being depends on the quality and breadth of our feelings, we may be led astray if our thinking becomes too focused on a few quantified self-rating variables. By insisting on measuring a broader range of feeling states, and by promoting the idea that optimal functioning is a separate category of human well-being, partly independent of feelings and evaluations, the intention of the FWBA is to help avoiding the perils of reductionism in happiness research.

The functional well-being approach is not an alternative to subjective well-being—it is a supplement. Few, if any, perspectives have added more to the scientific understanding of human well-being than the one offered by SWB researchers. Hence, the call from the FWBA is for future research not to abandon emotional or evaluative perspectives, but to broaden the theoretical scope so that it also reflects functional elements. By this route the science of happiness may continue to build an understanding of the mechanisms that cause human well-being to raise or shrink.

## References

Andrews, F. M., & Withey, S. B. (1976). *Social indicators of well-being*. New York, NY: Plenum Press.

Aspinwall, L. G., & Staudinger, U. M. (Eds.). (2003). *A psychology of human strengths: Fundamental questions and future directions for a positive psychology*. Washington, DC: American Psychological Association.

Barbano, M. F., & Cador, M. (2007). Opioids for hedonic experience and dopamine to get ready for it. *Psychopharmacology, 191*, 497–506.

Baumeister, R. F. (2005). *The cultural animal. Human nature, meaning, and social life*. Oxford, UK: Oxford University Press.

Baumeister, R. F., & Leary, M. R. (1995). The need to belong: Desire for interpersonal attachments as a fundamental human motivation. *Psychological Bulletin, 117*, 497–529.

Beebe-Center, J. G. (1965). *The psychology of pleasantness and unpleasantness*. New York, NY: Russell & Russell.

Bentham, J. (1948). *An introduction to the principles of moral and legislation*. New York, NY: Hafner. (Original work published 1789). (Available from http://www.econlib.org/library/Bentham/bnthPML1.html).

Berridge, K. C. (1995). Food reward: Brain substrates of wanting and liking. *Neuroscience & Biobehavioral Reviews, 20*, 1–25.

Berridge, K. C. (2003). Pleasures of the brain. *Brain and Cognition, 52*, 106–128.

Bowlby, J. (1969). *Attachment and loss*. New York, NY: Basic Books.

Bradburn, N. M. (1969). *The structure of psychological well-being*. Chicago, IL: Aldine.

Burgdorf, J., & Panksepp, J. (2006). The neurobiology of positive emotions. *Neuroscience & Biobehavioral Reviews, 30*, 173–187.

Cabanac, M. (2010). The dialectics of pleasure. In M. L. Kringelbach & K. C. Berridge (Eds.), *Pleasures of the brain* (pp. 113–124). Oxford, UK: Oxford University Press.

Campbell, A., Converse, P. E., & Rodgers, W. L. (1976). *The quality of American life*. New York, NY: Sage.

Carver, C. S. (2003). Pleasure as a sign you can attend to something else: Placing positive feelings within a general model of affect. *Cognition & Emotion, 17*, 241–261.

Caspi, A., & Roberts, B. W. (2001). Personality development across the life course: The argument for change and continuity. *Psychological Inquiry, 12,* 49–66.

Clark, D. A. (2006). The capability approach: Its development, critiques, and recent advances. In A. E. Clark (Ed.), *The Elgar companion to developmental studies.* Cheltenham, UK: Edward Elgar.

Clore, G. L., & Ortony, A. (2008). Appraisal theories: How cognition shapes affect into emotion. In M. Lewis, J. M. Haviland-Jones & L. F. Barrett (Eds.), *Handbook of emotions* (3rd ed., pp. 628–642). London, UK: The Guilford Press.

Cohn, M. A., & Fredrickson, B. (2009). Broaden-and-build theory of positive emotions. In S. J. Lopez (Ed.), *The encyclopedia of positive psychology* (Vol. I, pp. 105–110). Malden, MA: Wiley-Blackwell.

Csikszentmihalyi, M. (1975). *Beyond boredom and anxiety.* San Francisco, CA: Jossey-Bass.

Csikszentmihalyi, M. (2009). Flow. In S. J. Lopez (Ed.), *The encyclopedia of positive psychology* (Vol. I, pp. 394–400). Malden, MA: Wiley-Blackwell.

Damasio, A. (1999). *The feeling of what happens: Body and emotion in the making of consciousness.* New York, NY: Avon Books.

Damasio, A. (2004). Emotions and feelings. In A. S. R. Manstead, N. Frijda & A. Fischer (Eds.), *Feelings and emotions. The Amsterdam symposium* (pp. 49–57). Cambridge, UK: Cambridge University Press.

Deci, E. L., & Ryan, R. M. (2000). The "what" and "why" of goal pursuits: Human needs and the self-determination of behavior. *Psychological Inquiry, 11,* 227–268.

Diener, E. (1984). Subjective well-being. *Psychological Bulletin, 95,* 542–575.

Diener, E. (2006). Guidelines for national indicators of subjective well-being and ill-being. *Journal of Happiness Studies, 7,* 397–404.

Diener, E., Helliwell, J. F., & Kahneman, D. (Eds.). (2010). *International differences in well-being.* Oxford, UK: Oxford University Press.

Diener, E., Suh, E. M., Lucas, R. E., & Smith, H. L. (1999). Subjective well-being: Three decades of progress. *Psychological Bulletin, 125,* 276–302.

Eagly, A. H., & Chaiken, S. (1993). *The psychology of attitudes.* London, UK: HBJ.

Eckblad, G. (1981). *Scheme theory. A conceptual framework for cognitive-motivational processes.* London, UK: Academic Press.

Ellsworth, P. C. (1994). William James and emotion: Is a century of fame worth a century of misunderstanding? *Psychological Review, 101,* 222–229.

Ericsson, K. A. (Ed.). (2009). *Development of professional expertise. Toward measurement of expert performance and design of optimal learning environments.* Cambridge, UK: Cambridge University Press.

Ericsson, K. A., Krampe, R. T., & Tesch-Römer, C. (1993). The role of deliberate practice in the acquisition of expert performance. *Psychological Review, 100,* 363–406.

Field, J. (1981). *A life of one's own.* Los Angeles, CA: J. P. Tarcher. (Original work published 1934).

Fraley, R. C., & Roberts, B. W. (2005). Patterns of continuity: A dynamic model for conceptualizing the stability of individual differences in psychological constructs across the life course. *Psychological Review, 112,* 60–74.

Fredrickson, B. L. (2000). Extracting meaning from past affective experiences: The importance of peaks, ends, and specific emotions. *Cognition & Emotion, 14,* 577–606.

Frey, B. S., Benesch, C., & Stutzer, A. (2007). Does watching TV make us happy? *Journal of Economic Psychology, 28,* 283–313.

Frijda, N. H. (2007). *The laws of emotions.* Mahwah, NJ: Lawrence Erlbaum Associates.

Frijda, N. H. (2010). On the nature and function of pleasure. In M. L. Kringelbach & K. C. Berridge (Eds.), *Pleasures of the brain* (pp. 99–112). Oxford, UK: Oxford University Press.

Gergen, K. J. (1991). *The saturated self. Dilemmas of identity in contemporary life*. New York, NY: Basic Books.

Gewirth, A. (1998). *Self-fulfillment*. Princeton, NJ: Princeton University Press.

Grape, C., Sandgren, M., Hansson, L.-O., Ericson, M., & Theorell, T. (2003). Does singing promote well-being?: An empirical study of professional and amateur singers during a singing lesson. *Integrative Physiological & Behavioral Science, 38*, 65–74.

Griffin, J. (1986). *Well-being. Its meaning, measurement, and moral importance*. Oxford, UK: Clarendon Press.

Haidt, J. (2006). *The happiness hypothesis. Putting ancient wisdom and philosophy to the test of modern science*. London, UK: Arrow Books.

Harlow, H. F., & Suomi, S. J. (1979). Nature of love—simplified. *American Psychologist, 25*, 161–168.

Hellevik, O. (2008). *Jakten på den norske lykken. Norsk Monitor 1985–2007*. Oslo, Norway: Oslo Universitetesforlaget.

Helliwell, J. F., & Putnam, R. D. (2005). The social context of well-being. In F. Huppert, N. Baylis & B. Keverne (Eds.), *The science of well-being* (pp. 436–459). Oxford, UK: Oxford University Press.

Hetland, A., & Vittersø, J. (2012). The feelings of extreme risk: exploring emotional quality and variability in skydiving and BASE jumping. *Journal of Sport Behavior, 35*, 154–180.

Higgins, E. T. (2006). Value from hedonic experience *and* engagement. *Psychological Review, 113*, 439–460.

Humphrey, N. (2006). *Seeing red. A study in consciousness*. Cambridge, MA: The Belknap Press of Harvard University Press.

Johnson, J. T., Robinson, M. D., & Mitchell, E. B. (2004). Inferences about the authentic self: When do actions say more than mental states?. *Journal of Personality and Social Psychology, 87*, 615–630.

Johnston, V. S. (2003). The origin and function of pleasure. *Cognition & Emotion, 17*, 169–179.

Kagan, J. (2002). *Surprise, uncertainty, and mental structures*. New York, NY: Harvard University Press.

Kahneman, D. (1999). Objective happiness. In D. Kahneman, E. Diener & N. Schwarz (Eds.), *Well-being: The foundations of hedonic psychology* (pp. 3–25). New York, NY: Russell Sage Foundation.

Kahneman, D., Krueger, A. B., Schkade, D., Schwarz, N., & Stone, A. (2004). A survey method for characterizing daily life experience: The Day Reconstruction Method. *Science, 305*, 1776–1780.

Kahneman, D., Krueger, A. B., Schkade, D., Schwarz, N., & Stone, A. (2006). Would you be happier if you were richer? A focusing illusion. *Science, 312*, 1908–1910.

Kahneman, D., & Riis, J. (2005). Living, and thinking about it: Two perspectives on life. In F. Huppert, N. Baylis & B. Keverne (Eds.), *The science of well-being* (pp. 285–304). Oxford, UK: Oxford University Press.

Kahneman, D., Schkade, D. A., Fischler, C., Krueger, A. B., & Krilla, A. (2010). The structure of well-being in two cities: Life satisfaction and experienced happiness in Columbus, Ohio; and Rennes, France. In E. Diener, J. F. Helliwell & D. Kahneman (Eds.), *International differences in well-being* (pp. 16–33). Oxford, UK: Oxford University Press.

Keyes, C., L. M (1998). Social well-being. *Social Psychology Quarterly*, 61, 121–140.

Krueger, A. B., Kahneman, D., Fischler, C., Schkade, D., Schwarz, N., & Stone, A. A. (2009). Time use and subjective well-being in France and the USA. *Social Indicators Research*, 93, 7–18.

Lambie, J. A., & Marcel, A. (2002). Consciousness and the variety of emotion experience: A theoretical framework. *Psychological Review*, 109, 219–259.

Larsen, R. J., & Eid, M. (2008). Ed Diener and the science of subjective well-being. In M. Eid & R. J. Larsen (Eds.), *The science of subjective well-being* (pp. 1–13). New York, NY: Guilford Press.

Lazarus, R. S. (1991). *Emotion and adaptation*. Oxford, UK: Oxford University Press.

Lewis, M. D., & Granic, I. (Eds.). (2002). *Emotion, development, and self-organization. Dynamic systems approaches to emotional development*. Cambridge, UK: Cambridge University Press.

Leyton, M. (2010). The neurobiology of desire: Dopamine and the regulation of mood and motivational states in humans. In M. L. Kringelbach & K. C. Berridge (Eds.), *Pleasures of the brain* (pp. 222–243). Oxford, UK: Oxford University Press.

Litt, A., Khan, U., & Shiv, B. (2010). Lusting while loathing: Parallel counterdriving of wanting and liking. *Psychological Science*, 21, 118–125.

Løvoll, H. S., & Vitterso, J. (submitted). Can balance be boring? A critique of the "challenges should match skills" hypothesis in flow theory. Manuscript submitted for publication.

Magnusson, D., & Mahoney, J. L. (2003). A holistic person approach for research on positive development. In L. G. Aspinwall & U. M. Staudinger (Eds.), *A psychology of human strengths. Fundamental questions and directions for a positive psychology* (pp. 227–243). Washington, DC: American Psychological Association.

Markus, H., & Nurius, P. (1986). Possible selves. *American Psychologist*, 41, 954–969.

McGill, V. J. (1967). *The idea of happiness*. New York, NY: Frederick A. Praeger.

McGregor, I., & Little, B. (1998). Personal projects, happiness, and meaning: On doing well and being yourself. *Journal of Personality & Social Psychology*, 74, 494–512.

Melzack, R., & Wall, P. D. (1996). *The challenge of pain* (3rd ed.). London, UK: Penguin.

Nagel, T. (1974). What is it like to be a bat? *Philosophical Review*, 83, 435–450.

Nussbaum, M. C. (1992). Human functioning and social justice: In defense of Aristotelan essentialism. *Political Theory*, 20, 202–246.

Nussbaum, M. C., & Sen, A. (Eds.). (1993). *The quality of life*. Oxford, UK: Clarendon Press.

Oatley, K. (1992). *Best laid schemes. The psychology of emotions*. Cambridge, UK: Cambridge University Press.

Oatley, K. (1998). Emotion. *The Psychologist*, 11, 285–288.

Oatley, K., & Jenkins, J. M. (1996). *Understanding emotions*. Cambridge, MA: Blackwell.

Oishi, S., Diener, E., & Lucas, R. E. (2007). The optimum level of well-being: Can people be too happy? *Perspectives on Psychological Science*, 2, 346–360.

Oishi, S., & Koo, M. (2008). Two new questions about happiness. "Is happiness good?" and "Is happiness better?". In M. Eid & R. J. Larsen (Eds.), *The science of subjective well-being* (pp. 290–306). New York, NY: Guilford Press.

Panksepp, J. (1998). *Affective neuroscience. The foundations of human and animal emotions*. Oxford, UK: Oxford University Press.

Piaget, J. (1950). *The psychology of intelligence*. London, UK: Routledge & Kegan Paul.

Piaget, J. (1971). *Biology and knowledge. An essay on the relations between organic regulations and cognitive processes* (B. Walsh, Trans.). Edinburgh, UK: Edinburgh University Press.

Rogers, C. (1961). *On becoming a person*. Boston, MA: Houghton Mifflin Co.

Rogers, C. (1963). The actualizing tendency in relation to "motives" and to consciousness. In M. R. Jones (Ed.), *Nebraska symposium on motivation* (Vol. 11, pp. 1–24). Lincoln, NE: University of Nebraska Press.

Russell, J. A. (2003). Core affect and the psychological construction of emotion. *Psychological Review*, 110, 145–172.

Russell, J. A. (2009). Emotion, core affect, and psychological construction. *Cognition & Emotion*, 23, 1259–1283.

Ryan, R. M., & Deci, E. D. (2001). On happiness and human potentials: A review of research on hedonic and eudaimonic well-being. *Annual Review of Psychology*, 52, 141–166.

Ryan, R. M., & Huta, V. (2009). Wellness as healthy functioning or wellness as happiness: the importance of eudaimonic thinking (response to the Kashdan et al. and Waterman discussion). *Journal of Positive Psychology*, 4, 202–204.

Ryff, C. D. (1989). Happiness is everything, or is it? Explorations on the meaning of psychological well-being. *Journal of Personality & Social Psychology*, 57, 1069–1081.

Scherer, K. (2009). The dynamic architecture of emotion: Evidence for the component process model. *Cognition & Emotion*, 23, 1307–1351.

Schimmack, U., & Crites, S. L. (2005). The structure of affect. In D. Albarracín, B. T. Johnson & M. P. Zanna (Eds.), *The handbook of attitudes* (pp. 397–435). Mahwah, NJ: Lawrence Erlbaum.

Schlegel, R. J., Hicks, J. A., Arndt, J., & King, L. A. (2009). Thine own self: True self-concept accessibility and meaning in life. *Journal of Personality and Social Psychology*, 96, 473–490.

Schneider, K. J. (1999). *The paradoxical self: Toward an understanding of our contradictory nature*. Amherst, NY: Humanity Books.

Seligman, M. E. P. (2002). *Authentic happiness. Using the new positive psychology to realize your potential for deep fulfillment*. London, UK: Nicholas Brealey Publishing.

Sen, A. (2000). *Development as freedom*. New York, NY: Anchor Books.

Sheldon, K. M. (2007). Considering "The optimality of personality": Goals, self-concordance, and multilevel personality integration. In B. R. Little, K. Salmela-Aro & S. D. Phillips (Eds.), *Personal project pursuit. Goals, action, and human flourishing* (pp. 355–373). Mahwah, NJ: Lawrence Erlbaum.

Sheldon, K. M., Ryan, R. M., & Rawsthorne, L. J. (1997). Trait self and true self: Cross-role variation in the Big-Five personality traits and its relations with psychological authenticity and subjective well-being. *Journal of Personality & Social Psychology*, 73, 1380–1393.

Shizgal, P. (1999). On the neural computation of utility: Implications from studies of brain stimulation reward. In D. Kahneman, E. Diener & N. Schwarz (Eds.), *Well-being: The foundations of hedonic psychology* (pp. 502–526). New York, NY: Russell Sage Foundation.

Small, D. M., Zatorre, R. J., Dagher, A., Evans, A. C., & Jones-Gotman, M. (2001). Changes in brain activity related to eating chocolate. From pleasure to aversion. *Brain*, 124, 1720–1733.

Smith, C. A., & Ellsworth, P. C. (1985). Patterns of cognitive appraisal in emotion. *Journal of Personality & Social Psychology*, 48, 813–838.

Solomon, R. C. (2008). The philosophy of emotions. In M. Lewis, J. M. Haviland-Jones & L. F. Barrett (Eds.), *Handbook of emotions* (3rd ed., pp. 3–16). London, UK: The Guilford Press.

Straume, L. V., & Vittersø, J. (2012). Happiness, inspiration and the fully functioning person: Separating hedonic and eudaimonic well-being in the work place. *Journal of Positive Psychology*, 7, 387–398.

Sully, J. (1886). The feelings: Nature of feeling. In J. Sully (Ed.), *Teacher's handbook of psychology: On the basis of the "Outlines of psychology"* (pp. 279–302). New York, NY: D. Appleton & Co.

Sumner, L. W. (1996). *Welfare, happiness, and ethics*. Oxford, UK: Clarendon Press.

Valsiner, J. (1997). *Culture and the development of children's actions. A theory of human development* (2nd ed.). New York, NY: John Wiley & Sons.

Valsiner, J. (1998). The development of the concept of development: Historical and epistemological perspectives. In W. Damon & R. M. Lerner (Eds.), *Handbook of child psychology* (pp. 189–231). New York, NY: John Wiley & Sons.

Vittersø, J. (2009). Hedonics. In S. J. Lopez (Ed.), *The encyclopedia of positive psychology* (Vol. I, pp. 473–478). Malden, MA: Wiley-Blackwell.

Vittersø, J., Oelmann, H., & Wang, A. L. (2009). Life satisfaction is not a balanced estimator of the good life. Evidence from reaction time measures and self-reported emotions. *Journal of Happiness Studies, 10*, 1–17.

Vittersø, J., Overwien, P., & Martinsen, E. (2009). Pleasure and interest are differentially affected by replaying versus analyzing a happy life moment. *Journal of Positive Psychology, 4*, 14–20.

Vittersø, J., Søholt, Y., Hetland, A., Thorsen, I. A., & Røysamb, E. (2010). Was Hercules happy? Some answers from a functional model of human well-being. *Social Indicators Research, 95*, 1–18.

von Wright, G. H. (1963). *The varieties of goodness.* London, UK: Routledge.

Warholm, V., & Vittersø, J. (submitted). Good feelings and increased job performance: Pleasure and interest as predictors of skill improvement and work achievement. Manuscript submitted for publication.

Waterman, A. S. (2008). Reconsidering happiness: A eudaimonist's perspective. *Journal of Positive Psychology, 3*, 234–252.

Waterman, A. S., Schwartz, S. J., & Conti, R. (2008). The implications of two concepts of happiness (Hedonic enjoyment and eudaimonia) for the understanding of intrinsic motivation. *Journal of Happiness Studies, 9*, 41–79.

Wilson, T. D. (2002). *Strangers to ourselves: Discovering the adaptive unconscious.* Cambridge, MA: Belknap Press.

Wilson, T. D., & Dunn, E. W. (2004). Self-knowledge: Its limits, value, and potential for improvement. *Annual Review of Psychology, 55*, 493–518.

Zelazo, P. D., Moscovitch, M., & Thompson, W. (Eds.). (2007). *The Cambridge handbook of consciousness.* Cambridge, UK: Cambridge University Press.

# SECTION III

# PHILOSOPHICAL APPROACHES TO HAPPINESS

# CHAPTER 18

# INTRODUCTION TO PHILOSOPHICAL APPROACHES TO HAPPINESS

JAMES O. PAWELSKI

University of Pennsylvania, USA

HAPPINESS is one of the most central concerns of individual human experience and of collective human culture. It should come as no surprise, then, that it has been a perennial theme throughout the history of philosophical thought. For at least 2500 years, philosophers in the East and the West have paid considerable attention to the nature and cultivation of happiness. Most philosophers have agreed that happiness is an important part of human life, but they have disagreed widely on just what happiness is. Some have argued that happiness is pleasure, others that it is virtue, and still others that it is the fulfillment of human nature. Some have argued that happiness is our natural end; others, that it is something impossible for us to obtain. Some have argued that the pursuit of happiness should be our top priority; others, that we should not pursue happiness at all—and indeed that the pursuit of happiness is one of the greatest causes of human misery. With this long tradition of debate on the topic, philosophy has much to offer the contemporary study of happiness.

In addition to a rich collection of theories, definitions, and insights about happiness, philosophy also has much to contribute in the way of method. With its emphasis on clarity and precision, philosophical thinking can help us sort our way through the bewildering number of meanings happiness has taken on, and it may also help us develop more robust and satisfactory theories of happiness than are currently available.

This section on philosophical approaches to happiness is comprised of this introduction and seven other chapters. The following chapters are evenly balanced between historical and contemporary philosophical considerations, with the first chapters tending more toward historical topics and the later ones toward current philosophical analysis. Given the long history and conceptual complexity of philosophical investigations into happiness, this section can only hope, of course, to provide a sampling of some of this work.

In Chapter 19, Darrin M. McMahon writes on "The Pursuit of Happiness in History," presenting some key points in the intellectual history of the notion of happiness in Western culture. McMahon begins with an analysis of Ancient Greek perspectives on happiness, in which luck plays a key role. The happy person is one on whom fortune smiles. But given the reversibility of fortune, the truly happy person is one on whom fortune smiles over the course of the entire life span. With the rise of Classical Greek philosophy, McMahon points out, perspectives on happiness changed considerably. Socrates, Plato, Aristotle, and other philosophers argued that happiness is something noble souls can influence through their own efforts of philosophical reflection and virtuous activity. In the Christian era, attempts to achieve happiness on earth were often considered futile, or at best, reminders of our separation from the ultimate happiness that will be enjoyed only by the elect and only in the life to come. Later in the Christian era, thinkers like Aquinas saw earthly happiness as important in its own right but always as a very distant second to the joys of heaven. With the emphasis on reason and scientific investigation in the Enlightenment, perspectives on happiness shifted again, with the dominant view being that happiness is a right of all human beings, and that the proper kind of investigation and action will lead us to the full enjoyment of those rights. Indeed, in the United States Declaration of Independence, a document heavily influenced by the Enlightenment, the pursuit of happiness is identified as an inalienable right.

McMahon's analysis makes clear several important points about perspectives on happiness throughout history. First, these perspectives shift dramatically. What is taken for granted about happiness in one cultural context seems foreign in other cultural contexts. Second, because of these dramatic shifts, we must avoid the mistake of thinking that our current views on happiness necessarily hold true for cultural contexts different than our own. Third, these different perspectives can help us understand our own more deeply. Fourth, we must avoid mistakes others have made in the pursuit of happiness, mistakes like thinking that the attainment of happiness is easy, that we can force people to be happy, and that we can ignore paradoxes in the pursuit of happiness. Indeed, McMahon points out that, while there may be a dominant perspective in each cultural context, there are plenty of countervailing voices and paradoxical results of attempts to attain happiness. Perhaps the most obvious and the most tragic are the numerous post-Enlightenment revolutions that promised to bring happiness to the masses and instead brought widespread misery. McMahon concludes with a paradoxical claim from John Stuart Mill that perhaps the best way to achieve happiness is in the purposeful pursuit of something else.

While Chapter 19 concentrates on different cultural perspectives in Western thought, Chapter 20 shifts to an analysis of views of happiness in Eastern thought. Philip J. Ivanhoe writes about "Happiness in Early Chinese Thought," focusing particularly on Confucianism and Daoism. (For an analysis of happiness in Hindu and Buddhist thought, see Chapters 27, 28, and 29 in this volume.) Ivanhoe focuses on the views of two of the founding figures of these traditions: Kongzi (also known as Confucius) and Zhuangzi. Both the Confucians, as represented by Kongzi, and the Daoists, as represented by Zhuangzi, critique the common search for happiness through such things as wealth, power, and prestige. Instead, they teach that happiness consists in following the Dao (the "Way"), the patterns and processes of Nature. People who follow the Dao, argued Kongzi and Zhuangzi, will experience a state of joy that includes both a freedom from common human concerns, fears, and anxieties and a sense of being a part of something larger than the self. Ivanhoe observes that, although this latter point seems to involve a loss of the self, it is really only the loss of the narrow, small view we often have of the self. Much as these thinkers agree, Ivanhoe observes, there are also significant differences in their understanding of the Dao and of how it can best be followed. Kongzi tended to emphasize the importance of friends, family, and culture; whereas

Zhuangzi taught the importance of overcoming socialization in order to connect directly to what is most natural.

Chapter 21 explores the work of philosophers with much less sanguine views about happiness. In her piece entitled "Continental Contributions to our Understanding of Happiness and Suffering," Emmy Van Deurzen explores the views of continental philosophers such as Kierkegaard, Nietzsche, and Heidegger. For these thinkers, she argues, happiness is seen as an obstacle to the deeper goal of wisdom. To the extent that we try to focus on what is pleasant and easy, we ignore the realities of the human situation. It is only by facing up to these difficult realities and allowing ourselves to experience the attendant suffering that we can mature and become wise. This is certainly a devastating critique of forms of happiness that value unruffled pleasantness of experience over truth and wisdom, and it raises the question of how these continental philosophers might have responded to the more authentic, nuanced, and full-bodied conceptions of happiness explored in this volume.

In Chapter 22, Raymond Angelo Belliotti begins to answer this question by considering what he calls "worthwhile happiness." In his piece on "The Seductions of Happiness," he argues that Schopenhauer's critique of happiness—that it is an illusion whose pursuit is futile—is misguided, but that the popular understanding of happiness as "an accurate self-report of a person's predominantly positive state of mind" is overrated. Through a series of illustrative cases, Belliotti argues that happiness so conceived is often at odds with the good. For happiness to be worthwhile, he contends, it must be attained in the right way and connected properly to higher values. He then considers various philosophical perspectives on the connection between happiness and values, concluding that defining happiness as an accurate positive self-appraisal is the most effective of these approaches. Finally, he argues that even worthwhile happiness is not the greatest good, since a robustly meaningful, valuable life is even better than a life of worthwhile happiness. All things considered, Belliotti concludes, it is best to have a life of both worthwhile happiness and robust meaning, but if one can have only one or the other one should choose the life of robust meaning.

Daniel M. Haybron agrees with Belliotti on this point. In Chapter 23, "The Nature and Significance of Happiness," Haybron argues that virtue and right action are more important than happiness. He is quick to point out, however, that this does not mean happiness is unimportant. Happiness is pleasant, certainly, but more than that it helps determine how we will live our lives. The trajectory of our individual lives is heavily influenced by the level of happiness we experience, and the trajectory of nations and societies is guided by the dominant definitions of happiness they hold. Haybron distinguishes between the well-being sense of happiness (including hedonism, desire satisfaction, and objectivist accounts) and the psychological sense of happiness (including life satisfaction accounts and emotional state accounts), choosing to focus on the latter in this chapter. He critiques life satisfaction accounts of happiness on the grounds that they are dependent, not just on how one's life is going, but on the standards one uses to assess it. If I have high expectations for my life, then I may have lower life satisfaction than someone with lower expectations—even if my life is actually closer to my ideal than the other person's life is to theirs. So satisfaction with life may tell us less about one's life than about one's expectations for that life. Haybron explores emotional state views of happiness in some detail, arguing that they go far beyond one's mere feeling states to a condition of what he calls "psychic flourishing." Because of the complexity and nuances of different types of happiness, Haybron calls for more care in the measurement of happiness and implies that we may need more precise scales to measure these different types more accurately.

In Chapter 24 on "Philosophical methods in happiness research," Valerie Tiberius takes up the question of what philosophy can uniquely contribute to the investigation of happiness. She argues that although many questions about happiness (questions like how people define happiness) are in the domain of empirical researchers, normative questions about happiness (questions about how people should define happiness) cannot be answered through empirical methods alone and require the help of philosophers. She explores in detail philosophical methods that are important for addressing normative questions and creating adequate theories about happiness. (Where Haybron focuses on the psychological sense of happiness, Tiberius focuses on its well-being sense.) Tiberius describes in detail the method of "reflective equilibrium," which seeks to create theories that have both descriptive and normative adequacy by bringing into equilibrium ordinary judgments, putative normative principles, and background theories. In addition to discussing how this method is used in debates about theories of happiness, she also demonstrates the use of other specific methods as well, including thought experiments, intuition pumps, counter-examples, literary examples, and surveys. She concludes the chapter by emphasizing the importance of using philosophical and empirical methods in tandem, and thus of philosophers and psychologists continuing to work collaboratively in the ongoing study of happiness.

The final chapter in the section is "Happiness and its Opposites." In this chapter, I examine what happiness is by looking at what it is not. I point out that, although we typically think of happiness and unhappiness as opposites, empirical research is showing that they are not—at least not on the commonsense understanding of what opposites are. Different definitions of happiness have different opposites, but underlying all of them is the important insight that happiness is not simply the absence of unhappiness. This has important implications for the pursuit of happiness, since happiness involves both the presence of certain states or conditions and the absence of others. I examine the importance of these points for understanding philosophical advice on the pursuit of happiness, focusing on the works of Epictetus and Boethius. I also point out the need for more empirical study on the proper balance between the pursuit of happiness and the avoidance of unhappiness.

Much important work remains to be done in the philosophical investigation of happiness. With the rich tradition of philosophical debate on this topic for the last two-and-a-half millennia, there is an ongoing need for scholars to continue to analyze and understand that work. Such effort is important because it gives us access to the best ideas of thoughtful scholars in times and places other than our own. It is also important because it can help us avoid the dangers of presentism, a kind of temporal ethnocentrism that assumes our own views on happiness to be identical both to the views that have been held by others in the past and to those that will be held by others in the future. The avoidance of presentism is especially important when individuals and governments make decisions and adopt policies intended to increase the happiness of future generations. It is critical that this happiness be of the sort that those future generations will actually value. Related to this concern is the question of how the new knowledge being created about happiness will be applied in our own day. History is fraught with cases where knowledge was used for immoral purposes, and this is especially true in the domain of happiness. There will be much ethical work for philosophers to do to make sure, for example, that knowledge about happiness is not used to oppress others.

In addition to work in the history of philosophy, there is much yet to be done on the continued development and application of the philosophical methods explored in this section. Philosophical analysis can continue to help us disambiguate various definitions of happiness, render more precise the various dimensions of happiness studied as empirical constructs, develop more satisfactory theories of happiness, and generate suggestions for further empirical research.

Philosophers have many historical and methodological contributions to make to the study of happiness. Collaboration with other scholars coming from different traditions and using different types of methods will enable important progress in the continued study of a subject so central to human experience.

## Acknowledgments

I would like to thank Ilona Boniwell, Susan David, Daniel Haybron, and Valerie Tiberius for their suggestions on the overall plan for this section. I am especially indebted to Behdad Bozorgnia for help in making a variety of crucial editing decisions, and I am grateful to Xuan Gao for her keen eye in helping to prepare this section for publication.

# CHAPTER 19

# THE PURSUIT OF HAPPINESS IN HISTORY

## DARRIN M. MCMAHON
Florida State University, USA

If the pursuit of happiness is as old as history itself, then it is surely worth asking what the sources have to say about this perennial human quest. The time to do so is now. For at no other point in human history have so many men and women believed with such unquestioned certainty that they *should* be happy, that this is their inherent state and natural right. Thomas Jefferson's proud affirmation in the Declaration of Independence that the *pursuit of happiness* is a basic human entitlement—a truth at once God-given and self-evident—has slowly evolved into a much wider assumption about its capture and attainment. We deserve to be happy, Americans and many others now tend to believe, and we should be so.

In truth, the assumption that happiness is the natural human state is a relatively recent phenomenon—the product of a dramatic shift in human expectations carried out since the eighteenth century. Remembering that fact, and recalling, too, the received wisdom of some of the many historical observers who have pointed out the potential perils of pursuit may help us to view our own search for happiness in a slightly different light. In the end, I want to suggest, perhaps the best way to find happiness, paradoxically, may well be to look for something else.

## ANCIENT GREEK PHILOSOPHY OF HAPPINESS

But let us begin at the beginning—or at least with what scholars usually agree is the first work of history in the Western tradition, *The History* of Herodotus (1987), set down in Ancient Greece in the first half of the fifth century BCE. Croesus, the fabulously wealthy king of Lydia, has summoned before him the itinerant sage, Solon, lawgiver of Athens and a man who has traveled over much of the world in search of wisdom. The Lydian king lacks nothing, or so he believes, and he attempts to convince Solon of the fact, leading the wise Athenian round his stores of treasure so that he might marvel at their splendor. Ostensibly needing nothing, Croesus nonetheless reveals that he is in need, for he is overcome by a "longing" to know who is the happiest man in the world. Foolishly, Croesus believes that he himself might be that man, or that he might strive to become him.

Solon's wisdom, however, and the succession of distinctly unhappy events that follow, succeed in dispelling this illusion. When Solon observes cautiously that the "divine is altogether jealous and prone to trouble us" (Herodotus, 1987, p. 47), adding that in the span of a human life "there is much to see that one would rather not see and much to suffer likewise" Croesus is unmoved. And when Solon points out further that because of the unpredictability of human affairs, he cannot yet say if Croesus is, or will ever be, happy, for "man is entirely what befalls him," the proud Lydian is openly contemptuous, dismissing Solon as "assuredly a stupid man."

No sooner has he done so than Croesus receives a great visitation of evil. His son is killed in a freak hunting accident, Croesus himself misinterprets an oracle at Delphi and is lured into a disastrous war, and his kingdom is destroyed by invading Persian armies. Only as a captive, facing imminent death atop a funeral pyre whose flames lick at his feet, does Croesus realize the wisdom of Solon's words and the folly of his own presumption. "No one who lives is happy," he exclaims, calling out his own fate for the benefit of all who "are in their own eyes happy" (Herodotus, 1987, p. 74).

Now it may seem that this tragic tale of divine retribution and frustrated human aims is a particularly morbid introduction to history—any history—let alone a history of happiness. But in an era of inflated expectations, it is worth listening to precisely this sort of wisdom. For Solon's message that the relentless pursuit of happiness threatens always to subvert itself is one that resonates again and again.

Consider the very word that Herodotus (1987), employs to describe the elusive thing that his tragic hero seeks. In truth, Herodotus employs several terms—among them, the ancient Greek *olbios*, *eutychia*, and *eudaimon*,—which all, like their close cousin *makarios*, signify good fortune and blessedness, divine favor and prosperity. But it is above all *eudaimon*, and the noun *eudaimonia* (happiness) that features most prominently in Herodotus's work. In the succeeding 100 years it would emerge as an absolutely critical term in the lexicon of Greek philosophy.

Comprised of the Greek *eu* (good) and *daimon* (god, spirit, demon), *eudaimonia* contains within it a notion of fortune, for to have a good *daimon* on your side, a guiding spirit, is to be lucky. It also possesses a notion of divinity, for a *daimon* is an emissary of the gods, a personal spirit who watches over each of us, acting invisibly on the Olympians' behalf. But what is most interesting is that this *daimon* is an occult power, a hidden, spiritual force that drives human beings forward, where no specific agent can be named. It is this mysterious quality that helps account for that unpredictable "something" that impels Croesus along, driving him in pursuit of he knows not what. For though to have a good *daimon* means to be carried in the direction of the divine, to have a bad *daimon*—a *dysdaimon*—is to be turned aside, led astray, or countered by another. The gods, alas, are as capricious as mortals, as that unhappy wife of Shakespeare's Othello, Desdemona, learns to her dismay. Her name is simply a variation on the Greek word for unhappy, *dysdaimon*, as Shakespeare certainly knew. He was probably also aware that *daimon* is the Greek root of the modern word "demon," a fiend or an evil spirit who haunts and threatens us, who always has the power to do us wrong (Burkert, 1977/1985, p. 180).

Something of that vaguely sinister connotation lurks in *eudaimonia* itself. Thus, when Croesus asks, "Is the happiness (*eudaimonia*) that is mine so entirely set at naught by you…?"

(Herodotus, 1987, pp. 46–47). Solon responds that although Croesus's life may seem good now, it is far too early to predict where his *daimon* will finally lead him. In an uncertain world, life is unpredictable, less something to be made than to be endured. Only those who do so successfully—until the very end—can be deemed fortunate, blessed, happy.

Historians of Greek philosophy will point out that this emphasis on the chance or unpredictable nature of human affairs—an emphasis so central to the entire tradition of Greek Tragedy—was challenged in the centuries that followed (Nussbaum, 1994). From Socrates, Plato, and Aristotle in the 4th and 5th-centuries BC to the Epicureans and Stoics who enjoyed such favor throughout the Mediterranean world in the aftermath of the conquests of Alexander, lovers of wisdom and their devotees declared happiness (*eudaimonia*) to be the final aim of philosophical reflection and virtuous activity (Annas, 1993). To discover the secret of the flourishing life became for these men the *summum bonum*, the highest good, one that they were by no means willing to leave entirely to chance. On the contrary, they took as their point of departure the belief that human beings could exercise considerable control over the fate of their lives by living virtuously. Thus does Aristotle (1985), declare famously that happiness "is an activity of the soul expressing virtue" (p. 22). To the extent that we can learn to be good, he believed, we can learn to be happy.

All this is without question; it is also inspiring. Yet it would be wrong to assume that the Classical philosophers' stress on human virtue succeeded in banishing the demons from *eudaimonia*. "Someone might possess virtue," Aristotle (1985), himself concedes, but still "suffer the worst evils and misfortunes" (p. 7–8). He calls this the (bad) "luck of Priam," in reference to that unfortunate father of Hector in Homer's *Iliad*, who is forced like Croesus to endure the death of his beloved son and the destruction of his kingdom through no real fault of his own. To call such a person happy would be perverse, Aristotle insists, thereby acknowledging our inability to eradicate completely the uncertainty bound up with the pursuit of our highest end.

But Aristotle's reservations about the pursuit of happiness run deeper than this. Even if the virtuous man succeeds in running life's gauntlet without serious misfortune, he must deal with the paradoxical fact that the closer he comes to his end, the more cause he will have to regret what passes him by. "The more he has every virtue and the happier he is, the more pain he will feel at the prospect of death. For this sort of person, more than anyone, finds it worth while to be alive, and is knowingly deprived of the greatest goods, and this is painful" (Aristotle, 1985, p. 45). As the happiness of the happy man increases, so does his suffering at its loss.

Aristotle (1985), like the Stoics, counsels bravery in the face of this contradiction—recommending in effect that the virtuous man look death in the eye, grin, and bear it. We may find this admirable advice, but that it was not entirely satisfying to the denizens of antiquity is confirmed by the tremendous success of the next great philosophy of happiness to sweep the ancient world: Christianity. In this new faith, the paradoxes of pursuit were only further multiplied.

# Christianity's Philosophy of Happiness

"Blessed are those who mourn," (Matthew 5:4), we read in the Gospel of Matthew in the New King James Translation, or "Happy are those who are persecuted for righteousness's sake"

(Matthew 5:10–11). Similarly shocking to our received assumptions are the beatitudes of Luke. "Happy are you when people hate you, and when they exclude you, revile you …" (Luke 67:22–24). Those who weep are apparently "happy," like those who are hungry or are poor.

Admittedly, the critical word in question here is no longer *eudaimon*, but the Greek term *makarios*. Frequently rendered in English as "blessed," *makarios*, however, may just as validly be translated as "happy," as in fact it is in some other versions of the Bible. Many Greek authors, including Aristotle and Plato, used the two words (*eudaimon* and *makarios*) interchangeably. But this is not to deny that the Evangelists themselves meant something very different from what their Classical forebears intended by either term. Indeed, in some ways, their meaning is precisely the opposite. For if one can be genuinely "happy" or "blessed," in this new Christian sense, while mourning, or weeping, or starving—happy, in a manner of speaking, while sad—does it not follow that those who are "happy" in a more conventional sense are quite possibly flirting with the ultimate sorrow? The prosperous, the well-fed, those who feel good and are quick to laugh should beware, at the very least, that their earthly rejoicing is dangerously premature: God may well have other plans in store for them. Meanwhile, those who suffer unjustly in this world may take heart. "Now is your time of grief," Christ tells his disciples in the Gospel of John, "but I will see you again and you will rejoice, and no one will take away your joy" (John 16:22).

In one sense, this was simply the re-assertion of the wisdom of the tragic tradition. We should call no man happy until he is dead, Christians might legitimately claim, because God, who through his Providence controls both fate and fortune, may quickly bring our earthly striving to naught. As the monk in that classic account of Christian pilgrimage, Chaucer's *Canterbury Tales* reminds his fellow travelers as late as the fourteenth century:

> And thus does Fortune's wheel turn treacherously
> And out of happiness bring men to sorrow.
> (McMahon, 2006, p. 496)

The same admonition is repeated throughout the Middle Ages and the early Renaissance, the very period that gave rise to the modern words for "happiness" in the principal Indo-European languages (McMahon, 2006, pp. 136–137). It is hardly surprising that every one of these words—from the German *Glück* to the French *bonheur*—is linguistically related to good fortune or luck, what the Old English called "hap." Well after the coming of Christ, the earthly variety of "happiness" continued to depend on what *happened* to us, and this, good Christians knew, was ever prone, like Fortune's wheel, to take a turn for the worse.

But if in this respect the Christian world made a place for the older tragic understanding of happiness as divine fortune or good luck, it should also be clear that it considerably altered the meaning of the phrase "call no man happy until he is dead." Strictly speaking, happiness in the Christian conception *was* death (McMahon, 2006, p. 106). No longer considered a boundary marking off the conclusion of a life well lived, death was treated as a gateway that led from the inescapable striving and suffering of our earthly pilgrimage to the conclusion and rest of endless ecstasy, rapture, and bliss. Nothing, nothing at all, will be lacking in death's everlasting life, Saint Thomas Aquinas (1988), affirms typically in the *Summa Against the Gentiles*, for "in that final happiness every human desire will be fulfilled" (p. 9). In heaven, it seems, the saints will "inebriated" by the plenty of God's house, and shall drink of the "torrent" of God's pleasure. Quite literally, the saved will get drunk on God.

For all who suffer from the thirst of human dissatisfaction, this was—and remains—an inspiring prospect, providing what St Augustine (1984), termed the "happiness of hope." But as he fully appreciated, this same hope necessarily cast a dark shadow on the prospects for happiness on earth. If perfect happiness could only come in death by the grace of God, then it followed that the struggle to obtain earthly happiness was in vain. Pouring scorn on "all these [pagan] philosophers [who] have wished, with amazing folly, to be happy here on earth and to achieve bliss by their own efforts" (p. 852), Augustine (1984), argued at length in the *City of God* that "true happiness" was "unattainable in our present life." Due to the lasting consequences of original sin, we are condemned to suffer on earth—to yearn and long for a satisfaction that we can never as mere mortals know.

Adding yet another paradox to this already paradoxical history, Augustine (trans. 1984), and his Christian brethren thus imagined the pursuit of happiness as a form of punishment, a continual, nagging reminder of our banishment from the Garden of Eden and the consequent human inability to live contentedly without God's grace. According to this perspective, every time we long for happiness, we remind ourselves of our unworthiness and inability to attain it on our own, a vicious cycle whose necessary byproduct was guilt.

Which is not to suggest that there were no counter-veiling impulses in the Christian tradition. The antinomian ecstasies of the early messianic communities, who believed, with Matthew, that the kingdom of God was at hand, certainly had cause for rejoicing. And it is equally true that the Jewish tradition had long acknowledged a healthy place for the enjoyment of God's earth, giving Christian interpreters sunny precedents for their surmise (Tirosh-Samuelson, 2003). Similarly, St Francis observed cheerfully that "It is not right for the servant of God to show sadness and a dismal face" (Smith, 2001, p. 132). And both Luther and Calvin would later emphasize that happiness and good cheer may be viewed as the fruit of justification, a sign of the presence of God's redeeming grace (McMahon, 2006, pp. 164–175).

# Philosophy of Happiness in the Enlightenment

All this underscores the rather straightforward point that Christianity, like any religious tradition, is necessarily replete with rival tendencies and competing claims. Yet it is also fairly easy to show that this same tradition's more general misgivings about happiness succeeded in dampening human expectations for some time. It was only in the seventeenth century—at the dawn of the period that we now call the Enlightenment—that men and women in the West dared to think of happiness as something more than a divine gift or otherworldly reward, less fortuitous than fortune, less exalted than a millenarian dream (McMahon, 2006, p. 177). In the Enlightenment, for the first time in human history, comparatively large numbers of men and women were exposed to the novel prospect that they might not have to suffer as an unfailing law of the universe, that they could—and should—expect happiness in the form of good feeling and pleasure as a right of life.

The causes of this momentous transformation range from developments within the Christian tradition that gave greater sanction to earthly enjoyment and de-emphasized the impact of original sin; to new secular attitudes regarding the pleasures of pleasure; to the birth of consumer cultures able to offer an ever-expanding array of luxuries to ever-widening circles (McMahon, 2006, p. 205). Fascinating in their own right, these developments must cede their place in the present discussion, however, to what they wrought. For freed to think of happiness as something other than the superior striving of the happy few, men and women granted happiness on earth the privileged place they had once afforded to happiness hereafter. "Paradise is where I am," Voltaire (1736/2003), declared with his characteristically provocative wit in the first line of his 1736 poem "Le Mondain" (p. 303). By the century's end, his *bon mot* was more than just a happy phrase. Whereas, scarcely a century before, rulers had been enjoined to lead in the service of the faith and morals of their subjects—to lead in the service of salvation—they were now being asked to serve a different lord. "Happiness is in truth the only object of legislation of intrinsic value," the English utilitarian Joseph Priestley (Porter, 2000, p. 204), observed at the end of the eighteenth century, echoing Voltaire's own claim in a letter of 1729 that "the great and only concern is to be happy" (Craveri, 2005, p. 258). From the greatest happiness to the greatest number, this was the voice of a new age.

There was much to applaud in this new creed. If human beings were not required to look shamefacedly on enjoyment, they were increasingly free to seek their pleasures where they could. To dance, to sing, to enjoy our food, to revel in our bodies and the company of others—in short, to delight in a world of our own making—was not to defy God's will but to live as nature intended. This was our earthly purpose. Bringing with it a whole new range of attitudes that clashed with venerable taboos, the new bearing on happiness worked to overturn impediments to sexual pleasure, material prosperity, self-interest, and simple delight for simply standing in the way. At the same time, defenders of happiness focused their energy on "unnatural" barriers to our natural end. They assailed injustice and inhumanity, prejudice and superstition, barbarism and false belief for barring the way of the human pursuit (McMahon, 2006, p. 209). To the present day that same set of convictions remains at the heart of our closest-held humanitarian assumptions: that suffering is wrong and that it should be relieved wherever possible; that the enjoyment of life is, or ought to be, a basic human entitlement.

The liberating potential of this new creed notwithstanding, the belief that happiness was our natural condition entailed a vicious corollary. For if we *ought* to be happy, didn't it follow that when we were not, there was something wrong? For centuries Christianity had cast a pall over the prospect of happiness on earth, provoking guilt at the thought of worldly delight. But it also justified and made sense of human suffering and dissatisfaction. The long-term impact of the Enlightenment had precisely the opposite effect, creating guilt as a consequence of the failure to be happy, guilt at feeling sadness and pain (McMahon, 2006, p. 250).

It may well be that it is only now—when all must smile for the camera and sadness is treated as a disease—that human beings are experiencing the full force of this development. But even in the eighteenth century, keen observers were aware that the pursuit of happiness might have a dark side. "The time is already come," Samuel Johnson remarked in 1759, "when none are wretched but by their own fault" (1985, p. 87). If happiness were our natural condition, and if neither original sin nor the mystery of grace, the movement of the stars nor the caprice of fortune controlled our fate, then the failure to be happy would be just that—failure.

Was it really so clear, Johnson (1759/1985) wondered, that human beings were intended to be happy, and that they could make themselves so? The supposition itself, he understood, involved an assumption—an article of faith—about the purpose of human existence, about man's final destiny and end. And if this supposition were wrong, as he well believed, then it placed on human beings an awful burden: a responsibility that they could never entirely fulfill. "What ... is to be expected from our pursuit of happiness," one of his characters asks in his masterpiece, *Rassellas*, "when we find the state of life to be such, that happiness itself is the cause of misery?" (Johnson, 1759/1985, pp. 116–117). It was a disconcerting question, and it haunted others of the age. After the untimely death of his mistress, Madame de Châtelet, and the terrible shock of the Lisbon earthquake of 1755, which wiped out thousands in a day, Voltaire himself came to doubt his earlier optimism. In response, he penned his famous *Candide*, mocking the optimistic faith that "all is for the best in the best of all possible worlds." Jean-Jacques Rousseau (1782/1979b), shared his reservations. "I doubt whether any of us knows the meaning of lasting happiness" (p. 88), he despaired after a lifetime of pursuit, confirming a suspicion he had voiced earlier in his career: "Happiness leaves us, or we leave it" (Rousseau, 1762/1979a, p. 447).

Unlike Johnson, however, and unlike Voltaire, Rousseau refused to leave the matter at that. Child of the Enlightenment that he was in part, he remained adamant in his faith that happiness must be our natural end. Perhaps long ago, in a primitive state of nature, he mused, when our needs and faculties coexisted in harmony as they should, human beings were readily content. But that equilibrium had been upset long ago, with the balance further swayed in the direction of discontent by forces central to life as it was lived in the modern world. Presenting us with ever-greater possibilities and ever-expanding needs, modern commercial societies multiplied human desires, which ranged steadily ahead of our ability to fulfill them, creating envy and dissatisfaction in their wake. And so, Rousseau concluded, if human nature as constituted in the modern world rendered us incapable of achieving happiness, the world and human nature would have to be changed. "As soon as man's needs exceed his faculties and the objects of his desire expand and multiply, he must either remain eternally unhappy or seek a new form of being from which he can draw the resources he no longer finds in himself" (Rousseau, 1782/1994, Vol. 4, p. 82). To do that required radically altering the structure of society.

This was the task Rousseau set himself in his most famous work, *The Social Contract*, which proposed, in an infamous line, that human beings could be "forced to be free." To his credit, Rousseau never made the same claim about happiness, and in fact explicitly states elsewhere that "there is no government that can force the Citizens to live happily; the best is one that puts them in a condition to be happy if they are reasonable" (Rousseau, 1782/1994, Vol. 4, p. 41). Such qualifications, however, went unheeded. Distorting Rousseau's original intentions, men and women at the time of the French Revolution sought to bring his new man and society into being—with terrible results. As France and much of Europe reeled from war and the ghastly slaughter of the Terror, the Jacobin leader Saint-Just declared in the Spring of 1794 that happiness was "a new idea in Europe" (Saint-Just, 1984, p. 715). His colleague and fellow "terrorist," Joseph Marie Lequinio, went further, seeing fit to utter the words that Rousseau himself had eschewed. In a secular sermon delivered in the fall of 1793, Lequinio ended with a chilling invocation. "May the sacred love of the fatherland ... force every individual to take the only road that can lead them to the end they propose— the end of happiness" (Lequinio, 1793, p. 18–19). That "road," of course, was the road of the revolution; the "force" was provided by the guillotine; and the "end" was stated clearly in the first article of the Jacobin constitution: "the goal of society is common happiness" (McMahon, 2006, p. 261).

It is no exaggeration to say that this very same revolutionary promise—to remake human beings and their world in the service of happiness—lies behind every one of the terrible experiments in social engineering that have brought such misery to the post-Enlightenment world. The terrible history of these ventures is well known to us today. And perhaps, in the West at least, we can feel some confidence that this knowledge will help guard against similar experiments in the immediate future. To force human beings to be happy, it now seems clear, is no more practicable than to force them to be free.

## Pursuit of Happiness in the United States of America

But what of that other revolutionary experiment—and its liberal promise of freedom, the freedom to pursue happiness anyway we choose? Jefferson, it is worth stressing, placed the emphasis on the *pursuit* of happiness in the founding document of the United States not its attainment—and he was enough of a realist to doubt whether we could ever firmly grasp so slippery a thing. As his collaborator Benjamin Franklin is said to have observed: "The constitution only gives you the right to pursue happiness. You have to catch it yourself." The lines are undoubtedly apocryphal—for one thing, Franklin well knew that it was the Declaration, and not the Constitution, that conferred this right. But the sentiment itself is an apt approximation of the intent of the Founding Fathers. Governments must limit themselves to providing the basic conditions for the pursuit of happiness—civil liberties, peace and security, the protection of private property, the rule of law—and allow individuals to do the rest for themselves.

It was, and remains, a noble vision. But it is worth dwelling a little longer on just what this pursuit of happiness entailed. And here we should pause to consider the neglected term: pursuit. As the critic and historian Gary Wills (2002, p. 245) has emphasized, the word had a much harder meaning in the eighteenth-century than it does today, retaining a close link with its cognates, "prosecute" and "persecute." Thus, Samuel Johnson (1755) listed the word in his eighteenth-century *A Dictionary of the English Language* as:

> To Pursue... 1. To chase; to follow in hostility.
> Pursuit... 1. The act of following with hostile intention.

If one thinks of pursuing happiness as one pursues a fugitive (and indeed in Scottish law, criminal prosecutors were called "pursuers," a usage with which Jefferson was familiar), the "pursuit of happiness" takes on a somewhat different inflection. To pursue, in this sense, is to follow with hostile intention, chasing down a renegade wherever he might lead us, and growing ever-more frustrated as the sweat forms on our brow. Like the *daimon* who lurks in *eudaimonia*, happiness may lead us high and low, and often astray. And when it does, it is only natural to begin to resent the thing that continually eludes us.

Whether Jefferson himself and the other Founding Fathers made such conscious associations is far from clear. But it is hardly surprising to find perceptive observers who arrived at similar reflections. Think of Tocqueville who expressed such astonishment at the impatience and agitation of Americans. "No one could work harder to be happy," (Tocqueville, 1840/1988, Vol. 1, p. 243) he observed in *Democracy in America*, marveling repeatedly at the ceaseless, restless energy they expend in search of a better life. Rushing from one thing to the next, an American will travel hundreds of miles in a day. He will build a house in which to pass his old age and then sell it before the roof is on. He will continually change paths "for fear of missing the shortest cut leading to happiness" (Tocqueville, 1840/1988, Vol. 1, p. 243). Finally, though:

> Death steps in … and stops him before he has grown tired of this futile pursuit of that complete felicity which always escapes him. (Tocqueville, 1840/1988, Vol. 2, p. 536–537)

In dogged pursuit until the end, the restless American is brought up short only by death. And that, Tocqueville (1840/1988), concluded, in reference to America's related quest for an ever-elusive equality was "the reason for the strange melancholy often haunting inhabitants of democracies in the midst of abundance, and of that disgust with life sometimes gripping them in calm and easy circumstances" (Vol. 2, p. 538).

## John Stuart Mill's Insight

As the last line implies, Tocqueville (1840/1988) intended his reflections as a commentary not only on the specific case of America, but on liberal democracy more generally, which he deemed rightly was the inevitable wave of the future. It is striking, then, that his correspondent and contemporary, the equally astute John Stuart Mill, observed a similar phenomenon in that other great liberal empire of the nineteenth century, Great Britain. Indeed, Mill even observed the phenomenon in himself. Raised to be an apostle of the philosophy of his father's friend, Jeremy Bentham, the proponent of "felicific calculus" and the "greatest happiness of the greatest number," the young Mill made the attainment of happiness his life's work. And yet in his early manhood, having suffered a debilitating breakdown and an extended bout of depression, he hit upon a strange insight. As he confessed late in life in his gripping *Autobiography*:

> I now thought that this end [happiness] was only to be attained by not making it the direct end. Those only are happy (I thought) who have their minds fixed on some object other than their own happiness; on the happiness of others, on the improvement of mankind, even on some art or pursuit, followed not as a means, but as itself an ideal end. Aiming thus at something else, they find happiness by the way … Ask yourself whether you are happy, and you cease to be so. The only chance is to treat, not happiness, but some end external to it, as the purpose of life … This theory now became the basis of my philosophy of life. (Mill, 1873/1989, pp. 117–118)

This was a stunning avowal for one who continued throughout his life to hold happiness in the highest esteem. The way to reach it, he grasped, was to search for something else. Those who would capture happiness must pursue other things.

What are we to make of such talk from the vantage point of the early twenty-first century? It may be tempting to dismiss Mill's (1873/1989) reflections, along with those of many of the other thinkers examined here, as the abstractions of men of thought—fine *theories*, perhaps, but hardly grounded in solid research. And yet it is interesting to note that at least some solid research has helped to bear out Mill's reflections, echoing the wisdom of the ages that appears to suggest that those who pursue happiness directly should watch their step. In his well-known studies of the experience of "flow," the psychologist Mihaly Csikszentmihalyi (1990) has found that those engaged in purposeful, challenging activity, pursued for its own sake, are apt to live more satisfying—more satisfied—lives than those who don't, and that their reported levels of subjective well being reflect this fact. The work of many other positive psychologists would seem to confirm such findings. Csikszentmihalyi (1990) himself even goes so far as to invoke Mill directly, arguing that "we cannot reach happiness by consciously searching for it," (p. 2) but only indirectly, by the by.

Devoting ourselves to activities that we ourselves deem meaningful is of course a long way from the Classical belief that we can reach a god-like happiness by treading a single path of virtue. It falls short, too, of Mill's own unrealized dream that some other highest end—the promotion of liberty, say, or service to society—might carry us to happiness collectively. Nor will the pursuit of purposeful activity do much to surpass the limitations of our genes. This is a less exalted path, a round-about way, one that makes no claims to offer up good feeling and ready delight in the form of instant gratification—or in a pill. A long-term journey, the pursuit of purposeful activity is almost always difficult, requiring planning, sacrifice, and dedication to an end deemed worthy of devotion in and of itself.

This may not be a sensational revelation—the stuff of best-seller lists or "seven easy steps." But in an age of inflated expectations, fed by false promises and excessive claims, it is probably worth heeding some tempered advice. We could do worse than to take counsel from a man who also felt the pull of the promise of paradise on earth, but who then thought better of the prospect. When Voltaire's hero, Candide, returns from circling the globe, wiser but no more happy than when he began, he concludes simply that "we must cultivate our garden." Those seeking happiness—or something like it—in the twenty-first century, could do worse than to take up the hoe.

## References

Annas, J. (1993). *The morality of happiness*. New York, NY: Oxford University Press.

Aquinas, T. (1988). Summa contra gentiles. In P. E. Sigmund (Ed. & Trans.), *St. Thomas Aquinas on politics and ethics*. New York, NY: Norton. (Original work written 1258–1264).

Aristotle. (1985). *Nichomachean ethics*. (T. Irwin, Trans.). Indianapolis, IN: Hackett. (Original work written fourth century BCE.).

Augustine. (1984). *Concerning the city of God against the Pagans*. (H. Bettonson, Trans.). London, UK: Penguin Books. (Original work written circa 412–425).

Burkert, W. (1985). *Greek religion*. (J. Raffan, Trans.). Cambridge, MA: Harvard University Press. (Original work published 1977).

Craveri, B. (2005). *The age of conversation*. (T. Wangh, Trans.). New York, NY: New York Review of Books.

Csikszentmihalyi, M. (1990). *Flow: The psychology of optimal experience*. New York, NY: Harper & Row.

Herodotus. (1987). *History*. (D. Grene, Trans.). Chicago, IL: University of Chicago Press. (Original work written circa 440 BCE.).

Johnson, S. (1755). *A dictionary of the English language*. London, UK: Strahan.

Johnson, S. (1985). *The history of Rasselas, prince of Abissinia*. (D. J. Enright, Ed.). London, UK: Penguin Books. (Original work published 1759).

Lequinio, J.-M. (1793). *Du bonheur* [On happiness] Archives National F17 A1003, plaq. 3, no. 1263.

McMahon, D. M. (2006). *Happiness: A history*. New York, NY: Atlantic Monthly Press.

Mill, J. S. (1989). *Autobiography*. (J. M. Robson, Ed.). London, UK: Penguin Books. (Original work published 1873).

Nussbaum, M. (1994). *The therapy of desire: Theory and practice in Hellenistic ethics*. Princeton, NJ: Princeton University Press.

Porter, R. (2000). *Creation of the modern world: The untold story of the British enlightenment*. New York, NY: Norton.

Rousseau, J.-J. (1979a). *Emile*. (A. Bloom, Trans.). New York, NY: Basic Books. (Original work published 1762).

Rousseau, J.-J. (1979b). *Reveries of a solitary walker*. (P. France, Trans.). New York, NY: Penguin Books. (Original work published 1782).

Rousseau, J.-J. (1994). *The collected writings of Rousseau*. (J. R. Bush, R. D. Masters, & C. Kelley, Eds.; R. D. Masters & C. Kelly, Trans.). Hanover, NH: University Press of New England. (Original work published 1782).

Saint-Just, L. de. (1984). *Oeuvres completes de Saint-Just*. [The complete works of Saint-Just] (M. Duval, Ed.). Paris: Editions Gérard Lebovici.

Smith, L. (2001). Heavenly bliss and earthly delight. In S. McCready (Ed.), *Discovery of happiness* (pp. 116–136). London, UK: MQ Publications.

Tirosh-Samuelson, H. (2003). *Happiness in premodern Juadaism: Virtue, knowledge, and wellbeing*. Cincinnati, OH: Hebrew Union College Press.

Tocqueville, A. de. (1988). *Democracy in America* (J. P. Mayer, Ed.; G. Lawrence, Trans.). New York, NY: Harper Perennial. (Original work published 1840).

Voltaire, F. (2003). Le mondain [Man of the world]. In T. Besterman & W. H. Barber (Eds.), *The complete works of Voltaire. 16, Writings of 1736* (pp. 295–303). Oxford, UK: Voltaire foundation. (Original work published 1736).

Wills, G. (2002). *Inventing America: Jefferson's Declaration of Independence*. New York, NY: Mariner Books.

# CHAPTER 20

# HAPPINESS IN EARLY CHINESE THOUGHT

PHILIP J. IVANHOE

City University of Hong Kong, Hong Kong

> Formerly, when we studied with Zhou Dunyi, he always told us to look for passages that described the joy of Yanzi and Kongzi in order to discover what it was they took joy in.
>
> (H. Cheng & Y. Cheng, 1978)
>
> See how the little fish come forth and swim about at ease—this is the joy of fish!
>
> (Zhuangzi)

CONFUCIANISM and Daoism have had a profound and enduring influence on Chinese culture and every other culture in East Asia; their influence today is nothing less than global.[1] This essay presents the ideas of two of the founding figures of these traditions: Kongzi or "Confucius" (551–479 BCE) and Zhuangzi (c.399–295 BCE) in regard to their conceptions of the ideal life—what early Greek thinkers called *eudaimonia*. Eudaimonia often is translated "happiness," though in some respects this is unfortunate. In early philosophical writings, it most often means a sense of being blessed or favored by the gods, and while such a sense can give rise to what we might call a "happy" or satisfying psychological state, it is surely different from and more than most kinds of happy psychological states (McMahon, 2006, pp. 3–4, 68, etc.; Nussbaum, 1986, pp. 329–33). Among other things, it requires not just a feeling but a feeling grounded in a fairly complex judgment about how one's life is going, that one's life is good and fortunate not just on this or that occasion but *as a life*. The idea that *eudaimonia* implies one's life is going well inspires another common translation of the term: "flourishing." We shall follow convention by referring to Daoist and Confucian concern with "happiness" but mean by "happiness" a sense that one's life is going well (i.e., one is *flourishing*), as it should, and in accord with Heavenly patterns and processes. Daoists and Confucians agree that those who succeed in living such lives experience a special feeling of satisfaction, ease,

---

[1] For an introduction to these traditions and individual thinkers, see Schwartz (1985) and Graham (1989).

and delight or "joy" (*le* 樂); we will spend considerable time describing this feeling and what it connotes.[2]

## General Structure of Kongzi's and Zhuangzi's Views on Happiness

While Kongzi and Zhuangzi both maintain that happiness fulfills an objective description of the good life, they also believe that those who attain this ideal experience a special and valuable sense of satisfaction, fulfillment, and joy as part of the good life they lead. Neither understood such joy as just a feeling; it is an emotional state, in the sense that it involves rather complex cognitions and beliefs. This does not mean that complex cognitions and beliefs must be occurrant states of mind in order to experience such joy. As will be clear from the discussion that follows, such self-conscious reflection is by no means necessary and often can interfere or block the spontaneous experience of joy. What it does mean is that both Kongzi and Zhuangzi describe the pursuit of happiness in such terms and those who set out to realize happiness must at least begin by seeing this quest and its aim in such terms. For example, there is Kongzi's description of his own spiritual biography in *Analects* 2.4 or Cook Ding's account of how he learned to carve oxen in chapter three of the *Zhuangzi*. Nevertheless, as we shall see, Kongzi and Zhuangzi have very different views about the role such cognitions and beliefs play in the production of happiness and about the degree to which our ability to form such cognitions and beliefs is innate or acquired. They agree that happiness is not something one simply can decide upon for oneself; while in some important respects happiness is particular and context-sensitive it is not merely in the eye of the beholder; it is something about which one can be right or wrong, and most people get it wrong. This last point is particularly important. Many of the things they say about happiness focus on the folly, harm, and misery common misconceptions of happiness produce and the importance, for both self and others, of having the right view in this regard.

Kongzi and Zhuangzi both reject important aspects of their contemporary cultures; to a significant degree, they are social critics—though Zhuangzi's criticisms seem to extend to *any* form of social organization. This is not to say their projects are exclusively or primarily negative; both present a positive, alternative account of happiness. They are quite clear about the source and nature of happiness: happiness lies in following the "Way" (*Dao* 道), and a life lived in harmony with the Dao or Way results in a range of special and highly valued goods. Though they differ in their respective conceptions of the Dao and what a life in accord with it is like, they share a reliance on a conception of the Dao and a related ideal form of life to support both their ethical claims and their views about happiness. They believe that the forms of life they advocate hold the promise of certain highly desirable advantages, which are similar in their general features. On the one hand, a life in harmony with the Dao offers a sense of being free from a range of common human concerns, fears, and anxieties; on the

---

[2] Kongzi often described his conception of happiness in terms of the character 樂. Zhuangzi does not use the character as often but it does appear in important passages concerning happiness, such as the second epigraph to this essay. Whenever the English word "joy" appears in this essay as part of a quotation from a Chinese text, it is always a translation of the Chinese character *le* 樂.

other hand, it produces a sense of being part of something more grand and significant than any individual project or pleasure could possibly be.

This latter feature of the good life entails certain consequences that often have been misunderstood and as a result seem paradoxical or even unappealing. For example, Kongzi and Zhuangzi believe that true happiness requires one to recognize, value, and to some extent give oneself over to the patterns, processes, and rhythms of a certain kind of life: a life that hooks one up with the greater and deeper patterns, processes, and rhythms of the Dao. In other words, according with the Dao requires one, to some extent, to lose oneself in a form of life, and at first it seems odd to regard a *loss* of myself as the way to fulfill and *make myself happy*. This implication only appears paradoxical, because what they recommend is not properly thought of as a loss of the self per se, but the shedding of a narrow and overly self-centered conception of oneself.

Kongzi and Zhuangzi each describes a way to a grander, more comprehensive conception of the self that offers a profound and reliable way to happiness and is itself an important constituent of being happy. Those who are in harmony with the Dao experience a sense of *metaphysical comfort* (Ivanhoe, 2010a); they feel a profound and special sense of security, peace, and ease as part of and party to powers much greater and grander than anything one could muster on one's own. Such metaphysical comfort can but does not necessarily commit one to belief in a supernatural order, but, this point aside, it does bear significant similarities to William James' notion of "religious happiness" or "intimacy" (Slater, 2009, pp. 126–42). According with these powers opens new and unique sources of satisfaction and a unique sense of joy. In these ways, their conceptions of happiness are akin to eudaimonia's sense of being favored by the gods and indeed both Kongzi and Zhuangzi claim that the Way they advocate and value connects one with Heaven (*tian* 天). While neither conceives of Heaven as a personal deity or an entity that grants anything resembling grace, Kongzi certainly did view Heaven as conscious, intentional, and concerned with human welfare, and Zhuangzi did regard natural or Heavenly patterns and processes as normative and expressed a kind of faith in the Dao (Carr & Ivanhoe, 2010; Ivanhoe, 2007a, pp. 211–20). To varying degrees, though, the Confucian and Daoist views differ from most Western conceptions of *eudaimonia* in that both see a proper sense of self and satisfaction as more intimately and broadly connected with everyday aspects of the world. Instead of a sense of enjoying the personal good fortune of a god's favor or grace or emulating the activity of gods by exercising higher level cognitive faculties,[3] early Confucians such as Kongzi felt an intimate, *familial* connection to all human beings and a sense that they were playing a vital role in the welfare of the world as a whole. For example, the *Analects* teaches that a virtuous person regards all within the four seas as his brothers (see *Analects* 12.5). Other early Confucians, such as Mengzi and Xunzi, highlight different and broader aspects of this sense of connection to the world. For example, *Mengzi* 7A13 tells us that cultivated people "flow in the same stream as Heaven and earth," and Xunzi advocates the idea that human beings should form a triad with Heaven and earth (Ivanhoe, 1991, p. 309–322). One sees dramatic examples of this kind of idea in later Confucian works such as the opening sections of Zhang Zai's "Western Inscription"

---

[3] Kongzi and Zhuangzi did believe in destiny or fate (*ming* 命), which does provide individuals with a sense of having a mission or lot in life. These ideas are closer to later Western notions about having a special vocation or calling than the classical Greek sense of *eudaimonia*. Thanks to Erin M. Cline for pointing out the importance of early Chinese notions about fate for my topic.

(*Xi Ming* 西銘), which shows the profound influence of Daoist and Buddhist ideas. Another good example is Wang Yangming's ethical ideal of "forming one body with Heaven, earth, and all things" (*tiandi wanwu wei yi ti* 天地萬物為一體) as seen in his essay "Questions on the *Great Learning*." Zhuangzi extended this sense of community far beyond what we see in Kongzi's or Mengzi's philosophy; he sought to de-center the anthropomorphic nature of early Confucian thought. For Zhuangzi, there is a natural and radical *equality among all things* in the world; while this knocks humanity off the pedestal it enjoys in the Confucian view as "the most noble creature under Heaven" (*zui wei tianxia gui ye* 最爲天下貴也), it broadens and deepens the connections we feel with all the myriad creatures.[4] The Daoist sage was at home anywhere between Heaven and earth, rambled free and easy, and joyfully roamed the world as a fellow traveler and companion of the myriad creatures.

## Kongzi's Joy

To a large degree, Kongzi's conception of happiness can be grasped by attending to his use of the character 樂 (*le* "joy"), which, as noted earlier, is the special feeling that comes to those who follow the Way. In the *Analects*, this character never means an amoral feeling of pleasure derived from an individual's personal enjoyment of some thing or state or affairs. While always subjectively experienced, joy is not a private emotion or matter of taste. It is an ethical response to certain features of the world and primarily about how one is living life.[5] Such an attitude and orientation is not at all unique. Many reflective conceptions of happiness, from those of the early Greeks to the later Romantics, had strongly normative dimensions, which had little or nothing to do with personal pleasures (McMahon, 2006, pp. 234–7, 263–5, etc.).

One of the most prominent features of Kongzi's account of living well is his effort to distance himself from any thought that joy can be found in the kinds of personal pleasures or material well-being that, in his time as well as our own, often are thought to define happiness. Wealth and honor and material comforts of various kinds are good, but only when they come from a life lived in accord with the Way. Following the Dao is the necessary condition for enjoying these other goods and to a certain extent, though not completely, it is sufficient for a happy life. Kongzi is closer to Aristotle than Plato in this regard and for reasons that will become clear holds that a fully happy life requires a reasonable level of properly acquired material goods. These though should never be the primary concern of the good person and should rather be regarded as a matter of fate or fortune (*Analects* 12.5).

> The master said, "Eating coarse rice and drinking water, leaning upon my bent arm for a pillow—there is joy to be found in such things! Wealth and honor acquired in immoral ways are like floating clouds to me!" (*Analects* 7.15).

---

[4] The quote is from *Xunzi*, chapter 9 "The Regulations of a True King" (*Wang zhi* 王制). Xunzi had a more expansive view of the proper connection between self and world than either Kongzi or Mengzi, and this change reflects the influence of Zhuangzi.

[5] One might interpret the opening passage of the *Analects* as an exception to this generalization, but it should be clear that in these lines as well, what is being highlighted is a special kind of joy that is available only to those who are in harmony with the Dao.

The master said, "Worthy indeed was Hui! With a single bowl of food [to eat] and ladle of water to drink, living in a narrow lane—most could not have endured such hardship—but Hui never let it affect his joy. Worthy indeed was Hui!" (*Analects* 6.9)[6]

The second passage just quoted implies an idea Kongzi explicitly claims in other places: that those who are not virtuous not only cannot endure hardship for long, they cannot maintain a constant state of mind for very long, even if they enjoy all of the material things that commonly are thought to make one happy. It seems that without a proper foundation, without being grounded in the Dao, no form of joy proves stable or reliable. "The master said, 'Those who are not virtuous cannot maintain themselves for very long either in a state of want or joy'" (*Analects* 4.2). In contrast, those who embrace the Dao find in it a special reservoir of satisfaction and happiness that sustains them in the worst of times and nourishes, fulfills, and delights them when things go well. Kongzi describes various stages of understanding the Dao, but his goal always is a type of understanding that finds its joy in following the Way. "The master said, 'To understand [the Dao] is not as good as to delight in it; to delight in [the Dao] is not as good as to find joy in it'" (*Analects* 6.18; cf. 6.23). This and other passages show that the joy of following the Confucian Way arises in light of an understanding of what the good life is and a judgment that one has succeeded in attaining this ideal; true joy is fully experienced only when we wholeheartedly give ourselves over to the Way and lose ourselves in its spontaneous play. This is what Kongzi experienced when after fifty-five years of study and practice he could "follow whatever my heart desires without overstepping what is proper" (*Analects* 2.4).

In its most characteristic sense, Kongzi's joy is a quite particular emotional state that arises when we accord with something beyond ourselves; when we fit ourselves into a larger pattern or process and allow ourselves to be carried along, oriented, and guided by this grander and more meaningful structure. This sense of joy is a core feature of early Chinese conceptions of spontaneity and such spontaneity is described in two primary ways in early Chinese writings (Ivanhoe, 2010a). Early Chinese Confucians advocate "cultivated spontaneity," while Daoists favor "untutored spontaneity." Cultivated spontaneity concerns certain activities that arise out of a second, acquired nature. In our contemporary world, the spontaneous play of accomplished athletes, musicians, or dancers offer clear examples of this ideal; in Kongzi's society masters of ritual and music serve as primary examples.

Music was a prominent example of such spontaneity for early Confucians and music also "plays" a crucial role in their particular conception of joy. The notions were graphically as well as semantically related, as Xunzi noted, citing what was probably a well-known phrase, "Music is joy" (*Fu yue zhe le ye* 夫樂者樂也).[7] The connection between music and joy is much deeper and more subtle than this simple slogan might suggest. Consider the following passage from the *Mengzi*:

---

[6] "Hui" is the personal name of Yan Hui or Yanzi, Kongzi's favorite disciple who is mentioned in the first epigraph of this essay. Both these passages and others as well imply that Kongzi and his followers considered attending to the joy of certain kinds of actions and states of affairs as part of their spiritual training. Focusing our attention on certain goals and aspects of life constituted a kind of *practice*. This concern with where one finds joy and the idea that the ethical life of following the Dao is the only source of true joy is developed in the *Mengzi* and became an important part of neo-Confucian practice, as shown in the first epigraph. Thanks to Erin M. Cline for pointing out the importance of this aspect of Kongzi's teachings.

[7] See chapter 20, "On Music" (*Yue lun* 樂論), of the *Xunzi*, where the line appears twice. It also appears in the "Record of Music" (*Yueji* 樂記) chapter of the *Book of Rites* (*Liji* 禮記).

> Mengzi said, "The core of benevolence is serving one's parents. The core of righteousness is obeying one's elder brother. The core of wisdom is to understand these two and not depart from them. The core of ritual is to regulate and embellish them. The *core of music is to take joy in them*. When one takes joy [in them, they] begin to grow, and when they begin to grow they cannot be stopped. When they cannot be stopped, without realizing it, *one's feet begin to step in time* to them and *one's hands begin to dance* them out." (*Mengzi* 4A27)[8]

Among the most important points made in this passage is that music and joy share an intimate relationship: just as joy can give rise to music, music can give rise to joy, and the joy of music leads one to accord with the music spontaneously. Without fully realizing what one is doing, one begins to follow along, just as one begins to follow the proper standards of benevolence and righteousness because of the joy these produce. Music provides a proper pattern and moves us to step in time and dance along. *Part of the joy* of music consists in giving ourselves over to it, allowing it to infuse us and losing ourselves in its inviting rhythms and movements; this is an important part of the joy of acting morally as well: both invite us to experience a more expansive sense of ourselves. Acting morally and playing live music achieve this end simply by their shared social quality. A musician plays with and for those in her own age, often presenting or elaborating upon the compositions of others who lived in earlier times. Like morality, music connects us with other people, often in deep and emotional ways—joyful, sad, and otherwise.

The common phenomenon of losing oneself in the rhythms and movements of music and dance describe a crucial aspect of Kongzi's conception of happiness. As already noted, this is a state in which we give ourselves over to something greater than ourselves and as a result experience a sense of something grand, meaningful, and ultimately reassuring. As noted earlier, this involves gaining an expanded sense of self, while shedding a conventional, narrower, more self-centered perspective. This loss of the conventional self is one of the ways in which following the Dao frees one from common concerns, fears, and anxieties. For example, Kongzi's pursuit of the Dao led him to forget about more mundane concerns and even to lose the common human anxiety about his own mortality.

> The Duke of She asked Zilu what kind of man Kongzi is, but Zilu did not answer him. The master said, "Why did you not say I am the kind of man who in his eager pursuit of knowledge forgets about eating, who in his joy forgets about sorrow, and is unaware that old age is fast approaching?" (*Analects* 7.19; cf. 4.8)

Even when Kongzi writes about things we *should not* take joy in, the thought often is that we are according with or in these cases *abandoning* ourselves to some larger pattern or process; in such cases, some seductive source of temptation serves as a kind of Pied Piper, leading us astray.

> The master said, "People take joy in three things that help them and three things that injure them. To find joy in the regulation provided by ritual and music, to find joy in discussing the goodness of others, and to find joy in having many worthy friends—these things help. To take joy in extravagance, to find joy in desultory wandering, and to take joy in feasting—these things injure." (*Analects* 16.5)

---

[8] The same idea is seen throughout the early corpus. See for example the "Great Preface" (*Daxu* 大序) to the *Book of Odes* (*Shijing* 詩經) or the closing lines of the "Record of Music" chapter of the *Book of Rites*.

One of the reasons early Confucians were so concerned about certain types of morally bad music is precisely because such music too has the enchanting power to carry us away, and part of this power arises from our underlying desire to discover, fit into, and give ourselves over to something larger and more meaningful than our personal pleasures and desires (Ivanhoe, 2010b). Music, of any kind, is not just sound but regulated patterns of sounds,[9] and according with such patterns, identifying with and surrendering ourselves to them is a source of reassurance, solidarity, and a type of joy. This implies something that many thinkers have pointed out and that Daoists as well as Confucians were quite clear about: there are "joys" that should not be enjoyed.[10]

The theme of losing oneself in some larger and more meaningful pattern or process helps us understand Kongzi's views about the pleasures of wine. Kongzi enjoyed drinking in the company of others and saw social drinking as an important component of certain rituals and social interactions (*Analects* 10.6, 10.7). This aspect of his thought, though, should be understood in the context of his overall views about happiness. When done in proper moderation, sharing a few cups of wine can relax good friends or lower the inhibitions and boundaries that often separate people in new social settings; it can foster camaraderie and good cheer, even in the midst of competition.

> The master said, "The cultivated person never contends. [Perhaps someone will say] he must contend when he competes in ritual archery contests. On such occasions, though, he salutes and defers [to his companions] when he takes up his position and raises a glass to toast them, when he steps down. In so contending, he remains a cultivated person." (*Analects* 3.7)[11]

While Kongzi did not place any set limit upon how much one can drink, he makes very clear that one should not reach the point of drunkenness, for this would undermine the point of enjoying wine together (*Analects* 9.16, 10.6). Moderate amounts of wine promote and enhance harmonious social interaction; overindulgence inhibits and harms our relationships, selves, and society.

In summary, for Kongzi, joy is the feeling that comes with living well, a sense that one is properly aligned with the larger patterns and processes of the Dao. The Dao is a normative pattern much grander and more meaningful than anything an individual person could possibly achieve on her or his own. Being in accord with the Dao, moving along in harmony with the Way, redirects one's attention and reshapes one's sense of self. One is freed from a broad range of common concerns, fears, and anxieties and in their stead experiences a unique sense of comfort, ease, and peace, the feeling that one is properly oriented, situated, and playing one's role in the world. It is this experience and sensation that gives rise to Confucian joy.

---

[9] This idea is made very clear in a number of places in the early literature but especially so in the "Record of Music" chapter of the *Book of Rites*.

[10] In his splendid and stimulating book, Mihaly Csikszentmihalyi (1990) describes a sense of focused, optimal experience in which one loses oneself in the midst of certain kinds of activities, what I would call different kinds of spontaneity. One of vexing features of this phenomenon is that it does not seem to have any clear moral content: there is bad as well as good flow.

[11] In other words, he competes but does not contend. Compare 15.22. This passage or at least the idea is parodied in chapter four of the *Zhuangzi*.

## Zhuangzi's Joy

Like Kongzi, Zhuangzi did not especially look for or value the common types of happiness that most people sought and esteemed. In fact, Zhuangzi often criticizes more mundane forms of happiness as the source of considerable grief both to oneself and others. Because most human beings actively seek happiness by accumulating wealth, power, prestige and the like, they tend to treat each other and things badly and drive themselves to less contented and fulfilling lives. Zhuangzi presents the normal human search for happiness as sad, pathetic, and futile.

> Day after day they use their minds in strife, sometimes grandiose, sometimes sly, sometimes petty. Their little fears are mean and trembly; their great fears are stunned and overwhelming … They fade like fall and winter—such is the way they dwindle day by day. They drown in what they do—you cannot make them turn back. They grow dark. As though sealed with seals—such are the excesses of their old age. And when their minds draw near to death, nothing can restore them to the light. (Watson, 1968, p. 37)[12]

One of the first and greatest advantages enjoyed by those who follow the Dao is freedom from most of the concerns, fears, and anxieties that plague most people's lives. The Dao relieves one of many of the most vexing aspects of normal human life. Followers of the Dao are urged to abandon the frenzied and pointless rush to accumulate wealth, power, prestige and all the other goods commonly associated with "happiness." They are to do this by engaging in a process of "fasting" and "forgetting,"[13] in the course of which they empty their hearts and minds of these seductive but toxic ideals and goals. The Dao "gathers" in the empty and unstructured space created by this process.[14] While this relief from the troubles of ordinary human life is most welcome and desirable, it is not the ultimate aim of Zhuangzi's recommended form of life.[15] His true goal is to accord with the Dao and live a life characterized by the "free and easy wandering" (*xiaoyao you* 逍遙遊) that serves as the theme of the opening chapter of the text. Like the great Peng bird, we are to follow our spontaneous inclinations, accord with the patterns and processes of the natural world, and lose ourselves, secure in the comforting rhythms of the Dao. Instead of concerning ourselves with petty human goals and aspirations, we should trust in and accord with the Way. Zhuangzi often employs skillful exemplars to illustrate his ideal form of life and some have argued that such skillful living is Zhuangzi's ultimate aim. This, though, is only partly true. Skillfulness per se is not his goal, for that would allow all sorts of lives that are contrary to and disrupt the Dao. The only kind

---

[12] In other passages, Zhuangzi describes common emotions like joy and delight as highly transitory and unstable aspects of ordinary life. See, for example, the passage that begins immediately after the one quoted here.

[13] Zhuangzi describes these methods in considerable detail in several important passages in the text (Carr and Ivanhoe, 86–109). Compare the way Kongzi forgets about his troubles and even the approach of old age, discussed earlier.

[14] See the long dialogue between Kongzi and Yan Hui (Yanzi) in chapter four of the *Zhuangzi* (Watson, 58; Carr and Ivanhoe, 94–109).

[15] Paul Kjellberg offers an interesting discussion of the ways in which Zhuangzi's view includes something like the *ataraxia* of Sextus Empiricus (Kjellberg) but argues that this is not Zhuangzi's ultimate goal. See also Carr and Ivanhoe.

of life Zhuangzi advocates is one that leads one into harmony with the Dao. *Some* skillful lives achieve this end, and it is these he endorses (Carr & Ivanhoe, 2010, p. 48–62).

In one memorable passage, Zhuangzi criticizes his friend Huizi for trying to find some *practical* use for the gourds that grew from the seeds he was given by the king of Wei. Not finding any such application for the huge gourds, Huizi smashed them, prompting Zhuangzi to respond:

> You certainly are dense when it comes to using great things! … Now you had a gourd large enough to hold five piculs. Why didn't you think of making it into a great tub so you could go floating around the rivers and lakes, instead of worrying because it was too big and unwieldy to dip into things! (Watson, 1968, pp. 34–35)[16]

Huizi conceived of and evaluated the gourds on the standard of what the world finds "useful" and thereby was led to frustration and loss.[17] Instead, he should have climbed aboard them and cast himself adrift, confident that he would be led down the rivers and lakes to enjoy a free and easy excursion, safe and welcome within the bosom of the Dao.

The same idea is seen in one of the knack stories, which are among the most memorable features of the *Zhuangzi*. In the story of Cook Ding carving up and Ox for Lord Wen Hui, we find the marvelous cook guiding his chopper through the "openings" and "hollows" that are the joints and cavities of the ox, avoiding even the smallest "ligament or tendon much less a main joint."[18] By following the seams within the natural structure of the ox, the cook avoids forcing the human upon the Heavenly. Thus his work epitomizes the actions of one who follows the Dao. He makes this connection explicit when he tells Lord Wen Hui, "What I care about is the Way, which goes beyond skill." This is why after watching the cook and listening to his account of his work, Lord Wen Hui exclaims, "I have heard the words of Cook Ding and learned how to *care for life*!" Living according to the Dao is "the secret of caring for life," which is the title of this short chapter. Those who live such lives avoid harming themselves or others; like Cook Ding's chopper, they never collide with or bang up against the things of the world and so never wear themselves or others down. They remain, like the edge of his blade, clean and sharp as they slip around and pass by the obstacles that blunt and break the average person. Beyond this, though, followers of the Dao accord with and lose themselves in the Way; they dance along free and easy in the world, just as the cook's blade plays freely within the natural makeup of the ox. Cook Ding's movements make it appear "as though he were performing the dance of the Mulberry Grove or keeping time to the Jing Shou Symphony." Here, we see the same use of musical metaphors that we found and explored in the Confucian case. The skill and ease of one in accord with the Way has the same feel, attraction, and effect as enchanting music and dance. When Cook Ding completes his performance, he declares "I stand there completely satisfied and reluctant to move on …" Such is the special joy of one who follows the Way.

Those who follow the Dao feel part of something more grand and meaningful and this is the nature and source of their joy. Such a feeling is no longer a self-conscious aim but simply a natural result of spontaneously moving in accord with the Way. Giving oneself over to and losing oneself in the Dao offers the most satisfying and fulfilling of lives, but since this just

---

[16] Translation slightly emended.

[17] The theme of "the usefulness of the useless" is common in the *Zhuangzi*.

[18] The story is found in chapter three of the *Zhuangzi*, "The Secret of Caring for Life" (*Yang sheng* 養生). The following quotations all are from this section of Watson with some very minor changes.

means acting spontaneously and naturally, it gives the Daoist ideal an air of paradox. One fulfills the highest aspiration when one forsakes aspirations and just is as one is (*ziran* 自然) (Ivanhoe, 2007b, pp. 277–287, 2010a, 2010c).

> When the people of ancient times spoke of the fulfillment of aspiration (*de zhi*得志), they did not mean fine carriages and caps.[19] They meant simply that joy was so complete that it could not be made greater. Nowadays, how-ever, when people speak of the fulfillment of aspiration, they mean fine carriages and caps. But carriages and caps affect the body alone, not the inborn nature and fate. Such things from time to time may happen to come your way. When they come, you cannot keep them from arriving, but when they depart, you cannot stop them from going. Therefore, carriages and caps are no excuse for becoming puffed up with pride, and hardship and poverty are no excuse for fawning on the vulgar. You should find the same joy in one condition as in the other, and thereby be free of care, that is all. But now, when the things that happened along take their leave, you cease to be joyful. From this point of view, though you experience joy, it will always be fated for destruction. Therefore it is said, Those who destroy themselves in things and lose their inborn nature in the vulgar may be called, *upside-down people*. (Watson, 1968, p. 174)[20]

"Upside-down people" see and live in a world in which the priorities of all the most important values are reversed: such people intentionally pursue aims that violate the Way; they thereby undermine their own happiness and bring others to grief. Instead of their joy being "so complete that it could not be made greater" they live lives of constant fear, anxiety, and frustration. Since all their values are topsy-turvy, they turn away from true joy and embrace misery instead. The more widely and strongly these wrongheaded views take hold in society at large, the more difficult it is to see and make clear the Dao. People become accustomed to the misery they create and lose sight of their true nature, which is the only source of reliable and stable joy.

> As long as the world rests in the true form of its inborn nature and fate, it makes no difference whether these eight delights exist or not.[21] But if the world does not rest in the true form of its nature and fate, then these eight delights begin to grow warped and crooked, jumbled and deranged, and will bring confusion to the world. And if on top of that the world begins to honor them and cherish them, then the delusion of the world will be great indeed! You say these are only a fancy that will pass in time? Yet men prepare themselves with fasts and austerities when they come to describe them, kneel solemnly on their mats when they recommend them, beat drums and sing to set them forth in dance. What's to be done about it I'm sure I don't know! (Watson, 1968, p. 115)

Of course, Zhuangzi *does* know what to do or at least what would lead people away from the twisted, bumpy, and treacherous road that leads to human misery and the world's distress. We must "turn back" to our true nature and under its guidance follow the Way. If we come to succeed in this task, we will "forget" that we ever set about to complete it, for this path leads us back to spontaneity: "[So it is said,] the fish forget each other in the rivers and lakes, and human beings forget each other in the arts of the Way" (Watson, 1968, p. 87).[22]

---

[19] The word *zhi*志, translated here as "aspiration" is the same word that Kongzi uses in the famous passage that describes his spiritual autobiography: *Analects* 4.5, which begins, "At fifteen years of age I set my heart upon (*zhi yu*志於) learning."

[20] Translation slightly emended; italics added.

[21] The eight delights are human responses to colors, sounds, virtue, order, ritual, music, sages, and knowledge.

[22] Translation slightly emended.

Daoists are famous for their love of wine; here we see another similarity with Confucianism, but within such similarity lie important differences. Daoist love of wine is distinct from Confucian appreciation in at least two important respects. First, Daoists are willing to drink alone as well as in the company of others. Second, they see nothing wrong with drinking to the point of inebriation. Like Confucians, Daoists drink to lower the boundary between self and a greater world, but in the case of Daoism, what is sought is not the lowering of inhibitions *between people* but the boundaries between the human and the Heavenly or natural. This explains, first, why it does not matter whether one is alone or in the company of like-minded friends; in either case, wine can serve the purpose of effacing the boundary between self and Nature. Second, since enhancing and cherishing human relationships is not the goal of Daoists, they do not hesitate to drink lustily and carry on until carried away. Both of these characteristics are evident in the following passage from the *Zhuangzi*.

> When a drunken man falls from a carriage, though the carriage may be going very fast, he won't be killed. He has bones and joints the same as other men, and yet he is not injured as they would be, because his spirit is whole. He didn't know he was riding, and he doesn't know he has fallen out. Life and death, alarm and terror do not enter his breast, and so he can bang against things without fear of injury. If he can keep himself whole like this by means of wine, how much more can he keep himself whole by means of Heaven! (Watson, 1968, pp. 198–199)

Wine helps one forget oneself and brings one closer to the Dao. Nevertheless, as the passage makes clear, relying on wine is not as good as relying on Heaven.

We see the themes of how wine can help one forget oneself and bring one closer to the Dao in the works of one of the greatest Chinese poets, the Tang dynasty master, Li Bo (李白) (701–762). Consider the following lines, taken from the first and third of his *Four Poems on Wine* (Acker, 1965)[23]:

> Amidst the flowers
> a jug of wine—
> I pour alone
> lacking companionship,
> So raising the cup
> I invite the moon,
> Then turn to my shadow
> which makes three of us …
> … Once I am drunk
> losing Heaven and Earth,
> Unsteadily
> I go to my lonely pillow.
> Not to know
> that my self exists—
> Of all my joys
> This is the highest

Being without human company is not a loss for Li Bo; he has Heaven, earth, and the myriad creatures as his companions. Maintaining decorum is not a good and blurring the boundary between self and all the world is a most welcome effect of wine. Daoist love of wine, though,

---

[23] Thanks to Pauline C. Lee for suggesting Li Bo's works as an illustration of this aspect of Daoism.

is not Dionysian since Daoists do not think frenzy, madness, and ecstasy result when our true nature is allowed to manifest itself freely. Daoist lovers of wine are mellow; their natural setting is the bank of a slowly meandering stream, shaded by willows; their natural posture is reclining; their characteristic activities are chanting poetry, discussing the Dao, and communing with Nature. This is the Heavenly joy of the Daoist.

> So it is said, for him who understands Heavenly joy, life is the working of Heaven; death is the transformation of things. In stillness, he and the *yin* share a single Virtue; in motion, he and the *yang* share a single flow. Thus he who understands Heavenly joy incurs no wrath from Heaven, no opposition from man, no entanglement from things, no blame from the spirits… his emptiness and stillness reach throughout Heaven and earth and penetrate the ten thousand things. This is what is called Heavenly joy. Heavenly joy is the mind of the sage, by which he shepherds the world. (Watson, 1968, p. 174)[24]

## Conclusion

Kongzi's and Zhuangzi's views on happiness share important structural features. Neither conceived of happiness in terms of the kinds of personal pleasures that often are thought to define happiness, but both believed a special feeling of joy arises in those who live well. They further believed that living well consists in following the Way, though each offered his own distinctive view of what the Way is and where it is to be found. Kongzi and Zhuangzi agreed that the pleasures afforded by material goods, power, or fame are not a solid foundation for happiness and in fact offer at best semblances and often counterfeits of the true joy of life. Many philosophers have held such views and insisted that higher, more ethical, often more *cerebral* pleasures are the true source of happiness. In the Western tradition, Aristotle and J. S. Mill offer good examples of such views. Kongzi shares some similarities with Aristotle and Mill on this score; he believed that the cultivation of virtue and the pursuit of culture are important constituents of happiness. Nevertheless, he did not follow either Western philosopher in regard to the value of more cerebral pleasures. Contemplation and other purely intellectual pursuits do not figure significantly in his picture of the ideal, happy life. In contrast, he places much greater emphasis on the joys of familial relationships and a commitment to the enjoyment of a shared culture and tradition. These aspects of Kongzi's joy play a distinctive and central role in his conception of happiness and make such fulfillment available to a much broader range of people. He believed happiness is found primarily in the everyday activities of good familial and social life; the challenge is to live up to the demands of such a life and see it for what it is (*Analects* 11.24). In contrast, Aristotle's and Mill's discussions of happiness are dramatically more intellectually elitist and show a certain disdain for many of the joys of everyday life (McMahon, 2006, p. 353). Another difference between at least Mill and both the Chinese thinkers we are discussing is that Mill has no corresponding conception of metaphysical comfort. A helpful way of seeing this difference is to understand Kongzi as arguing for the *reframing* of everyday pleasures, incorporating ritual and proper social forms into such activities, so that they become integral parts of something of much greater significance, thereby serving as a source of metaphysical comfort. We need not turn

---

[24] Translation slightly emended.

away from or look down upon the more simple aspects of everyday life, just come to see them in a different and better light.[25]

At first glance, Zhuangzi is even more removed from thinkers like Aristotle and Mill in advocating certain kinds of skillfulness and Nature as opposed to family, tradition, and culture as the primary sources of joy and in often presenting a picture of the good life that appears to be more solitary and in some sense more stoic than Kongzi's—these last two features are also characteristic of the *Daodejing*. In a number of passages, Zhuangzi describes friends watching with apparent indifference as their companions are writhing with pain and in the throes of death. In one such passage friends even shoo away the grieving wife and children of one of the dying companions admonishing them with the words, "Get back! Don't disturb the process of change!" (Watson, 1968, p. 85; cf. 83–89) The text, though, is difficult to interpret in regard to how solitary and stoic the ideal Daoist really is supposed to be. Zhuangzi does mourn the death of his wife and clearly misses his friend Huizi after he dies (Watson, 1968, pp. 191–192, 269), so perhaps we should read the more dramatic passages about the death of friends as therapeutically aimed at loosening but not severing our connections to other people and their welfare. In any event, Zhuangzi's views about our connection with Nature form the core of his vision.

When the perplexing and challenging passages noted above are read against the greater context of Zhuangzi's teachings, they assume a different force, shape, and significance. In one passage, we find a description of Zhuangzi on the verge of death, and in it we see how his views about being a part and partner of the natural world enabled him to face death not only without fear, but with humor and his special form of joy.

> When Zhuangzi was dying, his disciples wanted to give him a lavish funeral. Said Zhuangzi, I have Heaven and earth for my outer and inner coffins, the sun and moon for my pair of jade discs, the stars for my pearls, the myriad creatures for my farewell gifts. Is anything missing from my funeral paraphernalia? What would you add to these?"
>
> "Master! We are afraid the crows and kites will eat you!" said one of his disciples.
>
> "Above ground I'll be eaten by the crows and kites; below ground I'll be eaten by the ants and mole-crickets. You rob from one to give to the other. How come you like them so much better?" (Zhuangzi)[26]

In different ways, both Kongzi and Zhuangzi are able to avoid the kind of alienation that is characteristic of modernity and the modern search for happiness. As many have noted, modern human beings often find themselves alienated from one another and the world at large because of what are thought to be distinctive features of their age. On the one hand, the rise of individualism has come to emphasize the pursuit of personal satisfaction and pleasure, which tends to break down interpersonal ties to family, friends, community, and tradition. More and more, people tend to work *for themselves*, but, paradoxically, this often results in lives that while materially rich are more isolated, solitary, and spiritually poor. On the other hand, the modern scientific disenchantment of the world tends to leave people without the larger schemes of value characteristic of pre-modern societies. People tend to see themselves less in terms of God's plan, part of a natural order, or great chain of being.

---

[25] Thanks to Justin Tiwald for suggesting this way of putting it.
[26] The passage is from chapter 32, "Lie Yukou" 列禦寇, of the *Zhuangzi*. The translation is my own. This passage offers a revealing contrast to *Analects* 9.12, which depicts Kongzi close to death. For a comparison of these stories, see Ivanhoe (2010d).

This trend too, tends to result in lives bereft of the companions, connections, and assurances that were key features of earlier conceptions of happiness and great sources of satisfaction. Kongzi's focus on family relationships and his advocacy of culture and tradition offer a distinctive response to this modern malaise. By emphasizing that a good deal of our identity and a special sense of joy lies in our relationships with others and our membership in community, culture, and tradition, his conception of happiness offers us a way to feel part of a temporally extended, expanding circle of meaning and importance. Zhuangzi too has a view that can remedy the modern condition. His insistence that we return to and never lose sight of our connections to the larger natural order of which we are a part and that in its patterns and processes we can find deep sources of fulfillment and joy can be understood as providing a conception of human beings as at home and in harmony with the natural world.

As parts of the Confucian and Daoist traditions respectively, Kongzi's and Zhuangzi's conceptions of the Dao often have been understood as in competition or at least in tension with one another. Nevertheless, many Chinese have seen great merit in both and sought to harmonize them in various ways, for example by understanding each as appropriate for and offering guidance in different, but complementary spheres of human life. Kongzi and Zhuangzi share a common concern with disabusing us of misconceived conceptions of happiness, which they see as widespread and deeply entrenched not only in their own cultures and times but also in certain errant tendencies in human nature. They both work to undermine the ideas that happiness is to be found in sensual or material pleasures or a narrow conception of the self. Though they have very different views about the proper form of the ideal life, they agree that aiming directly, exclusively, or even primarily at one's own happiness is the source of much grief not only for oneself but others as well.

Kongzi and Zhuangzi also agree in offering us the important lesson that happiness is to be found here in the world. We are to realize joy *in* life by living life a certain way.[27] Kongzi emphasizes the social aspects of the good life and highlights the joys of family, friends, and community on the one hand and ritual, culture, and tradition on the other. For him, there is a special joy in finding and fulfilling one's roles in the greater social order which arises when we begin to accord spontaneously with the greater, more meaningful patterns and processes of social life. As we assume our proper place in this larger, humanly constructed and Heavenly sanctioned order, we experience a special feeling of appropriateness, security, peace, and ease. This is the joy of Kongzi and his companion and disciple Yanzi.

Zhuangzi focuses upon our connections to the natural world and the unselfconscious surrender to certain pre-rational tendencies and inclinations. Among these natural intuitions is a sense of being part of the larger natural order—the Dao. Zhuangzi argues that socialization, with all its prohibitions and inhibitions, cuts us off and alienates us from the great Dao—just as modern society and technology often obscure our deep and complex connections to and need for Nature—and so we need to work our way back to a more innocent and uncluttered view of ourselves and the world. As we succeed in casting off our social baggage and freeing ourselves from its limitations and constrictions, we spontaneously begin to accord with grander natural patterns and processes. As we succeed in hearing and heeding these deep and subtle rhythms, we come to sense our connection to the Dao and

---

[27] Joel Kupperman (2002) has written revealing about the ways in which Kongzi is concerned with *style* as an important aspect of the good life. See also Olberding (2009, pp. 503–522).

experience a profound and distinctive sense of appropriateness, security, peace, and ease. This is the joy of Zhuangzi and also, as he well knew, the joy of fish.

While Kongzi's and Zhuangzi's views share these and other important similarities, in other respects they remain distinct and are not fully reconcilable. Confucians insist that culture is the core locus of value and human beings are unique: "the most noble" among creatures. In contrast, Daoists see the natural world as a realm in which "all things are equal." While there are important shared features between these two traditions and they can be seen as complementary, we should not reduce one to the other, see them both as expressions of some single higher truth, or obscure their differences in light of what they share. They offer two related but distinct perspectives on life. Nevertheless, many Chinese have believed that happiness can be found by embracing and harmonizing both views, playing upon, with, and within the tension between these two perspectives.

## Acknowledgments

Thanks to Erin M. Cline, Fan Ruiping, Paul Kjellberg, Pauline C. Lee, James O. Pawelski, Michael R. Slater, David W. Tien, and Justin Tiwald for comments and suggestions on earlier drafts of this essay. Thanks also to Timothy O'Leary and the other participants of the "Happiness East and West" conference held at the University of Hong Kong 10–December 11, 2009 for sharing their views on happiness.

## References

Acker, W. (1965). Four poems on wine. In C. Birch (Ed.), *Anthology of Chinese literature from early times to the fourteenth century* (Volume 1, pp. 230, 232). New York, NY: Grove Press.

Carr, K. L., & Ivanhoe, P. J. (2010). *The sense of antirationalism: The religious thought of Zhuangzi and Kierkegaard* (Revised 2nd ed.). Charleston, SC: CreateSpace.

Cheng, H., & Cheng, Y. (1978). *Extant works of the Cheng [brothers] from Henan* (*Henan Cheng shi yi shu* 河南程氏遺書). Taibei Shi, Taiwan: Taiwan shang wu yin shu guan.

Csikszentmihalyi, M. (1990). *Flow: The psychology of optimal experience*. New York, NY: Harper and Row.

Graham, A. C. (1989). *Disputers of the Tao: Philosophical argument in ancient China*. LaSalle, IL: Open Court.

Ivanhoe, P. J. (1991). A happy symmetry: Xunzi's ethical thought. *Journal of the American Academy of Religion*, 59, 309–322.

Ivanhoe, P. J. (2007a). Heaven as a source for ethical warrant in early Confucianism. *Dao: A Journal of Comparative Philosophy*, 6, 211–220.

Ivanhoe, P. J. (2007b). The paradox of *Wuwei*? *The Journal of Chinese Philosophy*, 34, 277–287.

Ivanhoe, P. J. (2010a). The values of spontaneity. In Y. Kam-por, J. Tao & P. J. Ivanhoe (Eds.), *Taking Confucian ethics seriously: Contemporary theories and applications* (pp. 183–207). Albany, NY: SUNY Press.

Ivanhoe, P. J. (2010b). The contemporary significance of Confucian views about the ethical values of music. In *Civilization and peace* (pp. 123–33). Edison, NJ: Jimoondang.

Ivanhoe, P. J. (2010c). The theme of unselfconsciousness in the *Liezi*. In R. Littlejohn & J. Dippmann (Eds.), *Riding the wind with Liezi: New essays on the Daoist classic* (pp. 129–52). Albany, NY: SUNY Press.

Ivanhoe, P. J. (2010d). Death and dying in the *Analects* 9.12. In A. L. Olberding & P. J. Ivanhoe (Eds.), *Mortality and traditional China* (pp. 137–51). Albany, NY: SUNY Press.

Kjellberg, P. (1996). Sextus Empiricus, Zhuangzi, and Xunzi on "Why Be Skeptical?" In P. Kjellberg & P. J. Ivanhoe (Eds.), *Essays on skepticism, relativism, and ethics in the Zhuangzi* (pp. 1–25). Albany, NY: SUNY Press.

Kongzi. (2009). *Collected Commentaries (on the "Analects") by He Yan.* (*He Yan ji jie* 何晏集解). Beijing, China: Beijing Ai ru sheng shu zi hua ji shu yan jiu zhong xin.

Kupperman, J. (2002). Naturalness revisited: Why western philosophers should study Confucius. In B. W. V. Norden (Ed.), *Confucius and the "Analects": New essays* (pp. 39–52). New York, NY: Oxford University Press.

McMahon, D. M. (2006). *Happiness: A history*. New York, NY: Atlantic Monthly Press.

Mengzi. (1992). *Collected Commentaries on the Mengzi.* (*Mengzi ji zhu* MM孟子集注). Jinan, China: Qi Lu shu she.

Nussbaum, M. C. (1986). *The fragility of goodness: Luck and ethics in Greek tragedy and philosophy*. Cambridge, UK: Cambridge University Press.

Olberding, A. (2009). Ascending the hall: Style and moral improvement in the *Analects*. *Philosophy East and West*, 59, 503–522.

Schwartz, B. I. (1985). *The world of thought in ancient China*. Cambridge, MA: The Belknap Press.

Slater, M. R. (2009). *William James on ethics and faith*. Cambridge, UK: Cambridge University Press.

Watson, B. (1968). *The complete works of Chuang Tzu*. New York, NY: Columbia University Press.

Xunzi. (2009). *Collected Commentaries on the Xunzi.* (*Xunzi ji jie* 荀子集解). Beijing, China: Beijing Ai ru sheng shu zi hua ji shu yan jiu zhong xin.

Zhuangzi. (2009). *Collected Explanations of the Zhuangzi.* (*Zhuangzi jishi* 莊子集釋). Beijing, China: Beijing Ai ru sheng shu zi hua ji shu yan jiu zhong xin.

# CHAPTER 21

# CONTINENTAL CONTRIBUTIONS TO OUR UNDERSTANDING OF HAPPINESS AND SUFFERING

EMMY VAN DEURZEN

Middlesex University and the New School of Psychotherapy and Counselling, UK

## INTRODUCTION

THIS chapter considers a number of contributions by continental philosophers who contrast the idea of happiness with the experience of suffering. In light of the fact there are other chapters in this volume dealing with classic philosophy as well as with early continental contributions, this chapter focuses exclusively on nineteenth- and twentieth-century philosophers and in particular on phenomenological and existential authors, excluding poststructural and postmodern contributions. The main theme of the chapter is whether the pursuit of happiness can be philosophically justified without taking its opposite of suffering into account. While the definition of happiness used is different for each of the authors discussed, they each argue against happiness as a valid objective of human existence. This chapter will argue that continental philosophers in line with Athenian philosophers have generally maintained that it is important to take a balanced view of happiness and suffering as the one is not possible without the other.

For the purpose of this chapter we shall define continental philosophy as the philosophies that have flourished on the continent of Europe from the beginning of the nineteenth century until the end of the twentieth century. This leaves out many important earlier continental contributions, as well as more recent continental philosophies under the broad umbrella of poststructuralism and postmodernism. The focus here will be on the movement of existential philosophy that revolutionized European thinking over the nineteenth and twentieth centuries by putting the human condition at the centre of its focus. These philosophies have returned firmly to the fundamental question of what human existence is and how it should be lived. Each of the authors considered in this chapter has defined the purpose of human living differently, though none has offered human happiness as a candidate for the purpose of life. This makes it difficult to give a definition of happiness from the standpoint of continental philosophy, though we shall attempt to do so in the conclusion.

These philosophies stand in sharp opposition to the analytic and positivistic traditions of Anglo-American thinking and thus propose a rather different take on happiness as well. In light of the current trend of positive psychology, which is deeply rooted in an Anglo-American framework of pragmatism and positivism and which is promoting a vigorously positivistic approach to the concept of happiness in the human sciences, continental philosophy has a very different perspective on offer, which may be both refreshing and much needed. Continental philosophy, as defined by Rosen (1998, p. 665), rejects scientism (i.e., the exclusive use of science as the ultimate authority on everything), tends towards historicism (i.e., the assumption that we define ourselves and our values in the process of living our lives), emphasizes the importance of human agency and of personal and moral transformation, and stresses the importance of meta-theory.

The question that continental philosophers would ask about current preoccupations with happiness as a prime objective of human living is whether happiness, pleasure, or well-being can ever be goals worth pursuing for their own sake. If there is any lesson to be learnt from the history of continental philosophy it is that happiness and well-being can never be singled out but need to be understood in relation to their counterpart of suffering and hardship.

Continental authors would ask questions such as: "How and when did we forget that happiness is not the ultimate objective in life? Why did we decide to pursue it so relentlessly in this new age of technology? When did we begin to think that the art of living could be reduced to the art of positive thinking that some people seem to equate with an understanding of what a good life entails? What seismic shift has separated us from the insights that were so hard earned by those who lived and thought about life long before us? Is it a reflection of the comfort-seeking nature of contemporary society that we let ourselves be lulled into the belief that happiness can and must be obtained?" Continental philosophies are deliberately unsettling in nature and challenging to the status quo.

One of the fundamental paradoxes that more recent continental philosophers have emphasized is that only to the extent that we are prepared to face difficulty, trouble, and suffering can we find ease and peace as well. It is only if we are prepared for the tension of existence that we can ever learn to master it. Kierkegaard prefigured most of these arguments.

# Kierkegaard's Up-Building and Stages on Life's Way

Søren Kierkegaard has often been called the father of existentialism and he contributed much to the description of human experience and the meaning of life. His philosophy was a critique of Hegel's grand view of the world which he considered to be too idealistic and out of touch with the reality of human existence. Kierkegaard studied and described his own subjective experience carefully and tried to come to grips with his internal world, even though, like Schopenhauer, he was soon aware that a sense of nothingness, coupled with anxiety and despair, were at the core of human experience when we face the abyss that reflected selfhood entails. Kierkegaard wrote detailed accounts of his personal struggles with unhappiness and spoke of the human tendency to isolate ourselves and "emigrate to a sixth continent where it is wholly sufficient to itself" (Kierkegaard, 1846/1941, p. 295).

Kierkegaard argued that we can paradoxically rise above the ordinary contradictions and difficulties of living only by facing them and not by trying to eliminate them. Kierkegaard's view is a dialectical one. Initially (Kierkegaard, 1843/1992) he suggested that we had to make up our minds and choose either to follow our aesthetic preferences, aiming for pleasure and happiness, or to follow our ethical inclination and live by the letter of the law and moral code. But later he proposed a dialectical overcoming of these options and suggested that we can go beyond these opposites by taking a leap of faith into a spiritual life instead (Kierkegaard, 1845/1940). Spirituality as defined by Kierkegaard is to think for ourselves rather than following our senses or the prescriptions of existing rules and regulations. We can only come to this if we allow for initial doubt:

> In the sphere of historical freedom, transition is a state. However, in order to understand this correctly, one must not forget that the new is brought about through the leap. (Kierkegaard, 1844/1980, p. 85)

The leap was only possible once we decided to have faith and to abandon the pursuit of aesthetic pleasures or the ethically correct living that was exacted by the Bible or other religious dogmas, but that ultimately could not satisfy. It is only when we started doubting, and thus thinking, that we could become aware of the possibility of falling into the abyss. This was the experience of anxiety (*Angst*) that made us fully aware of our existence and ourselves. It is then that we could encompass the tensions between infinity and finitude, possibility and necessity. And it was this that would make us feel dizzy with freedom:

> Anxiety is the dizziness of freedom, which emerges when the spirit wants to posit the synthesis and freedom looks down into its own possibility, laying hold of finiteness to support itself. Freedom succumbs in this dizziness. (Kierkegaard, 1844/1980, p. 61)

The rush towards happiness for Kierkegaard then was the exact opposite of grasping one's freedom. Wanting happiness was nothing but an attempt at not experiencing the contradictions and tensions of life. It was an attempt to return to the Garden of Eden, where all would be well ever after. But human beings owed themselves more than such ignorant freedom of tensions. The fall from paradise was the best thing that ever happened to us, in that it allowed us to discover the contradictions and tensions of life, recognizing the differences between good and evil, right and wrong, male and female. It is therefore not happiness we should pursue but rather the ability to fully come to life in awareness of our freedom and in awareness of our possibilities. This means that we should welcome anxiety, which wakes us from the comforting illusions of happiness.

> Whoever has learned to be anxious in the right way has learned the ultimate. (Kierkegaard, 1844/1980, p. 155)

# Nietzsche's Will to Power and the Love of Life

Nietzsche took this vigorous exploration of human existence one step further. He believed that suffering was a teacher and that looking for happiness was to look in the wrong place:

> The discipline of suffering, of great suffering—do you not know that only this discipline has created all enhancements of man so far? That tension of the soul in unhappiness which cultivates its strength, its shudders face to face with great ruin, its inventiveness and courage in enduring, persevering, interpreting, and exploiting suffering, and whatever has been granted to it of profundity, secret, mask, spirit, cunning, greatness—was it not granted to it through suffering, through the discipline of great suffering? (Nietzsche, 1886/1990, p. 225)

This is an even stronger argument against the pursuit of happiness, in the sense of our original definition, than we have heard before. The point Nietzsche made was that learning comes from experience, especially from the experience of stretching ourselves and improving ourselves, in order to bridge the gap between animal and god. Because he observed that God had been killed and that human beings were left to their own wits, we needed to reach out across the abyss between animal and divine and come into our own power, as the Superman (*Ubermensch*):

> Man is a rope, fastened between animal and Superman—a rope over an abyss. A dangerous going-across, a dangerous wayfaring, looking-back, a dangerous shuddering and staying still. What is great in man is that he is a bridge and not a goal; what can be loved in man is that he is a going-across and a down-going. (Nietzsche, 1883/1961, p. 43–44)

In order to become more like the superhuman who affirms his will to power and accepts his human destiny, human beings need to learn to accept their fate and love it: this is what Nietzsche referred to as "*amor fati*"—the love of fate. For him our combat is essentially a lonely one and we can certainly not learn if we pursue happiness as our goal. There can be no self-indulgence and we need to be tough and accepting of our destiny. For it is often because we are unready to accept difficulty and adversity that we fail to appreciate life. "Life has need of enmity and dying and martyrdoms" (p. 124), says Nietzsche's Zarathustra (1883/1961). It is only when we suffer that we are deepened and go down into the depth of life. Because of this it is only if we are willing to accept what life contains in reality that we can realize our will to power and live in a Dionysian way. Happiness is not something that we should be too keen on, for "Happiness and unhappiness are twins that grow up together" (Nietzsche, 1882/1974, p. 270).

We cannot have happiness on its own, for it will always come with its counterpart of unhappiness. To feel deeply we have to be willing to be open to both kinds of experiences. To pursue one in isolation is not to know life at all. This does not mean that we cannot feel joy, however. Exuberance is a hallmark of Nietzsche's *Ubermensch*. According to Nietzsche what one should aspire to is not the easy effortless happy life, but the life in which we are ready to do our work of living, the labour of life with all its challenges and difficulties:" My suffering and my pity – what of them! For do I aspire after happiness? I aspire after my work" (Nietzsche, 1883/1961, p. 336).

## Heidegger's Re-Owning of Life and Death

Kierkegaard and Nietzsche are the forerunners of modern and postmodern existential philosophy, which begins in earnest with the phenomenology of Husserl and his pupil Heidegger. Heidegger did not intend to write about ethics and his discourse is reserved for ontological descriptions of human existence. His philosophy is metaphysical in nature and he is not interested in the question of human happiness. But many of his ideas are directly relevant to an understanding of the concrete realities of human existence, nevertheless, and his work has been used to underpin new forms of existential psychotherapy (Deurzen, 2010) which very much do wonder how to use his ideas to enable people to live better lives.

Heidegger's (1927a/1962) ontological substratum is that of time. Human beings need to be understood in relation to the horizon of time they are thrown into, which implies that they are born in order to die. It also means that they are always no longer in the present they thought was theirs to keep, and not yet in the future that will be. Time constantly moves us and indeed moves through us. We are time and therefore we are historical, always in progress. This has important implications for our pretensions to a happy life, since happiness, even if it were achievable, would never be a steady presence, but would be fleeting. Everything passes and is in movement. There is no human certainty and human beings are mobile and homeless.

In fact one of the fundamental ontological givens, according to Heidegger, is that of our *Unheimlichkeit* (literally "not at homeness"), the unease that is with us from the outset and that can never be overcome as long as we are alive because human beings are defined by their existence rather than their essence and therefore are for ever doomed to worry about the projects of their life. With death, when our life is finally completed, we may eventually find safety and a home. Human beings, unlike objects, are in a constant process of becoming. We are projected, or thrown into the world towards the project that is our death (Deurzen, 2010, p. 55–56).

We are initially taken over by the world and we fall in with others, to such an extent that we find it hard to live for ourselves, as authentic individuals with awareness of the possibility of our death. Only when objects break down do we become properly aware of them and only when our relations with others become unsatisfactory are we able to start defining ourselves as separate from them. It is thus not the harmony and continuity of a happy and monotonous monochrome existence that makes us who we are, but rather the lack of these things, which invites us to become conscious by experiencing anxiety and guilt, leading to what Heidegger describes as the call of conscience.

It is because we cannot have full presence, but are always standing in what Heidegger terms the ecstasies of past, present, and future, that we can formulate and comprehend the idea of difference and therefore exist for real. The search for happiness in this context would be described as the search for oblivion and ease, for a time when the worry of our care is no longer required and we can sink into the simplicity of merging with all that is. Indeed such falling with others or with the world is the opposite of authentic life. Authentic living is about awareness and requires us to face finitude and reality.

> Impassioned freedom towards death [is] a freedom which has been released from the illusions of the "they" and which is factual, certain of itself, and anxious. (Heidegger, 1927a/1962, p. 266)

For Heidegger then a search for happiness would inevitably be a false, disowned inauthentic way of life, in which we would seek to hide and not own up to the realities of life, covering up the truths about time, death, and other frailties and conflicts of existence.

Of course, since human beings (*Dasein*, literally means being-there but might be best translated as human being) are always related to a world and part of it, absorbed by it, they will continuously worry about this world and this existence they are thrown into and have to stand out in. This worry, or care (*Sorge*) is an ontological given, which flows from the fact that we cannot be separate and are always in relation, so that what we relate to matters very much to us. Our worry only briefly gets covered up when we are in a state of self-deceptive rapture. Such rapture fools itself into the belief that it is aware when it is actually nothing but avoidance and denial of what is really the case. What is the case is that things matter to us and that we need to remain connected to that without which we are nothing. This is a direct consequence of the phenomenological fact of intentionality: i.e., that there can be no conscious life without an object of consciousness and that all is relationship and connectivity (Heidegger, 1927b/1981).

Heidegger sees the human capacity for alienation (*Entfremdung*), closing off (*Verschließen*), and forgetfulness (*Vergessen*) as the enemy of authentic existing. It can be argued that Heidegger's objective for *Dasein* is to have vision, which allows it to grasp past, present, and future at the same time and see the full reality of human existence in one blink of an eye. This moment of vision (*Augenblick*) far from being a moment of happiness is a moment of truth and requires resilient facing up to what is actually the case.

Heidegger moved from describing resolute facing and anticipating of death as the epitome of authentic living in his early work (Heidegger, 1927a/1962), to describing the human capacity for releasement (*Gelassenheit*), or letting be, which puts us in touch with *being* itself in his later work (Heidegger, 1954/1968, 1957, 1959/1966). Both the concepts of resolution and releasement, or letting be, are about disclosing existence more effectively; in essence, both are about opening ourselves up to what is already there. In the first case, we do this by being brave; in the second case, by yielding to Being. But it is never done by a mindless search for oblivion or for happiness and feeling good. Feelings for Heidegger only come into play as a guide to our better understanding and they are not cultivated in their own right, but translated into understanding, then articulated into language.

The feelings that help us find our way are anxiety and guilt as they point us towards that which we still owe to our existence and to Being. When we achieve this we can speak of *Ereignis*, which means literally happening or event, but also means renewal of ownership. We achieve this by deep, meditative thinking instead of calculative thinking or hiding. The goal of such thinking is to let the essence of being manifest. We now have become the guardians of being, allowing the complex interplay of the fourfold, which is that of Earth, Heavens, Divines, and Mortals (Henry, 1969; Heidegger, 1957).

> To be subject to the claim that presence makes is the greatest claim that a human being makes; it is what "ethics" is. (Heidegger, quoted in Boss, 1987/2001, p. 273)

For Heidegger then happiness is not even an option that has remote interest: the state of mind we aim for is openness and receptivity to what Being entails. If we can be true to Being we have done the best we can.

# The Existentialist Solution of Jean-Paul Sartre

Sartre reinterpreted Heidegger's ideas in a concrete and ontic manner. But he, too, had some difficulty in formulating ethical principles, at least initially. Camus and Beauvoir, and to some extent Merleau-Ponty, were more forthcoming on this point.

Sartre argued eagerly in his *Being and Nothingness* (Sartre, 1943/1956), that human beings are pure freedom, pure nothingness that tries to assert a way of being. We have to act in order to be anything at all. We are our actions and therefore we can manipulate our identity by either denying what we are, or pretending that we are something we are not. Interestingly this applies directly to the notion of happiness: the waiter in the café who gingerly maneuvers his towel and tray, is play-acting at being a waiter, but he could equally well play-act at being happy, wearing a cardboard smile on his face. The pursuit of happiness is like the pursuit of *l'homme serieux*, the man who takes himself too seriously and who believes that to make himself solidly happy once and for all is virtuous, or safe, when in fact it is a lie, because it betrays his true condition which is to be nothing and therefore free. We are free to be different things at different times: sometimes the mood takes us to be one thing and sometimes another. Sartre describes how we manipulate our moods to magically fall in with the beliefs that suit us.

The fundamental assumption Sartre makes is that human beings are essentially emptiness. They are not a something like a table or a chair. They are not defined once and for all—for they are fundamentally nothing. If we do not accept this basic idea we can imagine that happiness is the kind of fulfilment we wish to achieve and this is self-deceptive. If we do accept it we see immediately that the chasing of a particular state of mind, be it happiness or anything else, is bad faith (*mauvaise foi*) and is a way of alienating ourselves from our true nature, which is to be nothing and to resonate with the world.

> The human tragedy is that we aspire to being definite and fixed as objects are, while retaining total power and freedom at the same time. Human beings crave to be both in themselves (solid as objects) and for themselves (as self-determining consciousness). In other words, they aim at being substantial subjects. Interestingly, this idea of the combination of total solidity paired with absolute liberty is a classical definition of God. (Deurzen, 2010, p. 80)

Our consciousness is an indeterminate and open experience that gives us access to reflection and self-reflection. But we can also pretend not to have such abilities and choices, giving up our freedom and responsibility, behaving as if our consciousness were solid and set in stone. We can do all that, but the one choice we do not have is not to choose, for not choosing is also a choice.

We are capable of a wide range of choices and emotions and if we choose to settle for happiness, or any other particular emotion or experience, we are by the same token opting to eliminate the wide range of experiences we are in fact capable of and entitled to. If we let ourselves be beguiled by the idea of happiness we lose our capacity for attending to other things in the process. We could argue that such a search for happiness is a search for the end of consciousness, rather than the cultivation of that consciousness, for we can only be happy if we temporarily lose ourselves in the act of enjoyment. Such self-deceptive behaviour requires us to make ourselves one with an idealized image of reality and pretend it will be permanent. It is an act of bad faith in which we give up our capacity for self-reflective consciousness.

Such self-deception or bad faith is always an act of insecurity and fear. It requires that we deny the facts of the human condition, especially the fact that human beings can never be secure, solid, or happy.

It is this very fact of the emptiness and fragility of consciousness that is most important and its denial betrays our capacity for lucidity and transparency. Because of this Sartre's ethical work, which was only fully formulated posthumously, requires us to rethink moral and emotional matters minute by minute. There can never be a definitive ethical framework, nor can there be sure-fire ways towards a happy state.

> There is no abstract ethics. There is only an ethics in a situation and therefore it is concrete. An abstract ethics is that of the good conscience. It assumes that one can be ethical in a fundamentally unethical situation. (Sartre, 1983/1992, p. 17)

# Merleau-Ponty and Camus

Merleau-Ponty's "philosophy of ambiguity" (Kearney, 1986) goes down this same path as he reminds us to be alert to the tricks the mind plays on us. For Merleau-Ponty human life is so fundamentally about contradiction and opposites, which are mediated by the body, that we cannot escape from the ambiguity of sensations or feelings either.

> It is all too easy to let ourselves only be immersed in our embodied situation and not remember previous ones. If we are in a situation we are surrounded and cannot be transparent to ourselves, so that our contact with ourselves is necessarily achieved only in the sphere of ambiguity. (Merleau-Ponty, 1945/1962, p. 381)

We cast our own shadows and there cannot be a blue sky without a cloud. We may sometimes be immersed in the world in an aesthetically pleasing manner, but immediately experience ourselves as confused or out of touch with the very experience we aim to achieve. Unlike Sartre, who saw freedom as the basis of human action, Merleau-Ponty believes that our freedom is gained only from the way in which we act. There is no doubt, however, that both existentialist philosophers prefer freedom to happiness. Freedom opens the world I live in, whereas the pursuit of happiness closes it off and enslaves me to the pursuit of one single experience. Actions are commitments and we should not commit ourselves to anything that takes away the breadth and depth of experience. Experience may be demanding, but it is more worthwhile than stagnation in one state of mind.

Camus (1942/1975) goes a bit further, by describing human existence as a constant struggle, in which many people feel alienated and unsure. But for Camus, ultimately the challenge of life is not to find happiness but to grasp the freedom of having experiences and to persist no matter how difficult the challenges are. Our struggles may seem like Sisyphean tasks, but in accomplishing these tasks and relishing our destiny we can find satisfaction in the very experience of our journey and in the affirmation of our life. Camus's image of human life is that of a Dionysian experience which inspires us to strength even as we are tested and tried. His view is that it is not in spite of hardship that we awaken to our life, but because of it.

Courage and determination are far greater values than the pursuit of happiness. When Camus defines Sisyphus as happy, he means by this that Sisyphus is aware of challenge and struggle. This is clearly not a definition many would agree with.

## Beauvoir's Embrace of an Ethics of Ambiguity

Beauvoir, not unlike Camus, showed that people shape their own destiny in line with their project. She argued that it was crucial to keep such a project alive, renewing it constantly. She believed that when we lose the capacity to connect to our project, we lose ourselves. One way in which this may happen is when we become taken over by others and act out their desires for us, but it can also happen when we give up on our ability for creativity, for instance, when we are aging or when we consider ourselves condemned to a particular fate. She formulated the importance of living our lives passionately (Beauvoir, 1944/2004), without excusing ourselves from taking on board the predicaments we encounter. Human living is full of ambiguity, crisis, contradictions, and dilemmas; and to be fully alive is to be prepared to face these and rigorously work out on each count how best to face the challenges. Such is only possible if we allow ourselves full range of movement rather than confining ourselves to a happy medium where such questions may never arise because they have been suffocated out of life. She puts a premium on freedom, like her male colleagues Sartre, Merleau-Ponty, and Camus, but she shows how such freedom is best encountered and preserved by clear communication and a willingness to be fully present both in one's own life and in relation to others.

Beauvoir is fully aware of the burden of freedom, which does not allow us to rest on our laurels. We need to be prepared for the imperfections of the world, each other, and ourselves (Beauvoir, 1948/1970) and not ask for the guarantee of happiness and ease, but be prepared for whatever life brings on a daily basis and meet this with integrity. It is ultimately passion and commitment that make life worthwhile, not whether we have had a happy life. A happy life only exists in death.

> If it came to be that each man did what he must, existence would be saved in each one without there being any need of dreaming of a paradise where all would be reconciled in death. (Beauvoir, 1948/1970, p. 159)

## Jaspers's Comprehensive Boundary

Jaspers, a psychiatrist turned philosopher, came up with the important insight that life is essentially lived within a frame that has limits to it. To ignore these limits is foolish and yet most of us try to do just that.

> In our day-to-day lives we often evade them, by closing our eyes and living as if they did not exist. We forget that we must die, forget our guilt, and forget that we are at the mercy of chance. (Jaspers, 1951/1954, p. 20)

Jaspers argued that these limit situations should not be avoided, but faced because there is something about the fundamental limits and tragedy of human life that brings out the best in people as well. To be in despair makes one aware of things beyond this world. It is through our suffering and our finality that we become aware of what is not within our grasp and that we begin to aspire to improve ourselves while understanding our limits and finding peace and redemption within these. Jaspers claims that the source of philosophy is not just wonder, as Plato believed, but also doubt and the sense of forsakenness that we get when things go wrong or are hard. It is, in other words, uncertainty and suffering that bring us to life.

I am only myself when I become authentic by being willing to face up to my freedom and possibility as well as to my limitations and my loneliness. Only when I suffer do I find myself and communicate genuinely to others.

> Contrary to a life either without solid substance or a life in which this substance is never affected, only the enthusiastic attitude means a life awake, a life in totality and authenticity . . . Enthusiasm is becoming oneself in the act of devoting oneself. (Jaspers, 1938/1971, p. 119)

Man is inclined to self-forgetfulness. He must snatch himself out of this and not get lost in his work, and thoughtless habits. We need to dare get off the beaten track. One of the best ways to snatch myself out of forgetfulness and into existence is by encountering my limits. They abound. The world is full of them, so it is not hard to do if we let ourselves be unafraid in our encounter of the unusual and the difficult.

Such experiences are like ciphers—a secret text that we can interpret and make sense of. This leads us to live our lives with heroic intensity. Such lives are never lived in isolation. They are lived in the world and with others. Far from searching for happiness, we search for an understanding of all events, limits, and confrontations with difficulty—or even catastrophe.

## Conclusion

In conclusion, there can be little doubt that the tradition of continental philosophy is rather suspicious of the idea of happiness as a panacea of good living. There are no continental philosophers who have ever applauded the pursuit of happiness per se. Continental philosophy has never considered happiness a viable path towards an ethical life. While different authors may disagree on what the important pursuits of life are, they usually value enhanced consciousness, awareness, courage, freedom, truth, and the pursuit of purpose and meaning over the goal of easing one's life into a happy state.

If we are to follow in the steps of continental philosophers and deepen our understanding of human living, we shall have to aim for wisdom rather than for happiness. Wisdom, as defined particularly by Heidegger, means facing the conflicts, dilemmas, and paradoxes of the human condition and working out how best to live with these, whether or not fate smiles on us and whether or not we are fortunate. If Western philosophy is to rise to the global and intercultural challenges ahead, it may benefit from taking on board some of the views of continental philosophy, much as they may seem lacking in scientific rigor and positivity. Continental philosophers invite us to learn the lessons of life itself by throwing ourselves into our existence and feeling deeply and thinking passionately. Happiness then becomes redefined, as Camus pointed out, as the satisfaction of a radical reappraisal of what we might otherwise dismiss as mere challenge and struggle. This, in turn, may lead us to living a very individual and hard-earned, but profoundly meaningful life. The continental contribution to understanding the human plight is to realize that it is in the juxtaposition of good and bad experiences—including those of happiness and suffering—that we get to know life. It is this grappling with difficulty and with ups and downs that creates the possibility for the evolution of a consciousness that is awake and liberated, as it searches for truth, rather than for a state of harmony or happiness.

## REFERENCES

Beauvoir, S. de. (1970). *The ethics of ambiguity*. (B. Frechtman, Trans.). New York, NY: Citadel Press. (Original work published 1948).

Beauvoir, S. de. (2004). Pyrrhus and Cinéas. (M. Timmermann, Trans.). In M. A. Simons, M. Timmermann, & M. B. Mader (Eds.), *Philosophical writings* (pp. 89–149). Urbana, IL: University of Illinois Press. (Original work published 1944).

Boss, M. (2001). (Ed.). *Zollikon seminars: Protocols—conversations—letters*. (F. Mayr & Askay, Trans.). Evanston, IL: Northwestern University Press. (Original work published 1987).

Camus, A. (1975). *The Myth of Sisyphus* (J. O'Brien, Trans. 1955) London, UK: Hamish Hamilton. Reprinted 1975, Harmondsworth, UK: Penguin. (Original work published 1942).

Deurzen, E. V. (2010). *Everyday mysteries: A handbook of existential psychotherapy* (2nd ed.). London, UK: Routledge.

Heidegger, M. (1957). *Vorträge und Aufsätze*. Pfullingen, Germany: Neske.

Heidegger, M. (1962). *Being and time*. (J. Macquarrie & E. S. Robinson, Trans.). London, UK: Harper and Row. (Original work published 1927).

Heidegger, M. (1966). *Discourse on thinking*. (J. M. Anderson & H. Freund, Trans.). New York, NY: Harper and Row. (Original work published 1959).

Heidegger, M. (1968). *What is called thinking?* (G. J. Glenn, Trans.) New York, NY: Harper and Row. (Original work published 1954).

Heidegger, M. (1981). *The basic problems of phenomenology*. (A. Hofstadter, Trans.). Bloomington, IN: Indiana University Press. (Original work published 1927).

Henry, M. (1969). *L'Essence de la Manifestation*. Paris, France: PUF.

Jaspers, K. (1954). *The way to wisdom*. (R. Marsheim, Trans.). New Haven, CT: Yale University Press. (Original work published 1951).

Jaspers, K. (1971). *Philosophy of existence*. (R. F. Grabay, Trans.). Philadelphia, PA: University of Pennsylvania Press. (Original work published 1938).

Kearney, R. (1986). *Modern movements in European philosophy*. Manchester, UK: Manchester University Press.

Kierkegaard, S. (1940). *Stages on life's way*. (H. Hong & E. Hong, Trans.). Princeton, NJ: Princeton University Press. (Original work published 1845).

Kierkegaard, S. (1941). *Concluding unscientific postscript*. (D. F. Swenson & W. Lowrie, Trans.). Princeton, NJ: Princeton University Press. (Original work published 1846).

Kierkegaard, S. (1980). *The concept of anxiety*. (R. Thomte, Trans.). Princeton, NJ: Princeton University Press. (Original work published 1844).

Kierkegaard, S. (1992). *Either/or*. (A. Hannay, Trans.). London, UK: Penguin. (Original work published 1843).

Merleau-Ponty, M. (1962). *Phenomenology of perception*. (C. Smith, Trans.). London, UK: Routledge and Kegan Paul. (Original work published 1945).

Nietzsche, F. (1961). *Thus spoke Zarathustra*. (R. J. Hollingdale, Trans.). Harmondsworth, UK: Penguin. (Original work published 1883).

Nietzsche, F. (1974). *The gay science*. (W. Kaufmann, Trans.). New York, NY: Random House. (Original work published 1882).

Nietzsche, F. (1990). *Beyond good and evil*. (R. J. Hollingdale, Trans.). Harmondsworth, UK: Penguin. (Original work published 1886).

Rosen, M. (1998). Continental philosophy from Hegel. In A. C. Grayling (Ed.), *Philosophy 2: Further through the subject* (pp. 663–704). Oxford, UK: Oxford University Press.

Sartre, J. P. (1956). *Being and nothingness—An essay on phenomenological ontology*. (H. Barnes, Trans.). New York, NY: Philosophical Library. (Original work published 1943).

Sartre, J. P. (1992). *Notebooks for an ethics*. (D. Pellaner, Trans.). Chicago, IL: University of Chicago Press. (Original work published 1983).

# CHAPTER 22

# THE SEDUCTIONS OF HAPPINESS

## RAYMOND ANGELO BELLIOTTI

SUNY Fredonia, USA

With the exception of love, no human experience is celebrated more than happiness. We pursue wealth, success, honor, relationships, education, and the like because we believe they will lead to our happiness. Parents often say that what they want most for their children is happiness. The intuition is clear: our accomplishments, careers, relationships, the potentials we realize, are hollow if they do not make us happy (Belliotti, 2004).

However, throughout the history of philosophy, different definitions of "happiness," explanations of appropriate recipes for attaining happiness, and accounts of why these recipes make human beings happy abound. Until we understand precisely what someone means by "happiness," we cannot begin to answer the major questions: Is happiness attainable? If so, how might we attain it? How great a personal good is happiness? Are the best lives necessarily happy lives? Is happiness necessary for a good life, a meaningful life, a worthwhile life? Does it matter how we achieve happiness?

In this essay, I discuss and reject the possibility that happiness is an illusion, a fruitless goal whose pursuit underscores the desperation of the human condition. I then explain and evaluate happiness understood as a predominantly positive state of mind. I argue that such happiness can sometimes be attained in uninspiring ways that demonstrate the sense in which happiness is overrated. I then sketch contemporary philosophical views of happiness, highlighting their strategies and shortcomings. Finally, I relate the pursuit of happiness to the search for meaning and value. I conclude that leading a robustly meaningful, valuable life merits worthwhile happiness. But worthwhile happiness does not automatically follow from such a life. If we must choose, a robustly meaningful, valuable life is preferable to a merely happy life.

## Happiness as Illusion

Arthur Schopenhauer (1788–1860) (1818–1844/1948) was deeply skeptical that attaining happiness was even possible. Human life is beset with universal, unavoidable suffering which prevents fulfillment of basic needs and wants. Life itself, not merely mortality and fear of death, renders human existence problematic. Striving is the basic nature of the will, and no finished project can end striving. Schopenhauer envisions human beings as fastened to a punishing pendulum: Sensing a lack or deficiency we conjure, subconsciously or consciously, a desire. We pursue that desire and either attain it or fail to do so. If we fail, we become frustrated, disappointed, angry, and may even indulge self-pity. If we attain our goal, we experience a brief period of elation, followed swiftly by boredom. Attaining our goal never brings the glorious transformation we had imagined. Because striving is incapable of final serenity, we alternate between the lack of fulfillment we feel when not achieving temporary goals and the sense of letdown and boredom we feel when we attain them. In either case, we soon thereafter pursue new goals, obtusely hoping for a different result while repeating the same futile process.

Schopenhauer claims, then, that human desire is unquenchable. Much like Plato's tyrannical man, we create new desires soon after we fulfill earlier desires. We always want more regardless of how many desires we fulfill. Worse, a few "decoy birds" that seem to be happy lure us into mindlessly remaining on this self-defeating pendulum of desire. Schopenhauer concludes, along with the Buddhists, that we should minimize our attachments to this life and withdraw from it as much as possible. Our existence is cheeriest when we perceive it least. Philosophical contemplation, music, and art elevate us by allowing us to be disinterested spectators of life. But only specially gifted human beings can pursue such lofty activity and they will pay a price for their talents: They are more vulnerable to suffering and are estranged from the masses.

We should not jump aboard Schopenhauer's pessimistic bandwagon. He fails to see that value and meaning need not be permanent to be real; that process renders fulfillments independently of attaining goals; that the attainments of great effort and creation do not instantaneously produce emptiness; and that suffering is not inherently negative but can be transfigured for creative advantage.

What is the state to which Schopenhauer aspires? Does he secretly yearn for a condition of never-ending bliss? Does freedom from suffering require that we want nothing more? Many would find such a life deadening. A life devoid of new projects, adventures, journeys, and goals lacks creativity: bland contentment replaces vigorous thought and action. Perhaps suffering is produced not by the process of seeking fulfillment of new desires but by starving our desire-creating mechanism. Having unfulfilled desires need not be painful; it is often exhilarating. We imagine rewarding new situations and pursue them vigorously. We find fulfillments in the process and, often, in achieving the goal. Our insatiability ensures that we continue to imagine and pursue rewarding projects, instead of being limited to contemplating earlier fulfillments. Whether the new desires we create produce suffering depends on what they are and how we pursue them, not solely on their presence.

A crude dualism infects Schopenhauer's analysis. He separates human experience into desires and results. But human life is not experienced as a series of discrete pursuits of isolated goals. The process of striving itself yields satisfactions independently of attaining its goals. Upon being attained, goals propel us to new projects. Boredom results from inactivity, a loss of faith in life, and a lack of imagination. But human beings live in a continuous process of desires, finding appropriate means of satisfying those desires, and failing to achieve or attaining the ends we seek. As a continuous process, the categories of desires, means, and ends are fluid. What is called an end in relation to a particular means is itself a means to another end. What is an end with respect to a particular desire is itself a desire leading to pursuit of another end. The continuous process, at its best, energizes our spirit, manifests our faith in life, and reveals our imagination (Singer, 1982).

Schopenhauer talks of our incessant striving as if it were a disease to be eradicated through withdrawal. But human beings are not static characters trying to find a fixed point called "contentment." If contentment suggests inactivity, a final termination, or a mere savoring of the past then it does conjure terminal boredom or retreat from the world. If we understand contentment more robustly we will underscore its compatibility with continuous activity and self-creation. Contentment is not a final resting point, but a positive self-appraisal: an acknowledgment that we are on the proper course, a savoring of the past seasoned with hope for the future, a satisfaction with the self we are creating. Schopenhauer failed to understand that if we create an endless supply of rewarding projects, our lack of final satisfaction bears joyous tidings. Accordingly, human beings should not conclude that happiness is an illusion.

# Happiness as a Predominantly Positive State of Mind

The popular understanding of "happiness" is merely introspective and descriptive, an accurate self-report of a person's predominantly positive state of mind. If I report truthfully and accurately that I am happy—that I have a relatively enduring positive state of mind such as peace or exuberance—then I am happy. Happiness does not include a necessary normative element. This understanding of happiness is our prevalent cultural rendering and finds support in contemporary philosophical and psychological literature (Barrow, 1980; Von Wright, 1963).

While happiness so conceived is easily understood, its consequences are often ignored. Under the contemporary understanding, happiness cannot be the greatest personal good, is often not a great good, and is sometimes not a good at all.

*The successful immoralist.* While the possibilities of a thoroughly depraved, moral monster enjoying extended peace or exuberance are slim, morally unworthy people can attain the relatively enduring positive psychological state required for the contemporary understanding of happiness. Immanuel Kant (1724–1804) (1926, 1789/1943) argued that the morally unworthy do not deserve happiness, and that being morally worthy is a greater good than the happiness enjoyed by the unworthy villain. He was correct, at least insofar as the happiness of the villain is derived from unworthy deeds. We should not begrudge the happiness that the scoundrel gains from loving relationships, charitable acts, appreciation of the arts, and other worthy activities. To the extent, though, that the scoundrel wrongly benefits from villainy he or she does not deserve happiness. For Kant to say that the morally unworthy do not deserve to be happy, that the world would be better served if they were unhappy, resonates with our sense of justice. He understood the possibility of someone becoming unrighteously happy, being gratified by attaining wrongful goals. Such happiness is not a good.

*The master hypnotist.* Although Kant did not bring them to the forefront, his analysis suggests other ways that happiness would not be a great personal good. Suppose a master hypnotist charms a person into thinking he or she possesses a happy state of mind. The person thinks he or she is happy and, thus, is happy under the contemporary understanding of the term.

The state of mind, though, is false. It is not causally connected to the life the person has led, the character the person embodies, the choices the person has made, or accurate self-appraisals. The happiness is artificial because it is based only on an externally induced illusion. The same analysis holds true of a healthy person whose positive state of mind is induced externally by an injection of happiness serum.

*Virtual reality.* Robert Nozick (1974) imagines an experience machine that can give us any experience we desire. Our brains could be stimulated so we would think and feel that we were winning the Nobel Prize, having dinner with our favorite celebrity, breaking Barry Bonds's home-run record, engaging in a torrid love affair with the person of our dreams, or anything else we want to experience. All the while we would be floating in a tank with electrodes attached to our brains. We could, if we wished, plug into the machine for life and program our entire life's experiences. Or we could program some time out of the tank every 2 years or so to select the experiences for the next period of our lives. While in the tank we will not know we are there. We will think it is all actually happening. Assuming all other logistics could be resolved (for example, a team to monitor the tank, ways to fulfill our nutritional needs, required medical care, arranging the blissful death that must eventually come), would we choose to enter the tank for an extended period?

In an age of developing virtual realities, Nozick's thought experiment is less bizarre than might first seem. He argues that we would reject the experience machine for at least three reasons. First, doing things is more important than having the sensations of doing them. More matters to us than merely how our lives feel from within. Second, we want to become a certain type of person, not simply float in a tank as a bland receptacle of sensations. Third, the experience machine limits us to an artificial reality which prevents actual contact with any deeper reality. The experience machine lives our lives for us instead of helping us live our own life. However sophisticated we imagine the machine, its major function is to remove us from reality and prevent us from making any difference in the world. Our rejection of an experience machine that encloses us within a framework of just our own experiences, suggests that connecting with things and values beyond our individual experiences is more important to us than the artificial happiness spawned by the machine.

*Radical delusion.* Consider another case. A person enjoys extended bliss and attains the requisite psychological state that defines the contemporary notion of happiness. However, the person suffers from deep delusion: He sincerely believes he is living in the early nineteenth century and is Napoleon. His happiness is based on savoring his imagined power and his string of military triumphs, and hatching grandiose plans for the future. Yes, things could be worse. Better to be deluded Napoleon pleased by his imaginary lot than to be deluded Stalin dissatisfied by his imaginary life. Still, how can such a condition be good at all, much less a great personal good? If our positive state of mind is not connected to moral goodness, to valuable accomplishments, to continued intellectual growth, or even to reality, what is it worth?

*The accident victim.* Suppose you were the victim of a horrible automobile accident that rendered you incapable of any biographical life beyond that of a contented child. However, in your infantile condition you are happier than you were as a normal adult. True, after suffering a serious brain injury, a person is better off as an adult leading the life of a contented child than she would be leading the life of a miserable brat. But would we consider such a person fortunate? Would we hope to attain her situation?

*Trivial pursuits.* If you were strongly socialized, even brainwashed, into responding joyfully to small pleasures and minor enterprises but were unable to show courage, self-sufficiency, and boldness would we count you fortunate because you were happy? Ignorance, under certain circumstances, can be bliss. Such bliss is no more valuable than the ignorance that grounds it.

Friedrich Nietzsche (1844–1900) (1883–1885/1978) derided "the last man" as "the most contemptible and despicable" of creatures. Along with utilitarian philosophers, last men, Nietzsche's male-gendered notion of embodied banality, extol the values of hedonism. The highest ambitions of last men are comfort and security. They are the extreme case of the herd mentality: habit, custom, indolence, egalitarianism, self-preservation, and muted will to power prevail. Last men embody none of the inner tensions and conflicts that spur transformative action. They take no risks, lack convictions, avoid experimentation, and seek only bland survival. Such people lack deep convictions, inspiring projects, or significant purposes. They often attain happiness, but at an unacceptable cost.

With the proper imagination and appropriate details these examples can be more vividly and convincingly drawn. As it stands, I have sketched a host of happy people who enjoy a relatively enduring positive state of mind. None of these types exemplify an attractive lifestyle. Some deserve our pity, some our concern, others our contempt. Happiness so conceived is not the greatest personal good, or a great good, and in several cases not a good at all.

Note that as unalluring as the hypothetical lives appear, they are not the worst imaginable existences. To say that we would never prefer to adopt these lifestyles would be a mistake. Everything depends on our point of comparison. I would not prefer any of the hypothetical lives given my present situation. The lives depicted are all deficient. Some lack appropriate connection to reality. Some provide only muted meaning, significance, and value. Some are animated by extravagant psychological deficiencies. Such lifestyles neither warrant our allegiance nor inspire our confidence. Nevertheless, we can imagine even worse circumstances. We might prefer, for example, the simulated joys of the virtual reality machine to a life filled with enduring misery, oppression, and ignorance. That the hypothetical lives are not the worst imaginable existences is, though, faint consolation.

Consider the lives of the following: Ludwig van Beethoven, Joe DiMaggio, Emily Dickinson, Queen Elizabeth I, Abraham Lincoln, Emma Goldman, Jesus, Moses, Søren Kierkegaard, Michelangelo Buonarroti, and Vincent Van Gogh. These lives are paradigms of meaning, value, and significance in music, sports, literature, politics, religion, philosophy, and art. In terms of relatively enduring accomplishments, influences, excellences, creations, and social effects these lives are among the best in their fields.

Yet these people were not strikingly happy. While each of them flourished in many respects, none realized the extended peace or exuberance characteristic of happiness. Perhaps they demanded too much of themselves, saw reality too clearly, were unable to harbor self-flattering illusions, could not savor their feelings of pleasure, lacked the necessary biochemistry, or were too heroic to be happy. Robustly meaningful, valuable lives, then, are not necessarily happy lives (Belliotti, 2001).

Accordingly, some people who attain happiness understood as a predominantly positive state of mind lead unworthy lives and other people who lead worthy lives do not attain happiness. Thus, how we attain happiness is crucial to its value; to be a great personal good, happiness must be constituted by or connected to the higher values; a *worthwhile* happiness is more than merely a relatively enduring positive psychological state; and happiness gains value when it is earned, when the happy person is a worthy person.

# Contemporary Philosophical views of Happiness

Some contemporary philosophers argue that happiness is not merely an enduring positive state of mind. Happiness is not merely descriptive, but also normative. When we assert in good faith that we are happy we are not only reporting our psychological state but also positively evaluating our lives. We are saying that we are peaceful, contented, or exuberant and that we *deserve* these feelings given the lives we are leading. Our happiness is not capricious or fortuitous. It is merited by a life well lived.

Appeals to evaluation invite a question about standards: Whose standards supply the relevant criteria for appraisal? Standards can be purely objective or purely subjective or some combination of the two. By invoking a normative standard, philosophers hope to connect "happiness" to value. But each type of standard bears its own strengths and weaknesses.

## Purely objective standards

To invoke purely objective standards is to connect "happiness" most securely to value. We are happy if and only if our lives correlate to objective standards that define meaning, significance, and value. Under this view, the highest human end cannot merely be what a person chooses, but what all human beings must seek in order to be rational and moral. We must rationally apprehend and obey the imperatives of an external, metaphysical normative order (Finnis, 1985; Pieper, 1957/1958).

But objective standards of this kind are notoriously difficult to establish. Are they grounded in the dictates of a Supreme Being or embedded in Nature or in the proper application of Reason? All such claims are metaphysically dubious. And even if we could establish the existence of these metaphysical linchpins, we face the daunting problem of discerning which of our conclusions correspond to the imperatives of the Supreme Being, Nature, or Reason. That is, even if we know that an objective standard exists, how do we know when our judgments comply with that standard? Moreover, an objective standard might suggest implausibly that one ideal lifestyle and series of preferences exists for all of us. Also, if we react to these difficulties by claiming that the allegedly objective standards are more earth-bound, grounded only in our traditions and societal ideals, then they are accessible. But accessibility brings a stiff price. The objective standards reflect merely intersubjective agreement, perhaps over time. Such a standard urges us to conform to prevalent norms and dominant ideas. These invitations are redolent with the stench of mere conventionalism. Finally, even if we could resolve all these difficulties, would it not be possible to fulfill the purely objective standards of happiness yet not *feel* happy? Could we still be sad? If so, insisting that we are happy, although we do not know it, rings hollow.

## Purely subjective standards

The seemingly insurmountable difficulties faced by purely objective standards have led some thinkers to invoke purely subjective criteria: I am happy only if I am living up to my personal preferences about how I should live. This is the *happiness-as-positive-self-appraisal* view (Goldstein, 1973; Kraut, 1979). These preferences may or may not correlate to those of societal norms, alleged objective criteria embedded in the universe, or the imperatives of human reason.

By reconnecting reality with normative judgment, this view makes happiness more valuable than it sometimes is under the happiness-as-predominantly-positive-state-of-mind position. However, opponents of subjectivism lodge three primary objections. First, they argue that we might be mistaken in our evaluation that we have met our own standards. We could err in thinking that we are living up to our personal preferences when we are not. Under such circumstances, we think we are happy but we are not. Because the happiness-as-positive-self-appraisal philosophers add a normative component to the meaning of happiness, they must admit the possibility of mistakes in our appraisals. Therefore, our sincere reports of a positive, relatively enduring state of mind are not enough to establish that we are happy. We must also judge accurately that we are meeting our subjective standards about how our lives should be lived.

Note that this objection does not apply to the happiness-as-predominantly-positive-state-of-mind view. The social scientists and philosophers who hold this view claim happiness is purely descriptive: If I report truthfully that I am happy then I am happy. The causal link between my positive state of mind and what brought it about is unimportant for accurate claims to happiness. Deluded Napoleon, the person in the virtual reality machine, the modern version of Nietzsche's last man, and the rest of my hypothetical frolickers are all happy.

The happiness-as-positive-self-appraisal brigade must disagree. If I am deluded and merely think I am living up to my personal evaluative standards while I am not, then I wrongly think I am happy. So deluded Napoleon, assuming his personal evaluative standard is to conquer Europe, is not truly happy under this view (unless he antecedently desired to be deluded). He is not living up to his standards. He only thinks he is. If the hypnotized adult and person on the virtual reality machine have standards different from the lives they are actually leading then they are not happy even though they appear and claim to be happy. The modern version of Nietzsche's last man, though, could still be happy under this view, but only if his major desires focus on leading precisely the indolent life he exemplifies. Thus, the happiness-as-positive-self-appraisal view connects happiness to reality and to normative judgment. The position denies legitimacy to those whose claims to happiness are grounded in deep delusion, artificial inducement, or external imposition. The position forces us to evaluate, not merely describe, our psychological state. The position admits degrees of happiness and does not impose a particular ideal on everyone. Whether these differences are improvements or competing understandings of happiness is contestable.

Second, opponents of subjectivism argue that someone who fulfills internal standards that are immoral does not merit happiness. The happiness attained by such a reprobate strikes a sour note. Accordingly, merely fulfilling our subjective standards is neither sufficient nor necessary for happiness. We should examine the quality of internal standards, not merely take them as givens.

Third, critics point out that under this view happiness can be attained by meeting subjective standards that are uninspiring and effete, even if they are not immoral. Nietzsche's last man, steadfastly pursuing only comfort, security, conformity, and indolence, could easily be happy. A young adult who suffers a serious, irreversible brain injury and endures as a contented child thereafter could easily be happy. Such happiness, although not the worst alternative available, is not necessarily a great good. Nietzsche sneers contemptuously at the happiness of the last man. We would not cheer the brain injury of the young adult even if it made her "happier" than she was prior to the injury.

Again, I am not arguing that happiness-as-positive-self-appraisal fails to understand the real meaning of "happiness." Such arguments are not my concern. I argue only that happiness attained on these grounds cannot be the greatest personal good, is not necessarily a great good, and is sometimes not a good at all.

## Combining objective and subjective standards

Disturbed by the implications of invoking purely objective or purely subjective standards, some philosophers argue that a more reasonable objectivism is required (Griffin, 1986; Kekes, 1992; McFall, 1984). Such an objectivism demands an appeal both to subjective standards internal to a life and to objective standards grounded in shared community life.

The motivation of this view flows from a conviction that the happiness-as-positive-self-evaluation does not go far enough in connecting happiness and value. Although advocates of this view do not insist on one final good or a particular ideal lifestyle applicable to everyone, they resist the invitation of subjectivists to accept claims to happiness based on the satisfaction of immoral or unworthy desires. Again, opponents of subjectivism argue that someone who fulfills internal standards that are immoral or unworthy does not merit happiness. Accordingly, merely fulfilling our subjective standards is neither sufficient nor necessary for happiness. Our positive self-evaluation must be *accurate*; it must be based on a standard that is valuable, not merely a standard that happens to be *ours*.

Under this view, people may assert sincerely that they enjoy a relatively enduring positive psychological state and that they are meeting their subjective standards for living, but be mistaken that they are happy. Happiness also requires standards that are rationally justified. Some subjective standards will fail this test. This can happen for numerous reasons. A set of subjective standards might not fulfill the needs and basic wants of physical, emotion, and social life: a person might set standards that are dismally low. A set of subjective standards might be radically at odds with dominant, justified social morality: a person might have immoral standards. A set of subjective standards might not lead us to a good life, one embodying sufficient exercise of the best human capabilities: a person might set standards that dishonor uniquely human attributes, or that insufficiently animate robust self-creation. Although no single ideal or particular lifestyle must be fulfilled, not all subjective standards will foster a happy life. Human lives have no single, preordained *telos*, but some lives are rationally indefensible.

Happiness as *accurate-positive-self-appraisal* has its roots in Aristotelian and self-realization theory. Under this view, people whose dominant life goals are to collect bobby pins, to become a famous gangster, to luxuriate in a simulated, favorable environment, to derive contentment from deep delusion, and the like cannot be happy. Regardless of their extended peace, serenity, or exuberance, and their correct judgment that they are fulfilling their internal standards, such people lead rationally or morally indefensible lives. The collection of bliss-seekers described above falls short because leading a rationally and morally justified life is necessary to attain happiness under this view.

Beginning with sound intentions, this view strikes an imperialistic chord. The good intentions center on reconnecting happiness with value. Possessing a relatively enduring, positive psychological state grounded in adequately satisfying our subjective standards is not enough. Such happiness can be overrated, even dishonorable, irrational, or pathetic. Only reconnecting happiness with value, rationality, and higher human capabilities can re-establish its necessary worth.

The imperialistic chord resounds when we understand that this view dismisses sincere, accurate claims to happiness through semantic fiat. The advocate of happiness as predominantly positive-state-of-mind could object: "Why cannot happiness be grounded on simple pursuits, based on the exercise of limited capabilities, or correlated to our subjective expectations? Why say that the adult who suffers a terrible brain injury and who can live only the life of a contented child cannot be happy? Granted, such a life is less worthy than the lives to which we aspire, but sometimes we must play the cards we are dealt. Better, in the circumstances described, to live the life of a contented child than numerous other horrible imaginable lives. Why not say that the injured adult is happy, while recognizing that but for the injury he or she would have probably lived a much better life? As long as we do not insist that happiness is the greatest personal good, no problem arises. Sure, some happy lives are better lives overall than others on a host of dimensions, but that does not rule out the latter from being happy lives."

Again, we confront the tension in conceptions of happiness. As demonstrated, achieving happiness understood as a predominantly positive psychological state does not necessarily translate into a valuable life. Worthwhile happiness presupposes a connection to value, grounded either in metaphysically objective standards or in rational human appraisal. Why, though, must happiness be understood as accompanying only valuable lives?

Nietzsche (1883–1885/1978) disparaged the happiness of last men as unworthy of emulation, but he never denied that they were happy. Their happiness manifested acutely that a positive psychological state is not necessarily the highest value or even valuable. Nietzsche would agree with advocates of the instant view that a worthy happiness must be grounded in valuable attitudes and activities—although he would excoriate the conventionalism and appeal to societal norms upon which their rational and moral appraisals often depend. Nietzsche would also agree that self-direction was crucial and that a relatively enduring, positive psychological state is merited by those who live well. Happiness, though, for Nietzsche was not automatically a great good. The greatest good is the maximally affirmative attitude toward life, the values it exudes, the creative projects it undertakes, and the obstacles it vanquishes. A worthwhile happiness is often, but not invariably, an accompanying benefit.

Another possible objection to the happiness as accurate-positive-self-appraisal position is that it might rule out a social reformer such as Martin Luther King, Jr, from being considered happy because his values conflicted with those of the larger community. But the theory does not require a tight correlation between the values of individuals and those practiced by the larger community. The theory rules out only irrational, morally indefensible lifestyles. For example, in the case of King, to argue that he was insisting only that the larger community live up to its own professed ideals is plausible. Thus, the theory would not rule out the possibility of happiness for King. Still, this view bears a murky relationship to existing societal norms and is vulnerable to degenerating into mere conventionalism if applied clumsily.

In sum, the happiness as accurate-positive-self-appraisal position plausibly reconnects happiness with value. By going beyond happiness-as-positive-self-appraisal and requiring independent rational evaluation or minimal conditions of rational affirmation, the happiness as accurate-positive-self-appraisal position ensures that happiness is typically a good, often a great good. Yet it does not appeal to highly contestable metaphysical entities such as the dictates of a Supreme Being, the natural order built into the universe, or the imperatives of a fixed human nature. As a result, the position reasonably defines *worthwhile* happiness. My major misgiving is its aspiration to define happiness *as such*. A broad understanding of happiness is preferable to views that demand through definitional fiat that happiness *must* be valuable, even a great good.

## The Search for Meaning and Value

Nietzsche understood that greatness necessarily involves suffering and the overcoming of grave obstacles. He evaluated peoples, individuals, and cultures by their ability to transform suffering and tragedy to spiritual advantage. We cannot eliminate suffering, but we can use it creatively. Suffering and resistance can stimulate and nourish our highest creative energies. By changing our attitude toward suffering from pity to affirmation, we open ourselves to greatness. Nietzsche (1886/1966, 1882/1974, 1883–1885/1978) embraces the criterion of power: exertion, struggle, and suffering are at the core of overcoming obstacles, and human beings experience and truly feel their power only through overcoming obstacles. Higher human types joyfully embrace Nietzsche's "new happiness." We must acknowledge that final serenity or complete fulfillment is not available. The will to power is our second-order (general) desire from which all first-order (specific, determinant) desires flow. The will to power demands strong resistance, grand obstacles, and daunting challenges in the pursuit of first-order desires. The will to power aspires to overcome such resistance and obstacles in attaining first-order desires. But the will to power also desires continued resistance: eliminating all challenges and obstacles would prevent further growth and increased strength. Accordingly, the satisfaction of the will to power in regard to a particular first-order end implies dissatisfaction as well: a new first-order desire is required to renew the process. The core of the new happiness is continuous, insatiable striving in pursuit of self-overcoming and greater strength. Happiness, then, is a process—a particular type of activity—not a certain kind of condition or state. Progress is measured in terms of increased power in confrontation with more difficult challenges. In short, Nietzsche turns Schopenhauer on his head: our inveterate striving does not fasten us to a punishing pendulum, but opens transcendent possibilities for self-transformation and personal redemption.

In that vein, robustly meaningful lives do not necessarily include extended peace or exuberance, but they almost always include the ecstasy joined to great accomplishments and pursuits. But heroism and greatness often preclude happiness in non-Nietzschean senses because periods of savoring and contentment are more fleeting than in non-heroic meaningful lives. The hero confronts greater obstacles, expends his or her energies more extravagantly, and is less likely to survive than the non-hero.

Better to be Beethoven, DiMaggio, or Michelangelo unhappy than to be happy by minimally fulfilling the criteria of the happiness-as-accurate-positive-self-appraisal conception. Still, non-Nietzschean happiness is not everything, but it is something. Beethoven's life would have been better if he could have been happy, as well as being one of the world's greatest creators, but his life was still great and eminently worth living. DiMaggio's life would have been better if he could have been happy as well as being one of the world's greatest athletes, but his life was still great and eminently worth living. (A complicating factor: Is there a connection between unhappiness and exceptional creativity? Did Beethoven's and DiMaggio's perfectionist tendencies, psychological conflicts, and profound dissatisfactions contribute to their high creativity? Could they have been happy and still have produced what they did?)

Happiness remains valuable in most cases, but it is not the most important human aspiration. Robustly meaningful, valuable lives bring satisfaction and are typically accompanied by worthwhile happiness. Even if they cannot guarantee happiness, such lives are more valuable than happy, minimally meaningful lives. Even worthwhile happiness, then, is not the greatest personal good. A life lived well is a greater good than the deserved gratification that typically accompanies it: Better to live extraordinarily well and not be particularly happy, than to live less well and be deservedly happy. In sum, a happy life is not the same thing as a robustly meaningful, valuable life, although the two are often correlated. We are best off having it all—living happy, robustly meaningful, valuable lives. But if we must choose, a robustly meaningful, valuable life is preferable to a merely happy life.

In that vein, if our children lead robustly meaningful, valuable lives, they will deserve worthwhile happiness and often realize it. But even if they are not predominantly happy, they will have fought the good fight, fashioned a worthwhile biography, and added value to the world. We should all be so fortunate.

## Acknowledgements

Much of this article is adopted from my book *Happiness is Overrated* (Lanham, MD: Rowman & Littlefield Publishers, 2004) with permission of the publisher.

### References

Barrow, R. (1980). *Happiness and schooling*. New York, NY: St. Martin's Press.
Belliotti, R. A. (2001). *What is the meaning of human life?* Amsterdam, the Netherlands: Editions Rodopi.
Belliotti, R. A. (2004). *Happiness is overrated*. Lanham, MD: Rowman & Littlefield Publishers.
Finnis, J. (1985). Practical reasoning, human goods, and the end of man. *Proceedings of the American Catholic Philosophical Association*, 58, 23–36.
Goldstein, I. (1973). Happiness. *International Philosophical Quarterly*, 13, 523–534.
Griffin, J. (1986). *Well-being*. Oxford, UK: Clarendon Press.
Kant, I. (1926). *Critique of practical reason and other works on the theory of ethics*. (T.K. Abbot, Trans.). London, UK: Longmans, Green Publishers. (Original works written eighteenth century).
Kant, I. (1943). *Critique of pure reason*. (J. M. D. Meiklejohn, Trans.). New York, NY: John Wiley. (Original work published 1787).

Kekes, J. (1992). *The examined life.* University Park, PA: The Pennsylvania State University Press.

Kraut, R. (1979). Two conceptions of happiness. *Philosophical Review, 88,* 167–197.

McFall, L. (1984). Happiness, rationality, and individual ideals. *Review of Metaphysics, 38,* 595–613.

Nietzsche, F. (1966). *Beyond good and evil.* (W. Kaufmann, Trans.). New York, NY: Random House. (Original work published 1886).

Nietzsche, F. (1974). *The gay science.* (W. Kaufmann, Trans.). New York, NY: Random House. (Original work published 1882).

Nietzsche, F. (1978). *Thus spoke Zarathustra.* (W. Kaufmann, Trans.). New York, NY: Random House. (Original work written 1883–1885).

Nozick, R. (1974). *Anarchy, state, and utopia.* New York, NY: Basic Books.

Pieper, J. (1958). *Happiness and contemplation.* (R. Winston & C. Winston, Trans.). New York, NY: Pantheon Press. (Original work published 1957).

Schopenhauer, A. (1948). *The world as will and idea.* (R. B. Haldane & J. Kemp, Trans.). London, UK: Routledge & Kegan Paul. (Original work published 1818–1844).

Singer, I. (1982). *Meaning in life.* New York, NY: The Free Press.

Von Wright, G. H. (1963). *The varieties of goodness.* London, UK: Routledge & Kegan Paul.

# CHAPTER 23

# THE NATURE AND SIGNIFICANCE OF HAPPINESS

DANIEL M. HAYBRON

Saint Louis University, USA

## Introduction

THERE is no point trying to define "happiness" once and for all: the word has too many meanings for that. This chapter will focus just on the uses of "happiness" that have come to dominate scientific and popular discussions of well-being. Evidently a lot of people want to be happier, or less unhappy at any rate, and the masses are forking over quite a bit of cash to psychologists, and others peddling the wares of psychologists, to learn how. What exactly are they seeking? Roughly speaking, there are three main answers on offer: a favorable attitude toward one's life (the *life satisfaction* theory); a favorable emotional condition (the *emotional state* theory); or pleasure (*hedonism*). This chapter will discuss only the first two theories, as many of the points made here about emotional state extend to hedonism, and hedonism seems to this writer distinctly less promising than the other two views.[1] Both life satisfaction and emotional state conceptions of happiness find support in ordinary usage, so we could reasonably use "happy" and its cognates either way. But they are not at all equivalent, and in fact have radically different kinds of practical import.

This chapter will briefly examine these two ways of conceptualizing happiness, suggesting that only an emotional state view can sustain commonsense views about the significance of happiness. While it is not an abuse of the language to use terms like "happy" to denote life satisfaction, it can be highly misleading: life satisfaction is much less important than we ordinarily take happiness to be. Better, for most purposes, to understand happiness as a matter of a person's overall emotional condition. It matters less how we use the word "happiness",

---

[1] On the troubles with hedonism about happiness, see Haybron (2008). For an important recent defense of hedonism, see Feldman 2010.

however, than that we understand the very different sorts of significance of the different psychological conditions that go by that name, and that research on "happiness" respects these differences.

# Two Literatures on "Happiness," Two Subject Matters

We will not say much about Aristotle. Nor Plato, Aquinas, or Kant. The reason is that, as the popular media and most contemporary "happiness" researchers tend to use the term, these thinkers did not clearly *have* theories of happiness. Consider an example:

> George is generally very cheerful, highly satisfied with his life, and feels deeply fulfilled. He enjoys his life greatly and has a very pleasant experience on the whole. But he does not realize that his wife, children and friends can't stand him, ridiculing him behind his back. They pretend to love him only because he is wealthy. If he knew these things, he would be devastated. But he remains ignorant of the facts even into old age, and feels completely satisfied through the end of his life. He never learns the truth.

The reader may recognize this story as a variant of Robert Nozick's (1989) famous "experience machine" case, which involves plugging into a virtual reality device.[2] Was George happy? By many people's lights, yes, including all but three of the 39 undergraduates who assessed this vignette in a questionnaire.[3] Yet many find it implausible to think that George was doing very *well*, and indeed his predicament is likely to seem deeply unfortunate, even pathetic. Most philosophers also find it unintuitive to ascribe well-being to someone like George. A majority of students seem to have had a similar reaction, disagreeing with the suggestion that he was "fortunate," "enviable," "enjoyed a high level of well-being," or "flourished."

Interestingly, a slight majority of students (21 of 39) also did not think that George had a happy *life*. Yet virtually all of them also said he was *happy*. This result actually seems rather intuitive, and probably reflects a crucial ambiguity in the language of happiness: when speaking about whether a *person* is happy, we typically mean only to be describing the person's state of mind. Call this the *long-term psychological sense* of "happiness"—"long-term" to distinguish it from the short-lived emotion of *feeling* happy, which might be just one part, or no part at all, of *being* happy.

But when speaking of someone's leading a happy *life*, we seem not merely to be describing her mental state. For one thing, people's lives contain much more than mental states. Instead, we seem to be making a value judgment, evaluating how well the person's life is going for her. Is she fortunate, flourishing, doing well, enjoying a high level of well-being? The subject, in short, appears to be what philosophers tend to call *well-being*, welfare, or flourishing. Call this the *well-being sense* of "happiness". Most historical literature referring to "happiness", including translations of Aristotle, Aquinas, and so forth, employs the term in this way.

---

[2] This study was discussed in Haybron (2008), where a more extensive discussion of linguistic matters appears.

[3] The questionnaire was administered at the start of the semester to students in two sections of an introductory ethics course.

Given this impressive historical pedigree, the present chapter could with some justice have taken the well-being notion as its subject matter; it would then be a discussion of the ethical ideal of well-being, the best-known theories being hedonism, desire satisfaction views, and objectivist accounts such as Aristotelianism.[4] Yet the vast majority of contemporary research under the rubric of happiness, as well as most popular discussions of it, does not use the term this way: it concerns the purely psychological notion. Suppose that a paper on subjective well-being appears in a prestigious scientific journal, claiming that people in Utah, and every other state for that matter, exhibit higher levels of happiness than those in New York.[5] There is no reason to believe that the authors, in making this contention, would be taking themselves to be making a value judgment, or that they are thereby committing themselves to the highly tendentious proposition that Utahans are *better off* than New Yorkers. It is not hard to imagine a good proportion of Manhattanites allowing that people in Utah have more pleasant lives and so forth, but complaining that they are also idiots—or, as one blogger put it, "New Yorkers Unhappiest People in America (Because We Work Hard and Read Books, Unlike Lazy, Stupid Hicks)" (Edroso, 2009). The Utahans, for their part, might regard the New Yorkers as self-absorbed neurotics. Surely smart investigators who can get papers published in places like *Science* would not mean foolishly to embroil themselves in *that* controversy—which subjective well-being data alone couldn't possibly settle—even if they would side with the Utahans on this point. They are merely putting forth a psychological claim, in this case amounting to the contention that some people are more satisfied with their lives than others, and that this amounts in an important sense to being happier. This claim seems quite interesting enough, even if it does not try to settle Aristotle's question about which individuals are better off. Indeed, it says nothing that conflicts with Aristotle's writing at all.

This chapter follows the contemporary mainstream in focusing on happiness in the long-term psychological sense, and henceforth "happiness" and cognates will take that meaning. Returning to the Utah–New York paper, the relevant questions for our purposes are: Is the identification of happiness with life satisfaction—common in the empirical literature—plausible? How important is happiness, thus understood? What do self-reports of life satisfaction tell us about how happy people are, and about their well-being?

# What is Happiness?

## Life satisfaction

Earlier we set aside the hedonistic theory of happiness to focus on two other accounts: the emotional state (ES) and life satisfaction (LS) theories. In this section we will consider what each view amounts to and their relative merits, starting with LS.

---

[4] For discussion of happiness in the well-being sense see McMahon (Chapter 19, this volume) and Belliotti (Chapter 22, this volume). For an excellent survey of theories of well-being, see Crisp (2005).

[5] See, e.g., Oswald and Wu (2010). The authors cautiously avoid framing their central claims in terms of happiness. In the press release and in other work, however, they explicitly describe their results in terms of "happiness" (e.g., Oswald, 1997).

According to LS, happiness consists in being satisfied with one's life. This is normally understood as a *global attitude* encompassing all aspects of one's life over some period of time—typically that specified, vaguely, as "these days," though LS attitudes could range over shorter or longer time spans, including one's entire life. A typical LS measure might ask, "all things considered, how satisfied are you with your life as a whole now . . .?"[6] As well, LS is normally viewed as mainly a *cognitive* state; while it may well be taken to have affective components, and might even be deemed an emotion, it is not simply a feeling. Crucially, it embodies the individual's *judgment* about how her life is going.

These features of LS bear heavily on its appeal. We are rational creatures, with our own priorities in life, and it seems to matter a great deal how far those priorities are met. Arguably, the best measure of that is the priority-setter's own judgment, and LS may seem to accord with this intuition. We can understand why people should care about LS. We can also see how its significance differs from hedonistic happiness, or pleasure: whereas pleasure seems to matter because of how it feels, or what it's like, LS seems to matter because of its connection with whatever we happen to care about in our lives—be it pleasure or something else. (So the common practice of referring to LS research as "hedonic" is deeply misleading.) Moreover, the hedonist looks at our lives merely as the sum of many moments of pleasure or pain, whereas LS allows that a life may be other than the sum of its parts, and evaluates it holistically.

Yet LS theories of happiness face a number of objections.[7] Two will be mentioned only in passing: First, it is possible to be satisfied with one's life while, say, *depressed*, and many find it implausible to regard such a person as happy. Second, people's attitudes toward their lives may often be poorly *grounded*, reflecting only what comes most readily to mind at the moment, or even be nonexistent. The importance of such attitudes is questionable.

But here we will focus on a deeper threat to the importance of LS, one that stems from the very nature and point of LS attitudes. How satisfied you are with your life does not simply depend on how well you see your life going relative to your priorities. It also depends centrally on *how high you set the bar* for a "satisfactory" life: how good is "good enough?" Rosa might be satisfied with her life only when getting almost everything she wants, while Juliet is satisfied even when getting very little of what she wants—indeed, even when most of her goals are being frustrated. It can seem odd to think that satisfied Juliet, for whom every day is a new kick in the teeth, is better off than dissatisfied Rosa, who nonetheless succeeds in almost all the things she cares about but is more demanding.

More to the point, it is not clear why LS should be so important insofar as it is a matter of how high or low individuals set the bar. Suppose Rosa has a lengthy, and not inconsequential, "life list," and will not be satisfied until she has checked off every item on the list. It is not implausible that we should care about how well Rosa achieves her priorities—e.g., whether her goals are mostly met or roundly frustrated. But should anyone regard it as a weighty matter whether she actually gets *every last thing* on her list, and thus is satisfied with her life? It is doubtful, indeed, that *Rosa* should put much stock in it.

---

[6] From Veenhoven (1997). The most popular instrument, the Satisfaction With Life Scale, uses five related questions to get at life satisfaction attitudes (Diener, Emmons, et al. 1985). For a few examples of philosophical views making life satisfaction central to or exhaustive of "happiness," see Almeder (2000), Brülde (2007), Kekes (1982), Nozick (1989), Sumner (1996), Tatarkiewicz (1976), Telfer (1980). In some cases life satisfaction theories of "happiness" appear to concern the well-being sense of the term.

[7] This section builds on points discussed in Haybron (2007, 2008).

The point here is not simply that LS can reflect unreasonable demands, but that it depends on people's standards for a *good enough* life, and these bear a problematic relationship to people's well-being, depending on various factors that have no obvious relationship to how well people's lives are going for them. It may happen that Rosa comes to see her standards as unreasonably high and revises them downwards—not because her priorities change, but because she now finds it *unseemly* to be so needy. In this case, what drives her LS is, in part, the *norms* she takes to apply to her attitudes—how it is fitting to respond to her life. Such norms likely influence most people's attitudes toward their lives—a wish to exhibit virtues like fortitude, toughness, strength, or exactingness, non-complacency, and so forth. How satisfied we are with our lives partly depends, in short, on the norms we accept regarding how it is appropriate to respond to our lives. Note that most of us accept a variety of such norms, pulling in different directions, and it can be somewhat *arbitrary* which norms we emphasize in thinking about our lives. You may value both fortitude and not being complacent, and it may not be obvious which to give more weight in assessing your life. You may, at different times, vary between them.

Similarly, LS depends on the *perspective* one adopts: relative to what are you more or less satisfied? Looking at Tiny Tim, you may naturally take up a perspective on your life that makes your good fortune more salient, and so you reasonably find yourself pretty satisfied with things. Then you think about George Clooney, and your life doesn't look so good by comparison: your satisfaction drops. Worse, it is doubtful that any perspective is uniquely the *right* one to take: again, it is somewhat arbitrary. Unless you are like Rosa and have bizarrely—not to say childishly—determinate criteria for how good your life has to be to qualify as a satisfactory one, it will be open to you to assess your life from any of a number of vantage points, each quite reasonable and each yielding a different verdict.

Indeed, the very idea of subjecting one's life to an all-in assessment of satisfactoriness is a bit odd. When you order a steak prepared medium and it turns up rare, its deficiencies are immediately apparent and your dissatisfaction can be given plain meaning: you send it back. Or, you don't return to that establishment. But when your *life* has annoying features, what would it mean to deem it unsatisfactory? You can't very well send it back. (Well...) Nor can you resolve to choose a different one next time around. It just isn't clear what's at stake in judging one's life satisfactory or otherwise; lives are vastly harder to judge than steaks; and anyway, what counts as a reasonable expectation for a life is less than obvious since the price of admission is free—you're just born, and there you are. So it is hard to know where to set the bar, and unsurprising that people can be so easily gotten by trivial influences to move it (Schwarz & Strack, 1999). You might be satisfied with your life simply because it beats being dead. The ideal of life satisfaction arguably imports a consumer's concept, one most at home in retail environments, into an existential setting where metrics of customer satisfaction may be less than fitting. (It is an interesting question how far people spoke of life satisfaction before the postwar era got us in the habit of calling ourselves "consumers.")

In short, LS depends heavily on where you set the bar for a "good enough" life, and this in turn depends on factors like perspectives and norms that are substantially arbitrary and have little bearing on your well-being. The worry is not that LS fails to track some objective standard of well-being, but that we should expect that it will fail to track *any* sane metric of well-being, including the individual's own. To take one example: Studies suggest that dialysis patients report normal levels of LS, which might lead us to think they don't really mind it very much. Yet when asked to state a preference, patients said they would be willing to give up *half their remaining life-years* to regain normal kidney function (Riis et al., 2005; Torrance, 1976; Ubel & Loewenstein, 2008). This is about as strong as a preference gets. A plausible supposition is that people don't adjust their priorities when they get kidney disease so much as they adjust their standards for what they'll consider a satisfactory life. LS thus obscures precisely the sort of information one might expect it to provide—not because of errors or noise, but because it is not the sort of thing that is *supposed* in any straightforward way to yield that information. LS is not that sort of beast.

The claim is not that LS measures never provide useful information about well-being. In fact they frequently do, because the perceived welfare information is in there somewhere, and differences in norms and perspectives may often cancel out over large populations. They may not cancel out, however, where norms and perspectives systematically differ, and this is a serious problem in many contexts, especially cross-cultural comparisons using LS (Haybron, 2007, 2008).[8] But what the points raised in this section chiefly indicate about LS measures is that we cannot support conclusions about absolute levels of well-being with facts about LS. *That people are satisfied with their lives does not so much as hint that their lives are going well relative to their priorities.* If we wish reliably to assess how people see their lives going for them, we need a better yardstick than life satisfaction.

Life satisfaction theories may capture some uses of "happy", but the term, in its most compelling applications, seems primarily to concern emotional matters, as the next section will explain. Given that, and the difficulty LS theories have making sense of happiness' importance, it is misleading for researchers to couch life satisfaction claims as contentions about happiness. If the defeated, glue-sniffing residents of Mordonia report high levels of life satisfaction, but do so only because they deal with hardship by dropping the bar for a satisfactory life to the ground, it would be unenlightening at best to report one's findings by calling them *happy*. Would readers not tend to infer, on hearing that Mordonia's denizens are happy, that they are actually doing pretty well, and that life there is remarkably fulfilling? It would be wiser, it seems, to conceive of happiness in emotional state terms, at least regarding core uses of the word.

## Emotional state theories

The ES theory identifies happiness with a person's overall emotional condition: if one's emotional condition is sufficiently positive, one counts as happy. The theory differs from hedonism in two respects. First, it incorporates our emotional conditions in their entirety, including their non-conscious aspects. A depressed person is unhappy, not by virtue of experiencing the unpleasantness of depression, but by virtue of being *depressed*. Think of how depression involves so much more than simply having unpleasant experiences. It warps one's whole psyche, indeed one's personality. Second, the ES theory counts only affects that involve our emotional conditions. Trivial or "peripheral" affects, like merely sensory pains and pleasures, don't themselves impact how happy we are.[9] Consider the intense but sometimes unemotional pleasure of an orgasm—pleasant indeed, but one need not be any happier by virtue of it.

---

[8] For a vivid illustration of the problem, see Sen's discussion of self-reported health in India, which bears little relation to actual health (Sen, 2009).

[9] For further discussion of emotional state theories, and the contrast with hedonism, see Haybron (2008).

In its most basic form, an ES theory identifies happiness solely with an individual's moods and emotions. (In general, the account seems to center on mood-related states, understood broadly.) Some variants of the ES theory might incorporate, in addition, a person's *mood propensity*, which is to say her disposition to experience certain moods rather than others. You might, during a trying period of your life, be highly prone to anxiety, the slightest provocation tending to leave you tremendously anxious. Being so disposed arguably compromises your happiness, even when you aren't feeling anxious: your emotional condition is worsened. Or, similarly, you might generally be in good spirits, but only when you keep yourself busy; at day's end, when no longer distracted by the day's activities, you feel dispirited and depressed. This is a fairly standard portrait, in literature and film, of unhappiness. Interestingly, measures of depression and anxiety—which are essentially measures of certain kinds of unhappiness—often focus on dispositional states, such as "I can laugh and see the funny side of things" (Zigmond & Snaith, 1983).[10] Our emotional conditions run more deeply than our experienced moods and emotions, and so too, perhaps, does our happiness.

These considerations indicate that happiness, on an ES view, can amount to far more than simply being in a good mood or feeling happy. Indeed the greatest misconception about happiness, in ES terms, may be the common conflation of happiness with feeling happy. This is surely to take too narrow a view of happiness, and certainly of the potential resources of an ES theory. In fact it seems that someone could count as happy without *ever* feeling happy, say by enjoying a high degree of serenity. Intuitively, any psychological state that plays a role in defining a person's emotional condition could qualify as happiness-constituting on an ES view, and so the theory could encompass quite a broad range of psychic phenomena.

To illustrate, let's consider a conjecture about the varieties of emotional response. Correct or not, it will serve our purposes if it conveys a sense of the most important states involved in happiness and their diversity. Let's suppose that each emotional state instantiates one or more of three different modes of response, corresponding to different types of evaluation. (We are assuming that affects function as evaluations in some sense.) At the most basic level are responses pertaining to security or safety: are you taking up a vigilant and defensive posture, as to threatening or insecure circumstances? Emotional responses of this sort most obviously include states of tranquility versus anxiety, but may also include confidence and openness or expansiveness of mood, or a sense of freedom (as opposed to states of "compression," where you feel small and pressed-upon, or "pinched and hidebound," as Mill put it). The root idea here concerns being psychically at home in one's life, and we may call this dimension of happiness the *attunement* dimension.[11]

Assuming one's situation is secure, the next question is whether it merits investment or effort: are there opportunities to pursue, things worth doing? Here we can distinguish at least two sorts of affirmative response: vitality or exuberance, and flow. Flow is the state you experience when fully caught up in an activity, especially when "in the zone," as opposed say to boredom, whereas vitality concerns a high state of energy or enthusiasm. Both are stances conducive to heartily engaging with one's life, and so we can call this the *engagement* dimension of happiness. The importance of engagement comes to the fore in the case of depression,

---

[10] From the Hospital Anxiety and Depression Scale (HADS) (Zigmond and Snaith, 1983). In fact the HADS is arguably one of the better *happiness* measures, though it focuses inordinately on how the individual is doing now relative to her past condition.

[11] For an excellent illustration of happiness understood primarily as attunement, from a Buddhist perspective, see Ricard (2006).

which is not simply or even mainly sadness, but more centrally a profound form of psychic disengagement or withdrawal from one's life.

Finally, there is the question how to respond to good or bad events in one's life, which brings us to the *endorsement* dimension of happiness. Here we find the prototypical emotions, notably states of feeling happy or sad, cheerful or irritable. Most of what we think of when we think about emotions falls under this heading, and also most of what gets studied in research on happiness as an emotional phenomenon. Indeed, there seldom seems to be much recognition that our emotional lives, and certainly happiness, involve anything *but* endorsement-type affects. This is unfortunate, for three reasons. First, it is at least arguable that endorsement-type affects are the least important aspect of happiness. Historical ideals of living frequently center on states of attunement (e.g., Epicureans, Stoics, Buddhists) or engagement (e.g., Aristotle, Nietzsche), but not so much feeling happy or being cheerful (Democritus, perhaps). Joy gets a lot of attention, to be sure, but typically as a fleeting phenomenon; it is hard to sustain, at least in this life. Second, as just noted, endorsement states are highly sensitive to recent events, and hard to change over the long haul. This makes them both exceptionally prone to adaptation and less apt as objects of pursuit—again, mostly the wrong focus of well-being promotion. If your happiness research centers narrowly on these, you should not be surprised if happiness seems remarkably vulnerable to adaptation and hard to change, as many researchers have claimed. Third, many of our most pressing practical concerns relate to the other aspects of happiness. That Americans aren't cheerful enough has been rather less salient a social worry than that Americans may be too stressed, anxious, bored, weary, or depressed. These are all concerns about happiness, yet discussions of happiness often omit much of the story—indeed, perhaps the chief part of the story.

Whether this is the right way to conceptualize the emotional terrain is open to debate, but it should at least be clear that ES theories can take happiness far beyond the "smiley-face feeling" stereotypes. Indeed, happiness may not even be primarily a matter of feelings at all, but rather of the individual's *psychic orientation* or stance toward her life. Consider the way stress impacts our emotional conditions: not mainly through unpleasant feelings—it isn't usually that unpleasant—but by making us irritable and sapping our ability to enjoy life. This is, presumably, a fairly important phenomenon, and reducing it simply to unpleasant "feelings of stress" misses a rather large part of the picture.

Happiness, on an emotional state view, may best be seen, not on the model of feeling cheerful or happy, but more broadly as *psychic affirmation*—psychically responding to one's life as if things are going well. In more pronounced forms, as when a person is truly thriving, we might call it *psychic flourishing*. Needless to say, measures of happiness that focus only on good or bad feelings are omitting a large fraction of the story, and do little to dispel prejudices that happiness is simply a matter of cheery feelings, or being in a "good mood."

## Measuring Happiness

Our discussion carries an important moral for the study of happiness: measuring happiness demands a certain degree of rigor in specifying exactly what one is trying to measure. Note, first, that *asking people how happy they are is a nonstarter*. Even setting aside the "well-being" uses of the term, it is clear that common usage employs the term to denote at least two radically different psychological phenomena, with very different significance. Defenders of self-reported happiness will note that such measures exhibit nice psychometric properties, correlating decently with what you'd expect them to correlate with. (For reviews, see Pavot (2008) and Larsen and Fredrickson (1999).) Yet in matters of well-being, just about everything correlates decently with everything else. You might also get a passable happiness instrument by measuring stomachaches. We can do better. Alternatively, researchers might defend the practice on the grounds that it lets people decide what matters to them.[12] This is confused: seeking reports of life satisfaction in unambiguous language might be a way to let people judge their lives by their own standards. (Setting aside worries raised earlier.) But handing people a question of obscure meaning and letting them sort it out before answering whatever they guessed the query to be is a rather different project, and not obviously a good use of research money.

Happiness measures, then, require a prior decision about what psychological states are at issue. Happiness research does not require investigators to take a stand on the correct theory of happiness, so long as they make no explicit claims about "happiness." But it does demand that they decide exactly what states they are interested in and then apply the best feasible measures of those states. This will, *pace* the points above, probably never take the form of asking people how happy they are. Rather, it will involve applying explicit measures of life satisfaction, or emotional state, or whatever psychological states interest us. If we are interested in people's emotional conditions, then we will want to use, not "happiness" questions, but emotional state measures (e.g., HADS, or the Positive and Negative Affect Scale). In light of the broad spectrum of states potentially covered by an ES theory, it is a good question whether existing scales adequately cover this territory. Clearly, the breadth and richness of our emotional conditions belies any notion that happiness can easily be summed up in a single question. Indeed, it makes plain that even judging our own happiness is no simple affair: there is much to consider, some of it not even conscious, and a lot to overlook if we aren't careful—and maybe even if we are (Haybron, 2008).

## The Importance of Happiness

Given an ES view, happiness obviously matters a great deal, even if not quite as much as many have supposed. As we saw earlier, experience machine-type cases—among others, including "happy slave" cases involving extreme adaptation to deprivation—suggest that neither happiness nor any other mental state can suffice for well-being. But this hardly means that happiness isn't *important* for well-being. One response, which currently enjoys some popularity, is to identify well-being with happiness that is suitably grounded in the individual's life and values, or what L. W. Sumner calls "authentic happiness."[13]

---

[12] This seems to be a common sentiment among researchers, but is not often made explicit. But see, e.g., Carol Graham, "The Economics of Happiness," *The Washington Post*, January 3, 2010: "What makes the term so useful in research, allowing comparisons across countries and cultures, is that the definition is left up to the respondent."

[13] In recent years several theorists have proposed authentic happiness-centered theories of well-being (Brülde, 2007; Haybron 2008; Sumner, 1996; Tiberius & Plakias, 2010). Another possibility, of course, is to reject the intuitions taken to militate against pure mental state theories of well-being like hedonism (e.g., Crisp, 2006; Feldman 2004).

In fact happiness arguably qualifies as an important good, in most lives, on all major theories of well-being. Desire theories, for instance, should count happiness as a major good because most people so strongly desire it. Similarly, all plausible objectivist theories will accord substantial importance to happiness in some manner or other. Aristotle viewed well-being as a matter of virtuous activity, not happiness,[14] yet virtuous activity essentially involves pleasure—taking pleasure in acting well, for instance. Clearly *eudaimonia* for him includes being happy, on any plausible view of happiness, and Aristotle regards this as a crucial feature of his account. And so, too, do all major ideals of human well-being make it a matter of no small importance whether people are happy or unhappy.

This importance comes through in ordinary thinking about happiness, where happiness often appears to serve as a convenient proxy for well-being. That someone is happy arguably creates a presumption that she is doing well, while unhappiness signals the opposite. The presumption is defensible, for instance if we learn that the happy person has been lobotomized. But for the most part, happiness seems to correspond roughly with a person's overall well-being.

Why does happiness matter? The obvious answer is that it is *pleasant*. Beyond that, it plays a central role in *determining* how pleasant our experiences will be, and more broadly how we will respond to things in our lives; recall the earlier points about the dispositional aspects of happiness, and the way stress or anxiety can keep us from enjoying many of life's pleasures. In this respect happiness matters in much the way that health does. Third, happiness can be seen as a broad *evaluation* of the person's life: essentially an emotional counterpart to life satisfaction—the verdict of the individual's psyche on how he is living. Fourth, the pervasive impact of happiness on one's psychological condition suggests that happiness might be specially connected to the *self*: on one recent proposal, the facts about what ways of living make us (authentically) happy partly define who we are—our emotional selves or natures—and so (authentic) happiness can be seen as valuable, not only because it is pleasant, but also because it constitutes a kind of *self-fulfillment* (Haybron, 2008). (Think, by contrast, of a Jane-Austenesque woman trapped in a confining lifestyle that leaves her hollow, deflated, flat. Intuitively, the problem is that she's unable to fully express her nature, her self. Old friends might worry that she's a "shadow of her former self.") The ideal of self-fulfillment in turn belongs to a venerable tradition of thinking about human well-being, stretching from Aristotle through Mill to Maslow and the current school of "eudaimonic" psychology. So there are several plausible explanations of the role of happiness in well-being.

Yet, while happiness is a major part of human well-being, well-being itself may not be the only thing that matters in life. In fact most commentators take, not well-being, but virtue, to be the foremost element of a *good life*. The concept of a good life denotes a life that is desirable or choiceworthy all things considered—not just for the person's own benefit, but period. The notion of a good life thus encompasses all the values that matter in a life; whatever matters in life, matters for a good life. Whereas the concept of well-being more narrowly concerns what *benefits* a person (is good for her, serves her interests, or makes her better off).

In a good life we must above all act well, or at least decently: virtue is our first priority. On this point Utilitarians, Kantians, Aristotelians, and perhaps all other serious ethical thinkers agree. There is considerable dispute about whether virtue and well-being are distinct, and sometimes conflicting, elements of the good life, or whether well-being actually consists in

---

[14] Recall that we are using the word here purely as a psychological term, not in its well-being or *eudaimonia* sense.

virtue, as Aristotelians and Stoics maintain. But there is no dispute about whether virtue sometimes conflicts with happiness. While virtue surely is, on the whole, a better bet for happiness than immorality or the pursuit of worthless goals, there are times when acting well leaves us less happy. This point is crucial to bear in mind when thinking about the advancement of happiness. The fact that you would be happier with a divorce, for instance, does not by itself justify seeking one: it depends, at the very least, on what you owe to your children, and your spouse. Sometimes you just have to suck it up. Efforts to promote happiness, then, must be mindful of the limits that other values place on its pursuit. (For further discussion, see Belliotti (Chapter 22, this volume).)

Some commentators take such observations to vitiate happiness as a major practical concern. But that doesn't follow at all: happiness need not be the only thing that matters to merit a pretty lofty spot on the list. For example, one of the chief critiques that have been lodged against many contemporary societies, for instance, is that they seem to have traded the chief sources of happiness—social capital, companionship, a reasonable pace of life—for a bunch of stuff, the result being a lot of lonely, tense, rich people whose joyless lifestyles are taxing the biosphere. Billions of other aspiring consumers, meanwhile, see their own happiness in doing the same.

Or maybe not; the accuracy of this complaint is not our concern here. The point, rather, is that it matters whether our way of life makes us happy, or unhappy. Happiness matters.

# References

Almeder, R. (2000). *Human happiness and morality*. Buffalo, NY: Prometheus Press.
Brülde, B. (2007). Happiness theories of the good life. *Journal of Happiness Studies*, 8(1), 15–49.
Crisp, R. (2005). Well-being. In E. N. Zalta (Eds.), *The Stanford encyclopedia of philosophy*. Retrieved from http://plato.stanford.edu/entries/well-being/
Crisp, R. (2006). *Reasons and the good*. New York, NY: Oxford University Press.
Diener, E., Emmons, R. A., Larsen, R. J., & Griffin, S. (1985). The satisfaction with life scale. *Journal of Personality Assessment*, 49, 71–75.
Edroso, R. (2009, December 18). New Yorkers unhappiest people in America (because we work hard and read books, unlike lazy, stupid hicks). Retrieved from http://www.blogs.villagevoice.com.
Feldman, F. (2004). *Pleasure and the good life*. New York, NY: Oxford University Press.
Feldman, F. (2010). *What is this thing called happiness?* New York, NY: Oxford University Press.
Haybron, D. M. (2007). Life satisfaction, ethical reflection and the science of happiness. *The Journal of Happiness Studies*, 8, 99–138.
Haybron, D. M. (2008). *The pursuit of unhappiness: The elusive psychology of well-being*. New York, NY: Oxford University Press.
Kekes, J. (1982). Happiness. *Mind*, 91, 358–76.
Larsen, R. J., & Fredrickson, B. L. (1999). Measurement issues in emotion research. In D. Kahneman, E. Diener & N. Schwarz (Eds.), *Well-being: The foundations of hedonic psychology* (pp. 40–60). New York, NY: Russell Sage Foundation Press.
Nozick, R. (1989). *The examined life*. New York, NY: Simon and Schuster.
Oswald, A. J. (1997). Happiness and economic performance. *The Economic Journal*, 107(445), 1815–1831.

Oswald, A. J., & Wu, S. (2010). Objective confirmation of subjective measures of human well-being: Evidence from the US. *Science, 327*(5965), 576–579.

Pavot, W. (2008). The assessment of subjective well-being: Successes and shortfalls. In M. Eid & R. J. Larsen (Eds.), *The science of subjective well-being* (pp. 124–140). New York, NY: Guilford Press.

Ricard, M. (2006). *Happiness: A guide to developing life's most important skill*. New York, NY: Little, Brown and Co.

Riis, J., Loewenstein, G., Baron, J., Jepson, C., Fagerlin, A., & Ubel, P. A. (2005). Ignorance of hedonic adaptation to hemodialysis: A study using ecological momentary assessment. *Journal of Experimental Psychology: General, 134*(1), 3–9.

Schwarz, N., & Strack, F. (1999). Reports of subjective well-being: Judgmental processes and their methodological implications. In D. Kahneman, E. Diener & N. Schwarz (Eds.), *Well-being: The foundations of hedonic psychology* (pp. 61–84). New York, NY: Russell Sage Foundation Press.

Sen, A. (2009). *The idea of justice*. Cambridge, MA: Harvard University Press.

Sumner, L. W. (1996). *Welfare, happiness, and ethics*. New York, NY: Oxford University Press

Tatarkiewicz, W. (1976). *Analysis of happiness*. The Hague: Martinus Nijhoff.

Telfer, E. (1980). *Happiness*. New York, NY: St. Martin's Press.

Tiberius, V., & Plakias, A. (2010). Well-being. In J. M. Doris & the Moral Psychology Research Group (Eds.), *The moral psychology handbook* (pp. 401–431). New York, NY: Oxford University Press.

Torrance, G. (1976). Social preferences for health states: An empirical evaluation of three measurement techniques. *Socioeconomic Planning Science, 10*, 129–136.

Ubel, P. A., & Loewenstein, G. (2008). Pain and suffering awards: They shouldn't be (just) about pain and suffering. *The Journal of Legal Studies, 37*(s2), S195–S216.

Veenhoven, R. (1997). Advances in understanding happiness. *Revue Québécoise de Psychologie, 18*, 29–79.

Zigmond, A. S., & Snaith, R. P. (1983). The Hospital Anxiety and Depression Scale. *Acta Psychiatrica Scandinavica, 67*(6), 361–370.

CHAPTER 24

# PHILOSOPHICAL METHODS IN HAPPINESS RESEARCH

## VALERIE TIBERIUS
University of Minnesota, USA

## Introduction

PHILOSOPHERS do not typically run experiments, conduct surveys, or analyze data. So what do we do? To the outsider, it may seem as if "philosophical method" is just a term for glorifying what really amounts to sitting in one's armchair thinking about something. There is some truth to this stereotype of the philosopher, but it is also true that we employ methods in our armchairs, methods that are well suited to answering particular kinds of questions. In this essay I distinguish the kinds of questions that philosophical methods are designed to answer from the kinds of questions that the methods of empirical psychology are designed to answer, I give an overview of what philosophical methods are used in happiness research, and, finally, I say something about why this matters.

Psychological science is paradigmatically concerned with questions about cause and effect, questions like: What causes people to be happy? How does happiness affect individuals and communities? What are the effects of unhappiness on individuals and the communities to which they belong? These questions cannot be answered without conducting carefully controlled studies that allow us to quantify and interpret our observations of the world objectively. Philosophers and philosophical methods have no special privilege here.

But before we investigate how happiness is caused and what effects it has, we need to know what it *is*. When it comes to questions about the definition or the *nature* of happiness, philosophers have something to contribute. To see this, we need to distinguish different questions one might have about what happiness is. First, there are some questions about what happiness is that can be answered by scientific methods. For instance, "What do people mean when they use the word 'happiness'?" is a question that is best answered by interviewing subjects and conducting surveys. Questions about what people, in fact, want in their lives are also empirical questions. But there is another kind of question about the nature of happiness that cannot be answered purely by observation and investigation of the world.

This is the question "What is *happiness* such that it is a good thing to aim at in one's own life or to try to procure for others?" This is what philosophers call a *normative question*, that is, a question about what ought to be rather than what is. This is a question that we can't answer by surveying people, because it might be that what people think happiness is, what they want, and what they in fact aim at in their lives, do not track something worthwhile.

Of course, one might reject normative questions. One might think that there are no standards (or no good standards) for assessing whether something is worthwhile or good to aim at. One might think, in other words, that there are no methods for addressing normative questions and that the best we can do is to answer the empirical questions about how people use the concept of "happiness" and what they, in fact, aim at in their lives. This would be to reject ethics—a field whose business it is to employ philosophical methods to address normative questions. The rejection of ethics and, along with it, the assumption that at least some normative questions are tractable, seems an extreme and undesirable position to take. Moreover, this extreme position doesn't seem to be the one that most psychologists interested in happiness are inclined to take; indeed, questions about construct validity in happiness research seem to be questions about whether the way happiness gets operationalized really captures an important, normative notion. So, it is worth taking a look at the methods philosophy has to offer (see Tiberius and Hall (2010) for elaboration of the argument in this paragraph).

Before we turn to the main subject of this essay, a note about terminology is in order. "Happiness" has at least two different senses. It can refer to a positive psychological state as it seems to when we ask whether someone is "feeling happy". Or it can refer to a broader goal of life as it seems to when we talk about "the pursuit of happiness" or when we ask whether someone has had "a happy life". In this essay, I use "happiness" in the second sense (though the same points about philosophical methods could be made about "happiness" in the psychological sense). This is a deviation from some philosophers' usage (Haybron, 2008; Sumner, 1996), but it makes sense in this context because the peculiarly philosophical questions arise more clearly for happiness in the second sense. Because of the double meaning of "happiness", philosophers interested in the goal of life or what is good for a person often use the term "well-being" instead of "happiness". Therefore, I will sometimes discuss philosophers' views about well-being. The subtle differences between these concepts should not matter for the purposes of discussing philosophical methods.

# What Do We Want from a Philosophical Analysis?

I have said that the question about the nature of happiness is, at least in part, a normative question and that this means we cannot employ purely empirical methods to answer it. Having said that, it must also be acknowledged that the nature of happiness isn't something that floats free from our ordinary ideas about what it is. An analysis of happiness that identified it with a bizarre kind of life that no one actually has any interest in could not be correct. Happiness is something ordinary people have an interest in and this interest explains why research into happiness is so important. Therefore, even a philosophical analysis of happiness must pay attention to the ordinary concept and to actual human experiences of it.

Notice, though, that this makes things tricky. If ordinary views about happiness are numerous and conflicting, then paying attention to the ordinary concept and related experiences is not going to lead us to a univocal answer to the question "What is happiness?" Given this, according to most philosophers who work on this topic, what we need to do is to construct a theory of happiness that fits well with *some* ordinary uses of the concept and *some* experiences. Which parts of the ordinary concept and which ordinary experiences should be accommodated by our theory of happiness will be determined by the normative dimension of happiness. Dan Haybron (2008) calls this kind of analysis a "reconstructive analysis", the purpose of which "is not to explicate but to reconstruct: reworking rough-and-ready folk concepts to get something better suited to thinking clearly about the matters that concern us" (p. 47).

There are, then, two criteria for an adequate theory of happiness. L. W. Sumner (1996) has referred to these as *the criterion of descriptive adequacy* and *the criterion of normative adequacy*. Though different philosophers may interpret these criteria as demanding somewhat different things, the current consensus is that both are important. The former is typically taken to require that the theory fit our ordinary experiences and uses of the concept. Sometimes it has been taken to require, further, that the theory makes happiness something amenable to empirical investigation and measurement (Griffin, 1986; Tiberius & Plakias, 2010). The criterion of normative adequacy requires that a theory of happiness should justify claims about the value of happiness and explain why we have good reason to pursue it; it may also require that the resulting theory is adequate to playing a particular role in moral theory. For example, for Utilitarians, according to whom happiness is the central notion in moral theory, normative adequacy will mean that the theory of happiness should make happiness something that is up to this important job (Griffin, 1986).

## GENERAL METHODOLOGY

To construct a theory that meets the above two criteria, moral philosophers tend to employ the method of reflective equilibrium (Daniels, 1979). (My focus is on the method that predominates in contemporary analytic philosophy. Different methods are used in other philosophical traditions, some of which are discussed in other chapters in this volume.) According to this method, we construct normative theories by bringing into equilibrium ordinary judgments about particular cases (e.g., "Mary led a happy life, even though she didn't get everything she wanted"), putative normative principles (e.g., happiness is that which is to be promoted by beneficent action), and background theories (e.g., psychological theories about hedonic adaptation). We may not be able to save all of our intuitive judgments, and some of our principles may need to be modified or thrown out altogether, but the goal is to construct a theory that explains and systematizes as much of this large body of information as possible within the relevant theoretical constraints. We can see theoretical constraints as included in the forgoing list of things that must be brought into equilibrium. (For example, they might be theoretical principles, like simplicity and consistency, which are supported by a background conception of what counts as a good theory.) This methodology has obvious similarities to the scientific method: empirical theories are based on and aim to explain our observations, but sometimes a theory is well confirmed enough that a conflicting observation must be explained away and discounted. Similarly, when we use reflective equilibrium to defend a normative theory such as a theory of happiness we aim to systematize our intuitions, but there can be many reasons to discount intuitions when not all of them can be saved.

To see how the process goes it will be helpful to work through an example. Consider hedonism, the view that happiness is just pleasure and the absence of pain. (According to the philosopher Fred Feldman (2004), the process he uses to defend hedonism "is to attempt to get myself (and my patient and sympathetic reader) into reflective equilibrium with some form of hedonism" (p. 6).) Hedonism makes sense of many of our intuitions about cases: I think that my dog is happy when he gets his dinner because food is one of his major pleasures in life, I notice that my mother is happy when I telephone because it gives her pleasure to talk to me, I think that chemotherapy makes people unhappy because it is very unpleasant, and so on. Pleasure and happiness do seem to be closely related. But there are other intuitions about cases that conflict with hedonism. For example, imagine a life in which pleasure is the only thing it is possible to achieve. Do we think that a person living such a life—say, someone hooked up to a reliably pleasure-producing virtual reality machine—is living a happy life? Not everyone thinks so. (Robert Nozick's "experience machine" is a now infamous version of this argument against hedonism (Nozick, 1974, pp. 42–45).) Some people think a happy life, a life that is worth living, is one in which we actually achieve things, not just one in which we feel good.

What do we do about these conflicting intuitions? Guided by the method of reflective equilibrium, we could look to background theories or normative principles to help us. For example, consideration of the psychological theory of hedonic adaptation might lead us to think that pleasure can't be the goal of life, because it doesn't make sense to structure our lives around a goal that always eludes us. (Elijah Millgram (2000) makes an argument like this.) Further, the principle that happiness is that which ought to be promoted by beneficent action could lead us to think that hedonism is missing something on the grounds of additional intuitions about what benefits a person. When we start thinking about harming and benefiting others and we bring these thoughts to bear on the discussion of happiness, hedonism may begin to look like a theory that focuses too narrowly on one aspect of a person's life.

Philosophers in the Aristotelian tradition also use the method of reflective equilibrium to define *eudaimonia*, which they translate as happiness or (sometimes) flourishing. According to Richard Kraut (2006), Aristotle's method comprises five stages: (1) consult expert opinion about happiness and also opinions that are widely shared; (2) consider the puzzles that arise when opinions conflict; (3) discover the theory of happiness that best explains the puzzles and preserves as many opinions as possible; (4) with this theory in hand, return to the opinions to achieve a better understanding of them; and (5) subject the theory to the test of experience. We can see how this process is a form of reflective equilibrium insofar as it begins with intuitions or opinions and justifies taking some intuitions more seriously than others by trying to fit them into a coherent whole.[1] We can also see how this method leads to a theory that has normative significance, because the point of ethical inquiry according to

---

[1] Kraut (2006) suggests that Aristotle's method is foundational (as opposed to coherentist) because the theory of happiness that results from the process is a "foundational starting-point" (p. 89) that supports lower-order opinions. I would argue that the theory is also, in part, justified by opinion, which does make it a variety of reflective equilibrium.

Aristotle is to arrive at an understanding about how to live that provides a compelling answer to one's practical questions.

Aristotle's method has been adapted by his followers. For example, Martha Nussbaum (2001) uses a methodology that incorporates contemporary ideas about how reflective equilibrium should work. According to Nussbaum, happiness or flourishing is to be understood in terms of "human functional capabilities", which include: life; bodily health; bodily integrity; senses, imagination, and thought; emotions; practical reason; affiliation; play; and control over one's environment (Nussbaum, 2001, pp. 78–80). A flourishing person is one who develops these capabilities well. Nussbaum (2001) argues that her list of capabilities is in part justified by the "*overlapping consensus* [about the list] on the part of people with otherwise very different views of human life" (p. 76). Nussbaum adds a dimension of cross-cultural empirical inquiry to her method. Instead of relying entirely on her own intuitions or the intuitions of her students in her application of reflective equilibrium, she attempts to test the theory against the opinions of people across the world. In doing so, she is following Aristotle's advice to begin with opinions that are widely shared (as well as the opinions of experts).

It must be pointed out that Nussbaum does not think the opinions of the many—even opinions shared across cultures—*determine* the right view about human flourishing. She says "the primary weight of justification remains with the intuitive conception of truly human functioning and what that entails" (Nussbaum, 2001, p. 76). Here she is acknowledging the point I have been emphasizing that what people happen to think does not automatically answer normative questions about how we ought to live. More work must be done to construct a theory that makes sense of the various intuitions, to draw out the implications of this theory, and to evaluate the whole package in the light of principles, background theories and experience.

The method of reflective equilibrium functions to achieve both descriptive and normative adequacy. This back-and-forth process is not easy, but it is unclear how we would make progress in addressing questions that have a normative dimension without it. We would either be stuck with our pre-reflective, often conflicting opinions about happiness, or we would be forced to decide arbitrarily on a conception of happiness. Neither of these options supplies a satisfactory foundation for empirical study. I do not at all mean to suggest that current psychological research on happiness proceeds on confused or arbitrary assumptions. The point is that insofar as it doesn't this is because some reasonable method for deciding what to count as happiness or well-being has already been employed, either by the researchers themselves or by the philosophers on whom they rely. The method described here is one respectable method to which empirical researchers are likely to be sympathetic.

One might wonder, though, how respectable this method really is. Does what results from the reflective equilibrium process really counts as progress? Can reflective equilibrium *prove* that we ought to think of happiness in one way or another? Can it demonstrate that one theory is correct and the alternatives false? Why isn't this process arbitrary in just the way we hoped to avoid? These are deep questions that go beyond the scope of this chapter, but the basic strategy for defending the methodology is to insist that the demand for an incontrovertible proof about happiness is an illegitimate demand.

As Kraut (2006) puts it:

> Ethical inquiry is an attempt to become wiser about practical matters, not to convince a real or hypothetical opponent. It is part of one's own intellectual and moral development, not an

attempt to convince a hypothetical skeptic or to bring it about that more people think and act as one does. (p. 77)

We might say about the philosophical project of defending normative theories in general that the task is to construct a theory that makes the best sense of all the various ideas we have about happiness and that is compelling to those of us whose interests it is made to address. What we need, then, is not standards of *proof*, but criteria for making progress or for judging that one theoretical solution is better than another. These criteria are easiest to grasp by thinking about the dialectical method philosophers rely on in general. Philosophers typically proceed by generating hypotheses, considering objections, and rejecting or reformulating the original hypothesis. This general schema describes what happens when we use the method of reflective equilibrium: (1) we start with a theory that purports to make sense of all the relevant considerations (the various intuitions, principles and background theories, i.e., the data); (2) considerations that conflict with this theory are presented as objections to the theory; and (3) we modify the theory to meet the objections, explain why the objections needn't be heeded in the first place, or reject the theory entirely and start over. This process is repeated until we have answered all the objections and any further modification to the theory would result in conflict with other, more weighty considerations.

Notice that this process is not mechanical; what counts as a good objection, which considerations have the most weight, and what counts as a coherent solution are matters for discernment and cannot be decided by the numbers (it's not the case that *more* intuitions win). Relevant to these judgments are questions that are philosophical rather than empirical: What are the implications of accepting a particular intuition for other cases? How do the principles apply in different contexts? What other concepts might be disentangled from the target concept? Thus engaging in the three-stage process of reflective equilibrium requires reflection on principles, cases, concepts, and the inferential relations between them in addition to attention to the empirical facts.

Though there is no deductive proof of a theory of happiness, then, there is evidence for and against different theories and a standard for what counts as better. The best theory is the one that is favored by the preponderance of evidence from our intuitions about happiness, background theories about what human beings are like, reasonable principles, theoretical needs, and real-life experience. It is worth noting that the best conclusion to draw about happiness might turn out to be that there is no single theory that is suited for all of our purposes (Alexandrova, 2009).

## Specific Methods

As philosophers employ reflective equilibrium to arrive at a descriptively and normatively adequate theory of happiness, they also use some specific methods such as *thought experiments*. Psychologists also use these methods to support their normative assumptions (and for other purposes), though they may not conceive of themselves as using them to construct a normative theory. In this section I discuss some of the tools in the philosopher's toolbox and explain why these tools are particularly suited to the task of defending normative theories in reflective equilibrium.

In the context of reflective equilibrium, the overarching purpose of philosophical tools is to justify decisions about what to preserve and what to jettison in the construction of a theory of happiness. These tools are (in the terms familiar to psychologists) *methods* for gathering data that will add to the case for or against a particular hypothesis about the nature of happiness. For example, the claim that pleasure is the only thing good in itself is incompatible with the claim that there are other intrinsic goods; a coherent theory of happiness can't accept them both. Nozick's (1974) experience machine example (discussed in the following paragraph) is a method for generating more data (stronger and more numerous intuitions) on the side of rejecting the former.

Thought experiments, common tools in philosophy and the sciences, are "devices of the imagination used to investigate the nature of things" (Brown, 2007). In normative theory they are often used to investigate intuitions about specific features of a concept. For example, Nozick's (1974) thought experiment, which presents us a case in which you have to decide whether to hook up to a machine that some trustworthy super-duper neuroscientists will program to give you a very pleasant illusion of a life, is designed to ascertain intuitions about whether pleasure is the only thing we desire. The way Nozick sets up the case, all other factors are supposed to be eliminated by hypothesis. If this were real life, of course, one would wonder about the reliability of the machine, the trustworthiness of the scientists, and so on, but Nozick asks us to put these worries aside so that we can focus on whether pleasure is the only desirable thing.

People sometimes complain about philosophers' use of "crazy" science fiction cases, but these complaints ignore the difficulty in isolating intuitions. A more realistic example than Nozick's would be the case of someone who has the option of spending several hours each evening in a blissful, drug-induced state. But this example does not pit the value of pleasure against other possible values, because in real life drug use has seriously unpleasant long-term consequences and this fact clouds the issue.

Philosophers also use *intuition pumps* in order to argue for a particular theory or against alternative views that may conflict with it. For example, Amartya Sen's (1987) brief description of the lives of oppressed people evokes or "pumps" the intuition that subjective satisfaction with life cannot be all there is to living well:

> The hopeless beggar, the precarious landless labourer, the dominated housewife, the hardened unemployed or the over-exhausted coolie may all take pleasures in small mercies, and manage to suppress intense suffering for the necessity of continuing survival, but it would be ethically deeply mistaken to attach a correspondingly small value to the loss of their well-being because of this survival strategy. (pp. 45–46)

Sen's brief description of these four characters leads us to think that there is something unfortunate about their lives, despite the fact that they are satisfied. Drawing our attention to problem cases for a theory that takes happiness to consist solely in positive subjective attitudes stimulates intuitions on the other side and can lead us to change our view about what must be discarded in reflective equilibrium.

These two methods are related because thought experiments can serve as intuition pumps. For example, Nozick's thought experiment is meant to pump the intuition that being in touch with reality is valuable for its own sake. However, not all intuition pumps are thought experiments. One can pump an intuition by drawing the audience's attention to certain facts without asking them to engage in the imaginative exercise of considering a thought experiment.

Another method philosophers use to attack competing theories is *counter-exampling*. Counter-examples to a theory can be real-life examples or thought experiments and they are meant to pump intuitions against a particular theory, but what's special about this method is that it is a method of critique. Typically, it is used against theories that provide necessary and sufficient conditions for the application of a concept. To counter-example an analysis, one devises an example that meets all the necessary and sufficient conditions, yet intuitively seems not to be an example to which the concept in question applies. For example, according to one analysis, what is good for a person is what her fully informed self would want her actual self to want. This analysis, which has been quite popular in philosophy (Griffin, 1986; Railton, 1986), has been subject to numerous counter-examples. Here is one, aimed at a theory of practical reason according to which we have reason to do what we would want to do after vivid, informed, dispassionate reflection:

> Suppose an enthusiastic fan wants the Lakers to win the NBA championship and, largely because of her partisanship, she enjoys watching their games. But suppose further, what seems possible, that she would lose her partisanship and much of her enjoyment, if she vividly and dispassionately reflected on the facts about opposing players, their families, their desire to win, et cetera. She does not so reflect because she knows what would happen. (Hill, 1986, pp. 610–611)

The Lakers fan meets the theory's necessary conditions for someone who has a reason not to enjoy watching her team, because she would not desire to do so after reflection. Nevertheless, intuitively, Hill thinks we will be inclined to believe that there is nothing wrong with the Lakers fan enjoying the game. She has no reason not to watch and enjoy it. Hill's example is a counter-example to the informed desire theory.

One of the advantages of interdisciplinary study of happiness is that sometimes important counter-examples to a philosophical theory may come from the empirical literature. For example, the claim that people's overall life satisfaction varies with trivial factors such as the weather (Schwarz & Strack, 1999) presents a counter-example to the theory that identifies happiness with life-satisfaction on the assumption that happiness has greater stability. To defend a theory against counter-examples one either explains away the example so that it is revealed not to run counter to the theory, or one modifies the theory.[2] Tiberius and Plakias (2010) have argued that the life-satisfaction theory of well-being can be saved if we modify the theory to count only experiences of life-satisfaction that are responsive to what one values. Thus, they defend the Value-Based Life-Satisfaction theory of well-being in response to counter-examples that arise from psychology.

Whether pumping intuitions in favor of their own theory or critiquing a rival, it is clear from the foregoing discussion that philosophers often rely on examples or cases. Good examples focus the mind and make vivid the reasons to go this way rather than that in coming to an equilibrium. One might accept this strategy and yet wonder why philosophers are not more concerned to take examples from "real life". Of course, the fact that philosophers' examples are not from controlled experiments does not mean they aren't from real life. The examples we have discussed earlier—Sen's hopeless beggar, Hill's Lakers fan—come from the real life experiences of the authors. But philosophical examples are not (not typically anyway) case study reports of actual people. Moreover, they are often written in a literary

---

[2] In defense of hedonism against the experience machine thought experiment, Crisp (2006) uses the former strategy and Feldman (2004) the latter.

style or, indeed, come from literary works. For example, Alexandrova (2009) uses a fictionalized case study in order to argue for well-being "variantism," according to which what counts as well-being varies with the context. Haybron (2008) uses the character of Santiago from Hemingway's *Old Man and the Sea* as a paradigm case of happiness in order to lend support to his own emotional state theory of happiness: "… Santiago is not the image of happiness in the 'smiley-face' sense … Yet he is a model of what the ancients called *ataraxia*– tranquility, imperturbability – and Hemingway's exemplar, I suspect, of genuine happiness" (p. 110).

Haybron (2008) defends the use of literary examples and literary style by arguing that the complexity of happiness makes it difficult to describe analytically:

> The phenomenology of well-being is enormously rich, to put it mildly, leaving even poets at a loss to convey anything more than a hint of it … The process of verbal articulation distills the "blooming, buzzing confusions"[3] of lived experience down to the common currency of shared ideas, using as little of that currency as possible. Most of the information is, of necessity, lost in the transformation. Scientific language is more lossy still, since it trades only in the very narrow coinage of ideas that can be precisely defined, quantified and measured. (pp. 55–56)

The idea is that literary examples allow us to see something about human experience that would be very difficult to convey in precise philosophical or scientific language. In particular, literary examples can convey the attractiveness of a kind of life or the horror of another. Good literature can do this by causing us to identify or empathize with a character whose experience might be quite far from our own: a stark scientific description of Santiago the Cuban fisherman may not have the same effect as Hemingway's prose. So, the point of using literary style is not only that happiness is too complex to describe without it, but also that beautifully described examples can provide the reader a different kind of knowledge: knowledge of what it would be like to live a certain kind of life rather than just information about what happens to the person who lives it. This is important if we take our project in reflective equilibrium to be to survey all the relevant information and devise the theory that best fits it together. Surely, what it is like to live in different ways is relevant to the project of understanding happiness, and literature is particularly well suited to conveying information about what it is like to live a certain kind of life. Literary examples, then, give us more information but also information of a qualitatively different kind.

Finally, philosophers are beginning to use methods familiar to psychologists in the form of surveys designed to ascertain the conditions under which people will apply such concepts as "happiness" and "well-being". Phillips, Nyholm, and Liao (forthcoming), for example, have argued that the folk concept of happiness is moralized, because subjects are more likely to say that a person is happy if he is living a morally good life than if he is living a morally bad life. Building on this work, Phillips, Misenheimer, and Knobe (2011) show that evaluative judgments play a role in the application of the concept of "happiness", though not for the concept of "unhappiness". We can understand the point of these forays into what has come to be called "experimental philosophy" by seeing them in the context of the overall methodology of reflective equilibrium. Folk usage of the relevant concepts in the form of judgments (or intuitions) about particular cases is one source of information that must be brought into

---

[3] This three-word quote is from James, W. (1890/1981) *The Principles of Psychology*. Cambridge, MA: Harvard University Press, p. 462.

equilibrium. Of course, folk usage needn't carry the day: to arrive at a theory of happiness that is adequate to the role it must play in a moral theory, for example, we may need to conclude that sometimes people are mistaken about what happiness really is. (There may also be non-philosophical reasons for discounting the information we get about folk concepts from survey research. In particular, as psychologists are keenly aware, measurement problems such as misleading or confusing survey questions embedded in the methods can give us reason to reject the data.) But what people think about happiness is relevant, and experimental philosophers have realized that we don't know what people think unless we ask them.

## Working Together

Some of the methods I have described can be employed from the armchair. One can devise thought experiments and come up with explanations for why counter-examples aren't really counter-examples from the comfort of one's office. But the overall methodology of reflective equilibrium and many of the particular methods employed to serve this methodology are best employed by being engaged with the world and with the sciences. Psychological research can show us counter-examples we may not otherwise have thought of, studies of people's actual use of concepts can give us new data points in our attempt to find equilibrium, and background information about human psychology in general is relevant to the construction of the best-justified theory of happiness. Further, articulating a theory of happiness is only part of the important work that needs to be done. Theories need to be interpreted and applied and these steps demand empirical research.

That said, it is important to remember that reflective equilibrium is a philosophical methodology suited to constructing normative theories. If happiness is a normative notion that describes what it makes most sense to aim for in life, then how people happen to use the concept is not going to determine its nature, and information about the empirical study of happiness will be relevant as one strand in the mass of material that we must knit together. Other strands will come from reflection about what matters when we're seeing things clearly, what it means to see things clearly, and on the role that happiness plays in life and in our moral practice.

Philosophical work that aims to reach reflective equilibrium about happiness helps empirical investigators start from sound assumptions, and the results of the empirical investigations can help inform and deepen reflective equilibrium. Putting theories into practice requires empirical study, but philosophical reflection can be helpful here too when practice uncovers new questions about the nature of happiness. If these claims are correct, then we have reason to think that the best results in happiness research will be achieved if psychologists and philosophers work collaboratively. Perhaps it should come as no surprise that such a complex topic would require putting our heads together.

## Acknowledgments

I am grateful to Dan Haybron, James Pawelski and J. D. Walker for helpful comments on previous drafts of this essay.

# References

Alexandrova, A. (2009). *Doing well in the circumstances: A defense of wellbeing variantism.* Unpublished manuscript.

Brown, J. (2007). Thought experiments. *Stanford Encyclopedia of Philosophy.* Retrieved from http://plato.stanford.edu/entries/thought-experiment/#TypThoExp

Crisp, R. (2006). *Reasons and the good.* Oxford, UK: Clarendon Press.

Daniels, N. (1979). Wide reflective equilibrium and theory acceptance in ethics. *Journal of Philosophy,* 76(5), 256–82.

Feldman, F. (2004). *Pleasure and the good life: Concerning the nature, varieties, and plausibility of hedonism.* Oxford, UK: Clarendon Press.

Griffin, J. (1986). *Well-being: Its meaning, measurement and moral importance.* Oxford, UK: Clarendon Press.

Haybron, D. (2008). *The pursuit of unhappiness: The elusive psychology of well-being.* Oxford, UK: Oxford University Press.

Hill, T. (1986). Darwall on practical reason. *Ethics,* 96(3), 604–619.

James, W. (1981). *The principles of psychology.* Cambridge, MA: Harvard University Press. (Original work published 1890).

Kraut, R. (2006). How to justify ethical propositions: Aristotle's method. In R. Kraut (Ed.), *The Blackwell guide to Aristotle's Nicomachean Ethics* (76–115). Malden, MA: Blackwell Publishing.

Millgram, E. (2000). What's the use of utility? *Philosophy and Public Affairs,* 29(2), 113–136.

Nozick, R. (1974). *Anarchy, state, and utopia.* New York, NY: Basic Books.

Nussbaum, M. (2001). *Women and human development: The capabilities approach.* Cambridge, UK: Cambridge University Press.

Phillips, J., Nyholm, S., and Liao, S. (forthcoming). The good in happiness. In: Lombrozo, T., Nichols, S., & Knobe, J., eds., *Oxford studies in experimental philosophy 1.* New York, NY: Oxford University Press.

Phillips, J., Misenheimer, L., & Knobe, J. (2011). The ordinary concept of happiness (and others like it). *Emotion Review* 3, 320–322.

Railton, P. (1986). Moral realism. *Philosophical Review,* 95(2), 163–207.

Schwarz, N., & Strack, F. (1999). Reports of subjective well-being: Judgmental processes and their methodological implications. In D. Kahneman, E. Diener, & N. Schwarz (Eds.), *Well-being: The foundations of hedonic psychology* (pp. 61–84). New York, NY: Russell Sage Foundation.

Sen, A. (1987). *On ethics and economics.* Oxford, UK: Basil Blackwell.

Sumner, L. (1996). *Welfare, happiness and ethics.* Oxford, UK: Clarendon Press.

Tiberius, V., & Hall, A. (2010). Normative theory and psychological research: Hedonism, eudaimonism and why it matters. *Journal of Positive Psychology,* 5(3), 212–225.

Tiberius, V., & Plakias, A. (2010). Well-being. In J. M. Doris & the Moral Psychology Research Group (Eds.), *The moral psychology handbook* (pp. 401–431). Oxford: Oxford University Press.

# CHAPTER 25

# HAPPINESS AND ITS OPPOSITES

JAMES O. PAWELSKI

University of Pennsylvania, USA

HAPPINESS is notoriously difficult both to define and to obtain. In the first part of this chapter I will try to shed some light on what happiness means by examining what it does not mean—and more specifically, by examining its opposites. This will require, first, an exploration of what an opposite is and a description of different kinds of opposites. It will then require an analysis of the relation between different meanings of happiness and their opposites. A surprising result of this analysis will be that the relation between happiness and unhappiness is complex and that it can be deeply misleading simply to claim that these terms are opposites. In the second part of this chapter, I will argue that getting clear about the relation between happiness and its opposites has important implications for the pursuit of happiness. I will give several examples from the history of philosophy to show how getting clear about this relation can deepen our understanding of better philosophical advice on how to obtain happiness; I will also point out important implications for contemporary practice and suggest a program for further empirical study.

## UNDERSTANDING HAPPINESS AND ITS OPPOSITES

One way to understand what a term means is to get clear about what it does not mean. A child just learning language, for example, has to learn that the term "nose" refers to a certain part of the face only and not to the ears, cheeks, or mouth. A full understanding of the term "rock" includes the knowledge that it does not mean "flower," or "bird," or "cloud." In general, a correct definition includes everything to which a term refers and nothing to which it does not refer.

In some cases, the domain to which a term does not refer contains the term's opposite. An opposite is a special case of what a term does not mean. It has a particular logical relation to the original term, a relation we can call an inverse reference. Consider the term "light." "Light" refers to certain types of electromagnetic waves. It is what allows us to see the world when the sun comes up in the morning or when we make a fire at night. Clearly, there is a large domain of things not referred to by the term "light." This domain includes things like rain, squirrel, and molecule. If anyone thought that these were examples of light, we would conclude that they did not understand the meaning of the term. But there is one item in the domain of things to which "light" does not refer that bears a special logical relation to it. "Darkness" is clearly not an example of light, but it has a certain logical relation to it that rain, squirrel, and molecule do not. Darkness is the absence of light. So we say that darkness is the opposite of light. And we can see that "light" inversely refers to "darkness."

The term "opposite" comes from Latin and means "placed against." The Greek term for opposites in language is "antonym," meaning "against-name." Achievement tests sometimes have a section on antonyms as a way of testing the understanding of a term's meaning. Students who understand not only that to which a term refers directly, but also that to which it refers inversely, demonstrate a deeper understanding of the term.

Not all terms, of course, have opposites. We would be hard-pressed to come up with opposites for the terms mentioned in the first paragraph: nose, ears, cheeks, mouth, rock, flower, bird, or cloud. But there are many terms like "light" that do have opposites. Think of terms like cold, wet, tall, increase, and smooth. The opposites of these terms are easy to identify: hot, dry, short, decrease, and rough.

What does all of this have to do with happiness? Well, it makes sense that if happiness has an opposite, knowing what that opposite is may help us understand happiness more deeply. It is easy, of course, to identify the opposite of happiness. "Un-" is an English prefix which comes from Greek and Latin roots meaning "not." So for words like helpful, affordable, authorized, pleasant, grateful, loving, interesting, and many others, all we have to do is add the prefix 'un-" to arrive at their opposites: *un*helpful, *un*affordable, *un*authorized, *un*pleasant, *un*grateful, *un*loving, *un*interesting. The same is clearly true for happiness. By adding the same prefix to it, we arrive at its opposite: *un*happiness.

Upon further reflection, however, we can see that the situation is actually more complicated than this. Since opposites bear a logical relation to each other, it is important to understand that this relation can be of many different types. Some opposites, for example, are "binary opposites." That is, either one or the other opposite obtains, but not both. If I tell you that I am looking at someone across the street and that the person is male, you know that the person is not female. If I tell you the person is not male, you know automatically that the person must be female. This is because there are only two options, and everyone is either one or the other.[1] Other opposites are "continuum opposites." That is, the two terms are at the opposite ends of a single continuum. I have already mentioned that darkness is the opposite of light, since it is defined as its absence. If you have more darkness, by definition you have less light; if you have more light, by definition you have less darkness. Both binary opposites and continuum opposites belong to a larger class that I would like to call "contradictory opposites." They are contradictory, because the presence or absence of one automatically says something about the absence or presence of the other.

Not all opposites are contradictory opposites, however. A look at the Square of Opposition, with roots in Aristotle's logic (see *De Interpretatione*, 6–7), can help us identify some other types, as well. For those not already familiar with the Square of Opposition, it might be

---

[1] Since I am discussing "male" and "female" to illustrate a logical relation, I am leaving out the important exception of hermaphrodites.

easiest to begin with an example. Consider a room full of people. Here are some claims that can be made about them:

> AM = "All are male."
> AF = "All are female."
> SM = "Some are male."
> SF = "Some are female."

Which of these claims are contradictory opposites? There are two pairs of contradictory opposites in this group. AM and SF are contradictory opposites, since if all the people in the room are male, it is automatically false that some are female; and if some are female, it is automatically false that all are male. Similarly, if it is false that all are male, then it is automatically true that some are female; and if it is false that some are female, then it is automatically true that all are male. The truth or falsehood of either claim indicates automatically the falsehood or truth of the other. In just the same way, AF and SM are also contradictory opposites.

But consider the claims AM and AF. What is their relation? Clearly, if AM is true, then AF must be false. And if AF is true, then AM must be false. So far, they seem to be contradictory opposites. But notice what happens if AM is false. If AM is false, we do not know whether AF is true or false. This is because knowing that not all people in the room are males does not tell us whether they are all female, or only some female. And of course, by the same logic, if AF is false, we do not know whether AM is true or false. Aristotle calls claims of this type "contraries." Contraries can both be false, but they cannot both be true.

Finally, consider the claims SM and SF. If SM is false, then SF must be true. If it is not true that any of the people in the room are male, then some of them must be female. (In fact, all of them must be.) Similarly, if SF is false, then SM must be true. So far, these claims seem like contradictory opposites. But notice what happens if SM is true. If SM is true, we do not know whether SF is true or false. Knowing that some of the people in the room are male does not tell us whether or not some of them are female. (They could all be male, but we do not know that.) And by the same logic, if SF is true, we do not know whether SM is true or false. Claims of this type are called "subcontraries." Subcontraries can both be true, but they cannot both be false.

So what kind of opposites are happiness and unhappiness? The most obvious answer is that they are binary opposites. A person is either happy or unhappy about their life in general, or about some aspect of their life. We know how to recognize when a friend is happy or when he or she is unhappy. But a closer look at the situation shows that there are degrees of happiness and unhappiness. While getting my driver's license made me happy, getting married made me much happier. And while losing one of my contact lenses made me unhappy, getting mugged in New York City made me much unhappier. So perhaps happiness and unhappiness are continuum opposites, like light and darkness. Indeed, this is the common sense view: the more happy I am, the less unhappy I am, and vice versa. On this view, happiness automatically results from getting rid of unhappiness.

While we may initially think of happiness and unhappiness as binary or continuum opposites, there are actually good arguments to show that they are not contradictory opposites, at all. Seligman (2002) argues that in psychology the positive is not simply the absence of the negative. This is because there is a neutral point that divides them. For example, getting rid of negative emotions like anger, fear, and sadness may get us to a neutral emotional state, but that does not automatically bring us positive emotions like love, gratitude, and joy. In effect,

Seligman is arguing that it is possible to be neither happy nor unhappy. On this view, happiness and unhappiness are contrary opposites.

There is also good evidence, however, to believe that happiness and unhappiness are subcontrary opposites. That is, that it is possible to be both happy and unhappy. Indeed, it is rare to have an emotional state where we are experiencing positive emotions with no negative emotions at all mixed in; or where we feel only negative emotions with no hint of positive emotions at all. Most of us spend our time in a variety of states that contain mixtures of happiness and unhappiness.

These considerations seem to bring us to a dead end in our inquiry. If it is possible to be happy and not unhappy, or to be unhappy and not happy, or neither happy nor unhappy, or both happy and unhappy at the same time, then in what sense are these terms opposites at all? Is their opposition merely a verbal one? A trick of linguistic morphology?

To try to answer this question, it will be important to examine more closely how the addition of the prefix "un-" changes the meaning of a word. In fact, the addition of this prefix changes different words in different ways. Take two of the earlier examples: "affordable" and "pleasant." If something is affordable, it means I have enough money to buy it. If it is unaffordable, I do not. The way to make something affordable is simply to get rid of its unaffordability (find more money, get a discount). Unaffordability is a lack of affordability, and if we diminish this lack, we automatically render the thing affordable (or at least more so). But notice that the case is very different with the term "pleasant." If something is pleasant, it means it is enjoyable. If it is unpleasant, it is not enjoyable. But getting rid of the unpleasantness of a situation does not necessarily render the situation pleasant. Imagine lying in bed in the morning and suddenly being awakened by construction workers using a jack-hammer on the sidewalk in front of your next-door neighbor's house. You find the noise very unpleasant, and you get up and tell the construction workers it is too early for them to be making so much noise in the neighborhood. They agree to come back later in the day while you are at work, so as not to disturb you. You lie back down in bed to try to get some more sleep. You have gotten rid of the unpleasantness in your environment, but does this mean the unpleasantness has automatically been replaced by pleasantness? Not necessarily. As you drift back to sleep, you may find yourself returning to a neutral state, not feeling particularly pleasant or particularly unpleasant. Or you may find your unpleasant emotional reaction lingering, but mixing with the pleasantness of drifting off to sleep for another hour.

This example illustrates the claim that happiness and unhappiness are not merely existential opposites. By "existential opposites," I mean terms that simply mark the presence or absence of something. Affordable and unaffordable are existential opposites, as are light and darkness. Unaffordability is not anything in itself over and above a lack of affordability. Nor is darkness anything in itself over and above the absence of light. In spite of the misleading linguistic form of the two terms, happiness and unhappiness are not existential opposites. Rather, they are substantive opposites. By "substantive opposites," I mean that each term refers to something that exists in its own right. Male and female are substantive opposites. Despite the views of all-too-many individuals and cultures, masculinity is not simply the presence of something femininity lacks. Nor is it correct to say that femininity is a presence and masculinity is an absence. Masculinity and femininity are equally real metaphysically. What makes them opposites is the unique biological and genetic relations they have. Similarly, happiness and unhappiness are both substantive. They are both metaphysically real. So what is the unique relation they have that makes them opposites?

In order to answer this question, we need to consider different possible meanings of the term "happiness." We will see that these different meanings have different relations with the term "unhappiness" and that, accordingly, these terms can be seen to be opposites in different ways.

When we say we are happy, what we often mean is that we are experiencing positive emotions. One meaning of the term happiness, then, is the feeling of a positive emotion like joy. And the opposite of joy, of course, is sadness. Now, it is possible to experience joy but not sadness, or to experience sadness but not joy, or to experience neither joy nor sadness. It is even possible to experience both joy and sadness at the same time, as baseball player Kendry Morales of the Los Angeles Angels did when he hit a game-winning grand slam, then finished his tour of the bases with an ill-fated celebratory leap to home plate that twisted and broke his leg. This indicates that joy and sadness—and in general, positive and negative emotions—are two different things and not merely the flip side of the same thing. Although we no doubt think of them as opposites because of the contrasting ways we feel and behave when experiencing them, having (or lacking) one does not tell us whether we have (or lack) the other.

There is, however, one caveat I need to mention here. There is actually a low negative correlation between positive emotions and negative emotions. Researchers using the Positive and Negative Affect Schedule (PANAS) know that it is possible to score high on positive emotions and low on negative emotions, or low on positive emotions and high on negative emotions, or high on both positive and negative emotions, or low on both positive and negative emotions. But there is a tendency that if you are high on one, you will be low on the other. The correlation is moderate, about $r = -0.2$ (Watson, Clark, & Tellegen, 1988). So perhaps we should say that positive emotions and negative emotions are weak contradictory opposites. While having one does not guarantee not having the other, it does make it more likely that the other will be low. At the same time, they are strong substantive opposites, since one is not simply a lack of the other.

On the commonsense definition of happiness as positive emotion, it is clear that happiness is not the same thing as the absence of unhappiness, since positive emotion is not the same thing as the absence of negative emotion. A bit of reflection will show, however, that this commonsense notion of happiness is inadequate. We would not call someone happy if they had both strong positive emotions and strong negative emotions. This is because happiness involves both the presence of certain mental states and the absence of others. The mere presence of positive states or the mere absence of negative states is not sufficient to guarantee happiness.

This point is reflected in the work of key happiness researchers. Ed Diener (Diener & Biswas-Diener, 2008), for example, argues that happiness should be understood in terms of his construct of subjective well-being. He defines subjective well-being as the presence of high positive affect, low negative affect, and high life satisfaction. A person's level of subjective well-being is a composite of these three elements. Notice that subjective well-being is a function of both the presence of good emotions and the lack of negative emotions. Simply knowing that someone experiences lots of positive emotions is not sufficient evidence, according to Diener, to call someone happy. They could also have lots of negative emotions, and thus not be very happy. And knowing that someone has few negative emotions does not guarantee that they are happy, either. They could also have few positive emotions, and thus not be very happy. The fact that Diener includes positive affect and negative affect as two different elements in his scale indicates his understanding that they are substantive opposites and that they are not true contradictory opposites. Similarly, Barbara Fredrickson (2009) acknowledges that the mere presence of positive emotions or the mere absence of negative emotions does not guarantee happiness, or what she calls "positivity." For Fredrickson, the key is the ratio of positive states to negative states. She argues on the basis of empirical studies that happiness requires a ratio of at least three positive emotions for every negative emotion. The way she defines positive and negative emotions in terms of their different characteristics and functions makes it clear that she, too, understands them to be substantive opposites.

It is interesting to note what these last two definitions of happiness—as subjective well-being and as positivity—do to the relation between happiness and its opposites. Although they are each based on the substantive opposites of positive and negative emotions, their composite nature turns happiness into a continuum opposite. With positive and negative emotions, it is possible to have high levels of one or the other, both, or neither. This is not the case, however, with subjective well-being and subjective ill-being, or with positivity and negativity. Having high subjective well-being automatically means having low subjective ill-being (and vice-versa), and having high positivity automatically means having low negativity (and vice-versa). This is to be expected, of course, since scientific constructs of this sort typically are continuum opposites. In order to make accurate measurements, scientists need to disentangle complex states and try to measure one thing at a time.

The case is similar when we turn away from definitions of happiness that are so dependent on emotion. Another way we might think of happiness is in the sense parents have in mind when they say they want their children to be happy. They certainly want their children to experience joy and a whole range of other positive emotions and to avoid too much sadness or other negative emotions, but they also want them to have a virtuous character, good relationships, and a meaningful career. Parents want children to flourish in a way similar to what Aristotle meant by the term eudaimonia (for a fuller description of the meaning of this term, see McMahon, Chapter 19, this volume). So what is the opposite of eudaimonia, of flourishing? It is dysdaimonia, or languishing. And what kind of opposites are eudaimonia and dysdaimonia? If eudaimonia involves having a virtuous character, good relationships, and a meaningful career, then we might define dysdaimonia in terms of a vicious character, toxic relationships, and unemployment or—worse—a life of crime. Understood in this way, it seems that dysdaimonia is more than simply a lack of eudaimonia. More generally, having a terrible life involves very different things from simply not having a great life. So eudaimonia and dysdaimonia, it seems are substantive opposites.

This view is reflected in the work of Corey Keyes (2007) who argues for a "complete state" model of human mental health. His complete state model includes independent salutogenic and pathogenic scales. For Keyes, to be truly mentally healthy is to be mentally flourishing and free of mental illness. He defines mental flourishing in terms of positive emotions, positive psychological functioning, and positive social functioning, while mental illness is measured in accordance with the *Diagnostic and Statistical Manual of Mental Disorders* (American Psychiatric Association, 1994). He points to empirical data that indicates it is possible to be flourishing and not mentally ill, not to be flourishing and to be mentally ill, to be both flourishing and mentally ill, and to be neither flourishing nor mentally ill. Not surprisingly, though, there is a negative correlation between flourishing and mental illness. Like positive and negative emotions, flourishing and mental illness are weak contradictory opposites and strong substantive opposites. And just like Diener and Fredrickson, Keyes advocates measuring complete mental health on different scales of existential opposites. In addition to the *Diagnostic and Statistical Manual*, which presents ways for identifying the presence or absence of mental illness, Keyes proposes a different scale to measure the presence or absence of flourishing.

From this brief look at different ways of understanding happiness, we can see that different definitions of happiness have different types of opposites. Getting clear on what these opposites are can help us understand more clearly the notion of happiness we have in mind. Getting clear on what these opposites are can also help us be more effective in the pursuit of happiness. However we define happiness, it seems that it involves the presence of certain (positive) states or conditions and the absence of other (negative) states or conditions and that although these two sets of states or conditions may be negatively correlated, they can and often do coexist. So, as Seligman (2002) has argued, happiness is not the same thing as the absence of the negative. Nor, however, is it the same thing as the presence of the positive. These claims are not only important theoretically; they also have significant practical implications for the pursuit of happiness.

## Pursuing Happiness and Avoiding its Opposites

If the analysis in the first part of this paper is accurate, it follows that the successful pursuit of happiness must involve two different types of processes. It must involve processes for increasing positive states and conditions and processes for decreasing negative states and conditions. It can be instructive to see how this distinction plays out in the history of philosophy, particularly in understanding the advice philosophers have given on how to obtain happiness. I have room for just a few examples here.

Both the Stoics and the Epicureans, for example, emphasized the importance of decreasing the negative, of freeing ourselves from something. In the case of the Stoics, it was freeing ourselves from the control of the passions. They called the resulting state of freedom *apatheia*. Somewhat similarly, the Epicureans wanted freedom from worry, anxiety, and trouble. For them, the desired state was *ataraxia*, or tranquility. Although they had their differences, both the Stoics and the Epicureans emphasized getting rid of what we do not want as the path to happiness. As Martha Nussbaum points out in *The Therapy of Desire* (1994), members of these Hellenistic schools of philosophy followed the medical model of diagnosing and curing disease, conceiving of the philosopher as the doctor of the soul. Consider, for example, the teachings of the Stoic Epictetus. In the *Discourses*, Epictetus claims that "the lecture-room of the philosopher is a hospital; you ought not to walk out of it in pleasure, but in pain. For you are not well when you come ..." (Arrian, 1925, III. xxiii. 30).

This is not, however, the whole story as we have seen, this medical model of diagnosing and curing physical and mental illness is only part of what we need for health and flourishing. Reading Epictetus, we do find, it is true, passages where he makes use of the medical analogy, but there are many other passages in which he makes use of a quite different analogy, one that Martha Nussbaum does not consider. Epictetus frequently compares the student of philosophy to the athlete in training.[2] He says that "men who are engaged in the greatest of contests ought not to flinch, but to take also the blows; for the contest before us is not in wrestling or the pancratium ... but it is a contest for good fortune and happiness

---

[2] I am indebted to Luke Timothy Johnson for first having pointed this out to me.

itself" (Arrian, 1925, III. xxv. 3). Elsewhere, Epictetus (1925) points out that there are many costs to consider when becoming a philosopher and that it takes the same kind of dedication and perseverance to become a philosopher that it takes to be an Olympic athlete (*Encheiridion*, 29.2–7). What difference does it make if we think of the pursuit of philosophy as a training for the soul instead of as a cure for it? On the medical analogy, the soul is sick. There is a deficiency, a malfunction, a disease we want to get rid of. We are focused on what is wrong with us and how we can get rid of the problem. We find ourselves in a bad place, often in pain or even crisis, and we want to escape these things by finding a cure. On the training analogy, the situation is quite different. Here we are doing just fine. We are not seeking freedom from, but freedom to. We are not looking for freedom from illness, but rather, for freedom to develop our skills and to achieve. While training can require just as much hard work and discipline as therapy, the desired outcomes are very different. When sick, we feel compelled to find a cure, but when well, we can freely choose whether or not we want to subject ourselves to the instructions of the trainer. When focusing, not on a cure, but on choosing a training, we feel a greater sense of autonomy. We are focusing, not on what we want to get rid of, but on what we want to have more of in our lives. And this has a very different phenomenological feel to it.

A few centuries after Epictetus, Boethius (1999) brought together both of these perspectives, emphasizing the importance of both absence of illness and presence of health for those who would be truly happy. Boethius was the victim of a breathtakingly swift turn of the wheel of fortune that brought him from the highest levels of privilege and power in sixth-century Rome to a prison where he awaited his execution—falsely accused and convicted of treason. While awaiting execution, he wrote *The Consolation of Philosophy*. In this work, he pursued philosophy to try to moderate his misery. He imagined philosophy coming to him in the form of a woman who conversed with him about his present condition. Philosophy told him he was sick. She asked him questions so she could diagnose him and prescribe proper remedies. Without too much trouble, she was able to identify the cause of his sickness. He had forgotten his own identity and come to doubt that human affairs are justly ordered. He saw his unjust fall from power as "random and unguided." Philosophy noted that these symptoms were very serious. If not treated, they could lead to death.

Boethius's cure came in stages. Initially, Philosophy said, she must use lighter remedies "so that the hard swellings where the emotions have gathered may soften under a more caressing touch, and may become ready to bear the application of more painful treatment" (Boethius, 1999, I. 5. 12). The lighter remedies consisted in "soothing medicine with a pleasant taste" (Boethius, 1999, II. 1. 7). Philosophy used rhetoric, alternating with music, to persuade Boethius of the right attitude he should have toward Fortune.

Philosophy's first task was to show Boethius that he had no cause to complain in his present state, because Fortune is essentially fickle. Indeed, Fortune had brought him far more of her goods than she brings most people. But the kind of happiness Fortune brings is ephemeral, with no promise that the wealth, power, and fame she bestows will last. He had been free to enjoy these goods while he could, but surely he must have known that they were only loaned to him. He had no cause to complain when they were removed. Even so, Fortune had not removed all of her gifts from him. He still had the loyalty and support of his influential family, for example. Furthermore, if the wheel of fortune turned once, it could well turn again, and he could still have hopes that his lot would improve. Instead of having complained against misfortune in such a bitter and ungrateful way, Philosophy argued, it would have been more proper for Boethius to have counted his many blessings. Seeing that her arguments were having some effect on Boethius, Philosophy pressed further by claiming that, even if Fortune's gifts were not fleeting, they would not have yielded true happiness. Philosophy considered in turn five of Fortune's gifts (wealth, public office, regal power, fame, and physical pleasure) and showed how each is deficient.

To this point, Philosophy had been using lighter remedies to help calm Boethius and show him that he had been pursuing false goods that would not lead to happiness. At this stage, Philosophy turned to stronger remedies, medicines which are "bitter on the tongue, but sweet when swallowed" (Boethius, 1999, III. 1. 3–4). The goal of these stronger remedies was to show Boethius what happiness truly is. Philosophy led Boethius through a series of arguments whose conclusion is that true happiness does not come from a separate quest for self-sufficiency through wealth, or for respect and power through high office and kingship, or for true fame through the opinion of the mob, or for joy through bodily pleasures. Rather since true happiness is one, it can be found only by seeking that which makes a person "self-sufficient, powerful, venerable, famous, and joyful" all at the same time (Boethius, 1999, III. 9. 26–27). Philosophy argued that the true good and perfect happiness are one and that they are identical with God. "Hence every happy person is God; God is by nature one only, but nothing prevents the greatest possible number from sharing in that divinity" (Boethius, 1999, III. 10. 25).

Whatever we make of Boethius's Neoplatonic conclusions, it is instructive to observe that his cure came in two basic stages. First Philosophy needed to disabuse him of what she considered to be his false beliefs about happiness (that it was a gift of fortune). The intention was to remove something harmful to help Boethius gain freedom from beliefs that had been oppressing him. But Philosophy did not stop there. She moved on to a second stage which involved presenting Boethius with what she considered to be true beliefs about happiness (that it comes through sharing in God's divinity). The intention here was to inculcate something healthy to help Boethius gain the freedom to obtain true happiness.

In their own ways, Epictetus and Boethius illustrate the view I have argued for in this paper that happiness is not merely the opposite of unhappiness. Much work remains to be done to see how this view is supported by other figures in the history of philosophy and to see how ideas from the history of philosophy can help us develop this view more deeply. In the meantime, we can see that the relation between happiness and unhappiness is a complex one that depends on the definitions of the terms in question. But whatever definitions we use, it seems clear that happiness involves the presence of certain states or conditions and the lack of others and that the attainment of happiness involves both the cultivation of the former and the mitigation of the latter. This has implications for both the individual and the institutional pursuit of happiness. At the individual level, growing empirical evidence from the field of positive psychology indicates the importance of enjoying positive emotions, practicing strengths, and cultivating meaning, in addition to mitigating the effects of negative emotions, shoring up weaknesses, and fighting against angst. At the institutional level, we need to ask ourselves what we can do to increase social capital, altruism, and understanding, and not just what we can do to decrease hate, poverty, and crime. This seems consonant, for example, with the work of those who argue that national departments of defense are not sufficient to bring about the international harmony we desire. While departments of defense may help protect us from the dangers in the world, these persons argue, it may well be the case that we need departments of peace in each country to help move us closer to the positive opportunities we seek. Departments of peace, of course, would not obviate the need for departments of defense, but they may give them less to do.

In conclusion, I would like to point out further work that needs to be done in the investigation of happiness and its opposites. First, further theoretical work on different kinds of opposites can be useful. I have made distinctions here among contradictory opposites (including binary and continuum opposites), contrary opposites, and subcontrary opposites, as well as between existential and substantive opposites. These distinctions have proved helpful in understanding happiness. Identifying other kinds of opposites may prove useful, as well. Second, further textual work can be helpful. What insights about happiness and its opposites can we learn from looking to figures in the history of philosophy beyond Epictetus and Boethius? Conversely, what new insights might we find in philosophical writings if we look at them from the dual lenses of pursuing happiness and mitigating unhappiness? And there is no reason why this textual work need be limited to philosophy. What insights might we discover by using these questions to guide our readings of texts in literature, religion, and history? (See Charry, 2010; Pawelski & Moores, in press) What insights might we discover by using these questions to guide our interpretation of the visual arts, the performing arts, and music? Finally, this distinction opens up new empirical work to be done. If it is true that we need both constructive and mitigative approaches in the pursuit of happiness, to what degree should we rely on each? How much of our energy should go toward helping us increase our happiness, and how much of our energy should go toward helping us decrease our unhappiness? Under what conditions should we adopt a predominately constructive approach, and under what conditions should we adopt a predominately mitigative approach? These are important questions that can and should be operationalized and studied empirically. There is much further theoretical, textual, and empirical work to be done in understanding happiness and its opposites. If done carefully, this work will help create new knowledge about what happiness is (and is not) and provide fresh guidance for its effective pursuit.

## Acknowledgements

I would like to thank Behdad Bozorgnia for his help in the form of many discussions and much encouragement as I was thinking out many of the ideas for this chapter.

## References

American Psychiatric Association. (1994). *Diagnostic and statistical manual of mental disorders* (4th ed.). Washington, DC: American Psychiatric Association.

Aristotle. (1941). *De interpretatione* (E. M. Edgehill, Trans.). In R. McKeon (Ed.), *The basic works of Aristotle* (pp. 40–61). New York, NY: Random House. (Original work written fourth century B.C.E.).

Arrian. (1925). *Discourses of Epictetus* (W. A. Oldfather, Trans.). In J. Henderson (Ed.), *Epictetus* (2 vol.). Cambridge, MA: Harvard University Press. (Original work written circa AD 100).

Boethius. (1999). *The consolation of philosophy* (P. G. Walsh, Trans.). Oxford, UK: Oxford University Press. (Original work written circa AD 524).

Charry, E. (2010). *God and the art of happiness*. Grand Rapids, MI: William B. Eerdmans.

Diener, E., & Biswas-Diener, R. (2008). *Happiness: Unlocking the mysteries of psychological wealth*. Malden, MA: Blackwell.

Epictetus. (1925). *Encheiridion* (W. A. Oldfather, Trans.). In J. Henderson (Ed.), *Epictetus* (2 vol.). Cambridge, MA: Harvard University Press. (Original work written circa AD 125).

Fredrickson, B. (2009). *Positivity*. New York, NY: Crown Publishers.

Keyes, C. (2007). Promoting and protecting mental health as flourishing: A complementary strategy for improving national mental health. *American Psychologist, 62*, 95–108.

Nussbaum, M. C. (1994). *The therapy of desire: Theory and practice in Hellenistic ethics*. Princeton, NJ: Princeton University Press.

Pawelski, J. O., & Moores, D. J. (Eds.). (in press). *The eudaimonic turn: Well-being in literary studies*. Madison, NJ: Fairleigh Dickinson University Press.

Seligman, M. E. P. (2002). *Authentic happiness*. New York, NY: Free Press.

Watson, D., Clark, L. A., & Tellegen, A. (1988). Development and validation of brief measures of positive and negative affect: The PANAS scale. *Journal of Personality and Social Psychology, 54*, 1063–1070.

# SECTION IV

# SPIRITUAL APPROACHES TO HAPPINESS

# CHAPTER 26

# INTRODUCTION TO SPIRITUAL APPROACHES TO HAPPINESS

### JANE HENRY

Open University, UK

SPIRITUALITY is still central to most people's lives. In most countries the majority of the population believes in some form of the divine that is greater than themselves. In the USA, for example, around four-fifths of the public believe in God (e.g., Gallup, 2008) and over 90% believe in God or a higher power (e.g., Pew Forum, 2010).

For thousands of years spiritual traditions the world over have developed and refined a myriad of practices designed to help adults find wisdom, develop love (agape), and enhance well-being. While the conception of happiness in the West tends to emphasize positive emotion and personal fulfillment, spiritual conceptions of well-being tend to place greater emphasis on equanimity and a wholesome orientation to others. Until recently the study of spiritual approaches to development has been largely neglected by psychologists. Though contact with spiritual traditions, notably Eastern ones, influenced some humanistic self-inquiry practices both indirectly, and directly in cases such as visualization, as well as providing the impetus for transpersonal psychology. More recently the success of spiritually inspired attention training in ameliorating mental and physical health issues, offered in Western versions of mindfulness and other meditation practices, has seen this type of spiritual approach being taken on board by mainstream caring professionals.

Clearly, spiritual approaches to well-being cover a huge area and we can only address a subset of approaches here. We have chosen to offer some background to the spiritual approaches that are currently most influential in psychological development, i.e., the Eastern religious traditions of Buddhism and Hinduism. Most of the contributors are psychologists who have studied or have expertise in both spirituality and well-being.

In this section, two chapters (Ricard, Chapter 27, and Salagame, Chapter 29) offer accounts of spiritual approaches to well-being. Ricard provides an insider's view of the Buddhist understanding of and route to well-being. Salagame outlines the Hindu Advaita understanding of the truth of life and its approach to well-being. Two chapters (Kwee, Chapter 28, and Malinowski, Chapter 30) draw parallels between psychological and spiritual approaches to well-being. Kwee offers a clinical psychologist's take on Buddhism highlighting the relationship between the self and the wider world in which it sits. Malinowski points out the parallels between Buddhist and psychological approaches to flourishing, highlighting the role of mental balance. Two chapters (Mahoney, Pargament and Hernandez, Chapter 31, and Henry, Chapter 32) then look at psychological understandings of spiritual beliefs, experience, and development strategies. Mahoney et al. concentrate on the widespread sanctification of everyday life, highlighting both the positive and negative consequences. Henry discusses spiritual development practices highlighting parallels with practices ordinary people claim help them achieve lasting well-being. Other chapters in this book describe positive interventions that draw on spiritual practice, for example, Langer on mindfulness (Chapter 76) and Haynes on Acceptance and Commitment Therapy (Chapter 74).

Matthieu Ricard is a French neuroscientist who has been a Tibetan monk for over 30 years. Based in Nepal, he is the Dalai Lama's French translator and star subject in a series of brain scanning experiments investigating experienced meditators who can reliably maintain stable altered states. This quality is lacking in ordinary subjects and novice meditators. His books include the bestselling *The Monk and the Philosopher*, *Happiness*, and *The Art of Meditation*.

Pali and Sanskrit lack a separate word for emotion, rather emotion and cognition are seen as intertwined (a position mirrored in brain topography in that no separate area for emotion has been found). In his chapter, Ricard gives an elegant account of the Buddhist approach to happiness and how the mind is used to overcome and transform what we would call unwanted emotions. Ricard explains how Tibetan Buddhism uses the cultivation of positive emotion, such as altruistic love, to counteract negative emotions, such as hatred. The Buddhist sense of positive emotion contrasts with Anglo-Saxon notions in that it is essentially interpersonal in orientation. Well-being is seen as a state of mind but one that is associated with lasting fulfillment and equanimity.

Maurits Kwee is a clinical psychologist and prolific author who has long championed the potential for Buddhist inspired approaches within therapeutic endeavors. Here Kwee offers an existential account of Buddhism.

Buddhist psychology is centrally concerned with adult development and the nature of the self. Various commentators have noted the parallels between certain Buddhist practices, cognitive behavioral, and allied therapeutic strategies. However Buddhist conclusions about the best way to develop are quite different as reflection on mental phenomena and sensory experience leads Buddhists to the realization that our sense of identity as a skin-encapsulated being is erroneous. Appreciating that our thoughts, emotions, and actions are heavily influenced not just by our temperament and motivation but the ongoing relations we are engaged in and the environments we find ourselves in, Kwee argues that the Buddhist notion of dependent origination shares many features with a social constructionist perspective (a viewpoint that currently dominates much social science in Europe, though not all schools of psychology). Kwee also questions whether the Western use of meditation which tends to focus on redirecting attention and non-evaluative awareness goes far enough, as among adepts these are merely routes to developing insight into the way things are.

Kiran Salagame is a Professor of Psychology at Mysore University in India. He has a long-standing interest in Indian psychology, transpersonal psychology, and, more recently, the psychology of well-being. Here he outlines some of the thinking that underpins Hindu perspectives on spirituality and well-being, associating well-being with wholesome thought and action.

There are many different schools of Hinduism but the Advaita tradition and those drawing on the Vedas and Upanishads see the goal of spirituality as recognizing the ultimate truth of union with the divine. In terms of the loss of the egoic self and identification with a wider perspective there are clear parallels with Buddhism. In Hinduism, spiritual well-being is associated not just with peace and harmony but also great bliss. Salagame gives a telling example of a well-known guru who had achieved a blissful state even though this was not obvious to bystanders.

Hinduism has always accepted there are many different paths to the Divine and is perhaps unique in its understanding of the need for different routes to that goal. This led to a tolerance that traditionally accepted other religious traditions as equally legitimate paths. Hinduism recognizes spiritual practices ranging from working through the body and its energy systems, through worship, devotion and service, to control of the mind and knowledge. It recognizes an individual's need to choose a path suited to their temperament and character. In many spiritual traditions procedures for quieting the mind and developing virtues feature strongly. Salagame focuses on the impersonal but Hinduism recognizes both personal and impersonal aspects of the divine. It is seen as worth any hardness to achieve the goal of union with the divine. Negative circumstances may be welcomed as offering a great opportunity to learn about, and root out, one's weaknesses, and in this sense benefit the development of well-being.

Paul Malinowski is a German cognitive psychologist, neuroscientist, and Buddhist, currently based in the UK. He looks at the relationship between ideas in Buddhism and psychological work on flourishing. For example, both approaches see the need to reduce unhelpful experiences as well as increase helpful ones. He notes the variety of meditative practices and discusses mechanisms for their effectiveness in ameliorating psychological distress and promoting psychological health that involve an increase in positive emotion and enhanced positive resources. Drawing on Wallace and Shapiro (2006) he discusses the way in which meditative practice enhances well-being through greater mental, emotional, and attentional balance. He also warns against jumping to premature conclusions on the basis of cross-sectional studies.

In their chapter Annette Mahoney, Kenneth Pargamont, and Krystal Hernandez draw attention to aspects of ordinary life that can be viewed as spiritually sanctified.

Positive psychologists have begun to study the so called transcendent emotions—awe, elevation, forgiveness, gratitude, but these emotions are not unique to spiritual adherents. Pargament and Mahoney, who have been researching spirituality for many years, opt to focus on the sanctification of life, which they see as uniquely spiritual. Pargament characterizes spirituality as a search for the sacred—"a human yearning for a relationship with something sacred—something transcendent, boundless, and ultimate". A number of writers have expressed a concern that modern man has desanctified life but Mahoney et al.'s chapter shows that finding the sacred in everyday life is a very common experience. They examine the sanctification of striving, marriage, parenting, work, sex, the body, and nature; all areas that people imbue with a sense of the sacred whether from a belief in a divine presence in their life or a sacred quality. Generally they have found that areas imbued with sacred qualities are associated with enhanced positive functioning in those areas until something goes wrong. For some people the psychological costs at that point are greater because of their earlier investment, others rise to the occasion and find challenging experiences instructive. It is interesting that the sanctification of life is not necessarily associated with greater life satisfaction. Rather, in this chapter, as in the others in this section on spiritual approaches, well-being is associated with something greater than personal happiness and satisfaction.

Jane Henry is an applied psychologist based at the Open University in the UK. Her research concerns different paths of adult development and their relationship to lasting well-being. She has been active in the European positive psychology movement, co-organizing the first European conference on the topic. Here she reviews key aspects of spiritual experience, development, and practice, and contrasts these with lay understanding and psychological approaches. Spiritual traditions recognize many different spiritual experiences, including extremely positive and persistent states of bliss and joy and states where identity is experienced as much wider than our usual skin-encapsulated self. Notions of well-being in spiritual traditions are generally more concerned with contentment and equanimity than the more positive and upbeat notions of happiness that many psychologists address. One implication is that we could usefully redirect more effort to understand forms of well-being characterized by lower arousal, such as contentment. Spiritual approaches tend to differ from mainstream psychological interventions in their emphasis on retraining attention by quieting the mind. Henry's work investigating effective methods for enhancing long-term well-being suggests many people are well aware of the importance of relaxation, silence, and acceptance as routes to lasting contentment.

## Conclusion

One can view the spiritual and psychological approaches as interrelated concepts, or as complementary and dealing with different aspects of the self (e.g., Cortright, 2007) or see psychology as dealing with normal development and spirituality as addressing higher states of consciousness (e.g., Alexander, 1990). Whichever view is adopted, spiritual traditions talk of many different spiritual experiences yet to be recognized by psychology. What appears to be needed is a more detailed understanding of the nature of spiritual experiences and the beneficial effects of associated states of mind on both the experient and those around them.

The chapters in this section give a central place to contentment, equanimity, and balance in their conceptions of well-being, areas that seem to have received surprisingly little scrutiny in psychology to date. Positive psychologists could usefully direct more effort to studying the different varieties of optimal experience. Rather than talking of factors associated with well-being or happiness and effectively treating them as if they were a single state we need to differentiate between many different states of optimal experience, including neglected forms of well-being associated with lower arousal, such as contentment and equanimity.

Spiritual practice is very much concerned with a psychology of personal development. Spiritual development is generally undertaken with a master or mistress in the field who has already undergone some form of spiritual transformation which affords them special insight and influence. Gurus are often consulted by the lay public about life problems much as a psychological professional would be in the West. The advice they give tends to depend on the readiness of the individual and what is advised may vary significantly across individuals. This is very different from standard manual-based approaches sometimes encouraged in the West and offered by qualified but not necessarily particularly developed individuals.

There is also the question of how legitimate and advisable it is to advocate spiritual practices in non-spiritual settings. Some spiritual practices are esoteric or restricted to those advanced enough to be ready for them. Meditation, for example, may not be recommended until the adept has achieved a certain basic level of order and discipline in their life. Though proving to be very effective for many Westerners, it remains to be seen how widely we can usefully apply attention training drawn from spiritual practices like meditation and mindfulness.

Positive psychology has had great success in transforming the orientation of transformational psychology from an almost exclusive concentration on problem-based approaches to one that builds on strengths and positive experiences. At the same time, spiritually informed practices such as mindfulness-based stress reduction, mindfulness-based cognitive therapy, and allied approaches are having great success is raising the profile of approaches based on acceptance and detachment rather than striving and control. The articles in this section remind us that spiritual approaches also tend to place greater focus on the importance of a wholesome interpersonal orientation and the well-being of others. This shows a marked contrast with the focus on chasing personal goals found in many psychological interventions. However, interpersonal virtues such as gratitude, forgiveness, and compassion are beginning to take a more prominent role in some newer interventions (e.g., Gilbert, 2005).

More fundamentally, higher states of consciousness also seem to entail a much wider identification and with this the consequent dissolution of our normal psychological sense of self and much of the internal chatter associated with it. Were we to become spiritually developed much psychological endeavor could be redundant!

## References

Alexander, C. N., Davies, J. L., Dixon, C. A., Dilbeck, M. C., Drucker, S. M., Oetzel, R. M., … Orme-Johnson, D. W. (1990). Growth of higher stages of consciousness. In C. N. Alexander & E. Langer (Eds.), *Higher stages of human development* (pp. 286–341). Oxford, UK: Oxford University Press.

Cortright, B. (2007). *Integral psychology*. Albany, NY: SUNY.

Gallup (2008). *Belief in God far lower in the Western US*. Retrieved August 30, 2009 from http://www.gallup.com/poll/109108/belief-god-far-lower-western-us.aspx.

Gilbert, P. (2005). *Compassion: Conceptualisations, research and use in psychotherapy*. London, UK: Routledge.

Pew Forum (2010). *Religious landscape study findings*. Retrieved January 30, 2011 from http://religions.pewforum.org/pdf/report2religious-landscape-study-key-findings.pdf.

Wallace, B. A., & Shapiro, S. (2006). Mental balance and well-being: Building bridges between Buddhism and Western Psychology. *American Psychologist, 61*(7), 690–701.

# CHAPTER 27

# A BUDDHIST VIEW OF HAPPINESS

## MATTHIEU RICARD

Shechen Tennyi Dargyeling Monastery

A great majority of the European words for "happy" seem to imply "lucky" (with the exception of Welsh, where the word used first meant "wise"). The happy person is someone who has benefited from a lucky destiny and from favorable circumstances. In fact, instinctively most people put all their hopes and fear in the outer world.

In modern Western societies, happiness is often equated with a maximization of pleasure and some imagine that true happiness would consist of an interrupted succession of pleasurable experiences. This sounds more like a recipe for exhaustion than for genuine happiness and nothing is further away from the Buddhist notion of "sukha," which refers to an optimal way of being, an exceptionally healthy state of mind that underlies and suffuses all emotional states, that embraces all the joys and sorrows that come one's way (Dalai Lama, 1998, Ricard, 2007). *Sukha* is therefore a state of lasting well-being that manifests itself when we have freed ourselves of mental blindness and afflictive emotions. It is also the wisdom that allows us to see the world as it is, without veils or distortions. It is, finally, the joy of moving towards inner freedom and the loving kindness and compassion that radiates towards others.

In Buddhism, the word "reality" connotes the true nature of things, unmodified by the mental constructs we superimpose upon it. Such constructs open up a gap between our perception and that reality, and hence create a never-ending conflict with the world. We take for permanent that which is ephemeral and for happiness that which is but a source of suffering, and we imagine there being an independent self in the midst of the aggregates of the body and mind.

Under the influence of habitual tendencies, we perceive the exterior world as a series of distinct, autonomous entities to which we attribute characteristics that we believe belong inherently to them. This error, which Buddhism calls *ignorance*, gives rise to powerful reflexes of attachment and aversion that generally lead to suffering. The world of ignorance and suffering, *samsara*, is not a fundamental condition of existence, but a mental universe based on our mistaken conception of reality (Shantarakshita, 2005; Wallace, 2003).

The world of appearances is created by the coming together of an infinite number of ever-changing causes and conditions. Like a rainbow that forms when the sun shines across a curtain of rain and then vanishes when any factor contributing to its formation disappears, phenomena exist in an essentially interdependent mode and have no autonomous and enduring existence. Everything is *relation*; nothing exists in and of itself. Once this essential concept is understood and internalized, the erroneous perception of the world gives way to a correct understanding of the nature of things. This wisdom is not a mere philosophical construct. It emerges gradually and removes our mental blindness and the afflictive mental states it produces and, thus, the principal causes of our suffering.

Every being has the potential for authentic happiness and perfection, just as every sesame seed is permeated with oil. We are ignorant, unaware of that potential, like the beggar who is unaware of the treasure buried beneath his shack. Actualizing our true nature, coming into possession of that hidden wealth, allows us to live a life full of meaning. It is the surest way to find serenity and to let genuine altruism flourish (Kunsang Palden, 2007; Shantideva, 2006).

Yet, happiness does not come simply because we wish it to, or because we pray for it. It is not a gift that chance bestows upon us and a reversal of fortune takes back. Happiness is a skill that requires effort and time (Ricard, 2007, 2010).

As influential as external conditions may be, suffering, like well-being, is essentially a state of mind. It is the mind that translates good and bad circumstances into happiness or misery. The search for happiness is not about looking at life through rose-colored glasses or blinding oneself to the pain and imperfections of the world. It is the purging of mental toxins, such as hatred and compulsive desire, that literally poison the mind and, above all, of ignorance.

No one wakes up in the morning thinking: "I wish I could suffer all day, and if possible my whole life." We all strive, consciously or unconsciously, competently or clumsily, to be happier and suffer less. Yet, we so often confuse genuine happiness with merely seeking enjoyable feelings. To imagine happiness as the achievement of all our wishes and passions—and above all, to see it from an exclusively egocentric perspective—is to confuse the legitimate aspiration to inner fulfillment with a utopia that inevitably leads to frustration. The fact is that, without inner peace and wisdom, we have nothing we need to be happy. Happiness is a state of inner fulfillment, not the gratification of inexhaustible desires for outward things. As the Tibetan proverb says, "Seeking happiness outside ourselves is like waiting for sunshine in a cave facing north." Our desires are boundless and our control over the world is limited, temporary and, more often than not, illusory. If, conversely, happiness is a state that depends on inner conditions, each of us must recognize and bring those conditions together. Happiness is not given to us, nor misery imposed. At every moment we are at a crossroads and must choose the direction we are to take.

## Our happiness depends on that of others

Among all the clumsy, blind, and extreme ways we go about building happiness, one of the most sterile is egocentrism. The pursuit of selfish happiness is bound to fail. It is a lose–lose situation in which we make ourselves miserable and create misery around us. This does not mean that we should neglect our own happiness. Our desire for happiness is as legitimate as anyone else's. The goal here is to achieve a deep state of well-being and wisdom at all moments, accompanied by love for every sentient being, and not by the individual love that modern society relentlessly drums into us. True happiness arises from the essential goodness that wholeheartedly desires everyone to find meaning in their lives (Dilgo Khyentse, 2007).

## Happiness and pleasure

The most common error is to confuse pleasure for happiness. The fleeting experience of pleasure is dependent upon circumstance, on a specific location, or moment in time. It is unstable by nature and the sensation it evokes soon becomes neutral or even unpleasant. Likewise, when repeated it may grow insipid or even lead to disgust; savoring a delicious meal is a source of genuine pleasure, but we are indifferent to it once we've had our fill and would sicken of it if we were to continue eating.

Pleasure is exhausted by usage, like a candle consuming itself. It is almost always linked to an *activity* and naturally leads to lassitude by dint of being repeated. Listening to beautiful music requires a focus of attention that, minimal as it is, cannot be maintained indefinitely. Were we forced to listen for days on end, it would become unbearable.

Furthermore, pleasure can be joined to cruelty, violence, pride, greed, and other mental conditions that are incompatible with true happiness.

Unlike pleasure, genuine happiness and flourishing may be influenced by circumstance, but it isn't dependent on it. It actually gives us the inner resources to deal better with those circumstances. It does not mutate into its opposite, but endures and grows with experience. It imparts a sense of fulfillment that, in time, becomes second nature.

In brief, there is no direct relationship between pleasure and happiness. This distinction in no way suggests that we mustn't seek out pleasurable sensations. There is no reason to deprive ourselves of the enjoyment of a magnificent landscape, of swimming in the sea, or of the scent of a rose, so long as they do not alienate us. Pleasures become obstacles only when they are tainted with grasping and impede inner freedom, giving rise to avidity and dependence.

We may thus understand that even unpleasant experience, such as sadness in the face of a tragedy or an injustice are by no means incompatible with compassion, with a sense of direction and meaning in life, with inner strength and deep confidence in our resolve to bring about a better world. So even in sadness we can continue to pursue a most meaningful and constructive life, which characterizes genuine happiness.

## Suffering

Just as we distinguished between happiness and pleasure, we must also make the distinction between affliction and suffering. We *incur* suffering but we *create* unhappiness. The Sanskrit word *dukkha*, the opposite of *sukha*, does not define simply an unpleasant sensation, but rather reflects a fundamental vulnerability to suffering and pain that can ultimately lead to world-weariness, the feeling that life is not worth living because there is no way to find meaning in it.

Suffering can be triggered by numerous causes over which we sometimes have some power, and sometimes none. Being born with a handicap, falling ill, losing a loved one, or being caught up in war or in a natural disaster are all beyond our control. Unhappiness is altogether different; it is *the way in which we experience our suffering*. Unhappiness may indeed be associated with physical or moral pain inflicted by exterior conditions, but it is not *essentially* linked to it.

Just as it is the mind that translates suffering into unhappiness, it is the mind's responsibility to master its perception thereof. A modification, even a tiny one, in the way we manage our thoughts and perceive and interpret the world can significantly change our existence.

Buddhism also speaks of a pervasive form of suffering that stems from the blindness of our own minds, where it remains so long as we remain in the grip of ignorance and selfishness. Our confusion, born of a lack of judgment and wisdom, blinds us to what we must do and avoid doing to ensure that our thoughts, our words and our acts engender happiness and not suffering.

Is there any way to put an end to suffering? According to Buddhism, suffering will always exist as a *universal phenomenon*, but *every individual* has the potential for liberation from it.

Despite all that, this vision does not lead Buddhism to the view held by certain Western philosophers for whom suffering is *inevitable* and happiness out of reach. The reason for that is simple: unhappiness has causes that can be identified and acted upon.

The first mistake is believing that unhappiness is inevitable because it is the result of divine will or some other immutable principle and that it will therefore be forever out of our control. The second is gratuitously based on the idea that unhappiness has no identifiable cause, that it descends upon us randomly and has no relation to us personally. The third mistake draws on a confused fatalism that boils down to the idea that, whatever the cause, the effect will always be the same.

If unhappiness had immutable causes, we would never be able to escape it. If there were no cure for suffering, it would be pointless to make it worse by stressing over it. It would be better to accept it fully and to distract oneself so as to feel it less harshly.

But everything that occurs *does* have a cause. What inferno does not start with a spark, what war starts without thoughts of hatred, fear, or greed? What inner pain has not grown from the fertile soil of envy, animosity, vanity, or, even more basically, ignorance? Any active cause must itself be a changing one; nothing can exist autonomously and unchanging.

Genuine happiness results from creating new causes through cultivating various fundamental qualities, such as altruistic love, compassion, inner peace, strength, and freedom. Instead of being, like pleasure makes us, very vulnerable to outer circumstances, genuine happiness gives us the resources to deal with the inevitable ups and downs of life.

We all have the potential to sweep away the veils of ignorance, to purge ourselves of the selfishness and misplaced desires that trigger unhappiness, to work for the good of others and extract the essence from our human condition. It's not the magnitude of the task that matters, it's the magnitude of our determination.

## The Four Truths of Suffering

Over 2500 years ago, seven weeks after attaining enlightenment under the Bodhi tree, the Buddha gave his first sermon in the Deer Park outside Varanasi. There he preached the Four

Noble Truths. The first is the truth of suffering. The second is the truth of the causes of suffering—ignorance that engenders craving, malice, pride, and many other thoughts that poison our lives and those of others. Since these mental poisons can be eliminated, an end to suffering—the third truth—is possible. The fourth truth is the path that turns that potential into reality. The path is the process of using all available means to eliminate the fundamental causes of suffering. In brief, we must:

> Recognize suffering,
>
> Eliminate its source,
>
> End it
>
> By practicing the path.

## Contemplating the Nature of the Mind

The inability to manage our thoughts proves to be one of the principal causes of suffering. Learning to tone down the ceaseless racket of disturbing thoughts is a decisive stage on the road to inner peace.

We need to take a closer look at mind itself. The first things we notice are the currents of thought that are continuously flowing without our even being aware of them. Like it or not, countless thoughts born of our sensations, our memories and our imagination are forever streaming through our minds. But there is a quality of mind that is always present no matter what kind of thoughts we entertain. That quality is the primary consciousness underlying all thought. It is what remains in the rare moment when the mind is at rest, almost motionless, even as it retains its ability to know. That faculty, which we may call "pure consciousness" can exist in the absence of mental constructs.

When thoughts arise, can we assign them any inherent characteristics? Do they have a particular localization? No. A color? A shape? Neither. All we find is the quality of "knowing," but no intrinsic features of their own. In "pure consciousness" we experience the mind as "empty of inherent existence," which means that the mind is not a separate entity and is found to be devoid of any intrinsic characteristic, such as location, shape, color, etc.

When we understand that thoughts emerge from pure consciousness and are then reabsorbed in it, just as waves emerge from the ocean and dissolve into it again, we have taken a great stride towards inner peace. From that moment, our thoughts have lost a great deal of their power to disturb us.

## Emotions

If the passions are the mind's great dramas, the emotions are its actors. Throughout our lives they rush through our minds like an unruly river, determining countless states of happiness and unhappiness. Should we try to tame this river? Is it even possible, and if so, how? Some emotions make us flourish, others sap our well-being, others make us wither. Love directed towards the well-being of others, compassion focused on their suffering, in thought and deed, are examples of nourishing emotions that help to generate happiness. The hunger of obsessive desire, greed that latches onto the object of its attachment, and hatred are examples of draining emotions. How can we develop the constructive emotions while ridding ourselves of the destructive ones?

Despite its rich terminology for describing a wide range of mental events, the traditional languages of Buddhism have no word for "emotion" as such. That may be because, according to Buddhism, all types of mental activity, including rational thought, are associated with some kind of feeling, be it one of pleasure, pain, or indifference. And most affective states, such as love and hatred, arise together with discursive thought. Rather than distinguishing between emotions and thoughts, Buddhism is more concerned with understanding which types of mental activity are conducive to one's own and others' well-being, and which are harmful, especially in the long run (Ekman, Davidson, Ricard, & Wallace, 2005). This is actually quite consistent with what cognitive science tells us about the brain and emotion. Every region in the brain that has been identified with some aspect of emotion has also been identified with aspects of cognition. There are no "emotion centers" in the brain. The neuronal circuits that support emotions are completely intertwined with those that support cognition (Damasio, 1994; Davidson, 1999; Davidson & Irwin 2000).

If an emotion strengthens our inner peace and seeks the good of others, it is *positive*, or constructive; if it shatters our serenity, deeply disturbs our mind and is intended to harm others, it is *negative*, or afflictive. As for the outcome, the only criterion is the good or the suffering that we create by our acts, words and thoughts, for ourselves as well as for others. That is what differentiates, for instance, "holy anger"—indignation before injustice—from rage born of the desire to hurt someone. The former has freed people from slavery and domination and moves us to march in the streets to change the world; it seeks to end the injustice as soon as possible or to make someone aware of the error of his ways. The second generates nothing but sorrow.

We need to work on our thoughts one by one, analyzing the way they emerge and evolve and gradually learning to free them as they arise, defusing the chain reactions that allow thoughts to invade the mind. Furthermore, being able to repeatedly free oneself of such afflictive thoughts as they occur gradually erodes their very tendency to form again, until they stop appearing altogether. Just as our emotions, moods, and tendencies have been shaped by the accumulation of countless instantaneous thoughts, they can be transformed through time by dealing in a mindful way with such thoughts.

## What we Mean by "Negative Emotions"

The Tibetan word *nyön-mong* (*klesha* in Sanskrit) refers to a state of mental disturbance, torment, and confusion that "afflicts us from within." Consider hatred, jealousy, or craving at the moment they form—there is no question that they make us deeply uncomfortable. Moreover, the actions and words they inspire are usually intended to hurt others. Conversely, thoughts of kindness, affection, and tolerance give us joy and courage, open our minds and free us inside. They also spur us on to benevolence and empathy.

In addition, the disturbing emotions tend to distort our perception of reality and to prevent us from seeing it as it really is. Attachment idealizes its object, hatred demonizes it. These emotions make us believe that beauty or ugliness is inherent in people and in things, even though it is the mind that decides if they are "attractive" or "repulsive." This misapprehension opens a gap between the way things appear and the way they are, clouds the judgment and makes us think and act as if these qualities were not largely based on our how we see them.

On the other hand, "positive" emotions and mental factors strengthen the clarity of our thinking and the accuracy of our reasoning, since they are based on a more accurate appreciation of reality. Selfless love reflects some understanding of the intimate interdependence of beings, of our happiness and that of others, a notion that is attuned to reality, while selfishness opens an ever wider abyss between us and other people.

Buddhism's sole objective in treating the emotions is to free us from the fundamental causes of suffering. It starts with the principle that certain mental events are afflictive regardless of the intensity or context of their formation. That is particularly true for the three mental processes considered to be basic mental "poisons:" desire (in the sense of hunger or tormenting greed), hatred (the wish to harm), and delusion (which distorts our perception of reality.) Buddhism usually includes pride and envy as well; together, these are the five major poisons associated with some sixty negative mental states. The texts also refer to "84,000 negative emotions." These are not all specified in detail, but the symbolic figure gives a sense of the complexity of the human mind and helps us to understand that our methods of transforming the mind must be adapted to the enormous variety of mental dispositions. That is why Buddhism speaks of the "84,000 doors" that lead to inner transformation.

## Desire

No one would dispute the fact that it is natural to desire and that desire plays a driving role in our lives. But let us not confuse the deep aspirations of making oneself a better human being, of working for the good of others, or of achieving spiritual awakening, with the desire that is mere hunger and tortures the mind.

As natural as it is, desire degenerates into a "mental toxin" as soon as it becomes craving, an obsession or an unmitigated attachment. As the Buddha Shakyamuni taught: "Prey to desire, like a monkey in the forest you jump from branch to branch without ever finding any fruit, from life to life without ever finding any peace."

## Hatred

Of all the mental poisons, hatred is the most toxic. It is one of the chief causes of unhappiness and the driving force of all violence, all genocide, and countless assaults on human dignity. So long as one person's hatred generates another's, the cycle of resentment, reprisal and suffering will never be broken. "If hatred responds to hatred, hatred will never end," taught the Buddha Shakyamuni. Eliminating hatred from our mind stream is therefore a critical step in our journey to happiness.

Hatred exaggerates the faults of its object and ignores its good qualities. The mind, steeped in animosity and resentment, encloses itself in illusion and is convinced that the source of its dissatisfaction is entirely exterior to itself. We solidify the "evil" or "disgusting" attributes we see in them as being permanent and intrinsic traits, and turn away from any reevaluation of the situation. We thus feel justified in expressing our animosity and retaliating. Hence arises discrimination, wholesale condemnation, persecution, genocide, blind retaliation, and also the death penalty, the ultimate legal retaliation. By then, we have obscured the basic benevolence that makes us appreciate everyone's aspiration to avoid suffering and achieve happiness.

Our compassion and love usually depend on the benevolent or aggressive attitude of others towards us and our loved ones. That is why it is extremely difficult for us to feel compassionate towards those who harm us. Buddhist compassion, however, is based on the wholehearted desire for all beings without exception to be liberated from suffering and its causes, hatred in particular. Motivated by altruistic love, we can also go further by wishing that all beings, criminals included, may find the causes of happiness.

The only target of resentment left to us is hatred itself. It is a deceitful, relentless and unbending enemy that tirelessly disrupts and destroys lives. As appropriate as patience without weakness may be towards those we consider to be our enemies, it is entirely inappropriate to be patient with hatred itself, regardless of the circumstances.

## IGNORANCE: CLINGING TO THE NOTION OF SELF UNDERMINES HAPPINESS

According to Buddhism, among the many aspects of our mental confusion and ignorance, the most radically disruptive is the grasping onto the concept of a personal identity: the individual self.

The concept of personal identity has three aspects: the "I," the "person," and the "self." These three aspects are not fundamentally different from each other, but reflect the different ways we cling to our perception of personal identity.

The "I" lives in the present; it is the "I" that thinks, "I'm hungry" or "I exist." It is the locus of consciousness, thoughts, judgment and will. It *is* the experience of our current state.

The notion of the "person" is broader, a dynamic continuum of our experience and history extending through time and incorporating various aspects of our corporeal, mental and social existence. Its boundaries are more fluid (Galin, 2003).

But there is also a conceptual "self" shaped by the force of habit. We attribute various qualities to it and posit it as the core of our being, autonomous and enduring.

At every moment between birth and death, the body undergoes ceaseless transformations and the mind becomes the theater of countless emotional and conceptual experiences. And yet we assign qualities of permanence, uniqueness, and autonomy to the self. Furthermore, as we begin to feel that this self is highly vulnerable and must be protected and satisfied, aversion and attraction come into play—aversion for anything that threatens the self, attraction to all that pleases it, comforts it, boosts its confidence, or puts it at ease. These two basic feelings, attraction and repulsion, are the fonts of a whole sea of conflicting emotions.

We imagine that by retreating inside the bubble of ego, we will be protected. We create the illusion of being separate from the world, hoping thereby to avert suffering. In fact, what happens is just the opposite, since ego-grasping and disproportionate self-cherishing are powerful magnets to attract suffering.

Each of us is indeed a unique person, and it is fine to recognize and appreciate who we are and to aspire to happiness. But in reinforcing the separate identity of the self, we fall out of sync with reality. The truth is, we are fundamentally interdependent with other people and our environment.

Our experience is simply the content of the mental flow, the continuum of consciousness, and there is no justification for seeing the self as an entirely distinct entity within that flow. We are so accustomed to affixing the "I" label to that mental flow, however, that we come to identify with it and to fear its disappearance. There follows a powerful attachment to the self and thus to the notion of "mine"—my body, my name, my mind, my possessions, my friends, and so on—which leads either to the desire to possess or to the feeling of repulsion for the "other."

This erroneous sense of self forms the basis of all mental affliction, be it hatred, clinging, desire, envy, pride, or confusion. From that point on, we see the world through the distorting mirror of our illusions, which inevitably leads to frustration and suffering.

Let's consider what it is we suppose contributes to our identity. Our body? An assemblage of bones and flesh. Our consciousness? A continuous stream of instants. Our history? The memory of what is no more. Our name? We attach all sorts of concepts to it—our heritage, our reputation, and our social status—but ultimately it's nothing more than a grouping of letters (Dilgo Khyentse, 1993).

When we explore the body, the speech, and the mind, we come to see that this self is nothing but a word, a label, a convention, a designation. To unmask the ego's deception, we have to pursue our inquiry to the very end. When you suspect the presence of a thief in your house, you have to inspect every room, every corner, every potential hiding place, just to make sure there's really no one there. Only then can you rest easy.

Rigorous analysis leads us to conclude that the self does not reside outside the body, or in any part of the body, nor is it some diffuse entity permeating the entire body. We willingly believe that the self is associated with consciousness, but consciousness too is just a flow or experience: the past moment of consciousness is dead (only its impact remains), the future is not yet, and the present doesn't last. How could a distinct self exist, suspended between something that no longer exists and something that does not yet exist?

Thus, the self cannot be detected in either the body or the mind; it is neither a distinct entity in a combination of the two, nor an entity lying outside of them. No serious analysis or direct introspective experience can lead to a reasonable conviction that we possess a self. Buddhism therefore concludes that the self is just a convention, a name we give to a continuum, just as we name a river the Ganges or the Mississippi.

When the self ceases to be the most important thing in the world, we find it easier to focus our concern on others. The sight of their suffering bolsters our courage and resolve to work on their behalf, instead of crippling us with our own emotional distress.

## Is it Possible to Free Ourselves of Negative Emotions?

You might think that ignorance and negative emotions are inherent to the flow of consciousness, and that trying to rid yourself of them is like fighting against a part of yourself. But the most fundamental aspect of consciousness, the pure faculty of knowing—what we have called the "luminous" quality of the mind—contains no hatred or desire at its core. A mirror, for instance, will reflect both angry faces and smiling ones. The very quality of the mirror allows countless images to arise, yet none of them belongs to the mirror. In fact, if the angry face was intrinsic to the mirror, it could be seen at all times and would prevent other images from arising. Similarly, the most fundamental quality of cognition, the "luminous" quality of the mind, is what permits the arising of thoughts and underlies all of them. Yet none of these thoughts belongs intrinsically to the fundamental nature of the mind. The experience of introspection shows, on the contrary, that the negative emotions are transitory mental events that can be obliterated by their opposites, the positive emotions, acting as antidotes.

We have to gradually familiarize ourselves with each antidote—loving-kindness as antidote to hatred, for instance—until the absence of hatred becomes second nature. The Tibetan word *gom*, which is usually translated as "meditation," more precisely denotes "familiarization," while the Sanskrit word *bhavana*, also translated as "meditation" means "cultivation." It is about familiarizing oneself with a new vision of things, a new way to manage one's thoughts, of perceiving people and experiencing the world.

Buddhism teaches various ways of making this "familiarization" work. One method consists of applying a specific antidote to each negative emotion. Another one allows us to unravel or "liberate" the emotion by looking straight at it and let it dissolve as it arises. The choice of one method over another will depend on the moment, the circumstances and the capacities of the person using them. All share a common aspect and the same goal: to help us stop being victims of conflicting emotions.

## The use of antidotes

The first method consists of neutralizing afflictive emotions with a specific antidote, just as we neutralize the destructive effects of poison with anti-venom, or of acid with an alkali. One fundamental point emphasized by Buddhism is that two diametrically opposed mental processes cannot form *simultaneously*. We may fluctuate rapidly between love and hatred, but we cannot feel, *in the same instant of consciousness*, the desire to hurt someone and to do him good. The two impulses are as opposed to each other as water and fire.

In the same way, by habituating our minds to altruistic love, we gradually eliminate hatred, because the two states of mind can alternate but cannot co-exist at the same time. So the more we cultivate loving-kindness, the less there will space for hatred in our mental landscape. It is therefore important to begin by learning the antidotes that correspond to each negative emotion, and then to cultivate them.

Since altruistic love acts as a direct antidote to hatred, the more we develop it, the more the desire to harm will wither and finally disappear. It is a question not of suppressing hatred, but of turning the mind to something diametrically opposed to it: love and compassion.

It is equally impossible for greed or desire-passion, which has a strong binding aspect to coexist with inner-freedom, which allows us to taste mental peace and to rest in the cool shade of serenity. Desire can fully develop only when it is allowed to run rampant to the point where it monopolizes the mind.

As for anger, it will be neutralized by patience. This does not require us to remain passive, but to steer clear of being overwhelmed by destructive emotions. As the Dalai Lama explains: "Patience safeguards our peace of mind in the face of adversity ... It is a deliberate response (as opposed to an unreasoned reaction) to the strong negative thoughts and emotions that tend to arise when we encounter harm" (Dalai Lama, 1999, p. 109).

## Freeing the emotions

The second method consists in asking ourselves whether, rather than trying to stem each emotion that afflicts us with its specific antidote, there might be a *single* antidote that acts at a more basic level on all our mental afflictions. It is neither possible nor desirable to trammel the mind's natural activities, and it would be futile and unhealthy to try to block its thoughts. On the other hand, when we examine the emotions, we find that they are merely dynamic flows without any inherent substance of their own—what Buddhism calls the thoughts' "emptiness" of real existence. What would happen if, instead of counteracting a disturbing emotion with its opposite—anger with patience, for instance—we were simply to contemplate the nature of the emotion itself?

You are overwhelmed by a sudden tide of anger. You feel as if there's no choice but to let it sweep you away. But look closely. It is nothing more than a thought. When you see a great black cloud in a stormy sky, it seems so solid that you could sit on it. But when you approach it, there's nothing to grab on to. Instead of feeling one with the anger you experience, dissociate yourself as a person and experience anger as a transient phenomena. The more you look at anger in this manner, the more it evaporates under your gaze, like white frost under the sun's rays.

If we come to see that anger has no substance of its own, it rapidly loses all power. This is what Buddhism calls *liberation from anger at the moment it arises* by recognizing its emptiness, its lack of its own existence.

## Ethics as the science of happiness

What criteria allow us to qualify an act as good or bad? Buddhist ethics are not just ways of acting, but ways of being. A human being endowed with loving-kindness, compassion and wisdom will spontaneously act in an ethical way, because he or she is wise and "good at heart." In Buddhism, an act is essentially unethical if it is meant to cause suffering and ethical if is meant to bring genuine well-being to others. It is the motivation, altruistic or malicious, that colors the act as "good" or "bad," just as a crystal takes the color of the cloth upon which it rests. Ethics also affects our own well-being since making others suffer will bring suffering on to ourselves, either immediately or in the long term, while bringing happiness to others is ultimately the best way to guarantee our own. Through the interplay of the laws of cause and effect, which Buddhism calls *karma*—the laws governing the consequences of our actions—ethics are therefore intimately linked to well-being.

For Buddhism, as the Dalai Lama explains, "A meaningful ethical system divorced of an individual experience of suffering and happiness is hard to imagine." (Dalai Lama, 1999, p. 151). A dehumanized ethic built on abstract foundations has little utility.

Rather one needs mindfulness, wisdom and a basic altruistic disposition that, according to Buddhism, is deeply embedded in our minds, but needs to be cultivated throughout life. This has little to do with applying rules and principles but of being of a compassionate nature. One aspect of compassion is a spontaneous readiness to act for the benefit of others. Altruistic deeds will then naturally flow from such compassion.

Two main factors are decisive: motivation and the consequences of our acts. Even if we try to predict them to the best of our capacities, we have little control over the unfolding of external events, *but we can always adopt an altruistic motivation*. We therefore need to check our motivation again and again, as the Dalai Lama explains:

> Are we being broad-minded or narrow-minded? Have we taken in account the overall situation or are we considering only specifics? Is our view short-term or long-term? ... Is our motivation genuinely compassionate? ... Is our compassion limited just to our families, our friends and those we identify with closely? ... We need to think, think, think. (Dalai Lama, 1999, p. 154)

Our state of mind is thus the very core of ethics. It is only at the price of constant cultivation of wisdom and compassion that we can really become the guardians and inheritors of happiness.

## Where the Path Leads

Everybody (or almost everybody) is interested in happiness. But who is interested in enlightenment? The very word seems exotic, vague, and distant. And yet, ultimate well-being comes from fully eliminating delusion and mental toxins, and thus suffering. Enlightenment is what Buddhism calls the state of ultimate freedom that comes with a perfect knowledge of the nature of mind and of the world of phenomena. The sage has come to see that the individual self and the appearances of the world of phenomena have no intrinsic reality. He understands that all beings have the power to free themselves from ignorance and unhappiness, but that they don't know it. How, then, could he fail to feel infinite and spontaneous compassion for all those who, spellbound by ignorance, wander lost in the torments of *samsara*?

While such a state may seem very far removed from our daily concerns, it is certainly not beyond reach. But that doesn't happen by itself. Milk is the source of butter, but it won't make any if we simply leave it to its own devices; we have to churn it. The qualities of enlightenment are revealed through transformation at the far end of the spiritual path. Each stage is a step towards fulfillment and profound satisfaction. The spiritual journey is like traveling from one valley to another—beneath each pass lies a landscape more magnificent than the one behind it.

## Beyond Happiness and Suffering

In the bosom of Enlightenment, beyond hope and doubt, conceptual shadows dissolve in the light of the dawn of non-duality. From the point of view of absolute truth, neither happiness nor suffering has any real existence. They belong to the relative truth perceived by the mind so long as it remains in the grip of confusion. She who has come to understand the true nature of things is like a navigator landing on an island made entirely of pure gold; even if she looks for ordinary pebbles, she won't find any.

## References

Dalai Lama XIV, & Cutler, H. C. (1998). *The art of happiness: A handbook for living.* New York, NY: Riverhead Books.

Dalai Lama XIV. (1999). *Ancient wisdom, modern world, ethics for the next millennium.* London, UK: Little, Brown and Co.

Damasio, A. R. (1994). *Descartes' error.* New York, NY: Avon Books.

Davidson, R. J. (2000). Cognitive neuroscience needs affective neuroscience (and vice versa). *Cognition and Emotion, 42,* 89–92.

Davidson, R. J., & Irwin, W. (1999). The functional neuroanatomy of emotion and affective style. *Trends in Cognitive Science, 3,* 11–21.

Dilgo Khyentse. (1993). *The heart treasure of the enlightened ones: The practice of view, meditation, and action.* (Padmakara Translation Group, Trans.). Boston, MA: Shambhala Publications.

Dilgo Khyentse. (2007). *The heart of compassion: The thirty-seven verses on the practice of a Bodhisattva.* (Padmakara Translation Group, Trans.). Boston, MA: Shambhala Publications.

Ekman, P., Davidson, R. J., Ricard, M., & Wallace, B. A. (2005). Buddhist and psychological perspectives on emotions and well-being. *Current Directions in Psychological Science, 14,* 59–63.

Galin, D. (2003). The concepts of "self," "person," and "I," in Western psychology and in Buddhism. In B. Alan Wallace (Ed.), *Buddhism & science, breaking new ground* (pp. 107–144). New York, NY: Columbia University Press.

Kunzang Pelden. (2007). *The nectar of Manjushri's speech: A detailed commentary on Shantideva's way of the Bodhisattva.* (Padmakara Translation Group, Trans.). Boston, MA Shambhala Publications.

Ricard, M. (2007). *Happiness, a guide to developing life's most important skill.* Atlantic Books, London.

Ricard, M. (2010). *The art of meditation.* London, UK: Atlantic Books.

Shabkar. (2001). *The life of Shabkar: The autobiography of a Tibetan yogin.* Translated by Matthieu Ricard. Ithaca, NY: Snow Lion Publications.

Shantarakshita. (2005). *The adornment of the middle way: Shantarakshita's Madhyamakalankara with commentary by Jamgön Mipham.* (Padmakara Translation Group, Trans.). Boston, MA: Shambhala Publications.

Shantideva. (2006). *The way of the Bodhisattva: A translation of the Bodhicharyavatara.* (Padmakara Translation Group, Trans.). Boston, MA: Shambhala Publications.

Wallace, A. B. (2003). *Choosing reality: A Buddhist view of physics and the mind.* Ithaca, NY: Snow Lion Publications.

Yongey Mingyur Rinpoche & Swanson, E. (2007). *The joy of living: Unlocking the secret and science of happiness.* New York, NY: Harmony Books.

# CHAPTER 28

# RELATIONAL BUDDHISM: AN INTEGRATIVE PSYCHOLOGY OF HAPPINESS AMIDST EXISTENTIAL SUFFERING

G.T. MAURITS KWEE

University of Flores, Argentina; Institute for Relational Buddhism,
The Netherlands; Taos Institute, USA

A symbol of happiness known by many is the fat laughing Buddha whose statue radiating blissful delight can be found in Chinese restaurants. Although revered by almost every Chinese as a reminder that life is to be enjoyed, few people are familiar with the story of the monk Chi-Tze and the Buddhist values of kindness, compassion, and joy that he represents. Buddhists in the Far East regard him as the future embodiment of loving-kindness (Maitreya) which stands for the ideal of a cordial humankind. In the Sino-Japanese tradition, happiness does not come from the head but from the belly and to live from a big tummy means to be happy, joyful, and compassionate. Hotei is the Japanese name for this Chan/Zen figurehead who used to wander in the first half of the tenth century in the province of Fujien. He was known there as the hemp-bag monk as he carried a beggar's sack on his back. In his other hand he holds a gourd symbolizing "emptiness." His bag contains toys and sweets that he cheerfully gave away to children like a merry Santa Claus. He is often depicted surrounded by playful kids having fun. This conveys the message to celebrate life with a beginner's mind, i.e., by enjoying play and not worrying about winning or losing. Chi-Tze also exemplifies the idea that a serious subject can be addressed through humor. If there is no laughter, be suspicious.

He was eccentric, a quality in line with the Zen Buddhist love of absurd paradox. For example, when asked how old he is, he replied: "As old as space." His reply is taken to imply that life is to be lived mindfully here-and-now. Time is age-old but can only be experienced from moment to moment. One day he was in a village where someone asked him why he was wasting his time instead of teaching. He suddenly dropped his bag with a bang. People wondered: "What do you mean by that?" whereupon he said: "Drop your heavy burden, that's all!" Chi-Tze's bag was light; after all he only carried little presents, no burden of greed, hatred, or other woes of life. When the next question was fired: "Show us the way to awakening?" he immediately swung his bag on the shoulder and walked away with a gusty laugh, leaving the crowd puzzled behind. Picking up his bag indicates accepting that no-one can escape the suffering inherent in life, but by not allowing the world to live in our minds and by giving up clinging, grasping, and craving, we will be able to keep life's burden light and be happy. Chi-Tze's cosmic chuckle is a reminder that the ordinary man is unhappy because he does not know that he is already happy (Kwee, 1990).

The figure of Chi-Tze can also be found in the "ox-herding pictures" where he appeared in the tenth image depicting the happy-end of an awakening tale (Suzuki, 1956). The ox is a metaphor for the mind. The drawings help to explain the meditation stages. Briefly, the story tells of a seeker looking for Buddha-nature while he is already riding on it. While heading home on the ox in oblivion, the state of emptiness is unveiled to him. He mingles in the market place, indicating that an awakened person is not an escapist but lives a mundane social life. Clearing up the mind enables a happy life. Key aspects of the "bodyspeechmind" training required, as seen from the perspective of Zen Buddhism addressed later in the chapter, include the need to understand the monkey mind, the Buddha's "not-self" psychology, the shift to an integrative Buddhist psychology, the practice of mindfulness and other meditations, the karma of happiness, and a relational map to happiness.

## Monkey Mind

According to the Buddhist tradition the human predicament entails inescapable adversity, suffering, and non-satisfactoriness. As life is impermanent and imperfect it inheres in a state of being that is constantly unsatisfactory. In effect, we are all embarked on a ship with one destiny: sinking. The historical Buddha noted some 100 generations ago that existence is painful at birth and heads directly to death via illness and aging. According to the Buddha there is a way to overcome the painfulness of the gnawing mental imbalances that easily arise. In the spirit of free inquiry one needs to honestly ask oneself whether there is emotional balance here-and-now. If one is seriously unhappy and weakened due to a debilitating anxiety or a depressive condition, some form of "talking cure" or even medication might be necessary prior to learning meditation. Only after having regained inner strength will the chances of successfully accomplishing a trajectory of striving for joy and happiness be increased. This is in line with what is known of the Buddha's awakening. As narrated down the ages, the Buddha's awakening was preceded by his abandoning the extremes of self-indulgence and self-mortification. The Buddha endorsed instead a subtle and stable psychological composure which he considered a *conditio sine qua non* to understand the liberating practice that he disseminated. His teaching, known as the "ennobling middle way," comprises an eightfold entwined balancing practice to contentment. It is a path that balances: views, intentions, speech, action, living, effort, awareness, and attention.

Even after recovery from an emotional disorder through psychotherapy or other means the mind usually remains fuzzy and restless due to the hardships of life, particularly when defiled by ignorance of the workings of the mind, such as that manifested in the illusion of having a self and the delusion of believing in god(s) despite the extensive use of enticing god-like images by some Buddhist denominations. Buddhism does not involve any godhead and the Buddha dismissed metaphysics. He did not claim to be a prophet or assign people to worship him. By negating the existence of a god (theism) and negating the non-existence of a god (atheism), *non-theistic* emptiness remains which is to be filled by pro-social action. In effect, the Buddha considered both a "god in the sky" and a more impersonal supernatural "one-and-only" as a delusion of the ignorant. Indeed, religious beliefs often befuddle the mind with absolutisms, dichotomous thinking, and the illusion of a self or soul transmigrating to some paradise in the beyond. The run-of-the-mill mind plagued by daily emotional imbalances due to ignorant and detrimental views about self may well profit from balancing attention and awareness through Buddhist mindfulness meditation. Mindfulness is the all-embracing meditative process that can clear and prepare the mind to practice a dozen other meditations offered by the Buddha to help humanity gain insight into how to end the misery of emotional suffering. Mindfulness, a multifaceted term, may take the form of being attentive, aware, and alert or vigilant (*Appamada Sutta*).[1] The latter is found in the Buddha's admonishing to mindfully strive for discernment about what is wholesome and unwholesome. What is wholesome is not afflicted by greed (including fear and grief of loss), hatred (including anger and self-dejection), and ignorance (on how the mind works; illusions and delusions). Wholesomeness augments the relational qualities of loving-kindness, empathic compassion, shared joy, and relational equanimity of speech to eventually benefit humanity.

The Buddha meditated until he found the key to end mental misery and felt liberation. This key, which is of a non-dual nature, is ineffable, much like the concept of zero (emptiness) was for the ancient Greek mathematicians who allocated this "missing nothing" to the realm of the sacrosanct. We lack a linguistic foundation for understanding this, so words cannot replace what is experienced in meditation. Instead of worshipping the Buddha (nothing but a mere image or concept), one rather trains the mind to gain clarity on not-self and emptiness to pave the way toward happiness and become pro-social human beings. Indeed the fourteenth Dalai Lama declared that the purpose of life is to seek happiness and that his religion is loving-kindness.

Training the fuzzy, restless, or monkey mind, as it is often called in Buddhism, is to control the mind by accepting or rather audaciously allowing, tolerating, and enduring *experiencing* to happen, which is not a passive or apathetic undergoing. This might sound paradoxical for an urban mind but it is the meditative way to calm the mind toward balance, composure, and peacefulness. Externally inactive or active, an allowing mentality permits the mind to open up resources and redirect its focus to transcend the seemingly uncontrollable. Transcendence is not a goal as Buddhism is not directed towards esoteric spheres where joy is indefatigable and suffering is eliminated forever; rather, Buddhism is about self-transcendence which moves beyond a separated and isolated sense of self.

---

[1] For the Buddha's discourses, see http://www.metta.lk (*suttas*) and http://www.e-sangha.com (*sutras*).

## The Psychology of "Not-self"

All major psychologies in the West, whether psychoanalytic, cognitive behavioral, or existential/humanistic, endorse the idea of an abiding entity called self. This is in stark contrast to what the Buddha and Buddhist psychology put forward, namely that the self is an illusion and that the pivotal understanding of not-self is indispensable in working toward happiness. Not-self can be unveiled in Buddhist analytical and insight meditation. Anchored in biological and interpersonal processes and moving in a flux the so-called self comprises the modalities of action, affect, sensation, imagery-cognition, and consciousness (awareness). These modalities, interrelated in "dependent origination," arise and subside in concert impacting each other in circular causality. Ultimately there is no self because the modalities being in constant motion are empty even if reified and clung onto. Because there is no self to identify with, the Buddhist advice is not to attach to an illusory self. Notwithstanding, the advice to disattach from an eternal self or soul, the Buddha pragmatically acknowledged that there is a "provisional" (relative-empirical) self which is an indexing device serving practical purposes in society like having a name and an identity-card. Awakening to selflessness does not imply being out-of-orbit. On the contrary, "empty of self" one leads a meditative life full of affect, i.e. in kindness, compassion, and joy.

There is a convergence between the social constructionist and the Buddhist understanding of the self. Social constructionists might argue that in order to deal effectively with emotions one needs to appreciate them as relational performatives. The social constructional practice of viewing the other is based on the premise that whatever we do, think, or feel is infused by interpersonal meaning. Becoming deeply aware of this, it becomes clear that our "real" self consists of relational rather than self elements. If we nevertheless insist on having a self, the only feasible construction of self is a "relational self." This concurs with the Buddhist non-foundational provisional self. Obviously, we are not our names (speech), nor our bodies, nor our minds. The relational self, a social construction based on impermanence, is not eternal either. The only reality we have is the present moment. A relational view of self replaces the traditional emphasis on the isolated mind with a socialized mind and "relational being" (Gergen, 2009).

Psychology is central to Buddhism because dealing with the self and not-self is a core subject. The Buddha himself alluded to the central role of psyche and psychology when stating (*Rohitassa Sutta*): "In this fathom-long living body with perceptions and thoughts lays the world, the arising and cessation of the world." Unlike the proliferation of self psychologies, Buddhist psychology is the main not-self psychology to date. Its development can be discerned in four phases comprising an archaic, classical, modern, and postmodern period. The *archaic* period is a stage of philosophical psychology and starts with the discourses of the Buddha. It continues in the philosophical reflections as written down post the Buddha in a canonical book (the *Abhidhamma*). These "deeper" teachings were written by anonymous scholars up to the fifth century and seemingly left with an open end to be completed by successors. The *classical* period of Western interest is apparent in the late nineteenth century. William James (1890) was the first who recognized that Buddhism inheres in a psychology and who endorsed the notion of karma as the interplay of cognitive-affective intentions and manifest action. He also pointed to the value of meditation in mastering the mind. Rhys Davids coined the term "Buddhist psychology" in 1914.

The move to a *modern* Buddhist psychology is covered in numerous publications. For example, De Silva (1979/2005) and Kalupahana (1987) address Buddhist psychology from the Theravada tradition of Early Buddhism. Later texts stemming from Mahayana Buddhism (as from *c*.400 years after the Buddha) or "great vehicle" tradition have played a significant role in Buddhist psychology. They were introduced to a wider audience by among others D.T. Suzuki (1870–1966) from the Zen tradition and Chögyam Trungpa (1939–1987) from the Tibetan tradition. Various psychologists have expressed interest in Buddhist ideas including Jung (1875–1961), Maslow (1908–1970), Fromm (1900–1980), and Ellis (1913–2007). The present zeitgeist in psychotherapy is very much in favor of Buddhist-inspired approaches (e.g., Sugamura, Haruki, & Koshikawa, 2007; Wallace & Shapiro, 2006). Kabat-Zinn devised an 8-week outpatient mindfulness-based (MB) stress reduction training that, since 1979, has been applied with thousands of patients with various chronic and debilitating maladies (see Hsu & Langer, Chapter 76, this volume). Spin-offs include MB cognitive therapy, MB relapse prevention, and MB eating awareness training. Mindfulness is also included in "Dialectical Behavior Therapy" and in "Acceptance and Commitment Therapy" (Shapiro & Carlson, 2009).

More recently, the Mind and Life Institute offers an ongoing dialogue between scientists, including psychologists, and Tibetan Buddhist scholars and coordinates programs like the "Cultivating Emotional Balance" research project. Many others are committed to furthering Buddhist psychology. For example, the Transcultural Society for Clinical Meditation aims to integrate evidence-based data connecting Buddhism and psychology and establish a *postmodern* social constructional Buddhist psychology according to the principle of "skillful means" (*upaya*) (e.g., Kwee, 2012a, 2012b, 2012c; Kwee & Taams, 2006a).[2]

# A "New Buddhist Psychology"

New Buddhist psychology addresses the social, clinical, and neuropsychology of "bodyspeechmind" by linking work from first-, second-, and third-person perspectives. Within *neuropsychology* there are attempts to link neuroscience's third-person "objective" level of inquiry with Buddhist concepts and practices. Attempts to explain neuroscientific knowledge in Buddhist psychological terms were initiated by neurophysiologists such as Kasamatsu, Hirai, and Akishige in the 1950s. Half a century later, neuroscientists (e.g., the late F. Varela and R. Davidson) are still investigating the impact of Buddhist practices on hard-wired parameters. For a general review on the neuropsychology of consciousness, meditation, happiness, love, and wisdom, see Lutz, Dunne, and Davidson (2007), Hanson (2009), and Austin (2010). Notwithstanding the interesting findings, a social constructionist and relational Buddhist purview caution against any modernist claims based solely on "objective science." From a relational stance it is doubtful whether cortical data accrued by sophisticated techniques of brain scanning of reasoning and emotional response can open up the mind to inspection as human action is not intelligible in terms of neural activity. Although the cortex enables and limits activity, the human brain seems to primarily

---

[2] See http://www.relationalbuddhism.org

function as a tool of socially meaningful scenarios for action. To quote Gergen (2010, p. 814): "cultural life determines what we take to be the nature and importance of brain functioning."

*Clinical psychology,* a first-person "subjective" level of inquiry, draws on outcome studies as part of its evidence-based approach. To date, cognitive behavioral psychology practiced by mental health clinicians and corporate well-being coaches appears to be among the most effective and efficient interventions. Interestingly, the methods, concepts, and rationale of the cognitive behavioral approach coincide with the Buddhist *modus operandi* of meditation in a number of respects. This correspondence has been commented on a few decades back by frontrunners like W. Mikulas, P. De Silva, and M. Kwee (Kwee, 1990). Kwee and Taams (2010a) offer a recent account of Buddhist teachings as a cognitive behavioral psychology. As described earlier, the application of mindfulness based approaches is now increasingly common in therapeutic practice.

Sparked by research on MB Cognitive Therapy (Teasdale, 2000), A. T. Beck (the founding father of cognitive therapy) had a historical dialogue with the Dalai Lama at the 5th International Congress of Cognitive Psychotherapy (see Taams & Kwee, 2006). This groundbreaking summit included an extensive series of symposia on Buddhist psychology. The interface between Buddhist and cognitive behavioral psychology (e.g., Kwee & Ellis, 1998; Kwee & Taams, 2006b) paves the way for Buddhist happiness training. A number of approaches now found in positive psychology are arguably influenced by Buddhism, e.g., loving-kindness (Fredrickson, Cohn, Coffey, Pek, & Finkel 2008), compassion (Gilbert & Procter, 2006), and perhaps happiness and joy (Lyubomirsky, 2008).

A second-person "intersubjective" level of inquiry such as that found in much European social psychology, often employs a social constructionist meta-psychological viewpoint contending that there are no "Transcendental Truths" and that reality, facts, as well as much of existential suffering, are man-made. This postmodern stance views reality as a communally-based consensus within a culture. Science and authority are considered to be relative. This framework of "verstehen" (understanding), highlights the need to eradicate certain Eurocentric/colonial tendencies to shape the Buddhist teachings into metaphysics and a sky-god religion, and to re-install some Buddhist key terms and concepts into their original meaning, such as the "Four Ennobling Realities" (instead of "Noble Truths"), karma as intentional choice-action (instead of inevitable destiny or fate), or nirvana as arousal extinction (instead of a paradise in the beyond) (Kwee, 2010b). Humans are "bodyspeechmind": biochemical-sensing-moving-thinking-emoting-relational-constructs whose minds usually function at the pre-rational (child-like), irrational (foolish), and rational (scientific) levels, but seldom at the post-rational (wise) level, an aspect of which is to appreciate cultural relativity. On this level we are able to see and understand that to be means to "inter-be" and that to act is to "inter-act," implying that what comes about happens in dependent origination between people. This enables us to understand the pervasive interconnectedness of humanity. Thrown from the cradle to the grave into a social web, we cannot be self-contained. There is nothing that we can conceive of which is not injected by interpersonal meaning. Ensued from a history of interdependency, even "private worlds" are encapsulated in an inextricable relational network. Though we often take our socially embedded being for granted, interrelatedness is ubiquitous. Such a meta-vision views reality as a joint-venture, depicted in the Mahayana tradition as "Indra's Jewel Net" (*Avatamsaka Sutra*) a matrix with at each juncture mirrors/beings reflecting and interpenetrating each other *ad infinitum*. Truth is culture-bound and can only be provisional, linguistically co-constructed, and negotiated in a dance of meanings. In the end it is not about revealing the truth but about unveiling reality as constructed (imbued with meaning): happiness is a relational event!

## BUDDHIST MEDITATIONS: ONE FAMILY

Buddhist mindfulness as a means of accruing happiness, cultivated traditionally takes place in four frames of reference: the body, the body's activities (i.e. feelings: perceptions and emotions), the mind, and the mind's activities (i.e. thoughts: images and concepts) (*Mahasatipatthana Sutta*). It offers an overarching process to clear the mind as well as a skill to accompany various other meditations toward emptiness. These meditations refer to the body (breathing, behaviors, repulsiveness, elements, decomposing, and the senses) and to the mind (hindrances, modalities, perceptions, motivation, four ennobling realities, and an eightfold practice) (Kwee & Taams, 2010b). Formal meditation is generally practiced in a sitting position with the back held upright and if on a chair with the feet flat on the ground. Studies suggest that holding the back straight strengthens confidence and boosts positive mood, whereas a slouched posture invites or worsens dejection (Haruki, Homma, Umezawa, & Masaoka, 2001). The many other meditations include laughing, smiling, and singing meditations, and contemplations on kindness, compassion, and joy (see Ricard, Chapter 27, this volume). In effect, meditation is a *modus vivendi* to be applied throughout the day while sitting, lying, standing, and walking.

Buddhist mindfulness or "pristine mindfulness," which differs from the mindfulness in the "mindfulness-based" approaches (like MB stress reduction), offers a scaffold for a meditative way of life comprising the balancing of attention–concentration (to discipline a wandering mind) and awareness-introspection (to understand karma and not-self). Operating in the sensory modality, it can be a process of and produce the outcome of inward concentration; through: attention (to the changeable foreground presence), awareness (of the relatively changeable backdrop presence), and illuminating consciousness (of the relatively unchangeable backdrop presence). As a process of awareness, it is the alert and luminous introspection (monitoring) of the smallest units of experience (*dhammas*) toward clear comprehension (*sampajana*) of things as they become in dependent origination. The first step is to tame the mind by concentrating attention usually on breathing. Table 28.1 presents pristine mindfulness processes: calming (*samatha*) which engenders firming (*samadhi*)[3] and insight (*vipassana*) which engenders "emptiness" (*sunyata*).

The categories overlap slightly. The process from square 1 to 4 is a form of *social de-construction* (accompanied by Aha-experiences). Emptiness is not a goal in itself, a blank mind is a resetting point for electrifying the collaborative practice of *social re-construction*

---

[3] Csikszentmihalyi's "flow" (1990) could be seen as a rediscovery of *samadhi* because descriptions of their essential features overlap. Both are considered to be an optimal experience while performing a skilled task (or while meditating) characterized by intense concentration, energized focus, complete absorption, total involvement, no sense of time or self, enjoyable and gratifying for its own sake, and no distracting thoughts entering the mind due to a single-minded immersion. Zen Buddhists refer to the state of spontaneous rapture as "going with the flow while nothing remains undone" which is typified by oneness or non-dual experiencing where there is neither-perception-nor-non-perception and neither-thinking-nor-non-thinking, an effortless-effort and non-controlling control due to a merging of action and awareness (Kwee, 2010a).

## Table 28.1 Pristine mindfulness meditation quadrant

| **Remember to balance Body/Speech/Mind** to awaken from ignorance & to dissolve greed & hatred (emotional suffering) | **Bare attentiveness:** perception of the smallest phenomena of experience (knowledge by verbal description) | **Impartial awareness:** mind's apperception of feelings & thoughts (wisdom by non-verbal acquaintance) |
|---|---|---|
| **Relaxed/gentle/focused concentration** with zeal & diligence on an object (e.g., breathing) & its impermanent processes, from now-to-now | 1. CALMING (Body/Mind) toward composure/quiescence/equanimity, resulting in **tranquility** | 2. FIRMING (Body/Mind) by receptive absorption/flow-stabilization toward arousal extinction (aka **Nirvana**) |
| **Vigilant/alert/watchful observation–introspection** by wise reflection & clear comprehension to discern un/wholesome karma | 3. INSIGHT (Mind/Body) Understanding life's causality (e.g., feeling/thought/action) as they un/become in **dependent origination** | 4. EMPTINESS (Mind/Body) Liberating not-self in "luminous suchness": blank mind as a reset point (zeroness) & springboard to **loving-kindness** |

NB: The "mindfulness-based" approaches used in MB stress reduction and related approaches are limited to calming and firming.

by contemplating and embodying kindness, compassion, and joy (accompanied by HaHa-experiences), and realizing what we already are.[4] Mindfulness works like a *metonym*: "there is no way to mindfulness, mindfulness is the way." This is an insight that we are not going anywhere for we are "already there," therefore nothing needs to be done ("the grass grows by itself"). Containing means and goals, mindfulness implies an effortless effort of a beginner's mind with no aim and no agenda. However, at bottom mindfulness is purposeful as it furthers wise reflection on karma. It is advisable to practice mindfulness with a heedful introspection to the (un)wholesomeness of intentions and with illuminating insight. Impartial or "choiceless" awareness implies that there is no prejudice, sympathy, or antipathy for what appears in the space of "bodyspeechmind." Apperception is a pre-conceptual perception excluding preconceived ideas (by definition conceptual and judgmental).

Davidson and Kabat-Zinn (2004, pp. 150–152) explicitly de-contextualized their MB intervention by dismissing Buddhist psychology. They blatantly state that it "does not include Buddhist psychology." Indeed, we see that MB applications are limited to attention regulation and operate only in the first two quadrants of Table 22.1. Kabat-Zinn's (2003)

---

[4] These two processes are a relevant theme in the Mahayana teachings depicted on more than 1460 bas reliefs (panels of 2 ×1 meter) and by 504 sitting Buddha statues in ten circumambulatory corridors of an immense *stupa* structure or dome-like building called the Borobudur—a UNESCO protected world wonder stemming from the year 800—located on the island of Java (Indonesia) where this author was born. The visitor who ascends this huge pyramidal construction learns to meditate toward liberation as symbolized by the highest towering *empty* dome via the pictorial narratives and instructions on the panels. Once liberated, s/he begins the journey of descending back to the mundane world to fulfil the vow of practicing, in mindful equanimity, the social meditations of loving-kindness, compassion, and joy, and particularly the compassion meditation of offering (*kasih*) and receiving (*terima*), known in Tibet as *tonglen*, a legacy of Javanese Buddhism.

describes a non-judgmental attitude in his working definition of mindfulness as the awareness that emerges through paying attention on purpose in the present moment to the unfolding of experience. This "Buddhist-lite" mindfulness generally deprives the practitioner of the quintessential insight into dependent origination and not-self, and from the introspection and reversal of karma, which lie at the heart of Buddhism. De-contextualizing mindfulness from its original Buddhist origins and re-contextualizing it into western psychological paradigms is seen by many in the East as disrespectful to their tradition (e.g., Kwee, 2010a). A reductionist conversion of mindfulness (if taken from Buddhism) to a magic bullet is disapproved of as a *chutzpah*. Thus, controlled trials employing mindfulness without the Buddhist essence have got little to do with the original conception of mindfulness which is embedded in the whole teaching.

## Karma and "Dependent Origination"

Dependent origination, the Buddha's causality hypothesis and the crux of his awakening, contends that phenomena of the mind, things and events, arise, peak, subside, and cease to exist jointly. Focusing on events, psychologists, therapists, and coaches are interested in freedom from emotional suffering and in augmenting happiness (even if only to prevent relapse). This is in line with the Buddha's activity during his life as a "karmavadin," someone who deals with the "birth and rebirth of karmic episodes." Working with clients, the *modus operandi* is to tackle one emotional happening at a time in retrospect. Although this is when the damage is already done, there is no other way to prepare for the next potentially hurting event. The interpersonal context of daily agony is evident and the rethinking and replaying of the dialogued drama is aimed at rendering relational scenarios leading to emotional harmony and eventually sustainable happiness. Thus for instance, the cognitive-behavioral psychologist discusses emotional vicissitudes in collaborative practice with the client. In each instance the client is trained to accrue satisfying results by avoiding deficit discourse with an antagonist and by role playing a discourse which constructs the world and each other in a more promising way.

The cognitive behavioral notion of a stimulus–organism-response shows certain parallels with Buddhist ideas of karma. Karma also emphasizes cognition and behavior by highlighting intentional motivation/conation and behavioral (inter)action, here termed *intentional (inter)action*. These parallels are depicted in Table 28.2. The karma sequence starts with a sensory perception by one of the sense organs, immediately registered as sensory feeling relatively positive, neutral, or negative. This activating event on the input level of sensory feeling sparked by an external or internal stimulus can be discriminated as new or known. On the level of the organism, ignorance will result in irrational thoughts and beliefs: the illusion of self, the delusion of god(s), and unwholesome intentions and volitions (conation). They guide motivation by intensifying affect and emotions into unwholesome conduct and responses of greed-grasping and hatred-clinging which emanate from "bodyspeechmind" in an interpersonal context. Mindfulness can raise awareness of karmic activity which might consequently increase or decrease depending on the contingencies of learning. An emotional episode is part of a chain, preceded and followed by other episodes, thus forming vicious or virtual karmic cycles.

Table 28.2 Parallels between the cognitive behavioral and Buddhist micro-analytic approaches to emotional episodes

| Basic cognitive behavioral scheme | Multimodal & trimodal assessment | The Buddha's Karma sequence |
|---|---|---|
| **Stimulus** Discriminative Generalized | Sensation (*feeling*) | Awareness of sensory perception (*felt: +/0/−*) |
| **Organism** Cognitive Somatic | Cognition (*thinking*) Imagery (*thinking*) | Projections of ignorance: illusion of *self* & delusion of *god(s)* Intentional action planning: conation/volition/motivation |
| **Response** Emotional Behavioral | Affect (*feeling*) Behavior (*doing*) | Craving "musts" & consequent proclivity of Greed-grasping and/or Hatred-clinging |
| **Contingency** Reinforcement Punishment | Inter-relations (*doing*) Neurogenetic drives (biology) | To be mindfully aware of the interactivity of body/speech/mind in consciousness |

The *Dhammapada* (the Buddha's sayings in 423 verses), a gem of world literature, clarifies (Byrom, 2001, p. 3):

> We are what we *think*. All that we are arises with our *thoughts*. With our *thoughts* we make the world. *Speak* or *act* with an impure mind, and trouble will follow you as the wheel follows the ox that draws the cart.
>
> We are what we *think*. All that we are arises with our *thoughts*. With our *thoughts* we make the world. *Speak* or *act* with a pure mind, and happiness will follow you as your shadow, unshakable
>
> …

The art of turning the karma of drama into happiness lies in our own hands. In Buddhist lore karmic happiness is considered to be an epiphenomenon that occurs amidst adversity and while in the pursuit of awakening.

Positive psychology also sees a key place for intentional activity as a path to happiness, for example the application of strengths and virtues as a means of enabling individuals and communities to thrive. A well-known proposition suggests that sustainable happiness is determined by a genetic set-point (50%), circumstantial factors (10%), and intentional activity (40%) (Lyubomirsky, 2008).[5] The latter opens a window of opportunity for karmic happiness. If human beings are equipped with an idiosyncratic hardly modifiable set-point for happiness comparable with a set-point for weight or length, people with high set-points find it easier to be happy, and those with a lower set-point have to work harder to achieve and maintain happiness under similar conditions. Many studies suggest that circumstances like age, health, education, status, income, country, or religion determine only a small percentage

---

[5] Seligman's (2002) "happiness equation": H = S + C + V (Happiness = Set individual range + Circumstances of life + Voluntary controllable factors) similarly suggests that temperament and environment limit happiness and that certain actions accrue happiness.

of happiness (Veenhoven, Chapter 12, this volume). Happy people do not just sit around being happy but by making things happen intentionally, they can experience greater happiness than that suggested by their genetic set-point or set-range and life circumstances.

# Relational Buddhism

A social constructional Buddhist psychology offers a meta-psychological roadmap to happiness from the perspective of what I have coined "Relational Buddhism." This centers round the concept of "relational interbeing" which blends "interbeing," as relational awakening is called in the *Gandavyuha* Sutra (Thich Nhat Hanh, 1998), with Gergen's notions of "relational being" (2009). The idea of "relational interbeing" is derived from the awareness that human beings are interconnected. It focuses on individual being as the intersection of multiple relationships. A Buddhist stance implies that both our speech (inner talk and outer chatter) are directed toward a loving, empathic, and humorous outlook on life if we are to experience any happiness. Sagacity necessitates adherence to the relational scenarios of being kind, compassionate, and joyful with each other. From this perspective sustainable happiness is largely an interpersonal balancing experience and an epiphenomenon of harmonious relationships.

Relational Buddhism subscribes to the adage that "nobody is an island" and to the reality that we live in dependent origination with "the other" ubiquitously present in our minds. The individual-social binary is recast to lose the artificial qualification of the individual as a separate agency independent from social processes. Mind is not confined within an individual's subjective experience but is a continuous process between interacting individuals and from whom the experience derives its meaning. The attribution of meaning given to experience is (re)generated in co-action. Individual actors gain meaning through the enacted interpersonal process. Experience is a variety of relational action not unlike other actions. This view of experience as grounded in dialogical-narrative engagement does not mean the end of human conflict. However what we find psychologically painful can be transformed in collaborative practice dissolving the barriers of conflicting meanings. Rather than emphasizing deficiency we train people to talk positively, i.e. appreciatively.

The quest for happiness begins within our relational minds. Living in harmony (with)in our own relational selves offers the groundwork for interpersonal harmony. By demonstrating that the mind and mental processes are not so much in between the ears as within interactions and that the "spiritual" is to be found in-between people rather than in the sky, the hope is to open up a postmodern window for happiness and the sacred. Happiness is accrued as a by-product while pursuing a meaningful life and cannot be gained as an end in itself. Intelligible meaning is created by co-action, not by a single individual's solipsistic action. Thus, happiness necessitates awakened eyes that see our enmeshment in relationships through the language that we use. As there is no escape from relatedness, there is always someone in our actions. It is communal culture that determines our understanding of happiness. Whether an experience is happy or sad is shaped historically in the tradition we live by. Emotion and motivation are entwined in culturally immersed patterns. Relational contexts generate forestructures of experiential scenarios which make the subjective comprehensible. Hence, experiencing is part of a process of duplicating and replicating each other rather than an isolated phenomenon. It is through our dialogues that we give (re)birth to experience. By dismissing the subject–object duality as a foundation of experiencing, we might lift the self-other hiatus toward a deeper understanding and practice of relational interbeing.

While empiricists consider the person as autonomous, the validity of an independent agency is questionable. The individual actor in a continuing process of interpersonal dependence is inextricable from relational engagement. Relational interbeing implies that every individual action is embedded in a social network. If a private individual is held solely responsible for her/his action, one is positioned as an agent who takes a superior stance toward mortal others, the good, and the bad. Rather than relying on judgment of a human agency, action and responsibility are better viewed as the outcome of mutual relationships implanted in intertwined networks. Instead of owning responsibility, the impact of togetherness is emphasized by making the inextricability of relational enmeshment transparent. This relational responsibility corresponds with the Buddhist quintessence of dependent origination. Based on this reasoning, relational Buddhism submits that personal happiness arises through an interpersonal orientation rather than the other way around.

## In Conclusion

The art and science of sustainable happiness operate amidst existential suffering. This chapter argues for a social constructional perspective emphasizing the role of psychology in the transformation of cultural life. Psychology often offers the false promise that reality is controllable and that sufficient progress will alleviate suffering. Outcome results of specific therapeutic interventions for specific clients are insufficient. These studies have inherent flaws as there are simply too many variables to control (e.g., Ehrenreich, 2010; Mattes & Schraube, 2004; Toneatto & Nguyen, 2007). The Buddhist perspective of not-self/emptiness is non-foundational and practical. It views human functioning, including happiness, as a non-abiding cultural process of meaning creation. Shifting the location of the mind from behind the eyeballs to in-between interacting people shifts the focus on happiness to relational concerns. The Buddhist cultivation of a noble heart does not mean finding eternal cheerfulness but rather that one is turned-on to impartially infuse loving-kindness, compassion, and joy in much karmic activity.

We cannot all be a Chi-Tze, but perhaps the Buddhist spirit can be disseminated to those who are motivated (Kwee, 2010c). For the Buddhist activist the social is spiritual and to be pro-social is an immense task. The hope is that meditation-in-action based on the "Psychology of Relational Buddhism" will be able to secure down-to-earth happiness for all.

## References

Austin, J. H. (2010). Meditating selflessly. In M. G. T. Kwee (Ed.), *New horizons in Buddhist Psychology: Relational Buddhism for collaborative practitioners* (pp. 417–432). Chagrin Falls, OH: Taos Institute Publications.

Byrom, T. (Transl.). (2001). *The Dhammapada*. New York, NY: Bell Tower.

Csikszentmihalyi, M. (1990). *Flow.* New York, NY: Harper & Row.
Davidson, R. J., & Kabat-Zinn, J. (2004). Response to J.C. Smith. *Psychosomatic Medicine, 66,* 148–152.
De Silva, M. W. P. (2005). *An introduction to Buddhist psychology* (4th ed.). London: Palgrave-Macmillan.
Ehrenreich, B. (2010). *Smile or die: How positive thinking fooled America and the world.* London, UK: Granta.
Fredrickson, B. L., Cohn, M. A., Coffey, K. A., Pek, J., & Finkel, S. M. (2008). Open hearts build lives: Positive emotions, induced through loving kindness meditation, build consequential personal resources. *Journal of Personality & Social Psychology, 95,* 1045–1062.
Gergen, K. J. (2009). *Relational Being.* Oxford: Oxford University Press.
Gergen, K. J. (2010). The acculturated brain. *Theory & Psychology, 20,* 795–816.
Gilbert, P., & Procter, S. (2006). Compassionate mind training for people with high shame and self-criticism: Overview and pilot study of a group therapy approach. *Clinical Psychology & Psychotherapy, 13,* 353–379.
Hanson, R. (2009). *Buddha's brain: The practical neuroscience of happiness, love, and wisdom.* Oakland, CA: New Harbinger.
Haruki, Y., Homma, I., Umezawa, A., & Masaoka, Y. (2001). *Respiration and emotion.* Tokyo, Japan: Springer.
James, W. (1890). *Principles of psychology.* New York, NY: Holt.
Kabat-Zinn, J. (2003). Mindfulness-based stress reduction (MBSR). In M. G. T. Kwee & M. K. Taams (Eds.), Special issue: A tribute to Yutaka Haruki. *Constructivism in the Human Sciences, 2,* 73–106.
Kalupahana, D. J. (1987). *The principles of Buddhist psychology.* Albany, NY: State University of New York Press.
Kwee, M. G. T. (1990). *Psychotherapy, meditation & health.* London: East-West.
Kwee, M. G. T. (Ed.). (2010a). *New horizons in Buddhist psychology: Relational Buddhism for collaborative practitioners.* Chagrin Falls, OH: Taos Institute Publications.
Kwee, M. G. T. (2010b). The social construction of a New Buddhist Psychology. In M.G.T. Kwee (Ed.), *New horizons in Buddhist psychology: Relational Buddhism for collaborative practitioners* (pp. 29–50). Chagrin Falls, OH: Taos Institute Publications.
Kwee, M. G. T. (2010c). Relational Buddhism: On "Interhumane Multibeing" and Buddhist social action. In M. G. T. Kwee (Ed.), *New horizons in Buddhist psychology: Relational Buddhism for collaborative practitioners* (pp. 433–448). Chagrin Falls, OH: Taos Institute Publications.
Kwee, M. G. T. (2012a). Relational Buddhism: A psychological quest for meaning and sustainable happiness. In P.T.P. Wong (Ed.). *The human quest for meaning: Theories, Research and Applications* (2nd ed.) (pp. 249–274). New York: Routledge.
Kwee, M. G. T. (2012b). Buddhist Psychology. In A. Runehov & L. Oviedo (Eds.), *Encyclopedia of Sciences and Religions.* (Chapter 159). Dordrecht, Netherlands: Springer Science & Business Media..
Kwee, M. G. T., (2012c). Relational Buddhism: Wedding K.J. Gergen's Relational Being and Buddhism to create harmony in-between-selves. *Psychological Studies, 57*(2), 203–210.
Kwee, M. G. T., & Ellis, A. (1998). The interface between rational emotive behavior therapy (REBT) and Zen. *Journal of Rational-Emotive & Cognitive-Behavior Therapy, 16,* 5–44.
Kwee, M. G. T., & Taams, M. K. (2006a). A new Buddhist psychology: Moving beyond Theravada and Mahayana. In M. G. T. Kwee, K. J. Gergen, & F. Koshikawa (Eds.), *Horizons in Buddhist Psychology: Practice, research & theory* (pp. 435–478). Chagrin Falls, OH: Taos Institute Publications.

Kwee, M. G. T., & Taams, M. K. (2006b). Buddhist psychology and positive psychology. In A. Delle Fave (Ed.), *Dimensions of well-being: Research and intervention* (pp. 565–582). Milano, Italy: Franco Angeli.

Kwee, M. G. T., & Taams, M. K. (2010a). The collaborative practice of Karma Transformation: Cyclical emotional episodes and their sequential rebirths. In M. G. T. Kwee (Ed.), *New horizons in Buddhist psychology: Relational Buddhism for collaborative practitioners* (pp. 375–394). Chagrin Falls, OH: Taos Institute Publications.

Kwee, M. G. T., & Taams, M. K. (2010b). Karma functional analysis, strategic interventions, and mindfulness meditation. In M. G. T. Kwee (Ed.), *New horizons in Buddhist psychology: Relational Buddhism for collaborative practitioners* (pp. 395–416). Chagrin Falls, OH: Taos Institute Publications.

Lutz, A., Dunne, J. D., & Davidson, R. J. (2007). Meditation and the neuroscience of consciousness: An introduction. In P. D. Zelazo, M. Moscovitch, & E. Thompson (Eds.), *Cambridge handbook of consciousness* (pp. 499–555). New York, NY: Cambridge University Press.

Lyubomirsky, S. (2008). *The how of happiness: A scientific approach to getting the life you want.* New York, NY: Penguin.

Mattes, P., & Schraube, E. (2004). "Old-stream" psychology will disappear with the dinosaurs! Kenneth Gergen in conversation. *Forum: Qualitative Social Research*, 5, Article 27.

Seligman, M. E. P. (2002). *Authentic happiness.* New York, NY: Simon & Schuster.

Shapiro, S. L., & Carlson, L. E. (2009). *The art and science of mindfulness.* Washington, DC: American Psychological Association.

Sugamura, G., Haruki, Y., & Koshikawa, F. (2007). Building more solid bridges between Buddhism and western psychology. *American Psychologist*, 62, 1080–1081.

Suzuki, D. T. (1956). *Zen Buddhism.* New York, NY: Doubleday.

Taams, M. K., & Kwee, M. G. T. (2006). Himalaya Buddhism meets cognitive therapy: The Dalai Lama and Aaron T. Beck in dialogue, narrated by Marja Taams & Maurits Kwee. In M. G. T. Kwee, K. J. Gergen, & F. Koshikawa (Eds.), *Horizons in Buddhist Psychology: Practice, research & theory* (pp. 27–48). Chagrin Falls, OH: Taos Institute Publications.

Teasdale, J. (2000). Mindfulness-based cognitive therapy in the prevention of relapse and recurrence in major depression. In Y. Haruki & K. T. Kaku (Eds.), *Meditation as health promotion* (pp. 3–18). Delft, the Netherlands: Eburon.

Thich, N.H. (1998). *Interbeing.* Berkeley, CA: Parallax Press.

Toneatto, T., & Nguyen, L. (2007). Does mindfulness meditation improve anxiety and mood symptoms? A review of the controlled research. *Canadian Journal of Psychiatry*, 52, 260–266.

Wallace, B. A., & Shapiro, S. L. (2006). Mental balance and well-being: Building bridges between Buddhism and Western psychology. *American Psychologist*, 61, 690–701.

# CHAPTER 29

# WELL-BEING FROM THE HINDU/SANĀTANA DHARMA PERSPECTIVE

## KIRAN KUMAR K. SALAGAME
University of Mysore, India

INQUIRY into the nature of happiness and well-being has been one of the chief concerns of the wisdom traditions of India since antiquity. In Sanātana Dharma such an inquiry has progressed in the context of the dual nature of man recognized in Indian traditions. For instance, the ancient text *Hitopadesha* says that though hunger, sleep, fear, and sex are common to man and other animals, it is *jnāna*, reflective consciousness that specially characterizes man and that when humans lack it they are no different from animals. The *Aitareya Upanishad* states "man desires to attain the immortal through the mortal," and it is the "presence within him of this idea of perfection that makes man a spiritual being" (Hiriyanna, 1975, pp. 6–7). Such views result in approaching human behavior from both an "animal" and spiritual stance. This leads to a perspective on happiness and well-being that ranges from the ordinary to the non-ordinary, forming a continuum reflected in the concepts *preyas* and *shreyas*. For instance, in the Katha Upanishad, *preyas* stands for common pleasure and is distinguished from *sreyas* "or supreme bliss (and, by implication, all the higher values leading to it) which marks the goal of life" (Hiriyanna, 1975, pp. 17–18). This chapter focuses on the notion of happiness and well-being as enunciated in Sanātana Dharma (aka Hinduism).

## HINDUISM/SANĀTANA DHARMA—A NOTE ON HISTORY AND TERMINOLOGY

According to certain scholars and Indologists[1] two "patterns of life and thought" existed in ancient India—one non-Aryan, pre-Vedic and the other Aryan Vedic[2] known as the

---

[1] During the British rule in India many British scholars and other Europeans were interested in studying Indian history, civilization, and scriptures. They came to be known as Indologists and native scholars who showed such an interest also came to be known as such.

[2] The theory of the Aryan invasion to India is still a matter of controversy and debate. However, that does not invalidate the classification proposed by Dandekar.

*Muni-Yati* and *Rsi* traditions (Dandekar, 1981). The elements of the two traditions have mutually influenced each other and what is contemporarily known as Hinduism is a compound of both. "A large number of elements in the classical Hindu way of life and thought clearly betray a pre-Vedic non-Aryan origin" and "Aryan Vedism may be regarded as a grand interlude in the continuity of ancient Indian thought" (Dandekar, 1981, p. 339). To emphasize this continuity some scholars prefer to use the term *Sanātana dharma*.[3] The American scholar and Indologist David Frawley (1995) translated *Sanātana dharma* as "the eternal tradition" which literally means the "eternal or universal truth" and is "sometimes translated as the 'perennial wisdom' ... a tradition conceived as inherent in the cosmic mind, arising with creation itself... [it] is a set of teachings which comprehend Universal Life and Consciousness, including religion, yoga and mysticism, philosophy, science, art and culture as part of a single reality" (p. 18).

Frawley identified the following characteristics of *Sanātana dharma*: (1) It is not limited to any messiah, prophet, scripture, or church. (2) It is not restricted to any particular community or looking toward any particular historical end. (3) It embraces all aspiration toward the Divine or Supreme Being by all creatures, not only human beings but also plants and animals and the creatures, godly or ungodly, of subtle worlds beyond our physical senses. (4) It maintains our connection with the universal tradition through all worlds and all time, to the ancient past and the distant future "in the vision of a timeless self-renewing reality (Brahman)" (1995, pp. 20–21). Hence, what is known as Hinduism may be considered as a meta-perspective on the nature of reality, the universe, and the beings in it. In India inquiry concerning the nature of happiness and well-being has tended to proceed from this perspective.

## Concepts Related to Pleasure, Happiness, and Well-Being in the Indian Tradition

The Sanskrit language has many terms related to happiness and well-being that have percolated into other Indian languages. Those representing positive affect and common pleasure include *sukha* (agreeableness), *santosha* (happiness), *ullasa* (pleasant experience), *harsha* (joy), *shanti* (peace), *trpti* (satisfaction), and *tushti* (contentment). Each of these terms is used in specific contexts. The most widely used terms by lay people, as synonyms for happiness and well-being, are *sukha*, and *santosha*. The ancient seers and sages referred to this as *preyas*. All these concepts represent an individual's *sense of wellness in the ordinary states of consciousness*, associated with empirical reality and the bio-psycho-social self-sense as against a *state of happiness associated with spirituality or transcendence* which is referred to by the terms *ānanda* and *sthitaprajna* (Salagame, 2006a[4]). The term *sthitaprajana*, as

---

[3] References to this usage can be found in such ancient sources like *Matsyapurana* 143, 30–32, *Bhagavata* 7.11.2, *Brahmandapurana* 2.33.37–38 and also in Khānāpura plates of Mādhavavarma (vide *Epigraphica Indica*, vol. 27, p. 312) assigned to the sixth century AD (Harshananda, 2008).

[4] Note some references for Salagame, K. K. K may appear under Kumar, S. K. K in the original. The change corresponds to a switch to South Indian naming conventions.

described in the Bhagavad Gita indicates abiding firmly in one's Self. The sense of well-being associated with spirituality is known as *shreyas*.

In addition, there are terms that refer to physical or psychological health or of both. They include *ārogyam* (good health), *nirāmaya* (freedom from disease or illness), *swāsthyam* (sound state of body/mind), *shubha* (to shine, be splendid, and look beautiful or handsome; eminent, good, virtuous). The term *ārogyam* which means "good health" (Apte, 1988, p. 85) is used to refer both physical and mental health. The term *swāsthyam* is used to represent well-being. It has two components: *swa* in Sanskrit means "one's own, belonging to oneself, often serving as a reflexive pronoun; innate, natural, inherent, peculiar, inborn" (Apte, 1988, p. 630); *stha* means "standing, staying, abiding, being, existing" (p. 621). The two components put together indicate a state of abiding in one's self. While the Bhagavad Gita uses the term *sthitaprajana* to refer to this in a cognitive sense, Ayurveda defines *swāsthya*, as a condition of harmony in the functioning of soma, psyche and spirit. *Swāsthya* here refers to that condition of well-being in which the three *dosha* (body humors *vāta*, *pitta*, and *kapha*), two *agni* (digestive forces) and seven *dhātu* (bodily constituents) remain in balance and harmony along with proper eliminative functions (*malakriya*) and pleasantness (*prasanna*) of the sense organs (*indriya*), mind (*manas*), and self (*atma*). To achieve such a state Āyurveda prescribes a holistic lifestyle that gives due importance to diet, nutrition, exercise, psychological attitudes and values, social interactions, and spiritual practices. Ayurveda has guided much of the Indian life style in terms of food habits, religious practices, customs, and daily habits.

The contemporary distinction between hedonia and eudaimonia (Ryan & Deci, 2001) does not address the spiritual or transcendental dimension, though Aristotle's use of the latter emphasized happiness associated with virtuous living (Kristjá´nsson, 2010). Further, the tendency to consider them as two types of well-being has been questioned (Biswas-Diener, Kashdan, & King, 2009; Kashdan, Biswas-Diener, & King 2008). After an extensive review of literature related to contemporary well-being studies the authors point out that there is an element of hedonic pleasure even in eudaimonia and that there is far more overlap between the two models of well-being than was believed to be the case in the original philosophical conceptualizations. They caution thus: "We are concerned about the potential dangers of people misinterpreting a distinction between hedonic and eudaimonic happiness as meaning that there are two unrelated experiences of happiness (Biswas-Diener, Kashdan, & King, 2009, p. 210)." Unlike the contemporary researchers, in the Indian tradition, the distinction between preyas and shreyas is made based on whether desire springs from right philosophic knowledge (*vidya*) or not. That is, whether it will help us move forward in the attainment of the final goal of life (Hiriyanna, 1975), but not based on the affect quality involved.

# Preyas and Shreyas—the Nature of Pleasure in the Upanishads

A discussion of the nature of pleasure is found both in the *Brahadāranyka Upanishad* (Muni Kānda—Chapter IV, 3rd Brāhmana, 32nd sloka) and in the *Taittirya Upanishad* (Ānandavalli, Anuvāka 5 & 8). According to Upanishads the ultimate nature of reality is Existence (*sat*),

Consciousness (*chit*), and Bliss (*ānanda*). The Upanishads declare that the essence of human nature (Ātman) and the essence of the Universe (Brahman) are the same. In both sources, pleasure, termed as *ānanda*, is considered as intrinsic to nature itself. According to the *Taittirya Upanishad* when there are psychological barriers, this intrinsic pleasure does not manifest fully. Human beings erroneously think that objects in the external world are the source of pleasure, when in reality they only serve to remove the defenses for a while (Salagame, 2006b).

The term *ānanda* is used in the Upanishads in a generic sense to denote pleasure. To illustrate this the Upanishadic thinkers specify one unit of experienced intensity of human pleasure (*manushya ānanda* or *mānushānanda*) as that which is obtained by having all the good things one can aspire for—physical appearance and strength, youthfulness, scriptural education, character strength, intense desire to lead a worldly life, riches, and power that an emperor can have. This is the baseline of human pleasure. Then by providing, an exponential calculation raised to the power of 100 they indicate the different intensities of pleasure experienced by ten different orders of beings up to the peak of *Brahmānanda*, the ultimate spiritual happiness. It is equal to $100 \times 100 \times 100 \times 100 \times 100 \times 100 \times 100 \times 100 \times 100 \times 100$ *mānushānanda* (*Taittirya Upanishad* (Ānandavalli, Anuvāka 8, sloka 3). Compared to the one unit of human happiness defined by Upanishadic sages, all modern calculations of happiness are woeful!

According to the Upanishads everyday in deep sleep, we have a taste of *ānanda* momentarily, when there is no distinction between the experiencer and the experienced. To become aware of this essential pleasure in a conscious way during wakefulness is termed as *Ātma sākshātkāra*, Self-realization. The difference between a person who has not realized the Self and one who has realized is that the former "seeks" intrinsic pleasure in all kinds of things external and the latter "is in it." The idea that a "person who is in it and does not need to seek it elsewhere" is described in the Bhagavad Gita (Chapter II) as *sthitaprajna* (Pande & Naidu, 1992).

Certain non-Vedic traditions seem to have examined the issue of happiness from an existentialist point of view. Gautama the Buddha, for example, sought to find an answer for the questions that arose in him when he was exposed to human suffering and death. Gautama is known to have practiced all the available spiritual paths extant during his time to find an answer and finally got "enlightenment" when he stopped striving. "Buddha held that happiness may best be secured, when, not it, but its cause is aimed at" (Hiriyanna, 1975, p.17). The traditions of India converge on the point that we need to seek the source of happiness and well-being within, not in the external world. In this respect the approach of the wisdom traditions of India, differ from the contemporary approaches to studying well-being.

Modern sages echo ancient spiritual wisdom on the validity of Brahman and ānanda. For example Bhagavan Ramana Maharshi (1879–1950) states: "When I left home (in my seventeenth year), I was like a speck swept on by a tremendous flood. I knew not my body or the world, whether it was day or night. It was difficult even to open my eyes; the eyelids seemed to be glued down. My body became a mere skeleton. *Visitors pitied my plight as they were not aware how blissful I was.* It was after years that I came across the term 'Brahman' when I happened to look into some books on Vedanta brought to me. Amused, I said to myself, 'Is this known as Brahman?'"[5] (Vishwanatha Swami, 2001, p. 3). This episode in the life of

---

[5] Italics added for emphasis.

Ramana Maharshi illustrates several points: that *Brahman* is not a barren concept but rather a force to reckon with; when one is under its spell it seems nothing else matters, because one is in *ānanda*; one need not have heard or read about it to be seized by that force and the outward state of a person need not reveal anything about the inner condition.

## *SUKHA–DUHKHA*—PLEASURE AND PAIN

Sukha and duhkha is another pair of concepts that are relevant to well-being. While ānanda is used in a technical sense in the Upanishads, the term sukha has been used with a variety of connotations both in Sanskrit literature and in the day-to-day interactions. Apte (1988) listed the following English equivalents for this term: happiness, joy, delight, agreeable, sweet, charming, pleasant, virtuous, pious, comfort, prosperity, ease, health, welfare and well-being. However, the most common usage is in the sense of well-being without any misery and suffering. That is why it is paired with *duhkha*, suffering, which is the opposite of a healthy state (Anand, Srivastava, & Dalal, 2001; Lam & Palsane, 1997; Palsane & Lam, 1996).

Uddyotakara a philosopher of the Indian realist school, known as *Nyāya darshana*, considered that obtaining pleasure (*sukha-prāpti*) and the avoidance of pain (*duhkha-nivrtti*) was the object of human desire. According to him pleasure or the absence of pain is the key life value (Hiriyanna, 1975). However, it should be noted that the term *sukha*, is not limited to a hedonistic view and its use in the sense of pleasure is generic in significance. An ancient prayer of unknown authorship but still chanted today in all spiritual and religious congregation uses the term *sukha* to indicate well-being which is not just materialistic. It is a prayer that aspires for the welfare and well-being of each and everyone and that all avoid being afflicted with sorrow or suffering (*Sarve bhavantu sukhinah sarve santu nirāmayāha Sarve bhadrāni pashyantu mā kaschid dukkhabhāgbavet -Let everyone be happy, let everyone remain free from distress or illness and remain relaxed, let everyone perceive rightly, let not anybody be afflicted with suffering*).

Nevertheless, in the most popular sense the term *sukha* has acquired the connotation of the pleasure derived through a comfortable living suggesting the presence of greater positive affect and absence or little negative affect. Hence, one may consider that this term is synonymous with Diener's notion of subjective well-being (SWB). On the other hand, the term *ānanda* has acquired the connotation of bliss. For example, the names of all the monks of Sri Ramakrishna Mission end with the suffix *ānanda*, signifying its spiritual meaning (e.g., Swami *Vivekānanda*, Swami *Yateeshwarananda*, and so on). In the spiritual context, *ānanda* implies transcendence of pleasure and pain in the ordinary sense. Transcendence does not mean that the person does not undergo pain. Rather that he or she will be able to remain in a condition of equanimity and peace, without being subject to highs and lows associated with our normal living conditions. That is *sthitaprajna*. In Sanskrit *prajna* means state of awareness and *sthitha* means established. This term is used in Bhagavad-Gita, chapter 2. It refers to a person whose identity is established in a transcendental state of awareness. A description of the characteristics of such a person is provided in verses 55–72. In the Indian tradition this state is considered as an ideal state of well-being. In essence, it involves transcendental Self-realization; an ability to overcome desires, anger, hatred, and other negative emotions; the ability to regulate one's senses; non-attachment to situations and circumstances; and the ability to experience pain and pleasure with an equanimity.

## *PURUSHĀRTHA*—THE GOALS OF LIFE AND WELL-BEING

While *ānanda* and *sukha* represent the states of positive affect *purushārtha* represents the object of pleasure and well-being. The term *purushārtha* in Sanskrit literally means "what man desires"(*Purushaih arthayate iti*) and it "seems to express the general tendencies, of human nature" (Hiriyanna, 1975, p. 13, footnote 28). A person may desire material wealth (*artha*), sensory enjoyment (*kāma*), virtue (*dharma*) or transcendence and liberation from the cycle of birth and death (*moksha*). So the sense of well-being is seen as linked to what an individual desires.

Hiriyanna (1975) differentiates between "lower" and "higher values" and "empirical/secular" and "spiritual values" to refer to the four *purushārtha*. He notes that the lower or empirical/secular values are what a man "naturally seeks" and the higher/spiritual values are what he "ought to seek." Both are termed "human values" because they are consciously sought. Man has the potential to evolve to a higher stage. This means that a human being can strive towards perfection through the development of the virtues and strengths, which define humanness, *mānava dharma*. Indian thinkers went a step further and asserted that man can transcend all defining qualities to experience an identity beyond definitions, which they said is the real or true identity, known as *Ātman*, or Self. This is not an empty concept but a lived reality in the Indian tradition and a host of seer and sages of all ages and time periods have attested to the experience.

*Sanātana dharma* upheld the importance of higher values in experiencing sustainable well-being. The Indian thinkers observed that pursuit of lower values though natural, will not bring lasting sense of pleasure that endures because it is contingent upon the objects of the external world. Going after *artha* and *kāma* is like pouring oil into the fire, which only flares up the flame. They pointed out that if one keeps on fulfilling desires they continue to grow in strength. There is no end to seeking to maximize pleasure and avoid or minimize pain. Therefore, they advocated minimization of needs and eventually quelling of them. They regarded desires as the source of all misery and suffering, as the Buddha reiterated, and called upon people to overcome desires and to try to quell them completely rather than quenching them. Instead they said one can find satisfaction within one's self.

The objects of the world cannot provide the sustained feeling of well-being because they are impermanent (*a-nitya*) and perishable (*kshara*). In contrast, the experience of "pure consciousness," *Ātman*, the "Being within" is permanent (*nitya*) and imperishable (*a-kshara*) and its nature is *ānanda*. They thought it more prudent to seek that state of well-being which is intrinsic and natural to us and considered this the supreme goal of life. They advocated that it is wise for human beings to pursue *artha* and *kāma*, material wealth and pleasures guided by *dharma*, ethics and morality and strive towards *moksha*, liberation; like a train traveling to a destination being pushed from behind and pulled forward.

The contemporary distinction between SWB and psychological well-being (PWB) covers artha, kāma, and dharma. But moksha is a unique concept from Indian tradition. It is related to spiritual well-being. This author has discussed the similarities and differences between positive psychology and Indian viewpoints under *hedonic*, *collective*, and *transcendental* perspectives in detail elsewhere. These perspectives may be considered as associated with views of man as animal, human, and Divine or spiritual. Indian traditions accommodate all three views and make provision for dealing with them (see Salagame, 2003, 2004).

Dalal and Misra (2006, p. 99) have incorporated the ideas of ancient Indian thinkers into their "comprehensive model of health and well-being" which focuses on the "realization of the human potential for transcendent experiences and the cultivation of wisdom that touches the higher level of consciousness." A person who realizes such a potential: (1) works at the transpersonal level "by recognizing the continuity and inter-connectedness of the living beings and ecology"; (2) "the pain and suffering of such a person has no bounds as they are not personal"; (3) such an enlightenment "seeks the common ground and gazes at the issues for all beings (*jivas*) and for everyone (*sarva*)"; and (4) this demands "not only creativity but also a discipline of a very high order." Explicating on the nature of this "journey from fragmentation to integration or from self to Self" Dalal and Misra (2006, p. 99) observe that it is challenging but capable of bringing unparalleled joy and bliss. It entails a vision that celebrates the idea that "I am everywhere and everyone is in me." In this journey: (1) differentiation is set aside in favor of integration, (2) the person becomes more inward-looking, (3) is keen on transcending the physical environment and bodily concerns, (4) and focuses more and more on self-growth. In their opinion this aspect is a major contribution of Indian positive psychology.

Positive psychology though attempting to break free from the shackles of a pathology-oriented mind set still seems constrained by modern psychology's orientation to positivism. Researchers are guided by certain assumptions about the nature of the human being, reality, and the self. Misra (2009, p. 85) observes that the current approach to the study of happiness and well-being is situated in the context of a liberal individualism that is underpinned by the notion of an "independent self" that fosters a "kind of personhood which evolves in the direction of becoming more and more individualized." For such a self, happiness and well-being imply hedonic qualities such as joy, excitement, possessions, and achievements. This fits with a spirit of utilitarianism that entails increasing possessions and aspires to exercising greater control over the environment. Consumerism is a central feature of life in the twenty-first century and an emergent consequence of this approach. In contrast, ancient seer and sages recognized the limits and dangers of this type of orientation.

## *PANCHAKOSHA*—IDENTITY OR SELF-SENSE AND WELL-BEING

The *Taittiriya Upanishad* in which the concept *ānanda* is discussed provides a multidimensional model of human personality and self-sense that helps to elucidate the relationship between our self-sense and well-being. The Upanishad uses the metaphor of "sheath" (*kosha*) to conceptualize human personality. The human body as a material substance is compared to a sheath, called annamaya *kosha*,[6] within which we experience our identity or self-sense, or "I-feeling." Upanishadic sages spoke of four other sheaths viz., *prānamaya kosha*,

---

[6] The term *anna* means food and body and is considered as a sheath or covering made of food, in which our "I-feeling" throbs.

*manomaya kosha, vijñānamaya kosha* and *ānandamaya kosha*. The five sheaths are translated as physical, vital, mental, intuitive, and spiritual. Corresponding to these sheaths the Upanishad distinguishes five self-senses, *annamaya purusha, prāṇamaya purusha, manomaya purusha, vijñānamaya purusha* and *anandamaya purusha*. (The term *purusha* literally means man, but in the context of the Upanishad it refers to self-sense.)

It is possible to interpret the idea of *kosha* and corresponding *purusha* as different loci of identity. A person may identify their sense of self with a particular dimension and evaluate their sense of well-being with reference to that dimension. Ordinarily people feel their identities or self-sense with the *annamaya, prāṇamaya*, and *manomaya kosha* and remain established at that level. The evaluation of ill-being and well-being usually happen within this limited framework. However, some persons either spontaneously or through induction from meditation, yoga and other practices are able to move beyond these sheaths and narrow self-definitions. Spontaneous peak experiences, drug-induced states, and ecstatic and mystic experiences are instances of transcendence of the limitations of first three *koshas*. Therefore, our sense of well-being has an intrinsic relation to our self-definitions (Salagame, 2006b). The seers and sages of India have urged people to move beyond the limited self-definitions as a way of overcoming suffering and experiencing the dimension that is bliss itself.

The notion of *Ātman* is an inclusive concept that transcends the duality of subject-object and embraces the whole universe. Therefore, the Upanishadic seers and sages who were established in *Ātman* or in *anandamaya purusha* and lived in such a lofty height prayed for the universe and for the whole of the humanity. They believed the trick in achieving true happiness and well-being is not in limiting one's awareness, but in expanding it, which leads to an identity sense, rooted in a transcendental awareness.

Adam Curle (1972), a British psychologist, termed such an identity "awareness-identity" attained through "supraliminal awareness." This he contrasted with other types of identities. A second kind of "awareness-identity" is achieved through "psychological self-awareness" developed from various psychological interventions such as psychotherapy. The other "belonging-identity" develops from the process of identification with what we have and what we acquire, what we feel we belong to and what belongs to us.

Indian thinkers termed all types of personal identity that are rooted in some identification as *ahamkāra*, I, and *mamkāra*, Me or mine, and contrasted that with the *Atman*, awareness-identity centered in "pure consciousness" (Salagame, 2005). Sri Krishna said to Arjuna: "if one is without *ahamkāra* and *mamkāra* he/she will attain that Peace," (Bhagavad Gita, Chapter 2, verse 71), which is ultimate well-being. This is called the ultimate and supreme goal of human existence, *paramapuruṣhārtha*.

But how does one achieve this exalted state? It is through a continuous process of self-purification by following a path of virtue, which they called *dharma*. In practice this meant leading a life governed by a set of values that is conducive for one's own growth and the growth of the others. It involves overcoming our desires, attachments, regulation of our sensory cravings, and negative emotions in particular anger, jealousy, avarice, hatred, and pride. The Bhagavad Gita states that this can be achieved through the constant practice of self-reflection, non-attachment, meditation, and surrender to a higher power. Non-attachment, *anāsakti*, to the fruits/outcomes of one's actions is one of the important methods prescribed for attaining this (Naidu & Pande, 1999; Tewari, 2000)

## *GUNA* AND WELL-BEING

All the philosophical traditions of India refer to the important concept *guna* in describing mental and material phenomena. It is found in the Upanishads and later elaborated in the Sāmkhya system of philosophy. Subsequently this concept was accepted by all schools. In the traditional understanding *guna* constitutes *prakrti*, nature, and both mind and matter are manifestations of *guna*. There are three *guna* viz., *sattva, rajas*, and *tamas*. They constitute the fundamental operating principles of the universe and everything that happens—mental and material. *Sattva* represents the principle of illumination, *rajas*, the principle of energy, and *tamas*, the principle of inertia. What we call mind is predominated by the principle of illumination, *sattva*, and matter by the principle of inertia, *tamas*. *Rajas*, the principle of dynamism and energy is operating in both. Individual differences in behavior can be understood with reference to these three principles. The relationship of the three *guna* to happiness and well-being is explained in terms of the preponderance of *sattva* and ill-being is associated with *rajas* and *tamas* (Mathew, 1995, 2004; Murthy & Salagame, 2007). The emergence of positive psychology can be seen as an indication that modern psychology is moving away from *rajas* and *tamas* towards *Sattva* in its focus.

# EMPIRICAL INVESTIGATIONS OF THE TRADITIONAL CONCEPTS AND PERSPECTIVES

Various Indian psychologists are beginning to examine traditional concepts of well-being in Indian psychology. Wadhwa and Jain (1990) developed a scale, which measures the attitude of teachers towards the four *purushārtha*—material wealth (*artha*), sensory enjoyment (*kāma*), virtue (*dharma*) or transcendence and liberation from the cycle of birth and death (*moksha*). The 48-item scale has high reliabilities for each subscale: 0.70 (dharma), 0.80 (artha), 0.78 (kāma), and 0.96 (moksha). Dharma was found to significantly relate to artha and moksha, but not kāma. Moksha was negatively related with kāma. In another study of Hindus (aged 60–90 years) Rangaswami (1994) found that 93% believed in spiritual pursuit aimed at union with the universal Self as the ultimate goal of life.

Singh and Misra (2000) attempted to delineate the notion of "*santosha*" (contentment) in everyday discourse. The data were obtained through an open-ended measure pertaining to experiences related to contentment. The findings indicated that younger and older adults construed contentment in their collective life style as largely dominated by emotional bonding. In these samples materialistic desires prevailed alongside the pursuit of goals related to pleasure, enjoyment, happiness and contentment. "Saints" emerged as a separate category who shared a rational worldview but found contentment in different facets of life.

Effects of spirituality-based life styles have been investigated by some. Shinde (2001, 2002) studied a cohort who is known as "Swādhyāyee." Swādhyāya literally means self-study or discovery of Self. According to the founder of this movement swādhyāya is an attitude of the mind and it is the right perspective or the vision which enables one to understand and practice the deeper aspects of religion and culture (Shinde, 2001). The researcher explored the spiritual and material aspects of swādhyāyee with non-swādhyāyee families (age 25–50 years). He found that the swādhyāyee besides being high on spiritual orientation also showed superior social health and a higher level of interpersonal trust than the controls (Shinde, 2001). A comparison of the emotional maturity of the swādhyāyee and non-swādhyāyee youth showed that both males and females in the former group had higher levels of emotional maturity (Shinde, 2002).

Mohan, Prasad, and Rao (2004) studied the effects of the spiritually-based lifestyle change programme of Rishi Samskruti Vidya Kendra on individuals' well-being. They note that the idea that active participation in a lifestyle change program can bring about much desired positive changes in one's health and well-being is a concept that is being aggressively promoted. Results indicated that an overwhelming majority of the 200 participants experienced an increase in their sense of purpose/meaning for their lives and in their need to achieve higher consciousness.

Mohan, Mohan, Ray, Basu, and Viranjini (2004) explored the construct of spiritual well-being as understood and experienced by a broad section of an Indian population. The respondents felt spirituality to be a significant determinant of their sense of well-being. The findings revealed that it differed from "ordinary" well-being. It was seen as distinct from moral well-being or religiousness; was experienced to an extent independent of the outer conditions and circumstances; was considered as a "deeper" or "higher" source of the well-being; and was described in terms of various experiences and states of consciousness. Though the understanding of spiritual well-being differed amongst the various religious and spiritual groups, the deeper experiences were characterized by a closer harmony and similarity.

## STRATEGIES FOR ENHANCING PREYAS AND SHREYAS—DHARMA IS THE KEY

From what has been presented so far it may appear as though views of well-being in the Indian tradition are all spiritual with nothing material; but it is not so. Though Indian seers and sages postulated *moksha*, the liberation from the cycle of birth and death as the supreme goal of human existence—*parama purushārtha*, they were quite aware that it is not the cup of tea for all. Indian thinkers did recognize vast individual differences among human beings and accommodated the aspirations of all people in their worldview. Therefore, they devised different strategies for refining human beings, *samskāra*, and recommended them according to the person's level and *svadharma*, propensities.

Indian culture is rich with diversity in many aspects of life such as language, customs, dress, food habits, the kinds of enjoyment of material pleasures or wealth and faith in this or that god or goddess and so on. Sanātana dharma is as much concerned with material well-being as with spiritual well-being so to say. But what differentiates the Indian approach from the Western approach is the latter's overemphasis on the material as against the spiritual. Ultimate good life and well-being lies in harmonizing the two. To achieve this end, the Indian tradition laid utmost emphasis on *dharma*.

The term *dharma* in Sanskrit is derived from a root *dhr*, which means to uphold, to sustain, and to hold together. One leads life according to one's dispositions and inclinations (*svadharma*) but also harmonizes it with others at various stages of personal development (*āshrama*) from childhood to old age. Tips for living harmoniously with one's self and with others is primarily enunciated and elaborated in certain texts known as *dharma shāstra* and *grhya sūtra*, in the *Mahābhāratha*, and in other literary works like Bartrhari's *Neetishataka*, for example. It should be noted that it was the sage Vātsāyana who wrote the now world famous treatise on sexual life the *Kāmasūtra*. Kautilya, another thinker, wrote a magnum opus on economics and policy, *Arthashāstra*. Bharata, a dramatist, wrote his famous work on fine arts known as *Nātyashāstra*. There are many other works in other Indian languages, which throw light on achieving well-being in mundane existence.

Nevertheless, the main thrust in the Indian tradition has been on refinement of human beings. Spiritual practices of various kinds are aids in refining one's self. The practices that are now well known all over the world, such as the eight aspects of Patanjali Yoga; *karma yoga*, *bhakti yoga*, and *jnāna yoga*, are the strategies for developing oneself as a refined human being. Various types of meditation practice and forms of yoga were meant originally for this, not for deriving pleasure and bodily comfort per se. In an already refined human being *bhakti* (devotion) and *jnāna yoga* (knowledge) can lead to transcendence, *ānanda* and *stitaprajnatva*, the ideal state of well-being. In the endeavor to refine oneself one may willingly undergo any economic hardship, poverty, even hunger and any adverse circumstances of life.

Since the spiritual development of a person implies expanding one's consciousness seers and sages have tended to uphold *mānava dharma* (virtues and strengths that define humanness) as the most important aspect and encouraged the development of many positive traits. *Dharma Shaastra*, lists the following as defining qualities of a human being—contentment, forgiveness, self-control, abstention from unrighteous appropriating anything, following the rules of purification, disciplining the organs (sensory and motor), wisdom, knowledge, truthfulness, and abstention from anger. The *Artha Shaastra* of Kautilya emphasizes the following characteristics—harmlessness, truthfulness, purity, wisdom, freedom from spite, abstinence from cruelty, and forgiveness (Kuppuswamy, 1977). Fostering these positive traits is the way to achieve personal and collective well-being- according to Sanātana dharma.

## Conclusion

Pargament and Mahoney (2002) observe that researchers who study the relationship between spirituality and well-being tend to do so from a distance instead of developing a deeper understanding. According to them most modern psychological studies tend to adopt an approach to the enhancement of well-being that is control oriented where elements of religiosity like faith in God, attending religious services, frequency of prayer, etc., are seen as approaches that can enhance empowerment. They argue that spiritual traditions that address aspects of our lives that are beyond our control such as birth, developmental transitions, accidents, illnesses, and death, get little attention. They point out that spiritual concepts such as the sacred, transcendence, letting go, forbearance, suffering, faith, mystery, finitude, sacrifice, grace, and transformation are rarely addressed by psychologists. They advocate developing a deeper understanding of spirituality by studying it "closer-at-hand." This means getting to know spiritually-oriented people; learning about their worldview, values, and relationships; participating in and observing their institutions and settings; and, examining the specific resources and methods of spirituality in much greater detail. Study of Indian traditions particularly the ways of living associated with the pursuit of spirituality will help to illuminate the relationship between spirituality and well-being in the sense Pargament and Mahoney described earlier. Though there are few empirical investigations on well-being based in the Indian perspective, the findings show that the concepts and perspectives developed within the Indian tradition centuries ago are still relevant and potentially useful in understanding the nature of well-being.

## Acknowledgments

The author gratefully acknowledges the useful suggestions and comments received from Professor Anand Paranjpe and Professor Jane Henry on the initial drafts of this chapter.

## REFERENCES

Anand, J., Srivastava, A., & Dalal, A. K. (2001). Where suffering ends and healing begins. *Psychological Studies*, 46(3), 114–126.

Apte, V. S. (1988). *The student's Sanskrit English dictionary*. Delhi, India: Motilal Banarasidass.

Biswas-Diener, R., Kashdan, T. B., & King, L. A. (2009). Two traditions of happiness research, not two distinct types of happiness. *The Journal of Positive Psychology*, 4(3), 208–211.

Curle, A. (1972). *Mystics and militants: a study of awareness, identity and social action*. London, UK: Tavistock Publications.

Dalal, A. K., & Misra, G. (2006). Psychology of health and well-being: Some emerging perspectives. *Psychological Studies*, 51(2&3), 91–104.

Dandekar, R. N. (1981). *Exercises in Indology*. Delhi, India: Ajanta Publishers.

Dasgupta, S. N. (1927). *Hindu mysticism*. Delhi, India: Motilal Banrasidass.

Diener, E. (1984). Subjective well-being. *Psychological Bulletin*, 95, 542–575.

Frawley, D. (1995). *Hinduism—The eternal tradition (Sanātana Dharma)*. New Delhi, India: Voice of India.

Harshananda, S. (2008). *A concise encyclopedia of Hinduism, Vol. 3*. Bangalore, India: Ramakrishna Math.

Hawkins, B. K. (2004). *Asian religions*. New York, NY: Pearson Longman.

Hiriyanna, M. (1975). *Indian conception of values*. Mysore, India: Kavyalaya Publishers.

Kashdan, T. B., Biswas-Diener, R., & King L.A. (2008). Reconsidering happiness: The costs of distinguishing between hedonics and eudaimonia. *The Journal of Positive Psychology*, 3(4), 219–233.

Kristja´nsson, K. (2010). Positive psychology, happiness, and virtue: The troublesome conceptual issues. *Review of General Psychology*, 14(4), 296–310.

Kuppuswamy, B. (1977). *Dharma and society—A study in social values*. Delhi, India: The Macmillan Co. of India Ltd.

Lam, D. J., & Palsane, L. M. (1997). Research on stress and coping: Contemporary Asian approaches. In H.S.R. Kao & D. Sinha (Ed.), *Asian perspectives on psychology* (pp. 265–281). New Delhi, India: Sage.

Mathew, V. G. (1995). *IAS Rating Scale*. Trivandrum, India: Department of Psychology, University of Kerala.

Mathew, V. G. (2004). Personal growth and psychology in India. In K. Joshi & M. Cornelissen (Eds.), *Consciousness, Indian psychology and yoga* (pp. 248–256). New Delhi, India: Centre for Studies in Civilizations.

Misra, G. (2009). Self and well-being. *Psychological Studies*, 54(2), 85–86.
Mohan, Y., Mohan, K. K., Roy, G. Basu, S., & Viranjini, G. (2004). Spiritual well-being: An empirical study with yogic perspectives. *Journal of Indian Psychology*, 22(1), 41–52.
Mohan, K. K., Prasad, V. S., & Rao, P.V. K. (2004). Effectiveness of spiritually based lifestyle change programme on well-being. *Journal of Indian Psychology*, 22(1), 6–13.
Murthy, P. K., & Salagame, K. K. K. (2007). The concept of triguna: A critical analysis and synthesis. *Psychological Studies*, 52(2), 103–113.
Naidu, R. K., & Pande, N. (1999). Anāsakti: The Indian vision of potential human transcendence beyond mechanistic motivations. In G. Misra (Ed.), *Psychological perspectives on stress and health* (pp. 85–89). New Delhi, India: Concept Publishing Co.
Palsane, M. N., & Lam, D. J. (1996). Stress and coping from traditional Indian and Chinese perspectives. *Psychology and Developing Societies*, 8(1), 29–53.
Pande, N., & Naidu, R. K. (1992). Anāsakti and health: A study of non-attachment. *Psychology and Developing Societies*, 4(1), 89–104.
Pargament, K. I., & Mahoney, A. (2002). Spirituality: Discovering and conserving the sacred. In C. R. Snyder & S. J. Lopez (Eds.), *Handbook of positive psychology* (pp. 646–659). New York, NY: Oxford University Press.
Rangaswami, K. (1994). Self actualization and beyond: Union with universal self, the highest motive from Indian perspective. *Indian Journal of Clinical Psychology*, 21(2), 45–50.
Ryan, R., & Deci, E. (2001). On happiness and human potentials: A review of research on hedonic and eudaimonic well-being. *Annual Review of Psychology*, 52, 141–166.
Salagame, K. K. K. (2003). An Indian conception of well-being. In J. Henry (Ed.), *European positive psychology proceedings* (pp. 73–80). Leicester, UK: British Psychological Society.
Salagame, K. K. K. (2004). Perspectives on well-being in the Indian tradition. *Journal of Indian Psychology*, 22(2), 63–72.
Salagame, K. K. K. (2005). Concept ahamkāra: Theoretical and empirical analysis. In K.R. Rao & S. Marwah (Eds.), *Towards a spiritual psychology: Essays in Indian psychology* (pp. 97–122). New Delhi, India: Samvad India Foundation.
Salagame, K. K. K. (2006a). The role of spirituality in attaining well-being: Approach of Sanātana Dharma. In A. D. Fave (Ed.), *Dimensions of well-being. Research and intervention* (pp. 538–551). Milano, Italy: Franco Angeli.
Salagame, K. K. K. (2006b). Happiness and well-being in Indian tradition. *Psychological Studies*, 51(4), 105–112.
Shinde, V. R. (2001). Spiritual and material health associated with swādhyāyee and non-swādhyāyee families. *Behavioral Scientist*, 2(1), 3–10.
Shinde, V. R. (2002). Emotional maturity in swādhyāyee youths associated with divine brain trust and non-swādhyāyee youths. *Behavioral Scientist*, 3(2), 81–90.
Shukla, W. (2000). Body health, paganism and faith. *Psychological Studies*, 45(3), 131–135.
Singh J. K., & Misra G. (2000). Understanding contentment in everyday life. *I.P.R. Special Millennium Issue*, 54 & 55(4), 113–124.
Tewari, A. K. (2000). Anāsakti and mental health. *Psychological Studies*, 45(3), 156–166.
Vishwanatha, S. (2001). Reminiscences-I-At the feet of Bhagavan Ramana. In *Surpassing love and grace (An anthology of experiences and memories by the devotees)*. Tiruvannamalai, India: Sri Ramanasramam.
Wadhwa, B. S., & Jain, R. (1990). Attitudes of teachers towards four goals of life of Hindu morality—Dharma, artha, kāma and moksha. *Journal of Psychological Researches*, 34(1), 6–9.

CHAPTER 30

# FLOURISHING THROUGH MEDITATION AND MINDFULNESS

PETER MALINOWSKI

Liverpool John Moores University, UK

In recent years psychological research and practice have been enriched by two exciting developments which in combination add a new dimension to the quest for a meaningful and fulfilled life. The first development relates to the introduction of the concept of *flourishing*. The second concerns the growing recognition of the beneficial effects of *meditation* and *mindfulness practice* as clinical and non-clinical interventions. These two developments are slowly starting to cross-fertilize, providing new perspectives and practical approaches to the field of positive psychology.

In this chapter I will outline and discuss how these developments are interrelated and why meditation and mindfulness practices are considered to be useful tools for achieving a flourishing life. First attempts at conceptualizing the psychological mechanisms that are at work when meditation practices unfold their beneficial effects will be discussed, while also considering challenges that lie ahead.

## Flourishing

The American social psychologist Corey Keyes coined the term *flourishing* to describe a mental state that is characterized by the presence of positive feelings and positive functioning in life (Keyes, 2002, 2003). He furthermore argues that "mental health and mental illness are not opposite ends of a single measurement continuum" (Keyes, 2002, p. 209), but can rather be understood as two related but not identical continua. In a series of studies he provides evidence that exclusively focusing on mental disorders is insufficient for achieving genuine mental health (Keyes, 2005, 2007). In addition to the continuum of mental illness that ranges from severe mental disorders to states that are completely free of them, it would be important to also consider the continuum of mental health, ranging from a state of languishing to a state of flourishing. Complete mental health would be achieved if a person is free of mental disorders and is flourishing at the same time. Empirical evidence confirms that these are not just lofty ideas. Rather, languishing is related to increased measures of disability, of health care utilization and of chronic physical illness and is also related to lower psychosocial functioning. The importance of these findings becomes obvious when considering that the prevalence of flourishing in the adult US population is below 20% (Keyes, 2005, 2007). The situation in Europe is not much different. A study including 23 European nations revealed that in average only about 12% of the European population are in a state of flourishing, with marked differences between Northern Europe (22–33%) and Eastern Europe (6–13%) (Huppert, 2008; Huppert & So, 2009). Such data clearly indicate the potential for improving levels of flourishing in our Western societies. But while a broad spectrum of treatment approaches exist for alleviating mental disorders, ranging from psychopharmacological treatments to various forms of psychotherapy and counseling, tools that may foster flourishing have hardly been explored.

This is where meditation and mindfulness practices enter the picture. It is worth considering that the concept of complete mental health as a state that is free of mental disorders *and* is at the same time characterized by flourishing also lies at the heart of Buddhist psychology. For instance, it is clearly expressed in the Tibetan word *sangye* (*sangs rgyas* in Wylie transliteration), a central term frequently used when referring to the awakened state of Buddhahood, the ultimate goal of Buddhist practice. The first syllable *sang* can be translated as "removed," "purified" or "dissolved," while the second syllable *gye* means "developed," "evolved," "blossomed" or "flourished." Thus, according to Tibetan Buddhist understanding the state of a Buddha is reached when the mind is purified from all psychological disturbances or harmful mental tendencies and all mental, social and spiritual qualities are fully flourishing (Malinowski, 2010; Nydahl, 2008). It is at this point where contemporary psychological ideas of complete mental health and Buddhist ideas of the development and perfection of human qualities meet and overlap.

With her broaden-and-build theory Barbara Fredrickson provides a model how a state of flourishing and well-being can be achieved (Fredrickson, 2001, 2004, 2009; Fredrickson & Joiner, 2002) (see also Conway, Tugade, Catalino, & Fredrickson, Chapter 3, this volume). The central mechanisms proposed in this theory state that the experience of positive emotions broadens the available thought-action repertoires that subsequently leads to the building or strengthening of a variety of personal resources, a process that is linked to a marked improvement in well-being. Most interestingly for our topic, in a recent study that employed a randomized control group design Fredrickson and co-workers were able to show that the regular engagement with a loving kindness meditation, which is based on Buddhist principles of fostering love and compassion, lead to an increase in positive emotions, which in turn produced increases in a variety of personal resources that resulted in an increase in life satisfaction and a decrease in depressive symptoms (Fredrickson, Cohn, Coffey, Pek, & Finkel, 2008; see also Garland et al., 2010). This is considered to be the first empirical study to directly test a theory *how* meditation practice leads to an increase in personal resources, life satisfaction and flourishing. It should be noted, though, that within the conceptual framework of the broaden-and-build theory the loving kindness meditation was employed with the explicit aim of improving the experience of positive emotions. Within its original Buddhist context the aim of meditation practice, including loving kindness meditation, is considerably more far-reaching and is supposed to rely on other mechanisms than the mere increase of positive experiences. As a first approximation one may say that Buddhist meditation methods aim at fostering personal resources as for instance mindfulness or empathy, whereas accompanying fleeting emotional states (whether positive or negative) are considered less important. Linking meditation practice to the broaden-and-build theory constitutes a useful first step that can direct future research. It will, however, be important not to prematurely neglect the roots and philosophical background of these meditation practices, which are built on approximately 2500 years of practical experience (Kang & Whittingham, 2010; Wallace & Hodel, 2008).

## What is Meditation?

Several attempts have been made to define meditation from a psychological perspective. One approach taken for example by Cahn and Polich (2006) in their review of electrophysiological and neuroimaging studies of meditation defined it as "practices that self-regulate the body and mind, thereby affecting mental events by engaging a specific attentional set" (p. 180) and furthermore classified meditation as a subset of those practices that are "used to induce relaxation or altered states such as hypnosis, progressive relaxation, and trance-induction techniques" (p. 180). A definition like this does not help understanding the processes underlying meditation, as it avoids specifying many of the aspects that are central to meditation practice. Furthermore, relating meditation to the above mentioned group of practices can be confusing as the goals of the majority of traditional forms of meditation are neither relaxation, nor altered states of awareness or hypnosis, nor trance-inductions. The problem arises from attempts to capture the whole spectrum of meditation practices under one roof, an endeavor that must fail if one considers the sheer diversity of approaches and practices. Lutz et al. get to the heart of this by comparing the attempt of studying meditation without distinguishing between different meditation disciplines to investigating all types of sport as if they were essentially the same, which of course they are not (Lutz, Slagter, Dunne, & Davidson, 2008). Consequently, Lutz et al. restricted their studies to "Buddhist contemplative techniques and their clinical secular derivatives" (p. 163). As the majority of meditation techniques that are currently investigated fall into this category (including various forms of mindfulness practice) it seems a sensible approach, not least as this group of practices is large and diverse. The only addition I would make here is to also include non-clinical secular derivates as there is a growing interest in using secular meditation practices in non-clinical settings as for instance in staff development or education (e.g., Schonert-Reichl & Stewart Lawlor, 2010; Walach, et al., 2007). It is worth noting, though, that referring to these meditation practices as *contemplative techniques* may in itself be misleading, as contemplation implies active engagement with specific thought contents, whereas many forms of Buddhist meditation practice actually aim at non-engagement with the specific content of experience (Chiesa & Malinowski, 2011). Furthermore, the term meditation itself is used with different meanings. So far we have discussed it in the sense of a mental training regime or a technique that is employed. But let us consider a definition given by the Buddhist meditation master Lama Ole Nydahl. He explains "In the state of meditation one does not produce anything but instead rests consciously in the perception of what is. Thus one […] remains without stress in the multiplicity of what is going on, and feels joyful and conscious during the moment of experience." (Nydahl, 2004, p. 121) Here, meditation is not understood as a form of practice or training, but as the state of mind that is the outcome of such practice: One practices to reach a state of meditation.

Thus, it is important to keep in mind that we are confronted with a large variety of methods, while equipped with a psychological vocabulary that has not yet sufficiently evolved to capture the richness of these methods and the variety of states of minds and aspects of psychological, social and spiritual functioning they are thought to bring about.

Bearing the difficulties in defining meditation in psychological terms in mind it might be useful to consider its roots. The Sanskrit term *bhāvanā* that is commonly translated as meditation actually means "cultivating" and the Tibetan equivalent *sgom* (pronounced "gom") may translate as "getting used to" or "familiarizing oneself." Although depending on the philosophical background and the aim of the specific form of meditation these terms are interpreted in slightly different ways, one can generally assume that they convey the idea of cultivating a certain state of mind or mental habit (as for instance to be focused, mindful or compassionate; see also Ricard, Chapter 27, this volume). A slightly different picture emerges when seen from the *Vajrayana* or Diamond Way perspective of Buddhism where meditation can be understood as the process of familiarizing oneself with the ever-present but usually unnoticed ultimate qualities of mind that are summarized in the idea of Buddha nature (Gampopa, 1998; Maitreya/Asanga, 1985; Nydahl, 2004, 2008). Simply put, the meditation practice would help getting used to one's own perfect (though hidden) qualities.

In light of the breadth of Buddhist meditation practices that reach from cultivating stable attention to resting the mind in its own ultimate qualities it becomes obvious that any attempt at summarizing them all under one concise definition would be an impossible feat. Nevertheless, for getting a general idea about some underlying principles one may want to rely on a systematization used within Tibetan Buddhism, transmitted to Tibet by the Indian master Kamalaśīla in the eighth century CE (Kamalaśīla, 1997). According to this system, Buddhist meditation practices can be subdivided into aspects that aim at calming the mind (calm abiding meditation, Sanskrit: *śamatha*, Tibetan: *shiney*) and aspects that aim at gaining insight into the nature of all phenomena and mind itself (insight meditation, Sanskrit: *vipaśyanā*, Tibetan: *lhagthong*). Both aspects of meditation can be trained separately or in combination, depending on the specific meditation system. But it is generally understood that the development of a calm, focused and stable mind through the practice of calm abiding meditation is a prerequisite for progressing with insight meditation (Wangchug Dorje, 2009). The practice of calm abiding essentially consists of focusing the mind on an object and practicing to keep the focus of attention with this object. Typically, the sensation of one's own breathing is taken as an object, but there are many varieties and in principle every meditation that includes non-elaborative focusing of attention contains the aspect of calm abiding (see, for instance, Wallace, 1999). Quite obviously, insight meditation, where one trains the mind in directly seeing the nature of phenomena instead of their superficial appearances requires some mental stability developed through calm abiding. Again there exists a huge variety of practices, some of them analytical, to gain this insight (Bokar, 1992; Kamalaśīla, 1997; Shamar, 2009). Concerning flourishing and well-being, calm abiding meditations in themselves are considered to only bring temporal improvements, whereas insight meditation that breaks through (or dissolves) the usual mental patterns of likes and dislikes and the various misconceptions of reality has the potential to lead to an experience of bliss that does not depend on specific inner and outer conditions, and is thus also described as non-conditioned happiness (Nydahl, 2008; Ricard, 2006, see also Ricard, Chapter 27, this volume).

## Mindfulness

The idea of mindfulness is derived from Buddhist traditions and is closely related to Buddhist meditation practice. It is thus not surprising that similar concerns regarding terminology and definitions also apply to the term mindfulness, which is frequently used to refer to a construct, a mental state or a number of practices designed to achieve this state (Chambers, Gullone, & Allen, 2009; Rapgay & Bystrisky, 2009). Dorjee (2010) provides an overview of the breadth of meaning that is currently condensed under this single term and highlights the importance of more conceptual clarity (see also Malinowski, 2008).

Mindfulness has nevertheless been a success story regarding the integration of Buddhist principles and practices into mainstream psychology. The foundation was laid with the introduction of the mindfulness-based stress reduction (MBSR) program by Jon Kabat-Zinn approximately 30 years ago (Kabat-Zinn, 1982, 1990, 2003), followed by an ever growing number of evaluation studies that provide increasing evidence of the efficacy of mindfulness-based interventions in treating several clinical conditions (Brown & Ryan, 2003; Chiesa & Serretti, 2011; Grossman, Niemann, Schmidt, & Walach, 2004). Within that context mindfulness has been described as "the awareness that emerges through paying attention on purpose, in the present moment, and nonjudgmentally to the unfolding of experience moment by moment" (Kabat-Zinn, 2003, p. 145) and is "characterized by dispassionate, non-evaluative and sustained moment-to-moment awareness of perceptible mental states and processes. This includes continuous, immediate awareness of physical sensations, perceptions, affective states, thoughts, and imagery" (Grossman, et al., 2004, p. 36). Brown et al. condense these to define mindfulness as "a receptive attention to and awareness of present events and experience" (Brown, Ryan, & Creswell, 2007, p. 212). In most of the psychological applications of mindfulness, meditation practice plays a central role in developing the described levels of awareness (Malinowski, 2008). Practices usually focus on training the ability to maintain a level of non-judging awareness.

## Flourishing and Meditation

As we have seen, current psychological and traditional Buddhist views agree that a mind free of disturbances and mental problems and full of positive human qualities and resources is required for achieving a meaningful and fulfilled life. However, the majority of mindfulness-based applications currently focus on the treatment of disorders and diseases. Its ability to influence positive states of mind and contribute to flourishing has barely been explored.

# Psychological Approaches to Meditation and Mindfulness

## Intention, attention, attitude

Shauna Shapiro and co-workers suggested a three-component model to explain the main mechanisms of how mindfulness meditation can promote positive change (Shapiro, Carlson, Astin, & Freedman, 2006). In addition to the two widely discussed components of (1) developing one's attentional abilities combined with (2) a certain non-evaluative attitude towards the experiences one attends to (e.g., Bishop et al., 2004), they add the third component of *intention* to the mix, highlighting that the personal motivation or vision as to why somebody engages in meditation and mindfulness practice will have an important impact on the outcome. According to this model one would expect that people who engage in mindfulness practice to deal with health-related problems may succeed in achieving this aim but may not necessarily progress to a state of flourishing and complete mental health. One early study in this area confirms that the outcome usually corresponds to the intentions of the practitioner but also suggests that the aim of individuals practicing meditation may shift from more health-related to more self-reflective or spiritual topics (Shapiro, 1992). This is certainly what participants in our *mindfulness@work* staff development courses (Malinowski, unpublished) commonly report, where they tend to initially seek a way of dealing with (work-related) stress but find out that their practice brings up more fundamental, sometimes live-changing issues.

In line with Shapiro's three-component model, also classical Buddhist conceptions of practice and development emphasize the importance of intention. Within Tibetan Buddhist traditions this is expressed as part of the training of *view* (which includes motivation and intention), *meditation* and *action* (Khyentse, 1992; Nydahl, 2008), similarly in *Theravada* Buddhism, where the Noble Eightfold Path is condensed into the threefold training of Higher Virtue (communication, action, livelihood), Higher Mind (concentration, mindfulness, effort) and Higher Wisdom (including view and intention) (Harvey, 1990). Both conceptions of a complete way of practicing thus stress the importance of the view and intention in one's practice, but in addition also emphasize the aspect of activity in supporting ones meditation practice and of translating its results into actual socially beneficial activity (see Ricard, Chapter 27, this volume).

In current meditation research the role of intention and even more that of activity have so far been largely neglected, but as definitions of flourishing also include psychosocial functioning one can expect that with the introduction of this new perspective this is going to change.

## The neuroscience of Buddhist meditation

Another perspective on meditation comes from neuroscience where an increasing number of studies are investigating trait and state effects of meditation practice (Cahn & Polich, 2006; Lutz, Slagter, et al., 2008). So far the majority of findings have to be considered preliminary with regards to the question of what the neural effects of meditation practice are and how they come about, because with only very few exceptions only cross-sectional designs, comparing meditators to non-meditators, were employed. Furthermore, a variety of meditation types were used and often not sufficiently specified. This research is nevertheless encouraging and a variety of publications in high-profile journals sparked widespread interest in this new field of research. While the cross-sectional studies cannot answer the question whether (or how) meditation practice *causes* the observed differences between meditators and non-meditators, they provide information where possible effects might be found and thus lay the foundation for more rigorous longitudinal studies.

## Meditation, mindfulness, and mental balance

One of the most detailed and direct attempts to integrate Western psychological and Buddhist perspectives on well-being puts the idea of mental balance at its heart. According to this model comprehensive well-being and flourishing is the result of achieving a balanced mind. In bringing both views together, the authors identified four kinds of mental balance: conative, attentional, cognitive, and affective (Wallace & Shapiro, 2006). These are thought to "encapsulate the major processes involved in training the mind to achieve exceptional levels of health and well-being" (p. 693). Imbalances in these four areas are described in terms of deficits, hyperactivities and dysfunctions. A brief overview of these four mental balances combined with some empirical evidence of their relation to meditation and mindfulness practice provides an indication of their relevance. This model can also serve as a framework to structure existing psychological research on how meditation might promote well-being.

### *Conative balance*

Conation relates to motivation, volition, and intention. Our vision and motivation in life will determine in what kind of activities we engage and underpins meditation practice in important ways. It provides the underlying drive for developing the other three mental balances and will in turn be strengthened when these are developed. Matthieu Ricard (Chapter 27, this volume) eloquently explained the Buddhist perspective on real happiness and its causes, which lie in the cultivation of altruistic love, compassion, inner peace, strength, freedom and in overcoming self-centredness (see also Ekman, Davidson, Ricard, & Wallace, 2005). A conative deficit thus occurs when people have no drive to find happiness or meaning for themselves and others, which may for example express itself in existential indifference, where a particular disinterest in anything that would give meaning to one's life exist. Based on a representative sample it is estimated that approximately 35% of the German population do not see any meaning in life, but at the same time are not concerned with it nor consider it a problem (Schnell, 2010). Conative hyperactivity would express itself as an obsession with certain goals that obscure the ability to experience the present reality, as for instance extreme forms of craving. A dysfunction would be present if ones motivation and energy are directed towards goals that are detrimental to one's own or others' flourishing and well-being.

### *Attentional balance*

Developed and refined attentional abilities as for instance the ability to voluntarily orient and sustain ones attention and to flexibly engage or disengage it, is important for any goal directed activity. It is a crucial aspect for mental balance as a whole, because it is a prerequisite for developing and sustaining cognitive and affective balance. But this should be understood as a reciprocal process, as more emotional and affective balance will in turn also support the development of attentional balance. Attentional imbalances are not limited to attention related disorders such as attention-deficit/hyperactivity disorder but are wide-spread. Many participants in our *mindfulness@work* courses report difficulties to fully focus on one task and are easily distracted by outer events (as for instance the incoming flood of e-mails) or their own thoughts and emotions. An attentional deficit is characterized by the inability to vividly and continuously focus on a chosen object. Attentional hyperactivity would be present when the mind gets easily and excessively attracted, distracted and over-aroused, thus not allowing one to maintain the focus of attention. A dysfunction would be present when one engages and focuses in a way that is not useful to one's own or others' health and well-being. I remember a friend who used to excessively engage in every new video game of his preferred genre to the extent that he had problems keeping on top of his work commitments, and keeping social relationships and his partnership alive.

The link between Buddhist meditation practice and attentional functions has so far received the most attention in psychological and neuroscientific research into meditation (see Lutz, Slagter, et al., 2008 for a review), most likely because the refinement of attention is integral to all forms of Buddhist meditation and also because cognitive psychology and neuroscience provide well-developed theories of attentional functions and an arsenal of tools for investigating them. Several studies suggest that people who regularly engage in meditation and mindfulness practice have improved attentional functions, evidenced for instance by an improved ability to flexibly engage and disengage attention, improved processing speed and the ability to bring automatic responses under voluntary control (Moore & Malinowski, 2009). Such findings are corroborated by evidence of increased activation of the anterior cingulate cortex and the dorsal medial prefrontal cortex in both hemispheres in *vipaśyanā* meditators compared to a control group, suggesting an increased involvement of attentional control processes during meditation (Hölzel, et al., 2007). Another investigation of *vipaśyanā* meditators suggests that the cognitive resources of meditators may be less bound when a stimulus is perceived, with the effect that more resources remain available for processing additional information (Slagter et al., 2007; Slagter, Lutz, Greischar, Nieuwenhuis, & Davidson, 2009). In yet another study *vipaśyanā* meditators exhibited higher oscillating EEG-activity in the gamma frequency range (35–45 Hz), especially over parieto-occipital brain areas, interpreted by the authors as a signature for increased awareness of sensory information (Cahn, Delorme, & Polich, 2010). Finally, one interesting study revealed marked differences in the activation of the brain network typically involved in sustaining attention. During focused meditation expert meditators (Tibetan Buddhism) with an average of 19,000 hours of practice had more activation than age-matched meditation beginners, but experts with an average of 44,000 hours had less activation in this sustained attention network (Brefczynski-Lewis, Lutz, Schaefer, Levinson, & Davidson, 2007). Although due to the cross-sectional nature of the study caution in interpreting the results is required, it suggests that when meditators reach very high levels of expertise (44,000 hours equals 10 years of 12 hours meditation per day) the ability to maintain sustained attention becomes highly automated and does not require any effort anymore.

Thus, there is growing evidence that, indeed, regular meditation practice might improve attentional performance in line with the idea of attentional balance, which also seems to be reflected in related changes in neural function.

## Cognitive balance

Cognitive balance is related to the way we conceptualize our experience. In Buddhist terms it is the ability to experience without imposing our own ideas and assumptions and thus without distortions. A cognitive deficit would be absent-mindedness, where experiences do not fully enter one's conscious awareness. Cognitive hyperactivity would be present when somebody is caught up in their own assumptions, expectations or fantasies while failing to perceive them as such. In extreme forms this hyperactivity could manifest as hallucination or psychosis. A cognitive dysfunction can appear in many ways, whenever we mistake an object (or experience) for something it is not. From a Buddhist perspective the most profound form is to misapprehend the self and outer phenomena as really, independently existent (see Ricard, Chapter 27, this volume).

Research into the link between cognition and meditation/mindfulness is less well developed. Pilot data from our research group indicate that there might be a link between mindfulness and ones thought patterns. Participants who score high on the non-judging subscale of the Five-Facet Mindfulness Questionnaire (Baer, Smith, Hopkins, Krietemeyer, & Toney, 2006) score low on a scale that measures the habit of negative self-thoughts (Habit Index of Negative Thinking, Verplanken, Friborg, Wang, Trafimow, & Woolf, 2007), indicated by a correlation of $r = -0.42$ ($N = 84$, $p < 0.01$). In Buddhist meditators from various traditions their self-reported levels of optimism were correlated to their experienced meditation depth (Piron, 2001) ($r = 0.62$, $N = 59$, $p < 0.001$) suggesting a link between meditation practice and a positive conceptualization of life.

## Affective balance

Affective balance is here defined as the mental freedom from excessive emotional states, strong emotional fluctuations, emotional apathy or inappropriate emotions and would be the natural outcome when the three other balances are achieved. An affective deficit could express itself in emotional coldness and indifference towards others. Emotional hyperactivity would be characterized by extreme emotional states swinging between hope and fear, elation and depression etc. The German term *Schadenfreude* captures one possible emotional dysfunction where somebody would take delight in the problems or pains of somebody else.

The role mindfulness practice can play in improving affective reactivity is evidenced by its effective use in treating depression and anxiety as part of MBSR and mindfulness-based cognitive therapy (Chiesa & Serretti, 2011). Neuroscientific evidence suggests that evoking altruistic states of mind through a loving kindness meditation might change the brain networks involved in empathic responses, showing higher activities during sounds expressing distressing states of others in experienced meditators than in meditation beginners (Lutz, Brefczynski-Lewis, Johnstone, & Davidson, 2008). One experimental approach combined the investigation of cognitive and affective aspects. Compared to a control group, participants in an 8-week MBSR program showed a more pronounced reduction of activity in the medial prefrontal cortex during a task focusing on present-moment experiences relative to a task with self-related attention (Farb et al., 2007), indicating that through mindfulness practice the self across time and the present-moment self may dissociate. Furthermore, MBSR participants showed higher activity in a network lateralized to the right hemisphere, comprising of the right prefrontal cortex and several viscerosomatic areas. A subsequent study qualified the role of this network in mindfulness practice. During induction of sadness the same network was recruited more strongly in MBSR participants than in controls, although self-reported sadness did not differ between groups (Farb et al., 2010). Thus, mindfulness practice might foster the ability to balance affective and sensory neural networks leading to a more detached observation of events and thus reduced vulnerability to negative affect.

In sum, Wallace and Shapiro's model of mental balance provides a useful framework for investigating the processes how meditation practice might improve different aspects of psychological function. It highlights the role these four balances play and thus provides a general roadmap for further research.

## Conclusions

As this short overview showed, Western psychological studies of meditation are still in their infancy. Some encouraging steps have been made and there is growing evidence that clinical and non-clinical secularized mindfulness-based interventions are efficacious. Several neuroscientific studies provide encouraging results that justify thorough and rigorous studies to investigate causal relationships between meditation practice and assumed effects on the neural system. Concerning happiness and well-being the link between flourishing and Buddhist meditation practices appears to be most promising, as the classical deficit oriented approach of various psychological disciplines may not be well equipped for capturing the extraordinary levels of human strengths, virtues and perfection Buddhist meditation practices aim at. Furthermore, Buddhist expertise in mapping out and developing human potential can make a significant, arguably unique, contribution to positive psychology and the question how the good life and flourishing can be achieved. While current psychological models of meditation and mindfulness mechanisms now also include intention (or conation), it is worth noting that the question how meditation practice (or mental balance) improves the active participation in one's social environment, and how this activity supports meditation practice and mental balance has not yet been addressed. Linking research into flourishing and meditation can thus contribute this additional useful perspective.

## References

Baer, R. A., Smith, G. T., Hopkins, J., Krietemeyer, J., & Toney, L. (2006). Using self-report assessment methods to explore facets of mindfulness. *Assessment, 13*, 27–45.

Bishop, S. R., Lau, M. A., Shapiro, S. L., Carlson, L. E., Anderson, N. D., Carmody, J., ... Devins, G. (2004). Mindfulness: A proposed operational definition. *Clinical Psychology: Science and Practice, 11*(3), 230–242.

Bokar, R. (1992). *Meditation: Advice to beginners*. San Francisco, CA: Clear Point Press.

Brefczynski-Lewis, J. A., Lutz, A., Schaefer, H. S., Levinson, D. B., & Davidson, R. J. (2007). Neural correlates of attentional expertise in long-term meditation practitioners. *Proceedings of the National Academy of Sciences of the United States of America, 104*(27), 11483–11488.

Brown, K. W., & Ryan, R. M. (2003). The benefits of being present: Mindfulness and its role in psychological well-being. *Journal of Personality and Social Psychology, 84*(4), 822–848.

Brown, K. W., Ryan, R. M., & Creswell, J. D. (2007). Mindfulness: Theoretical foundations and evidence for its salutary effects. *Psychological Inquiry, 18*(4), 211–237.

Cahn, B. R., Delorme, A., & Polich, J. (2010). Occipital gamma activation during Vipassana meditation. *Cognitive Processing, 11*(1), 39–56.

Cahn, B. R., & Polich, J. (2006). Meditation states and traits: EEG, ERP, and neuroimaging studies. *Psychological Bulletin, 132*(2), 180–211.

Chambers, R., Gullone, E., & Allen, N. B. (2009). Mindful emotion regulation: An integrative review. *Clinical Psychology Review, 29*(6), 560–572.

Chiesa, A., & Malinowski, P. (2011). Mindfulness based interventions: are they all the same? *Journal of Clinical Psychology, 67*(4), 404–424.

Chiesa, A., & Serretti, A. (2011). Mindfulness based cognitive therapy for psychiatric disorders: A systematic review and meta-analysis. *Psychiatry Research, 187*(3), 441–453.

Dorjee, D. (2010). Kinds and dimensions of mindfulness: Why it is important to distinguish them. *Mindfulness, 1*(3), 152–160.

Ekman, P., Davidson, R. J., Ricard, M., & Wallace, B. A. (2005). Buddhist and psychological perspectives on emotions and well-being. *Current Directions in Psychological Science, 14*(2), 59–63.

Farb, N. A., Anderson, A. K., Mayberg, H., Bean, J., McKeon, D., & Segal, Z. V. (2010). Minding one's emotions: Mindfulness training alters the neural expression of sadness. *Emotion, 10*(1), 25–33.

Farb, N. A., Segal, Z. V., Mayberg, H., Bean, J., McKeon, D., Fatima, Z., & Anderson, A. K. (2007). Attending to the present: Mindfulness meditation reveals distinct neural modes of self-reference. *Social Cognitive and Affective Neuroscience, 2*(4), 313–322.

Fredrickson, B. L. (2001). The role of positive emotions in positive psychology. The broaden-and-build theory of positive emotions. *American Psychologist, 56*(3), 218–226.

Fredrickson, B. L. (2004). The broaden-and-build theory of positive emotions. *Philosophical Transactions of the Royal Society B: Biological Sciences, 359*(1449), 1367–1378.

Fredrickson, B. L. (2009). *Positivity: Groundbreaking research reveals how to embrace the hidden strength of positive emotions, overcome negativity, and thrive*. New York, NY: Crown.

Fredrickson, B. L., Cohn, M. A., Coffey, K. A., Pek, J., & Finkel, S. M. (2008). Open hearts build lives: Positive emotions, induced through loving-kindness meditation, build consequential personal resources. *Journal of Personality and Social Psychology, 95*(5), 1045–1062.

Fredrickson, B. L., & Joiner, T. (2002). Positive emotions trigger upward spirals toward emotional well-being. *Psychological Science, 13*(2), 172–175.

Gampopa (1998). *The Jewel Ornament of Liberation: The wish-fulfilling gem of the noble teachings* (K. R. Khenpo Könchog Gyaltsen, Trans.). Ithaca, NY: Snow Lion Publications.

Garland, E. L., Fredrickson, B., Kring, A. M., Johnson, D. P., Meyer, P. S., & Penn, D. L. (2010). Upward spirals of positive emotions counter downward spirals of negativity: Insights from the broaden-and-build theory and affective neuroscience on the treatment of emotion dysfunctions and deficits in psychopathology. *Clinical Psychology Review, 30*, 849–864.

Grossman, P., Niemann, L., Schmidt, S., & Walach, H. (2004). Mindfulness-based stress reduction and health benefits. A meta-analysis. *Journal of Psychosomatic Research, 57*, 35–43.

Harvey, P. (1990). *An introduction to Buddhism: Teaching, history and practices*. Cambridge, MA: Cambridge University Press.

Hölzel, B. K., Ott, U., Hempel, H., Hackl, A., Wolf, K., Stark, R., & Vaitl, D. (2007). Differential engagement of anterior cingulate and adjacent medial frontal cortex in adept meditators and non-meditators. *Neuroscience Letters, 421*(1), 16–21.

Huppert, F. A. (2008). *Foresight mental capital and wellbeing project: Making the most of ourselves in the 21st century: State-of-Science Review: SR-X2. Psychological wellbeing: Evidence regarding its causes and consequences.* London, UK: The Government Office for Science.

Huppert, F. A., & So, T. T. C. (2009). *What percentage of people in Europe are flourishing and what characterises them?* Paper presented at the OECD/ISQOLS Meeting "Measuring subjective well-being: an opportunity for NSOs?".

Kabat-Zinn, J. (1982). An outpatient program in behavioral medicine for chronic pain patients based on the practice of mindfulness meditation: Theoretical considerations and preliminary results. *General Hospital Psychiatry*, 4, 33–47.

Kabat-Zinn, J. (1990). *Full catastrophe living: Using the wisdom of your body and mind to face stress, pain and illness.* New York, NY: Bantam Doubleday Dell Publishing.

Kabat-Zinn, J. (2003). Mindfulness-based interventions in context: Past, present, and future. *Clinical Psychology: Science and Practice*, 10(2), 144–156.

Kamalaśīla (1997). *Bhāvanākrama* (P. Sharma, Trans.). New Delhi, India: Aditya Prakashan.

Kang, C., & Whittingham, K. (2010). Mindfulness: A dialogue between Buddhism and clinical psychology. *Mindfulness*, 1(3), 161–173.

Keyes, C. L. M. (2002). The mental health continuum: From languishing to flourishing in life. *Journal of Health and Social Behavior*, 43(2), 207–222.

Keyes, C. L. M. (2003). Complete mental health: An agenda for the 21st century. In C. L. Keyes & J. Haidt (Eds.), *Flourishing: Positive psychology and the life well-lived* (pp. 293–312). Washington, DC: American Psychological Association.

Keyes, C. L. M. (2005). Mental illness and/or mental health? Investigating axioms of the complete state model of health. *Journal of Consulting and Clinical Psychology*, 73(3), 539–548.

Keyes, C. L. M. (2007). Promoting and protecting mental health as flourishing: A complementary strategy for improving national mental health. *American Psychologist*, 62(2), 95–108.

Khyentse, D. R. (1992). *Heart treasure of the enlightened ones.* Boston, MA: Shambala Publications.

Lutz, A., Brefczynski-Lewis, J., Johnstone, T., & Davidson, R. J. (2008). Regulation of the neural circuitry of emotion by compassion meditation: Effects of meditative expertise. *PLoS ONE*, 3(3), e1897.

Lutz, A., Slagter, H. A., Dunne, J. D., & Davidson, R. J. (2008). Attention regulation and monitoring in meditation. *Trends in Cognitive Sciences*, 12(4), 163–169.

Maitreya/Asanga (1985). *The changeless nature: Mahayana uttara tantra sastra* (K. Holmes & K. Holmes, Trans.). Eskdalemuir, UK: Karma Kagyu Trust.

Malinowski, P. (2008). Mindfulness as psychological dimension: Concepts and applications. *Irish Journal of Psychology*, 29(1), 155–166.

Malinowski, P. (2010). *Flourishing—Welches Glück hätten Sie gern?: Positive Eigenschaften kultivieren und Schwierigkeiten meistern.* München, Germany: Random House/Irisiana.

Malinowski, P. (unpublished). *Mindfulness @ work: A staff-development programme.*

Moore, A., & Malinowski, P. (2009). Meditation, mindfulness and cognitive flexibility. *Consciousness and Cognition*, 18(1), 176–186.

Nydahl, O. (2004). *The great seal—Limitless space & joy: The Mahamudra view of Diamond Way Buddhism.* San Francisco, CA: Fire Wheel Publishing.

Nydahl, O. (2008). *The way things are: A living approach to Buddhism.* US: O-Books.

Piron, H. (2001). The Meditation Depth Index (MEDI) and the Meditation Depth Questionnaire (MEDEQ). *Journal for Meditation and Meditation Research*, 1, 69–92.

Rapgay, L., & Bystrisky, A. (2009). Classical mindfulness: an introduction to its theory and practice for clinical application. *Annals of the New York Academy of Sciences*, 1172, 148–162.

Ricard, M. (2006). *Happiness: A guide to developing life's most important skill.* London, UK: Little, Brown and Co.

Schnell, T. (2010). Existential indifference: Another quality of meaning in life. *Humanistic Psychology, 50*(3), 351–373.

Schonert-Reichl, K. A., & Stewart Lawlor, M. (2010). The effects of a mindfulness-based education program on pre- and early adolescents' well-being and social and emotional competence. *Mindfulness, 1*(3), 137–151.

Shamar, R. (2009). *The path to awakening: A commentary on Ja Chekawa Yeshé Dorjé's "seven points of mind training."* New Delhi, India: Motilal Banarsidass Publishers.

Shapiro, D. H. (1992). A preliminary study of long term meditators: Goals, effects, religious orientation, cognitions. *Journal of Transpersonal Psychology, 24*(1), 23–39.

Shapiro, S. L., Carlson, L. E., Astin, J. A., & Freedman, B. (2006). Mechanisms of mindfulness. *Journal of Clinical Psychology, 62*(3), 373–386.

Slagter, H. A., Lutz, A., Greischar, L. L., Francis, A. D., Nieuwenhuis, S., Davis, J. M., & Davidson, R. J. (2007). Mental training affects distribution of limited brain resources. *PLoS Biology, 5*(6), e138.

Slagter, H. A., Lutz, A., Greischar, L. L., Nieuwenhuis, S., & Davidson, R. J. (2009). Theta phase synchrony and conscious target perception: Impact of intensive mental training. *Journal of Cognitive Neuroscience, 21*(8), 1536–1549.

Verplanken, B., Friborg, O., Wang, C. E., Trafimow, D., & Woolf, K. (2007). Mental habits: Metacognitive reflection on negative self-thinking. *Journal of Personality and Social Psychology, 92*(3), 526–541.

Walach, H., Nord, E., Zier, C., Dietz-Waschkowski, B., Kersig, S., & Schüpbach, H. (2007). Mindfulness-based stress reduction as a method for personnel development: A pilot evaluation. *International Journal of Stress Management, 14*(2), 188–198.

Wallace, B. A. (1999). The Buddhist tradition of samatha: Methods for refining and examining consciousness. *Journal of Consciousness Studies, 6*(2–3), 175–187.

Wallace, B. A., & Hodel, B. (2008). *Embracing mind: The common ground of science and spirituality.* Boston, MA: Shambala Publications.

Wallace, B. A., & Shapiro, S. (2006). Mental balance and well-being: Building bridges between Buddhism and Western Psychology. *American Psychologist, 61*(7), 690–701.

Wangchug Dorje, K. (2009). *Mahamudra: Ocean of true meaning.* Münster, Germany: Edition Octopus.

# CHAPTER 31

# HEAVEN ON EARTH: BENEFICIAL EFFECTS OF SANCTIFICATION FOR INDIVIDUAL AND INTERPERSONAL WELL-BEING

ANNETTE MAHONEY, KENNETH I. PARGAMENT, AND KRYSTAL M. HERNANDEZ

Bowling Green State University, USA

SCIENTIFIC evidence that religion and spirituality facilitates well-being is proliferating and becoming more sophisticated (Paloutzian & Park, 2005; Pargament, Exline, & Jones, in press; Pargament, Mahoney, & Shafranske, in press). Researchers have gone beyond predicting well-being with a few general questions about religiousness, such as type of religious affiliation or attendance at services. Of particular interest to positive psychology, scientists have begun to tie constructs that have been rooted historically in theological systems of meaning and promoted by diverse faith communities, such as virtues, to personal and relational happiness. This handbook, for example, highlights recent scientific evidence on the benefits of forgiveness, compassionate love, and gratitude. Yet laudable virtues may be tied only loosely, or not at all, to religion or spirituality. For example, virtuous conduct may be readily evident in the lives of individuals who consider themselves "neither religious nor spiritual." This raises the question as to whether we can identify constructs that are fundamentally spiritual in substance and that function to promote individual and interpersonal well-being. In this chapter, we identify and discuss one such construct, sanctification, which refers to perceiving an aspect of life as having divine significance and character.

We start with our approach to defining spirituality and sanctification. We then discuss ways people may come to view an aspect of life as sanctified. Next we highlight evidence that sanctification enhances and is, in turn, enhanced by positive psychosocial functioning. This evidence comes from studies on the sanctification of strivings, marriage, marital and non-marital sexuality, parenting, work, the body, and nature. We close by discussing the paradoxical darker side of sanctification, which can be seen when people are challenged to radically alter their perceptions about a sacred aspect of life.

## SANCTIFICATION: CONCEPTUALIZATION AND OPERATIONALIZATION

The construct of sanctification grows out of our definition of spirituality as "the search for the sacred" (Pargament, 2007; Pargament & Mahoney, 2009). "The search" component refers to three dynamic and recursive stages of discovering, maintaining, and transforming one's experience of the sacred across the life span. Discovery refers to a proactive process of developing an understanding of what the sacred is and how the sacred operates. Maintenance involves seeking ways to conserve one's understanding and experience of the sacred during the ups and downs of daily life. Transformation refers to fundamentally altering one's experience of the sacred, typically prompted by life events that deeply challenge one's basic assumptions about the sacred. In our view, "the sacred" centrally involves perceptions of the divine, God or transcendent reality, but may extend to any aspect of life that takes on divine character and significance by virtue of its association with divinity (Mahoney, Pargament, & DeMaris, 2009; Pargament & Mahoney, 2005). Thus, as seen in Fig. 31.1, "the sacred" consists of a core that involves individuals' perceptions of the divine, God or transcendent reality and a ring that holds different constellations of sacred objects across different individuals.

### Defining sanctification

Considerable research has addressed how people construe and relate to the core of the sacred (Pargmant, 2007). For example, some people speak of having a personal relationship with an external deity who has well-delineated features. Other people speak of experiencing profound connections to a spark of divinity within the self or to depersonalized supernatural forces that permeate life. People also travel along diverse cognitive and behavioral pathways—from the solitary exploration to engagement in religious social networks—to foster their felt connections to the divine, within and outside the self. Further, people often turn to the divine to cope in times of trouble (Pargament, 1997).

In our view, however, the sacred can extend beyond an understanding of the divine to virtually any aspect of seemingly mundane life. As Durkheim (1915) wrote: "By sacred things one must not understand simply those personal beings which are called gods or spirits; a rock, a tree, a pebble, a piece of wood, a house, in a word anything can be sacred" (p. 52). We use the term "sanctification" to refer to the process by which people appraise an aspect of life as having divine[1] character and significance (Pargament & Mahoney, 2005). It is important

---

[1] In our initial study on sanctification of marriage, we defined sanctification as perceiving as aspect of life as having *spiritual* character and significance, but we subsequently replaced the word "spiritual" with "divine." We have initiated a distinct line of research on perceiving as aspect of life as possessing overtly negative spiritual qualities (e.g., unholy, demonic, or cursed).

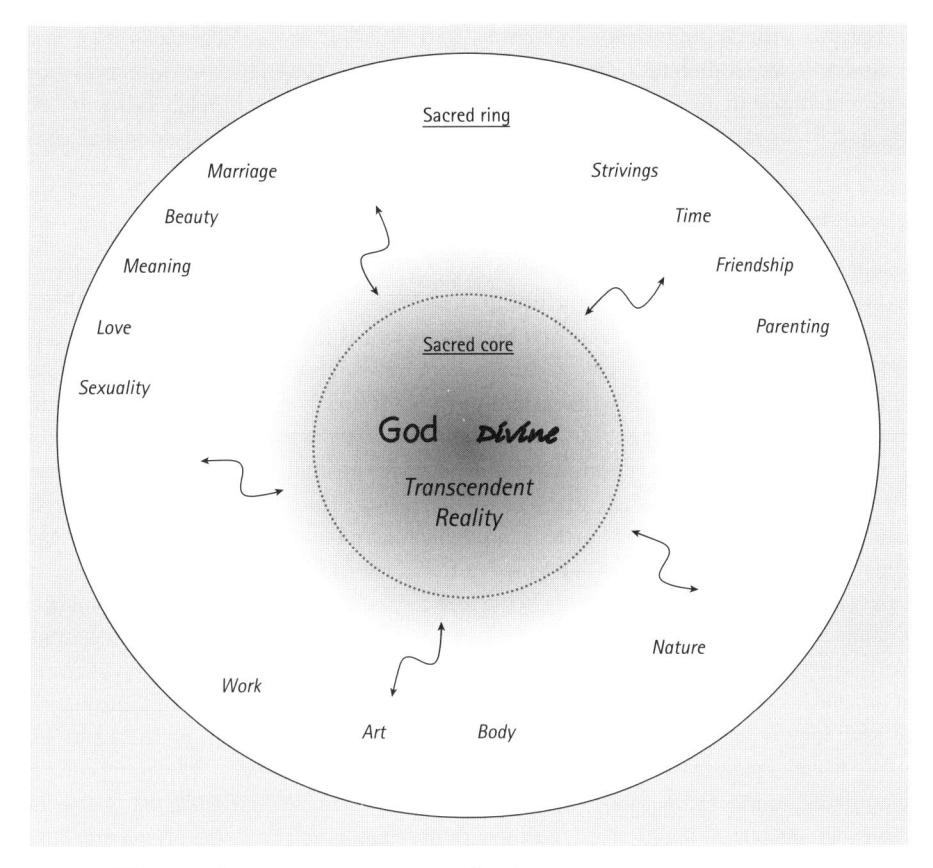

FIG. 31.1 The sacred encompasses a core and a ring.

to note that our concept of "sanctification" differs from theological meanings that vary across religious traditions. For example, from a Christian vantage point, sanctification is an inherently mysterious process through which God transforms profane objects into sacred entities. In contrast, our definition of sanctification is "psychospiritual," not theological, in nature. It is spiritual because of its point of reference, the sacred. It is psychological because it: (1) focuses on human perceptions of the sacred, and (2) is studied with social scientific methods.

## Theistic sanctification

To operationalize sanctification for scientific research, we differentiate between theistic and non-theistic forms of sanctification. Theistic sanctification is defined as appraising an aspect of life as a manifestation of one's images, beliefs, or experiences of God. This is illustrated by the five items that 178 couples drawn from mid-sized community in the Midwest who were pregnant with their first child most often said applied to their marriage to some degree[2]:

[2] Lichter and Carmalt (2009) slightly modified five items from a 14-item Manifestation of God in Marriage subscale from Mahoney et al. (1999) to assess the sanctification of marriage (personal communication,

"God played a role in how I ended up being married to my spouse" (86% of wives; 79% of husbands); "I see God's handiwork in my marriage" (84%, 74%); "I sense God's presence in my relationship with my spouse" (81%, 71%), "My marriage is a reflection of God's will" (80%; 72%), and "In mysterious ways, God touches my marriage" (79%; 74%; Mahoney et al., 2009).

## Non-theistic sanctification

Non-theistic sanctification is defined as perceiving an aspect of life as having sacred qualities often associated with divinity, including attributes of transcendence, ultimate value and purpose, and boundlessness. In our first two efforts to assess sacred qualities, we asked participants to rate pairs of opposing adjectives (e.g., holy–unholy, blessed–cursed, spiritual–secular) on a seven-point scale with endpoints of "very closely describes" and a midpoint of "neutral" (Mahoney et al., 1999; Murray-Swank, Mahoney, & Pargament, 2006). We found that participants very rarely reported that the negative spiritual qualities "slightly," "closely," or "very closely" described their marriage or parenting. Thus, we subsequently shifted to asking participants to rate how much each positive sacred quality applied to a given aspect of life ("not at all" to "very much"), and we initiated another line of research on perceiving stressful life events, such as divorce, as being imbued with demonic qualities or influence by the devil (e.g., Krumrei, Mahoney, & Pargament, 2011). In addition, in our most recent non-theistic sanctification of marriage scale, we used complete statements to tap into cognitions that couples who were pregnant had about the non-theistic sanctification of their marriage (see Mahoney et al., 2009); the following five items were most often endorsed to some degree: "My marriage is sacred to me" (93% of wives; 90% of husbands); "My marriage seems like a miracle to me" (88%, 73%), "My marriage connects my spouse and me to something greater than ourselves" (84%, 78%), "Being with my spouse feels like a deeply spiritual experience" (74%; 63%), and "This marriage is part of a larger spiritual plan" (75%; 70%).

While sanctification can occur theistically and/or non-theistically, neither perception appears to be unusual or outdated, at least in the USA. The prevalence rates just cited involved couples drawn from a Midwestern community who in 2005 were, on average, 28 years old, and the wives' frequency of religious attendance was similar to a nationally representative sample of married, first-time pregnant couples (Mahoney et al., 2009). Further, in a 2006 survey of married Americans, the average rating of five sanctification of marriage items fell at 2.8 on a scale with "4" equal to "strongly agree" and "1" equal to "strongly disagree" (Litcher & Carmalt, 2009). Such perceptions also apply to non-martial relationships as seen in 2006 national survey where 55% of US adults involved in a steady dating relationship and cohabiting "strongly agreed" that "God is at the center of my relationship" (Henderson, Ellison, & Glenn, 2010). In another national survey, most Americans said they often or very often saw God's presence in life (75%), saw evidence of God in nature in creation (78%), sensed that their spirit was part of God's spirit (68%), and sensed God's presence moving in their relationships with others (56%; Pargament, 2007, p. 38). Other community-based studies on sanctification likewise indicate that people often view various

July 18, 2009). Although these authors refer to the construct as "religious centrality, i.e., the importance of religion to the marital relationship" (p. 174), we use "sanctification of marriage" to refer their findings with Lichter's agreement. A chart of various theistic sanctification items used across studies can be found at http://www.bgsu.edu/departments/psych/page31068.html, along with additional suggestions for how to assess sanctification in different domains.

aspects of life through a sacred lens. A complete list of samples and items used to assess sanctification can be found at http://www.bgsu.edu/departments/psych/spirituality/

## Discovery: Coming to See an Aspect of Life Through a Sacred Lens

People vary in which aspects of life they view as having a divine dimension. For instance, in a study on the sanctification of life strivings, diverse endeavors in life were perceived as sacred to some degree, including family relationships (e.g., working at one's marriage), self-development (e.g., learning), work and money (e.g., being successful at work), physical health (e.g., exercising), and existential concerns (e.g., seeking inner peace; Mahoney, Pargament, et al., 2005). This sample wasn't religiously atypical for the US; it consisted of adults from a Midwestern community who, as a group, showed the same range and frequency of attending religious services as Americans as a group. What might account for differences in spiritual acuity? To date, little research has focused on factors that contribute to coming to see various objects as falling within the ring of the sacred (see Fig. 31.1). Nevertheless, theological literature highlights two pathways that people often follow to discover the sacred in daily life. First, people may stumble unexpectedly upon experiences that lead them to perceive sacred phenomena as forces which have, in essence, come to them (Hardy, 1979). They may experience the invisible made visible, a light shed on a dark mystery, a revelation of the divine. Similarly, Eliade (1957/1959) speaks of the sacred revealing itself to people through a particular kind of experience, a "hierophany," in which the sacred dimension "erupts" into the world. Such spiritual awakenings could happen outside the context of organized religion and be triggered by significant or unexpected life events that could be attributed to divine forces. Likely examples include falling in love unexpectedly, giving birth or adopting a child, or stumbling upon a new career path. Second, people may perceive sacred matters as something they themselves and their social networks, especially religious communities, have had a hand in finding and nurturing. In this vein, Eliade (1957/1959) goes on to note that "by reactualizing sacred history, by imitating divine behavior, man puts and keeps himself close to the gods – that is, in the real and the significant" (p. 202). Some may wonder if the origin of what is sacred lies in God or the human mind, individually or collectively. This ultimate theological question falls beyond the grasp of science. We cannot determine whether God "makes sacred" or people do. We can, however, draw on scientific theories and methods to identify measurable factors that facilitate people's discovery of what is sacred, both "encountered" and "constructed" (Paden, 1992).

Presumably, a variety of behavioral, emotional, and social experiences help to impart divine meaning and significance to particular aspects of life. For example, in Christian and Jewish wedding rituals, the couple's union is sanctified by verbal (e.g., vows, prayers) and non-verbal behaviors (e.g., exchange blessed rings) in a social context (e.g., clergy, family, friends) that can elicit strong emotions (e.g., joy, trepidation). Thus, while viewing an aspect of life through a sacred lens may be a cognitive process, certain religious or spiritual experiences may elicit and strengthen such beliefs. In one qualitative study, religious couples reported that the wedding ceremony itself, particularly the vows, intensified the spouses' sense that God was an active third party in their marriage (Lambert & Dollahite, 2008).

In addition, an experimental study found that the assigned behavioral task to pray for a romantic partner's well-being caused increases over time in the perception that the relationship was sanctified (Fincham, Lambert, & Beach, 2010). We have also identified spiritual emotions and behaviors centered on marriage as two factors that reciprocally shape the cognitive appraisal of marriage as sacred, beyond the influence of religious attendance, prayer, or Biblical conservatism (Mahoney et al., 2009). Of course, the overall salience of religion or spirituality in one's life may feed into sanctification. In this vein, spouses who generally rate themselves as more "religious" or "spiritual," and engage in more private (e.g., prayer) and public (e.g., religious attendance) religious activities are more likely to view their marriage as sanctified (DeMaris, Mahoney, & Pargament, 2010; Litcher & Carmalt, 2008; Mahoney et al., 1999, 2009). Studies of other domains likewise show that higher general religiousness and spirituality are modestly correlated with higher sanctification ratings (e.g., Mahoney, Carels, et al., 2005, Mahoney, Pargament, et al., 2005; Walker, Jones, Wuensch, Aziz, & Cope, 2008).

# Maintenance: Sustaining Reciprocity Between a Sacred Aspect of Life and Psychosocial Benefits

Once individuals develop the belief that an aspect of life is connected to God or imbued with sacred qualities, they are likely to strive to maintain its sacred status. Such efforts may include investing disproportional time and energy in the domain, and acting to preserve and protect the domain in coping with the ups and downs of daily life. In turn, people are likely to report better functioning in that domain and view this area of life as a source of personal strength and self-efficacy. Positive psychosocial functioning in a domain may, in turn, reinforce the belief that a given aspect of life is part of the sacred realm. We now summarize evidence that sanctification is associated with psychosocial benefits. Due to space constraints, we highlight selective findings from the 26 studies on sanctification we located.

## Sanctification of strivings

Within a sample of Midwestern adults whose general religiousness was similar to other Americans, greater sanctification of personal strivings was linked to greater investment of psychological and pragmatic resources that could sustain the pursuit of strivings (Mahoney, Pargament, et al., 2005). This included greater perceived importance of, commitment to, longevity of, social support for, confidence about, and internal locus of control attached to strivings. People also devoted more time and energy to their most versus least sanctified strivings based on two phone calls assessing their behaviors in the past 24 hours. Higher sanctification was also tied to greater joy and meaning derived from pursuit of sacred strivings. Yet sanctification was not linked to greater life satisfaction, lower depression, and better physical health. The overall pattern of findings was consistent with a core message found in many world religions, namely that people should move beyond goals that are personally gratifying to pursue goals that may involve sacrifice and effort. Therefore, individuals may persist in and find fulfillment in strivings they believe have transcendent purposes, even if this sometimes exposes them to stress that triggers sadness, compromises physical health, and fosters difficult life circumstances. At other times, such costs may be offset by the self-enhancing benefits tied to strivings that are believed to be sacred. Paradoxically, then, religion's answer to the question of what makes life goals meaningful, valuable, and purposeful may not necessarily guarantee personal satisfaction and well-being.

## Sanctification of marriage and couples' relationships

Three qualitative studies suggest that perceptions of a romantic union as sacred can enhance the quality of that relationship. For example, most highly religious couples in long-term marriages reported that God played an influential and constructive role in their marriage, either directly or indirectly via other people's actions (Goodman & Dollahite, 2006). Further, most couples from a southern US state who obtained a covenant marriage license indicated their non-egalitarian gender roles in marriage reflected God's intentions, and the sacred structure of their traditional roles facilitated communication and follow-through on their respective marital responsibilities (Baker, Sanchez, Nock, & Wright, 2009). Similarly, nearly all same-sex couples from the mid-South region of the US saw their union as being imbued with divine significance and indicated this enhanced their communication dynamics and long-term commitment (Rostosky, Riggle, Brodnicki, & Olson 2008).

Four rigorous quantitative studies also help substantiate that sanctification is tied to relational benefits for couples. In a national survey, higher sanctification of marriage by both spouses, and especially husband–wife similarity in sanctification, predicted greater marital satisfaction and commitment, after controlling for demographic variables, general religiousness of spouses, and unmeasured characteristics of the couples' relationship (Lichter & Carmalt, 2009). Similar findings emerged using a community sample of Midwestern couples where higher sanctification by one or both spouses were associated with less marital conflict and dysfunctional communication strategies in (Mahoney et al., 1999). In addition, in a community sample of married Midwestern couples pregnant with their first child, sanctification of marriage neutralized the tendency for perceived unfairness between spouses to elicit marital dissatisfaction, marital conflict or personal anxiety (DeMaris et al., 2010). This buffering of the negative effects of perceived inequity on relational and personal adjustment was especially strong for wives who felt they were receiving more benefits from husbands than they were giving to husbands. Fourth, in a national sample of adults in a cohabiting or steady dating relationship, greater belief that God was at the center of the relationship was tied to greater relationship satisfaction (Henderson et al., 2010); this link persisted after controlling for acts of kindness, consideration, and criticism between partners and demographic characteristics. Overall, sanctification of marriage has been tied to greater relational happiness and positive relationship processes for couples involved, on average, in organized religion about as much as other American couples.

## Sanctification of marital and non-marital sexuality

Consistent with long-standing religious prohibitions against adultery, two qualitative studies with highly religious couples suggest that greater sanctification of marriage may strengthen commitment to sexual fidelity. For instance, couples reported that certain religious beliefs and practices facilitated viewing their marriage as sacred and connected to God's purposes which improved marital quality; higher marital quality, in turn, promoted sexual fidelity (Dollahite & Lambert, 2007). A related study with this sample found that couples believed they were more committed to each other because they had engaged in past (e.g., exchanging vows in religious wedding ceremony) and ongoing spiritual experiences (e.g., worship services) that reminded them of the sanctity of their union (Lambert & Dollahite, 2008). These observations from qualitative interviews dovetail with several national surveys where higher religious attendance predicted lower levels of infidelity (Mahoney, 2010). Further, using a rigorous experimental design with undergraduates, Fincham et al. (2010) found that praying for romantic partner's well-being increased perceptions of their intimate relationship as sacred. Further, these increases in the sanctification of the relationship accounted for the causal links that were found between praying for their partner and decreased sexual infidelity, in thought or action, over time. These initial studies suggest that perceiving marriage or an intimate relationship is sacred can discourage sexual infidelity.

Remarkably, almost no controlled research exists on whether spirituality may enhance marital sexuality, not merely suppress extramarital affairs (Hernandez, Mahoney, & Pargament, 2011). Three recent studies on the sanctification of marital sexuality are beginning to fill gaps in understanding the intersection of spirituality, sex, and marriage. In a Midwestern community sample of newlyweds, greater sanctification of marital sexuality related strongly to greater sexual satisfaction, sexual intimacy, marital satisfaction, and spiritual intimacy after controlling for demographic variables, frequency of religious attendance and prayer, and Biblical conservatism (Hernandez et al., 2011). Even more striking, greater sanctification of sexuality predicted more frequent sexual intercourse, and greater sexual and marital satisfaction 1 year later after accounting for initial levels of marital satisfaction (Hernandez & Mahoney, 2009). In an additional study, greater sanctification of marital sexuality has been tied to greater sexual satisfaction for married individuals, over and above the role of personality traits and feelings of shame, guilt or pride about sex (Murray-Swank & Brelsford, 2009). Further, manifestation of God in marital sexuality is tied to lower sexual dysfunction, especially for spouses who endorse conservative views of the Bible.

The salutary outcomes associated with sacred sex for married couples may also extend to undergraduates involved in premarital relationships that they perceive as loving (Murray-Swank, Pargament, & Mahoney 2005). Specifically, undergraduates at a state university in the Midwest who more often ascribed sacred qualities to sex with their partner reported they had more satisfying and positive feelings about their sexual relationship. Unexpectedly, undergraduates (with or without a current romantic partner) who imbued the act of sexual intercourse in a loving relationship with greater sacred qualities reported a greater likelihood of ever having sexual intercourse, more lifetime partners, more frequent intercourse in the past month, and a varied history of sexual experiences. These results stand in contrast to national surveys linking higher religious attendance to lower levels of premarital sexual activities (Murray-Swank et al., 2005). The findings indicate that while some markers of spirituality, such as religious attendance, may inhibit sexual activity, imbuing sexuality with sacred meaning may enhance a sense of sexual desire and fulfillment.

## Sanctification of parenting

Descriptive accounts indicate that many new parents imbue parenthood with spiritual significance and purpose (Mahoney et al., 2009). Yet, controversy exists within and across religious subcultures about the emphasis parents should place on fostering children's obedience versus autonomy (for review, see Mahoney, 2010). Likewise, debate exists within religious circles about the blend of parenting techniques that should be used to socialize children, with some subcultures advocating spanking. Thus, it is perhaps not surprising that in one initial small scale study of mothers from a Midwestern community, higher sanctification of parenting translated into different patterns of parenting practices toward young children by mothers, depending on their degree of Biblical conservatism (Murray-Swank, Mahoney, & Pargament, 2006). For mothers who endorsed more literal interpretations of the Bible, higher sanctification was tied to more spanking and positive interactions with their children. Such findings are consistent with national surveys that indicate parents with a conservative Christian orientation tended both to spank more and be more affectionate with young children (Mahoney, 2010). For mothers with more liberal views of the Bible, higher sanctification was tied to less spanking and did not alter relatively high levels of positive interactions with their children. For all mothers, higher sanctification of parenting related to less verbal hostility and more self-reported consistency in parenting. In another small-scale study of married Midwestern couples (Volling, Mahoney, & Rauer, 2009), higher sanctification of parenting related to greater use of positive parenting strategies by mothers and fathers (e.g., praise, induction) to elicit young children's moral conduct. Also, positive parenting techniques were especially likely to predict children's conscience development when fathers viewed parenting as connected to God. This implies that parents who view parenting as a sacred mission may be more motivated to use positive parenting strategies to instill in their children a sense of personal responsibility for their actions. Finally, in a sample of parents from a low-income, urban setting, sanctification of parenting related to greater investment in parenting, but not parenting satisfaction or efficacy, after controlling for demographics and child problems (Dumas & Nissley-Tsiopinis, 2006). Parents who believed parenting was a sacred task were also more likely to report spiritual struggles, such as feeling punished or abandoned by God when faced with parenting problems, and such spiritual struggles predicted more parental disengagement. These interesting results hint at the possible risks of sanctification when situations arise that conflict with expectations that people should not experience failure in a more sacred aspect of life (see more later in this chapter).

## Sanctification of work

For centuries, the word "calling" has been understood in Western religious contexts as being "'called' by God to do morally and socially significant work (Steger, Pickering, Shin & Dik, 2010). Increasingly, however, the term "calling' is losing its spiritual connotation in scientific circles and is used simply to refer to deriving a sense of personal fulfillment and meaning from work (Steger et al., 2010). Yet studies that have directly assessed whether people view work as a spiritual endeavor highlight the possible benefits of such perceptions. For example, Walker et al. (2008) found that greater sanctification of work by full-time employees holding a variety of jobs correlated with greater job satisfaction, higher organizational commitment, and lower intention to leave the job after controlling for demographics and global religiousness. Carroll (in press) replicated these findings using a large sample of male and female educators working in religiously affiliated middle and secondary schools. Further, in a sample of 200 working mothers with a post-college degree who were recruited from Christian organizations, greater sanctification of work related to greater satisfaction with work, subjective well-being and positive mood, and less internal conflict about balancing work and parenting roles, net of demographic factors and general levels of religiousness. Such findings echo those from a qualitative study on the sanctification of one's career among evangelical Christian, female professors and mothers; those who saw their career as a spiritual enterprise and part of a greater plan reported less guilt and less tension about juggling the multiple roles of wife, mother, and professional because both their paid and unpaid work roles were imbued with sacred purposes (Oates, Hall, & Anderson, 2005). Hopefully, more research will be done to reveal the benefits and drawbacks of having work that men and women perform in and out of the home infused with spiritual significance (Hernandez & Mahoney, in press).

## Sanctification of the material world: the body and nature

Broadly speaking, conflicting theological views exist as to whether the realm of the body and earth has equal spiritual status with the realm of spirit and heaven. For instance, Christians have hotly debated whether people's physical bodies should be eschewed as a source of sin or celebrated as a conduit of the Holy Spirit (Mahoney, Carels, et al., 2005). Theological debates have also persisted about the intersection of spirituality and nature (Tarakeshwar, Swank, Pargament, & Mahoney, 2001). Three published studies shed initial light on the psychosocial implications of imbuing the material world with divine significance.

Regarding the physical body, greater sanctification of one's body by college students at a Midwestern state university related to more health-protective behaviors (eat sensibly, get enough sleep, wear a seat belt, greater satisfaction with one's body) and disapproval of illicit drug use, even after controlling for demographics and general religiousness (Mahoney, Carels, et al., 2005). In elderly individuals from the Midwest, greater sanctification of the body related to greater body satisfaction for men, but not women, after taking into account the centrality of religion in one's life (Boyatzis & Homan, 2009). Yet, in both studies, significant ties between many other health-related factors and sanctification disappeared after controlling for overall general religiousness (e.g., religious attendance). This suggests that certain religious beliefs centered on the body may attenuate or intensify the impact of sanctification of the body on health outcomes due to differing perceptions of God's mandates about the care of one's physical body. With regard to nature, a national survey of members, elders, and clergy affiliated with the Presbyterian Church found that a stronger belief in the sanctification of nature was associated with greater pro-environmental beliefs and willingness to invest personal funds in the environment (Tarakeshwar et al., 2001). These results are consistent with theological teachings that nature itself is a transcendent and holy object, and merits reverence and care because it is a creation of God. Conversely, greater Biblical conservatism was associated with lower care for the environment, a finding consistent with the theological stance that humans have dominion over the earth and securing a place in heaven takes precedence over caring for the environment. These contrasting findings again suggest that viewing the material world as sacred may have different psychosocial implications based on varying spiritual ideals that people hold about how humans should relate to nature, including various beliefs about God's will.

# Transformation: Dealing with Fundamental Threats to a Sacred Aspect of Life

It is important to recognize that perceiving an aspect of life as sacred can carry potential psychosocial risks, not merely benefits. This paradoxical side of sanctification emerges when negative life events challenge people to relinquish a sacred object. In an initial study on this topic, adults from a Midwestern region indicated the extent to which a traumatic event within the past 2 years (e.g., serious illness, accident, natural disaster, divorce) led to a perceived loss (i.e., sacred loss) or violation (i.e., desecration) of a sanctified aspect of life (Pargament, Magyar, Benore, & Mahoney, 2007). Higher sacred loss and desecration both related to more intrusive, distressing thoughts about the event. In addition, sacred loss was related to greater depression whereas desecration tied to greater anger. Thus, people seem to experience more unhappiness when a sacred object is harmed. Yet, the more that a traumatic event was experienced as a sacred loss, the more people also reported personal and spiritual growth due to the trauma. This implies that letting go of a sacred object may paradoxically spur the discovery of new sacred objects as people rework their constellation of sanctified objects and redefine the strivings that they hold sacred. On the other hand, if someone or something is perceived as intentionally injuring a sacred object, these perceptions seem to elicit added anger toward the source of the threat. Along these lines, when Christians view Jews (Pargament, McConnell, Mahoney, & Silberman, 2007) or Muslims (Raiya, Pargament, Mahoney & Trevino, 2008) as desecrating their faith tradition, they are more likely to report anti-Semitic or anti-Muslim attitudes, respectively. Further, recent research indicates that perceptions of sacred loss and desecration almost always unfold concurrently for some life events, such as one's own divorce (Krumrei, Mahoney, & Pargament, 2009) or parental divorce (Warner, Mahoney, & Krumrei, 2009). Moreover, these negative spiritual interpretations of divorce added both to the psychological distress and spiritual growth that family members experienced in trying to come to terms with the event. Taken together, these findings suggest that when objects fall from their sacred pedestals, people are challenged to transform their understanding of what aspects of life are imbued with divine significance.

# Summary

Emerging research on sanctification reveals that people often find the sacred within the inner workings of their day-to-day lives. Indeed, virtually any aspect of life could be perceived as a manifestation of God's presence (theistic sanctification) or imbued with sacred qualities independent of a belief in a deity (non-theistic sanctification). For instance, researchers have discovered that people commonly view major life strivings, marriages, sexuality, parenting, careers, bodies, and nature through a sacred lens. Such perceptions fit well with teachings found in most religious traditions that God is concerned with earthly as well as heavenly matters, and that seemingly profane matters can take on a sacred aura.

Hopefully, empirical work will be extended on viewing other domains through a sacred lens, such as the sanctification of art, beauty, science, love, or friendship (see Cohen, Gruber, & Keltner, 2010).

Interpreting an aspect of life as possessing a sacred dimension is reciprocally tied to several benefits, including: (1) greater commitment to and investment in that aspect of life; (2) stronger efforts to preserve and protect what has been sanctified; (3) greater access to resources for strength, support, and sustenance; and (4) greater satisfaction and happiness derived from that realm (Pargament & Mahoney, 2005). Examining possible links between sanctification and virtues, such as hope, gratitude, and forgiveness is another promising avenue for psychologists interested in well-being and spirituality. Not surprisingly, the benefits associated with sanctification seem to raise the costs when a sanctified object is lost or violated. Paradoxically, however, situations that challenge people to let go of broken sacred vessels may also spur personal and spiritual growth as they seek alternative sacred objects. In sum, emerging research suggests that the study of sanctification offers one fruitful, direct approach to understanding the benefits and risks of integrating spirituality into daily life.

## Acknowledgments

This chapter was supported in part by a grant from the John Templeton Foundation.

## References

Baker, E. H., Sanchez, L. A., Nock, S. L., & Wright, J. D. (2009). Covenant marriage and the sanctification of gendered marital roles. *Journal of Family Issues, 30,* 147–178.

Boyatzis, C. J., & Homan, K. J. (2009). Body image in older adults: Links with religion and gender. *Journal of Adult Development, 16,* 230–238.

Carroll, S. T. (in press). The role of sanctification of work, religiosity, and spirituality as predictors of work-related outcomes for individuals working at religiously affiliated institutions. Manuscript under review.

Cohen, A. B., Gruber, J., & Keltner, D. (2010). Comparing spiritual transformations and experiences of profound beauty. *Psychology of Religion and Spirituality, 2,* 127–135.

DeMaris, A., Mahoney, A., & Pargament, K. I. (2010). Sanctification of marriage and general religiousness as buffers of the effects of marital inequity. *Journal of Family Issues, 31,* 1255–1278.

Dollahite, D. C., & Lambert, N. M. (2007). Forsaking all others: How religious involvement promotes marital fidelity in Christian, Jewish, and Muslim couples. *Review of Religious Research, 48,* 290–307.

Dumas, J., & Nissley-Tsiopinis, J. (2006). Parental global religiousness, sanctification of parenting, and positive and negative religious coping as predictors of parental and child functioning. *International Journal for the Psychology of Religion, 16,* 289–310.

Durkheim, E. (1915). *The elementary forms of the religious life.* New York, NY: Free Press.

Eliade, M. (1959). *The sacred and the profane: The nature of religion.* (W. R. Trask, Trans.). New York, NY: Harcourt, Brace. (Original work published 1957).

Fincham, F. D., Lambert, N. M., & Beach, S. R. H. (2010). Faith and unfaithfulness: Can praying for your partner reduce infidelity? *Journal of Personality and Social Psychology, 99,* 649–659.

Goodman, M. A., & Dollahite, D. C. (2006). How religious couples perceive the influence of God in their marriage. *Review of Religious Research, 48,* 141–155.

Hardy, A. (1979). *The spiritual nature of man: A study of contemporary religious experience.* Oxford, UK: Clarendon Press.

Henderson, A. K., Ellison, C. G., & Glenn, N. D. (2010). *Religion and relationship quality among cohabiting and dating couples.* Manuscript submitted for publication.

Hernandez, K. M., & Mahoney, A. (2009). *Sex through a sacred lens: The longitudinal effects of sanctifying marital sexuality.* Working paper located at National Marriage & Family Research center website. Retrieved from http://ncmr.bgsu.edu/data/workingpapers.html.

Hernandez, K., M., & Mahoney, A. (2012). Balancing sacred callings in career and family life. In P. Hill & B. Dik (Ed.), *Advances in workplace spirituality: Theory, research and application* (pp. 135–155). Information Age Publishing.

Hernandez, K. M., Mahoney, A., & Pargament, K. I. (2011). Sanctification of sexuality: Implications for newlyweds' marital and sexual quality. *Journal of Family Psychology*, 25(5), 775–780.

Krumrei, E. J., Mahoney, A., & Pargament, K. I. (2009). Divorce and the divine: The role of spirituality in adjustment to divorce. *Journal of Marriage and Family*, 71, 373–383.

Krumrei, E. J., Mahoney, A., & Pargament, K. I. (2011). Demonization of divorce: Prevalence rates and links to postdivorce adjustment. *Family Relations*, 60, 90–103.

Lambert, N. M., & Dollahite, D. C. (2008). The threefold cord—Marital commitment in religious couples. *Journal of Family Issues*, 29, 592–614.

Lichter, D. T., & Carmalt, J. H. (2009). Religion and marital quality in low-income couples. *Social Science Review*, 38, 168–187.

Mahoney, A. (2010). Religion in families 1999–2009: A relational spirituality framework. *Journal of Marriage and Family*, 72, 805—827.

Mahoney, A., Carels, R. A., Pargament, K. I., Wachholtz, A., Leeper, L. E., Kaplar, M., & Frutchey, R. (2005). The sanctification of the body and behavioral health patterns of college students. *The International Journal of the Psychology of Religion*, 15, 221–238.

Mahoney, A., Pargament, K. I., Cole, B., Jewell, T., Magyar, G. M., Tarakeshwar, N., … Phillips, R. (2005). A higher purpose: The sanctification of strivings. *The International Journal of the Psychology of Religion*, 15, 239–262.

Mahoney, A., Pargament, K. I., & DeMaris, A. (2009). Couples viewing marriage and pregnancy through the lens of the sacred: A descriptive study. *Research in the Social Scientific Study of Religion*, 20, 1–45.

Mahoney, A., Pargament, K. I., Jewell, T., Swank, A. B., Scott, E., Emery, E., & Rye, M. (1999). Marriage and the spiritual realm: The role of proximal and distal religious constructs in marital functioning. *Journal of Family Psychology*, 13, 321–338.

Murray-Swank, N. A., & Brelsford, G. (2009, April). *Sex and soul: The sanctification of sexuality in married individuals.* Paper presented at the annual meeting of the American Psychological Association, Division 36, Mid-Year Research Conference on Religion and Spirituality, Columbia, Maryland.

Murray-Swank, A., Mahoney, A., & Pargament, K. I. (2006). Sanctification of parenting: Links to corporal punishment and parental warmth among biblically conservative and liberal mothers. *The International Journal of the Psychology of Religion*, 16, 271–287.

Murray-Swank, N. A., Pargament, K. I., & Mahoney, A. (2005). At the crossroads of sexuality and spirituality: The sanctification of sex by college students. *The International Journal of the Psychology of Religion*, 15, 199–219.

Oates, K. L., Hall, M.E., & Anderson, T. L. (2005). Calling and conflict: A qualitative exploration of interrole conflict and the sanctification of work in Christian mothers in academia. *Journal of Psychology and Theology*, 33, 210–223.

Paden, W. E. (1992). *Interpreting the sacred: Ways of viewing religion.* Boston, MA: Beacon Press.

Paloutzian, R. F., & Park, C. L. (2005). *Handbook of the psychology of religion and spirituality.* New York, NY: Guilford Press.

Pargament, K. I. (1997). *The psychology of religion and coping: Theory, research, practice.* New York, NY: Guilford Press.

Pargament, K. I. (2007). *Spiritually integrated psychotherapy: Understanding and addressing the sacred.* New York, NY: Guilford Press.

Pargament, K. I., Exline, J. J., & Jones, J. W. (Eds.) (in press). *APA handbook of psychology, religion, and spirituality* (Vol I). Book in preparation.

Pargament, K. I., Magyar, G. M., Benore, E., & Mahoney, A. (2005). Sacrilege: A study of sacred loss and desecration and their implications for health and well-being in a community sample. *Journal of Personality and Social Psychology, 44,* 59–78.

Pargament, K. I., & Mahoney, A. (2005). Sacred matters: Sanctification as vital topic for the psychology of religion. *The International Journal of the Psychology of Religion, 15,* 179–198.

Pargament, K. I., & Mahoney, A. (2009). Spirituality: The search for the sacred. In S. J. Lopez (Eds), *Handbook of positive psychology* (2nd ed., pp. 611–620). New York, NY: Oxford University Press.

Pargament, K. I., Mahoney, A., & Shafranske, E. P. (Eds.) (in press). *APA handbook of psychology, religion, and spirituality* (Vol. II). Book in preparation.

Pargament, K. I., McConnell, K., Mahoney, A., & Silberman, I. (2007). They killed our Lord: The perception of Jews as desecrators of Christianity as a predictor of anti-Semitism. *Journal for the Scientific Study of Religion, 46,* 143–158.

Raiya, H. A., Pargament, K. I., Mahoney, A., & Trevino, K. (2008). When Muslims are perceived as a religious threat: Examining the connection between desecration, religious coping, and anti-Muslim attitudes. *Basic and Applied Social Psychology, 30,* 311–325.

Rostosky, S.S., Riggle, E. B., Brodnicki, C., & Olson A. (2008). An exploration of lived religion in same-sex couples from Judeo-Christian traditions. *Family Process, 47,* 389–403.

Steger, M. F., Pickering, N. K., Shin, J. Y., & Dik, B. J. (2010). Calling in work secular or sacred? *Journal of Career Assessment, 18,* 82–96.

Tarakeshwar, N., Swank, A. B., Pargament, K. I., & Mahoney, A., (2001). Theological conservatism and the sanctification of nature: A study of opposing religious correlates of environmentalism. *Review of Religious Research, 42,* 387–404.

Volling, B. L., Mahoney, A., & Rauer, A. J. (2009). Sanctification of parenting, moral socialization, and young children's conscience development. *Psychology of Religion and Spirituality, 1,* 53–68.

Walker, A. G., Jones, M. N., Wuensch, K. L., Aziz, S., & Cope, J. G. (2008). Sanctifying work: Effects on satisfaction, commitment, and intent to leave. *The International Journal for the Psychology of Religion, 18,* 132–145.

Warner, H. L., Mahoney, A., & Krumrei, E. J. (2009). When parents break sacred vows: The role of spiritual appraisals, coping and struggles for young adults' adjustment to parental divorce. *Psychology of Religion and Spirituality, 1,* 233–248.

# CHAPTER 32

# QUIETING THE MIND AND LOW AROUSAL ROUTES TO HAPPINESS

## JANE HENRY

Open University, UK

Psychology has only recently turned its gaze to investigate happiness and well-being while spiritual traditions have been scrutinizing this area for millennia. Spiritually-based psychologies of adult development tend to have different emphases than those in mainstream Western psychology. This chapter introduces aspects of spiritual experience, psychospiritual development, and spiritual practice pertinent to enhancing well-being. It contrasts lay, psychological, and spiritual approaches to happiness, looks at how spiritual approaches have influenced psychological interventions, and advocates further research on contentment and equanimity.

## Religious Belief

Religious belief is still common, for example, around 80% of the US population believes in God. However religion and spirituality are often differentiated. Religion is generally associated with belief systems that accept a higher power such as God, institutions like the church, and associated rituals, such as regular attendance at a place of worship or ceremonies focused towards higher being(s). In contrast spirituality is associated with mystical experience, higher states of consciousness and practices designed to facilitate these states, such as meditation or yoga.

Psychologists interested in the quality of life have found that religious belief appears to confer an advantage. George, Ellison, and Larsen (2002) have shown religious observance to have a positive effect on well-being. Believers attending religious institutions rate themselves as slightly happier than non-believers (Inglehart, 1990; Myers, 2000). They compare favorably with the general population on various other measures including number of health issues (Comstock & Partridge, 1972), recovery from health issues (Argyle, 1987), and social relationships, for example, reporting happier marriages (Argyle, 2003; Chesser, 1956).

The positive life outcomes associated with religious belief have been explained by scientists in three main ways: a sense of meaning and purpose, social support and a healthy lifestyle. A religious belief system offers the comfort of making sense of some of the vagaries of life, giving meaning to life (Freedman, 1978), and often helping make sense of difficult life circumstances (Pargament, 1996). Witter, Okun, Stock, & Haring's (1984) meta-analysis of US studies supports meaning as one independent element in the benefits of religious belief. The social advantages conferred by membership of religious groups include a sense of belonging arising from being part of a social group, social support and some life structure, and social embeddedness is known to be central to well-being. The health advantages have been explained by the healthier lifestyle often advocated and practiced by religious believers. Chapter 27 (this volume) by David Myers elaborates. It must be added that many spiritual practitioners (though not all Buddhists) believe in a supernatural realm and attribute many of their apparent life benefits to grace deriving from contact with that realm.

## Spiritual Experience

Down the ages people have reported many forms of exceptional experience including spiritual, parapsychological and peak experiences (e.g., White, 1994). Spiritual experiences seem to be quite common, Hardy (1966), Greely (1975), and Hay (1987) all found about a third of the population had had one or more experiences they perceived as religious or spiritual.

Central to notions of spirituality are experiences people associate with something larger than themselves, for example, experiences of oneness or unity where everything seems connected. Most collections of spiritual experiences are positive in character and feature strong positive emotions notably exultation, awe, bliss, love, joy, and sometimes ecstasy, along with a sense of peace and often great clarity and insight. Only a small percentage of reported spiritual experiences feature fear or a sense of evil, for example, in Hardy's (1979) studies only 4% of their large collection were negative in character. Spiritual experiences sometimes appear to involve contact with another realm. This may involve visions of spiritual being(s) (e.g., James, 1961) or a more diffuse presence or guiding hand. For example, Hay's modern Western collection of experiences people perceive as spiritual, drawn from a UK sample, includes a sense of God's presence, a response to a prayer, a guiding presence and a sacred presence in nature (Hay & Heald, 1987).

Spiritual experiences often have a marked impact and can be life changing. Savage, Fadiman, Mogar, and Allan (1995) found they tended to have a lasting positive effect, enhancing confidence, sense of meaning, and purpose. Greely's (1975) survey found a moderately high correlation of 0.6 between 'being bathed in the light' and positive affect. Pahnke (1966) found that even spiritual experiences induced through psychedelic drugs enhanced happiness up to 6 months later.

# Transcendent Emotions and Interpersonal Virtues

Spiritual experiences are associated with transcendent emotions and interpersonal virtues. These may entail uplifting experiences like awe and elevation, an appreciative attitude such as gratitude and interpersonally-oriented virtues like forgiveness and compassion.

Though transcendent emotions and interpersonal virtues are not unique to believers, work in this area has partly been inspired by spiritual concerns.

Positive psychology has addressed positive emotions such as happiness and joy but until recently had less to say about transcendent emotions and the more interpersonal virtues. However Haidt (2002) has begun to study elevation, Keltner (2003) awe, Fuller (2006) wonder, Snyder (2002) hope, Emmons and Crumpler (2000) gratitude, and McCullough et al. (2001) forgiveness.

Haidt (2002) argues that uplifting experiences such as elevation and appreciation feature prominently in spiritual life. Awe entails an appreciation of vastness whether of great beauty or understanding. Elevation happens when people feel touched, moved or inspired. It is characterized by a warm openness that occurs with a strong but relatively calm appreciation of beauty, nature, ideas or others. Haidt (2002) notes that people often touch their heart area when they feel elevated and feel a relaxation there. He speculates that elevation may involve the parasympathetic system. Haidt (2006) has shown experimentally that uplifting activities such as watching a Mother Teresa video was more likely to motivate people to help others than viewing happy videos. The latter were more likely to motivate them to pursue their own goals suggesting that while happiness and joy can motivate constructive self-interest transcendent emotions inspire generosity to others.

A spiritual orientation often embodies noble values. Haidt (2002) suggests there is a neglected dimension of social life relating to purity of the self where elevating, positive, noble feelings can be seen at one end of a dimension with disgust, degradation, and pollution at the other. He argues the impetus to noble action found among the spiritually oriented has been neglected but may be as fundamental to social life as the much better researched dimensions of social status and belonging.

Appreciation and gratitude are dispositions that are prized in theistic and non-theistic traditions around the world. Regular appreciation of their lot was also one of the features that reportedly characterized Maslow's (1970) self-actualizers. Several newish interventions make a point of building from an appreciative stance; appreciative inquiry is one such well-known change intervention (Cooperrider & Whitney, 2005).

Interventions drawing on appreciation, gratitude, forgiveness, and compassion seem to be very effective. Evidence is building that a sense of gratitude leaves people feeling contented. In a 1998 Gallup survey, the vast majority of the teenage respondents agreed expressing gratitude made them feel happy. Seligman et al. (2005) have found that making a point of letting someone else know you are grateful for their actions was rated as one of the most effective positive psychology exercises both in terms of enhancing well-being and in reducing depression. Emmons and Crumpler (2000) offer experimental support for the link between gratitude and happiness. Health psychology undergrads were asked to keep a

10-week log of emotions, physical symptoms, health behavior (exercise, drug taking), and coping strategies. One-third were also asked to record up to five major events that affected them, another third to record five minor hassles that occurred each week, and the remaining third to note five things they were grateful for. Those in the gratitude group felt better about their lives and were more optimistic about the following week. A follow-up study involving completing a journal for 21 days showed those completing the gratitude journal scored higher on measures of well-being, and were more likely to have offered emotional support to or helped another person.

Religious traditions generally expect more than gratitude and commonly stress the importance of altruism and interpersonal virtues, the need to cultivate a kind and understanding orientation, and practice forgiveness of others. Christians are urged to turn the other cheek and Buddhists to develop loving kindness. Forgiveness seems to be good for the forgiver, for example, Manger et al. (1996) report that the more forgiving among us report less negative affect like anxiety and hostility. Fortunately people tend to become more forgiving as they get older and wiser (e.g., Girard & Mullet, 1997) possibly because they develop more understanding about others' motives and their own failings. Practical applications of forgiveness can be found in the reconciliation programs in South Africa and Northern Ireland. A key feature of these programs is to understand rather than judge the motivation and experience of the other party.

Spiritual traditions have practices designed to cultivate laudable qualities. Tibetan Buddhism, for example, is known for contemplative practices designed to enhance compassion. One practice moves out from initially imagining compassionate feelings to people one feels close to towards feeling compassion for all sentient beings including those that have wronged you. Tibetan Buddhism also prescribes particular practices to counter particular failings, loving kindness meditation as an antidote for hatred, for example (see Ricard, Chapter 27, this volume). Gilbert's (2005) compassion training offers an intervention that begins with the development of compassion for the self.

These more interpersonally-oriented interventions develop interpersonal virtues long prized in spiritual traditions and psychological research is beginning to provide support for the spiritual assertion that a greater interpersonal orientation enhances one's own well-being.

## Spiritual Development

Many spiritual traditions have detailed accounts of the different spiritual experiences likely to be encountered as one practices. Spiritual adherents report experiences that lead to various states of bliss, understanding, compassion, and certainty that over time leave them with a changed sense of self, awareness, and understanding and as much more effective, centered, and happy people. Various spiritual commentators from Plotinus to Aurobindo (1957) have described the different levels of consciousness that underpin such experiences. These are often pictured as a series of vertical stages sequenced in a hierarchy (Alexander & Langer, 1990). There are parallels in the stages of spiritual development found in Hindu, Buddhist, and certain Western esoteric traditions. For example, Brown and Engler (1986) show parallels across the Tibetan Mahayana and Pali Theravaddin traditions with the Hindu Yoga Sutras and Chirban (1986) shows parallels across the experiences of Christian Eastern orthodox saints.

Many psychological theories of adult development also treat development as a hierarchical process that advances through a series of stages (e.g., Kegan, 1982). Commentators such as Mahoney (1991) have elaborated on the parallels in stage schemes of psychological development. The number of stages can be variously elaborated but many commentators see stages of psychological development broadly in line with Piaget (1977) and Kohlberg (1981)—briefly an egocentric preconventional stage focused on the self, and a conventional group oriented conforming phase focused more on the group one identifies with, followed by a postconventional more autonomous stage featuring a wider identification and more pluralistic perspective.

Spiritual schemes add various so called transpersonal states or stages of development. Drawing on Vedantic sources Wilber (2000) has popularized the higher spiritual states as psychic, subtle, causal, and non-dual. In the higher states the focus of attention and sense of identification changes. In the non-dual state, for example, people cease to identify their experience with a sense of personal identity—the I that the normal mind constructs and much of a person's conventional psychological sense of self drops away. They become more absorbed in the present and are without the narrative of incessant internal chatter about themselves, their past, and future that typically occupies the normal mind and accompanies daily activity. Rather people are left to enjoy a more present-centered consciousness as it happens in them.

One interpretation is that psychology deals with the early stages of adult development, essentially the preconventional, conventional, and postconventional stages, and spirituality deals with higher stages of development barely or not recognized in Western theories of adult development. From this perspective Western psychology can be seen a form of developmental arrest that has yet to discover the higher states of mind long detailed in spiritual traditions. In support of this view, Wilber (e.g., 2000) and others have elaborated on the correspondences across various psychological and spiritual schemes of development. Appealing though the idea of apparent parallels in stages across different traditions may be, the validity of such cross-correspondences has been questioned. For example, Cortright (2007) argues there is little correspondence between Wilber and Aurobindo's schemes past the second stage.

Critics of the idea of a staged scheme of spiritual development argue that spiritual experiences are too different in character to be classed along a single dimension and that the different practices and approaches found in different spiritual traditions lead to different spiritual states. For example, Rawlinson (2000) sees a fundamental distinction between experiences of other, such as revelation and grace found in magical, shamanistic, and theistic traditions, and approaches associated with quieter, more introverted forms of spiritual transformation featuring self-realization through meditation and contemplation. Meditation practice and intent also varies across tradition, for example, Zen's open presence, Hindu going within, and Tibetan Buddhist loving kindness meditation. Neuroscientists need to define what form of meditation they are investigating as they find different neurological reactions to different forms of meditation (Lutz et al. 2007).

In addition the hierarchical image of staged development does not readily accommodate situations where people have deep spiritual experiences spontaneously, for example,

St. Paul's conversion on the road to Damascus or children's spiritual experiences. Combs and Wilber have offered an alternative perspective that views spiritual states of experience as orthogonal to psychological stages of development (e.g., Combs & Krippner, 2003). This also deals more satisfactorily with the situation where people are more developed in one area of life than another. What is agreed is that spiritual traditions describe beneficial states of awareness and well-being not yet recognized by psychology.

## Spiritual Practice

Much spiritual practice is designed to help prepare people for these states. Such practices are many and varied and range from working on the body and attendant energy systems, through worship, service to others, and devotion to higher being(s), to procedures that help develop insight and understanding and control the mind to enable it to experience higher states. In Hinduism these are known respectfully as hatha, karma, bhakti, jnana, and raja yoga (Aurobindo (1957) elaborates). Hinduism openly acknowledges that there are many different paths to spiritual development, recognizes that different people are attracted to different approaches, and offers practices suited to those of varying temperaments and stages of development. Some examples follow.

Physical routes to spiritual development are found in the use of endurance by sadhus, repetitive dancing and drumming in shamanistic traditions, postures and breathing exercises in hatha yoga, Sufi use of circle dancing, and Chinese development of chi through movement, for example. Such practices serve to get people beyond thought and facilitate enlightening visions. Fadiman has speculated that the unidirectional turning in Sufi circle dancing may even enhance brain function and lift mood through entraining the left hemisphere, over and above any effect that exercise may have on endorphins.

Chinese and Indian traditions have detailed maps of the "spiritual" energy channels that prana/kundalini/chi energy takes through the body and ideas about how far it extends outside the body. Practices such as acupuncture, shiatsu, and kundalini aim to rebalance this energy and allow it to flow more beneficially. Though these energies are not yet recognized by Western science, major junctures like chakras parallel major organs and differences in skin resistance have been identified at expected acupuncture points. Further empirical support is suggested by successful medical trials of acupuncture (e.g., Turban & Ulrich, 1978).

The more caring amongst us may be drawn to a path of service. Virtually all religious traditions advocate living a moral and ethical life and emphasize the need to care for others: Christianity encourages us to "love your neighbor as yourself" and undertake charitable service; Islam encourages tithing and looking after the poor; and Tibetan Buddhism's emphasizes developing compassion and lauds Bodhisattvas, enlightened ones who vow to return to earth until all sentient beings are free.

Religious ceremonies and rituals of worship such as church service, pujas, and prostrations that believers are expected to adhere to offer an expression of faith and encourage discipline. Haidt (2002) has suggested they encourage a purity of mind he associates with a spiritual mentality. Spiritual adherents often show great devotion to a guru. This entails humility and egoic surrender, admired qualities in Eastern traditions.

Intellectuals may be more attracted to traditions that emphasize the study of sacred texts and contemplation as a route to spiritual realization. Most religions also have esoteric practices that are not necessarily made available to all. These practices may involve meditation, mindfulness, and contemplation designed to help practitioners control their mind, quiet its chattering, develop insight into the way things are, and sometimes special powers.

The psychologist Roger Walsh (1999) sought to identify the commonality in spiritual practices and specify those that might be of use to ordinary people. He concluded that seven psychological practices were common to various spiritual traditions. These are: to redirect motivation and follow intuitive prompting, refine awareness to reduce craving, cultivate love and gratitude through the practice of service, reduce fear and anger to transform emotion, live ethically, retrain attention by quieting the mind, and foster wisdom by developing subtle senses.

Many spiritual traditions also recognize the need for individualized attention to spiritual development. In the East most serious adepts are attached to a particular master who has already undergone a spiritual transformation. The standardized manual-based interventions beloved of modern psychology sit rather uncomfortably with traditions that recognize how very different individuals are and the consequent need to personalize their route to development. What research there is on individual responses to different approaches supports the idea that individuals vary considerably in the approach that they find beneficial (e.g., Fordyce, 1983; Henry, 2006).

# Calming the Mind

Spiritual practices such as meditation are designed to develop consciousness to a point where it recognizes spiritual realities the normal mind misses. Western psychological interventions are increasingly drawing on spiritual meditation practices as a way of redirecting attention more fruitfully and calming anxiety. Meditation teaches people to understand and calm the mind and see more clearly. It does this by training attention, balancing emotions and transforming consciousness. Four common approaches are concentrative meditation where one focuses on an object such as a mantra, the breath or the body, mindfulness where attention is open and an attitude of attentiveness is encouraged to whatever is experienced, contemplation around a quality such as compassion and intuitive apprehension where the practitioner waits for an answer to emerge to a particular question.

Meditation is associated with a state of relaxation but heightened alertness suggested by increased cerebral blood flow and alpha electroencephalogram (e.g., Wallace, 1986). Davidson et al. (2003) have shown that meditation seems to enhance activity in the left prefrontal cortex and that more activity in the left cortex than right is associated with greater happiness. Regular practice substantially reduces fearful thoughts (Lutz et al., 2007). Many meditation studies have focused on its effects in ameliorating various health conditions (Miller & Thorenson, 2003). It has been shown to be an effective intervention for conditions ranging from heart problems, through chronic pain (Kabat-Zhin, 1982) to anxiety (Miller et al., 1996) as well as reducing the likelihood of relapse among the clinically depressed

(Teasdale, Segal, & Williams, 1995). Of course the original purpose of meditation was to develop insight into the nature of reality, wisdom, understanding, compassion and well-being. Relatively few studies have investigated the positive benefits of meditation as a development tool, but Murphy et al. (1997) suggest those that have found increased concentration, greater empathy, sense of coherence, and autonomy.

The meditation practice that has had most impact on psychological interventions in recent decades is mindfulness (e.g., Hsu & Langer, Chapter 76; Kwee, Chapter 28; Malinowski, Chapter 32, this volume). Long championed by the likes of De Silva (1979), Kabat-Zhin (1990, 2003), and Teasdale et al. (1995). Its recent take up by therapists effectively offers a paradigm shift in approaches to treating the mentally troubled now recognized as the third wave in psychotherapeutic circles. Elements of mindfulness feature in Kabat-Zhin's (1990) mindfulness-based stress reduction therapy (MBSR), Teasdale et al.'s (1995) mindfulness-based cognitive therapy (MBCT), acceptance and commitment therapy (Hayes, Chapter 74, this volume), and dialectical therapy.

Mindfulness focuses on ways of redirecting attention to the present, typically encouraging people to attend non-judgmentally. It makes us sensitive to what is happening in the here and now and diminishes the tendency to evaluate things, whether these are perceived as positive or negative. This entrains an attitude of acceptance of experienced emotions along with less attachment to them. Experiencing more of the present people tend to let go of much rumination about the past and fears for the future, this in turn leads to a form of non-judgmental discernment. The approach shifts the goal from decreasing anxiety to accepting it. Teasdale and Williams have shown clearly that MBCT has a better success rate than conventional treatment at interrupting the rumination and negative self-evaluation that can easily trap someone disposed to depression (Teasdale et al., 1995).

Research by Henry (2000) suggests many people are well aware of the centrality of a quiet mind for a contented soul and value routes to well-being that have more in common with the spiritual practice of finding time for silence and retraining attention. In Henry's (2006) studies of adults' perceptions of key factors in achieving a lasting improvement in their own well-being the most valued approach is some form of quieting the mind. This is the most commonly cited approach mentioned by about a third of respondents.

The quieting practice may be meditation, mindfulness, or contemplation but for others (often unfamiliar with spiritual discourse) it took a more informal form such as finding time in the day for a period of quiet. For some it was more a question of relaxing, for example, spending an afternoon fishing. In the UK, angling is the most popular sport. People sit still by a river, canal, or pond for hours, often alone, and rarely catch a fish. This is an activity that engenders a quiet absorption in the present. Many people had learnt to follow their intuitions as to the way forward, some made a point of "following their bliss"—the things that felt intuitively right and made them feel good. Others would go to sleep at night confident that the way forward will be clear the next morning. By bypassing conscious analysis of problems these approaches avoid the danger of negative rumination central to depressive thinking patterns. Others had learnt to be kinder and more gentle with themselves, to let go of certain goals and strivings, and/or concerns about others evaluations. Their route had been one of quiet self-acceptance. Self-surrender is central to many spiritual traditions.

Other valued approaches included physical activity such as walking or being out in nature and social support which was mentioned by around a fifth of the sample. Interestingly talking about problems was one of the most commonly cited practices seen as least effective (Henry, 2000).

# Contentment

Psychological and spiritual understandings of happiness have different associations. In Anglo-Saxon countries happiness is associated with positive experience and high arousal. Extraversion, a known correlate of happiness, is associated with positive experience and active engagement and in Five Factor personality theory these are defining qualities in instruments such as NEO (e.g., McCrae and Costa, 2003).

The spiritual understanding of happiness is associated more with contentment, a state characterized by lower arousal. The ordinary man in the street also seems to associate well-being with contentment (Boniwell, 2006; Henry, 2000). A 2005 UK poll conducted by NOP showed that over half the thousand respondents associated well-being with contentment and peace of mind. Boniwell (2006) reports that relationships, contentment, transcendence, fulfillment, security and health were the six main categories participants volunteered as representing their understanding of well-being. Contentment, the second most commonly cited category after relationships, was mentioned by three-quarters of the sample.

Spiritual well-being seems to rest more in an inner equanimity than positive experience. Contentment and equanimity perhaps derive more from balance, coherence, an interpersonal orientation and non-personal identification than positive arousal, goal seeking, and a personal orientation and identification. In Buddhism for example, flourishing is seen to result from mental balance rather than positive arousal and developing peace of mind is central to much spiritual practice.

To date, psychologists have studied very few states of optimal experience and those that they have studied tend to be associated with positive experience and high arousal, and personal strengths; for example, Frederickson's studies of positive emotion and Peterson's studies of personal strengths. Contentment and other states of well-being associated with lower forms of arousal have been largely neglected. Csikszentmihalyi's (1988) studies of the state of mind known as flow does address a state of contented absorption in the present. However the theory of flow describes it as a form of optimal experience with high but obtainable challenge and skill such as learning new things or playing with children. This demotes pleasurable activities, like gardening or watching a beautiful sunset, that require little skill but are still highly satisfying.

Psychological studies of subjective well-being also often treat it as if it were a single state. Various characteristics and necessary conditions to explain subjective well-being have been suggested including positive experience, personal mastery, active engagement, personal meaning, coherence between goals and actions, autonomy, and relatedness. In contrast, spiritual traditions tend to acknowledge many different states of consciousness, including blissful, non-dual, and unusually wise and perceptive states. There is a case for more investigation into the many different kinds of optimal experience including contentment and peace of mind.

Contentment and peace of mind entail acceptance. This may involve accepting internal feelings, desisting from criticizing oneself and getting angry with others, letting go of any sense of not feeling good enough or being superior, detaching enough to loose concern about any discrepancy between what one might wants and gets. This does not mean being passive or detaching from the world as spiritual adepts often exhibit a form of relaxed attention that allows exceptionally efficient active engagement. Being better able to detach from outcomes such people often seem to have a clarity of perception that makes it easier for them to do the right thing.

## Psychological and Spiritual Routes to Well-Being

The routes psychology and spirituality advocate to achieve lasting well-being differ. Western development, caring, and positive psychology has largely focused on personal development to help the client strive to make themselves a better, happier, and more fulfilled person. (Perhaps not surprisingly as much psychology is dominated by Anglo-Saxon conceptions, a culture known for its individualistic sense of self.) In spiritual traditions the focus tends to be more on interpersonal virtues involving forgiveness, self-less action, and compassion towards others. Eastern spiritual practices tend to be more concerned with releasing expectations, living in the present, and surrendering to a higher good.

Psychological approaches to development (whether coaching, counseling, psychotherapy, or self-help) often takes the form of talking therapy that focuses on the contents of consciousness. People are encouraged to externalize what they want and led to believe they can control their behavior. Cognitively-based therapies, for example, are concerned with changing thoughts as a route to a more satisfactory emotional experience. Self-awareness and insight are often gleaned through explicit analysis of problematic areas, negative thoughts may be challenged in cognitive therapy and plans for action developed in coaching, for example.

Parallels have been drawn between specific Buddhist practices and certain cognitive behavioral techniques (e.g., Claxton, 1996); both encourage challenging our interpretations of events and have similar thought stopping tactics, for example. However, many Buddhist, Hindu and some Christian practices are more concerned with refining the instrument of perception by widening and redirecting attention than addressing unmet desires or building on positive experiences. Such approaches generally bypass much of the usual Western psychological focus on problems and/or goals.

The spiritual route to development often involves attention training designed to quiet the chattering mind, as learning to silence the mind is seen as a key skill on the path to well-being. The focus in mindfulness, for example, is on establishing non-evaluative awareness rather than making plans for first steps towards pursuing particular goals. Over time spiritual practice seems to enhance emotional balance, develop intuitive discernment, and refine insight.

Positive psychology redirects the therapeutic focus on fixing problems and ameliorating deficiencies to building on strengths and enhancing positive experience and positive emotion. However many of its interventions, such as Seligman's learned optimism and Fava's well-being therapy, also adopt an essentially cognitive approach.

The role of positive experience as a route to well-being seems to be less central in many Eastern spiritual traditions. Where positive psychology seeks to maximize positive emotion, the importance of detaching from fleeting emotions features prominently in Buddhism and Hinduism. Hinduism also asserts that it is possible for individuals to be content in very trying conditions. A colleague tells the tale of it being impossible to be unhappy in the presence of his guru despite the fact that he was suffering from gangrene at the time. The spiritually-oriented may even welcome unpleasant interactions as much as more positive ones as the former can offer a test of the extent to which they have developed a pure generosity and the opportunity to learn where they need to refine their reactions and remove unbalancing mindsets.

# Conclusion

Eastern mysticism documents many different higher states of consciousness which often leave the recipient in a state of joyful, perceptive, equanimity. Western notions of happiness tends to be associated with high arousal whereas the contentuen and equanimity found in spiritual practice represent states of well-being associated with lower arousal. Psychologists could usefully spend more time examining different states of optimal experience and well-being, in particular those associated with low arousal such as contentment.

Spiritual psychologies advocate living ethically and stress the importance of an interpersonal orientation and the value of quieting the mind. Spiritual practice often encourages people to go within, root out their failings, and develop the capacity to attend to others kindly. There is a greater focus in Eastern spiritual practice on acceptance and detachment from desires than the seeking and striving after goals found in many Western forms of psychological development. An increasingly number of new interventions, such as mindfulness, compassion therapy, and reconciliation, draw on spiritual practice for inspiration. The marriage of psychological and spiritual approaches shows great promise.

## References

Alexander, C. N., & Langer, E. (1990). *Higher stages of human development*. Oxford, UK: Oxford University Press.

Alexander, C. N., Davies, J. L., Dixon, C. A., Dilbeck, M. C., Drucker, S. M., Oetzel, R. M., ... Orme-Johnson, D. W. (1990). Growth of higher stages of consciousness. In C. N. Alexander and E. Langer (Eds.), *Higher stages of human development* (pp. 286–387). Oxford: Oxford University Press.

Argyle, M. (1987). *The psychology of happiness*. London, UK: Methuen.

Argyle, M. (2003). Causes and correlates of happiness. In D. Kahneman, E. Deiner, and N. Schwarz (Eds.), *Well-being* (pp. 307–322). New York, NY: Russell Sage Foundation.

Aurobindo, S. (1957). *The synthesis of yoga*. Pondicherry, India: Sri Aurobindo Ashram.

Boniwell, I. (2006, May). The undervalued component of happiness. Retrieved from http://news.bbc.co.uk/1/hi/programmes/happiness_formula/4888706.stm

Brown, D. P., & Engler, J. (1986). The stages of mindfulness meditation: A validation study. In K. Wilber, J. Engler, & D. P. Brown (Eds.), *Transformations of consciousness* (pp. 161–190). London, UK: Shambala.

Chesser, E. (1956). *The sexual, marital and family relationships of English women*. London, UK: Hutchinson.

Chirban, J. (1986). Developmental stages in eastern orthodox Christianity. In K. Wilber, J. Engler, & D. P. Brown (Eds.), *Transformations of consciousness* (pp. 258–314). London, UK: Shambala.

Claxton, G. (Ed.). (1996). *Beyond therapy: The impact of eastern religions on psychological theory and practice*. Sturminster Newton, UK: Prism Press. (Original edition 1986 Wisdom Publications.)

Comstock, G. W., & Partridge, K. B. (1972). Church attendance and health. *Journal of Chronic Diseases*, 25, 665–72.

Combs, A., & Krippner, S. (2003). Process, structure and form: an evolutionary transpersonal psychology of consciousness. *International Journal of Transpersonal Studies*, 22, 47–60.

Cooperrider, D., & Whitney, D. (2005). *Appreciative inquiry: A positive revolution in change*. San Francisco, CA: Berrett-Koehler Publishers.

Cortright, B. (2007). *Integral psychology*. Albany, NY: SUNY.

Csikszentmihalyi, M., & Csikszentmihalyi, I. (1988). *Optimal experience: studies in the flow of consciousness*. Cambridge, UK: Cambridge University Press.

Davidson, R. J., Kabat-Zhin, J., Schumacher, J., Rosenkranz, M., Muller, D., & Santorelli, S. (2003). Alteration in brain and immune function produced by mindfulness meditation. *Psychosomatic Medicine*, 65, 564–70.

De Silva, P. (1979). *An introduction to Buddhist psychology*. London, UK: Macmillan.

Emmons, R. A., & Crumpler, C. A. (2000). Gratitude as a human strength: Appraising the evidence. *Journal of Social and Clinical Psychology*, 19, 56–69.

Fordyce, M. W. (1983). A program to increase happiness: Further studies. *Journal of Counseling Psychology*, 30, 483–98.

Freedman, J. L. (1978). *Happy people*. New York, NY: Harcourt Brace Jovanovich.

Fuller, R.C. (2006). Wonder and the religious sensibility: A study in religion and emotion. *The Journal of Religion*, 86, 3, 364–384.

Girard, M., & Mullet, E. (1997). Propensity to forgive in adolescents, young adults, older adults and elderly people. *Journal of Adult Development*, 4, 209–20.

George, L. K., Ellison, C. G., & Lason, D. B. (2002). Explaining the relationships between religious involvement and health. *Psychological Inquiry*, 13, 190–200.

Gilbert, P. (2005). *Compassion: Conceptualisations, research and use in psychotherapy*. London, UK: Routledge.

Greeley, A. M. (1975). *The sociology of the paranormal*. London, UK: Sage.

Haidt, J. (2002). Elevation and positive psychology. In C. L. Keyes & J. Haidt (Eds.), *Flourishing* (pp. 275–290). Washington, DC: American Psychological Association.

Haidt, J. (2006). *The happiness hypothesis*. London, UK: Arrow.

Hardy, A. (1966). *The divine flame*. London, UK: Collins.

Hardy, A. (1979). *The spiritual nature of man: a study of contemporary religious experience*. Oxford: Clarendon Press.

Hay, D. (1987). *Exploring inner space*. Harmondsworth, UK: Penguin.

Hay, D., & Heald, G. (1987). Religion is good for you. *New Scientist*, 80, 20–22.

Henry, J. (2000). Effective change strategies. *Consciousness and Experiential Psychology*, 5, 6–13.

Henry, J. (2006). Strategies for achieving well-being. In Csikszentmihalyi, M. & Csikszentmihaly, I.S. (Eds.), *A life worth living* (pp. 120–142). Oxford, UK: Oxford University Press.

Huxley, A. (1946). *The perenniel philosophy*. London, UK: Chatto and Windus.
Inglehart, R. (1990). *Culture shift in advanced societies*. Princeton, NJ: Princeton University Press.
James, W. (1961). *The varieties of religious experience*. New York, NY: Macmillan.
Kabat-Zinn, J. (1982). An outpatient program in behavioral medicine for chronic pain based on the practice of mindfulness meditation. *General Hospital Psychiatry*, 4, 33–47.
Kabat-Zhin J. (1990). *Full-catastrophe living*. New York, NY: Delacorte.
Kabat-Zhin, J. (2003). Mindfulness-based interventions in context: past, present and future. *Clinical Psychology: Science and Practice*, 10, 144–56.
Kegan, R. (1982). *The evolving self*. Cambridge, MA: Harvard University Press.
Keltner, D., & Haidt, J. (2003). Approaching awe, a moral, spiritual and aesthetic emotion. *Cognition and Emotion*, 17(2), 297–314.
Kohlberg, L. (1981). *Essays on moral development*. New York, NY: Harper and Row.
Lutz, A., Dunne, J. D., & Davidson, R. J. (2007). Meditation and the neuroscience of consciousness. In P. D. Zelato, M. Moscovitch, & E. Thompson, (Eds.), *Cambridge handbook of consciousness* (pp. 499–555). New York, NY: Cambridge University Press.
McCrae, R. R., & Costa, P. T. (2003). *Personality in adulthood: A five-factor perspective* (2nd ed.). New York, NY: Guildford Press.
McCullough, M. E., Kilpatrick, S. D., Emmons, R. A., & Larson, D. B. (2001). Is gratitude a moral affect? *Psychological Bulletin*, 127, 249–66.
Mahoney, M. (1991). *Human change processes*. New York, NY: Basic Books.
Maslow, A. (1970). *Towards a psychology of being*. Princeton, NJ: Van Nostrand.
Mauger, P. A., Saxon, A., Hamill, C., & Pannell, M. (1996). The relationship of forgiveness to interpersonal behaviour. Presented to SE Psychological Association Annual Convention, Norfolk, VA. Quoted in M. E. McCullough & C. V. Witvliet (2002). The psychology of forgiveness. In C. R. Snyder & S. J. Hope, S. J. (Eds.), *The positive psychology handbook* (p.456). Oxford UK: Oxford University Press.
Miller, T. Q., Smith, T. W., Turner, C. W., Guijarro, M. L., & Hallet, A. J. (1996). A meta-analytic review of research on hostility and physical health. *Psychological Bulletin*, 119, 322–48.
Miller, W. E., & Thoresen, C. E. (2003). Spirituality, religion and health: An emerging field. *American Psychologist*, 58, 24–35.
Murphy, M. (1993). *The future of the body*. San Francisco, CA: Tarcher.
Murphy, M., Donovan, S., & Taylor, E. (1997). *The physical and psychological effects of meditation*. Sausilito, CA: Institute of Noetics.
Myers, D. (2000). The funds, friends and faith of happy people. *American Psychologist*, 55, 56–7.
Pahnke, W. H. (1966). Drugs and mysticism. *International Journal of Parapsychology*, 8, 295–314.
Pargament, K. I. (1996). Religious methods of coping: Resources for the conservation and transformation of significance. In E. P. Shafranske (Ed.), *Religion and clinical practice in psychology* (pp. 215–239). Washington, DC: American Psychological Association.
Piaget, J. (1977). *The essential Piaget* (H. E. Gruber & J. J. Voneche, Eds.). New York, NY: Basic Books.
Rawlinson, A. (2000). A model of experiential comparative religion. *International Journal of Transpersonal Studies*, 19, 99–108.
Rozin, P., Haidt, J., & MacCauley, C. R. (2000). Disgust. In M. Lewis & J. M. Haviland-Jones (Eds.), *Handbook of emotions* (2nd ed., pp. 637–653). New York, NY: Guildford Press.

Savage, C., Fadiman, J., Mogar, R., & Allan, M. (1995). The effects of psychedelic therapy on values, behaviour and personality. *International Journal of Neuropsychiatry*, 2, 241–54.

Seligman, M., Park, N., & Peterson, C. (2005). Positive psychology progress: Empirical validation of interventions. *American Psychologist*, 60(5), 411–21.

Snyder, C. R., & Hope, S. J. (Eds.). (2002). *The positive psychology handbook*. Oxford, UK: Oxford University Press.

Teasdale, J., Segal, B., & Williams, M. (1995). How does cognitive therapy prevent depressive relapse and why should attention control mindfulness training help. *Behavioural Research and Therapy*, 33, 25–39.

Turban, E., & Ulrich, S. (1978). The evaluation of therapeutic acupuncture. *Social Science and Medicine*, 12, 39–44.

Wallace, R.K. (1986). The Maharishi technology of the unified field: The neurophysiology of enlightenment. Fairfield IA: MIU Neuroscience Press. Quoted in Shapiro, S.L. Walsh, R Britton W.B (2003). An analysis of recent meditation research and suggestions for future direction, *Journal of Meditation and Meditation Research*, 3, 69–90.

Walsh, R. (1999). *Essential spirituality: The 7 central practices to awaken heart and mind*. New York, NY: Wiley.

White, R. A. (Ed.). (1994). *Exceptional human experience*. New Bern, NC: EHE Network.

Wilber, K. (2000). *Integral Psychology*. Boston, MA: Shambala.

Witter, R. A., Okun, M. A., Stock, W. A., & Haring, M. J. (1984). Education and subjective well-being: A meta-analysis. *Educational Evaluation and Policy Analysis*, 6, 163–73.

# SECTION V

# HAPPINESS AND SOCIETY

# CHAPTER 33

# INTRODUCTION TO HAPPINESS AND SOCIETY

SAM THOMPSON

University of Liverpool, UK

It has become a cliché—but no less meaningful for being so—to follow John Donne in noting that "no man is an island, entire of itself." We live our lives as social beings, interacting not just with one another, but with the systems, institutions, and norms that comprise what we understand as "society."

Psychologists, especially clinical psychologists, work in what has become known as the *biopsychosocial* paradigm. In essence, this paradigm contends that people's experience of their lives, be it good or bad, results from a dynamic interplay between three forces. The first is biological endowment, influenced (although, as contemporary research makes increasingly clear, not *determined*) by genetics. The second are those relatively stable (but, again, not fixed) aspects of individual psychology, variously characterized as personality, IQ, strengths, attitudes, values, and so on. The third is the social, in the wide-ranging influence that is exerted on individuals by the society and culture in which they grow up and are a part.

It would not be unfair to contend that, in practice, the "social" in the biopsychosocial model receives the least attention. This is not because its importance per se is doubted (although it has certainly been underplayed by some traditions of psychological thinking). Rather, it is because the society-level determinants of people's mental states are harder to isolate and study than the individual-level determinants. By putting someone in a laboratory and subjecting them to carefully controlled experimentation, it is possible to tease apart subtleties in how they respond to certain stimuli, or reason when faced with particular problems. But no such approach is possible for exploring the impact of society and culture. *Everything*—even the business of doing "psychology"—is infused with assumptions, influences, and tacit understandings that have their origin in the social and cultural situation.

Crucially, moreover, social determinants of happiness and unhappiness are hard for psychologists to influence. The archetypal psychological and psychiatric interventions—talking therapies and psychoactive medication, respectively—act at the level of the individual and are usually developed in order to ameliorate specific problems. What if an individual's unhappiness stems not from any biological or psychological "fault," but from the wider socioeconomic conditions in which they find themselves living—in an area with extreme deprivation and inequality, say, or a faltering economy? Psychologists and psychiatrists may be able to alleviate suffering and perhaps even restore happiness to such individuals, but the job of reshaping the conditions that led to unhappiness in the first place typically falls to others: policy-makers, business people, community leaders, advertisers, and so on.

Of course, this brings a political element into the discussion. The fact that certain aspects of a society influence the happiness of those living within it is a relatively uncontroversial claim. But what does this imply for governance? To what extent should those in public office actively seek to shape society *in order* to promote the happiness of citizens? A plethora of recent books and think-tank reports have argued that politicians should give more explicit consideration to happiness, and perhaps even use the latest scientific findings in order to develop policies specifically aimed at promoting subjective well-being (Bok, 2010; Diener, Lucas, Schimmack & Helliwell 2009; Layard, 2011; Shah & Marks, 2004;). This is a highly controversial area. Different conceptions of happiness relate directly to centuries-old problems in political philosophy; in particular, to the question of the proper role of the state in relation to the individual's happiness and to the balance between individual liberty and the collective good. These debates shape our public discourse today.

To give a specific example, consider the case of unemployment. Unemployment is already seen as an undesirable outcome of policy, because it hurts individuals economically and requires extra government spending on welfare. Most governments tolerate a certain amount of unemployment because of its trade-offs with inflation and productivity; striking this balance requires making political judgments about where priorities lie. But data on subjective well-being and happiness shed light on these decisions, showing that unemployed people report levels of happiness substantially below what might be expected merely from the loss of income (Clark, 2010). Moreover, longitudinal research suggests that unemployment has a "scarring" effect, whereby a well-being deficit remains even after people have become re-employed (Clark, Georgellis, & Sanfey, 2001). Psychologists, understandably, do not regard labor market policy as within their professional jurisdiction. However, it is evident that decisions made at this macro level, and which are at least partly driven by political considerations, have considerable consequences for the happiness of many people. In turn, they influence the kinds of problems that psychologists and other mental health professionals are called upon to help deal with.

Elsewhere in this book, the biological and psychological underpinnings of happiness are considered in detail. The aim of the present section is to explore some of the ways in which people's happiness is influenced by the social, economic, and environmental forces that operate beyond the level of the individual. In doing so, it aims to relate the study of happiness to some contemporary social concerns: politics, economics, consumerism, environmental sustainability, inequality, and more.

Of all the society-wide influences on happiness, one of the most significant—or, at least, the most comprehensively studied—is that of economic circumstances. Few findings in the happiness literature have had more impact, and aroused more controversy, than the notorious "Easterlin paradox." Named for Richard Easterlin, the Californian economist who first identified it in a famous article (Easterlin, 1974), the paradox suggests that whilst there is a positive relationship between income and happiness within a country at any given moment, overall levels of happiness do not increase even as national wealth (measured by gross domestic product) rises over time. In Chapter 34, economists Bruno Frey and Alois Stutzer provide an insightful introduction to the economics of happiness. As well as discussing some of the paradigmatic findings in the literature—including the Easterlin paradox—they consider how the study of happiness has begun to influence the discipline of economics itself. Has the "dismal science" become a bit more cheerful? And if so what might be the implications?

Growing appreciation of the role of society and culture on happiness has brought with it a good deal of public interest in the notion that some countries may be happier places than others. The idea that Denmark is "the happiest country in the world" has entered popular folklore. But what is the source of this claim and what does it really tell us? In Chapter 35 on cross-national comparisons of happiness, William Tov and Evelyn Au deconstruct this and other findings. Whilst not disputing the value of cross-national happiness surveys, they show how methodological difficulties of the kind generally ignored in popular reporting have serious implications for how data from such surveys should be interpreted. If recent efforts to bring a consideration of happiness into the mainstream of policy-making are to succeed, these issues must be tackled head-on.

Next, in Chapter 36, Dimitris Ballas and Danny Dorling consider geographical influences on happiness. To the extent that different countries, regions, and local areas *do* differ in terms of happiness, what are the driving factors? A particular focus of this chapter is the issue of inequality, not only of income but of space and place. If we want a happier society, Ballas and Dorling argue, we must be prepared to confront deeply entrenched causes of inequality, even if that leads in some cases to uncomfortable conclusions.

In the following chapter, Aaron Ahuvia and Elif Izberk-Bilgin turn their attention to a characteristic feature of modern Western society: consumerism. Lauded by some as an exemplar of human progress, the society characterized by abundant choice is derided by others for its supposedly detrimental impacts on happiness. Ahuvia and Izberk-Bilgin provide a nuanced summary of these arguments, outlining the critiques that have been advanced from different theoretical perspectives and challenging us to consider whether there is a trade-off between happiness and individual sovereignty, at least insofar as it is expressed through consumer behavior.

It has often been argued that the consumer society is, itself, a significant driving force in the environmental problems that are of increasing concern to policy-makers and the public alike. To what extent is people's desire for happiness and well-being in their own lives compatible with achieving environmental sustainability? In Chapter 38, Sam Thompson, Nic Marks, and Tim Jackson review the arguments for considering sustainability and happiness together, before presenting a new conceptual model that aims to unpack the complex interrelationship between the state of the environment and the way in which people utilize environmental resources in order to support their well-being.

In the final chapter of this section, leading UK policy analyst Geoff Mulgan reflects on the difficulty of building a consideration of happiness and well-being into the business of day-to-day policy-making. Drawing on a number of case studies from the UK and elsewhere, Mulgan shows how many of the social and economic factors likely to influence our happiness fall wholly or partially within the remit of policy-makers, and yet at the same time are extremely difficult for them to influence in predictable ways. This is a new area and Mulgan argues that policy-makers must be bold enough to experiment with innovative ideas, running the risk of failure, in order to discover what really works.

## REFERENCES

Bok, D. (2010). *The politics of happiness: What government can learn from the new research on well-being.* Princeton, NJ: Princeton University Press.

Clark, A. (2010). Work, jobs and well-being across the millennium. In E. Diener, J. Helliwell, & D. Kahneman (Eds.). *International differences in well-being* (pp. 436–464) New York, NY: Oxford University Press.

Clark, A. E., Georgellis, Y., & Sanfey, P. (2001). Scarring: The psychological impact of past unemployment. *Economica, 68,* 221–41.

Diener, E., Lucas, R., Schimmack, U. & Helliwell, J. (2009). *Well-being for public policy.* New York, NY: Oxford University Press.

Easterlin, R. A. (1974). Does economic growth improve the human lot? Some empirical evidence. In P. A. David & M. W. Reder (Eds.). *Nations and households in economic growth: Essays in honour of Moses Abramowitz.* New York, NY: Academic Press.

Layard, R. (2011). *Happiness: Lessons from a new science* (2nd ed.). London, UK: Penguin.

Shah, H., & Marks, N. (2004). *A well-being manifesto for a flourishing society.* London: nef.

CHAPTER 34

# ECONOMICS AND THE STUDY OF INDIVIDUAL HAPPINESS

BRUNO S. FREY[1] AND ALOIS STUTZER[2]

[1]University of Zurich, Switzerland; [2]University of Basel, Switzerland

WITHIN economics a remarkable new development is underway: the theoretical and empirical economic analysis of individual well-being or happiness.[1] This development transcends the borders of standard economics in various ways. The economics of happiness argues that the measurable concepts of happiness or life satisfaction allow us to proxy the theoretical concept of utility in a satisfactory way. This approach provides new insights into how human beings value goods and services and more general social and economic conditions, and suggests new policies that significantly deviate from what has been proposed so far. These developments could even be called "revolutionary" in that they change the way society is looked at from an economics point of view (Frey, 2008). Happiness economics has the potential to change economics substantially in the future, both with respect to analysis of economic problems and the policy recommendations intended to solve them. Our argument rests on three pillars: measurement, new insights, and policy consequences.

## MEASUREMENT

The measurable concept of happiness or life satisfaction allows us to proxy the concepts of *utility* or *individual welfare* in a satisfactory way. Utility is a term used in economics to represent the relative satisfaction derived from, or the desirability of pursuing, one course of action rather than another. Oftentimes, it is meant to capture what people obtain from consuming goods and services. Life satisfaction proposes the opposite of something that was

---

[1] There are several surveys of the state of economic research on subjective well-being available in the form of journal articles (e.g., Di Tella & MacCulloch, 2006; Dolan et al., 2008; Frey & Stutzer, 2002b; Stutzer and Frey 2010), books (e.g., Frey, 2008; Frey & Stutzer, 2002a; Layard, 2005; van Praag & Ferrer-i-Carbonell, 2004) and readers (Bruni & Porta, 2007; Easterlin, 2002).

considered a revolution in the 1930s, when Sir John Hicks, Lord Lionel Robbins, and others claimed that utility could not and need not be measured. Their approach opened the way to a fruitful application of microeconomics to economic issues, and more recently to issues far beyond economics.[2] But the situation has changed dramatically since the 1930s. Psychologists have taught us how to measure subjective well-being and thus give life to the concept of utility.

The ability to measure happiness allows us to extend economic theory into new areas. For instance, it enables us to analyze biases in decision-making. Standard economic theory equates the utility expected when deciding between alternative actions or consumption bundles (e.g., spending holidays in the Alps or at the sea) with the utility experienced when realizing the plan or consuming the bundle. In contrast, happiness research suggests that individuals make biased decisions when choosing between alternatives (for an introduction to utility misprediction in economics see Stutzer & Frey, 2007). As a result of these biases in judgment, they find themselves less satisfied with life than they could be according to their own evaluation. Similarly, individuals' utility is lower when they are subject to significant self-control problems. They allow themselves to undertake activities (such as eating candy) which appear attractive to them but which turn out to raise their utility only in the short run. The individuals, after the fact, realize that they would have been better off had they resisted the temptation (Stutzer, 2009).

Happiness research enables us not only to acknowledge these aspects of human behavior but also to analyze them empirically and therewith to evaluate their importance for explaining human behavior. This is not possible in standard theory based on "revealed preference," which presumes that observed behavior is the result of a utility-maximizing calculus in which individuals do not make any systematic mistakes.

## New Insights

The economic analysis of subjective well-being teaches us how human beings value goods and services, as well as how they value social conditions. This applies, in particular, to the effects of income, unemployment, and other economic factors on well-being. The new insights go beyond economics to include non-material values, such as the value of autonomy, social relations in the family, etc. Moreover, individuals derive utility from *processes*, not just from outcomes. For instance, they are more satisfied with a court decision if they feel that they have been well treated by the judge, even if the outcome is less favorable for them (Frey, Benz, & Stutzer, 2004). It is understood that economic activity is certainly not an end in itself, but only has value insofar as it contributes to human happiness.[3]

---

[2] Areas of non-market economics include, e.g., the economics of the arts, sports economics, the economics of terrorism, etc.

[3] There is, of course, the fundamental issue of whether happiness is the ultimate goal to be pursued. Other valid goals, for instance, may be loyalty, responsibility, self-esteem, freedom, or personal development.

# Policy Consequences

Taking a constitutional perspective, there are two levels at which policy decisions are made: (1) in the current politico-economic process, within a given framework of rules; and (2) at the constitutional level, where the rules of the game as such are determined. Economic happiness research is relevant for both levels. For instance, the life satisfaction approach enables policy-makers to capture individuals' preferences and individuals' welfare for public goods in a novel way. As a consequence, insights from happiness research increase political competition in the current politico-economic process. Moreover, aggregate happiness indicators may become a relevant macro input in the political discourse. At the constitutional level, happiness research can be applied to comparative institutional analyses of, for example, democracy and federalism. We argue that it is mistaken to jump to the conclusion that governments should pursue a happiness policy maximizing an aggregate happiness indicator conceived to be a social welfare function.

In the following pages, we will provide a primer on how economists use information about happiness as a new approach to measuring individual welfare. Next we will discuss the relationship between two important economic variables and subjective well-being, i.e., income and unemployment. For income, we emphasize the role of income aspirations in the notion of relative utility. For unemployment, we contrast the views that it occurs as a voluntary or an involuntary act. We then address challenges to the rational consumer hypothesis due to limited will power and utility misprediction that can be studied based on reported welfare judgments.

# A Primer on the Economic Analysis of Happiness

The economic study of individual happiness is based on a subjective view of utility, which recognizes that everyone has his or her own ideas about happiness and the good life, and that observed behavior is an incomplete indicator of individual well-being. Fortunately, observed behavior is not the only way to capture individual well-being. Consistent with a sensible tradition in economics to rely on the judgment of the persons directly involved, individuals' welfare can be captured and analyzed by asking the person how satisfied he is with his life. Since people are reckoned to be good judges of the overall quality of their life, this is a straightforward strategy.

Much happiness research in economics takes reported subjective well-being as a proxy measure for individual welfare. "Subjective well-being" is the scientific term used in psychology for an individual's evaluation of the extent to which he or she experiences positive and negative affect, happiness, or satisfaction with life.[4]

---

[4] The empirical study of subjective well-being used to be the province of hedonic psychology (for reviews, see Diener, Suh, Lucas & Smith, 1999; Kahneman, Diener & Schwarz, 1999).

There are a number of different measurement techniques available to capture subjective well-being (see also Chapters 10, 13, and 14). These can be distinguished along two dimensions: cognition, the evaluative or judgmental component of well-being (usually assessed with questions asking about satisfaction with life overall); and affect, the pleasure–pain component of well-being (Diener, 1984). With regard to the latter, it is common to distinguish further between positive affect (e.g., happiness, joy) and negative affect (e.g., anger, sadness), treating them as independent. It is also useful to distinguish between measures that attempt to capture a person's level of subjective well-being in general, as opposed to those that focus on the proportion of time spent in one, rather than another, mental state. Because people's satisfaction with their lives tends to be relatively stable from moment to moment, duration measures usually focus on affect (Kahneman & Krueger, 2006). A primary example of a duration measure is the U-index, which measures the proportion of time an individual spends in an unpleasant state (Kahneman & Krueger, 2006).

The measures may be elicited through a variety of methods, including: (1) global self-reports in surveys, (2) the Experience Sampling Method, which collects information on individuals' actual experiences in real time in their natural environments, and (3) the Day Reconstruction Method, which asks people to reflect on how satisfied they felt at various times during the day (on the latter two techniques, see Kahneman, Krueger, Schkade, Schwarz, and Stone (2004) and Stone, Shiffman, and De Vries (1999)).

Provided that self-reported subjective well-being is a valid and empirically adequate measure for human well-being, statistical analyses can be conducted that allow for exploration of the relationship between known determinants such as socioeconomic and sociodemographic characteristics and well-being.[5] This approach has been successfully applied in numerous studies on the correlates of subjective well-being and has given rise to many interesting findings, including the relationship between individual well-being and economic conditions such as income, unemployment, inflation and inequality (for reviews see the references in footnote 1). We discuss some specific results on the relationship between happiness and income as well as unemployment in the following two sections.

## Income and Happiness

Persons with higher income have more opportunities to attain whatever they desire: in particular, they can buy more material goods and services. Standard economics therefore takes as self-evident that higher income and consumption levels provide higher well-being. This conclusion also follows from the concept of utility in economics, which is based on the notion that people's utility depends on what they have in absolute terms. Research on subjective well-being allows us to test this notion empirically.

---

[5] Technically, subjective well-being is modeled in a microeconometric function $W_{it} = \alpha + \beta X_{it} + \varepsilon_{it}$. In this model, $W_{it}$ is the true well-being of individual i at time t. $X = x_1, x_2, ..., x_n$ are known variables, like sociodemographic and socioeconomic characteristics, or environmental, social, institutional, and economic conditions for individual i at time t. Multiple regression analyses are conducted to estimate the model parameters and, as the dependent variable is measured on a ranking scale, normally ordered logit or probit estimation techniques are applied.

## Paradoxical empirical findings

The relationship between income and happiness measured at a particular point in time and place is the subject of a large empirical literature. As a robust and general result, it has been found that richer people, on average, report higher subjective well-being (see Clark, Frijters, & Shields, 2008 for a review). The relationship between income and subjective well-being proves to be statistically (usually highly) significant, even when a large number of other factors are controlled for. This evidence from happiness research seems to confirm the standard economic view.

However, there is a second way to study the relationship between income and happiness, namely to ask whether an increase in income over time raises reported subjective well-being. A striking and curious relationship is observed: people in some industrialized countries do not appear to be becoming happier over time, despite economic growth. This was first observed and documented by Easterlin (1974), and has been repeatedly found ever since (Blanchflower & Oswald, 2004; Easterlin, 1995, 2001; Easterlin & Angelescu, 2009). As these two findings on the relationship between income and happiness cannot easily be aligned, they are often referred to as the Easterlin paradox.

The Easterlin paradox has provoked reactions in two directions. One reaction is to challenge the empirical findings. Stevenson and Wolfers (2008), for instance, argue that some of the data on which the analyses of Easterlin and others rely should be dismissed due to changes in methodology (e.g., in Japan different survey questions have been used to measure subjective well-being in different years). Others document that there are Western countries like Denmark, Germany, and Italy that experienced substantial real per capita income growth as well as a (small) increase in reported satisfaction with life in the 1970s and 80s (Diener et. al. 2000). Moreover, the relationships presented between income and happiness over time are often not analyzed ceteris paribus. In other words, it is difficult to examine income and happiness in isolation, and additional factors that also change over time may contribute to observed outcomes. However, for the USA, a negative trend in subjective well-being over time is found even when individual characteristics are controlled for (Blanchflower & Oswald, 2004).

Given the current state of empirical data, it is difficult to reject, on statistical grounds, any hypothesis about the relationship or non-relationship between income and subjective well-being over time. Perhaps the safest position is to accept that there is no clear-cut trend, positive or negative, in self-reported subjective well-being over periods of 20–30 years in rich countries. Of course, this is interesting in itself; it indicates that there is more to subjective well-being than just the absolute level of income.

## The role of income aspirations

In order to shed light on the apparent paradox highlighted by Easterlin, happiness research in economics has sought to develop a concept of utility that is more psychologically sound. Two processes are emphasized. First, it is noted that whilst additional material goods and services initially provide extra pleasure, this is usually only transitory. Happiness with material things wears off, whereas satisfaction depends on change and disappears with continued consumption (Stutzer & Frey, 2007). This process, or mechanism, that reduces the hedonic effects of a constant or repeated stimulus, is called adaptation.

Second, people make social comparisons with relevant others and hence it is not the absolute level of income that matters most, but rather one's position relative to other individuals. Indeed, several economists in the past (e.g., Duesenberry, 1949; Veblen, 1899) have noted that individuals compare themselves to significant others with respect to income or consumption. Higher income people also have a higher *relative* income compared to others, and therefore a higher status in society (Frey & Stutzer, 2002a). Socially comparative or even competitive processes in consumption complement processes of hedonic adaptation.

It is suggested that the two processes make people strive for ever higher aspirations. Together, they can also explain why persons with high income at a given point in time report higher subjective well-being than those with low income. This is the social comparison effect suggesting that individuals derive utility from being superior to others. In contrast, there is no clear statistical relationship between income per capita and average life satisfaction in industrialized countries over time. This is the adaptation effect, which suggests that people get used to a higher income and therefore do not derive any additional utility from it after some time has passed (Frank, 1999).

There is now direct empirical evidence for the important role of income aspirations in individual welfare from two empirical studies for Germany and Switzerland (Stutzer, 2004; Stutzer & Frey, 2004). This is made possible by using two data sets that both include individual data on reported satisfaction with life, as well as income evaluation measures as proxies for people's aspiration levels.[6] It is found that higher income aspirations reduce people's satisfaction with life. In Switzerland and the New German Laender, the negative effect on subjective well-being of an increase in income aspiration level is of a similar absolute magnitude as the positive effect on well-being of an equal increase in income (Stutzer, 2004). This suggests that subjective well-being depends largely on the gap between income aspirations and actual income and not on the income level as such. Thus, the higher the ratio between aspired income and actual income, the less satisfied people are with their life, ceteris paribus. This supports the notion of relative income, which describes that individuals do not focus on the absolute income level but rather compare their income to the income of other individuals.

What are the consequences of the research insights relating to relative income? The empirical basis is still too small to be able to draw firm implications for economic theory and economic policy, and caution is required because such implications might be far-reaching. However, it would be interesting to study in greater depth how income aspirations relate to, for instance, redistributive taxation or public policy in general.

## Unemployment and Happiness

Standard economics has always considered unemployment a social bad with negative consequences for society. The economic policy proposals made by Keynes and his followers

---

[6] The income evaluation question in the German Socio-Economic Panel reads as follows: "Whether you feel an income is good or not so good depends on your personal life circumstances and expectations. In your case – the net household income _____ DM is just sufficient income." The reported amount is taken as a proxy for people's income aspirations.

were an effort to overcome this ill and to establish full employment. However, the assessment changed dramatically with the advent of new classical macroeconomics (see e.g., Snowdon & Vane, 2005). This school argued that unemployment is largely voluntary: most of those not working just refuse to do so at the prevailing wage rate. In this view, an important reason why the reservation wage is higher than the prevailing wage is that unemployment benefits are too high. People prefer not to work and to cash in these benefits. Happiness research in economics offers a new approach to this debate about the individual and social costs of unemployment.

## Unemployment reduces subjective well-being

The basic finding from happiness data is that unemployment reduces the individual well-being of those personally affected. Following their innovative work in Britain, Clark and Oswald (1994, p. 655) summarize this result as follows: "Joblessness depresses well-being more than any other single characteristic including important negative ones such as divorce and separation." In Germany, Winkelmann and Winkelmann (1998) found a negative effect of personal unemployment on life satisfaction that would require a sevenfold increase in income to compensate. Importantly, in these two analyses, indirect effects like income losses that may, but need not, accompany personal unemployment are kept constant. Being unemployed therefore has psychological costs over and above those due to potential decrease in material living standards (see Clark, 2003; Frey & Stutzer, 2002a, pp. 95–109; Stutzer & Lalive, 2004).

High unemployment rates also have non-negligible effects on people who are not personally affected by unemployment. Based on survey data from population samples from European Union member countries between 1975 and 1992, Di Tella et al. (2003) show that aggregate unemployment decreases average reported life satisfaction even if personal unemployment is taken into account. The question that naturally arises is why even people who are employed feel less satisfied with their lives when unemployment rates increase.

## Costs of high unemployment for the employed

The potential reasons that explain why workers' well-being decreases when unemployment rates increase can be divided into two broad categories (Luechinger et al. 2010). First, a high rate of unemployment may have general negative effects on society that affect everyone in a region. Such reasons include not only the direct effects of unemployment on crime and public finances, but also the general increase in income inequality within a society—an increase that may have the effect of triggering workers' empathy with the unemployed. Moreover, high unemployment rates affect factors specific to people's individual workplaces such as, for instance, changes in working hours and salaries (Frey, 2008).

Second, high unemployment also affects anticipated economic distress. For instance, the probability that a worker may himself experience a spell of unemployment in the future increases. A large literature documents the importance of self-reported job security on individuals' well-being (see e.g., De Witte, 1999; Duncan, White, Cheng, & Tomlinson, 1998; Green, 2006). Moreover, people may also expect salary decreases, reduced promotion opportunities and fewer possibilities to change jobs.

In an empirical study, Luechinger, Meier, and Stutzer (2010) isolate the negative anticipatory feelings of angst and stress due to economic insecurity. In order to distinguish between general negative externalities of unemployment and changes in economic risks to individuals, workers were studied in two sectors of the economy that differ fundamentally in their exposure to economic shocks—people working in the private sector and those working in the public sector. Public sector employees usually work in organizations that very rarely go bankrupt, and enjoy extended protection from dismissal. Thus, for institutional reasons these workers face a reduced risk of losing their jobs in comparison with workers in the private sector. For Germany, the researchers found that the subjective well-being of people working in the private sector was affected more strongly by general economic shocks than that of people working in the public sector, suggesting that a substantial fraction of the psychological costs brought about by general unemployment is due to increased economic insecurity.

In sum, research on happiness has identified two major aspects of unemployment that are largely neglected in standard economics. The first is that unemployment is not simply an underutilization of resources and not simply a decision between choosing to stay employed (at a low wage) and becoming unemployed (with unemployment benefits). Rather, unemployed individuals experience a loss in psychological well-being that goes beyond the reduction in income involved. The second major difference to standard economics is that the experience of utility losses goes beyond the persons actually unemployed. Persons with a job are also negatively affected by a higher unemployment rate; this is due in part to an increase in economic insecurity.

## Happiness Research Challenges the Rational Consumer Hypothesis

Neoclassical economic theory relies on revealed behavior—that is, on the actual choices people make—in order to evaluate the utility generated by the option chosen in a particular decision. This assumes that individuals are perfectly informed about what will bring them how much utility, and that they are perfectly capable of maximizing their utility given the options available to them. Further, this implies that people do not make any systematic mistakes when making decisions and that, if mistakes occur, individuals will correct them in the long run by learning. Scitovsky (1976) criticized this view as "unscientific" because "it seemed to rule out – as a logical impossibility – any conflict between what man chooses to get and what will best satisfy him" (p. 4).

Research on happiness has given rise to two insightful extensions of neoclassical economics' traditional emphasis on ex ante (that is, before the event) evaluation and observed decision. First, the standard economic concept of decision utility can be extended by using the concept of subjective well-being to indicate individual welfare judgments (similar to the concept of experienced utility by Kahneman et al. (1997)). This separation of concepts makes it possible to distinguish between the utility gained from experiences and the utility derived from observed behavior. The second extension is closely related to the first. It emphasizes that individuals may not be fully rational when they take decisions. Rather, their rationality may be imperfect with respect to the cognitive processes involved. The crucial question is:

How do people fare after they have made decisions? This is particularly relevant if people have limited self-control, i.e., are subject to restricted willpower.

## Limited self-control and individual well-being

In standard economics people are considered to have no self-control problems; they are able to make decisions that are concordant with their long-term preferences. Viewed this way, consuming goods and pursuing activities that some people consider addictive, such as smoking cigarettes, taking cocaine or watching TV, are considered a rational act. Contrary to this view, many people judge their own and other people's behavior as irrational in the sense that they think that they would be better off if they behaved differently and cared more for their future well-being.

Based on revealed preference, it is difficult, if not impossible, to discriminate between the view of consumers as rational actors and consumers mispredicting utility or facing self-control problems. However, with a measure of individual well-being, competing theories can be distinguished that make the same predictions concerning individual behavior, but differ in what they put forward as individual utility levels. This kind of test is a powerful tool in challenging theories that proved resistant to a multitude of observed behavior patterns.

The new approach is briefly illustrated for a specific issue, namely cigarette smoking. Other possible illustrations would be TV viewing (Benesch, Frey, & Stutzer, 2010; Frey, Benesch, & Stutzer, 2007) or obesity (Oswald & Powdthavee, 2007; Stutzer, 2009).The standard economic model predicts that recent increases in cigarette taxes and tighter restrictions on smoking reduce smoking and make individuals worse off. Smokers could always voluntarily refrain from smoking; the additional restrictions are only perceived as a reduction of the choice set. However, some smokers may have limited willpower to quit smoking. Such persons may welcome smoking restrictions and higher taxes as a kind of self-control mechanism. An approach that incorporates limited willpower into the process of decision-making thus predicts that smoking is reduced while individuals feel better off.

Research on happiness contributes to this debate by directly analyzing the effect of tobacco taxes on people's subjective well-being. Two longitudinal analyses across US and Canadian states used data from the General Social survey to study the effect of changes in state tobacco taxes on the reported happiness of people who were predicted to engage in smoking at the prevailing tax rates (Gruber & Mullainathan, 2005). It was found that a cigarette tax of 50 cents (in real terms) significantly raised the likelihood of being happy among those who tend to be smokers. In fact, with this tax they would be just as likely to report being happy as those not predicted to be smokers (i.e., the proportion of smokers in the lowest happiness category would fall by 7.5 percentage points). This result favors models of time-inconsistent smoking behavior, in which people have problems with self-control. Moreover, the result shows that price increases can serve as a self-commitment device by forcing individuals to reduce smoking as this activity has become more expensive.

## The misprediction of utility

Standard economics *assumes* people can successfully predict future utility—that is, how they will feel about future events. In contrast, in many careful experiments and surveys, psychologists have actually studied whether people are successful in forecasting utility (for reviews, see Hsee et al. 2012; Kahneman & Thaler, 2006; Loewenstein & Schkade, 1999; Wilson & Gilbert, 2003). While they find that people accurately predict whether an experience will primarily elicit good or bad feelings, people often hold incorrect intuitive theories about the determinants of happiness; that is, they overestimate the impact of specific life events on their experienced well-being with regard to intensity, as well as with regard to duration. For instance, many people predict that a win of their favored soccer team would leave them in a happy mood for days. In fact, every day events take over and determine people's mood such that the joy over the win is short term, if there is elation at all.

The standard economic model of consumer decisions is probably appropriate for most goods and activities and for most situations. It also applies when individuals make random prediction errors. There are, however, situations in which people have to make trade-offs between different activities, goods, or options that differ systematically in the extent to which their future utility can be predicted. If this is the case, systematic economic consequences emerge (Frey & Stutzer, 2008). There are options, or attributes of options, that are more salient than others when making a decision, and are thus relatively overvalued. If people choose options according to this evaluation, their experienced utility is lower than what they expected and lower than what they could have experienced had they not mispredicted their utility. Moreover, they consume different goods with different attributes and pursue different activities than in a situation where no option in the choice set would have special salience.

There are four major sources for systematic over- and undervaluation of choice options that can be distinguished: (1) the underestimation of adaptation,[7] (2) distorted memory of past experiences, (3) the rationalization of decisions, and (4) false intuitive theories about the sources of future utility (Frey & Stutzer, 2008).

Future research may further explore the tensions people face when they have to trade off material and non-material or social goods and activities. Misprediction of utility might be more likely across these two categories of options. When people face various possible alternatives, material factors get more attention and are overvalued due to the neglect of adaptation, rationalization and memory biases. This would imply consequences with regard to behavior (material goods are over-consumed) and with regard to individual well-being (people are less well off than they would be without mispredicting utility).

# The Use of Happiness Research for Public Policy

From a constitutional point of view (Buchanan & Tullock, 1962; Mueller, 1996), there are two levels at which policy decisions are taken: (1) in the current politico-economic process within given rules; and (2) at the constitutional level, where the rules of the game as such

---

[7] The aspect of underestimated adaptation to new situations has been neatly introduced in theoretical models of intertemporal decision-making (Loewenstein et al. 2003). Based on their model of projection bias, various phenomena can be modeled, like the misguided purchase of durable goods or consumption profiles with too much consumption early on in life. Misprediction of utility thus provides an alternative to seemingly irrational saving behavior that is usually addressed in a framework of self-control problems.

are determined. We briefly inquire how the insights gained from happiness research affect public policy at the two levels.

# Happiness research for the current politico-economic process

One of the major contributions of happiness research, directly relevant for public policy, refers to the new instruments that enable individuals' preferences and welfare to be captured. As a consequence, insights from happiness research increase political competition in the current politico-economic process. There is a demand for happiness research by politicians, public officials, and representatives of special interest groups as they hope to strengthen their position in the competition for votes or in bargaining for government policies. As we will explore in this section, a point of interest is the valuation of public goods and public bads. There are also hopes that a complementary indicator of aggregate happiness might guide policy making more towards citizens' preferences than indicators of aggregate national income alone. In the following, we discuss happiness research in these two areas.

## *Valuation of public goods*

The provision of public goods (e.g., clean air, security) is a central function of government agencies. More and more often, government agencies are required to provide cost–benefit analyses to back their proposals for government programs. However, the benefits derived from public goods are inherently difficult to measure because they are not exchanged on markets. In reaction to the demand by public agencies and private actors, a wide variety of methods related to stated and revealed preference have been developed for the valuation of public goods (see, e.g., Freeman, 2003).

Within happiness research, another promising method is emerging. It is called the Life Satisfaction Approach (LSA) (see Frey, Luechinger, & Stutzer, 2010). With reported subjective well-being as a proxy measure for individual welfare, public goods can be directly evaluated in utility terms. The marginal utility of public goods or the disutility of public bads is estimated by correlating the amount of public goods or public bads with individuals' reported subjective well-being. By measuring the marginal utility of a public good or the marginal disutility of a public bad, as well as the marginal utility of income, the tradeoff ratio between income and the public good can be calculated.

This approach avoids some of the major difficulties inherent in both the stated preference and the revealed preference methods. For instance, the contingent valuation method (Freeman, 2003)—asking people how much, in principle, they would be willing to pay for some non-market good—often faces the problem of the hypothetical nature of the questions asked and the unfamiliarity of the task. People may, for instance, be asked how much they would be willing to pay to preserve a particular kind of fish in the North Sea. Moreover, one cannot exclude the failure of respondents to consider the effect of their budget constraints and substitutes. Symbolic valuation in the form of attitude expression and superficial answers is likely to result (Kahneman & Knetsch, 1992). Similarly, the problem of strategic answers (in order to bias the result in the respondent's preferred direction) can be addressed only to a limited extent. The LSA is not affected by either of these problems. It does not rely on respondents' ability to consider all relevant consequences of a change in the provision of a public good. It suffices if respondents state their own life satisfaction with some degree of precision. Moreover, there is no reason to expect strategic answering behavior. A more detailed comparison of the LSA with the standard non-market valuation techniques can be found in Kahneman and Sugden (2005) and Dolan and Metcalfe (2008).

The LSA has, for example, been used to value air pollution (Luechinger, 2009; Welsch, 2006), airport noise nuisance (van Praag & Baarsma, 2005), terrorism (Frey et al., 2009), droughts (Nick et al., 2009), and flood hazards (Luechinger & Raschky, 2009). Recent studies applying the LSA have already reached a high standard, and preconditions for its application are better understood and formulated. What has so far been an academically driven development of a new method may soon become an empirical tool that is in demand in the political process.

## Aggregate happiness indicators as complements to gross national product

Happiness indicators are increasingly accepted as complements to the long-established measures of national income as a way to infer aggregate welfare within a nation, thus following the lead of the social indicators approach and of the capabilities approach (e.g., Sen, 1999). The Human Development Index, e.g., measures social welfare by aggregating per capita income, longevity, and school participation rates, attributing each one equal weight. The capabilities approach inquires to what extent the individuals have actual access to goods and services. The UK and Australia as well as some other countries are committed to producing national measures of well-being. Recently, a specific module was added to the European Social Survey generating comparative information on a wide range of aspects of individual well-being (Huppert et al., 2009). Aggregate happiness indicators have several interesting qualities in comparison to traditional measures of economic activity. First, measures of happiness include *non-material* aspects of human well-being such as the influence of social relations, autonomy, and self-determination. These are excluded, or most insufficiently included, in the traditional national accounts. Second, measures of happiness consider *outcome* aspects of components already included in gross national product (GNP) via input measures. This holds in particular with respect to the vast area of government activity (measured in GNP by the costs of material and of labor). Third, measures of happiness look at *subjectively* evaluated outcomes in line with the basic methodological approach of economics. In contrast, the capabilities approach and the United Nations Human Development Index look at objectively observable functioning (Sen, 1999).

In sum, aggregate happiness indicators provide new and complementary information about preference satisfaction that could become a relevant input into political discourse. So far, robust effects of unemployment and inflation on the popularity and re-election support of governments have been documented (for a review, see Lewis-Beck & Paldam, 2000). This research is based on the idea that voters hold governments responsible for the state of the economy and thereby also fuel political competition providing incentives to governments for a sound economic policy. An aggregate happiness indicator might intensify this competition as politicians get incentives to justify their actions in terms of a broader and better indicator of individual welfare. However, not too much should be expected. Aggregate happiness indicators are relatively cheap to assemble. While this allows replicating surveys that seem rigged, it also allows parties with special interests to easily come up with yet another measure serving those interests but confusing voters. A group active in the construction industry may, for instance, propose a social welfare indicator which attributes great weight to the quality of housing. As a result, such an aggregate happiness index indicates a rise in social welfare when more houses are built even if other aspects of welfare are treated lightly.

## Happiness research for the constitutional level of policy

Happiness research can also provide valuable insights on the constitutional level of public policy. However, this requires that research questions be chosen that relate institutions to reported subjective well-being in a comparative manner. This provides the public with access to information about the institutions that might best allow them to pursue their idea of the good life. Some insights have already been produced, which can be brought into the political discussion process. They include policy issues such as, for example, the role of direct democratic decision making in citizens' well-being (Frey & Stutzer, 2000), the effect of mandatory retirement and mandatory schooling on happiness (Charles, 2004; Oreopoulos, 2007), the consequences of social work norms and birth control rights on women's well-being (Lalive & Stutzer, 2010; Pezzini, 2005) or the relation between working time regulation and people's subjective well-being (Alesina, Glaeser, & Sacerdote, 2005). However, to our mind, happiness research has so far only skimmed the surface of what promises to become a challenging area of comparative institutional research.

## Concluding Remarks

This chapter has presented only a selection of possible applications and recent advances in the economic study of individual happiness. Many more have been undertaken. No attempt has been made to be comprehensive. Rather, the intention is to convey to the reader that happiness data offers a useful proxy measure for individual welfare. It therewith points to new ways of tackling old questions, and opens the possibility of exploring issues that have previously been seen as difficult, or even impossible, to address empirically. The examples provided cover several fields of study, ranging from income aspirations and unemployment to limited willpower and utility misprediction, suggesting that the new approach may be useful for many different issues in economic research. Time will show whether the potential of economic research on subjective well-being is enough to make it part of a new core of economics.

## References

Alesina, A., Glaeser, E., & Sacerdote, B. (2005). Work and leisure in the United States and Europe: Why so different? In M. Gertler & K. Rogoff (Eds.), *NBER Macroeconomics Annual 2005* (pp. 1–100). Cambridge, MA: MIT Press.

Benesch, C., Frey, B. S., & Stutzer, A. (2010). TV channels, self control and happiness. *The BE Journal of Economic Analysis and Policy, 10*, Article 86.

Blanchflower, D. G., & Oswald, A. J. (2004). Well-being over time in Britain and the USA. *Journal of Public Economics, 88*(7–8), 1359–1386.

Buchanan, J. M., & Tullock, G. (1962). *The calculus of consent. Logical foundations of constitutional democracy*. Ann Arbor, MI: University of Michigan Press.

Carroll, N., Frijters, P., & Shields, M. A. (2009). Quantifying the costs of drought: New evidence from life satisfaction data. *Journal of Population Economics*, 22(2), 445–461.

Charles, K. K. (2004). Is retirement depressing? Labor force inactivity and psychological well-being in later life. In Polachek, Solomon W. (Ed.), *Accounting for worker well-being. Research in labor economics vol. 23* (pp. 269–299). Amsterdam, the Netherlands: Elsevier.

Clark, A. E. (2003). Unemployment as a social norm: Psychological evidence from panel data. *Journal of Labor Economics*, 21(2), 323–51.

Clark, A. E., & Oswald, A. J. (1994). Unhappiness and unemployment. *Economic Journal*, 104(424), 648–659.

Clark, A., Frijters, P., & Shields, M. (2008). Relative income, happiness and utility: An explanation for the Easterlin paradox and other puzzles. *Journal of Economic Literature*, 46(1), 95–144.

De Witte, H. (1999). Job insecurity and psychological well-being: Review of the literature and exploration of some unresolved issues. *European Journal of Work and Organizational Psychology*, 8(2), 155–77.

Di Tella, R., & MacCulloch, R. (2006). Some uses of happiness data in economics. *Journal of Economic Perspectives*, 20(1), 25–46.

Di Tella, R., MacCulloch, R. J., & Oswald, A. J. (2003). The macroeconomics of happiness. *Review of Economics and Statistics*, 85(4), 809–27.

Diener, E. (1984). Subjective well-being. *Psychological Bulletin*, 95(3), 542–575.

Diener, E., & Oishi, S. (2000). Money and happiness: Income and subjective well-being across nations. In E. Diener & E. M. Suh (Eds.), *Culture and subjective well-being* (pp. 185–218). Cambridge, MA: MIT Press.

Diener, E., Suh, E. M., Lucas, R. E., & Smith, H. L. (1999). Subjective well-being: Three decades of progress. *Psychological Bulletin*, 125(2), 276–302.

Dolan, P., & Metcalfe, R. (2008). *Comparing willingness-to-pay and subjective well-being in the context of non-market goods. Centre for Economic Performance Discussion Paper No. 0890*. London, UK: LSE.

Duesenberry, J. S. (1949). *Income, savings and the theory of consumer behavior*. Cambridge, MA: Harvard University Press.

Duncan, G., White, M., Cheng, Y., & Tomlinson, M. (1998). *Restructuring the employment relationship*. New York, NY: Oxford University Press.

Easterlin, R. A. (1974). Does economic growth improve the human lot? Some empirical evidence. In P. A. David & Reder, M. W. (Eds.), *Nations and households in economic growth: Essays in honour of Moses Abramowitz* (pp. 89–125). New York, NY: Academic Press.

Easterlin, R. A. (1995). Will raising the incomes of all increase the happiness of all? *Journal of Economic Behavior and Organization*, 27(1), 35–48.

Easterlin, R. A. (2001). Income and happiness: Towards a unified theory. *Economic Journal*, 111(473), 465–484.

Easterlin, R. A. (Ed.). (2002). *Happiness in Economics*. Cheltenham, UK: Edward Elgar.

Easterlin, R A., & Angelescu, L. (2009). *Modern economic growth and quality of life: Cross sectional and time series evidence*. Mimeo, CA: University of Southern California.

Frank, R. (1999). *Luxury fever: Why money fails to satisfy in an era of excess*. New York, NY: Free Press.

Freeman, A. M., III. (2003). *The measurement of environmental and resource values: Theory and methods*. Washington, DC: Resources for the Future.

Frey, B. S. (2008). *Happiness: A revolution in economics*. Cambridge, MA: MIT Press.

Frey, B. S., & Stutzer, A. (2000). Happiness, economy and institutions. *Economic Journal*, 110(466), 918–938.

Frey, B. S., & Stutzer, A. (2002a). *Happiness and economics: How the economy and institutions affect well-being*. Princeton, NJ: Princeton University Press.

Frey, B. S., & Stutzer, A. (2002b). What can economists learn from happiness research? *Journal of Economic Literature*, 40(2), 402–435.

Frey, B. S., & Stutzer, A. (2008). *Economic consequences of mispredicting utility*. WWZ Discussion Paper No. 01/08, University of Basel.

Frey, B. S., Benesch, C., & Stutzer, A. (2007). Does watching TV make us happy? *Journal of Economic Psychology*, 28(3), 283–313.

Frey, B. S., Benz, M., & Stutzer, A. (2004). Introducing procedural utility: Not only what, but also how matters. *Journal of Institutional and Theoretical Economic*, 160(3), 377–401.

Frey, B. S., Luechinger, S., & Stutzer, A. (2009). The life satisfaction approach to the value of public goods: The case of terrorism. *Public Choice*, 138(3–4), 317–345.

Frey, B. S., Luechinger, S., & Stutzer, A. (2010). The life satisfaction approach to environmental valuation. *Annual Review of Resource Economics*, 2, 139–160.

Green, F. (2006). *Demanding work. The paradox of job quality in the affluent economy*. Princeton, NJ: Princeton University Press.

Gruber, J. H., & Mullainathan, S. (2005). Do cigarette taxes make smokers happier? *Advances in Economic Analysis and Policy*, 5(1), 1–43.

Hsee, C. K., Rottenstreich, Y., & Stutzer, A. (2012). Suboptimal choices and the need for experienced individual well-being in economic analysis. Forthcoming in the *International Journal of Happiness and Development*.

Huppert, F. A., Marks, N., Clark, A., Siegrist, J., Stutzer, A., Vittersø J., & Wahrendorf, M. (2009). Measuring well-being across Europe: Description of the ESS well-being module and preliminary findings. *Social Indicators Research*, 91(3), 301–315.

Kahneman, D., & Knetsch, J. L. (1992). Valuing public goods: The purchase of moral satisfaction. *Journal of Economics and Management*, 22(1), 57–70.

Kahneman, D., & Krueger, A. B. (2006). Developments in the measurement of subjective well-being. *Journal of Economic Perspectives*, 20(1), 3–24.

Kahneman, D., & Sugden, R. (2005). Experienced utility as a standard of policy evaluation. *Environmental and Resource Economics*, 32(1), 161–81.

Kahneman, D., & Thaler, R. H. (2006). Anomalies: Utility maximization and experienced utility. *Journal of Economic Perspectives*, 20(1), 221–234.

Kahneman, D., Wakker, P. P., & Sarin, R. (1997). Back to Bentham? Explorations of experienced utility. *Quarterly Journal of Economics*, 112(2), 375–405.

Kahneman, D., Diener, E., & Schwarz, N. (Eds.). (1999). *Well-Being: The Foundations of Hedonic Psychology*. New York, NY: Russell Sage Foundation.

Kahneman, D., Krueger, A. B., Schkade, D. A., Schwarz, N., & Stone, A. A. (2004). A survey method for characterizing daily life experience: The day reconstruction method. *Science*, 306(5702), 1776–1780.

Lalive, R., & Stutzer, A. (2010). Approval of equal rights and gender differences in well-being. *Journal of Population Economics*, 23(3), 933–962.

Layard, R. (2005). *Happiness: Lessons from a new science*. New York, NY: Penguin.

Lewis-Beck, M. S., & Paldam, M. (2000). Economic voting: An introduction. *Electoral Studies*, 19(2–3), 113–121.

Loewenstein, G., & Schkade, D. A. (1999). Wouldn't it be nice? Predicting future feelings. In D. Kahneman, E. Diener and N. Schwarz (Eds.), *Well-being: The foundation of hedonic psychology* (pp. 85–105). New York, NY: Russell Sage Foundation.

Loewenstein, G., O'Donoghue, T., & Rabin, M. (2003). Projection bias in predicting future utility. *Quarterly Journal of Economics*, 118(4), 1209–1248.

Luechinger, S. (2009). Valuing air quality using the life satisfaction approach. *The Economic Journal*, 119(536), 482–515.

Luechinger, S., & Raschky, P. A. (2009). Valuing flood disasters using the life satisfaction approach. *Journal of Public Economics*, 93(3–4), 620–633.

Luechinger, S., Meier, S., & Stutzer, A. (2010). Why does unemployment hurt the employed? Evidence from the life satisfaction gap between the public and the private sector. *Journal of Human Resources*, 45, 998–1045.

Mueller, D. C. (1996). *Constitutional Democracy*. Oxford, UK: Oxford University Press.

Oreopoulos, P. (2007). Do dropouts drop out too soon? Wealth, health, and happiness from compulsory schooling. *Journal of Public Economics*, 91(11–12), 2213–2229.

Oswald, A. J., & Powdthavee, N. (2007). Obesity, unhappiness, and the challenge of affluence: Theory and evidence. *Economic Journal*, 117(521): 441–454.

Pezzini, S. (2005). The effect of women's rights on women's welfare: Evidence from a natural experiment. *Economic Journal*, 115(502), C208–C227.

Scitovsky, T. (1976). *The joyless economy: An inquiry into human satisfaction and consumer dissatisfaction*. New York, NY: Oxford University Press.

Sen, A. K. (1999). *Development as freedom*. New York, NY: Alfred Knopf.

Snowdon, B., & Vane, H. R. (2005). *Modern macroeconomics: Its origin, development and current state*. Cheltenham, UK: Elgar.

Stevenson, B., & Wolfers, J. (2008). Economic growth and subjective well-being: Reassessing the Easterlin paradox. *Brookings Papers on Economic Activity*, Spring.

Stone, A. A., Shiffman, S. S., & DeVries, M. W. (1999). Ecological momentary assessment. In D. Kahneman, E. Diener, & N. Schwarz (Eds.), *Well-being: The foundations of hedonic psychology* (pp. 26–39). New York, NY: Russell Sage Foundation.

Stutzer, A. (2004). The role of income aspirations in individual happiness. *Journal of Economic Behavior and Organization*, 54(1), 89–109.

Stutzer, A. (2009). Happiness when temptation overwhelms willpower. In A. K. Dutt & B. Radcliff (Eds.), *Happiness, economics, and politics: Toward a multi-disciplinary approach* (pp. 97–126). Cheltenham, UK: Edward Elgar.

Stutzer, A., & Frey, B. S. (2004). Reported subjective well-being: a challenge for economic theory and economic policy. *Schmollers Jahrbuch: Zeitschrift für Wirtschafts- und Sozialwissenschaften* 124(2), 191–231.

Stutzer, A., & Frey, B. S. (2007). What happiness research can tell us about self-control problems and utility misprediction. In Bruno S. Frey and Alois Stutzer (Eds.), *Economics and psychology. A promising new cross-disciplinary field* (pp. 169–195). Cambridge, MA: MIT Press.

Stutzer, A., & Frey, B. S. (2010). Recent advances in the economics of individual subjective well-being. *Social Research* 77(2), 679–714.

Stutzer, A., & Lalive, R. (2004). The role of social work norms in job searching and subjective well-being. *Journal of the European Economic Association*, 2(4), 696–719.

van Praag, B. M. S., & Baarsma, B. E. (2005). Using happiness surveys to value intangibles: The case of airport noise. *Economic Journal, 115*(500), 224–246.

van Praag, B. M. S., & Ferrer-i-Carbonell, A. (2004). *Happiness quantified—A satisfaction calculus approach.* Oxford, UK: Oxford University Press.

Veblen, T. (1899). *The theory of leisure class.* New York, NY: Modern Library.

Welsch, H. (2006). Environment and happiness: Valuation of air pollution using life satisfaction data. *Ecological Economics, 58*(4), 801–813.

Wilson, T. D., & Gilbert, D. T. (2003). Affective forecasting. In M. Zanna (Ed.), *Advances in Experimental Social Psychology* (Vol. 35, pp. 345–411). New York, NY: Elsevier.

Winkelmann, R., & Winkelmann, L. (1998). Why are the unemployed so unhappy? Evidence from panel data. *Economica, 65*(257), 1–15.

# CHAPTER 35

# COMPARING WELL-BEING ACROSS NATIONS: CONCEPTUAL AND EMPIRICAL ISSUES

## WILLIAM TOV AND EVELYN W. M. AU

Singapore Management University, Singapore

THE past decade has witnessed a growing interest in well-being indicators and their potential for informing public policy (Diener & Tov, 2011; Dolan & White, 2007; Kahneman, Krueger, Schkade, Schwarz, & Stone, 2004). A number of factors have contributed to this trend. First, a substantial body of research on subjective well-being (SWB) has fostered increasing confidence in the validity of well-being measures (Diener, Suh, Lucas, & Smith, 1999; Veenhoven, 1996). A traditional concern is that happiness means different things to different people and that, consequently, people's ratings of how happy they are cannot be compared in any meaningful way. This problem is potentially magnified when comparing people from different cultures. In fact, over the past half-century, cross-national research on SWB has provided important evidence *against* these objections (e.g., Diener, Diener, & Diener, 1995). In showing that societal levels of well-being *are* related to socioeconomic conditions, cross-national studies provide evidence that well-being judgments are not completely relative and that meaningful comparisons are possible.

Another factor contributing to the prominence of well-being measures in discussions of public policy is increased scrutiny over economic indicators, especially their limitations for providing a complete picture of the quality of life in society. Economists have suggested that rising economic growth can sometimes be accompanied by negative effects across society. These negative "externalities" can include pollution from increased manufacturing and lack of family stability from greater geographic mobility (Layard, 2005). Oswald (1997) observed that job satisfaction in the USA and UK remained stagnant despite rising income from the 1970s to the 1990s. Although economic variables are related to well-being, other factors such as social relationships and a sense of mastery (i.e., feeling that one is developing and is using valuable skills) are also important (Tay & Diener, 2011). Consequently, several economists have begun to advocate for *subjective* measures of well-being to supplement objective indicators that have traditionally informed public policy (Blanchflower & Oswald, 2011; Stiglitz, Sen, & Fitoussi, 2009; see also Cummins, Chapter 14, this volume). Layard (2005) has suggested that such measures could help improve cost–benefit analyses of policy decisions. Instead of considering costs solely in financial terms (such as people's willingness-to-pay for goods), well-being measures could expand the notion of costs and benefits to how people's quality of life might be affected. However, the ability to make use of such information is likely to hinge on the sufficiency and cautious interpretation of survey data. Though the most relevant surveys for policymakers will be those involving their constituents, on occasion, cross-national data may also be useful because social conditions and policies often vary more between countries than within. That said, such data must be interpreted cautiously lest faulty policy recommendations will be made.

In this chapter, we review cross-national survey studies of SWB. We begin with a short history of the concept of SWB and examine how it has been measured in national surveys. We then review some findings on well-being at the level of societies and individuals. The former concerns how the economic and social conditions of *countries* are related to their average level of happiness and life satisfaction. The latter considers how the characteristics of happy and unhappy *individuals* may differ across cultures. Next we discuss important issues in research design and analysis of cross-national data, and in the measurement of well-being across cultures. Advances in psychometrics and cross-cultural psychology have raised the standards for measuring constructs across cultures, and initial applications to well-being measures are examined. We close with an assessment of future directions for cross-national research on well-being.

# The Concept of Subjective Well-Being

SWB refers to the myriad ways in which people experience and evaluate their own lives positively (Diener, 1984). Due to the breadth of the concept, survey studies have measured SWB in different ways. An early measure was the self-anchoring scale (Kilpatrick & Cantril, 1960), which uses a pictorial ten-step ladder. Participants are first asked to define for themselves the top and bottom of the ladder (i.e., the best and worst possible lives). Then they indicate where on the ladder their current life is. Another common measure asks people to report how often they experienced various positive and negative feelings (or affect; Bradburn, 1969). An *affect balance* score is then computed by subtracting the negative affect score from the positive affect score. Alternatively, people might be asked how they feel about various domains of life (Andrews & Withey, 1974) such as their family, job, and health.

This initial body of work led to a distinction between cognitive and affective aspects of SWB (Diener, 1984; Diener et al., 1999). The cognitive components include overall judgments of life satisfaction as well as more specific domain satisfactions (e.g., satisfaction with working life, economic situation, health and so on), whereas the affective components consist of positive and negative emotions. One can also distinguish global measures of SWB from more specific types of measures (Diener & Tov, 2011; Kim-Prieto, Diener, Tamir,

Table 35.1 Types of SWB measures in survey studies

|  | Cognitive | Affective |
|---|---|---|
| Global | Life satisfaction<br>Overall quality of life<br>Life evaluation<br>(e.g., best possible life) | Overall happiness<br>General depression |
| Time-inclusive | Satisfaction with the past day | Past month depression<br>Frequency of happiness in past week<br>Previous day emotions |

Scollon, & Diener, 2005; Robinson & Clore, 2002). Global measures require an overall assessment of well-being, generalized over one's life (such as overall happiness). In contrast, *narrow* measures might focus on specific areas of life (e.g., job satisfaction). There are also *momentary* measures that ask people to report their on-line (current) feelings and moods, and *time-inclusive* (or retrospective) measures that ask people how they felt over a certain period of time (e.g., depression in the past week).

Thus, the different components of well-being can be measured in various ways (see Table 35.1). Cognitive well-being can be assessed at a global level or at a more specific, time-inclusive level (e.g., satisfaction with the past week). Similarly, affective well-being can be measured in an overall sense or with reference to specific periods. Different SWB measures have distinct advantages. Kahneman et al. (2004) noted that global SWB measures were more susceptible to memory biases than were measures of recent feelings. On the other hand, global measures are more likely than momentary measures to capture cultural differences in well-being (Diener & Lucas, 2000; Robinson & Clore, 2002), and may be more reflective of enduring societal conditions. However, not all types of SWB measures have been emphasized in cross-national surveys.

# THE NATURE OF SUBJECTIVE WELL-BEING MEASURES IN CROSS-NATIONAL SURVEYS

To assess the types of well-being that have been measured in cross-national surveys, we turned to the World Database of Happiness (WDH; Veenhoven, n.d.). The WDH provides a well-updated compendium of well-being scores for over 160 societies based on survey studies from 1946 to the present. Our analysis includes data up to 2009. Large portions of the data are taken from cross-national surveys such as the Eurobarometer, the World Values Survey (WVS), and the Gallup World Poll, as well as smaller scale national studies. Because we were interested in the *totality of information* in the WDH, our basic unit of analysis was the single data point (e.g., average happiness for France in 1995). We included nations that are no longer formally in existence (e.g., Yugoslavia) because we were interested in how SWB has been measured throughout the history of survey research. However, to maintain a consistent level of analysis, we excluded data that were aggregated into "super regions" (e.g., the European Union), as well as data on specific states within the United States.

For each data point, we classified the measure according to the framework in Table 35.1. Although we initially distinguished between cognitive and affective measures, some measures were a mixture of both. For example, the delighted–terrible scale (Andrews & Withey, 1974) was considered a mixed measure because the response labels included both cognitive (e.g., mostly satisfied) and affective (e.g., unhappy) terms. We classified mixed measures separately. Three measures in the database did not clearly reflect affective or cognitive well-being per se and were excluded. These were measures of success in achieving one's goals and how well a person's happiness can be judged.

We also grouped the countries into subregions (United Nations, 2000). These groupings were predominantly geographical rather than cultural or ideological. For example, the UN classifies both Georgia and Jordan as part of Western Asia, instead of Eastern Europe and the Middle East, respectively. As our intention is to provide a rough assessment of world representation in the WDH, the UN categories serve our purpose.

Table 35.2 presents the distribution of data points across subregions and sorted according to type of SWB. Ninety percent of the cross-national data available in the WDH consists of global measures of well-being. This is not surprising given that survey researchers are often interested in broad topics such as political attitudes and economic conditions rather than the nuances of daily experience. Even so, most global measures focused on *cognitive* SWB rather than affective SWB (67% versus 22%). The cognitive measures included life satisfaction judgments, overall perceptions of the quality of life, and the self-anchoring ladder. All measures of general, affective well-being asked respondents to rate their overall happiness.

Only 10% of WDH data involved time-inclusive measures that specified a recent period of time (e.g., the previous day or the past week). The Affect Balance Scale (ABS; Bradburn, 1969)—which assesses feelings in the past few weeks—accounted for nearly one-third (28%) of time-inclusive affective measures. The majority of time-inclusive affect measures (64%) were from the Gallup World Poll (GWP; Gallup, Inc., 2008), which measured previous-day affect. In contrast to global measures, the time-inclusive measures included more negative affect items such as depression and anger. The small percentage of data using time-inclusive mixed measures is based on a single item from the GWP asking respondents if they would like "more days like yesterday." This item is mixed as both cognitive evaluations and affective experience could influence responses to this question.

Both global and time-inclusive measures provide researchers with distinct information. For example, Diener, Kahneman, Arora, Harter, and Tov (2009) observed that gross domestic product (GDP) per capita correlated more strongly with global well-being measures than previous-day affect balance. Although people in poor countries are generally less satisfied in an overall sense, they still report positive experiences in their daily life. The distinction between global cognitive SWB and time-inclusive affective SWB may also have implications for how countries are ranked. In Table 35.3, we present the top and bottom five countries on two measures of well-being from the 2008 GWP (as compiled by the WDH). The first measure is global life satisfaction; the second measure is previous-day affect balance. We only included countries with data on both measures (N = 65) to ensure that the rankings were based on a consistent set. As a result, some countries (e.g., USA, China, and Denmark) were excluded. In terms of life satisfaction, four of the top five countries are in Europe, and all of the bottom five countries are in Africa. In contrast, the rankings for previous-day affect

Table 35.2 Number of data points in the World Database of Happiness by region and type of well-being

| UN Region | General | | | Time-inclusive | | | Total | Pct (%) |
| --- | --- | --- | --- | --- | --- | --- | --- | --- |
| | Cog | Aff | Mix | Cog | Aff | Mix | | |
| Africa, Eastern | 43 | 1 | | | 13 | 10 | 67 | 2 |
| Africa, Middle | 13 | | | | 7 | 2 | 22 | 1 |
| Africa, Northern | 22 | 5 | | | 8 | 3 | 38 | 1 |
| Africa, Southern | 23 | 10 | | | 6 | 2 | 41 | 1 |
| Africa, Western | 51 | 6 | | | 14 | 10 | 81 | 2 |
| America, Central | 93 | 15 | | | 10 | 7 | 125 | 3 |
| America, Caribbean | 17 | 4 | | | 7 | 5 | 33 | 1 |
| America, Northern | 187 | 119 | 8 | | 29 | 2 | 345 | 9 |
| America, Southern | 144 | 30 | | | 15 | 10 | 199 | 5 |
| Asia, Eastern | 137 | 42 | 9 | | 13 | 5 | 206 | 5 |
| Asia, South-Central | 62 | 25 | | | 17 | 11 | 115 | 3 |
| Asia, South-Eastern | 45 | 30 | | | 11 | 7 | 93 | 2 |
| Asia, Western | 112 | 29 | | | 24 | 12 | 177 | 4 |
| Europe, Eastern | 341 | 121 | 26 | | 29 | 12 | 529 | 13 |
| Europe, Northern | 434 | 163 | | | 31 | 9 | 637 | 16 |
| Europe, Southern | 353 | 86 | 1 | | 26 | 11 | 477 | 12 |
| Europe, Western | 561 | 182 | 3 | | 21 | 6 | 773 | 19 |
| Oceania | 40 | 17 | 6 | | 4 | 2 | 69 | 2 |
| Total | 2678 | 885 | 53 | 0 | 285 | 126 | 4027 | 100 |
| Pct (%) | 67 | 22 | 1 | 0 | 7 | 3 | 100 | |

Aff, affective measure; Cog, cognitive measure; Mix, mixed measure.
A data point is defined as a mean well-being score for a single country from a single survey-year. Countries are grouped according to regions defined by the United Nations (2000).
Data are taken from Veenhoven (n.d.).

balance are more diverse: the top five countries include both Western European and African countries, and the bottom five countries span Europe, Africa, and the Middle East.

An important insight from Table 35.3 is that the "happiest" nation in a cognitive sense may not necessarily be the happiest nation in terms of emotional experiences, and vice versa. This distinction should be borne in mind when rankings of the "happiest countries" are reported in the media. For example, Denmark is frequently cited as the happiest country in the world (Safer, 2008; Weir & Johnson, 2007). This label has been met with mixed reaction ranging from tongue-in-cheek reflection (Christensen, Herskind, & Vaupel, 2006) to skepticism. A puzzled Danish columnist remarked that "People [in Denmark] are not looking

Table 35.3 Top and bottom five countries on two measures of well-being

|  |  | General life satisfaction | | Previous day affect balance | |
| --- | --- | --- | --- | --- | --- |
|  |  | Nation | Score | Nation | Score |
| Top 5 |  | Ireland | 8.14 | Iceland | 66 |
|  |  | Norway | 8.09 | Djibouti | 62 |
|  |  | Finland | 8.02 | Kenya | 62 |
|  |  | Sweden | 7.90 | Ireland | 60 |
|  |  | Australia | 7.88 | Mali | 60 |
| Bottom 5 |  | Liberia | 3.43 | Lebanon | 23 |
|  |  | Benin | 3.02 | Algeria | 21 |
|  |  | Burundi | 2.94 | Armenia | 21 |
|  |  | Zimbabwe | 2.83 | Georgia | 19 |
|  |  | Tanzania | 2.45 | Iraq | 14 |

very happy in the street" (Dorset, quoted in Safer, 2008). As Safer (2008) reports, the happiness of Danes may be better characterized by contentment rather than over-flowing ebullience.

What tends to be overlooked in these reports is that a major source of these data is the WDH. As we noted earlier, the majority of data in the WDH (67%) are global cognitive measures of well-being such as life satisfaction. Thus, what the media (and often well-being researchers themselves) have referred to as "happiness" rankings may be a misnomer. The term *happiness* (in contrast to *life satisfaction*) connotes an experience that is emotional and momentary; it conjures up images of smiling, laughing people. How does Denmark score on happiness? The WDH does not contain an exact measure of momentary happiness; however, it contains two measures that are relevant. First, in 2007, Denmark's score on previous-day affect balance was 60, which would place it in the top six in Table 35.3. However, the extent to which the affect balance score captures *happiness* per se is not clear because participants were not specifically asked how much happiness they felt (Veenhoven, n.d.). A second measure asks respondents how happy they are "taking all things together." Although this is not a momentary measure, it makes a clear reference to happiness. Using data from 1999, Denmark ranked 10th out of 70 on overall happiness. That same year, Denmark ranked 2nd in life satisfaction (after Puerto Rico). Thus, although Denmark is consistently high in terms of cognitive well-being, its ranking is somewhat lower in terms of emotional well-being. These subtleties in well-being measures must be appreciated before claiming that people in a society are happy or unhappy.

In addition to the types of SWB measures that have been emphasized, we also examined *where* well-being data have been collected. Table 35.2 breaks down the percentage of WDH data from different subregions of the world. Much of the data come from European

Table 35.4 Representation of UN macro-regions in World Database of Happiness and world population

| UN macro-region | Total data points in WDH | % of data in WDH | Population (in millions) | % of world population |
|---|---|---|---|---|
| Africa | 249 | 6 | 934.50 | 14 |
| Asia | 591 | 15 | 3998.42 | 61 |
| Europe | 2416 | 60 | 729.86 | 11 |
| Latin America | 357 | 9 | 568.07 | 9 |
| North America | 345 | 9 | 334.66 | 5 |
| Oceania | 69 | 2 | 33.56 | 1 |

WDH, World Database of Happiness (Veenhoven, n.d.).
Population figures come from the *World Factbook* (Central Intelligence Agency, 2007). Macro-regions are defined according to the United Nations (2000).

and North American nations, and few data points are available from African nations. In Table 35.4, we aggregated the data into macro-regions, as defined by the UN (2000). We also compiled population estimates (Central Intelligence Agency, 2007) for each macro-region. Two discrepancies are worth noting. First, although 11% of the world's population lives in Europe, almost 60% of the WDH data come from this macro-region. Second, the reverse pattern is observed for Asia which makes up 61% of the world's population, but represents only 15% of the data in the WDH.

These discrepancies reflect the longer history of national surveys in the industrialized nations of Europe. Since the late 1940s, early public opinion surveys in these countries included questions on happiness. Because each data point in our analysis reflects a single country from a single survey-year, the longer history of data collection in the West contributes to the "overrepresentation" of these nations in the WDH. Data for Asian countries accumulated sparsely after the 1960s. Well-being data were unavailable for many Asian countries until the recent decade (2000–2010). Thus, regarding the current record of SWB data, we know far less about the well-being of people from the Asian continent compared with those from Western nations. To a smaller degree, African countries are also underrepresented in the WDH. Moreover, though the Oceanic countries seem to be well-represented, all data points from this region are from Australia and New Zealand; none are from the South Pacific island nations. As research infrastructure improves in these areas, the discrepancies among macro-regions may reduce.

# Types of Cross-National Comparisons

There are two types of comparisons that are commonly made using cross-national SWB data: societal-level and person-level comparisons. Some examples from the literature are presented next.

## Comparing societal well-being

Several studies have examined the correlates of societal well-being. For example, average life satisfaction tends to be higher in wealthier countries (Diener et al., 1995), and average well-being is higher where there are greater civil rights (Diener et al., 1995; Schyns, 1998). Scholars have also investigated the relation between societal well-being and cultural values such as individualism–collectivism. It appears that individualist countries (e.g., the Netherlands) have higher levels of life satisfaction and happiness than collectivist countries (e.g., East Asian nations; Diener et al., 1995; Schyns, 1998). Japan, for instance, has lower SWB than would be expected based on its level of wealth. One explanation is that social norms in individualist cultures promote individual happiness to a greater extent than in collectivist cultures, where emphasis is placed on social harmony and self-criticism (Suh, 2000).

When such correlational data are reported, people are often tempted to conclude, for instance, that greater wealth (e.g., GDP) *causes* societal levels of well-being to rise. Such claims have intuitive appeal, but they are not *proven* by correlational, cross-sectional (measured at a single point in time) data, because the direction of causality is unclear. Greater GDP could increase societal well-being (assuming that a stronger economy improves conditions for the majority of the population). On the other hand, greater well-being could improve productivity and spur economic growth. Alternatively, both GDP and societal well-being could be caused by a third factor, such as greater economic or political freedom, which might facilitate the development of trade and business along with well-being. Longitudinal analyses can help clarify these ambiguities. Recent cross-national time-series analyses suggest societal SWB *does* increase with economic growth (Stevenson & Wolfers, 2008), although the exact nature and significance of the relationship is still a matter of considerable dispute (Easterlin & Angelescu, 2010).

Even when economic changes appear to predict changes in societal well-being, many questions remain. Wealthy nations tend to have several other qualities (e.g., greater civil liberties, less gender inequality, greater individualism) making it difficult to pinpoint what exactly it is about economic growth that predicts increases in well-being. The answers to these questions are crucial if well-being data are to provide guidance on policy issues. Numerous hypotheses have been proposed to explain why some nations are happier than others (Bond, 2003). For example, Kristof (2010) attributed the high well-being of Costa Rica to a disbanded military and investment in education. These hypotheses can best be answered with data collected over time, across nations, and using a consistent set of items.

## Comparing person-level correlates of well-being

Not only do nations differ in their average levels of SWB, they also differ in the correlates of *individual* well-being. For example, financial satisfaction and income are more strongly related to life satisfaction in poorer nations (Bonini, 2008; Oishi, Diener, Lucas, & Suh, 1999). It is not that income is unimportant in wealthier nations, only that the relationship between income and life satisfaction is not as strong as it is in poorer countries. The relationship between SWB and social attitudes such as generalized trust and confidence in government also differs across nations. People with high levels of SWB are more likely to be trusting and confident where economic inequality and violence are low (Diener & Tov, 2007;

Tov, Diener, Ng, Kesebir, & Harter, 2009). This is contrary to the dystopic vision depicted in Huxley's (1932/1998) *Brave New World* in which a dominant world government enslaves its citizens by breeding them to be happy and encouraging the use of drugs. Happiness is portrayed as a state of care-free hedonism that blinds people to the oppressive rule of the "World State". In contrast, Tov et al.'s (2009) research suggests that the positive attitudes generally associated with happy people are actually constrained by the social realities they face.

Cross-national comparisons of person-level correlates lead to more nuanced understandings of well-being. These approaches permit an understanding that the correlates of well-being may be both universal (e.g., "Income is generally associated with greater SWB") and culturally variable (e.g., "The relation is stronger in poorer countries"). These insights notwithstanding, it is important to bear in mind that these studies are cross-sectional in nature, and do not establish causality any more than those that examine the correlates of *societal* well-being.

# Conceptual and Methodological Issues in Cross-National Comparisons

On balance, it appears that SWB measures are meaningfully related to societal conditions. Nevertheless, when making cross-national comparisons, there are several issues that consumers of research should be aware of.

## Conceptual issues

Although societal well-being is often computed by averaging the ratings of individual respondents, it is important to remember that it reflects the happiness of a *nation* and not any particular person. The factors that affect the average well-being in a country do not always affect a single person's well-being. Thus, in discussing the happiness of nations, there is a danger in confusing this aggregate-level phenomenon with individual-level processes— what has been called the ecological fallacy. For example, in response to the high life satisfaction ranking of Denmark, a Danish journalist wryly remarked, "I really wonder about the suicide rates in Denmark … I mean is it that we're so happy we kill ourselves?" (quoted in Taylor, 2006). Likewise, a report on the happiness of Singapore carried the subheading "Citizens Willing to Trade Civil Liberties for a Cleaner, Safer, Efficient Society" (Weir, 2008). These comments assume a perfect relation between societal conditions and individual well-being. We do not dispute the impact that macro-level factors may have on personal well-being; however it is important to understand that the overall relation is likely to be indirect and dependent upon intervening factors. An increase in GDP is not likely to improve a person's well-being if he or she remains unemployed. Similarly, suicide rates may not affect well-being if they apply to a limited segment of society rather than one's close friends and family. Incidentally, Denmark's suicide rate is lower than several countries in Eastern Europe and East Asia (World Health Organization, 2009).

Moreover, we cannot assume from high societal levels of SWB that people are perfectly aware and contented with *all* aspects of their society. These claims should be scrutinized empirically when possible. For example, the notion that Singaporeans are content to give up civil liberties is debatable. When asked which of four societal goals is more important, 86% of Singaporeans ranked maintaining order in the nation either first or second (World Values Survey, 2005). However, the majority of these respondents (62%) also ranked having more say in how things are done as important, and a considerable proportion (18%) endorsed protecting freedom of speech.[1] The point is that we must not make assumptions about the individual motives and desires of *all* people in a country based on societal SWB alone.

Similar caution applies when interpreting macro-level variables that are empirically correlated with societal well-being. For example, at the individual level, married people report greater well-being than those who are not married (Bonini, 2008; Diener, Gohm, Suh, & Oishi, 2000). However, at the societal level, the *percentage* of people married in a country correlates positively with average depression (van Hemert, van de Vijver, & Poortinga, 2002) and divorce rates correlate positively with national SWB (Diener et al., 1995). These findings are puzzling unless one considers that marriage and divorce rates reflect cultural norms. Societies with high divorce rates may prioritize individual rights and goals over collective obligations and relationships. Alternatively, lower divorce rates in collectivist countries may reflect greater social pressure to stay together. Thus, interpreting aggregated data requires a shift in perspective toward broad, societal conditions and norms.

## Sample size

The issue of sample size applies to both the number of *individuals* used to estimate the mean SWB of a country, and the number of *countries* included in cross-national analyses. In terms of individual respondents, smaller samples produce less reliable estimates of mean SWB because random individual differences are more likely to affect the overall score. Many cross-national surveys collect data from at least 1000 respondents per country, providing very precise estimates of mean SWB.

The number of nations available for analysis of cross-national data should also be considered. When the sample of nations is small, spurious relationships may arise from just one or two nations. The latter argument was used by Easterlin (1974) in his examination of Cantril's (1965) data on income and well-being in 14 countries. Easterlin noted that ten countries differed widely on gross national product, but barely differed in well-being—implying that the positive association was driven primarily by four countries. In contrast, Stevenson and Wolfers (2008) had access to well-being data from 131 nations; they were able to conclude that economic development was positively associated with mean SWB.

## Representativeness

A related but distinct issue from sample size is the representativeness of the sample. The ability to make claims about the overall well-being of a nation rests on how well respondents represent the nation as a whole. This is ultimately a question of validity, not reliability. One

---

[1] The exact proportion of Singaporeans who ranked these goals as first or second were as follows: maintaining order (first = 68%; second = 18%); having more say (first = 20%; second = 42%); protecting freedom of speech (first = 5%; second = 13%).

thousand respondents from New York will provide a precise, *reliable* estimate of mean SWB, but not necessarily a *valid* estimate of the entire USA. This is a basic issue of which survey researchers are well-aware. Probability samples are often carried out and sample weights may be applied to ensure that the data are representative. When the representativeness of the sample varies across nations, results should be interpreted cautiously. For example, in their analysis of depression across nations, van Hemert et al. (2002) observed that the mean for Israel was unusually high relative to data for other countries. Although the mean was based on a large sample of 574 respondents, all were Palestinian. Some cross-national studies rely on college student samples (e.g., Kuppens, Ceulemans, Timmerman, Diener, & Kim-Prieto, 2006). Such samples control for differences in education and may serve basic research purposes. However, they may not always provide representative estimates of societal SWB (Cummins, 2003).

The time period in which data are collected should be representative as well. Unusual circumstances (e.g., a recent natural disaster) could artificially inflate or deflate people's moods. Time-inclusive measures are particularly sensitive to such events. However, global well-being can also be affected if conditions are prolonged. In 1962, the Dominican Republic's mean score was 1.6 on the self-anchoring ten-step ladder. This extensive misery has been attributed to political turmoil that followed the assassination of the dictator Rafael Trujillo (Bond, 2003; Easterlin, 1974). A noteworthy approach taken by the European Social Survey has been to maintain a log of national and international events that occurred during data collection (Jowell & Eva, 2009). This does not solve the problem of bias but helps current and future researchers identify possible influences on responses—enabling a more cautious interpretation of the data.

## Ensuring equivalence of measurement

An assumption behind comparisons of societal SWB and person-level correlates is that the same concept is measured across nations. If two people—one from Denmark, the other from Zimbabwe—both say they are satisfied with their life, are they talking about the same thing? This issue is absolutely critical for efforts to include measures of *subjective* well-being as indicators of progress and quality of life across nations (Marks et al., 2006; Stiglitz et al., 2009). The concept of gross national happiness (GNH), for example, implies that self-reported ratings of well-being in one country can be compared with those in another country. If GNH is to be a meaningful metric, policymakers must be able to conclude that people in high-GNH countries (e.g., Denmark) truly are happy and satisfied, whereas those in low-GNH countries (e.g., Zimbabwe) are truly miserable. Cross-national researchers may address measurement equivalence through careful translation before data collection, and statistical assessment after data collection.

### *Translation*

To ensure equivalence of meaning, the survey instrument is often translated from a standard language into other languages. The translations might then be back-translated into the original standard language, and the process repeated to minimize any loss in meaning (Gallup Organization, 2006). Studies in which people from the same country report their well-being in either English or another language have shown minimal language effects (Tov & Diener,

2007). For example, the happiness of French-Canadians is more similar to English-speaking Canadians than to the French in Europe (Veenhoven, 2008). These findings suggest that self-reported SWB may reflect societal conditions more than language per se.

Despite these promising results, translation equivalence cannot be assumed; it must be evaluated for each society. A puzzling finding from the fourth wave of the WVS (1999–2004) is that Tanzania ranked 2nd (out of 70 nations) on general happiness (behind Nigeria), but 70th on general life satisfaction! Although happiness and life satisfaction reflect distinct aspects of SWB such stark discrepancies raise several questions discussed earlier. We examined the data file (World Values Survey, 2005) and technical information for the Tanzanian sample (World Values Survey, 2001). The sample size for Tanzania (N = 1171) was adequate and random sampling procedures were used to ensure a representative sample. However, the technical notes reported that there was difficulty translating the term *happiness* into Kiswahili, and back-translation procedures were not used. Although the technical notes did not clarify the nature of these difficulties, future well-being research in Tanzania should be aided by careful linguistic study to improve translation.

## Response styles

Even if SWB items are understood similarly across nations, another potential issue is that responses are influenced by an overall tendency to agree (acquiescent response style) or be neutral. If this overall tendency occurs more often in one culture than another, then societal differences in SWB scores would not represent true differences in well-being. Chen, Lee, and Stevenson (1995) observed a tendency for Japanese and Taiwanese high school students to use the midpoint of rating scales relative to their North American peers. In contrast, the latter were more likely to use the end points of rating scales.

It is not clear to what extent response styles affect SWB scores across nations. For example, different from the research described earlier, Diener, Suh, Smith, and Shao (1995) did not observe a neutral-response tendency in the self-reported emotional experience of Asian college students. Furthermore, Chen et al. (1995) noted that the effects of response styles were small, and controlling for these tendencies did not remove cultural differences in attitude items. Smith (2004) observed greater acquiescence in collectivist cultures. This would imply that Asian respondents are more likely to agree (give higher ratings) on SWB items. However, cross-national data are inconsistent with this idea, as average SWB is often lower in Asian countries relative to Western countries (Tov & Diener, 2007). Smith suggested that response styles may reflect substantive differences in cultural attitudes rather than noise that must be removed from responses. This issue awaits further conceptual and methodological refinement.

## Measurement invariance

Advanced statistical methods can be used to evaluate the equivalence or "invariance" of well-being measures across cultures. Suppose there are five items measuring life satisfaction, as in the Satisfaction With Life Scale (SWLS; Diener, Emmons, Larsen, & Griffin, 1985). Example items are "I am satisfied with my life" and "The conditions of my life are excellent." If all five items tap into the same concept (life satisfaction), then responses to the items should correlate strongly with each other—people who agree with one item should also agree with the others. That is, a single *factor* (a person's life satisfaction) should underlie responses to the items. If responses to the items correlate strongly among Italians but weakly among Ghanaians, the two groups may have interpreted the items differently. The researchers' definition of life satisfaction might apply to Italians but not to Ghanaians. Vittersø, Røysamb, and Diener (2002) conducted analyses on college student samples in 41 nations (including those in Latin America, Africa, and Asia) and concluded that the five items were adequately represented by a single factor in all nations. However, results were more consistent in wealthy nations (e.g., Italy) compared with less wealthy nations (e.g., Ghana), perhaps because of greater familiarity with surveys in the former. A similar explanation was offered by Tucker, Ozer, Lyubomirsky, and Boehm (2006), who compared Americans and Russians using structural equation modeling (SEM). Responses to the SWLS were comparable between the two groups when college students were used, but not when community samples were used. Russian community members may have been less familiar with taking multi-item surveys.

An alternative approach to evaluating measurement invariance is item response theory (IRT). An assumption of IRT is that people with the same level of well-being should be equally likely to agree with any particular well-being item. For instance, if a Chinese and an American respondent are *equally satisfied with life* (i.e., they have the same overall score), they should be equally likely to agree with the SWLS item "If I could live my life over, I would change almost nothing." In one study (Oishi, 2006), Chinese were actually less likely than Americans to agree with this particular item even when their overall well-being was equated. This suggests that the item measures life satisfaction differently in the two cultures. When such differences are found, the items may be discarded or a statistical adjustment might be made in computing the overall score. Chinese respondents still reported lower mean life satisfaction than Americans after such adjustments were made.

One can also ask whether the affective components of SWB are equally distinguishable across cultures. Kuppens et al. (2006) examined the frequency of various emotions experienced by college students in 48 nations. They confirmed that positive and negative emotions were distinguishable across nations. Using similar data, Lucas and Diener (2008) showed that positive and negative emotions were also distinct from life satisfaction. The factor structure held both at the level of individual responses and nation-level means across 40 countries. These results are promising; however more cross-national studies are desirable—especially in representative samples.

Advanced statistical methods hold promise for improving SWB measures and the validity of cross-national comparisons. To date, however, their application to survey data is rare. One limitation is that SWB measures in large-scale surveys have traditionally been single-item measures. Approaches such as SEM and IRT require that constructs be measured with multiple items. Future surveys should employ multi-item measures of SWB (e.g., Huppert et al., 2009). Another limitation is that these approaches have typically been applied to a limited number of groups at a time. Methods for evaluating measurement equivalence across many nations are still in their infancy. Stringent measurement approaches to well-being pose many challenges for cross-national researchers, but they are worth the effort. Until more sophisticated methods are available for assessing equivalence at a large-scale, analyses that compare the equivalence of SWB measures in smaller groups of nations can contribute to their improvement.

## FUTURE DIRECTIONS

Our review of the cross-national data on SWB suggests three key developments for the future. First, it is important to fill in the gap in our existing knowledge of well-being in African and Asian societies. No doubt there are challenges to gathering data in countries in which the research and transportation infrastructure have been weakened by instability or are expanding slowly. If representative samples are not possible, convenience samples will have to do for the time being. *Some* information is better than no information at all.

Second, measures of SWB could be improved in several ways. Multiple items should be used to measure the affective and cognitive components of well-being. Moreover, a diversity of measures is desirable, as SWB is a broad construct. Most survey measures of SWB have been global, cognitive measures. Time-inclusive measures would add to our understanding of more immediate experiences of well-being. These measures should complement, not replace global measures.

Third, measurement equivalence of SWB measures should be assessed—even if applicable data are only available for a few countries. This development must go hand in hand with increased administration of multi-item measures. Collecting data from non-student samples and improving measures for the general population is critical if national indices of well-being are to be used to guide public policy.

## CONCLUSION

Cross-national studies of SWB have generated many important insights into the nature and measurement of well-being. Measuring any concept across the world is not an easy task. Although there are certainly many factors that can influence responses to SWB measures, existing studies show that societal levels of well-being are meaningfully related to macro-level social and economic conditions. Thus, the noisy process of cross-cultural measurement is indeed picking up a signal. As policymakers become increasingly interested in the utility of SWB indicators, developing better measures of well-being will be critical. We remain optimistic that current and future researchers will meet this challenge.

## REFERENCES

Andrews, F. M., & Withey, S. B. (1974). Developing measures of perceived life quality: Results from several national surveys. *Social Indicators Research*, 1(1), 1–26.

Blanchflower, D. G., & Oswald, A. J. (2011). International happiness: A new view on the measure of performance. *The Academy of Management Perspectives*, 25(1), 6–22.

Bond, M. (2003). The pursuit of happiness. *New Scientist*, 180(2415), 40–43.

Bonini, A. N. (2008). Cross-national variation in individual life satisfaction: Effects of national wealth, human development, and environmental conditions. *Social Indicators Research*, 87(2), 223–236.

Bradburn, N. M. (1969). *The structure of psychological well-being*. Oxford, UK: Aldine.

Cantril, H. (1965). *The pattern of human concerns*. New Brunswick, NJ: Rutgers University Press.

Central Intelligence Agency. (2007). *CIA—The world factbook*. Retrieved August 3, 2007, from https://www.cia.gov/library/publications/the-world-factbook/

Chen, C., Lee, S., & Stevenson, H. W. (1995). Response style and cross-cultural comparisons of rating scales among East Asian and North American students. *Psychological Science*, 6(3), 170–175.

Christensen, K., Herskind, A. M., & Vaupel, J. W. (2006). Why Danes are smug: Comparative study of life satisfaction in the European Union. *British Medical Journal*, 333(7582), 1289–1291.

Cummins, R. A. (2003). Normative life satisfaction: Measurement issues and a homeostatic model. *Social Indicators Research*, 64(2), 225–256.

Diener, E. (1984). Subjective well-being. *Psychological Bulletin*, 95(3), 542–575.

Diener, E., Diener, M., & Diener, C. (1995). Factors predicting the subjective well-being of nations. *Journal of Personality and Social Psychology*, 69(5), 851–864.

Diener, E., Emmons, R. A., Larsen, R. J., & Griffin, S. (1985). The satisfaction with life scale. *Journal of Personality Assessment*, 49(1), 71–75.

Diener, E., Gohm, C. L., Suh, E., & Oishi, S. (2000). Similarity of the relations between marital status and subjective well-being across cultures. *Journal of Cross-Cultural Psychology*, 31(4), 419–436.

Diener, E., Kahneman, D., Arora, R., Harter, J., & Tov, W. (2009). Income's differential influence on judgments of life versus affective well-being. In E. Diener (Ed.), *Assessing well-being: The collected works of Ed Diener*. Social indicators research series; 1387–6570 (pp. 233–245). New York, NY: Springer Science & Business Media.

Diener, E., & Lucas, R. E. (2000). Explaining differences in societal levels of happiness: Relative standards, need fulfillment, culture and evaluation theory. *Journal of Happiness Studies*, 1(1), 41–78.

Diener, E., Suh, E. M., Lucas, R. E., & Smith, H. L. (1999). Subjective well-being: Three decades of progress. *Psychological Bulletin*, 125(2), 276–302.

Diener, E., Suh, E. M., Smith, H., & Shao, L. (1995). National differences in reported subjective well-being: Why do they occur? *Social Indicators Research*, 34(1), 7–32.

Diener, E., & Tov, W. (2007). Subjective well-being and peace. *Journal of Social Issues*, 63(2), 421–440.

Diener, E., & Tov, W. (2011). National accounts of well-being. In K. C. Land, A. C. Michalos, & M. J. Sirgy (Eds.), *Handbook of social indicators and quality-of-life research* (pp. 137–158). New York, NY: Springer.

Dolan, P., & White, M. P. (2007). How can measures of subjective well-being be used to inform public policy? *Perspectives on Psychological Science*, 2(1), 71–85.

Easterlin, R. A. (1974). Does economic growth improve the human lot? In P. A. David & M. W. Reder (Eds.), *Nations and households in economic growth: Essays in honor of Moses Abramovitz* (pp. 89–125). New York, NY: Academic Press.

Easterlin, R. A., & Angelescu, L. (2010). Happiness and growth the world over: Time series evidence on the happiness–income paradox. In R. A. Easterlin (Ed.), *Happiness, growth, and the life cycle* (pp. 111–129). New York. Oxford University Press.

Gallup Organization. (2006). *Gallup World Poll research design*. Princeton, NJ: Gallup Organization. Retrieved from http://media.gallup.com/muslimwestfacts/PDF/MWResearchDesign030207.pdf

Gallup, Inc. (2008). *World Poll questions.* Washington, DC: Gallup, Inc. Retrieved from http://media.gallup.com/dataviz/www/WP_Questions_WHITE.pdf

Huppert, F. A., Marks, N., Clark, A., Siegrist, J., Stutzer, A., Vittersø, J., & Wahrendorf, M. (2009). Measuring well-being across Europe: Description of the ESS well-being module and preliminary findings. *Social Indicators Research, 91*(3), 301–315.

Huxley, A. (1998). *Brave new world.* New York, NY: HarperCollins Publishers. (Original work published 1932).

Jowell, R., & Eva, G. (2009). Happiness is not enough: Cognitive judgements as indicators of national wellbeing. *Social Indicators Research, 91*(3), 317–328.

Kahneman, D., Krueger, A. B., Schkade, D. A., Schwarz, N., & Stone, A. A. (2004). Toward national well-being accounts. *American Economic Review, 94*(2), 429–434.

Kilpatrick, F. P., & Cantril, H. (1960). Self-anchoring scaling: A measure of individuals' unique reality worlds. *Journal of Individual Psychology, 16,* 158–173.

Kim-Prieto, C., Diener, E., Tamir, M., Scollon, C., & Diener, M. (2005). Integrating the diverse definitions of happiness: A time-sequential framework of subjective well-being. *Journal of Happiness Studies, 6*(3), 261–300.

Kristof, N. D. (2010, January 6). The happiest people. *The New York Times.* Retrieved from http://www.nytimes.com/2010/01/07/opinion/07kristof.html?_r=1&em

Kuppens, P., Ceulemans, E., Timmerman, M. E., Diener, E., & Kim-Prieto, C. (2006). Universal intracultural and intercultural dimensions of the recalled frequency of emotional experience. *Journal of Cross-Cultural Psychology, 37*(5), 491–515.

Layard, R. (2005). *Happiness lessons from a new science.* New York, NY: Penguin Press.

Lucas, R. E., & Diener, E. (2008). Can we learn about national differences in happiness from individual responses? A multilevel approach. In F. J. R. van de Vijver, D. A. van Hemert, & Y. H. Poortinga (Eds.), *Multilevel analysis of individuals and cultures.* (pp. 223–248). New York, NY: Taylor & Francis.

Lucas, R. E., Diener, E., & Suh, E. (1996). Discriminant validity of well-being measures. *Journal of Personality and Social Psychology, 71*(3), 616–628.

Marks, N., Abdallah, S., Simms, A., & Thompson, S. (2006). *The Happy Planet Index.* London, UK: New Economics Foundation.

Oishi, S. (2006). The concept of life satisfaction across cultures: An IRT analysis. *Journal of Research in Personality, 40*(4), 411–423.

Oishi, S., Diener, E., Lucas, R. E., & Suh, E. M. (1999). Cross-cultural variations in predictors of life satisfaction: Perspectives from needs and values. *Personality and Social Psychology Bulletin, 25*(8), 980–990.

Oswald, A. J. (1997). Happiness and economic performance. *Economic Journal, 107*(445), 1815–1831.

Robinson, M. D., & Clore, G. L. (2002). Episodic and semantic knowledge in emotional self-report: Evidence for two judgment processes. *Journal of Personality and Social Psychology, 83*(1), 198–215.

Safer, M. (2008, June 15). And the happiest place on Earth is...Morley Safer on why the Danes are considered the happiest people on Earth. *60 Minutes – CBS News.* Retrieved April 7, 2010, from http://www.cbsnews.com/stories/2008/02/14/60minutes/main3833797.shtml

Schyns, P. (1998). Crossnational differences in happiness: Economic and cultural factors explored. *Social Indicators Research, 43*(1/2), 3–26.

Smith, P. B. (2004). Acquiescent response bias as an aspect of cultural communication style. *Journal of Cross-Cultural Psychology, 35*(1), 50–61.

Stevenson, B., & Wolfers, J. (2008). Economic growth and subjective well-being: Reassessing the Easterlin paradox. *Brookings Papers on Economic Activity*, 1–87.

Stiglitz, J. E., Sen, A., & Fitoussi, J.-P. (2009). *Report by the commission on the measurement of economic performance and social progress*. [White paper]. Retrieved from http://www.stiglitz-sen-fitoussi.fr/documents/rapport_anglais.pdf

Suh, E. M. (2000). Self, the hyphen between culture and subjective well-being. In E. Diener & E. M. Suh (Eds.), *Culture and subjective well-being* (pp. 63–86). Cambridge, MA: MIT Press.

Tay, L., & Diener, E. (2011). Needs and subjective well-being around the world. *Journal of Personality and Social Psychology*, 101(2), 354–365.

Taylor, J. (2006, August 1). Denmark is the world's happiest country – official. *Independent*. Retrieved from http://www.independent.co.uk/news/world/europe/denmark-is-the-worlds-happiest-country--official-410075.html

Tov, W., & Diener, E. (2007). Culture and subjective well-being. In S. Kitayama & D. Cohen (Eds.), *Handbook of cultural psychology* (pp. 691–713). New York, NY: Guilford Press.

Tov, W., Diener, E., Ng, W., Kesebir, P., & Harter, J. (2009). The social and economic context of peace and happiness. In R. S. Wyer, C. Chiu, & Y. Hong (Eds.), *Understanding culture: Theory, research, and application* (pp. 239–255). New York, NY: Psychology Press.

Tucker, K. L., Ozer, D. J., Lyubomirsky, S., & Boehm, J. K. (2006). Testing for measurement invariance in the satisfaction with life scale: A comparison of Russians and North Americans. *Social Indicators Research*, 78(2), 341–360.

United Nations. (2000). United Nations world macro regions and components. Retrieved December 1, 2009, from http://www.un.org/depts/dhl/maplib/worldregions.htm

van Hemert, D. A., van de Vijver, F. J. R., & Poortinga, Y. H. (2002). The Beck Depression Inventory as a measure of subjective well-being: A cross-national study. *Journal of Happiness Studies*, 3(3), 257–286.

Veenhoven, R. (1996). Developments in satisfaction-research. *Social Indicators Research*, 37(1), 1–46.

Veenhoven, R. (2008). Comparability of happiness across nations. *School of Sociology and Social Work Journal*, 104, 211–234.

Veenhoven, R. (n.d.). Happiness in nations. *World Database of Happiness*. Retrieved November 30, 2009, from http://worlddatabaseofhappiness.eur.nl/hap_nat/nat_fp.php

Vittersø, J., Røysamb, E., & Diener, E. (2002). The concept of life satisfaction across cultures: Exploring its diverse meaning and relation to economic wealth. In E. Gullone & R. A. Cummins (Eds.), *The universality of subjective wellbeing indicators: A multi-disciplinary and multi-national perspective* (pp. 81–103). Dordrecht, the Netherlands: Kluwer Academic Publishers.

Weir, B. (2008, January 9). Has Singapore Found the Secret to Satisfaction? *ABC News*. Retrieved April 30, 2010 from http://abcnews.go.com/print?id=4097264

Weir, B., & Johnson, S. (2007, January 8). Denmark: The happiest place on Earth. *ABC News*. Retrieved from http://abcnews.go.com/2020/story?id=4086092&page=1#.T8NyXeg2-uI

World Health Organization. (2009). Suicide rates per 100,000 by country, year and sex (Table). Retrieved May 2, 2010 from http://www.who.int/mental_health/prevention/suicide_rates/en/index.html

World Values Survey. (2001). *Tanzania [2001]* [Technical specification document, 1999–2004 wave]. Retrieved from http://www.wvsevsdb.com/wvs/WVSTechnical.jsp?Idioma=I

World Values Survey. (2005). *Values survey official aggregate datafile, 1995 & 1999/2000 waves* [Computer file]. Madrid, Spain: APES/JDS [distributor]. Retrieved February 22, 2006 from http://www.worldvaluessurvey.org/services/index.html

CHAPTER 36

# THE GEOGRAPHY OF HAPPINESS

DIMITRIS BALLAS AND DANNY DORLING
University of Sheffield, UK

## INTRODUCTION

DOES geography matter when it comes to happiness? To what extent does *where* we live affect *how* we feel and *why*? These questions have not yet received the attention they deserve in the growing body of interdisciplinary research on the determinants of subjective happiness and well-being. While a considerable number of happiness studies are now approaching the issue from various perspectives, there is a paucity of work by geographers on this topic. This is surprising, given the importance of geographical context in understanding and measuring subjective happiness and well-being.

From a measurement point of view, it has long been argued that there are cultural (Lu & Gilmour, 2004; Tiberius, 2004; Uchida, Norasakkunkit & Kitayama, 2004) as well as possible linguistic (Veenhoven, 1993) issues affecting the responses to happiness questions in surveys. People living in societies where personal modesty is valued over individualism may understate their levels of happiness, whereas happiness may be overstated by those living in societies that encourage individuals to "stand out from the crowd." It is often suggested, for example, that Americans have a tendency to say that they are "very happy" because salient happiness is so positively valued in the USA, whereas in countries like France the exact opposite may be the case (Frey & Stutzer, 2002).

In addition to cultural characteristics, there are a number of additional geographical factors that influence the extent to which people appear to feel happy or satisfied with their lives. These include climate and the physical environment (Brereton, Clinch, & Ferreira, 2008; Ferrer-i-Carbonelli & Gowdy, 2007; Mitchell & Popham, 2008), as well as social and spatial inequalities (Alesina, Di Tella, & MacCulloch, 2004; Ballas, Dorling, & Shaw, 2007; Dorling & Barford, 2009; Frank, 2007; Wilkinson, 2005; Williamson & Pickett, 2009).

A comprehensive geographical approach to subjective happiness and well-being is needed to address the extent to which subjective happiness may be attributed to "individual" (e.g., employment status, age group), "household" (e.g., household income, accommodation type and size), and/or wider "contextual" (e.g., climate, socioeconomic environment) circumstances and characteristics across the world, and to establish the relative importance of such characteristics in different countries and within regions and cities in a country. This chapter considers some of the key geographical contextual issues that may be particularly important when measuring and explaining variation in subjective happiness across cities, regions, and nations.

First, we provide a brief review of the ways in which happiness has been conceptualized in different geographical regions. The subsequent section critically reviews work on the geography of happiness across different countries in the world and discusses the problems of comparing self-rated happiness and, in particular, issues pertaining to the impact of inequality. This is followed by a consideration of place and space at the smaller area level. The final section of the chapter offers concluding comments and outlines a possible research agenda for the better understanding of the geography of happiness.

## Perceptions and Theories of Happiness Through Time and Space

When we look at the world's great thinkers . . . [we] find them different in time, different in place, different in language and culture. Yet inevitable though these differences are, they cannot obscure the deep similarities in how we search for happiness. (Schoch, 2007, p. 13)

The meaning of happiness varies through space and time. The first known attempts to understand and define happiness began in the Far East around 600 BC, with the Chinese schools of Confucianism, Mo Ti, Buddhism, and Taoism (Fung, 1985; Tam 2010). Confucianism placed emphasis on societal quality of life and social relationships, arguing that a positive attitude towards knowledge, learning and responsibility are of central importance for happiness (Legge, 1971; Zhang & Veenhoven, 2007). The followers of Mo Ti, a Chinese philosopher who, unlike Confucius, was from the laboring class, argued for reciprocity and equality (Tam, 2010, pp. 12–13, 74). On the other hand, Taoism emphasized the individual and suggested that social conditions do not affect the ability of individuals to be happy. A Taoist might have argued against the development of knowledge and wisdom and suggested that the good life is a "simple life," implying that children are the happiest human beings (Zhang & Veenhoven, 2007). Buddhism also placed emphasis on the individual and introduced the concept of Nirvana: "a state of saintliness, that is characterized by perfect inner peace, enlightenment and the abolition of all wants" (Zhang & Veenhoven, 2007, p. 8).

A few decades after the Eastern philosophies of happiness took form, and 4000 miles to the West, the "Golden Age" of Greek philosophy began. Aristotle, in the *Nicomachean Ethics*, argued that happiness was the highest good achievable by human action and suggested that the attainment of happiness involves the satisfaction of the human desires through living a full and rich life (Annas, 1993; Lear, 1988; Ryff & Singer, 2006; Tam, 2010). However, Aristotle believed that the question of what is a full and rich life could not be answered in abstraction from the society in which people lived (Lear, 1988). Moreover, he argued that the achievement of human happiness relies upon the realization of an individual's true potential, which is consistent with earlier views, widely attributed to Socrates, that the "unexamined life is not worth living." In other words, happiness involves "doing well" rather than the attainment of actual pleasure, implying that social and geographical context matters when asking the question of happiness.

A new wave of happiness philosophy was formulated during the Hellenistic period, running from 323 BC, the year of the death of Alexander the Great, until the establishment of the Roman Empire in 31 BC (Bergsma, Poot, & Liefbroer, 2007; Tarn, 1952). This was a time of great change: city-states were losing their prominence, more people were traveling around a vast empire characterized by authoritarianism but also cosmopolitanism, commitment to civic and political activities was on the decline (Bergsma et al., 2007; Russell, 1990), and individualism was on the rise. These changes were accompanied by increases in feelings of insignificance and insecurity and the emergence of the new philosophies of Stoicism, Scepticism, and Epicureanism. While Stoicism "addressed the more highly educated and aristocratic citizens with its focus on public life" (Bergsma et al., 2007, p. 8) the ideas of the philosopher Epicurus appealed mostly to the fearful and oppressed citizens, the ones that felt very uncomfortable in the new world order (Bergsma et al., 2007; Tarn, 1952). Epicurus advised that the best way to lead a good life, characterized by the absence of pain and fear, is by living a modest and contemplative life in friendly communities (Annas, 1993; Bergsma et al., 2007; Tam, 2010). Epicurus advocated a quiet life as a way of achieving happiness, emphasizing individual self-sufficiency in the context of small groups of like-minded friends who are indifferent about the feelings of other people in society (Schoch, 2007). Thus, "Epicureans in the west and Taoists in the east encouraged people to withdraw from public life to seek enjoyments in their own spheres of life" (Tam, 2010, 18).

It can be argued that, despite the years and distance between them, the Eastern and Western philosophical traditions, briefly reviewed here, share the idea that happiness is something that is achieved through human effort. As a philosopher based in the British Empire 2000 years after the Hellenistic period, Bertrand Russell also argued that happiness is something for which we must strive and work hard, and that it does "not just happen to us like ripened fruit falling effortlessly into the mouth" (Russell, 1930; cited in Ryff & Singer, 2006, p. 19). While there is little argument as to the role of effort in the achievement of happiness, there is a divergence in the way these schools of thought address social and geographical context; namely, how they address issues such as whether the feelings, actions and circumstances of *other* people affect *our* own happiness.

In the fourth and fifth century AD, discussion of the "good life" was heavily influenced by theological concerns and the belief that true happiness could only be attained after death. The focus shifted from how to achieve happiness in the present, to how life should be led in order to accomplish ultimate happiness in the afterlife (for a detailed review of how both religious and philosophical perspectives influenced thinking on the definition of happiness, see McMahon (Chapter 19, this volume) and Schoch (2007)). Amongst the most comprehensive systematic attempts to examine the meaning of happiness in this context are the works of Thomas Aquinas, Abu Hamid al-Ghazali, and Al-Farabi (Schoch, 2007).

In Britain, it was not until decades after the seventeenth-century European Enlightenment that the focus for understanding of happiness shifted to how people actually felt as they went about their earthly lives. This, in turn, gave rise in the eighteenth century to the idea that happiness was something that could be measured, cultivated, and consequently, linked to public policy. Jeremy Bentham (1789/1983) argued that all human actions should aim at producing the greatest happiness for the greatest number of people (Layard, 2005; Frey and Stutzer, 2002).

As this brief review shows, the concept of happiness has been historically understood, valued, and explained by different schools of thought that emerged in different times, places, and cultures. This is not merely of historical interest, for these differences are reflected, at least to some extent, in how happiness is understood and valued today by people with different cultural and geographical upbringings. This can be further demonstrated by using an example of qualitative research of happiness by Lu and Gilmour (2004), highlighting how cultural background may be affecting the alternative ways in which happiness is defined. They present and discuss the following extracts of essays on the meaning of happiness by university students of the same age but with different backgrounds (the first two extracts were from essays of Chinese students and the last two from essays of American students):

> a. Happiness is a mental state. Only when the spirit is rich, the mind is peaceful and steady, is happiness possible.
>
> b. For me, happiness can be defined in four aspects: (1) free of physical sufferings, illnesses or disabilities; (2) being socially acceptable, getting along well with other people, being respected and cared for, not being isolated; (3) free of worries and hardships, being able to live a carefree and joyful life; and (4) possessing a healthy, normal mind, being accepted by the society.
>
> c. Happiness is absolutely great and one of the most important states of being a person or living thing could ever pursue. The pursuit of happiness is one of my supreme goals in life.
>
> d. To me happiness is doing and being who I want to be without being held back by the restrictions of society. Happiness is a reward for all the hard work you employ.
>
> (Lu & Gilmour, 2004, pp. 269–270)

It is evident that the meanings of "happiness," as well as perceptions of its determinants, have varied through time and space, influencing patterns of divergence that are observable today. However, recent advances in relevant socioeconomic and geographical data allow these issues to be investigated empirically, and thus provide a geographically-oriented perspective on subjective happiness and well-being. The remainder of this chapter reviews some of the empirical evidence on the extent to which *space* and *place* matter to subjective happiness and well-being.

# Happiness, Space, and Place

There are now a number of national surveys across the world containing a range of subjective happiness and well-being measures (Tov & Au, Chapter 35, this volume). These survey data have been used extensively by social scientists to conduct individual level studies of happiness and its determinants in each nation, as well as to compare aggregate happiness levels between nations (see Veenhoven (1993, 2000) for a review of more studies, and for survey data see Veenhoven (2009)). Very few examinations of these data have been explicitly concerned with the difference place makes; instead they have focused on how factors that are place-related may influence how happy people appear to be. They consider composition instead of context.

It is important to more fully understand why *where* someone lives may affect *how* they respond to happiness questions in surveys, in other words, how place and space affect the measurement of people's feelings. In this chapter, "place" is determined by the physical and cultural environment, whereas "space" is determined by the possible links between sociospatial processes (e.g., migration), states (e.g., socioeconomic spatial polarization; social and spatial inequalities) and subjective happiness.

As many philosophers and economists have noted, the position that a person has in her society, as well as the overall level of status inequalities, strongly influences her subjective experience, including happiness and unhappiness. Adam Smith famously wrote: "By necessities, I understand not only the commodities which are indispensably necessary for the support of life, but whatever the customs of the country renders it indecent for creditable people, even of the lower order, to be without. A creditable day labourer would be ashamed to appear in public without a linen shirt" (Smith, 1759, p. 383). Karl Marx (1847) identified the importance of relative social position via the impact of inequality and social comparisons upon human well-being in a social justice context. Veblen (1899) and Duesenberry (1949) highlighted the importance of social comparison of how people live and what (and how much) they consume. Runciman (1966) argued that people compare themselves most with their "near equals" and, more recently, Layard (2005) has suggested that people tend to compare themselves to their colleagues, friends and neighbors, with consequences for both happiness and health.

Most of the empirical studies that have examined comparison effects in relation to happiness have focused on relative income (a person's income in relation to the income of others) and income-rank. The logic here is that income is a means of communicating relative status in a social hierarchy (Alesina et al., 2004; Frank, 1985, 1999, 2007; Layard, 2005), and thus an individual's position in the income distribution is also an indicator of how much they are "valued." In practice, it is difficult to know a person's income without explicitly asking them, and so it is estimated by evaluating personal factors like consumption patterns, job titles and even residential addresses.

It has long been known that there is a moderate positive correlation of subjective well-being with real income per capita within a country. However, it has been shown that, for the wealthiest countries, further increases in overall income per capita do not markedly affect aggregate happiness (Frey & Stutzer, 2002). As Clark, Frijters, and Shields (2008) note, there is broad agreement that this finding reflects "the importance of relative considerations in the utility function, where higher income brings both consumption and status benefits to an individual" (p.137). In other words, once most people's material needs have been met, across the board growth in income fails to increase average happiness since status is zero-sum.

However, a good deal of recent and compelling evidence suggests that there is a relationship between the degree of *inequality* within a society and various health and social issues that are known to influence happiness, including physical and mental health, trust and community life (see, for instance, Fig. 36.1; Wilkinson & Pickett, 2009). Even within wealthy Western nations, outcomes in these and other areas appear to be substantially worse in societies that are more unequal (in terms of income and wealth inequalities and social cohesion). These findings highlight the role of social and geographical context with regard to a wide range of factors that are associated with happiness.

These findings have been the subject of lively debate, which is of particular relevance to the geography of happiness. For instance, Jen, Jones, and Johnston (2009) have offered

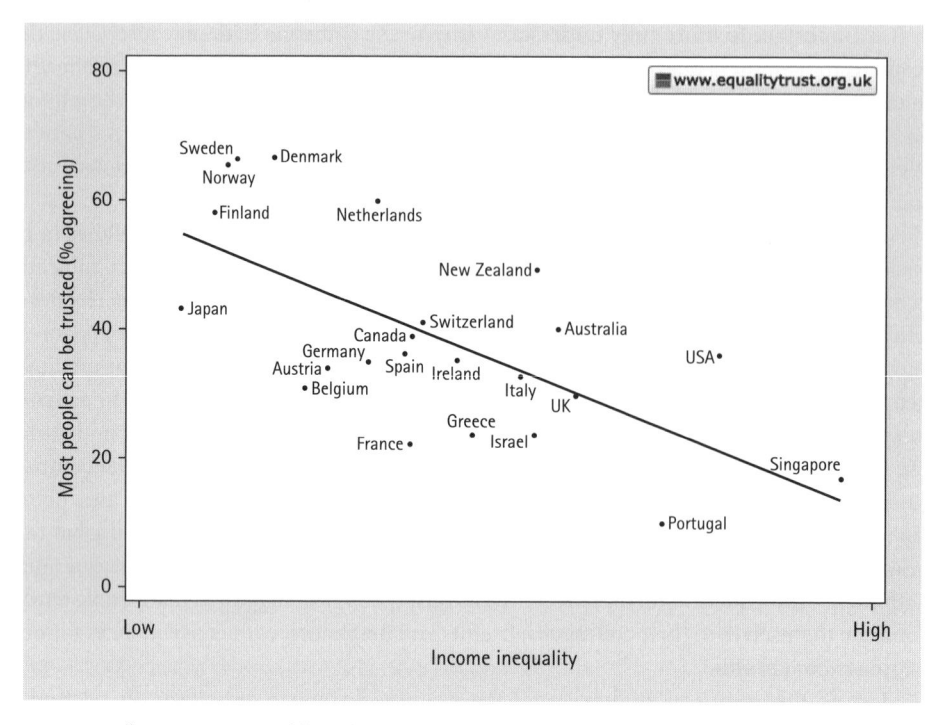

FIG. 36.1 "Community Life" and income inequality.

criticism on the basis of empirical analyses of the relationship between measures of self-rated health and income inequality. They found that self-rated health is better in more unequal countries, which seems surprising given that numerous studies have shown life expectancy to be lower in more unequal countries. However, Dorling and Barford (2009) argue in response that measurements of "self-rated health" are themselves subject to cultural bias. There have long been studies showing that people's ratings of their health are affected by social position, choice of reference group and gender (e.g., see Idler & Benyamini, 1997).

Recently, Wilkinson and Pickett (2009) have presented their "Spirit Level" hypothesis, according to which the relationship between income distribution and well-being is mediated through psychosocial pathways by the impacts of economic structure upon social relationships. In this model, lower income inequality is seen to result in societies with more cohesion, greater trust, and cooperation and lower social stress. Therefore, it can be argued that the level of inequality within a society has a direct impact on the way in which people perceive and report their health. If relative social position is an important influence on self-rated health, then, in more equal societies, fewer people occupy extreme positions in the social hierarchy and each person's frame of reference for comparing themselves to other people is likely to be wider and hence include more people. Importantly, people may be less inclined to make comparisons with peers who are "above" when, in a more equal society, such differences are so much less important.

It also seems plausible that in more unequal societies, which are characterized by more status competition (Frank, 2007), people may more frequently and obviously need to reassure themselves of their health and well-being and their potential to succeed. Asserting that one has "excellent" or "very good" health might be part of maintaining one's self-image. Relatedly, it could be that people in more equal societies may be less inclined to rate themselves at the top of a scale. Perhaps growing up in a more egalitarian society means that people are less likely to label themselves as "the best" or "excellent." Also, as noted in the introduction, social context and cultural norms (e.g., societies that value personal modesty and collectivism over individualism, or a desire to "stand out from the crowd"), may influence responses to survey questions (Abdallah, Thompson, & Marks, 2007).

Wilkinson and Pickett (2009) suggest that one way to cope with living in an extremely unequal affluent society is to feign optimism: to convince yourself that you are strong, you will survive and prosper, even though you realize that most around you will not (Dorling & Barford, 2009). Linking this discussion to the impact of "place," consider the experience of living in Harlem in New York City, which has both a high murder rate and a low suicide rate. Wilkinson and Pickett (2009) argue that individuals are unlikely to do well in an unequal environment like Harlem if they internalize their concerns. Better to attribute blame for one's own problems to external factors, let your anger out, and when asked how you are, say you are doing "'just great'". Conversely, Wilkinson and Pickett (2009) hypothesize that it is harder to blame others—or "the system"—for your woes in places that are more socially equal. People in such areas may be more likely to internalize their concerns and not lash out, to blame themselves more and be less inclined to "talk themselves up." If this is the case, it may be that people would be likely to admit their own health to be poor; poorer than it actually is in relation to others living in more unequal countries, but perhaps poor as far as they see it (Dorling & Barford, 2009; Wilkinson & Pickett, 2009).

The previous discussion is relevant to cross-country comparisons of happiness: it illustrates the possibility of obtaining survey responses at the international level that contradict actual physical experience. Thus, international variation in reported levels of happiness can clearly be affected by cultural differences in expression, in the same way that cultural influences seem to affect how people express their perceptions of health. Such effects can even be found within a single country. For instance, in Britain, levels of reporting long-term illness, all else being equal, are higher in Wales than in England, and lower in Scotland than in England. In other words, people in Scotland do not report being ill as much as those elsewhere in Britain given the same levels of actual health; the opposite is true of Wales. This may well be beneficial to the Welsh, who tend to be treated earlier as a result of actual illnesses being diagnosed more frequently (Mitchell, 2005).

Despite these results, cultural and geographical contextual influences with regards to the measurement of subjective happiness and well-being are much weaker when looking at differences in places within nations and regions (including within countries as unequal as Britain). For instance, Oswald and Wu (2010) tested the validity of reported well-being at the state level within the USA using a recent sample of one million American citizens. They found that the subjective responses traced out a similar pattern of quality of life as previously calculated using objective measures of well-being. Based on a sample of 100,000 individuals in Britain, Blanchflower and Oswald (2009) found a strong relationship between blood pressure by region and the level of reported mental strain. Therefore, it could be argued that comparing subjective measures of happiness and well-being within countries is much less problematic than performing international comparisons.

Nevertheless, the geographical level at which contextual factors matter with regards to determining the actual objective (rather than self-reported subjective) happiness is much less clear. As noted previously, inequality matters because people compare themselves with their "peer groups." But do they compare themselves to "peer groups" in their neighborhood, city, region, country, or possibly to diaspora groups in other countries or with peoples of whom they know little, but who appear on television? It is far from clear how reference groups are constituted. There are many other kinds of non-geographical groups to which we may compare ourselves and with whom we consider ourselves to be of a similar social standing. Given this confusion, some have elected to simply focus on inequality in more local areas (e.g., neighborhood or community areas), aiming to capture social comparisons within that level, without reference to the wider social structure (Wilkinson and Pickett, 2006). Wilkinson (1997) has argued that income inequality in small areas (such as streets, wards, or even towns) is affected by the degree of residential segregation of rich and poor. He proposes that the health of people in materially deprived neighborhoods is poorer not because of the inequality within their neighborhoods, but because they are deprived in relation to the wider society as measured at the national level (also see Ballas et al., 2007).

Most significantly, Wilkinson and Pickett (2006) compiled a list of 155 published peer-reviewed reports of research on the relation between income distribution and measures of population health. They classified these studies as "wholly supportive" or "unsupportive" according to whether they were international studies, using data for whole countries, whether their data were for large subnational areas such as states, regions, and metropolitan areas or whether they were for smaller units such as counties, census tracts, or parishes. The proportion of analyses classified as wholly supportive falls from 83% (of all wholly supportive or unsupportive) in the international studies to 73% in the large subnational areas, to 45% among the smallest spatial units. The implication is that the spatial scale at which people make their social comparisons is more likely to be the nation state (arguably reflecting socioeconomic position) than it is to be locality (reflecting position within neighborhood). In Wilkinson and Pickett's (2006) words:

> ... the broad impression is that social class stratification establishes itself primarily as a national social structure, though there are perhaps also some more local civic hierarchies – for instance within cities and US states. But it should go without saying that classes are defined in relation to each other: one is higher because the other is lower, and vice versa. *The lower class identity of people in a poor neighbourhood is inevitably defined in relation to a hierarchy which includes a knowledge of the existence of superior classes who may live in other areas some distance away* (p. 1774, our emphasis).

Despite the local evidence being weakest, there is a need for more empirical studies that explore the geographical and socioeconomic factors affecting individual happiness at different geographical scales. Studies of happiness at local levels are relatively limited due to the paucity of relevant data, although there are some exceptions. Propper et al. (2005) examined the association between neighborhood-level variables and mental health disorders in Britain. Their analysis included the estimation of multilevel models of "level-changes" (such as individual level, household level, and area level) and 5-year changes of common mental disorders, and suggested that individual and household-level characteristics, not place, appear to be most important in terms of predicting mental health disorders.

A number of studies have examined the role of income and employment in local well-being. Luttmer (2005) matched individual level happiness data to information about average earnings in geographical areas of 150,000 inhabitants on average (the so-called US Public Use Microdata areas) to investigate whether individuals feel worse off when others around them earn more. He found that, on average, higher earnings of neighbors are associated with lower levels of self-reported well-being. Clark (2003) used data from the British Household Panel Survey (a national annual survey of the adult population of the UK, drawn from a representative sample of over 5000 households) to show that the well-being of unemployed people is strongly positively correlated with reference group unemployment at the regional and household level, suggesting that "unemployment hurts, but it hurts less when there are more unemployed people around." Similarly, Powdthavee (2007) used cross-sectional data from South Africa to examine the role of social norms in the relationship between happiness and unemployment and reported that unemployment appears to be less detrimental to happiness in regions where the rate of unemployment is high.

Morrison (2007) used survey data to compare subjective well-being in 12 different locations in New Zealand, and used single-level regression models to explore the extent to which "place" has an effect upon individual well-being. He found that, even after controlling for characteristics of individuals known to influence subjective well-being, there were considerable "place effects," suggesting that the characteristics of local areas may have an independent impact on well-being. Ballas and Tranmer (2012) employed multilevel modeling on a combination of census and survey microdata in Britain and found that happiness and well-being was not significantly different between metropolitan districts in the UK, once a full set of individual, household and area characteristics is controlled for. Nevertheless, it is interesting to note that this analysis suggested that, on average, the longer an individual has lived at their address, the higher their well-being. This finding may be likely to be associated with the extent of individuals' social and support networks.

As noted earlier, there are very limited data on happiness and well-being for small areas. Nevertheless, it is possible to use small area data to build formal indices of "local well-being," for instance, the index of "anomie" (the sociological term to describe, according to some interpretations, the feeling of "not belonging"). Such measures can also be described as "loneliness indices." Recently Dorling, Vickers, Thomas, Pritchard, and Ballas (2008) calculated such an index to explore the geography of "loneliness" or "anomie" in Britain in a study commissioned by the BBC which aimed at comparing BBC radio and TV regions. The index used was based on a scale and weightings which have now been widely employed in many pieces of research (Congdon, 1996). Specifically, the index is calculated based on weighted sums of non-married adults, one person households, people who have moved to the area within the last year and people renting privately.

The data used to calculate the index are readily available in Britain for small areas from the census of population and it can be argued that they represent a number of variables that are associated with happiness and well-being. For instance, it has long been suggested that single people appear to be on average less happy than married couples (Frey and Stutzer, 2002; Helliwell, 2003; Inglehart, 1990) and in general there is evidence that stable and secure intimate relationships are beneficial for happiness. In contrast, the dissolution of such relationships is damaging (Dolan et al., 2007; Myers, 1999). In this context the census variables "number of 1-person households" and "numbers of non-married adults" could be considered suitable to measure at the local level. Also, as noted earlier, length of time at current address and social networks have an impact on well-being. The census variables "number of people who have moved to their current address within the last year" and "number of people renting privately" capture, to some extent, the degree to which people are integrated to the local community and may feel that they "belong." This variable also implicitly incorporates in the analysis the spatial process of migration (as it provides the number of in-migrants in the area within the year before the census date).

Dorling et al. (2008) collected these data from the British censuses for the years 1971, 1981, 1991, and 2001 to compare the "anomie" index levels between different regions (using the BBC radio regions as the geographical unit of analysis). They mapped this proxy of social fragmentation or "local well-being" across Britain using both conventional maps and human cartograms that show areas in proportion to their populations (see Fig. 36.2). Fig. 36.3 shows the spatial distribution of the "social fragmentation" index in 1971, and Fig. 36.4 depicts the same variable in 2001. The gap between the index extreme values has grown over time (other than during the 1970s). Fig. 36.5 shows the spatial distribution of anomie index change between 1971 and 2001. This follows similar patterns with regards to economic and social polarization and political disaffection (Dorling et al., 2008). Young adults, who have increasingly moved to more affluent cities for work, especially to London, are moving further away

**FIG. 36.2** (Also see Color plate 1.) The BBC radio regions map and human cartogram. Courtesy: the Social and Spatial Inequalities (SASI) Group, Department of Geography, University of Sheffield, UK.

Social fragmentation (Anomie) 1971

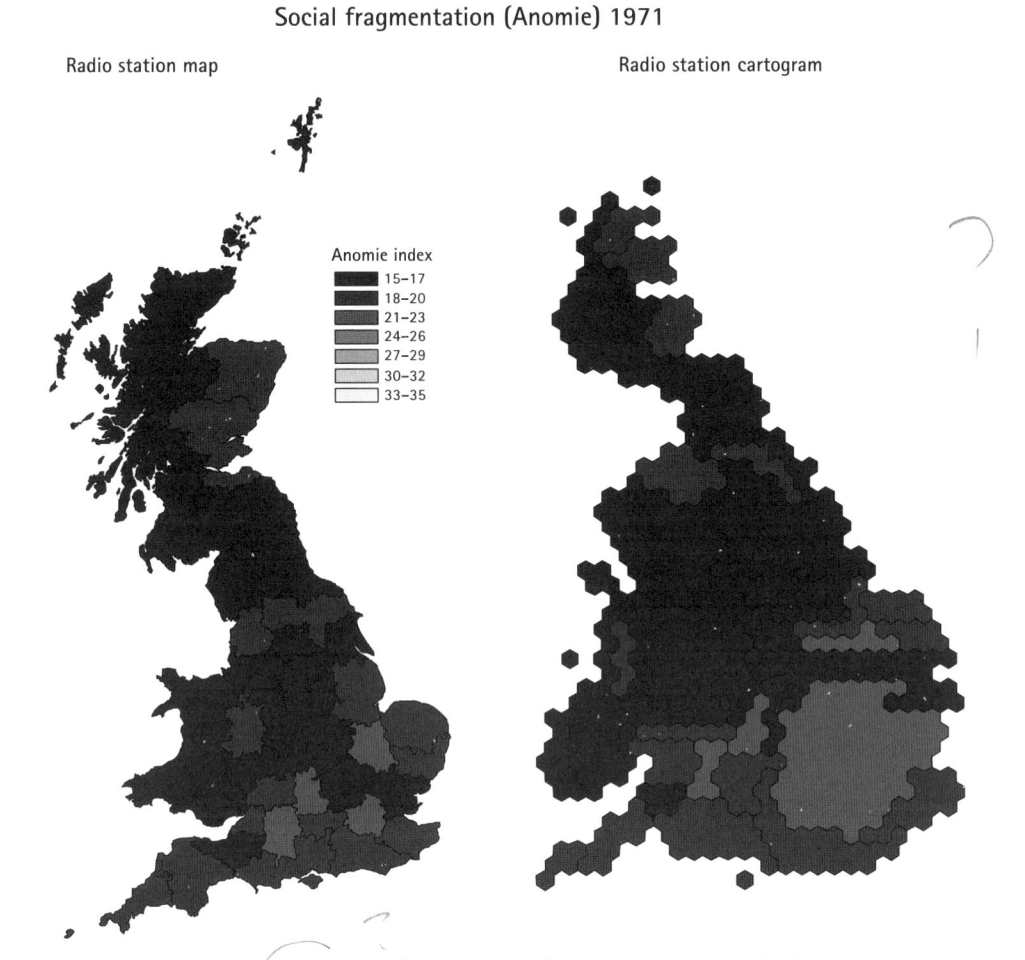

Radio station map    Radio station cartogram

Anomie index
- 15–17
- 18–20
- 21–23
- 24–26
- 27–29
- 30–32
- 33–35

FIG. 36.3 (Also see Color plate 2.) Spatial distribution of anomie index in 1971. Courtesy: the Social and Spatial Inequalities (SASI) Group, Department of Geography, University of Sheffield, UK.

from both younger and older generations. As they do so, however, they are also moving into increasingly socially fragmented cities. Areas they feel they belong to less and less.

## Concluding comments

This chapter has highlighted a number of conceptual issues pertaining to geographical determinants of happiness and unhappiness, and reviewed some empirical work in this area. There is a strong need to build on extant work in order to explore the "between level" interactions and the role of social rank and its impact upon local community life and well-being (Clark et al., 2009; Dorling, 2010; Dorling & Thomas, 2004; Dorling et al., 2007; Wilkinson

## Social fragmentation (Anomie) 2001

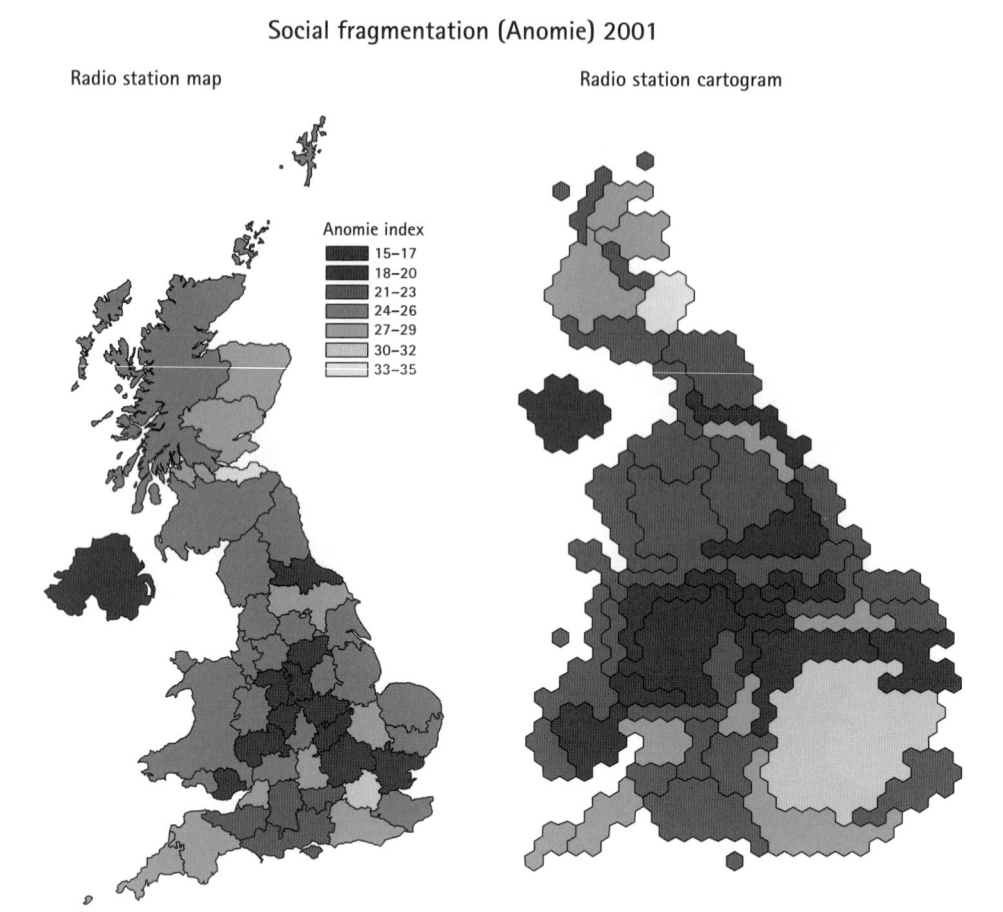

Radio station map

Radio station cartogram

Anomie index
- 15–17
- 18–20
- 21–23
- 24–26
- 27–29
- 30–32
- 33–35

FIG. 36.4 (Also see Color plate 3.) Spatial distribution of anomie index in 2001. Courtesy: the Social and Spatial Inequalities (SASI) Group, Department of Geography, University of Sheffield, UK.

& Pickett, 2009). In addition, there is a need to revisit the concept of "local social well-being" by building on new understandings resulting from how we measure concepts of "trust," "social cohesion," "social fragmentation," "belonging" and "social well-being" at the local level (Dorling et al., 2008). It is also important to explore the possible relationships between demographic segregation, socioeconomic polarization, social fragmentation and well-being. There is an increasing availability of data at the local and regional levels that enable us to identify the individual and household-level behaviors that appear to result in different geographical population patterns (such as decisions to migrate and to move house in the city to secure access to better schools and other services). This kind of work can also be linked to relevant findings on the relationship between individual choice and happiness (e.g., see Lane, 2000; Ott, 2001; Schwartz, 2004; Veenhoven, 1999). In the future, research could explore the relationship between subjective well-being, happiness, and choice with

Anomie change 1971–2001

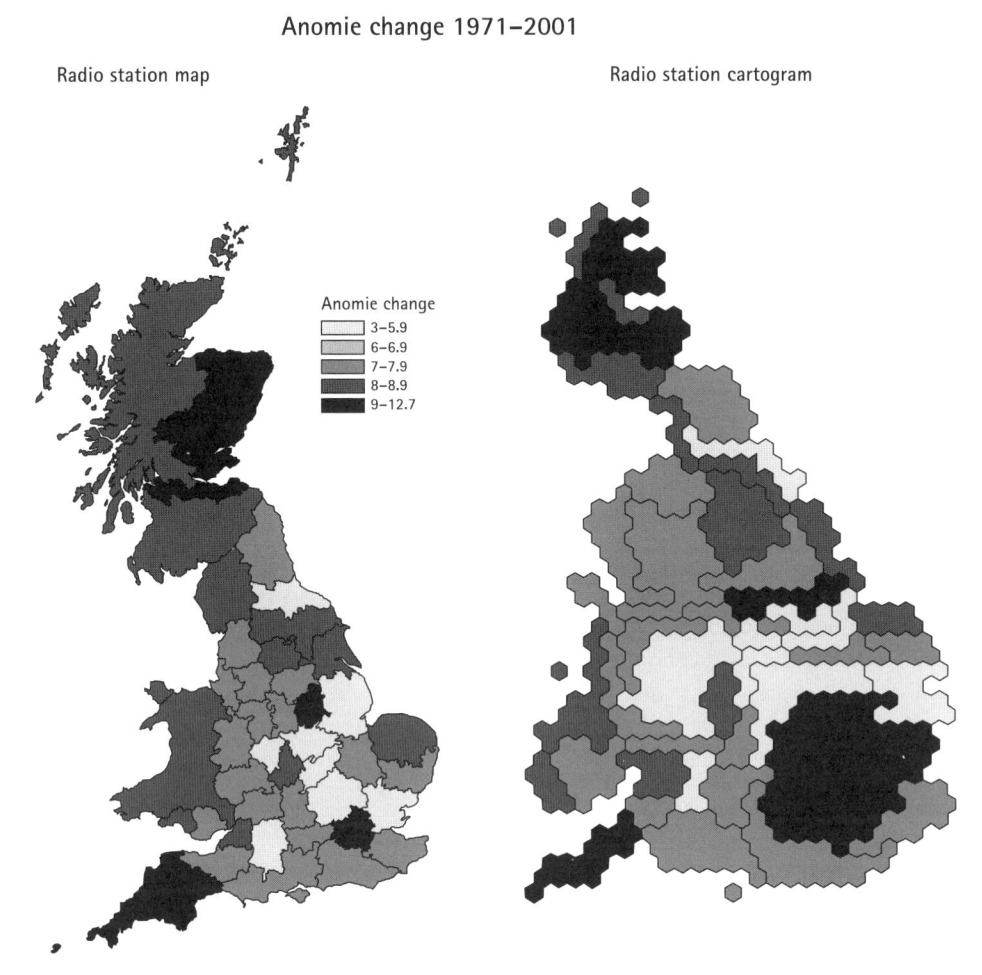

Radio station map        Radio station cartogram

Anomie change
- 3–5.9
- 6–6.9
- 7–7.9
- 8–8.9
- 9–12.7

FIG. 36.5 (Also see Color plate 4.) Spatial distribution of anomie index difference between 1971 and 2001. Courtesy: the Social and Spatial Inequalities (SASI) Group, Department of Geography, University of Sheffield, UK.

regards to different services (such as education and health) and the degree to which "more choice" may be beneficial or detrimental to human well-being (Offner, 2006). From the geographical point of view, abundant choice could also result in a more socioeconomically polarized and segregated society in which everyone becomes more psychologically worse-off. In this context it will also be important to examine individual-group conflicts; that is, conflicts between individual and collective choice and the relationship between well-being and the so called "smart for one, dumb for all" behaviors (Frank, 1999, 2007).

It is also important to explore the impact of local, regional, and global environmental and socioeconomic factors simultaneously, building on the relatively limited work in this area (Ballas & Fritz, 2008; Brereton et al., 2008; Ferrer-i-Carbonelli & Gowdy, 2007). Possible future research could explore the ways in which global issues such as climate change and its impacts are related to concepts of well-being including people's health, happiness and community relations (Cato, 2009). It would, for example, be interesting to explore the relationship between choosing "environmental" individual behaviors and consumption practices (e.g., recycling, choosing to cycle or walk to work, or use a car), and their impact upon the well-being of the individual and the collective. Such research might identify conflicts between alternative behaviors, and could provide guidance for designing government economic policies (e.g., provide incentives to recycle and disincentives to commuting by car) and environmental policies (e.g., coastal retreat policies, energy policies) that could affect these behaviors (see Thompson, Marks & Jackson, Chapter 38, this volume).

Finally, there is growing potential for interdisciplinary research that could address issues pertaining to links between environmental change and well-being at different scales ranging from the individual to the household, neighborhood, regional, and larger areas. Of particular importance are the potential conflicts between individual interests and group interests that arise from alternative behavior choices.

## Acknowledgments

The authors would like to thank the editors and two anonymous reviewers for their very useful comments and suggestions on an earlier draft. Dimitris Ballas and Danny Dorling were funded by the UK Economic and Social Research Council (research fellowship grant number RES-163-27-1013) and the British Academy and Leverhulme Trust (British Academy Research Leave Fellowship and Leverhulme Trust grant) respectively, while conducting the research and literature reviews upon which this chapter was based.

## References

Abdallah, S., Thompson, S., & Marks, N. (2007). Estimating worldwide life satisfaction. *Ecological Economics, 65*, 35–47.

Alesina, A., Di Tella, R., & MacCulloch, R. (2004). Inequality and happiness: Are Europeans and Americans different? *Journal of Public Economics, 88*, 2009–2042.

Annas, J. (1993). *The morality of happiness*. New York, NY: Oxford University Press.

Ballas, D. (2008). Geographical modelling of happiness and well-being. *British Urban and Regional Information Systems Association Newsletter, 177*, 12–17.

Ballas, D. (2010). Geographical simulation models of happiness and well-being. In J. Stillwell, P. Norman, C. Thomas, & P. Surridge, P. (Eds.), *Spatial and social disparities: Understanding population trends and processes (Volume 2)*. New York, NY: Springer.

Ballas, D., Dorling, D., & Shaw, M. (2007). Social inequality, health, and well-being. In J. Haworth & G. Hart (Eds.), *Well-being: Individual, community, and social perspectives* (pp. 163–186). Basingstoke, UK: Palgrave.

Ballas, D., & Fritz, S. (2008). *Geographical modelling of happiness and well-being using population surveys and remote sensing data*. Paper presented at Studying, Modeling and Sense Making of Planet Earth (UNESCO) international conference, Department of Geography, University of the Aegean, Greece, June 1–6.

Ballas, D., & Tranmer, M. (2012). Happy people or happy places? A multilevel modelling approach to the analysis of happiness and well-being. *International Regional Science Review, 35*, 70–102.

Bentham, J. (1983). An introduction into the principles of morals and legislation. In: *The collected works of Jeremy Bentham*. Oxford, UK: Clarendon Press. (Original work published 1789).

Bergsma, A., Poot, G., & Liefbroer, A. C. (2007). Happiness in the Garden of Epicurus. *Journal of Happiness Studies, 9*, 397–423.

Blanchflower, D., & Oswald, A. (2009). *Hypertension and happiness across regions.* Working paper, June 25, 2009. Retrieved from http://www2.warwick.ac.uk/fac/soc/economics/staff/academic/oswald/hypertensionregionsblanchos.pdf

Brereton, F., Clinch, J. P., & Ferreira, S. (2008). Happiness, geography and the environment. *Ecological Economics, 65*, 386–396.

Cato, M. S. (2009). *Green economics.* London, UK: Earthscan.

Clark, A. E. (2003). Unemployment as a social norm: Psychological evidence from panel data. *Journal of Labor Economics, 21*, 324–351.

Clark, A. E., Frijters, P., & Shields, M. A. (2008). Relative income, happiness, and utility: An explanation for the Easterlin paradox and other puzzles. *Journal of Economic Literature, 46*, 95–144.

Clark, A., Kristensen, N., & Westergård-Nielsen, N. (2009). Economic satisfaction and income rank in small neighbourhoods, *Journal of the European Economic Association, 7*, 519–527.

Congdon, P. (1996). Suicide and parasuicide in London: A small-area study. *Urban Studies, 33*(1), 137–158.

Di Tella, R., MacCulloch, R., & Oswald, A. (2001). Preferences over inflation and unemployment: Evidence from surveys of happiness. *American Economic Review, 91*, 335–341.

Dolan, P., Peasgood, T., & White, M. (2007). Do we really know what makes us happy? A review of the literature on the factors associated with subjective well-being. *Journal of Economic Psychology, 29*, 94–122.

Dorling, D. (2010). *Injustice: Why social inequality persists.* Bristol, UK: Policy Press.

Dorling, D., & Barford, A. (2009). The inequality hypothesis: Thesis, antithesis, and a synthesis? *Health & Place, 15*, 1166–1169.

Dorling, D., Rigby, J., Wheeler, B., Ballas, D., Thomas, B., Fahmy, E., Gordon, D., & Lupton, R. (2007). *Poverty, wealth and place in Britain, 1968 to 2005.* Bristol, UK: Policy Press.

Dorling, D., & Thomas, B. (2004). *People and Places: A census atlas of the UK.* Bristol, UK: Policy Press.

Dorling, D., Vickers, D., Thomas, B., Pritchard, J., & Ballas, D. (2008). *Changing UK: The way we live now.* Report commissioned for the BBC. Retrieved from http://news.bbc.co.uk/1/shared/bsp/hi/pdfs/01_12_08_changinguk.pdf

Duesenberry, J. S. (1949). *Income, saving and the theory of consumer behaviour.* Cambridge, MA: Harvard University Press.

Easterlin, R. A. (1974). Does economic growth improve the human lot? Some empirical evidence. In P. A. David & M. W. Reder (Eds.), *Nations and households in economic growth: Essays in honor of Moses Abramovitz.* New York, NY: Academic Press.

Ferrer-i-Carbonella, A., & Gowdy, J. M. (2007). Environmental awareness and happiness. *Ecological Economics, 60*, 509–516.

Frank, R. H. (1985). The demand for unobservable and other nonpositional goods. *American Economic Review, 75*, 101–116.

Frank, R. H. (1999). *Luxury fever: Money and happiness in an era of excess.* New York, NY: Princeton University Press.

Frank, R. H. (2007). *Falling behind: How rising inequality harms the middle class.* Berkeley, CA: University of California Press.

Frey, B., & Stutzer, A. (2002). *Happiness and economics.* Princeton, NJ: Princeton University Press.

Fung, Y-L. (1985). *Short history of Chinese philosophy.* New York, NJ: The Free Press.

Helliwell, J. F. (2003). How's life? Combining individual and national variables to explain subjective well-being. *Economic Modelling, 20,* 331–360.

Idler, E. L., & Benyamini, Y. (1997). Self-rated health and mortality: A review of twenty-seven community studies, *Journal of Health and Social Behavior, 38*(1), 21–37.

Inglehardt, R. (1990). *Culture shift.* Princeton, NJ: Princeton University Press.

Jen, M. H., Jones, K., Johnston, R. (2009). Compositional and contextual approaches to the study of health behaviour and outcomes: Using multi-level modelling to evaluate Wilkinson's income inequality hypothesis. *Health & Place, 15,* 198–203.

Jencks, C. (2002). Does inequality matter? *Daedalus, Winter,* 49–65.

Johnston, R., Jen, M., & Jones, K. (2009). On inequality, health, scientific progress and political argument: A response to Dorling and Barford. *Health & Place, 15,* 1163–1165.

Lane, R. E. (2000). *The loss of happiness in market democracies.* New Have, CT: Yale University Press.

Layard, R. (2005). *Happiness: Lessons from a new science.* London, UK: Penguin.

Lear, J. (1988). *Aristotle: The desire to understand.* Cambridge, UK: Cambridge University Press.

Legge, J. (1971). *Translation of Confucian analects.* New York, NY: Dover Publications.

Lu, L., & Gilmour, R. (2004). Culture and conceptions of happiness: Individual oriented and social oriented SWB. *Journal of Happiness Studies, 5,* 269–291.

Luttmer, E. F. P. (2005). Neighbors as negatives: Relative earnings and wellbeing. *Quarterly Journal of Economics, 120,* 963–1002.

Lynch, J., Davey Smith, G., Harper, S., Hillemeier, M., Ross, N., Kaplan, G. A., & Wolfson, M. (2004). Is income inequality a determinant of population health? Part 1: A Systematic review. *Millbank Quarterly, 82,* 5–99.

Marmot, M. (2004). *Status Syndrome.* London, UK: Bloomsbury.

Marx, K. (1847). *Wage, Labour and Capital,* [on-line document]. Marx/Engels Internet Archive (http://www.marxists.org) 1993, 1999. Retrieved September 15, 2006 from http://www.marxists.org/archive/marx/works/1847/wage-labour/index.htm.

Mitchell, R. (2005). Commentary: The decline of death—How do we measure and interpret changes in self-reported health across cultures and time? *International Journal of Epidemiology, 34,* 306–308.

Mitchell, R., & Popham, F. (2008). Effect of exposure to natural environment on health inequalities: An observational population study. *The Lancet, 372,* 1655–1660.

Morrison, P. (2007). Subjective well-being and the city. *Social Policy Journal of New Zealand, 31,* 74–103.

Myers, D. G. (1999). Close relationships and quality of life. In D. Kahneman, E. Diener, & N. Schwarz (Eds.), *Well-being: foundations of hedonic psychology.* New York, NY: Russell Sage Foundation Press.

Offner, A. (2006). *The challenge of affluence: Self-control and well-being in the United States and Britain since 1950.* Oxford, UK: Oxford University Press.

Ott, J. (2001). Did the market depress happiness in the US? *Journal of Happiness Studies, 2,* 433–434.

Oswald, A., & Wu, S. (2010). Objective confirmation of subjective measures of human well-being: Evidence from the US. *Science, 327*, 576–579.

Powdthavee, N. (2007). Are there geographical variations in the psychological cost of unemployment in South Africa? *Social Indicators Research, 80*, 629–652.

Propper, C., Jones, K., Bolster, A., Burgess, S., Johnston, R., & Sarker, R. (2005). Local neighbourhood and mental health: Evidence from the UK. *Social Science and Medicine, 61*, 2065–2083.

Putnam, R. (2000). *Bowling alone: The collapse and revival of American community*. New York, NY: Simon and Schuster.

Runciman, W. G. (1966). *Relative deprivation and social justice*. Henley, UK: Routledge and Kegan Paul.

Russel, B. (1930). *The conquest of happiness*, London, UK: George Allen & Unwin.

Ryff, C. D., & Singer, B. H. (2006). Know thyself and become what you are: a eudaimonic approach to psychological well-being. *Journal of Happiness Studies, 9*, 13–3.

Schoch, R. (2007). *The secrets of happiness: Three thousand years of searching for the good life*. London, UK: Profile Books.

Schwartz, B. (2004). *The paradox of choice. Why more is less*. New York, NY: Harper & Collins.

Smith, A. (1759). *The theory of the moral sentiments*. Edinburgh, UK: A. Kincaid and J. Bell.

Tarn, W. W. (1952). *Hellenistic civilisation*. London, UK: E. Arnold.

Tam, H. (2010). *Against power inequalities: Reflections on the struggle for inclusive communities*. London, UK: Birkbeck, London University.

Tiberius, V. (2004). Cultural differences and philosophical accounts of wellbeing. *Journal of Happiness Studies, 5*, 293–314.

Uchida, Y., Norasakkunkit, V., & Kitayama, S. (2004). Cultural constructions of happiness: Theory and empirical evidence. *Journal of Happiness Studies, 5*, 223–239.

Veblen, T. (1899). *The theory of the leisure class*. New York, NY: MacMillan.

Veenhoven, R. (1993). *Happiness in nations: Subjective appreciation of life in 56 nations 1946–1992*. Rotterdam, the Netherlands: Erasmus University Press.

Veenhoven, R. (1999). Quality-of-life in individualistic society: A comparison in 43 nations in the early 1990s. *Social Indicators Research, 48*, 157–186.

Veenhoven, R. (2000). Freedom and happiness: A comparative study in forty-four nations in the early 1990s. In E. Diener & M. E. Suh (Eds.), *Culture and subjective wellbeing*. Cambridge, MA: MIT Press.

Veenhoven, R. (2009). *World database of happiness*. Erasmus University Rotterdam. Retrieved December 1, 2009 from http://worlddatabaseofhappiness.eur.nl.

Wilkinson, R. (1997). Socioeconomic determinants of health: Health inequalities: Relative or absolute material standards? *British Medical Journal, 314*, 591–595.

Wilkinson, R. (2005). *The impact of inequality: How to make sick societies healthier*. New York, NY: The New Press.

Wilkinson, R. G., & Pickett, K. E. (2006). Income inequality and population health: A review and explanation of the evidence. *Social Science & Medicine, 62*, 1768–1784.

Wilkinson, R. G., & Pickett, K. E. (2009). *The spirit level: Why more equal societies almost always do better*. London, UK: Penguin.

Zhang, G., & Veenhoven, R. (2007). Ancient Chinese philosophical advice: Can it help us find happiness today? *Journal of Happiness Studies, 9*, 425–443.

CHAPTER 37

# WELL-BEING IN CONSUMER SOCIETIES

AARON AHUVIA AND ELIF IZBERK-BILGIN

University of Michigan, USA

DEBATES on the relationship between consumption and well-being predate the emergence of consumer societies by thousands of years. Ancient religious thinkers preached the folly of materialistic aspirations, and philosophers such as Epicurus expressed views that would be quite acceptable in today's voluntary simplicity movement, a perspective that espouses adopting practices to simplify one's lifestyle and reduce one's consumption. Yet these debates have intensified with growing concerns about global warming and new data on the subjective aspects of well-being.

This chapter reviews how two broadly defined research orientations in consumer behavior have approached well-being. The first research tradition is often called qualitative or interpretive because it generally uses qualitative research methods such as depth interviews or ethnography to collect data, which is then interpreted by the researcher. But we will use the more recent term consumer culture theory (CCT) in a broad sense to refer to this large and diverse body of work, which has one foot in the social sciences and the other foot in the humanities. While CCT research sometimes talks about "well-being," more often it addresses distinct issues which are vital to well-being, such as the construction of community and personal identity, or the ways in which consumption both frees and restricts human possibility.

The second research tradition has often been called quantitative because it generally uses surveys or experiments to collect data, which is analyzed statistically as part of the interpretive process. But we will use the term "neo-positivist" research for this work, bearing in mind the important caveat that this refers to a wide range of research which descended from the positivist tradition, but frequently differs in important ways from the original positivist vision. Neo-positivist research has one foot in the social sciences and the other in the natural sciences, and tends to utilize experimental research, quantitative surveys, and neurological research. Findings from this research can be usefully discussed in terms of objective (external) and subjective (internal) aspects of well-being. Objective aspects of well-being include income, education, longevity, health, crime rates, political freedom, etc. These objective aspects of well-being are not "objective" in the sense of being value neutral, since treating something as an indicator of well-being is always a values statement. Rather, they are "objective" in that they describe the external circumstances of a person's life. In contrast, the "subjective" aspects of well-being such as happiness, life satisfaction, and life meaning or purpose, describe how a person subjectively or internally experiences the circumstances of their life.

We begin our review with a discussion of consumer society. We then highlight criticisms and defenses of marketing and consumer societies as discussed within CCT. Next, we discuss objective indicators of well-being within consumer societies, particularly as debated within economics, quantitative sociology, and the environmental sciences. The final sections of the chapter outline key findings from positive psychology and related research on subjective well-being within consumer societies, with a particular focus on income, materialism, and consumer behavior.

## Consumer Societies

Consumer societies exist across the globe, but are best exemplified by Europe and North America after the Industrial Revolution, and particularly from the latter half of the twentieth century to the present. One obvious difference between a consumer society and other ways of life is the sheer quantity of purchasing, using, and disposing that pervades our daily lives; not to mention the time we spend working for the income to make these purchases, and thinking about what we will buy and how we will use it (C. Campbell, 1987).

Not only do people in *non*-consumer societies have far less stuff and purchase far fewer services (Bonsu & Belk, 2003; Sridharan & Viswanathan, 2008; Viswanathan, Gajendiran, & Venkatesan, 2008), but more of what they do have tends to be produced in the home rather than purchased in a marketplace. In a consumer society marketplace exchanges are, in principle at least, impersonal (Slater, 1997) in that one person's $10 is worth as much as the next person's $10. In contrast, in non-consumer societies goods are often allocated based on family relationships or social roles. And even when goods are bought or bartered the transactions are usually shaped by an ongoing social relationship between the buyer and seller, with no expectation that the same deal would be offered to all.

Consumer societies began emerging in Europe as early as the sixteenth century with the boom in trade and the development of fashion (Slater, 1997). Their development gathered steam in the eighteenth century as the Industrial Revolution made the consumption of commercially produced goods and services accessible to the middle classes. Consumer societies brought with them a hedonistic ethos regarding consumption, which became widely visible in the 1880s as shopping emerged as a mass leisure activity (Laermans, 1993). And while advertising dates back to the ancient world, its relentless assault on every moment of human consciousness began in consumer societies with the growth of advertising funded mass media in the 1920s.

Although communism tried—largely unsuccessfully—to create its own version of consumer societies, America emerged as the sole superpower with the fall of the Berlin Wall in 1989, resulting in the spread of global capitalism throughout the world. This, in turn, brought consumerism into "more and more aspects of more and more people's lives" (Kasser & Kanner, 2002, p. 3). Finally, the social trends variously labeled postmodernism or late modernism have further heightened the importance of consumption choices in defining individuals' sense of identity in consumer societies (Ahuvia, 2005; Ahuvia & Izberk-Bilgin, 2011; Brown, 1995; Firat & Venkatesh, 1995; Holt, 1997; Thompson & Troester, 2002). This final point, on the centrality of consumer choices in helping people fashion their sense of identity, is so important to understanding consumer society that it bears further elaboration.

In traditional preconsumer societies much of one's identity is determined by existing circumstances. For example, in medieval Europe, one's profession, religion, political views (such as they were), clothing style, diet, musical taste, and religion were largely a function of what family and social class one was born into (Slater & Tonkiss, 2001). In contrast, in today's consumer societies, identity is much less assigned than it is achieved. One's religious views, political views, entertainment preferences, diet, clothing preferences, home location, profession, marital partner (if any), number of children, etc. are all significantly matters of individual choice. Baumeister sums up this position: "To put it crudely, society stopped telling people who they were, and instead it was left up to the individual to construct his or her own identity" (1991, p. 95). In this project of constructing a desired sense of identity, factors such as one's job, one's social circle, and one's political and/or religious commitments are often more important to one's identity than are one's consumption habits.

Nonetheless, one's consumer choices and how one thinks and/or talks about those choices (Holt, 1997, 1998) are also very important aspects of this ongoing identity project. As Featherstone comments, "Rather than unreflexively adopting a lifestyle, through tradition or habit, the new heroes of consumer culture make lifestyle a life project and display their individuality and sense of style in the particularity of the assemblage of goods, clothes, practices, experiences, appearance and bodily dispositions they design together into a lifestyle" (1991, p. 86). This construction of identity is not an easy task. As Giddens (1991) writes, in pursuing the "project of the self,[1] the narrative of self-identity is inherently fragile. The task of forging a distinct identity may be able to deliver distinct psychological gains, but it is clearly also a burden" (p. 186). Therefore, "experience which seems to tell about the self, to help define it, develop it or change it, has become an overwhelming concern" (Sennett, 1977, p. 219). Since both what we purchase and refuse to purchase plays an important role in defining our sense of identity, consumer choices also become an overwhelming concern.

This ability of people within consumer societies to play a leading role in shaping and maintaining a sense of identity brings us to the topic of well-being. For those raised within a consumer culture, the idea that most (or even all) decisions can be based on what will produce the most personal happiness can seem natural and inevitable. But in preconsumer societies decisions were often based on tradition, honor, or other factors; the pursuit of personal happiness was often relegated to a secondary concern. It is only with the transition from assigned to achieved identities that the pursuit of happiness becomes an overriding personal mission and a cultural fixation (Ahuvia, 2002). The ideas that (1) people can and should choose their own identity, and (2) people can and should pursue their personal happiness (within some ethical limits), are closely linked. This is because doing what will provide deep and lasting personal happiness (i.e. following your bliss; J. Campbell, 1988) is often presented within achieved identity cultures as the best basis for determining what one's "true" identity is.

---

[1] In this literature, the terms "self" and "identity" are largely synonymous.

Claiming that activities which make one happy also express one's authentic self is an easy argument to make within individualistic cultures, where people are taught that one's true self lies "within" and can best be reached through introspection (Markus & Kitayama, 1991). This argument is somewhat less compelling within collectivist cultures in which one's true identity is believed to be located in one's social roles and relationships (Markus & Kitayama, 1991). Japan, Hong Kong, and other economically successful Southeast Asian societies have created thriving consumer cultures based on the interdependent self-concept: enacting one's social role, rather than pursuing individual happiness, is the driving force behind high levels of consumption (Wong & Ahuvia, 1998). However, unless these collectivist cultures break the long-established patterns of history, widespread affluence will slowly push them towards a more individualistic culture based on an independent self-concept in which personal happiness is seen as a guide to actualizing one's authentic self (Wong & Ahuvia, 1998). Hence, the type of widespread popular interest in happiness, which makes the publication of a vast literature on this topic possible, is particularly characteristic of a consumer culture.

# WELL-BEING AND CONSUMER CULTURE THEORY

CCT is a branch of consumer research which is linked in theory and method with sociology, anthropology, history, literary theory and related disciplines (Arnould & Thompson, 2005). CCT researchers have investigated a host of different factors related to well-being, including possessions and personal relationships (Costley, Friend, Meese, Ebbers, & Wang 2007), addiction (Hirschman, 1992), overconsumption (Moisio & Beruchashvili, 2010), environmentally friendly consumption habits (Dobscha & Ozanne, 2001), marketplace ideologies (Thompson, 2004; Thompson & Troester, 2002), consumer disempowerment (Henry, 2005), credit card debt (Bernthal, Crockett, & Rose, 2005), and ritualistic consumption (Bonsu & Belk, 2003). Some studies explicitly address well-being (Pancer, 2009); others contribute to an ongoing debate about the ways in which consumer culture liberates the people who participate in it (Firat & Venkatesh, 1995; Fiske, 1989) versus the ways in which consumer culture is itself a "hegemonic" force from which people need liberation (Murray, 2002; Murray & Ozanne, 1991).

The Consumer Society Reader (Schor & Holt, 2000) provides an overview of these debates, and identifies aspects of consumer society which its authors believe compromise well-being. For example, Holt and Schor (2000) argue that the unprecedented spending habits of the rich have led to anxieties and stress in those who do not have the economic means to participate in a consumption bonanza; this view is gaining strong empirical support in economics (Clark & Senik, 2010). Holt and Schor point out that homelessness, hunger, and poverty continue to be the most pressing societal problems threatening our collective well-being, even as a wealthy class of individuals enjoys an opulent lifestyle. They also critique consumer culture's tendency to commoditize everything from health, education, news, entertainment, public space, culture, to religion; such that "little remains sacred, and separate from the world of the commodity. As a result people become ever more desperate to sacralize the profane consumer world around them, worshipping celebrities, collections, and brand logos" (Holt and Schor, 2000, p. ix).

These concerns are part of an ongoing critical discourse whose modern manifestations hark back to the Frankfurt school, a Neo-Marxist interdisciplinary social theory (Geuss, 1981), and to early critics of advertising such as Vance Packard (1957). Critics of consumerism have suggested that advertising creates "false needs" and anxieties by first problematizing completely natural aspects of human existence (e.g., sweating), then offering their products as solutions to these invented problems, leaving consumers no better off than they were before the cycle started (for a review of these critical schools of thought see Izberk-Bilgin, 2010a). Today, Klein (2000) is one of the best-known voices speaking from this perspective. In her book *No Logo* she suggests that consumer culture takes over and commercializes public space (*no space* argument), reduces freedom of choice to the number of marketplace offerings (*no choice* argument), and eliminates local jobs for cheaper production overseas (*no jobs* argument) (see also Bauman, 2007; Gabriel & Yang, 1995, 2008; Markus & Schwarts, 2010).

Blumer (1969) explained how consumer tastes tend to shift as they reflect the changing economic climate and cultural zeitgeist. Holt and Schor (2000) apply this logic to the social criticism of consumer culture itself, noting that criticism of consumer society disappears during economic downturns, but becomes visible again when "prosperity seems secure, cultural transformation is too rapid, or environmental disasters occur" (p. vii). Indeed, in times of economic malaise, voracious consumption is portrayed as a civic obligation. For example, Cohen (2004, p. 236) demonstrates how in postwar America "business leaders, labor unions, government agencies, the mass media, advertisers, and many other purveyors of the new postwar order" collaborated to declare consumerism a patriotic duty. Similarly, following the terrorist attacks of September 11 2001, consumerism was once again packaged as a patriotic act which sustains our collective well-being.

Human well-being depends upon strong and vibrant communities, and the weakening of community is also a frequent criticism raised against the individualistic tendencies of American consumer culture (Putnam, 2004). For many people in consumer cultures, finding common bonds with others over a favorite brand is an important source of social connection. But are these social groupings, based around favorite brands, merely "counterfeit communities" (Freie, 1998)? Muniz and O'Guinn (2001, p. 426) respond to the criticism that consumer culture threatens communal relations and thus jeopardizes well-being by stating that:

> A brand community is neither any more nor less real than many other forms of community, and is simply an essential form humans invariably employ in their social existence ... brand communities are a response to the postindustrial age. Consumers seek communal affiliation and are likely to foster it wherever they can. Given consumption's undeniable centrality in contemporary culture, to either ignore these communities of commerce or to dismiss them entirely as yet another of late capitalism's excesses diminishes the phenomenon and the experience to banality and entirely denies the humanity to be found where commerce resides.

Of course, not everyone agrees with Muniz and O'Guinn (2001). In fact, for a significant counterculture within consumer societies, rejection of most brands itself becomes a source of communal affiliation. For example, Kozinet's ethnographic study of the annual Burning-Man festival finds an idealized community among the participants who form friendships, share belongings, and present gifts to individuals who were complete strangers at the onset of the festival. The festival brings together people who generally share a strong dislike for commercial consumer culture, and enables participants "to gather and focus their critiques and to assert their common agency against the interests of producer communities. In so doing, consumer communities can provide some of the foundations necessary for consumers to direct their own consumption meanings, practices, roles, and identities." Yet Kozinets (2002, p. 33) adds that "if we look, we can (also) find these qualities in commercial consumption-celebrating gatherings such as fan-run *Star Trek* conventions (Kozinets, 2001) and Harley-Davidson rallies (Schouten & McAlexander, 1995)."

# Consumer Society and the Objective Aspects of Well-Being

In this and the following sections we shift from the CCT approach, which primarily utilizes qualitative/interpretive methodologies, to research that generally utilizes experimental or quantitative survey methods. This includes approaches from psychology, consumer research, sociology and behavioral economics.

Well-being is comprised of both the objective/external circumstances of a person's life as well as his or her subjective experience of that life. To date, consumer societies have done very well on objective indicators of well-being. Economic development leads to the emergence of consumer culture (Ahuvia, 2002) as well as marked improvements in many objective well-being indices such as increased education, longevity, and transportation; greater political, religious, and artistic freedom; more varied choice in entertainment, foodstuffs and recreation; as well as increased physical comforts too plentiful to catalog.

With regard to these objective indicators of well-being, the main critiques of consumer society focus on inequality, and question the ecological sustainability of high consumption lifestyles. Criticisms of inequalities within consumer societies are as old as the consumer societies themselves (Marx, 1867/1976). But recent concerns about global warming have led the debate about consumer culture, at least within consumer societies, to focus more on ecological degradation than on economic inequalities.

Creating high levels of consumption produces massive amounts of pollution and quickly depletes finite natural resources (Princen, Maniates, & Conca, 2002). While politicians debate how we should best move towards cleaner renewable energy, natural resource experts often argue for the much less politically popular idea that only significant cutbacks in the total level of consumption will allow us to stave off dire ecological consequences (Princen et. al., 2002). Although still a countercultural movement, growing numbers of people within consumer societies are voluntarily reducing their overall level of consumption. Known variously as ethical consumption, responsible consumption, downshifting, or voluntary simplicity (Elgin, 1993; Schor, 1998); these consumers react against what they see as a materialist lifestyle which brings diminishing quality of life and courts ecological disaster (Soper, 2007; Thompson & Coskuner-Balli, 2007; Trentmann, 2007). Whether in postindustrial economies or the developing world (Izberk-Bilgin, 2010b), anticonsumerist activists are embracing the moral aspects of self-limited consumption, thereby forging a new civic understanding of consumer society and well-being (Kozinets, 2002; Thompson & Arsel, 2004; Thompson, Rindfleisch, & Arsel, 2006; Varman & Belk, 2009).

While there is much debate about the ecological costs of maintaining consumer cultures and the distribution of resources within those cultures, there is widespread agreement among researchers that consumer cultures go hand-in-hand with material progress, and corresponding increases in objectively measurable indicators of well-being. However, the extent to which objective indicators of well-being translate into subjective well-being, including happiness, overall life satisfaction and a sense of meaning and purpose in one's life is much less clear. Hence, the relationship between consumer culture and subjective well-being (SWB) will be the focus of the rest of this chapter.

## Materialism and Subjective Well-Being

One of the most common criticisms of consumer culture is that it leads to materialism. To a certain extent, materialism is an inevitable part of being raised in a culture where earning, shopping and owning are central parts of daily life. Advertising has long been subject to criticism for promoting materialism (Pollay, 1986; Richins, 1996). Pollay (1986) likened any given advertisement to a rain drop which has little effect on a person, but living in a consumer culture is like an advertising thunderstorm which has a major influence on individuals and their societies. These critiques have developed into *cultivation theory*, which holds that personal values are shaped (or "cultivated") over a long period of time in childhood and adolescence, and it is the cumulative effect of repeated exposure to the mass media which gradually influences peoples' value priorities and world views as adults (Besley, 2008). While this research literature has not let advertising off the hook, it has generally moved from a narrow focus on advertising to a broader focus on "media effects" including, for example, the combined effects of both television advertisements and the television shows they are embedded in (e.g., Benmoyal-Bouzaglo & Moschis, 2010; Speck & Roy, 2008). Studies tend to be generally supportive of cultivation theory in that media is one (among several) influences on our values. However, because it deals with small changes to people over many years (e.g., Besley, 2008) and cannot easily be studied using experiments, it is difficult for studies to produce conclusive results.

There are three widely used definitions of materialism. Belk and colleagues (e.g., Belk, 1985; Ger & Belk, 1996) see materialism as a combination of possessiveness, non-generosity, and envy. Richins and colleagues (reviewed in Richins & Rudmin, 1994) see materialism as (1) having possessions and money play a central role in one's life, (2) believing that money brings happiness, and (3) judging one's own and others' success based on income and possessions. Kasser and colleagues (reviewed in Kasser, 2002) see materialism as part of a larger tendency to place a relatively high priority on extrinsic goals rather than intrinsic goals (explained later in this section).

In all three approaches to materialism, higher levels of materialism have been shown to be correlated with lower levels of subjective well-being across a broad range of measures. Data on the relationship between how consumers spend (or save) their money and SWB also suggests that materialism is not a wise strategy for people wanting to be happy. Spending money has been shown to produce the most lasting happiness when the money is spent on (1) charitable donations (Dunn, Aknin, & Norton, 2008), (2) things which help foster social relationships (Lyubomirsky, 2007), and (3) experiences as opposed to physical objects (Van Boven

& Gilovich, 2003), so long as the experience was purchased with the primary goal of acquiring a life experience. Apparently, watching television is not such an experience, as it is negatively associated with well-being (Frey, Benesch, & Stutzer, 2007). Finally, there is also evidence that a good way to turn money into happiness is not to spend it at all, as savings is a good psychic investment (Headey, Muffels, & Wooden, 2008).

When examining what objects consumers list as their favorite possessions, Richins (1994) finds that materialists are less likely than other consumers to cherish objects which facilitate interpersonal relationships or help them have fun. She also finds that materialists are more likely than other consumers to highly prize objects which help them look good, cost a lot of money, and thereby convey prestige upon their owner. Consistent with this theme, Fitzmaurice (2008) found that when making a splurge purchase, materialists are more likely than other consumers to buy expensive items that are used in public settings, and after the purchase materialists are more likely to feel irresponsible and guilty about their actions, as compared to less materialistic consumers who also make splurge purchases.

Kasser (2002) applies self-determination theory to materialism. Kasser sees materialism as a particular instance of a larger value system in which people prioritize extrinsic goals (e.g., money, fame, good looks) over intrinsic goals (e.g., having close social relationships, improving oneself as a person, making a contribution to one's community). A nutrition analogy may be helpful in explaining the concepts of intrinsic and extrinsic goals. Just as the body has certain nutritional needs to be healthy, the mind has certain "psychological nutrition" needs—called *intrinsic* needs or goals—which must be met to be mentally healthy and happy. Extrinsic goals such as gaining social prestige through conspicuous consumption are the equivalent of mental desserts—attractive but lacking in psychological nutrition. Therefore pursuing these mental desserts is of no lasting psychological value once the initial taste has faded.

Hence in this needs-based view, simply desiring something is not a good indicator that attaining it would make one lastingly happy and psychologically healthy. This needs-based theory is in marked contrast to the typical consumer decision making models in economics which hold that consumers are excellent judges of what is in their own interest. After all, if achieving our financial ambitions or other extrinsic goals failed to produce lasting happiness, wouldn't people figure this out and stop pursuing those goals? Logical as this may sound, it is now a well documented aspect of human decision making that we consistently miss-estimate how much lasting happiness or unhappiness future events in our lives will bring us. Yet we don't seem to learn from our mistakes, and we repeat these errors over and over again (Wilson & Gilbert, 2003).

Although materialism is frequently equated with a strong desire for money, the situation is more complex. Studies find that desiring money is problematic when people want the money to achieve extrinsic goals (e.g., showing off or gaining power over others) rather than intrinsic goals (e.g., improving oneself as a person) or even pragmatic goals which are not clearly extrinsic or intrinsic, such as saving for retirement or supporting one's family (Carver & Baird, 1998; Srivastava, Locke, & Bartol, 2001). The desire for happiness itself plays a complicated role in this process: while the desire to be happy may seem like the quintessential intrinsic goal, the desire for money because one believes that money will make one happier is particularly strongly associated with reduced subjective well-being (Gardarsdóttir, Dittmar, & Aspinall, 2009).

All of these theories of materialism argue that less materialistic value systems are healthier for human beings than are highly materialistic value systems. Any claim that one value system is inherently superior to another value system will court controversy, and the evidence about this controversy is inconsistent. We can say with a high degree of confidence that on average people who prioritize extrinsic goals over intrinsic goals tend to suffer disproportionately from a host of maladies including anxiety, depression, physical symptoms, unpleasant emotions, drug abuse, alcohol abuse, behavioral disorders, lower levels of self-actualization, less vitality, less life satisfaction and fewer pleasant emotions (Emmons, 1996; Kasser, 2002). This evidence is strong enough to conclude that cultivating a less materialistic value system is probably wise. But there are still significant gaps in our knowledge about the extent to which materialism causes these problems, and whether it causes problems for all people or in all situations. For example, children whose parents divorce are more likely to become compulsive consumers, and slightly more likely to be highly materialistic than are children from intact homes at the same income level (Kasser, Ryan, Couchman, & Sheldon, 2002; Rindfleisch, Burroughs, & Denton, 1997). Thus, some of the problems correlated with materialism may actually result from childhood stressors such as divorce, rather than directly from materialism itself.

Materialism is clearly psychologically harmful on average, but conflicting evidence exists as to whether materialism is bad for all people and in all situations. Some studies have suggested that materialistic goals are fine so long as one achieves them (Oishi, Diener, Suh, & Lucas, 1999; Sagiv & Schwartz, 2000). However, Sheldon and Kasser (1998) tracked subjects' experiences over time and found that even when extrinsic goals were achieved subjective well-being did not improve. These two sets of conflicting results have yet to be reconciled.

Researchers have also investigated whether materialism is always negative, by looking at two forms of value conflicts: value conflicts between an individual and their community, and value conflicts within an individual. Sagiv and Schwartz (2000) presented data suggesting that highly materialistic people would not tend toward unhappiness if their materialistic values were supported by their social group. However, two follow-up studies found data contradicting this view (Kasser & Ahuvia, 2001; Vansteenkiste, Simons, Soenens, & Duriez, 2003). Burroughs and Rindfleish (2002) looked at conflicting values within the individuals and found that materialism causes psychological stress within an individual because materialistic values conflict with "collective" values which promote the welfare of the group. This study also found that for people low on these collective values, materialism does not cause them internal psychological conflict and hence does not reduce their well-being.

This last finding may be good news for materialistic individuals who aren't burdened with concerns about the welfare of others, but it also suggests that materialism may be linked to problems for society as a whole, and not just for the materialistic individual. Research suggests that simply thinking about money reduces prosocial behaviors like helping others or donating to charity (Dunn, Aknin, & Norton, 2008). Materialism also promotes high levels of consumption which, as discussed above, leads to global warming and other environmental problems ultimately harming human welfare (Ahuvia, 2008b; Princen et al., 2002; Shaw & Newholm, 2002). Finally, materialists tend to engage in less environmentally friendly behaviors (Saunders & Munro, 2000) and to be shortsighted in their management of natural resources, at least in experimental settings (Sheldon & McGregor, 2000).

# INCOME AND SUBJECTIVE WELL-BEING

The literature on materialism addresses the question: Does believing "money leads to happiness" make you unhappy? The literature on income and SWB addresses a different question: Is the belief that money leads to happiness correct?

Studies generally find a curvilinear relationship between income and happiness in which additional income is strongly correlated with increased SWB among the poor (Biswas-Diener & Diener, 2001), but very weakly correlated with SWB among the non-poor (Ahuvia, 2008a and 2008b). The influence of increased income on SWB among the non-poor is an especially hot political topic that is sometimes presented with a lot of "spin." Proponents of the idea that wealth leads to happiness among the non-poor correctly state that statistically significant correlations between income and happiness have been found for every income level in almost every study on the topic (for the few exceptions, see Arthaud-Day and Near (2005, pp. 518–519)). However, most studies suggest that among the non-poor, and especially among those comfortably in or above the middle class, increased income has an extremely small impact on happiness (for a somewhat larger impact, see Stevenson and Wolfers (2008)), so that the time and effort put into increasing income would yield more happiness if invested in, say, improving social relationships (Argyle, 1999; Lyubomirsky, Tkach, & DiMatteo, 2006; Myers, 1999) or even just getting enough sleep (Dement & Vaughan, 2000).

There is also substantial evidence that these correlational studies linking income to happiness overstate the influence of income on the experience of daily life (Kahneman, Krueger, Schkade, Schwarz, & Stone, 2004). Similarly, to the extent that income and happiness are correlated, this may not be due to higher levels of income causing high levels of SWB. Rather, some third variable may be causing both higher income and more happiness. For example, high-paying jobs tend to have other rewards such as autonomy and relatively interesting work, which are associated with SWB (Argyle, 1996). Unemployment brings both a loss in income, and strong negative effects on happiness over and above the associated loss of wages (Clark, Georgellis, & Sanfey, 1999; Oswald, 1997). Variables other than the level of one's consumption, like crime and single-parent families, may decrease the happiness of poorer people. One of the great benefits of higher income is that it increases one's options, and increased choice is seen as one of the core benefits provided by consumer societies. However, even with regards to increased choice, research is finding that it's easy to get too much of a good thing, as large numbers of choices become burdensome and can lead to dissatisfaction (Schwartz, 2005). Finally, strange as it may at first sound, rather than income causing happiness, *happiness may cause income.* Some aspects of a happy personality, such as optimism, lead to higher incomes (Argyle, 1996; Diener & Lucas, 1999; Myers & Diener, 1995). The influence of personality variables can be so powerful that when income is included in models along with psychological variables such as optimism, control, and self esteem, income does not show unique significance (Cummins, 2000).

As the literature advances, studies are moving away from a one-size-fits-all approach to this issue, and asking if the relationship between income and happiness might be stronger in some people than in others. In general, studies find that the strength of the relationship between income and happiness does increase somewhat among people who are highly materialistic, see wealth as an important part of a happy life, tend to compare their income to others, or have major life goals that income can help them attain (Clark & Senik, 2010; Diener & Fujita, 1995; Dolan, Peasgood, & White, 2008; Georgellis, Tsitsianis, & Yin, 2009; Rojas, 2007). These findings can be interpreted in two different, but equally valid, ways: (1) materialistic and extrinsically oriented people would benefit psychologically from higher incomes, or that (2) people can become happier at moderate income levels by becoming less materialistic and less extrinsically oriented. The evidence clearly shows, however, that for people who are not poor, increasing one's income is a highly inefficient strategy for increasing one's happiness.

## Conclusions

Consumer societies are spreading around the globe in no small part because they are highly attractive to many people. Consumer societies are wealthy societies, and tend to come with many objective indicators of well-being such as education and healthcare. Consumer societies also do well in international studies of subjective well-being (Ahuvia, 2002). However, evidence suggests that the *consumer* part of consumer societies (by which we mean buying, owning and/or using an abundance of commercially produced goods and services, beyond what meets one's basic needs) is not directly responsible for these higher self-reported levels of subjective well-being (Alesina, Di Tella, & MacCulloch, 2001; Helliwell, 2003). Ecological issues now pose a serious challenge to the sustainability of these societies. And materialism, which might be described as an excessive enthusiasm for consumer society, has itself been shown to be closely associated with negative outcomes for the materialists themselves and the people with whom they interact. For citizens of consumer societies, the question remains, where to go from here?

## References

Ahuvia, A. C. (2002). Individualism/collectivism and cultures of happiness: A theoretical conjecture on the relationship between consumption, culture and subjective wellbeing at the national level. *Journal of Happiness Studies*, 3, 23–36.

Ahuvia, A. C. (2005). Beyond the extended self: Loved objects and consumers' identity narratives. *Journal of Consumer Research*, 32(1), 171–184.

Ahuvia, A. C. (2008a). Wealth, consumption and happiness. In A. Lewis (Ed.), *The Cambridge Handbook of Psychology and Economic Behaviour* (pp. 199–226). Cambridge, UK: Cambridge University Press.

Ahuvia, A. C. (2008b). If money doesn't make us happy, why do we act as if it does? *Journal of Economic Psychology*, 29(4), 491–507.

Ahuvia, A. C., & Izberk-Bilgin, E. (2011). Limits of the McDonaldization thesis: eBayization and ascendant trends in post-industrial consumer culture. *Consumption Markets and Culture*, 14(4), 361–384.

Alesina, A., Di Tella, R., & MacCulloch, R. (2001). *Inequality and happiness: Are Europeans and Americans different?* National Bureau of Economic Research (NBER) working paper 8198.

Argyle, M. (1996). Subjective well-being. In A. Offer (Ed.), *Pursuit of the Quality of Life* (pp. 18–45). New York, NY: Oxford University Press.

Argyle, M. (1999). Causes and correlates of happiness. In D. Kahneman, E. Diener, & N. Schwarz (Eds.), *Well-Being: The foundations of hedonic psychology* (pp. 353–373). New York, NY: Russell Sage Foundation.

Arnould, E., & Thompson, C. (2005). Consumer culture theory (CCT): 20 years of research. *Journal of Consumer Research, 31* (March), 868–882.

Arthaud-Day, M. L., & Near, J. P. (2005). The wealth of nations and the happiness of nations: Why "accounting" matters. *Social Indicators Research, 74,* 511–548.

Bauman, Z. (2007). Collateral casualties of consumerism. *Journal of Consumer Culture, 7*(1), 25–56.

Baumeister, R. F. (1991). *Meanings in life.* New York, NY: The Guilford Press.

Belk, R. W. (1985). Materialism: Trait aspects of living in the material world. *Journal of Consumer Research, 12,* 265–280.

Benmoyal- Bouzaglo, S., & Moschis G. P. (2010). Effect of family structure and socialization on materialism: A life-course study in France. *Journal of Marketing and Practice, 18*(1), 53–69.

Bernthal, M. J., Crockett, D., & Rose, R. L. (2005). Credit cards as lifestyle facilitators. *Journal of Consumer Research, 32*(1), 130–145.

Besley, J. C. (2008). Media use and human values. *Journalism and Mass Communication Quarterly, 85,* 311–330.

Biswas-Diener, R., & Diener, E. (2001). Making the best of a bad situation: Satisfaction in the slums of Calcutta. *Social Indicators Research, 55,* 329–352.

Blumer, H. (1969). Fashion: From class differentiation to collective selection. *Sociological Quarterly, 10,* 275–291.

Bonsu, S. K., & Belk, R. W. (2003). Do not go cheaply into that good night: Death-ritual consumption in Asante, Ghana. *Journal of Consumer Research, 30,* 41–55.

Brown, S. (1995). *Postmodern Marketing.* New York, NY: Routledge.

Burroughs, J. E., & Rindfleisch, A. (2002). Materialism and well-being: A conflicting values perspective. *Journal of Consumer Research, 29* (December), 348–370.

Campbell, C. (1987). *The romantic ethic and the spirit of modern consumerism.* Cambridge, MA: Blackwell Press.

Campbell, J. (1988). *The power of myth.* New York, NY: Doubleday & Co.

Carver, C. S., & Baird, E. (1998). The American dream revisited: Is it what you want or why you want it that matters? *Psychological Science, 9* (July), 289–292.

Clark, A., Georgellis, Y., & Sanfey, P. (1999). *Scarring: The psychological impact of past unemployment.* Orleans, France: Laboratoire d'Economie d'Orleans.

Clark, A. E., & Senik, C. (2010). Who compares to whom? The anatomy of income comparisons in Europe. *The Economic Journal, 120,* 573–594.

Cohen, L. (2004). A consumers' republic: The politics of mass consumption in postwar America. *Journal of Consumer Research, 31,* 236–239.

Costley, C., Friend, L., Meese, E., Ebbers, C., & Wang, L.-J. (2007). Happiness, consumption, and being. In R. W. Belk and J. F. Sherry (Eds.), *Consumer culture theory, Vol. 11* (pp. 209–240). Bingley, UK: Emerald Group Publishing Limited.

Cummins, R. A. (2000). Personal income and subjective well-being: A review. *Journal of Happiness Studies, 1,* 133–158.

Dement, W. C., & Vaughan, C. (2000). *The promise of sleep: A pioneer in sleep medicine explores the vital connection between health, happiness, and a good night's sleep.* New York, NY: Dell Publishing Company.

Diener, E., & Fujita, F. (1995). Resources, personal strivings, and subjective well-being: A nomothetic and idiographic approach. *Journal of Personality and Social Psychology, 68,* 926–935.

Diener, E., & Lucas, R. E. (1999). Personality and subjective well-being. In D. Kahneman, E. Diener & N. Schwarz (Eds.), *Well-Being: The foundations of hedonic psychology* (pp. 213–229). New York, NY: Russell Sage Foundation.

Diener, E., Wolsic, B., & Fujita, F. (1995). Physical attractiveness and subjective well-being. *Journal of Personality and Social Psychology, 69,* 120–129.

Dobscha, S., & Ozanne, J. L. (2001). An ecofeminist analysis of environmentally sensitive women using qualitative methodology: The emancipatory potential of an ecological life. *Journal of Public Policy and Marketing, 20,* 201–214.

Dolan, P., Peasgood, T., & White, M. (2008). Do we really know what makes us happy? A review of the economic literature on the factors associated with subjective well-being. *Journal of Economic Psychology, 29,* 94–122.

Dunn, E. W., Aknin, L. B., & Norton, M. I. (2008). Spending money on others promotes happiness. *Science, 319,* 1687–1688.

Elgin, D. (1993). Voluntary simplicity and the new global challenge. In J. B. Schor & D. B. Holt (Eds.), *The consumer society reader* (pp. 397–414). New York, NY: The New Press.

Emmons, R. A. (1996). Striving and feeling: Personal goals and subjective well-being. In P. M. Gollwitzer & J. A. Bargh (Eds.), *The pychology of action: linking cognition and motivation to behavior* (pp. 313–337). New York, NY: Guilford Publications.

Featherstone, M. (1991). *Consumer culture and postmodernism.* Newbury Park, CA: Sage.

Firat, F. A., & Venkatesh, A. (1995). Liberatory postmodernism and the reenchantment of consumption. *Journal of Consumer Research, 22,* 239–267.

Fiske, J. (1989). *Understanding popular culture.* Boston, MA: Unwin Hyman.

Fitzmaurice, J. (2008). Splurge purchases and materialism. *The Journal of Consumer Marketing, 25,* 332–338.

Freie, J. F. (1998). *Counterfeit community: The exploitation of our longings for connectedness.* Lanham, MD: Rowman & Littlefield Publishers, Inc.

Frey, B. S., Benesch, C., & Stutzer, A. (2007). Does watching TV make us happy? *Journal of Economic Psychology, 28,* 283–313.

Gabriel, Y., & Lang, T. (1995). *The unmanageable consumer: Contemporary consumption and its fragmentations.* Thousand Oaks, CA: Sage Publications.

Gabriel, Y., & Lang, T. (2008). New faces and new masks of today's consumer. *Journal of Consumer Culture, 8,* 321–340.

Gardarsdóttir, R. B., Dittmar, H., & Aspinall, C. (2009). It's not the money, it's the quest for a happier self: The role of happiness and success motives in the link between financial goals and subjective well-being. *Journal of Social and Clinical Psychology, 28,* 1100–1128.

Georgellis, Y., Tsitsianis, N., & Yin, Y. (2009). Personal values as mitigating factors in the link between income and life satisfaction: Evidence from the European Social Survey. *Social Indicators Research, 91,* 329–344.

Ger, G., & Belk, R. W. (1996). Cross-cultural differences in materialism. *Journal of Economic Psychology, 17,* 55–77.

Gergen, K. J. (1991). *The saturated self: Dilemmas of identity in contemporary life.* New York, NY: Basic Books.

Geuss, R. (1981). *The idea of a critical theory. Habermas and the Frankfurt school.* Cambridge, UK: Cambridge University Press.

Giddens, A. (1991). *Modernity and self-identity.* Stanford, CA: Stanford University Press.

Helliwell, J. F. (2003). How's life? Combining individual and national variables to explain subjective well-being. *Economic Modeling, 20*, 331–360.

Headey, B., Muffels, R., & Wooden, M. (2008). Money does not buy happiness: Or does it? A reassessment based on the combined effects of wealth, income and consumption. *Social Indicators Research, 87*, 65–82.

Henry, P. C. (2005). Social class, market situation, and consumers' metaphors of (dis)empowerment. *Journal of Consumer Research, 31*, 766–778.

Hirschman, E. (1992). The consciousness of addiction: Toward a general theory of compulsive consumption. *Journal of Consumer Research, 19* (September), 155–179.

Holt, D. B. (1997). Post-structuralist lifestyle analysis: Conceptualizing the social patterning of consumption in postmodernity. *Journal of Consumer Research, 23* (March), 326–350.

Holt, D. B. (1998). Does cultural capital structure American consumption? *Journal of consumer research, 25*, 1–25.

Holt, D. B., & Schor, J. B. (2000). Introduction: Do Americans consume too much? In J. B. Schor and D. B. Holt (Eds.), *The consumer society reader* (pp. vii–xxiii). New York, NY: The New Press.

Izberk-Bilgin, E. (2010a). An interdisciplinary review of resistance to consumption, some marketing interpretations, and future research suggestions. *Consumption, Markets, and Culture, 13*(3), 299–323.

Izberk-Bilgin, E. (2010b). Lifting the veil on infidel brands: Islamist discourses of anticonsumerism. *Advances in Consumer Research, 37*, 686–687.

Kahneman, D., Krueger, A. B., Schkade, D., Schwarz, N., & Stone, A. (2006). Would you be happier if you were richer? A focusing illusion. *Science, 312*, 1908–1910.

Kasser, T. (2002). *The high price of materialism*. Boston, MA: MIT press.

Kasser, T., & Ahuvia A. C. (2001). Materialistic values and well-being in business students: An empirical reply to Sagiv & Schwartz (2000). *European Journal of Social Psychology, 32*, 137–146.

Kasser, T., Ryan, R. M., Couchman, C. E., & Sheldon, K. M. (2002). Materialistic values: Their causes and consequences. In T. Kasser & A. Kanner (Eds.), *Psychology and the culture of consumption* (pp. 11–28). Washington, DC: American Psychological Association Press.

Klein, N. (2000). *No logo*. New York, NY: Picador.

Kozinets, R. V. (2001). Utopian enterprise: Articulating the meanings of Star Trek's culture of consumption. *Journal of Consumer Research, 28*, 67–88.

Kozinets, R. V. (2002). Can consumers escape the market? Emancipatory illuminations from Burning Man. *Journal of Consumer Research, 29*, 20–38.

Laermans, R. (1993). Learning to consume: Early department stores and the shaping of the modern consumer culture (1800-1914). *Theory, Culture, and Society, 10*, 79–102.

Lyubomirsky, S., & Ross, L. (1997). Hedonic consequences of social comparison: a contrast of happy and unhappy people. *Journal of Personality and Social Psychology, 73*, 1141–1157.

Lyubomirsky, S., Tkach, C., & DiMatteo, M. R. (2006). What are the differences between happiness and self-esteem? *Social Indicators Research, 78*, 363–404.

Markus, H. R., & Kitayama, S. (1991). Culture and the self: Implications for cognition, emotion, and motivation. *Psychological Review, 98*, 224–253.

Markus, H. R., & Schwartz, B. (2010). Does choice mean freedom and well-being? *Journal of Consumer Research, 37*, 344–355.

Marx, K. (1976). *Capital*. Volume 1. New York, NY: Penguin Books. (Original work published 1867).

Moisio, R., & Beruchashvili, M. (2010). Questing for well-being at Weight Watchers: the role of the spiritual-therapeutic model in a support group. *Journal of Consumer Research, 36*, 857–875.

Muniz, A. M., Jr., & O'Guinn, T. C. (2001). Brand Community. *Journal of Consumer Research, 27* (March), 412–432.

Murray, J. B. (2002). The politics of consumption: A re-inquiry on Thompson and Haytko's (1997) "Speaking of Fashion". *Journal of Consumer Research, 29* (December), 427–440.

Murray, J. B., & Ozanne, J. L. (1991). The critical imagination: emancipatory interests in consumer research. *Journal of Consumer Research, 18*, 129–144.

Myers, D. G. (1999). Close relationships and quality of life. In D. Kahneman, E. Diener, & N. Schwarz (Eds.), *Well-Being: The foundations of hedonic psychology* (pp. 353–373). New York, NY: Russell Sage Foundation.

Myers, D. G., & Diener, E. (1995). Who is happy? *Psychological Science, 6*, 10–19.

Oishi, S., Diener, E., Suh, E., & Lucas, R. E. (1999). Value as a moderator in subjective well-being. *Journal of Personality, 67*, 157–184.

Oswald, A. J. (1997). Happiness and economic performance. *The Economic Journal, 107* (November), 1815–1831.

Packard, V. (1957). *The hidden persuaders.* London, UK: Longmans, Green.

Pancer, E. (2009). *What is consumer well-being?: An historical analysis.* Conference on Historical Analysis & Research in Marketing, Leicester, United Kingdom, May 28–31.

Pollay, R. W. (1986). The distorted mirror: Reflections on the unintended consequences of advertising. *Journal of Marketing, 50*, 18–35.

Princen, T., Maniates, M., & Conca, K. (2002). *Confronting consumption.* Cambridge, MA: MIT Press.

Putnam, R. D. (2004). *Democracies in Flux: The evolution of social capital in contemporary society.* New York, NY: Oxford University Press.

Richins, M. L. (1991). Social comparison and the idealized images of advertising. *Journal of Consumer Research, 18*, 71–83.

Richins, M. L. (1996). Materialism, desire, and discontent: Contributions of idealized advertising images and social comparison. In R. P. Hill (Ed.), *Marketing and consumer research in the public interest* (pp. 109–132). Thousand Oaks, CA: Sage.

Richins, M. L., & Rudmin, F. W. (1994). Materialism and economic psychology. *Journal of Economic Psychology, 15*, 217–231.

Rindfleisch, A., Burroughs, J. E., & Denton, F. (1997). Family structure, materialism, and compulsive consumption. *Journal of Consumer Research, 23*(March), 312–325.

Rojas, M. (2007). Heterogeneity in the relationship between income and happiness: A conceptual-referent-theory explanation. *Journal of Economic Psychology, 28*, 1–14.

Sagiv, L., & Schwartz, S. H. (2000). Value priorities and subjective well-being: Direct relations and congruity effects. *European Journal of Social Psychology, 30*, 177–198.

Saunders, S., & Munro, D. (2000). The construction and validation of a consumer orientation questionnaire (SCOI) designed to measure Fromm's (1955) 'marketing character' in Australia. *Social Behavior and Personality, 28*, 219–240.

Schor, J. B. (1998). *The overspent american: upscaling, downshifting, and the new consumer.* New York, NY: Basic Books.

Schor, J. B. (1999). Towards a new politics of consumption. In J. B. Schor & D. B. Holt (Eds.), *The consumer society reader* (pp. 446–463). New York, NY: The New Press.

Schor, J. B., & Holt, D. B. (Eds.). (2000). *The consumer society reader.* New York, NY: The New Press.

Schouten, J. W., & McAlexander, J. H. (1995). Subcultures of consumption: An ethnography of the new bikers. *Journal of Consumer Research, 22*, 43–61.

Schwartz, B. (2005). *The paradox of choice: Why more is less.* New York, NY: Harper Perennial.
Sennett, R. (1977). *The fall of public man.* Cambridge, UK: Cambridge University Press.
Shaw, D., & Newholm, T. (2002). Voluntary simplicity and the ethics of consumption. *Psychology & Marketing, 19,* 167–185.
Sheldon, K. M., & Kasser, T. (1998). Pursuing personal goals: skills enable progress, but not all progress is beneficial. *Personality and Social Psychology Bulletin, 24,* 1319–1331.
Sheldon, K. M., & McGregor, H. A. (2000). Extrinsic value orientation and 'The Tragedy of the Commons'. *Journal of Personality, 68,* 383–411.
Slater, D. (1997). *Consumer Culture and Modernity.* Cambridge, UK: Polity Press.
Slater, D., & Tonkiss, F. (2001). *Market society: Markets and modern social theory.* Malden, MA: Blackwell Publishers.
Soper, K. (2007). Re-Thinking the 'Good Life': The citizenship dimension of consumer disaffection with consumerism. *Journal of Consumer Culture, 7,* 205–229.
Speck, S. K. S., & Roy, A. (2008). The interrelationship between television viewing, values, and perceived well-being: A global perspective. *The Journal of International Business Studies, 39,* 1–23.
Sridharan, S., & Viswanathan, M. (2008). Marketing in subsistence marketplaces: consumption and entrepreneurship in a South Indian context. *Journal of Consumer Marketing, 25,* 455–462.
Srivastava, A., Locke, E. A., & Bartol, K. M. (2001). Money and subjective well-being: It's not the money, it's the motives. *Journal of Personality and Social Psychology, 80,* 959–971.
Stevenson, B., & Wolfers, J. (2008). Economic growth and subjective well-being: Reassessing the Easterlin paradox. *Brookings Papers on Economic Activity 2008, 1,* 1–87.
Thompson, C. J. (2004). Marketplace mythology and discourses of power. *Journal of Consumer Research, 31,* 162–180.
Thompson, C. J., & Arsel, Z. (2004). The Starbucks brandscape and consumers' (anticorporate) experiences of glocalization. *Journal of Consumer Research, 31,* 631–642.
Thompson, C. J., & Coskuner-Balli, G. (2007). Enchanting ethical consumerism: The case of community supported agriculture. *Journal of Consumer Culture, 7,* 275–303.
Thompson, C. J., Rindfleisch, A., & Arsel, Z. (2006). Emotional branding and the strategic value of the Doppelgänger brand image. *Journal of Marketing, 70,* 50–64.
Thompson, C. J., & Troester, M. (2002). Consumer value systems in the age of postmodern fragmentation: The case of the natural health microculture. *Journal of Consumer Research, 28,* 550–571.
Trentmann, F. (2007). Citizenship and consumption. *Journal of Consumer Culture, 7,* 147–158.
Van Boven, L., & Gilovich, T. (2003). To do or to have? That is the question. *Journal of Personality and Social Psychology, 85,* 1193–1202.
Varman, R., & Belk, R. W. (2009). Nationalism and ideology in an anticonsumption movement. *Journal of Consumer Research, 36,* 686–700.
Viswanathan, M., Gajendiran, S., & Venkatesan, R. (2008). *Enabling consumer and entrepreneurial literacy in subsistence marketplaces.* New York, NY: Springer.
Wilson, T. D., & Gilbert, D. T. (2003). Affective forecasting. In M. P. Zanna (Ed.), *Advances in experimental social psychology* (Vol. 35, pp. 345–411). New York, NY: Academic Press.
Wong, N., & Ahuvia, A. C. (1998). Personal taste and family face: Luxury consumption in confucian and western societies. *Psychology and Marketing, 15,* 423–441.

# CHAPTER 38

# WELL-BEING AND SUSTAINABLE DEVELOPMENT

SAM THOMPSON[1], NIC MARKS[2], AND TIM JACKSON[3]

[1]University of Liverpool, UK; [2]**nef** (the new economics foundation), UK;
[3]University of Surrey, UK

WHILST it may be too simplistic to say that "development," at the level of nations and societies, is synonymous with economic growth, it is hardly an exaggeration that economic growth is assumed to be a necessary prerequisite for development. Economic growth, defined by rising levels of gross domestic product (GDP), has contributed to advances in healthcare, increasing rates of employment, and rising levels of education. It has created the wealth that, in turn, has increased personal freedoms and opportunities, and met community needs and national goals.

At the same time, the increased demand for energy, food, services and consumer goods that has driven economic growth (at least since the industrial revolution) has also been the key driver of environmental change. Such material consumption relies on the use of planetary resources—oil, gas, coal, minerals and metals, land, water, and so on. This is sustainable only if the rate at which resources are being depleted or damaged is less than the rate at which they can be replenished, repaired by natural processes or, in the case of carbon dioxide ($CO_2$) emissions, absorbed. It is, by now, hardly controversial to claim that our current rate of use of resources is unsustainable. The Millennium Ecosystem Assessment (MEA), a major United Nations initiative involving more than 1300 experts worldwide, suggested that about 60% of ecosystem services are currently being degraded or used unsustainably. According to calculations made using the Ecological Footprint (Wackernagel & Rees, 1996), global levels of resource use became unsustainable around the mid-1980s and have steadily become more so over the past decades (Simms, 2009).

It is this simple observation—that consumption growth has led to our environmental problems—that underpins the concept of *sustainable development*. In the well-known definition put forward by the Bruntland Commission (WCED, 1987), sustainable development is that which "meets the needs of the present without compromising the ability of future generations to meet their own needs." Sustainable development is often regarded as a challenge to orthodox economic development. But it is also—and perhaps primarily—a call to pursue a different pathway towards maximizing human well-being and happiness.

The relationship between well-being and environmental sustainability hinges on the nature of consumption; specifically, whether the kinds of consumer behavior promoted by prevailing social, economic, and political forces act to support, or interfere with, the satisfaction of underlying needs. According to economic theory, consumer demand is a key driver of economic growth. It is also strongly related to individuals' well-being, because in a growing economy people are increasingly affluent and able to purchase goods and services that enhance their quality of life in a number of ways, three of which are worth noting here.

Firstly, fulfilling basic physical needs for subsistence and protection requires access to a variety of goods and services including food, adequate housing, shelter, clothing, and so on. Because consumer goods and services play a functional role in the satisfaction of basic needs, greater access to goods and services should, in principle, improve our ability to satisfy these needs; and by extension improve well-being.

Secondly, commodities play important social and psychological roles in people's lives (Jackson, 2005a, 2006). After subsistence needs have been met, the psychological needs of well-being—which can be characterized as a sense of autonomy, competence, and relatedness to others (Deci & Ryan, 2000)—are all mediated, to a greater or lesser extent, through our relationship to material artefacts. As development economist Amartya Sen (1984) points out, some societies require a "more expensive bundle of goods and services" than others to effect needs satisfaction.

Thirdly, incomes carry symbolic value; higher incomes represent higher social status. The evidence on the relationship between income and happiness illustrates this point very clearly. Easterlin (1974) first showed that relative income has a bigger impact than absolute income on levels of reported life-satisfaction, a result that has been consistently borne out since (Diener & Seligman, 2004; Layard, 2005). Recently, there has been some convergence on the idea that the relatively weak, but nonetheless clear relationship between subjective life satisfaction and income within a country is predominantly a function of status effects (for a review, see Clark, Frijters, & Shields, 2006).

To summarize: in the conventional economic account, if people are more affluent they are able to purchase goods and services that enhance their quality of life and happiness. But now let us assume that this Western model of "development," regarded as paradigmatic by much of the world, is essentially unsustainable from an environmental perspective. Now, there seem to be only two possible outcomes for well-being:

1. Compromised well-being for future generations, as rising material consumption leads inexorably to serious and irreversible resource depletion.
2. Compromised well-being *now*, as consumption is severely curtailed in an effort to reverse environmental degradation.

This would be a bleak choice indeed, were it the only one. In recent years, however, this understanding of the relationship between economic growth and well-being has been increasingly challenged. Most notably, the surge of interest in happiness and subjective well-being has appeared to offer a radically new approach to understanding and, critically, to *measuring* people's happiness and well-being that does not rely on economic proxies such as income. In turn, this has raised questions about the real relationship between material consumption and well-being. A particularly influential finding is that after a certain—surprisingly low—level of GDP has been reached, the strength of its relationship to reported well-being at the population level declines markedly, such that increases in GDP do not lead to overall increases in reported well-being (Easterlin, 1995).

Nonetheless, in terms of public discourse, the well-being and sustainability debates have been held at some distance from one another. To date, research and thinking on well-being has often emphasized the contribution of psychological and psychosocial factors over actual material circumstances (such as individual wealth), with very little explicit consideration of the role of the environment or of ecological behavior. Conversely, popular debate about sustainable development is conducted largely at the national policy level. Where reference is made to the impact of environment on individuals' well-being, it is usually to "future generations" rather than those living now.

However, the potential of well-being for those promoting environmental sustainability is clear. If current forms of unsustainable consumption were found to be *detrimental* to well-being in some regard, this would represent an extremely powerful argument in favor of explicitly pro-environmental policies. Conversely, if it could be demonstrated that there was a potential "double dividend" (Jackson, 2005a), in which increasing sustainability might actually improve well-being, this again would present a compelling argument for persuading people to change their incumbent behaviors and assumptions.

# Pathways between Environmental Sustainability and Well-Being

In the previous section, we gave a brief overview of the arguments that have led recently to a degree of convergence between the sustainable development and well-being agendas. To advance this thinking, however, it is necessary to theorize in more detail the relationship between environmental sustainability and individual well-being and happiness. The lines of causation are of various types and do not fall easily into a scheme of classification. In the remainder of this chapter we present and elaborate upon a schematic model that provides—we think—a useful way to begin unpacking the relationship between sustainability and happiness. This is shown in Fig. 38.1.

The model lays out three different kinds of causal pathway between the environment and the individual. *Transparent* pathways are those in which the relationship between environmental sustainability and well-being is direct and immediate. *Semi-transparent* pathways are those in which a direct relationship is mediated by environmentally relevant values and behaviors. Finally, *Opaque* pathways are those in which a relationship exists but is wholly or largely indirect.

Because they are not mediated by the individual's behavior, transparent pathways operate *from* the environment *to* the individual. In other words, changes in the environment or exposure to some aspect(s) of it influence the individual; an example of this might be the impact of increasing levels of ambient air pollution on physical and psychological well-being. Semi-transparent and opaque pathways, meanwhile, operate largely in the opposite direction, namely *from* the individual *to* the environment. In both cases, individuals'

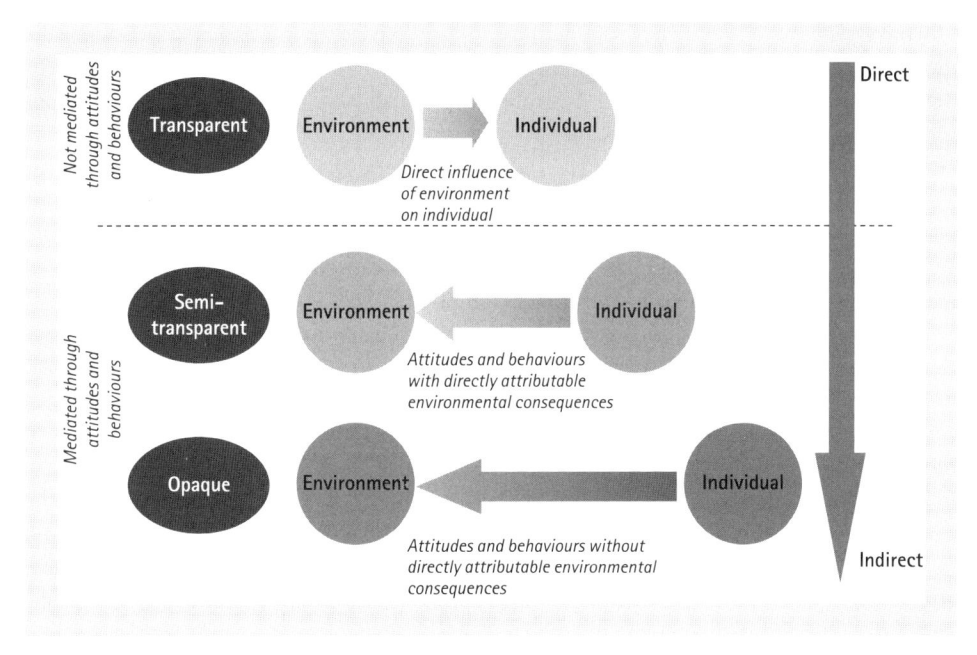

FIG. 38.1 (Also see Color plate 5.) Pathways between the environment and the individual.

attitudes and behaviors influence the environment either directly, or through some mediating process; here, an example might be the environmental impact of an individual's decision to drive to work rather than take the bus.

In the following sections, we review a range of empirical evidence illustrating how each kind of pathway might operate in practice. This is not intended to be an exhaustive review; rather, the aim is to begin to flesh-out the model and provide a useful basis for future work.

## Transparent pathways

### Local environmental conditions

Many writers have noted that local environmental conditions can have positive impacts on the psychological well-being of individuals (e.g., Kaplan & Kaplan, 1989; Burns, 2005). The benefits of spending time in green space are well documented; Mace, Bell, and Loomis (2004) even suggest that policy interventions to preserve natural parks can be justified on the basis of proven psychological effects. Pretty et al. (2005) argue for wider-ranging policy intervention to promote green space on the grounds of psychological and physical well-being benefits, stressing in particular the need to encourage active engagement with green spaces, through educational activities in school and partnership with the sport and leisure industry. More dramatically, it has recently been suggested that benefits may extend beyond the individual to the community level. Availability of communal green spaces in highly urbanized areas can have a significant impact on community cohesion and social interaction amongst neighbors (Kuo, Sullivan, Coley, & Brunson, 1998) and may even be associated with lower crime rates (Kuo & Sullivan, 2001).

Conversely, there is evidence that damage to local environments can be psychologically detrimental. Connor, Albrecht, Higginbotham, Freeman, and Smith (2004) studied residents of the Upper Hunter Valley in Australia, an area that has suffered centuries of environmental degradation as the result of intense resource exploitation, in particular coal mining and land clearance for agriculture. The researchers found that environmental decline was associated with significant expressions of psychological distress, and also linked to negative changes in participants' sense of place and perceptions of autonomy. The researchers dub this condition *solastalgia*, namely "the specific distress caused by the negatively perceived transformation of one's home and sense of belonging" (p. 55; see also Albrecht, 2005).

A negative psychological impact can be observed in response to environmental changes that happen over much shorter time periods. Baum and Fleming (1993) gathered longitudinal data on people living near the Three Mile Island nuclear power station and a number of other hazardous waste sites. In addition to physical problems (e.g., long-term increases in blood pressure), psychological symptoms of distress and anxiety were frequently observed, in addition to poorer performance on standard psychological tasks. Importantly from the perspective of psychological well-being, many participants in the study reported a perceived loss of control relative to those not exposed to such hazards, leading to distress and heightened arousal associated with uncertainty and concerns about future health. Similar results have been found for people living near the site of the Chernobyl nuclear disaster (Havenaar et al, 1996).

## Wider environmental conditions

There is some, albeit relatively slight, evidence for a relationship between wider environmental conditions and psychological well-being. Vemuri and Costanza (2006) found that a country's natural capital (that is, its stock of ecosystem resources, measured by a composite indicator such as the Ecosystem Services Product) was strongly associated with aggregate life satisfaction across countries, and was a better predictor than social capital. At the within-country level, Welsch (2002) demonstrated a statistical relationship between happiness ratings and environmental pollution. Using cross-sectional data from the World Database of Happiness (Veenhoven, 2005), he included self-reported life satisfaction as an explanatory variable in an analysis of the "cost" of air pollution, enabling the implied valuation to be expressed both in terms of monetary value and in terms of life satisfaction. Welsch's analysis suggested that if levels of nitrogen dioxide in Germany were to rise to the levels found in Japan, nearly 10% of the German population would experience a significant decrease in life satisfaction (one category lower, on a four-point scale). He describes this, somewhat delicately, as "probably not ... a trivial event to society."

In a later publication, Welsch (2006) used panel data (i.e., information gathered from the same people over a period of time) on life satisfaction from ten European countries, comparing this with levels of GNP, air pollution, and a host of additional controlling variables. Using these data, it was possible to calculate implied valuation of improvements in air quality over the period 1990–1997. Air pollution (in particular nitrogen dioxide and lead) was found to be a significant predictor of differences in life satisfaction both between countries and over time.

Rehdanz and Maddison (2005) used regression methods to compare reported levels of life satisfaction from the World Database of Happiness with comprehensive data on temperature and precipitation in each country. Higher average temperatures in the warmer months were associated with lower levels of self-reported life satisfaction, whereas higher average temperatures in the cooler months were positively associated with life satisfaction. These results held even when a number of other variables, including GDP per capita, were held constant. Notably, annual average temperature was not significantly related to happiness, suggesting that the effect is attributable to weather extremes. The authors infer from this analysis that climate change, as currently forecast, will differentially impact on well-being in different countries. In high latitude countries, winter temperatures will rise, leading to increased levels of well-being. In low latitude countries, by contrast, temperatures in the summer months will rise higher still, leading to negative health outcomes.

## Summary

There is suggestive—albeit not conclusive—empirical evidence that interaction with the natural environment brings positive psychological benefits. There is also evidence that negative changes to a local environment have a negative psychological impact on inhabitants, although these may be mediated through changes in perceived autonomy and an acute sense of loss rather than by direct effects. Furthermore, there is some (limited) evidence of a relationship between wider environmental factors, such as air quality, on psychological well-being, although it is unclear precisely how such effects are caused.

This evidence suggests that sustainable development could contribute to preventing negative psychological outcomes. There is, however, an important caveat: the well-being "pay-off" from such policies will lag significantly, since substantive changes to the environment will happen only over the relatively long term.

## Semi-transparent pathways

In a well-known essay, Hardin (1968) described what he saw as the impossibility of increasing both global population and quality of life for all within the limits of finite planetary resources. In Hardin's view this is a paradox, because individuals' rational desire to enhance their own quality of life by consuming more resources is incommensurate with the common good, which requires limited, and increasingly scarce, resources to be preserved. He dubbed this the "tragedy of the commons"—"tragedy" because it is an inevitable consequence of human nature.

The tragedy of the commons is an example of a *social dilemma*, namely a situation in which the rational course of action for individuals within a group is detrimental to the group as a whole (see, e.g., Dawes, 1980). Social dilemmas are central to the relationship between environmental sustainability and well-being, and exist in a number of semi-transparent pathways: namely, those where an individual engages in behaviors that are not "intentioned" towards the environment yet which have a direct impact on environmental sustainability. In other words, these are situations in which the net environmental effect would change if the individual behaved differently, but it is not in their rational interests to do so.

There are many examples of these kinds of behaviors. Personal transport choice is perhaps the most obvious, but others include recycling and awareness of household resource use. These situations can be thought of as social dilemmas because an action that is rational for the individual—say, driving to work rather than getting the bus—has a net detrimental impact on the environment, and hence, ultimately, on all individuals.

## Transport choice

Private car use makes a significant contribution to $CO_2$ emissions, as well as other environmental pollutants. Moreover, because the actual amount of car use is under the individual's direct control, this has been considered fertile ground for instigating behavior change. Policies such as "green" taxes and schemes where by drivers pay for the use of certain roads (such as, for instance, central London's "congestion charge") aim to encourage voluntary reductions in car use. However, such policies are often met with resistance because, for many people, car use is virtually synonymous with autonomy (Stradling, 2007). Unlike public transport, cars are seen as convenient, fast, clean, and safe and, critically, something over which the individual can exercise personal control (Wardman, Hine, & Stradling, 2001).

It is typically assumed that reductions in private car use would lead to a concomitant reduction of individual well-being, manifest through a perceived loss of autonomy for people who have grown to value, and so to demand, the flexibility and convenience that cars provide. Transport is essential to the extent that people need it to access their places of work, shops, and other services and leisure opportunities. Without personal transport, the day-to-day lives of many people—especially those in rural communities—would be appreciably more difficult. In the longer term it could be argued (for instance, on the basis of Welsch, 2006) that everyone would benefit from improvements in air quality resulting from reduced emissions, but this is somewhat speculative and certainly not likely to persuade many people to give up their cars. It could be posited that those who switch from driving to cycling or walking will experience relatively little loss of autonomy, and perhaps even a well-being benefit mediated through increased physical fitness. Unfortunately, in many regions of the world transport policy does not support genuine alternatives to car use, however substantial the benefits may be. Cycling and walking are simply not feasible alternatives for a majority of people as a means of going about their daily business.

A key element to changing car use behavior may thus be public transport. A report from the UK's Royal Automobile Club (RAC Report on Motoring, 2006) found that most UK motorists agreed that tougher measures were required to address the problems of congestion, with 40% in favor of charging a levy to motorists who use particularly congested roads. However, over two-thirds of respondents also said that their support for any such road charging schemes was contingent on visible improvements in public transport provision.

Moreover, availability of good public transport may be necessary but not sufficient. Psychological research on motivations for car use has tended to stress the role of pro-environmental attitudes or "value norms" (e.g., Marell, Davidsson, & Girling, 1995; Nordlund & Garvill, 2002; 2003). In one study, Joireman, van Lange, and van Vugt (2004) found that preference for using public transport was positively correlated with beliefs about the environmental damage of cars. However, this was only the case for those people who reported high levels of concern for future consequences of environmental change—there was no correlation for people who did not express such concern.

## Air travel

Air travel, another major contributor to $CO_2$ emissions, is a somewhat different case. Relatively few people in the UK *need* to fly, either to access essential services or as part of their employment. Most flights in the UK are taken for leisure, as a means of reaching holiday destinations (Civil Aviation Authority, 2009). Given the reasonable assumption that foreign holidays increase rather than reduce well-being for most people, then, as with car use, it is not obvious how a reduction in flying would lead to well-being benefits. At best, it may be that people would adapt to taking holidays within their own countries, or at least within the distance of a reasonable train journey, and suffer no long-term reduction in well-being as a result. However, it seems likely that moves to seriously curb air travel would be met with resistance.

An additional aspect of air travel relevant to well-being is noise pollution. Van Praag and Baarsma (2005) gathered data from a large sample of Amsterdam residents, some of whom lived directly on the flight path to Schiphol airport. Data included subjective well-being, ratings of noise exposure from various sources, objective measures of noise experienced, and a range of detailed demographic information. The resulting analysis demonstrated, firstly, that life satisfaction was negatively related to the amount of airport noise experienced, all else being equal. Secondly, and more significantly, it showed that the detrimental impact of noise pollution on life satisfaction was greater than would have been predicted by using conventional economic valuation techniques, such as assuming that the difference in market price between more and less noisy properties reflected the amount of money required to compensate for the noise. Using this information, the researchers were able to build a model for estimating appropriate levels of monetary compensation as a function not just of the extent to which house prices explain noise differences, but also the actual noise level experienced, household income and the amount of noise insulation in the home.

## Ecological behaviors in the home

Many behaviors in the home—in particular those that are water and energy intensive—represent a semi-transparent relationship between environmental sustainability and well-being. On the one hand, these behaviors appear to have well-being benefits for the individual: using the dishwasher rather than washing-up by hand, having a long hot bath rather than a quick shower, or keeping the heating turned up rather than wearing more layers of clothing. On the other, most people are aware of environmental issues surrounding their own behavior, and are willing in principle to "do their bit" as long as it is convenient and cost-effective (Holdsworth, 2003) and they feel that it is part of a wider effort (SCR, 2006).

Nevertheless, obvious barriers exist. Kurz, Donaghue, Rapley, and Walker (2005) conducted a qualitative analysis of interviews with homeowners in Perth (Australia) on the subject of water and energy conservation in the home. A notable finding was the frequently observed dichotomy between people's (claimed) personal desire to save water and perceived social "obligations," such as to keep up appearance of the garden and maintain accepted standards (e.g., of hygiene). McMakin, Malone, and Lundgren (2002) studied the motivation of household residents to conserve energy in the home without financial incentives. They found that sustainable behavior change arose from a variety of motivations, including pro-environmental altruism. However, altruistic motivations were more likely when people felt a sense of autonomy and control (see also Geller, 1995; de Young, 1996).

These results imply that some aspects of psychological well-being may in fact be precursors to ecological behavior, or at least that psychological well-being and pro-environmental behavior might be correlated. Several studies provide evidence to support this. Kasser and Sheldon (2002) demonstrated that Americans who reported more satisfaction and less stress at Christmas time also engaged in more environmentally-friendly holiday behaviors like using organic or locally-grown foods and giving environmentally friendly presents. Brown and Kasser (2005) found a positive correlation between the happiness of American adolescents and how much they reported engaging in environmentally-friendly behaviors such as turning off electric lights, recycling, and reusing paper, aluminum foil, and plastic bags. They also found that Americans who experienced high life satisfaction reported significantly more engagement in ecologically-sustainable behaviors and had significantly lower ecological footprints.

Generally, de Young (1996) emphasizes that attempts to increase the likelihood of individuals engaging in environmentally sustainable behaviors should not overlook the psychological need for competence and efficacy. Whilst, for instance, recycling household waste appropriately is not difficult, neither is it obvious or intuitive at first. Attempts to promote recycling, for instance, must therefore not only encourage people's motivations to act, but should recognize that many individuals will not feel especially competent when they try activities that are new to them. This feeling of incompetence, in turn, is likely to interfere both with their persistence at the new behaviors and with their personal well-being.

## Environmental concern

It is broadly accepted in the environmental psychology literature that "environmentally friendly" behavior is predicted to some extent—although perhaps not especially strongly (Olli, Grendstad, & Wollebaek, 2001)—by attitudes towards the environment. This raises the question of whether the presence or absence, or the phenomenological character, of attitudes towards the environment has a relationship with psychological well-being. In one of very few studies to consider this directly, Villacorta, Koestner, and Lekes (2003) administered an inventory of environmental attitudes, along with various standard measures of autonomy, motivation, and aspiration. They found that pro-environmental attitudes were associated with likelihood of engaging in ecological behaviors. However, they were also associated with personal autonomy and motivations such as concern for one's community, and with the experience of "positive affect" and the absence of frequent "negative affect" (which, under some definitions, are key components of well-being; Diener et al. 1999).

Ferrer-i-Carbonell and Gowdy (2007) used regression methods to analyze attitudinal data from the British Household Panel Survey. Using a dichotomous variable of concerned/not concerned, they found a negative relationship between well-being and concern about ozone depletion, but a positive relationship between well-being and concern about biodiversity loss. Both of these results held when potentially confounding variables were controlled for (i.e., individual personality traits, actual levels of pollution in the respondent's area and their propensity to engage in outdoor pursuits). Individuals who reported concern about both ozone depletion and biodiversity showed no effect on well-being. These results are interesting because they suggest: (1) that concerns about environmental issues can have a significant impact on well-being; and (2) that different types of concerns might affect well-being in different directions.

## Summary

The very existence of social dilemmas in the cases of car use, air travel and similar behaviors suggests that, at a minimum, people perceive that changing their behavior patterns might lead to a decrease in their well-being. It is obviously not true that everyone who flies regularly, or drives to work rather than takes the bus, holds antienvironmental views, or is indifferent towards the natural world. However, it probably is true that many people assume—reasonably—that their own actions have such negligible environmental impact that there is no appreciable benefit in them acting alone, especially when they suspect that their well-being would be compromised as a result. In fact, they are very likely wrong about this latter point; the psychological principle of adaptation (Helson, 1964; and supported since by copious empirical evidence) suggests that people soon become used to quite radical changes in their physical and material circumstances and ultimately end up no less (and sometimes more) happy. But, at least from the perspective of policy-making, telling people that their intuitions are wrong and that they will "get used to it" is an unappealing basis for persuading them to make significant lifestyle changes.

Much research shows that a person's values and attitudes towards the environment play key roles in influencing their ecological behaviors (although there is some disagreement about exactly how this influence is operationalized). Of more interest in the present context, some studies have shown a positive association between psychological well-being and environmental attitudes and behaviors. Such an association, if found to be robust, would provide a powerful argument in support of the kinds of behavior change—especially so-called "downshifting" whereby people consciously adopt simple, lower-consumption lifestyles—that are widely assumed to be required for a really substantive effect on the environment.

Essentially, to yield a positive well-being payoff from pro-environmental behavior, people have to want to behave differently. However, society-wide shifts in values are extremely difficult to instigate, slow to take hold, and even slower to yield widespread changes in behavior (see, e.g., Abramson & Inglehart, 1995). The environmental sustainability benefit would be very significantly delayed—indeed, it would probably not be evident at all until some critical mass of individuals made appreciable and persisting lifestyle changes. However, any well-being pay-off resulting from psychological affinity with the environment and the subsequent reward from engaging in pro-environmental behaviors would also emerge gradually over time. It would certainly occur concurrently with, or sometime after, the initial dip in well-being resulting from curtailing previously desirable behaviors.

# Opaque pathways

As noted earlier in this chapter, it is broadly accepted in the sustainable development literature that rising per capita consumption has a negative environmental impact. If this is true, however, then it is important to consider two key aspects of the relationship of individual well-being to consumption and economic growth, both of which have been marshaled as possible explanations for the failure of subjective well-being to rise with GDP: (1) values and attitudes associated with consumption; and (2) the impact a consumption-based economy itself has on social structures and institutions. We describe these pathways as "opaque" because the relationship of individuals' behavior on the environment is typically obscured by a complex of mediating processes.

## *Materialism and sources of motivation*

For our growth-based economy to function, people have to want to consume, and to keep consuming after their basic physical needs have been met. For this, in turn, they have to believe that consumption will make them (in the broad sense) happier. The very goal of the advertising and marketing professions is to persuade people that they need more goods and services for a complete and fulfilling life. There is little doubt that such tactics are successful, for instance, research suggests that people who watch a lot of television (and are thus exposed to a large amount of advertising) are likely to have a more strongly materialist outlook and be more dissatisfied with their standard of living (Sirgy et al., 1998).

However, for some time a number of psychologists, ecologists, and philosophers have argued that the entire project of consumption growth rests on a fundamental misunderstanding of human nature. Far from making us happier, according to this critique, the pursuit of material things can be psychologically damaging. Beyond the satisfaction of our basic physical needs for housing, clothing, and nutrition, the pursuit of material consumption merely serves to entrench us in unproductive status competition, disrupt our work-life balance, and distract us from those things that offer meaning and purpose to our lives (Csikszentmihalyi, 2000; Scitovsky, 1976; Wachtel, 1983). These theoretical arguments are now supported by a significant body of recent empirical research, which purports to demonstrate that holding a strongly materialist value orientation is, all else being equal, detrimental to well-being (see, e.g., Burroughs & Rindfleisch, 2002; Chan & Joseph, 2000; Diener & Oishi, 2000; Kasser & Ryan, 1993; Stutzer, 2004; Tatzel, 2002)

Why should this be? One popular explanation relates to individuals' motivations. Psychologists Kasser and Ryan (1996) distinguish between two types of pursuits in life: "intrinsic" and "extrinsic" goals. Intrinsic goals are inherently rewarding, because they satisfy psychological needs. Extrinsic goals, on the other hand, are typically pursued as a means to some other end, perhaps financial success, image or popularity/status. In other words, extrinsic goals are not inherently satisfying of needs; rather, they are motivations to pursue ends that people believe will satisfy their needs.

Across multiple studies and in a variety of cultures (e.g., Grouzet et al., 2005) it has been consistently demonstrated that intrinsic and extrinsic goals are distinguishable, and in psychological opposition to each other. Further, studies have demonstrated that such pursuits differentially relate to personal well-being and to ecological behavior. Kasser (2002) reviewed a variety of studies demonstrating that individuals with goals that are highly extrinsic and materialistic report lower personal well-being, whereas those with strong intrinsic values are happier and healthier. Other research shows how materialistic, extrinsic goals are associated directly with more ecologically-degrading attitudes and behaviors: materialistic people have less concern for other living things (Richins & Dawson, 1992), engage in fewer environmentally sustainable behaviors, and, in resource-dilemma games, report being more motivated by greed and use up more limited resources (Sheldon & McGregor, 2000).

Kasser (2006) proposed that in order to decrease materialism, a threefold strategy is necessary that works to: (1) decrease the likelihood that people will be exposed to materialistic messages (e.g., by banning advertisements to children or by removing tax write-offs for advertising); (2) increase people's resilience to the materialistic messages that remain in the environment (e.g., by building intrinsic values or by teaching individuals how to decode advertisement messages); and (3) help people to act more consistently with the intrinsic goals that they may value (e.g., by encouraging ethical consumption and investments). Strategies that follow these paths are likely to help shift people's values and goals, and thus behaviors, in ways that may ultimately improve well-being and ecological-sustainability.

## Structural relationships between the economy and the individual

Not everyone is convinced by the argument that valuing wealth and material possessions is both detrimental to well-being and also the underlying root of unsustainable consumption. Nonetheless, even amongst those who are skeptical of such claims, the lack of a linear relationship between GDP and subjective well-being has been regarded as serious enough to demand explanation. The conclusions arrived at are, in some cases, even more radical, and more critical of the conventional economic model than those that depend on individual psychological explanations.

For example, in an attempt to construct an international index of quality of life, *The Economist's* Intelligence Unit (EIU) put forward what amounts to a profound structural critique of the conventional model (EIU, 2005). Attempting to explain the apparent paradox of diminishing returns to rising consumption, they suggested that "there are factors associated with modernization that, in part, offset its positive impact" (p. 3). Specifically, they argue that alongside consumption growth:

> [a] concomitant breakdown of traditional institutions is manifested in the decline of religiosity and of trade unions; a marked rise in various social pathologies (crime, and drug and alcohol addiction); a decline in political participation and of trust in public authority; and the erosion of the institutions of family and marriage. (p. 3)

Three elements of the cultural changes highlighted by the EIU seem significant. The first is that they involve factors known to be closely correlated with well-being, in particular, feelings of social and community relatedness and trust. The second is that the changes which have occurred in these factors are in the "wrong" direction; in other words they act to undermine well-being. Thirdly, the suggestion implicit in *The Economist's* article is that these changes have occurred as a direct result of the modernization process, based on consumption growth. In other words, the pursuit of consumption has systematically undermined not only the environmental conditions on which future well-being depends, but also certain social conditions (e.g., family, friendship, community, trust) that are critically important for well-being *now*.

It is clearly worth asking why this trade-off might have occurred, and it turns out that sociologists and social philosophers have preoccupied themselves with almost precisely the same question for well over a century—an early landmark is Durkheim's (1951/1897) study of suicide in turn of the century Europe in which he identified forces of alienation aligned specifically with the emerging capitalist model of social organization. Some of the answers which have been put forward within this literature are distinctly challenging for the existing model of economic development. A key responsibility for undermining well-being, for example, has been placed on processes of commodification—through which previously public or informal goods and services become the object of commercial markets—and individuation—the gradual separation of people's individual identities and interests from the interests of the social group (as argued by Robert Putnam in his well-known book from 2000, *Bowling Alone*).

As many critics of modernity have pointed out, modern economies have a structural need for individualist, consumerist values in order to sustain demand for consumption (see, e.g.,

Baudrillard, 1970/1997; Bauman, 1998, 2001; Douthwaite, 1992; Fromm, 1976; Illich, 1977). This structural need arises, specifically, because of the role that material consumption plays in economic stability. In a system in which the stability of the economy depends on continued consumption, it becomes increasingly important to maintain the social and psychological momentum of consumption. The continuing expansion of the market into new areas, and the continuing allegiance of people as consumers appear to be vital.

The suggestion that certain critical aspects of society are undermined by relentless consumption is lent further support by sociological work on trends in cultural attitudes and perceptions of quality of life. Studies since the mid 1990s, both qualitative and quantitative, reveal levels of anger and moral anxiety about changes in society that were not apparent 30 years ago (Eckersley, 2005, 2006). They show that many people are concerned about the materialism, greed, and selfishness they believe drive society today, underlie social ills, and threaten their children's future. For instance, a 1995 US study, *Yearning for Balance*, underscores Americans' worries about their way of life (Harwood Group, 1995). Based on focus group discussions and a national survey, the study found that people shared a deep and abiding concern with the core values driving their society and "the frenzied, excessive quality of American life today."

Some studies make quite explicit the tension between concerns about quality of life and the political emphasis on growth. For example, surveys have shown that 87% of Britons and 83% of Australians agree that their societies are "too materialistic, with too much emphasis on money and not enough on the things that really matter" (Hamilton, 2002, 2003). An Australian survey revealed that "having extra money for things like luxuries and travel" ranked last in a list of seven items judged "very important" to success, well behind the top-scoring "having a close and happy family." And in contrast to government priorities, "maintaining a high standard of living" ranked last in a list of sixteen critical issues; educational access, children and young people's well-being, and health care were at the top (Bagnall, 1999).

## Summary

As Jackson (2005b) points out, "individual behaviours are deeply embedded in social and institutional contexts" (p. 2). The result is that people become "locked-in" to patterns of behavior consistent with the entrenched belief that consumption is the route to well-being. This is a good thing from an economic perspective, since it drives the consumption growth on which the economy depends. However, it is a bad thing for the environment, since it also drives the exploitation of natural resources and disregard for long-term environmental impacts that are responsible for unsustainability.

A growing body of evidence suggests that, at least in some respects, materialist values may also be a bad thing for individual well-being (for summaries, see Kasser, 2002, 2006). More profoundly, it has been argued that ever-greater consumption has been achieved only through increasing emphasis on the individual as distinct from society, in turn leading to the breakdown of certain social structures and institutions known to be important to well-being. Whether such feelings underlie increasing rates of suicide (as Durkheim suggested a century ago) and depression or drive negative trends in people's perceptions about society is, of course, a matter for debate. But future research needs to take seriously the suggestion that changes in society which have a detrimental effect on well-being are, in part, caused by aspects of the incumbent, environmentally unsustainable economic model.

# Conclusion

The review presented here is, by necessity, partial and incomplete. Moreover, the model we present is—like any model—a simplification. Nevertheless, it is notable that the nature of the economic system itself lies at the nexus of all three pathways. Transparent pathways do not depend on the attitudes or behaviors of individuals and are completely mediated by changes to the environment; but, to the extent that such changes are largely attributable to increased resource use required to meet consumption demand, then it is possible to argue that consumption growth ultimately underlies these pathways.

Opaque pathways, meanwhile, are entirely mediated through the prevailing socio-economic system—they concern how people's attitudes to their lives, to themselves, their goals and their beliefs about what will make them happy will impact on their well-being. As such, they are the very drivers of material consumption.

Semi-transparent pathways occupy a middle ground in which individuals' personal attitudes towards the environment mediate behaviors with directly attributable environmental consequences. Yet these, too, must be seen in the wider context of a consumption-focused economy. Energy use in the home has risen dramatically as the "bundle of goods" (Sen, 1984) required for an acceptable standard of living has increased. To the extent that few of these goods are essential in any "basic needs" sense (no-one's survival depends on owning a dishwasher) and that the well-being benefits they yield are usually minimal and short-lived (because of the effects of adaptation; see, e.g., Easterlin, 2003), it becomes clear that the personal consumption decisions are driven by other needs. At least some of these are likely to be psychosocial in nature, relating to perceived social expectations and lay beliefs about the well-being gains from consumption.

What to make of the evidence that well-being has not increased in line with growing consumption, and indeed that by some measures it has begun to decrease? On the one hand, no-one seriously doubts that economic growth of some form is essential to reduce levels of absolute poverty and improve living conditions in the developing world. Neither would it be easy—or sensible—simply to abandon the current socio-economic model in the developed world. On the other hand, because consumption behaviors ultimately mediate the key pathways between environmental sustainability and individual well-being, the potential need for dramatic change must be taken seriously. Jackson (2009) has argued that this kind of analysis leads, ultimately, to the need for a new understanding of "prosperity"—one that does not depend inexorably on economic growth.

In conclusion, then, analysing the relationship between happiness and sustainability leads us to take seriously the suggestion that, in some significant respects, modern society may be adrift in its pursuit of well-being. But equally, this well-being deficit suggests the possibility of some hope for the future. Namely, that it might be possible to deliver well-being without materialism, and thus without the associated material throughput and environmental impact: to live better by consuming less.

## Acknowledgments

This chapter is based on sections of a paper commissioned by the UK government's Department for Environment, Food and Rural Affairs (Marks, Thompson, Eckersley, Jackson, & Kasser, 2006).

## REFERENCES

Abramson, P. R., & Inglehart, R. F. (1995). *Value Change in Global Perspective*. Ann Arbor, MI: University of Michigan Press.

Albrecht, G. A. (2005). "Solastalgia": A new concept in health and identity. *PAN: Philosophy, Activism, Nature, 3*, 41–55.

Bagnall, D. (1999). Reasons to be cheerful. *The Bulletin, 29*, 36–39.

Baudrillard, J. (1970/1997). *The consumer society: myths and structures*. (G. Ritzer, Trans.). London, UK: Sage Publications. (Original work published 1970).

Baum, A., & Fleming, I. (1993). Implications of psychological research on stress and technological accidents. *American Psychologist, 48*, 665–671.

Bauman, Z. (1998). *Work, consumerism and the new poor*. Buckingham, UK: Open University Press.

Bauman, Z. (2001). Consuming life. *Journal of Consumer Culture, 1*, 9–29.

Brown, K. W., & Kasser, T. (2005). Are psychological and ecological well-being compatible? The role of values, mindfulness, and lifestyle. *Social Indicators Research, 74*, 349–368.

Burns, G. (2005). Naturally happy, naturally healthy: The role of the natural environment in well-being. In F. A. Huppert, N. Baylis, & B. Keverne (Eds.), *The science of well-being* (pp. 407–431). Oxford: Oxford University Press.

Burroughs, J. E., & Rindfleisch, A. (2002). Materialism and well-being: A conflicting values perspective. *Journal of Consumer Research, 29*, 348–70.

Civil Aviation Authority. (2009). *UK business air travel: Traffic trends and characteristics*. London, UK: Civil Aviation Authority.

Chan, R., & Joseph, F. (2000). Dimensions of personality, domains of aspiration, and subjective well-being. *Personality and Individual Differences, 28*, 347–354.

Clark, A. E., Frijters, P., & Shields, M. (2006). *Income and happiness: Evidence, explanations and economic implications*. PSE, Discussion Paper 2006-24.

Co-Operative Bank. (2005). *The ethical consumerism report 2005*. Manchester, UK: The Co-Operative Bank.

Connor, L., Albrecht, G. A., Higginbotham, N., Freeman, S., & Smith, W. (2004). Environmental change and human health in upper hunter communities of New South Wales, Australia. *EcoHealth, 1*(Suppl. 2), 47–52.

Csikszentmihalyi, M. (2000). The costs and benefits of consuming. *Journal of Consumer Research, 27*, 267–272.

Dawes, R. M. (1980). Social dilemmas. *Annual Review of Psychology, 31*, 169–193.

Deci, E. L., & Ryan, R. M. (2000). The "what" and "why" of goal pursuits: Human needs and the self-determination of behavior. *Psychological Inquiry, 11*, 227–268.

de Young, R. (1996). Some psychological aspects of reduced consumption behavior: The role of intrinsic satisfaction and competence motivation. *Environment and Behavior, 28*, 358–409.

Diener, E., & Oishi, S. (2000). Money and happiness: Income and subjective well-being across nations. In E. Diener, & E. M. Suh (Eds.), *Culture and subjective well-being* (pp. 185–218). Cambridge, MA: MIT Press.

Diener, E., & Seligman, M. E. P. (2004). Beyond money: Toward an economy of well-being. *Psychological Science in the Public Interest*, 5, 1–31.

Diener, E., Suh, E. M., Lucas, R. E., & Smith, H. E. (1999). Subjective well-being: Three decades of progress. *Psychological Bulletin*, 125, 276–302.

Douthwaite, R. (1992). *The growth illusion*. Devon, UK: Green Print.

Durkheim, E. (1951/1897). *Suicide*. (J. A. Spalding & G. Simpson, trans.) New York, NY: Free Press.

Easterlin, R. A. (1974). Does economic growth improve the human lot? In P. A. David & M. W. Reder (Eds.), *Nations and households in economic growth: Essays in honor of Moses Abramovitz* (pp. 89–125). New York, NY: Academic Press, Inc.

Easterlin, R. A. (1995). Will raising the incomes of all increase the happiness of all? *Journal of Economic Behavior and Organization*, 27, 35–47.

Easterlin, R. A. (2003). Explaining happiness. *Proceedings of National Academy of Science of the United States of America*, 100, 11176–11183.

Eckersley, R. (2005). *Well & good: Morality, meaning and happiness* (2nd edn). Melbourne, Australia: Text Publishing.

Eckersley, R. (2006). What's wrong with the official future? In Hassan, G. (Ed.), *After Blair: Politics after the New Labour decade* (pp. 172–184). London, UK: Lawrence and Wishart.

EIU. (2005, January). *Economist Intelligence Unit's Quality of Life Index*. London, UK: The Economist.

Ferrer-i-Carbonella, A., & Gowdy, J. M. (2007). Environmental awareness and happiness. *Ecological Economics*, 60, 509–516.

Fromm, E. (1976). *To have or to be?* London, UK: Jonathon Cape.

Geller, E. S. (1995). Actively caring for the environment: An integration of behaviorism and humanism. *Environmental and Behavior*, 27, 184–195.

Grouzet, F. M. E., Kasser, T., Ahuvia, A., Fernandez-Dols, J. M., Kim, Y., Lau, S., ... Sheldon, K. M. (2005). The structure of goal contents across 15 cultures. *Journal of Personality and Social Psychology*, 89, 800–816.

Hamilton, C. (2002). *Overconsumption in Australia: The rise of the middle-class battler. Discussion paper no. 49*. Canberra: The Australia Institute.

Hamilton, C. (2003). *Overconsumption in Britain: A culture of middle-class complaint. Discussion paper no. 57*. Canberra: The Australia Institute.

Hardin, G. (1968). The tragedy of the commons. *Science*, 162, 1243–1248.

Harwood Group. (1995). *Yearning for balance: Report for Merck family fund*. Retrieved from http://www.iisd.ca/consume/harwood.html.

Havenaar, J. M., Van den Brink, W., Van den Bout, J., Kasyanenko, A. P., Poelijoe, N. W., & Wholfarth, T. (1996). Mental health problems in the Gomel region (Belarus): An analysis of risk factors in an area affected by the Chernobyl disaster. *Psychological Medicine*, 26, 845–855.

Helson, H. (1964). *Adaptation level theory: An experimental and systematic approach to behavior*. New York, NY: Harper & Row.

Holdsworth, M. (2003). *Green choice, what choice?* London, UK: National Consumer Council.

Illich, I. (1977). *Towards a history of needs*. New York, NY: Pantheon Books.

Jackson, T. (2005a). Live better by consuming less? Is there a double dividend in sustainable consumption? *Journal of Industrial Ecology, 9*, 19–36.

Jackson, T. (2005b). *SDRN briefing one: Motivating sustainable consumption*. London, UK: Sustainable Development Research Network.

Jackson, T. (2006). Consuming paradise? Towards a social and cultural psychology of sustainable consumption. In T. Jackson (Ed.), *Earthscan reader in sustainable consumption*. London, UK: Earthscan.

Jackson, T. (2009). *Prosperity without growth*. London, UK: Earthscan.

Joireman, J. A., van Lange, P. A. M., & van Vugt, M. (2004). Who cares about the environmental impact of cars? Those with an eye toward the future. *Environment and Behavior, 36*, 187–206.

Kaplan, R., & Kaplan, S. (1989). *The experience of nature: A psychological perspective*. New York, NY: Cambridge University Press.

Kasser, T. (2002). *The high price of materialism*. Cambridge, MA: MIT Press.

Kasser, T. (2006). Materialism and its alternatives. In M. Csikszentmihalyi & I. S. Csikszentmihalyi (Eds.), *A life worth living: Contributions to positive psychology*. Oxford, UK: Oxford University Press.

Kasser, T., & Ryan, R. M. (1993). A dark side of the American Dream: Correlates of financial success as a central life aspiration. *Journal of Personality and Social Psychology, 65*, 410–422.

Kasser, T., & Ryan, R. M. (1996). Further examining the American dream: Differential correlates of intrinsic and extrinsic goals. *Personality and Social Psychology Bulletin, 22*, 280–287.

Kasser, T. & Sheldon, K. M. (2002). What makes for a Merry Christmas? *Journal of Happiness Studies, 3*, 313-329.

Kuo, F. E., Sullivan, W. C., Coley, R. L., & Brunson, L. (1998). Fertile ground for community: Inner-city neighborhood common spaces. *American Journal of Community Psychology, 26*, 823–851.

Kuo, F. E., & Sullivan, W.C. (2001). Environment and crime in the inner city: Does vegetation reduce crime? *Environment and Behavior, 33*, 343–367.

Kurz, T., Donaghue, N., Rapley, M., & Walker, I. (2005). The ways that people talk about natural resources: Discursive strategies as barriers to environmentally sustainable practices. *British Journal of Social Psychology, 44*, 603–620.

Layard, R. (2005). *Happiness: Lessons from a new science*. London, UK: Allen Lane.

Mace, B. L., Bell, P. A., & Loomis, R. J. (2004). Visibility and natural quiet in natural parks and wilderness areas: Psychological considerations. *Environment and Behavior, 36*, 5–31.

McMakin, A. H., Malone, E. L., & Lundgren, R. E. (2002). Motivating residents to conserve energy without financial incentives. *Environment and Behavior, 34*, 848–863.

Marell, A., Davidsson, P., & Girling, T. (1995). Environmentally friendly replacement of automobiles. *Journal of Economic Psychology, 16*, 513–529.

Marks, N., Thompson, S., Eckersley, R., Jackson, T., & Kasser, T. (2006). *Sustainable development and well-being: Relationships, challenges and policy implications*. London, UK: Department for Environment, Food and Rural Affairs.

Nordlund, A., & Garvill, J. (2002). Value structures behind proenvironmental behaviour. *Environment and Behavior, 34*, 740–756.

Nordlund, A., & Garvill, J. (2003). Effects of values, problem awareness, and personal norm on willingness to reduce personal car use. *Journal of Environmental Psychology, 23*, 339–347.

Olli, E., Grendstad, G., & Wollebaek, D. (2001). Correlates of environmental behaviours: Bringing back social context. *Environment and Behavior, 33*, 181–201.

Pretty, J., Griffin, M., Peacock, J., Hine, R., Sellens, M., & South, N. (2005). *A countryside for health and wellbeing: The physical and mental health benefits of green exercise*. Sheffield: Countryside Recreation Network.

Putnam, R. D. (2000). *Bowling alone: The collapse and revival of American community*. New York, NY: Simon & Schuster.

RAC Report on Motoring. (2006). *The future of motoring: A clear road map, or collision course?* London, UK: RAC.

Rehdanz, K., & Maddison, D. (2005). Climate and happiness. *Ecological Economics, 52*, 111–125.

Richins, M. L., & Dawson, S. (1992). A consumer values orientation for materialism and its measurement. *Journal of Consumer Research, 19*, 303–316.

Scitovsky, T. (1976). *The joyless economy: An inquiry into human satisfaction and consumer dissatisfaction*. Oxford, UK: Oxford University Press.

SCR. (2006). *I will if you will: Towards sustainable consumption (Report from the Sustainable Consumption Roundtable)*. London, UK: NCC/SDC.

Sen, A. (1984). The living standard. *Oxford Economic Papers, 36*. (Augmented version reprinted as Chapter 16 in D. Crocker & T. Linden (Eds.), *The ethics of consumption*. New York, UK: Rowman and Littlefield.

Sheldon, K., & MacGregor, H. (2000). Extrinsic value orientation and the tragedy of the commons. *Journal of Personality, 68*, 383–411.

Sirgy, M. J., Dong-Jin Lee, Kosenko, R., Meadow, H. L., Rahtz, D., Cicic, M., ... Wright, N. (1998). Does television viewership play a role in the perception of quality of life? *Journal of Advertising, 27*, 125-142.

Simms, A. (2009). *Ecological debt: Global warming and the wealth of nations* (2nd rev ed.). London, UK: Pluto Press.

Stradling, S. G. (2007). Determinants of car dependence. In T. Garling & L. Steg (Eds.), *Threats to the quality of urban life from car traffic: Problems, causes and solutions*. Oxford, UK: Elsevier.

Stutzer, A. (2004). The role of income aspirations in individual happiness. *Journal of Economic Behavior and Organization, 54*, 89–109.

Tatzel, M. (2002). "Money worlds" and well-being: An integration of money dispositions, materialism and price-related behaviour. *Journal of Economic Psychology, 23*, 103–126.

van Praag, B. M. S., & Baarsma, B. E. (2005). Using happiness surveys to value intangibles: The case of airport noise. *The Economic Journal, 115*, 224–246.

Veenhoven, R. (2005). *Average Happiness in 91 Nations 1995–2005: World Database of Happiness*. Retrieved from http://www.worlddatabaseofhappiness.eur.nl.

Vemuri, A. W., & Costanza, R. (2006). The role of human, social, built, and natural capital in explaining life satisfaction at the country level: Toward a National Well-Being Index (NWI). *Ecological Economics, 58*, 119–133.

Villacorta, M., Koestner, R., & Lekes, N. (2003). Further validation of the motivation toward the environment scale. *Environment and Behavior, 35*, 486–505.

Wachtel, P. (1983). *The Poverty of Affluence—A psychological portrait of the American way of life*. New York, NY: The Free Press.

Wackernagel, M., & Rees, W. E. (1996). *Our ecological footprint: Reducing human impact on the earth*. Gabriola Island, Canada: New Society Publishers.

Wardman, M., Hine, J., Stradling, S.G. (2001). *Interchange and travel choice (Volumes 1 & 2)*. Edinburgh, UK: Scottish Executive Central Research Unit.

WCED. (1987). *Our common future.* Oxford, UK: Oxford University Press.

Welsch, H. (2002). Preferences over prosperity and pollution: environmental valuation based on happiness surveys. *Kyklos, 55,* 473–495.

Welsch, H. (2006). Environment and happiness: Valuation of air pollution using life satisfaction data. *Ecological Economics, 58,* 801–813.

# CHAPTER 39

# WELL-BEING AND PUBLIC POLICY

## GEOFF MULGAN

The National Endowment for Science, Technology and the Arts (NESTA), UK

## INTRODUCTION

INCREASING public happiness has become an overt goal of public policy in many countries, sitting, sometimes uneasily, alongside more familiar goals such as economic growth, national security, and social justice. This has been the result of many factors, including the growing body of research on the causes of happiness and the rise of public concern for quality of life issues.

As I will show in this chapter, policy-makers are beginning to test specific policies to improve well-being in fields ranging from schools and family policy to healthcare and the environment. However, there is little hard evidence on how particular public policies influence happiness. This remains a field in its infancy with, as yet, relatively little agreement on the long-term policy implications of new knowledge.

Despite its novelty as a field supported by evidence, promoting public happiness has been an overt goal of government for much of recorded history. In ancient Athens, Socrates described the aim of the commonwealth as being "not to make any one class especially happy but to secure the greatest possible happiness for the community as a whole." Ashoka, the great Mauryan Emperor of northern India, described himself in one of his edicts as desiring "safety, self-control, justice and happiness for all beings." Al Farabi, one of Islam's most influential political philosophers, wrote that "happiness is the good desired for itself; it is never desired to achieve by it something else and there is nothing greater beyond it that a human being can achieve" (Mahdi, 2001, p. 128). An influential Chinese thinker of the twelfth century, Chen Liang, argued in a similar vein the rightness of whatever "satisfied the reasonable desires and needs of the people."

Similar ideas came to the fore as modern democracy took shape in the West. The United States Declaration of Independence promised "life liberty and the pursuit of happiness," while the French constitution of 1793 committed the new nation to the statement that "the purpose of society is the common happiness." In Britain, the utilitarianism of Jeremy

Bentham, who argued that the good state is one that achieves the greatest happiness for the greatest number, had extensive influence on the then British Empire. Two hundred years later the small Asian state of Bhutan even committed its government to maximizing gross national happiness, an alternative to the gross domestic product.

Commitments to public well-being can be found in many different contexts and civilizations. Yet these views have always been contested. The Aristotelian tradition sees well-being as deriving from excellence or virtuous activity, rather than from pleasure. Many religions have emphasized happiness in the hereafter rather than on earth. The modern liberal position was put succinctly by Benjamin Constant in the early nineteenth century when he wrote that governments should "confine themselves to being just. We shall assume the responsibility of being happy for ourselves." Others have argued that dissatisfaction is essential to human progress and creativity; indeed, there is evidence that the happiest decile succeed less than the next happiest (Oishi, Diener, & Lucas, 2007).

Contrasting views on well-being have given policy-makers reason to pause. The first challenge has been to decide whether promoting well-being is indeed an appropriate goal for governments.

## Is Well-Being a Coherent or Valid Goal for Policy?

As has been made clear in preceding chapters, "happiness" has many different meanings and interpretations: different policies will result if the goal is to maximize pleasure or present happiness, life satisfaction, or some other "well-being" measure such as fulfillment. How a government defines well-being will influence, for example, how much weight is given to feelings of safety relative to opportunities for fun, whether to promote tranquility or vitality, how much to emphasize overall satisfaction in life, or whether to stretch people (i.e. seeing some dissatisfaction now as necessary for greater fulfillment later; Diener, Nickerson, Lucas, & Sandvik, 2002). Well-being also has to be situated alongside, and sometimes in tension with, other goals such as national security, the interests of future generations, or moral virtue.

Notwithstanding contrary views, there are obvious reasons why democratic governments should be interested in actions that might increase the well-being of their citizens, as well as the implications of new evidence about what shapes well-being. The problem faced by policy-makers has been how to translate this evidence into clear directions for action. First, however, it has been necessary to identify systems of measurement.

## Can Well-Being be Measured?

Modern governments have become attached to measurement and formal targets when developing and tracking public policy. Fortunately, happiness measures have grown in number and sophistication over the last decade. Measures of self-reported happiness correlate well with other measures (such as perceptions from friends and family), and are now increasingly used by statistical offices (see, for instance, the UK Office for National Statistics' Measuring National Well-being program).[1] Detailed analysis of how populations break down in terms of well-being, pain, or feelings of autonomy and relatedness, provide useful and often novel insights for policy-makers. Promising work is also underway on designing new national accounts for well-being (see, e.g., Michaelson, Abdallah, Steuer, Thompson, & Marks, 2009).

Unfortunately, there remains considerable disagreement about how to measure different dimensions of well-being. Some cross-national studies have found low levels of correlation between measures of life satisfaction and positive affect; this has led researchers to argue that more weight should be given to hedonic measures and measures of how people spend their time day-to-day rather than focusing just on overall evaluations of life satisfaction (Krueger, Kahneman, Schkade, Schwarz, & Stone, 2009). Comparisons between countries are also problematic. Recent research has found that the USA appears to have significantly higher levels of life satisfaction than France, yet more detailed analysis of happiness levels day by day shows Americans doing worse than the French, pointing to the power of cultural norms in the USA that encourage people to present their lives in a positive light (Kahneman & Riis, 2005).

Despite these difficulties, many governments have concluded that well-being can be measured, and can be used as an indicator of policy efficacy. The problems of measurement are not inherently greater than those facing other key indicators, notably gross domestic product (GDP). The Organisation for Economic Co-operation and Development's (OECD) program, *Measuring the Progress of Societies*, successfully brought together a wide body of work to operationalize well-being measures, and French President Sarkozy's commission into measuring progress in 2009 added impetus to the drive to complement or adapt GDP. Moreover, some researchers are now demonstrating how life satisfaction measures can be used to help with specific policy decisions. One approach is to use surveys of life satisfaction and income to judge social projects and programs in terms of how much extra income people would need to achieve an equivalent gain in life satisfaction (e.g., van Praag & Baarsma, 2005; Welsch, 2002). An imaginative study of a regeneration scheme, for example, showed that modest investments in home safety which cost about 3% as much as home repairs generated four times as much value in terms of life satisfaction (Dolan & Metcalfe, 2008).

# Do governments have the power to influence well-being?

Even if well-being can be measured, it may not be possible to influence it. It is generally accepted that genetic factors explain a significant proportion of variation in individual well-being—perhaps around 50% (Lyubomirsky, Sheldon, & Schkade, 2005). The evidence that most people have a fairly constant (although not completely fixed; Lucas, 2007) set point for well-being also appears to suggest that policy influence is likely to be slim. Yet there is also evidence that the overall conditions of governance—factors such as the presence of the rule

---

[1] http://www.ons.gov.uk/well-being.

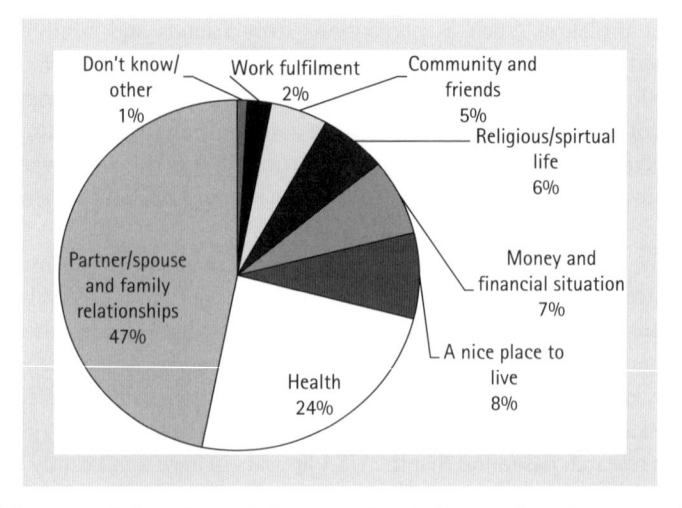

FIG. 39.1 (Also see Color plate 6.) Factors that influence happiness: results of a poll conducted for the BBC. Data from a poll undertaken for the BBC by GfK NOP during October 2005. Results available at http://news.bbc.co.uk/nol/shared/bsp/hi/pdfs/29_03_06_happiness_gfkpoll.pdf.

of law, democracy, and low levels of corruption—correlate with well-being. Helliwell (2003) compared happiness rates in some 50 countries and found that around 80% of the variation could be explained with six variables, including the quality of government, trust, and corruption. The World Bank's regular surveys of government point in a similar direction: countries that perform best on the six dimensions of governance (including democratic voice, effectiveness, regulation, law, stability, and control of corruption) also perform well in terms of well-being.

Over the last decade, various books and manifestos have brought together ideas about how to promote well-being (e.g., Shah & Marks, 2004). However, even if the overall quality of governance can enhance well-being, it is not clear that the fields in which governments are active are the ones that matter most for well-being. Fig. 39.1 shows a widely replicated picture of what contributes to well-being, with relationships paramount. Fig. 39.2 shows public views from across Europe about what people say matters to their well-being when they are asked. Clearly, governments' ability to influence some of these factors is limited.

## SPECIFIC POLICY FIELDS

Thus far, much of the most interesting work on policies for well-being has been led by local rather than national governments. However, national governments are beginning to engage more seriously, with a tendency to focus on a small number of fields where evidence suggests a causal impact on variations in well-being. These include marriage and family, social relationships, employment, health, and the quality of governance. There is also considerable interest in how education can influence well-being. The influence of the environmental movement in promoting alternatives to GDP has brought a particular interest in how to

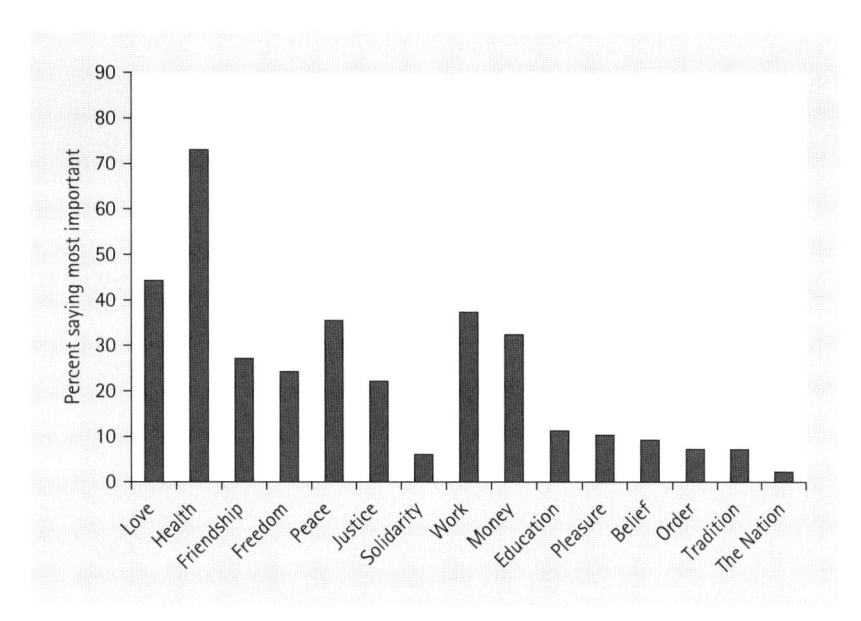

FIG. 39.2 Perceptions of "what is important" across 27 EU countries.[1] From Eurobarometer 69, available at http://ec.europa.eu/public_opinion/archives/eb/eb69/eb69_values_en.pdf accessed November 9, 2009. © European Union, 1995–2012.

combine green goals with the promotion of well-being, even though these are often in tension (see, e.g., Marks, Abdallah, Simms & Thompson, 2006). In addition, there remain unresolved arguments about the relationship between income distribution and happiness. In what follows I review the position, and arguments, in each area.[2]

## Family policy

The data on happiness consistently point to the importance of relationships and family, and the potentially damaging impact of long-term trends toward increases in family dissolution. Recent statistics from the UK's Office of National Statistics (ONS) show that the rate of divorce in England and Wales has increased over the last 26 years (though the rate had fallen slightly in 2007).[3] A third of UK 16-year-olds now live apart from their biological fathers, and in the USA the equivalent figure is half. Recent surveys highlight the fact that many developed countries fare poorly in terms of child well-being (OECD, 2009; UNICEF). It seem at least possible, therefore, that family policy could have a positive impact on well-being.

Public policy has emphasized support for parenting skills (see, e.g., Department for Education, Skills and Families, 2007), and in some cases has begun to address parental well-being as well as children's interests (Bacon, Brophy, & Roberts, 2009). There have also been

---

[2] *Eurobarometer 69*, available at http://ec.europa.eu/public_opinion/archives/eb/eb69/eb69_values_en.pdf accessed November 9, 2009.

[3] http://www.ons.gov.uk/ons/rel/vsob1/divorces-in-england-and-wales/2010/stb-divorces-2010.html.

significant moves in many countries to make it easier for parents to spend time with their children, whether through rights to parental leave or more flexible work schedules.

Beyond this, however, there is little agreement on how policy should respond to research that reveals the importance of stable families for well-being. For example, there is strong evidence of the positive relationship between marriage and well-being, but no proof that any particular policy significantly influences decisions to marry. Should governments promote or incentivize marriage, or invest heavily in counseling services to reduce the proportion of marriages that fail. Should policies encourage closer links between extended family members, for example, through housing allocations, or subsidies for grandparents providing childcare? The combination of strongly held, often ideologically grounded views and inconclusive evidence in this field suggests that there is little immediate prospect of a consensus on how to support well-being through family policy.

## Education

Policies in education have been somewhat less contested, with overt attention to well-being in many countries. Schools, colleges, and universities have long been aware of their role in contributing to student development, well-being, and resilience, and in preparing young people for life and not just exams. Contributing to pupil well-being became a statutory requirement for UK schools in 2007, with the Education and Inspections Act placing a duty on schools to promote the well-being of their pupils. The government has since developed both qualitative and quantitative school-level indicators to enable more effective self-evaluation and to support external inspections.

Within schools, many have opted for dedicated class time for personal development. One example is the UK Resilience Programme (UKRP), which is being piloted with 2000 pupils across 22 schools. The program draws on models developed and tested rigorously by the University of Pennsylvania, USA that are designed to improve the emotional resilience of 11–13-year-olds by enhancing a number of important life skills to enable them to deal constructively with daily problems and challenges (Cutuli, Chaplin, Gillham, Reivich, & Seligman, 2006). Evaluation of the program found that it was popular with both pupils and teachers, and that there was some evidence of positive impacts on pupils' depression and anxiety symptom scores (Challen, Noden, West, & Machin, 2011). Many other methods promise similar results, usually by encouraging greater self-awareness and empathy. Given the trends in many countries towards earlier and worsening incidence of depression amongst teenagers, programs of this kind are likely to spread.

## Work

Research on happiness has consistently shown the disastrous impact that unemployment can have (Clark, 2003; Clark, Georgellis, & Sanfey 2001; Clark & Oswald, 1994). Happiness levels decline sharply following involuntary unemployment and may take years to recover; unemployment also often leads to symptoms of mental illness and even suicide (Classen & Dunn, 2012). It has a negative impact on well-being, less because of the loss of income than because of the loss of work itself, with its accompanying sense of usefulness and recognition (Layard, 2005). It seems that people do not get used to unemployment (though it hurts less if other people are also out of work; Clark, 2003), and even when they are back at work, the negative psychological effects are long-lasting (Clark et al., 2001; Lucas, Clark, Georgellis, & Diener, 2004). Economist Andrew Oswald has estimated that you would have to give someone UK£23,000 per month (or £250,000 per year) to compensate for the loss of happiness from being unemployed—far more than even the most generous benefit system (reported in Donovan and Halpern, 2002; the large figure partly reflects the relatively small impact of income per se on subjective well-being). Arguably, this research has reinforced policy moves during the economic crisis of 2008–10 to give more weight to unemployment, including heavy public investment in job creation programs (e.g., in the UK and Australia), and policies to share work as an alternative to unemployment (notably in Germany).

For people who are employed, the quality of the work experience influences overall well-being. Since the majority of people will work from the age of 18 through to retirement, spending between 1200–2000 hours a year at work, the positive relationship between job satisfaction and life satisfaction is unsurprising. Job satisfaction is associated with opportunity for personal control and skill use; internally generated goals; variety; job security and income; physical security; supportive supervision; opportunity for interpersonal contact and social status (Donovan & Halpern, 2002). However, the policy implications of these findings are less clear. Tight labor markets encourage employers to put more emphasis on the quality of work experience, as do strong trade unions or professional bodies. However, many have used their market power to emphasize financial rewards more than job satisfaction.

If policy attended more to good work it might start with encouraging greater transparency about different work experiences. Csikszentmihalyi (1990) argues that work is at its most fulfilling when people are in a state of "flow," a deep focus that occurs when people engage in tasks with intense concentration and commitment. There is a sense of control; sense of self vanishes and time stops (Peterson & Seligman, 2004). The American *Good Work Project* (http://www.goodworkproject.org) has emphasized the importance of "good work"—work that it is technically excellent, personally meaningful or engaging, and carried out in an ethical way. The project has shown the wide variations between different sectors, some of which have a close alignment between work and values, while others show a sharp disconnect. These findings are relevant to the management of rewards. Recent work by Helliwell, Huang, and Putnam (2009) showed that within workplaces, trust in management has a much greater impact on happiness than pay or incentives. However, here too, the implications are clearer for managers than they are for governments.

A partial exception is the evidence on working hours and work arrangements. Working hours on the whole have decreased in most Western countries.[4] Flexible and part-time working has increased, the proportion of workplaces where non-managerial staff work from home has risen from 16% in 1998 to 28% in 2004.[5] This has a positive impact on individuals' work–life balance, and therefore on their well-being. Employee satisfaction in the UK has increased from 64% in 1998 to 70% in 2004.[6] However, there is evidence that work is having

---

[4] Office for National Statistics (2009). *Labour force survey: Employment status by age and occupation, April-June 2009*. [online] London, UK: ONS. Retrieved from http://www.ons.gov.uk/ons/search/index.html?pageSize=50&sortBy=none&sortDirection=none&newquery=labour+force+survey+working+hours+2009

[5] http://www.berr.gov.uk/whatwedo/employment/research-evaluation/wers-2004/#.

[6] http://www.berr.gov.uk/whatwedo/employment/research-evaluation/wers-2004/#.

a damaging impact on life satisfaction for some groups and in some countries. Research links long commutes to lower levels of frustration tolerance and job stability, as well as with poor health, and increased work absences (Navaco & Collier, 1994). There is also conflicting evidence, suggesting that for some groups, mainly those with substantial autonomy, very long working hours are associated with higher levels of satisfaction. The role of public policy varies according to national contexts. In some countries there are extensive regulations governing contracts, time, and pay. In others, government avoids direct involvement in the workplace. Social norms in relation to work hours also vary substantially between countries, as well as between sectors.

## Health

The improvement of mortality rates across a host of countries has encouraged many healthcare systems to turn their attention to well-being. For example, a recent report from Germany describes a shifting "emphasis on physical, mental and social welfare as the future task of its health policy rather than a mere increase in life expectancy" (Kurth, 2005, p. 1). Even with advancements in health care, many countries fare poorly in terms of obesity, smoking, alcohol and drug consumption, and mental illness—all of which damage individuals' and societies' well-being. The WHO estimates that half of all people with poor physical health have poor mental health. Mental health has worsened in developed countries in recent years, and, in the UK, prescriptions for antidepressants have increased threefold from 1991–2007. In addition to those formally diagnosed as "mentally ill," there are a large number of people who are anxious, lonely, or suffering from mild depression. As Parks, Seligman, and Steen (2004) argue, "we know very little about how to improve the lives of people whose days are free of overt mental dysfunction but are bereft of pleasure, engagement and meaning" (p. 1379).

However, the links between well-being and physical and mental health are strong. A higher level of well-being at the national level is associated with longer life expectancy, even when controlling for national income and infant mortality. Older women considered to have higher levels of "eudaimonic" well-being (well-being associated with self-development, personal growth, and purposeful engagement) demonstrate a number of positive health traits, including low waist to hip ratio and low cholesterol (Ryff, Singer, & Love, 2004).

A recent UK Government's report on "promoting mental capacity and mental well-being" (Foresight, 2008) highlights some of the difficult policy choices that follow. One is the practical issue of how to shift the focus away from cure to preventative mental health interventions without major increases in spending, at least in the medium term. A second is whether policy should focus on improving the mental well-being of the many, or address the chronic mental disorders of the few.

## Ageing

The ageing of populations is likely to be one of the major challenges of the century. Often it is presented as a problem, threatening the affordability of pensions systems and healthcare. Yet growing older can be a positive experience for many. In the "U-shaped" curve of happiness across a lifespan, well-being reaches its nadir in the mid-forties and then climbs (Blanchflower & Oswald, 2008). "Younger old" baby boomers are enjoying good pensions and the benefits of decades of inflation in the price of their homes. A physically fit 70-year-old is on average as happy as a 20-year-old (Jha, 2008). Mental, physical, and emotional decline is no longer an inevitable consequence of growing older, albeit that older people are more likely to face physical and/or cognitive decline, as well as social and financial exclusion.

Until recently, governments focused largely on improving the physical health and independence of older people. Comparatively little attention was paid to mental health disorders such as depression, which have relatively high prevalence in later life (Lee, 2006). Physical activity, mental health and cognition are inextricably linked—particularly for the older age ranges (see, e.g., Willis et al., 2006)—and policy-makers are increasingly looking at how to improve diet and exercise amongst the elderly. A high-profile example is the North Karelia project in Finland, where levels of physical health increased dramatically over several decades following a systematic, community-wide initiative incorporating both individual-level behavior change interventions and interventions focused on changing the social environment (Puska, Vartiainen, Laatikainen, Jousilahti, & Paavola, 2009).

Increased longevity is often linked to increases in loneliness and shrinking social networks which can lead to lower life satisfaction, particularly when an older person is less financially well-off, in ill health, living in unfit housing, or living in a care home (Layard, 2005). The result is growing interest in befriending schemes or social networks that can provide informal support alongside the formal support of health services and welfare providers.

"Active" or "productive" ageing is already becoming a common language in the policy world (Kalache & Gatti, 2003), reflecting a turn away from the assumption that ageing can only be seen as a problem. In fact, a growing body of research shows that the opportunity to make a contribution has an important impact on an older person's life satisfaction. People are ageing productively and simultaneously maintaining their well-being by engaging in work, volunteering, and by remaining involved in the community.

## The arts, sports, and culture

Enjoyment of, and participation in, sports and the arts can contribute to emotional and physical health (Galloway, 2006; Hamilton & Scullion, 2006). The links between exercise and well-being are well-established (Department of Health, 2004). However, the links between well-being and watching sports or the arts are much less clear. Indeed, there is no evidence that well-being is enhanced by a city or nation hosting major sports and arts events; followers of particular teams or sports stars are as likely to experience dejection when they lose as elation when they win.

More encouraging evidence comes from the ways in which sports and arts activities help people gain life skills which then help them cope with setbacks more effectively. Team sports tend to improve team working and communication, and both arts and sports projects can improve empathy and motivation (Sonstroem, Harlow, & Josephs, 1994).

The bulk of government funding for sports and arts is spent on supporting performances, training performers and sports men and women, and funding sporting events. Maximizing the well-being impact of arts, cultural, and sports spending, by contrast, would imply a shift in spending from spectator sports and arts to participation.

## Social capital

There is now extensive evidence linking social trust and social capital to well-being (Hothi, Bacon, Brophy, & Mulgan, 2008), both at the level of whole nations and in localities. Strong neighborhood networks can have a significant impact on quality of life. Data from the British Household Panel Survey highlights a strong link between personal well-being and talking to neighbors.[7] There is also evidence that the existence of social networks is linked to lower levels of crime, and improved educational achievement and health. Volunteering and giving are also strongly correlated with well-being (Office for National Statistics, 2001).

Moreover, people who feel that they can influence their immediate environment have higher levels of well-being. Direct democracy, for example, in which every citizen is able to participate in decision-making, e.g., through referendums, has been shown to improve well-being of citizens (Frey & Stutzer, 2000). The same is true of higher levels of "collective efficacy," meaning that residents feel able to respond to and manage local problems (Innes & Jones, 2006).

This trend is played out in international comparisons, with those countries with greater levels of "everyday democracy" reporting higher levels of life satisfaction (Skidmore & Bound, 2008). Everyday democracy encapsulates not only democratic practice in formal structures, but also structures in the private sphere such as families, schools, and local communities. Evidence of this kind supports policies that provide greater devolution of power, as well as attention to the fine grain of social relationships, and more spending to help community activities such as local media, websites, and festivals.

## Safety

The negative effect of fear of crime on well-being is similar to the effects of being an actual victim of crime. Research shows that residents who feel safe score higher on mental and social well-being measures (Green, Gilbertson, & Grimsley, 2002). One of the policy implications of these findings is that police forces should be judged in terms of fear of crime, as well as apparently more objective measures of crime. Where this has been done, the day-to-day practices of the police have tended to change, giving greater priority to reducing antisocial behavior, while encouraging community engagement.

## The environment

Well-being and environmental sustainability are often linked in debates about how to measure societal progress. However, the relationship between well-being and environmental sustainability agendas is not always an easy one (see Thompson, Marks & Jackson, Chapter 38, this volume). Although often mutually reinforcing (for example, cycling to work decreases carbon emissions and pollution and is also good for mental and physical well-being), they sometimes clash. A common assumption is that green lifestyles involve sacrifice and/or extra expense, for example, cutting down on long haul flights, using public transport rather than driving, or buying organic or locally-sourced food.

---

[7] BHPS, "Waves Spanning the years 1997-2001 and 2002-2003," made available by the University of Essex through ESRC UK Longitudinal studies Centre data archives.

Research has found that people who live a more eco-friendly lifestyle tend to score significantly higher in subjective well-being assessments (Brown & Kasser, 2005). Many initiatives demonstrate the positive impact of green initiatives on physical, mental, economic, and community well-being. For example, increased engagement with nature and the outdoors is associated with higher levels of concentration, lower levels of aggression, lower levels of stress, and higher levels of well-being (Newton, 2007), and linked with a variety of health outcomes, including faster recovery times among hospital patients, decreased mortality among senior citizens, and fewer sick calls for prisoners (Lavin, Higgins, Metcalfe, & Jordan, 2006; Maller, Townsend, Pryor, Brown, & St Leger, 2006). "Green exercise" is an expanding movement that advocates a range of physical activities in the outdoors that aim to improve mental health (Newton, 2007). Green initiatives that are group based improve social networks, sense of belonging and social capital (Kweon, Sullivan, & Wiley, 1998; Hothi et al., 2008). What is more, recent research has shown that the presence of vegetation can reduce crime in inner-city housing (Kuo & Sullivan, 2001). This evidence suggests that a greater density of everyday initiatives connecting well-being and environmental goals may create more favorable conditions for policies involving sacrifice.

## Redistribution, growth, and happiness

One of the main catalysts for greater interest in policies for well-being has been the now familiar evidence on the complexity of the relationship between well-being and income (Layard, 2005). Many governments have presumed that their primary obligation is to promote economic growth, and then to invest some of the proceeds of growth into social provision. However, Richard Easterlin (1974) and others have been showing for several decades that once a population's basic material needs are met, economic growth does not necessarily lead to a corresponding increase in life satisfaction. While countries with a higher GDP per capita generally reflect a higher level of life satisfaction, the association with increases in wealth and life satisfaction is much greater in poorer countries than richer economies (Haller & Hadler, 2006). Once incomes rise above the level needed to pay for basic needs, well-being is influenced by relative income—how people see their situation compared to others—more than by absolute income (Luttmer, 2005). Comparisons with neighbors, neighboring countries, or an individual's own past contribute to shaping perceptions (Bjørnskov, Gupta, & Pedersen, 2008; Diener & Seligman, 2004). Moreover, very unequal societies seem to perform worse on a wide range of counts, from crime and health to life satisfaction, to such an extent that even the well-off do worse in unequal societies than the well-off in more equal ones (Wilkinson & Pickett, 2009).

Awareness of relativity is part of the explanation why growth has not led to greater happiness. But in the 1970s, the economist Fred Hirsch suggested another explanation for the lack of influence of rising wealth on happiness (Hirsch, 1976). He argued that once material needs have been satisfied, a greater proportion of consumption is motivated by its "positional" effect—the status and value that accrue from having access to things which are inherently scarce and high status, such as ownership of stately homes or enjoyment of luxury holidays. Some positional goods can be opened up—as cheap air travel has democratized access to holiday destinations and rights of way have opened up previously exclusive areas of the countryside. But Hirsch suggests that the competition for relative position is bound to lead to both greater stress and greater disappointment.

The policy implications of these kinds of analysis are potentially profound. They can be used to justify significantly more redistributive policies for both income and capital, not least because the impact of marginal income on happiness will be much greater for the poor than the rich. They can be used to justify regulatory moves to constrain the emergence of positional goods, as well as heavy taxation of such goods (since demand will tend to be inelastic). Taxation can be made not only progressive in terms of income (i.e. taxing higher earners more) but also progressive in terms of hours worked so as to promote better work-life balance (Layard, 2005).

However, many of these conclusions are contested. The evidence that higher income does not lead to greater happiness is matched by similar evidence that rising public spending (in both absolute terms, and as a share of GDP) does not correlate with greater happiness either. Very happy countries include ones with relatively small public sectors such as Switzerland and Iceland, as well as the high-spending Scandinavians. Recent data has also challenged the common view that inequality tends to be associated with less happiness. Work by Alesina, Di Tella, and MacCulloch (2004) suggested that growing inequality in the USA has not made Americans less satisfied; nor has it led to a wider distribution of happiness, a finding corroborated in several other countries by Veenhoven (2005). At this stage the argument remain unresolved: clearly in some countries, including the USA, the public are willing to accept high levels of inequality. In most countries, however, there do seem to be strong links between inequality and poorer life satisfaction, and strong grounds for believing that some greater redistribution of resources would increase average, and total, well-being.

## Conclusions

This brief survey confirms that the translation of evidence about well-being into policy is only just beginning. There are, as yet, no widely shared metrics for well-being; no widely shared frameworks for designing and implementing policy; and no widely accepted lessons from experience. However, progress is being made rapidly, particularly in health and education, along with greater understanding of the subtleties and complexity of well-being. What the field now needs more than anything is healthy experimentation, testing out different models, measuring their impact, and incorporating the results into refined theories. A politician or official would have to be very brave to claim, confidently, that they have the answers to the question of how policies can best improve happiness. But, as the evidence accumulates, it will be increasingly foolhardy for any politician or official to claim that the question is an irrelevant one.

## References

Alesina, A., Di Tella, R., & MacCulloch, R. (2004). Inequality and happiness: Are Europeans and Americans different? *Journal of Public Economics, 88*, 2009–2042.

Bacon, N., Brophy, M., & Roberts, Y. (2009). *Parenting and wellbeing: Knitting families together.* London, UK: The Young Foundation.

Bjørnskov, C., Gupta, N., & Pedersen, P. (2008). Analysing trends in subjective wellbeing in 15 European countries, 1973–2002. *Journal of Happiness Studies, 9*, 317–330.

Blanchflower, D. G., & Oswald, A. J. (2008). Is wellbeing U-shaped over the life cycle? *Social Science & Medicine, 66*, 1733–1749.

Brown, K. W., & Kasser, T. (2005). Are psychological and ecological well-being compatible? The role of values, mindfulness, and lifestyle. *Social Indicators Research, 74*, 349–368.

Challen, A., Noden, P., West, A., & Machin, S. (2011). *UK resilience programme evaluation: Final report*. London, UK: Department for Education.

Clark, A. E. (2003). Unemployment as a social norm: Psychological evidence from panel data. *Journal of Labour Economics, 21*, 323–51.

Clark, A. E., Georgellis, Y., & Sanfey, P. (2001). Scarring: The psychological impact of past unemployment. *Economica, 68*, 221–41.

Clark, A. E., & Oswald, A. (1994). Unhappiness and unemployment. *Economic Journal, 104*, 648–659.

Classen, T. J., & Dunn, R. A. (2012). The effect of job loss and unemployment duration on suicide risk in the United States: A new look using mass-layoffs and unemployment duration. *Health Economics, 21*, 338–350.

Csíkszentmihályi, M. (1990). *Flow: The psychology of optimal experience*. New York, NY: Harper and Row.

Cutuli, J. J., Chaplin, T. M., Gillham, J. E., Reivich, K. J., & Seligman, M. E. P. (2006). Preventing co-occurring depression symptoms in adolescents with conduct problems: The Penn Resiliency Program. *New York Academy of Sciences, 1094*, 282–286.

Department for Education and Skills (now Department for Children, Schools and Families). (2007). *Every parent matters*. London, UK: Crown Copyright.

Department for Environment, Food and Rural Affairs. (2010). *Measuring progress: Sustainable development indicators 2010*. London, UK: Crown Copyright.

Department of Health. (2004). *At least five a week: Evidence on the impact of physical activity and its relationship to health*. London, UK: Crown Copyright.

Diener, E., Nickerson, C., Lucas, R. E., & Sandvik, E. (2002). Dispositional affect and job outcomes. *Social Indicators Research, 59*, 229–59.

Diener, E., & Seligman, M. (2004). Beyond money: Toward an economy of wellbeing. *Psychological Science in the Public Interest, 5*, 1–31.

Dolan, P., & Metcalfe, R. (2008). *The impact of subjective wellbeing on local authority interventions* (Working paper). Imperial College London.

Donovan, N., & Halpern, D. (2002). *Life satisfaction: The state of knowledge and the implications for government*. London, UK: Prime Minister's Strategy Unit.

Easterlin, R. A. (1974). Does economic growth improve the human lot? In P. David & M. Reder (Eds.), *Nations and households in economic growth: Essays in honor of Moses Abramovitz* (pp. 89–125). New York, NY: Academic Press.

Ellwood, D. T., & Jencks, C. (2004). The spread of single-parent families in the United States since 1960. In D. P. Moynihan, T. M. Smeeding & L. Rainwater (Eds.), *The future of the family* (pp. 25–65). New York, NY: Russell Sage Foundation.

Foresight. (2008). *The foresight project on mental capital and wellbeing: Making the most of ourselves in the 21st century*. London, UK: Government Office for Science.

Frey, B. S., & Stutzer, A. (2000). Happiness, economy and institutions. *The Economic Journal, 110*, 918–938.

Galloway, S. (2006). *Well-being and quality of life: Measuring the benefits of culture and sport—A literature review*. Edinburgh, UK: Scottish Executive Social Research.

Green, G., Gilbertson, J., & Grimsley, M. (2002). Fear of crime and health in residential tower blocks: A case study in Liverpool, UK. *European Journal of Public Health*, 12, 10–15.

Haller, M., & Hadler, M. (2006). How social relations and structures can produce happiness and unhappiness: An international comparative analysis. *Social Indicators Research*, 75, 169–216.

Hamilton, C., & Scullion, A. (2006). *Well-being and quality of life: Measuring the benefits of culture and sport—A think-piece*. Edinburgh, UK: Scottish Executive Social Research.

Helliwell, J. F. (2003). How's life? Combining individual and national variables to explain subjective well-being. *Economic Modelling*, 20, 331–360.

Helliwell, J. F., Huang, H., & Putnam, R. D. (2009). How's the job? Are trust and social capital neglected workplace investments? In V. O. Barktus & J. H. Davis (Eds.), *Social capital: Reaching out, reaching in* (pp. 87–144). Cheltenham, UK: Edward Elgar.

Hirsch, F. (1976). *Social limits to growth*. Cambridge, MA: Harvard University Press.

Hothi, M., Bacon, N., Brophy, M., & Mulgan, G. (2008). *Neighbourliness + empowerment = wellbeing*. London, UK: The Young Foundation.

Innes, M., & Jones, V. (2006). *Neighbourhood security and urban change*. London, UK: Joseph Rowntree Foundation.

Jha, A. (2008, January 29). Happiness is being young or old, but middle age is misery. *The Guardian*.

Kalache, A., & Gatti, A. (2003). Active ageing: A policy framework. *Advances in Gerontology*, 11, 7–18.

Kahneman, D., & Riis, J. (2005). Living, and thinking about it: Two perspectives on life. In F. Huppert, N. Baylis & B. Keverne (Eds.), *The science of wellbeing* (pp. 185–304). Oxford, UK: Oxford University Press.

Krueger, A. B., Kahneman, D., Schkade, D., Schwarz, N., & Stone, A. A. (2009). National time accounting: The currency of life. In A. B. Krueger (Ed.), *Measuring the subjective well-being of nations: National accounts of time use and well-being*. Chicago, IL: University of Chicago Press.

Kuo, F. E., & Sullivan, W. C. (2001). Environment and crime in the inner-city: Does vegetation reduce crime? *Environment and Behavior*, 33, 343–67.

Kurth, B-M. (2005). *KIGGS: The German health survey for children and adolescents*. Berlin, Germany: Robert Koch Institute.

Kweon, B. S., Sullivan, W. C., & Wiley, A. R. (1998). Green common spaces and the social integration of inner-city older adults. *Environment and Behavior*, 30, 832–58.

Lavin, T., Higgins, C., Metcalfe, O., & Jordan, A. (2006). *Health impacts of the built environment: A review*. Dublin, Ireland: Institute of Public Health in Ireland.

Layard, R. (2005). *Happiness: Lessons from a new science*. London, UK: Penguin Press.

Lee, M. (2006). *Promoting mental health and well-being in later life: A first report from the UK inquiry into mental health and well-being in later life*. London, UK: Age Concern and The Mental Health Foundation.

Lucas, R. E. (2007). Adaptation and the set-point model of subjective well-being: Does happiness change after major life events? *Current Directions in Psychological Science*, 16, 75–80.

Lucas, R. E., Clark, A. E., Georgellis, Y., & Diener, E. (2004). Unemployment alters the set point for life satisfaction. *Psychological Science*, 15, 8–13.

Luttmer, E. F. P. (2005). Neighbors as negatives: Relative earnings and well-being. *Quarterly Journal of Economics*, 120, 963–1002.

Lyubomirsky, S., Sheldon, K. M., & Schkade, D. (2005). Pursuing happiness: The architecture of sustainable change. *Review of General Psychology, 9*, 111–131.

Mahdi, M. (2001). *Al Farabi and the foundation of Islamic political philosophy*. Chicago, IL: University of Chicago Press.

Maller, C., Townsend, M., Pryor, A., Brown, P., & St Leger, L. (2006). Healthy nature healthy people: "Contact with nature" as an upstream health promotion intervention for populations. *Health Promotion International, 21*, 45–54.

Marks, N., Abdallah, S., Simms, A., & Thompson, S. (2006). *The (un)happy planet index: An index of human well-being and environmental impact*. London, UK: nef (the new economics foundation).

Michaelson, J., Abdallah, S., Steuer, N., Thompson, S., & Marks, N. (2009). *National accounts of well-being: Bringing real wealth onto the balance sheet*. London, UK: nef (the new economics foundation).

Navaco, R. W., & Collier, C. (1994). *Commuting stress, ridesharing, and gender: Analyses from the 1993 State of the Commute Study in Southern California*. Irvine, CA: Institute of Transportation Studies, University of California.

Newton J. (2007). *Wellbeing and the natural environment: a brief overview of the evidence*. London, UK: Department for Environment, Food and Rural Affairs.

OECD. (2009). *Doing better for children*. Paris, France: OECD Directorate for Employment, Labour and Social Affairs.

Oishi, S., Diener, E., & Lucas, R. (2007). The optimal level of wellbeing: Can people be too happy? *Perspectives on Psychological Science, 2*, 346–7.

Office for National Statistics. (2001). *Social capital: A review of the literature*. London, UK: Social Analysis and Reporting Division, Office for National Statistics.

Parks, A., Seligman, M., & Steen, T. (2004). A balanced psychology and a full life. *Philosophical Transactions of the Royal Society B: Biological Sciences, 359*, 1379–1381.

Peterson, C., & Seligman, M. (2004). *Character strengths and virtues: A handbook and classification*. New York, NY: Oxford University Press.

Puska, P., Vartiainen, E., Laatikainen, T., Jousilahti, P., & Paavola, M. (Eds.). (2009). *The North Karelia project: From North Karelia to national action*. Helsinki, Finland: National Institute for Health and Welfare.

Ryff, C., Singer, B., & Love, G. (2004). Positive health: Connecting wellbeing with biology. *Philosophical Transactions of the Royal Society London B: Biological Sciences, 359*, 1383–1394.

Shah, H., & Marks, N. (2004). *A wellbeing manifesto for a flourishing society*. London, UK: nef (the new economics foundation).

Skidmore, P., & Bound, K. (2008). *The everyday democracy index*. London, UK: Demos.

Sonstroem, R. J., Harlow, L. L., & Josephs, L. (1994). Exercise and self-esteem: Validity of model expansion and exercise associations. *Journal of Sport & Exercise Psychology, 16*, 29–42.

UNICEF. (2007). *An overview of child well-being in rich countries: A comprehensive assessment of the lives and well-being of children and adolescents in the economically advanced nations*. Florence, Italy: UNICEF Innocenti Research Centre.

van Praag, B. M. S., & Baarsma, B. E. (2005). Using happiness surveys to value intangibles: The case of airport noise. *The Economic Journal, 115*, 224–246.

Veenhoven, R. (2005). Return of inequality in modern society? Test by dispersion of life satisfaction across time and nations. *Journal of Happiness Studies, 6*, 457–487.

Welsch, H. (2002). Preferences over prosperity and pollution: Environmental valuation based on happiness surveys. *Kyklos, 55*, 473–495.

Wilkinson, R., & Pickett, K. (2009). *The spirit level: Why more equal societies almost always do better*. London, UK: Allen Lane.

Willis, S. L., Tennstedt, S. L., Marsiske, M., Ball, K., Elias, J., Mann Koepke, K., ... Wright, E. (2006). Long-term effects of cognitive training on everyday functional outcomes in older adults: The ACTIVE study. *Journal of the American Medical Association, 296*, 2805–2814.

Wolfson, M., Rowe, G., & Sharpe, A. (2009). *"Good life time": Health, income, and the time to enjoy them. A new framework and index for measuring social progress*. Paper presented at the 3rd OECD World Forum on Statistics, Knowledge and Policy: Charting Progress, Building Visions, Improving Life. Busan, Korea, October 27–30, 2009.

# SECTION VI
# POSITIVE EDUCATION

# CHAPTER 40

# INTRODUCTION TO POSITIVE EDUCATION

## ILONA BONIWELL

The University of East London, UK;
Positran, Paris, France

> The true measure of a nation's standing is how well it attends to its children—their health and safety, their material security, their education and socialization, and their sense of being loved, valued, and included in the families into which they are born.
>
> (UNICEF, 2007)

It is likely that the first decade of the twenty-first century will be viewed by historians as a landmark time for the explicit development of children's well-being. Once implicit in the education of children, well-being has now become an overt government agenda in many countries across the world. For instance, the primary objective of the UK Government's "Every Child Matters" initiative, underpinned by the Children Act 2004, is to "Safeguard children and young people, improve their life outcomes and general well-being" (DfES, 2007, p. 35). More recently, the UK's Department for Children, Schools and Families published *The Children's Plan,* setting ten new targets to improve children's wellbeing by 2020, through nurturing "happy, capable and resilient children" (DCSF, 2007, p. 5).

The reasons for the focus on the development of well-being and happiness in children are twofold. On the one hand, Western countries are facing an unprecedented increase in childhood and adolescent depression. At any point in time, approximately 2% of children aged 11–15 and 11% of youth aged 16–24 in the UK suffer a major depressive disorder (Green, McGinnity, Meltzer, Ford, & Goodman, 2005). Anxiety disorders, which often precede and co-occur with depression, are found in approximately 3% of children aged 5–15 and 15% of youth aged 16–24 (Green et al., 2005). In the USA, approximately one in five adolescents has a major depressive episode by the end of high school (Lewinsohn, Hops, Roberts, & Seeley, 1993), with a similar picture observed in Australia (Noble & McGrath, 2005). Children and adolescents who suffer from high levels of depressive symptoms or depressive disorders are more likely to have academic and interpersonal difficulties. They are more likely to smoke, use drugs and alcohol, and attempt suicide (Covey, Glassman, & Stetner, 1998; Garrison, Schluchter, Schoenbach, & Kaplan, 1989).

The wealth of Western countries appears to provide relatively little protection for their youth. Recent international attempts to directly measure child well-being offer a worrying picture. The 2007 UNICEF report, which presents an overview of child well-being in rich countries, shows France, the USA, and UK occupying the bottom third in the list of 21 industrialized countries (UNICEF, 2007). Of primary importance to this report is Dimension 5—Subjective well-being—in which children ranked their opinion of their health, their liking for school, and their subjective view of their personal well-being. The UK came in last in this dimension, causing a rich debate over the success of current welfare and education policies. Bob Reitemeier, the chief executive of The Children's Society, reported in *The Guardian* on February 14, 2007: "Unicef's report is a wake-up call to the fact that, despite being a rich country, the UK is failing children and young people in a number of crucial ways."

Although the case for positive education can be made purely on the basis of prevention of ill-health, depression, anxiety, and other mental health disorders, there is at least as much value in appreciating the benefits that happiness can bring. A substantial body of research documents advantages of well-being and positive individual characteristics. Research demonstrates that happy people are successful across multiple life domains, including marriage, relationships, health, longevity, income, and work performance. They are more creative, able to multitask and endure boring tasks, more trusting, helpful, and sociable (Lyubomirsky, King, & Diener, 2005). Those able to identify, develop, and use their strengths are more likely to be high achievers (Buckingham & Coffman, 1999), whilst higher levels of grit or self-discipline in children predict academic success over and above their IQ levels (Duckworth & Seligman, 2005).

Positive education aims to develop the skills of well-being, flourishing, and optimal functioning in children, teenagers, and students, as well as parents and educational institutions. It therefore adopts both the preventative and enabling or developmental functions. Importantly, positive education is underpinned by the principles and methods of empirical validation, which is what differentiates it from self-help initiatives.

The first chapter in this section looks into establishing a philosophical case for well-being as the focus for educational policy. Challenging the widespread assumption that the main focus of schooling is the transmission of knowledge, Professor John White talks about the importance of teaching children to acquire appropriate habits whilst also understanding their own basic needs (Chapter 41). This is the foundation for flourishing. Going further, the chapter discusses four perspectives on what can be considered a "worthwhile pursuit," ranging from a religious one and Bethamite hedonism, to the positions Professor White calls "autonomous desire satisfaction" and "beyond individual preferences." Discussing how the pursuit of individual well-being can be integrated with concern for others, he charges the school with the caring for the child's well-being in a way that penetrates its very ethos, rather than simply offering "happiness lessons."

The next chapter by Dr Nash Popivic (Chapter 42) takes a different position on "happiness lessons," arguing instead for the necessity of introducing a structured personal development education into schools' curricula. Highlighting the problems with the whole-school and cross-curricula approaches, the chapter shows how timetabled lessons can offer more comprehensive, systematic, consistent, unbiased, and focused education than their diffuse counterparts.

Moving on from a philosophical debate to the practice of happiness education, in Chapter 43 Professor Toni Noble and Helen McGrath offer a fascinating historical narrative on the evolution of parenting and well-being education throughout the twentieth century. The authors demonstrate the gradual transformation of the self-esteem movement of the 1970s, based on the core principles of humanistic psychology, into the current Social and Emotional Learning (SEL) movement, supported by explicit initiatives to teach resilience and student well-being. Offering a well-researched and expert-derived definition of student well-being, Noble and McGrath go further to identify some guidelines for the effective implementation of SEL programs in schools.

Jennifer Fox Eades, Carmel Proctor, and Martin Ashley offer supplementary historical insights, followed by a review of a number of current educational initiatives to increase happiness and well-being in Chapter 44. They focus on the school-wide programs, the Celebrating Strengths framework and the Strengths Gym, and review the emerging evidence for the effectiveness of these approaches. The chapter concludes by discussing the role of unhappiness amidst the happiness initiatives and argues for the importance of considering well-being of teachers in the creation of happy schools.

Chapter 45 presents a strong case for embedding well-being teaching within other subjects, identifying both the principles and specific techniques that can be utilized by educators with the view to enhance students' emotional and intellectual development. Topic by topic, Laura McInerney demonstrates how research on positive emotions, emotional intelligence, humor, flow, and playfulness can be used to achieve concentration, engagement, enhanced motivation, or creative problem solving, depending upon the objectives of the lesson. The concluding pages of the chapter also point out the dangers of happiness teaching, highlighting not only the already familiar problems with raising self-esteem, but also the danger of focusing on positive rather than purposeful emotions.

Focusing on one of the major aspects of happiness education, Dr Jane Gillham and her colleagues Drs Rachel Abenavoli, Steven Brunwasser, Karen Reivich, and Professor Martin Seligman, make a strong case for teaching resilience as part of the school curriculum, as a preventative measure for the development of depression and other disorders (Chapter 46). The chapter offers an overview of Penn's two flagship programs—the Penn Resiliency Program (PRP) and the High School Positive Psychology Program. The PRP has been developed and researched for over 16 years and consequently has acquired a solid base of evidence. The evidence from 19 controlled studies suggests that it prevents both depression and anxiety and has long-lasting effects. The positive psychology program of 17 lessons, each 2 hours in length, was developed to introduce the science of happiness to high school students. Developed around Martin Seligman's Authentic Happiness (2002) ideas and including a substantial resilience component, the program incorporates several tested and innovative positive psychology interventions, such as savoring, gratitude letters, counting blessings, forgiveness, and letting go of grudges. The emergent evidence for the effectiveness of this program is also discussed.

Happiness, as defined in this volume, spans from so-called hedonic approaches, concerned with feeling good, to eudaimonia, concerned with doing well, contributing to humanity and the acquisition of a common good. In Chapter 47, Professor Robert Stenberg discusses the Wisdom Curriculum that encourages the moral development of children through the medium of mainstream subjects. Drawing on the example of the recent worldwide economic collapse, he vividly demonstrates the limits of even superior intellectual functioning when an individual's objectives centre primarily on their own short-term interests.

Whereas the previous two chapters discussed distinctive classroom-based happiness programs (as broadly defined), the last two chapters in this section focus on case studies of two prominent educational establishments. Ian Morris introduces us to the Wellington College experience of education as happiness and educating for happiness in Chapter 48. In September 2006, Wellington College—a private coeducational school in the UK—introduced a 2-year Skills of Well-Being program for its pupils. Skills of Well-Being has attracted unprecedented media coverage, placing the well-being debate firmly in the heart of the British political agenda. The course is delivered fortnightly to Years 10 and 11 (ages 14–16) with the specific aim of redressing the imbalance in modern education caused by an emphasis on exam results and measured outcomes. The ultimate aim of the course is to give Wellington College pupils practical skills for living well that are useful, easily understood, and can be applied on a daily basis. The passionate desire to deliver these skills is driving an ongoing review and development of the course. This is coupled with an intention to avoid a "myopic" approach and broaden the breadth and depth of the course to include knowledge from positive psychology, drawing on the latest evidence-based research and practical interventions.

In the final chapter of this section, Dr Mathew White introduces us to the Positive Education initiative at Geelong Grammar School, Australia's leading coeducational boarding and day school. Developed in collaboration with Professor Martin Seligman and his team of positive psychology experts, the initiative combines the structured PRP-based resilience and the positive psychology-based lessons, with the more indirect happiness teaching through mainstream subjects. Based on the "seven pillars" of creativity, emotion, gratitude, mindfulness, resilience, self-efficacy, and strengths, all of these underpinned by empathy, it is hoped that the positive education approach will help the students combat future depression and anxiety.

With governments around the world taking an active interest in children's well-being, as well as the availability of research and science in positive psychology and a multitude of initiatives, happiness education is set for a positive future. Nevertheless, it is important to recognize that we are still at the very beginning of the journey. For these programs and interventions to succeed, research needs to continue. Until then, the reader is invited to learn more about positive education by engaging with the chapters in this section.

# References

Buckingham, M., & Coffman, C. (1999). *First, break all the rules: What the world's greatest managers do differently*. New York, NY: Simon Schuster.

Covey, L. S., Glassman, A. H., & Stetner, F. (1998). Cigarette smoking and major depression. *Journal of Addictive Diseases, 17*, 35–46.

DCSF (2007). *Children and young people today: Evidence to support the children's plan*. London, UK: Department for Children, Schools and Families.

DfES (2007). *Social and emotional aspects of learning for secondary schools (SEAL): Guidance Booklet*. London, UK: Department for Children, Schools and Families.

Duckworth, A. L., & Seligman, M. E. P. (2005). Self discipline outdoes IQ in predicting academic performance of adolescents. *American Psychological Society, 16*, 939–944.

Garrison, C. Z., Schluchter, M. D., Schoenbach, V. J., & Kaplan, B. K. (1989). Epidemiology of depressive symptoms in young adolescents. *Journal of the American Academy of Child and Adolescent Psychiatry, 28*, 343–351.

Green, H., McGinnity, A., Meltzer, H., Ford, T., & Goodman, R. (2005). *Mental health of children and young people in Great Britain 2004.* London, UK: Office for National Statistics.

Lewinsohn, P. M., Hops, H., Roberts, R., & Seeley, J. (1993). Adolescent psychopathology: I. Prevalence and incidence of depression and other DSM-III-R disorders in high school students. *Journal of Abnormal Psychology, 102*, 110–120.

Lyubomirsky, S., King, L. A., & Diener, E. (2005). The benefits of frequent positive affect: Does happiness lead to success? *Psychological Bulletin, 131*, 803–855.

Noble, T., & McGrath, H. (2005) Helping children and families 'bounce back', *Australian Family Physician, 9*, 34.

UNICEF Innocenti Research Centre. (2007). *Child poverty in perspective: An overview of child well-being in rich countries.* Retrieved from http://www.unicef-irc.org.

# CHAPTER 41

# EDUCATION AND WELL-BEING

## JOHN WHITE
Institute of Education, London, UK

## Introduction

What should schools and families do to help children to lead a flourishing life? The question opens up not one can of worms, but several. What *is* a flourishing life? Is there consensus on this? If not, won't parents and teachers be imposing their own conception of it on their charges? Should they be getting involved, in any case, with this goal? Shouldn't they be turning children's attention on to wider and nobler things than the pursuit of their own interests? And as far as the school is concerned, don't we know already that its specialized function is to pass on knowledge of one's mother tongue, mathematics, science, history, and other forms of understanding? Outside the intellectual area, shouldn't personal development be left to parents, not teachers?

On this last point, just because schools have traditionally confined themselves, by and large, to the transmission of knowledge, that is no reason why they should continue to do so. In any case, why have they traditionally gone for knowledge? It is hard not to see pupil well-being as part of the answer. A century and a half ago, people held that curriculum subjects develop a range of mental faculties, like memory or demonstrative reasoning, all beneficial to the learner. Nowadays, a more common justification for a broad, knowledge-based, curriculum is that it gives pupils a basis for choosing the career and way of life they prefer. This second argument holds more water than the first. But it also threatens its own position, that schooling is about knowledge alone. For if promoting personal well-being is the underlying aim, why should schools stick only to academic tasks? Living a fulfilled life requires personal qualities that go far beyond these: resilience, for instance, the proper regulation of one's emotions, cooperativeness, good judgment in practical affairs. Schools can do something to nurture these, too.

Since the millennium, schools in Britain have been moving in this broader direction, partly under the *Every Child Matters* initiative, that seeks to enhance children's well-being across the whole range of children's services (Department for Children, Schools and

Families, (2008)). New statutory aims for the whole curriculum have appeared, including the development of "confident individuals." A new school subject called "Personal wellbeing" has been introduced (Department for Children, Schools and Families/Qualifications and Curriculum Authority, 2007)). How, more systematically and more globally, might schools, as well as families, educate for personal well-being?

## Basic Needs

There are two aspects of well-being. The first is that, if you are to lead a flourishing life at all, certain basic requirements have to be met (Griffin, 1986, Chapter 3; Raz, 1986, Chapter 12.2; Sumner, 1996, Chapter 3.2). Some of these are material prerequisites, many of them necessary not only for flourishing, but more fundamentally for survival: things like food and drink, shelter, clothing, income, exercise, a certain level of health. You also need practical intelligence and the good judgment this brings with it. You need to live in a society that is relatively peaceful and respects your freedom of action, provided this is not harmful to others; and—as a priority of increasing urgency—to live in a world that takes the gathering ecological crisis seriously and finds ways to circumvent it. You also need good luck: a road accident, a natural disaster, or an unexpected death of a close family member, are likely to diminish your well-being.

Schools and families may not be able to do much, at least directly, to guarantee a peaceful society, renewable resources, or a minimum income; or to eliminate bad luck. But they *can* help children to think flexibly about means to ends, to develop nuanced judgment in making decisions where conflicting values are at stake. They can help them to acquire appropriate habits when it comes to eating and drinking sensibly, taking exercise, and looking after their health more generally. They can encourage them in the proper regulation of their emotions, like fear, anger, contempt, sympathy; and of their bodily desires, including their sexual desires.

Inextricable from acquiring appropriate habits is acquiring the knowledge on which they depend—e.g., about diet, the human body, and how one's own and other people's minds work. Both schools and families have something to contribute here. They can also help children to understand why other basic needs like peace, income, the environment, freedom, and luck are important to their flourishing. And not only to theirs. Education for well-being can focus learners' attention—not only intellectually, but also as agents of change—on basic needs more generally, as a vital element in all human flourishing. There are implications here for pupils' education in global citizenship.

## Worthwhile Pursuits: Four Approaches

I turn to the second aspect of personal well-being. This is more complicated. Suppose all your basic needs are met. Is this enough for your life to be a thriving one? Surely not. Even though you are well fed, well off, healthy, and untouched by bad luck, you may spend most of your time on worthless or unsuccessful pursuits.

This is where the difficulties start. The last point suggests that a thriving life should be built around pursuits that are, to a large extent, both worthwhile and successful. The second of these is fairly straightforward. If I spend a lot of my time gardening, but produce only weed patches, I do worse for myself than my neighbor with her immaculate lawns and borders.

The bigger question is: what counts as a worthwhile pursuit? This is especially important for parents and teachers, since they have to know what activities they have to acquaint children with, or induct them into, if they are to lead a fulfilled life.

Historically, there have been different kinds of answers to this question.

## Approach [i]: a religious perspective

In a more universally religious age, the most devout located fulfillment is not in this mortal world, but in heaven. Our earthly life is a site only for meeting the moral obligations that God lays upon us, including, in some Protestant theologies, unremitting hard work in his service. These obligations also include nurturing our spiritual powers of reflection, since it is these that will persist into our eternal life.

Secular schools in a country like Britain, and perhaps the USA, their historical roots tapping into a religious subsoil, are still places of dutiful endeavor and industriousness, even though they have long lost from view the original rationale for this. The same may be true of their traditional focus on a comprehensive initiation into all the major forms of knowledge. To the great seventeenth-century educationalist Comenius (1907, p. 41), for whom an encyclopedic education develops our spiritual powers, given that man is the image of an omniscient God, this focus was self-evident. It is far from that today.

Some faith schools today still work with an other-worldly conception of well-being, seeing this-world pursuits as no more than preparation for the next. But in Britain, at least, most religiously affiliated schools (a third of the total) have much more time for this-world fulfillment, however they may conceive its relationship to the transcendental.

## Approach [ii]: Benthamite hedonism

At the end of the eighteenth century, Jeremy Bentham's hedonism understood a flourishing life as one filled with pleasure and minimally painful. Although much media and advertising output seems to reinforce this message, no school's aims, to my knowledge, have been built round it. This is not surprising. John Stuart Mill (1861, Chapter 2) argued that it allowed in, as the most flourishing life, one based only on the physical pleasures we share with other animals. For Mill himself, fulfillment has much to do with the "pleasures of the mind," that is, with intellectual and artistic pursuits. His stance fits hand in glove with what many of us now think of as the proper office of the school, assuming we broaden this from the more austere version that restricts its aims to knowledge alone. We will come back to this.

## Approach [iii]: autonomous desire satisfaction

Members of most human communities have lived by local mores, some, presumably, thriving better than others. But in recent times it has become, for many of us, all but impossible to detach the notion of personal well-being from the notion of personal autonomy (Raz, 1986, Chapters 12 and 14; Brighouse, 2006). We take it as read that, if we are to flourish, we must be in charge of our own lives, making our own decisions about our work, our relationships, what religion, if any, we follow, where we live, and so on. In one version of this modern ideal, the goals we autonomously adopt are entirely up to us. We are sovereign choosers.

Our ideas of education have been massively influenced by this ideal. So as to become able to make such major choices in their lives, young people have to understand alternative possibilities from which to select. This is not about doing whatever you want—for some wants, the desire to smoke, for instance, you may prefer to be without. It is about making *informed* choices (Sumner, 1996, Chapter 5.2). Parents make the first moves in opening their children's eyes to the myriad opportunities ahead of them. Teachers continue their work, introducing them to more recondite kinds of understanding and experience.

On this view, it is not up to teachers, parents, or anyone else, to steer children towards particular kinds of major choices: they are not to direct them as to whom to marry, what religion to adopt, what career to follow. But it does permit some steering of a different sort. In the basic needs area, since health is good for well-being, upbringers have a good reason, as we have seen, for encouraging children to eat well and take exercise. Moral constraints are also crucial. The informed choices for which children are being equipped exclude becoming a gangster, a bully, a liar, or a con artist.

In one variant that falls under the ideal under discussion, that is the end of the matter. Educators have no right to compel children to study this or that, if the latter have no inclination to do so. Compulsion, it is claimed, involves paternalism.

This is challenged by those, the overwhelming majority, who argue that leaving children free to attend lessons or not is a poor preparation for a life of autonomous informed choices. For this, they must be able to read and write, experience the delights of various art forms, understand the society they live in, and the science and mathematics that underpin it, and so on. Learning of these and other sorts is non-negotiable. Pupils must be teacher-directed today so that they can become self-directed tomorrow. The same argument applies also to personal qualities. If such things as persistence, good judgment, or being able to bounce back from reverses, are valuable dispositions to have if one is to flourish, parents and perhaps teachers, too, have reason to nurture them.

## Approach [iv]: beyond individual preferences

From yet another perspective, the view just outlined is defective. It makes the individual the final authority on what constitutes his or her well-being. But is this defensible? It is possible, if admittedly not very likely, that someone could make an informed choice to live a life of playing slot machines. Would he not be leading a misspent life, rather than a flourishing one?

On the defective view, again, educational institutions and those of the High Street are in the same line of business (White, 2005, Chapter 12). Both are helping individuals to realize their informed preferences, whatever these may be. Can this be right? Are schoolteachers and ad men *really* on the same wavelength? Considerations like these lead some to conclude that not everything goes. What human fulfillment is cannot be left to the individual to decide.

Why might we want to rule out a life devoted to slot machines? On perspective [iv] there is nothing—or perhaps next to nothing—worthwhile about it. We are happy to rule it out, because we *already* have some sort of idea of what makes for a flourishing life. We know that close, loving relationships do so; as do worthwhile activities—gardening, photography, or teaching, for instance—if these are fully absorbing and successfully conducted (Raz, 1994, Chapter 1).

Will this do? Who is the gatekeeper who lets in the things just mentioned and excludes others? Isn't there still the danger of paternalism unless people are allowed to do what they want, assuming no harm to others?

There is a muddle here. Our topic is well-being, not liberty. No one is saying that people should be *prevented* from engaging in activities and relationships that have nothing worthwhile about them. Even so, the gatekeeper problem remains. Who is to say what counts as worthwhile?

For part of the answer, one approach looks to history. We live in a culture that has witnessed the creation—especially over the last few centuries, as secular notions of well-being have been replacing religious ones—of a proliferating array of activities and relationships that human beings have found give meaning to their lives. Take the arts. Music, literature, painting, architecture, dance have all developed new genres and subgenres. Think of the novel in its various overlapping forms: historical, comic, romantic, works of social criticism, detective stories, science fiction. As time goes on, new forms and exemplars of valuable activity are bequeathed from one generation to the next. This is true in domain after domain. Think of the three activities I mentioned earlier, gardening, photography, and teaching. Each of them comes down to us with the same kind of history, the same burgeoning of variety.

The same applies to relationships. Take the growth of the idea of marriage as based on mutual love and autonomous choice among equals, rather than on parental wishes, or male domination; non-married partners, gay relationships, companionate marriages; friendships founded on common interests, face-to-face friendships, friendship by correspondence, web-based friendships across continents; cooperative relations with colleagues, also, in a complex modern society, taking countless shapes. In both activities and relationships, so many of us can now tap into a cornucopia of opportunities far beyond the dreams of even the most privileged a century or two ago.

Although, according to this account, well-being is culturally indebted (Raz, 2003); that is not to say that its values are culturally relative. The aesthetic worth of Mozart's music did not pass away with the princely culture for which it was created.

To come back to gatekeepers. Who is a reliable authority on what counts as a worthwhile activity? Two or three centuries ago, when nearly everyone in a country like Britain was living near subsistence level, only a few more affluent people had anything like a wide experience of the worthwhile pursuits and relationships then available, and so might have had views worth listening to on what makes for a fulfilling life. Today, nearly all of us are somewhere on the scale, and many of us quite far along it. There are no individual authorities on worthwhileness, despite guru-figures who would have us believe otherwise. The relevant understanding is now more widely diffused among the population—not as a static attainment, but as a shared possession open to modification in the light of constant, on-going discussion, at every level, about what makes life worth living (White, 2007).

# Relevance for education

What bearing does perspective [iv] have on education for personal well-being? With autonomy in mind, we can keep the idea, already mentioned, that schools introduce learners to a whole array of options, and ways of understanding their world, against which background they can make informed choices. Now, however, the underlying aim is not that they choose whatever they like, without restriction; but that they are equipped to lead a life of wholehearted and successful engagement in activities and relationships of a worthwhile sort.

A narrower view than [iv] follows J. S. Mill in confining the worthwhile activities, or at least the most important of them, to intellectual, including artistic, pursuits pursued for their own sake (Peters, 1966, Chapter 5). This provides a ready justification for the academic curriculum often associated with a grammar- or public-school education. But it faces a problem. Why the restriction to intellectual activities, important as they are? This demotes others like engineering, nursing, construction work, many craft activities, in all of which people can find success and lose themselves in a totally absorbing way. Coming back to the broader view, in [iv], there is a strong case for schools' keeping their notion of worthwhile activities and relationships wide enough to allow all who pass through them, and not just an academically inclined minority, to enjoy a fulfilling life. How this should be embodied in a curriculum is a further question. There is a "basis for choice" argument for having a broad range of offerings, but the end-result might well be different from the familiar academic version of this.

For one thing, there is a case for putting weight on the likely pulling power of an activity as a major constituent of well-being throughout a learner's life. Even with a good early grounding in the subjects, I suspect few people spend much time on advanced mathematical or geographical activity—especially if, like most of us, they are not in a job that involves such specialisms. Yet vastly more of us easily get engrossed in one or other of the arts—hardly surprisingly, given the seductive devices creative artists use to draw us into their work. Considerations like this may lead us to rethink current curriculum priorities. For education for well-being is partly a matter of learning from experience *what it is like* to get wholeheartedly and successfully caught up in an activity: and this involves habituation into fulfilling ways of being. Do the proliferating enjoyments that the arts bring with them entitle them to a greater place in education than our somewhat austere traditional attitude towards them has allowed (White, 2005, Chapter 15)?

A further word about worthwhile *relationships*. These make an enormous contribution to human flourishing, but schools have traditionally left them largely off their agenda. Today, the conception of pupils assimilating items of knowledge as isolated and competing learners is increasingly under challenge from more collaborative forms of pedagogy; and discussion about friendships and sexual attachments is often built into the curriculum. More space for the arts in school, not least the literary arts, could also help to underline the centrality of relationships to well-being and the need to foster discernment in this area.

The point made earlier about gatekeepers and authorities is also educationally relevant. The more that children become immersed in worthwhile pursuits, the more capable they become of joining the on-going discussion, mentioned previously, about what makes life worth living. Schools have every reason to build such discussion into their programs.

## Objections

Will [iv] do as an account of personal well-being, applicable to education in the ways just described? Not everyone will buy it. For some, it gives much too much space to the pursuit of self-interest. The more you are intent on bettering yourself, the less room you will have in your life for altruism and morality. As for education, some would say that this should not be about self-advancement, but about immersion in curricular subject-matter, ideally for its own sake.

There are multiple difficulties about the central objection here (Raz, 1999, Chapters 12 and 13). Approach [iv] has not in fact mentioned the pursuit of self-interest. It is about what it is to lead a flourishing life, and this is a different topic. Take someone who has an enjoyable job and all sorts of enthralling interests, as well as deep, loving relationships with friends and family members. There is nothing to say that she must have been guided in her choices by the thought "what is in this for me?" She may have *found herself* in this way of life, having been drawn further into its component pursuits as they have become increasingly satisfying to her. This is no less true of her work than of other things: there are all sorts of reasons apart from self-interest why people take on jobs.

There is also an error in the implied contrast between personal well-being on the one hand and morality or altruism on the other. What is part of my flourishing may also be part of other people's. The fulfillment I get from teaching children also helps them to thrive. Many of the worthwhile activities I may choose to engage in are, like teaching, collaborative ones. The benefits that accrue from my participation in them—not only attaining their palpable goals (e.g., pupils' learning), but also working with others with admirable or attractive personal qualities—are not my benefits alone, in some atomic way, but are benefits shared with collaborators (MacIntyre, 1981, Chapter 14). In doing well what the work requires of me, I am directly helping them, too, to lead a fulfilling life.

In close personal relationships, a line between what is good for me and what is good for the other is especially hard to draw. When acting altruistically for my friend, my lover, my child, I am—in fact, but not in intention—promoting my own well-being. Where morality comes more centrally into the picture, in cases, for example, of helping the afflicted or rectifying an injustice, again there need be no opposition with one's own good. These are equally worthwhile activities, and can be carried out as wholeheartedly and successfully, as reading poetry or playing with one's children.

What is the educational upshot of all this? It is that in equipping children for a flourishing personal life, we are not *ipso facto* turning them into people who think first of Number One, who put their own interests ahead of others'. We are bringing them, on the contrary, to see that what is good for one person is not hermetically sealed off from what is good for another, and that in the worthwhile pursuits and personal bonds that make up a fulfilled life, these goods overlap and interpenetrate at point after point.

It is especially odd for a critic to suggest that educators should not aim at furthering pupils' well-being, but should rather be immersing them in curricular subject-matter, preferably for its own sake. For immersion of this kind—provided the curriculum activities are suitable—is, as we saw earlier, a large part of *what it is* to educate for well-being.

## Education and success

This is a convenient point at which to turn the spotlight on to education and success. There is an irony in one version of the idea that schools should be getting pupils to enjoy learning for its own sake. This is where it is well known that the more a secondary student gets caught up in the delights of science or Latin, the better her chances of doing well in public examinations, getting to university, and landing a well-paid and well-regarded job. Intrinsic interest in learning is *extrinsically* valuable here as a means to a successful life.

A successful life, that is, as conventionally understood. Personal well-being, at least on version [iv], requires one's life to be successful, but in a different sense. It is hard to uncouple the conventional sense from the fact that, in a society with limited resources, if there are winners, there are also losers. Schooling has long been a device for winnowing out those on the road to success from the less fortunate. One ancient root of this in Protestant countries may be the association between overcoming ignorance and putting oneself in the best position to achieve salvation. Has the prospect of privileged happiness in this life rather than the next become a secular motivator as compelling as its religious predecessor?

Version [iv]'s linkage of education and success is less divisive. There is no reason in principle why *everyone*, barring ill-luck, should not live a life full of absorbing worthwhile activities and relationships in which they successfully engage. Schools could contribute to this ideal by giving the overall well-being of each pupil equal weight, and giving up their role as handmaidens of a divided society.

Many of the goods favored in society as it is, are, from the point of view of version [iv], dubious. Much energy is spent in pursuit of so-called "positional goods," that is, things valued because only some can possess them, like, in some cases, wealth, luxury goods, or celebrity. The dubiousness lies in the fact that possessing these goods is no guarantee of the kind of fulfillment found in version [iv]. One can be rich or famous and have disastrous relationships with others, or flit from pleasure to pleasure without ever getting drawn into anything worthwhile.

Interestingly, if we go back from [iv] to [iii], there is no reason, in that account of well-being, why the pursuit and enjoyment of positional goods should raise any doubts. Suppose what a person most wants, having reflected on alternatives, is to have wealth she can flaunt, or to make it as a household name; and suppose she succeeds in her ambition: according to [iii], this must be good for her. We have already seen good reason to abandon [iii]. I suspect, though, that many educational institutions implicitly follow it, perhaps on grounds of neutrality: it is outside their proper remit, they believe, to steer pupils towards or away from any preferred life-ideal, provided, as always, that it is not harming others.

Even if we take the more stringent attitude towards positional goods implied in [iv], this is not to deny that wealth and fame have *some* connection, and perhaps an unavoidable connection, with well-being. In more modest forms than those associated with positional goods, they are both basic requirements of it. We need a certain amount of material prosperity in order to flourish. Just how much it is reasonable for us each to have is a question that will become increasingly salient over the next decades, in the light of threats to world resources.

Fame is inflated recognition. We each of us need recognition as part of our flourishing. We expect our friends and colleagues, our teachers and our students, to respect us, to value us for what we are and what we can contribute; and we treat them in the same way ourselves. Virtually all of us are appreciated in this way in small circles of acquaintance; others' virtues and achievements are known more broadly. But none of us need the millions-wide recognition given to media stars and other celebrities. Given their popularity in schoolchildren's pictures of the best life, the place of wealth and celebrity in this could and should be a discussion topic in schools.

## Life-planning

Some people plan out their lives in some detail. They know they want to live abroad for a few years, then become a travel writer, marry, and have a family. Others let themselves be more directed by circumstances. Some philosophers have taken life-planning to be a necessary part of personal well-being (Rawls, 1971, Chapter 7); others (Williams, 1981, p. 35) have questioned this.

The latter appear to be on firmer ground, at least if the weight is on wholeheartedness of engagement rather than conventional notions of success; for taking life as it comes can be—for some people, by no means all—the path to fulfillment. Schools often seem to be biased towards the life-planning model, not only in their explicitly vocational education, but also in the feeling they create in students, as they move upwards through the exam structure, that they are on the first rungs of a ladder that will continue long into their adulthood. Those who cannot or don't want to climb the ladder may well be seen as failures. Like schools' attachment, in some cases, to comprehensive knowledge and to a conventional notion of success in life, the idea of vocation, especially where this is seen as realizing one's innate gifts or talents, seems to have now-forgotten religious roots. Whatever the truth on this matter, schools would do well to make discussions of the pros and cons of life-planning more prominent in their work. The education system as a whole could also consider tilting its energies and resources more towards responding to a passion for learning, whenever it happens to occur.

## Education and work

Talk of vocation leads us neatly into the wider topic of the place of work in well-being and the implications of this for education. Work, characterized most generally, is activity that leads to some end-product. It includes paid employment as well as non-paid work like getting meals ready and writing letters. Many kinds of work—teaching, for instance, making a garden pond, engineering, painting watercolors—can feature among the worthwhile activities that an autonomous person might choose wholeheartedly to engage in, on a par with non-work activities like strolling through the countryside, chatting with friends, listening to music. Call this kind of work "autonomous"; and work which would not be chosen in this way "heteronomous." Examples of the latter might be: picking cotton on a slave plantation; working long hours on a supermarket till. From the perspective of enabling as many people as possible to lead a fulfilling life, there is good reason to increase the availability of autonomous work and decrease the amount of heteronomous work, not least by reducing individuals' working hours.

What place does work have in education for well-being (White, 2005, Chapter 11)? As schools are now, for all but the youngest children, and increasingly so for them, they are mainly places where work goes on throughout the day and spills over, as homework, into the evening. Much of this work is heteronomous. Pupils have not chosen, but are obliged to do it. In some cases the work they have to do becomes a fascination, and is transmuted into the autonomous activity.

Is the amount of heteronomous work that schools require justifiable, given their role in nurturing well-being? There is an underlying cultural factor at work here. The radical Protestant insistence on a life of hard work as a religious obligation has withered since its heyday in Victorian times, but its secularized shadow still lies long across our schools. But should we see the school as a site primarily of work, or of learning? The two do not necessarily go together. Children, like the rest of us, can acquire knowledge about their world, and develop desirable dispositions, through non-work activities, sometimes guided, sometimes not, like conversation, reading books, watching films, looking at things going on around them, playing with toys. Conversely, they can spend time on schoolwork—on mechanical exercises in arithmetic, or painting pictures, for instance—and learn nothing. If school is for learning, should non-work activities have higher priority? For obvious reasons, work must always be salient; but should the balance tip away from the heteronomous sort, and towards the autonomous? If so, does this speak for more student choice of subjects studied? Or is comprehensive learning across the board of such high value as to justify insisting that learners study everything, whether they like it or not?

# CONCLUSION

There is much more to say about schools' aims and practices (Marples, 1999). Equipping pupils for a flourishing life is not their only valid purpose (Brighouse, 2006). Schools have responsibilities to society as a whole, perhaps indeed to the world as a whole, not just to individuals. Education has moral, civic, and economic aims as well as personal ones. While this is unchallengeable, there are two points that must be made about it. First, these trans-individual aims cannot trump the promotion of personal fulfillment. If any of them are such that any individual's well-being is sacrificed to their pursuit, we move beyond the frontiers of a liberal-democratic society into an authoritarian one. Trans-individual aims must be consonant with the aim of well-being for all.

Fortunately—and this brings us to the second point—there are ways of bringing them into line with each other. As we have seen, the concern for others that is at the basis of morality is not at odds with one's own well-being. Neither, *a fortiori*, is its civic dimension: work for the community, local, national or global, is one source of personal fulfillment. Economically, there is still much more to do in making everyone's paid work a contribution to, rather than a detraction from, their well-being; in a country like Britain, we have come a long way from the harshnesses of the nineteenth century, but further reduction of working hours, more flexible arrangements, and greater worker involvement in the running of enterprises, are still desirable. Economically, too, with mounting evidence that, beyond a certain point, reported levels of well-being do not increase with increased real income per head (Layard, 2005, Chapter 3), the easy assumption that economic growth is a good thing is now facing serious challenge. A cultural shift from the desire-satisfaction notion of well-being in [iii] to the more restrictive account in [iv] should help to slow down the incessant drive for more and more goods, including positional goods, and turn our energies towards what really makes our lives go well.

Twenty-first century schools are now becoming more responsive to the demands of well-being, at some cost to their traditional confinement to academic goals. So-called "happiness lessons" are one sign of this (Suissa, 2008). As this handbook entry has made clear, however, well-being is not a curriculum item that can be totally slotted into a series of 50-minute lessons, despite the contribution these may make. Care for the child's well-being has to pervade the whole *raison d'être* of the school (White, 2011).—Not only this, but also the way we think about the education system as a whole.

## REFERENCES

Brighouse, H. (2006). *On education*. London, UK: Routledge.

Comenius, J. (1907). *The great didactic*. (M. W. Keatinge, Trans.). London, UK: Adam and Charles Black.

Department for Children, Schools and Families (2008). *Schools' role in promoting pupil well-being*. London, UK: Department for Education.

Department for Children, Schools and Families/Qualifications and Curriculum Authority (2007). *The National Curriculum Statutory requirements for key stages 3 and 4*. London: HMSO.

Griffin, J. (1986). *Well-being*. Oxford, UK: Clarendon Press.

Layard, R. (2005). *Happiness: lessons from a new science*. London, UK: Allen Lane.

MacIntyre, A. (1981). *After virtue*. London, UK: Duckworth.

Marples, R. (Ed.). (1999). *The aims of education*. London, UK: Routledge.

Mill, J. S. (1861). *Utilitarianism, liberty and representative government*. London, UK: Everyman.

Peters, R. S. (1966). *Ethics and education*. London, UK: Allen and Unwin.

Rawls, J. (1971). *A theory of justice*. Oxford, UK: Clarendon Press.

Raz, J. (1986). *The morality of freedom*. Oxford, UK: Clarendon Press.

Raz, J. (1994). *Ethics in the public domain*. Oxford, UK: Clarendon Press.

Raz, J. (1999). *Engaging reason*. Oxford, UK: Oxford University Press.

Raz, J. (2003). *The practice of value*. Oxford, UK: Clarendon Press.

Suissa, J. (2008). Lessons from a new science? On teaching happiness in schools. *Journal of Philosophy of Education, 42*, 575–590.

Sumner, L.W. (1996). *Welfare, happiness and ethics*. Oxford, UK: Clarendon Press.

White, J. (2005). *The curriculum and the child*. London, UK: Routledge.

White, J. (2007). Wellbeing and education: issues of culture and authority. *Journal of Philosophy of Education, 41*(1), 17–28.

White, J. (2011). *Exploring well-being in schools: a guide to making children's lives more fulfilling*. London, UK: Routledge.

Williams, B. (1981). *Moral luck*. Cambridge, UK: Cambridge University Press.

# CHAPTER 42

# SHOULD EDUCATION HAVE HAPPINESS LESSONS?

## NASH POPOVIC

University of East London, UK

> The principal problem is no longer the fight with the adversities of nature but the difficulty of understanding ourselves if we want to survive.
>
> (Eugene Wigner)

THIS chapter is an attempt to tackle head-on this fundamental but certainly controversial question. There is no shortage of those who would passionately argue for and against "happiness lessons." Despite some vocal opponents (Craig, 2009; Ecclestone & Hayes, 2008; Suissa, 2008) this type of program is proliferating in British schools and, it seems, with a good reason. If you ask parents and young people what they want from life, the most frequent answer would be "to be happy" (see, e.g., Snyder, 2010). So, should not education contribute, in fact, should it not be a prerogative of education to help children achieve what really matters to them and to their parents? This seems to make sense, but there is something odd about teaching happiness. Imagine that we have a machine or vaccine that can make children permanently happy. Would we want to use it? The answer is probably no. Even if such a vaccine or machine could induce lasting good feelings, this would impoverish human experience. Perhaps, as somebody puts it, happiness is "not a destination to arrive at, but the way of traveling."

For this and other reasons happiness is nowadays often replaced with the term "well-being." This does not solve all the problems, though. Most mainstream subjects are fairly well defined: for example, science or math classes even in such diverse countries as Britain and Iran are recognizably similar. A very different picture emerges when we talk about well-being. Even within a small group, well-being may mean different things for different students (Craig, 2009). Some people are only happy when in company; others need some time on their own. For some, well-being requires peace of mind, for others, the excitement of risk taking. A balance between leisure, work, and family life is important for well-being, but where that balance lies differs from person to person. In other words, well-being may legitimately have very different meaning for different people, and if we try to impose a universal definition, we are in a danger of doing Procrustean psychology with young people.

So, shall we abandon lessons on happiness or well-being? Far from it. We just need to be clear what such lessons should be about. Rather than teaching young people how to be happy, they can be equipped with skills and ways of understanding how to make their own autonomous choices and put them into practice. To make a somewhat crude analogy, learning to drive is about learning to drive well, safely, and with consideration for other drivers. It is not about a destination. No driving instructor is concerned with where you will drive once you learn how to do it. The point is to learn to drive well enough so that you can go anywhere you want.

If this point is taken—namely that we should teach children how to navigate through their lives rather than where to arrive, such lessons may appear hugely relevant for a number of reasons that will be discussed in this chapter. To emphasize the process, this type of education will be called Personal Development Education (PDE).

There is a striking imbalance in present education between the amount of time, resources, and attention dedicated to the study of the world on the one hand, and to the areas that constitute personal life and experience on the other. Young people have opportunities to learn about mathematics, literature, geography, physics, etc., but little chance to learn about themselves and the ways they can experience and relate to their environment. In the 14 volumes (over 8000 pages) of the *International Educational Encyclopaedia*, for example, there is not a single entry on either personal or social education, and there are only four pages on moral education. Such an attitude may have served well the purpose of education in the past, but its inadequacy in the modern world is becoming increasingly apparent.

There is a profound awareness that we are living in a time of rapid and dramatic changes (Ingelhart, 1977, 1990). Such "transition periods" have happened many times in history, but this one stands out for its intensity and rapidity. According to Giddens, "one of the most obvious characteristics separating the modern era from any other period preceding it is modernity's extreme dynamism" (1991, p. 16). Some of these changes are summarized by The Citizenship Foundation as "the increasingly complex nature of our society, the greater cultural diversity and the apparent loss of a value consensus, combined with the collapse of traditional support mechanisms such as extended families" (as cited in Qualifications and Curriculum Authority, 1998, p. 17). Although such transition periods are an important factor in the development of a society, they also bring feelings of increased responsibility, insecurity, anxiety and, most of all, the need for self-reliance, which is a challenge for many individuals, groups or indeed whole societies.

Social structures based on tradition, religion, family, and culture that once provided support, guidance, and a reference point for most people seem no longer sufficient to assist personal development in the complex society in which we live:

> We live in a pluralistic society in an age of rapid social and technological change. The tradition, customs and practices—and the assumptions, attitudes and institutions which stand behind them—of the various communities which make up our society are frequently called into question. (Inner London Education Authority, 1987, p.5)

On the other hand, working parents often do not have enough time, knowledge, or experience (and sometimes energy and motivation) to assist the personal development of their offspring adequately. At the Cornell University symposium in 1993, Kate Bronfenbrenner stated:

> In the absence of good support systems, external stresses have become so great that even strong families are falling apart. The hecticness, instability and inconsistency of daily family life are rampant in all segments of our society; including the well-educated and well-to-do. (1993, as cited in Goleman, 1995, p. 234)

We have to rely on ourselves more than ever. As the French historian Fernand Braudel put it, we live in a period that "breaks the old cycles and the traditional customs of man" (1980, p. 215). In such a situation, people can be easily influenced by forces that do not have their well being as a priority (e.g., media) or choose solutions that provide short-term security and relief even if they are destructive and self-defeating in the long run. Alcohol and drug abuse, delinquency, extremism and violence are on the increase, especially among adolescents (Green et al., 2004).

Not surprisingly, school counselors are more and more in demand, but as Professor van Deurzen-Smith suggests, "Although it is a good thing that counselors are here to help those who have got lost on the way, it would be much better if we could get to a position from where prevention and education were of the order of the day rather than crisis intervention and cure." (1994, pp. 20–21). It seems that there is an urgent and ever-increasing need for an approach that will be able to reach the majority of young people and be of a preventive and educational rather than remedial nature.

Introducing an education which expands theoretical, reflective, and practical knowledge of ourselves will be beneficial not only for individuals but for society in general. People simply need a better understanding of themselves in order to deal with the challenges of modern life. Hopson & Scally's conclusion still seems relevant:

> . . . we are living through a period of transition—and the demands on young people and adults will be similar. People will need to be adaptable, flexible, and more personally competent than at any other time in our history. (1981, p. 6)

Education focused on people themselves is no longer a luxury but a necessity.

Admittedly, this is not something terribly new. Since the late 1960s, it has been recognized that post-industrial society requires a new educational agenda. The interest in personal education among officials, teachers, parents, and students has been steadily increasing. Her Majesty's Inspectorate (HMI; 1979, p. 12) observes that "teachers generally acknowledge . . . the need to provide more personal education in the curriculum of all pupils." Elliott (1981, pp. 40–57) writes that for parents, "children's personal and social development at school is at least as important as their academic development." MacBeath (1988, p. 11) also acknowledges that parents wish to see more of personal education in schools. The *Human Behaviour Curriculum Project* survey concludes that "the pupils want a psychology that will teach them about themselves, about their emotions, relationships, personal power, consciousness, pain and depression" (Sprinthall, 1980, p. 346). HMI concludes "[t]he personal and social development of the pupils is one way of describing the central purpose of education." (1980, p. 206). The literature on Personal and Social Education (PSE) points in the same direction. Murray, for example, writes:

> More specific writing on PSE (Hargreaves et al., 1988; David 1983; Pring, 1984) also suggest that rapid and profound social changes most notably the erosion of traditional values,

breakdowns in family childrearing practices, and massive contraction in the youth labour market, render it ever more important for schools to intervene in the social processes defining the transition from adolescence to adulthood. (1998, p. 29)

In fact, very few would take a wholesale opposition to this type of education. The idea that schools should or could make a "surgical cut" and focus only on some aspects of their charges—such as developing their intellectual capacities—had its day. Nevertheless, the worthwhile British education initiative "Every Child Matters" should perhaps be accompanied with "The Whole Child Matters" to make this explicit.

A far more contentious issue though is how best to deliver such education. Broadly speaking there are three options: the so called "whole-school" approach, the cross-curricular approach, and discrete lessons. This chapter argues that all three are necessary and should complement each other.

## The Whole-school Approach

There are a number of educators (Hamblin, 1978; Marland, 1974; Pring, 1984) who believe that the best way to convey this type of education is not through a specific course but through the atmosphere and attitude of the whole school. It is known as the "caught, not taught" argument. Brown, for example, writes:

> There was a time when few schools put PSE on the timetable. They would have claimed that personal education arose out of relationships between pupils and the teacher, especially in extra-curricular activities, and that social education was achieved through the experience of schooling itself: learning to live with others, to share experience in sport, drama etc., to develop loyalty and a sense of pride and identity. (1995, p. 107)

There is no doubt that school atmosphere and teachers' attitudes are important factors for pupils' personal development. It should not be forgotten that "classroom atmosphere, the active mode of learning, relationships between teacher and pupil (i.e. authoritarian or non-authoritarian), and the strategies for involving pupils in deliberation and reflective learning" (Pring, 1984, p. 121) are factors that primarily depend on and should be a concern of overall school policy and every teacher irrespective of his or her subject. However, there are several reasons why the whole-school approach may not be sufficient.

*It is not comprehensive and systematic.* This is the biggest problem with relying only on this approach. It can help pupils to develop some social skills or increase their self-esteem, but this cannot be considered comprehensive personal development education. Although the atmosphere of the school and attitude of teachers can greatly affect the learning process, they do not in themselves provide systematic education. For example, a non-authoritarian atmosphere may facilitate personal development better than an authoritarian atmosphere. However, this will not necessarily touch on every aspect of pupils' lives. There is much to be learned about emotions, thinking, perception, relationships, decisions, etc. that can be of great practical value for students and that cannot be fully and systematically captured only from school atmosphere.

*It is difficult to organize and appraise.* Because it is blended with other aspects of school life it is hard to pinpoint its domain and easy to leave it to "spontaneous" processes. Aware of this, Hellwig warns:

> When schools attempt to take a major concept on board without working it through . . . the result is similar to playing a game without knowing the rules, or the object of the game. (1989, p. 9)

*It is rarely consistent and it can be biased.* Even if a school has an agreed policy, it is likely that different teachers will have different, sometimes contradictory, attitudes. Also, it would be too idealistic to expect teachers to care for every pupil equally. They naturally like some pupils more than others, and do not like some at all. Moreover, the behavior and attitudes of others are not always good examples, they are often inconsistent and people (including teachers) do not always care how their behavior and attitude influence others ("do what I say, not what I do" can be still heard in schools).

*It is limited.* This approach does not prepare students for situations out of and after school, where they will be exposed to different (often harsher) experiences. Furthermore, we should not overestimate the effect of observation and identification (many people spend hours watching football and yet very few play well). McNiff rightly comments that "teachers who assume that the children will 'learn by example' or 'pick it up as they go along' do their children a disservice" (1985, p. 27).

David summarizes the growing awareness of the insufficiency of this approach:

> The complexities of a changing society make it essential that schools attempt to develop all the inner resources of students, emotional as well as intellectual. This development cannot be achieved in an *ad hoc* manner, or by dependence on the ethos of the school alone. It requires constructive thinking and planning, and properly structured programmes. (1983, p. 9)

Despite its appeal, it does not seem that the whole-school approach on its own is enough for the whole-person education. This is not to say that the atmosphere and ethos of the school can be neglected. No personal education program can be effective if it goes against the tide of the school climate. If the whole school does not foster self-respect and mutual respect, open-mindedness and autonomy, trust and self-awareness, it is unlikely that a timetabled personal development education can achieve much. However, even the best "whole school approach" does not make the need for some time specifically designated for children' personal development obsolete.

## The Cross-curricular Approach

Some educators agree that this type of education should be taught, but only within other academic subjects. However, there are a number of objections to this view, too.

*There is not enough time.* It is unlikely that teachers will pay sufficient attention to personal education if it is at the expense of time designated for their own subjects. Preparation for exams will sooner or later have priority and take over. This concern is confirmed by the National Confederation of Parent-Teacher Associations (NCPTA, 1991) survey of 2051

Parent-Teachers Associations that shows that 64% of these do not consider that staff have adequate time to develop pastoral contact with pupils, and that this is one of the most important problems facing schools. More recently, 75% of respondents to OFSTED survey (2009) agreed or strongly agreed that a school can be reasonably held to account for its contribution to pupil well-being.

*It is haphazard, uncoordinated, and unorganized.* Pring vividly depicts a difficulty with having coherent personal education taught within other subjects:

> Presumably the English teacher introducing *Middlemarch*, the history teacher dealing with the social consequences of the civil War, the R. E. teacher explaining various religious ideals, the house tutor helping a pupil through some emotional difficulty, the P. E. teacher persuading the rugger team to grit their teeth in the face of fierce opposition—all would claim with justification to be contributing to the personal and social development of the pupils. How can one make coherent curriculum sense out of such a wide range of classroom activities, teaching objectives, sought-for skills, attitudes, habits, values? (1982, p. 136)

Yet, the personal and social development of children is far too important to be left to accidental and haphazard occurrences.

*Fragmentation, omissions, and duplications.* As Andrews points out "[t]he 10 national curriculum subjects do not represent the totality of human experience" (1990, p. 39). If we rely only on these subjects, some areas of personal education are missed completely, some are duplicated and most of them are dealt with in a fragmented way. MacBeath also highlights this problem:

> The add-in approach is limited because … [it is not] always easy to find a home within the traditional subject structure and existing expertise of teachers for many of the emerging issues. (1988, pp. 10–11)

*Nobody takes responsibility for it.* When the position is taken that PSE is the responsibility of *all* teachers, it is all too easy for PSE to become the responsibility of none.

*The focus is always somewhere else.* Curriculum subjects inevitably deal with personal education from their specific perspectives. And yet, as Mosher and Sprinthall rightly noticed "learning about Macbeth's emotions is not … systematically learning about one's own emotions" (1970, p. 915).

To conclude, it is true that all the subjects *contribute* to the personal and social development of pupils and students, but they do not provide comprehensive PDE. Murray points out that "[t]here is limited evidence of successful integration of PSE with National Curriculum subjects." (1998, p. 31). There are many areas that can be dealt with in a cross-curricular manner. But only timetabled PDE with clear boundaries can satisfy the necessary conditions for this type of work: comprehensiveness, structure and organization, high quality and equal status. It needs to be emphasized though, that this certainly does not imply exclusion of elements of personal education from whole school policy and other subjects. A CCOSS (1984, 3.9.37) report states:

> The function of a separate course in personal and social education is not to evacuate other subjects of the elements of personal and social education which they doubtless contain. Rather its function is to bring many aspects of personal and social education into a more coherent shape and to serve as an important linking device between the wide range of subjects followed by pupils.

Many schools nowadays already accept that they need to dedicate some time specifically to personal development of young people. However, there are number of concerns that need to be addressed. The following reservations about a systematic approach to this type of education are collected from the literature or informal and formal conversations with teachers, pupils, parents and other researchers.

## Some General Concerns About the Timetabled Personal Development Education

### Academic subjects will suffer

There is a concern that personal development education will take time from subjects that will be tested and reduce the results.

It is worthwhile considering that the "loss" of 1–2 hours a week may be well compensated by the gains that this education can bring. Academic achievement does not depend only on the amount of hours that students spend studying curriculum subjects and PDE can have a positive impact on it. We are all aware that many other factors contribute to success in this respect, such as self-discipline, dealing with anxiety, an ability to concentrate, motivation and interest—all topics of PDE, none of which are directly addressed within the existing subjects.

### Separate lessons could "ghettoize" personal and social education

One of the main objections to a specific program has been that it isolates personal and social education in the school curriculum. MacBeath, for example, is concerned that timetabled classes would be "releasing the ordinary classroom teacher from the responsibility for the personal education of her pupils" (1988, p. 107).

To address this concern, we need to make sure that PDE has a well-defined content which does not overlap with other subjects (and there is enough material for this) and make clear that it is nothing more and nothing less than *education*, not a substitute for care.

### Unqualified staff

Numerous studies (see, e.g., Quicke, 1986) show the inadequacy of teachers drawn from other subject disciplines. Lee is right to caution that "the combination of non-specialist teachers... and low-status work is not conducive to good teaching" (1982, p. 14). However, it is unrealistic to expect that we will have enough qualified teachers to run such programs soon, so we need to accept that the staff will be drawn from other subjects. Any program needs to take this into account and provide the best possible training to teachers. Moreover, the materials need to be designed in such a way so as not to undermine teachers' confidence and minimize the difference from other subjects in terms of its delivery. We also need to be clear that teachers are not expected to take the role of psychologists and psychotherapists or do anything beyond their role.

## Impracticability

Another widespread objection to these programs is that personal and social aspects are all-pervading, so they cannot be taught as a separate subject.

This does not hold water, though: some other subjects are also all-pervasive, but nobody objects to teaching them as separate subjects. David writes that this objection "does not preclude the need for specific provision in school any more than a global concept of 'language across the curriculum' obviates the need for the special work of the English and languages departments" (1983, p. 15). Having some time to focus specifically on personal and social aspects of life would certainly be just as worthwhile.

# Some Specific Concerns About the Practice

The following concerns are not related to these types of lessons in general, but to existing practice and need be taken seriously. Rather than ignoring them or making counter-arguments, they should be embraced as signposts that can help us modify and improve such education if we want it to be widely accepted.

## Personal education can undermine pupils

Askew criticizes personal education on the basis that it is apparently "a deficit model" (1995, p. 65), which assumes that young people lack some personal knowledge and skills.

To some extent the whole educational system is based on a "deficit model" and in this respect PDE is not different from other subjects. However, there is more to this objection. Askew uses the example of programs that aim to increase children's self-esteem, which clearly implies a deficit assumption that may well be counterproductive. However, if we move away from such end-goals to the process, as suggested at the beginning of this chapter, this can be avoided. The aim could be, rather than increasing self-esteem, to increase awareness about self-esteem and its effects, and the ability to exercise a certain level of self-control over it. PDE should never be considered a compensatory mechanism for the disadvantaged, but a part of education for all pupils.

## The individualistic position

There is a claim that we are so unique that it is impossible to develop a universally applicable PDE. Craig (2009) writes: "Human beings are complex. This is why a programmatic approach to this type of work is short-sighted. What is appropriate for one pupil may be different for another." One teacher has put it in this way: "How can you teach me about myself?"

In this postmodernist climate it is often forgotten that we are much more similar than different. We all have common basic faculties like thinking, feeling, communicating, deciding, doing, relating to others, etc., although we differ to what end and how we use them. Concentrating on universal aspects of these abilities will not restrict their expression in particular ways. In fact, if we pay attention to these "fundamentals" we will be in a better position to develop our individuality and originality. To use an example from a different field, in order to be a creative writer one needs to, first of all, master a grammar, syntax, etc. Without this, one is not original but illiterate. Again, if the objective of PDE is to help pupils to know better and be more in charge of themselves, rather than teaching them what they should be, it should be compatible with respect for individual differences.

## Inadequacy

This objection is rarely spelt out, but it is often behind skepticism about personal education. It may be summarized in this way: we do not know enough how human beings operate; scientific detachment and objectivity are not always applicable, so there cannot be an authority in this field.

There are two responses to this view: firstly, the rapid development of human science and other disciplines in recent years (e.g., positive psychology) have provided us with useful knowledge that can be, and should be imparted to pupils and students. Secondly, PDE does not need to be authoritative and "all-knowing" in order to be effective. Encouraging reflection and discussion can be beneficial and sufficient if we are not trying to impose a particular trajectory upon students.

## Personal education could be intrusive

A number of people from different walks of life are concerned that this type of education could intrude upon their private lives. One student commented "My well-being is my own businesses." The author of this chapter has a lot of sympathy with this view; however, the problem is that the lives of young people are already affected by many other agencies that have mainly instrumental interest in them (TV and other media, commercial industry, some political and religious groups, peer groups, etc.). Moreover, as with any other self-education, personal development left to "spontaneous" process is usually sporadic, patchy, and disorganized. The majority, left to themselves, just inertly get by, or adopt a "philosophy" from others around them, which if not thought through, is inflexible and unproductive, especially in new situations. So, there is no doubt that this type of education can be useful, but special attention should be paid to avoid infringing on privacy of individuals. There is much to be learned without making students "open up." We should always bear in mind that PDE should be about education, never to be confused with group therapy or something similar.

## Fear of indoctrination

There is a fear that a systematic PDE might become an instrument of social control that could be counterproductive for individual development and lead to conformity (see Craig, 2009).

It is true that education has been used too often to indoctrinate students. Nevertheless, nowadays, in liberal societies, the danger of indoctrination within mainstream education is somewhat exaggerated. Pupils and students simply do not "buy" it. This does not mean that we can be lenient on this issue. On the contrary, we have to insure that every trace of indoctrination is rigorously eradicated if we want PDE to be accepted. The fact that attempts at covert indoctrination are still present even among some liberal educators might be one of the reasons why well-being or happiness programs have not achieved greater popularity among pupils.

For example, Craig criticizes the flagship British program SEAL (Social and Emotional Aspects of Learning) for starting from certain assumptions, such as that it is good to express one's emotions. She is right to do so. Expressing emotions may be good is some situations and inappropriate in others. Reticence and suppression may sometimes be a better response. Rather than starting from such assumptions, we can teach young people about these and other possible ways to respond emotionally and thus help them increase their choice and control over these responses. So, as in other cases, this concern can be met too, if we focus on the process rather than a pre-set goal.

## The values problem

Alexander points out that "the area is acknowledged to be central yet value-saturated. The solution to this dilemma is usually to dodge it" (1984, p. 54).

No education, even in natural science, is completely value-free. PDE too cannot be value-free, but it does not need to be more value-burdened than other subjects. The fact that it concentrates (among other things) on values themselves does not mean that it must be selling a *particular* set of values beyond those already accepted as a part of school ethos (e.g., respecting and listening to each other). This issue again depends on how the aim and purpose of this type of education are defined. If we focus on the personal development of students (the process), rather than a predefined destination (e.g., well-being or happiness as conceived by an authority), it does not need to be value-loaded.

## Low status and assessment

The unfortunate reality is that subjects that are not tested acquire a lower status among teachers and pupils than those that are tested. This may be one of the main reasons why the SEAL initiative made an attempt to introduce an assessment of students. This aspect of SEAL has been probably criticized more than any other. Learning outcomes such as "I know how to express my feelings appropriately" (DfES, 2005, 2007) are indeed something that make many people uneasy. However, there is perhaps a way to avoid the Scylla of the low status and the Charybdis of the tests by being creative with the assessment. Here is one example: personal development modules based on Personal Synthesis Program (Popovic, 2005) have been run at the University of East London for a number of years now, gaining a considerable popularity among students. However, rather than having an exam, students are required to compile their personal development portfolio, which consists of some theory, reflections, and practical steps taken to assist their personal development. The assignment does not require self-disclosure or any personal revelations. Moreover, the assessment is not based on predefined answers and outcomes, but on an evidence of progress as defined by students themselves. Judging by students' feedback, many have found this assignment beneficial beyond getting their grades. Such an assessment that avoids intrusion and can covert indoctrination can be easily adapted for use in secondary schools.

In conclusion, it should be acknowledged that concerns regarding this type of lessons are legitimate and need to be taken seriously, but we should not throw out the baby with the bathwater. We can see that many objections can be met. However, in order to do so we need to re-examine our assumptions, aims and practices, the most important of which is shifting focus from an end goal to the process. Focusing on an end goal would go against the grain of liberal education as a whole (Suissa, 2008). When we teach literacy and numeracy we do not have an end goal in mind. We are not concerned whether the pupils will use their knowledge or skills to write books or "cook the books." We simply believe that every child has right to learn to read, write, and count. The same should apply to PDE. Young people have right to learn how to be in charge of their own lives, how to be in the driving seat, without imposing on them where they should drive. Perhaps the argument in this chapter can be summarized in the following way: the specific time designed for pupils and students' personal development can be immensely beneficial as long as it is about happiness of pursuit rather than the pursuit of happiness.

## REFERENCES

Alexander, R. (1984). *Primary teaching*. London, UK: Holt, Rinehart and Winston.
Andrews, D. (1990, May 15). Finding the thread. *Times Educational Supplement*, *3840*, 32.
Askew, S. (1995). Self-esteem as a goal of self-empowerment: critical appraisal. In Askew, S. and Carnell, E. (Eds.), *Developing the personal-social curricula*. Bristol, UK: Avec Designs.
Braudel, F. (1980). *On history*. London, UK: Weidenfeld and Nicolson.
Brown, C. (1995). PSE: timetable ghetto or whole-school practice. In Askew, S. and Carnell, E. (Eds.), *Developing the personal-social curricula*. Bristol, UK: Avec Designs.
CCOSS. (1984). *Improving secondary schools*. London, UK: Inner London Education Authority.
Craig, C. (2009). *The curious case of the tail wagging the dog: well-being in schools*. Retrieved from http://www.centreforconfidence.co.uk/projects.php?p=cGlkPTU2JmlkPTYzMw
David, K. (1983). *Personal and social education in secondary schools*. York, UK: Longman.
Department for Education and Skills (2005). *Primary national strategy: Excellence and enjoyment: Social and emotional aspects of learning*. London, UK: DfES Publications.
Department for Education and Skills (2007). *Social and emotional aspects of learning for secondary schools (SEAL)*. London, UK: DfES Publications.
Deurzen-Smith, E. van (1994). *Can counselling help?* Durham, UK: School of Education, University of Durham.
Ecclestone, K., & Hayes, D. (2008). *The dangerous rise of therapeutic education*. London, UK: Routledge.
Elliott, J. (1981). How do parents choose schools. In Elliott, J. (Ed.), *School accountability*. London, UK: Grant McIntyre.
Giddens, A. (1991). *Modernity and self-Identity*. Cambridge: Polity Press.
Goleman, D. (1995). *Emotional intelligence: Why it can matter more than IQ*. New York, NY: Bantam Books.
Green, H., McGinnity, A., Meltzer, H., Ford, T., & Goodman, R. (2004). *Mental health of children and young people in Great Britain*. Crown Copyright. Basingstoke, UK: Palgrave Macmillan.
Hamblin, D. (1978). *The teacher and pastoral care*. Oxford, UK: Basil Blackwell.
Hargreaves, A., Baglin, E., Henderson, P., Leeson, P., & Tossell, T. (1988). *Personal and Social Education: choices and challenges*. Oxford, UK: Blackwell.
Hellwig, E. (1989). Pastoral care for the 1990s and beyond: a visitor viewpoint. *Pastoral Care in Education*, *7*(1), 6–13.

Her Majesty's Inspectorate. (1979). *Aspects of secondary education in England.* London, UK: HMSO.
Her Majesty's Inspectorate. (1980). *A view of the curriculum.* London, UK: HMSO.
Hopson, B., & Scally, M. (1981). *Lifeskills teaching.* London, UK: McGraw-Hill.
Inner London Education Authority. (1987). *The teaching of controversial issues in schools.* London, UK: Inner London Education Authority.
Inglehart, R. (1977). *The silent revolution.* Princeton, NJ: Princeton University Press.
Inglehart, R. (1990). *Culture shift in advanced industrial society.* Princeton, NJ: Princeton University Press.
Lee, R. (1982). *Beyond coping.* York, UK: Longman.
MacBeath, J. (1988). *Personal and social education.* Edinburgh, UK: Scottish Academic Press.
Marland, M. (1974). *Pastoral care.* London, UK: Heinemann Educational Books.
McNiff, J. (1985). *Personal and social education: A teachers' handbook.* Cambridge, UK: CRAC/Hobsons Press.
Mosher, R. L., & Sprinthall, N. (1970). Psychological education in secondary schools: a program to promote individual and human development. *American Psychologist, 25*(10), 911–924.
Murray, L. (1998). Research onto the social purposes of schooling: Personal and Social Education in secondary schools in England and Wales. *Pastoral Care in Education, 16*(3), 28–35.
NCPTA (1991). *The state of schools in England and Wales.* Gravesend: NCPTA.
OFSTED (2009) *Indicators of a school's contribution to well-being*, Retrieved from http://www.ofsted.gov.uk/Ofsted-home/Publications-and-research/Browse-all-by/Documents-by-type/Consultations/Indicators-of-a-school-s-contribution-to-well-being2.
Popovic, N. (2005). *Personal synthesis.* London, UK: PWBC.
Pring, R. (1982). Personal and Social Education. In Ward L. O. (Ed.), *The ethical dimension of the school curriculum.* Swansea, UK: Pineridge.
Pring, R. (1984). *Personal and social education in the curriculum.* London, UK: Hodder and Stoughton.
Qualifications and Curriculum Authority. (1998). *Education for citizenship and the teaching of democracy in schools.* London, UK: Qualifications and Curriculum Authority.
Quicke, J. (1986). Personal and Social Education: a triangulated evaluation of an innovation. *Educational Review, 38*(3), 217–228.
Snyder, T. (2010). *What parents want for their children.* Retrieved from http://www.lifemodification.com/personal-improvement/well-being/what-parents-want-for-their-children/.
Sprinthall, N. (1980). Psychology for secondary schools: the saber-tooth curriculum revisited. *American Psychologist, 35*(4), 335–347.
Suissa, J. (2008). Lessons from a new science? On teaching happiness in schools. *Journal of Philosophy of Education, 42*(3–4), 574–590.
Wigner, E. (1967). *Symmetries and reflections.* Bloomington, IN: Indiana University Press.

# CHAPTER 43

# WELL-BEING AND RESILIENCE IN EDUCATION

TONI NOBLE[1] AND HELEN McGRATH[2]

[1]Australian Catholic University, Australia; [2]Deakin University, Australia

## INTRODUCTION

For all of us, life is an exciting and often unpredictable journey that provides joys, satisfactions, and highlights, but also, along the way, some difficulties, challenges, disappointments, and hard times. Through successfully meeting life's challenges we develop a sense of well-being and become more resilient. This chapter provides an overview of the emergence of the constructs of student well-being and resilience in education, offers a definition of student well-being to inform educational initiatives, and identifies evidence-informed guidelines for developing and implementing social and emotional learning programs in schools that have the potential to enhance student well-being and resilience.

Young people have always needed coping skills to deal with life's challenges, but there is an ever-increasing body of evidence from different disciplines that indicates that today's youth are less well equipped and less well situated than previous generations to effectively cope with the challenges, disappointments, and adverse circumstances that inevitably occur in most people's life journey. The challenges they face are different and the conditions in which they have been raised have changed significantly compared to previous generations (Weissberg, Walberg, O'Brien, & Kuster, 2003).

Some of the changes over the last 50 years that present significant challenges to the well-being of young people today include higher levels of family break-up, family relocation, and blended families; more pressure to complete higher levels of education; cybersafety issues; easier access to drugs; less time with parents and more family stress from increases in dual-career families; more loneliness and isolation as a result of being part of smaller families; and the experience of less connection or sense of belonging to their local community.

Previous generations born and raised in the late nineteenth century and the first half of the twentieth century also faced challenges, but different kinds of challenges. They often struggled to survive poverty, economic recessions, and wars. Yet they often belonged to families that were usually part of a close-knit and supportive community, and were comforted during difficult times by their strong commitment to their country, their family, and their religious community. Their childhood experiences promoted the core values of loyalty, honor, and duty. These "World War" parents taught their children to expect that life could be difficult as it had been for them. They modeled stoicism and taught their children the skills and attitudes that would help them to become independent and be able to survive. Their childhood experiences appear to have led to parenting for resilience for their children, the so-called "baby boomers" born between 1946 and 1965 (McKay, 1997).

However, unlike their parents, the baby boomers were raised in relatively prosperous times in a world that was expected to improve. When they became parents there was increasingly easy access to reliable birth control that resulted in smaller families and in most children being "wanted" rather than contributing to the family economic burden. Unlike their parents they did not have to struggle to survive and were much better educated. The baby boomers' parenting was strongly influenced by the self-esteem movement of the 1970s/1980s and focused on providing their children with opportunities for "personal growth," "self-expression," and "being oneself." The baby boomers' change in parenting style can also be considered to be a negative reaction to their parents' parenting style that focused on duty, conformity, and placing the needs of the community above the needs of the individual (Twenge, 2007).

Now the children of baby boomers are becoming or have become parents. The previous generation's "parenting for self-esteem" appears to be morphing into "parenting for safety and happiness," still encompassing a focus on the development of self-esteem but with an additional emphasis on minimizing risks or threats to their children's safety. New terms such as "helicopter" parents (who hover over their children) and "cotton-wool" children (who are not allowed to be "unhappy" or take any risks) have emerged. Current parents are more likely to drive their child to school rather than let them walk, insist they only play on plastic play equipment, and enroll them at a later age in school so that they will not be disadvantaged.

Intergenerational research across three generations compares the results of personality tests, self-esteem, and other measures given to people under 30 years of age (Twenge, 2007). The results indicate that the children of the baby boomers (those born after 1970) appear to be more narcissistic. A narcissistic approach to life has the potential to adversely affect long-term relationships, reduce empathy and honesty, decrease impulse control, and increase aggressive responses, especially in response to criticism or perceived lack of respect (LaPorta, 2009; Twenge & Campbell, 2009). These researchers suggest that young people's current enthusiastic participation in social networking sites, Twitter, and YouTube reflects their desire to be the focus of attention.

Since the 1960s this intergenerational research comparison shows a 50% increase in people under 30 having an "external" locus of control belief system, i.e., today's young people are less likely to believe they are in control of their own lives and they think their lives are more determined by others or by "fate" (Twenge, Zhang, & Im, 2004). This type of thinking has been shown to contribute to depression and anxiety (Gillham & Reivich, 2004; Seligman, 1998), a tendency to become stressed easily, and lower levels of effort and lower educational attainment (Dweck, 2006). Current studies of the mental health of young people suggest that an increasing number of them suffer from anxiety, depression, and disorders related to substance abuse. Being depressed makes it even more difficult for some young people to cope with the normal setbacks, hardships, and difficulties in life. The World Health Organization (WHO) predicts that depression will be the world's leading cause of disability by 2020 and is also expected to be the second most important determinant of the burden of human disease in the world (Andrews, Szabó, & Burns, 2001).

Twenge's (2007) research also indicates that today's young people may be lonelier and more isolated than those in previous generations. This generation will have to try and cope alone with the collapse of comfortable opportunities to meet people and date, later marriage and a high divorce rate, shared custody and step-parenting, and more frequent geographical relocations as a result of work and study demands.

> One of the strangest things about modern life is the expectation that we [i.e. those of us born after 1970] will stand alone, negotiating breakups, moves, divorces, and all manner of heartbreak that previous generations were careful to avoid. This may be the key to the low rate of depression among older generations: despite all the deprivation and war they experienced, they could always count on each other. (Twenge, 2009, p. 11)

# The Emergence of Student Well-being and Resilience

## The self-esteem movement

The social and emotional lives of school-aged young people became a focus in education in the 1970s with the emergence of the self-esteem movement. This movement was derived from the core principles of humanistic psychology. From the 1970s, the self-esteem movement began to impact on teachers' practices in the classroom and parents' childrearing practices. Classroom self-esteem programs typically focused on the importance of helping children gain a sense of achievement in a relatively non-competitive and failure-free learning environment and engage in self-expression. Children were encouraged by both teachers and parents to see themselves as special and unique. "Low self-esteem" was promoted as an explanation for many social "ills" such as juvenile crime, out-of-wedlock pregnancy, substance abuse, and low academic achievement. Yet Twenge (2009) documents increases in anxiety amongst young people since the 1970s that she links with systematic techniques used in schools to "boost" self-esteem.

Concern about the self-esteem movement's focus on "feeling good" and individualism is also shared by Martin Seligman (2007b), a founder of the positive psychology movement. He claims that the movement has probably contributed to the increase in depression in young people.

> Armies of . . . teachers, along with . . . parents, are straining to bolster children's self esteem. That sounds innocuous enough, but the way they do it often erodes children's sense of worth. By emphasizing how a child feels, at the expense of what the child does—mastery, persistence, overcoming frustration and boredom and meeting a challenge—parents and teachers are making this generation of children more vulnerable to depression. (Seligman, 2007b, p.27)

Seligman argues that if children are not allowed to fail or be disappointed with themselves and if they receive less-than-genuine praise, then they are deprived of opportunities to develop frustration tolerance and persistence and are less motivated to work harder. He also argued that if people believe that they are special and unique individuals who are *entitled* to happiness, they find it more difficult to perceive themselves as part of a larger community. They are less likely to be able to put things in perspective and more likely to believe that what happens to *them* is the only thing that matters. This can result in their becoming overwhelmed and unable to cope with the setbacks and disappointments that are a normal part of most people's lives. It also means they will be less motivated to helping others and contributing to a sense of community.

A review of the self-esteem literature has shown that it is difficult to find strong evidence that developing young people's self-esteem makes significant differences to student academic achievement, their mental health, or societal problems (e.g., Baumeister et al., 2003; Emler, 2003; Kahne, 1996). Baumeister was a former proponent of the self-esteem movement but concluded from the results of his own studies and his analysis of earlier studies that the assumption that artificially enhancing self-esteem would reduce young people's problems and increase their achievement was false. Despite these findings the self-esteem movement continued for many years and is only now beginning to fade.

> While the self-esteem movement has been largely debunked, we are just now reaping what it has sown. The generation raised under these conditions is entering the workforce and has been described as difficult and that their expectations far exceed those of their predecessors in entry level positions. The praise they have been given all of their lives is still expected, even if they have not done anything to earn it and they lack the resiliency to deal with real disappointment and the realities of life. (LaPorta, 2009, p. 5)

## The construct of resilience

There are many different definitions of resilience but all refer to the capacity of the individual to "overcome odds" and demonstrate the personal strengths needed to cope with some kind of hardship or adversity. Resilience has been described as "the ability to persist, cope adaptively and bounce back after encountering change, challenges, setback, disappointments, difficult situations or adversity and to return to a reasonable level of wellbeing" (McGrath & Noble, 2003, 2011). Benard (2004) suggests resilience is also a set of qualities or protective mechanisms that give rise to successful adaptation by a young person despite high risk factors during the course of their development.

The construct of resilience emerged about 40 years ago, almost by accident, from longitudinal developmental studies of "at-risk" children. This research showed that, despite encountering many major life stressors as they grew up, some children survived and even thrived (Werner & Smith, 1992). The well-being and resilience research has shifted the focus from those children who are casualties of these risk factors to those children who manage to bounce back from stress, trauma, and risk in their lives. The resiliency construct is a dramatic change in perspective from a deficit model of young people "at risk" to a model that focuses on teaching the personal skills and developing the environmental contexts that help young people withstand high levels of "risk." Research has now been able to identify the most significant coping skills and protective life circumstances that help young people to become more resilient (e.g., Benard 2004). Next to families, schools are the most likely place where students can experience the protective environmental conditions and learn the social-emotional skills that enhance resilience. For young people who do not experience family support, school may be the only place where they can learn those skills. Teaching these skills can also inoculate them against the possibility of not coping when faced with future difficulties or adversity, just as vaccinations can inoculate them against the possibility of being adversely affected by exposure to future disease.

## *The social and emotional learning movement*

Over the last 15 years the social and emotional learning (SEL) movement has been slowly replacing the self-esteem movement. Daniel Goleman popularized the notion of emotional intelligence in the 1990s (Goleman, 1995). In his work he drew on Howard Gardner's earlier ground-breaking work on the Multiple Intelligences model, (Gardner, 1983, 1999) and Salovey and Mayer's (1990) work on "emotional intelligence." The SEL model developed by CASEL (Collaboration for Academic and Social-Emotional Learning) at the University of Illinois, USA, is based on Goleman's framework. SEL differs from the self-esteem movement in many ways but, most importantly, there is research evidence to support the claim that school-based SEL programs can increase student achievement, build their connection to school, improve their interpersonal attitudes and behaviors, and decrease negative behaviors such as violence and substance abuse, and that these outcomes occur across a wide range of diverse students and settings and persist over time (Zins, Payton, Weissberg, & O'Brien, 2007). A recent meta-analyses of school-based universal interventions in social-emotional learning found that SEL participants demonstrated significantly improved social and emotional skills, attitudes, behavior, and academic performance that reflected an 11-percentile point gain in achievement compared to controls (Durlak, Weissberg, Dymnicki, Taylor, & Schellinger, 2011).

The SEL movement links closely with the construct of resilience in that most of the following social and emotional skills identified by CASEL (2007) have also been identified as key ingredients of resilient behavior. They are:

- *Self-awareness*: accurately assessing one's feelings, interests, values, and strengths; maintaining a well-grounded sense of self-confidence.
- *Self-management*: regulating one's emotions to handle stress, control impulses, and persevere in overcoming obstacles; setting and monitoring progress toward personal and academic goals; expressing emotions appropriately.
- *Social awareness:* being able to take the perspective of and empathize with others; recognizing and appreciating individual and group similarities and differences; recognizing and using family, school, and community resources.
- *Relationship skills*: establishing and maintaining healthy and rewarding relationships based on cooperation; resisting inappropriate social pressure; preventing, managing, and resolving interpersonal conflict; seeking help when needed.
- *Responsible decision-making*: making decisions based on the consideration of ethical standards, safety concerns, appropriate social norms, respect for others, and the likely consequences of various actions; applying decision-making skills to academic and social situations; contributing to the well-being of one's school and community.

# Student Well-being

Initiatives to explicitly teach social-emotional learning skills to young people in schools are designed to enhance student well-being and resilience and improve student learning outcomes. A comprehensive and systematic review of the research literature between 1930 and 2008 reveals a gradual shift in both research and school practices away from the concept of *student welfare*, with an emphasis on individual assistance and support, and towards the concept of *student well-being*, with an emphasis on universal prevention and the development of positive behaviors (Noble, McGrath, Roffey, & Rowling, 2008). As early as 1947, the WHO constitution defined health as a state of complete physical, mental and social well-being and not merely the absence of disease or infirmity (WHO, 2007).

The potential of even a small improvement in well-being to help decrease mental health problems and help young people flourish is highlighted in the Foresight UK (2008) initiative. A stronger focus on well-being in general and on student well-being in particular has evolved from the positive psychology movement. Like the self-esteem movement positive psychology incorporates some of the principles of humanistic psychology. However, unlike the self-esteem movement, positive psychology is significantly supported by research (Seligman, 2007a). Positive education is a new term (Seligman, 2009) that applies the principles of positive psychology to education. Positive psychology, as the name implies, focuses on positives, namely those strengths and behaviors that enable people to have robust levels of well-being and enable individuals, groups, and organizations to thrive. Positive psychology researchers study the positive effects of a range of factors on well-being/happiness including: positive emotions (Fredrickson & Joiner, 2002); engagement and "psychological flow" (Csikszentmihalyi, 2002); the identification and building of personal character strengths (Peterson & Seligman, 2004) and intellectual strengths (Gardner, 1999; McGrath & Noble, 2005); optimistic thinking (Seligman, 1998); and having a sense of meaning and purpose (Seligman, 2002) and accomplishment (Seligman, 2011).

## Defining student well-being

A robust definition of student well-being is required to guide educational policy and practices. Different professional disciplines have taken different perspectives on well-being. The clinical and health perspective tends to define well-being as the absence of negative conditions such as depression, anxiety, or substance abuse. Contemporary psychologists tend to operationalize well-being in terms of happiness and satisfaction with life (Kahnemann, Diener, & Schwartz 1999; Seligman, 2002) and/or as the presence of a significant number of positive self-attributes (Keyes, 1998; Ryff & Singer, 1996). Sociologists and community workers have focused on well-being in terms of "broader meanings and difficulties in social processes in young people's lives and how these impact on individual behaviour" (Bourke & Geldens, 2007, p. 42).

Student well-being is assumed to be a school-based outcome. Although a child's family, home, and community environment all significantly impact on student well-being, a student well-being perspective focuses the school community's attention on the actions that schools can take in the school context to enhance student well-being. Levels of student well-being are indicated by the degree to which a student demonstrates effective academic and social and emotional functioning and appropriate behavior at school.

One clear conclusion from a review of the research literature is that student well-being significantly influences academic engagement and success in learning (Noble et al., 2008). Weissberg and O'Brien (2004) have described the broad mission of schools as developing students who are "knowledgeable, responsible, healthy, caring, connected and contributing." In a series of focus groups held with 26 teacher educators from two Australian universities, all either agreed or strongly agreed that enhancing student well-being is a core business of schools (Noble et al., 2008).

Whilst most educators and psychologists support the importance of student well-being for academic achievement and social-emotional adjustment, there is very little consensus on what student well-being actually is (Fraillon, 2004). An analysis of the research literature on the construct of well-being identified 30 general definitions of well-being but only three definitions of student well-being. The five most common characteristics identified in these general definitions of well-being were (in order of frequency of being mentioned): positive affect (the characteristic mentioned most often), resilience and adaptivity, satisfaction with relationships, effective functioning, and the maximization of one's potential and satisfaction with other dimensions of one's life.

On the basis of this literature review, a draft definition of student well-being was developed as part of a scoping study into student well-being (Noble et al., 2008). A modified Delphi methodology was used to seek clarification and agreement on the components of this draft definition. The first stage of the Delphi process involved contacting 30 worldwide experts and asking them to participate in the process. The people selected as experts were researchers, theorists, and/or writers around the world who had made substantial and relatively recent contributions to the field of "well-being." Twenty-six of them accepted the invitation to participate and they represented key people working in the field of well-being and/or student well-being from a range of countries including Australia, Denmark, UK, Italy, New Zealand, Portugal, and the USA. These respondents then made comments (in an online survey) on each component of the draft definition and indicated their level of agreement with each component and the overall definition. The experts' responses were collated after the first round and the key findings summarized and returned to them in stage 2 for further comments and to seek consensus. There was significant but not total agreement amongst the experts on each component and on the wording of the final definition, which is:

> *Optimal student wellbeing is a sustainable emotional state characterised by (predominantly) positive mood and positive relationships at school, resilience, self-optimisation and a high level of satisfaction with learning experiences.*
>
> 'Optimal student well-being' is the desirable level of well-being for all students and the level most likely to lead to positive student learning outcomes.
>
> A 'sustainable state' is a relatively consistent mental or emotional condition that is pervasive (ie it affects most aspects of a student's learning and functioning at school) and is able to be maintained over time despite minor variations triggered by life events.
>
> 'Predominantly positive mood, and positive relationships at school' implies mainly positive feelings and an optimistic approach to school plus high-quality and pro-social relationships with peers and teachers at school that engender social satisfaction and support.
>
> 'Resilience' is the ability to cope and bounce back after encountering negative events, difficult situations or adversity and then return to almost the same level of emotional well-being. It is

also the capacity to respond adaptively to difficult circumstances and still thrive (McGrath & Noble, 2003, 2011).

'*Self-optimisation*' refers to a student's willingness to strive to get the best out of themselves based on their realistic and mostly positive judgments of their abilities, strengths, behavior and learning capacity.

'*Satisfaction with learning experiences at school*' describes a student's satisfaction with the nature, quality and relevance of their learning experiences at school. Suldo, Shaffer, and Riley (2008) have identified that children's own perceptions of the quality of aspects of their life is an important indicator of their level of well-being.

## Effective programming for student well-being

An integration of the SEL movement, the discipline of positive psychology/positive education and the constructs of resilience and student well-being offers a school-based framework for fostering student well-being. Such a framework incorporates social and emotional learning initiatives that have a strong focus on coping skills and resilience, and provide students with opportunities to optimize their strengths, build positive relationships, and experience a sense of meaning and purpose.

The available research evidence strongly indicates the following guidelines for the effective implementation of social and emotional learning programs in schools.

### *Whole-school programs are more effective*

A whole-school program that is embedded in the curriculum and in the general life of the classroom and the school is more effective that an "add-on" program (Scheckner, Rollin, Kaiser-Ulery, & Wagner, 2002; Wells, Barlow, & Stewart-Brown, 2003). A whole-school program involves all classes and students as well as connecting to the students' families and the community (Dryfoos, 1990; Greenberg et al., 2003). When a program is embedded, the skills, concepts, and understandings in the program are linked to other curriculum areas and applied in a variety of classroom and playground contexts. The key principles of the program influence the school vision, structures, organization, and school and classroom practices, and teachers endeavor to act in accordance with the social-emotional skills and concepts they are teaching.

### *Programs that are taught by class teachers and integrated with academic learning are more likely to be effective*

Academic improvement as well as social and emotional improvement is more likely when teachers (rather than external consultants or professionals) implement a social-emotional learning program (CASEL, 2007; Weissberg & O'Brien, 2004). It would appear that SEL programs delivered by teachers can be more readily incorporated into routine educational practices (Durlak et al., 2011).

### *The program should be acceptable to teachers*

A school-based program that is acceptable to the teachers who teach the program is more likely to be effective (Eckert & Hintz, 2000; Elliott, Witt, & Kratochwill, 1991; McDougal,

Clonan, & Martens, 2000; Truscott, Cosgrove, Meyers, & Eidle-Barkman, 2000). Teacher acceptability reflects their perception that the program is perceived to be worth their time and effort, feasible, socially valid (Gresham & Lopez, 1996) and consistent with their educational, psychological and social perspectives and classroom practices. It also reflects their perception that they have the necessary competencies to teach it and that it has some degree of flexibility (Nastasi, 2002).

## Universal programs are more effective

A universal program is delivered to all students and not just those who are identified as "at risk" for mental health difficulties (Durlak et al., 2011). Universal programs delivered at the primary/elementary school level are especially likely to be effective (Diekstra, 2008). A universal program reflects the paradigm shift in education, social welfare, and psychology from just targeting students at risk to the protective factors that schools can put in place and the coping skills that can be taught (Benard 2004; CASEL, 2007; Greenberg, Domitrovich, and Bumbarger, 2001; National Health and Medical Research Council, 1996). Universal programs can also incorporate options for additional targeted learning with indicated students.

## Programs that are long-term and multiyear have more chance of success

Short-term preventive interventions produce time-limited benefits. Multiyear programs are more likely to produce enduring benefits and are more sustainable especially when taught across age levels (Greenberg et al., 2001, 2003; Wells et al., 2003).

## A multistrategic approach is more effective than a single highly-focused approach

A multistrategic approach involves the inclusion of a collection of coordinated "active ingredients" rather than a single focus (Greenberg et al., 2001; Kellerman, Fuqna-Whitely, Rivara, and Mervy, 1998; Resnick et al., 1997). Effective programs contain at least five different aspects of social and emotional learning (Catalano, Haggerty, Oesterle, Flemming, and Hawkins, 2003) and focus on both promoting positive behavior and reducing anti-social behavior (Catalano, Haggerty, Gainey, Hoppe, & Brewer, 1998). In their meta-analyses of a range of SEL programs, Durlak et al. developed the acronym SAFE to identify the multistrategic practices essential to effective outcomes; Sequenced activities, Active learning, Focused teaching of personal and social skills, and Explicit guidelines on how to teach the skills.

## Effectiveness is enhanced when children are first introduced to the program early in their schooling

Most reviews of preventive research stress that programs which start when students are very young are more likely to be effective (Greenberg et al., 2003; O'Shaugnessy, Lane, Gresham, and Beebe-Frankenberg, 2003) Reivich (2005) has identified that children develop the habit of thinking optimistically or pessimistically by the end of primary school, indicating the importance of teaching optimistic skills from early childhood.

## *An effective program includes a significant component of skills derived from cognitive behavior approaches*

There is substantial research support for the efficacy of cognitive behavior therapy (CBT) in constructively changing feelings and behavior (e.g., Andrews et al., 2001, 2002; Scheckner et al., 2002). CBT, which was originally developed by Aaron Beck (Beck, 1979), is based on the understanding that *how you think affects how you feel* which in turn influences *how you behave*. The premise is that by adopting more positive and rational thinking you can help yourself to change your behavior. Two specific sophisticated applications/refinements of the basic model of CBT are Albert Ellis' rational emotive behavior therapy (Ellis & Harper, 2008) and Martin Seligman's learned optimism (Seligman, 1995; 1998). A meta-analysis of research on the Penn Resiliency Program (PRP) based on learned optimism found that in 13 randomized controlled trials the program can prevent symptoms of depression (Gilham et al., 2007). However, in the PRP studies sample sizes are relatively small and despite the manualized curriculum, the PRP team recommend trained facilitators.

## *The program should incorporate evidence-based teaching strategies*

If a whole-school program is to be successfully embedded in the curriculum, then it must not only include evidence-based psychological approaches but also incorporate evidence-based teaching strategies. Cooperative learning has extensive evidence support for improving academic outcomes as well as building positive relationships, class cohesion and social-emotional learning (e.g., Hattie, 2009; Marzano, Pickering, & Pollock, 2001; Roseth, Johnson, & Johnson, 2008). The use of high-quality literature as an entry point for discussions on well-being topics can also serve to meet literacy outcomes as well as being a powerful tool for teaching about relationships, values, courage, and resilience. Other teaching strategies such as educational games tournaments (in which students play in pairs against other pairs in the class (e.g., McGrath & Noble, 2010)) and circle time, where all children sit in a circle and participate in class discussion of student well-being issues (McCarthy, 2009; Roffey, 2006) can also actively engage students in learning, develop positive relationships, and teach social-emotional skills.

# Two Examples of National Initiatives in Student Well-being

## Social and Emotional Aspects of Learning

The Primary SEAL program is a UK social and emotional whole-school program for K-6 students which involves classroom teachers teaching social and emotional skills in order to enhance student relationships, attendance, behavior, learning, and emotional well-being (Department for Education and Skills, 2005). It was adopted in 80% of British schools (Humphrey et al., 2008). SEAL is a universal approach but also includes early intervention with small learning groups for students who are deemed to need extra support and follow-up individual interventions with those students who do not appear to have benefited from either the whole-class program or the small group early interventions (Department for

Education and Skills, 2005). The themes in the program are New Beginnings (emotional literacy), Going for Goals (self-regulation and empathy), Getting On and Falling Out (social skills), Say No to Bullying, and Good to Be Me. So far only the small-group component has been evaluated but results look to be promising (Humphrey et al., 2008)

## KidsMatter (Kidsmatter.org.au)

KidsMatter is an Australian Primary Schools Mental Health Initiative which is supported by a partnership between the Commonwealth Department of Health and Ageing, Beyond Blue: The National Depression initiative, The Australian Psychological Society, Principals Australia, and Australian Rotary Health. It aims to improve the mental health and well-being of primary school students, reduce mental health problems amongst primary-aged students, and achieve greater support for students experiencing mental health problems. In 2007 and 2008 grants were provided to 100 schools to implement the social and emotional learning program they selected from a program booklet that had evaluated all potential programs according to CASEL SEL criteria (CASEL, 2007). The evaluation of the effectiveness of the KidsMatter initiative indicated that there were significant and positive changes in the schools, teachers, parents/caregivers, and students over the 2-year trial. In particular there were statistically and practically significant improvements in students' measured mental health in terms of both reduced mental health difficulties and increased mental health strengths. The impact of KidsMatter was especially apparent for students who were rated as having higher levels of mental health difficulties at the start of the trial (Dix, Owens, Skrzypiec, & Spears, 2009). The program will be continued and a pre-school version is also being piloted.

### *An example of a student well-being program: Bounce Back!*

Bounce Back! was selected by 64% of the KidsMatter schools that chose to implement a whole school well-being program. It was also implemented in 16 primary schools in the Perth and Kinross area in Scotland where it has been shown to enhance student well-being as well as teacher well-being (Axford, Blythe, & Schepens 2010; Axford, Schepens, & Blythe, 2011). The program (McGrath & Noble 2003, 2011) has been developed for children from kindergarten (5 years old) to early adolescence (14 years old) and has three levels of age-appropriate resources. It is a whole-school universal and CBT-based program that takes a literature-based approach to teaching well-being and resilience and incorporates the following nine curriculum units:

- The *Core Values* unit encourages children to be honest, fair, kind, cooperative, respectful of self and others, and accepting of differences.
- The *People Bouncing Back* unit incorporates the Bounce Back! acronym of 10 coping statements based on cognitive behavioral and counseling principles.
- *Looking on the Bright Side* teaches optimistic thinking and gratitude.
- The *Courage* unit discriminates between "everyday" courage of having a go at something that is challenging for you despite experiencing fear or anxiety and heroism or foolhardy behavior.
- The *Emotions* unit teaches children ways to amplify positive emotions, to have empathy for others as well as ways to manage strong negative emotions.

- The *Relationships* unit teaches strategies for making and keeping friends as well as managing conflict.
- The *Humor* unit incorporates ideas for building class fun through a giggle gym and other strategies and explains the differences between humor that is helpful and humor that is hurtful or trivializes a difficult situation
- The *No Bullying* unit helps children discriminate between bullying behavior and other kinds of antisocial behavior and teaches skills in acting confidently and assertively as well as skills in supporting others who are being bullied.
- The *Success* unit helps children to identify their character and ability strengths, to set and maintain realistic goals and to gain a sense of meaning and purpose through class and community activities.

An abbreviated version of Bounce Back! was trialed in eight Year 5/Year 6 classes (10–12-year-olds) in eight schools (McGrath & Anders, 2000). The teachers reported marked improvements and greater confidence in their ability to counsel and support their students. They perceived that their use of the initiative facilitated better communication with their students, which helped in the students' management of personal issues as well as schoolwork issues. All teachers reported that teaching the program improved their own personal and professional resilience and their capacity to cope with difficult times. The students demonstrated an increase in resilient thinking, especially optimistic and helpful thinking. They also demonstrated skills in transferring their learning to situations outside the classroom and at home. Teachers reported their observations of students spontaneously using the Bounce Back! statements in real-life stressful situations and in supporting their classmates and friends.

## Conclusions and Future Directions

This chapter reviewed the research literature that indicates that children and young people today appear to be less resilient than those of previous generations. One reason offered is the failure of the self-esteem movement that has focused parental and teacher attention on helping children and young people "feel good" in order to boost their self-esteem at the expense of their learning to be resilient. Although the vision statement of many schools highlights the importance of fostering student well-being there has been very little clarity to date in the research literature about the construct of student well-being in the school context. A practical and robust operational definition of student well-being is outlined in this chapter. This definition evolved from the consensus-seeking research process with "experts in the field." Furthermore the evidence-based active ingredients and guidelines for the successful implementation of school-based student well-being and social and emotional learning initiatives are identified. This definition and guidelines for programming offer clear directions and support to schools in their ongoing commitment to the promotion of student well-being and resilience.

## References

Andrews, G., Szabó, M., & Burns, J. (2001). *Avertable risk factors for depression*. Report for beyond blue: the Australian National Depression Initiative.

Andrews, G., Szabo, M., & Burns, J. (2002). Preventing major depression in young people. *British Journal of Psychiatry*, 181, 460–462.

Axford, S., Blythe, K., & Schepens, R. (2010). *Can we help children learn coping skills for life? A study of the impact of the Bounce Back programme on resilience, connectedness and wellbeing of children and teachers in sixteen primary schools in Perth and Kinross, Scotland.* Retrieved from http://www.pkc.gov.uk/Education+and+learning/Schools/Schools+-+health

Axford, S., Schepens, R., & Blythe, K. (2011). Did introducing the Bounce Back programme have an impact on resilience, connectedness, and well-being of children and teachers in 16 primary schools in Perth and Kinross, Scotland? *Educational Psychology in Scotland*, 12(1), 2–5.

Baumeister, R.F., Campbell, J.D., Krueger, J.I., & Vohs, K.D. (2003). Does high self-esteem cause better performance, interpersonal success, happiness or healthier lifestyles. *Psychological Science in the Public Interest*. 4 (1), 1–44.

Beck, A.T. (1979). *Cognitive therapy and the emotional disorders*. New York, NY: Penguin.

Beck, J. S. (1995). *Cognitive therapy: Basic and beyond*. New York, NY: Guilford Press.

Benard, B. (2004). *Resiliency: What we have learned*. San Francisco, CA: WestEd.

Bender, T.A. (1997). Assessment of subjective well-being during childhood and adolescence. In G. Phye (Ed.), *Handbook of classroom assessment: Learning, achievement and adjustment* (pp. 199–225). San Diego, CA: Academic Press.

Bourke, L., & Geldens, P.M. (2007). What does wellbeing mean? Perspectives of wellbeing among young people and youth workers in rural Victoria. *Youth Studies Australia*, 6(1), 41–49.

CASEL (Collaboration for Academic and Social-Emotional Learning) (2007). *CASEL brief: Background on social and emotional learning*. Retrieved on September 4, 2012 from http://casel.org/publications/what-is-sel/

Catalano, R. F., Haggerty, K. P., Oesterle, S., Fleming, C. B., & Hawkins, J. D. (2003). *The importance of bonding to school for healthy development: Findings from the Social Development Research Group*. Paper presented at Wingspread Conference on School Connectedness, June, Racine, WI.

Catalano, R. F., Haggerty, K. P., Gainey, R. R., Hoppe, M. J., & Brewer, D. D. (1998). Effectiveness of prevention interventions with youth at high-risk of drug abuse. In W. J. Bukoski, & R. I. Evans (Eds.), *NIDA research monograph: Vol. 176. Cost– benefit/cost-effectiveness research of drug abuse prevention: implications for programming and policy*, pp. 83–110. Rockville, MD: National Institute on Drug Abuse.

Csikszentmihalyi, M. (2002). *Flow: The classic work on how to achieve happiness*. London, UK: Rider.

Department for Education and Skills (UK) (2005). *Primary National Strategy. Excellence and enjoyment: Social and emotional aspects of learning*. Nottingham, UK: DfES Publications.

Diekstra, R. (2008). Effectiveness of school- based social and emotional education programmes (Part One and Part Two). In D. Goleman (Ed.), *Social and emotional education: An international analysis* (pp 285–312). Santander, Spain: Fundacion Marcellino Botin.

Dix, K. L., Owens, L., Skrzypiec, G., & Spears, B. (2009). *KidsMatter evaluation executive summary*. Beyond Blue. Retrieved January 7, 2010 from www.kidsmatter.edu.au/primary/uploads/2009/10/kidsmatter-exec-summary-report-web.pdf

Dryfoos, J. G. (1990). *Adolescents at risk. Prevalence and prevention*. New York, NY: Oxford University Press.

Durlak, J. A., Weissberg, R. P., Dymnicki, A. B., Taylor, R. D., & Schellinger, K. B. (2011). The impact of enhancing students' social and emotional learning: A meta-analysis of school-based universal interventions. *Child Development*, 82, 405–432.

Dweck, C. S., (2006). *Mindset. The new psychology of success*. New York, NY: Random House.

Eckert, T. L., & Hinze, J. M. (2000). Behavioral conceptions and applications of acceptability: Issues related to service delivery and research methodology. *School Psychology Quarterly*, 15, 123–148.

Elliott, S. N., Witt, J. C., & Kratochwill, T. R. (1991). Selecting, implementing and evaluating classroom interventions. In G. Stoner, M. R. Shinn, & H. M. Walker (Eds.), *Interventions for achievement and behavior problems* (pp. 99–135). Silver Springs, MD: National Association of School Psychologists.

Ellis, A., & Harper, R.A. (1961). *A new guide to rational living.* Hollywood, CA: Wilshire Book Company.

Ellis, A. & Harper, R. (2008). *A new guide to rational living*, 3rd edition. Hollywood, CA: Wilshire Book Company.

Emler, N. (2003). Does it matter if young people have low self esteem? In K. Richards (Ed.), *Self-esteem and youth development* (pp. 1–26). Ambleside, UK: Brathay Hall Trust.

Foresight Mental Capital and Wellbeing. (2008). *Making the most of ourselves in the 21st century*. Government Office of Science, UK. Retrieved from #http://www.bis.gov.uk/assets/bis-partners/foresight/docs/mental-capital/mentalcapitalwellbeingexecsum.pdf

Fraillon, J. (2004). *Measuring student wellbeing in the context of Australian schooling.* Discussion paper. Retrieved 6 February, 2010 #http://www.mceetya.edu.au/verve/resources.

Fredrickson, B., & Joiner, T. (2002). Positive emotions trigger upward spirals toward emotional well-being. *Psychological Science*, 13, 172–175.

Fredrickson, B., & Tugade, M. (2004). Resilient individuals use positive emotions to bounce back from negative emotional experiences. *Journal of Personality & Social Psychology*, 86, 320–333.

Gardner, H. (1983) *Frames of mind: The theory of multiple intelligences.* New York, NY: Basic Books.

Gardner, H., (1999). *Intelligence reframed: Multiple intelligences for the 21st century*. New York, NY: Basic Books.

Gillham, J., & Reivich, K. (2004). Cultivating optimism in childhood and adolescence. *Annals of the American Academy of Political and Social Science*, 591, 146–163.

Gillham, J. E., Brunwasser, S. M., & Freres, D. R. (2007). Preventing depression in early adolescence. In J. R. Z. Abela & B. L. Hankin (Eds.), *Handbook of depression in children and adolescents* (pp. 309–332). New York, NY: Guilford Press.

Goleman, D. (1995). *Emotional intelligence.* New York, NY: Bantam Books.

Greenberg, M., Weissberg, R., O'Brien, M., Zins, J., Fredericks, L., Resnik, H., & Elias, M. (2003). Enhancing school-based prevention and youth development through coordinated social, emotional, and academic learning. *American Psychologist*, 58, 466–474.

Greenberg, M.T., Domitrovich, C., & Bumbarger, B. (2001). *Preventing mental disorders in school-age children: A review of the effectiveness of prevention programs*. Rockville, MD: Center for Mental Health Services (CMHS), Substance Abuse Mental Health Services Administration, US Department of Health and Human Services.

Gresham, F. M., & Lopez, M. F. (1996). Social validation: A unifying concept for school-based consultation. *School Psychology Quarterly*, 11, 204–227.

Hattie, J. (2009). *Visible learning: A synthesis of over 800 meta-analyses relating to achievement.* London, UK: Routledge.

Huebner, E. S. (1994). Preliminary development and validation of a multidimensional life satisfaction scale for children. *Psychological Assessment*, 6(2), 149–158.

Humphrey, A., Kalambouka, A., Bolton, J., Lendrum, A., Wigelsworth, M., Lennie, C., & Farrell, P. (2008), *Primary social and emotional aspects of learning (SEAL)—Evaluation of small group work.* Retrieved from http://www.dcsf.gov.uk/research/data/uploadfiles/DCSF-RB064.pdf.

Kahne, J. (1996). The politics of self-esteem. *American Education Research Journal*, 33, 3–22.

Kahnemann, D., Diener, E., & Schwartz, N. (1999). *Well-being: The foundations of hedonic psychology.* New York, NY: The Russell Sage Foundation.

Kellerman, A. L., Fuqua-Whitley, D. S., Rivara, F. P., & Mervy, J. (1998). Preventing youth violence: What works? *Annual Review of Public Health*, *19*, 271–292.

Keyes, C. (1998). Social well-being. *Social Psychology Quarterly*, *61*, 121–140.

LaPorta, L.D., (2009). Twitter and YouTube: Unexpected consequences of the self-esteem movement? *Psychiatric Times*, *26*(11), 1–6.

Marzano, R. J., Pickering, D. J., & Pollock, J. E. (2001). *Classroom instruction that works: Research-based strategies for increasing student achievement*. Alexandria, VA: Association for Supervision and Curriculum Development.

McCarthy, F. (2009). *Circle time solutions: Creating caring school communities*. Sydney, Australia: Report for NSW Department of Education.

McGrath, H. & Anders, E. (2000). *The BOUNCE BACK! program. Turning the tide in schools drug education project*. Melbourne, Australia: Victorian Department of Education.

McGrath, H., & Noble, T. (2003). *BOUNCE BACK! A classroom resiliency program.* (Teacher's Handbook. Teacher's Resource Books, Level 1: K-2; Level 2: Yrs 3–4; Level 3: Yrs 5–8). Sydney, Australia: Pearson Education.

McGrath, H., & Noble, T. (2005). *Eight ways at once. Book one: Multiple intelligences + Bloom's revised taxonomy = 200 differentiated classroom strategies*. Sydney, Australia: Pearson Education.

McGrath, H., & Noble, T. (2011). *BOUNCE BACK! A wellbeing & resilience program*. Lower Primary K-2; Middle Primary: Yrs 3–4; Upper Primary/Junior Secondary: Yrs 5–8. Melbourne, Australia: Pearson Education.

McGrath, H., & Noble, T. (2010). *HITS and HOTS. Teaching + thinking + social skills*. Melbourne, Australia: Pearson Education.

McKay, H. (1997). *Generations: Baby boomers, their parents and their children*. Sydney, Australia: Angus and Robertson.

McDougal, J. L., Clonan, S. M., & Martens, B. K. (2000). Using organizational change procedures to promote the acceptability of prereferral intervention services: The School-Based Intervention Team Project. *School Psychology Quarterly*, *15*, 149–171.

Nastasi, B. K. (2002). Commentary: The realities of large-scale change efforts. *Journal of Educational & Psychological Consultation*, *13*(3), 219–226.

National Health and Medical Research Council's Health Advancement Committee. (1996). *Effective school health promotion: Towards health promoting schools*. Canberra, Australia: National Health and Medical Research Council.

Noble, T., McGrath, H., Roffey, S., & Rowling, L. (2008). *A scoping study on student wellbeing*. Canberra, Australia: Australian Government Department of Education, Employment & Workplace Relations.

Peterson, C., & Seligman, M. E. P. (2004). *Character strengths and virtues: A handbook and classification*. Oxford, UK: Oxford University Press.

O'Shaughnessy, T. E., Lane, K. E. Gresham, F. E., & Beebe-Frankenberg, M. E. (2003). Children placed at risk for learning and behavioural difficulties. Implementing a school-wide system of early identification and intervention. *Remedial & Special Education*, *24*(1), 27–35.

Reivich, K. (2005). Optimism lecture. In *Authentic Happiness Coaching Course*. University of Pennsylvania, PA.

Resnick, M. D., Bearman, P. S., Blum, R. W., Bauman, K. E., Harris, K. M., Jones, J., … Udry, J. R. (1997). Protecting adolescents from harm: Findings from the national longitudinal study on adolescent health. *JAMA*, *278*, 823–832.

Roffey, S. (2006). *Circle time for emotional literacy*. London, UK: Sage/Paul Chapman.

Roseth, C., Johnson, D., & Johnson, R. (2008). Promoting early adolescents' achievement and peer relationships: the effects of cooperative, competitive and individualistic goal structures. *Psychological Bulletin*, *134*, 223–246.

Ryff, C. D., & Singer, B. (1996). Psychological wellbeing: Meaning, measurement and implications for psychotherapy research. *Psychotherapy and Psychosomatics, 65*, 14–22.

Salovey, P., & Mayer, J.D. (1990). Emotional intelligence. *Imagination, Cognition, and Personality, 9*, 185–211.

Scheckner, S., Rollin, S. A., Kaiser-Ulery, C., & Wagner, R. (2002). School violence in children and adolescents: A meta-analysis of the effectiveness of current interventions. *Journal of School Violence, 1*(2), 5–32.

Seligman, M. (2009). Positive psychology and positive education. Workshop notes: *Mind & Its Potential Conference*, Sydney, December.

Seligman, M. E. P. (2007a). Coaching and positive psychology, *Australian Psychologist, 42*(4), 266–267.

Seligman, M. E. P. (2007b), *The optimistic child: A proven program to safeguard children against depression and build lifelong resilience*. New York, NY: Houghton Mifflin, Harcourt.

Seligman, M. E. P. (1998). *Learned optimism*. New York, NY: Pocket Books (Simon and Schuster).

Seligman, M. E. P. (2002). *Authentic happiness: Using the new positive psychology to realize your potential for lasting fulfillment*. New York, NY: Free Press.

Seligman, M. E. P. (2011). *Flourish: A visionary new understanding of happiness and well-being*. New York, NY: Free Press.

Seligman, M. E. P., Reivich, K., Jaycox, L., & Gillham, J. (1995). *The optimistic child*. New York, NY: Houghton Mifflin

Suldo, S., Shaffer, E. J., & Riley, K. N. (2008). A social-cognitive-behavioral model of academic predictors of adolescents' life satisfaction. *School Psychology Quarterly, 23*(1), 56–69.

Terry, T., & Huebner, E. S., (1995). The relationship between self-concept and life satisfaction in children. *Social Indicators Research, 35*(1), 39–52.

Truscott, S. D., Cosgrove, G., Meyers, J., & Eidle-Barkman, K. A. (2000). The acceptability of organizational consultation with prereferral intervention teams. *School Psychology Quarterly, 15*, 172–206.

Twenge, J. M. (2007). *Generation me: Why today's young Americans are more confident, assertive, entitled—and more miserable than ever before*. New York, NY: Free Press.

Twenge, J. M., & Campbell, W. K. (2009). *The Narcissism epidemic: Living in the age of entitlement*. New York, NY: Free Press.

Twenge, J. M., Zhang, L., & Im, C. (2004). It's beyond my control: A cross-temporal meta-analysis of increasing externality in locus of control, 1960–2002. *Personality and Social Psychology Review, 8*, 308–319.

Weissberg, R. P., & O'Brien, M. U. (2004). What works in school-based social and emotional learning programs for positive youth development. *Annals of the American Academy of Political and Social Science, 591*, 86–97.

Weissberg, R. P., Walberg, H. J., O'Brien, M. U., & Kuster, C. B. (2003). *Long-term trends in the well-being of children and youth*. Washington, DC: CWLA Press.

Wells, J., Barlow, J., & Stewart-Brown, S. (2003). A systematic review of the universal approaches to mental health promotion in schools. *Health Education, 103*(4), 197–220.

Werner, E., & Smith, R. (1992). *Overcoming the odds: high risk children from birth to adulthood*. New York, NY: Adams, Bannister and Cox.

WHO (2007). *Fact sheet No.220*. Retrieved from http://www.who.int/mediacentre/factsheets/fs220/en/.

Zins, J. E., Payton, J. W., Weissberg, R. P., & O'Brien, M. U. (2007). Social and emotional learning and successful school performance. In G. Matthews, M. Zeidner, & R. D. Roberts (Eds.), *Emotional intelligence: Knowns and unknowns*. New York, NY: Oxford University Press.

Radio area labelled maps

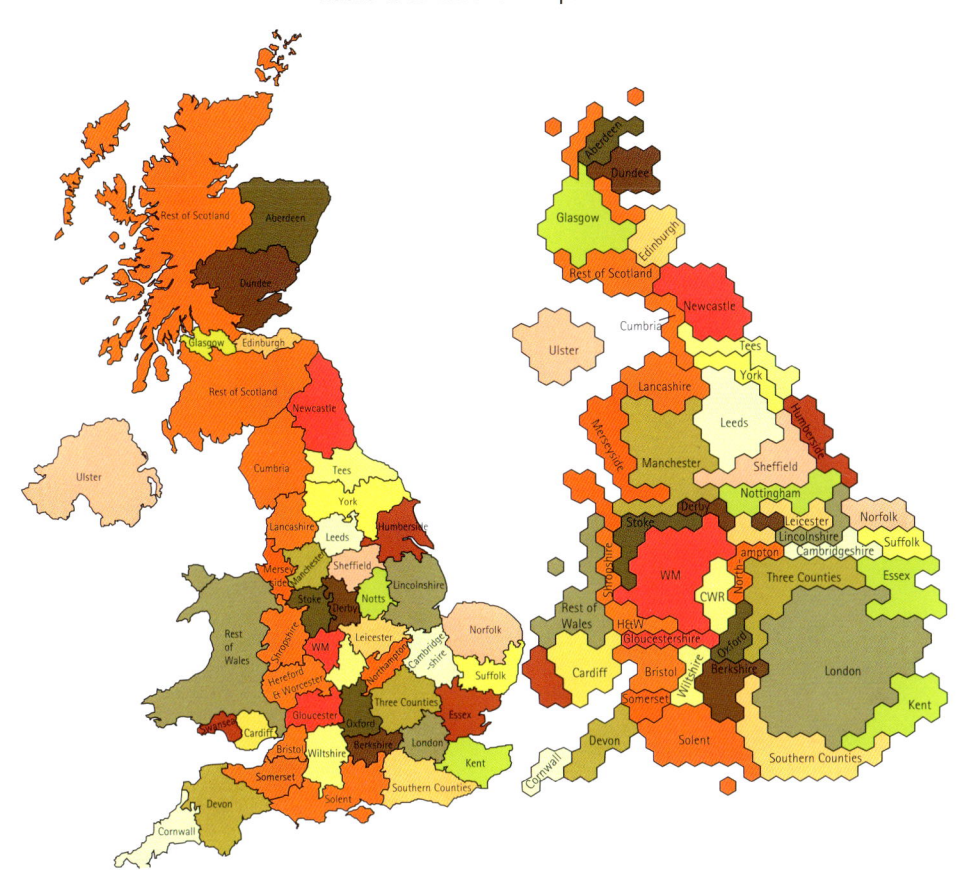

PLATE 1 (Also see Fig. 36.2.) The BBC radio regions map and human cartogram. Colors have no meaning here other than to differentiate areas. Areas are colored the same on both map and cartogram. Courtesy: the Social and Spatial Inequalities (SASI) Group, Department of Geography, University of Sheffield, UK.

## Social fragmentation (Anomie) 1971

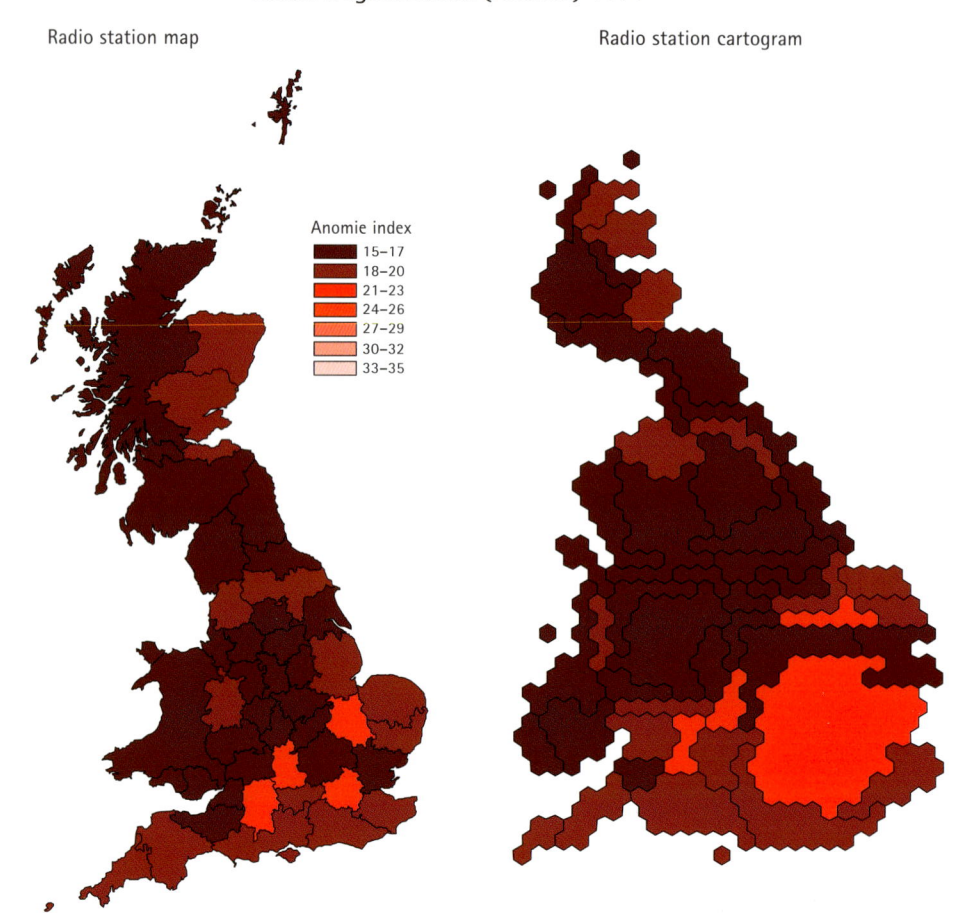

Radio station map

Radio station cartogram

Anomie index
- 15–17
- 18–20
- 21–23
- 24–26
- 27–29
- 30–32
- 33–35

PLATE 2 (Also see Fig. 36.3.) Spatial distribution of anomie index in 1971. Colors become lighter as rates of anomie increase. Areas are colored the same on both map and cartogram. Courtesy: the Social and Spatial Inequalities (SASI) Group, Department of Geography, University of Sheffield, UK.

## Social fragmentation (Anomie) 2001

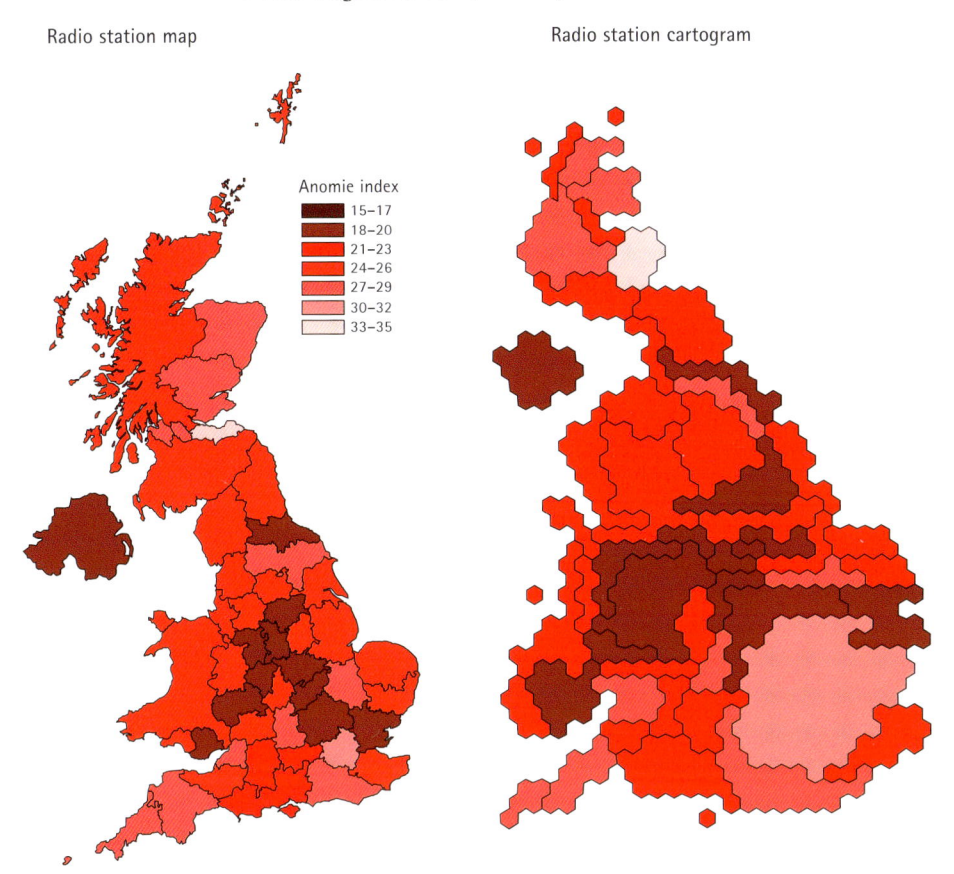

Radio station map · Radio station cartogram

Anomie index
- 15–17
- 18–20
- 21–23
- 24–26
- 27–29
- 30–32
- 33–35

**PLATE 3** (Also see Fig. 36.4.) Spatial distribution of anomie index in 2001. Colours become lighter as rates of anomie increase. Areas are coloured the same on both map and cartogram. Courtesy: the Social and Spatial Inequalities (SASI) Group, Department of Geography, University of Sheffield, UK.

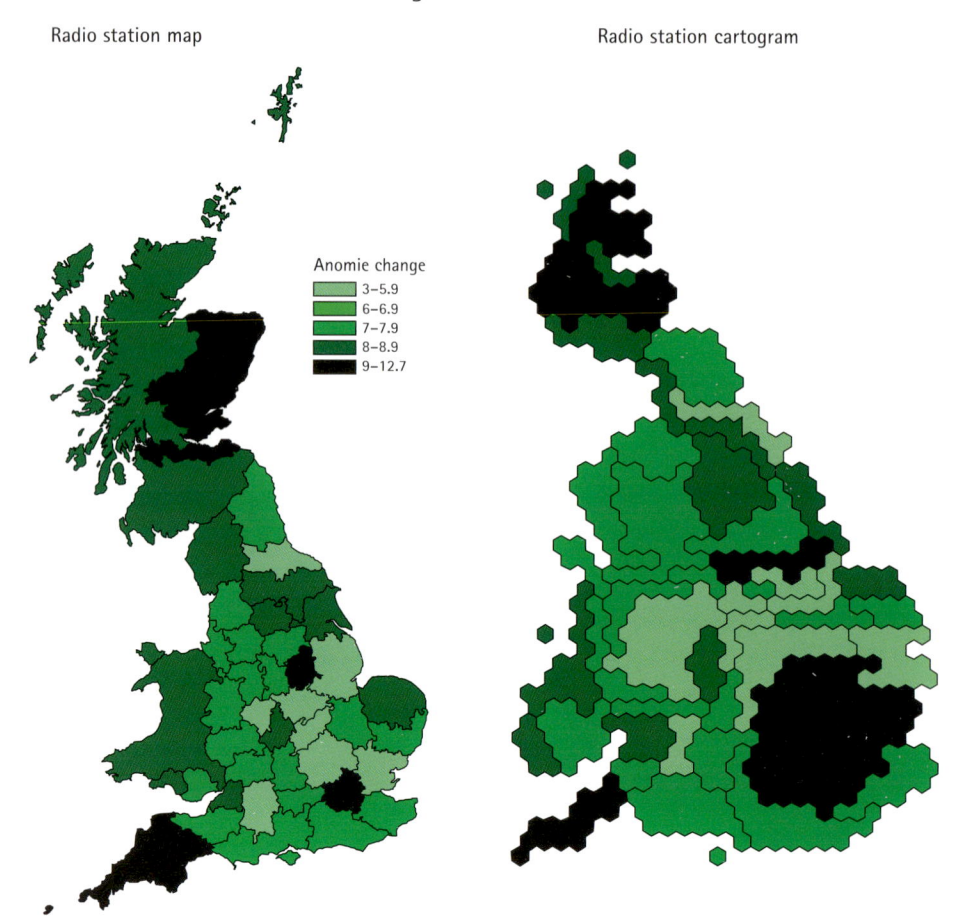

PLATE 4 (Also see Fig. 36.5.) Spatial distribution of anomie index difference between 1971 and 2001. Colors become darker for greater increases in anomie over time. Areas are colored the same on both map and cartogram. Courtesy: the Social and Spatial Inequalities (SASI) Group, Department of Geography, University of Sheffield, UK.

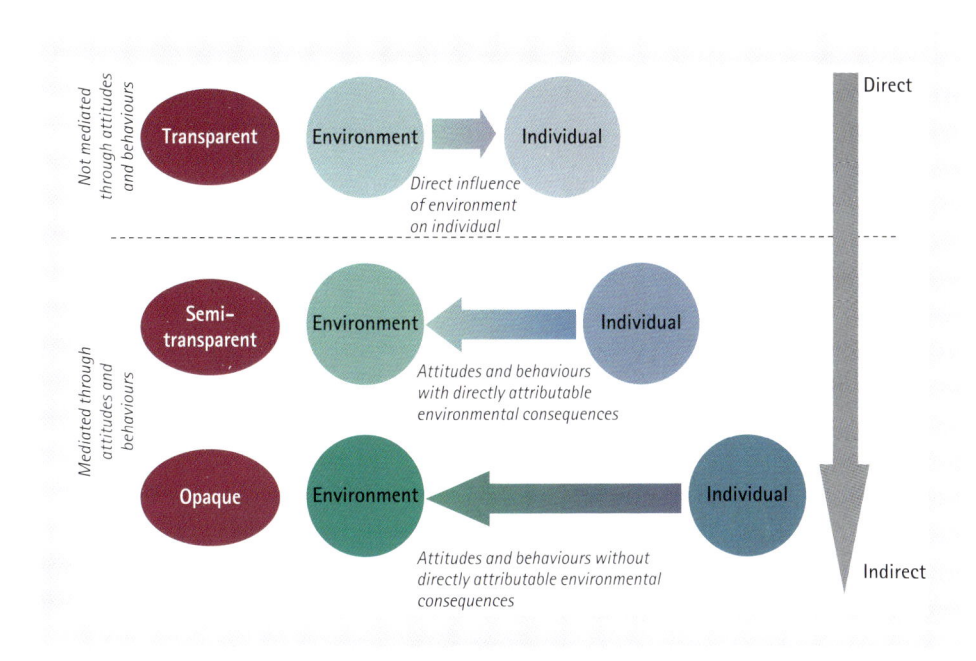

**PLATE 5** (Also see Fig. 38.1.) Pathways between the environment and the individual.

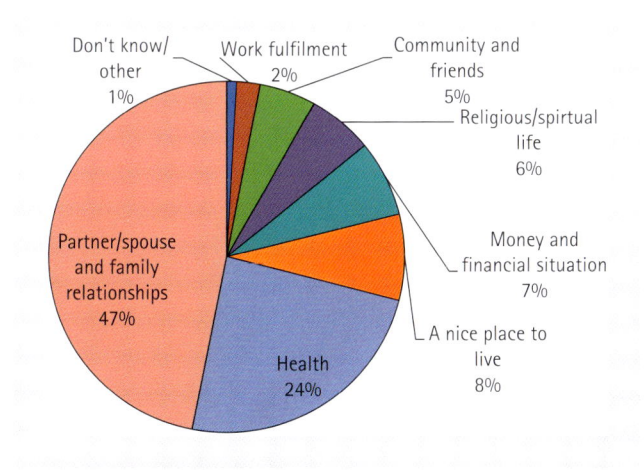

**PLATE 6** (Also see Fig. 39.1.) Factors that influence happiness: results of a poll conducted for the BBC. Data from a poll undertaken for the BBC by GfK NOP during October 2005. Results available at http://news.bbc.co.uk/nol/shared/bsp/hi/pdfs/29_03_06_happiness_gfkpoll.pdf.

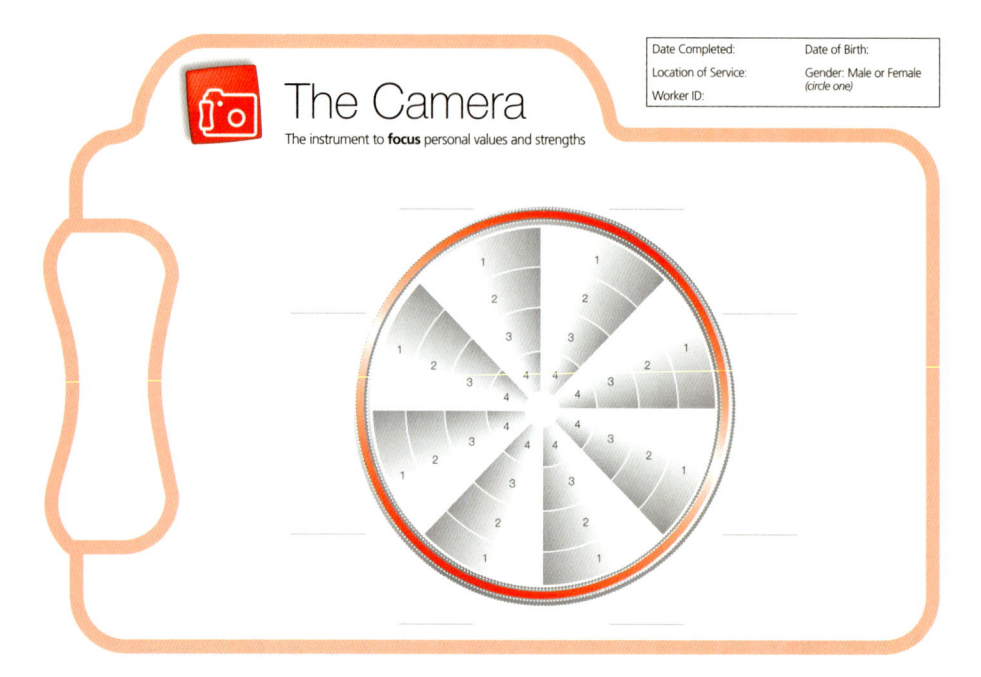

PLATE 7 (Also see Fig. 78.2.) The Camera values and strengths use coaching tool. Oades, L.G., Crowe, T.P. & Nguyen, M. (2009). Leadership coaching transforming mental health systems from the inside out: The Collaborative Recovery Model as person-centred strengths based coaching psychology. *International Coaching Psychology Review*, 4(1), 64–75. Reproduced with permission (© University of Wollongong).

# The Compass

The instrument to know where you are and **where you are going**

| Date Completed: | Date of Birth: |
|---|---|
| Location of Service: | Gender: Male or Female *(circle one)* |
| Worker ID: | |

## My personal life vision is:

*(e.g. what would you call a photo album of photos taken by your camera – values and strengths)*

Please list in order of importance up to 3 **valued life directions** towards which you are typically trying to orient yourself in your daily life (blue areas). On the review date, rate the level of success you feel you've attained within this **valued direction** (orange areas).

| | Valued direction A | Attainment Score (tick one at review) | Valued direction B | Attainment Score (tick one at review) | Valued direction C | Attainment Score (tick one at review) |
|---|---|---|---|---|---|---|
| Higher level goal attainment | Write goal here | score = 2 | Write goal here | score = 2 | Write goal here | score = 2 |
| Target goal attainment >70% confident | Write goal here / Target goal importance A (A+B+C must = 10) | score = 1 | Write goal here / Target goal importance B (A+B+C must = 10) | score = 1 | Write goal here / Target goal importance C (A+B+C must = 10) | score = 1 |
| Lower level goal attainment | Write goal here | score = 0 | Write goal here | score = 0 | Write goal here | score = 0 |
| | Coordinate A | | Coordinate B | | Coordinate C | |

**Calculating Coordinates:** For each Valued direction, multiply the Attainment score by the Target goal importance, to get a Coordinate.
**Calculating Success Coordinates:** Add Coordinates A, B and C. Multiply this number by 5. This is your Success coordinate out of 100.

Success Coordinate

**PLATE 8** (Also see Fig. 78.3.) The Compass valued direction and goal striving coaching tool. Oades, L.G., Crowe, T.P. & Nguyen, M. (2009). Leadership coaching transforming mental health systems from the inside out: The Collaborative Recovery Model as person-centred strengths based coaching psychology. *International Coaching Psychology Review, 4*(1), 64–75. Reproduced with permission (© University of Wollongong).

# The MAP

My Action Plan: The instrument to plan **what to do next**

| Valued Direction (from Compass) | Target goal (from Compass) | | |
|---|---|---|---|
| **Action name:** Eg walking | **Action Description:** What specific action is required to achieve the target level goal? Eg Walking briskly on the oval next door three times a week in the morning | | |
| **Date Set:** | How often | When | Where |
| **Social support** | **Resources** Who can give me practical help? With what? | **Information** Who can give me information when needed? What information? | **Emotional** Who can listen to and support me? |
| **Monitoring actions** | How will I monitor actions? (eg diary, calendar recording what you have done) | | |
| **Barriers** | What are my barriers? (eg financial, time, motivation) | | |
| **Solutions** | What are some solutions or backup plans? | | |
| **Confidence** (circle level of confidence) | Not at all confident  0 10 20 30 40 50 60 70 80 90 100  Very confident Specific action listed above. Repeat if not over 70% confident. | | |
| **Review date:** Make as soon as possible | **Review outcome:** | | |

Date Completed:   Location of Service:   Worker ID:   Date of Birth:   Gender: Male or Female (circle one)

PLATE 9 (Also see Fig. 78.4.) The MAP action planning coaching tool. Oades, L.G., Crowe, T.P. & Nguyen, M. (2009). Leadership coaching transforming mental health systems from the inside out: The Collaborative Recovery Model as person-centred strengths based coaching psychology. *International Coaching Psychology Review*, 4(1), 64–75. Reproduced with permission (© University of Wollongong).

# CHAPTER 44

# HAPPINESS IN THE CLASSROOM

JENNIFER M. FOX EADES[1], CARMEL PROCTOR[2], AND MARTIN ASHLEY[1]

[1]Edge Hill University, UK; [2]Positive Psychology Research Centre, UK

There is great interest today in the subject of happiness and well-being. In December 2009 policy-makers from 100 countries traveled to Brazil to consider ways of creating policies that focus on happiness instead of economic growth (Grainger, 2010). This concern for happiness extends to the field of education. Schools all over the world are focusing on topics such as emotional literacy, resilience, and well-being. The second Australian Positive Psychology and Well-being Conference in 2010 had an entire section devoted to positive education while psychologists such as Martin Seligman suggest that well-being should be taught in schools alongside traditional subjects (Seligman, Ernst, Gillham, Rievich, & Linkins, 2009).

It might be argued that schools should concern themselves less with happiness and more with learning. However, there is no contradiction between a concern for happiness and a concern for learning. We agree with Noddings's (2003) contention that "happiness and education are, properly, intimately related: Happiness should be an aim of education and a good education should contribute significantly to personal and collective happiness" (p. 1). This chapter is grounded in the belief that happiness is an appropriate aim of education and also a tool for facilitating effective education because how we feel has a direct impact on how we learn. Happiness in the classroom however extends beyond merely "feeling good" and includes feeling competent, challenged, autonomous, respected, and engaged in meaningful activities. For children and young people "happiness" will encompass the highest possible standards of education, a high level of challenge and ample opportunities to develop as active and ethical citizens. This chapter will give examples of classroom practice that include a focus on happiness or well-being. It will argue that an appropriate concern for the happiness of both students and teachers will ultimately enhance learning and in no way detract from this core purpose.

# An Idea with History

There are educational traditions that have focused on the well-being and happiness of the child for many years. Montessori (2008) emphasized intrinsic motivation and "spontaneous concentration" and argued for the creation of a classroom environment that would integrate both freedom (autonomy) and a high level of challenge (Shernoff & Csikszentmihalyi, 2009). Soka Education, developed by Japanese philosopher and educator Tsunesaburo Makiguchi (1871–1944), was founded on the principle that the purpose of education is the lifelong happiness of the learner (Jaffe, 1993). More recently the Dalai Llama has sponsored an educational initiative (informed by Tibetan Buddhist traditions) called The 16 Guidelines (Murdoch & Oldershaw, 2008). These guidelines encourage teachers and students to focus on 16 positive qualities known to enhance one's quality of life and relationships. The education of the whole child is a goal that has also been held by other religious traditions. For example, in a recent book by Christopher Jamison (2008), the Abbot of Worth Abbey and former Head Teacher of Worth School, he argues that well-being in its deepest sense has always been at the heart of the Christian monastic tradition.

While a concern with happiness in the classroom cannot be said to be new, the understanding that emotions are intimately bound up with cognition and learning, coupled with concern at apparently growing rates of depression among young people, has led to increased interest in the subject of well-being within schools and colleges in recent years (Craig, 2007). The field of positive psychology is helping to provide a growing body of evidence about what contributes to happiness and why it is important. It is argued that whilst the human tendency to preference the negative aspects of our experience has had evolutionary value, directing excessive attention towards such experiences compromises our happiness and impedes our ability to learn (Seligman, 2002). Positive psychologists propose that this negative attentional bias can be deliberately and effectively balanced by a focus on the positive. Evidence emerging from the field supports the work of teachers in considering the "whole child" and in adopting positive approaches to education. For example, work on the effects of positive emotion on learning, creativity, and memory (Frederickson, 2001; Isen, 2000) strongly suggests that happy students are likely to learn more effectively. Research such as this is helpful for cultivating classroom practices and curricula that will promote happiness and well-being, whilst also providing excellent educational opportunities.

# Promoting Happiness Alongside Educational Excellence

The following example illustrates how concepts from positive psychology can be applied creatively by teachers to simultaneously promote educational excellence and student well-being. Whilst the case study represents an unpublished piece of action research, it is described here to illustrate how positive psychology may be used to benefit students of varying ability.

The Milestone School is a school for students with severe learning difficulties (aged 2–16 years) which runs a project called "Making Listening Special" (Thompson, 2009). The project uses concepts from Gentle Teaching (McGee & Menolascino, 1991), an approach to working with special needs that explicitly focuses on well-being. The aim of the project has been to increase the happiness, confidence, and sense of belonging of a class of children on the autistic spectrum. It does this by putting the strengths of the children at the heart of curriculum planning and classroom organization. Daily planning is informed by both the curriculum content and the extent to which activities enhance student self-worth and are perceived as meaningful. The staff achieve this via direct observation of students (to detect personal strengths) and then plan daily activities that are designed to utilize those strengths. Activities that allow children to enter "flow" and feel calm are typically given priority and are often used at the start of each day to increase positive emotions (such as serenity). The explicit aim of the project has been to improve learning and deal with the educational challenges of students by maximizing their choices and involving them in decision-making. For example, a common difficulty in class is turn taking and sharing. To address this challenge a weekly session was planned that drew on students' favorite activities and incorporated choices about how they would work on the skills of "wait and share." Not only did these skills develop quickly as a result of these sessions, the staff also noticed a transferring of these skills back into the classroom. As a result, the staff have realized that taking the time to listen and observe students is key to gaining an understanding of their individual strengths and needs. Indeed, listening to the students and involving them more in decision-making, appears to have been a potent combination in increasing students' levels of participation, confidence, understanding, and co-operation, whilst also enabling the students to influence the culture and organization of the school.

# What Kind of Happiness Matters in the Classroom?

Ricard (2003/2006) argues that happiness is not simply the absence of unhappiness. Indeed the construct of happiness is a complex one. Seligman (2002) distinguishes between three kinds of happiness, which lead respectively to what he calls the pleasant life, the engaged life, and the meaningful life. All three kinds of happiness are relevant in the classroom and there is considerable overlap between them in educational contexts. Based on this conceptualization, one can argue that a happy classroom is not the same as a flourishing classroom.

## The pleasant life (or hedonic happiness)

This is perhaps what most people think of when the word "happiness" is used. Positive emotion has an important impact on our ability to learn in the present moment and on our longer-term well-being. Frederickson (2001) highlights the effect of positive emotions like gratitude, joy, serenity, and delight on memory, verbal dexterity, openness in social relationships, and creativity. Creating a positive mood at the start of a school day or a class lesson (e.g., through play, laughter, savoring a happy memory or a piece of food) is likely to have a positive impact on learning (the rationale use by the Milestone School). Research has also shown that positive reminiscence about the past increases happiness in the present (Bryant, Smart, & King, 2005) and that expressing gratitude can lead to increased optimism and satisfaction with life (Lyubomirsky, 2008). These insights are potentially helpful for teachers in shaping curricula that allow students time to focus on the positive, through activities like writing about happy memories or writing thank you letters. This also emphasizes the educational value of making space during school days to stop and savor one's experiences (a practice that is likely to also shape school culture).

## The engaged life (or fulfillment)

This dimension of happiness has obvious relevance to the classroom. Mihalyi Csikszentmihalyi (1990) has identified the state of flow as a combination of concentration, interest, and enjoyment. Flow is best described as a state of optimal functioning in which an individual is fully immersed and absorbed in the task at hand, to the extent that they fail to notice the passage of time (Csikszentmihalyi, 1990). According to Csikszentmihalyi (1990), flow emerges during periods where the challenge of a task and a person's skill level are at a point of equilibrium and subsides whenever they are not. Accordingly, challenging activities attempted with too little skill typically result in anxiety and frustration, and skill levels that exceed the level of challenge typically result in boredom or disinterest. The challenge for educators is to design activities that balance skill and challenge and to facilitate in older students the total absorption often seen in the very young (who appear to enter flow states easily and regularly). Results of studies conducted in the USA indicate that high school students are less engaged and experience less flow in the classroom than anywhere else. Shernoff and Csikszentmihalyi (2009) found that students experience greater enjoyment, motivation, self-esteem, and engagement when they perceive themselves to be in control, active, and competent. During after school activities, students experienced a greater variety of instructional techniques than in the classroom and reported more flow and more engagement. Engagement and enjoyment were also higher in mixed adult/student groups than for students alone.

Oral story telling is one practical way of increasing flow in the classroom. When a teacher tells a story well and is completely focused both on the story and the audience they are likely to approach a state of flow. The listeners are also in flow, recreating the story for themselves in their imaginations and totally absorbed in the present moment. It is rare for students not to fully engage with a well-told story. When students learn to tell stories for themselves they become fully engaged in the task at hand, relishing the experience of being in control in deciding how to retell a story: what to include, what to leave out, what words to use, whether to use props or gestures. Full concentration is both essential in storytelling and a precondition for flow.

Mindfulness is another construct with relevance to engagement. Whilst flow is characterized by the narrowing of attention (on the task at hand) and diminished awareness of non-task related information (e.g., situational factors, bodily sensations, etc), mindfulness, by contrast, is associated with an expanding of awareness and an ability to direct one's attention towards present moment experience without becoming enmeshed in it (or captured by it). These are clearly important skills to promote in any classroom. A student's ability to pay attention to the task in hand has a direct bearing on their success and mindfulness practice has been shown to improve a variety of perceptual and cognitive abilities related to the quality of attention (Murphy, Donovan, & Taylor, 1997). Hart (2004) gives examples of simple practices that can integrate mindfulness into the classroom from preschool to university level. For example, teachers at Milestone School hold a basic intention to be mindful and seek to develop their ability to reflect, to monitor their emotions and to teach "with love, kindness, and compassion" (Thompson, 2009).

The Mindfulness in Schools Project in the UK is currently trialing a number of mindfulness training programs within different educational contexts with encouraging results (Burnet, 2009; Morris, 2009). Whilst not all schools will feel equipped to teach mindfulness in a formal sense, at the simplest form mindfulness can be promoted by encouraging students to become more aware of themselves and of others. Other classroom programs such as Celebrating Strengths (Fox Eades, 2008) and Strengths Gym (Proctor & Fox Eades, 2009) both utilize a teaching technique called a community of enquiry (Lipman, 2003) that cultivates mindfulness in students. A community of enquiry is a structured discussion in which participants can speak without interruption and where time is spent in silent reflection. Used thoughtfully and regularly, a community of enquiry will help students to become more aware of their own thought processes, more attentive to their peers, and consequently more mindful.

## The meaningful life

Whilst this is perhaps the most difficult dimension of happiness to apply in the classroom, it is possibly the most crucial. This is the dimension that aligns most closely to the Buddhist conception of happiness. Ricard (2003/2006) argues that while pleasure is important, it is fleeting and focused on the individual. Buddhist notions of happiness, however, regard it as a form of lasting well-being, with selflessness an integral part. According to Seligman (2002) meaningful happiness includes values and strengths, a sense of belonging or social connectedness, and satisfaction with life. It might also include a focus on spirituality and ethics. As Montessori (2008) discovered, meaningful activities are essential to fostering intrinsic motivation, whilst concentration, attentiveness, and student engagement have all been found to be significantly higher when learning is perceived as both challenging and relevant (Shernoff, Csikszentmihalyi, Schneider, & Shernoff, 2003). As mentioned earlier, the Milestone School found that allowing students to choose meaningful activities increased classroom participation levels. Other studies have confirmed this observation. For example, a pilot study conducted by Frost and Stenton (2010) involved students in the management of their schools (by giving them meaningful activities and some operational responsibilities) and observed a "radical shift" in the attitudes of participating students.

Whilst all the dimensions of happiness discussed overlap significantly, all make unique contributions to the flourishing classroom. The examples in this chapter reflect a small sample of the range of creative work being done in schools around the world.

# Happy Students or Happy Schools?

Whilst schools are principally concerned with the academic achievement and well-being of individuals, teaching most typically occurs within groups and a broader educational context that influences happiness. The question can therefore be asked: Are educators best to focus on the happiness of individuals in classrooms or on whole classrooms and the wider institution? Positive psychology has been criticized in the past for an overemphasis on the individual and a neglect of what is required to create positive institutions (Gable & Haidt, 2005). Ideally, a focus on happiness in the classroom will consider both the individual and the wider institution of which individuals are part.

Much of the work in education inspired by positive psychology has, indeed, focused on individuals rather than on institutions. A pilot study by Ewen (2009) found that a 10-week positive psychology group coaching program for Year 5 students resulted in significant increases in goal striving, hope, and well-being. The students completed the Values in Action (VIA) Inventory of Strengths for Youth (Park & Peterson, 2006) and created "Strengths Shields" for display in the classroom. They also learned about goal setting, completed mindfulness exercises, wrote gratitude letters, and told a story about themselves at their very best. Similarly, a high school study by Green, Grant, and Rynsaardt (2007) found that ten individual coaching sessions, facilitated by a trained teacher-coach, resulted in significant increases in cognitive hardiness and hope and decreases in depression for a group of female students (n = 28). Another individually focused program is The Penn Resiliency Program (PRP), which aims to reduce hopelessness, anxiety, and depressive symptoms and to increase students' ability to withstand the common problems of adolescence (Gillham, Brunwasser, & Freres, 2007). Designed and researched by psychologists over the past 20 years using control studies, PRP delivers a series of structured lessons designed to teach realistic thinking (Gillham, Brunwasser, et al., 2007; Gillham, Reivech, et al., 2007). Research has shown that this program is optimized when it is facilitated by either psychologists or by teachers who have undergone intensive training and supervision.

By contrast, the Geelong Grammar School in Australia is currently attempting to embed positive psychology into the practice and curriculum of the whole school (Seligman et al., 2009). Starting in January 2008, teachers at the school received intensive training from a team of psychologists over a period of months in topics such as resilience, strengths, gratitude, and positive communication. The school has introduced stand alone courses (across several grades) on subjects like strengths and supplemented them with whole-school practices, such as students starting the day with a focus on "what went well" (WWW) the previous day (Fox Eades, 2006). In addition, teachers are developing their own methods of applying the principles they have learned. For example, a sports coach using a character strengths framework to debrief teams following a game (Seligman et al., 2009).

## Celebrating Strengths—A Focus on the Institution

One institution-wide approach is the Celebrating Strengths framework (Fox Eades, 2008), which takes a whole-school view of well-being. One of the unique features of this approach is that it focuses as much on the adults as it does on the students in a school, and as much on the school environment as it does on the content of lessons. The approach is built upon the belief that a flourishing classroom requires a flourishing teacher, recognizing that a highly stressed, unhappy teacher will find it hard to create the conditions needed for students to flourish. Developed in collaboration with teachers and students in the UK, Celebrating Strengths started as a pilot project designed to promote mental health in classrooms through a focus on oral storytelling and regular community celebrations.

A wide range of traditional stories, told by students and teachers alike, are connected to seven annual celebrations. Particular strengths are then associated with each celebration and students learn to "strengths spot" in themselves, in the stories they hear, and in one another. Story telling, like strengths, crosses the entire curriculum so it enables positive concepts like courage and kindness to be embedded into the daily life and the curriculum of the school. Schools using the Celebrating Strengths approach do not have dedicated lessons on positive psychology. This was partly to avoid adding to an already overcrowded curriculum, and partly because the aim was to embed principles of positive mental health into the existing curriculum, organization, and daily life of the school.

An unpublished evaluation of Celebrating Strengths found that the project had affected teachers as well as students (Linley & Govindji, 2008). Pilot schools reported increases in student confidence, self-esteem, and social and emotional intelligence. They also reported increases in teacher engagement, work enjoyment, and resilience. One teacher reported a renewed sense of vocation. In addition, student behavior and especially teamwork improved and students realized, sometimes for the first time, that their peers with special educational needs also had strengths. According to the findings from this pilot study, a focus on the whole institution resulted in increases in happiness for individuals (Linley & Govindji, 2008). Encouraged by these preliminary findings, several other institutional interventions are currently being piloted with the aim of developing strengths-based school cultures and increasing teacher satisfaction, student academic performance, and the well-being of students and teachers.

An example of this work is the development of Strengths Gym (Proctor & Fox Eades, 2009). Originally conceptualized as a component of the Celebrating Strengths framework, Strengths Gym is now a program in its own right[1] and is being used by students between the ages of 11–14. The aim of Strengths Gym is to encourage students to build their strengths, learn new strengths, and to recognize strengths in themselves and others. Student booklets contain descriptions of 24 strengths, based on the VIA inventory of strengths classification (Peterson & Seligman, 2004) and a selection of exercises, called "Strengths Builders" and "Strengths Challenges," that encourage students to reflect on the strengths they see most in themselves and to use those strengths in different ways. Designed to be used flexibly, these exercises can be completed by students working alone or in class and may be applied in school-wide initiatives (such as focusing on a particular strength for a day). The Strengths Gym handbook provides teachers with brief theoretical rationale for each strength, along with ideas for lesson plans. It also provides stories, historical or contemporary, that illustrate the strengths being used in real life. Preliminary research has found that participation in the program is associated with significant increases in life satisfaction among students (Proctor, Tsukayama, Wood, Maltby, Fox Eades, & Linley, 2010).

To complement the use of Strengths Gym with younger students, work in one high school that piloted the program also focused on engaging the staff and older students in trying to embed strengths-based ways of working into all levels of school life. This included having senior leaders participate in strengths-based coaching conversations designed to deepen their awareness of their own strengths and setting time aside at leadership meetings to engage in development work that focused explicitly on strengths. A range of initiatives were developed, including strengths-based careers preparation for older students, a strengths-based student leadership program, cross-curricular links to strengths, school wide "traditions" with a

---

[1] Please see: http://www.strengthsgym.co.uk for more details.

focus on strengths, and reflective and strengths-based assemblies. While the initiatives were wide ranging, all were underpinned by the following core principles: (1) the focus on strengths applied to staff and students equally; (2) students were to be involved in the planning and implementation of projects wherever practical; (3) teachers and students were the "experts" in their own school, and (4) teacher well-being was central to the success of the project.

## Creating the Conditions for Happiness

Self-determination theory (Ryan & Deci, 2000) proposes that well-being derives from the satisfaction of three basic human needs: autonomy, competence, and relatedness. All of the work that has been described in this chapter may be seen as fulfilling one or more of these needs. For example, evidence-based coaching interventions (e.g., Ewen, 2009; Green, Grant & Rynsaardt, 2007) and programs like the PRP (Seligman et al., 2009) which teach skills like goal setting, explanatory style, or active constructive responding, increase students' sense of competence and their perceived ability to face challenges. Similarly, work at the Milestone School (Thompson, 2009) has adopted "student as expert" as one of its guiding principles, purposefully maximizing student choice and thus promoting autonomy for children with severe learning difficulties. It also promoted student competence, by respecting and making space for students' strengths, and relatedness through a focus on warm accepting relationships with the teacher. As such, it appears that (in line with the basic predictions of self-determination theory) an explicit focus on strengths may create conditions that enhance well-being through the satisfaction of basic psychological needs for autonomy, competence, and confidence (Linley & Harrington, 2006).

Another crucial element of the "happy classroom" is the provision of meaningful activities. Montessori education is a good example of a tradition that places "meaning" at the heart of education. Students engaged in what they regard as pointless exercises will struggle to concentrate or to feel any degree of engagement with what they do. Epstein (2007) argues that much of the "problem" with teenagers in the West today stems from the fact that our culture deprives them of autonomy and meaningful activity. Indeed, research has demonstrated that schools which foster student autonomy, responsibility, and egalitarian staff–student relationships report higher levels of student engagement than traditional schools with more controlling staff and more rigid, irrelevant curriculum (Shernoff & Csikszentmihalyi, 2009).

Teachers are the single most important factor in creating happiness in the classroom so the well-being and happiness of each teacher is of great importance. Meaningful challenge is certainly crucial to student engagement, but whether challenge is perceived as positive or negative by students is directly related to the classroom climate created by the teacher. A focus on process rather than outcome, on effort rather than attainment, and on the positive value of risk taking and mistakes produce a high level of motivation and enjoyment for students (Turner & Meyer, 2004). Turner and Meyer (2004) also argue that this emphasis on challenge, effort, and student accountability must be accompanied by positive affect and enthusiasm on the part of the teacher. For this reason, any program that promotes happiness for students but which neglects the happiness of staff is not likely to be a successful long term strategy. As Noddings (2004) points out, "if children are to be happy in schools, their teachers should also be happy. Too often we forget this obvious connection." (p. 261) A focus on student happiness needs therefore to be underpinned by a whole school philosophy that respects and promotes autonomy, competence, and relatedness for staff and students alike. Controlling management practices, deficit-based performance review, rigid learning schemes that allow no place for teacher creativity or student initiative will undermine or limit the effectiveness of any number of happiness programs. A focus on the individual will therefore ideally be balanced by a genuine and authentic whole school ethos that promotes well-being for all members of the community.

## Imposing Happiness?

The challenge for leaders, coaches, or psychologists wishing to promote applied positive psychology innovation in schools is that imposed change can lead to demoralization and a perceived lack of autonomy and competence in staff. A recent study by Grenville-Cleave (2009) found that UK teachers had less perceived control—and less well-being—than other professionals. As Frost and MacBeath (2010) point out, "Teachers have, for decades, been at the receiving end of so many demands and 'brilliant' but ephemeral ideas, so that any impetus for sustained change has to be understood within the context and developmental history of the school" (p. 28). A top-down, expert-led initiative can be counter productive if it imposes rigid structures on teachers and does not acknowledge their expertise. As such, the challenge for researchers and practitioners becomes: How can new ideas be introduced into classrooms in a way that affirms the existing strengths and expertise of staff and students?

Strengths Gym (Proctor & Fox Eades, 2009) is an example of a program that, despite being designed by "experts," seeks to satisfy the autonomy, relatedness, and competence needs of both students and staff. For students choice is an integral part of the program, with options being provided within each lesson. For example, students can choose to work individually or in groups. They are considered to be the "experts" on the strengths they possess and are invited to lead classes whenever their strengths become a focus of study. For the teachers, they are encouraged to engage in activities alongside students as co-learners, not experts. Their handbooks present Strengths Gym as a flexible framework, rather than a blueprint, and provide suggestions and ideas, rather than prescriptions. In addition, stories are provided in the handbook for each lesson because story telling is considered a key pedagogical tool, an inherently respectful teaching method, and a powerful means of building positive relationships (see Fox Eades, 2006, 2008).

Another approach that offers great potential in this area is Appreciative Inquiry (AI; Cooperrider, Whitney, & Stavros, 2008), as the use of AI at the institution level would involve seeking to identify what is already being done to enhance happiness in schools and then to build upon the best elements of such work. In so doing, an institution's current efforts become a platform for transformative initiatives that emerge from within the institution itself (even though they may be enhanced by theories or knowledge derived from other disciplines, like positive psychology). Though not widely known in education, some schools are already using AI to bring about effective change at the level of the institution (Adamson, Samuels, & Willoughby, 2002).

## Making Room for Unhappiness?

It is perhaps unfortunate that schools in the UK are now assessed on how well they promote student well-being. Creating happiness targets alongside targets for achievement in English, maths, and science was perhaps not the best way of recommending well-being to the UK's teachers. There is a danger that happiness becomes yet another target for both staff and students to fail at and it is too important for that. As Parke (2007) notes, "nothing truly valuable can ever be made into a target."

Recently Ben-Shahar (2002) has called for "permission to be human," emphasizing the fact that we all feel a full range of emotions at some point, including occasionally feeling discouraged or low. A school or classroom that promotes a meaningful level of happiness, as opposed to simply pleasure, will be one where both students and teachers can be authentic, however they are feeling. Students learn regardless of how well or unhappy they are feeling because they are remarkably resilient. Teachers teach effectively however much stress they may be under because they are competent professionals. One of the reasons Celebrating Strengths (Fox Eades, 2008) has always used traditional stories in the classroom is that they make space for the negative or uncomfortable emotions (like anger, fear, and hate) in a safe and containing way. All emotional life is relevant to the flourishing classroom. Moreover, sometimes, as Bushe (2007) argues, "the motivation underlying 'keeping the focus on the positive" (p.4) is to avoid the anxiety of dealing with real concerns or to suppress the expression of dissent." Neither is desirable. A classroom or a school that takes happiness seriously will stifle neither debate nor the appropriate expression of any human emotion.

## Recommendations for Practice

The following recommendations can be made for practitioners interested in promoting happiness within educational contexts:

- Change initiatives must take the well-being of staff into account.
- Involve students and staff in considering how to apply positive principles in a school.
- Focus on the whole-school culture as well as the individual.
- Practice positive psychology in lessons and life, don't just teach about it.
- Positive practices need to be modeled by the adults within the school.
- Make space for unhappiness—it is part of being human.

## Conclusion

Ricard (2003/2006) points out that happiness, in the sense of a deep, lasting well-being, is a skill that can be learned with committed effort. Whilst teachers cannot guarantee their students happiness, they can ensure that they create conditions (both at the classroom and school levels) that allow their students to flourish and learn the skills required to be happy. The conditions that promote happiness in the classroom—autonomy, relatedness, competence, meaningful activities, a focus on strengths, mutual respect, and positive regard—are also the conditions that promote creativity, curiosity, love of learning, and intrinsic motivation. A focus on happiness is not an "add on" to the real business of education, but a necessary condition for fostering the lifelong love of learning that is the goal for every school. Moreover, for schools to realize that goal, it is not enough for teachers to be concerned with the well-being of their students; school leaders, politicians, and society as a whole must also consider the well-being of teachers. Schools where teachers and students feel valued and able to flourish, will be effective schools, as well as happy ones.

## References

Adamson, J., Samuels, N., & Willoughby, G. (2002). Changing the way we change at heathside school. *Managing Schools Today, March*, 24–27.

Ben-Shahar, T. (2002). *The question of happiness*. London, UK: Writers Club Press.

Bryant, F. B., Smart, C. M., & King, S. P. (2005). Using the past to enhance the present: Boosting happiness through positive reminiscence. *Journal of Happiness Studies*, 6(3), 227–260.

Burnet, R. (2009). *Mindfulness in schools, learning lessons from the adults-secular and Buddhist*. Unpublished manuscript.

Bushe, G. R. (2007). Appreciative inquiry is not (just) about the positive. *OD Practitioner*, 39(4), 30–35.

Cooperrider, D. L., & Srivasta, S. (1987). Appreciative inquiry in organizational life. *Research in Organizational Change and Development*, 1, 129–169.

Cooperrider, D. L., Whitney, D., & Stavros, J. M. (2008). *Appreciative inquiry handbook* (2nd ed.). Brunswick OH: Crown Custom Publishing, Inc.

Craig, C. (2007). *The potential dangers of a systematic, explicit approach to teaching social and emotional skills (SEAL)*. Glasgow: Centre for Confidence and Wellbeing.

Csikszentmihalyi, M. (1990). *Flow: The psychology of optimal experience*. New York, NY: Harper and Row.

Deci, E. L., & Flaste, R. (1995). *Why we do what we do*. London, UK: Penguin.

Epstein, R. (2007). *The case against adolescence: Rediscovering the adult in every teen*. Sanger, CA: Quill Driver Books.

Ewen, W. (2009). *The strong kids programme*. Unpublished manuscript.

Fox Eades, J. M. (2006). *Classroom tales: Using storytelling to build emotional, social and academic skills across the primary curriculum*. London, UK: Jessica Kingsley Publishers.

Fox Eades, J. M. (2008). *Celebrating strengths: Building strengths-based schools*. Coventry, UK: CAPP Press.

Frederickson, B. L. (2001). The role of positive emotions in positive psychology: The broaden-and-build theory of positive emotions. *American Psychologist*, 56, 218–226.

Frost, D., & MacBeath, J. (2010). *Learning to lead: An evaluation*. Cambridge, UK: Leadership for Learning, University of Cambridge Faculty of Education.

Frost, D., & Stenton, S. (2010). *Leading to lead: The story so far*. Cambridge and Wells, UK: University of Cambridge Faculty of Education/Learning to Lead CIS.

Gable, S. L., & Haidt, J. (2005). What (and why) is positive psychology? *Review of General Psychology*, 9(2), 103–110.

Gillham, J. E., Brunwasser, S. M., & Freres, D. R. (2007). Preventing depression early in adolescence: The Penn Resiliency Program. In J. R. Z. Abela, & B. L. Hankin (Eds.), *Handbook of depression in children and adolescents* (pp. 309–332). New York, NY: Guildford Press.

Gillham, J. E., Reivich, K. J., Freres, D. R., Chaplin, T. M., Shatté, A. J., Samuels, B., ... Martin, E. P. (2007). School-based prevention of depressive symptoms: A randomized controlled study of the effectiveness and specificity of the Penn resiliency program. *Journal of Consulting and Clinical Psychology*, 75(1), 9.

Grainger, L. (2010, January 2). A happier measure. *The Times*.

Green, S., Grant, A., & Rynsaardt, J. (2007). Evidence-based life coaching for senior high school students: Building hardiness and hope. *International Coaching Psychology Review*, 2(1), 24–32.

Grenville-Cleave, B. (2009). *UK teachers in 2008: Surviving or thriving?* Unpublished manuscript.

Hart, T. (2004). Opening the contemplative mind in the classroom. *Journal of Transformative Education*, 2(1), 28–46.

Ikeda, D. (2001). *Soka education: A Buddhist vision for teachers, students and parents*. Santa Monica, CA: Middleway Press.

Isen, A. M. (2000). Positive affect and decision-making. In M. Lewis, & J. M. Haviland-Jones (Eds.), *Handbook of emotions* (pp. 417–435). New York, NY: Guildford.

Jaffe, C. (1993). Tsunesaburo Makiguchi: Teacher, philosopher, value creator. *Teaching Education*, 5(2), 101–105.

Jamison, C. (2008). *Finding happiness: Monastic steps for a fulfilling life*. London, UK: Weidenfeld & Nicolson.

Linley, P. A., & Govindji, R. (2008). *An evaluation of celebrating strengths*. Unpublished manuscript.

Linley, P. A., & Harrington, S. (2006). Strengths coaching: A potential-guided approach to coaching psychology. *International Coaching Psychology Review*, 1(1)

Lipman, M. (2003). *Thinking in education*. Cambridge, UK: Cambridge University Press.

Lyubomirsky, S. (2008). *The how of happiness*. London, UK: Penguin Press.

McGee, J., & Menolascino, F. J. (1991). *Beyond gentle teaching: A nonaversive approach to helping those in need*. New York, NY: Plenum Press.

Montessori, M. (2008). *The Montessori method*. USA: BN Publishing

Morris, I. (2009). *Teaching happiness and well-being in schools: Learning to ride elephants* London, UK: Continuum International Publishing Group Ltd.

Murdoch, A., & Oldershaw, D. (2008). *16 guidelines for a happy life, the basics*. London, UK: Essential Education.

Murphy, M., Donovan, S., & Taylor, E. (1997). *The physical and psychological effects of meditation: A review of contemporary research 1991–1996* (2nd ed.). Petalum, CA: Institute of Noetic Sciences.

Noddings, N. (2003). *Happiness and education*. New York, NY: Cambridge University Press.

Noddings, N. (2004). *Happiness and education* (New ed.). New York, NY: Cambridge University Press.

Park, N., & Peterson, C. (2006). Moral competence and character strengths among adolescents: The development and validation of the values in action inventory of strengths for youth. *Journal of Adolescence*, 29(6), 891–909.

Park, N., Peterson, C., Seligman, M. E. P., & Steen, T. A. (2005). Positive psychology progress: Empirical interventions. *American Psychologist, 60*(5), 410–421.

Parke, S. (2007). *The beautiful life: Ten new commandments because life could be better.* London, UK: Bloomsbury.

Peterson, C., & Seligman, M. E. P. (2004). *Character strengths and virtues: A classification and handbook.* Washington, DC: American Psychological Association.

Proctor, C., & Fox Eades, J. (2009). *Strengths Gym.* St. Peter Port, Guernsey: Positive Psychology Research Centre.

Proctor, C., Tsukayama, E., Wood, A. M., Maltby, J., Fox Eades, J., & Linley, P. A., (2010). Strengths Gym: The impact of a character strengths-based intervention on the life satisfaction and well-being of adolescents. *Journal of Positive Psychology, 6,* 377–388.

Ricard, M. (2003/2006). *Happiness: A guide to developing life's most important skill.* (J. Browner, Trans.). London, UK: Atlantic Books. (Work originally published in 2003).

Ryan, R. M., & Deci, E. L. (2000). Self-determination theory and the facilitation of intrinsic motivation, social development, and well-being. *American Psychologist, 55*(1), 68–78.

Santorelli, S. (1999). *Heal thy self.* New York, NY: Three Rivers Press.

Seligman, M. E. P. (2002). *Authentic happiness.* London, UK: Nicholas Brealey Publishing.

Seligman, M. E. P., Ernst, R. M., Gillham, J., Rievich, K., & Linkins, M. (2009). Positive psychology and classroom interventions. *Oxford Review of Education, 35*(3), 293–311.

Shernoff, D. J., Csikszentmihalyi, M., Schneider, B., & Shernoff, E. S. (2003). Student engagement in high school classrooms from the perspective of flow theory. *School Psychology Quarterly, 18,* 158–176.

Shernoff, D. J., & Csikszentmihalyi, M. (2009). Flow in schools, cultivating engaged learners and optimal learning environments. In R. Gilman, E. S. Huebner & M. J. Furlong (Eds.), *Handbook of positive psychology in schools* (pp. 131–145). New York, NY: Routledge.

Thompson, J. (2009). *Making listening special.* Unpublished manuscript.

Turner, J. C., & Meyer, D. K. (2004). A classroom perspective on the principle of moderate challenge in mathematics. *The Journal of Educational Research, 97,* 311–318.

# CHAPTER 45

# APPLYING HAPPINESS AND WELL-BEING RESEARCH TO THE TEACHING AND LEARNING PROCESS

### LAURA McINERNEY

Positive Psychology UK, UK

Classrooms are good places to find examples of happiness and the positive consequences of motivation and hard work. Students develop confidence, skills, and abilities through teachers who use their knowledge of pedagogy to plan and facilitate learning activities. When this works well, students grow and exhibit not only their new found capacity but also their satisfaction and pleasure at the results, as is touchingly displayed in any graduation hall.

Yet, as a school teacher, the author is also aware that learning can be a painful experience. Learning anything requires a student to start at ignorance before working towards competence. Getting to competence involves the learner actively engaging with new materials and completing tasks they cannot initially do. Learning therefore comes with the potential for failure, humiliation and frustration. When these negative emotions are felt by learners they may react aggressively, outwardly expressing their negative emotions or otherwise withdrawing from the situation (Claxton, 2002). Seeing their well-intentioned plans dissolving, many teachers also panic, experience anxiety, and then negatively express their own emotions. In these instances, the happy productive classroom becomes a miserable environment. "Happiness" research and the literature of well-being have the potential to guide educators in understanding the factors contributing to this careful balance.

By applying research on well-being to the classroom educators can facilitate a more positive learning environment. This chapter will outline ways that happiness research has commonly been applied to classrooms before suggesting new ways to incorporate research into all learning environments and ending on a defense against those who argue happiness is not a legitimate focus for educators.

# A Short History of Well-being Programs in Education

Since the late 1800s educators have been conflicted about education's purpose and its potential for the academic, moral, emotional, and social development of learners. For much of the twentieth century, Western countries focused on traditional conceptions of knowledge based on academic subject groups, e.g., math, geography, and music. Increasingly educators felt the emotional aspects of learning were neglected, prompting school leaders to reconsider the curricula needs of young people. Programs were developed to meet particular needs arising as new social issues arose or "soft-skills" were needed. Examples include school programs developing knowledge on HIV/AIDs during the 1980s (Kirby, Laris, & Rolleri, 2007) or teaching students the basics of cookery in the UK due to a rise in obesity (Office for Standards in Education, Children's Services and Skills (Ofsted), 2006). Concerns about the mental health of young people and their ability to cope in a modernizing world have led to several programs focused on improving student mental well-being. Specific facets of positive mental-functioning, e.g., self-esteem or resilience, have been the main focus of most programs.

One example of a school program focused on one aspect of well-being is the Penn Resilience Program, an American program teaching the cognitive behavioral and problem-solving skills of resilient individuals to elementary and middle school students (Gillham, Hamilton, Freres, Patton, & Gallop, 2006). Over a series of lessons learners complete role plays, skits, and stories illustrating techniques that resilient individuals tend to use. Once the skills are understood, students practice the skill using hypothetical situations. The program has been extensively evaluated with results varying widely. A meta-analysis of 17 controlled evaluations of the program found participants reported fewer depressive symptoms up to 1 year after the program in comparison to young people who received no intervention (Brunwasser, Gillham, & Kim, 2009). However, the Penn Resilience Program is essentially preventative in nature with the expressed aim of reducing depression among teenagers. For students whose future functioning is more positive the program is beneficial, however, it is difficult to ascertain whether it is beneficial for students not at risk of depression.

An alternative program, "Zippy's Friends," is an international 24-week school curriculum that teaches all students a set of coping skills designed to improve future relationships and mental well-being. Meta-analysis of the program's evaluation reports at least small positive effects for each implementation of the program (Durlak & Wells, 1997). However evaluated programs tend to have small sample sizes and use "expert" teachers for implementation (Mishara & Ystgaard, 2006). Given that research clearly shows that the quality of a teacher impacts on student well-being and achievement regardless of the subject it is difficult to discern whether positive student outcomes from Zippy's Friends are due to the content of the lessons on coping skills or whether it is due to students receiving the attention of a high-quality teacher (Hattie, 2003).

The quality of teachers may also be a key factor in the positive outcomes of UK-based well-being curricula. For example, English schools teach "Personal, Social, Health & Economic Education" as part of the National Curriculum entitlement for 11–16-year-olds.

Included in the curriculum are skills of communication, negotiation, and collaboration across a range of social situations in order to promote physical and mental health. A recent report from the Schools Inspectorate Ofsted attributed the quality of student learning and outcomes in this subject to the skills of teachers and the time dedicated to the program. If poor quality teachers deliver the program then the outcomes are less positive even when lessons are carefully pre-planned by a trained coordinator (Ofsted, 2010). Initial findings of the UK Resilience Programme across 22 schools in the UK also found that beneficial outcomes for students were mediated by the effectiveness of the delivery team and the quality of teachers (Challen, Noden, West, & Machin, 2009).

A second problem besets the traditional curriculum approach to improving student well-being and happiness. Students may learn the rules of punctuation at school but this does not guarantee they will become great writers; likewise, teaching the skills of happiness does not necessarily translate into happy, highly-functioning individuals. This inability to transfer desired behaviors through school lessons is demonstrated by the many carefully researched and implemented youth pregnancy prevention programs still failing to achieve success in reducing pregnancy among teenagers (DiCenso, Guyatt, Willan, & Griffith, 2002; Franklin, Grant, Corcoran, Miller, & Bultman, 1997). While formal curricula can support the teaching of resilience, a school program alone is unlikely to replace all negative behaviors with positive ones. The successful translation of such skills appears to require teachers who continually model skills—such as negotiation and resilience—as well as an atmosphere of positive peer relationships across the school (Mellanby, Newcombe, Rees, & Tripp, 2001; Nation et al., 2003). After all, students learn their "real-world values" by watching the way adults in schools make value choices (Jackson, 1968). In my classroom I could deliver an academically rigorous lesson clearly explaining techniques for improving resilience, but if I continually lose my temper and fail to model the skills I explain then the students are unlikely to develop the required attitude or skills. In fact, they are more likely to feel dissatisfaction at the inauthentic message portrayed. But, if I can model positive behaviors students absorb these positive messages information and work to live up to expectation (Thornberg, 2009). Curriculum approaches are therefore important, but are undermined if wider school policies do not model the lessons being taught. To fully increase positive behaviors all educational environments should be infused with adults modeling positive skills and promoting well-being whether the subject is math, psychology, or an after-school sports club.

## Applying Happiness and Well-being Research to all Learning Environments

The good news is that research on well-being can be used to improve the effectiveness of teaching in any subject. Teachers have used psychological research on cognitive development for many years to structure appropriately difficult learning activities—for example, beginning with simple concrete ideas before having students attend to more creative tasks including abstract concepts (Bruner, 1966). Research on happiness and well-being should also be used by practitioners in order to structure activities that attend to the emotional as well as intellectual, growth of their students.

# Applying positive emotion research to the learning environment

Getting students to begin the learning process is difficult if they do not feel ready. Humans use their emotions as a way to judge whether or not to enter novel situations. Positive emotions signal safety and prompt "approach-mode" behaviors, so if a student enters a classroom feeling positively they will more readily attend to new problems (Davidson, 1993). On the other hand, negative emotions signal that situations are unsafe and our brain responds by prompting withdrawal behaviors, e.g., if the learner feels threatened they may refuse to complete a worksheet. Given the potential for failure when learning, students may feel unpleasant emotions in anticipation of this failure and therefore reject participation in a learning task. It is therefore crucial that teachers carefully plan activities that will engage positive emotions and elicit approach-mode behaviors, particularly at the beginning of class.

Positive emotions not only encourage students to begin learning, they can also impact productivity as demonstrated in Barbara Fredrickson's "broaden-and-build" theory (Fredrickson & Brannigan, 2005). Fredrickson showed that participants primed with positive images responded more productively to the question "How many uses are there for a brick?" than participants in a second group primed with negative images. This is because negative images narrow thinking whereas the positive images increase divergent thinking resulting in more creative problem-solving. Experiments also show that people high in positive emotions have a more global visual processing style, make greater word associations, and are more flexible in their categorizations of objects, all findings supporting the idea that positive emotions promote creativity (Isen, Johnson, Mertz, & Robinson, 1985; Isen, Niedenthal, & Cantor, 1992; Kimchi & Palmer, 1982). The impact of this for teachers was highlighted recently by a teacher colleague I watched describing his own experience of this phenomena to a group of trainee teachers. Having struggled in a previous topic to capture the attention of his rowdy class of 14-year-olds, he planned a lesson on crime and punishment that began with an attention-grabbing slide show graphically depicting lynch mobbings, stonings, and a public hanging. Predictably the students sat in quiet fascination all through the slides but afterwards they sincerely struggled to attempt the main learning of creating arguments "for" and "against" the death penalty. My colleague guiltily explained that while his behavior management technique of "shock" had achieved the aim of pacifying the class's behavior he had unwittingly sent his students into "withdraw-mode" moments before a learning activity that required creative thinking. Emotional manipulation can therefore be an asset in the classroom but it requires careful thought if one is to gain the most beneficial atmosphere.

In order to test my colleague's findings I rewrote the slides I first show students arriving into my class. When teaching women's voting rights for several years I started my lesson with an image of Emily Davies, an English suffragette, being trampled by a horse in during a protest for women's rights in the early 1900s. Students are prompted to brainstorm questions to ask about the picture and we discuss the possible answers to their queries. Though students were often interested in the picture, many also seemed nervous; sometimes students would stay at a physical distance from the picture, pulling away as they entered the room and discussions were often briefer than I expected given the intriguing nature of the subject. After rewriting I now show pictures of women in the United Arab Emirates and Switzerland voting in their countries for the first time (in 2006 and 1990 respectively).

Immediately upon making the switch students asked more questions and, unexpectedly, were more likely to offer personal opinions and debate with others in the class about their answers. Although initially counterintuitive I now regularly reframe activities so they focus on the most positive, rather than the most negative aspects, of the concept I am trying to teach.

Positive emotions are not, however, the only emotion required for a beneficial learning environment. Research shows that a positive mood can reduce other abilities—for example, reducing student performance on reasoning tests (Oaksford, Morris, Grainger, & Williams, 1996), the Stroop Test (Phillips, Bull, Adams, & Fraser, 2002), and complex problem-solving (Spering, Wagener, & Funke, 2005). Unlike tasks with open answers that require creativity, some problems require concentration and discernment therefore benefiting most from a neutral to negative mood.

In either case, teachers limit student potential if they only plan for happy environments. Focusing on the flexibility and context-usefulness of emotions creates the best quality teaching environment. Although researchers tend to treat emotions as static "one-off," in reality emotions work more like the links in a bicycle chain by overlapping and continually moving. The most successful students will be those who best regulate their emotions, moving between "concentration" and mild frustration through to being "optimistic" or "joyful." Good educators teach students how best to self-manage these emotional links.

# Applying emotional intelligence research to the learning environment

Teaching emotional regulation was recently highlighted to school leaders through Daniel Goleman's (1998) popular book on emotional intelligence (EI). Goleman argues that using our emotions intelligently is more important than cognitive ability for career and scholastic success. In the UK, the Department for Children, Schools & Families created a school-wide program of SEAL—"Social and Emotional Aspects of Learning" (DfEeS, 2005)—based on Goleman's conclusions and drawing on psychological research showing that negative emotions block learning and that emotions interplay with cognitive abilities as they help guide prioritization and decision-making (Damasio, Everitt, & Bishop, 1996). The Department's report for the program pointed to curricula that had been taught in schools and had improved student behavior (Marshall & Watt, 1999). However, the SEAL program authors recognized that the limited time and resources available for ensuring specific lessons of SEAL were delivered meant a "holistic" approach would better help students manage their emotions. Problematically the report provided few detailed strategies for achieving this holistic nature and while follow-up evaluations show that many teachers were positive about the implementation of SEAL (Hallam, 2009) the evidence that it reduced truancy or the type of poor behaviors that lead to school exclusion are limited (Craig, 2007) The issue appears to be that SEAL focused on improving the self-esteem of children and making them feel more positive, rather than improving student's ability to self-regulate their emotions in ways appropriate to the situation. Though EI could be usefully implemented in schools, so far this has not clearly been the case in the UK.

The wider research picture on EI is, however, useful to classroom teachers seeking to improve the learning environment they create for learners. The Mayer–Salovey model of EI

(Salovey & Mayer, 1990) outlines EI as the ability to: identify emotions, use those emotions to solve problems, understand what causes and changes emotions, and manage our emotions so that decisions are based on our understanding of emotions. This is similar to the need for flexibility shown in classroom observations. Sansone and Thoman (2005) found that when a student is given stimulus materials—for example, an article about children living in slums—the material may first invoke disgust, then interest, until finally, when completing a task related to the article, the student feels relaxed. In this chain of events all the emotions are perfectly appropriate for maintaining interest and motivation. The disgust occurred when creative thinking was not required, but the student pushed themselves past it and became curious before, finally, when they felt safe they began the task. The emotionally intelligent individual is therefore the one who can regulate their emotions during tasks using emotion-regulation strategies such as "self talk" which will beneficially affect their performance (Aydin & Emmioglu, 2008).

The critical question is how can teachers encourage students to self-regulate emotions in the most beneficial way possible? Teaching strategies such as biofeedback, mindfulness, and internal talk all help students develop the emotional self-regulation skills demonstrated by emotionally intelligent people. As per the Mayor–Salovey model, helping students first identify their emotions is the initial way to improve their ability to change emotions. Biofeedback is particularly useful at this stage. Experiments show that participants in a condition observing their physiological responses—e.g., heart rate and blood pressure—are more able to change into a productive calmer state and make better decisions than participants who cannot see their physical state (Katkin, Wiens, & Öhman, 2001). In my classroom, students cannot continually monitor physiology through technology but I can teach students to recognize the physical sign of their emotions. I can do this explicitly by getting students to measure their heart rate before and during a competitive math challenge. If I have a class that struggles to settle down, particularly after playing sport during their breaks, I will ask the students to try and purposely lower their heart rates through concentration. Many students are skeptical that this can be done but most achieve it simply by being told that it is possible and allowing them the time to practice this skill. Beyond my own classroom, psychological research shows that teaching students the physical signs of emotions through meditation and conscious breathing exercises improves their ability to notice their emotional state and hence they can slowly begin changing it (Schutz & Davis, 2000).

In addition to biofeedback, mindfulness techniques also enhance students' ability to recognize and manipulate their emotional state. Evidence suggests that mindful meditation can improve self-actualization, empathy, increase autonomy, moral maturity, concentration, and attention (Shapiro, Schwarzt, & Santerre, 2002). Wachelka and Katz (1999) worked with a group of vulnerable students and taught progressive muscle relaxation, guided imagery, and self-instruction training and study skills. In comparison to a control group, the students taught these techniques decreased their level of text anxiety but instead demonstrated an increase in self-esteem. Although not going to the lengths of a full-blown program, I have watched several lessons were teachers use a "mindfulness" entry activity to calm learners. One particularly lively group of underperforming boys tried to concentrate on a paper cup for 1 minute. The boys clearly struggled with the task, though most remained quiet, but almost all reported enjoying the experience and wrote in their reflections that this was one of the activities they most enjoyed. Over the year the teacher was able to extend the time of the activity until the boys were able to sit quietly, looking at the cup, for up to 10 minutes of time. When re-telling this story some colleagues have criticized the teacher for using learning time to teach a basic skill. Before the meditations, however, the students struggled to sit through teacher demonstrations and were often removed from exam halls. The mindfulness activity was not only a positive experience for students but they gradually became more able to sit quietly in other contexts, e.g., exam halls, meaning their overall learning achievements increased.

A final way to improve EI is through the educator's own modeling of self-regulation in the face of their classroom conflicts. Developmental psychologists explain that children's emotional development occurs as a "co-construction" with their caregiver (Bretherton, 1993). When a conflict occurs, a child's ability to self-regulate their emotion usually reflects the pattern of regulation demonstrated by their caregiver in dialogues between the pair. Teachers are not parents but, especially with young learners, teachers may interact the child for several hours each day during a period when children are still making sense of their emotions and how best to use them. A caregiver who is focused on suppressing their own emotion tends to devalue a child's emotional experience in their dialogue and limits the child's ability to recognize and change their emotions in the future. Adults who identify and accept their own emotions before resolving to make changes model this in conversation to their children, prompting problem and emotion-focused coping approaches in their child (Thompson, 2006). In school I use this idea with trainee teachers who wish to keep students back to discuss an incident during the lesson. Quite reasonably, teachers are often angry at students whose behavior results in the teacher feeling embarrassed or threatened. In this heightened emotional state inexperienced teachers sometimes try to provoke embarrassment or fear in their students, which then results in the student also becoming angry. A more useful approach is having both the student and teacher write about the incident explaining what happened, how they felt, the consequence of these feelings, and providing suggestions for the future. In doing so, both parties are working through the Mayor–Salovey EI process of identifying, understanding, and creating ways to change the emotions. This process helps the teacher became calmer and more able to deal with the situation while also modeling positive emotion regulation to the student. Some educators may feel this process undermines the role of the teacher as it brings both student and teacher to the same level; however, it supports students' ability to regulate themselves flexibly in the future and will therefore lead to a more positive classroom in the future.

## Applying humor research to the learning process

A more straightforward approach to improving the learning environment is using humor and its evidenced impact on well-being and learning. Humor is a specific subset of positive emotion, where laughter signals a person's internal positive emotion. Laughter correlates with greater physiological health as shown in experiments where participants increased their production of salivary antibody immunoglobulin A, suggesting humor increases functioning of a person's immune system (Dillon, Minchoff, & Baker, 1985). But humor is not only beneficial for physical health, it also impacts the mental well-being of students and their capacity for learning (Wanzer & Frymier, 1999).

Laughter acts as an all-clear sign, signaling to others in our group that a novel experience does not require a stress reaction (Gervais & Wilson, 2005). Hence, we laugh if a person slips and falls in a way clearly showing they are not badly hurt, but we tend not to laugh if the person has broken a limb. The all-clear signal means the body relaxes and can remain in a neutral, or approach-mode state. In the classroom, teachers can create laughter by surprising students with novel situations that seem strange but are safe. Costumes, silly voices, or actions and props provide "safe shocks" bringing about laughter and the associated relaxed and positive emotional state.

The positive state induced by humor enables students to learn more quickly and effectively (Gorham & Christophel, 1990). If used early in a lesson, humor promotes student participation providing an early opportunity for successful learning, meaning students are more likely to remain engaged in the learning process. Humor is therefore a useful learning aid although it has two problems. Firstly, in a meta-analysis of humor research Martin (2007) explains that most humor research does show humor positively impacts health and well-being but only in the short term. It is therefore useful for engaging students positively at the beginning of lessons, but should not be relied on as a lasting strategy for learning. A more important issue is that humor is highly personal with a potential dark side if used for sarcasm or bullying. Humor in the classroom is not appropriate if some students become the topic of the joke or are excluded due to the humor. For these reasons many teachers may be uncomfortable with the use of humor in the classroom and seek other ways to create a positive environment.

## Applying research on play and flow to student motivation

If positive emotion inducement and humor are limited strategies for creating positive learning environments a more sustainable strategy involves increasing students' internal motivation so that even when the learning process becomes difficult or frustrating the learner continues regardless. Many teachers rely on the use of sanctions and rewards to motivate students through difficult periods in their learning journey. However extrinsic motivators applied by classroom teachers can weaken students' natural curiosity and their intrinsic desire to learn (Deci, Koestner, & Ryan, 1999). When creating a positive learning environment it is more beneficial to fuel students' intrinsic desire to learn so that they choose to continue with their learning tasks.

Research shows that the quality and quantity of student motivation varies depending on the way learners are first introduced to tasks. In one experiment participants were given a series of activities to complete including menial tasks categorizing odd and even numbers mixed with creative tasks such as changing words in a joke to change its meaning. All participants completed the same tasks. However, for half of the participants their instructed referred to the tasks as "work" while the other half read instructions referring to the tasks as a "game." Once the tasks finished, participants described how often their mind wandered during the tasks. Participants in the "work" condition stated that their minds wandered twice as often as those in the play condition (Langer, 1997). Follow-up studies show that participants continue activities for longer periods of time when the task is presented as "play" versus "work" even though the tasks are identical in content (Sandelands, 1988). The conclusion drawn from these tasks is that "play" is associated with a more freeing, lower-stakes environment, engaging the brain in approach-mode behaviors encouraging participants to continue the task for longer periods than participants who negatively perceive the "work" as something to be quickly withdrawn from. Exams are often equated with "work" by students, hence when a teacher introduces the concept students sometimes disengage. But there is no reason why exams cannot be playful, especially in subjects with written answers. Encouraging students to "play" with their answers—by using interesting metaphors, diagrams, or language challenges (e.g., no words beginning with "e")—adds a sense of play to the task. Students are much more likely to remain engaging and develop creative thinking skills than if the exam is presented as inevitable "work."

Over the long term, maintaining a sense of "playfulness" can be quite exhausting and I have seen it lead to students devaluing their work as they start to believe that "fun" is more satisfying than progress in their learning. Where this occurs, a second approach to increasing motivation is to replace "fun" in the classroom with "flow", a state where people are deeply engrossed in a task, working at it for long periods of time and deeply enjoying the process. Flow is associated with higher levels of well-being, including a better self-concept (Jackson, 2001) and higher levels of commitment and achievement at school (Carli, Fave, & Massimini, 1988). After interviewing and observing many people in flow states Csikszentmihalyi (2000) concluded two conditions are vital for the occurrence of a flow state:

- There is a perceived challenge stretching beyond current capabilities, and
- Immediate feedback available on the aims of the task.

If a teacher can create these conditions in the classroom then the motivated state of "flow" will occur, meaning students become engaged in developing mastery of the target skill. Learning to drive is an example of a "class" where flow conditions easily occur. Initial tasks are easy—e.g., driving in a straight line—before gradually becoming more complex as the driver is encouraged into increasingly novel situations such as car parks or highways. Immediate feedback is given by the reactions of other drivers' physical closeness to other cars in parking tasks. Learning to drive can, however, be an intensely frustrating experience due to initial failures being experienced in public places. However, if the instructor can keep the learner feeling positive, and flexibly regulating how they feel while also providing the learner with the correct level of challenge and feedback, the learner is likely to become deeply engrossed in the learning process.

In a driving lesson flow conditions occur easily due to the learner's immersion into a "real-world" scenario. Arranging these conditions in a school classroom or lecture theatre is more difficult. A teacher may begin with a specific task—for example, simplifying fractions—but if the challenge is too high or too low learners may reject or not even begin if the potential for embarrassment is too high (Ryan, Connell, & Plant, 1990). By starting a lesson with open questions that have several correct answers, teachers can avoid panicking students and instead enable students to set their own challenge bar appropriately. For example, "Which fraction problem looks the hardest to solve?" can be accessed by all learners as it relies on personal opinion and learners with the greatest grasp on fractions are likely to discuss more complex reasons for their answers. Open questions provide comfort and enable students to find their own level of challenge but given that learners start at different levels of understanding, to keep students in flow teachers must provide opportunities for students to progress through activities at all levels of challenge but without being overwhelming. Computer games are particularly successful at providing this kind of learning. Designers program games so they become progressively more difficult as the player gains skills—for example, by decreasing the time available, encouraging multi-skilling, or requiring development of new abilities (Rieber, 1996). Computer games keep the challenge non-threatening by providing extra lives or re-entry points into the game when a failure occurs. Computer games also combine this with immediate feedback meaning that flow occurs because "skills and challenges are progressively balanced, goals are clear and feedback is unambiguous" (Bowman, 1982, p.15) Gamers therefore readily enter a state of flow being both challenged and able to continually correct mistakes.

Similar to the progressive difficulty in computer games, teachers learn to "differentiate," a process of adapting activities so that different students can access some learning (Petty, 2004). Differentiation can occur by task, outcome, or time allowed. For example, I have seen colleagues use differentiation technique involves color-coding an "activity menu" from which learners pick a "starter, main, & dessert" activity. In the "starter" menu a choice of tasks will be available, each requiring a different skill (e.g., drawing versus writing), time allocation, or level of understanding of the material. Students move through the menu at a pace appropriate to their needs, checking answers at each stage against answer-sheets before moving onto the next part of the menu. When discussing this lesson with trainee teachers, many were afraid their learners would always pick the "easiest" option. But, when pushed, they admit they have never seen a teenager continually play the same easy level on a computer game. When playing video games, young people often become obsessed with reaching higher and harder tasks. If students pick only the easy tasks this suggests that, for whatever reason, the student believes easy success is more valued than learning, or they find the task intrinsically demotivating or irrelevant (Jensen, 2008). In my colleague's case, by encouraging the student to complete all parts of the menu and explaining that the value was in continually attempting the tasks, all her students eventually challenged themselves to the harder tasks. By framing the tasks in this way each student could personalize the challenge, helping to bring about flow conditions.

Clear feedback is also an important motivator in the teaching and learning process. Since 1968, evidence has shown a relationship between effective teacher praise and a reduction in disruptive student behavior (Madsen, Becker, & Thomas, 1968). The quantity and the quality of feedback matters. In the early stages of learning, praise or positive corrective feedback is needed every 10 minutes to be effective with the frequency fading as a skill is developed. Alternatively teachers might use a "praise ratio" with some studies suggesting teachers use ten praise statements against each negative statement for maximum student engagement (Nafpaktitis, Mayer, & Butterworth, 1985). The content of the feedback is also important for motivation and developing student resilience. Experiments show that different types of praise impact students. Students were asked to complete a task and then praised differently afterwards. One group were praised for their innate abilities ("Wow. You got a high score. You must be smart at this."). A second group were praised for their efforts during the learning task ("You must have worked really hard to get that score."). Students were then asked to choose one of two tasks to do next. One task was challenging but students would learn a lot regardless of their success at the task. The other task was easier with assured success but provided less opportunity for learning. Ninety percent of the children praised for their effort completed the challenging task, whereas those praised for being intelligent only attempted the easier task (Mueller & Dweck, 1998). By praising innate ability the teacher inadvertently leads students to believe task outcomes reflect their personality and fails to encourage students to see that the process of learning is the most important part for success. The learner therefore begins to believe that future failures would reflect their personality and so seeks to avoid this situation, preferring immediate success over the longer-term benefits of hard work. In the long term, praise given for personality rather than effort or the demonstration of specific skills can lead to greater feelings of pseudo-incompetence causing procrastination and task avoidance in adult life (Clarkson, 1994). Therefore, if wishing to increase flow in the classroom and improve future mental well-being, teachers should provide timely, specific, and targeted praise helping the learner know where they were successful or where their work was wrong.

# Addressing Potential Dangers of Happiness in the Classroom

Undoubtedly, new strategies for promoting happiness in the classroom make some teachers uncomfortable. Over a 20-year career an average teacher personalizing 20 lesson plans per week, will plan over 15,000 lessons. Changing a process that you have completed 15,000 times is likely to be difficult and could prompt anxieties. Beyond fear of change, however, legitimate concerns are raised about the appropriateness of happiness in the classroom and the potential for ironic effects such that by focusing on happiness we actually reduce rather than increase its presence (Wegner, 1994). It is important to address these dangers and incorporate suggestions into practice where necessary.

## The danger of over-burdening teachers

Most teachers experience high-levels of stress throughout their day (Kyriacou, 1987). Physically, the levels of stress on teachers impacts their immune system leading to mental pressures such as cynicism, apathy, absenteeism, and even exit from the field (Guglielmi & Tatrow, 1998). Additional pressures are unlikely to ease this situation and evidence shows how the more teachers are controlled and forced to achieve specific learning outcomes, the more those teachers then over-control and negatively impact student learning (Deci, 1982). Making teachers responsible for the emotional lives of students is likely to add to this stressful workload.

Research into teacher professional development supports the idea that most teachers want to improve their teaching and learning environment and are happy to listen to new ideas if they are discussed through supportive networks and in a whole-school focus on practice (McLaughlin & Talbert, 2006). Teacher-led research communities can provide a "collective mindfulness" that not only improves teaching but can support feelings of belonging and staff retention, often used as key indicators of well-being (Weick, Sutcliffe, & Obstfeld, 1999). Happiness research can therefore add to classroom practice best if it is used as a discussion starting point in mentoring meetings, teacher-led groups, or staff development sessions rather than an anxiety-inducing prescriptive set of standards to be addressed in each lesson.

## The danger of "positive" rather than "purposeful" emotions

Positive emotions are not always the most appropriate emotion to induce in learning and students need to feel a range of emotions to remain psychologically healthy. Inexperienced teachers often confuse happy learners with productive ones and so focus on positive feelings as an outcome in its own right. Skeptics of "happiness" in education point out that positive feelings are not an end-point and under broader definitions of well-being such as *eudemonia*, happiness is derived from living the "worthwhile" life rather than constantly feeling pleasurable emotions (Smith, 2008). No research presented here opposes this claim. Learning often requires a neutral mood and teachers must be able to manage difficult emotions, such as frustration or embarrassment, from their pupils without trying to suppress or reduce those emotions. Only by working through them are students able to achieve and gain feelings of satisfaction. But, if built into school life well-being encourages active social engagement in civic life (Thornberg, 2009).

## The dangers of increasing self-esteem

The vigorous debate regarding the dangers or benefits of increasing self-esteem is sometimes introduced in discussions about happiness in learning as a way of diminishing the evidence base for applying well-being research into classrooms (Craig, 2007). Self-esteem has become a slippery concept but most debators in the argument conceptualize it as beliefs students hold about themselves, but rather than being based on judgments about ability (as per self-efficacy) it also incorporates the value judgments we make about our self-worth and what we are entitled to feel and demand from others. Helping students protect their self-esteem may reduce harmful mental disorders and promote happiness (Baumeister, Campbell, Krueger, & Vohs, 2003; Seligman, Reivich, Jaycox, & Gillham, 1995). Therefore several self-esteem programs implemented new educational practices in schools supporting the development of student self-esteem. For example, using aspirational grading and helping young people value their unique skills (Twenge & Im, 2007). A backlash has since developed against this approach, arguing that the evidence base for a link between self-esteem and higher achievement is limited and, contrary to expectation, low self-esteem does not contribute to violence, bullying, or risky behaviors such as alcohol or drug abuse (Emler, 2001; Twenge, 2006). Research also shows people undertaking risky behaviors tend to have high levels of self-esteem coupled with low levels of competence and also exhibit signs of narcissism and unhealthy materialism (Crocker & Park, 2004; Morf & Rhodewalt, 2001). It is therefore contended that changing educational practices to incorporate self-esteem was unfounded and based on flawed research. Both sides of the debate provide impressive arguments; however, it is important to recognize that schools have moved beyond simple notions of "self-esteem" and teachers are becoming more aware of all needs—cognitive, emotional, and social. The most important message is not that teaching self-esteem "went wrong," but that the picture is more complex than first thought, meaning school policies and materials should be adapted in response.

# Conclusion

Any teacher must work with the current curriculum and educational trends of their time, but among the changes that may occur in the education systems, teachers can always maximize student learning by taking the time to create a positive educational environment.

Doing so can be difficult due to practical constraints—time and resources—but also because we are not always sure what factors make the difference to learning. Research on cognitive developments has always informed pedagogy, but research on happiness and well-being also enhances our understanding of students' emotional relationship to learning and provides practical ways to improve our practice and increase student learning. This does not mean simply creating "happiness lessons" in which we transmit our knowledge about well-being to learners; instead we can, and we should, apply this knowledge to all parts of the teaching environment. After all, there is little point watching the usually touching scene of a graduation hall if everyone has achieved a broadening of the mind but happiness and well-being had to be sacrificed to achieve it.

# References

Aydin, Y. C., & Emmioglu, E. (2008). *High school students' emotions and emotion regulation during test taking*. European Conference on Educational Research, Goteberg.

Bandura, A. (1982). Self-efficacy mechanism in human agency. *The American Psychologist*, 37(2), 122–147.

Baumeister, R. F., Campbell, J. D., Krueger, J. I., & Vohs, K. D. (2003). Does high self-esteem cause better performance, interpersonal success, happiness or healthier lifestyles? *Psychological Science in the Public Interest*, 4(1), 1–44.

Berk, L. S., Tan, S. A., Fry, W. F., Napier, B. J., Lee, J. W., Hubbard, R. W., … Eby, W. C. (1989). Neuroendocrine and stress hormone changes during mirthful laughter. *The American Journal of the Medical Sciences*, 298(6), 390–396.

Bowman, J. (1982). A "Pac-Man" theory of motivation: Tactical implications for classroom instruction. *Educational Technology*, 22(9), 14–16.

Bretherton, I. (1993). From dialogue to internal working models: The co-construction of self in relationships. *Memory and Affect in Development*, 26, 237–263.

Bruner, J., Olver, R., & Greenfield, P. (Eds.). (1966). *Studies in cognitive growth*. New York, NY: Wiley.

Brunwasser, S. M., Gillham, J. E., & Kim, E. S. (2009). A meta-analytic review of the penn resiliency program's effect on depressive symptoms. *Journal of Consulting and Clinical Psychology*, 77(6), 1042–1054.

Carli, M., Fave, A. D., & Massimini, F. (1988). The quality of experience in the flow channels: Comparison of Italian and US students. In M. Csikszentmihalyi & I. Csikszentmihalyi (Eds.), *Optimal experience: Psychological studies of flow in consciousness* (pp. 288–306). New York, NY: Cambridge University Press.

Csikszentmihalyi, M. (2000). *Beyond boredom and anxiety: Experiencing flow in work and play*. San Francisco, CA: Jossey Bass.

Challen, A., Noden, P., West, A., & Machin, S. (2009). *UK resilience programme evaluation—Interim report*. London, UK: Department for Children, Schools & Families.

Clarkson, P. (1994). *The Achilles syndrome: Overcoming the secret fear of failure*. Shaftesbury, UK: Element.

Claxton, G. (2002). *Building learning power*. Bristol, UK: TLO limited.

Craig, C. (2007). *The potential dangers of a systematic, explicit approach to teaching social and emotional skills (SEAL)*. Glasgow, UK: Centre for Confidence & Well-Being.

Crocker, J., & Park, L. (2004). The costly pursuit of self-esteem. *Psychological Bulletin*, 130(3), 392–414.

Damasio, A. R., Everitt, B., & Bishop, D. (1996). The somatic marker hypothesis and the possible functions of the prefrontal cortex [and discussion]. *Philosophical Transactions: Biological Sciences*, 351(1346), 1413–1420.

Davidson, R. J. (1993). Parsing affective space: Perspectives from neuropsychology and psychophysiology. *Neuropsychology*, 7, 464–464.

Deci, E. L. (1982). Effects of performance standards on teaching styles: Behavior of controlling teachers. *Journal of Educational Psychology*, 74(6), 852–859.

Deci, E. L., Koestner, R., & Ryan, R. M. (1999). A meta-analytic review of experiments examining the effects of extrinsic rewards on intrinsic motivation. *Psychological Bulletin*, 125, 627–668.

DfES (2005). *Excellence and enjoyment: Social and emotional aspects of learning guidance*. London: Department for Education & Skills.

DiCenso, A., Guyatt, G., Willan, A., & Griffith, L. (2002). Interventions to reduce unintended pregnancies among adolescents: Systematic review of randomised controlled trials. *British Medical Journal*, 324(7351), 1426.

Dillon, K. M., Minchoff, B., & Baker, K. H. (1985). Positive emotional states and enhancement of the immune system. *The International Journal of Psychiatry in Medicine*, 15(1), 13–18.

Durlak, J. A., & Wells, A. M. (1997). Primary prevention mental health programs for children and adolescents: A meta-analytic review. *American Journal of Community Psychology*, 25(2), 115–152.

Emler, N. (2001). *Self esteem: The costs and causes of low self worth*. York, UK: The Joseph Rowntree Foundation.

Franklin, C., Grant, D., Corcoran, J., Miller, P. O. D., & Bultman, L. (1997). Effectiveness of prevention programs for adolescent pregnancy: A meta-analysis. *Journal of Marriage and the Family*, 59(3), 551–567.

Fredrickson, B. L., & Brannigan, C. A. (2005). Positive emotions broaden the scope of attention and thought-action repertoires. *Cognition and Emotion*, 19, 313–332.

Gervais, M., & Wilson, D. S. (2005). The evolution and functions of laughter and humor: A synthetic approach. *The Quarterly Review of Biology*, 80(4), 395–430.

Gillham, J. E., Hamilton, J., Freres, D. R., Patton, K., & Gallop, R. (2006). Preventing depression among early adolescents in the primary care setting: A randomized controlled study of the Penn resiliency program. *Journal of Abnormal Child Psychology*, 34(2), 195–211.

Glasser, W. (1998). *Choice theory: A new psychology of personal freedom* New York, NY: Harper Collins.

Goleman, D. (1998). *Working with emotional intelligence*, New York, NY: Random House, Inc.

Gorham, J., & Christophel, D. M. (1990). The relationship of teachers' use of humor in the classroom to immediacy and student learning. *Communication Education*, 39(1), 46–62.

Guglielmi, R. S., & Tatrow, K. (1998). Occupational stress, burnout, and health in teachers: A methodological and theoretical analysis. *Review of Educational Research*, 68(1), 61–99.

Hallam, S. (2009). An evaluation of the social and emotional aspects of learning (SEAL) programme: Promoting positive behaviour, effective learning and well-being in primary school children. *Oxford Review of Education*, 35(3), 313–330.

Hattie, J. (2003). *Teachers make a difference: What is the research evidence?* Paper presented at the Australian Council for Educational Research Annual Conference on Building Teacher Quality, Melbourne, October.

Isen, A. M., Johnson, M. M., Mertz, E., & Robinson, G. F. (1985). The influence of positive affect on the unusualness of word associations. *Journal of Personality and Social Psychology*, 48(6), 1413.

Isen, A. M., Niedenthal, P. M., & Cantor, N. (1992). An influence of positive affect on social categorization. *Motivation and Emotion, 16*(1), 65–78.

Jackson, P. W. (1968). *Life in classrooms.* New York, NY: Holt, Rinehart, and Winston.

Jackson, T., Thomas, P. R., Marsh, H. W., & Smethurst, C. J., (2001). Relationships between flow, self-concept, psychological skills, and performance. *Journal of Applied Sport Psychology, 13,* 129–153.

Jensen, E. (2008). *Brain-based learning: The new paradigm of teaching* San Diego, CA: Corwin Press.

Katkin, E. S., Wiens, S., & Öhman, A. (2001). Nonconscious fear conditioning, visceral perception, and the development of gut feelings. *Psychological Science, 12*(5), 366.

Kimchi, R., & Palmer, S. E. (1982). Form and texture in hierarchically constructed patterns. *Journal of Experimental Psychology: Human Perception and Performance, 8*(4), 521–535.

Kirby, D. B., Laris, B. A., & Rolleri, L. A. (2007). Sex and HIV education programs: Their impact on sexual behaviors of young people throughout the world. *Journal of Adolescent Health, 40*(3), 206–217.

Kyriacou, C. (1987). Teacher stress and burnout: An international review. *Educational Research, 29*(2), 146–152.

Langer, E. (1997). *The Power of Mindful Learning.* New York, NY: Perseus Publishing.

Madsen Jr, C. H., Becker, W. C., & Thomas, D. R. (1968). Rules, praise, and ignoring: Elements of elementary classroom control. *Journal of Applied Behavior Analysis, 1*(2), 139.

Marshall, J., & Watt, P. (1999). *Child behaviour problems: A literature review of the size and nature of the problem and prevention interventions in childhood.* Perth, Australia: Interagency Committee on Children's Futures.

Martin, R. A. (2007). *The psychology of humor: An integrative approach.* London, UK: Academic Press.

McCutcheon, G. (1981). On the interpretation of classroom observations. *Educational Researcher, 10*(5), 5–10.

McLaughlin, M. W., & Talbert, J. E. (2006). *Building school-based teacher learning communities: Professional strategies to improve student achievement.* New York, NY: Teachers College Press.

Mellanby, A., Newcombe, R., Rees, J., & Tripp, J. (2001). A comparative study of peer-led and adult-led school sex education. *Health Education Research, 16*(4), 481.

Mishara, B. L., & Ystgaard, M. (2006). Effectiveness of a mental health promotion program to improve coping skills in young children: Zippy's friends. *Early Childhood Research Quarterly, 21*(1), 110–123.

Morf, C. C., & Rhodewalt, F. (2001). Unravelling the paradoxes of narcissism: A dynamic self-regulatory processing model. *Psychological Inquiry, 12*(4), 177–196.

Morgan, W., & Streb, M. (2001). Building citizenship: How student voice in service-learning develops civic values. *Social Science Quarterly, 82*(1), 154–169.

Mueller, C. M., & Dweck, C. S. (1998). Praise for intelligence can undermine children's motivation and performance. *Journal of Personality and Social Psychology, 75,* 33–52.

Nafpaktitis, M., Mayer, G. R., & Butterworth, T. (1985). Natural rates of teacher approval and disapproval and their relation to student behavior in intermediate school classrooms. *Journal of Educational Psychology, 77*(3), 362–367.

Nation, M., Crusto, C., Wandersman, A., Kumpfer, K. L., Seybolt, D., Morrissey-Kane, E., & Davino, K. (2003). What works in prevention: Principles of effective prevention programs. *American Psychologist, 58*(6/7), 449–456.

Oaksford, M., Morris, F., Grainger, B., & Williams, J. M. G. (1996). Mood, reasoning, and central executive processes. *Journal of Experimental Psychology: Learning, Memory, and Cognition, 22*(2), 476–492.

Ofsted (2006). *Healthy schools, healthy children? The contribution of education to pupils' health and well-being.* London, UK: Ofsted.

Ofsted (2010). *Personal, social, health and economic education in schools.* London, UK: Ofsted.

Petty, G. (2004). *Teaching today: A practical guide.* London, UK: Nelson Thornes.

Phillips, L. H., Bull, R., Adams, E., & Fraser, L. (2002). Positive mood and executive function: Evidence from Stroop and fluency tasks. *Emotion, 2*(1), 12–22.

Rathunde, K., & Csikszentmihalyi, M. (2005). Middle school students' motivation and quality of experience: A comparison of Montessori and traditional school environments. *American Journal of Education, 111*(3), 341–371.

Rieber, L. P. (1996). Seriously considering play: Designing interactive learning environments based on the blending of microworlds, simulations, and games. *Educational Technology Research and Development, 44*(2), 43–58.

Ryan, R., & Deci, E. L. (2000). Self-determination theory and the facilitation of intrinsic motivation, social development, and well-being. *American Psychologist,* (65), 529–566.

Ryan, R. M., Connell, J. P., & Plant, R. W. (1990). Emotions in nondirected text learning. *Learning and Individual Differences, 2*(1), 1–17.

Ryan, R. M., Deci, E. L., & Grolnick, W. S. (1995). Autonomy, relatedness, and the self: Their relation to development and psychopathology. In D. Cicchetti & D. J. Cohens (Eds.), *Developmental psychopathology: Vol 1. Theory and Methods* (pp. 618–655). New York, NY: Wiley.

Salovey, P., & Mayer, J. D. (1990). Emotional intelligence. *Imagination, Cognition and Personality, 9*(3), 185–211.

Sandelands, L. E. (1988). Effects of work and play signals on task evaluation. *Journal of Applied Social Psychology, 18*(12), 1032–1048.

Sansone, C., & Thoman, D. B. (2005). Interest as the missing motivator in self-regulation. *European Psychologist, 10*(3), 175–186.

Schutz, P. A., & Davis, H. A. (2000). Emotions and self-regulation during test taking. *Educational Psychologist, 35*(4), 243–256.

Seligman, M. E. P., Reivich, K., Jaycox, L., & Gillham, J. (1995). *The optimistic child.* New York, NY: Harper Perennial.

Shapiro, S. L., Schwart, G. E. R., & Santerre, C. (2002). Meditation and positive psychology. In C. R. Snyder & S. J. Lopez (Eds.), *Handbook of positive psychology* (pp. 632–645). New York, NY: Oxford University Press.

Smith, R., (2008). The long slide to happiness. *Journal of Philosophy of Education, 42*(3–4), 559–573.

Spering, M., Wagener, D., & Funke, J. (2005). The role of emotions in complex problem-solving. *Cognition and Emotion, 19*(8), 1252–1261.

Thompson, R. A. (2006). Conversation and developing understanding: Introduction to the special issue. *Merrill-Palmer Quarterly, 52*(1), 1–16.

Thornberg, R. (2009). The moral construction of the good pupil embedded in school rules. *Education, Citizenship and Social Justice, 4*(3), 245–261.

Twenge, J. M. (2006). *Generation me.* New York, NY: Free Press.

Twenge, J. M., & Im, C. (2007). Changes in the need for social approval, 1958–2001. *Journal of Research in Personality, 41*(1), 171–189.

Wachelka, D., & Katz, R. C. (1999). Reducing test anxiety and improving academic self-esteem in high school and college students with learning disabilities. *Journal of Behavior Therapy and Experimental Psychiatry, 30*(3), 191–198.

Wanzer, M. B., & Frymier, A. B. (1999). The relationship between student perceptions of instructor humor and students' reports of learning. *Communication Education, 48*(1), 48–62.

Wegner, D. M. (1994). Ironic processes of mental control. *Psychological Review, 101*, 34–34.

Weick, K. E., Sutcliffe, K. M., & Obstfeld, D. (1999). Organizing for high reliability: Processes of collective mindfulness. *Research in Organizational Behavior, 21*, 23–81.

# CHAPTER 46

# RESILIENCE EDUCATION

JANE E. GILLHAM [1,2], RACHEL M. ABENAVOLI[5],
STEVEN M. BRUNWASSER[3], MARK LINKINS[4],
KAREN J. REIVICH[2], AND MARTIN E. P. SELIGMAN[2]

[1]Swarthmore College, Swarthmore, PA, USA; [2]Psychology Department and Positive Psychology Center, Pennsylvania State University, Philadelphia, USA; [3]University of Michigan, USA; [4]VIA Institute on Character, Cincinnati, USA; [5]Human Development & Family Studies, Pennsylvania State University, University Park, USA

> The aim of education should always transcend the development of academic competence. Schools have the added responsibility of preparing fully-functioning and resilient individuals capable of fulfilling their hopes and their aspirations. To do so, they must be armed with optimism, confidence, self-regard, and regard for others, and they must be shielded from unwarranted doubts about their potentialities and capacity for growth.
>
> Pajares (2009, p. 158)

## INTRODUCTION

ONE of the most striking findings in developmental and clinical research is that children who have been exposed to trauma, poverty, community violence, and other serious risk factors often reach, and sometimes surpass, normal developmental milestones. Research has identified many qualities in individuals and their social environments that promote resilience, and many of these qualities are malleable. That is, individuals can learn specific skills that contribute to resilience, and social environments can be structured in ways that promote resilience.

As a primary learning and social environment for most children, schools have tremendous potential to—and responsibility for—promoting resilience and well-being in children. This chapter reviews the rationale for focusing on resilience in education and illustrates some of the ways that schools can promote resilience in young people. Although resilience education can also encompass academic or educational resilience, we focus primarily on the power of schools to promote students' social and emotional well-being and provide examples from our team's work on school-based resilience and positive psychology interventions. As we hope to show, resilience education holds great promise in promoting the well-being of all students.

## Resilience

Many children who are exposed to harmful experiences and environments are remarkably resilient (Luthar, Cicchetti, & Becker, 2000; Masten, 2001). These children do not suffer the negative consequences that are expected for them. They adapt. Many of them thrive.

Such resilience does not imply that risk factors such as poverty, violence, and trauma are benign or should be accepted. The phenomenon of resilience does imply, however, that psychologists' understanding of children's development has been deficient. For many decades, clinical and developmental research focused on how children are damaged by adversity and ignored the capacity for positive development and growth even in the worst circumstances.

Resilience has been defined as a "dynamic process of positive adaptation or development in the context of significant adversity" (Luthar et al., 2000, p. 543). Youth who show resilience display "good outcomes in spite of serious threats to adaptation or development" (Masten, 2001, p. 228). As researchers have expanded their focus from predicting negative outcomes to also predicting positive outcomes and adaptation, they have discovered many qualities within people, families, and communities that can promote resilience. Although some qualities are especially important for children in high risk contexts, many promote children's social and emotional well-being in general (Collaborative for Academic, Social, and Emotional Learning (CASEL), 2003; Goleman, 1995; Luthar, 2006; Zins, Bloodworth, Weissberg, & Walberg, 2004). Fig. 46.1 lists many of these promotive qualities.

Some of the personal strengths and skills that are frequently mentioned across the resilience literature include: emotional competence (emotion awareness and regulation), self-regulation (impulse control, goal setting, self-discipline, perseverance), problem-solving and decision-making (being able to think creatively, flexibly, and realistically about the problems one encounters), social awareness (perspective taking, empathy, respect for others), social competence (communication, social engagement, teamwork, conflict management, giving and receiving help), self-efficacy, optimism, and a sense of purpose or meaning (for reviews, see Benard, 2004; CASEL, 2003; Goleman, 1995; Luthar, 2006; Reivich & Shatté, 2002; Zins et al., 2004). For example, personal skills and strengths such as self-control, problem-solving, and optimism are linked to higher academic achievement, to more positive relationships, and to greater emotional well-being (Duckworth & Seligman, 2005; Fincham & Bradbury, 1993; Seligman, 1991). These personal qualities include many of the character strengths identified in recent research in positive psychology (Park & Peterson, 2006; Peterson & Seligman, 2004).

Family, school, and community environments also promote resilience. Some of the environmental factors that foster resilience include caring relationships, safety, prosocial norms, high expectations, structure and guidance, and opportunities to contribute or to matter (Benard, 2004; Benninga, Berkowitz, Kuehn, & Smith, 2006; CASEL, 2003; Eccles, Flanagan, Lord, Midgley, Roeser, & Yee, 1996; Luthar, 2006; Reivich & Shatté, 2002; Wang, 2009;

```
┌─────────────────────────────────────┐
│ Personal Strengths and Skills       │
│ Emotional competence                │
│ Self-control                        │
│ Problem-solving & decision-making   │
│ Social awareness                    │       ┌─────────────────────────────────┐
│ Social competence                   │──┐    │ Positive outcomes               │
│ Self-efficacy                       │  │    │ Emotional well-being            │
│ Optimism                            │  │    │ Positive behavior               │
│ Purpose                             │  ├───▶│ Positive relationships          │
└─────────────────────────────────────┘  │    │ Engagement in school            │
              ▲                          │    │ Achievement                     │
              │                          │    │ Reductions in depression,       │
              ▼                          │    │   anxiety, substance use,       │
┌─────────────────────────────────────┐  │    │   behavioral problems, and other│
│ Nurturing Environments              │──┘    │   negative outcomes             │
│ Caring Relationships                │       └─────────────────────────────────┘
│ Safety                              │
│ Prosocial norms                     │
│ High expectations                   │
│ Structure and guidance              │
│ Opportunities to contribute         │
└─────────────────────────────────────┘
```

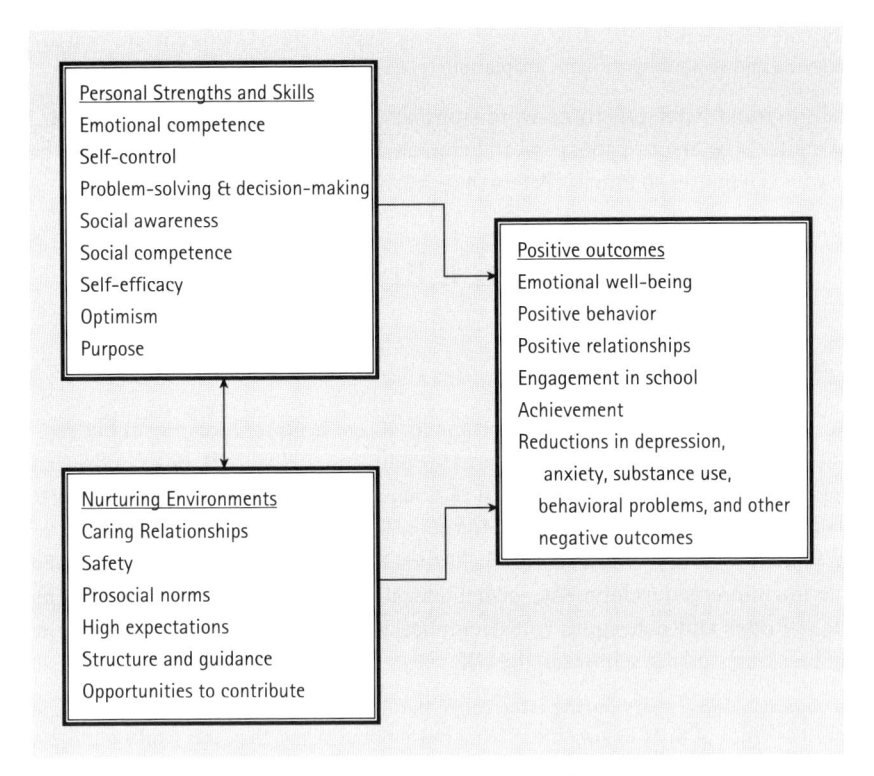

FIG. 46.1 Personal and social qualities that promote resilience.

Zins et al., 2004). Students with strong connections to school and to family are less likely than their peers to develop depression and to engage in substance use, violence, and other risky behaviors (Benard, 2004; Resnick et al., 1997; Rutter, Maughan, Mortimore, & Ouston, 1982; Wang, 2009). These connections may be especially important to children who are growing up in communities plagued by poverty and violence (Rutter et al., 1982; Wang, Haertel, & Walberg, 1994).

Positive environments and adaptive personal characteristics can be mutually reinforcing. Nurturing environments encourage the development of children's strengths. For example, teachers who convey high expectations and who help students to reach their potential promote optimism, self-efficacy, and persistence in their students. Children's strengths also shape their environments. Students who can control impulses help to create a safe school environment. Students who are kind help to create a nurturing and supportive environment. Over time, these different personal and environmental qualities interact and work together to promote resilience. Some qualities are linked to specific outcomes or are especially important in particular contexts. Thus, Fig. 46.1 presents a simplified model.

Research suggests that the characteristics of children's social environments are stronger predictors of resilience than children's personal qualities. In her review of the last 50 years of resilience research, Luthar (2006) concludes:

> The first major take-home message is this: Resilience rests, fundamentally, on relationships. The desire to belong is a basic human need and positive connections with others lie at the

very core of psychological development; strong, supportive relationships are critical for achieving and sustaining resilient adaptation. (p. 42)

This calls to mind Peterson's three-word summary of positive psychology research: "Other people matter" (Peterson, 2006, p. 249). Peterson also reminds us that "we are all the other people who can matter so much" (Peterson, 2008, np).

# Resilience Education

## The role of schools

Next to family, school is the most important social environment for most children. In the USA, more than 94,000 public schools provide education to more than 47 million students (Snyder & Hoffman, 2003). An additional 28,000 private schools provide education to more than 5 million children (Snyder, Tan, & Hoffman, 2006). Children and teens spend, on average, more than 30 hours a week at school (Juster, Ono, & Stafford, 2004). Because of its central role in children's development, formal education has enormous potential to promote resilience. Rutter and colleagues (1982) emphasize this potential in the opening to their ground breaking study of schools in the UK:

> For almost a dozen years during a formative period of their development, children spend almost as much of their waking life at school as at home. Altogether, this works out to some 15,000 hours (from the age of five until school leaving) during which schools and teachers may have an impact on the development of children in their care. (p. 1)

Schools can promote resilience by providing nurturing environments and by cultivating students' personal skills and strengths. Schools that provide children with safe and caring learning environments make a profound difference in children's lives, especially when these qualities are lacking or inconsistent in children's communities or families (Rutter et al., 1982; Wang et al., 1994). Schools are an ideal place for children to learn self-regulation and social skills such as empathy and teamwork that are essential for positive relationships and achievement. And because interpersonal and academic challenges are a regular part of life for most students at one time or another, there is ample opportunity to teach coping and problem solving skills in schools. Ultimately, education that focuses on resilience has the potential to promote students' growth and well-being both in and out of school, and long after students' participation in formal education has ended.

## Overlap with other educational initiatives

Resilience education (education that aims to foster students' resilience) overlaps with educational initiatives that promote good character (Berkowitz & Bier, 2004; Elias, Wang, Weissberg, Zins, & Walberg, 2002) and social and emotional learning (CASEL, 2003, 2007), as well as psychosocial interventions that aim to prevent psychopathology, substance use, and other negative outcomes (National Research Council and Institute of Medicine, 2009; Weissberg, Kumpfer, & Seligman, 2003). For example, CASEL defines social and emotional learning as "the process of acquiring the skills to recognize and manage emotions, set and achieve positive goals, appreciate the perspectives of others, establish and maintain positive relationships, make responsible decisions, and handle interpersonal situations effectively" (CASEL, 2007, p. 1). Similarly, Elias and colleagues define social emotional learning as "the process through which we learn to recognize and manage emotions, care about others, make good decisions, behave ethically and responsibly, develop positive relationships, and avoid negative behaviors" (Elias et al., 1997, as cited in Zins et al., 2004, p. 4). These behaviors and skills are central to resilience as well as to social and emotional well-being more generally. Resilience education is a component of "positive education" (Seligman, Ernst, Gillham, Reivich, & Linkins, 2009) and of positive youth development (Catalano, Berglund, Ryan, Lonczak, & Hawkins, 2004).

## The need for resilience education

Many psychologists and educators have argued that resilience skills are more important for children today than ever before (e.g., Greenberg et al., 2003). The number of children exposed to major adversity is staggering. In the USA, close to 50% of youth are exposed to violence each year, including 19% who witness a violent act within their community (Finkelhor, Turner, Ormrod, Hamby, & Kracke, 2009). Nearly 10% of youth witness violence between family members each year and nearly 10% of children are victims of physical or emotional abuse or neglect (Finkelhor et al., 2009). About 20% of children under 18 live in poverty (US Census Bureau, 2009). Children who live in poverty are more likely to experience other family and community risk factors such as violence, parental depression, parental conflict, abuse, and neglect (Evans, 2004). They are more likely than children from middle class or affluent communities to attend struggling schools and to be exposed to pollution and other environment risk factors (Evans, 2004). Thus, multiple risk factors converge in the lives of many children.

Psychological and behavioral difficulties are also very common among children. In a given year, about 20% of children will have diagnosable psychological disorders, such as depression or anxiety, that create at least mild impairment in functioning (US Department of Health and Human Services, 1999). Each year, about 5–9% of children are classified as having a "serious emotional disturbance" (US Department of Health and Human Services, 1999). Many adolescents experience elevated symptoms of depression, anxiety, and other psychological difficulties that do not reach the threshold for clinical diagnoses (Nolen-Hoeksema, Girgus, & Seligman, 1986). In a recent Centers for Disease Control and Prevention study, 28.5% of youth reported feeling so sad or hopeless that they stopped their normal activities at some point in the past year, and 11.3% had made a plan to commit suicide (Centers for Disease Control and Prevention, 2008).

There is some evidence that rates of psychological problems have increased during the last century. For example, research by Twenge and colleagues indicates that narcissistic and antisocial personality traits, depression, and anxiety have increased substantially over the last 50–70 years (Twenge, 2000; Twenge & Foster, 2010; Twenge et al., 2010). These findings are controversial; other research suggests that the rates of depression and other disorders have not increased substantially (Costello, Erkanli, & Angold, 2006). Nevertheless, mental health and public health experts agree that psychological and behavioral difficulties are extremely prevalent among school-age youth, especially during adolescence. Adolescents who develop depression and substance dependence are at high risk for future episodes and the associated difficulties throughout adulthood (Harrington, Fudge, Rutter, Pickles, & Hill,

1990; Kim-Cohen et al., 2003). Thus, programs that promote resilience during adolescence could have an enormous impact across a life time.

## Teaching resilience broadly

### Relevant to all students

Recent studies suggest that prevention programs that target youth at high risk are particularly beneficial (Conduct Problems Prevention Research Group, 2007; Horowitz & Garber, 2006; Stice, Shaw, Bohon, Marti, & Rohde, 2009), but educational initiatives that aim to reach all children are also important. Many risk factors are common and many children (even those believed to be at "low risk") will experience significant stressors or distress at some point during their school years. In addition, our knowledge of risk factors is incomplete. Significant risk factors may exist and even be common in environments that have traditionally been viewed as "low risk." For example, recent research suggests that many youth from backgrounds that are traditionally considered to be privileged are at high risk for anxiety, substance use, and other problems, perhaps because of the intense pressures to achieve and limited time with parents (Luthar & Latendresse, 2005).

### Applicable to a range of challenges

When people think about resilience, major adversities typically come to mind, for example, the child who performs well in school and who develops close connections to others despite enduring years of abuse and neglect. While such outcomes clearly signify resilience, our research team conceptualizes resilience more broadly. The process of resilience is also reflected in positive adaptation in response to everyday stressors (e.g., conflicts with peers, low marks in school) and common life transitions (e.g., the birth of a sibling, the break-up of relationship during adolescence). This broader definition appears justified given the evidence that both major life events and daily stressors contribute to depression and other difficulties (Bockting, Spinhoven, Koeter, Wouters, & Schene, 2006; Kwon & Laurenceau, 2002; Libby & Glenwick, 2010; Sund, Larsson, & Wichstrom, 2003; Thompson et al., 2007). Over time, responses to everyday events can develop into habits that either promote or detract from well-being, relationships, and ability to reach one's goals.

### Consistent with comprehensive education

Resilience education is consistent with a broad view of the purpose of education, as preparing youth to become lifelong learners who are productive, caring, and responsible members of the community (Cohen, 2006; Elias et al., 2002; Seligman et al., 2009). This broader view of education is supported by many parents and educators. For example, recent surveys indicate that two-thirds of adults in the USA believe that schools should be responsible for dealing with the social, emotional, and behavioral needs of their students (Rose & Gallup, 2007). About 85% want schools to focus more on the prevention of drug and alcohol abuse (Rose & Gallop, 2000). Respondents also gave high ratings to educational goals such as preparing youth to become responsible citizens, improving social conditions, enhancing happiness, and enriching people's lives (Rose & Gallup, 2000). More than 70% of respondents wanted schools to focus more on promoting racial and ethnic understanding and tolerance (Rose & Gallup, 2000). Creating the conditions necessary to meet these expectations should be a focus of our educational system.

## Approaches and findings

Two general approaches to enhancing resilience are through: (1) teaching skills and cultivating strengths and (2) promoting a nurturing school climate or culture. Initiatives that focus on teaching resilience skills and cultivating strengths often use curricula and formal instruction, explicit modeling, and/or coaching. Initiatives that focus on school climate may focus on instructional practices; school rules, policies, goals, and aspirations; support networks such as counseling and advisory; and increased collaborations with families and with individuals and organizations in the community that serve youth (Benard, 2004; Cohen, McCabe, Michelli, & Pickeral, 2009). Several approaches may be combined to weave resilience education into the fabric of the school.

### Research findings

There is considerable evidence for benefits from curricula and other school-based interventions that are designed to promote resilience in youth. For example, the Coping with Stress Course, which teaches coping and problem solving to adolescents with elevated symptoms of depression, prevents the onset of depressive disorders (Clarke et al., 1995). The Social Decision Making and Social Problem Solving Program, a curriculum that teaches self-control, social awareness, problem-solving, and decision-making, increases prosocial behavior and reduces behavioral problems in students (Elias, 2004). The Promoting Alternative THinking Strategies (or PATHS) program, which teaches emotional awareness, social competence, and problem-solving, improves social skills and prevents behavior problems and symptoms of anxiety and depression (Greenberg, Kusché, & Riggs, 2004). The Seattle Social Development program, a program for 1st through 6th graders that promotes a positive classroom environment and teaches social competence and problem-solving skills, prevents aggression, violence, substance use, and other high-risk behavior through adolescence (Hawkins, Smith, & Catalano, 2004).

Programs that teach resilience and promote students' social and emotional development have a wide range of positive effects. CASEL recently reviewed the relevant research literatures for: (1) universal programs (often delivered to whole classrooms), designed for implementation with all students, (2) indicated programs (typically small group interventions), designed for students who are showing early signs of behavioral or emotional problems, and (3) after-school programs (Payton et al., 2008). Together these reviews included more than 300 studies with about 300,000 students. On average, these programs significantly improved students' emotional well-being, social skills, classroom behavior, attitudes about school, and achievement. All three types of programs (universal, indicated, after-school) were beneficial relative to control. These findings are consistent with those of other recent reviews of school and community programs designed to promote social and emotional development and prevent psychological and behavioral problems (e.g., Catalano et al., 2004; Greenberg et al., 2003; Zins et al., 2004).

The CASEL review also found that children from different geographic, socioeconomic, and racial, ethnic, and cultural backgrounds benefited from school-based programs. Findings from CASEL's reviews of universal and indicated programs suggest that these programs are effective when delivered by school staff, and not just by external research teams that may take the lead in developing and evaluating them. This is a promising finding that suggests that programs that promote social and emotional skills can be effectively incorporated into regular educational practice.

## Benefits for learning and achievement

Despite the common concern that devoting resources to students' social and emotional well-being may detract from efforts to promote student achievement, recent reviews confirm what many teachers and resilience researchers have long argued: the personal and environmental qualities that promote social and emotional resilience also promote students' learning and engagement in school. For example, self-regulation and optimism predict success at school, even when controlling for past achievement or scores on intelligence tests (Duckworth & Seligman, 2005; Schulman, 1995). Students who feel more connected to school have better attendance and higher achievement (Christenson & Havsy, 2004; Goodenow, 1993; Gottfredson & Gottfredson, 1989). Indeed, these personal and environmental factors may be at least as important to achievement as intellectual capacity alone (Lopes & Salovey, 2004). For example, Duckworth and Seligman (2005) found that self-discipline was a stronger predictor than IQ of adolescents' grades. Sternberg and colleagues (2001) estimate that IQ accounts for less than 30% of grades, job performance, and other real-world outcomes, meaning that other individual and environmental factors play a crucial role in achievement.

Attending to social and emotional well-being may also prevent disengagement from school, which is common in adolescence. Children's enjoyment of school often declines during middle school and high school (Eccles et al., 1996). In the USA, more than 10% of students leave school without obtaining a high school diploma or its equivalent. Only about 74% of students graduate from high school on time (Snyder & Tan, 2005). Some students are pulled away from school by work, family, and other pressures. Research suggests, however, that factors that push students away (such as difficulties getting along with teachers and peers) are even more important (Christenson & Havsy, 2004; Jordan, McPartland, & Lara, 1999).

This disengagement coincides with changes in school environment that make it difficult to maintain a positive school culture. For example, as children make the transition from elementary school to middle school, they encounter larger schools, larger classes, more distant relationships with teachers and peers, and feedback systems that focus on performance relative to others rather than effort and self-improvement (Eccles et al., 1996). It is not surprising that students' perceptions of school become more negative during this time. In a recent survey of youth in California, 61% of 5th graders reported their schools provided caring relationships and 62% reported that their schools provided high expectations. By 11th grade, these numbers had dropped to 29% and 35%, respectively. Few students across all grades reported meaningful opportunities to participate (Benard & Slade, 2009). Thus, the social qualities that promote resilience appear to be lacking in many high schools. Programs that promote positive connections to school can enhance engagement in learning. For example, the Check & Connect program, which provides caring mentors from within the school community to students at risk for school failure, reduces students' behavioral problems and suspensions, and increases attendance and achievement (Christenson & Havsy, 2004). Programs that promote students' social and emotional skills can also enhance their academic achievement (CASEL, 2007; Elias et al., 2002; Greenberg et al., 2003; Seligman et al., 2009; Zins et al., 2004). For example, several substance use and violence prevention programs that promote problem-solving, coping, and social competence also improve grades, graduation rates, standardized test scores, as well as specific reading, math, writing, and cognitive skills (Substance Abuse and Mental Health Services Administration, 2009; Wilson, Gottfredson, & Najaka, 2001). The CASEL reviews found significant benefits on achievement for universal, indicated, and after-school programs (Payton et al., 2008).

# Two Programs for Children and Adolescents

For the past 15 years, our research team has been developing, evaluating, and (more recently) disseminating school-based interventions designed to promote resilience and well-being in children and adolescents. Much of this work has focused on two types of interventions: programs designed to promote resilience by teaching problem solving and coping skills, and programs intended to increase students' positive emotions, personal strengths, and sense of meaning and fulfillment. Here we briefly review two of our programs for school-age youth.

## The Penn Resiliency Program

The Penn Resiliency Program (PRP; Gillham, Reivich, & Jaycox, 2008) is a school-based, group program for late elementary through middle-school age students (approximately 10–14 years old). PRP grew out of cognitive behavioral theories and interventions used to treat psychological disorders, especially depression (Beck, 1976; Beck, Rush, Shaw, & Emery, 1979; Ellis, 1962; Seligman, 1991).

PRP is delivered in a small group format by teachers and counselors. The program uses a variety of teaching methods. Group leaders introduce concepts and skills through skits, discussions, and didactic instruction. Students then practice these skills through role plays and other hands-on activities, first using hypothetical scenarios. Group leaders then help students apply the skills to their own experiences. Each lesson ends with assignments that encourage students to use the skills in real life situations. For a detailed description of PRP see Gillham, Brunwasser, and Freres (2008).

PRP fosters several personal strengths and skills that are related to resilience (Reivich & Gillham, 2010; Reivich & Shatté, 2002):

- Emotional competence—being able to identify, label, and express emotions, and control emotions when appropriate.
- Self-control—being able to identify and resist impulses that are counterproductive for a given situation or for reaching long-term goals.

- Problem-solving and decision-making—especially the skills of flexibility (being able to consider a range of possible interpretations, to see situations from multiple perspectives, and to generate a variety of solutions to problems) and judgment (being able to make informed decisions based on evidence).
- Social awareness—being able to consider others' perspectives and empathize with others.
- Social competence—being able to work through challenges in important relationships.
- Self-efficacy and realistic optimism—confidence in one's abilities to reach goals and to identify and implement coping and problem-solving skills that are suited to a situation.

PRP includes two major components: cognitive skills and problem-solving. The cognitive component teaches a variety of skills that help students to become more aware of their emotions and to think more flexibly and accurately about problems. Ellis's ABC model is central to this component: when *A*ctivating events (or adversities) occur, our *B*eliefs or interpretations largely determine the event's emotional and behavioral *C*onsequences. Thus, in the same situations, different sets of beliefs may lead people to respond in very different ways.

In PRP, students learn to identify their emotional experiences, to monitor their interpretations (or "self-talk"), and to identify habitual patterns in their thinking (e.g., pessimism) that may be inaccurate or maladaptive. A major goal of the cognitive component is to interrupt self-defeating thought-behavior patterns. Pessimistic beliefs (e.g., "I'm stupid") often lead to maladaptive behaviors (e.g., not studying), which then increase the likelihood of negative outcomes (e.g., poor grades). The negative outcomes then reinforce the person's initial pessimistic belief, creating a self-fulfilling prophecy. These downward spirals are often visible in achievement contexts but play an important role in social interactions as well (see Figs 46.2 and 46.3). Once they are able to identify self-talk, students learn to challenge negative or maladaptive interpretations by evaluating the accuracy of their beliefs and by

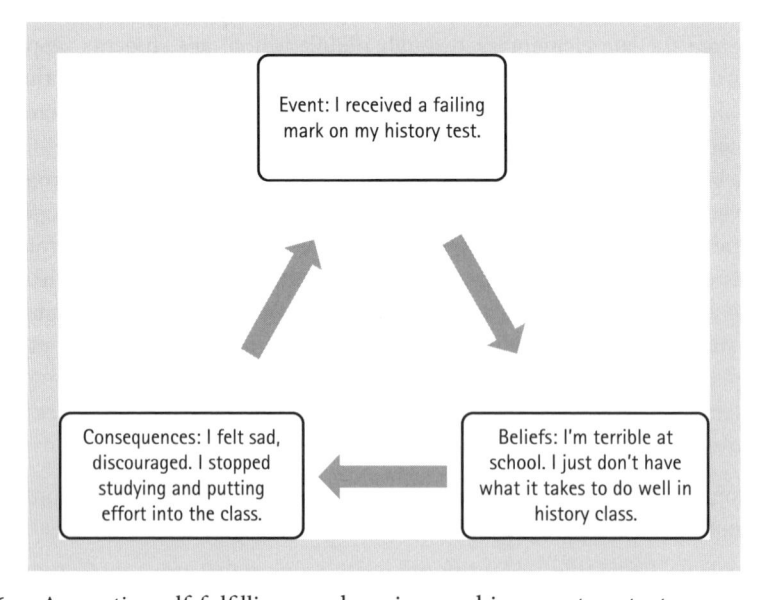

FIG. 46.2 A negative self-fulfilling prophecy in an achievement context.

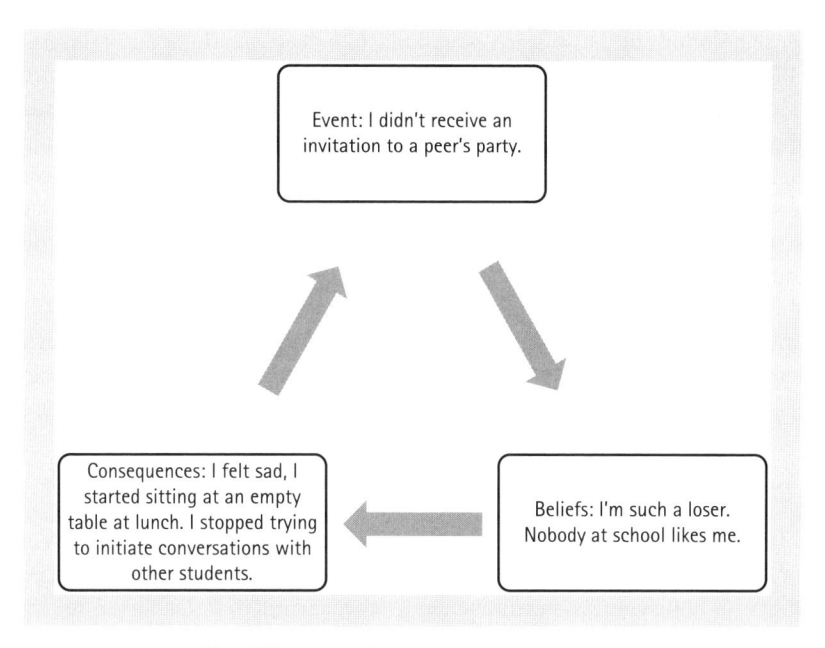

FIG. 46.3 A negative self-fulfilling prophecy in a social context.

considering alternative interpretations. These twin skills, accuracy and flexibility, are at the heart of PRP.

Our goal is not simply to swap a pessimistic thinking style with an optimistic one. Rather, we want to help students detect patterns in their self-talk, feelings, and behaviors that may be counterproductive. Often, the skills of flexibility and accuracy lead to greater optimism. But sometimes they can lead students to recognize that they are at least partly responsible for a problem. By learning to interpret problems more accurately, students can begin to solve them. The cognitive component can also promote social awareness as students apply their knowledge of emotions and self-talk to understand the perspectives of others.

The second component of PRP teaches a variety of problem-solving skills. Students learn to set realistic goals and subgoals and to develop plans for reaching them. Assertiveness training helps students to express their needs respectfully without escalating conflicts. The negotiation skill incorporates assertiveness as well as active listening and creative brainstorming to find solutions that work for both parties. PRP teaches a five-step approach to problem-solving that is based on Dodge's and Crick's (1990) social information processing model and incorporates many of the other PRP skills. When problems arise, students are encouraged to: (1) stop and think, especially about their goals, (2) evaluate the situation (look for clues, consider others' perspectives), (3) brainstorm about solutions creatively (generate a list of possible solutions), (4) decide what to do (consider the pros and cons of different options and how they affect short- and long-term goals), and (5) go for the goal (enact the solution and evaluate the outcome; if the solution didn't work try the process again). The creative brainstorming and decision-making steps apply the cognitive skills (e.g., flexibility, accuracy, and critical thinking) learned in previous lessons to one's outward behavior.

Finally, PRP also teaches skills for managing difficult emotions and for coping with negative events that are beyond one's control. Students share their personal methods of coping with intense emotions and also learn new skills, like deep breathing and relaxation techniques. PRP emphasizes the importance of seeking help and support from friends and family. Although the second component focuses on behavioral skills (or what students can do when problems happen), students continue to apply the cognitive skills throughout the program. For example, they examine and challenge beliefs that can interfere with effective problem-solving, that fuel procrastination, or that lead to aggression or passivity and interfere with assertiveness. The problem-solving and coping skills target behaviors that often contribute to downward spirals (see Figs 46.2 and 46.3).

In addition to teaching specific cognitive, coping, problem solving, and social skills, PRP's group format also provides opportunities for students to receive support from teachers and for students to support and help each other. Thus, although PRP primarily develops personal skills and strengths, it may also help to create a nurturing social environment.

*Research findings*

PRP has been evaluated extensively. Recent meta-analytic reviews identified 19 controlled studies of PRP, including 17 that evaluated PRP's effects on depression and 15 that evaluated PRP's effects on hopelessness, pessimism, and other cognitive styles linked to depression (Brunwasser & Gillham, 2008; Brunwasser, Gillham, & Kim, 2009). Together, these studies evaluated PRP with more than 2000 children from a wide variety of geographic, cultural, and socioeconomic backgrounds. Findings from these reviews indicate that PRP significantly improves thinking styles. Students who participated in PRP were more optimistic than controls and these effects endured for at least 1 year (the last assessment examined in the meta-analysis). Similarly, PRP significantly reduced and prevented depressive symptoms and these effects also endured for at least 1 year. Although fewer studies have examined PRP's long-term effects, findings from some of these studies are promising. For example, the first study of PRP found that the benefits on depression lasted for 2 years and the benefits on optimism lasted for at least 3 years (Gillham & Reivich, 1999; Gillham, Reivich, Jaycox, & Seligman, 1995). A few recent studies have found positive effects on anxiety symptoms and behavioral problems (for a review, see Gillham, Brunwasser, & Freres, 2008). Research on PRP's effects on academic achievement is underway. A similar resilience program developed by our team for older adolescents and young adults has also been found to improve optimism and reduce and prevent symptoms of anxiety and depression (Seligman, Schulman, DeRubeis, & Hollon, 1999; Seligman, Schulman, & Tryon, 2007).

## The high school positive psychology program

Like many programs designed to promote resilience and positive youth development, PRP focuses extensively on students' responses to setbacks and challenges. Our team's high school positive psychology curriculum (Reivich et al., 2007) is based on recent work in positive psychology (Peterson & Seligman, 2004; Seligman, 2002) which offers an alternative, complementary approach to resilience. Positive psychology highlights the importance of enhancing well-being more broadly, and not simply in response to stressors. Schools can also promote resilience by helping students to develop close relationships, to identify and use their strengths, to experience positive emotions, and to engage in activities that are meaningful to them. Interventions that target these outcomes improve life satisfaction and reduce depression (Seligman, Rashid, & Parks, 2006; Seligman, Steen, Park, & Peterson, 2005; Sin & Lyubomirsky, 2009). Ultimately, we believe that educational initiatives that integrate both perspectives will be most helpful.

The high school positive psychology curriculum is based largely on Seligman's (2002) three pathways to happiness. The program includes three units: The Pleasant Life, the Engaged Life, and The Meaningful Life. Many of the program's skills and activities have been used and tested in other positive psychology interventions (e.g., Seligman et al., 2005, 2006). The Pleasant Life unit focuses on increasing positive emotion. Lessons focus on savoring, gratitude, and optimism. For example, a gratitude lesson encourages students to think about people who have helped them but whom they have not yet thanked. Students write a letter expressing gratitude and are encouraged to share it in person. A lesson on "counting our blessings" encourages students to think about the good things that happen each day and to log them in a journal each evening. These activities can counter negative thinking styles that are targeted in PRP and so they are likely to reduce negative emotions. But they go far beyond this. They actively promote positive emotions like contentment and joy, and may deepen interpersonal relationships.

The Engaged Life unit is the largest. It promotes strengths (e.g., kindness, creativity, perseverance, integrity) that are valued across time and throughout history (Dahlsgaard, Peterson, & Seligman, 2005; Peterson & Seligman, 2004). The program encourages students to identify their personal (or signature) strengths and to use them more in their everyday lives. Students identify their strengths through several activities including completing the Values in Action Inventory of Strengths for Youth (Park & Peterson, 2006), and by reflecting on past experiences when they were "at their best." They develop action plans for using signature strengths and for developing other strengths that are important to them. The family tree of strengths activity encourages students to interview family members and find out about strengths that run through their family tree.

During the Meaningful Life unit, students reflect on life purpose and meaning. Rather than focus on meaning in the abstract sense (i.e., What is the meaning of life?), teachers encourage students to think about what makes life meaningful for *them*. Teachers engage students in discussions about meaning, and students read relevant passages from literature and from the personal reflections of others. We've used excerpts from *The Meaning of Life* (Friend & the Editors of *Life*, 1991), which contains short essays by philosophers, writers, artists, politicians, spiritual leaders, sports figures, comedians, and others. Students reflect on how these different perspectives fit with their own views on life meaning. Students and their parents then complete a back-and-forth meaning journal in which they dialogue about the meaning of life. In our experience, students' discussions of meaning typically center on the importance of connections to others, institutions, and values that are larger than the self.

The positive psychology curriculum is designed to be delivered by teachers in a small- or large-class format. The program uses a variety of teaching methods. Teachers introduce concepts and skills through in-class activities and discussions. Most lessons end with assignments that encourage students to apply the positive psychology concepts and strategies in their everyday lives. Students write reflections about their experiences when using the positive psychology strategies. Lessons typically begin with a discussion of students' experiences and reflections.

We developed our positive psychology program to target well-being broadly, rather than resilience specifically. But we now believe that these concepts and skills are as essential to resilience as the skills covered in PRP. By promoting students' capacity for positive emotions, to use strengths such as kindness, teamwork, humor, and creativity, and to experience strong connections with other people and with purposes outside the self, positive psychology provides a strong foundation that can help youth cope with adversity. Research indicates that positive emotions enhance problem-solving (Fredrickson, 2001). Also, many studies over many decades document the power of close relationships to protect against depression and other psychological and physical health problems (Leavy, 1983; Uchino, Cacioppo, & Kiecolt-Glaser, 1996). The positive psychology program aims to promote upward spirals; it promotes flourishing by helping students to build upon what they do well.

## Research

We have nearly completed our first scientific evaluation of the high school positive psychology program. In that study, 347 9th grade students were randomly assigned to regular grade Language Arts classes or to Language Arts classes that included the positive psychology curriculum. We followed students for 4 years, until graduation from high school. Preliminary analyses examining effects through students' 11th grade year suggest two major areas of benefit (Gillham, Linkins, & Reivich, 2009; Seligman et al., 2009). The positive psychology program improved students' social skills (e.g., empathy, cooperation, assertiveness, and self-control) according to both teachers' and mothers' reports. It also improved students' engagement in school, according to teacher reports. The findings on teachers' report measures are especially encouraging. Teachers who completed questionnaires did not deliver the curriculum and were not informed about students' condition assignments. Thus, they are unlikely to be biased by an awareness of students' participation in the positive psychology program. There was no overall effect on students' achievement, but follow-up analyses indicated that the positive psychology program significantly improved Language Arts achievement among students with average and low (but not high) levels of achievement at baseline. Contrary to our expectations, we found no effects on students' symptoms of depression or anxiety although other positive psychology interventions have been successful at reducing depressive symptoms (Seligman et al., 2006; Sin & Lyobomirsky, 2009).

# School community and culture

Curricula like PRP and our high school positive psychology program appear to promote well-being in students. Such programs are likely to be most effective when delivered as part of a school's comprehensive focus on social and emotional well-being and resilience. Reviews of research on positive youth development, social and emotional learning, prevention, and character education converge on the conclusion that isolated curricula are not as helpful as approaches that are embedded into school culture and delivered over many years in a child's life (e.g., CASEL, 2003; Gottfredson, 2000). This finding is consistent with research documenting the importance of social contextual factors in promoting resilience in youth (Luthar, 2006).

Recently, our team's work has increasingly focused on promoting resilience through the classroom, school, and other contexts where children live. In our trainings for teachers and counselors who deliver our programs, we first encourage teachers to apply the concepts and skills to their own lives so that they can experience first-hand the benefits of the resilience and positive psychology skills. We hope that our approach to training teachers leads to a strong personal connection with the concepts and skills, increasing the likelihood that they will be effective models for students both in and out of the classroom. In some of our school collaborations, we are consulting with teachers, counselors, and other staff to develop curricula for all ages and to infuse resilience education into everyday interactions and instruction across disciplines. Integrating resilience and positive psychology skills explicitly through formal instruction also helps to create common language and practices among educators and students that contribute to a culture of resilience education.

Given the daily stress and challenges they face, teachers who are resilient and use their strengths are likely to be more effective (Stanford, 2001). Even in the absence of formal resilience curricula for students, supportive work environments and professional development for teachers can go a long way in the promotion of resilience and learning in the students that they teach. When schools support teachers in their own social and emotional development, for example, those teachers can more effectively model social and emotional skills for students (Elias et al., 1997). A teacher's optimism can motivate a child to persist through a challenging assignment; a teacher's own flexible thinking about problems can encourage students to think through conflicts from multiple perspectives. In addition, teachers who can regulate their own impulses and emotions may be skilled in classroom management and creating environments conducive to student learning and well-being. Indeed, teachers who approach classroom management with respect for students' perspectives and appreciate the importance of group cohesion ultimately have more time for academic subjects throughout the school year (Elias et al., 1997).

Both life satisfaction and grit, or perseverance toward long-term goals, determine teacher effectiveness as measured by student learning (Duckworth, Quinn, & Seligman, 2009). The hard work of gritty teachers pays off in terms of student learning and achievement. Duckworth and colleagues also suggest that "teachers higher in life satisfaction may be more adept at engaging their pupils, and their zest and enthusiasm may spread to their students" (p. 545). More broadly, a positive school culture that cultivates strengths enables teachers to bring the best of themselves to their professions. As a result, increased teacher engagement can promote students' learning in the classroom as well as foster the meaningful teacher-student relationships that nurture positive development in students.

Recent reviews of social and emotional learning programs highlight the importance of strengthening ties between home and school, as well as between school and the larger community. We have developed a resilience program for parents that teaches them the core PRP skills so they can apply them in their own lives and support their children's use of these skills. Several activities in the positive psychology curriculum (e.g., family tree of strengths, meaning journals) create opportunities for students and parents to work together, and for parents to provide guidance as students identify their personal strengths and what makes life most meaningful. Many parents appreciate the opportunity to share their values so openly with their children. Students' reflections suggest that they are grateful for the deeper connection to parents and the life lessons learned.

Other activities help to strengthen connections to the larger community. For example, in the paragons of strengths activity, students interview members of the larger community who exemplify different strengths. Community service projects help youth put many of their strengths to use. These projects can provide youth with meaningful opportunities to connect with others and make a positive difference in the world. Community service may also lead to long-term benefits in well-being (Bowman, Brandenberger, Hill, Lapsley, & Quaranto, 2010).

## Conclusions

Positive psychology and resilience research have identified many qualities of individuals and social contexts that enable people to adapt and to thrive in their everyday lives and when confronted with adversity. Given their central role in students' lives, schools have enormous potential (and, many argue, responsibility) to promote social and emotional well-being and resilience in youth both within and outside of school settings.

Many educators are understandably skeptical of curricula that purportedly foster well-being in students, as many isolated programs—even some that have been implemented widely—either have not been evaluated rigorously or have not shown positive effects. Recent reviews, however, suggest that comprehensive and well-integrated programs do, in fact, contribute to well-being in children and adolescents, and research has identified several programs that can significantly reduce emotional or behavioral problems and dramatically cultivate social skills, strengths, positive relationships, and achievement.

As we have shown, integrating resilience into education through explicit instruction can equip students with the skills needed to rise above and grow from major challenges and daily struggles. Simultaneously, embedding principles of resilience and positive psychology into educational practices can help to create a school climate that contributes to student learning and positive development in non-academic domains. Perhaps now more than ever before, resilience education has the power to help students successfully navigate the academic and non-academic demands they juggle, as well as grow and thrive in the face of adversity and the challenges of childhood and adolescence.

### Disclosures

The University of Pennsylvania has licensed the Penn Resiliency Program to Adaptiv Learning Systems. Drs. Reivich and Seligman own Adaptiv stock and could profit from the sale of this program. None of the other authors has a financial relationship with Adaptiv.

## References

Beck, A. T. (1976). *Cognitive therapy and the emotional disorders.* New York, NY: International Universities Press.
Beck, A. T., Rush, A. J., Shaw, B. F., & Emery, G. (1979). *Cognitive therapy of depression.* New York, NY: Guilford Press.
Benard, B. (2004). *Resiliency: What we have learned.* San Francisco, CA: WestEd.
Benard, B., & Slade, S. (2009). Listening to students: Moving from resilience research to youth development practice and school connectedness. In R. Gilman, E. S. Huebner, & M. J. Furlong (Eds.), *Handbook of positive psychology in schools* (pp. 353–369). New York, NY: Routledge/Taylor & Francis Group.
Benninga, J. S., Berkowitz, M. W., Kuehn, P., & Smith, K. (2006). Character and academics: What good schools do. *Phi Delta Kappan, 87,* 448–452.

Berkowitz, M. W., & Bier, M. C. (2004). Research-based character education. *Annals of the American Academy of Political and Social Science*, *591*, 72–85.

Bockting, C. L. H., Spinhoven, P., Koeter, M. W., Wouters, L. F., & Schene, A. H. (2006). Prediction of recurrence in recurrent depression and the influence of consecutive episodes on vulnerability for depression: A 2-year prospective study. *Journal of Clinical Psychiatry*, *67*, 747–755.

Bowman, N. A., Brandenberger, J. W., Hill, P. L., Lapsley, D. K., & Quaranto, J. C. (2010). Serving in college, flourishing in adulthood: Does community engagement during the college years predict adult well-being? *Applied Psychology: Health and Well-Being*, *2*, 14–34.

Brunwasser, S. M. & Gillham, J. E. (2008, May). *A meta-analytic review of the Penn Resiliency Program*. Paper presented at the Society for Prevention Research, San Francisco, CA.

Brunwasser, S. M., Gillham, J. E., & Kim, E. S. (2009). A meta-analytic review of the Penn Resiliency Program's effects on depressive symptoms. *Journal of Consulting and Clinical Psychology*, *77*, 1042–1054.

Catalano, R. F., Berglund, M. L., Ryan, J. A. M., Lonczak, H. S., & Hawkins, J. D. (2004). Positive youth development in the United States: Research findings on evaluations of positive youth development programs. *Annals of the American Academy of Political and Social Science*, *591*, 98–124.

Centers for Disease Control and Prevention. (2008). *Youth risk behavior surveillance: United States, 2007* (MMWR Publication No. SS-4). Atlanta, GA: Coordinating Center for Health Information and Service.

Christenson, S. L., & Havsy, L. H. (2004). Family-school-peer relationships: Significance for social, emotional, and academic learning. In J. E. Zins, R. P. Weissberg, M. C. Wang, & H. J. Walberg (Eds.), *Building academic success on social and emotional learning: What does the research say?* (pp. 59–75). New York, NY: Teachers College Press.

Clarke, G. N., Hawkins, W., Murphy, M., Sheeber, L. B., Lewinsohn, P. M., & Seeley, J. R. (1995). Targeted prevention of unipolar depressive disorder in an at-risk sample of high school adolescents: A randomized trial of group cognitive intervention. *Journal of the American Academy of Child & Adolescent Psychiatry*, *34*, 312–321.

Cohen, J. (2006). Social, emotional, ethical, and academic education: Creating a climate for learning, participation in democracy, and well-being. *Harvard Educational Review*, *76*, 201–237.

Cohen, J., McCabe, L., Michelli, N. M., & Pickeral, T. (2009). School climate: Research, policy, practice, and teacher education. *Teachers College Record*, *111*, 180–213.

Collaborative for Academic, Social, and Emotional Learning (CASEL). (2003). *Safe and sound: An educational leader's guide to social and emotional learning programs*. Chicago, IL: Author. Retrieved from http://casel.org/publications/safe-and-sound-an-educational-leaders-guide-to-evidence-based-sel-programs/

Collaborative for Academic, Social, and Emotional Learning (CASEL). (2007). *The benefits of school-based social and emotional learning programs: Highlights from a forthcoming CASEL report*. Chicago, IL: Author. Retrieved from http://www.melissainstitute.org/documents/weissberg-3.pdf

Conduct Problems Prevention Research Group (2007). Fast track randomized controlled trial to prevent externalizing psychiatric disorders: Findings from grades 3 to 9. *Journal of the American Academy of Child & Adolescent Psychiatry*, *46*, 1250–1262.

Costello, E. J., Erkanli, A., & Angold, A. (2006). Is there an epidemic of child or adolescent depression? *Journal of Child Psychology and Psychiatry*, *47*, 1263–1271.

Dahlsgaard, K., Peterson, C., & Seligman, M. E. P. (2005). Shared virtue: The convergence of valued human strengths across culture and history. *Review of General Psychology, 9*, 203–213.

Dodge, K. A., & Crick, N. R. (1990). Social information-processing bases of aggressive behavior in children. *Personality and Social Psychology Bulletin, 16*, 8–22.

Duckworth, A. L., Quinn, P. D., & Seligman, M. E. P. (2009). Positive predictors of teacher effectiveness. *The Journal of Positive Psychology, 4*, 540–547.

Duckworth, A. L., & Seligman, M. E. P. (2005). Self-discipline outdoes IQ in predicting academic performance of adolescents. *Psychological Science, 16*, 939–944.

Eccles, J. S., Flanagan, C., Lord, S., Midgley, C., Roeser, R., & Yee, D. (1996). Schools, families, and early adolescents: What are we doing wrong and what can we do instead? *Journal of Developmental and Behavioral Pediatrics, 17*, 267–276.

Elias, M. J. (2004). *Strategies to infuse social and emotional learning into academics.* In J. E. Zins, R. P. Weissberg, M. C. Wang, & H. J. Walberg (Eds.), *Building academic success on social and emotional learning: What does the research say?* (pp. 113–134). New York, NY: Teachers College Press.

Elias, M. J., Wang, M. C., Weissberg, R. P., Zins, J. E., & Walberg, H. J. (2002). The other side of the report card: Student success depends on more than test scores. *American School Board Journal, 189*, 28–30.

Elias, M. J., Zins, J. E., Weissberg, R. P., Frey, K. S., Greenberg, M. T., Haynes, N. M., … Shriver, D. P. (1997). *Promoting social and emotional learning: Guidelines for educators.* Alexandria, VA: Association for Supervision and Curriculum Development.

Ellis, A. (1962). *Reason and emotion in psychotherapy.* New York, NY: Lyle Stuart.

Evans, G. W. (2004). The environment of childhood poverty. *American Psychologist, 59*, 77–92.

Fincham, F. D., & Bradbury, T. N. (1993). Marital satisfaction, depression, and attributions: A longitudinal analysis. *Journal of Personality and Social Psychology, 64*, 442–452.

Finkelhor, D., Turner, H., Ormrod, R., Hamby, S., & Kracke, K. (2009). *Children's exposure to violence: A comprehensive national survey.* Washington, DC: US Department of Justice, Office of Justice Programs.

Fredrickson, B. L. (2001). The role of positive emotions in positive psychology: The broaden-and-build theory of positive emotions. *American Psychologist, 56*, 218–226.

Friend, D., & the Editors of *Life*. (1991). *The meaning of life: Reflections in words and pictures on why were are here.* New York, NY: Little, Brown and Company.

Gillham, J. E., Brunwasser, S. M., & Freres, D. R. (2008). Preventing depression in early adolescence: The Penn Resiliency Program. In J. R. Z. Abela & B. L. Hankin (Eds.), *Handbook of depression in children and adolescents* (pp. 309–332). New York, NY: Guilford Press.

Gillham, J. E., Linkins, M., & Reivich, K. J. (2009, June). *Teaching positive psychology to 9th graders: Results through 11th grade.* Paper presented at the first World Congress of the International Positive Psychology Association, Philadelphia, PA.

Gillham, J. E., & Reivich, K. J. (1999). Prevention of depressive symptoms in school children: A research update. *Psychological Science, 10*, 461–462.

Gillham, J. E., Reivich, K. J., & Jaycox, L. H. (2008). *The Penn Resiliency Program (also known as The Penn Depression Prevention Program and The Penn Optimism Program).* Unpublished manuscript, University of Pennsylvania.

Gillham, J. E., Reivich, K. J., Jaycox, L. H., & Seligman, M. E. P. (1995). Prevention of depressive symptoms in schoolchildren: Two-year follow-up. *Psychological Science, 6*, 343–351.

Goleman, D. (1995). *Emotional intelligence.* New York, NY: Bantam Books.

Goodenow, C. (1993). Classroom belonging among early adolescent students: Relationships to motivation and achievement. *The Journal of Early Adolescence, 13*, 21–43.

Gottfredson, D. G. (2000). *School climate, population characteristics, and program quality.* Washington, DC: Department of Justice, Office of Juvenile Justice and Delinquency Prevention. (ERIC Document Reproduction Service No. ED446312).

Gottfredson, G. D., & Gottfredson, D. C. (1989). *School climate, academic performance, attendance, and dropout.* Washington, DC: Office of Educational Research and Improvement. (ERIC Document Reproduction Service No. ED308225).

Greenberg, M. T., Kusché, C. A., & Riggs, N. (2004). The PATHS curriculum: Theory and research on neurocognitive development and school success. In J. E. Zins, R. P. Weissberg, M. C. Wang, & H. J. Walberg (Eds.), *Building academic success on social and emotional learning: What does the research say?* (pp. 170–188). New York, NY: Teachers College Press.

Greenberg, M. T., Weissberg, R. P., O'Brien, M. U., Zins, J. E., Fredericks, L., Resnik, H., & Elias, M. J. (2003). Enhancing school-based prevention and youth development through coordinated social, emotional, and academic learning. *American Psychologist, 58*, 466–474.

Harrington, R., Fudge, H., Rutter, M., Pickles, A., & Hill, J. (1990). Adult outcomes of childhood and adolescent depression. *Archives of General Psychiatry, 47*, 465–473.

Hawkins, J. D., Smith, B. H., & Catalano, R. F. (2004). *Social development and social and emotional learning.* In J. E. Zins, R. P. Weissberg, M. C. Wang, & H. J. Walberg (Eds.), *Building academic success on social and emotional learning: What does the research say?* (pp. 135–150). New York, NY: Teachers College Press.

Horowitz, J. L., & Garber, J. (2006). The prevention of depressive symptoms in children and adolescents: A meta-analytic review. *Journal of Consulting and Clinical Psychology, 74*, 401–415.

Jordan, W. J., McPartland, J., & Lara, J. (1999). Rethinking the causes of high school dropout. *The Prevention Researcher, 6*, 1–3.

Juster, F. T., Ono, H., & Stafford, F. P. (2004). *Changing times of American youth: 1981–2003.* Ann Arbor, MI: University of Michigan Institute for Social Research. Retrieved from http://www.ns.umich.edu/Releases/2004/Nov04/teen_time_report.pdf

Kim-Cohen, J., Caspi, A., Moffitt, T. E., Harrington, H., Milne, B. J., & Poulter, R. (2003). Prior juvenile diagnoses in adults with mental disorder: Developmental follow-back of a prospective-longitudinal cohort. *Archives of General Psychiatry, 60*, 709–717.

Kwon, P., & Laurenceau, J. (2002). A longitudinal study of the hopelessness theory of depression: Testing the diathesis-stress model within a differential reactivity and exposure framework. *Journal of Clinical Psychology, 58*, 1305–1321.

Leavy, R. L. (1983). Social support and psychological disorder: A review. *Journal of Community Psychology, 11*, 3–21.

Libby, C. J., & Glenwick, D. S. (2010). Protective and exacerbating factors in children and adolescents with fibromyalgia. *Rehabilitation Psychology, 55*, 151–158.

Lopes, P. N., & Salovey, P. (2004). Toward a broader education: Social, emotional and practical skills. In J. E. Zins, R. P. Weissberg, M. C. Wang, & H. J. Walberg (Eds.), *Building academic success on social and emotional learning: What does the research say?* (pp. 76–93). New York, NY: Teachers College Press.

Luthar, S. S. (2006). Resilience in development: A synthesis of research across five decades. In D. Cicchetti & D. J. Cohen (Eds.), *Developmental psychopathology: Vol. 3. Risk, disorder, and adaptation* (pp. 739–795). Hoboken, NJ: John Wiley & Sons, Inc.

Luthar, S. S., Cicchetti, D., & Becker, B. (2000). The construct of resilience: A critical evaluation and guidelines for future work. *Child Development, 71*, 543–562.

Luthar, S. S., & Latendresse, S. J. (2005). Children of the affluent: Challenges to well-being. *Current Directions in Psychological Science, 14*, 49–53.

Masten, A. S. (2001). Ordinary magic: Resilience processes in development. *American Psychologist, 56*, 227–238.

National Research Council and Institute of Medicine. (2009). *Preventing mental, emotional, and behavioral disorders among young people: Progress and possibilities*. Washington, DC: The National Academies Press.

Nolen-Hoeksema, S., Girgus, J. S., & Seligman M. E. P. (1986). Learned helplessness in children: A longitudinal study of depression, achievement, and explanatory style. *Journal of Personality and Social Psychology, 51*, 435–442.

Pajares, F. (2009). Toward a positive psychology of academic motivation: The role of self-efficacy beliefs. In R. Gilman, E. S. Huebner, & M. J. Furlong (Eds.), *Handbook of positive psychology in schools* (pp. 149–160). New York, NY: Routledge/Taylor & Francis Group.

Park, N., & Peterson, C. (2006). Moral competence and character strengths among adolescents: The development and validation of the Values in Action Inventory of Strengths for Youth. *Journal of Adolescence, 29*, 891–909.

Payton, J., Weissberg, R. P., Durlak, J. A., Dymnicki, A. B., Taylor, R. D., Schellinger, K. B., & Pachan, M. (2008). *The positive impact of social and emotional learning for kindergarten to eighth-grade students: Findings from three scientific reviews*. Chicago, IL: Collaborative for Academic, Social, and Emotional Learning (CASEL).

Peterson, C. (2006). *A primer in positive psychology*. New York, NY: Oxford University Press.

Peterson, C. (2008). Other people matter: Two examples. *Psychology Today*. Retrieved from http://www.psychologytoday.com/blog/the-good-life/200806/other-people-matter-two-examples

Peterson, C., & Seligman, M. E. P. (2004). *Character strengths and virtues: A handbook of classification*. Washington, DC: American Psychological Association.

Reivich, K., & Gillham, J. (2010). Building resilience in youth: The Penn Resiliency Program. *Communiqué, 38*, 1, 17–18.

Reivich, K. J., Seligman, M. E. P., Gillham, J., Linkins, M., Peterson, C., Schwartz, B., … Geraghty, T. (2007). *Positive psychology program for high school students: Lessons for the pleasant life, the good life, and the meaningful life*. Unpublished manuscript, Wallingford-Swarthmore School District, University of Pennsylvania, and Swarthmore College.

Reivich, K., & Shatté, A. (2002). *The resilience factor: 7 essential skills for overcoming life's inevitable obstacles*. New York, NY: Broadway Books.

Resnick, M. D., Bearman, P. S., Blum, R. W., Bauman, K. E., Harris, K. M., Jones, J., … Udry, J. R. (1997). Protecting adolescents from harm: Findings from the National Longitudinal Study on Adolescent Health. *Journal of the American Medical Association, 278*, 823–832.

Rose, L. C., & Gallup, A. M. (2000). The 32nd annual Phi Delta Kappa/Gallup poll of the public's attitudes toward the public schools. *Phi Delta Kappan, 82*, 41–52.

Rose, L. C., & Gallup, A. M. (2007). The 39th annual Phi Delta Kappa/Gallup poll of the public's attitudes toward the public schools. *Phi Delta Kappan, 89*, 33–48.

Rutter, M., Maughan, B., Mortimore, P., & Ouston, J. (1982). *Fifteen thousand hours: Secondary schools and their effects on children*. Cambridge, MA: Harvard University Press.

Schulman, P. (1995). Explanatory style and achievement in school and work. In G. M. Buchanan & M. E. P. Seligman (Eds.), *Explanatory style* (pp. 159–171). Hillsdale, NJ: Lawrence Erlbaum Associates, Inc.

Seligman, M. E. P. (1991). *Learned optimism*. New York, NY: Knopf.
Seligman, M. E. P. (2002). *Authentic happiness: Using the new positive psychology to realize your potential for lasting fulfillment*. New York, NY: Free Press.
Seligman, M. E. P., Ernst, R. M., Gillham, J., Reivich, K., & Linkins, M. (2009). Positive education: Positive psychology and classroom interventions. *Oxford Review of Education, 35*, 293–311.
Seligman, M. E. P., Rashid, T., & Parks, A. C. (2006). Positive psychotherapy. *American Psychologist, 61*, 774–788.
Seligman, M. E. P., Schulman, P., DeRubeis, R. J., & Hollon, S. D. (1999). The prevention of depression and anxiety. *Prevention & Treatment, 2*, np.
Seligman, M. E. P., Schulman, P., & Tryon, A. M. (2007). Group prevention of depression and anxiety symptoms. *Behaviour Research and Therapy, 45*, 1111–1126.
Seligman, M. E. P., Steen, T. A., Park, N., & Peterson, C. (2005). Positive psychology progress: Empirical validation of interventions. *American Psychologist, 60*, 410–421.
Sin, N. L., & Lyubomirsky, S. (2009). Enhancing well-being and alleviating depressive symptoms with positive psychology interventions: A practice-friendly meta-analysis. *Journal of Clinical Psychology, 65*, 467–487.
Snyder, T. D., & Hoffman, C. M. (2003). *Digest of Education Statistics: 2002* (NCES 2003-060). Washington, DC: US Government Printing Office.
Snyder, T. D., & Tan, A. G. (2005). *Digest of Education Statistics: 2004* (NCES 2006-005). Washington, DC: US Government Printing Office.
Snyder, T. D., Tan, A. G., & Hoffman, C. M. (2006). *Digest of Education Statistics: 2005* (NCES 2006-030). Washington, DC: US Government Printing Office.
Stanford, B.H. (2001). Reflections of resilient, persevering urban teachers. *Teacher Education Quarterly, 28*, 75–87.
Sternberg, R. J., Grigorenko, E., & Bundy, D. A. (2001). The predictive value of IQ. *Merrill-Palmer Quarterly, 47*, 1–41.
Stice, E., Shaw, H., Bohon, C., Marti, C. N., & Rohde, P. (2009). A meta-analytic review of depression prevention programs for children and adolescents: Factors that predict magnitude of intervention effects. *Journal of Consulting and Clinical Psychology, 77*, 486–503.
Substance Abuse and Mental Health Services Administration (SAMHSA). (2009). *SAMHSA Model Programs: Model Prevention Programs Supporting Academic Achievement*. Retrieved from http://www.p12.nysed.gov/sss/ssae/schoolsafety/sdfsca/AcadAchievement.html
Sund, A. M., Larsson, B., & Wichstrom, L. (2003). Psychosocial correlates of depressive symptoms among 12–14-year-old Norwegian adolescents. *Journal of Child Psychology and Psychiatry, 44*, 588–597.
Thompson, K. N., Phillips, L. J., Komesaroff, P., Yuen, H. P., Wood, S. J., Pantelis, C., … McGorry, P. D. (2007). Stress and HPA-axis functioning in young people at ultra high risk for psychosis. *Journal of Psychiatric Research, 41*, 561–569.
Twenge, J. M. (2000). The age of anxiety? The birth cohort change in anxiety and neuroticism, 1952–1993. *Journal of Personality and Social Psychology, 79*, 1007–1021.
Twenge, J. M. & Foster, J. D. (2010). Birth cohort increases in narcissistic personality traits among American college students, 1982–2009. *Social Psychology and Personality Science, 1*, 99–106.
Twenge, J. M., Gentile, B., DeWall, C. N., Ma, D., Lacefield, K., & Schurtz, D. R. (2010). Birth cohort increases in psychopathology among young Americans, 1938–2007: A cross-temporal meta-analysis of the MMPI. *Clinical Psychology Review, 30*, 145–154.

Uchino, B. N., Cacioppo, J. T., & Kiecolt-Glaser, J. K. (1996). The relationship between social support and physiological processes: A review with emphasis on underlying mechanisms and implications for health. *Psychological Bulletin, 119*, 488–531.

US Census Bureau. (2009). *Income, poverty, and health insurance coverage in the United States: 2008* (Current Population Reports No. P60-236). Washington, DC: US Government Printing Office.

US Department of Health and Human Services. (1999). *Mental health: A report of the Surgeon General*. Rockville, MD: US Department of Health and Human Services, Substance Abuse and Mental Health Services Administration, Center for Mental Health Services, National Institutes of Health, National Institute of Mental Health.

Wang, M. (2009). School climate support for behavioral and psychological adjustment: Testing the mediating effect of social competence. *School Psychology Quarterly, 24*, 240–251.

Wang, M. C., Haertel, G. D., & Walberg, H. J. (1994). Educational resilience in inner cities. In M. C. Wong & E. W. Gordon (Eds.), *Educational resilience in inner-city America: Challenges and prospects* (pp. 45–72). Hillsdale, NJ: Lawrence Erlbaum Associates, Inc.

Weissberg, R. P., Kumpfer, K., & Seligman, M. E. P. (2003). Prevention that works for children and youth. *American Psychologist, 58*, 425–432.

Wilson, D. B., Gottfredson, D. C., & Najaka, S. S. (2001). School-based prevention of problem behaviors: A meta-analysis. *Journal of Quantitative Criminology, 17*, 247–272.

Zins, J. E., Bloodworth, M. R., Weissberg, R. P., & Walberg, H. J. (2004). The scientific base linking social and emotional learning to school success. In J. E. Zins, R. P. Weissberg, M. C. Wang, & H. J. Walberg (Eds.), *Building academic success on social and emotional learning: What does the research say?* (pp. 3–22). New York, NY: Teachers College Press.

# CHAPTER 47

# TEACHING FOR WISDOM

### ROBERT J. STERNBERG

Oklahoma State University, USA

In October of 2008, the world entered into a recession unequaled since the Great Depression of 1929. Many people, including economists, thought that such a recession was no longer even possible. What made the recession particularly odd is that it came after, not before, investment banking started attracting the best and the brightest among the graduates of the top universities in the world. Bankers had created dizzyingly complex mathematical formulas that had brought them enormous profits and that seemed to have no downside. The top investment banks, at least in the USA, only recruited in the top universities in the country. In this way, they hoped to ensure the growth but at the same time the security of the world's financial system. How could such smart people have created so much misery for so many people? Even more curiously, how could these smart people have then tried to profit from the misery they created, so ignorant of its repercussions that the CEO of Goldman Sachs, Lloyd Blankfein, referred to the company as doing "God's work?" This was the same company that later was revealed to be betting its own funds against the funds of clients who paid Goldman Sachs for financial advice. This unbridled arrogance—on the part of bankers, politicians, and others—is probably what led to the loss in January, 2010, by the US Democratic Party, of the Senate seat held by Ted Kennedy. Scott Brown, a formerly practically unknown state senator, won the election. The state of Massachusetts had not elected a Republican senator since 1972. The question, which also forms the title of a book, is one of "Why smart people can be so stupid" (Sternberg, 2002).

I will argue in this chapter that smart people can be so stupid, or to be exact, foolish, because they are unwise. Having intelligence is not tantamount to being wise. People in particular and the world in general will experience greater happiness when schools place more emphasis upon the acquisition of wisdom, and not just upon the accumulation of knowledge.

## What is Wisdom?

Wisdom has many definitions, none of which are entirely agreed on by laypersons or scholars alike. It has been noted as the ability to make proper judgments, a wealth of philosophic or scientific learning, the possession of insight, the ability to discern inner qualities and relationships, and good sense. How do these general definitions relate to more developed theoretical models of wisdom?

Historically, the concept of wisdom has been the object of philosophical as well as psychological inquiries (Birren & Svensson, 2005; Osbeck & Robinson, 2005; Robinson, 1990; Staudinger, 2008) since the Platonic dialogues in *The Republic*. More recently, with the emergence of psychology as a field of study separate from philosophy, the concept of wisdom has also been studied as a psychological construct, and a number of psychologists have attempted empirical investigation of the concept of wisdom and its manifestations (see reviews in Karelitz, Jarvin, & Sternberg, 2010; Staudinger, 2008; Sternberg, 1990, 2008; Sternberg & Jordan, 2005). Wisdom has been studied from a range of psychological perspectives (a summary of the major approaches to understanding wisdom, and references for further reading, can be found in Sternberg (2001) and Sternberg and Jordan (2005)). Some researchers (see Clayton 1975, 1982; Holliday & Chandler, 1986; or Sternberg, 1990) have focused on implicit theories of wisdom, that is, on trying to understand how the layperson perceives and defines wisdom (Bluck & Glueck, 2005). Other researchers have adopted a developmental perspective to investigate how wisdom develops or fails to develop. Most noticeably, empirical work in this area has been conducted by Paul Baltes and his colleagues at the Max Planck Institute (Baltes & Smith, 2008; Baltes & Staudinger, 1993, 2000; Kunzmann & Baltes, 2005; Smith & Baltes, 1990). Another developmental approach to defining wisdom is to view it as postformal–operational thinking, extending beyond the traditional Piagetian stages of intelligence (Piaget, 1972).

Several researchers and theoreticians have focused on the importance of integration and balance in wisdom. Labouvie-Vief (1990), for example, has emphasized the balance between different kinds of thinking, suggesting that wisdom constitutes a balance of *logos*, which are objective and logical processes, and *mythos*, which represent subjective and organismic processes. Kramer (1990, 2000) has focused on the balance between various self-systems such as the cognitive, conative, and affective, arguing that wisdom involves integration of cognition and affect, resulting in a well-balanced personality, where the conscious and unconscious interact in harmony. Still others insist on the balance between different points of view (Kitchener & Brenner, 1990), or on "a balance between the opposing valences of intense emotion and detachment, action and inaction, knowledge and doubts" (Birren & Fisher, 1990, p. 326). This essay will focus on a theory of wisdom first proposed by Sternberg (1998), which builds on previous theories emphasizing the importance of integration and balance in wisdom.

## The Balance Theory of Wisdom

Sternberg defines wisdom as the use of one's intelligence, creativity, and knowledge and as mediated by positive ethical values toward the achievement of a common good through a balance among: (1) intrapersonal, (2) interpersonal, and (3) extrapersonal interests, over the (a) short and (b) long terms (Sternberg, 2001, 2003, 2004, 2009).

Let us examine the different components of this definition one by one.

First, wise decisions do not just require intelligence and explicit knowledge, they typically draw on or tacit, or implicit, knowledge gained through experience as well. The term *tacit knowledge* was first introduced by Polanyi (1966) and describes knowledge that is: (1) implicit, or acquired without instructional support or even conscious awareness, (2) procedural, or "knowing how" rather than "knowing what," and (3) instrumental to obtaining a particular goal (Sternberg et al., 2000). Tacit knowledge allows people to appreciate the nuances of a given situation that are not obtainable from any formalized, or even verbalized, set of rules. Tacit knowledge is not a substitute for other types of knowledge, such as declarative or explicit procedural knowledge. Rather, tacit knowledge helps to inform wise decision making in combination with other types of explicit knowledge. It provides the advantage to a seasoned diplomat over a freshman student in political science.

Second, the definition draws heavily on the idea of *balance*: the balance among multiple interests, immediate and lasting consequences, and environmental responses. What are these different interests and responses? *Intrapersonal interests* affect only the individual. They have to do with one's own sense of identity and may include such things as the desire for self-actualization, popularity, prestige, power, prosperity, or pleasure. *Interpersonal interests* involve other people. They relate not only to one's sense of self but also to desirable relationships with others. *Extrapersonal interests* are those that affect a wider organization, community, country, or environment. In addition to multiple interests, the consequences of each decision are assessed in order to balance short- and long-term objectives.

Importantly, the balance in Sternberg's theory of wisdom does not mean that each interest, consequence, or response is weighted equally. The relative "weightings" are determined by the extent to which a particular alternative contributes to the achievement of a common good.

Choosing the right balance depends on one's system of ethical values. In fact, *positive ethical values* can, or at least should, lie at the core of wise decision making, and not only in the balance theory described here. According to Csikszentmihalyi and Rathunde (1990, p. 32), "wisdom becomes the best guide for what is the *summum bonum*, or 'supreme good'" (see also Csikszentmihalyi & Nakamura, 2005). Pascual-Leone (1990) also considers "moral feelings and ethical evaluations (right–wrong or bad–good judgments) of motives and possible acts (e.g., morality)" as an important component of wisdom (p. 267; see Sternberg & Stemler, 2004). In Sternberg's theory, positive ethical values not only establish what constitutes the common good, they also influence the relative weightings of the various interests, conflicting consequences, and alternative responses to environment.

The central place of positive ethical values in Sternberg's theory brings up the question of who determines what the "right" positive ethical values are. We know that people's ethical values differ in different cultures and at different points in history. In fact, our own democratic values dictate that we respect others' differences in deciding what is right or wrong. But certain ethical values seem to transcend cultures and the world's great ethical systems, such as honesty, reciprocity, fairness, and justice.

When faced with a problem, wise individuals rely on their ethical values and knowledge to help them find a solution that balances conflicting intrapersonal, interpersonal, and extrapersonal interests over short and long terms. This conceptual model of wisdom, however, is not merely an esoteric intellectual exercise. Rather, it is oriented toward *action*. Applying relevant ethical values and knowledge, together with considering multiple interests and consequences, must lead to choosing a particular behavior (Reznitskaya & Sternberg, 2004; Sternberg, Jarvin, & Reznitskaya, 2008; Sternberg, Reznitskaya, & Jarvin, 2007). Although the balance theory of wisdom cannot determine a wise answer to any problem, it can help to assess how well a particular solution meets the theory specifications in a given context.

It could be rightly argued that formulating a wise solution to a problem may not necessarily lead to actually acting on it (Paris, 2001). Perkins (2002) describes several strategies for confronting behaviors that one considers unwise, but nevertheless finds too irresistible to abandon. For example, behaviors such as impulsiveness, procrastination, indulgence, or indecisiveness can be diminished and even eliminated with the use of deliberate conditioning and self-management techniques (Perkins, 2002).

Considering the complexity of the theoretical framework, and the possible obstacles to finding wise solutions and acting wisely, *can* and *should* schools teach in a manner to increase wise thinking in their students?

## Should we Teach for Wisdom?

Teaching for wisdom not only enhances students' thinking skills—their ability to reason reflectively, dialogically and dialectically—it also helps educators to develop more integrated curriculum units. Integrated units are beneficial because they help students see the bigger picture and understand how literature is related to history, how science and scientific discoveries and facts are embedded in a specific time and place (history), how social science and social-policy relate to history and geography, how economics are influenced by philosophical and political beliefs as well as by climate and geography, or how foreign language is inseparable from culture. Even within disciplines, far more integration is needed for students to acquire a complete and complex understanding of a topic.

Why should schools include instruction in wise-thinking skills in their curriculum? Consider four reasons.

First, knowledge is insufficient for wisdom and certainly does not guarantee satisfaction or happiness. Wisdom seems a better vehicle to the attainment of these goals. Second, wisdom provides a mindful and considered way to enter thoughtful and deliberative values into important judgments. One cannot be wise and at the same time impulsive or mindless in one's judgments. Third, wisdom represents an avenue to creating a better, more harmonious world. Dictators such as Adolph Hitler and Joseph Stalin may have been knowledgeable and may even have been good critical thinkers, at least with regard to the maintenance of their own power. Given the definition of wisdom, however, it would be hard to argue they were wise. Fourth and finally, students—who later will become parents and leaders—are always part of a greater community and hence will benefit from learning to judge rightly, soundly, or justly on behalf of their community.

We especially should teach for wisdom because smart people are especially susceptible to foolishness, that is, lack of wisdom. Foolish behavior, I suggest, is due largely, although certainly not exclusively, to six fallacies in thinking. These fallacies resemble those we might associate with adolescent thinking, because they are the kind of thinking often seen in adolescents (Sternberg, 2005).

1. *The unrealistic optimism fallacy.* This fallacy occurs when one believes one is so smart or powerful that it is pointless to worry about the outcomes, and especially the long-term ones, of what one does because everything will come out all right in the end—there is nothing to worry about, given one's brains or power. If one simply acts, the outcome will be fine. Bill Clinton tended to repeat sexual behavior that, first as Governor and then as President, was likely to come to a bad end. He seemed not to worry about it.

2. *The egocentrism fallacy.* This fallacy arises when one comes to think that one's own interests are the only ones that are important. One starts to ignore one's responsibilities to other people or to institutions. Sometimes, people in positions of responsibility may start off with good intentions, but then become corrupted by the power they yield and their seeming unaccountability to others for it. John Edwards, for example, seemed to let egocentrism get the better of him when he ran for president at the same time he was having an extramarital affair from which he fathered a child out of wedlock.

3. *The omniscience fallacy.* This fallacy results from having available at one's disposal essentially any knowledge one might want that, is, in fact, knowable. With a phone call, a powerful leader can have almost any kind of knowledge made available to him or her. At the same time, people look up to the powerful leader as extremely knowledgeable or even close to all-knowing. The powerful leader may then come to believe that he or she really is all-knowing. So may his or her staff.

4. *The omnipotence fallacy.* This fallacy results from the extreme power one wields, or believes one wields. The result is overextension, and often, abuse of power. Sometimes, leaders create internal or external enemies in order to demand more power for themselves to deal with the supposed enemies. In Zimbabwe, Robert Mugabe has turned one group against another, with the apparent goal of greatly expanding and maintaining his own power.

5. *The invulnerability fallacy.* This fallacy derives from the presence of the illusion of complete protection, such as might be provided by a large staff. People and especially leaders may seem to have many friends ready to protect them at a moment's notice. The leaders may shield themselves from individuals who are anything less than sycophantic. The Republican win in Massachusetts in 2010, mentioned earlier, showed Democrats they were not invulnerable at the polls, despite the decisive win in 2008.

6. *The ethical-disengagement fallacy.* This fallacy occurs when one starts to believe that ethics are important for other people but not for oneself. Many leaders of countries and corporations alike have seemed to think themselves exempt from the ethical standards to which they hold others. Kim Jong Il of North Korea comes to mind.

## How can we Teach for Wisdom?

Western education in the past couple of centuries has typically focused on imparting content knowledge and developing cognitive skills in students. Schools promote intelligent—but not necessarily wise—students. These students may have admirable records in school, yet make poor judgments in their own lives and in the lives of others. An important goal of educators, I believe, is to help prepare students to lead happy, satisfying, and productive lives. An increasing number of both researchers and policy makers share this belief that schools must foster both the cognitive and the moral development of their students (Reznitskaya & Sternberg, 2004). Leading a successful life inevitably involves the ability to solve difficult and uncertain everyday life problems. The problems people are exposed to vary depending on their environment and the responsibilities they carry, but all people will at one point or another be exposed to situations in which they have to rely on wisdom to make the right decision. We therefore believe that school *should* help enhance these wise thinking skills in students. How can teachers help their students develop all the explicit and implicit insights requisite for the display of wisdom?

The goal of teaching for wisdom can be achieved by providing students with educational contexts where students can formulate their own understanding of what constitutes wise thinking. In other words, teaching for wisdom is not accomplished through a didactic method of "imparting" information *about wisdom* and subsequently assessing students with multiple-choice questions. Instead, students need to actively experience various cognitive and affective processes that underlie wise decision making. In other words, teachers can provide scaffolding for the development of wisdom and case studies to help students develop wisdom, but a teacher cannot teach particular courses of actions, or give students a list of do's and don'ts, regardless of circumstances.

What are the processes underlying wise thinking that students have to acquire, and how can they be introduced into the classroom? Sternberg (2001) outlined 16 pedagogical principles and six procedures derived from the theory of wisdom, described in Tables 47.1 and 47.2. The fundamental idea behind all these educational guidelines is that the instructor teaches children not *what* to think, but, rather, *how* to think.

## Procedures for teaching for wisdom

Consider six procedures for teaching for wisdom (see also Table 47.2).

*Procedure 1:* Whenever possible, encourage students to engage in *reflective thinking*, to reflect on their own functioning to increase their metacognition (Flavell, 1987), that is, their awareness of their cognitions, emotions, and beliefs. The process of making a wise decision is strategic and goal-oriented, and therefore requires an ongoing monitoring of selected strategies, as well as an ability to modify less successful strategies to better fit the situational demands. Teachers can help students to practice reflective thinking by designing instructional activities that allow students to explore and shape their own ethical values. Also, students can be explicitly instructed in useful metacognitive strategies such as self-questioning or the use of self-monitoring checklists. Wisdom also helps in cultivating the habit of recognizing the influence of one's immediate emotions, desires, preferences or biases on one's judgments or reactions.

*Procedure 2:* Engage students in class discussions, projects, and essays that encourage them to discuss the lessons they have learned from the literary and philosophical works they've read, and how these lessons can be applied to their own lives and the lives of others. A history curriculum, for example, should make salient the relationships between history and personally relevant everyday experiences.

Table 47.1 Sixteen principles for teaching for wisdom (Sternberg, 2001).

| Principles 1–8 | Principles 9–16 |
| --- | --- |
| 1. Explore with students the notion that conventional abilities and achievements are not enough for a satisfying life. Many people become trapped in their lives and, despite feeling conventionally successful, feel that their lives lack fulfillment. Fulfillment is not an alternative to success, but rather, is an aspect of it that, for most people, goes beyond money, promotions, large houses, and so forth. | 9. Wise judgments are dependent in part on selecting among adaptation to, shaping of, and selection of environmental responses. |
| 2. Demonstrate how wisdom is critical for a satisfying life. In the long run, wise decisions benefit people in ways that foolish decisions never do. | 10. Encourage students to form, critique, and integrate their own ethical values in their thinking. |
| 3. Teach students the usefulness of interdependence and of interacting minds. | 11. Encourage students to think dialectically, realizing that both questions and their answers evolve over time, and that the answer to an important life question can differ at different times in one's life (such as whether to go to college). |
| 4. Role model wisdom because what you do is more important than what you say. Wisdom is action-dependent and wise actions need to be demonstrated. | 12. Show students the importance of dialogical thinking, whereby they understand interests and ideas from multiple points of view. |
| 5. Have students read about wise judgments and decision making so that students understand that such means of judging and decision making exist. | 13. Teach students to search for and then try to reach the common good—a good where everyone wins and not only those with whom one identifies. |
| 6. Help students to learn to recognize their own interests, those of other people, and those of institutions. | 14. Encourage and reward wisdom. |
| 7. Help students learn to balance their own interests, those of other people, and those of institutions. | 15. Teach students to monitor events in their lives and their own thought processes about these events. One way to learn to recognize others' interests is to begin to identify your own. |
| 8. Teach students that the means by which the end is obtained matters, not just the end. | 16. Help students understand the importance of inoculating oneself against the pressures of unbalanced self-interest and small-group interest. |

Reproduced from Robert J. Sternberg, Why Schools Should Teach for Wisdom: The Balance Theory of Wisdom in Educational Settings, Educational Psychologist, 36 (4), pp. 227–45 © 2001, Taylor and Francis, with permission.

| Table 47.2 Six procedures for teaching for wisdom (Sternberg, 2001) |
| --- |
| Procedures |
| 1  Encourage students to engage in *reflective thinking*, to reflect on their own functioning to increase their metacognition |
| 2  Engage students in class discussions, projects, and essays that encourage them to discuss the lessons they have learned from these works and how they can be applied to their own lives and the lives of others. A particular emphasis should be placed on dialogical (see principle 12) and dialectical (see principle 11) thinking. |
| 3  Encourage students to study not only "truth," but ethical values, as developed during their reflective thinking. |
| 4  Place an increased emphasis on critical, creative, and practical thinking in the service of good ends that benefit the common good. |
| 5  Encourage students to think about how almost *any* topic they study might be used for better or for worse ends, and about how important that final end is. |
| 6  Remember that a teacher is a role model! To role model wisdom, the teacher should adopt a Socratic approach to teaching, and invite students to play a more active role in constructing learning—from their own point of view and from that of others. |

Reproduced from Robert J. Sternberg, Why Schools Should Teach for Wisdom: The Balance Theory of Wisdom in Educational Settings, *Educational Psychologist*, 36 (4), pp. 227–45 © 2001, Taylor and Francis, with permission.

Teachers should engage students in dialogical and dialectical thinking, in addition to the reflective thinking described earlier. What is dialogical thinking (principle 12)? When one is faced with a complex problem involving several points of view, it is often necessary to take into account different frames of reference and various perspectives to find the best possible solution. What may at first appear as the right answer may turn out to be the wrong choice when the long term is considered, or when the interests of the community as a whole are taken into account. In dialogical thinking, one uses multiple frames of reference to generate and deliberate about various perspectives on the issue at hand (Kuhn, Shaw, & Felton, 1997; Reznitskaya et al., 2001).

What is dialectical thinking (principle 11)? Whereas dialogical thinking involves the consideration and weighing of multiple points of view, *dialectical thinking* emphasizes the consideration and *integration* of two opposing perspectives. The first perspective considered is the *thesis*. For example, one can be a radical pacifist and opposed to any military presence or intervention, whatever the circumstances. A second perspective, an *antithesis* (a negation of the original statement) is then considered. For example, one can argue that a people can only live freely and in peace if their borders are protected by armed forces. Finally, a *synthesis* or reconciliation of the two seemingly opposing statements is developed. For example, one might decide that borders under dispute should be protected by a third party, such as an international army, rather than having the opposing countries measure their military strength against each other. The process does not stop when the two opposing view are reconciled; on the contrary, each synthesis becomes a new thesis, which can then be integrated in a new round of dialectical thinking. In the classroom, dialectical thinking can be encouraged through opportunities to study different sources, enabling students to build their own knowledge, or through writing assignments that explicitly call for a thesis, antithesis, and synthesis. Empirical studies have investigated the impact of developing such a fluid and dynamic concept of knowledge, where the source of knowledge is not the "authority" (the teacher or the book), but rather, the student. Such conceptions of knowledge have been shown to relate to active engagement in learning (e.g., McDevitt, 1990), persistence in performing a task (e.g., Dweck & Leggett, 1988), and deeper comprehension and integration of the material taught (e.g., Qian & Alvermann, 2000; Songer & Linn, 1991).

*Procedure 3:* Encourage students to study not only "truth," but ethical values, as developed during their reflective thinking. The problems of major corporate fiascos such as Enron, WorldCom, Global Crossing, and more recently, a series of failed banks beginning with Bear-Stearns and continuing through Lehman Brothers and other major banks, began with the rejection of positive ethical values.

*Procedure 4:* Place an increased emphasis on critical, creative, and practical thinking in the service of good ends that benefit the common good. In the typical classroom, teachers encourage critical thinking skills in their students. Some teachers also aim to develop creative and practical thinking skills (Sternberg & Grigorenko, 2007; Sternberg, Jarvin, & Grigorenko, 2009) by engaging students in activities that lead them to go beyond the content they have studied (creative thinking) to apply this knowledge to their environment (practical thinking). To enhance wise thinking, however, students should also be encouraged to consider the outcome of their thinking, and to keep in mind that the best solution is not the one that benefits only the individual doing the thinking, but rather the one that helps others as well. The common good should be the guiding principle in choosing between different possible solutions.

*Procedure 5:* Encourage students to think about how almost *any* topic they study might be used for better or worse ends, and about how important that final end is. As described under Procedure 4, students should be encouraged to seek different solutions and to choose the one that benefits the common good rather than the individual. They should also be brought to realize that, just as there are different solutions benefiting different people, a given concept or point of knowledge can be used to a good or poor end. A stereotypical example is that the knowledge of nuclear physics can be applied to constructing bombs or to develop sources of energy. The end to which one chooses to apply one's knowledge matters greatly.

*Procedure 6:* Remember that a teacher is a role model! To role model wisdom, the teacher adopts a Socratic approach to teaching, and invites students to play a more active role in constructing learning—from their own point of view and from that of others. Wise thinking is not a set of rules or decisions that the teacher can outline for students to copy down; it is a type of thinking that the students themselves need to adopt and master. The most effective way to encourage wise thinking skills is not through memory drills but through student participation and teacher modeling. For example, a teacher can capitalize on a negative event, such as two students getting into a fight, as a way to demonstrate how one can approach a similar situation in a more constructive way. The teacher can model wise thinking by saying: "When I get into the situations like this, I try to see the dispute from the perspective of the other person and think about whether my own behavior contributed to the situation. Was there anything I could have done differently to prevent this confrontation? Is there a solution to our disagreement that is acceptable to both of us?" Also, teachers should not miss the opportunity to recognize and praise good judgments made by students, such as when they show consideration for others and their ideas, or when they offer a solution that benefits the class as a whole rather than themselves as individuals.

## Applications of the procedures

In science teaching, dialectical thinking can be applied to illustrate to students the notion that scientific facts are not eternal or immutable, but rather the state of affairs as we perceive them at this very specific point in time. Indeed, science often is presented as though it represents the end of a process of evolution of thought, rather than one of many midpoints (Sternberg, 1998). Students could scarcely realize from this kind of teaching that the paradigms of today, and thus the theories and findings that emanate from them, will eventually be superseded, much as the paradigms, theories, and findings of yesterday were replaced by those of today. Further, students must learn that, contrary to the way many textbooks are written, the classical "scientific method" is an ideal rather than a reality, and that scientists are as susceptible to fads as is anyone else. How many scientists in his time considered as scientific evidence the data presented by Galileo Galilei to demonstrate that the Earth evolved around the Sun, and not vice versa?

Wise thinking skills can also be applied in the literature classroom. Literature is often taught in terms of the standards and context of the contemporary American scene. Characters often are judged in terms of our contemporary standards rather than in terms of the standards of the time and place in which the events took place. Imagine if students were routinely encouraged to approach the study of literary works with a dialogical mindset, studying literature in the context of history. Censorship and the banning of books often reflect the application of certain contemporary standards to literature, standards of which an author from the past never could have been aware.

The foreign language classroom is another terrain for enhancing students' wise thinking skills. Foreign languages should be taught in the cultural context in which they are embedded, requiring students to engage in reflective and dialogical thinking to truly grasp the foreign culture and to position themselves and their experiences in relation to this culture. It tends to be more common in Europe to speak one or several languages beyond one's mother tongue. Perhaps American students have so much more difficulty learning foreign languages than do children in much of Europe not because they lack the ability, but because they lack the motivation and the exposure. An American student would probably much more readily see the need to learn a foreign language if each of the 50 states spoke a different language, much like the member states of the European Union do. We would also do our students a service by teaching them to understand other cultures rather than just to expect people from other cultures to understand them. Learning the language of a culture is a key to understanding it, and the two can not be taught separately, or by viewing culture as an appendix to language rather than the context in which it is deeply rooted.

Teaching of history also provides an important vehicle for teaching for wisdom, and is what we have used in our own teaching for wisdom program (Reznitskaya & Sternberg, 2004; Sternberg, Jarvin, & Reznitskaya, 2008; Sternberg, Reznitskaya, & Jarvin, 2007). For example, students can put themselves in the place of famous historical leaders and ask what decisions they would have made had they been those leaders? Should Napoleon have invaded Russia? Should Abraham Lincoln have fought the Civil War or sought a negotiated settlement with the South to prevent bloodshed? Should King George III have let the American colonies go their own way, or fought them? When are settlers, settlers, and when are they invaders?

## Conclusion

In conclusion, schools cannot teach wisdom, but they can teach for wisdom. The balance theory provides one of many bases by which teachers can teach for wisdom. The important goal is to teach knowledge not for its own sake, but for its use to promote the common good by balancing intrapersonal, interpersonal, and extrapersonal interests over the short and long terms through the mediation of positive ethical values. Individual and group happiness depend far more on the acquisition of wisdom than they do on the accumulation of knowledge. Knowledge can destroy the world, as the sophistication of terrorist bombs and attacks has shown us; wisdom can only make it better.

## Acknowledgments

I am grateful to Elena Grigorenko, Linda Jarvin, Jennifer Jordan, Tzur Karelitz, Jill Pousty, and Alina Reznitskaya for the collaborations that made this work possible.

## References

Baltes, P. B., & Smith, J. (2008). The fascination of wisdom: Its nature, ontogeny, and function. *Perspectives on Psychological Science*, 3(1), 56–64.

Baltes, P. B., & Staudinger, U. (1993). The search for a psychology of wisdom. *Current Directions in Psychological Science*, 2, 75–80.

Baltes, P. B., & Staudinger, U. (2000). Wisdom: A metaheuristic (pragmatic) to orchestrate mind and virtue toward excellence. *American Psychologist*, 55, 122–136.

Birren, J. E., & Fisher, L. M. (1990). The elements of wisdom: Overview and integration. In R. J. Sternberg (Ed.), *Wisdom: Its nature, origins, and development* (pp. 317–332). New York, NY: Cambridge University Press.

Birren, J. E., & Svensson, C. M. (2005). Wisdom in history. In R. J. Sternberg, & J. Jordan (Eds.), *A handbook of wisdom: Psychological perspectives* (pp. 3–31). New York, NY: Cambridge University Press.

Bluck, S., & Glueck, J. (2005). From the inside out: People's implicit theories of wisdom. In R. J. Sternberg, & J. Jordan (Eds.), *A handbook of wisdom: Psychological perspectives* (pp. 84–109). New York, NY: Cambridge University Press.

Clayton, V. (1975). Erickson's theory of human development as it applies to the aged: Wisdom as contradictory cognition. *Human Development*, 18, 119–128.

Clayton, V. (1982). Wisdom and intelligence: The nature and function of knowledge in the later years. *International Journal of Aging and Development*, 15, 315–321.

Czikszentmihalyi, M., & Nakamura, J. (2005). The role of emotions in the development of wisdom. In R. J. Sternberg, & J. Jordan (Eds.), *A handbook of wisdom: Psychological perspectives* (pp. 220–242). New York, NY: Cambridge University Press.

Csikszentmihalyi, M., & Rathunde, K. (1990). The psychology of wisdom: An evolutionary interpretation. In R. J. Sternberg (Ed.), *Wisdom: Its nature, origins, and development* (pp. 25–51). New York, NY: Cambridge University Press.

Dweck, C. S., & Leggett, E. L. (1988). A social–cognitive approach to motivation and personality. *Psychological Review, 95*, 256–273.

Flavell, J. H. (1987). Speculations about the nature and development of metacognition. In F. E. Wienert & R. H. Kluwe (Eds.), *Metacognition, motivation, and understanding* (pp. 21–29). Hillsdale, NJ: Erlbaum.

Holliday, S.G., & Chandler, M. J. (1986). *Wisdom: Explorations in adult competence*. Basel, Switzerland: Karger.

Karelitz, T. M., Jarvin, L., & Sternberg, R. J. (2010). The meaning of wisdom and its development throughout life. In W. Overton (Ed.), *Handbook of lifespan human development* (pp. 837–881). New York, NY: Wiley.

Kitchener, K. S., & Brenner, H. G. (1990). Wisdom and reflective judgment: Knowing in the face of uncertainty. In R. J. Sternberg (Ed.), *Wisdom: Its Nature, origins, and development* (pp. 212–229). New York, NY: Cambridge University Press.

Kramer, D. A. (1990). Conceptualizing wisdom: The primacy of affect–cognition relations. In R. J. Sternberg (Ed.), *Wisdom: Its nature, origins, and development* (pp. 279–313). New York, NY: Cambridge University Press.

Kramer, D. A. (2000). Wisdom as a classical source of human strength: Conceptualization and empirical inquiry. *Journal of Social and Clinical Inquiry, 19*, 83–101.

Kuhn, D., Shaw, V., & Felton, M. (1997). Effects of dyadic interaction on argumentative reasoning. *Cognition and Instruction, 15*, 287–315.

Kunzmann, U., & Baltes, P. B. (2005). The psychology of wisdom: Theoretical and empirical challenges. In R. J. Sternberg, & J. Jordan (Eds.), *A handbook of wisdom: Psychological perspectives* (pp. 110–135). New York, NY: Cambridge University Press.

Labouvie-Vief, G. (1990). Wisdom as integrated thought: Historical and developmental perspectives. In R. J. Sternberg (Ed.), *Wisdom: Its Nature, origins, and development* (pp. 52–83). New York, NY: Cambridge University Press.

McDevitt, T. M. (1990). Mothers' and children's beliefs about listening. *Child Study Journal, 20*, 105–128.

Osbeck, L. M., & Robinson, D. N. (2005). Philosophical theories of wisdom. In R.J. Sternberg, & J. Jordan, *A handbook of wisdom: Psychological perspectives*. New York, NY: Cambridge University Press.

Paris, S. G. (2001). Wisdom, snake oil, and the educational marketplace. *Educational Psychologist, 36*, 257–260.

Pascual-Leone, J. (1990). An essay on wisdom: Toward organismic processes that make it possible. In R. J. Sternberg (Ed.), *Wisdom: Its nature, origins, and development* (pp. 244–278). New York, NY: Cambridge University Press.

Perkins, D. (2002). The engine of folly. In R. J. Sternberg (Ed.), *Why smart people can be so stupid* (pp. 233–243). New Haven, CT: Yale University Press.

Piaget, J. (1972). *The psychology of intelligence*. Totowa, NJ: Littlefield-Adams.

Polanyi, M. (1966). *The tacit dimensions*. Garden City, NY: Doubleday.

Qian, G., & Alvermann, D. E. (2000). Relationship between epistemological beliefs and conceptual change learning. *Reading & Writing Quarterly, 16*, 59–74.

Reznitskaya, A., Anderson, R. C., McNurlen, B., Nguyen-Jahiel, K., Archodidou, A., & Kim, S. (2001). Influence of oral discussion on written argument. *Discourse Processes, 32*, 155–175.

Reznitskaya, A., & Sternberg, R. J. (2004). Teaching students to make wise judgments: The "teaching for wisdom" program. In P. A. Linley, & S. Joseph (Eds.) *Positive psychology in practice* (pp. 181–196). New York, NY: Wiley.

Robinson, D. N. (1990). Wisdom through the ages. In R.J. Sternberg (Ed.), *Wisdom: Its nature, origins, and development* (pp. 13–24). New York, NY: Cambridge University Press.

Smith, J., & Baltes, P. B. (1990). Wisdom-related knowledge: Age/cohort differences in response to life-planning problems. *Developmental Psychology*, 26, 494–505.

Songer, N. B., & Linn, M. C. (1991). How do views of science influence knowledge integration. *Journal of Research in Science Teaching*, 28, 761–784.

Staudinger, U. M. (2008). A psychology of wisdom: History and recent developments. *Research in Human Development*, 5, 107–120.

Sternberg, R. J. (1998). A balance theory of wisdom. *Review of General Psychology*, 2, 347–365.

Sternberg, R. J. (Ed.). (1990). *Wisdom: Its nature, origins, and development*. New York, NY: Cambridge University Press.

Sternberg, R. J. (1990). Understanding wisdom. In R. J. Sternberg (Ed.), *Wisdom: Its nature, origins, and development*. New York, NY: Cambridge University Press.

Sternberg, R. J. (1998). A balance theory of wisdom. *Review of General Psychology*, 2, 347–365.

Sternberg, R. J. (2001). Why schools should teach for wisdom: The balance theory of wisdom in educational settings. *Educational Psychologist*, 36, 227–245.

Sternberg, R. J. (Ed.). (2002). *Why smart people can be so stupid*. New Haven, CT: Yale University Press.

Sternberg, R. J. (2003). *Wisdom, intelligence, and creativity synthesized*. New York, NY: Cambridge University Press.

Sternberg, R. J. (2004). Teaching for wisdom: What matters is not what students know, but how they use it. In D. R. Walling (Ed.) *Public education, democracy, and the common good* (pp. 121–132). Bloomington, IN: Phi Delta Kappan.

Sternberg, R. J. (2005). Foolishness. In R. J. Sternberg & J. Jordan (Eds.), *Handbook of wisdom: Psychological perspectives* (pp. 331–352). New York, NY: Cambridge University Press.

Sternberg, R. J. (2008). Schools should nurture wisdom. In B. Z. Presseisen (Ed.), *Teaching for intelligence* (2nd ed., pp. 61–88). Thousand Oaks, CA: Corwin.

Sternberg, R. J. (2009). Wisdom. In S. J. Lopez (Ed.) *Encyclopedia of positive psychology*. (Vol. 2, pp. 1034–1037) New York, NY: Wiley-Blackwell Publishing.

Sternberg, R. J., Forsythe, G. B., Hedlund, J., Horvath, J. A., Wagner, R. K., & Williams, W. M., ... Grigorenko, E. L. (2000). *Practical intelligence in everyday life*. Cambridge, MA: Cambridge University Press.

Sternberg, R. J., & Grigorenko, E. L. (2007). *Teaching for successful intelligence* (2nd ed.). Thousand Oaks, CA: Corwin.

Sternberg, R. J., Jarvin, L., & Grigorenko, E. L. (2009). *Teaching for wisdom, intelligence, creativity, and success*. Thousand Oaks, CA: Corwin.

Sternberg, R. J., Jarvin, L., & Reznitskaya, A. (2008). Teaching of wisdom through history: Infusing wise thinking skills in the school curriculum. In M. Ferrari & G. Potworowski (Eds.), *Teaching for wisdom* (pp. 37–57). New York, NY: Springer.

Sternberg, R. J., & Jordan, J. (Eds.). (2005). *Handbook of wisdom: Psychological perspectives*. New York, NY: Cambridge University Press.

Sternberg, R. J., Reznitskaya, A., & Jarvin, L. (2007). Teaching for wisdom: What matters is not just what students know, but how they use it. *The London Review of Education*, 5(2), 143–158.

Sternberg, R. J., & Stemler, S. E. (2004). Wisdom as a moral virtue. In T. A. Thorkildsen, & H. J. Walberg (Eds.), *Nurturing morality* (pp. 187–197). New York, NY: Kluwer Academic/Plenum Publishers.

# CHAPTER 48

# GOING BEYOND THE ACCIDENTAL: HAPPINESS, EDUCATION, AND THE WELLINGTON COLLEGE EXPERIENCE

### IAN MORRIS

Wellington College, Berkshire, UK

In the first few chapters of Charles Dickens's novel *Hard Times*, we are presented with a disquieting, reductionist, and utilitarian vision of education that demands nothing of children other than they be receptacles for facts imparted to them by their teachers. In this vision, the teachers are cold and hard, referring to children by surname only, or worse, by number: Sissy Jupe is "girl number twenty." The architect of this vision of education, Thomas Gradgrind, routinely humiliates children for their failure to accumulate facts and as Dickens himself put it, this approach to education murders innocents and dispatches childhood:

> . . . [Gradgrind] seemed a kind of cannon loaded to the muzzle with facts, and prepared to blow them clean out of the regions of childhood at one discharge. He seemed a galvanizing apparatus, too, charged with a grim mechanical substitute for the tender young imaginations that were to be stormed away. (Dickens, 1854/1994, p. 2)

It is not just the children in Gradgrind's educational system who are subjected to his reductionist vision of being human, it is the teachers too. Mr M'Choakumchild, a recent graduate of teacher training according to the Gradgrind method, knew so many facts about so many things that he was unable to relate to the children as anything other than pitchers that he was required to fill.

The children of Gradgrind's "model school" will eventually emerge as citizens of Coketown, a miserable industrial town concerned solely with what it can produce with no regard for the happiness of its workforce:

> [Coketown] contained several large streets all very like one another, inhabited by people equally like one another, who all went in and out at the same hours, with the same sound

upon the same pavements, to do the same work, and to whom every day was the same as yesterday and to-morrow, and every year the counterpart of the last and the next. (Dickens, 1854/1994, p. 19)

We recoil from Gradgrind's vision of education perhaps for two reasons. Primarily, it is objectionable because we know from our own experiences that a philosophy and praxis of education that reduces and dehumanizes is an education that fails. Coketown and the "model school" prevent happiness because they treat persons as automata fit only for the accumulation of facts or the performance of tasks which contribute to production. Thomas Gradgrind's vision of education is one that stymies and diminishes young people. When we think about our own favorite teachers, they were those who took an especial interest in us and were able to elicit the best from us in a variety of ways. We thrive and flourish in education when it goes much further than the mere imparting of knowledge, to a deeper level of education that addresses the fundamental questions of what it means to be human. The second reason we recoil, is we know at an instinctive level that education of this sort will not lead to happiness (in fact, in *Hard Times* it leads to considerable unhappiness for Gradgrind's own children) and at an instinctive or more intellectual level, we know that something is amiss if education and human happiness are not interwoven. Education, if it is to live up to its etymological root "to lead out," must do the opposite: it must equip young people with the ability to bring about their own flourishing.

But what is the nature of the relationship between happiness and education and why do some commentators suggest that the teaching of happiness has no place in education?

## "Education as Happiness" and "Educating for Happiness"

Children are happy in schools when their needs are being met, when they have positive relationships with peers and teachers, when they enjoy and are challenged by the activities that they are engaging in, and when they can see reward, meaning, and purpose in what they are doing. It seems so simple, but these are the key challenges that teachers and schools face. Schools have a twofold role in the promotion of happiness. Firstly, the school itself must be a happy place to be. The basic needs of the pupils need to be met, the curriculums (formal, informal, and hidden[1]) must enable pupils to discover and develop their physical, intellectual, and social strengths and abilities and, above all, the school must create the conditions for excellence and allow its pupils to discover a sense of meaning and purpose that will carry them well beyond the school gates. This might be termed "*education as happiness*." Secondly, schools should give explicit guidance to their pupils on how happiness might be achieved in life and not just assume that happiness will result from the ordinary activities of school life; this might be termed "*educating for happiness*." It is this second suggested role that is controversial and that has attracted a great deal of media attention in recent times.

---

[1] Formal curriculum: the provision of subjects and lessons; informal curriculum: extracurricular activities such as sport and drama; hidden curriculum: the ethos and values of the school that shape the experience that the members of the community encounter.

## Should Happiness be an Aim of Education?

There have been a number of critical reactions to the suggestion that happiness should be a function and aim of education and they vary from being simplistic and reactionary to being reasoned contributions that will help develop a sophisticated understanding of how happiness and education might go together. What is often most interesting about the more reactionary criticisms of the role of happiness in education (and indeed anywhere), is that they are themselves often uncritical about definitions of happiness (and terms which critics choose to associate with it such as "optimism," "positivity," and "well-being") and tend to assume that the reader knows exactly what is meant by them.[2] If we are to argue for a relationship between education and happiness, should we not at least be clear about exactly what we are discussing? As is explained elsewhere in this volume, there are myriad theories of happiness and for the sake of simplicity this article will make use of Diener's 1984 classic *Subjective Well-Being*, which classifies approaches to happiness (Diener, 2009). Of the six categories Diener describes, one in particular seems to have the strongest connection to education, namely the *activity* theory of happiness.[3] Activity theories of happiness suggest that happiness is experienced as a by-product of human activity and Diener cites the Aristotelian vision of happiness which suggests that happiness arises from excellence, from doing something well in line with a commonly agreed set of virtues (Aristotle, 2004). Activity views of happiness reject the idea that happiness is something that can be aimed at per se and can only be experienced as a result of the activities we choose to engage in.

If, when education and happiness are put together, we are required to infer what type of happiness is being discussed, the less sophisticated objections are bound to recur. Critics are right to be suspicious of an education system which promotes the simple, utilitarian pursuit of pleasures over pain as proposed by hedonistic approaches to happiness because it would promote triviality as opposed to engagement and meaning-making. They are also right to be suspicious of an education system that promotes "positivity" and "self-esteem" at all costs, as can be seen with the catastrophic failure of the self-esteem movement in the education system in the USA (Roberts, 2009; Seligman, 1995). They are also right to be wary of approaches to happiness that advocate social or material comparison. James (2007) and Schwartz (2004) have put forward persuasive arguments that the contemporary Western culture of competitive consumerism and the myth that we are happy so long as we are keeping up with and outpacing the Joneses is a widespread and profound cause of unhappiness. It is incumbent on those of us who wish to advocate educating for happiness to be clearer about our meanings

---

[2] Take, for example, Julian Baggini's article "State of Joy: Why your country needs you to be happy" published in *The Independent* newspaper on January 6 2010, where the term "happiness" is left unexamined and "optimism" is used only in keeping with popular connotations of being cheerful in the face of adversity, rather than its more specific sense of having the cognitive resources to adapt and thrive under pressure.

[3] The other six categories are: *Telic theories*, where happiness is achieved when some goal is met; *Pleasure and Pain theories*, the hedonic view of happiness where a preponderance of pleasure over pain affects happiness; *Top-down and Bottom-up theories*, the former suggesting that happiness results from a sum of small pleasures, the latter suggests that there is a "global propensity to experience things in a positive way"; *Associationistic theories*, which suggest that happiness results from making positive associations and learning to react in particular ways and *Judgment theories*, where happiness results from a comparison between a judgment and actual conditions (Diener, 2000, pp. 38–47).

and to base our arguments upon robust rather than popular conceptions of happiness. It is also incumbent upon the critics to take note of these definitions and avoid simplifying the debate in order to gather support for their own arguments.

One of the most useful critiques of the place of happiness in education comes from Suissa (2009). She suggests that some approaches to happiness education rely too heavily on the new academic discipline of positive psychology which, she argues, presents a view of happiness which is more concerned with empirical verification than with philosophical discussions of the nature of happiness. Suissa includes Wellington College in this critique and uses it for concrete examples of what she is railing against. Her examples are based upon a ten-item plan for well-being which was aimed to provide advice at a popular level and is a small aspect of the well-being program at Wellington and unrepresentative of our philosophy as a whole. As with so many critiques of happiness education, the author homed in on a narrow aspect of our practice and used it to make more general philosophical observations which as it turns out, are not at odds with much of what we are trying to achieve at Wellington.

Importantly, Suissa goes on to argue that happiness is complex and individual and should not be reduced to packages of skills or techniques whose effectiveness is readily measurable. Focusing on measurable happiness interventions risks eliminating normative philosophical questions of the good life and of meaning and values from the discussion, which is in her view *anti*-educational. Suissa also argues that happiness education fails when it is dictatorial: just because there has been shown to be a correlation between certain behaviors and self-reports of subjective well-being, this does not mean that we should prescribe certain behaviors for individuals. Suissa's paper is a vital contribution to the debate about the role of measurable outcomes in education, including in happiness education, and their potential to act as a trap rather than an ameliorative influence.

## Education as Happiness

Three strong advocates of the activity approach to developing happiness in schools are Claxton, Brighouse, and Roberts. All three argue that schools can and should do more to enable young people to be happier, enjoy enhanced well-being, and flourish.

In his book *What's the Point of School?*, Claxton argues that if schools were better able to help children to learn and engage with the process of learning in the first place, then education would make children happier:

> Happiness is better seen as a by-product of having done something challenging and worthwhile. Happiness is a mixture of pride, satisfaction and the sense of effectiveness and value that arises when we have stretched ourselves to achieve something we care about. In other words, happiness is the fruit of worthwhile learning. In my view, too much stress and unhappiness in young people's lives comes from the fact that they do not know how to learn, nor what it is that they want to learn about. If we can help them to discover the things they most passionately want to get better at, and to develop the confidence and capability to pursue those passions, then I think more happiness and less stress will be the result. (Claxton, 2008, pp. 193–194)

As it stands, Claxton argues, current educational provision, especially in the UK, leaves many school leavers stressed and anxious with its focus on testing and accumulating qualifications.

For him, modern education does not connect children to the fundamental joys of learning and has missed the opportunity to use the school years as what he calls an "epistemic apprenticeship," where children learn to become learners. Too often, he argues, children spend time learning *about* learning and accumulating an ineffective language of learning, rather than actually learning *to* learn. Schools have been hamstrung by accountability and are afraid of allowing children to take risks as learners, to explore real-life, meaningful and challenging material without the close teacher control that arises when a certain percentage of A*–C grades has to be achieved. Claxton's solution is an approach called "Building Learning Power," or "The Learning Gymnasium," where children spend time developing their "learning muscles" (i.e. learning how to learn) and discovering that they delight in learning. In Claxton's view, an education system with the child, not political concerns, at its centre would lead to children who experience happiness through the activity of learning.

However, Claxton stops short of advocating *educating for happiness*. For him, lessons of this sort, which have only operated at a superficial level in the past, would become superfluous if the formal curriculum was delivered properly, as is also argued by Suissa. This view is at odds with the conclusions reached in this section. As Noddings (2003, p. 23) puts it:

> Education by its very nature should help people to develop their best selves...A large part of our obligation as educators is to help students understand the wonders and complexities of happiness, to raise questions about it, and to explore promising possibilities responsibly.

Brighouse (2008) argues that we need to replace what has become the predominant aim of education, the provision of a skilled workforce, with an aim that operates at a deeper human level; the development of flourishing individuals. For Brighouse, using education to produce skilled workers falls short of its potential to transform individuals and societies.

> If quality of life is the reason that economic stability and growth matter, and growth does not systematically improve quality of life, then education should be guided not solely or primarily by economic considerations, but directly by the value of human flourishing. It should aim to improve children's prospects for leading flourishing lives. (Brighouse, 2008, p. 59)

Given what sociology, psychology, and the human sciences are now revealing about the causes of and impediments to human flourishing, Brighouse argues that education is strongly placed to make use of this research to focus *primarily* on the flourishing of those who pass through the system. The formal curriculum, for example, is not just there to provide skills for the job market but so:

> that children have an interest – entirely independent of whatever interest they have in being equipped with job-related skills – in being acquainted with the greatest cultural goods that our civilization has produced, goods that can help them lead fully flourishing human lives in multiple dimensions, not just economic. (Brighouse, 2008, p. 65)

For Brighouse, the entirety of school communities from the formal curriculum provision through to the values and ethos of the school should have *flourishing* as their purpose. Brighouse also advocates *educating for happiness*, although expresses a note of caution that lessons of that sort are more vulnerable to teachers "inappropriately bring[ing] their own biases and experiences into the classroom" than other subject areas. In Brighouse's article, we see a philosophy of education that has enormous support in the educational world and which returns us to the fundamental reason that many people choose education as a profession.

In her paper *Grit*, Roberts (2009) takes a slightly different approach to Claxton and Brighouse. For Roberts, there is no doubt that we need curriculum reform of the sort suggested by Claxton and schools need to develop the building of what she calls "SEED skills" (SEED being an acronym standing for; Social and emotional competencies, Emotional resilience, Enterprise innovation and creativity and Discipline) but where she parts company with Claxton[4] and Brighouse and to an extent with the philosophy of this article is, for her, this reform is needed, in large part, to prepare young people for an increasingly dynamic and uncertain job market. It would be reckless to ignore the fact that the education system has a responsibility to enable young people to make an enduring contribution to society and that much of this contribution will be made through their working lives. However, we should be wary of arguments that advocate the introduction of programs that cover SEED-type skills in order to meet the needs of employers. To do so is to subordinate fundamental human skills such as resilience to an instrumental level when they are goods per se. Alongside the argument against introducing happiness education as an instrument of economic good, runs the argument against introducing it for reasons of pathology. Much is made of the "epidemic of childhood depression" or the "epidemic of adolescent substance misuse," when statistics inform us that the vast majority of young people enter adulthood without mental health or addiction problems.[5] To introduce lessons to address specific but high profile problems neglects the experiences that most young people have and misses an opportunity to educate for flourishing, rather than mere prevention.

Of enormous significance in Roberts's paper is her emphasis on the need for education to focus not just on the traditional academic disciplines and not just on social and emotional skills, but on helping students to develop the two qualities of grit and resilience:

> This paper focuses on these two in particular because of the remarkable gap between what's known about their importance and current practice in schools. Their meanings are very familiar from daily life. One group of academics, for example, describes grit as: 'working strenuously towards challenges, maintaining effort and interest over years despite failure, adversity and plateaus in progress. The gritty individual," they explain: "approaches achievement as a marathon: his or her advantage is stamina. Whereas disappointment or boredom signal to others that it is time to change trajectory and cut losses, the gritty individual stays the course." (Roberts, 2009, p. 15)

For Roberts, a significant cause of unhappiness amongst young people is their lack of grit and resilience. Roberts cites numerous examples of research conducted by academics such

---

[4] Claxton writes: Another reason for attending school is that in these globally cut-throat economic times, the country needs them to be a part of a "world-class, highly skilled, adaptable workforce." Whilst this might be a good reason as far as the government is concerned, "contributing to the national economy" is not a very inspiring reason to get out of bed and pack your school-bag on a cold February morning. The idea that children go to school to be shaped into serviceable cogs in a giant economic machine doesn't really do it for young people—nor, it is to be hoped, for the majority of their parents and tutors (Claxton, 2008, p.33).

[5] "At any point in time, approximately 2% of children aged 11-15 and 11% of youth aged 16-24 in Great Britain have a major depressive disorder (Green, McGinnity, Meltzer, Ford, & Goodman, 2005; Singleton, Bumpstead, O"Brien, Lee, & Meltzer, 2001)', quoted in Karen Reivich et al., the Penn Resiliency Project Executive Summary, March 2009: this of course leaves 98% and 89% of 11–15- and 16–24-year-olds respectively *without* major depressive disorders. According to the NHS, only 14% of 15-year-olds are regular smokers; more young people than ever report never having had an alcoholic drink and the numbers of 11–15-year-olds reporting having had an alcoholic drink is down nine percentage points from 61% in 2003 to 52% in 2008; only 7% of 15-year-olds reported having taken drugs on more than 10 occasions in the last year in 2008 (source http://www.ic.nhs.uk, accessed January 7, 2010).

as Seligman and Dweck, and experimental approaches to education such as the Studio Schools, to show that it is possible to equip young people with these skills and that an education system that focuses on teaching to exams deprives its students of the opportunity to take risks as learners and develop grit and resilience in the process. For Roberts, a sound education involves not only equipping young people with a mastery of academic or technical skills, but doing so in such a way that they derive satisfaction from school because it engenders skills of grit and resilience. On top of this, comes an education in the vital SEED skills: the skills that go beyond the mere mastery of a discipline, but the human skills that enable us to translate mastery of a discipline into human flourishing through creativity, perseverance and the ability to build sound relationships.

*Education as happiness*, as Claxton, Brighouse, and Roberts suggest, arises when children derive satisfaction and fulfillment from the business of being at school, not because school gives them a sheaf of qualifications that may be traded for something else, but because school helps young people to develop those essential human skills of learning which will enable them to flourish in all areas of school life, from the classroom to the playground, sports-field to the stage, structure of the day to the paintings on the walls:

> *This* is a school! A place where people together learn to live together and love one another, where people learn to reason, learn to understand and above all learn to think for themselves. School was not invented for little people to become the same as big people, but for the pupils to learn how to live and let live. (Judith, thirteen). (Claxton, 2008, p. 28)

But what of *educating for happiness*? We have seen glimpses already of what this may involve, and it is now time to explore what it might look like in more detail.

## Educating for happiness

As mentioned earlier, happiness education involves not only helping young people to be happy as they learn, but helping them to learn how to make themselves happier. There is considerable current, reliable, and meaningful research into the ingredients of a happy life and young people should be given the opportunity to engage critically with that research. I am arguing for a tandem approach to happiness education where not only does the curriculum itself generate happiness (education as happiness), but also where students are given the opportunity to question what it is about their education that makes them happy and what else they could be doing in life to maximize their happiness (educating for happiness). In short, every opportunity must be given to young people to learn how to bring about their own flourishing. Furthermore, as educators we should be arguing for *educating for happiness* not because it will benefit the labor market directly through increased productivity, or because it will benefit young people incidentally by making them happy at work or less likely to take drugs, but because to learn how to flourish as a human being is a major entitlement of young humans.

Since 2006, we have been pioneering lessons in happiness at Wellington College. From their arrival and for the first 3 years they are at Wellington, all students receive discrete happiness lessons. The aim of our course is to put students in touch with the wealth of research that has gone into what causes human flourishing and to give them the opportunity to put the fruits of this research to the test in their own lives. Our happiness lessons focus on what it means to be a human being, what our students can do to make the best of their human resources and most importantly what it might mean to lead a flourishing life. In this way, alongside the provision of a well-delivered formal curriculum, a varied program of extra-curricular activities, the pastoral care provided by a boarding environment, and a clear ethos supporting the holding of values, happiness lessons join up *education as happiness* with *educating for happiness*.

Sometimes education of this sort (traditionally called something like "Personal Social and Health Education" in the UK) descends either into lessons in prohibition where adults tell children what harmful things not to do; or they begin with a fabulous list of concepts, but with none of the conceptual underpinning or practical application that would enable students to do something with them, leaving students with a cozy chat about feelings which doesn't effect change in behavior. For us, the lessons firstly had to be aspirational: consideration of how life ought to be lived and secondly, practical, providing real guidance on how to flourish based on reliable research, rather than bad science. Clearly, there is a need to signpost students to particular dangerous activities such as substance abuse and unsafe sex, and commentators such as Ehrenreich (2009) have lambasted those who advocate positivity at all costs and ignore obvious dangers citing this as a cause of amongst other things, the economic downturn caused by the collapse of the subprime property market. This is an important critique, but in developing a pedagogy of happiness, educators should be mindful of the work of researchers such as Magruder-Watkins and Mohr (2001) who caution against excessive focus on the negative in trying to effect change and Seligman (2003) who talks about flourishing not as a removal of ills but as a promotion of goods.

## The Methodology

Each 1-hour lesson follows a similar structure. A typical lesson begins with "awareness," something to bring the lesson topic to life for the students; this could be anything from a short video clip to a game or even just a question or a picture; something to capture the interest of the students and that will provoke discussion and the sharing of ideas and the asking of questions. Once the students are on board with the topic, the awareness continues by enhancing their understanding of a particular aspect of being human. This may involve looking at (or perhaps rehearsing) a psychological experiment that reveals aspects of human nature or looking at somebody else's experiences and comparing them with our own. One of our students' favorite lessons involves re-enacting Walter Mischel's famous delayed gratification experiment where they have to employ strategies to resist jelly babies for the lesson.

We then move into the "intervention" part of the lesson, where the students learn a specific skill that might help them to maximize their happiness: for example, in the lessons on physical health (described in the following section), students learn techniques to help them sleep, advice on how to maximize learning, or ways of managing stress. It is important that students have the opportunity to try the interventions out together and learn through experience. It is all too easy to just tell students "if you want to achieve X, then do Y" but unless students have an opportunity to try these ideas out with guidance when needed, the interventions simply won't get used by them.

The third section of the lesson, "evaluation," is where we encourage the students to evaluate the intervention they have just learned and they do this in between the lessons. All students are provided with a happiness journal where they write down their reflections on the usefulness of the interventions we teach, or keep notes on how what they are learning in the lessons is impacting upon their subjective well-being. This element of the methodology is vital, because it offers the students the opportunity to provide reasons why they accept or *reject* what they have learned. Happiness is ultimately subjective and the activities that we choose to engage in to promote our own happiness have to have subjective value based on individual reasoning. The more prescriptive and dictatorial we become about happiness the more we undermine the validity of what we are doing.

## Course Content: The Six Strands

Our course is divided up into six strands which we believe cover the range of knowledge of the causes of human flourishing, deriving from disciplines such as the human sciences, psychology, philosophy, and theology. The strands are as follows:

1. Physical health.
2. Positive relationships.
3. Perspective: building psychological capital.
4. Character strengths.
5. The world: learning to live sustainably in a consumer culture.
6. Meaning and purpose.

There is insufficient room to go into comprehensive detail for each strand, but what follows will give a sense of what is taught and the justifications for teaching it.[6]

The course is delivered by a hand-picked team of teachers over the course of 3 years in the 1 hour per fortnight lesson allocated by the curriculum. It begins with "Physical health" and an examination of the physical factors that can help to promote flourishing. Lessons in this strand look at basic care of the physical self through sensible diet, sleep, and exercise and build on common knowledge in these areas by introducing the students to research that they may not be familiar with by people such as Gesch, Hammond, Hampson, Eves, and Crowder (2002), who have studied the effect of nutrition on young offenders[7] and by Ratey (2008) who has written extensively on the benefits of exercise for combating low mood and improving learning and creativity in his books *Spark* and *A User's Guide to the Brain*. This strand also devotes time to exploring exactly what happens in the brain when we learn (and contains a lovely lesson where students make neuronal connections with modeling clay) and how to resist temptation. The lesson on learning aims to emphasize the idea of neuroplasticity to the students as well as giving them practical advice on how to maximize their chances of learning. Many young people fall into the trap of thinking that learning ability is fixed by genetics and it is important to show them just how powerful the effect of behaviors such as exercise, diet, and sleep is on learning. The lesson on resisting temptation fits in with recent

---

[6] For a more detailed explanation not only of the theory underpinning the new discipline of happiness and well-being lessons, but also ideas on how to teach it, see further *Learning to Ride Elephants: Teaching Happiness and Well-Being in Schools*, by Ian Morris (2009).

[7] See further *They Are What You Feed Them*, by Alex Richardson (2006).

work on delayed gratification and executive function and gives students advice on how to use incentives and distractions to try to resist unhelpful temptations.

The second strand, "Positive relationships," looks at techniques for the better management of relationships, with a focus on experiential learning. For example, trust is explored using games from drama; altruism and gratitude are explored by practicing random acts of kindness and keeping a gratitude journal; attentiveness is explored by trying out Active Constructive Responding,[8] and long term relationships are considered using a charity called *Explore*, who bring married couples into schools to talk about their experiences of being in a long-term relationship[9]. This strand also pays attention to emotional recognition and management.

The third strand, "Perspective," provides students with strategies to help them successfully adapt and function in the face of challenge or trauma: in short, building resilience and grit, or what Daniel Gilbert (2007) has called the *"psychological immune system."* So many of us are hampered by our thinking patterns and this unit owes its existence to the brilliant insights of people such as Aaron Beck, Martin Seligman, and Carol Dweck, who not only describe how our thoughts and misperceptions can limit us but also offer us practical strategies for overcoming those limitations. Perspective lessons cover techniques such as getting an accurate perspective on events and challenging unhelpful patterns of thinking, challenging the "fixed mindset" view that ability and talent is the result of genetics by emphasizing neuroplasticity, the role of effort in achievement, and self-efficacy beliefs. We bring these cognitive ideas to life with stories such as Aesop's fable of the hare and the tortoise, Roald Dahl's story of Fantastic Mr Fox, exploding super-hero myths surrounding the athlete Usain Bolt, or looking at how climber Joe Simpson overcame enormous adversity to survive a horrendous climbing accident. Lessons in perspective are complemented by the teaching of philosophy, which similarly attempts to develop an accurate perspective on the world.

The fourth strand, "Strengths," really goes to the heart of the purpose of education, which is to discover and draw out our best selves. In this unit, students explore how to discover and nurture character strengths and abilities using the VIA Signature Strengths Inventory,[10] and also look at the research of Mihaly Csikszentmihalyi into flow (2002). Again, in these lessons the emphasis is upon the experiential and the reflective: one of the most powerful strengths lessons is where students talk to each other about times when they have used their character strengths, in other words where they get to talk about being at their best, which sadly is often a rarity in schools as our target setting and exam result culture often has them skip over achievement to focus on areas of weakness, which are given undue weight.

The fifth strand, "The World," looks at how to survive in a culture which tends to advocate conspicuous consumerism at the expense of more sustainable forms of living. Here we rely on suggestions made by Schwartz (2004) and James (2007) on how to resist the consumer culture and by an organization called *Adbusters* on how to be more media critical. This strand also explores how the beauty of the natural and man-made world can be used to elevate us.

---

[8] Based on the work of Shelly Gable at the University of California, who using research to show that those who are better connected to others are healthier and happier, has developed the technique of "Active Constructive Responding" which focuses on building meaningful responses to others when they communicate with us.

[9] More information can be found at http://www.theexploreexperience.co.uk

[10] Available to take for free at http://www.authentichappiness.org.

The course finishes by spending time reflecting on meaning and purpose and this moment comes just before the students are due to sit their first series of major public examinations and start to make decisions about directions in life. This unit takes its inspiration from Viktor Frankl, who in *Man's Search for Meaning* suggests that there is no one meaning of life, but that it is down to the individual to find and express their own meaning and purpose. We spend time looking at what life might hold for the students (using the Eriksonian structure found in George Vaillant's work (2003)), what skills they will need to bring about their own flourishing and how what they know of themselves so far can help to carry them there.

This is, as mentioned, only a snapshot of what we teach as part of *educating for happiness* and much of what we are doing is echoed in work done in other schools. What we believe is unique, however, is the breadth of approach that we take towards teaching happiness: rather than homing in on one area such as resilience or social and emotional intelligence, we cover numerous factors leading to human flourishing. It has also been important to couch our work in research that can be relied upon and to provide students with real, practical skills that they can use: the challenge of this kind of education is to go beyond a superficial discussion of concepts to the acquisition of skills that can bring about change.

## Happiness Education as an Entitlement

Earlier, we noted that one of the objections to happiness education is that it can become simplistic, dictatorial, and prescriptive. It may well be the case that some forms of happiness education involve deliberate attempts to engineer very specific behavioral outcomes in those who participate, perhaps motivated by an extreme religious, social or political agenda. It should be clear that the philosophy of happiness education advocated here strongly opposes any approach which attempts to impose contentious or debatable norms of behavior on others, especially the young, or which entreats them to uncritically accept pre-packaged advice on the happy life.

The alternative to the dictatorial objection is a liberal laissez-faire approach which in the interests of protecting the complexity of the human experience forbids us from legislating for happiness. But this just won't do as the logical extension of this view is that happiness is somehow intuitively discovered. You only have to look around you to see that's not true. There is a middle ground in happiness education which preserves complexity and also equips young people with the building blocks to begin developing their own approaches to finding happiness and making meaning.

As a human community, we *know* that certain freely chosen activities or habits of mind will greatly increase one's chances of experiencing what can be described as happiness or flourishing in life. There exists a wealth of empirical studies to show what those things are and many of them are discussed elsewhere in this volume. Children are *entitled* to know what they can freely choose to do in their lives that will increase their chances of happiness; they are entitled to know about the benefits of exercise, about how to build trusting relationships, about how to develop the cognitive skills of resilience, about how to discover and employ their strengths, and so on, just as they are entitled to be told that smoking tobacco will do them harm and just as they are entitled to find out about photosynthesis and sonnets. Happiness, at least on the activity conception of it, results from freely chosen activities and if children don't know what to freely choose, how can they choose to be happier? Alongside this lies the debate about the nature of happiness which stretches back through the course of human history. Just as young people are entitled to find out what might make them happy, they are entitled to find out what that happiness might be.

It is important that education starts to shore up the view that happiness arises from living skillfully, from making informed choices based on the fruits of well-conducted research, or from the collective store of anecdotes about how to live well. As educators, living for happiness should feature most prominently in the list of skills we want to equip our young people with, alongside speaking foreign languages, solving logical problems, and understanding the world through science. This is not interference, oppression or over simplification of the human experience, it is a duty of education that has been lost amidst focus on measurable performance and accountability and it is an entitlement of the young people who progress through our education system.

## The teacher of happiness

If we accept the dual responsibility of the education system to provide *education as happiness* and to *educate for happiness*, there are significant implications for teachers. Primarily, restoring happiness in education should serve to refocus us on why we enter the classroom in the first place: is it to earn a living, is it to inspire a love of our subject, is it to equip children with qualifications, or is it something that transcends these motivations and in turn which ties them together? To re-state Noddings (2003, p. 23) definition of education, it ". . . by its very nature should help people to develop their best selves": we must therefore accept that every teacher is not just a teacher of math, English, or chemistry, but a teacher of happiness and flourishing. We must also remember that children look to us as teachers for more than just how to solve quadratic equations or decline verbs. Children adopt teachers as role models without first asking permission and the way that we conduct our relationships with those that we teach is being closely studied whether we like it or not. This assertion is not new and as mentioned above, we all remember our greatest teachers because they gave us clues about how life ought to be lived that went beyond the teaching of their subject, just as we remember those awful teachers, like Thomas Gradgrind, who managed to use education as an instrument of torture.

Above all, if we adopt happiness, well-being, flourishing, call it what you will, as a central aim of education and use that aim to inform everything that takes place in a school community from the way that lessons are taught to how we deal with undesirable behavior, we are all of a sudden, amidst our modern culture of endless educational initiatives and using schools to provide band-aid solutions to social ills, returned to what draws idealistic young graduates to work in education rather than a career in banking: to help people to develop their best selves.

### REFERENCES

Aristotle. (2004). *The Nicomachean ethics*. (J. A. K. Thompson, Trans.). London, UK: Penguin. (Original work published fourth century BCE).

Brighouse, H. (2008). Education for a flourishing life. In J. R. Wiens & D. L. Coulter (Eds.), *Why do we educate? 2008 NSSE Yearbook—Volume Two* (pp. 58–71). Chichester, UK: Blackwell-Wiley.

Claxton, G. (2008). *What's the point of school? Rediscovering the heart of education*. Oxford, UK: OneWorld.

Csikszentmihalyi, M. (2002). *Flow*. London, UK: Random House.

Dickens, C. (1994). *Hard times*. London, UK: Penguin. (Original work published 1854).

Diener, E. (2009). *The science of well-being: The collected works of Ed Diener*. New York, NY: Springer.

Dweck, C. S. (2000). *Self-theories*. Philadelphia, PA: Taylor & Francis.

Dweck, C. S. (2008). *Mindset*. New York, NY: Ballantine.

Gilbert, D. (2007). *Stumbling on happiness*. London, UK: Harper Perennial.

Ehrenreich, B. (2009). *Bright-sided*. New York, NY: Henry Holt and Company.

Frankl, V. (2004). *Man's search for meaning*. London, UK: Rider.

Gesch, C. B., Hammond, S. M., Hampson, S. E., Eves, A., & Crowder, M. J. (2002). Influence of supplementary vitamins, minerals and essential fatty acids on the antisocial behaviour of young adult prisoners. Randomised, placebo-controlled trial. *British Journal of Psychiatry*, *181*, 22–28.

James, O. (2007). *Affluenza*. London, UK: Random House.

Magruder-Watkins, J., & Mohr, B. (2001). *Appreciative inquiry: Change at the speed of imagination*. San Francisco, CA: John Wiley and Sons.

Morris, I. (2009). *Learning to ride elephants: Teaching happiness and well-being in schools*. London, UK: Continuum.

Noddings, N. (2003). *Happiness and education*. New York, NY: Cambridge University Press.

Ratey, J. (2001). *A user's guide to the brain*. New York, NY: Random House.

Ratey, J. (2008). *Spark*. New York, NY: Little, Brown and Company.

Richardson, A. (2006). *They are what you feed them*. London, UK: HarperCollins.

Roberts, Y. (2009). *Grit: The skills for success and how they are grown*. London, UK: The Young Foundation.

Schoch, R. (2006). *The secrets of happiness*. London, UK: Profile.

Schwartz, B. (2004). *The paradox of choice*. New York, NY: HarperCollins.

Seligman, M. E. P., Reivich, K., Jaycox, L., & Gillham, J. (1995). *The optimistic child*. New York, NY: HarperCollins.

Seligman, M. E. P. (2003). *Authentic happiness*. London, UK: Nicholas Brealey.

Suissa, J. (2009). Lessons from a new science? On teaching happiness in schools. In R. Cigman & A. Davies (Eds.) *New philosophies of learning* (pp. 205–220). Chichester, UK: John Wiley & Sons.

Vaillant, G. E. (2003). *Aging well*. New York, NY: Little, Brown and Company.

Willoughby, G., & Samuels, N. (2009). *Brilliant: The Heathside story*. Chichester, UK: Kingsham Press.

CHAPTER 49

# POSITIVE EDUCATION AT GEELONG GRAMMAR SCHOOL

MATHEW A. WHITE

The University of Melbourne, Australia

This chapter summarizes the introduction of positive education at Geelong Grammar School, Australia's leading coeducational boarding and day school, and its collaboration with Martin Seligman. The chapter outlines the landscape for adolescent mental health in Australia, a brief history of Geelong Grammar School, its structure, a summary of the positive education program and its approach, the seven pillars of the positive education approach at the school, and the development of its scope and sequence, and a summary of possible future directions in research and practice.

## Introduction

Over the past 10 years there has been an increase in development of proactive approaches to adolescent well-being in Australia. The paradox between increasing levels of depression and anxiety in Australian youth and increased levels of economic stability (despite the recent global financial crisis) has been recorded as a significant issue challenging school communities from a diversity of socioeconomic backgrounds (Beyond Blue, 2009; Black Dog Institute, 2009).

One in five Australians experiences a mental illness within a 12-month period. In 2007, almost half (45%) of all Australians had experienced a mental disorder at some point in their lifetime. It has been noted that mental health problems affect 14% of children and adolescents in Australia (Beyond Blue, 2009). As the Australian national depression initiative Beyond Blue notes:

> Depression and anxiety are the most common mental health problems in young people. At any point in time, up to five percent of adolescents experience depression that is severe enough to warrant treatment, and around 20% of young people will have experienced

significant depressive symptoms by the time they reach adulthood (Beyond Blue, 2009; National Health and Medical Research Council, 1997).

Norrish and Vella-Brodrick (2009) provided an excellent summary of significant initiatives based in the areas of positive psychology and well-being in Australia and highlight that despite being in its early days there is a growing body of evidence for further support for the development of positive psychology-based educational programs.

## Defining positive education

Positive education is defined by Seligman, Ernst, Gillham, Reivich, & Linkins (2009) as an approach to education for both traditional skills and for happiness (Norrish & Vella-Brodrick, 2009). Emerging 9 years after the umbrella term of positive psychology or the scientific study of subjective well-being was defined, positive education has sparked international interest as evidenced at the First World Congress on Positive Psychology in Philadelphia (Seligman et al., 2009). At policy level, adolescent well-being is understood to play a pivotal part in student engagement and connectedness with school (Department of Education, 2008). Nevertheless, in Australia as numeracy and literacy emerge as central pillars to an Australian National Curriculum agenda, well-being remains an overlooked area in its own right. The paradox is that schools are increasingly being asked to take on more responsibility for many issues of adolescent well-being that were traditionally the purview of the family.

This societal shift in the role of the school places substantial ethical obligations on our institutions. It is no longer satisfactory that schools prepare students to read and write. Schools have the potential to act as places that prepare students in a proactive way to be able to engage with issues of mental health to equip them with the best possible life choices into the future.

Debate about positive education and its merits evokes a diversity of reactions from principals and teachers, parents and students, academics and policy-makers with divergent educational agendas. The American educationalist Noddings (2003, pp. 1–5) comments on the paradox of learning arguing that: "[. . .] happiness and education don't go together! [. . .] but children learn best when they are happy." Critics question the scientific basis of positive psychology, asserting that it makes too many claims based on small samples sizes, that it is an American import (Lazarus, 2003; Boniwell, 2006). However, there are an increasing number of educationalists who are articulating that this could be an important step towards in helping young people lead a more engaged life and real life benefits (DEEWR, 2008).

## Positive education at Geelong Grammar School

In 2005 Geelong Grammar School commenced the first steps towards a significant development in its educational history. A pioneer in educational innovation since its foundation in 1855, Geelong Grammar School is Australia's largest coeducational boarding and day school. Geelong Grammar School today has around 1200 students across five campuses.

Given its heritage, it is easy to assume that Geelong Grammar School is only associated with results, high-stakes competition, league tables, and sporting events. However, the Geelong Grammar School community recognized there was more to character education and positive youth development than traditional learning. Education in its broadest sense encompassed the development of character, service, and deep engagement in society's issues and the resilience and self-efficacy to make a difference. In 2007, spearheaded by Geelong Grammar School's Principal Stephen Meek, Vice-Principal and Head of Corio Charles Scudamore, Director of Learning Debbie Clingeleffer-Woodforde, and Director of Student Welfare John Hendry, Australia's largest coeducational boarding school started to incorporate positive psychology principles and practices across all aspect of the school life.

This lighthouse program has attracted much attention throughout the world. In 2008 over 15 MAPP graduates and scholars associated with the Positive Psychology Center converged on Geelong Grammar School to teach the skills of positive psychology to over 100 faculty members over a 9-day course. Following this program led by the father of positive psychology, Martin Seligman, Seligman lived in residence at the school with his family for 6 months to help establish the first phase of the program and the school launched the evolution of an approach known as positive education (Seligman et al., 2009).

During 2008 many of the world's leading thinkers in positive psychology completed residencies at Geelong Grammar School including: self-control experts Roy Baumeister and Dianne Tice; former distinguished Chief Executive of the American Psychological Association Raymond Fowler; public intellectual and expert in medical ethics Stephen G. Post; Frank Mosca; Director of The Well-being Institute at the University of Cambridge, UK; Felicia Huppert, leading research on positive emotions; Barbara Fredrickson; co-authors of *Character Strengths and Virtues* Christopher Peterson and Nansook Park; and psychiatrist and Harvard professor George Vaillant.

Each scholar visited classrooms, met with the school's faculty, collaborated with teachers on ideas and approaches, and shared their expertise to help develop a positive education approach at Geelong Grammar School. Throughout the year 2 curriculum experts, Randy Ernst and Mark Linkins, were in residence to help guide the early stages of the development of positive education.

## A positive education approach

Geelong Grammar School's positive education approach combines the explicit teaching of positive psychology programs written by evidence-based researchers and teachers for the Positive Psychology Center at the University of Pennsylvania, USA, and an implicit approach to principles and practices applied across all aspects of school life: academic subjects, pastoral life, and the co-curriculum program as developed by Geelong Grammar School staff (Seligman et al., 2009; White, 2009). It is a strengths-based approach to the practice of teaching based on the work of Seligman, Fredrickson, and others and combines this with specific pedagogical actions that aim to: increase the experience of positive emotions in staff and students; encourage staff and students to engage their signature strengths for personal and community goals; seek staff and students to lead meaningful lives to find purpose and make a difference to our communities at large; encourage staff and students to strive towards positive accomplishment.

Geelong Grammar School's positive education approach is not happyology. It is not about simplifying academic content in classes. Positive education seeks to engage students to engage with the full kaleidoscope of positive and negative emotion in their studies, co-curriculum, and pastoral life. Positive education does not downplay competition and achievement; instead it aims to broaden and build the school's understanding of what it labeled as success.

Positive education celebrates positive accomplishment and encourages students to seek engagement in their academic work. Many parents and teachers share similar ambitions for the children in their care. Parents hope that their children will be happy and lead engaged and fulfilled lives. Similarly, teachers also want their students to be engaged in the subjects that they teacher, the sport that they play, and the relationships they develop with friends at school.

## Six pillars for a positive education approach

Geelong Grammar School's positive education approach encourages students to explore and actively develop:

- Their aspirations for the future (Lyubomirsky, 2009)
- Articulate and explore gratitude (Park & Peterson, 2009)
- Hope based on goal setting (Lopez, Rose, Robinsons, Marquez, & Pais-Ribeiro, 2009)
- Experience and engender positive emotion (Fredrickson, 2009)
- Highlight and develop resilience in themselves and each other (Reivich and Shatté, 2002)
- Embrace a strength base to living in a community (Peterson & Seligman, 2004).

Geelong Grammar School chose two pathways to develop the staff's teaching methodology to achieve positive education at the school: an explicit program of lessons taught to students based on the work of Seligman et al. (2009) and an implicit approach to teaching and learning drawn into all aspects of school life. The explicit teaching of positive education classes for 12–13-year-olds and 15–16-year-olds was embedded into the school's daily timetable in the same way that English, mathematics, science, or history is taught.

Based on these theoretical foundations the staff at Geelong Grammar School identified six pillars central to the development of a positive education approach. These pillars include: strengths, emotion, creativity, self-efficacy, mindfulness, and gratitude (Fig. 49.1). The objective for the identification of these pillars was to enable a conceptual model for faculty to begin to align existing curriculum documentation with a positive education approach. The objective of this structure was to guide faculty discussion across a diversity of theoretical pillars at age-appropriate levels that encouraged faculty to focus on the clinical practice linked with the theories identified.

To enable this structure to flourish, Geelong Grammar School established a Positive Education Department. The rationale for this structure was to mirror the way we engage with well-being rather than compartmentalize well-being into a particular subject discipline. The foundation Positive Education Department was created with teachers drawn from six departments including Literature, Languages other than English, History, Geography, Experimental Sciences, and Mathematics. Within the department there are members of the school's senior management: the Director of Learning, Director of Student Welfare, Senior Chaplain, International Baccalaureate, and VCE Coordinators.

Since 2009, Geelong Grammar School students have completed positive education classes in year 10 studying the Strath Haven Positive Psychology Curriculum and in Year 7 the Penn Resiliency Program. The efficacy of the Strath Haven Positive Psychology Course is still under review and details are available at http://www.positivepsych.org/; however, the Penn

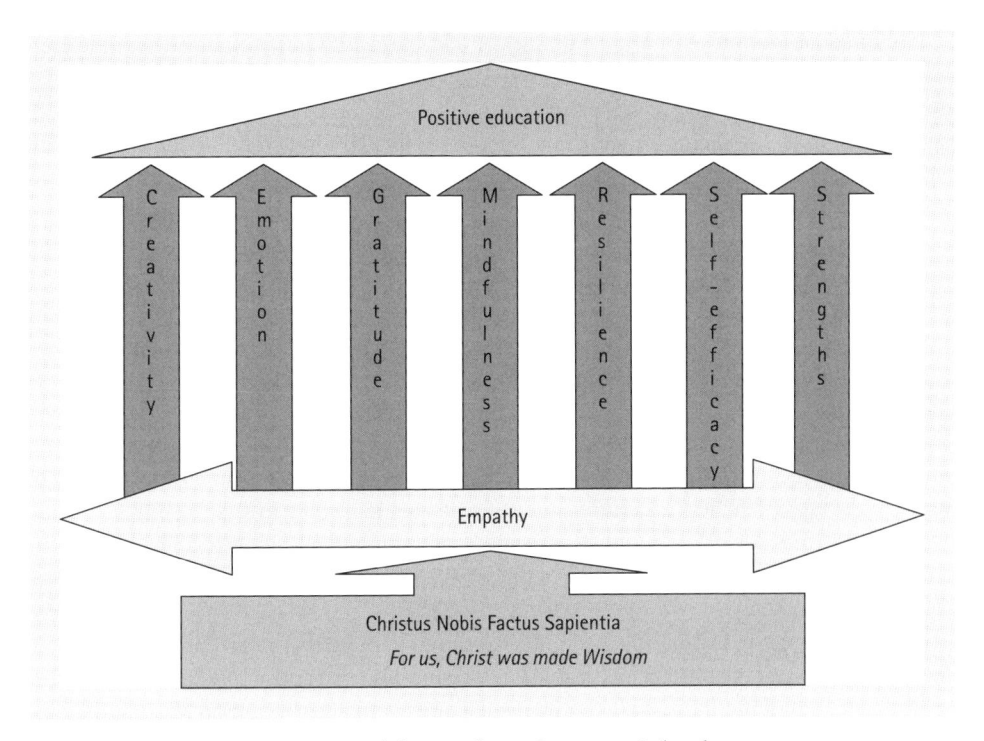

FIG. 49.1 Positive education model at Geelong Grammar School 2009.

Resiliency Program has been discussed by Brunwasser, Gillham, and Kim (2009) in the USA and in the UK by Challen, Noden, and West (2009).

## A scope and sequence for positive education

After a 12-month consultation period with Geelong Grammar School staff led in 2008 by master-teachers Randal Ernst and Mark Linkins from the USA, Mathew White identified six pillars drawn from the literature on positive psychology that provided the conceptual framework for discussion about positive education (outlined in Fig. 49.1).

In order to create a whole-school approach, the rationale for the choice of these pillars grew from discussion held over two whole school curriculum summits that included staff from each Geelong Grammar School campus and were held at the school to explore methods to incorporate positive psychology practices as a whole-school approach. All members of the school community were invited to these summits to participate to help develop the framework for discussion. The aim was to link the theory of positive psychology principles and practices into teaching action in the pre-existing curriculum.

Using Kotter's (1996) change model the positive education scope and sequence was based on the school's core value of empathy captured in the school's motto Christus Nobis Factus Sapientia (For us, Christ was made wisdom) a foundation of empathy underscored the pillars that helped to support the creation of a whole-school approach from the early years of schooling (aged 4) to year 12 (18 years). A program based on a series of "booster" programs developed by Reivich et al. (2007) was to be included for the senior years. Geelong Grammar

School in collaboration with Mark Linkins also developed an individualized set of leadership modules based on a strengths-based approach to leadership that encouraged all students to engage with and develop their strengths.

An audit of all well-being programs at the school was conducted following three teaching team summits held in July 2008 and twice in 2009, the pillars identified by the Geelong Grammar School positive education team provided the framework for an audit of positive psychology literature. From a survey of recent publications from positive psychology, a scope and sequence document was created with teachers from the youngest years of schooling to year 10 that incorporated documentation of existing practice across the school.

The use of the VIA Character Strengths has been a powerful method used by teachers to engage students from a diversity of cultural backgrounds and has been particularly helpful in engaging students in discussion about their own strengths, the strengths of their peers, and the dynamics that they bring with the experience with their peer groups. The VIA Strength data gave teachers and tutors quantifiable data to be able to analyze, interpret, and develop strategies for growth and development of student well-being in their care in the same way a teacher might develop individualized approaches to teaching and learning for literacy and numeracy.

Geelong Grammar School has been able to develop strengths-based information about each day and boarding house. It has enabled discussion amongst and across year levels. Before the introduction of the VIA Character Strengths questionnaire, discussion about individual students, or the strengths of student groups was based on the knowledge of experienced teachers. The advantage of this approach is that it has provided the pastoral care team with a unified language and approach that is based on students' strengths. Students have also been able to take part in this discussion because they also have access to this language.

For example, following students completing the VIA Character Strengths Questionnaire in 2008 and 2009, the school discovered that year 12 students' top signature strengths include gratitude, curiosity, and playfulness, appreciation of beauty, and excellence and creativity. A similar program was undertaken in the Middle School and the school found that gratitude, humour/playfulness, zest, citizenship/teamwork, honesty, curiosity, and appreciation of beauty were their strengths. In the Early Learning Centre (ELC), year 2 class teachers have encouraged students and teachers to identify personal strengths and passions, focusing on learning styles in years 3 and 4 and signature strengths in years 5 and 6.

Given that schools can act as crucibles that have the capacity to forge the strengths of our students and teachers for future challenges, the identification of each year levels of character strengths has been a significant method to engage all students in a discussion based on positive emotion and strengths. In the classroom, on the sports field, and in the orchestra, life strengths and their science can buttress the science of good teaching and building self-efficacy in our students. There is much to be gained for searching for the blaze of light in every word in the darkest text of Shakespeare to the brilliance of the music of Brahms, the poetry of Keats, and the beauty in motion of Cathy Freeman and these discussions have become central in many classes in English, history, and studies in religion.

For example, the English Department and the Religious Education Department used the language of the VIA Character Strengths classification to discuss the strengths of individual characters and their relationships in texts. For instance, in the teaching of *King Lear,* students and teachers explored Lear's lack of self-regulation and his capacity to love and be loved as the character faced his adversities. This was compared and contrasted with students' individual character strengths profiles to encourage them to engage more deeply with character strengths.

Peterson and Seligman (2004) claim that understanding one's strengths and an awareness of these qualities stimulates greater awareness of our place in the world, greater levels of creativity, and increased levels of meaningful engagement.

A positive education approach could help students and teachers navigate their roles and encourage them to take the road less travelled, to develop the resources and self-efficacy when they are called to the most significant of tests. As a teaching approach in the classroom, a strengths-based approach to teaching and building communities means that students and teachers, teachers and parents understand the significance of strategies to counter the role negativity bias plays in the character development of Geelong Grammar School students and teachers. Geelong Grammar School has found the science of positive psychology provides a common language and the tools to be able to help their students and teachers' understand this to a greater degree in their own lives and builds on the tradition of pastoral care at the school.

Critics such as Wilson (2008) have suggested that an unbalanced approach to positive psychology has the potential to be shallow and overlook the role that melancholy has played in the development of Western literature. However, a balanced positive education approach is not an attempt to eradicate sadness. It does not mean that we overlook the work of Beethoven, Wordsworth, Blake, Keats, and Rothko because they do not fit into a "happiness" equation. It is a method designed to provide students and teachers with skills crafted into specific lessons captured in the year 7 Penn Resiliency Programe (Gillham et al., 2006) and the year 10 Strath Haven Positive Psychology Curriculum that we have commenced teaching at Geelong Grammar School.

Some of the Penn Resiliency Program skills encouraged upon completing the program are the ability to understand and act on:

- The link between thoughts and feelings
- Thinking styles
- Challenging belief, generating alternatives and evidence
- Evaluating thoughts and putting them into perspective
- Assertiveness and negotiation
- Coping strategies
- Decision-making and social problem-solving.

Positive education could allow students to be able to heighten their awareness of their emotional thermostat, giving them skills to be able to regulate their internal locus of control, providing a greater range of vocabulary to engage with, explore, consider, and reflect on emotional experience. Another achievement is that it provides students and teachers with a framework of skills and exercises through a scientifically validated tool allowing them to navigate the map of their emotional responses.

## Resilience through creativity

Examples from the curriculum units on resilience in art, music, and literature is central to the study of what it means to be human and something that needs to be implicitly and explicitly taught. Resilience is not about being tough. It is not about being strong. It is about rebuilding, creating opportunities to muddle through, to move forward and through this to the reward of the future. The topic of resilience in art, music, and literature is central to the story of what it means to be human—and service to others (Reivich & Shatté, 2002). The Geelong Grammar School year 7 and year 10 curriculums are designed to engage students and teachers in developing skills of resiliency including: better proficiency in problem solving; more moderate temperament; adaptability; self-efficacy; and a positive outlook.

As resilience is characterized by positive adaption in adversity there were several practical applications that Geelong Grammar School needed to strengthen to build resilience: a focus on developing students' self-efficacy in teaching and learning; teaching coping strategies to students; nurturing positive relations across all aspects of school life, in the boarding house, on the sports field, in an art class, or orchestra.

The power to create can transform lives long after an emotional event has taken place. It is the cusp of an opportunity to act as the catalyst for change. Aristotle, Descartes, Shakespeare, Beethoven were all concerned with the positive in the creation, imagination, and creativity. The Greeks pursued creativity in all areas of poetry—sacred and profane.

Spearheaded by the Head of the Visual Arts Department (Margot Anwar) and her colleagues, students and teachers from ELC—year 12 were led on the development of an embedded unit on the emotion of optimism that explored a range of responses to optimism directly engaging with the science of positive psychology. The culmination was an exhibition titled "Cusp" that explored the emotion of optimism. Students from the ELC to year 6 have been integrating strengths and optimism in creative and performing arts subjects with their classroom curriculum, focusing on the development of critical and creative thinking skills, and Geelong Grammar School teachers have been shaping learning assessment tasks to harness creative talents and abilities.

Transformative approaches to creativity are at the core of everything. They are essential for interaction between mind, body, and soul and critical on the thermostat of well-being. It is one thing to walk to the well-being centre, it is another thing to admire the creativity of Geelong Grammar School senior schools and their art that links between mind, body, and spirit which have been curated to capture the spirit of Geelong Grammar School enterprise. The transformative power of the artists highlights awareness of emotion, order, chaos, and beauty, finding the link with these is the role of the arts and the power of the opportunity to creation of a positive education. Creativity must be at the centre of everything, for to create is to be alive.

## What is the role of self-efficacy?

Dweck (2006) suggests that the skills that enable confidence, effort, and persistence are significant and should be taught. Some powerful truths in teaching and learning are connected with the simplest truths. Self-efficacy (not self-esteem) is one example. Geelong Grammar School's ELC—year 6 teachers are moving away from self-esteem-based education and are starting to introduce the concept of "who I am and what skills I have" in their interaction with our students and teachers. This shift in their approach was based on research that identified in the Australian Federal Government's Department of Education, Employment and Workplace Relations (2008) scoping study into approaches to student well-being, that self-esteem no longer has the impact it had in schools. Seligman et al. (1995) highlighted the limitations of the self-esteem construct:

> [. . .] teachers, along with . . . parents, are straining to bolster children's self-esteem. That sounds innocuous enough, but the way they do it often erodes children's sense of worth. By emphasizing how a child feels, at the expense of what the child does – mastery, persistence, overcoming frustration and boredom and meeting a challenge – parents and teachers are making this generation of children more vulnerable to depression (Seligman et al., 1995, p. 27).

In Geelong Grammar School's year 7 and 10 curriculums the topic of self-efficacy in the context of our students' lives is explained as the belief that people through their own efforts will bring about change. In Geelong Grammar School's pastoral care systems in boarding and day boarding houses, the relationship between Head of House, tutor, and student are important factors impacting self-efficacy. We have seen this start to emerge more systematically in Geelong Grammar School's sports coaching. In particular, a strengths and self-efficacy-based approach has been adopted in the coaching of Geelong Grammar School's football and rowing teams environments that are responsive to the child's actions are important. It impacts their sense of personal agency.

## Gratitude

Peterson (2004) highlights the importance gratitude plays in overall levels of well-being. Year 10 students have recently completed lessons in gratitude as part of the positive psychology course. Geelong Grammar School's teachers guided students through a series of exercises including writing gratitude letters after scaffolded lessons created by the Penn team. A world without gratitude would be unbearable (Schwarz, 1971, p. 168). Emmons and Shelton (2002) note that gratitude has attracted significant interest in popular culture. Look on the shelves of a bookstore and you will discover in the self-help section books specifically discussing gratitude usually marketed to particular groups. Reflections, journals—they are often argued to be the cure for all ills.

However, should we teach children to be more grateful in schools—does this fit with the core concerns of schools? Gratitude is a topic that has fascinated writers across all cultures— it is central to Christian, Islamic, Buddhist, Hindu, and Jewish thought; it is captured by the simple words "thank you"—but these are words that do not always come very easily for many people when they should appear to be second nature. Why is it that we often do not find it so straightforward to express gratitude?

Given the universal agreement that gratitude is an important emotion, it often remains left out of the lexicon of psychologists. This is because there is widespread ambiguity and uncertainty about it. Is it possible to develop a culture of gratitude and is this desirable? This is a question for the interior world or the world of reflection. Can gratitude be helpful?

Geelong Grammar School's aims of this method are to increase the experience of positive emotions in our students and teachers; encourage students and teachers to engage their signature strength for personal and community goals; live meaningful lives to find a purpose; and make a difference to our communities at large.

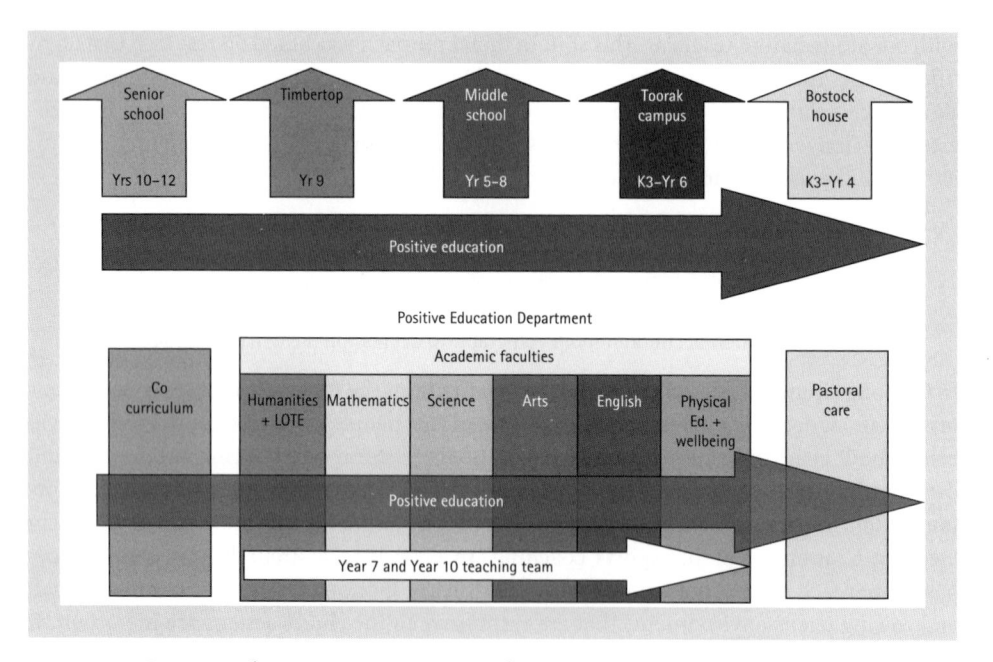

FIG. 49.2 Positive education structure at Geelong Grammar School 2009.

## Future directions

The development of effective measurement of positive education will be critical for the progress of this younger sibling of the positive psychology movement, coupled with further development in the area of clinical practice. Positive psychology mirrors the goals of teachers (Fineburg, 2004). Speak to teachers and they will outline that they went into teaching to make a difference, to have an effect. Seligman and Csikszentmihalyi (2000, p. 6) note that positive psychology embraced:

> Positive individual traits: the capacity for love and vocation, courage, interpersonal skills, perseverance, forgiveness, originality, future mindedness, spirituality, high talent, wisdom. At the group level, it is about civic virtues and the institutions that move individuals towards better citizenship: responsibility, [. . .], altruism, tolerance and work ethic.

What teacher has not wanted the best for her students? The developments of method are central to this. Socrates, one of the West's great teachers, asserted that the examined life is not worth living. The potential for our teachers emerging from pre-service teacher training in the future, skilled in a positive education strength-based approach founded in the science of positive psychology, is an opportunity gap that is waiting to be filled. The next step is to formalize this approach, not as an elective subject as part of a well-being course, but as an interdisciplinary approach.

We must not underestimate the power of the pursuit of happiness and the significance of genuine empathy for others—it is the pursuit and its journey that creates, broadens, builds, and transforms schools from being schools into enabling institutions that encourage their students to understand the theory of well-being in the same way they understand literacy and numeracy.

Positive education has the potential to buttress Geelong Grammar School and a generation of students who will be playing their part in a world where the odds are stacked against them. In a speech delivered at the school, Seligman (2006) asserted that

> Geelong Grammar School is the pioneer in the world in taking steps to introduce this type of learning through all aspects of an educational curriculum. In doing so, I believe that Geelong Grammar students who go through the program will be less likely to suffer from depression—which is increasing in epidemic proportions in many western countries, including Australia—and will lead more positive and fulfilling lives.

Geelong Grammar School waits with anticipation to see the contribution this generation will make to Australian and international life, like the Grammarians who have gone before them.

## Acknowledgments

All correspondence about the Positive Education Program at Geelong Grammar School should be directed to HeadOfPosEd@ggs.vic.edu.au. This chapter is based on a lecture delivered by Mathew White to launch the 2009 Richard and Janet Southby Visiting Fellows Program. The author acknowledges the collaboration and feedback of the Geelong Grammar School Positive Education Department and staff; the input of Professor Martin Seligman and the late Professor John Abela is also acknowledged. An audio recording of the lecture is available at http://www.ggs.vic.edu.au/Positive-Education/Resources/Lectures-2009.aspx.

## References

Beyond Blue (2009, February 27). *Fact sheet.* Melbourne, Australia: Beyond Blue.

Black Dog Institute (2009). http://www.blackdoginstitute.org.au/.

Boniwell, I. (2006). *Positive psychology in a nutshell.* Hertford, UK: Stephen Austin.

Brunwasser, S., Gillham, J., & Kim, E. S. (2009). A meta-analytical review of the Penn Resiliency Program's effect on depressive symptoms. *Journal of Consulting and Clinical Psychology, 77*(6), 1042–1054.

Challen, A., Noden, P., & West, A. (2009). *UK Resilience Programme evaluation. Research report No DCSF-RR094.* London, UK: London School of Economics.

Department of Education (2008). *Scoping study into approaches to student wellbeing. Report to the Department of Education, Employment and Workplace Relations.* Canberra, Australia: Department of Education.

Dweck, C. S. (2006). *Mindset.* New York, NY: Random House.

Emmons, R. A., & Shelton, C. M. (2002). Gratitude and the science of positive psychology. In C. R. Snyder and S. J. Lopez (Eds.), *Handbook of positive psychology* (pp. 459–471). New York, NY: Oxford University Press.

Fineburg, A. (2004). Introducing positive psychology to the introductory psychology student. In P. A. Linley & S. Joseph (Eds.), *Positive psychology in practice* (pp. 197–209). Hoboken, NJ: Wiley.

Gillham, J. E., Reivich, K. J., Freres, D. R., Lascher, M., Litzinger, S., Shatté, A., & Seligman, M.E.P. (2006). School-based prevention of depression and anxiety symptoms in early adolescence: A pilot of a parent intervention component. *School Psychology Quarterly, 21*, 323–348.

Kotter, J. (1996). *Leading change.* Boston, MA: Harvard Business Press.

Lazarus, R. S. (2003). Does the positive psychology movement have legs? *Psychological Inquiry: An International Journal for the Advancement of Psychological Theory, 14*(2), 93–109.

Lopez, S., Rose, S., Robinsons, C., Marquez, S., &. Pais-Ribeiro, J. (2009). Measuring and promoting hope in schoolchildren. In R. Gilman, E. &. Scott Huebner (Eds.), *Handbook of positive psychology in schools.* New York, NY: Routledge.

Lyubomirsky, S. (2009). *The how of happiness: A practical approach to getting the life you want.* London, UK: Piatkus.

National Health and Medical Research Council (1997). *Depression in young people: Clinical practice guidelines.* Canberra: Australian Government Publishing Service.

Noddings, N. (2003). *Happiness and education.* New York, NY: Cambridge University Press.

Norrish, J., & Vella-Brodrick, D. (2009). Positive psychology and adolescents: Where are we now? Where to from here? *Australian Psychologist, 44*(44), 270–278.

Peterson, C., & Seligman, M. (2004). *Character strengths and virtues: A handbook and classification.* New York, NY: Oxford University Press.

Reivich, K., & Shatté, A. (2002). *The resilience factor.* New York, NY: Three Rivers Press.

Schwarz, B. (Ed.). (1972). *The human person and the world of values; a tribute to Dietrich Von Hildebrand by his friends in philosophy.* Westport, CN, Greenwood Press.

Seligman, M. E. (2000). Positive psychology: An introduction. *American Psychologist, 55*(5), 5–14.

Seligman, M. (2004). Foreword. In P. A. Liney & S. Joseph (Eds.), *Positive psychology in practice* (xi–xiii). Hoboken, NJ: John Wiley.

Seligman, M. (2006). *Positive psychology at Geelong Grammar School.* Melbourne, Australia: Geelong Grammar School, Positive Education.

Seligman, M. E. P., & Csikszentmihalyi, M. (2000). Positive psychology: An introduction. *American Psychologist, 55,* 5–14.

Seligman, M., Enst, R. M., Gillham, J., Reivich, K. & Linkins, M. (2009). Positive education: Positive psychology and classroom interventions. *Oxford Review of Education, 35*(3), 293–311.

Seligman, M. E., Reivich, K., & Jaycox, L. (1995). *The optimistic child.* New York, NY: Houghton Mifflin Press.

Seligman, M., & Steen, T. A. (2005). Positive psychology programs: Empirical validation of interventions. *American Psychologist, 60,* 410–421.

Wilson, E. (2008). *Against happiness: In praise of melancholy.* New York, NY: Farrar, Straus and Giroux.

White, M. (2009, March). Why teach positive education in schools? *Curriculum Leadership Journal, 7*(7).

# SECTION VII

# HAPPINESS AND ORGANIZATIONS

CHAPTER 50

# AN INTRODUCTION TO HAPPINESS AND ORGANIZATIONS

ARRAN CAZA[1] AND KIM S. CAMERON[2]

[1]Griffith University, Australia; [2]University of Michigan, USA

THIS section considers happiness in the context of positive psychology's "third pillar," the study of positive institutions (Seligman & Csikszentmihalyi, 2000). In examining the nature and dynamics of happiness in organizations, the chapters in this section draw upon and extend the emerging domain of positive organizational scholarship (POS), which is focused specifically on the study of especially positive outcomes, processes, and attributes of organizations and their members (Cameron & Spreitzer, 2011). POS is an organizational response to positive psychology, in that the use of "positive" in the label of POS declares an affirmative bias and an orientation toward exceptional, virtuous, life-giving, and flourishing phenomena (Cameron, Dutton, & Quinn, 2003). POS is premised on the belief that individuals and their organizations are inherently eudaimonic, that they seek goodness for its intrinsic value (Dutton & Sonenshein, 2009).

It should, however, be noted that the declared positive bias of POS is not without controversy in organizational studies (Caza & Carroll, 2011). While positive psychology emerged in response to a predominance of negatively-focused psychological research (Seligman & Csikszentmihalyi, 2000), it is not as clear that organizational studies had a similarly negative focus. Although some have noted a tendency toward negativity in the organizational literature (Caza & Caza, 2008; Roberts, 2006), others disagree, and as such have questioned the need for adopting an explicitly "positive" focus (Fineman, 2006; Hackman, 2009). It is certainly true that various positive outcomes have always been a part of organizational studies, and while happiness per se has not been a frequent focus of research, the field does have a long history of examining closely related phenomena, including job satisfaction, job involvement, organizational commitment, engagement, social concern, collective morale, and intrinsic motivation.

Despite these concerns, however, the recent focus on positivity in organizations appears to have made important contributions, uncovering relationships and phenomena that had not previously been examined, thereby advancing organizational studies (Cameron & Spreitzer, 2011). For example, Bono and Ilies (2006) described a series of studies showing that leaders who express more positive emotion engender the same responses in followers. Similarly, military leaders who expressed love fostered greater well-being, commitment, and productivity among followers (Fry, Vitucci, & Cedillo, 2005). Happiness in organizations has been linked to employees making personal sacrifices for the sake of clients, even though these sacrifices were neither required nor rewarded by the organization (O'Donohoe & Turley, 2006). In a study of management teams, Losada and Heaphy (2004) found that the highest performing organizations were characterized by a ratio of five displays of happiness or other positive communications for every negative communication. These and other studies suggest that there are important insights to be gained by explicitly studying happiness and positivity in organizations.

Nonetheless, these insights do not invalidate the concerns raised by skeptics. An exclusive focus on happiness and positivity could be problematic for organizational studies (Caza & Cameron, 2008). The reality of life in organizations includes opposition, obstacles, and challenges, and these matters need to be included in the study of happiness in organizations. In fact, Ellis and colleagues' (2006) lab study confirmed that a singularly positive focus is not helpful for task learning. They used a computer-based business simulation to test the effect of different after-event review strategies. Participants completed the simulation, and then took part in facilitated interventions to help them improve their performance. There were three interventions, each one focused on previous successes, failures, or both success and failure. The results from a second round of the simulation showed that those who focused only on success did no better than a control group with no intervention, and that an analysis of failures tended to produce the greatest increase in subsequent performance. These results support the observation that "all sunshine makes a desert," and that it is important to recognize the importance of the positive and the negative in understanding organizations (Fredrickson, 2009).

The chapters in this section do so, examining both the opportunities and the threats associated with happiness in organizational life. The following eight chapters in this section advance POS by illuminating organizational factors and processes that are closely associated with the happiness and well-being of employees. They provide reviews of the extant work in their areas, and advance those literatures by helping to frame and reorient the discussion.

Cameron and Caza (Chapter 51) examine virtues at the organizational level and their relationships with happiness. The authors review evidence in support of the notion that virtuousness can be an aspect of collectives as well as individuals. They describe three processes—amplification, buffering, and heliotropism—that create the possibility of virtuousness propagating at the organizational level and subsequently contributing to the happiness of organizational members.

In Chapter 52, Caza and Wrzesniewski consider how working in organizations influences individuals' physical, psychological, and social well-being. They integrate prior research in these areas to discuss how work can be both helpful and harmful to well-being. The outcomes associated with work, the nature of one's work, and the context in which work is conducted are identified as key factors in happiness, and their complex relationships with well-being are described.

Searle and Parker (Chapter 53) adopt a work design perspective to examine how work can contribute to proximal and enduring psychological outcomes. In so doing, they combine organizational and individual perspectives, to highlight how organizations can influence happiness through top-down job design and how individuals can influence their own happiness in a bottom-up fashion. In addition, they highlight the reciprocal relationship between job design and happiness, such that happiness is not only a consequence of job design, but also a potential determinant of the implementation and interpretation of various work characteristics.

Next, in Chapter 54, Warr examines the link between work and happiness by integrating two approaches that have historically been distinct. He notes that most studies of job-related happiness have emphasized either the nature of the job or the characteristics of the individual job holder; rarely have the two been combined. Warr's chapter provides a summary of work in both approaches, and then develops possibilities for combining them in an integrated understanding of how jobs contribute to specific individuals' happiness at work.

Youssef and Luthans explore the mechanisms by which employees' psychological capital can contribute to happiness in Chapter 55. Psychological capital refers to a stable set of resources that previous research has linked to multiple positive outcomes in organizations. In this chapter, the authors describe how psychological capital can contribute to happiness through its effect on interpretations, affective states, goal-related behavior and social connections.

In Chapter 56, Morgan-Roberts describes the reflected best self and its potential influence on happiness and vitality at work. The reflected best self refers to individuals' dynamic self-construal of themselves when they are performing to the best of their capabilities. Morgan-Roberts explains the identity process by which one's reflected best self is developed, and defines four means—purposeful engagement, strength-based engagement, authentic engagement, and relational affirmation—by which individuals' reflected best self can contribute to positive outcomes in organizations.

Wright (Chapter 57) reviews the historical tradition of studying health in organizational studies. This highlights the relatively recent inclusion of happiness and psychological well-being in organizational conceptions of health, which have more often focused primarily on financial considerations when defining health. However, as the review shows, expanding the definition beyond financial health provides important insights, as happiness at work has been linked to many outcomes including physical health and work performance.

In recognition of the important influence that leaders have on their organizations, Quick and Quick focus on the well-being of executives in the final chapter of this section, Chapter 58. They identify five sources of positive well-being among executives: character strength, self-awareness, motivation, self-reliance and professional support. The authors also discuss the significant threats to well-being among executives, and the persistent asymmetry in well-being between male and female executives.

Together, these eight chapters contribute to the understanding of happiness in organizations. They review and integrate prior work, providing clarity to existing findings. Each chapter also suggests important directions for future investigation, all of which have the potential to advance the "positive institutions" pillar of positive psychology. Moreover, while each chapter's suggestions are particular to the domain under discussion in that chapter, there are some common themes among them which suggest general directions for the study of happiness in organizations.

The most apparent of these themes is the need for more complex theorizing about happiness in organizations. Because a specific focus on happiness is relatively new to organizational studies, much of the related theory is still being developed. As such, there is a clear need for more complex models, such as ones that recognize the interactions among antecedents of happiness, and which distinguish the potentially additive or substitutive consequences of different aspects of happiness and well-being. Similarly, there is growing evidence in support of non-linear relationships among happiness and other phenomena, with the attendant need to develop theory accommodating such non-linearity. In a related point, several of the chapters note reciprocal relationships among constructs, such that happiness may simultaneously be a cause and a consequence. The field of organizational studies will need to develop theories of happiness that reflect these complexities.

The second theme among the suggested directions concerns the need for richer research and data collection designs. Longitudinal data is rare in the work reviewed. Indeed, even at a theoretical level, there is a need for more consideration of the role of time. For example, there are likely to be important differences in the processes involved in episodic interventions versus the maintenance of an ongoing relationship between happiness and work.

Finally, both richer theory and richer research design will require the development of associated tools for their implementation. Models and measures that reflect the complex, multidimensional, and non-linear nature of happiness in organizations will need to be developed. Similarly, for the most part, the practical interventions associated with these models and existing findings remain to be created. However, as the exciting developments in these chapters show, such advancements may be on the horizon. The work required to respond to critics of studying happiness in organizations is well underway.

## References

Bono, J. E., & Ilies, R. (2006). Charisma, positive emotions and mood contagion. *Leadership Quarterly*, 17, 317–334.
Cameron, K. S., Dutton, J. E., & Quinn, R. E. (Eds.). (2003). *Positive organizational scholarship: Foundations of a new discipline*. San Francisco, CA: Berrett-Koehler Publishers Inc.
Cameron, K. S., & Spreitzer, G. M. (Eds.). (2011). *Handbook of positive organizational scholarship*. New York, NY: Oxford University Press.
Caza, A., & Cameron, K. S. (2008). Positive organizational scholarship: What does it achieve? In S. R. Clegg & C. L. Cooper (Eds.), *SAGE handbook of organizational behaviour* (Vol. II, pp. 99–116). Thousand Oaks, CA: Sage.
Caza, A., & Carroll, B. (2011). Critical theory and positive organizational scholarship. In K. S. Cameron & G. M. Spreitzer (Eds.), *Handbook of positive organizational scholarship* (pp. 965–978). New York, NY: Oxford University Press.
Caza, B. B., & Caza, A. (2008). Positive organizational scholarship—A critical theory perspective. *Journal of Management Inquiry*, 17, 21–33.
Dutton, J. E., & Sonenshein, S. (2009). Positive organizational scholarship. In S. J. Lopez (Ed.), *Encyclopedia of Positive Psychology* (pp. 737–742). Malden, MA: Blackwell Publishing.
Ellis, S., Mendel, R., & Nir, M. (2006). Learning from successful and failed experience: The moderating role of kind of after-event review. *Journal of Applied Psychology*, 91, 669–680.
Fineman, S. (2006). On being positive: Concerns and counterpoints. *Academy of Management Review*, 31, 270–291.
Fredrickson, B. L. (2009). *Positivity*. New York, NY: Crown Books.
Fry, L. W., Vitucci, S., & Cedillo, M. (2005). Spiritual leadership and army transformation: Theory, measurement, and establishing a baseline. *Leadership Quarterly*, 16, 835–862.
Hackman, J. R. (2009). The perils of positivity. *Journal of Organizational Behavior*, 30, 309–319.

Losada, M., & Heaphy, E. (2004). The role of positivity and connectivity in the performance of business teams: A nonlinear dynamics model. *American Behavioral Scientist, 47,* 740–765.

O'Donohoe, S., & Turley, D. (2006). Compassion at the counter: Service providers and bereaved consumers. *Human Relations, 59,* 1429–1448.

Roberts, L. M. (2006). Shifting the lens on organizational life: The added value of positive scholarship—Response. *Academy of Management Review, 31,* 292–305.

Seligman, M. E. P., & Csikszentmihalyi, M. (2000). Positive psychology: An introduction. *American Psychologist, 55,* 5–14.

CHAPTER 51

# VIRTUOUSNESS AS A SOURCE OF HAPPINESS IN ORGANIZATIONS

KIM S. CAMERON[1]
AND ARRAN CAZA[2]

[1]University of Michigan, USA; [2]Griffith University, Australia

IN this chapter, we examine the relationship between virtuousness and happiness in organizations. More specifically, we examine how virtuousness may contribute to and enable happiness in organizational settings. Our review confirms prior evidence about the relationship between virtuousness and individual happiness (i.e., positive affect) and between happiness and individual behavior (e.g., engagement), but we find that the relationship between these factors and organization-level performance and collective happiness has been largely absent in past research. We address this link in this chapter.

To begin, it is important to be clear about the definitions of the two key concepts examined in this chapter, namely "happiness" and "virtuousness." Happiness has been defined in a variety of ways (Kesebir & Diener, 2008; Kristjansson, 2010), but the two primary approaches to happiness refer to "hedonic" happiness—denoting durable subjective well-being consisting of life satisfaction and a preponderance of positive feelings and relatively few negative feelings (e.g., Diener, Suh, Lucas, & Smith, 1999)—and to "eudaimonic" happiness—denoting doing what is right or virtuous and pursuing meaningful, enduring, growth-producing goals (Seligman, 2002; Sheldon & Elliott, 1999; Warr, 2007). Hedonic happiness is similar to life-satisfaction, whereas eudaimonic happiness is similar to life-fulfillment. Hedonic happiness may be equated with pursuing the pleasurable life, whereas eudaimonic happiness may be equated with pursuing the good life (Gavin & Mason, 2004; Seligman, 2002).

The concept of virtuousness has also been defined in a variety of ways, for example, as goodness for its own sake, as the best of the human condition, as the most functional attributes for the human species, and as personal and social betterment (Chapman, & Galston, 1992; Comte-Sponville, 2001; Dent, 1984; MacIntyre, 1984; Weiner, 1993). Rooted in the Latin word *virtus,* or the Greek *arête*, meaning excellence, virtuousness was described by Plato and Aristotle as the desires and actions that produce personal and social good.

More recently, virtuousness has been described as the best of the human condition, the most ennobling behaviors and outcomes of people, the excellence and essence of humankind, and the highest aspirations of human beings (Cameron, 2011). The meaning of virtuousness has shifted, in other words, from being a means to another more desirable outcome to representing an ultimate good itself.

It seems reasonable that virtuousness and happiness would be strongly associated with one another inasmuch as they share an emphasis on eudaimonism, which is the assumption that an inclination exists in all human beings toward excellence or goodness for its own sake (Aristotle, *Metaphysics*; Dutton and Sonenshein, 2007). Another similarity between happiness and virtuousness is that both have been the focus of relatively little research in the organizational studies literature. However, as described next, there is reason to believe that both are relevant concerns for organizational studies. As such, this chapter reviews what is known about the connections between happiness and virtuousness in organizations and uses that review to suggest future directions for research.

In keeping with this goal, we focus on the organization level of analysis. That is, we examine these two concepts at the collective level, so that the manifestations of happiness and of virtuousness are in organizations, and not solely within single individuals. In organizational research, proxies for organizational happiness have included job satisfaction, engagement, thriving, flourishing, positive affect, morale, and positive climate (Fisher, 2010; Warr, 2007). In organizational research, proxies for virtuousness have included corporate social responsibility, business ethics, prosocial behavior, and citizenship (George, 1991; McNeeley & Meglino, 1994; Piliavin & Charng, 1990). None of these latter terms is exactly synonymous with organizational virtuousness, however, so we will clarify the definition of organizational virtuousness before proceeding.

## Organizational Virtuousness

An important aspect of the original Greek term for virtue (*arête*) is that it can be applied at both the individual and collective level (Schudt, 2000). That is, while one could refer to a virtuous individual, it is equally valid to refer to a virtuous family or group. Consistent with this interpretation, there is a substantial body of research that examines virtuousness at the collective level, particularly in families (McCubbin, Thompson, Thompson, & Fromer, 1998; Sandage & Hill, 2001; Stinnett & Defrain, 1986; Walsh, 2006). The notion of collective virtuousness has since been extended to organizations on the basis that other kinds of collectives also can be more or less virtuous (Bright, Cameron, & Caza, 2006; Cameron, Bright, & Caza, 2004; Cameron & Caza, 2002).

Virtuousness *in* organizations refers to the behavior of individuals in organizational settings, and a growing literature on this topic is emerging in the field of positive psychology (Baer & Lykins, 2011; Peterson & Seligman, 2004). The manifestation and consequences of hope, gratitude, wisdom, forgiveness, compassion, resilience, and other similar virtues are receiving substantial attention in the psychological literature (Emmons, 1999; Harker & Keltner, 2001; McCullough, Pargament, & Thoreson, 2000; Peterson & Bossio, 1991; Seligman, 2002; Snyder, 1994; Sternberg, 1998). For example, individual virtuousness has been found to predict desired outcomes such as individual's commitment, satisfaction, motivation, positive emotions, effort, physical health, and psychological health (Andersson, Giacalone, & Jurkiewicz, 2007; Cameron & Caza, 2004; Dutton, Worline, Frost, & Lilius, 2006; Emmons, 1999; Fry, Vitucci, & Cedillo, 2005; Giacalone, Paul, & Jurkiewicz, 2005; Gittell, Cameron, Lim, & Rivas, 2006; Grant et al., 2007; Harker & Keltner, 2001; Kellett, Humphrey, & Sleeth, 2006; Luthans, Avolio, Avey, & Norman, 2007; McCullough, Pargament, & Thoreson, 2000; Peterson & Bossio, 1991; Seligman, 2002; Snyder, 1994; Sternberg, 1998).

Virtuousness *through* organizations refers to the role of formal groups in fostering and sustaining eudemonic action. Virtuousness through organizations has rarely been examined, and the manifestation of collective virtuousness has only recently been investigated in organizational research. Although studies of business ethics, corporate social responsibility, and citizenship behavior have been conducted, virtuousness is unique from these concepts—as we explain in the next section—and organizational manifestations of virtuousness and its consequences remain under-developed both theoretically and empirically. This chapter reviews what is known about virtuousness through organizations.

## THE IRONY OF ORGANIZATIONAL VIRTUOUSNESS

One of the key attributes of virtuousness is that it is not a means to obtain another end, but it is considered to be an end in itself (Bright, Cameron, & Caza, 2006; Ilies, Nahrgang, & Morgeson, 2007). Virtuousness is most closely associated with what Aristotle labeled goods of first intent—in other words, "that which is good in itself and is to be chosen for its own sake" (*Metaphysics* XII, p. 3). In fact, virtuousness in pursuit of another more attractive outcome ceases, by definition, to be virtuousness (Comte-Sponville, 2001). Forgiveness, compassion, and courage in search of recompense are not virtuous. If kindness toward employees is demonstrated in an organization solely to obtain compliance or an economic advantage, for example, it ceases to be kindness and is, instead, manipulation. Virtuousness is associated with social betterment, but this betterment extends beyond self-interested benefit. Virtuousness creates social value that transcends the instrumental desires of the actor (Aristotle, 1998). Virtuous actions produce advantage to others in addition to, or even exclusive of, recognition, benefit, or advantage to the actor (Cawley, Martin, & Johnson, 2000).

This intrinsic aspect of virtuousness in organizations distinguishes it from participation in normatively prescribed corporate social responsibility, sponsoring environmentally friendly programs, or utilizing renewable resources (Bollier, 1996). Whereas some activities included in the corporate social responsibility and corporate citizenship domains may represent organizational virtuousness, these activities are typically understood to be motivated by instrumental benefit or exchange relationships. That is, engagement in these actions is initiated to benefit the firm, or the actions result from a reciprocal arrangement between stakeholders (Batson, 1994; Fry, Keim, & Meiners, 1982; Moore & Richardson, 1988; Piliavin & Charng, 1990; Sánchez, 2000). Exchange, reciprocity, and self-serving motives, however, are inconsistent with virtuousness. Barge and Oliver (2003) and Gergen (1999) argued that associating an instrumental motive with organizational virtuousness changes the nature of the relationships among organization members and causes the behavior to evolve into "another technique of manipulation and discipline" (Barge & Oliver, 2003, p. 11). Of course, virtuousness does not stand in opposition to concepts such as citizenship and social responsibility, but it extends beyond them.

The same is true of ethics. To date, the dominant (although not exclusive) emphasis in the ethics literature has been on avoiding harm, fulfilling contracts, and obeying the law (Handselsman, Knapp, & Gottlieb, 2002). In practice, ethics are understood and implemented as duties (Rawls, 1971). They are usually specifications designed to avoid injury or to prevent damage (Orlikowski, 2000). Virtuousness, on the other hand, represents the highest aspirations of human kind and the pursuit of excellence or eudaimonism, not just avoiding harm.

The irony in virtuousness, therefore, is that while it does not require a visible, instrumental pay-off to be of value, attention to virtuousness usually becomes subservient to the demands of enhancing financial return and organizational performance (Davis, 2008; Jensen, 2002). Few leaders invest in practices or processes that do not produce higher returns to shareholders, profitability, productivity, and customer satisfaction. In other words, without tangible benefit, those who manage organizational resources tend to ignore virtuousness. If organizational virtuousness is to be pursued, evidence of pragmatic utility must usually be provided. This creates a motive for investigating the relationships between virtuousness and tangible outcomes in organizations. Only a few studies have explored these relationships, and the key results of those investigations are summarized next.

## Virtuousness and Happiness-Related Outcomes

In the organizational studies literature, happiness per se is not a commonly studied outcome. Instead, proxies are used that measure elements related to happiness, such as job satisfaction, positive affect, engagement, positive climate, and organizational commitment (Fisher, 2011). As mentioned earlier, these outcomes have most frequently been studied at the individual level of analysis where an extensive literature documents the effects of individuals' virtuous behaviors on others. For example, one study found that experiences of hope and gratitude prompted workers to feel more responsibility to care for coworkers and society as whole but had no effect on their felt responsibility toward economic performance (Andersson et al., 2007; also see O'Donohoe & Turley, 2006). Another study linked character strengths and virtuousness to concern about corporate social performance (Giacalone, et al., 2005). For example, the traits of spirituality (transcendent ideals and a desire for meaning in community) and generativity (concern for future generations) were associated with inclinations toward involvement in social responsibility. In addition to one's own virtue evaluations, the behaviors and expressed beliefs of others have been found to have an important influence on individual behavior (Bandura, 1986; Collins, 1996; Festinger, 1954; Wheeler & Miyake, 1992), so that one person's virtuous action can shape the experiences and behavior of others in the organization (Giacalone & Promislo, 2010; Tangney et al., 2007). Such studies are examples of virtuousness *in* organizations.

In contrast to this growing literature, investigations of virtuousness *through* organizations have been comparatively rare. One series of studies examined the effects of virtuousness in organizations on the consequences of downsizing. Cameron and colleagues (Cameron, Bright, & Caza, 2004; Cameron & Caza, 2002) conducted a series of studies in which indicators of virtuousness and of performance were assessed in organizations. One study investigated eight independent business units randomly selected within a large corporation in the transportation industry. All eight units had recently downsized, so that the well-documented negative effects associated with downsizing were expected to ensure deteriorating performance and unhappiness among all groups of stakeholders (Cameron, 1994, 1998). Organizational virtuousness scores for each business unit were measured by survey items measuring *compassion, integrity, forgiveness, trust,* and *optimism* (concepts included on lists of universally valued virtues, such as in Chun, 2005; Peterson & Seligman, 2004). Organizational performance outcomes consisted of objective measures of organization performance (e.g., productivity, efficiency, customer claims) as well as proxies for happiness (e.g., commitment and satisfaction). The results revealed significant relationships between organizational virtuousness scores and both performance outcomes and happiness indicators.

Consistent results were reported by those authors' other studies. For example, the same dimensions of virtuousness in organizations were linked to positive outcomes in a study of recently downsized firms in 16 different industries. Indicators of happiness among employees, happiness among customers, and organizational performance were all significantly higher in organizations demonstrating the most virtuousness.

In still another investigation, Bright, Cameron, and Caza (2006) distinguished between *tonic* virtuousness (virtuousness that occurs irrespective of conditions, such as trust and meaningfulness) and *phasic* virtuousness (virtuousness that depends on the occurrence of negative circumstances, such as forgiveness when harm is done or courage when danger is present) at the organizational level. They found that both served a buffering function against the negative effects associated with downsizing. Buffering refers to enhancing an organization's capacity to absorb shocks, recover, and heal relationships. Where organizations scored high in virtuousness, they were also more proficient at maintaining morale (happiness) and performing effectively in spite of the challenges associated with downsizing. Virtuousness was found to provide a form of resilience in organizations (Sutcliffe and Vogus, 2003).

A different kind of downsizing study was conducted in the USA airline industry after the tragedy of September 11, 2001 (Gittell et al., 2006). The tragedy of 9/11 led to enormous financial losses for US airline companies, and this study examined the extent to which different firms handled those financial setbacks in virtuous ways. Following 9/11, all US airline companies felt compelled to downsize in order to survive, but some did so in ways that were more virtuous than others (e.g., reduced hours, voluntary leave, or pay cuts rather than terminations and layoffs). Virtuousness in this study was defined as implementing practices and strategies that preserved human dignity, supported individual development, and provided an environment in which employee well-being was a priority. Controlling for unionization, fuel price hedging, and financial reserves, the study found that the correlation between the companies' virtuousness during the crisis and financial return (as measured by stock price gains) was very high ($r = 0.80$) over the next 5 years. The more virtuousness the organization demonstrated in responding to financial losses caused by 9/11, the better was its financial performance. Employee satisfaction (happiness) scores followed this same pattern and were argued to be a key explanatory mechanism in the relationship between virtuousness and performance.

The studies reviewed thus far have offered relatively strong initial support for a link between organizational virtuousness and the outcomes of happiness and performance. However, they were all cross-sectional studies. As a result, the question of causality remains unanswered. Does virtuousness produce happiness and higher performance, or is the relationship reversed (e.g., happy employees collectively perceive and enact more virtuousness)? Two studies, conducted by Cameron, Mora, Leutscher, and Calarco (2011) have explored this issue.

In both studies, virtuous practices were defined as collective behaviors characteristic of organizations in six categories: *caring* (people care for, are interested in, and maintain responsibility for one another as friends), *compassionate support* (people provide support for one another including kindness and compassion when others are struggling), *forgiveness* (people avoid blaming and forgive mistakes), *inspiration* (people inspire one another at work), *meaning* (the meaningfulness of the work is emphasized, and people are elevated and renewed by their work), and *respect* (people treat one another with respect and express appreciation for one another as well as trusting one another to maintain integrity). The two studies examined the time-lagged associations between these six virtues and various outcomes to assess causality.

The first study investigated 40 financial service organizations. Monetary returns and a win-at-all-costs climate are typically characteristic of this business sector (Burrough & Helyar, 1990; Jensen, 2002; Korten, 2001; McLean & Elkind, 2003), which might seem to argue against benefits from virtuousness. Nonetheless, employees' ratings of the organizations' virtue practices predicted happiness and performance outcomes 1 year later. Time 1 virtuousness was linked to Time 2 proxies for happiness (e.g., employee retention, positive organizational climate), as well as with time 2 measures of financial performance. Organizations that supported and maintained virtuous practices produced greater happiness and higher performance 1 year later.

In the second study, 29 organizations in the healthcare industry were investigated to determine if changes in virtuousness scores would produce changes in organizational outcomes. Two findings of interest emerged from this study. One was that organizations with higher scores in virtuousness also had better subsequent outcomes, including patient satisfaction, employee satisfaction, employee retention, interpersonal relationship quality, employee engagement, working climate, and external evaluations of quality of care. These results were similar to those found in financial service organizations. The second important finding was that organizations which improved their virtuousness scores over a 2-year period also experienced significant improvement in the outcomes above, subsequent to the gains in virtuousness. Organizations improving the most in virtuousness also produced the most gain in outcomes during subsequent years.

These studies provide supportive evidence that virtuousness in organizations is associated with, and may even produce, outcomes related to happiness—such as employee satisfaction, retention, interpersonal relationship quality, work engagement, and positive working environment—as well as outcomes related to organizational performance—such as profitability, productivity, and quality. Of course, as stated earlier, the worth of virtuousness in organizations does not require that it be associated with other outcomes; virtuousness is of inherent worth. Nonetheless, the pragmatic utility associated with virtuous organizational practices may assist leaders in their efforts to maintain or pursue virtue when faced with stakeholder demands for measurable results, when helping organizations find ways to improve mandated performance measures, or when trying to lead an organization through trying times.

# Explanations for the Virtuousness– Happiness Connection

At least three explanations have been advanced for how organizational virtuousness contributes to happiness and performance: *amplifying effects*, *buffering effects*, and *heliotropic effects*. Whereas these explanatory mechanisms have not been tested directly, each is grounded in existing literature which provides a rationale for their role in linking virtuousness to happiness in organizations. Each appears to have both social and biological foundations (Kok & Fredrickson, 2010; Lawrence & Norhia, 2002).

## Amplifying effects

Organizational virtuousness provides an amplifying effect because of its association with positive emotions and with social capital (Cameron, Bright, & Caza, 2004). Several authors have reported that exposure to virtuousness produces positive emotions in individuals, which, in turn, leads to elevation in individual performance in organizations (Fineman 1996; Fredrickson, 1998; Seligman, 2002; Staw, Sutton, & Pellod, 1994; Tutu, 1999). When organization members observe compassion, experience gratitude, or witness forgiveness, for example, they experience positive emotions and a mutually reinforcing cycle begins. Fredrickson (2003, p. 173) reported that since "elevation increases the likelihood that a witness to good deeds will soon become the doer of good deeds, then elevation sets up the possibility for some sort of upward spiral . . . and organizations are transformed into more compassionate and harmonious places." This effect is also well documented in the social networks literature (Christakis & Fowler, 2009). Virtuousness tends to increase individual happiness, which leads to more virtuous behavior, which, in turn, fosters increased happiness.

A second rationale for the amplifying effects of virtuousness is its association with social capital formation (Baker, 2000; Coleman, 1998). Social capital in organizations refers to the relationships among individuals through which information, influence, and resources flow (Adler & Kwon, 2002; Leana & Van Buren, 1999; Nahapiet & Ghoshal, 1998). Several researchers have reported that when employees observe displays of virtuousness among fellow employees—for example, sharing, loyalty, advocacy, caring—the results are increased liking, commitment, participation, trust, and collaboration (Koys, 2001; Podsakoff, MacKensie, Paine, & Bachrach, 2000; Walz & Niehoff, 2000). Staw and Barsade (1993) found, for example, that improved cognitive functioning, better decision making, and more effective interpersonal relationships occurred when social capital is high. Employees were more helpful to customers, more creative, and more attentive and respectful to one another (George 1998; Sharot, Riccardi, Raio, & Phelps, 2007). These behaviors tended to propagate themselves throughout the organization via social capital.

These enhanced relationships serve as the social capital upon which organizational performance is built. That is, the positive emotions (or happiness) that emerge from exposure to virtuousness produce the necessary social capital that organizations need to effectively perform. Organizational effectiveness is therefore likely to be enhanced, because amplifying virtuousness fosters greater degrees of social capital in the form of collaboration, growth-producing interpersonal relationships, and respectful engagement. This form of capital amplifies itself and elevates organizational performance.

## Buffering effects

Virtuousness also buffers the organization from the negative effects of trauma or distress by enhancing resiliency, solidarity, and a sense of efficacy (Masten et al., 1999; Weick, Sutcliffe, & Obstfeld, 1999). Seligman and Csikszentmihalyi (2000) pointed out that the development of virtuousness serves as a buffer against dysfunction and illness at the individual and group levels of analysis. They reported that compassion, courage, forgiveness, integrity, and optimism prevent psychological distress, addiction, and dysfunctional behavior (also see Seligman, Schulman, DeRubeis, & Hollon, 1999). This buffering enhances happiness and performance by reducing, or even preventing, the diminishing effects of otherwise deleterious environmental events.

At the group and organization levels, virtuousness enhances the ability to absorb threat and trauma and to bounce back from adversity (Dutton, Frost, Worline, Lilius, & Kanov, 2002; Wildavsky, 1991), including absorbing work related stress (Cohen, 2003; Kaplan, 2003; Kiecolt-Glaser, 2003), and healing from traumatic events (Powley & Cameron, 2006). Virtuousness serves as a source of resilience and "toughness" (Dienstbier & Zillig, 2002), in other words, it helps to preserve relationships and collective efficacy (Sutcliffe & Vogus, 2003), as well as to strengthen, replenish, and limber organizations (Worline et al., 2003). It serves as a buffering agent that protects and inoculates organizations, permitting them to bounce back from misfortune and to avoid deteriorating happiness.

## Heliotropic effects

Virtuousness also possesses attributes consistent with heliotropism (Drexelius, 1627/2009). The heliotropic effect is the attraction of all living systems toward positive energy and away from negative energy, or toward that which is life-giving and away from that which is life-depleting (D'Amato & Jagoda, 1962; Mrosovsky & Kingsmill, 1985; Smith & Baker, 1960). Organizations characterized by virtuousness foster positive energy among members, and positive energy produces elevated performance (Cameron, 2008b; Dutton, 2003; Erhardt-Siebold, 1937).

Several explanations have been proposed for why heliotropic tendencies exist in human beings and their systems. Erdelyi (1974) explained positive biases as a product of individual cognitive development. Perceptual defense mechanisms (e.g., denial, displacement) emerge to counteract the effects of negative information, so inclinations toward positivity develop in the brain. In brain scan research, Sharot et al. (2007) found that the human brain tends toward optimistic and positive orientations in its natural state, and that more areas of the brain activate when positive and optimistic images are processed compared to negative or pessimistic images. Unkelbach, Fiedler, Bayer, Stegmuller, & Danner (2008) reported a series of studies showing that the human brain processes positive information faster and more accurately than negative information, so human productivity and performance are elevated by the positive more than the negative. Learning theorists (e.g., Skinner, 1965) explain positive biases as being associated with reinforcement. Activities that are positively reinforcing are repeated while activities that are punishing or unpleasant are extinguished.

The eudaimonic tendency in human beings leads people toward helping or contributing behaviors (Krebs, 1987), and when others observe these behaviors they feel compelled to join with and build upon those contributions (Sethi & Nicholson, 2001). Gouldner (1960) proposed that role modeling and social norm formation create this link between virtuousness and happiness in that positive social processes are more likely to survive and flourish over the long run than negative social processes because they are functional for the group. Collectives survive when they rely on positive norms, and these norms are a direct product of demonstrated virtuousness. Evolutionarily, the dysfunctional effects of non-virtuousness eventually cause them to become extinguished.

As we have shown, the literature provides at least three potential explanations for why virtuousness is predictive of happiness in organizations. Cognitive, emotional, behavioral, physiological, and social evidence suggests that human systems naturally prefer exposure to virtuousness, so it not surprising that happiness and organizational performance would be enhanced.

# Future Research

Because the quantity and scope of research on virtuousness in organizations has been limited, a variety of important research questions remain to be investigated. Among the key areas of needed research are: (1) the measurement of virtuousness, (2) the predictive power of virtuousness, and (3) the moderators and mediators of the effects of virtuousness on outcomes.

## Measurement

To date, no standardized measures have been developed for assessing the concept of organizational virtuousness or its component elements. Two different instruments have been used in the studies mentioned in this chapter, but both measured a limited selection of specific virtues. The psychometric analyses that have been conducted to date (e.g., Cameron, Bright, & Caza, 2004; Cameron et al., 2011) have not provided a rationale for why some virtues are assessed and others are excluded. More generally, the conceptual boundaries and nomological network have yet to be precisely established for the concept of virtuousness, and, therefore, the groundwork for theories of virtuousness has not yet been fully established. Clarifying the nature and measurement of organizational virtuousness is an important challenge for future research.

## Prediction

Clarifying the relationships among organizational virtuousness and various outcomes is another important area to be addressed. The surveys used to assess organizational virtuousness to date might be referred to as "blunt" instruments in that they provide aggregated ratings of virtuous practices in organizations. Thus far, aggregated virtuousness scores in companies have been found to predict outcomes, but no single virtue appears to account for a great deal more variance than others. This may be a product of imprecise measurement, or it may be a product of virtues not being displayed in isolation from one another. If the latter is true, then investigations of which clusters of virtues occur naturally together in organizations would be useful.

Moreover, identifying which virtues (or clusters) are most closely associated with which outcomes is also an important area for study. For example, one might ask whether tonic virtues (such as love and integrity) are more or less predictive of happiness than phasic virtues (such as forgiveness and compassion). Experimental manipulations and carefully designed organizational interventions will help to clarify the various effects of organizational virtuousness.

Further, in the studies reviewed which described investigations of causal associations, interventions occurred that exposed organizations to virtuous practices, and some organizations subsequently improved their scores. It is not clear, however, which specific interventions were most helpful in raising organizational virtuousness scores in which domains. Determining explicitly how to assist organizations in becoming more virtuous is an area of needed investigation.

In addition, consistent with Gladwell's (2002) concept of a "tipping point," it is important to understand how much virtuousness is sufficient. Is there a ratio—such as the now well-established 3:1 ratio of positive to negative emotions which predicts flourishing outcomes (Fredrickson, 2009)—that also maximizes the happiness associated with organizational virtuousness? How much virtuousness is enough?

## Moderators and mediators

Another set of issues has to do with the extent to which virtuousness has direct or moderated effects on outcomes. Some studies have been cited that directly link organizational virtuousness with happiness and other outcomes, but causal associations and explanations have not yet been examined. Cameron (2003) summarized literature suggesting that virtuousness elevates positive emotions which, in turn, fosters higher performance. Virtuousness also enhances social capital which reduces transaction costs, facilitates communication and cooperation, enhances employee commitment, fosters individual learning, and strengthens relationships and involvement. Given these observations, it may be true that organizational virtuousness contributes to happiness by enhancing the number and quality of relationships that employees have at work. Alternatively, since virtuousness also fosters prosocial behavior, the amplifying or "contagious" nature of virtuous behavior may be the key to explaining why employees in virtuous organizations appear to be happier.

Similarly, other factors may moderate the effects of virtuousness in organizations, but to date, almost no attention has been paid to what these factors might be. For example, differences such as the size of an organization, its culture, the demographic make-up of the top management team, the explicit goals and strategy of the organization, or certain industry dynamics may influence the relationship between virtuousness and happiness. Investigating which factors, if any, serve as moderators and mediators of the organizational virtuousness-happiness relationship will certainly be a fruitful area for future investigations.

## Conclusion

At the individual level, it has been established empirically that virtuousness produces happiness, at least as measured by proxies such as satisfaction with work, personal well-being, reduced intention to quit, reduced conflict, and social satisfaction (Cooper, Okamura, & Gurka, 1992; Donovan, 2000; Foster et al., 2004; Lyubomirsky, King, & Diener, 2005; Van Katwyk, Fox, Spector, & Kelloway, 2000;). For example, engaging in virtuous action leads to increased positive affect and reduced negative affect (Fineman, 1996; Fredrickson, 1998; Seligman, 2002; Staw, Sutton, & Relled, 1994; Tutu, 1999). In fact, the emotional power of virtuous action is such that simply witnessing another's deeds can increase one's positive affect (Christakis & Fowler, 2009; Fredrickson, 2003). Moreover, positive emotion tends to produce increased cognitive functioning, better decision making, creativity, and physical health (Cohn & Fredrickson, 2006; Fredrickson, 2001; Johnson, Waugh, & Fredrickson, 2010; Sharot et al., 2007; Staw & Barsade, 1993), all of which can in turn contribute to increased happiness, or satisfaction with aspects of one's life (Kesebir & Diener, 2008; Lyubomirsky et al., 2005).

It has also been established that happiness (as measured by positive emotions) affects individual performance at work by increasing job performance, support provision, and social interactions while also reducing work withdrawal and counterproductive work behavior (Baldassare, Rosenfield, & Rook, 1984; Donovan et al., 2000; George, 1995; Harter, Schmidt, & Keyes, 2002; Jundt & Hinsz, 2001; Philips, 1967). Luthans and colleagues (2007) found, for example, that psychological capital (i.e., resilience, hope, optimism, and self-efficacy) produced happiness in employees which, in turn, predicted motivation, commitment, and intention to stay.

The questions that remain to be answered concern the dynamics between virtuousness and happiness at a collective level. This chapter has summarized the arguments for virtuousness as a collective phenomenon and the preliminary empirical data linking organizational virtuousness to happiness and to organizational performance. Evidence suggests that when organizations implement and encourage virtuous practices, desired performance and employee happiness increases. However, much work is left to be done in this area before it is clear how the collective aspects of virtuousness influence the happiness of employees, other stakeholders, and organizational outcomes.

## References

Adler, P. S., & Kwon, S. (2002). Social capital: Prospects for a new concept. *Academy of Management Review*, 27, 17–40.

Andersson, L., Giacalone, R. A., & Jurkiewicz, C. L. (2007). On the relationship of hope and gratitude to corporate social responsibility. *Journal of Business Ethics*, 70(4), 401–409.

Aristotle. (1998). *Metaphysics*. New York, NY: Penguin Books.

Baer, R. A. & Lykins, E. L. B. (2011). Mindfulness and positive psychological functioning. In K. M. Sheldon, T. B. Kashdan, & M. F. Steger (Eds.) *Designing positive psychology* (pp. 335–348). New York, NY: Oxford University Press.

Baker, W. E. (2000). *Achieving success through social capital*. San Francisco, CA: Jossey-Bass.

Baldassare, M., Rosenfield, S., & Rook, K. S. (1984). The types of social relations predicting elderly well-being. *Research on Aging*, 6, 549–559.

Bandura, A. (1986). *Social foundations of thought and action: A social cognitive theory.* Englewood Cliffs, NJ: Prentice Hall.

Barge, J. K., & Oliver, C. (2003). Working with appreciation in managerial practice. *The Academy of Management Review*, 28(1), 124–142.

Batson, C. D. (1994). Why act for the public good? Four answers. *Personality and Social Psychology Bulletin*, 20, 603–610.

Bollier, D. (1996) *Aiming higher: 25 Stories of how companies prosper by combining sound management and social vision.* New York, NY: Amacom.

Bright, D., Cameron, K. S., & Caza, A. (2006). The amplifying and buffering effects of virtuousness in downsized organizations. *Journal of Business Ethics*, 64(3), 249–269.

Burrough, B., & Helyar, J. (1990) *Barbarians at the gate.* New York, NY: Harper & Row.

Cameron, K. S. (1994). Strategies for successful organizational downsizing. *Human Resource Management*, 33(2), 189–211.

Cameron, K. S. (1998). Strategic organizational downsizing: An extreme case. *Research in Organizational Behavior*, 20, 185–229.

Cameron, K. S. (2003). Organizational virtuousness and performance. In K. S. Cameron, J. E. Dutton, & R. E. Quinn (Eds.), *Positive organizational scholarship: Foundations of a new discipline* (pp. 48–65). San Francisco, CA: Berrett-Koehler Publishers Inc.

Cameron, K. S. (2008). Positively deviant organizational performance and the role of leadership values. *Journal of Values Based Leadership*, 1, 67–83.

Cameron, K. S. (2011). Virtuousness in organizations. In K. S. Cameron & G. M. Spreitzer (Eds.) *Oxford handbook of positive organizational scholarship.* New York, NY: Oxford University Press.

Cameron, K. S., Bright, D., & Caza, A. (2004). Exploring the relationships between organizational virtuousness and performance. *American Behavioral Scientist*, 47(6), 766–790.

Cameron, K. S., & Caza, A. (2002). Organizational and leadership virtues and the role of forgiveness. *Journal of Leadership and Organizational Studies*, 9(1), 33–48.

Cameron, K. S., Mora, C., Leutscher, T., & Calarco, M. (2011). Effects of positive practices on organizational effectiveness. *Journal of Applied Behavioral Science*, 47, 1–43.

Cawley, M. J., Martin, J. E., & Johnson, J. A. (2000). A virtues approach to personality. *Personality and Individual Differences*, 28, 997–1013.

Caza, A., Barker, B. A., & Cameron, K. S. (2004). Ethics and ethos: The buffering and amplifying effects of ethical behavior and virtuousness. *Journal of Business Ethics*, 52(2), 169–178.

Chapman, J. W., & Galston, W. A. (1992). *Virtue.* New York, NY: New York University Press.

Christakis, N. A., & Fowler, J. H. (2009). *Connected: The surprising power of our social networks and how they shape our lives.* New York, NY: Little, Brown and Company.

Chun, R. (2005). Ethical character and virtue of organizations: An empirical assessment and strategic implications. *Journal of Business Ethics*, 57(3), 269–284.

Cohen S. (2003). *The social environment and susceptibility to infectious disease.* Conference on The Role of Environmental Influences on Health and Performance: From Organism to Organization. University of Michigan, September.

Cohn, M. A., & Fredrickson, B. L. (2006). Beyond the moment, beyond the self: Shared ground between selective investment theory and the broaden-and-build theory of positive emotion. *Psychological Inquiry*, 17(1), 39–44.

Coleman, J. S. (1998). Social capital in the creation of human capital. *American Journal of Sociology*, 94, S95–S120.

Collins, R. L. (1996). For better or worse: The impact of upward social comparison on self-evaluations. *Psychological Bulletin, 119*(1), 51–69.

Comte-Sponville, A. (2001). *A small treatise on the great values.* New York, NY: Metropolitan Books.

Cooper, H., Okamura, L., & Gurka, V. (1992). Social activity and subjective well-being. *Personality and Individual Differences, 13,* 573–583.

D'Amato, M. R., & Jagoda, H. (1962). Effect of early exposure to photic stimulation on brightness discrimination and exploratory behavior. *Journal of Genetic Psychology, 101,* 267–271.

Davis, G. F. (2008). The rise and fall of finance and the end of the society of organizations. *Academy of Management Perspectives, 23,* 27–44.

Dent, N. (1984). *The moral psychology of the virtues.* New York, NY: Cambridge University Press.

Diener, E., Suh, E. M., Lucas, R. E., & Smith, H. L. (1999). Subjective well-being: Three decades of progress. *Psychological Bulletin, 125,* 276–302.

Dienstbier, R. A., & Zillig, L. M. P. (2002). Toughness. In C. R. Snyder & S. J. Lopez (Eds.), *Handbook of positive psychology* (pp. 515–527). New York, NY: Oxford University Press.

Donovan, M. A. (2000). Cognitive, affective, and satisfaction variables as predictors of organizational behaviors: A structural equation modeling examination of alternative models. *Dissertation Abstracts International, 60* (9-B), 4943. (UMI #AA19944835).

Drexelius, J. (2009). *The heliotropium, or conformity of the human will to the divine* (R. N. Shutte, Trans.). New York, NY: The Devin-Adair Company. (Original work published 1627).

Dutton, J. E. (2003). *Energize your workplace.* San Francisco, CA: Jossey-Bass.

Dutton, J. E., Frost, P. J., Worline, M. C., Lilius, J. M., & Kanov, J. M. (2002). Leading in times of trauma. *Harvard Business Review, January,* 54–61.

Dutton, J. E., & Heaphy, E. D. (2003). The power of high-quality connections. In K. Cameron, J. E. Dutton, & R. E. Quinn (Eds.). *Positive organizational scholarship: Foundations of a new discipline* (pp. 263–278). San Francisco, CA: Berrett-Koehler Publishers Inc.

Dutton, J. E., Worline, M. C., Frost, P. J., & Lilius, J. (2006). Explaining compassion organizing. *Administrative Science Quarterly, 51*(1), 59–96.

Dutton, J. E., & Sonenshein, S. (2007). Positive organizational scholarship. In S. Lopez & A. Beauchamps (Eds.), *Encyclopedia of positive psychology* (pp. 732–747). Malden, MA: Blackwell Publishing.

Emmons, R. A. (1999). *The psychology of ultimate concerns: Motivation and spirituality in personality.* New York, NY: Guilford Press.

Erdelyi, E. H. (1974). A new look at a new look: Perceptual defense and vigilance. *Psychological Review, 81,* 1–25.

Erhard-Seibold, E. V. (1937). The heliotrope tradition. *Orisis, 3,* 22–46.

Festinger, L. (1954). A theory of social comparison processes. *Human Relations, 7,* 117–140.

Fineman, S. (1996). Emotion and organizing. In S. R. Clegg, C. Hardy, & W. R. Nord (Eds.), *Handbook of organizational studies* (pp. 543–564). London, UK: Sage.

Fisher, C. D. (2011). Happiness at work. *International Journal of Management Reviews, 12,* 384–412.

Foster, J. B., Hebl, M. R., West, M., & Dawson, J. (2004). *Setting the tone for organizational success: The impact of CEO affect on organizational climate and firm-level outcomes.* Paper presented at the 17th annual meeting of the Society for Industrial and Organizational Psychology, Toronto, Canada.

Fredrickson, B. L. (1998). What good are positive emotions? *Review of General Psychology, 2,* 300–319.

Fredrickson, B. L. (2001). The role of positive emotions in positive psychology: The broaden-and-build theory of positive emotions. *American Psychologist*, 56, 218–226.

Fredrickson, B. L. (2003). Positive emotions and upward spirals in organizations. In K. S. Cameron, J. E. Dutton, & R. E. Quinn (Eds.), *Positive organizational scholarship: Foundations of a new discipline* (pp. 163–175). San Francisco, CA: Berrett-Koehler Publishers Inc.

Fredrickson, B. L. (2009). *Positivity*. New York, NY: Crown.

Fry, L. W., Keim, G. D., & Meiners, R. E. (1982). Corporate contributions: Altruistic or for-profit? *Academy of Management Review*, 25, 94–106.

Fry, L. W., Vitucci, S., & Cedillo, M. (2005). Spiritual leadership and army transformation: Theory, measurement, and establishing a baseline. *Leadership Quarterly*, 16, 835–862.

George, J. M. (1998). Salesperson mood at work: Implications for helping customers. *Journal of Personal Selling and Sales Management*, 18, 23–30.

George, J. M. (1991). State or trait: Effects of positive mood on prosocial behaviors at work. *Journal of Applied Psychology*, 76, 229–307.

George, J. M. (1995). Leader positive mood and group performance: The case of customer service. *Journal of Applied Social Psychology*, 25, 778–794.

Gergen, K. J. (1999). *An invitation to social constructionism*. London, UK: Sage.

Giacalone, R., & Promislo, M. (2010). Unethical and unwell: Decrements in well-being and unethical activity at work. *Journal of Business Ethics*, 91(2), 275–297.

Giacalone, R. A., Paul, K., & Jurkiewicz, C. L. (2005). A preliminary investigation into the role of positive psychology in consumer sensitivity to corporate social performance. *Journal of Business Ethics*, 58(4), 295–305.

Gittell, J. H., Cameron, K., Lim, S., & Rivas, V. (2006). Relationships, layoffs, and organizational resilience: Airline industry responses to September 11. *Journal of Applied Behavioral Science*, 42(3), 300–329.

Gladwell, M. (2002). *The tipping point. How little things can make a big difference*. New York, NY: Little, Brown and Company.

Gouldner, A. (1960). The norm of reciprocity: A preliminary statement. *American Sociological Review*, 25, 161–179.

Grant, A. M., Campbell, E. M., Chen, G., Cottone, K., Lapedis, D., & Lee, K. (2007). Impact and the art of motivation maintenance: The effects of contact with beneficiaries on persistent behavior. *Organizational Behavior and Decision Processes*, 103, 53–67.

Handelsman, M. M., Knapp, S., & Gottlieb, M. C. (2002). Positive ethics. In C. R. Snyder, & S. J. Lopez (Eds.), *Handbook of positive psychology* (pp. 731–744). New York, NY: Oxford University Press.

Harker, L. A., & Keltner, D. (2001). Expressions of positive emotion in women's college yearbook pictures and their relationship to personality and life outcomes across adulthood. *Journal of Personality and Social Psychology*, 80, 112–124.

Harter, J. K., Schmidt, F. L., & Keyes, C. L. M. (2002). Well-being in the workplace and its relationship to business outcomes: A review of the Gallup studies. In C. L. Keyes & J. Haidt (Eds.), *Flourishing: The positive person and the group life* (pp. 205–224). Washington DC: American Psychological Association.

Ilies, R., Nahrgang, J. D., & Morgeson, F. O. (2007). Leader-member exchange and citizenship behaviors: A meta-analysis. *Journal of Applied Psychology*, 92, 269–277.

Jensen, M. C. (2002). Value maximization, stakeholder theory and the corporate objective function. *Business Ethics Quarterly*, 12, 235–256.

Johnson, K. J., Waugh, C. E., & Fredrickson, B. L. (2010). Smile to see the forest: Facially expressed positive emotions broaden cognition. *Cognition & Emotion*, 24(2), 299–321.

Jundt, D., & Hinsz, V. B. (2001). *Are happier workers more productive workers? The impact of mood on self-set goals, self-efficacy, and task performance.* Paper presented at the annual meeting of the American Psychological Association, Chicago.

Kaplan J. (2003). *Status, stress, and atherosclerosis: The role of environment and individual behavior.* Conference on The Role of Environmental Influences on Health and Performance: From Organism to Organization. University of Michigan, September.

Kellett, J. B., Humphrey, R. H., & Sleeth, R. G. (2006). Empathy and the emergence of task and relations leaders. *Leadership Quarterly, 17*(2), 146–162.

Kesebir, P., & Diener, E. (2008). In pursuit of happiness: Empirical answers to philosophical questions. *Perspectives on Psychological Science, 3*(2), 117–125.

Kiecolt-Glaser, J. (2003). *The effect of environmental factors on health: Wound healing as a model.* Conference on The Role of Environmental Influences on Health and Performance: From Organism to Organization. University of Michigan, September.

Kok, B. E., & Fredrickson, B. L. (2010). Upward spirals of the heart: Autonomic flexibility, as indexed by vagal tone, reciprocally and prospectively predicts positive emotions and social connectedness. *Biological Psychology, 85*, 432–436.

Korten, D. C. (2001). *When corporations rule the world.* San Francisco, CA: Berrett Koehler.

Koys, D. J. (2001). The effects of employee satisfaction, organizational citizenship behavior, and turnover on organizational effectiveness. *Personnel Psychology, 54*, 101–114.

Krebs, D. (1987). The challenge of altruism in biology and psychology. In C. Crawford, M. Smith, & D. Krebs (Eds.), *Sociobiology and psychology* (pp. 81–118). Hillsdale, NJ: Lawrence Erlbaum Associates.

Kristjansson, K. (2010). Positive psychology, happiness, and virtue: The troublesome conceptual issues. *Review of General Psychology, 14*, 296–310.

Lawrence, P. R., & Nohria, N. (2002) *Driven: How human nature shapes our choices.* San Francisco, CA: Jossey Bass.

Leana, C. R., & Van Buren, H. J. I. (1999). Organizational social capital and employment practices. *Academy of Management Review, 24*(3), 538–555.

Luthans, F., Avolio, B. J., Avey, J. B., & Norman, S. M. (2007). Positive psychological capital: Measurement and relationship with performance and satisfaction. *Personnel Psychology, 60*(3), 541–572.

Lyubomirsky, S., King, L., & Diener, E. (2005). The benefits of frequent positive affect: Does happiness lead to success? *Psychological Bulletin, 131*(6), 803–855.

MacIntyre, A. (1984). *After virtue: A study in moral theory* (2nd ed.). Notre Dame, IN: University of Notre Dame Press.

Masten, A. S., Hubbard, J. J., Gest, S. D., Tellegen, A., Garmezy, N., & Ramirez, M. (1999). Competence in the context of adversity: Pathways to resilience and maladaptation from childhood to late adolescence. *Development and Psychopathology, 11*, 143–169.

McCubbin, P. H. I., Thompson, D. E. A., Thompson, D. A. I., & Fromer, D. J. E. (1998). *Stress, coping, and health in families: Sense of coherence and resiliency.* Thousand Oaks, CA: Sage Publications, Inc.

McCullough, M. E., Pargament, K. I., & Thoreson, C. (2000). *Forgiveness: Theory, research, and practice.* New York, NY: Guilford.

McLean, B., & Elkind, P. (2003). *The smartest guys in the room.* New York, NY: Penguin.

McNeeley, B. L., & Meglino, B. M. (1994). The role of dispositional and situational antecedents in prosocial organizational behavior: An examination of the intended beneficiaries of prosocial behavior. *Journal of Applied Psychology, 79*, 836–844.

Merton, R. K. (1968). *Social organization and social structure*. New York, NY: Free Press.
Moore, C., & Richardson, J. J. (1988). The politics and practice of corporate responsibility is Great Britain. *Research in Corporate Social Performance and Policy*, 10, 267–290.
Mrosovsky, N., & Kingsmill, S. F. (1985). How turtles find the sea. *Zeitschrift Fur Tierpsychologie-Journal of Comparative Ethology*, 67(1–4), 237–256.
Nahapiet, J., & Ghoshal, S. (1988). Social capital, intellectual capital, and the organizational advantage. *Academy of Management Review*, 23, 242–266.
O'Donohoe, S., & Turley, D. (2006). Compassion at the counter: Service providers and bereaved consumers. *Human Relations*, 59(10), 1429–1448.
Orlikowski, W. J. (2000). Using technology and constituting structures: A practice lens for studying technology in organizations. *Organization Science*, 11(4), 404–428.
Peterson, C., & Bossio, L. M. (1991). *Health and optimism*. New York, NY: Free Press.
Peterson, C., & Seligman, M. E. P. (2004). *Character strengths and virtues: A handbook and classification*. New York, NY: Oxford University Press.
Philips, D. L. (1967). Mental health status, social participation, and happiness. *Journal of Health and Social Behavior*, 8, 285–291.
Piliavin, J. A., & Charng, H. (1990). Altruism: A review of recent theory and research. *Annual Review of Sociology*, 16(1), 27–65.
Podsakoff, P. M., MacKenzie, S. B., Paine, J. B., & Bachrach, D. G. (2000). Organizational citizenship behaviors: A critical review of the theoretical and empirical literature and suggestions for future research. *Journal of Management*, 26(3), 513–563.
Powley, E., & Cameron, K. S. (2006). Organizational healing: Lived virtuousness amidst organizational crisis. *Journal of Management, Spirituality and Religion*, 3, 13–33.
Rawls, J. (1971). *A theory of justice*. Cambridge, MA: Harvard University Press.
Sánchez, C. M. (2000). Motives for corporate philanthropy in El Salvador: Altruism and political legitimacy. *Journal of Business Ethics*, 27, 363–375.
Sandage, S. J., & Hill, P. C. (2001). The virtues of positive psychology: The rapprochement and challenges of an affirmative postmodern perspective. *Journal for the Theory of Social Behaviour*, 31(3), 241–260.
Schudt, K. (2000). Taming the corporate monster: An Aristotelian approach to corporate virtues. *Business Ethics Quarterly*, 10, 711–723.
Seligman, M. E. P. (2002). *Authentic happiness: Using the new positive psychology to realize your potential for lasting fulfillment*. New York, NY: Free Press.
Seligman, M. E. P., & Csikszentmihalyi, M. (2000). Positive psychology: An introduction. *American Psychologist*, 55, 5–14.
Seligman, M. E. P., Schulman, B. S., DeRubeis, R. J., & Hollon, S. D. (1999). The prevention of depression and anxiety. *Prevention and Treatment*, 2, Article ID 8a.
Sethi, R., & Nicholson, C. Y. (2001). Structural and contextual correlates of charged behavior in product development teams. *Journal of Product Innovation Management*, 18(3), 154–168.
Sharot, T., Riccardi, A. M., Raio, C. M., & Phelps, E. A. (2007). Neural mechanisms mediating optimism bias. *Nature*, 450, 102–106.
Sheldon, K.M., & Elliot, A.J. (1999). Goal striving, need satisfaction, and longitudinal well-being: The self-concordance model. *Journal of Personality and Social Psychology*, 76, 482–497.
Skinner, B. F. (1965). *Science and human behavior*. New York, NY: Free Press.
Smith, J. C., & Baker, H. D. (1960). Conditioning in the horseshoe crab. *Journal of Comparative and Physiological Psychology*, 53, 279–281.

Snyder C. R. (1994). *The psychol...  ...e.* New York, NY: Free Press.
Staw, B. M., & Barsade, S. G., ... ...nd managerial performance: A test of the sadder-but-wiser versus happi... ...theses. *Administrative Science Quarterly, 38,* 304–331.
Staw, B. M., Sutton, ... ...loyee positive emotion and favorable outcomes at the...
Sternberg, J. J. ... ...*General Psychology, 2,* 347–365.
Stinnett, N.,... ...MA: Little Brown & Co.
Sutcliffe, ... ...S. Cameron, J. E. Dutton, & R... ...s of a new discipline (pp. 94...
Tangney, J. P., ... ...behavior. *Annual Review of Psyc...*
Tutu, D. (1999). *No fu... ...y.*
Unkelbach, C., Fiedler, ... ...D. (2008). Why positive information is processed ... ...nal of Personality and Social Psychology, 95,* 36–49.
Van Katwyk, P.T., Fox, S., Spector, P... ...00). Using the job-related affective well-being scale to investigate affect... ...ork stressors. *Journal of Occupational Health Psychology, 52,* 219–230.
Vannette, D., & Cameron, K.S. (2008). *Imp... ...ting positive organizational scholarship at Prudential.* Ross School of Business, University of Michigan. Distributed by the William Davidson Institute.
Walsh, F. (2006). *Strengthening family resilience.* New York, NY: Guilford Press.
Walz, S. M., & Niehoff, B. P. (2000). Organizational citizenship behaviors: Their relationship to organizational effectiveness. *Journal of Hospitality and Tourism Research, 24,* 301–319.
Warr, P. (2007). *Work, happiness, and unhappiness.* Mahwah, NJ: Lawrence Erlbaum.
Weick, K. E. (1999) *The social psychology of organizing.* Reading, MA: Addison-Wesley.
Weick, K. E., Sutcliffe, K. M., & Obstfeld, D. (1999). Organizing for high reliability: Processes of collective mindfulness. In B. M. Staw & R. I. Sutton (Eds.), *Research in Organizational Behavior* (pp. 81–123). Stamford, CT: JAI Press.
Weiner, N. O. (1993). *The harmony of the soul: Mental health and moral virtue reconsidered.* Albany, NY: State University of New York Press.
Wheeler, L., & Miyake, K. (1992). Social comparison in everyday life. *Journal of Personality and Social Psychology, 62*(5), 760–773.
Wildavsky, A. (1991). *Searching for safety.* New Brunswick, NJ: Transaction Books.
Worline, M. C., Dutton, J. E., Frost, P. J., Kanov, J., Lilius, J., & Maitlis, S. (2003). *Creating fertile soil: The organizing dynamics of resilience.* Working paper, University of Michigan School of Business.

# CHAPTER 52

# HOW WORK SHAPES WELL-BEING

BRIANNA BARKER CAZA[1] AND
AMY WRZESNIEWSKI[2]

[1]Wake Forest University, USA; [2]Yale School of Management, USA

> There is work that is work and there is play that is play; there is play that is work and work that is play. And in only one of these lies happiness.
>
> (Gelett Burgess)

WORK has long held a significant role in people's lives (Ciulla, 2000; Gini, 2001; Kohn & Schooler, 1982; Rosso, Dekas, & Wrzesniewski, 2010). This is, in part, because of the ways in which work influences well-being. In much of the developmental lifecycle people are likely to be engaged in varied, rich, and complex relationships with the world of work—whether preparing for it, entering into it, or contemplating their exit from it (Erikson, 1968). For example, at the tender age of 5, children have a working practical model of what work is and what role they expect it to play in their life (Berti & Bombi, 1988). In childhood, work is often idealized as children dream about what they may become. Upon entering the work force, many find that the realities of working life lead them to reconceptualize work as simply a way of meeting their needs (Brief & Aldag, 1989; Brief & Atieh, 1987; Brief, Brett, Futter, & Stein, 1997). Early career professionals may find that they thrive on the challenge and excitement of work. New parents learn about both the value and cost of their jobs to their families. After retirement, some retirees struggle to reconstruct their lives in the absence of the structure that work provides. While some people find deep fulfillment in their work, others feel a strong disdain for it, and still others find their relationship with their work vacillating over time and contexts. Though the meaning of work varies widely, that it has an impact on people's lives is well-established (Campbell, Converse, & Rodgers, 1976). In a variety of ways, work matters to everyone (Warr & Wall, 1975).

Work can be a source of sustenance, wealth, joy, frustration, deep meaningfulness, and boredom. In recognition that work is a domain of life that shapes how people experience their lives in a broad sense, scholars have invested considerable effort in understanding the relationship between work and well-being. While some have studied the impact of work on life domains such as family and leisure (e.g., Edwards & Rothbard, 2000; Greenhaus & Beutell, 1985; Rothbard, 2001), others have examined the role that these life domains play in the general experience of work (Snir & Harpaz, 2002). Though we touch on both literatures, we are primarily focused on understanding how work shapes well-being. First, we define well-being and explain why work has a hand in determining general well-being. Second, we explain how work shapes well-being, and what factors affect whether the relationship is generally positive or negative. In the third section we discuss the individual and contextual variables that may moderate the relationship between work and well-being.

## Defining Well-Being

Other chapters in this book have already provided an in-depth understanding of general well-being (see Section II). We will therefore only briefly review our conceptualization of well-being and the assumptions that underlie it. Well-being is often used synonymously with wellness, health, and happiness. While different types and domains of well-being have been proposed, in the research literature there has been convergence regarding three core dimensions of well-being: psychological, physical, and social (Diener & Seligman, 2004). Further, while researchers have studied both objective and subjective indicators of well-being, in this chapter, we are focusing on the latter. Subjective well-being (SWB) is defined as a "broad category of phenomena that includes people's emotional responses, domain satisfactions, and global judgments of life satisfaction" (Diener, Suh, Lucas, & Smith, 1999, p. 277) and includes positive emotion, engagement, satisfaction, and meaning (Seligman, 2002). SWB refers to a set of constructs and experiences, rather than a single construct reflecting happiness or satisfaction (Myers & Diener, 1995; Ryff, 1989).

As Myers and Diener (1995) point out, high SWB reflects a "preponderance of positive thoughts and feelings about one's life" (p. 11) and includes a sense of satisfaction with life that comprises satisfaction with major life domains, including work, family, health, finances, and self. Lucas, Diener and Suh (1996) suggest that SWB has two facets, cognitive and affective SWB. The affective component of SWB consists of the presence of positive affect (e.g., joy, elation, happiness, and contentment) and the absence of negative affect (e.g., guilt, sadness, anxiety, anger) (Diener et al., 1999). The cognitive component is an information-based appraisal of life in which people judge the extent to which their life measures up to expectations and resembles their ideal. Cognitive evaluations of satisfaction with each domain of life and life as a whole play an important role in SWB.

Research shows that both cognitive and affective well-being are influenced by work, using various terms such as *employee well-being*, *working well-being*, and *work-related well-being* to refer to individual experiences of and functioning within the work domain. Many studies have defined well-being predominantly in terms of domain-specific satisfaction (i.e., job satisfaction; Weiss, 2002), while others have adopted a broader definition that encompasses the overall quality of functioning at work (Warr, 1987). In this chapter, we build upon and extend these literatures by considering how one's work experiences influence their generalized feelings and cognitions about life. We begin doing so in the next section by considering why work shapes well-being.

# The Influence of Work on Well-Being

Among the domains of life to which people dedicate their time and energy, work holds a special place. This is partly due to the sheer number of hours dedicated to it—most adults spend one-third of their waking lives working (Wrzesniewski, McCauley, Rozin, & Schwartz, 1997). Beyond the time invested in work, there are important economic (Brief & Aldag, 1989), social (Dutton & Ragins, 2006), and psychological (Rosso et al., 2010) functions of work that underscore the "central place that work plays in life and society" (Warr & Wall, 1975, p. 10). People experience significant ties to work, both physically and psychologically (Ciulla, 2000). It often determines where people live and even shapes what they do during non-working hours (Meissner, 1971). The way people think about themselves and feel about their lives is significantly impacted by their work for several reasons.

The first is the time devoted to work over the course of life. Most adults spend the bulk of their waking hours engaged in some form of work. This time commitment can lead to the blurring of boundaries between home and work, allowing individuals' feelings and thoughts about their work to spill over into other areas of life. Scholars have argued that these blurred boundaries have reshaped the nature of work itself (Arthur & Rousseau, 1996; Barley 1996; Bridges 1994). Work has largely retained its definition as activities done for pay (Brief & Nord, 1990), but the form, timing, and structural arrangements of these activities have undergone significant changes, particularly for knowledge workers (e.g., Arthur & Rousseau, 1996; Barley & Kunda, 2004; Wiesenfeld, Raghuram, & Garud, 1999). These changes to the nature of work serve to further blur the boundary between work and non-work domains for many knowledge workers, who are increasingly expected to work from any location at any time. While scholars have made several predictions about how these changes affect the nature of work (e.g., Schor, 1991; Sennett, 1998, 2008), the influence of these changes on well-being is not well understood.

Second, where people live (and how they live) depends in large part on where they work. While it used to be more common for people to find work in the local environment in which they lived, it is now the case that—particularly in the USA—increasing numbers of people move to locales based on their jobs (Blackburn, 2009; Sennett, 1998). Furthermore, the job often dictates the way in which people spend their days and nights, and the leisure time they have available. Adjusting to the demands of our society, many people do not work a traditional 9-5 job for 40 hours a week. Some employees take on positions in which they work nights, while others work for days, weeks, or even months without a break. As a result, work schedules significantly impact family life, hobbies, and even physical health.

It is not only the geography of life that is influenced by work: for most, the material trappings of life are dictated by the means that work provides. Mortgages, rent levels, forms of transportation, and creature comforts are largely a function of what one can afford—which is, in turn, a direct outcome of what one earns. The possibilities offered by one's work range from unsustainable (Leana, Mittal, & Stiehl, 2012) to luxurious. Work defines the mode of life experiences far beyond the physical realities of the job.

Third, people invest a significant amount of time in work even before they actually begin their jobs; work is typically a domain for which people prepare themselves for some time. While relatively few pursue the career of their childhood fantasies, it is assumed that most children will work when they complete their schooling. This assumption fuels investments in education and training in order to make the school-to-work transition a success. Whether educated in vocational-technical programs, colleges, or postgraduate university settings, most people grow up with the expectation that they will work in adulthood. As such, people make significant investments in what they do for a living even before they are working.

Fourth, people experience strong psychological ties to their work. People's sense of themselves is intimately connected to their work (Lawler & Hall, 1970). Consider the first things people tell others about themselves upon meeting at a party. Work, and in particular, the identity implications of work, are salient in how people come to think of themselves. Scholars suggest that this cognitive bond with work is increasing (Casey, 1995; Rosso et al., 2010; Sennett, 2008). For better or for worse, work is an important element of what defines people (Gini, 2001). This is true even in the most direct sense; research suggests that the kind of work people do influences their cognitive structures over time (Kohn & Schooler, 1982).

Fifth, work also helps satisfy many psychological needs for achievement and individual purpose (Warr & Wall, 1975). A sense of purpose in work is one of the ways in which work comes to be seen as meaningful (Rosso et al., 2010). Ryff (1989) defines purpose as a sense of directedness and intentionality in life, building on a tradition that suggests that pursuing a purpose in life or work, brings meaning to life (Aristotle, 2000; Dalai Lama & Cutler, 1998; Seligman, 2002). At the extreme end of this argument, Frankl (1959) has argued that having a sense of purpose in life is necessary for survival. For those who pursue their life's purpose through work (e.g., Bunderson & Thompson, 2009), the importance of work for a basic sense of well-being is indisputable.

Sixth, the social bonds of our lives are intimately connected to work. Whether others at work are friends, mentors, colleagues, or general acquaintances, research suggests that our sense of who we are is informed by the social landscape at work (Bradbury & Lichtenstein, 2000; Wrzesniewski, Dutton, & Debebe, 2003). It is telling that when offering depictions of their jobs, people often offer depictions of their work interactions and relationships instead (Sandelands & Boudens, 2000). The rootedness of social bonds at work is evidenced in part by the number and importance of celebrated social events that cross into the work domain. People come together with their work colleagues around hiring, promotions, retirements, and other markers of entry into, progress within, or exit from the work domain. That people experience strong social bonds at work is cause for celebration—the Gallup organization notes that having even one "best friend" at work is a predictor of positive well-being (Harter, Schmidt, & Keyes, 2003). However, if people make significant social investments at work, there exists the potential for conflict between the work and home domains. Considerable research on the conflict between work and home suggests that clarity in how one is investing one's time in social bonds and obligations between these two spheres is important.

Seventh, work influences well-being because it is a domain that is infused with affect. Whether in the context of the work itself (Hochschild, 1983; Margolis & Molinsky, 2008) or the interactions and relationships that compose the job (Dutton, 2003; Porath & Erez, 2007; Wrzesniewski et al., 2003), people experience a range of emotions of varying strength at work (Barsade, 2002; Bartel & Saavedra, 2000). To the extent that well-being is informed by affect, the sign and power of the charge left by one's work is an important component to understanding well-being. As Campbell and colleagues (1976) point out, 20% of the variance in overall well-being is explained by well-being related to one's work. When work is a source of joy, this bond between the self and work can be powerful and positive. As Maslow notes about his own work, "I think I am just most happy, and most fulfilled, and most myself, and most being as if that's where I were meant to be when I am involved in my work" (Frick, 1971, p. 31). Research on people's experience of the emotional spillover from work to other domains of life, such as family and leisure, suggests that whether work is a positive or negative experience matters for how people engage in and experience the non-work domains of life (Rothbard, 2001; Williams & Alliger, 1994).

This summary of research on the interface between the work and life domains suggests that any understanding of well-being must take into account the role of work in people's lives. Work shapes people's physical, emotional and cognitive experiences, influencing every aspect of life. Research on unemployment underscores the critical role of work for general well-being. Nationally, high levels of unemployment are a strong negative predictor of well-being (Frey & Stutzer, 2002a, 2002b). At the individual level, unemployment can be devastating to well-being (Helliwell, 2003). By studying what happens to people who have lost a job, Jahoda's (1982) influential work suggests that work fulfills both manifest and latent functions in life. In addition to enabling people to earn a living, work also provides a temporal structure to the day, allows people to participate in a collective effort, and gives them some measure of status and identity from their work roles. In the next section, we consider the direct pathways through which work shapes well-being.

# How Work Shapes Well-Being

Work influences well-being in three ways. First, from an economic perspective, the work contract affects well-being. Second, the work itself has psychological and physiological implications for well-being. Third, the work context influences well-being in a variety of ways. We take each kind of influence in turn, describing the evidence of its impact and the implications for its role in well-being.

## Work as a contract

In its most basic form, work is an exchange of effort for compensation. It is an essential means through which people meet their basic needs of shelter and food. Being able to meet these needs is essential for well-being. As such, economics plays an important role in shaping one's quality of life, in that the specific terms of the employment contract influence well-being. This influence operates in two ways: in a literal sense and in a psychological sense.

In the literal sense, the employment contract matters to well-being because it determines whether or not people are able to meet their basic needs and aspirations. A key element of the employment contract is pay. It is often assumed that the greater the pay, the greater the resulting well-being must be. In some of the world's poorest nations, this assumption holds, however the relationship becomes less strong as national wealth increases. In wealthy Western societies, research suggests that while income is positively correlated with well-being (Diener & Diener, 1995), the relationship is moderate, with correlations of only 0.13 (Diener, Sandvik, Seidlidz, & Diener, 1993). Some research has suggested that income is not related to emotional well-being at all (Kahneman & Deaton, 2010). Other evidence suggests that income may have a *negative* relationship with other life domains that influence well-being. Moreover, while the average salary in wealthy nations has grown steadily in the past 50 years, so have rates of anxiety and depression (Diener & Seligman, 2004). In light of this complex relationship Diener and Seligman (2004) explain that, "Money is an inexact surrogate for well-being, and the more prosperous a society becomes, the more inexact a surrogate income becomes" (p. 2). This research suggests that the context influences how people evaluate their own well-being. Those living in a modernized, wealthy society in which "the good life" is a cultural ideal will have very different standards and aspirations for well-being than will individuals living in poorer nations.

Well-being is also influenced by how people evaluate the fairness of their employment contracts. Assessments of fairness have three main roots: the distribution of resources (distributive justice), the fairness of decision-making procedures (procedural justice), and the type of interpersonal treatment a person receives (interactional justice) (Colquitt, Greenberg, & Zapata-Phelan, 2005). Given the focus of employment contracts on the relationship between effort, or inputs, and rewards, or outputs, perceptions of fairness in this exchange are important for well-being. Equity theory has demonstrated that people need to sense that their inputs are equal to their perceived outputs in order to feel fairly treated (Adams, 1965).

Perceptions of fairness in the work contract have been linked to employee well-being (Lawson, Noblet, & Rodwell, 2009). When employees feel that they are treated fairly they enjoy higher job satisfaction and better physical health, are more committed to and trusting of their organization, perform better, and engage in more voluntary citizenship behaviors (Colquitt, Conlon, Wesson, Porter, & Ng, 2001; Cropanzano, Bowen, & Gilliland, 2007; Liden, Wayne, Kraimer, & Sparrowe, 2003). Conversely, when employees perceive a lack of fairness, they experience poorer psychological and physical health (Caza & Cortina, 2008), highlighting another link between work and well-being.

## The work itself

Attributes of the work itself also influence well-being in both positive and negative ways (e.g., Bowling & Beehr, 2006; Harned, Ormerod, Palmieri, Collinsworth, & Reed, 2002; Maslach, 1982; Meyer & Allen, 1991). These effects can be generally understood through two established approaches to understanding subjective well-being: hedonic and eudaimonic traditions (Keyes, Shmotkin, & Ryff, 2002; Ryan & Deci, 2001). The hedonic tradition focuses on the experiences of happiness, while the eudaimonic tradition focuses on fulfillment and personal growth (Keyes et al., 2002). Viewed this way, hedonic approaches to understanding the influence of work on well-being focus on the relationship between the job itself and employees' experienced job satisfaction, defined as the subjective judgments employees make about their work situation (Locke, 1976). In contrast, eudaimonic approaches to understanding the influence of work on well-being focus on how work can shape perceptions of meaningfulness and fulfillment.

Several characteristics of work impact people's evaluations of their jobs, which spill over into perceptions of their lives. For instance, when people perceive their jobs as having high levels of autonomy, skill variety, task identity, and task significance, they experience increased well-being (Fried & Ferris, 1987; Hackman & Lawler, 1971). More recent research on job design suggests that well-being can be boosted through the reorganization of the work itself (see Grant, Christianson, & Price, 2007 for a review). The relationship between job characteristics and general well-being may be partially explained by job satisfaction. The more satisfied people are with their work, the more positive their satisfaction with life, a key component of well-being (Campbell et al., 1976; Rice, Near, & Hunt, 1980).

Other research suggests that over and above job satisfaction, the perceived meaningfulness of work will influence general well-being. Specifically, meaningful work has been linked with several key outcomes, including engagement (May, Gilson, & Harter, 2004), empowerment (Spreitzer, 1996), and personal fulfillment (Kahn, 2007).Work also affects well-being through its impact on how people perceive themselves in relation to their life's aspirations. To the extent that it provides people with a sense of challenge and accomplishment, work will positively influence well-being (Diener & Seligman, 2002).

Finally, the temporal structure of work may also influence well-being through both psychological and physiological means. Work is a primary source of structure for people's hours, days, and weeks. This can have a positive influence on well-being if the structure of work is compatible with people's non-work aspirations. For example, the routine of work provides a sense of control and structure, but can be problematic if it conflicts with other aspects of life. Work is especially problematic if it is non-traditional in form, such as with shift work. Over 20% of the population works nights, and while society has made adjustments to accommodate these individuals (e.g., 24-hour stores and gyms), there are several aspects of shift work that compromise their well-being. Research has linked shift work with increased work-to-family conflict and poorer physical and mental well-being (Barnes-Farrell et al., 2008; Driesen, Jansen, Kant, Mohren, & van Ameslvoort, 2010; Wilson, Chen, & Fernandes, 2007). The negative physical health effects appear to be linked to the development of circadian rhythm desynchronization, which results in sleep disturbances, gastrointestinal dysfunction, and a less effective immune system (LaDou, 1982). More recent research has shown that individual differences in internal time (chronotype) play a key role in people's ability to adjust to shift work, making it possible for some to avoid the more negative physiological effects of working at night (Kantermann, Juda, Vetter, Roenneberg, 2010).

The temporal structure of work may also affect the ability to engage in non-work activities. Non-work activities are an important way that people recover from work (Sonnentag, 2003). It is essential for people to recover from stresses and fatigue caused by work in order to maintain physical, social, and mental health (Rook & Zijstra, 2006). In particular, people whose jobs involve shift work or late nights may not have the same recreational or family opportunities as do those with more traditional jobs. As a result, shift workers experience reduced social opportunities and alienation from their communities (Rosenthal & Howe, 1984). These complications with other domains of life are likely to decrease general well-being.

## The work context

As described earlier, the economic results and content of work are critical inputs to well-being. However, the setting in which one works, whether the organization, the other people encountered in the course of the job, or the physical setting of work itself, also matters for well-being. Next, we describe the potential for these factors to influence well-being.

Most people who work do so in organizations. Whether employees work in offices, on the road, at home, or at client sites, the organizations that employ them can be significant sources of meaning in work (Rosso et al., 2010). Organizations provide employees with a social group to which they belong (Bartel & Dutton, 2001), which can help to address a basic human need for belongingness (Baumeister & Leary, 1995). Employees also benefit from their identification with their organizations and draw a sense of community from the bonds they experience with others there. In particular, Brickson (2005, 2007) points out that organizations themselves have identity orientations, and can be understood as individualistic, relational, or collectivistic in their identity and their approach to a variety of constituents, including employees. To the extent that employees feel their own identities are congruent with the identity orientation of their organization (i.e., individualistic, relational, or collectivistic) a sense of belongingness and well-being can result. And, of course, those who are members of organizations held in high esteem by the self and others experience benefits from their ability to experience that part of their identity that is defined by membership in the organization.

Within organizations, employees work together to achieve a variety of work goals. The opportunities people have to create meaningful relationships with those they work with represent one of the most salient ways in which organizations contribute to well-being. While relationships with others at work can range from positive and supportive (Dutton, 2003) to abusive (Tepper, 2000) and uncivil (Porath & Erez, 2007)—indeed, Hughes observed that those encountered at work "can do the most to make life sweet or sour" (1950, p. 321)—they represent important social ties that inform general well-being. Dutton (2003) has detailed the positive impact that high-quality connections at work can have on both employees and their organizations. Literature on social support has revealed the myriad benefits of relationships (or even interactions) with others that provide symbolic or concrete support (e.g., Cropanzano et al., 1997). Social support at work has emerged as a key variable for explaining positive outcomes for people at work (e.g., Randall, Cropanzano, Bormann, & Birjulin, 1999). Whether through the smallest glance or gesture or through powerful demonstrations of support, people encountered on the job give employees a variety of cues from which their understanding of how others see them, their job, and their role in the organization is composed (Wrzesniewski et al., 2003). Thus, to the extent that well-being is influenced by the nature of interactions and relationships with others, it is clear that work is a major arena of life in which others contribute to well-being.

The physical environment of work is another important input to well-being. The effect of the work environments on individuals' well-being begins with the safety and security of the workplace. In a basic sense, the physical environment at work must be safe and secure in order for employees to experience positive well-being (Barling & Frone, 2004). But more than guarantees of a work environment in which one need not worry about injuries, mishaps, or exposure to danger, it turns out that simple factors in the physical environment can make a significant difference to well-being.

For instance, the ways in which work environments are organized can influence employees' psychological and physical well-being. Specifically, whether work environments are set up to incorporate the outdoors and other aspects of nature can have a significant effect on general well-being. One of the most examined aspects of workplace design is the use of windows. Research suggests that windows are an essential element to well-being at work; 90% of employees who work in windowless offices are dissatisfied with their work environments, feel depressed, and lack stimulation (Ruys, 1970). Researchers have demonstrated that a window can help restore depleted attention processes (Kaplan & Kaplan, 1989) and balance hormone production and regulation (Kuller & Lindsten, 1992).

The effects of work on well-being vary widely, from an important and positive input to well-being to a source of negativity and dysfunction. We have considered some of the most important pathways through which work shapes well-being. Our treatment of work and well-being may seem to suggest that the effects of work on well-being are fixed across individuals. However, research suggests that people vary in their experience of the work they do in predictable ways, and that their general orientation toward work may predict how they feel about their work. In the following section, we consider the role of the individual as it moderates the relationship between work and well-being.

# Individual Patterns in the Experience of Work

For decades, scholars of organizations waged a debate over the question of whether the situation or the person mattered more in determining work attitudes and experience (e.g., Davis-Blake & Pfeffer, 1989; Staw, Bell, & Clausen, 1986). In the end, both sides won; scholars now (mostly) agree that the attributes of the situation matter—including the nature of the work itself, the organizational context, and people encountered on the job—*and* attributes of the person matter as well. Indeed, current research tends to account for and include both categories of inputs in order to reflect that both are likely to have an impact on the relationships being studied.

Past research has argued that attitudes toward work are determined in large part by stable individual differences such as personality (Alderfer, 1972; Staw et al., 1986). According to this view, individual factors like social class, demographic factors, and needs influence the experience of work. By marshaling research evidence across situations and time, there is stability in how individuals rate their well-being related to their work (Arvey, Bouchard, Segal, & Abraham, 1989; Staw et al., 1986), scholars have supported a view that underscores the importance of individual differences in shaping the experience of work.

More recently, research on work orientation (Wrzesniewski, 2003; Wrzesniewski et al., 1997) has suggested that people can experience their work in one of three ways: as a job, a career, or a calling (Bellah, Madsen, Sullivan, Swidler, & Tipton, 1985). Those with job orientations primarily view work as a means to a financial end, and work to support their lives outside of the job. In contrast, those with career orientations work primarily to advance in their occupation, whether within or between organizations, and to reap the benefits of the increased standing and power that comes with advancement. Finally, those with calling orientations work not for financial ends or for career advancement but for the fulfillment that the work itself brings them. Those with callings tend to view work as inseparable from the rest of their lives and feel that their work contributes to making the world a better place. Researchers have described callings as work that is one's duty and destiny (Bunderson & Thompson, 2009), a source of fulfillment that is important to one's identity (Berg, Grant, & Johnson, 2010; Wrzesniewski et al., 1997), a social contribution to the wider world (Wrzesniewski, 2003; Wrzesniewski et al., 1997), expressive of one's purpose (Hall & Chandler, 2005), and comprises one's passion, identity, urgency, engulfing consciousness, longevity, sense of meaning, and domain-specific self-esteem (Dobrow, 2006a).

Given the relationship between well-being and domain-specific and general satisfaction, work orientation matters for understanding well-being. While job and career orientations have been associated with lower levels of well-being on the job and off, calling orientation has emerged in a number of studies as a strong positive correlate of well-being. Research on work orientations suggests that they are associated with work and life satisfaction (Wrzesniewski et al., 1997). Several positive outcomes have been associated with having a calling, such as work, life, and health satisfaction (Dobrow, 2006a; Wrzesniewski et al., 1997) and lower absenteeism from work (Wrzesniewski et al., 1997). Callings have also been associated with more satisfaction from the work domain than other major life domains, such as leisure time (Wrzesniewski et al., 1997). People with callings have more passion for and enjoyment of their work (Novak, 1996; Vallerand et al., 2003), stronger identification and engagement with their work (Bunderson & Thompson, 2009; Dobrow, 2006a), and perform at higher levels than those without callings (Hall & Chandler, 2005).

A calling may even serve as a buffer against markers of negative functioning. Bunderson and Thompson (2009) describe research indicating that those with callings are less likely to suffer from stress, depression, and conflict between work and the rest of life (Oates, Hall, & Anderson, 2005; Treadgold, 1999). While most of the extant research seems to paint a positive picture of viewing work as a calling, researchers are beginning to assess drawbacks associated with callings (Bunderson & Thompson, 2009; Dobrow, 2006b). For example, Bunderson and Thompson (2009) suggest that a calling is a "double-edged sword" that involves profound experiences of sacrifice and vigilance among those who feel their work is a sacred duty they must perform. Callings also hold the possibility of leading to depletion and burnout when they become an all-consuming activity in life (Caza & Cardador, 2009; Maslach, Schaufeli, & Leiter, 2001).

Overall, it appears that work orientations offer a helpful window to understanding how people experience their work in ways that are likely to directly affect well-being, as well as interact with the likelihood that their job design and work contexts will promote well-being. Future research will likely explore how moderating factors such as work orientation may transform the relationship between inputs to the job and the experience of well-being that results. In the next section, we consider evidence of the positive and negative impact of work on well-being.

# The Helpful and Harmful Effects of Work on Well-Being

We began this chapter by describing seven reasons why work is an important factor in shaping well-being. We then went on to detail how the work contract, the work itself, and the work context influence well-being through their effects on psychological, physical, and social variables. Through this we have established that a variety of aspects of work influence well-being. Generally, many aspects of work seem to have a largely positive impact on well-being (e.g., increased meaningfulness), some have a largely negative impact on well-being (e.g., shiftwork), and still others have a complicated relationship with well-being (e.g., income). However, a variety of individual-level moderators are likely to influence the relationship between work and well-being. Additionally, there may also be broader temporal effects than those considered here. Specifically, the relationship between work and well-being may vary across the lifespan as the meaning of work shifts within the broader context of life.

A large literature on work-to-family conflict suggests that how people manage work and family roles has major implications for well-being, job performance, and family functioning (Gareis, Barnett, Ertel, & Berkman, 2009). Traditionally, the interface between work and family has been viewed in largely negative terms. While work provided people with the economic means to provide for their families, it also caused psychological and physical distance within families. For people who are trying to balance competing priorities of work and family life, a deficit-based perspective on work and family can be fairly troubling. Early research on work-family conflict has established that failure to balance competing priorities and demands can result in sacrificed well-being (Greenhaus & Beutell, 1985).

However, this relationship between work and family roles and well-being is not always negative (Rothbard, 2001). In fact, research has supported the concept of work–family enrichment, defined as the extent to which experiences in one role improve the quality of life in the other role (Greenhaus & Powell, 2006, p. 73). Toward this end, researchers have explored the ways that resources and experiences gained from one's work role can improve performance and quality of life in one's family role, and vice versa (Carlson, Kacmar, Wayne, & Grzywacz, 2006; Rothbard, 2001). Recent support for this argument comes from a rather unexpected population: new parents. Research with new working parents suggests that work remains an important influence on well-being even when life priorities are readjusted. Specifically, many new mothers decrease the number of hours they work (or stop working altogether) and many new fathers increase the number of hours they work, a trend that involves drawbacks (Keizer, Dykstra, & Poortman, 2010). It is this change in work hours that accounts in part for decreased partner satisfaction and increased negative affect—mothers who remained in their jobs or increased working hours showed decreased negative affect. These findings confirm that during critical family life transitions, when the work–family interface seems to have the most potential for conflict, work can provide important benefits that increase the quality of one's life.

## Conclusion and Future Directions

There are a number of important future research directions that hold promise for increasing understanding of the powerful and complex relationship between work and well-being. First, researchers can do more to explore the dynamic nature of the relationship between work and well-being. In this chapter, we have considered how a series of variables influence well-being. However, these variables do not exist in isolation; it is essential to understand how they interact to influence well-being. For instance, do aspects of a fair work contract mitigate the effects of a poor working environment? Does shift work dampen the effect of meaningful work on well-being? In general, how do the variables that contribute to increased or decreased well-being interact with one another in ways that suggest important information about their relative strength?

A second related research question is to understand how individuals and organizations can sustain a positive relationship between work and well-being over time. There are obviously many benefits to well-being for individuals, such as increased physical health and longevity (Diener et al., 1999), but there are also a number of benefits to organizations (Diener & Seligman, 2004). For instance, employee well-being is related to customer satisfaction and loyalty (Fleming, 2000; Harter, Schmidt & Hayes, 2002), and decreased turnover and shirking (Diener & Seligman, 2004). Thus, it is essential to better understand how to sustain positive spillovers of work to well-being.

However, sustaining a positive relationship between work and well-being over time may be difficult. Working life often spans several decades. As people move through their life trajectory, they may be looking for different things from their work. For example, young professionals gain materially from employment, but are likely to gain psychologically as well (Diener & Seligman, 2004). As young professionals make the transition into parenthood, the influence of work on well-being is likely to change. Work may become a place for adult connections, satisfaction, and feelings of competence and belongingness (Keizer et al., 2010). As people move into later stages of their careers, they may find that their well-being is more influenced by the ability to make contributions to others in their work and lives (Erikson, 1968). At any one stage, it seems that there is a potential for both positive and negative effects of work on well-being. It is important to understand how the influence of work on well-being waxes and wanes between being a positive or negative force in the various life-stages through which individuals work. Building from this, future research should explore the ways that people can shape their work to continually get positive benefits from it as the meaning of the work shifts throughout their lives.

## References

Adams, J. S. (1965). Inequity in social exchange. *Advances in Experimental Social Psychology*, 62, 335–343.

Alderfer, C. (1972). *Existence, relatedness, and growth*. New York, NY: Free Press.

Aristotle. (2000). *Nicomachean ethics* (R. Crisp, Trans.). Cambridge, UK: Cambridge University Press.

Arthur, M. B., & Rousseau, D. M. (1996). *The boundaryless career: A new employment principle for a new organizational era*. New York, NY: Oxford University Press.

Arvey, R. D., Bouchard, T. J., Segal, N. L., & Abraham, L. M. (1989). Job satisfaction: environmental and genetic components. *Journal of Applied Psychology*, 74, 187–192.

Barley, S. R. (1996). *The new world of work*. Washington, DC: National Planning Association.

Barley, S. R., & Kunda, G. (2004). *Gurus, hired guns and warm bodies: Itinerant experts in a knowledge economy*. Princeton, NJ: Princeton University Press.

Barling, J., & Frone, M. (Eds.). (2004). *The psychology of workplace safety*. Washington, DC: American Psychological Association.

Barnes-Farrell, J., Davies-Schrils, K., McGonagle, A., Walsh, B., Di Milia, L., Fischer, F. , … & Tepas, D. (2008). What aspects of shift work influence off-shift well-being of healthcare workers? *Applied Ergonomics*, 39, 589–596.

Barsade, S. (2002). The ripple effect: Emotional contagion and its influence on group behavior. *Administrative Science Quarterly*, 47, 644–675.

Bartel, C., & Dutton, J. (2001). Ambiguous organizational memberships: Constructing organizational identities in interactions with others. In M. Hogg & D.J. Jerry (Eds.), *Social identity processes in organizational contexts* (pp. 115–130). Philadelphia, PA: Psychology Press.

Bartel, C. A., & Saavedra, R. (2000). The collective construction of work group moods. *Administrative Science Quarterly 45*, 197–231.

Baumeister, R. F., & Leary, M. R. (1995). The need to belong: Desire for interpersonal attachments as a fundamental human motivation. *Psychological Bulletin, 117*(3), 497–529.

Bellah, R. N., Madsen, R., Sullivan, W. M., Swidler, A., & Tipton, S. M. (1985). *Habits of the heart.* Berkeley, CA: University of California Press.

Berg, J. M., Grant, A. M., & Johnson, V. (2010). When callings are calling: Crafting work and leisure in pursuit of unanswered occupational callings. *Organization Science, 21*, 973–994.

Berti, A. E., & Bombi, A. S. (1988). *The child's construction of economics.* Cambridge, MA: Cambridge University Press.

Blackburn, M. L. (2009). Internal migration and the earnings of married couples in the USA. *Journal of Economic Geography, 10*, 87–111.

Bowling, N. A., & Beehr, T. A. (2006). Workplace harassment from the victim's perspective: A theoretical model and meta-analysis. *Journal of Applied Psychology, 91*, 998–1012.

Bradbury, H., & Lichtenstein, B. M. B. (2000). Relationality in organizational research: Exploring the space between. *Organizational Science, 11*(5), 551–64.

Brickson, S. L. (2005). Organizational identity orientation: Forging a link between organizational identity and organizations' relations with stakeholders. *Administrative Science Quarterly, 50*, 576–609.

Brickson, S. L. (2007). Organizational identity orientation: The genesis of the role of the firm and distinct forms of social value. *Academy of Management Review, 32*(3), 864–888.

Bridges, W. (1994). *Job shift.* Reading, MA: Addison-Wesley Publishing.

Brief, A. P. (2008). *Money and the meaning of work.* Paper presented at the All-Academy Symposium: Changing the questions we ask: New directions in the meaning of work, Academy of Management Annual Meeting, Anaheim, CA.

Brief, A. P., & Aldag, R. J. (1989). The economic functions of work. In K. Rowland & G. R. Ferris (Eds.), *Research in personnel and human resources management.* Greenwich, CT: JAI Press.

Brief, A. P., & Atieh, J. M. (1987). Studying job stress: Are we making mountains out of molehills? *Journal of Occupational Behavior, 8*, 115–126.

Brief, A. P., Brett, J. F., Futter, D., & Stein, E. (1997). Feeling economically dependent on one's job: Its origins and functions with regard to worker well-being. *Journal of Applied Social Psychology, 27*, 1303–1307.

Brief, A. P., & Nord, W. R. (1990), *Meanings of occupational work.* Lexington, MA: Lexington Books.

Bunderson, J. S., & Thompson, J. A. (2009). The call of the wild: Zookeepers, callings, and the dual edges of deeply meaningful work. *Administrative Science Quarterly, 54*, 32–57.

Campbell, A., Converse, P. E., & Rodgers, W. L. (1976). *The quality of American life.* New York, NY: Russell Sage Foundation.

Carlson, D. S., Kacmar, M. K., Wayne, J. H., & Grzywacz, J. G. (2006). Measuring the positive side of the work-family interface: Development and validation of a work-family enrichment scale. *Journal of Vocational Behavior, 68*, 1, 131–164.

Casey, C. (1995). *Work, self and society: After industrialism.* London, UK: Routledge.

Caza, B. B., & Cardador, T. (2009). *Sustaining a calling orientation toward work: The case for healthy vs. unhealthy callings.* Paper presented at Academy of Management Meetings, Chicago, IL.

Caza, B. B., & Cortina, L. (2008). From insult to injury: Explaining the impact of incivility in social settings. *Basic and Applied Social Psychology, 29*(4), 335–350.

Ciulla, J. B. (2000). *The working life: The promise and betrayal of modern work*. New York, NY: Three Rivers Press.

Clydesdale, T. T. (1997). Family behaviors among early USA baby boomers: Exploring the effects of religion and income change, 1965–1982. *Social Forces, 76*, 605–635.

Colquitt, J. A., Conlon, D. E., Wesson, M. J., Porter, C. O. L. H., & Ng, K. Y. (2001). Justice at the millennium: A meta-analytic review of 25 years of organizational justice research. *Journal of Applied Psychology, 86*, 425–445.

Colquitt, J. A., Greenberg, J., & Zapata-Phelan, C. P. (2005). What is organizational justice? A historical overview. In J. Greenberg & J. A. Colquitt (Eds.), *The handbook of organizational justice* (pp. 3–56). Mahwah, NJ: Erlbaum.

Cropanzano, R., Bowen, D. E., & Gilliland, S. W. (2007). The management of organizational justice. *Academy of Management Perspectives, 21*(4), 34–48.

Cropanzano, R., Howes, J. C., Grandey, A. A., & Toth, P. (1997). The relationship of organizational politics and support to work behaviors, attitudes, and stress. *Journal of Organizational Behavior, 18*, 159–180.

Dalai Lama, & Cutler, H. C. (1998). *The art of happiness: A handbook for living*. London, UK: Hodder & Stoughton.

Davis-Blake, A., & Pfeffer, J. (1989). Just a mirage: The search for dispositional effects in organizational research, *Academy of Management Review, 15*, 385–400.

Diener, E., & Diener, M. (1995). Cross-cultural correlates of life satisfaction and self-esteem. *Journal of Personality and Social Psychology, 68*, 653–663.

Diener, E., Sandvik, E., Seidlitz, L., & Diener, M. (1993). The relationship between income and subjective well-being: Relative or absolute? *Social Indicators Research, 28*, 195–223.

Diener, E., & Seligman, M. E. P. (2002). Very happy people. *Psychological Science, 13*(1), 81–84.

Diener, E., & Seligman, M. E. P. (2004). Beyond money: Toward an economy of well-being. *Psychological Science in the Public Interest, 5*(1), 1–31.

Diener, E., Suh, E. M., Lucas, R. E., & Smith, H. E. (1999). Subjective well-being: Three decades of progress. *Psychological Bulletin, 125*, 276–302.

Dobrow, S. R. (2006a). *Having a calling: A longitudinal study of young musicians*. Doctoral dissertation, Harvard University.

Dobrow, S. R. (2006b). *The dark side of calling: Career tunnel vision*. Paper presented at the Academy of Management Annual Meeting, Atlanta, GA.

Driesen, K., Jansen, N. W. H., Kant, I., Mohren, D., & van Ameslvoort, L. G. P. M. (2010). Depressed mood in the working population: Associations with work schedules and working hours. *Chronobiology International, 27*(5), 1062–1079.

Dutton, J. E. (2003). *Energize your workplace: How to build and sustain high-quality connections at work*. San Francisco, CA: Jossey-Bass Publishers.

Dutton, J. E., & Ragins, B. R. (Eds.). (2006). *Exploring positive relationships at work: Building a theoretical and research foundation*. Mahwah, NJ: Lawrence Erlbaum Associates, Inc.

Edwards, J. R., & Rothbard, N. P. (2000). Mechanisms linking work and family: Clarifying the relationship between work and family constructs. *Academy of Management Review, 25*, 178–199.

Erikson, E. H. (1968). *Identity, youth and crisis*. New York, NY: Norton.

Fleming, J. H. (2000). Relating employee engagement and customer loyalty to business outcomes in the retail industry. *The Gallup Research Journal, 3*(1), 103–115.

Frankl, V. E. (1959). *Man's search for meaning*. Boston, MA: Beacon Press.

Fried, Y., & Ferris, G. R. (1987). The validity of the job characteristics model: A review and meta-analysis. *Personnel Psychology, 40*, 287–322.

Frey, B. S., & Stutzer, A. (2002a). *Happiness and economics: How the economy and institutions affect well-being.* Princeton, NJ: Princeton University Press.

Frey, B. S., & Stutzer, A. (2002b). What can economists learn from happiness research? *Journal of Economic Literature, 40*(2), 402–435.

Frick, W. B. (1971). *Humanistic psychology: Interviews with Maslow, Murphy, and Rogers.* Columbus, OH: Merrill.

Gareis, K. C., Barnett, R. C., Ertel, K. A., & Berkman, L. F. (2009) Work-family enrichment and conflict: Additive effects, buffering, or balance? *Journal of Marriage and Family, 71*, 696–707.

Gini, A. 2001. *My job, my self: Work and the creation of the modern individual.* New York, NY: Routledge.

Grant, A. M., Christianson, M. K., & Price, R. H. (2007). Happiness, health, or relationships? Managerial practices and employee well-being tradeoffs. *Academy of Management Perspectives, 21*, 51–63.

Greenhaus, J. H., & Beutell, N. J. (1985). Sources of conflict between work and family roles. *Academy of Management Review, 10*, 76–88.

Greenhaus, J. H., & Powell, G. N. (2006). When work and family are allies: A theory of work-family enrichment. *Academy of Management Review, 31*, 72–92.

Hackman, R. J., & Lawler, E. E. (1971). Employee reactions to job characteristics. *Journal of Applied Psychology, 55*, 259–286.

Hall, D. T., & Chandler, D. E. (2005). Psychological success: When the career is a calling. *Journal of Organizational Behavior, 26*, 155–176.

Harned, M. S., Ormerod, A. J., Palmieri, P. A., Collinsworth, L. L., & Reed, M. (2002). Sexual assault by workplace personnel and other types of sexual harassment: A comparison of antecedents and consequences. *Journal of Occupational Health Psychology, 7*, 174–188.

Harter, J. K., Schmidt, F. L., & Hayes, T. L. (2002). Business-unit-level relationship between employee satisfaction, employee engagement, and business outcomes: A meta-analysis. *Journal of Applied Psychology, 87*, 268–279.

Harter, J. K., Schmidt, F. L., & Keyes, C. L. M. (2003). Well-being in the workplace and its relationship to business outcomes: A review of the Gallup studies. In C. L. M. Keyes & J. Haidt (Eds.), *Flourishing: Positive psychology and the life well lived* (pp. 205–224). Washington, DC: American Psychological Association.

Helliwell, J. (2003). How's life? Combining individual and national variables to explain subjective well-being. *Economic Modelling, 20*(2), 331–360.

Hochschild, A. R. (1983). *The managed heart: Commercialization of human feelings.* Berkeley, CA: University of California Press.

Hughes, E. C. (1950). Work and the self. In J. H. Rohrer & M. Sherif (Eds.), *Social psychology at the crossroads* (pp. 313–323). New York, NY: Harper.

Jahoda, M. (1982). *Employment & unemployment: A social-psychological analysis.* New York, NY: Cambridge University Press.

Kahn, W. A. (2007). Meaningful connections: Positive relationships and attachments at work. In J. E. Dutton & B. R. Ragins (Eds.), *Exploring positive relationships at work: Building a theoretical and research foundation.* (pp. 189–206). Mahwah, NJ: Lawrence Erlbaum Associates.

Kahneman, D., & Deaton, A. (2010). High income improves evaluation of life but not emotional well-being. *Proceedings of the National Academy of Sciences of the United States of America. 107*(38), 16489–16493.

Kantermann, T., Juda, M., Vetter, C., & Roenneberg, T. (2010). Shift-work research: Where do we stand, where should we go? *Sleep and Biological Rhythms, 8*(2), 95–105.

Kaplan, R., & Kaplan, S. (1989). *The experience of nature: A psychological perspective*. New York, NY: Cambridge University Press.

Keizer, R., Dykstra, P., & Poortman, A. (2010). The transition to parenthood and well-being: The impact of partner status and work hour transitions. *Journal of Family Psychology*, 24(4), 429–438.

Keyes, C. L. M., Shmotkin, D., & Ryff, C. D. (2002). Optimizing well-being: The empirical encounter of two traditions. *Journal of Personality and Social Psychology*, 82, 1007–1022.

Kohn, M. L., & Schooler, C. (1982). Job conditions and personality: A longitudinal assessment of their reciprocal effects. *American Journal of Sociology*, 87(6), 1257–1286.

Kuller, R., & Lindsten, C. (1992). Health and behavior of children in classrooms with and without windows. *Journal of Environmental Psychology*, 12, 305–317.

LaDou, J. (1982). Health effects of shift work. *Western Journal of Medicine*, 137(6), 525–530.

Lawler, E. E. III, & Hall, D. T. (1970). Relationship of job characteristics to job involvement, satisfaction, and intrinsic motivation. *Journal of Applied Psychology*, 54, 305–312.

Lawson, K. J., Noblet, A. J., & Rodwell, J. J. (2009). Promoting health in the public sector: The relevance of organisational justice. *Health Promotion International*, 24(3), 223–233.

Leana, C., Mittal, V., & Stiehl, E. (2012). Organizational behavior and the working poor. *Journal Organization Science*, 23, 888–906.

Liden, R. C., Wayne, S. J., Kraimer, M. L., & Sparrowe, R. T. (2003). The dual commitments of contingent workers: An examination of contingents' commitment to the agency and the organization. *Journal of Organizational Behavior*, 24, 609–625.

Locke, E. A. (1976). The nature and causes of job satisfaction. In M. D. Dunnette (Ed.), *Handbook of industrial and organizational psychology* (pp. 1297–1349). Chicago, IL: Rand McNally.

Lucas, R. E., Diener, E., & Suh, E. (1996). Discriminant validity of well-being measures. *Journal of Personality and Social Psychology*, 71, 616–628.

Margolis, J. D., & Molinsky, A. L. (2008). Navigating the bind of necessary evils: Psychological engagement and the production of interpersonally sensitive behavior. *Academy of Management* Journal, 51, 847–872.

Maslach, C. (1982). *Burnout: The cost of caring*. New York, NY: Prentice-Hall.

Maslach, C., Schaufeli, W. B., & Leiter, M. P. (2001). Job burnout. *Annual Review of Psychology*, 52, 397–422.

May, D. R., Gilson, L., & Harter, L. M. (2004). The psychological conditions of meaningfulness, safety and availability and the engagement of the human spirit at work. *Journal of Occupational and Organizational Psychology*, 77, 11–37.

Meissner, M. (1971). The long arm of the job: A study of work and leisure. *Industrial Relations*, 10, 239–260.

Meyer, J. P., & Allen, N. J. (1991). A three component conceptualization of organizational commitment. *Human Resource Management Review*, 1, 61–89.

Novak, M. (1996). *Business as a calling: Work and the examined life*. New York, NY: The Free Press.

Myers, D. G., & Diener, E. (1995). Who is happy? *Psychological Science*, 6(1), 10–19.

Oates, K. L. M., Hall, M. E. L., & Anderson, T. L. (2005). Calling and conflict: A qualitative exploration of interrole conflict and the sanctification of work in Christian mothers in academia. *Journal of Psychology and Theology*, 33, 210–223.

Porath, C. L., & Erez, A. (2007). Does rudeness matter? The effects of rude behavior on task performance and helpfulness. *Academy of Management Journal*, 50, 1181–1197.

Randall, M. L., Cropanzano, R., Bormann, C. A., & Birjulin, A. (1999). Organizational politics and organizational support as predictors of work attitudes, job performance, and organizational citizenship behavior. *Journal of Organizational Behavior, 20*(2), 159–174.

Rice, R. W., Near, J. P., & Hunt, R. G. (1980). The job satisfaction/life satisfaction relationship: A review of empirical research. *Basic and Applied Social Psychology, 1*, 37–64.

Rook, J., & Zijlstra, F. (2006). The contribution of various types of activities to recovery. *European Journal of Work and Organizational Psychology, 15*(2), 218–240.

Rosso, B. D., Dekas, K. H., & Wrzesniewski, A. (2010). On the meaning of work: A theoretical integration and review. *Research in Organizational Behavior, 30*, 91–127.

Rosenthal, L., & Howe, M. (1984). Activity patterns and leisure concepts: A comparison of temporal adaptation among day versus night shift workers. *Occupational Therapy in Mental Health, 4*(2), 59–78.

Rothbard, N. P. (2001). Enriching or depleting? The dynamics of engagement in work and family roles. *Administrative Science Quarterly, 46*, 655–684.

Ruys, D. (1970). *Windowless offices*. Unpublished master's thesis, University of Washington, Seattle, Washington.

Ryan, R. M., & Deci, E. L. 2001. On happiness and human potentials: A review of research on hedonic and eudaimonic well-being. In S. Fiske (Ed.), *Annual review of psychology, 52*, 141–166. Palo Alto, CA: Annual Reviews, Inc.

Ryff, C. (1989). Happiness is everything, or is it? Explorations on the meaning of psychological well being. *Journal of Personality and Social Psychology, 57*, 1069–1081.

Sandelands, L. E., & Boudens, C. J. (2000). Feelings at work, emotions in organizations. In S. Fineman (Ed.), *Emotions in organizations* (2nd ed., pp. 46–63). London, UK: Sage.

Schor, J. B. (1991). *The overworked American*. New York, NY: Basic Books.

Seligman, M. E. P. (2002). *Authentic happiness*. New York, NY: Free Press.

Sennett, R. (1998). *The corrosion of character: The personal consequences of work in the new capitalism*. New York, NY: W.W. Norton & Company.

Sennett, R. (2008). *The craftsman*. New Haven, CT: Yale University Press.

Sonnentag, S. (2003). Recovery, work engagement, and proactive behavior: A new look at the interface between work and non-work. *Journal of Applied Psychology, 88*, 518–528.

Snir, R., & Harpaz, I. (2002). Work-leisure relations: Leisure orientation and the meaning of work. *Journal of Leisure Research, 34*(2), 178–203.

Spreitzer, G. M. (1996). Social structural characteristics of psychological empowerment. *Academy of Management Journal, 39*(2), 483–504.

Staw, B. M., Bell, N. E., & Clausen, J. A. (1986). The dispositional approach to job attitudes: A lifetime longitudinal test. *Administrative Science Quarterly, 31*, 56–77.

Tepper, B. J. (2000). Consequences of abusive supervision. *Academy of Management Journal, 43*, 178–190.

Treadgold, R. (1999). Transcendent vocations: Their relationship to stress, depression, and clarity of self-concept. *Journal of Humanistic Psychology, 39*, 81–105.

Vallerand, R. J., Blanchard, C., Mageau, G. A., Koestner, R., Ratelle, C., Léonard, M., … & Marsolais, J. (2003). Les passions de l'ame: On obsessive and harmonious passion. *Journal of Personality and Social Psychology, 85*(4), 756–767.

Warr, P. B. (1987). *Work, unemployment, and mental health*. Oxford, UK: Clarendon Press.

Warr, P. B., & Wall, T. D. (1975). *Work and well-being*. Harmondsworth, UK: Penguin.

Weiss, H. M. (2002). Deconstructing job satisfaction: Separating evaluations, beliefs and affective experiences. *Human Resource Management Review, 12*, 173–194.

Wiesenfeld, B. M., Raghuram, S., & Garud, R. (1999). Communication patterns as determinants of organizational identification in a virtual organization. *Organization Science, 10*(6), 777–790.

Williams, K., & Alliger, G. (1994). Role stressors, mood spillover, and perceptions of work-family conflict in employed parents. *Academy of Management Journal, 37*, 837–868.

Wilson, M., Polzer-Debruyne, A., Chen, S., & Fernandes, S. (2007). Shift work interventions for reduced work-family conflict. *Employee Relations, 29*(2), 162–177.

Wrzesniewski, A. (2003). Finding positive meaning in work. In K. S. Cameron, J .E. Dutton, & R. E. Quinn (Eds.), *Positive organizational scholarship: Foundations of a new discipline* (pp. 296–308). San Francisco, CA: Berrett-Koehler.

Wrzesniewski, A., Dutton, J. E., & Debebe, G. (2003). Interpersonal sensemaking and the meaning of work. In R. M. Kramer & B. M. Staw (Eds.), *Research in organizational behavior, 25*, 93–135.

Wrzesniewski, A., McCauley, C., Rozin, P., & Schwartz, B. (1997). Jobs, careers, and callings: People's relations to their work. *Journal of Research in Personality, 31*, 21–33.

# CHAPTER 53

# WORK DESIGN AND HAPPINESS: AN ACTIVE, RECIPROCAL PERSPECTIVE

### BEN J. SEARLE[1] AND SHARON K. PARKER[2]

[1]Macquarie University, Australia; [2]University of Western Australia, Australia

> To business that we love we rise betime, and go to't with delight.
> (William Shakespeare, *Antony and Cleopatra*, Act IV scene iv).

TEDIOUS administrative tasks, unhelpful co-workers, vague and inconsistent direction from the boss ... Any discussion about work is likely to generate a multitude of factors that can make a person miserable at work. Since we spend much of our lives in the workplace, and potentially derive much of our identity from our work role, the negative aspects of work are a matter of legitimate concern, as reflected in both popular discussion and academic research on work design. Until recently, there has been less attention to those aspects of work that promote positive outcomes like happiness and thriving. Yet the opening quote from Shakespeare demonstrates how long it has been recognized that happiness and other positive states can be closely tied to our experience of work. This chapter explores a range of ways in which characteristics of a job and work role relate to the happiness of the job holder.

Much research indicates that well-being is strongly influenced by *work design*, or the way that job roles and mental, interpersonal, and physical tasks are organized, enacted, and experienced. As we will discuss later, traditional models of work design suggest that characteristics endemic to the work role or job, such as decision-making freedom, workload, and support from co-workers, are directly responsible for the psychological states experienced by employees, and in turn their well-being and performance. However, as we seek to demonstrate in this chapter, more contemporary approaches to work design conceptualize employees not just as passive recipients of their latent work characteristics but as more active influencers of their job characteristics and roles. Once we see employees as active agents, we will also see that the relation between work design and happiness does not always flow from work design to happiness, but also from happiness to work design. In this chapter, therefore, we discuss how traditional models of work design apply to happiness, but we will also develop an understanding as to how happiness can shape perceived and actual characteristics of work.

## Happiness at Work

There are many ways of conceptualizing and operationalizing well-being at work. Concepts and measures range from those focused on symptoms of psychological ill health (e.g., anxiety, depression, strain, and burnout) to those focused on positive aspects such as engagement and vigor. Warr (1987, 1990) described a useful way of making sense of the many concepts that relate to well-being. First, he focused on affective states (moods and emotions) as key indicators of well-being. Most relevant for considering work affect is the two-dimensional affect circumplex (Russell, 1980) that has considerable support within the mood and emotion literature (Weiss, 2002). This framework has two separate dimensions of affect: pleasure (how positive or negative one feels) and activation (how aroused or energized one feels). All affective states can be viewed in terms of these two dimensions. To illustrate, contentment and satisfaction would be characterized as high on pleasure but low on activation, while enthusiasm and joy would be high on both dimensions. Feelings like "depressed" and "gloomy" are low on both dimensions, whereas feelings like "anxious" and "tense" are low on pleasure but high on activation.

We suggest that using the affect circumplex provides valuable information beyond variables like job satisfaction. First, whereas job satisfaction includes affect, it also is highly cognitive because it encapsulates evaluations about one's job and workplace (e.g., Moorman, 1993). Second, even affective measures of job satisfaction assess a relatively "passive" form of well-being, relating to affective valence (good or bad) with little or no consideration of activation (Warr, 1997). For example, Bruggeman, Groskurth, and Ulich (1975) argued that employees can experience a sense of "resigned job satisfaction" in which they have lowered their level of aspiration and have become resigned to a job. Most job satisfaction concepts do not distinguish such passive forms from more active forms of job satisfaction. Yet more activated forms of positive affect are important, especially for prompting behaviors like proactivity (Parker, Bindl, Strauss, 2010), as we will explain later. This emphasis on more activated affect dovetails with the recent growth in interest in engagement (Macey & Schneider, 2008) defined, for example, as a positive, fulfilling state of mind that has vigor as one of its elements (a form of activated positive affect) as well as dedication and absorbtion (Schaufeli & Bakker, 2004).

Beyond affective well-being, Warr (1987) identified the following types of mental health: positive self-regard (e.g., high self-esteem); competence (e.g., effective coping); aspiration (e.g., goal directedness); autonomy/independence (e.g., proactivity), and integrated functioning (i.e., states involving balance, harmony, and inner-relatedness). These components of mental health can affect one's well-being (e.g., effective coping can reduce negative affect), but they are also important in their own right. First, they are potentially more enduring aspects than affective well-being. Second, outcomes such as competence, aspiration, and autonomy represent more active states and behaviors than many existing measures of well-being.

Warr's (1987) approach to mental health parallels thinking in the positive scholarship literature that aims to identify psychological states that are more enduring than moods. In their description of the meta-construct of psychological capital, Luthans and Youssef (2004) outlined four state-like constructs: self-efficacy, resilience, hope, and optimism. Self-efficacy, one's beliefs about one's capability to perform to a given level (Bandura, 1986), overlaps with Warr's construct of competence. Resilience, the capacity to recover from adversity (Luthans, 2002), is more distinct, but also involves personal competence. Hope shares features with Warr's construct of aspiration: it is a motivational state comprised of a sense of goal-directed energy (agency) and plans to meet goals (Snyder, Irving, & Anderson, 1991). Optimism shares some features with Warr's construct of positive self-regard. It is an attributional style that explains positive events (e.g., accomplishing a task) in terms of personal, permanent, and pervasive causes, and negative events (e.g., getting taken off a project) in terms of external, temporary, and situation-specific factors (Seligman, 1998). Thus, current thinking in positive psychology scholarship is consistent with earlier views that there are positive psychological experiences that last longer than the simple moods we typically associate with the words "happiness," and which can have important effects.

Another approach to conceptualizing well-being is to look at stable personality traits. Dispositional affectivity has been identified as a key individual difference variable. Thus far, much of the research has focused on trait negative affectivity, the tendency to experience negative emotions and emotional instability (DeNeve & Cooper, 1998; McCrae & Costa, 1991), which is broadly equivalent to neuroticism or trait anxiety. While less closely examined, trait positive affectivity, the tendency to experience positive emotions and perceive situations optimistically, has been linked to greater job satisfaction, and also greater job performance (Cropanzano, James, & Konovsky, 1993). Core self-evaluations represent a higher-order personality factor characterized by high self-efficacy across performance domains, high self-esteem, low neuroticism, and an internal locus of control (Judge, Locke, & Durham, 1997). People who experience more positive core self-evaluations not only experience greater happiness (in such forms as job satisfaction), they also appear to perform better at work (Judge & Bono, 2001).

In sum, happiness can be usefully considered as a form of positive affect. Our focus here is on relatively more activated forms of positive affect (e.g., enthusiasm, vigor). Other activated forms of well-being like self-efficacy and resilience, as well as traits like dispositional positive affect, can be seen as additional forms of happiness.

## Effects of Work Design on Happiness

The effect of work design on happiness can be usefully understood by contrasting traditional and contemporary approaches. Traditional theories have focused on the impact of job characteristics, while more contemporary approaches consider how an individual employee actively shapes the design of his or her job.

## Traditional "top-down" approaches to work design

Many theories have emphasized the impact of work design on both the individual and the organization. A century ago, work activities were broken down into simple elements to reduce training times and maximize labor flexibility, with managers closely controlling the nature of work (Taylor, 1911). Not surprisingly, work design theories emerging in response to these simple and impersonal jobs mainly focused on work characteristics that might lead to motivation and favorable job attitudes. Herzberg, Mausner, and Snyderman (1959) proposed that "motivator" factors, such as level of recognition, lead to job satisfaction, while an absence of extrinsic "hygiene" factors, such as salary, lead to job dissatisfaction. Although research has failed to support this two-factor theory (e.g., Hulin & Smith, 1967), it inspired the practice of job enrichment, or the creation of challenging and responsible jobs to promote motivation and performance (Paul, Robertson, & Herzberg, 1969).

The principle of job enrichment was further supported by the *job characteristics model*, or JCM (Hackman & Oldham, 1976). One of the most influential models of its kind, it proposed that desirable individual and organizational outcomes are more common in the presence of five job characteristics: task variety, task significance, task identity, feedback, and autonomy. Increasing these characteristics in a work role is known as job enrichment. The JCM further proposed that positive outcomes of job characteristics are achieved via three mediating psychological states: experienced meaningfulness, felt responsibility, and awareness of the impact of one's actions. For example, a "good" work design characteristic—such as having a wide variety of tasks—would promote happiness to the extent that it encouraged an employee to experience work as meaningful. These critical psychological states overlap to some degree with psychological empowerment, the motivational state of experiencing meaning, impact, competence (or self-efficacy), and a sense of choice (or self-determination) (Conger & Kanungo, 1988; Spreitzer, 1995; Thomas & Velthouse, 1990). Like meaningfulness, psychological empowerment mediates relations between work characteristics and positive outcomes (Parker & Ohly, 2008). Experienced meaningfulness has also been linked with activated forms of happiness, such as engagement (May, Gilson, & Harter, 2004; Olivier & Rothmann, 2007).

While the initial focus of the JCM was on motivation and performance, research has also supported links between job characteristics and positive states associated with happiness, such as aspirations, self-efficacy, and feelings of competence (Parker, 2003); de-activated forms of positive affect such as job satisfaction and contentment (Loher, Noe, Moeller, & Fitzgerald, 1985; Saavedra & Kwun, 2000); activated positive affect such as vigor and enthusiasm (Saavedra & Kwun, 2000; Shraga & Shirom, 2009); and flow and engagement (Csikszentmihalyi, 1991; Saks, 2006). While autonomy and significance are typically identified as having the strongest impact, Saavedra and Kwun's (2000) study demonstrated that these characteristics predicted only activated positive affect. De-activated positive affect was experienced more in the presence of high feedback and low skill variety. Different work characteristics appear to impact different types of happiness.

Two early meta-analytic studies supported the core propositions of the JCM, showing the five job characteristics collectively relate to attitudinal outcomes such as job satisfaction and motivation, and to a lesser extent, ratings of work effectiveness and absenteeism (Fried & Ferris, 1987; Loher et al., 1985). A more recent meta-analysis supported the importance of work characteristics affecting these outcomes, as well as other outcomes (such as organizational commitment and role perceptions), and identified experienced meaningfulness as the most important mediating factor (Humphrey, Nahrgang, & Morgeson, 2007). This meta-analysis also documented the importance of social characteristics of jobs, such as interdependence and social support, which received little attention in the traditional job characteristics model (see Grant & Parker (2009) for a further extended discussion of social job characteristics).

Another influential model of work and well-being is the *job demands-control* (JDC) model (Karasek, 1979). Karasek predicted well-being will be harmed by highly demanding work (tasks involving high physical and/or cognitive workloads) as well as by work lacking decision latitude (control over work tasks and autonomy regarding job-relevant decisions). Moreover, it was proposed that control would moderate the impact of demands, such that the impact of high demands would be substantially reduced in the presence of sufficient control. Karasek argued that, as demands increase, so too does stress or "potential energy" (p. 287), but that higher control over work would allow people to convert this into a more beneficial "energy of action" (p. 287). Karasek also proposed that high demands, when combined with high levels of control, could promote enthusiasm and positive energy, which would have benefits for motivation and learning. In the context of Warr's (1990) two-dimensional approach to affect, this seems to be a prediction that –in the face of stressful demands—the amount of autonomy experienced in a work role can determine whether an employee experiences activated negative affect or activated positive affect.

A recent adaptation of the job demands-control model, the *job demands-resources* (JDR) model, broadened the control category to include demand-reducing and growth-promoting phenomena such as social supports, role clarity, and skill variety. For example, Bakker, Hakanen, Demerouti, and Xanthopoulou (2007) showed that work resources such as control, support, and information directly influenced the engagement components of vigor, dedication and absorption for teachers. Similar effects have been observed elsewhere (Schaufeli & Bakker, 2004) with the evidence indicating that work resources promote positive motivational states and can protect employees from negative effects of work demands (Bakker & Demerouti, 2007). A key element of the job demands-resources model is that different types of work characteristics affect different psychological systems (Bakker & Demerouti, 2007). Work demands are thought to primarily affect strain and behavior outcomes by influencing negative psychological states (burnout mechanism), while work resources have more positive impacts due to their impact on positive psychological states (motivation mechanism). This is consistent with findings from the stress literature, which has shown that work demands, rather than resources, are strongly related to burnout (Lee & Ashforth, 1996). Thus, the reason why work resources are beneficial may have less to do with reducing unhappiness than with increasing happiness.

A related approach is the *challenge–hindrance stressor framework* (Cavanaugh, Boswell, Roehling, & Boudreau, 2000). Influenced by the conceptual models of stress as an appraisal phenomenon (Lazarus & Folkman, 1984) that can be positive (Selye, 1982), Cavanaugh and colleagues categorized stressors according to their potential to support an employee's goals ("challenge" stressors, such as workload and task complexity) and their potential to obstruct goal attainment ("hindrance" stressors, such as role ambiguity and resource inadequacies). In contrast to most previous research linking all such stressors to negative outcomes, challenge stressors were associated with more satisfaction and less intention to leave, while the opposite pattern was true of hindrance stressors. Research has replicated and extended these findings through new studies, such as LePine, LePine, and Jackson's (2004) observation that challenge stressors had stronger effects on learning motivation while hindrance stressors had stronger effects on exhaustion. In two meta-analyses, LePine, Podsakoff, and LePine (2005) and Podsakoff, LePine and LePine (2007) re-classified findings from previous stress research using the challenge–hindrance framework. While both challenge and hindrance stressors appeared to increase psychological strain, challenge stressors were positively (and hindrance stressors negatively) related to job satisfaction, organizational commitment, motivation and performance. Thus, in contrast to the JDC or JDR models, work demands are seen as having the potential to impact employee happiness positively, rather than negatively.

The research reviewed here shows that work characteristics are highly relevant to employee happiness. Where jobs are lacking the five characteristics described by Hackman and Oldham (1976), particularly autonomy (following Karasek, 1979), or where they lack resources described in the job demands–resources model (Bakker & Demerouti, 2007), then some or all of these characteristics should be adjusted through an organizational intervention. Moreover, in order to maximize activated forms of happiness, such interventions should focus on increases in autonomy, task significance, feedback, and other resources and challenges. It should be noted that the inclusion of a high proportion of studies with cross-sectional designs in reviews and meta-analyses, combined with the limited number of studies with experimental or quasi-experimental intervention designs, raises the question of whether such interventions are genuinely likely to affect happiness. However, the few intervention studies tend to support the above conclusions. For example, Griffin's (1991) study of bank tellers who had their roles enriched showed the intervention improved job satisfaction almost immediately, and ultimately improved job performance. It is interesting to note that the effects on job satisfaction were relatively short-lived. This may be due to the fact that the intervention also increased variety, which Saavedra and Kwun (2000) found to be negatively related to deactivated positive affect. In contrast, Parker's (2003) study of job deskilling in a manufacturing company that introduced a moving assembly line showed the reduction in enrichment also reduced employees' commitment and self-efficacy. These longitudinal studies support the notion that job design can directly influence employee happiness and related psychological states.

## Contemporary "bottom-up" approaches to work design

Traditional work design research emerged in a context where manufacturing was a dominant industry in Western nations, and work design was the responsibility of plant designers and supervisors. However, with growth in service and knowledge work, and the increased pace of change in competitor activity, legislation, and customer expectations, it is less feasible to identify the precise tasks and behaviors required in each situation for employees to support an organization's goals (Griffin, Neal, & Parker, 2007). Organizations need jobs and roles to develop over time to address emergent demands and opportunities (Ilgen & Hollenbeck, 1991). The advent of global work, virtual work, tele-work, and self-managing teams has replaced static jobs with dynamic roles, tasks, and projects. As such, the meaning of performance in organizations is changing. Managers now rely on employees to both adapt to and initiate changes in their work (Frese & Fay, 2001; Griffin et al., 2007; Morrison & Phelps, 1999).

Whereas work design researchers have sought to study how jobs, roles, and tasks can be structured to encourage and support proactive behaviors, with the implication being that job design occurs in a "top down" manner, other researchers examine the different ways in which employees themselves take initiative to modify their own jobs, roles, and tasks (Grant & Parker, 2009). This notion has theoretical roots in research on role innovation and role transition, which suggest that employees actively engage in efforts to modify their roles (Baker & Faulkner, 1991; Callero, 1994; Katz & Kahn, 1966; Nicholson, 1984; Van Maanen & Schein, 1979). Building on Nicholson's (1984) work, Black and Ashford (1995) studied how, in the socialization process, many employees seek to "make jobs fit" by adjusting their jobs to match their values, skills, and preferences. Similarly, Ashford and colleagues found that employees do not just wait for feedback to be provided but they actively seek out feedback from supervisors and others (Ashford, Blatt, & VandeWalle, 2003; Ashford & Cummings, 1983, 1985). Employees also actively adjust their work environments (Dawis & Lofquist, 1984), take initiative to improve faulty tasks (Staw & Boettger, 1990) and take charge to bring about change (Morrison & Phelps, 1999). Parker, Bindl, and Strauss (2010) referred to these concepts as proactive behaviors because they are future-focused, self-starting, and aimed at bringing about change.

One type of employee adjustment is job crafting, a concept that Wrzesniewski and Dutton (2001) introduced in order to "capture the actions employees take to shape, mold, and redefine their jobs" (p. 180). In contrast to job design or redesign, which entails the organizational manipulation of work features to control processes, manage behavior and influence employee attitudes, Wrzesniewski and Dutton (2001) characterized job crafting as an often invisible process where an employee, intrinsically motivated by personal needs, adjusts their job content, job meaning, and/or job relationships. These scholars questioned assumptions that only those individuals with highly autonomous, complex roles have the opportunity to adjust the characteristics of their work. Rather, they highlighted how employees would be more motivated to craft jobs in less meaningful roles. They cite the example of hospital cleaning staff who sought out opportunities to expand the task, cognitive, and relational boundaries of their roles by providing social support to patients and visitors. Consistent with this prediction, Berg, Wrzesniewski, and Dutton (2010) reported that staff at higher ranks in the organization reported less engagement in job crafting compared to those in lower ranks, even though the higher ranked individuals had higher autonomy. The crafting of those in higher ranked positions appeared to be stifled by excess work demands.

Hornung, Rousseau, Glaser, Angerer, and Weigel (2010) describe customizing jobs through "I-deals" as a further way to redesign work that is mid-way between the extremes of top down redesign and bottom up job crafting. I-deals are idiosyncratic deals that employees negotiate with employers for non-standard arrangements, such as flexible working hours or expanded levels of autonomy. The authors argue that top-down work redesigns are not only difficult to implement and potentially costly, but they also do not necessarily allow individually-optimized work characteristics. In comparison to Wrzesniewski and Dutton's (2001) expectation that job crafting occurs outside of organizational structures and awareness, I-deals enable customizing of job content to an individual's needs and capabilities in a way that is acceptable to supervisors and within the culture and practices of an organization.

Grant and Parker (2009) summarized four pathways by which proactive behaviors like job crafting, I-deals, and taking charge influence work characteristics: (1) changing the tasks and methods (e.g., increasing task variety by negotiating involvement in a broader set of projects); changing either (2) the context within which work is performed by changing systems (e.g., reducing work demands by introducing a more efficient technology) or (3) the relational aspects of work (e.g., increasing autonomy by taking charge, resulting in greater autonomy and responsibility being awarded by a supervisor); and (4) changing aspects of the individual that then influence perceived or actual work characteristics (e.g., increasing experienced meaning through job crafting, resulting in greater perceived autonomy). Grant and Parker (2009) discussed how positive spirals can emerge in which proactive measures taken by employees change their work characteristics, prompting yet more proactivity and further change in work characteristics. For example, in a four-wave study, Frese, Garst, and Fay (2007) showed that job control and complexity influenced control orientations, which in turn affected personal initiative, and this went on to influence later control orientations and work characteristics. Likewise, Weigl et al. (2010) reported that job control and other such resources promoted engagement, which in turn promoted more control and resources.

# Happiness Effects on Work Design

In considering how happiness can affect work design and vice versa, we draw on Daniels' (2006) framework that distinguishes among latent, enacted, and perceived work design. Latent work design includes the characteristics embedded in the nature of an occupation or work environment, and reflects the typical content, processes and actions required in a certain type of work role. Changing such latent characteristics is the goal of traditional top down forms of work redesign discussed above. Enacted work design refers to the experiences and choices employees face on a daily basis, the unexpected challenges and hindrances they try to manage, and the unrequired actions they take. Enacted work design is what is affected by proactive crafting and shaping of one's role, also discussed above. Finally, perceived work design is an employee's appraisal of his/her work. Daniels outlined how latent work design influences perceived work design as well as opportunities for variation in enacted work design (as outlined above and depicted in Fig. 53.1).

From the perspective of latent work design, it would be difficult to imagine how employee psychological states like happiness could influence job content and work processes. After all, work characteristics from this perspective are relatively fixed and independent of employee characteristics. However, as we show in our reciprocal model (Fig. 53.1), we believe that individual differences in happiness-related states and traits play an important role in career choice and progression, which in turn affects latent characteristics of work. Moreover, as discussed earlier, individuals can change their enacted work characteristics, and happiness can play a role in whether and how individuals engage in this active shaping of one's job. Finally, happiness can influence how we perceive situations, and thereby perceived work design. We elaborate these pathways next.

## Influence of happiness on latent work design

The idea that individual differences can influence job choice is neither new nor controversial (Kristof, 1996). Our contribution is to contextualize this point within research on happiness

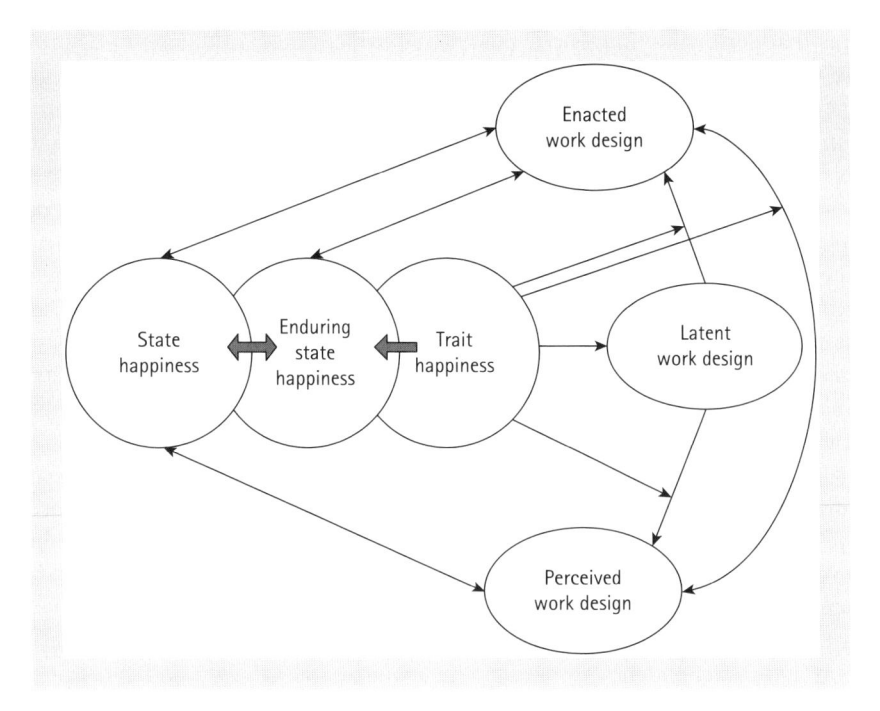

FIG. 53.1 The reciprocal model of work design and happiness. Trait happiness refers to dispositional factors such as positive core self-evaluations. Enduring happiness states include phenomena such as self-efficacy, aspiration, and optimism, which are less stable than dispositions but persist longer than state happiness in the form of activated positive affect (e.g., enthusiasm) or deactivated positive affect (contentment). Latent work design refers to relatively stable characteristics of work within the occupation or organization one works in, while enacted work design refers to those characteristics that vary from day to day and are amenable to job crafting. Perceived work design refers to the manner in which an individual appraises and interprets latent and enacted characteristics.

and work design. Thus we propose (see Fig. 53.1) that more enduring states, and even traits linked to happiness, affect job opportunity and choice, and thereby the latent work designs that individuals are likely to be exposed to within a career or occupation. We develop these arguments drawing on Schneider's (1987) attraction–selection–attrition framework, which identified psychological factors that can result in homogeneity of employees within an organization.

People are differentially attracted to careers as a function of their individual qualities, such as personality, interests, and capabilities (Holland, 1985). For example, people with positive core self-evaluations have been observed to hold jobs objectively assessed as higher in complexity (Judge, Bono, & Locke, 2000). One could argue, consistent with Kohn and Schooler (1982), that this may represent a long-term effect of complex work design on personality. However, Srivastava, Locke, Judge, and Adams (2010) found that people with higher core self-evaluations voluntarily chose higher levels of complexity on work tasks, which increased their task satisfaction. This suggests that trait happiness may well influence preferred types of work. Judge and Cable (1997) showed in a survey of nearly two thousand students that personality influenced the relative attractiveness of different organizational culture types. For example, innovative work cultures, thought to involve high degrees of change, autonomy, and risk-taking, while lacking security and stability, were less attractive to neurotic individuals. An enduring tendency to experience positive emotions and hold positive self-beliefs may therefore encourage self-selection into jobs and careers with opportunities to make decisions independently, to learn new skills, and to rise to challenges. Such an explanation does not contradict suggestions that these work characteristics affect state happiness; it merely positions this effect as subsequent to the effect of trait happiness on work choice and latent work design.

Following Schneider's (1987) attraction–selection–attrition model further, happiness is also likely to influence a candidate's chance of being selected into an organization, and remaining there once selected, as a consequence of the happiness of other employees. Schneider argued that organizations are likely to preferentially select job candidates who seem similar to those currently employed within the organization, and that employees who are more different from their peers will experience less psychological "fit" and be more likely to leave. Thus over time, organizations with latent work designs more attractive to happier employees are likely to preferentially select happier job candidates and see higher attrition rates among unhappy employees.

Another way that happiness can influence selection decisions involves emotional contagion, the automatic tendency to mimic others' non-verbal behavior and consequently to experience their emotions (Hatfield, Cacioppo, & Rapson, 1992). Ashforth and Saks (2002) argued that displays of enthusiasm by interviewers can increase the attractiveness of the organization from the candidate's point of view. The interviewee's enthusiasm is likely to have a similar effect on the interviewer. Indeed, countless sources for potential job candidates advise of the importance of displaying self-confidence and a cheerful attitude in job interviews (Huczynski, 1996). A study by Fox and Spector (2000) demonstrated that candidate positive affect does in fact play a critical role on selection decisions. Candidates who displayed greater positive affect received higher ratings by interviewers in terms of willingness to hire and perceived qualifications, perhaps because they were also more likely to be liked by and to seem similar to the interviewer. This suggests that happier candidates are more likely to be offered *any* job, regardless of their actual organizational fit.

As for attrition, intent to leave an organization is strongly linked to affective well-being. Meta-analyses (e.g., Hellman, 1997; Tett & Meyer, 1993) have shown strong and consistent links between employees' dissatisfaction and their intention to leave. Studies (e.g., Chiu & Francesco, 2003; Cropanzano et al., 1993) have also shown that dispositional affectivity influences intention to quit, and that this relation is mediated by job satisfaction. Considering Srivastava et al.'s (2010) finding that complex jobs were unpopular among those high in negative affectivity (i.e., more negative core self-evaluations) alongside findings that employees high in negative affectivity react more negatively to work demands (e.g., Bolger & Schilling, 1991; Moyle, 1995; Parkes, 1990), it seems likely that those low in trait happiness would be more likely to leave challenging work roles.

In summary, the attraction–selection–attrition framework describes three mechanisms whereby happiness can influence latent work design. Happiness affects what types of jobs and organizations we seek out, our likelihood of being selected into them, and how long we remain there. These processes mean that the occupations and organizations to which we belong, and their associated characteristics of work, are likely to reflect our affective tendencies, as shown in Fig. 53.1 by the direct path from trait happiness to latent work design. However, affect can also influence enacted characteristics of work, as we describe in the next section.

## Influence of happiness on enacted work design

We described earlier how contemporary approaches to work design acknowledge that employees can and do take active steps to shape their roles in order to be happier at work. Here we propose that trait affect, positive self-beliefs, and even state happiness can be an antecedent to these proactive role-shaping efforts, with resulting impacts on enacted forms of work design.

Neuroticism, defined as an enduring tendency to experience negative emotional states such as anxiety, has been negatively associated with job performance (Barrick, Mount, & Judge, 2001) and well-being, especially in demanding roles (Moyle, 1995; Parkes, 1990). Neuroticism is associated with increased threat appraisals (Chan & Lovibond, 1996), as well as avoidant coping behaviors, with more neurotic individuals being motivated to avoid situations that elicit negative emotions (McCrae & Costa, 1987). Since role adjustments that enhance skill variety and increase work autonomy have the potential to increase task difficulty, workload and risk of errors (Clegg & Spencer, 2007), those high in neuroticism are more likely to perceive such role adjustment opportunities as threats or hindrances. Employees with positive core self-evaluations, on the other hand, feel more in control of their environments, feel more capable of handling higher levels of autonomy (Judge et al., 1997; Schaubroeck & Merritt, 1997), and are more likely to take active steps to cope with work challenges (Kahn & Byosiere, 1992). Positive core self-evaluations support the development of more positive domain-specific efficacy beliefs (Yeo & Neal, 2006), which have been identified as critical in models of role adjustment (e.g., Clegg & Spencer, 2007) and proactive behavior (Parker, Williams, & Turner, 2006). People with more positive core self-evaluations engage in more social network-building (Johnson, Kristof-Brown, Van Vianen, De Pater, & Klein, 2003), a further type of proactive behavior.

Happiness can also influence how an employee interprets and enacts job goals and tasks. Those experiencing more positive affect are known to set themselves more challenging goals (Ilies & Judge, 2005). Dalal, Lam, Weiss, Welch, and Hulin (2009) found that day-level positive affect was associated with citizenship behaviors, and negative affect was associated with counter-productive behaviors. This suggests that affect can influence how employees undertake tasks outside their prescribed job roles, and may even influence how they perceive the boundaries of that role. Positive affect has also been linked to adopting more proactive approaches to existing work tasks, such as patient care (Bindl, Parker, Johnson, Groth, & Collins, 2009). Parker, Bindl, and Strauss (2010) identified activated positive affect (such as feelings of enthusiasm) as a key driver of proactive work behaviors that shape and stretch people's work roles.

Happiness can also influence relational aspects of enacted work design. Interpersonal relationships are thought to be maintained through contribution and reciprocation—when I do something for my friend, she feels a need to reciprocate (Berkowitz, 1968). According to social exchange theory, people are likely to provide social supports to others to the degree that they anticipate reciprocation of equivalent supports (Buunk & Hoorens, 1992). Someone who generally displays happiness and confidence might therefore be seen as a good "investment" for social support, even under difficult circumstances, since the expectations of reciprocation would be high. Conversely, someone who rarely displays happiness or confidence might frequently feel the need of support, yet might be perceived as unable to reciprocate such investments. This prediction is supported by Daniels and Guppy's (1994) observation that accountants' state positive affect was associated with subsequent levels of support from others.

## Influence of happiness on perceived work design

Work design is often conceptualized as objectively verifiable characteristics of an environment or occupation. Intervention studies (e.g., Griffin, 1991; Parker, 2003), experimental studies (e.g., Jimmieson & Terry, 1998; 1999; Searle, Bright, & Bochner, 1999; 2001), and even some longitudinal survey studies using objective grades or categories of jobs (e.g., Karasek, Theorell, Schwartz, Pieper, & Alfredsson, 1982; Marmot et al., 1991; Shaw & Riskind, 1983) together provide strong evidence that objective characteristics of work influence employee well-being. However, others have argued that perceptions of work situations, rather than objective characteristics, have greater utility in well-being research (Perrewé & Zellars, 1999).

According to transactional theory, an individual's stress response is governed not just by the external environment but more proximally by how he or she perceives, or appraises, the situation (Lazarus, 1966; Lazarus & Folkman, 1984). Affective states are a consequence of this appraisal process. According to Scherer (1999), "A central tenet of appraisal theory is the claim that emotions are elicited and differentiated on the basis of a person's subjective evaluation ... of a situation" (p. 637). Indeed, the importance of subjective evaluation is evidenced by scientific research: health psychology studies show that indicators of heart disease are linked to an individual's style of appraisal (Fontana & McLaughlin, 1998), while experimental studies indicate that different appraisals of the same task conditions can affect outcomes like task performance (Drach-Zahavy & Erez, 2002).

Studies using both subjective and objective approaches have supported the notion that these approaches assess different constructs and predict different outcomes (Daniels, 2006; Ganster, 2008). Some studies suggest that objective features, such as assessments of job descriptions made by independent evaluators or use of pre-existing job classifications, have a stronger impact on outcomes, particularly non-subjective outcomes such as absences or visits to a doctor (North, Syme, Feebey, Shipley, & Marmot, 1996; Roelen, Weites, Koopmans, van der Klink, & Groothoff, 2008). Other studies find the reverse to be true (Frese & Zapf, 1999). Spector and Jex (1991) compared multiple types of work characteristic assessments, including "objective" occupational classification data, ratings based on job descriptions, and self-report ratings. Results showed that occupational classification information was associated with self-report ratings (e.g., $r = 0.18$ for autonomy; $r = 0.39$ for complexity) but was more strongly related to the ratings based on job descriptions ($r = 0.59$ for both autonomy and complexity). Self-reports of work characteristics were associated with self-reported well-being, although the number of visits to a doctor was associated with the independent classifications and ratings. This seems to suggest that subjective measures of work design are more useful for predicting happiness.

However, the direction of the effect in such studies is often unclear. If we assume that self-reports of work characteristics are more than an indication of latent work design, other factors must influence these perceptions. Recognized influences on perceptions include personality, beliefs, attitudes, and emotional states, with the common thread of affect connecting many of these explanations.

A key aspect of personality linked to situational appraisals is neuroticism. Neurotic people appear to be more adversely affected by demands (e.g., Bolger & Schilling, 1991; Moyle, 1995; Parkes, 1990), consistent with the theory that neuroticism produces a heightened reactivity to stressors (Spielberger, Gorsuch, & Lushene, 1970). In terms of transactional theory, the suggestion is that during the first (primary) stage of appraisal—where the potential impact of the situation is judged—those high in neuroticism are more likely to interpret ambiguous situations as threatening (Chan & Lovibond, 1996) and thus perceive characteristics of work more negatively, with consequences for affective well-being (Moyle, 1995). Conversely, positive affect may positively influence appraisals and perceptions. Employees with positive core self-evaluations have been shown to make more positive self-reports of job characteristics (Judge et al., 2000) and perceive more intrinsic value in their work (Judge, Locke, Durham, & Kluger, 1998). This may be because happiness promotes less threat appraisal and greater belief in one's capacity to cope with challenges. For example, optimism is believed to enhance employees' perception that a positive outcome will be achieved (Carver, Scheier, & Segerstrom, 2010).

Another explanation for these effects can be found in models of affect and cognition, such as affect priming (Forgas & Bower, 1987). An individual in a negative affective state is likely to recall negative experiences involving similar stressors and is therefore more likely to appraise the stressors as threats (Forgas, 2001) or hindrances. In a mood-manipulation experiment, Cohen, Towbes, and Flocco (1988) demonstrated that people in activated positive moods recalled fewer stressful life events than those in neutral or depressed moods, while those in depressed moods perceived that they had less social support. In addition, moods may serve as a heuristic to deciding how to interpret and respond to situations, as predicted in affect-as-information models (Clore, Schwarz, & Conway, 1994). Forgas and Locke (2005) found that positive affect influenced how experienced school teachers judged vignettes about work events. Those experiencing happy moods were inclined to be more optimistic and lenient in their judgments of those involved in the events, even when the events involved negative outcomes.

Fredrickson's (2001) broaden-and-build theory proposes that positive emotions expand individual's thought-action repertoires and build their enduring personal resources. In other words, the happier one feels, the easier it is to consider a wide variety of new ideas and alternative courses of action. In the context of the appraisal process, this may mean the individual is able to identify more resources and coping responses, making it more likely that problems will seem solvable, and resulting in a better chance of success and preservation of the positive mood. This is somewhat consistent with affect priming models in that successful strategies are more likely to be recalled in happy moods, while failures are more likely to be recalled in depressed moods (Forgas & Locke, 2005). The broadening process is thought to build enduring personal resources that can function as reserves for future circumstances or threats (Fredrickson, 2001).

Direct evidence of the role of affect in judgments of work characteristics can be seen in a study by Kraiger, Billings, and Isen (1989). Student participants evaluated the characteristics of enriched and unenriched versions of a work task, and commented on their satisfaction with the task. Those induced into happy moods gave higher scores when rating the task on standard job characteristics scales, regardless of the objective task characteristics (Hackman & Oldham, 1975; Sims, Szilagyi, & Keller, 1976). Scores were particularly high in relation to skill variety and feedback. The study also showed a direct relationship between happiness and satisfaction: the happier the participant, the more satisfied he or she was with the task. In this case, it is not clear whether the findings could be attributed to affect priming, to affect as informational heuristic, or to some combination of these mechanisms. However, it does suggest that the happier we are, the more positively we will perceive the latent and emergent characteristics of our work (shown as moderating effects in Fig. 53.1), which can, in turn, influence affect and behavior.

## Happiness and Work Design: Where to from Here?

We have examined relations between job or work design—the content, context and characteristics of one's work—and employee happiness. We conceptualized happiness broadly, whilst at the same time identifying the different specific types of happiness that have been studied. We have argued that it is important to recognize the potential of activated forms of positive affective states, such as enthusiasm and engagement, which are most likely to promote the active work behaviors that bring value to modern work organizations (Parker et al., 2010). Stable individual differences associated with happiness are also important, since relatively enduring attitudes and beliefs such as self-efficacy and optimism, and stable traits such as positive core self-evaluations can have long-lasting effects on workplace behavior.

Based on many years of research, we can conclude that jobs designed to be high in enriched work characteristics are not only associated with fewer negative outcomes but also greater employee happiness. For example, more enriched work characteristics affect employee beliefs and attitudes (such as their self-efficacy, role orientations, and resilience), and these in turn increase the likelihood of experiencing positive affective states.

While this top-down pathway is important, it is also valuable to recognize work design as a dynamic and enacted phenomenon. The way in which individuals actively shape their work roles is another path through which work design influences happiness. The opportunity to craft one's own job role will occur more naturally in some jobs than in others: this gives rise to the possibility that improvements in employee well-being can be achieved through training employees to actively shape their roles. Indeed, Grant and Parker (2009) suggested that integrating crafting-oriented training with more traditional work redesign might be the best of both worlds, enabling individuals to capitalize on the advantages of traditional approaches whilst helping employees recognize that proactive efforts can facilitate further changes. Such combined interventions have yet to be examined.

The interpersonal effects of affective states also warrant further investigation. For example, at a team-level of analysis, the affective states of supervisors or co-workers might represent important work design characteristics—or resources, to use job demands-resources terminology. Research on emotional contagion suggests that others' moods influence affective well-being and behavior at work. For example, Lord, Brown and Freiberg (1999) proposed that supervisors likely influence employees' affective states through their non-verbal behavior. Studies have linked supervisor moods to team absenteeism and performance (George, 1990; George & Bettenhausen, 1995). Evidence suggests that positive moods can be influenced in this manner as well as negative moods (Neumann & Strack, 2000). Seeing happiness as a work resource further extends traditional approaches to work design, and has further implications for interventions—this time, at the level of the supervisor rather than the employee. If managers could be more effective in displaying and encouraging positive moods at the team-level, this might contribute to psychological and relational work designs that prompt valued affective states, situational perceptions and workplace behaviors.

We have argued that happiness is not just an outcome of work design, but that positive beliefs, attitudes, and affective states also influence work designs. This "bottom-up" effect manifests in different ways for latent, enacted, and perceived work characteristics. As depicted in Fig. 53.1, we expect that the most stable forms of happiness (such as core self-evaluations) have the most direct influences on latent aspects of work design, such as those achieved through career decisions. Thus, trait affect influences the attractiveness of jobs and organizations, as well as the likelihood of being selected into and remaining within those jobs and organizations. This in turn affects the type of latent work designs available to an employee throughout his or her career.

Positive attitudes and beliefs, such as self-efficacy and optimism, can have direct influences on enacted work design: happier employees seek out more meaningful and fulfilling work, and are more likely to engage in role innovation and job crafting. States of activated positive affect can also influence enacted work design, with feelings of enthusiasm prompting citizenship, proactivity and role expansion.

We recommend further research into these reciprocal relationships between work design and happiness. Closer investigation could reveal upward spirals, whereby latent work designs containing enriched work characteristics promote positive activated affect, which in turn results in role innovation. Thus by providing a positive job design, one attracts happier people, promotes enthusiasm at work, and stimulates employee engagement in role innovation and job crafting to make their work even more interesting and meaningful, creating further happiness in a positive spiral. By this argument, we would also expect to see downward spirals whereby less enriched jobs potentially attract more cynical or helpless employees and then promote negative affect, which in turn likely discourages employees from role innovation or crafting. Such situations could even prompt contraction of roles, whereby employees seek to avoid challenging tasks they might otherwise be expected to perform.

In sum, our argument is that a 'good' job design is much more than simply satisfying. Rather a good job design, by virtue of its positive influence on affect and associated developmental changes, can promote self-initiated work redesign which, in turn, generates further positive affect, development and job redesign, in a positive virtuous cycle. Work design is thus a more powerful force for positive individual outcomes than traditional theory and research suggests.

# References

Ashford, S. J., Blatt, R., & VandeWalle, D. (2003). Reflections on the looking glass: A review of research on feedback-seeking behavior in organizations. *Journal of Management*, 29, 769–799.

Ashford, S. J., & Cummings, L. L. (1983). Feedback as an individual resource: Personal strategies of creating information. *Organizational Behavior and Human Performance, 32*, 370–398.

Ashford, S. J., & Cummings, L. L. (1985). Proactive feedback seeking: The instrumental use of the information environment. *Journal of Occupational Psychology, 58*, 67–79.

Ashforth, B. E., & Saks, A. M. (2002). Feeling your way: Emotion and organizational entry. In R. G. Lord, R. J. Klimoski, & R. Kanfer (Eds.), *Emotions in the workplace: Understanding the structure and role of emotions in organizational behavior* (pp. 331–369). San Francisco, CA: Jossey-Bass.

Baker, W. E., & Faulkner, R. R. (1991). Role as resource in the Hollywood film industry. *American Journal of Sociology, 97*, 279–309.

Bakker, A. B., & Demerouti, E. (2007). The job demands-resources model: State of the art. *Journal of Managerial Psychology, 22*, 309–328.

Bakker, A. B., Hakanen, J. J., Demerouti, E., & Xanthopoulou, D. (2007). Job resources boost work engagement, particularly when job demands are high. *Journal of Educational Psychology, 99*, 274–284.

Bandura, A. (1986). *Social foundations of thought and action: A social cognitive theory*. Englewood Cliffs, NJ: Prentice-Hall.

Barrick, M. R., Mount, M. K., & Judge, T. A. (2001). Personality and performance at the beginning of the new millennium: What do we know and where do we go next? *International Journal of Selection and* Assessment, 9, 9–30.

Berg, J. M., Wrzesniewski, A., & Dutton, J. E. (2010). Perceiving and responding to challenges in job crafting at different ranks: When proactivity requires adaptivity. *Journal of Organizational Behavior, 31*, 158–186.

Berkowitz, L. (1968). Responsibility, reciprocity, and social distance in help-giving: An experimental investigation of English social class differences. *Journal of Experimental Social Psychology, 4*, 46–63.

Bindl, U. K., Parker, S. K., Johnson, A., Groth, M., & Collins, C. G. (2009). Disentangling the motivational drivers of nurses' voice and proactive care. Paper presented at the 2009 Industrial and Organizational Psychology Conference, Sydney, Australia.

Black, J. S., & Ashford, S. J. (1995). Fitting in or making jobs fit: Factors affecting mode of adjustment for new hires. *Human Relations, 48*, 421–437.

Bolger, N., & Schilling, E. A. (1991). Personality and the problems of everyday life: The role of neuroticism in exposure and reactivity to daily stressors. *Journal of Personality, 59*, 355–386.

Bruggeman, A., Groskurth, P., & Ulich, E. (1975). *Arbeitszufriedenheit*. Bern, Switzerland: Huber.

Buunk, B. P., & Hoorens, V. (1992). Social support and stress: The role of social comparison and social exchange processes. *British Journal of Clinical Psychology, 31*, 444–457.

Callero, P. L. (1994). From role playing to role-using: Understanding role as resource. *Social Psychology Quarterly, 57*, 228–243.

Carver, C. S., Scheier, M. F., & Segerstrom, S. C. (2010). Optimism. *Clinical Psychology Review, 30*, 879–889.

Cavanaugh, M. A., Boswell, W. R., Roehling, M. V., & Boudreau, J. W. (2000). An empirical examination of self-reported work stress among USA managers. *Journal of Applied Psychology, 85*, 65–74.

Chan, C. K., & Lovibond, P. F. (1996). Expectancy bias in trait anxiety. *Journal of Abnormal Psychology, 105*, 637–647.

Chiu, R. K., & Francesco, A. M. (2003). Dispositional traits and turnover intention: Examining the mediating role of job satisfaction and affective commitment. *International Journal of Manpower, 24,* 284–298.

Clegg, C., & Spencer, C. (2007). A circular and dynamic model of the process of job design. *Journal of Occupational and Organizational Psychology, 80,* 321–339.

Clore, G. L., Schwarz, N., & Conway, M. (1994). Affective causes and consequences of social information processing. In R. S. Wyer & T.K. Srull (Eds.), *Handbook of social cognition* (2nd ed., pp. 323–341). Hillsdale, NJ: Erlbaum.

Cohen, L. H., Towbes, L. C., & Flocco, R. (1988). Effects of induced mood on self-reported life events and perceived and received social support. *Journal of Personality and Social Psychology, 55,* 669–674.

Conger, J. A., & Kanungo, R. N. (1988). The empowerment process: Integrating theory and practice. *Academy of Management Review, 13,* 471–482.

Cropanzano, R., James, K., & Konovsky, M. A. (1993). Dispositional affectivity as a predictor of work attitudes and job performance. *Journal of Organizational Behavior, 14,* 595–606.

Csikszentmihalyi, M. (1991). *Flow: The psychology of optimal experience.* New York, NY: Harper & Row.

Dalal, R. S., Lam, J., Weiss, H. M., Welch, E. R., & Hulin, C. L. (2009). A within-person approach to work behavior and performance: Concurrent and lagged citizenship-counterproductivity associations, and dynamic relationships with affect and overall job performance. *Academy of Management Journal, 52,* 1051–1066.

Daniels, K. (2006). Rethinking job characteristics in work stress research. *Human Relations, 59,* 267–290.

Daniels, K., & Guppy, A. (1994). Occupational stress, social support, job control, and psychological well-being. *Human Relations, 47,* 1523–1544.

Dawis, R. V., & Lofquist, L. H. (1984). *A psychological theory of work adjustment.* Minneapolis, MN: University of Minnesota Press.

DeNeve, K., & Cooper, H. (1998). The happy personality: A meta-analysis of 137 personality traits and subjective well-being. *Psychological Bulletin, 124,* 197–229.

Drach-Zahavy, A., & Erez, M. (2002). Challenge versus threat effects on the goal-performance relationship. *Organizational Behavior and Human Decision Processes, 88,* 667–682.

Fontana, A., & McLaughlin, M. (1998). Coping and appraisal of daily stressors predict heart rate and blood pressure in young women. *Behavioral Medicine, 24,* 5–16.

Forgas, J. P. (Ed.). (2001). *The handbook of affect and social cognition.* Mahwah, NJ: Erlbaum.

Forgas, J. P., & Bower, G. H. (1987). Mood effects on person-perception judgments. *Journal of Personality and Social Psychology, 53,* 53–60.

Forgas, J., & Locke, J. (2005). Affective influences on causal inferences: The effects of mood on attributions for positive and negative interpersonal episodes. *Cognition and Emotion, 19,* 1071–1081.

Fox, S., & Spector, P. E. (2000). Relations of emotional intelligence, practical intelligence, general intelligence and trait affectivity with interview outcomes: It's not all just 'G'. *Journal of Organizational Behavior, 21,* 203–220.

Fredrickson, B. L. (2001). The role of positive emotions in positive psychology: The broaden-and-build theory of positive emotions. *American Psychologist,* **56,** 218–226.

Frese, M., & Fay, D. (2001). Personal initiative: An active performance concept for work in the 21st century. *Research in Organizational Behavior, 23,* 133–187.

Frese, M., Garst, H., & Fay, D. (2007). Making things happen: Reciprocal relationships between work characteristics and personal initiative in a four-wave longitudinal structural equation model. *Journal of Applied Psychology, 92*, 1084–1102.

Frese, M., & Zapf, D. (1999). On the importance of the objective environment in stress and attribution theory. Counterpoint to Perrewé and Zellars. *Journal of Organizational Behavior, 20*, 761–765.

Fried, Y., & Ferris, G. R. (1987). The validity of the job characteristics model: A review and meta-analysis. *Personnel Psychology, 40*, 287–322.

Ganster, D. C. (2008). Measurement challenges for studying work-related stressors and strains. *Human Resource Management Review, 18*, 259–270.

George, J. M. (1995). Leader positive mood and group performance: The case of customer service. *Journal of Applied Social Psychology, 25*, 778–794.

George, J. M., & Bettenhausen, K. (1990). Understanding prosocial behavior, sales performance, and turnover: A group-level analysis in a service context. *Journal of Applied Psychology, 75*, 698–709.

Grant, A. M., & Parker, S. K. (2009). Redesigning work design theories: The rise of relational and proactive perspectives. *Academy of Management Annals, 3*, 317–375.

Griffin, R. W. (1991). Effects of work redesign on employee perceptions, attitudes, and behaviors: A long-term investigation. *Academy of Management Journal, 34*, 425–435.

Griffin, M. A., Neal, A., & Parker, S. K. (2007). A new model of work role performance: Positive behavior in uncertain and interdependent contexts. *Academy of Management Journal, 50*, 327–347.

Hackman, J. R., & Oldham, G. R. (1975). Development of the Job Diagnostic Survey. *Journal of Applied Psychology, 60*, 159–170.

Hackman, J. R., & Oldham, G. R. (1976). Motivation through the design of work: Test of a theory. *Organizational Behavior & Human Decision Processes, 16*, 250–279.

Hatfield, E., Cacioppo, J.T., & Rapson, R. (1992). Primitive emotional contagion. In M. S. Clark (Ed.), *Emotion and social behavior. Review of personality and social psychology* (Vol. 14, pp. 151–177). Thousand Oaks, CA: Sage.

Hellman, C. M. (1997). Job satisfaction and intent to leave. *Journal of Social Psychology, 137*, 677–689.

Herzberg, F., Mausner, B., & Snyderman, B. (1959). *The motivation to work.* Oxford, UK: Wiley.

Holland, J. L. (1985). *Making vocational choices.* Englewood Cliffs, NJ: Prentice Hall.

Hornung, S., Rousseau, D. M., Glaser, J., Angerer, P., & Weigl, M. (2010). Beyond top-down and bottom-up work redesign: Customizing job content through idiosyncratic deals. *Journal of Organizational Behavior, 31*, 187–215.

Huczynski, A. (1996). *Influencing within organisations.* Hemel Hempstead, UK: Prentice Hall.

Hulin, C. L., & Smith, P. A. (1967). An empirical investigation of two implications of the two-factor theory of job satisfaction. *Journal of Applied Psychology, 51*, 396–402.

Humphrey, S. E., Nahrgang, J. D., & Morgeson, F. P. (2007). Integrating motivational, social, and contextual work design features: A meta-analytic summary and theoretical extension of the work design literature. *Journal of Applied Psychology, 92*, 1332–1356.

Ilgen, D., & Hollenbeck, J. (1991). The structure of work: Job design and roles. In M. D. Dunnette & L. M. Hough (Eds.), *Handbook of industrial and organizational psychology* (Vol. 2, pp. 165–208). Palo Alto, CA: Consulting Psychologists Press.

Ilies, R., & Judge, T. A. (2003). On the heritability of job satisfaction: The mediating role of personality. *Journal of Applied Psychology, 88*, 750–759.

Ilies, R., & Judge, T. A. (2005). Goal regulation across time: The effects of feedback and affect. *Journal of Applied Psychology, 90*, 453–467.

Jimmieson, N. L., & Terry, D. J. (1998). An experimental study of the effects of work stress, work control, and task information on adjustment. *Applied Psychology: An International Review, 47*, 343–369.

Jimmieson, N. L., & Terry, D. J. (1999). The moderating role of task characteristics in determining responses to a stressful work simulation. *Journal of Organizational Behavior, 20*, 709–736.

Johnson, E. C., Kristof-Brown, A. J., Van Vianen, A. E. M., De Pater, I. E., & Klein, M. R. (2003). Expatriate social ties: Personality antecedents and consequences for adjustment. *International Journal of Selection and Assessment, 11*, 277–288.

Judge, T. A. & Bono, J. E. (2001). Relationship of core self-evaluations traits—self-esteem, generalized self-efficacy, locus of control, and emotional stability—with job satisfaction and job performance: A meta-analysis. *Journal of Applied Psychology, 86*, 80–92.

Judge, T. A., Bono, J. E., & Locke, E. A. (2000). Personality and job satisfaction: The mediating role of job characteristics. *Journal of Applied Psychology, 85*, 237–249.

Judge, T. A., & Cable, D. M. (1997). Applicant personality, organizational culture, and organizational attraction, *Personnel Psychology, 50*, 359–394.

Judge, T. A., Locke, E. A., & Durham, C. C. (1997). The dispositional causes of job satisfaction: A core evaluations approach. *Research in Organizational Behavior, 19*, 151–188.

Judge, T. A., Locke, E. A., Durham, C. C., & Kluger, A. N. (1998). Dispositional effects on job and life satisfaction: The role of core evaluations. *Journal of Applied Psychology, 83*, 17–34.

Kahn, R. L., & Byosiere, P. (1992). Stress in organizations. In M. D. Dunnette & L. M. Hough (Eds.), *Handbook of industrial and organizational psychology* (Vol. 3, pp. 571–650). Palo Alto, CA: Consulting Psychologists Press.

Karasek, R. A. J. (1979). Job demands, job decision latitude, and mental strain: Implications for job redesign. *Administrative Science Quarterly, 24*, 285–308.

Karasek, R. A., Theorell, T. G. T., Schwartz, J., Pieper, C., & Alfredsson, L. (1982). Job, psychological factors and coronary heart disease. *Advanced Cardiology, 29*, 62–67.

Katz, D., & Kahn, R. L. (1966). *The social psychology of organizations.* New York, NY: Wiley.

Kohn, M. L., & Schooler, C. (1982). Job conditions and personality: A longitudinal assessment of their reciprocal effects. *The American Journal of Sociology, 87*, 1257–1286.

Kraiger, K., Billings, R. S., & Isen, A. M. (1989). The influence of positive affective states on task perceptions and satisfaction. *Organizational Behavior and Human Decision Processes, 44*, 12–25.

Kristof, A. L. (1996). Person-organization fit: An integrative review of its conceptualizations, measurement, and implications. *Personnel Psychology, 49*, 1–49.

Lazarus, R. S. (1966). *Psychological stress and the coping process.* New York, NY: McGraw-Hill.

Lazarus, R. S., & Folkman, S. (1984). *Stress, appraisal, and coping.* New York, NY: Springer.

Lee, R. T., & Ashforth, B. E. (1996). A meta-analytic examination of the correlates of the three dimensions of job burnout. *Journal of Applied Psychology, 81*, 123–133.

LePine, J. A., LePine, M. A., & Jackson, C. (2004). Challenge and hindrance stress: Relationships with exhaustion, motivation to learn, and learning performance. *Journal of Applied Psychology, 89*, 883–891.

LePine, J. A., Podsakoff, N. P., & LePine, M. A. (2005). A meta-analytic test of the challenge stressor-hindrance stressor framework: An explanation for inconsistent relationships among stressors and performance. *Academy of Management Journal, 48*, 767–775.

Loher, B. T., Noe, R. A., Moeller, N. L., & Fitzgerald, M. P. (1985). A meta-analysis of the relation of job characteristics to job satisfaction. *Journal of Applied Psychology, 70*, 280–289.

Lord, R. G., Brown, D. J., & Freiberg, S. J. (1999). Understanding the dynamics of leadership: The role of follower self-concepts in the leader/follower relationship. *Organizational Behavior and Human Decision Processes, 78*, 167–203.

Luthans, F. (2002). The need for and meaning of positive organizational behavior. *Journal of Organizational Behavior, 23*, 695–706.

Luthans, F., & Youssef, C. M. (2004). Human, social, and now positive psychological capital management: Investing in people for competitive advantage. *Organizational Dynamics, 33*, 143–160.

Macey, W. H., & Schneider, B. (2008). The meaning of employee engagement. *Industrial and Organizational Psychology: Perspectives on Science and Practice, 1*, 3–30.

Marmot, M. G., Davey Smith, G., Stansfeld, S., Patel, C., North, F., Head, J., Feeney, A. (1991). Health inequalities among British civil servants: The Whitehall II study. *The Lancet, 337*, 1387–1393.

May, D. R., Gilson, R. L., & Harter, L. M. (2004). The psychological conditions of meaningfulness, safety and availability and the engagement of the human spirit at work. *Journal of Occupational and Organizational Psychology, 77*, 11–37.

McCrae, R. R., & Costa, P. T., Jr. (1987). Validation of the five-factor model of personality across instruments and observers. *Journal of Personality and Social Psychology, 52*, 81–90.

McCrae, R. R., & Costa, P. T. (1991). Adding liebe und arbeit: The full five-factor model and well being. *Personality and Social Psychology Bulletin, 17*, 227–232.

Moorman, R. H. (1993). The influence of cognitive and affective based job satisfaction measures on the relationship between satisfaction and organizational citizenship behavior. *Human Relations, 46*, 759–776.

Morrison, E. W., & Phelps, C. (1999). Taking charge: Extra-role efforts to initiate workplace change. *Academy of Management Journal, 42*, 403–419.

Moyle, P. (1995). The role of negative affectivity in the stress process: Tests of alternative models. *Journal of Organizational Behavior, 16*, 647–668.

Neumann, R., & Strack, F. (2000). Approach and avoidance: The influence of proprioceptive and exteroceptive cues on affective processing. *Journal of Personality and Social Psychology, 79*, 39–48.

Nicholson, N. (1984). A theory of work role transitions. *Administrative Science Quarterly, 29*, 172–191.

North, F. M., Syme, L., Feeney, A., Shipley, M., & Marmot, M. (1996). Psychosocial work environment and sickness absence among British civil servants: The Whitehall II study. *American Journal of Public Health, 86*, 332–340.

Olivier, A. L., & Rothmann, S. (2007). Antecedents of work engagement in a multinational oil company. *SA Journal of Industrial Psychology, 33*, 49–56.

Parker, S. K. (2003). Longitudinal effects of lean production on employee outcomes and the mediating role of work characteristics. *Journal of Applied Psychology, 88*, 620–634.

Parker, S. K., Bindl, U. K., & Strauss, K. (2010). Making things happen: A model of proactive motivation. *Journal of Management, 36*, 827–856.

Parker, S. K., & Ohly, S. (2008). Designing motivating work. In R. Kanfer, G. Chen, & R. D. Pritchard (Eds.), *Work motivation: past, present, and future* (pp. 233–384). New York, NY: Routledge.

Parker, S. K., Wall, T. D., & Jackson, P. R. (1997). "That's not my job": Developing flexible employee work orientations. *Academy of Management Journal, 40*, 899–929.

Parker, S. K., Williams, H. M., & Turner, N. (2006). Modeling the antecedents of proactive behavior at work. *Journal of Applied Psychology, 91*, 636–652.

Parkes, K. R. (1990). Coping, negative affectivity, and the work environment: Additive and interactive predictors of mental health. *Journal of Applied Psychology, 75*, 399–409.

Paul, J. P., Robertson, K. B., & Herzberg, F. (1969). Job enrichment pays off. *Harvard Business Review, 47*, 61–78.

Perrewé, P. L., & Zellars, K. L. (1999). An examination of attribution and emotions in the transactional approach to the organizational stress process. *Journal of Organizational Behavior, 20*, 739–752.

Podsakoff, N. P., LePine, J. A., & LePine, M. A. (2007). Extending the challenge stressor-hindrance stressor framework: A meta-analytic test of differential relationships with job attitudes and retention criteria. *Journal of Applied Psychology, 92*, 438–454.

Roelen, C. A. M., Weites, S. H., Koopmans, P. C., van der Klink, J. J. L., & Groothoff, J. W. (2008). Sickness absence and psychosocial work conditions: A multilevel study. *Occupational Medicine, 58*, 425–430.

Russell, J. A. (1980). A circumplex model of affect. *Journal of Personality and Social Psychology, 39*, 1161–1178.

Saavedra, R., & Kwun, S. K. (2000). Affective states in job characteristics theory. *Journal of Organizational Behavior, 21*, 131–146.

Saks, A. M. (2006). Antecedents and consequences of employee engagement. *Journal of Managerial Psychology, 21*, 600–619.

Schaubroeck, J., & Merritt, D. (1997). Divergent effects of job control on coping with work stressors: The key role of self-efficacy. *Academy of Management Journal, 40*, 738–754.

Schaufeli, W., & Bakker, A. B. (2004). Job demands, job resources, and their relationship with burnout and engagement. *Journal of Organizational Behavior, 25*, 293–315.

Scherer, K. R. (1999). Appraisal theories. In T. Dalgleish & M. Power (Eds.), *Handbook of cognition and emotion* (pp. 637–663). Chichester, UK: Wiley.

Schneider, B. (1987). The people make the place. *Personnel Psychology, 40*, 437–453.

Searle, B. J., Bright, J., & Bochner, S. (1999). Testing the 3-factor model of occupational stress: The impact of demands, control and social support on a mail sorting task. *Work and Stress, 13*, 268–279.

Searle, B. J., Bright, J., & Bochner, S. (2001). Helping people sort it out: The role of social support in the job strain model of occupational stress. *Work and Stress, 15*, 328–346.

Seligman, M. E. P. (1975). *Helplessness: On depression, development, and death*. San Francisco, CA: W.H. Freeman.

Seligman, M. E. P. (1998). *Learned optimism* (2nd ed.). New York, NY: Simon and Schuster.

Selye, H. (1982). History and present status of the stress concept. In L. Goldberger & S. Breznitz (Eds.), *Handbook of stress: Theoretical and clinical aspects* (pp. 7–20). New York, NY: The Free Press.

Shaw, J. B., & Riskind, J. H. (1983). Predicting job stress using data from the position analysis questionnaire. *Journal of Applied Physiology, 68*, 253–261.

Shraga, O., & Shirom, A. (2009). The construct validity of vigor and its antecedents: A qualitative study. *Human Relations, 62*, 271–291.

Sims, H. P., Szilagyi, A. D., & Keller, R. T. (1976). The measurement of job characteristics. *Academy of Management Journal, 19*, 195–212.

Snyder, C. R., Irving, L. M., & Anderson, J. R. (1991). Hope and health. In C. R. Snyder & D. R. Forsyth (Eds.), *Handbook of social and clinical psychology: The health perspective* (pp. 285–305). Elmsford, NY: Pergamon.

Spector, P. E., & Jex, S.M. (1991). Relations of job stressors, job characteristics, and job analysis ratings to affective and health outcomes. *Journal of Applied Psychology, 76*, 46–53.

Spielberger, C. D., Gorsuch, R. C., & Lushene, R. E. (1970). *Manual for the state trait anxiety inventory*. Palo Alto, CA: Consulting Psychologists Press.

Spreitzer, G. M. (1995). Psychological empowerment in the workplace: Dimensions, measurement, and validation. *Academy of Management Journal, 38*, 1442–1465.

Srivastava, A., Locke, E. A., Judge, T. A., & Adams, J. W. (2010). Core self-evaluations as causes of satisfaction: The mediating role of seeking task complexity. *Journal of Vocational Behavior, 77*, 255–265.

Staw, B. M., & Boettger, R. D. (1990). Task revision: A neglected form of work performance. *Academy of Management Journal, 33*, 534–559.

Taylor, F. W. (1911). *The principles of scientific management*. New York, NY: W. W. Norton.

Tett, R. P., & Meyer, J. P. (1993). Job satisfaction, organizational commitment, turnover intention, and turnover: Path analyses based on meta-analytic findings. *Personnel Psychology, 46*, 259–293.

Thomas, K. W., & Velthouse, B. A. (1990). Cognitive elements of empowerment: An 'interpretive' model of intrinsic task motivation. *Academy of Management Review, 15*, 666–681.

Van Maanen, J., & Schein, E. H. (1979). Toward a theory of organizational socialization. *Research in Organizational Behavior, 1*, 209–264.

Warr, P. (1987). *Work, unemployment, and mental health*. Oxford, UK: Clarendon Press.

Warr, P. B. (1990). The measurement of well-being and other aspects of mental health. *Journal of Occupational Psychology, 52*, 129–148.

Warr, P. B. (1994). A conceptual framework for the study of work and mental health. *Work and Stress, 8*, 84–97.

Warr, P. B. (1997). Age, work, and mental health. In K. W. Schaie & C. Schooler (Eds.), *The impact of work on older adults* (pp. 252–296). New York, NY: Springer.

Weigl, M., Hornung, S., Parker, S. K., Petru, R., Glaser, J., & Angerer, P. (2010). Work engagement and accumulation of task, social, and personal resources: A three-wave structural equation model. *Journal of Vocational Behavior, 77*, 140–153.

Weiss, H. M. (2002). Conceptual and empirical foundations for the study of affect at work. In R. G. Lord, R. J. Klimoski, & R. Kanfer (Eds.), *Emotions in the workplace* (pp. 20–63). San Francisco, CA: Jossey-Bass.

Wrzesniewski, A., & Dutton, J. E. (2001). Crafting a job: Revisioning employees as active crafters of their work. *Academy of Management Review, 26*, 179–201.

Yeo, G., & Neal, A. (2006). An examination of the dynamic relationship between self-efficacy and performance across levels of analysis and levels of specificity. *Journal of Applied Psychology, 91*, 1088–1101.

CHAPTER 54

# JOBS AND JOB-HOLDERS: TWO SOURCES OF HAPPINESS AND UNHAPPINESS

## PETER WARR

Institute of Work Psychology, University of Sheffield, UK

PERSPECTIVES on the sources of happiness (sometimes viewed as "well-being") may be distinguished in terms of their primary emphasis—either on features in the environment or on people's thoughts and feelings. Much research in industrial-organizational psychology and occupational health psychology has been based on the first of those, examining the impact of job or organizational features (e.g., Hackman & Oldham, 1975; Schaufeli & Bakker, 2004), and relatively few publications have instead focused on workers and their cognitive and affective processes (e.g., Warr, 2006). Associated intervention studies have concentrated mainly on the environment (e.g., redesigning jobs and organizations) and less on the worker (e.g., managing negative thoughts and establishing positive routines).

Each approach has its value, but happiness and unhappiness clearly derive from both sources. Increased understanding in this area thus requires a combination of environment-centered and person-centered frameworks. This chapter will illustrate some possible ways to bring together research of the two kinds. The first two sections will separately cover environmental features and within-person mental processes, and a third section will examine the combined operation of those two kinds of variable. The emphasis will be on happiness with a medium conceptual focus, at the level of "domain-specific" (here job-related) happiness rather than broader "context-free" happiness (e.g., life satisfaction) or narrower "facet-specific" happiness (e.g., satisfaction with one's boss or pay).

# An Environment-Centered Perspective: Job Characteristics and Happiness

Within the environment-centered approach to worker happiness, there is a core need for appropriate classification of influential job features. The framework set out in Table 54.1 identifies the 12 principal characteristics of a job that have been widely shown to be associated with employee happiness or unhappiness. Items are preceded by "E" to indicate their environmental reference, and sub-components of each are illustrated in the second column.

A job that is psychologically "good" scores well on at least some of those features. The fact that the environmental sources of happiness or unhappiness are broadly the same in any domain gave rise to Warr's (1987, 2007) framework to account for experiences associated with employment, unemployment and retirement in the same terms. For example, the opportunity for personal control (E1 in the table) is essential in any setting for meeting personal goals, for

Table 54.1 Principal job characteristics affecting happiness or unhappiness

| Job feature | Themes and illustrative subcomponents |
| --- | --- |
| E1. Opportunity for personal control | Personal influence, autonomy, discretion, decision latitude, participation |
| E2. Opportunity for skill use and acquisition | A setting's potential for applying and developing expertise and knowledge |
| E3. Externally-generated goals | External demands, challenge, underload and overload, task identity, role conflict, required emotional labor, competition from others, work-home conflict |
| E4. Variety | Changes in task content and social contacts, varied work location |
| E5. Environmental clarity | Predictable outcomes, clear requirements, role clarity, task feedback, low future ambiguity |
| E6. Contact with others | Amount of social contact, quality of social relationships, dependence on others, team working |
| E7. Availability of money | Available income, pay level, payment for results |
| E8. Physical security | Working conditions, degree of hazard, quality of equipment |
| E9. Valued social position | Significance of a task or role, contribution to society, status in valued groups |
| E10. Supportive supervision | Consideration by bosses, fair treatment by supervisor, concern for one's welfare |
| E11. Career outlook | Job security, the opportunity to gain promotion or shift to other roles |
| E12. Equity | Justice within one's organization, fairness in the organization's relations with society |

sustaining a sense of personal agency, and for reducing feelings of helplessness. Environmental clarity (E5) is generally desired both to reduce anxiety about the future and to make it possible to plan and regulate actions. Nine of the characteristics in Table 54.1 are important in roles of all kinds (including unemployment, retirement, and home-making), and three of them (E10, E11, and E12) specifically concern jobs. See also Warr and Clapperton (2010).

## Non-linear associations and the vitamin analogy

The importance of these 12 environmental features has been demonstrated by research in many countries, but the precise nature of particular processes requires further examination. For example, it seems likely that the level of an environmental feature is associated with happiness in a non-linear fashion, specifically in a pattern analogous to the effect of vitamins on bodily condition. Vitamins are important for physical health up to but not beyond a certain level. At low levels of intake, vitamin deficiency gives rise to physiological impairment and ill-health (sometimes referred to in a medical context as "deficiency disease"), but after a moderate level has been reached (the "recommended, or guideline, daily allowance") there is no benefit from additional quantities. In a similar manner, it may be that the absence of a primary environmental characteristic leads to certain forms of unhappiness, but that its presence beyond a certain level does not further increase happiness.

In addition, some vitamins become toxic in very large quantities, so that the association between increased vitamin intake and physical health becomes negative beyond moderate amounts. This relationship may also occur for certain aspects of the environment, particularly with respect to context-free (rather than more restricted forms of) happiness. The possibility is summarized in Fig. 54.1, where low ("deficiency") values of an environmental feature are depicted as particularly harmful and those in the middle range are shown as

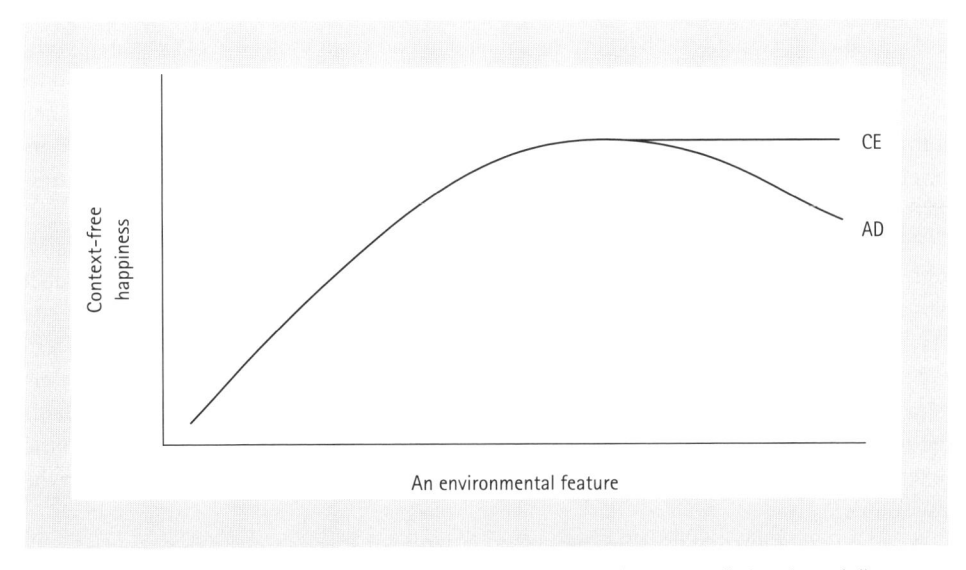

FIG. 54.1 The vitamin analogy: proposed "additional decrement" (AD) and "constant effect" (CE) relationships between environmental features and context-free happiness. For context-specific and facet-specific happiness see the text.

having a constant beneficial effect on happiness. A second, smaller decrement is proposed at particularly high ("toxic") values for certain environmental features (labeled as "AD") but not for others ("CE").

These two labels are also based on abbreviations in the vitamin analogy. There are no toxic consequences from very high intakes of certain vitamins: deficiency causes ill-health, but additional doses beyond a moderate amount have a constant effect. Vitamins C and E are of that kind. The abbreviation "CE" in Fig. 54.1 reflects this pattern, and can also stand for "constant effect." On the other hand, vitamins A and D are toxic at very high levels, and "AD" in the figure may be read as an "additional decrement."

The vitamin model suggests that six of the primary environmental features considered so far may be viewed as analogues of vitamins A and D, and that the other six instead parallel vitamins C and E. Suggested AD vitamins are E1 to E6 in Table 54.1: opportunity for personal control, opportunity for skill use and acquisition, externally-generated goals, variety, environmental clarity, and contact with others. The CE features thought to have a constant effect beyond moderate levels are E7 to E12: availability of money, physical security, valued social position, supportive supervision, career outlook, and equity (Warr, 2007; Warr & Clapperton, 2010).

Why should certain features of the environment (E1 to E6), desirable at moderate levels, become harmful when extremely high? The "too much of a good thing" pattern seems likely for both intrinsic reasons and because of associated effects from other features. Very high levels of some environmental characteristics can become punishing in themselves, and they are likely also to be accompanied by extremely high levels of other features that themselves yield an additional decrement.

Thus features identified as "opportunities" (for control and for skill use; E1 and E2) are expected to yield happiness decrements at the right-hand side of Fig. 54.1 as the "opportunity" becomes an "unavoidable requirement" at very high levels; behavior is then coerced rather than being encouraged or facilitated. For example, environments that call for unremitting control (a very high level of feature E1) through extremely difficult decision-making and sustained personal responsibility, or which demand continuous use of extremely complex skills (E2), can give rise to overload problems as very high demands exceed personal capabilities (e.g., Burger, 1989). In part, those problems of excess arise from an associated shift to a particularly high level of externally-generated goals (E3). As those goals become extremely difficult and/or numerous, demands may become complex and internally contradictory, beyond a person's ability to cope (e.g., Warr, 2007, chapter 6).

Extremely high variety in the environment (E4) requires constant switching of attention and activity, with resulting low concentration and limited attainment of single goals; conflict between contradictory goals may then be present (an aspect of E3), and extreme diversity may prohibit the development and use of skills (E2). E5 (environmental clarity) appears also to be of this "additional decrement" (AD) kind. At extremely high levels, there is no uncertainty about the future, events are entirely predictable and never novel, and a fixed set of role requirements permits no new experiences. Such settings prevent risk-taking, contain little potential for skill development, and provide no opportunity to expand one's control over the environment.

A similar down-turn of the happiness curve is expected at very high levels of contact with other people (E6). Very large social inputs can impair well-being through overcrowding and lack of privacy in high-density situations, or through a lack of personal control, frequent interruptions, and the prohibited initiation of valued activities because of other people's continuing demands. Behavioral procedures and physical structures to prevent excessive social contact have been created in cultures of all kinds (e.g., Altman & Chemers, 1980).

Several environmental features in the vitamin model are thus assumed to be of the "additional decrement" kind, with their positive association with happiness not only leveling off across the moderate to high range but also becoming reversed at very high levels; research evidence about jobs will be illustrated below. Harmful effects at very high "toxic" levels are likely to be less severe than at very low levels, since deficiencies in a feature (at the left of Fig. 54.1) carry particularly negative implications for the person; and even excessively high levels retain some of the benefits provided in the moderate range. The additional decrement (AD) assumption about context-free happiness as a function of certain environmental features thus takes the form of an asymmetrical, flattened, inverse U-shaped association.

This average pattern for context-free happiness is likely to be slightly different for narrower forms—domain-specific or facet-specific happiness. At the context-free level, additional features from multiple domains (e.g., family or social life as well as merely from a job) cumulatively bear upon happiness, in different ways for different people and with potentially inconsistent or conflicting impacts; the relationship between context-free happiness and a single environmental feature is also determined by other aspects of life. However, more focused forms of happiness are less subject to a wide range of different influences, and happiness of those kinds is less likely to level off and then decline as an environmental feature becomes increasingly positive. The general possibility in Fig. 54.1 is thus likely to vary slightly between different levels of happiness scope. Specifically, the mid-range plateau shown in the figure is expected to be progressively shorter as one moves from context-free to facet-specific experiences, with environment-happiness associations at the facet-specific level tending to be most linear; see Warr (2007, chapter 4).

The vitamin model also proposes that, beyond medium levels, differences in the other six features in Table 54.1 (E7 to E12) are on average unrelated to (especially context-free) happiness, exhibiting a "constant effect" (CE) across all the higher range. Although extremely high levels of these features can create unhappiness in particular cases, increases within the high range are on average unlikely to have an incrementally negative effect for people as a whole. The high-range negative impact proposed for "additional decrement" features (see earlier) was suggested to arise from two sources: each one's inherent harmful impact, and associated harm from other variables. Neither of those impacts is expected on average for high levels of the identified "constant effect" features. Instead, it is assumed that high to very high values of those characteristics are on average accompanied by similar levels of context-free happiness.

In all cases, a non-linear association between the level of an environmental feature and people's happiness is thus proposed. Environmental increments of a certain size at lower values (to the left of Fig. 54.1) are suggested to give rise to greater increases in happiness than do increments of the same magnitude at moderate to high values. Some non-linearity of this kind appears to be logically necessary, since affects are inherently limited in their intensity; it is not possible for them to continue to increase at the same rate without limit.

To what extent have research findings in occupational settings been consistent with these proposals? Only a tiny proportion of studies in this area have examined possible departures from linearity, and many of those are unsuitable for the task since their environmental scores are restricted in range and do not extend fully from very low to very high levels. Linked to that, research into several job characteristics has intentionally examined only a limited section of scores, for example covering only low or only high levels of skill use, variety or demands. In addition, the common statistical practice in this area of including a variety of non-linear functions within the same multiple regression is inappropriate. That simultaneous analysis tests a multivariate hypothesis that is different from the primary one discussed here. To learn about a single variable's non-linearity, we should not previously have extracted the variance linked to other variables' non-linearity.

Empirical evidence about Fig. 54.1 relationships is thus both scarce and often inadequate. However, "additional decrements," as proposed for the first six "vitamins," have been observed in several studies of job-related well-being. In respect of E1 (opportunity for personal control), Baltes, Bauer, Bajdo, and Parker (2002) recorded an AD pattern for job satisfaction, and a leveling-off beyond medium levels was found in studies described by Warr (2007). (An absence of extremely high levels of personal control in typical research samples may be relevant here.) Findings across a wide range of scores are not available for E2 (opportunity for skill use and acquisition), but overlaps of that feature with E1 and E3 suggest that a similar pattern is present.

In respect of externally-generated goals (E3), research restricted to either low or high scores (sometimes referred to as "underload" and "overload" respectively) has shown that well-being is associated in opposite directions at the two extremes of the horizontal axis in Fig. 54.1. "Additional decrement" patterns across a wider range of E3 have been demonstrated by, for instance, Karasek (1979) and Warr (1990). Other studies have observed an AD pattern for particular forms of happiness or in specific subsamples (e.g., De Jonge, Reuvers, Houtman, Bongers, & Kompier, 2000).

For role clarity (an aspect of E5), significant non-linearity with a decrement at the highest levels was observed by Baltes et al. (2002). In respect of E6, research has examined both the quantity and the quality of social contact. In terms of quantity, very low social density can of course yield feelings of loneliness and personal isolation; and very high levels of input from other people have been shown to be undesirable in work settings through studies of open-plan offices (e.g., Brennan, Chugh, & Kline, 2002). The importance of quality of interaction (rather than merely its quantity) has been confirmed by research into bullying (e.g., Zapf, Einarsen, Hoel, & Varti, 2003) and social support (e.g., Viswesvaran, Sanchez, & Fisher, 1999) in the low or higher ranges of that feature respectively. "Additional decrement" effects also occur at higher levels of E6. A laboratory experiment by Deelstra, Peeters, Schaufeli, Stroebe, Zilstra, and van Doornen (2003) arranged for workers in a simulated office setting to receive instrumental assistance from a co-worker, who was in fact a confederate of the investigators. Extremely high levels of social support of this kind led to a down-turn in affect, as illustrated in Fig. 54.1. That pattern was also observed in an organizational sample by de Jonge et al. (2000).

In respect of the other environmental features in Table 54.1, only a few studies have examined possible non-linearity. However, stabilization of association after moderate quantities has frequently been demonstrated in respect of income (E7) and context-free happiness. A standard increment in income, which can provide a major benefit to people in poverty, yields a smaller benefit to happiness in the wealthy. This "constant effect" pattern has been found in comparisons between individuals within a single country (e.g., Diener, Sandvik, Seidlitz, & Diener, 1993) and in terms of average scores for entire nations (e.g., Frey & Stutzer, 2001). Non-linearity in respect of this feature appears not to have been tested in organizational research, although Kornhauser (1965) reported a stronger association between pay and happiness among lower-skilled employees.

Examining supervisors' considerate behavior (E10), non-linearity at the group level (rather than in respect of individuals themselves) was observed by Fleishman and Harris (1962). They found that subordinates' grievances and turnover were correlated with this environmental feature at low levels of consideration but not at higher levels. For equity (E12), Schaufeli's (2006) review identified non-linear patterns in several studies. For example, Taris, Kalimo, and Schaufeli (2002) found that, once a threshold of acceptability had been reached, further increments had no further impact. This "constant effect" pattern appears likely on conceptual grounds to be widely found: above a moderately high level of features E7 to E12, small gains (important at low levels) are expected to be of little average consequence.

Discussion so far has concerned individual aspects of a job, the 12 "vitamins" in Table 54.1. Jobs do of course involve several features in combination, and it might be expected that compounds of either "additional decrement" or "constant effect" elements will also yield the patterns in Fig. 54.1. No study has examined non-linearity across an entire subset of "vitamins" (either all AD or all CE together), but Xie and Johns (1995) observed the asymmetric inverted-U in a study combining four assumed AD features and one of the "constant effect" kind.

Job features may also combine with each other in an interactive manner, yielding non-linear patterns only in certain combinations. For example, Chung-Yan (2010) found an inverted-U relationship between job complexity and job satisfaction for workers whose job autonomy was low but not for higher-autonomy workers: the tipping point at which additional complexity became undesirable to a job-holder was lower when the freedom to handle that complexity was also low.

In overview, the environmental vitamin model proposes non-linearity of association between job content and worker happiness or unhappiness, with different forms of non-linearity in two sets of job features. Additionally but not detailed here because of space limitations, the model contains different predictions for different indices of happiness. For example, very high job demands are expected and found to have a particularly negative impact in respect of job-related anxiety-contentment rather than for depression-enthusiasm (see Warr, 2007). Another implication of this non-linear account concerns between-study differences. If an examined sample is mainly to the right of Fig. 54.1 in, say, job demands (E3), a negative association between that feature and happiness is expected. However, if the sample happens to be more widely spread or located mainly in the middle of the range, a correlation around zero is likely. Observed demands-happiness patterns are expected to vary somewhat between investigations, and that is indeed the case.

# A Person-Centered Perspective: Mental Processes and Happiness

Although environmental sources are important as already considered, happiness and unhappiness also derive from within a person himself or herself. Two aspects are important: longer-term characteristics, such as dispositional or demographic features, and also an individual's way of attending to and thinking about particular situations as they are experienced.

In the former respect, personality traits such as neuroticism, extraversion and conscientiousness are significantly related to many happiness indicators including job satisfaction (e.g., Judge, Heller, & Mount, 2002) and job engagement (Inceoglu & Warr, 2011); and associations of well-being with age (e.g., Clark, Oswald, & Warr, 1996) and gender (e.g., Warr, 2007) are often also significant. In regard to shorter-term influences, happiness is partly a function of several comparative judgments, concerned with where one has been, where one might be instead, how the future might develop, and assessments of self-efficacy, novelty and personal salience. Ten judgments of those kinds are summarized in Table 54.2, together with questions that people might ask themselves in respect of each one.

In respect of judgment J1 in Table 54.2, it is regularly found in non-organizational research that "downward" comparisons with other people (i.e., judgments made relative to people who are worse-off in the relevant respect) tend to enhance a person's own happiness (e.g., Wheeler, 2000). Some studies in employment settings have adopted the framework of equity theory to examine social comparisons of several kinds, finding that perceived input-output ratios in comparison with other people's ratios affect feelings; happiness can depend in part on perceptions of fairness in relation to other people. For example, satisfaction with pay received (an "output") has been shown to depend on perceived comparisons with other

Table 54.2 Multiple judgments of a situation within a person-centered approach to happiness or unhappiness

| Type of mental process | Illustrative self-questions |
| --- | --- |
| J1. Comparisons with other people | J1. "How does my situation compare with that of another individual/group or of the average person?" |
| J2. Comparisons with other situations | |
| J2A. Expected situation | J2A. "How does my situation compare with the situation I expected?" |
| J2B. Counterfactual situation(s) | J2B. "How might the situation have developed in other ways?" |
| J3. Comparisons with other times | |
| J3A. Previous trend | J3A. "Up to now, has the situation deteriorated, improved, or remained unchanged?" |
| J3B. Likely future trend | J3B. "From now on, is the situation likely to deteriorate, improve, or remain unchanged?" |
| J4. Assessments of situation-related self-efficacy | J4. "Was/is my performance effective in this situation?" |
| J5. Assessments of novelty or familiarity | J5. "Is the situation unusual or is it routine?" |
| J6. Assessments of personal salience | |
| J6A. Rated importance of role membership | J6A. "Do I want to be in this role?" |
| J6B. Rated importance of a role characteristic | J6B. "Do I value this feature?" |
| J6C. Rated attractiveness of core tasks in the role | J6C. "Do I like the things I have to do?" |

people's pay relative to their effort, skill, and other "inputs" (e.g., Adams 1965). Schaufeli (2006) has documented similar themes in respect of social exchange in organizations, and comparative processes of this kind are likely in respect of several other environmental contributors in Table 54.1.

Comparisons with other situations (J2 in Table 54.2) can be of two kinds—in relation to situations that were expected, or relative to those that otherwise might have occurred. In these ways, job-related well-being sometimes derives in part from judgments based on a person's prior expectations (J2A) or on assessments of other situations, known or imagined (J2B). In the first case, laboratory studies have confirmed that events that are unexpected have a greater impact on happiness or unhappiness than do those that were expected. The J2B comparison involves consideration of either poorer or better counterfactual alternatives, those which are contrary to the facts. People may focus upon ways in which their current situation might instead have developed, for example judging that the situation could be a lot worse or better than it is.

Upward counterfactual judgments (relative to a more attractive possibility) tend to evoke unpleasant feelings, whereas downward comparisons (which consider an alternative that is worse than reality) can increase a person's happiness (Olson, Buhrman, & Roese, 2000). The process was illustrated by Medvec, Madey, and Gilovich (1995) in a study of Olympic medalists. Those receiving silver medals for achieving second place tended to be less happy with their position than were bronze medalists in third place. Many second-place winners appeared to base their feelings in part on upward counterfactual comparisons ("I failed to be the best"), whereas athletes in third place were more likely to make downward comparisons, being pleased to have reached the medal positions ("I did better than all the rest").

Third in Table 54.2 are assessments of previous and likely future trends (J3). For example (J3A), has this stressful situation been getting better or worse? Have I moved adequately towards a goal? Given that goals may be defined as "internal representations of desired states" (Austin & Vancouver, 1996, p. 338), good progress towards a goal (a "desired state") is generally associated with better well-being, and low or negative progress gives rise to reduced well-being (e.g., Lyubomirsky, Sheldon, & Schkade, 2005). Linked to that, employees' attainment of work goals can contribute to their job-related happiness and context-free well-being (Harris, Daniels, & Briner, 2003; Wiese & Freund, 2005).

Table 54.2 also draws attention to the possible impact on well-being of expectations about a future trend (J3B). This has sometimes been examined as perceived probability of success, and positive expectations of that kind are significantly associated with subjective well-being (e.g., Emmons, 1986); in everyday terms, happiness is often felt to depend in part on "having something to look forward to." One implication is that in negative situations, for instance during job stress, it can be predicted that employees' unhappiness will be in part a function of expected future levels of that stress. Examining the extent to which employees mentally "switch off" after a working day, Sonnentag and Bayer (2005) concluded it is not primarily the amount of time pressure that one has faced at work that makes psychological detachment difficult, but rather the anticipation that time pressure will continue during the working days to come.

The appraisal judgments reviewed so far (J1 to J3) have their impact on happiness or unhappiness through comparisons with reference standards that are external to the person. J4 to J6 in Table 54.2 operate instead in relation to a person's own bench-marks, in terms of self-efficacy, novelty and personal salience.

Self-efficacy reflects a person's perception that he or she is competent in relation to present demands (J4 in Table 54.2). Both retrospective and prospective judgments about situation-related self-efficacy are likely to influence happiness. In the first case, recent behavior is compared against one's bench-mark level of competence, in response to questions like "Have I coped well?" or "Have I made a mess of this?." For example, an employee's perception that he or she has failed to prevent a controllable negative event might give rise to even more unhappiness. Scheck and Kinicki (2000) found that employees' positive assessments of their self-efficacy during organizational change were linked to lower perceptions of threat and potential harm. In addition, future-oriented beliefs about one's personal efficacy in a situation (such as "I'm going to be able to handle this" or "I'm not going to cope") are expected to influence current happiness, even when a perceived ability to exercise control over that situation is in fact illusory (e.g., Bandura & Locke, 2003). As in other cases, relevant investigations in job settings are still required.

Also important are a person's assessments of the novelty or familiarity of a current situation (J5 in Table 54.2). Continued exposure to a situation tends to reduce its affective potential, either negative or positive, so that more familiar inputs come to generate feelings that are less extreme. In effect, you evaluate your position partly in terms of what you are used to.

Biological and psychological processes of habituation have been widely observed, when responses to a stimulus become diminished after repeated presentation of that stimulus. Such a change may be viewed in terms of a raised adaptation level, when exposure to earlier stimuli establishes a higher standard against which later stimuli are judged. Over time, instances of a particular stimulus have to exceed that increased threshold in order to influence well-being to the same degree. For example, judgmental thresholds may be indexed as the average pleasantness of recent experiences (Parducci, 1995). An increase across time in this average pleasantness implies that a later event or situation has to be more pleasurable (exceeding the raised judgmental standard) before it has the same impact on well-being.

Much research has demonstrated that positive feelings in response to a constant or repeated environmental stimulus can gradually become reduced or even give way to indifference. For example, Brickman, Coates, and Janoff-Bulman (1978) reported adaptation across time in people who had won large sums of money in a state lottery, and also found that victims of serious accidents did not appear as unhappy as might have been expected. They drew attention to a common perceptual error, when observers see victims of misfortune as more distressed than do those people themselves.

Forms of hedonic adaptation have been illustrated in several projects in organizations. Boswell, Boudreau, and Tichy (2005) studied well-being changes longitudinally among employees voluntarily moving into a new job. Overall job satisfaction was found to increase immediately after entry into a new position, but in subsequent years it declined significantly as individuals became adapted to the realities of their role. Daniels and Guppy (1997) examined employees' strain as a function of particular environmental stressors, finding that experienced strain was less from those stressors that had previously been encountered.

Processes of adaptation may thus contribute to an increased ability to handle environmental demands after a period of exposure to those demands. In that respect, everyday experience suggests that many people's capacity to manage a substantial workload becomes "ratcheted up" after a period of coping with increased pressure; a workload that would otherwise cause difficulties and strain can more easily be handled after a person has become adapted to a raised level. The impact of workload itself (an environmental feature) is not fixed—it depends in part on judgments about one's situation.

Adaptation can operate through the application of other judgments in the framework. For example, changes in J1 and J2B (comparisons with other people and with other possible situations) can contribute to adaptation, as people over time come to reinterpret their situation through new social comparisons or by emphasizing different counterfactual possibilities. In addition, adaptation can give rise to changes in the impact of environmental features considered earlier. For example, environmental clarity (E5 in Table 54.1) can increase as knowledge develops, and contact with others (E6) may be modified as mutual learning occurs between an individual and people in his or her changed setting. Adjustment to a situation may also involve shifts in externally-generated goals (E3), as different activities are undertaken or a person's ability to attain particular goals becomes enhanced or reduced.

The happiness or unhappiness of employees whose job features have improved or deteriorated is for these reasons likely to return towards an equilibrium level, perhaps being held under personal homeostatic control (Cummins, 2000). The "dynamic equilibrium model" of Headey and Wearing (1992) proposed that each person has a customary level of well-being, and that changes from that level are likely to be only temporary as subsequent adaptation occurs. Headey and Wearing observed this pattern in a community sample across a 6-year period. The longitudinal pattern reported for job-changers by Boswell et al. (2005) also illustrated a return to people's baseline happiness levels after a temporary increase in happiness. Within banking organizations, Griffin (1991) found that, although the content of employees' jobs remained enhanced for several years after job redesign, their overall job satisfaction increased only temporarily before falling back to its earlier level. This tendency for happiness and unhappiness to stabilize around a person's baseline level is reflected in significant associations with personality traits (illustrated earlier) and in consistency of, for instance, satisfaction across time (e.g., Bowling, Beehr, Wagner, & Libkuman, 2005).

Finally in Table 54.2 are judgments about the personal salience of an environmental feature (J6). Research in this area has used two sets of descriptive labels, which are conceptually and empirically interdependent. On the one hand, the salience of a situation or environmental feature has been examined in terms of the degree to which it is viewed as personally important, significant, or of concern (i.e., how much it "matters to" a person). In other studies, descriptions have been in terms of a person's wants, preferences or values—the extent to which he or she would like the feature to be present.

Judgments of personal salience are likely to have a moderating influence on happiness in many domains of life. Table 54.2 points out that relevant themes may be viewed at three levels of generality—concerned with the salience of role membership (e.g., the strength of one's commitment to having a job, J6A), the salience of role characteristics (e.g., how much one values personal autonomy in a job, J6B), or the salience of core tasks (e.g., how much one is attracted to working with animals in a job, J6C). Occupational research at all three levels has been reviewed by Warr (2007); the present focus (illustrated in the following section) will be restricted to J6B, the perceived desirability of job features.

In overview, the present section has emphasized that happiness or unhappiness in jobs and elsewhere depends on the person as well as the environment. Personal influences on well-being can derive from long-term attributes and dispositions, and in addition research has pointed to the importance of certain kinds of thought about a current situation. Both long-term personal features and situation-specific mental processes require inclusion in studies of work and happiness. However, most occupational research has focused only on the job or organizational environment, and conversely the few person-oriented studies that do examine within-worker variables have typically excluded the environment, reporting merely associations between, for instance, personality traits and outcomes irrespective of possible impacts from characteristics of an individual's job. Findings to date are thus one-sided and incomplete.

# A Combined Perspective: Happiness as a Function of Both Job and Personal Characteristics

How might these two perspectives—environment-centered and person-centered—be brought together? Several forms of joint operation can be envisaged. For example, the two kinds of variable might both affect happiness but operate independently of each other. Alternatively, they might work together through some form of mediation, perhaps such that the environment has its impact partly or entirely through personal variables. Or the two may have a moderating impact on each other, with one's association depending on the level of the other. In addition, mutual impact can develop across time, for example, as individuals' cognitive, physical, or personality attributes encourage a transition into certain forms of employment or a concentration on certain job activities, which then affect happiness. Joint operation of those kinds can involve personal variables that are either relatively long-term (e.g., dispositional traits) or shorter-term (as in situation-specific judgments).

## Longer-term personal influences

Mediation of a personality-happiness link through aspects of job content has been illustrated by Judge, Bono, and Locke (2000) and Grant and Langan-Fox (2007), and across-time processes are reflected in a significant longitudinal association between negative affectivity and key job characteristics a year later (Houkes, Janssen, de Jonge, & Bakker, 2003). Evidence is also growing about the moderation of job–happiness associations by relevant aspects of personality; job features can have either more or less impact depending on certain dispositional traits.

For example, Kahn, Wolfe, Quinn, and Snoek (1964) and Keenan and McBain (1979) showed that the correlation of role ambiguity with aspects of happiness differed between workers with low and high ambiguity-tolerance. Vroom's (1959) study found that the autonomy-satisfaction correlation depended on a worker's low authoritarianism and preference for independence. Other job-related instances of personality moderation have been reported by Bond, Flaxman, and Bunce (2008), Dijkstra, van Dierendonck, Evers, and de Dreu (2005), Rego, Souto, and Cunha (2009), and Rogelberg, Leach, Warr, and Burnfield (2006). Workman and Bommer (2004) described an experimental study in which call center jobs were redesigned to increase team-based interaction; job satisfaction increased most for those employees with a stronger preference for working in a group.

Moderation of this kind has also been demonstrated in respect of workers' continuing preferences (a form of value-judgment) for particular job features. Individuals who value a particular job characteristic are more likely to be affected by the degree to which it is present or absent (e.g., Rice, Gentile, & McFarlin, 1991). This pattern has also been shown for groups of job features, for which preferences have been recorded as "growth need strength"

(GNS—the extent to which a worker values a mix of intrinsic job features such as personal autonomy, new learning, and so on.). Much research has confirmed that correlations between relevant job features and job satisfaction are greater for high-GNS employees than for those who value the features less (e.g., Loher, Noe, Moeller, & Fitzgerald, 1985).

Personal dispositions are expected also to affect the linearity or non-linearity of associations between job features and happiness. For example, the same level of high task demands can overload less able workers (yielding an AD pattern as described earlier) while their more able colleagues cope with those demands and may seek still more challenge. A down-turn in well-being is thus expected to accompany still-greater demands at more moderate levels for less able individuals. Similarly, low scorers on a particular personality trait will sooner reach a tipping point for trait-relevant job features; they do not want still-higher levels of those features in the way that high-trait individuals do. For example, Rego et al. (2009) found that workers with a lower need to belong showed greater non-linearity in the association between degree of social support and affective well-being than did high-need workers; for individuals with a lower need for interpersonal inputs, high levels of support more readily yielded "additional decrements" than for workers who more sought that support.

## Shorter-term personal influences

It is clear (see earlier) that environmental features are associated with happiness or unhappiness to different degrees and in different ways according to the nature of an individual, for example in respect of his or her personality traits and continuing values. This pattern is presumably linked to disposition-related differences in ways of thinking and feeling about one's environment, and shorter-term mental processes of that kind require inclusion in studies and models of well-being. Staw and Cohen-Charash (2005) have illustrated how the experience of job satisfaction derives from several within-person information-processing steps—recognition and evaluation of work features, memory and retrieval, element-aggregation, and the expression of feelings. Aspects of those occur within the ten forms of situational judgment in Table 54.2, but mental processes of those kinds have rarely been investigated in job settings.

A key research need in this area is for the creation of thought-process measures that can be incorporated in studies of the environment. There are undoubtedly problems in the accurate measurement of cognitive activity, and the reliability and validity of retrospective self-reports is open to question. Nevertheless, given that observed correlations between job features and happiness indicators are often only moderate and that causal mechanisms can depend on the mental processes involved, it is essential to include measures of at least some of the Table 54.2 judgments in well-being research. For example, the nature of a worker's relevant social or counterfactual comparisons (J1 and J2B) should be explored, and job-feature preferences (J6B) should routinely be recorded within studies of job characteristics and their outcomes. Given that the degree of discrepancy between job content and a worker's preferences is in general linked to job-related well-being (e.g., Ostroff & Judge, 2007), more research into specific forms of misfit and different aspects of well-being would be valuable (Warr & Inceoglu, 2012).

It is also important to learn about factors linked to the occurrence or non-occurrence of each type of Table 54.2 judgment. Their prevalence, and thus potential impact, is likely to be associated with factors such as the nature of a setting, personality traits, age, and gender. Furthermore, differences in cognitive emphasis are likely to depend in part on local norms in a work-group or wider culture (Warr, 2006).

## Person-oriented interventions

In addition to environment-and-person studies that examine potentially important longer-term and shorter-term personal variables (described earlier), a third combined approach is through individual-level interventions to enhance well-being. Counseling procedures to reduce strain in a particular setting may seek to encourage relaxation, meditation, stress awareness, more appropriate assertiveness, or improved time management and goal-setting. Some programs have applied themes from cognitive behavioral therapy, in which a trainer and a client work together to identify a worker's negative thoughts and seek to replace those by more constructive routines.

Occupational strain management programs have proved to be effective across at least several subsequent weeks (e.g., Richardson & Rothstein, 2008), especially for workers with high initial levels of distress (Flaxman & Bond, 2010). Positive findings in non-job settings have been brought together by Lyobomirsky (2008) and applied to happiness at work by Warr and Clapperton (2010). Person-centered studies of this kind, introducing and monitoring change, are in effect experiments into the impact of potentially important cognitive and affective variables. They take us more directly to potential within-person causal explanations, and can go beyond the limitations of research which merely examines correlations between well-being and its possible sources. Worker-oriented interventions are therefore desirable for both practical and theoretical reasons—both to reduce strain and also to develop and test models about person-level processes underlying happiness or unhappiness in particular environmental conditions.

Intervention studies can sometimes be strengthened by the inclusion of person-oriented themes from the two previous sections, covering longer-term attributes or situational judgments. In that way, dispositional, demographic, and judgmental variables found in correlational research to be associated with happiness or unhappiness can helpfully be incorporated in intervention projects, providing by means of experiment more detailed information about causal processes. For example, Bond and Bunce (2000) found that workers' willingness to accept undesirable thoughts and feelings mediated the beneficial impact of an emotion-focused intervention on distress and depression. Intervention studies that change environmental variables as well as processes within an individual are particularly desirable, in part because adjustments to a work setting can themselves be important in implementing and maintaining person-level changes.

# CONCLUSION AND FUTURE DIRECTIONS

This chapter has emphasized that, in order to understand and enhance worker happiness, it is essential to examine aspects of the person as well as features of a job and organization. Within that overall need, the following developments are advocated:

- Investigate the possible mediation or moderation of environment–outcome links by personality dispositions and personal values and by situation-specific mental processes.
- Explore the presence of non-linear relationships between job features and happiness or unhappiness, and examine how non-linearity may differ between individuals with different characteristics.

- Develop models and measures of job-relevant judgments of the kind illustrated in Table 54.2.
- Expand person-oriented intervention research in job settings, to enhance well-being and to learn more about key causal processes.

Other themes merely mentioned within the chapter's space limitation also point to desirable action requirements. For example, it is essential to distinguish conceptually and empirically between different forms of happiness and unhappiness (e.g., Spector, Chen, & O'Connell, 2000, p. 216): each one has its own partly distinct sources and consequences (e.g., Warr, 2007; Warr & Inceoglu, 2012; Warr, Bindl, Parker, & Inceoglu, 2012). And the joint investigation in a single study of our discipline's two key outcomes—performance as well as well-being—remains extremely rare. It is essential to learn more about how those might affect each other. For instance, procedures to enhance well-being might sometimes impair productivity, or personal or organizational efforts to improve performance might give rise to greater anxiety and tension before raised well-being becomes possible. In addition, a mental and behavioral trade-off may occur, as individuals seek to regulate one in relation to the other; why work any harder if that will make you anxious, exhausted or even ill? Joint performance-and-happiness issues of these kinds provide exciting opportunities for future research.

# References

Adams, J. S. (1965). Inequity in social exchange. In L. Berkowitz (Ed.), *Advances in experimental social psychology* (pp. 267–299). San Diego CA: Academic Press.

Altman, I., & Chemers, M. (1980). *Culture and environment.* Monterey, CA: Brooks Cole.

Austin, J. T., & Vancouver, J. B. (1996). Goal constructs in psychology: Structure, process, and content. *Psychological Bulletin, 120,* 338–375.

Baltes, B. B., Bauer, C. C., Bajdo, L. M., & Parker, C. P. (2002). The use of multitrait-multimethod data for detecting non-linear relationships: The case of psychological climate and job satisfaction. *Journal of Business and Psychology, 17,* 3–17.

Bandura, A., & Locke, E. A. (2003). Negative self-efficacy and goal effects revisited. *Journal of Applied Psychology, 88,* 87–99.

Bond, F. W., & Bunce, D. (2000). Mediators of change in emotion-focused and problem-focused worksite stress management interventions. *Journal of Occupational Health Psychology, 5,* 156–163.

Bond, F. W., Flaxman, P. E., & Bunce, D. (2008). The influence of psychological flexibility on work redesign: Mediated moderation of a work reorganization intervention. *Journal of Applied Psychology, 93,* 645–654.

Boswell, W. R., Boudreau, J. W., & Tichy, J. (2005). The relationship between employee job change and job satisfaction: The honeymoon-hangover effect. *Journal of Applied Psychology, 90,* 882–892.

Bowling, N. A., Beehr, T. A., Warner, S. H., & Libkuman, T. M. (2005). Adaptation-level theory, opponent process theory, and dispositions: An integrated approach to the stability of job satisfaction. *Journal of Applied Psychology, 90,* 1044–1053.

Brennan A., Chugh, J. S., & Kline, T. (2002). Traditional versus open office design: A longitudinal field study. *Environment and Behavior, 34,* 279–299.

Brickman, P., Coates, D., & Janoff-Bulman, R. (1978). Lottery winners and accident victims: Is happiness relative? *Journal of Personality and Social Psychology, 36,* 917–927.

Burger, J. M. (1989). Negative reactions to increases in perceived personal control. *Journal of Personality and Social Psychology, 56,* 246–256.

Chung-Yan, G. A. (2010). The nonlinear effects of job complexity and autonomy on job satisfaction, turnover, and psychological well-being. *Journal of Occupational Health Psychology, 15,* 237–251.

Clark, A. E., Oswald, A., & Warr, P. B. (1996). Is job satisfaction U-shaped in age? *Journal of Occupational and Organizational Psychology, 69,* 57–81.

Cummins, R. A. (2000). Objective and subjective quality of life: An interactive model. *Social Indicators Research, 52,* 55–72.

Daniels, K., & Guppy, A. (1997). Stressors, locus of control, and social support as consequences of affective psychological well-being. *Journal of Occupational Health Psychology, 2,* 156–174.

De Jonge, J., Reuvers, M. M. E. N., Houtman, I. L. D., Bongers, P. M., & Kompier, M. A. J. (2000). Linear and non-linear relations between psychosocial job characteristics, subjective outcomes, and sickness absence: Baseline results from SMASH. *Journal of Occupational Health Psychology, 5,* 256–268.

Deelstra, J. T., Peeters, M. C. W., Schaufeli, W. B., Stroebe, W., Zijlstra, F. R. H., & van Doornen, L. P. (2003). Receiving instrumental support at work: When help is not welcome. *Journal of Applied Psychology, 88,* 324–331.

Diener, E., Sandvik, E., Seidlitz, L., & Diener, M. (1993). The relationship between income and subjective well-being: Relative or absolute? *Social Indicators Research, 28,* 195–223.

Dijkstra, M. T. M., van Dierondonck, D., Evers, A., & de Drew, C. K. W. (2005). Conflict and well-being at work: The moderating role of personality. *Journal of Managerial Psychology, 20,* 87–104.

Emmons, R. A. (1986). Personal strivings: An approach to personality and subjective well-being. *Journal of Personality and Social Psychology, 51,* 1058–1068.

Flaxman, P. E., & Bond, F. W. (2010). Worksite stress management training: Moderated effects and clinical significance. *Journal of Occupational Health Psychology, 15,* 347–358.

Fleishman, E. A., & Harris, E. F. (1962). Patterns of leadership behavior related to employee grievances and turnover. *Personnel Psychology, 15,* 43–56.

Frey, B., & Stutzer, A. (2001). *Happiness and economics: How the economy and institutions affect well-being.* Princeton, NJ: Princeton University Press.

Grant, S., & Langan-Fox, J. (2007). Personality and the occupational stressor-strain relationship: The role of the Big Five. *Journal of Occupational Health Psychology, 12,* 20–33.

Griffin, R. W. (1991). Effects of work redesign on employee perceptions, attitudes, and behaviors: A long-term investigation. *Academy of Management Journal, 34,* 425–435.

Hackman, J. R., & Oldham, G. R. (1975). Development of the Job Diagnostic Survey. *Journal of Applied Psychology, 60,* 159–170.

Harris, C., Daniels, K., & Briner, R. B. (2003). A daily diary study of goals and affective well-being at work. *Journal of Occupational and Organizational Psychology, 76,* 401–410.

Headey, B., & Wearing, A. (1992). *Understanding happiness: A theory of subjective well-being.* Melbourne, Australia: Longman Cheshire.

Houkes, I., Janssen, P. P. M., de Jonge, J., & Bakker, A. B. (2003). Personality, work characteristics, and employee well-being: A longitudinal analysis of additive and moderating effects. *Journal of Occupational Health Psychology, 8,* 20–38.

Inceoglu, I., & Warr, P. B. (2011). Personality and job engagement. *Journal of Personnel Psychology, 10,* 177–181.

Judge, T. A., Bono, J. E., & Locke, E. A. (2000). Personality and job satisfaction: The mediating role of job characteristics. *Journal of Applied Psychology, 85,* 237–249.

Judge, T. A., Heller, D., & Mount, M. K. (2002). Five-factor model of personality and job satisfaction: A meta-analysis. *Journal of Applied Psychology, 87*, 530–541.

Kahn, R. L., Wolfe, D. M., Quinn, R. P., & Snoek, J. D. (1964). *Organizational stress: Studies in role conflict and ambiguity*. New York, NY: Wiley.

Karasek, R. A. (1979). Job demands, job decision latitude, and mental strain: Implications for job design. *Administrative Science Quarterly, 24*, 285–308.

Keenan, A., & McBain, G. D. M. (1979). Effects of type A behaviour, intolerance of ambiguity, and locus of control on the relationship between role stress and work-related outcomes. *Journal of Occupational Psychology, 52*, 277–285.

Kornhauser, A. W. (1965). *Mental health of the industrial worker: A Detroit study*. New York, NY: Wiley.

Loher, B. T., Noe, R. A., Moeller, N. L., & Fitzgerald, M. P. (1985). A meta-analysis of the relation of job characteristics to job satisfaction. *Journal of Applied Psychology, 70*, 280–289.

Lyubomirsky, S. (2008). *The how of happiness*. New York, NY: Penguin.

Lyubomirsky, S., Sheldon, K. M., & Schkade, D. (2005). Pursuing happiness: The architecture of sustainable change. *Review of General Psychology, 9*, 111–131.

Medvec, V. H., Madey, S. F., & Gilovich, T. (1995). When less is more: Counterfactual thinking and satisfaction among Olympic athletes. *Journal of Personality and Social Psychology, 69*, 603–610.

Olson, J. M., Buhrman, O., & Roese, N. J. (2000). Comparing comparisons: An integrative perspective on social comparison and counterfactual thinking. In J. Suls and L. Wheeler (Eds.), *Handbook of social comparison: Theory and research* (pp. 379–398). New York, NY: Kluwer/Plenum.

Ostroff, C., & Judge, T. A. (Eds.). (2007). *Perspectives on organizational fit*. New York, NY: Erlbaum.

Parducci, A. (1995). *Happiness, pleasure, and judgment*. Mahwah, NJ: Erlbaum.

Rego, A., Souto, S., & Cunha, M. P. (2009). Does the need to belong moderate the relationship between perceptions of spirit of camaraderie and employees' happiness? *Journal of Occupational Health Psychology, 14*, 148–164.

Rice, R. W., Gentile, D. A., & McFarlin, D. B. (1991). Facet importance and job satisfaction. *Journal of Applied Psychology, 76*, 31–39.

Richardson, K. M., & Rothstein, H. R. (2008). Effects of occupational stress management intervention programs: A meta-analysis. *Journal of Occupational Health Psychology, 13*, 69–93.

Rogelberg, S. G., Leach, D. J., Warr, P. B., & Burnfield, J. (2006). "Not another meeting!" Are meeting time demands related to employee well-being? *Journal of Applied Psychology, 91*, 83–96.

Schaufeli, W. B. (2006). The balance of give and take: Toward a social exchange model of burnout. *Revue Internationale de Psychologie Sociale, 19*, 87–131.

Schaufeli, W. B., & Bakker, A. B. (2004). Job demands, job resources, and their relationship with burnout and engagement: A multi-sample study. *Journal of Occupational Health Psychology, 25*, 293–315.

Scheck, C. L., & Kinicki, A. (2000). Identifying the antecedents of coping with an organizational acquisition: A structural assessment. *Journal of Organizational Behavior, 21*, 627–648.

Sonnentag, S., & Bayer, U.-V. (2005). Switching off mentally: Predictors and consequences of psychological detachment from work during off-job time. *Journal of Occupational Health Psychology, 10*, 393–414.

Spector, P. E., Chen, P. Y., & O'Connell, B. J. (2000). A longitudinal study of relations between job stressors and job strains while controlling for prior negative affectivity and strains. *Journal of Applied Psychology, 85*, 211–218.

Staw, B. M., & Cohen-Charash, Y. (2005). The dispositional approach to job satisfaction: More than a mirage, but not yet an oasis. *Journal of Organizational Behavior, 26*, 59–78.

Taris, T. W., Kalimo, R., & Schaufeli, W. B. (2002). Inequity at work: Its measurement and association with worker health. *Work and Stress, 16*, 287–301.

Viswesvaran, C., Sanchez, J. I., & Fisher, J. (1999). The role of social support in the process of work stress: A meta-analysis. *Journal of Vocational Behavior, 54*, 314–334.

Vroom, V. H. (1959). Some personality determinants of the effects of participation. *Journal of Abnormal and Social Psychology, 59*, 322–327.

Warr, P. B. (1987). *Work, unemployment, and mental health*. Oxford, UK: Oxford University Press.

Warr, P. B. (1990). Decision latitude, job demands and employee well-being. *Work and Stress, 4*, 285–294.

Warr, P. B. (2006). Differential activation of judgments in employee well-being. *Journal of Occupational and Organizational Psychology, 79*, 225–244.

Warr, P. B. (2007). *Work, happiness, and unhappiness*. Mahwah, NJ: Erlbaum.

Warr, P. B., & Clapperton, G. (2010). *The joy of work? Jobs, happiness, and you*. New York, NY: Routledge.

Warr, P. B., & Inceoglu, I. (2012). Job satisfaction, job engagement, and contrasting associations with person-job fit. *Journal of Occupational Health Psychology, 17*, 129–138.

Warr, P. B., Bindl, U., Parker, S., & Inceoglu, I. (2012). Four-quadrant investigation of job-related affects and behaviours. Submitted for publication.

Wheeler, L. (2000). Individual differences in social comparison. In J. Suls and L. Wheeler (Eds.), *Handbook of social comparison: Theory and research* (pp. 141–158). New York, NY: Kluwer/Plenum.

Wiese, B. S., & Freund, A. M. (2005). Goal progress makes one happy, or does it? Longitudinal findings from the work domain. *Journal of Occupational and Organizational Psychology, 78*, 287–304.

Workman, M., & Bommer, W. (2004). Redesigning computer call center work: A longitudinal field experiment. *Journal of Organizational Behavior, 25*, 317–337.

Xie, J. L., & Johns, G. (1995). Job scope and stress: Can job scope be too high? *Academy of Management Journal, 38*, 1288–1309.

Zapf, D., Einarsen, S., Hoel, H., & Vartia, M. (2003). Empirical findings on bullying in the workplace. In S. Einarsen, H. Hoel, D. Zapf, & C. Cooper (Eds.), *Bullying and emotional abuse in the workplace: International perspectives in research and practice* (pp. 103–126). London, UK: Taylor and Francis.

# CHAPTER 55

# MANAGING PSYCHOLOGICAL CAPITAL IN ORGANIZATIONS: COGNITIVE, AFFECTIVE, CONATIVE, AND SOCIAL MECHANISMS OF HAPPINESS

CAROLYN M. YOUSSEF[1] AND FRED LUTHANS[2]

[1]Bellevue University, USA; [2]University of Nebraska–Lincoln, USA

HAPPINESS and well-being have always been of interest to organized civilizations. However, recently they have received renewed attention not only because of increased uncertainties and even threats people are currently facing around the world, but also in the academic world because of the advent of positive psychology. There is now a heightened awareness and realization of the importance of happiness and well-being at the individual, organizational, and even national levels. For example, positive psychologists such as Diener (2000) have proposed a national index of happiness, raising its visibility and status to a level comparable with economic, social, and political indices that have traditionally received much more emphasis. The same trend is occurring in today's organizations, as evidenced in the chapters in this section of the handbook.

The value of happiness, and more specifically well-being, is receiving increased attention by the management of today's organizations. Although some positive psychologists make a distinction between happiness and well-being (for a summary review of the theoretical background and studies on these distinctions, see Snyder, Lopez & Teramoto Pedrotti (2011, pp. 128–139)), we will follow the view of Diener and colleagues (Diener, 2000, Diener & Biswas-Diener, 2008; Diener & Seligman, 2002) that treats well-being as a synonym for happiness. Moreover, when applied to the workplace, well-being tends to be preferred and used more than happiness and recognizes the important role that one's positive psychological resources, or overall positive mindset, play in one's well-being (see Avey, Luthans, Smith, & Palmer, 2010). This organizational concern for well-being stems from socioeconomic factors such as high unemployment rates and escalating healthcare costs, as well as concern for physical and emotional factors such as stress, which is associated with the drive for high performance inherent in the hyper-competitive global economy. This emphasis on employees' well-being is also being fueled by increasing evidence that physical and mental states have quantifiable implications for organizations' financial outcomes (Cascio & Boudreau, 2008).

The conventional wisdom that "happy workers are productive workers" goes back to the beginning of the field of organizational behavior and human resource management (e.g., see Maslow, 1954). However, in the ensuing years there has generally been a lack of rich theoretical development and supporting empirical research testing this hypothesis until the stimulation provided by the positive psychology movement (Lopez & Snyder, 2009; Seligman & Csikszentmihalyi, 2000). Now, both organizational scholars and practitioners are beginning to have renewed interest in the role that employees' positive psychological resources and positive mindset have on their well-being and their performance.

In this chapter, we focus on better understanding the emerging domain of positive organizational behavior (POB) and specifically the core construct of psychological capital (PsyCap), which consists of the positive psychological resources of hope, efficacy, resilience, and optimism (see Luthans, 2002a, 2002b; Luthans, Youssef, & Avolio, 2007). We start by introducing what is meant by POB and defining PsyCap. We then present processes in which PsyCap may contribute to better theoretical understanding of employee well-being through cognitive, affective, conative, and social mechanisms. Implications and future directions conclude the chapter.

# Positive Organizational Behavior and Psychological Capital

Drawing from positive psychology, POB seeks to focus on the important role that positive psychological resources and a positive mindset play in organizational studies. POB is defined as "the study and application of positively oriented human resource strengths and psychological capacities that can be measured, developed, and effectively managed for performance improvement" (Luthans, 2002b, p. 59). POB focuses on positive, developmental psychological resources that are backed by theoretical understanding and scientific research, have valid and reliable measurement, are open to development and change, and have a recognized performance impact in the workplace (Luthans, 2002a). To date, we have identified four specific positively-oriented psychological capacities that best fit these inclusion criteria.

The first of these identified psychological resources included in POB is hope, which is defined as "a positive motivational state that is based on an interactively derived sense of successful (1) agency (goal-directed energy) and (2) pathways (planning to meet goals)" (Snyder, Irving, & Anderson, 1991, p. 287). Agency represents the willpower and determination required to achieve goals, while pathways represent the "waypower" or ability to generate alternative pathways and overcome obstacles in the pursuit of these goals. Hope's fit with the POB inclusion criteria is evident in its extensive theoretical foundation, reliable and valid measurements, and developmental potential (see Snyder (2000) for a comprehensive review), as well as its relationship to a wide range of desired work attitudes and performance (Peterson & Byron, 2008; Youssef & Luthans, 2007).

The second positive psychological resource included in POB is efficacy, or confidence, which is defined as: "one's belief about his or her ability to mobilize the motivation, cognitive resources, and courses of action necessary to execute a specific action within a given context" (Stajkovic & Luthans, 1998b, p. 66). Probably best at meeting the POB inclusion criteria, efficacy draws from the widely recognized social cognitive theory (Bandura, 1997), has reliable and valid measures, has been clearly shown to be open to development and management, and is one of the strongest predictors of performance in the workplace (Stajkovic & Luthans, 1998a), as well as in numerous other life domains (see Luthans, Youssef, & Avolio, 2007, chapter 2, for a comprehensive review).

Third is resilience, which draws from the extant developmental psychology research (Masten, 2001; Masten & Reed, 2002), and is defined as "the developable capacity to rebound or bounce back from adversity, conflict, and failure," (Luthans, 2002a, p. 702). Importantly, not only is there this bounce back capacity, but those with high levels of resilience often learn and grow from the adversity they have overcome. In addition to the established theory, research, measurement, and developmental potential of resilience and its desirable outcomes in "at-risk" populations, there has been a significant recent growth in interest and applications to organizational settings (Sutcliffe & Vogus, 2003). This attention is due, in part, to the recent turbulent times and dramatic changes in the economic, ethical and sociopolitical landscape facing today's organizations. Resilience has been shown to be significantly related to job performance (for comprehensive reviews see Luthans & Youssef, 2007; Luthans, Youssef, & Avolio, 2007, chapter 4; and studies such as Luthans, Avolio, Avey, & Norman, 2007; Luthans, Avolio, Walumbwa, & Li, 2005) as well as to satisfaction, commitment and happiness at work (Youssef & Luthans, 2007).

Finally, there is optimism, which has been conceptualized both as a generalized positive expectancy (Carver & Scheier, 2002) and a positive explanatory style of attributing positive events to personal, permanent and pervasive causes and negative events to external, temporary and situational ones (Seligman, 1998). Optimism has been supported, both conceptually and empirically, as a measurable, learned capacity with a recognized performance impact in various contexts, including the workplace (for comprehensive reviews see Luthans and Youssef, 2007; Luthans, Youssef, and Avolio, 2007, chapter 4; and studies such as Youssef and Luthans, 2007.

We use the acronym HERO to represent the identified positive psychological resources of hope, efficacy, resilience and optimism that best meet our POB inclusion criteria, but it is important to note that these four are only intended as a representative set, rather than an exhaustive taxonomy. Luthans, Youssef, and Avolio (2007, chapters 6 and 7) comprehensively review and assess numerous other positive psychological constructs for their relative fit with the POB inclusion criteria. Examples of these include the cognitive resources of creativity and wisdom; the affective resources of flow and humor; the social resources of gratitude, forgiveness, and emotional intelligence; and the higher-order resources of spirituality, authenticity and courage.

Psychological capital, or simply PsyCap, comprises the criteria-meeting psychological resources of POB and is specifically defined as "an individual's positive psychological state of development that is characterized by: (1) having confidence (self-efficacy) to take on and put in the necessary effort to succeed at challenging tasks; (2) making a positive attribution (optimism) about succeeding now and in the future; (3) persevering toward goals and, when necessary, redirecting paths to goals (hope) in order to succeed; and (4) when beset by problems and adversity, sustaining and bouncing back and even beyond (resiliency) to attain success" (Luthans, Youssef, et al., 2007, p. 3). PsyCap has been found to be a valid and measurably reliable higher order, latent multidimensional core construct (Luthans, Avolio, et al., 2007). In addition, there is a clearly demonstrated empirical relationship (see the recent meta-analysis by Avey, Reichard, Luthans, and Mhatre (2011) and studies such as Luthans, Avolio, et al. (2007)) and beginning causal evidence (e.g., Luthans, Avey, Avolio, & Peterson, 2010; Peterson, Luthans, Avolio, Walumbwa, & Zhang, 2011) between employees' PsyCap and their organizationally desirable attitudes, behaviors, and performance. PsyCap has also been empirically found to contribute added value over more established positive traits such as personality dimensions, self-evaluations, and demographics in predicting desirable work attitudes and behaviors (Avey, Luthans, & Youssef, 2010). However, PsyCap also relates to positive outcomes beyond immediate performance and goal achievement, which makes it particularly relevant for long term, sustainable well-being. For example, a recent study supports the relationship between PsyCap and well-being over time (Avey, Luthans, Smith, et al., 2010).

Although PsyCap as a core construct has been empirically demonstrated to be a better predictor of desirable outcomes than each of the four resources that make it up (Luthans, Avolio, et al., 2007), conceptually, the underlying theoretical mechanism shared among PsyCap's four constituent psychological resources is represented by "one's positive appraisal of circumstances and probability for success based on motivated effort and perseverance" (Luthans, Avolio, et al., 2007, p. 550). These positive appraisals can be viewed as the driving force for a hopeful effort investment toward the pursuit (and taking alternative pathways when necessary) of meaningful and challenging goals, confident behavioral intentions and actions, resilient processing and bouncing back from obstacles and setbacks, and an optimistic outlook. Taken together, these HERO components of PsyCap are working in concert and compensating for one another to increase the chances of future success. This success can materialize both objectively, in terms of goal attainment and tangible performance accomplishments, as well as subjectively in terms of higher levels of well-being. We will discuss this further, but for now it is sufficient to say that we believe that PsyCap is a driving force not only for desired work attitudes, behaviors and performance, but also, based on initial empirical evidence, that it also may have a positive impact on other key components of well-being such as relationships and health (Luthans, Youssef, Sweetman & Harms, in press).

Before discussing the proposed theoretical mechanisms for understanding PsyCap's relationship with well-being, it is important to note that there are other emerging positively-oriented scientific movements as well. We end this section by briefly distinguishing PsyCap from these related initiatives in order to help clarify the meaning and theoretical position of PsyCap. As discussed earlier, POB and PsyCap focus on positively-oriented, theory-driven, micro-level positive psychological resources that can be measured, developed, and managed in the workplace, and that have been empirically demonstrated to yield desirable work-related outcomes. In comparison, positive psychology scholars identify many individual-level positive character strengths and virtues that tend to develop over extended periods of time or across one's lifespan (see Peterson & Seligman (2004) for comprehensive reviews of many of these strengths and virtues such as wisdom, courage, humanity, and justice). Studies are also starting to emerge that demonstrate how these character strengths relate to desired work outcomes (e.g., see Avey, Luthans, Hannah, Sweetman, & Peterson, 2012; Peterson, Park, Hall, & Seligman, 2009). While important, these positive traits cannot be as readily developed in organizational settings through short training micro-interventions as is the case with PsyCap (Luthans et al., 2006; Luthans, Avey, Avolio, et al., 2010; Luthans, Avey & Patera, 2008). On the other hand, these character strengths can be captured and nurtured in organizational settings through careful selection of individuals that exhibit them, intentional utilization of effective mentoring practices over time, and organizational policies emphasizing retention and career-long learning.

Similarly, the organizational literature supports a wide range of positive constructs. Most of these are considered to be quite stable or "trait-like." For example, the Big Five personality traits (conscientiousness, extroversion, neuroticism, agreeableness, openness to experience), while strongly related to work performance (Barrick & Mount, 1991), are not as malleable, and thus open to development, as PsyCap. The same applies to core self evaluations (generalized efficacy, locus of control, self-esteem, emotional stability) (Judge & Bono, 2001). Our research has empirically demonstrated that both the personality trait of conscientiousness and core self-evaluations were relatively more stable over time than was the PsyCap of study participants (Luthans, Avolio, et al., 2007). On the other hand, these stable, trait-like characteristics have been long recognized as valid, reliably-measured, performance-related, and thus legally defensible as selection criteria in human resource management.

We utilize the term "trait-like" to distinguish between these character, personality, or self-evaluation dimensions, which may undergo lifespan development and growth processes, and the largely genetically-determined "pure" traits such as intelligence or temperament. While such distinctions may be debatable and have "gray areas," we view these characterizations as ranges on a continuum of stability and malleability (see Luthans, Avey, Avolio et al., 2010; Luthans & Youssef, 2007 for a comprehensive review). On the opposite end of the continuum, we place "pure" states, such as momentary pleasure, moods, and transient emotions. Again, while important, particularly for happiness, the short-lived temporal nature of these "pure" states limits the return on investment in their formal, deliberate development in the workplace. In fact, a major problem with a significant share of the popular positivity literature and consulting practices is that they tend to focus on short-lived, "feel good" positive approaches, that is, "pure" states. PsyCap, on the other hand, is considered to be "state-like," more malleable than the pure traits and the trait-like characteristics, but relatively more stable than pure states (e.g., our research indicated that the PsyCap of study participants was relatively more stable than their positive emotions; Luthans, Avolio, et al., 2007).

Similar to individuals, organizations can be positive, neutral, or negative. They can be flourishing, passively languishing, or even toxic. A positive organizational context is critical for the development and performance of positive managers and employees (Luthans,

Norman, Avolio, & Avey, 2008). This macro level of analysis is given relatively greater attention in positive organizational scholarship (POS) research (e.g., see Cameron & Caza, 2004; Cameron, Dutton, & Quinn, 2003; Cameron & Lavine, 2006). However, we would also assert that positive managers and employees are certainly instrumental for creating and sustaining such a positive organizational context (Avey, Wernsing, & Luthans, 2008).

Empirical findings to date support this complex and dynamic relationship between individual and organizational positivity. For example, while employees' PsyCap is directly related to their performance, leader PsyCap and a service-oriented organizational climate have been found to moderate this relationship (Walumbua, Peterson, Avolio, & Hartnell, 2010). Other recent organizational leadership studies have found that leaders' PsyCap is related to their followers' PsyCap and performance (Avey, Avolio, & Luthans, 2011) and also impacts their perceived trust and evaluation of their leader (Norman, Avolio, & Luthans, 2010). Employee positivity (specifically PsyCap, positive emotions, mindfulness) has been found to facilitate positive organizational change through change-oriented attitudes and behaviors (Avey, Wernsing, et al., 2008), and employees' PsyCap was determined to be a mediator between a supportive organizational climate and their performance (Luthans, Norman, et al., 2008). PsyCap has also been supported at the group level. In recent studies, collective PsyCap was found to mediate the relationships between authentic leadership and both group performance and citizenship behaviors (Walumbua, Luthans, Avey, & Oke, 2011) and the collective PsyCap of top management teams was related to their business unit performance (Peterson & Zhang, 2011).

# Using Psychological Capital's Mechanisms to Help Explain Happiness and Well-Being

Positive perspectives from psychology, POB, and POS explain happiness and well-being with slightly different theoretical lenses and mechanisms. While other chapters in this volume address these approaches, in this chapter we propose that PsyCap can contribute to the explanations of happiness and well-being through its cognitive, affective, conative, and social process mechanisms.

## The cognitive mechanism of psychological capital

As described earlier, PsyCap and its HERO components can directly influence how people interpret situations. In turn, these interpretations can influence their well-being. The cognitive contribution of PsyCap to well-being is evident in the positive appraisals it enables individuals to make regarding their current circumstances, as well as their future expectations of success. Such positive subjective appraisals have been demonstrated to be stronger predictors of well-being than objective life events (Emmons & Diener, 1985; Kim-Prieto, Diener, Tamir, Scollon, & Diener, 2005). Positive cognitive appraisals can facilitate more favorable (or less unfavorable) assessments of events by helping to buffer the human negativity bias (Baumeister, Bratslavsky, Finkenauer, & Vohs, 2001). For example, employees with high PsyCap may appraise an undesirable job assignment as a challenge and opportunity for advancement or as an indicator of management's confidence in their unique capabilities to get the job done, rather than as a demotion or indicator of failure.

This is not to say that such positive cognitive appraisals can alone predict one's well-being. There are also affective and conative predictors of well-being (discussed next). However, positive appraisals can trigger the selective memory processes involved in the retention of positive affective states, allowing their impact to be sustained and to materialize into higher and more sustainable levels of well-being (Levine, 1997; Levine, Prohaska, Burgess, Rice, & Laulere, 2001). For example, employees assigned "bad" jobs who have more positive appraisals of their experience to draw from will likely cause them to retain more positive than negative memories of the ensuing events throughout the undesirable assignment. This positive experience in turn can be conducive to higher well-being after the assignment has been completed. On the other hand, negative appraisals of experience can negatively bias employees' perceptions and attributions of subsequent events, causing them to hold a grudge and become bitter. Such negativity can lead to unhappiness and compromise the employees' physical, mental and emotional well-being, not to mention the impact on future productivity and attitudes toward the organization.

## The affective mechanism of psychological capital

No discussion of happiness and well-being would be complete without including the indispensable role of affect, specifically positive emotions. We have found PsyCap is related to positive emotions (Avey, Wernsing, & Luthans, 2008) and propose that these affective states contribute to one's well-being. We draw from Barbara Fredrickson's (2001, 2003, 2009) broaden-and-build model to help explain this affective process. This model can be used to highlight the role of PsyCap in triggering, and as mentioned earlier, relating to and sustaining positive emotions, which in turn contribute to well-being. Specifically, in Fredrickson's model, positive emotions have a broadening impact on one's thought–action repertoires, as well as a building impact for physical, social, and psychological resource reserves that can be drawn upon in subsequent times of negativity.

We posit that PsyCap's affective contribution to well-being operates through creating positive affective emotional states that can be instrumental in facilitating both the broaden and the build dimensions. In terms of broadening, positive appraisals, expectancies, challenge-seeking and endurance can motivate individuals to target their energies and resources at a broader range of goals, aspirations and courses of action, all of which have been shown to be conducive to positive emotions (Bandura, 2008; Snyder, Ilardi, Michael, & Cheavens, 2000). In terms of building, the developmental nature of PsyCap (discussed next) allows for growth in overall positivity, and in turn happiness and well-being, as the psychological resources and overall PsyCap are developed. The developing PsyCap of employees allows them to gain the confidence and tools they need to pursue more challenging and meaningful goals and persevere in the face of obstacles with resulting performance improvement. The increased PsyCap may help employees build a wide range of positive emotions. The enhanced PsyCap of employees can also buffer the impact of negativity as they learn to overcome the emotional toll of overwhelming feelings of inadequacy and defeat. In turn, the positive emotions generated throughout the PsyCap development process can help build a broader range of psychological (as well as physical and social) resources, which in turn can not only enhance happiness, but also induce motivation toward even more challenging goals.

This cognitive-affective growth cycle is comparable to the "upward spirals" of flourishing discussed in the POS literature (Cameron et al., 2003). This growth cycle is also highly applicable to organizational applications of well-being, as it is not entirely reliant on transient moods and fleeting emotions, which are difficult to manage in the workplace. Research has shown that PsyCap can also counteract negative affective states that are so detrimental to today's organizations such as stress (Avey, Luthans, & Jensen, 2009), cynicism and deviance (Avey, Werning, & Luthans, 2008).

## The conative mechanism of psychological capital

Drawing from Bandura's (2008) perspective of positive psychology, the primary underlying theoretical mechanism of PsyCap has been identified to be agentic in nature (Luthans, Avolio, et al., 2007; Youssef & Luthans, in press). This agentic foundation of PsyCap is rooted in awareness of the current actual self, positive self-evaluations that can yield positive beliefs and expectancies about one's future possible self, and self-regulation toward the achievement of the desired possible self (Avolio & Luthans, 2006; Luthans & Avolio, 2003). Thus, we propose that besides cognition and affect, the classic, but overlooked in recent times, process of conation can also be used to explain the contribution that PsyCap can make to well-being.

Psychology's three primary foundational explanatory processes of cognition, affect and conation have long been recognized (Hilgard, 1980). Often ignored in favor of the easier-to-define and measure cognitive and affective psychological processes, conation refers to "the mental process that activates and/or directs behavior and action … the personal, intentional, planful, deliberate, goal-oriented, or striving component of motivation, (and) the proactive (as opposed to reactive or habitual) aspect of behavior" (Huitt & Cain, 2005, p. 1). Atman (1987, p. 15) further defined conation as "vectored energy: i.e., personal energy that has both direction and magnitude."

PsyCap's internally generated, agentic drive has the capacity to mobilize psychological resources (including cognitive and affective resources) and activate goal-directed courses of action. In other words, agency is exercised at the conscious discretion of the individual. Agency selectively determines the nature and magnitude of cognitive and affective resource investment toward various goals, which embedded as a mechanism in PsyCap, can in turn help explain one's level of well-being. For example, related to conation and agency is the concept of self-determination (Deci & Ryan, 1985), which posits that people have a fundamental need to feel in control. PsyCap's conative mechanism can contribute to well-being through providing the motivation and efficacy to confidently choose to take action in relation to important and challenging personal goals, which can facilitate and satisfy this need for control. This self-control can, in turn, contribute to one's well-being.

PsyCap's conative, agency mechanism motivates positive cognitions, emotions, energy, and resources to be voluntarily enlisted in the pursuit of important and aligned organizational and personal goals. This intentional, willful and deliberate approach is clearly distinguishable from "getting caught up in the times" or simply "going through the motions" at work, or from the "emotional labor" experienced when employees outwardly exhibit unfelt emotions in order to meet the expectations of their roles (Morris & Feldman, 1996). The difference between being a "pawn" in the system and intentional agentic, conative action inherent in one's PsyCap is evident not only in terms of performance, but also in terms of important employee outcomes such as experiencing vitality, engagement, flow, and ultimately higher levels of happiness and well-being (Csikszentmihalyi, 1997, 2003; Ryan & Fredrick, 1997). Specifically, it has been empirically determined that about 40% of one's level of happiness is the result of deliberate, intentional activity (i.e., conation), compared to one's largely uncontrollable nature and nurture derived set point (about 50%) and situational circumstances (about 10%) (Lyubomirsky, 2007).

## The social mechanism of psychological capital

In addition to PsyCap's cognitive, affective, and conative contributions to one's well-being, we also propose a social mechanism. We contend that PsyCap builds upon and goes beyond social capital (Luthans & Youssef, 2004), represented by one's breadth and depth of relationships, connections, and interpersonal networking capabilities. However, the role of social support and relationships is also integral in building PsyCap and its constituent capacities. Research has found that employees' PsyCap mediates the relationship between a supportive social climate and their performance (Luthans, Norman, et al., 2008). In addition, vicarious learning and social persuasion are widely recognized mechanisms for building efficacy (Bandura, 1997), and social support is identified as a very critical asset for sustaining resilience (Masten, 2001). Social support from managers and coworkers is also recognized as being vital to better work performance and well-being (Glaser, Tatum, Nebeker, Sorenson, & Aiello, 1999). More directly, highly positive social relationships have been found to consistently characterize very happy people (Diener & Seligman, 2002). The extant literature on the spillover and crossover effects across work and non-work domains also supports the presence of these linkages (Bakker, Westman, & Van Emmerik, 2009; Judge & Ilies, 2004).

We propose, and have initial empirical evidence (Luthans, Youssef, et al., in press), that PsyCap can make significant contributions to social relationships in highly meaningful ways and can magnify the impact of social relationships on well-being. For example, positive cognitive and affective appraisals of relationships can make them more meaningful and fulfilling, and intentional activities aimed at improved relationships can increase the chances of success. This success can materialize directly in terms of better relationships and drawing valuable social support that is instrumental for well-being, as well as in achieving other significant personal and professional goals through richer and more diversified interpersonal networks, which can also contribute to well-being.

# Developing Psychological Capital

Besides PsyCap's theoretical mechanisms contributing to the better understanding of happiness and well-being, its state-like nature has important implications for practical application. Specifically, as discussed earlier, one of the unique characteristics of PsyCap is that it lends itself to development and performance management in the workplace. Successful training interventions have empirically supported the developmental potential of PsyCap in work settings (Luthans, Avey, Avolio, Norman, & Combs, 2006; Luthans, Avey, et al., 2010; Luthans, Avey, & Patera, 2008). The effectiveness of these PsyCap development interventions has been empirically supported using quasi-experimental designs utilizing random assignment and control groups, which helps establish internal validity and causal linkages between the PsyCap training intervention and performance back on the job (Luthans, Avey, et al., 2010). In line with the scientific inclusion criteria emphasized throughout this chapter, these PsyCap training interventions build on established theory and research foundations in efficacy-building, behavioral modeling, goal setting, contingency planning, risk-management, coping, positive self-talk, and others, all of which directly contribute to the cognitive, affective, conative, and social mechanisms described earlier.

In addition to the research directly testing PsyCap development, parallels can be drawn between the PsyCap development process and the ways to increase happiness and well-being recently presented in the positive psychology literature. For example, Fredrickson (2009) recommends disputing negative thinking, breaking the grip of rumination, and finding positive meaning in current circumstances and visualizing future success, all of which are foundational for positive self-talk. Such deliberate positive self-talk strategies can be instrumental in building confidence, developing optimism, and overcoming learned helplessness (Schneider, 2001; Seligman, 1998). Similarly, Lyubomirsky (2007) recommends cultivating optimism and strategies for coping with stress, hardship and trauma (i.e., resilience), and committing the motivation and effort toward goal pursuit. The impact of positive appraisals on affect and memory retention described earlier has also been supported as instrumental for increased well-being (Diener & Biswas-Diener, 2008). These recommendations, backed by an extensive tradition in psychological research and practice, support the potential impact of PsyCap development on happiness and well-being.

As indicated, with more valid measurement and demonstrated performance impact, there may be other positive psychological constructs and accompanying developmental approaches to increasing well-being which represent an adequate fit with the POB inclusion criteria. In the future, these may be incorporated into PsyCap development interventions. For example, gratitude and forgiveness are highly relevant in interactions with others in the workplace, and successful interventions for their development over relatively short time periods have been implemented (e.g., Baskin & Enright, 2004). Similarly, experiencing flow in the workplace is conceptually linked to work engagement, and work can provide excellent opportunities for frequent experiences of flow given effective person-job fit in terms of having employees with considerable skills doing challenging work (see Nakamura & Csikszentmihalyi, 2009; Luthans, Youssef, et al., 2007).

## Future Directions

A number of questions pertinent to theory-building, research, and application remain to be explored in the emerging domain of positive mindset in general, and PsyCap in particular. We conclude this chapter with several suggested directions for future research and practice.

- *A positive mindset as an antecedent, process, and outcome in organizations.* While PsyCap has been generally treated as an antecedent or mediator of work-related outcomes, its constituent psychological resources are sometimes treated as outcomes in the positive psychology literature, and at the organizational level in the POS literature.

Similarly, whether well-being itself is treated as an antecedent, process, or an outcome of success and goal achievement has also been debated (see Lyubomirsky, King, & Diener, 2005). We suggest that these relationships are likely reciprocal in nature. However, future research needs to emphasize the development of the theoretical frameworks and mechanisms underlying the "positioning" of PsyCap, well-being, and other positive constructs within an explicit or implied causal chain. Furthermore, even though recent research has found within-individual change in employees' PsyCap over time with causal impact on their performance (Peterson et al., 2011), there is a need for more longitudinal designs (Avey, Luthans, & Mhatre, 2008) and the inclusion of time as a variable in positive organizational behavior research (Wright, 1997). This type of research is particularly needed in testing PsyCap development interventions. It can help shed more light on PsyCap's malleability, and the causality and sustainability of the impact on employee well-being and specific organizational outcomes over time.

- *Which is more important at work? To be happy, or to be realistic?* It is hard to argue against the overall benefits of higher levels of happiness and well-being. However, in the work context, there is some support for moderate levels of happiness as being optimal for success. For example, research has found that moderate, as opposed to high levels of happiness may better promote career development and growth (Oishi, Diener, & Lucas, 2007). PsyCap's integration of hope, efficacy, resiliency, and optimism is intended to offer a balanced perspective of positivity that is particularly relevant for the workplace. While false hope, over-confidence, excessive hardiness, and unrealistic optimism have all been shown in the literature to represent "too much of a good thing," we propose that the cognitive, affective, conative, and social mechanisms associated with PsyCap allow it to hold these extremes in check. These processes can result in an optimal, but still realistic, level of well-being at work. Future research needs to verify and differentiate these dynamic mechanisms that we propose may be used by individuals to optimize their levels of PsyCap and well-being in work and non-work domains. Such research can potentially have important implications for human resource practices. As it stands, even the most conservative organizations seem to operate under the assumption that their managers and employees are seeking to maximize, not optimize, their levels of well-being at work. This may or may not be the case, nor necessarily should be the case.

- *To have a job, and enjoy it, too!* While enjoying one's job is undoubtedly instrumental for well-being, recent economic conditions render just having a job and maintaining a stable source of income an important goal for many. For example, Gallup's recent world polls consistently find that most people rate having a good job over political ideals or material things (Clifton, 2011). Moreover, unemployment has been shown to result in long-term changes to well-being, and even to one's overall "set point" (Lucas, Clark, Georgellis, & Diener, 2004). These findings seem to imply that having an unsatisfying job may be less detrimental on PsyCap and well-being than not having a job at all. While circumstances alone may only determine a seemingly small portion of one's well-being (Lyubomirsky, 2007; Lyubomirsky, Sheldon, & Schkade, 2005), having a job is critical for the agentic pursuit of many other personal, social, and professional goals. Perceived goal frustration (e.g., due to unemployment or underemployment) and loss of control (Deci & Ryan, 1985) may lead to lowered levels of well-being (Kim-Prieto et al., 2005). On the other hand, unless significantly degrading or demeaning (Biswas-Diener &

Diener, 2001), jobs and income may have diminishing marginal utility in favor of a more balanced life (Diener, Ng, & Tov, 2009). In other words, it is possible that lack of employment operates on well-being through different mechanisms than the type of employment one has. Each affects PsyCap and well-being through different mechanisms, both within and beyond the workplace. For example, being unable to provide for one's dependents due to unemployment may diminish well-being through the conative mechanism. On the other hand, being unable to spend adequate quality time with loved ones due to a demanding job, even if cognitively engaging and affectively satisfying, may diminish well-being through the social mechanism. Future research and practice should challenge the underlying conceptual and empirical assumptions of linearity in well-being research in general, and particularly in its applications to organizational settings.

## References

Atman, K. (1987). The role of conation (striving) in the distance learning enterprise. *The American Journal of Distance Education*, 1(1), 14–28.

Avey, J. B., Avolio, B. J., & Luthans, F. (2011). Experimentally analyzing the impact of leader positivity on follower positivity and performance. *The Leadership Quarterly*, 22, 282–294.

Avey, J. B., Luthans, F., Hannah, S. T., Sweetman, D., & Peterson, C. (2012). Impact of employees' character strengths of wisdom on stress and creative performance. *Human Resource Management Journal*, 22, 165–181.

Avey, J. B., Luthans, F., & Jensen, S. (2009). Psychological capital: A positive resource for combating employee stress and turnover. *Human Resource Management*, 48, 677–693.

Avey, J. B., Luthans, F., & Mhatre, K. H. (2008). A call for longitudinal research in positive organizational behavior. *Journal of Organizational Behavior*, 29, 705–711.

Avey, J. B., Luthans, F., Smith, R., & Palmer, N. (2010). Impact of positive psychological capital on employee well-being over time. *Journal of Occupational Health Psychology*, 12, 17–28.

Avey, J. B., Luthans, F., & Youssef, C. M. (2010). The additive value of psychological capital: Predicting positive and negative work attitudes and behaviors. *Journal of Management*, 36, 430–452.

Avey, J. B., Reichard, R., Luthans, F., & Mhatre, K. (2011). Meta-analysis of the impact of positive psychological capital on employee attitudes, behaviors and performance. *Human Resource Development Quarterly*, 22, 127–152.

Avey, J. B., Wernsing, T. S., & Luthans, F. (2008). Can positive employees help positive organizational change? *The Journal of Applied Behavioral Science*, 44, 48–70.

Avolio, B. J., & Luthans, F. (2006). *The high impact leader: Moments matter in accelerating authentic leadership development*. New York, NY: McGraw-Hill.

Bakker, A. B., Westman, M., & Van Emmerik, I. J. H. (2009). Advances in crossover theory. *Journal of Managerial Psychology*, 24, 206–219.

Bandura, A. (1997). *Self-efficacy: The exercise of control*. New York, NY: Freeman.

Bandura, A. (2008). An agentic perspective on positive psychology. In S. J. Lopez (Ed.), *Positive psychology: Exploring the best in people*, (vol. 1, pp. 167–196). Westport, CT: Greenwood Publishing Company.

Barrick, M. R., & Mount, M. K. (1991). The big five personality dimensions and job performance: A meta-analysis. *Personnel Psychology*, 44, 1–26.

Baskin, T., & Enright, R. (2004). Intervention studies on forgiveness: A meta-analysis. *Journal of Counseling & Development, 82*, 79–90.

Baumeister, R. F., Bratslavsky, E., Finkenauer, C., & Vohs, K. D. (2001). Bad is stronger than good. *Review of General Psychology, 5*, 323–370.

Biswas-Diener, R., & Diener, E. (2001). Making the best of a bad situation: Satisfaction in the slums of Calcutta. *Social Indicators Research, 55*, 329–352.

Cameron, K. S., & Caza, A. (2004). Contributions to the discipline of positive organizational scholarship. *American Behavioral Scientist, 47*, 731–739.

Cameron, K. S., Dutton, J. E., & Quinn, R. E. (Eds.). (2003). *Positive organizational scholarship*. San Francisco, CA: Berrett-Koehler.

Cameron, K. S., & Lavine, M. (2006). *Making the impossible possible: Leading extraordinary performance: The Rocky Flats story*. San Francisco, CA: Berrett Koehler.

Carver, C., & Scheier, M. (2002). Optimism. In C. R. Snyder & S. Lopez (Eds.), *Handbook of positive psychology* (pp. 231–243). New York, NY: Oxford University Press.

Cascio, W., & Boudreau, J. (2008). *Investing in people: Financial impact of human resource initiatives*. Upper Saddle River, NJ: Pearson/FT Press.

Clifton, J. (2011). *The coming jobs war*. New York, NY: Gallup Press.

Csikszentmihalyi, M. (1997). *Finding flow*. New York, NY: Basic Books.

Csikszentmihalyi, M. (2003). *Good business*. New York, NY: Penguin Books.

Deci, E., & Ryan, R. (1985). *Intrinsic motivation and self-determination in human behavior*. New York, NY: Plenum Press.

Diener, E. (2000). Subjective well-being: The science of happiness, and a proposal for a national index. *American Psychologist, 55*, 34–43.

Diener, E., & Biswas-Diener, R. (2008). *Happiness: Unlocking the mysteries of psychological wealth*. Malden, MA: Blackwell.

Diener, E., Ng, W., & Tov, W. (2009). Balance in life and declining marginal utility of diverse resources. *Applied Research in Quality of Life, 3*, 277–291.

Diener, E., & Seligman, M. E. P. (2002). Very happy people. *Psychological Science, 13*, 80–83.

Emmons, R. A., & Diener, E. (1985). Factors predicting satisfaction judgments: A comparative examination. *Social Indicators Research, 16*, 157–168.

Fredrickson, B. L. (2001). The role of positive emotions in positive psychology: The broaden-and-build theory of positive emotions. *American Psychologist, 56*, 218–226.

Fredrickson, B. L. (2003). Positive emotions and upward spirals in organizations. In K. S. Cameron, J. E. Dutton, & R. E. Quinn (Eds.), *Positive organizational scholarship* (pp. 163–175). San Francisco, CA: Berrett-Koehler.

Fredrickson, B. L. (2009). *Positivity*. New York, NY: Crown/Random House.

Glaser, D. N., Tatum, B. C., Nebeker, D. M., Sorenson, R. C., & Aiello, J. R. (1999). Workload and social support: Effects on performance and stress. *Human Performance, 12*, 155–176.

Hilgard, E. R. (1980). The trilogy of mind: Cognition, affection, and conation. *Journal of the History of the Behavioral Sciences, 16*, 107–117.

Huitt, W., & Cain, S. (2005). An overview of the conative domain. *Educational Psychology Interactive*. Valdosta, GA: Valdosta State University. Retrieved August 2, 2010 from http://www.edpsycinteractive.org/papers/conative.pdf

Judge, T. A., & Bono, J. E. (2001). Relationship of core self-evaluations traits—self-esteem, generalized self-efficacy, locus of control, and emotional stability—with job satisfaction and job performance: A meta-analysis. *Journal of Applied Psychology, 86*, 80–92.

Judge, T. A., & Ilies, R. (2004). Affect and job satisfaction: A study of their relationship at work and at home. *Journal of Applied Psychology, 89*, 661–673.

Kim-Prieto, C., Diener, E., Tamir, M., Scollon, C. N., & Diener, M. (2005). Integrating the diverse definitions of happiness: A time-sequential framework of subjective well-being. *Journal of Happiness Studies: An Interdisciplinary Periodical on Subjective Well-Being, 6*, 261–300.

Levine, L. J. (1997). Reconstructing memory for emotions. *Journal of Experimental Psychology General, 126*, 165–177.

Levine, L. J., Prohaska, V., Burgess, S. L., Rice, J. A., & Laulere, T. M. (2001). Remembering past emotions: The role of current appraisals. *Cognition and Emotion, 15*, 393–417.

Lopez, S., & Snyder, C. R. (Eds.). (2009). *Oxford handbook of positive psychology* (2nd ed.). New York, NY: Oxford University Press.

Lucas, R. E., Clark, A. E., Georgellis, Y., & Diener, E. (2004). Unemployment alters the set point for life satisfaction. *Psychological Science, 15*, 8–13.

Luthans, F. (2002a). The need for and meaning of positive organizational behavior. *Journal of Organizational Behavior, 23*, 695–706.

Luthans, F. (2002b). Positive organizational behavior: Developing and managing psychological strengths. *Academy of Management Executive, 16*, 57–72.

Luthans, F., Avey, J. B., Avolio, B. J., Norman, S. M., & Combs, G. M. (2006). Psychological capital development: Toward a micro-intervention. *Journal of Organizational Behavior, 27*, 387–393.

Luthans, F., Avey, J. B., Avolio, B. J., & Peterson, S. J. (2010). The development and resulting performance impact of positive psychological capital. *Human Resource Development Quarterly, 21*, 41–67.

Luthans, F., Avey, J. B., & Patera, J. L. (2008). Experimental analysis of a web-based training intervention to develop positive psychological capital. *Academy of Management Learning and Education, 7*, 209–221.

Luthans, F., & Avolio, B. (2003). Authentic leadership: A positive development approach. In K. S. Cameron, J. E. Dutton, & R. E. Quinn (Eds.), *Positive organizational scholarship* (pp. 241–258). San Francisco, CA: Berrett-Koehler.

Luthans, F., Avolio, B. J., Avey, J. B., & Norman, S. M. (2007). Psychological capital: Measurement and relationship with performance and satisfaction. *Personnel Psychology, 60*, 541–572.

Luthans, F., Avolio, B. J., Walumbwa, F. O., & Li, W. (2005). The psychological capital of Chinese workers. *Management and Organization Review, 1*, 247–269.

Luthans, F., Norman, S. M., Avolio, B. J., & Avey, J. B. (2008). The mediating role of psychological capital in the supportive organizational climate-employee performance relationship. *Journal of Organizational Behavior, 29*, 219–238.

Luthans, F., & Youssef, C. M. (2004). Human, social, and now positive psychological capital management. *Organizational Dynamics, 33*, 143–160.

Luthans, F., & Youssef, C. M. (2007). Emerging positive organizational behavior. *Journal of Management, 33*, 321–349.

Luthans, F., Youssef, C. M., & Avolio, B. J. (2007). *Psychological capital: Developing the human competitive edge*. Oxford, UK: Oxford University Press.

Luthans, F., Youssef, C. M., Sweetman, D., & Harms, P. D. (in press). Psychological capital and employee well-being: Impact of satisfaction with work, relationships and health. *Journal of Leadership and Organizational Studies*.

Lyubomirsky, S. (2007). *The how of happiness: A new approach to getting the life you want*. New York, NY: Penguin.

Lyubomirsky, S., King, L., & Diener, E. (2005). The benefits of frequent positive affect: Does happiness lead to success? *Psychological Bulletin, 131,* 803–855.

Lyubomirsky, S., Sheldon, K. M., & Schkade, D. (2005). Pursuing happiness: The architecture of sustainable change. *Review of General Psychology, 9,* 111–131.

Maslow, A. (1954). *Motivation and personality.* New York, NY: Harper.

Masten, A. S. (2001). Ordinary magic: Resilience process in development. *American Psychologist, 56,* 227–239.

Masten, A. S., & Reed, M. J. (2002). Resilience in development. In C. R. Snyder & S. J. Lopez (Eds.), *Handbook of positive psychology* (pp. 74–88). New York, NY: Oxford University Press.

Morris, J. A., & Feldman, D. C. (1996). The dimensions, antecedents, and consequences of emotional labor. *Academy of Management Review, 21,* 986–1010.

Nakamura, J., & Csikszentmihalyi, M. (2009). Flow theory and research. In S. J. Lopez & C. R. Snyder (Eds.), *Oxford handbook of positive psychology* (2nd ed.) (pp. 195–206). New York, NY: Oxford University Press.

Norman, S. M., Avolio, B. J., & Luthans, F. (2010). The impact of positivity and transparency on trust in leaders and their perceived effectiveness. *The Leadership Quarterly, 21,* 350–364.

Oishi, S., Diener, E., & Lucas, R. (2007). The optimum level of well-being: Can people be too happy? *Perspectives on Psychological Science, 2,* 346–360.

Peterson, C., Park, N., Hall, N., & Seligman, M. E. P. (2009). Zest and work. *Journal of Organizational Behavior, 30,* 161–172.

Peterson, C., & Seligman, M. (2004). *Character strengths and virtues: A handbook and classification.* New York, NY: Oxford University Press.

Peterson, S. J., & Byron, K. (2008). Exploring the role of hope in job performance: Results from four studies. *Journal of Organizational Behavior, 29,* 785–803.

Peterson, S. J., Luthans, F., Avolio, B. J., Walumbwa, F. O., & Zhang, Z. (2011). The impact of psychological capital on employee performance: A latent growth modeling approach. *Personnel Psychology, 64,* 427–450.

Peterson, S. J., & Zhang, Z. (2011). Examining the relationships between top management team psychological characteristics, transformational leadership, and business unit performance. In M. A. Carpenter (Ed.), *Handbook of top management team research.* (pp. 127–149). New York, NY: Elger.

Ryan, R. M., & Frederick, C. (1997). On energy, personality, and health: Subjective vitality as a dynamic reflection of well-being. *Journal of Personality, 65,* 529–565.

Schneider, S. L. (2001). In search of realistic optimism. *American Psychologist, 56,* 250–263.

Seligman, M. E. P. (1998). *Learned optimism.* New York, NY: Pocket Books.

Seligman, M. E. P., & Csikszentmihalyi, M. (2000). Positive psychology. *American Psychologist, 55,* 5–14.

Snyder, C. R. (2000). *Handbook of hope.* San Diego, CA: Academic Press.

Snyder, C. R., Ilardi, S., Michael, S. T., & Cheavens, J. (2000). Hope theory: Updating a common process for psychological change. In C. R. Snyder, & R. E. Ingram (Eds.), *Handbook of psychological change: Psychotherapy processes and practices for the 21st century* (pp. 128–153). New York, NY: John Wiley & Sons.

Snyder, C. R., Irving, L., & Anderson, J. (1991). Hope and health: Measuring the will and the ways. In C. R. Snyder & D. R. Forsyth (Eds.), *Handbook of social and clinical psychology* (pp. 285–305). Elmsford, NY: Pergamon.

Snyder, C. R., Lopez, S. J., & Teramoto Pedrotti, J. (2011). *Positive psychology* (2nd ed.). Los Angeles, CA: Sage.

Stajkovic, A. D., & Luthans, F. (1998a). Self-efficacy and work-related performance: A meta-analysis. *Psychological Bulletin*, *124*, 240–261.

Stajkovic, A. D., & Luthans, F. (1998b). Social cognitive theory and self-efficacy: Going beyond traditional motivational and behavioral approaches. *Organizational Dynamics*, *26*, 62–74.

Sutcliffe, K. M., & Vogus, T. J. (2003). Organizing for resilience. In K. S. Cameron, J. E. Dutton, & R. E. Quinn (Eds.), *Positive organizational scholarship*. (pp. 94–110). San Francisco, CA: Berrett-Koehler.

Walumbwa, F. O., Luthans, F., Avey, J. B., & Oke, A. (2011). Authentically leading groups: The mediating role of collective psychological capital and trust. *Journal of Organizational Behavior*, *32*, 4–24.

Walumbwa, F. O., Peterson, S. J., Avolio, B. J., & Hartnell, C. A. (2010). An investigation of the relationship between leader and follower psychological capital, service climate and job performance. *Personnel Psychology*, *63*, 937–963.

Wright, T. A. (1997). Time revisited in organizational behavior. *Journal of Organizational Behavior*, *18*, 201–204.

Youssef, C. M., & Luthans, F. (2007). Positive organizational behavior in the workplace: The impact of hope, optimism, and resilience. *Journal of Management*, *33*, 774–800.

Youssef, C. M., & Luthans, F. (in press). Psychological capital theory: Toward a positive holistic model. In A. Bakker (Ed.), *Advances in positive organizational psychology*. Bingley, UK: Emerald.

# CHAPTER 56

# REFLECTED BEST SELF ENGAGEMENT AT WORK: POSITIVE IDENTITY, ALIGNMENT, AND THE PURSUIT OF VITALITY AND VALUE CREATION

LAURA MORGAN ROBERTS

Antioch University, Yellow Springs, OH, USA

DID *you bring your best self to work today?* This question, infused with considerable subjectivity, also elegantly captures a wide range of personal aspirations, motives, and evaluations regarding the experience of being extraordinary at work. Yet the notion of "bringing one's best self to work" has received more attention in the popular domain than it has in scholarly examinations of happiness, fulfillment, and performance at work. A plethora of self-help, personal growth, and leadership resources encourages people to be their best self through optimal thinking, relationship building, soaring on strengths, and living their best life. The dearth of scholarly examinations of such claims limits understanding of the core elements of the best self and leaves the construct of the "best self" subject to various loose interpretations that lack theoretical grounding. Moreover, many of the proclaimed tools and interventions for becoming one's best self have not been scientifically validated or supported by extant empirical research. It is thus incumbent upon scholars to establish the conceptual parameters, preconditions, and impact of becoming one's best self.

The topic of best self engagement is ripe for scholarly investigation, particularly within organizational studies. As positive organizational scholars, my colleagues[1] and I have begun

---

[1] This chapter is written in acknowledgement and appreciation of the Center for Positive Organizational Scholarship and my affiliated colleagues, with whom I have explored the theoretical and practical implications of RBS engagement: Brianna Caza, Jane Dutton, Emily Heaphy, Janet Max, Robert Quinn, Ryan Quinn, Shawn Quinn, Steven Shafer, Gretchen Spreitzer, and Lynn Wooten.

to explore the theoretical underpinnings of the mass appeal to become extraordinary by engaging one's best self. The purpose of this chapter is to extend our work on best-self engagement. I situate the reflected best self as a conceptual anchor for understanding how individuals might increase their extraordinary experiences at work. The phrase, reflected best self (RBS), signifies that this form of self construal is a product of reflected appraisals and personal reflection on lived experiences of being at one's best. In keeping with the overarching theme of this handbook, this chapter associates the RBS with happiness at work, wherein happiness is a form of subjective well-being that is manifested through enhanced vitality and value creation at work. I employ a deliberately broad frame on the manifestations of happiness at work, given the varied definitions of the construct itself (Peterson, Park, & Seligman, 2005). Viewing happiness as an indicator of subjective well-being, I focus on optimal functioning, or vitality within an individual, as well as the generative state of value creation, in which the individual's vitality is externally directed to strengthen a social system. Given the importance of multilevel theorizing about organizing and work, I place equal importance on vitality and value creation as potentially related, but distinct indicators of personal and social well-being in work organizations.

This chapter will review the organizational research on positive identity development and alignment at work to illuminate critical pathways for RBS engagement that also increase vitality and value creation. The chapter is organized as follows. First, I define the RBS and position it in related discussions of development and engagement at work. Second, I describe identity processes for discovering one's RBS, based on recent research on the RBS and positive identity construction at work. Third, I present four alignment-based pathways for activating the RBS at work: purposeful engagement, strength-based engagement, authentic engagement, and relational affirmation. Studies in positive psychology, positive organizational scholarship, and organizational behavior provide evidence for the potency of each of these four pathways for promoting extraordinary outcomes at work. This chapter contributes to these literatures by explaining how the RBS is a theoretically useful construct for understanding how positive identity construction and alignment increase vitality and value creation at work. Finally, I conclude with a discussion of future research directions on the RBS and its impact on individual and collective well-being in organizations.

# THE REFLECTED BEST SELF AS A THEORETICAL CONSTRUCT

The RBS is a changing self-knowledge structure about who we are when we are at our best that cuts across multiple domains and provides a template for action (Roberts, Dutton, Spreitzer, Heaphy, & Quinn, 2005a). The RBS serves as an "anchor and a beacon, a personal touchstone of who we are and a guide for who we can become" (Roberts et al., 2005a, p. 712). This means that the RBS represents a fusion of the reality of lived experience (who I have been at my best) with the idealized sense of possibility for who one can be(come) when one fully embodies his or her best self. Further, the RBS is a relational representation—it reflects a person's self understanding as a valuable contributor to a social system, as informed by social experiences. RBS construals vary in terms of content and clarity; each person's RBS is unique, and some people are more cognizant of their RBS characteristics and are better able to articulate the conditions that invoke RBS episodes than are others (Roberts et al., 2005b).

The RBS construal, or "portrait", is also a representation of an action-oriented state of being that involves "actively employing strengths to create value, actualize one's potential, and fulfill one's sense of purpose, which generates a constructive experience (emotional, cognitive, or behavioral) for oneself and for others" (Roberts et al., 2005a, p. 714). Research on the RBS does not examine evaluative comparisons across people or attempt to identify *the best* person in a particular domain or task. The emphasis here is on the extent to which any individual identifies with and activates his or her RBS in a given situation.

This current chapter emphasizes how and why a person might express his or her RBS during a given moment at work. I use the term "reflected best self (RBS) engagement" to describe the state of being, in which, an individual knowingly activates his or her RBS. Engagement refers to the expression of a particular self during a given moment at work (Kahn, 2007), and the psychological state when one is working at full capacity (Nakamura & Csikszentmihalyi, 2002). There are two facets of reflected best self engagement at work: discovery (i.e., composing a RBS portrait that increases salience, clarity and identification with one's RBS in a given moment) and alignment (i.e., deliberate attempts to act in accordance with or embody one's RBS during a given moment). The next two sections will review each facet of reflected best self engagement and its association with vitality and value creation at work.

# Discovering One's Reflected Best Self: A Pathway for Positive Identity Construction

Discovering one's RBS is a central pathway in the process of positive identity construction. A positive identity is a self-view that a person deems valuable or desirable in some way (for reviews, see Dutton, Roberts, & Bednar, 2010; Roberts & Creary, 2011). Certain jolts (i.e., discrepant or surprising events) are likely to prompt positive identity changes involved in RBS discovery (Roberts et al., 2005a). Both affirmative and challenging jolts can prompt people to modify and enhance their self-view by helping them to see themselves as a meaningful contribution to a social system, and therefore promote greater awareness and understanding of the RBS. Affirmative jolts call attention to the positive aspects of one's identity and enhance feelings of self-regard, while challenging jolts make salient one's strength and capacity to exceed expectations. For example, the Reflected Best Self Exercise[2] is an affirmative jolt; the exercise involves soliciting "contribution stories" from work colleagues, family, and friends about times when a person added value or made an important contribution by activating his or her RBS. The RBS exercise helps people to experience others' appreciation of their contributions, thus enhancing their sense of significance within a social system. Challenging jolts also help people to learn more about who they are at their best, by providing stretch opportunities that reveal one's capacity to lead, endure or adapt in

---

[2] See http://www.bus.umich.edu/positive.

difficult situations. These challenging jolts can also help people to develop a deeper sense of significance and capacity for effective action, generally speaking.

Affirmative and challenging jolts may also prompt people to change the content or increase the clarity of their RBS portrait to include more precise descriptors of Dutton et al.'s (2010) prominent bases of positive identity cultivation: virtuous, favorably regarded, developing, and complex yet balanced and whole. For example, contribution stories may help to illuminate the specific virtues that are enacted when a person engages his or her RBS, while also making salient feelings of appreciation, admiration and positive regard for another person. Challenging jolts, such as extending oneself in an act of community service, can also call forth the character strengths and virtues that reflect one's best self and thus promote positive identity cultivation (Dutton et al., 2011). Given that people compose RBS portraits on a holistic canvas, drawing from personal and professional experiences and incorporating both their past and present, affirmative and challenging jolts raise awareness of how the core elements of one's RBS may manifest in work-related tasks, in social outings, through civic engagement, and with family. As such, the formation of the RBS portrait helps to reinforce a positive identity structure; rather than seeing oneself as fragmented or fractured, the RBS discovery process likely generates complementarity and balance across life domains.

The process of RBS discovery also reinforces the cultivation of a more positive developmental identity, as one comes to see oneself as evolving, maturing and adapting in a positive direction. An emphasis on discovering and embodying one's RBS can promote self-actualization (Maslow, 1954), by providing concrete examples of maximizing one's potential to create value and experience vitality. RBS episodes are peak moments, and reflecting upon them may increase awareness of one's capacity to optimize his or her existence. Jolts that catalyze the discovery of one's RBS also provide an alternate pathway for personal growth and professional development via the constructive application of strengths (Spreitzer, 2006).

Rather than focus on weaknesses, deficits, or shortcomings, the RBS discovery process features strengths as a platform for growth and development. An emphasis on development is critical here; overused, inflated or insincere praise is often rejected (Rath & Clifton, 2004) and can actually decrease well-being (Spreitzer, Stephens, & Sweetman, 2009), which could explain why people are often reticent to focus on strengths when developing themselves or others. The RBS discovery process supports a learning orientation (Grant & Dweck, 2003) and an incremental view of development; it is based on the assumption that strengths can be cultivated, and that there is greater value in learning than in winning. Greater understanding of the identity development processes involved in RBS discovery may help to articulate how individuals, like groups, can grow from good to great and develop in their areas of greatest strength.

## Proposed impact of reflected best self discovery on vitality and value creation

The RBS discovery process increases vitality through its links to positive affect and well-being. Writing about one's best possible future self (relative to writing about other topics) is more strongly associated with immediate and long-term effects on positive mood, subjective well-being, and illness prevention (King, 2001; Sheldon & Lyubormirski, 2006).

Similarly, the RBS Exercise, which provides only strength-based feedback from professional and personal counterparts, promotes vitality via enhanced positive emotions. After receiving RBS feedback, young adults reported higher levels of positive emotions in best self portraits and action plans than study participants who: (1) received strengths feedback from only professional contacts, or (2) received more traditional (strength- and improvement-based) feedback (Spreitzer et al., 2009). Positive emotional states are particularly important for enhancing vitality because they "broaden-and-build" thought–action repertoires, which facilitate the building of other resources and enhances well-being (Fredrickson, 2001).

The RBS discovery process also increases vitality through the cultivation of more positive identities. Embodying certain character strengths and virtues (e.g., hope, zest, gratitude, love, and curiosity) has a positive impact on life satisfaction (Park, Peterson, & Seligman, 2004a, 2004b). Increasing one's sense of self-regard is associated with higher life satisfaction and lower depression and hopelessness (Crocker, Luhtanen, Blaine, & Broadnax, 1994). Feelings of personal growth and striving toward an optimal existence promote well-being (Ryan & Deci, 2001; Ryff, 1989; Waterman, 1993). Developing a more positive identity structure that embraces complexity is particularly important for increasing access to the various coping resources that multiple identities provide, and building resilience in stressful situations (Caza, 2007; Caza & Wilson, 2009; Thoits, 1983).

The RBS discovery process builds relational resources in the form of broader, more diverse or higher quality relationships with others, which fulfill human needs for belongingness (Baumeister & Leary, 1995; Lawrence & Nohria, 2002) and are associated with better physical and psychological health (Heaphy & Dutton, 2008; Ryff & Singer, 2001) and thriving at work (Spreitzer, Sutcliffe, Dutton, Sonenshein, & Grant, 2005). An RBS exercise field experiment supported that the RBS discovery process builds social resources by promoting the expression of love/attachment and kindness/generosity in RBS portraits (i.e., written descriptions of one's RBS) (Spreitzer et al., 2009). The interpersonal interactions that help people to learn more about their valued contributions also help to strengthen people with social support, trust, intimacy, and feelings of being loved (Roberts, 2007a). The related positive identity effects of the RBS discovery process that I described previously are also likely to promote the building of such social resources that, in turn, can increase vitality (Dutton et al., 2010).

Composing RBS portraits also promotes value-creation, by increasing a sense of agency, such that people feel more confident in their ability to exercise control over events that affect their lives (Roberts et al., 2005a; Spreitzer et al., 2009). For example, writing about one's best future self increases motivation to persist with self-concordant goals (Sheldon & Lyubormirski, 2006). The RBS discovery and identity development process can also help people to exhibit resilience and optimism in the face of difficulty with a larger reservoir of positive emotions (Fredrickson, 2009). The building of positive identities are also beneficial for social systems when people act in accordance with self-defined virtues and character strengths (Aquino & Reed, 2002; Peterson & Park, 2006), increase openness to relationship-building across dimensions of difference (Dutton et al., 2010; Johnson & Fredrickson, 2005), and exhibit more creativity at work (Cheng, Sanchez-Burks, & Lee, 2008). Thus, as the RBS discovery process helps people to construct more positive identities, it is directly and indirectly generating increased vitality (e.g., positive emotions) and value-creation (e.g., agency, resilience, building social resources, promoting virtuous behavior, and fostering creativity).

# ACTIVATING ONE'S BEST-SELF: ALIGNMENT-RELATED PATHWAYS

The second facet of RBS engagement at work is alignment: deliberate attempts to act in accordance with or embody one's RBS during a given moment or within a given context. The discovery process increases the salience, clarity and identification with one's RBS in a given moment. As this self-understanding becomes clearer and more refined, it is more accessible as part of the working self-concept (Markus & Wurf, 1987), and thus more easily activated or engaged in work situations. Yet people must still engage in deliberate action to bring their best self to work. Not all work environments are conducive to one's RBS, and ego-preservation desires often lead people to act in ways that undermine RBS engagement at work. Conscious actors who place a higher priority on contribution than gratification are able to achieve optimal states of functioning and leadership in organizations (Cameron, 2008; Quinn, 2004).

Discovering one's RBS enables an individual to be a social architect—one who co-creates the conditions in which the RBS can flourish (Roberts et al., 2005a). Four key alignment-based pathways for activating the RBS at work—purposeful engagement, strength-based engagement, authentic engagement, and relational affirmation—enable individuals to co-create the conditions that enliven the RBS by increasing the degree of alignment between their RBS and their work activities, context, and relationships.

## Purposeful engagement at work

The first pathway for aligning one's RBS with work activities is via strengthening one's connection to work-related tasks. I term this pathway purposeful engagement at work, because it encompasses both the experience of work-related tasks as meaningful and engaging, and the evaluation that work-related effort is worthwhile according to personally held values. Purposeful engagement in work activates the RBS by increasing motivation to put forth extra effort on work tasks and strive beyond mediocrity to embody one's full potential for contributing and self-actualizing in the context of work.

Purposeful engagement in work is scientifically grounded in the study of motivation, job design, task engagement, meaning, and work orientation. In accordance with expectancy theory (Porter & Lawler, 1968; Vroom, 1964), a person will expend effort toward RBS engagement at work if one associates such effort with desired results and valued rewards. Job enrichment theory (Hackman, Oldham, Janson, & Purdy, 1975) points to the importance of three additional job characteristics that stimulate engagement and commitment by producing desired results and rewards: experienced meaningfulness ("perceiving work as worthwhile or important by some system of values [s]he accepts"), experienced responsibility (believing "[s]he is personally accountable for the outcomes of his [or her] efforts"), and knowledge of results (being "able to determine, on some fairly regular basis, whether or not the outcomes of his [or her] work are satisfactory"). More recent research on work motivation, job design and prosocial helping and giving behaviors consistently shows that (even remote) contact with a beneficiary of one's work activities increases the meaningfulness of work and persistence and productivity for workers in a variety of occupations, including call center employees, fundraisers and lifeguards (see Grant et al., 2007; Grant & Parker, 2009, for examples). Further, those with calling orientations, defined, in a secular sense, as the belief that one's work contributes to the greater good and makes the world a better place, report higher levels of enjoyment and satisfaction with work and life (Wrzesniewski, 2003; Wrzesniewski, McCauley, Rozin, & Schwartz, 1997). Moreover, people who pursue protean careers with a self-guided, adaptive, self-actualizing approach also experience positive career outcomes (Hall, 2002; Ibarra, 2003). Research on job crafting provides additional evidence for how social architects deepen their sense of purpose at work, by actively altering and/or deriving meaning from the tasks they perform and the relationships they build while performing such tasks (Berg, Wrzesniewski, & Dutton, 2010; Wrzesniewski & Dutton, 2001). For example, a hospital cleaner may define her job responsibility as creating an atmosphere for healing, and a project manager may create new methods for database management to make his job more efficient and less repetitive. Thus, meaningful work can increase purposeful engagement, and therefore, foster the activation of the RBS toward valued pursuits.

## Strength-based engagement with work

The second pathway for aligning one's RBS with work activities is via strength-based engagement. The exhortation to "focus on strengths" has inspired scholars and practitioners across the globe to examine their own practices for sources of individual and collective excellence. The focus on strengths is consistent with the broader intention of becoming one's best self. As defined earlier, the RBS is activated when one engages strengths in ways that promote vitality and value creation. Thus, strengths are at the core of best self engagement.

Strength-based engagement has a more enduring positive impact on subjective well being than merely reflecting on a best self episode (Seligman, Steen, Park, & Peterson, 2005). People who used their core strengths in new ways over a 1-week period were more likely to display higher well-being outcomes 6 months later than were people who wrote a best self story and re-read it every night for 1 week (Seligman et al., 2005). This research suggests that merely reflecting on one's best self is not sufficient for long-term enhancements to vitality; people also need to intentionally activate their best selves by putting their strengths to work. Theories of human resource management, talent management, and leadership development espouse that organizations should hire, promote and retain individuals who possess the core competencies required to meet an organization's strategic aims. In this light, strength-based engagement not only promotes RBS activation, it also enriches an organization's reservoir of accessible human capital. Organizations benefit when employees exercise their strengths, showing 1.4 times higher productivity than typical organizations, lower turnover, higher employee satisfaction, and higher customer satisfaction (Harter & Schmidt, 2002; Harter, Schmidt, & Hayes, 2002).

Yet, the opportunity to develop into one's RBS by engaging strengths may be neglected, overlooked or devalued in comparison to deficit reduction (Spreitzer, 2006). While competency building is critical for developing well-rounded, capable contributors who meet task requirements, researchers from the Gallup Institute advocate that the greatest areas for growth and contribution lie in identifying and utilizing one's core strengths (Hodges & Clifton, 2004). Eighty percent of workers, globally, do not exercise their strengths at work, and are therefore less emotionally engaged on the job. This means that they are more likely to report: dreading going to work, having more negative than positive interactions with colleagues, treating customers poorly, telling friends what a miserable company they work for, achieving less on a daily basis, and having fewer positive and creative moments (Rath, 2007). However, people who do exercise their strengths regularly at work are six times more likely to be engaged in their jobs and three times more likely to report having an excellent quality of life in general (Rath, 2007). They also claim fewer sick days, file fewer workers' compensation claims, and have fewer accidents while on the job (Buckingham & Clifton, 2001). The Center for Applied Positive Psychology (CAPP) also reports that using one's strengths is associated with higher levels of energy and vitality (Govindji & Linley, 2007), less stress (Wood, Linley, Maltby, & Hurling, 2010), and greater goal achievement, which results in psychological need satisfaction and increased happiness (Linley, Nielsen, Wood, Gillett, & Biswas-Diener, 2010). The Values in Action (VIA) Institute also surveyed over 13,000 US, Swiss and German adults and found that several character strengths independently predicted life satisfaction, and that love, hope, curiosity, gratitude and zest were most highly linked to life satisfaction (Beerman, Park, Peterson, Ruch, & Seligman, 2007; Park et al., 2004a, 2004b). By leading people to desire and pursue the good, or to do the right thing (Peterson & Park, 2006), character strengths thus promote both vitality and value creation, and serve as a critical resource for organizations (Peterson & Park, 2006). These findings support a link between strength-based engagement, vitality, and value creation.

## Authentic engagement at work

The first two pathways to increasing alignment—purposeful engagement and strength-based engagement—align the RBS with work-related activities. The third pathway, authentic engagement at work, aligns one's RBS with his or her work context. Specifically, it examines the extent to which one's values and background are consistent with one's expressed style and organizational culture. The authentic engagement pathway is especially critical in diverse work settings, and for people who are marginal, that is people who differ from the majority or historically dominant group, in a salient and meaningful way.

Becoming more authentic involves increasing the subjective experience of alignment between internal experiences and external expressions (Avolio & Gardner, 2005; Erikson, 1995; Harter, 2002; Roberts, 2007b). Internal experiences include thoughts, feelings, values, and behavioral preferences; external expressions refer to outward behavior, including verbal disclosures and nonverbal behavior, as well as displays such as attire and office décor (Roberts, Cha, Hewlin, & Settles, 2009). The authentic experience reflects an individual's gestalt or overall feeling of having sufficiently communicated and acted upon his or her genuine internal experiences in the workplace (Liedtka, 2008). Authenticity has been associated with fewer physical and depressive symptoms, lower anxiety, lower stress, and greater subjective vitality (e.g., Lopez & Rice, 2006; Ryan, LaGuardia & Rawsthorne, 2005). When one behaves authentically, this behavior fosters a sense of virtuousness, higher self regard, and the feeling that one is living in accordance with the daimon or true self (Roberts et al., 2009).

The lack of authenticity at work bears substantial emotional and productivity costs for individuals, work groups, and organizations in the form of stress (Hochschild, 1983), inhibited creativity, cohesion, and group decision-making (Avery & Steingard, 2008; Milliken, Morrison, & Hewlin, 2003). For example, people who attempt to alter or mute their cultural expressions or perspectives for the sake of assimilating into the organization's dominant culture may also experience stress, diverting cognitive resources to cope with identity conflict (Bell, 1990; Hewlin, 2003; Settles, 2006). Assimilation may also limit the quality of creativity and group decision-making (Ely & Thomas, 2001).

Authentic engagement requires self-awareness and moral courage. To fully express one's RBS, a person must be willing to engage with critical participation in life and to counter his or her tendencies to suppress counternormative thoughts, feelings, values, and behaviors. Critical participation in life means understanding the context, questioning contradictions inherent in that context, and then owning one's values and beliefs because they reflect one's personal experience, not because they are socially or politically appropriate (Heidegger, 1962; Shamir & Eilam, 2005). Moral courage in the face of the discomfort of dissension, disapproval, or rejection is required to remove masks, or public personae, that deny internal experiences or deceive others about thoughts, feelings, values or behavioral preferences in order to increase their stature, protect their image, or avoid conflict in relationships. For women and minorities, peeling off masks may involve displaying aspects of one's cultural heritage, even when they do not conform to mainstream stylistic preferences, in order to enhance authenticity and foster eudaimonia (Roberts & Roberts, 2007). In these circumstances, becoming more authentic means finding ways to integrate one's gendered and cultural experiences into the values and practices of their work environment, perhaps even drawing upon such aspects of one's background as a source of strength that enhances the quality of one's work and relationships (Bell & Nkomo, 2001; Cha & Roberts, 2011; Roberts, 2007b). In short, authentic engagement calls for people to engage in positive deviance, by exhibiting "intentional behaviors that depart from the norm of a reference group in honorable ways" (Spreitzer & Sonenshein, 2003, p. 209) in order to fully activate the RBS in work contexts.

## Relational affirmation

I have heretofore reviewed alignment between the RBS and work-related activities (purposeful engagement and strength-based engagement) and alignment between the RBS and the work context (authentic engagement at work). The fourth alignment pathway, relational affirmation, points to the critical role that relationships play in RBS engagement.

Relational affirmation refers to the act of enhancing another person's sense of being known and understood for what he or she contributes to a relationship and to the social environment more generally. When both parties in a relationship feel that they are known and understood, they are more likely to trust, respect and like one another (Dutton & Heaphy, 2003; Kahn, 2007; Miller & Stiver, 1997; Polzer, Milton, & Swann, 2002), to proactively seek performance feedback because they have fewer impression management concerns (Ashford, Blatt, & Van de Walle, 2003), and to trust that positive and negative feedback is accurate and well-intended (Cohen, Steele, & Ross, 1999). Even visualizing close, positive relationships makes people more receptive to additional feedback about newly discovered performance and intellectual deficiencies (Kumashiro & Sedikides, 2005).

People can increase RBS engagement by cultivating affirming relationships, which is a process of mutual discovery. The quality of that connection, and the enduring nature of affirmation, may also depend on people's capacity for perspective taking. Perspective taking fosters relational affirmation by helping people to recognize external circumstances that can lead to failure and to acknowledge the internal characteristics that enable another's success

(Galper, 1976; Parker & Axtell, 2001). Perspective-taking also helps people to see more commonalities between themselves and others, and thus reduces the likelihood of stereotyping (Davis, Conklin, Smith, & Luce, 1996; Galinsky, Ku, & Wang, 2005; Galinsky & Moskovic, 2000). Adopting another's perspective also enables one to learn which aspects of the other's identity are most valued and to affirm those aspects of identity (Polzer et al., 2002; Roberts, 2007a).

The amount of positive feedback, relative to negative feedback, also determines important relational and well-being outcomes. Research on positive emotions, relationships and well-being reveals that human flourishing, team performance, and marital satisfaction are predicted by a ratio of 3:1 for positive to negative affect or interactions (Fredrickson & Losada, 2005; Gottman, 1994; Losada & Heaphy, 2004). There is an upper limit, however; if the positive outweighs the negative by a factor of 13 or more, there may be harmful effects on individuals and relationships (Fredrickson, 2009). Based on this finding, affirming relationships do not require that one refrain from any "negative" exchange, but that the positive outweigh the negative by a factor of 3 to 9. Cultivating affirming relationships in this way can promote vitality via enhanced self-esteem, positive emotions, and resilience for RBS engagement, while also promoting value creation through the establishment of affirming social practices that enliven others' reflected best selves.

# FUTURE RESEARCH

As stated at the beginning of this chapter, the question of bringing one's best self to work generates a host of questions for scholarly investigation. This chapter has drawn upon research in organizational behavior, positive psychology, and positive organizational scholarship to define the RBS as a socially constructed self-construal, to describe four pathways for RBS engagement, and to offer several theories and empirical studies that support the potency of RBS engagement in promoting vitality and value-creation in organizations. However, many of these proposed links call for additional empirical testing to further explore the boundary conditions and mechanisms by which RBS engagement facilitates such positive outcomes.

The relationship between challenging jolts, affirmative jolts, and positive identity construction should be further examined. Event sampling techniques might allow for investigations of the source, timing, magnitude and impact of jolts that people experience on a daily basis, with respect to cultivating the RBS and other types of potentially related positive identities (i.e., seeing oneself as virtuous, favorably regarded, whole, balanced, and growing or adapting in a positive direction). The alignment pathways proposed should be examined for their unique and combined impact on RBS engagement, vitality, and value creation. A scale of RBS engagement should be developed, and survey research should be used to test the strength of relationships between RBS engagement and purposeful engagement, strength-based engagement, authentic engagement, and the cultivation of affirming relationships at work. Additional alignment pathways may exist as well.

Despite the wealth of evidence substantiating the claims that RBS engagement promotes well-being and performance, it is important to identify the boundary conditions for such relationships. For example, using strengths *in new ways* appears to have a stronger impact on vitality than does using strengths with intention or merely reflecting on a single best self episode. A combination of RBS awareness (i.e., discovering one's best self) and situated action (i.e., being at one's best more often) may have the most potent and durable impact on vitality and value creation. This proposition should be examined with experimental research methodologies.

Value creation often requires personal and situational changes. A sense of self as "becoming" (i.e., positive identity development) and the motivation to grow and develop oneself in areas of strength and weakness (i.e., make one's best self even better) may be critical for gaining the maximal benefit from RBS engagement. Qualitative research may be best suited for capturing narratives of growth in one's RBS. Critics of strength-based engagement and relational affirmation often (mis)construe positive scholarship as promoting narcissism and complacency. It is important to determine the personal and situational characteristics that foster eudaimonia, or self-optimization with RBS engagement, versus those that foster hedonism or pleasure-seeking.

This chapter has focused primarily on the individual's actions in (co)creating the conditions in which the RBS is activated at work. Yet the research on affirming relationships indicates that significant others can enable (or inhibit) RBS engagement, the research on purposeful engagement suggests that job design might impact RBS engagement, and the research on authentic engagement establishes that the culture of the work environment also influences RBS engagement. Multilevel analyses would allow researchers to parse out the effects of individual characteristics (e.g., positive identity descriptors, personal agency), leader behaviors (e.g., strength-based feedback, provision of developmental opportunities), and organizational context (e.g., job design, organizational culture, diversity, and inclusion of minorities) on RBS engagement and other psychological and performance-related outcomes.

It is also important to develop a deeper understanding of people's varying levels of tolerance for being out of alignment with their best selves. Not all people work because it is their calling; many derive a sense of purpose from the ability to provide financially for their family. Yet if a job requires the underutilization of strengths, the suppression of valued identities, or frequent interactions with toxic, uncivil coworkers, the amount of money that one earns may not be sufficient to override the deleterious impact on RBS engagement, vitality, or value creation. There are likely individual differences in the valuation of each area of alignment with the RBS.

Finally, the importance of voice is evident in the authentic engagement pathway to RBS activation. Ironically, some critics of positive organizational scholarship contend that this project of enabling people to bring their best selves to work may be a form of subtle exploitation. Prescribing RBS engagement as an organizational mandate or job requirement, it may feed into a dysfunctional performance culture. People may seek status enhancements and rewards, rather than the intrinsic motivation of self-actualization, pursuing the daimon, and maximizing contributions. It is thus important that organizations recognize people materially and immaterially (e.g., through appreciation, developmental opportunities) for RBS engagement. Each individual must also maintain the freedom and autonomy to self-determine his or her optimal level of RBS engagement in the service of promoting vitality and value creation.

# References

Aquino, K., & Reed, A. (2002). The self-importance of moral identity. *Journal of Personality and Social Psychology, 83*, 1423–1436.

Ashford, S. J., Blatt, R., & VandeWalle, D. (2003). Reflections on the looking glass: A review of research on feedback-seeking behavior in organizations. *Journal of Management, 29*, 773–799.

Avery, D., & Steingard, D. (2008). Achieving political trans-correctness: Integrating sensitivity and authenticity in diversity management education. *Journal of Management Education, 32*, 269–293.

Avolio, B., & Gardner, W. (2005). Authentic leadership development: Getting to the root of positive forms of leadership. *The Leadership Quarterly, 16*, 315–338.

Baumeister, R. F., & Leary, M. R. (1995). The need to belong: Desire for interpersonal attachments as a fundamental human motivation. *Psychological Bulletin, 117*, 497–529.

Beerman, U., Park, N., Peterson, C., Ruch, W., & Seligman, M. (2007). Strengths of character, orientations to happiness and life satisfaction. *The Journal of Positive Psychology, 2*, 149–156.

Bell, E. L. (1990). The bicultural life experience of career-oriented black women. *Journal of Organizational Behavior, 11*, 459–477.

Bell, E. L., & Nkomo, S. M. (2001). *Our separate ways: Black and white women and the struggle for professional identity*. Boston, MA: Harvard Business School Press.

Berg, J. M., Wrzesniewski, A., & Dutton, J. E. (2010). Perceiving and responding to challenges in job crafting at different ranks: When proactivity requires adaptivity. *Journal of Organizational Behavior, 31*, 158–186.

Buckingham, M., & Clifton, D. (2001). *Now, discover your strengths*. New York, NY: The Free Press.

Cameron, K. (2008). *Positive leadership: Strategies for extraordinary performance*. San Francisco, CA: Berrett-Koehler Publishers, Inc.

Caza, B. B. (2007). *Experiences of adversity at work: Toward an identity-based theory of resilience*. Unpublished doctoral dissertation, University of Michigan, Ann Arbor.

Caza, B. B., & Wilson, M. G. (2009). Me, myself, and I: The benefits of work-identity complexity. In L. M. Roberts & J. E. Dutton (Eds.), *Exploring positive identities and organizations: Building a theoretical and research foundation* (pp. 99–123). New York, NY: Routledge.

Cha, S. E., & Roberts, L. M. (2011). *Navigating race: Asian American journalists' engagement of identity-related resources at work*. Working paper. McGill University and Antioch University.

Cheng, C., Sanchez-Burks, J., & Lee, F. (2008). Connecting the dots within: Creative performance and identity integration. *Psychological Science, 19*, 1178–1184.

Cohen, G. L., Steele, C., & Ross, L. (1999). The Mentor's dilemma: Providing critical feedback across the racial divide. *Personality and Social Psychology Bulletin, 25*, 1302–1318.

Crocker, J., Luhtanen, R., Blaine, B., & Broadnax, S. (1994). Collective self-esteem and psychological well-being among White, Black, and Asian college students. *Personality and Social Psychology Bulletin, 20*(5), 503–513.

Davis, M., Conklin, L., Smith, A., & Luce, C. (1996). Effect of perspective-taking on the cognitive representation of persons: A merging of self and other. *Journal of Personality and Social Psychology, 70*, 713–726.

Dutton, J. E., & Heaphy, E. D. (2003). The power of high quality connections. In K. S. Cameron, J. E. Dutton, & R. E. Quinn (Eds.), *Positive organizational scholarship: Foundations of a new discipline* (pp. 263–278). San Francisco, CA: Berrett-Koehler.

Dutton, J. E., Roberts, L. M., & Bednar, J. S. (2010). Pathways for positive identity construction at work: Four types of positive identity and the building of social resources. *Academy of Management Review*, *35*, 265–293.

Dutton, J. E., Roberts, L. M., & Bednar, J. S. (2011). Prosocial practices, positive identity, and flourishing at work. In S. I. Donaldson, M. Csikszentmihalyi, & J. Nakamura (Eds.), *Applied positive psychology: Improving everyday life, schools, work, health, and society* (p. 155–170). New York, NY: Taylor & Francis Group.

Ely, R. J., & Thomas, D. A. (2001). Cultural diversity at work: The effects of diversity perspectives on work group processes and outcomes. *Administrative Science Quarterly*, *46*, 229–273.

Erikson, R. (1995). The importance of authenticity for self and society. *Symbolic Interaction*, *18*, 121–144.

Fredrickson, B. (2001). The role of positive emotions in positive psychology: The broaden-and-build theory of positive emotions. *American Psychologist*, *56*, 218–226.

Fredrickson, B. L. (2009). *Positivity: Groundbreaking research reveals how to embrace the hidden strength of positive emotions, overcome negativity, and thrive.* New York, NY: Crown.

Fredrickson, B., & Losada, M. (2005). Positive affect and the complex dynamics of human flourishing. *American Psychologist*, *60*, 678–686.

Galinsky, A., Ku, J., & Wang, C. (2005). Perspective-taking and self-other overlap: Fostering social bonds and facilitating social coordination. *Group Processes and Intergroup Relations*, *8*, 109–124.

Galinsky, A., & Moskovic, G. (2000). Perspective-taking: Decreasing stereotype expression, stereotype accessibility, and in-group favoritism. *Journal of Personality and Social Psychology*, *78*, 708–724.

Galper, R.E. (1976). Turning observers into actors: Differential causal attributions as a function of "empathy". *Journal of Research in Personality*, *10*, 328–335.

Gottman, J. (1994). *Why marriages succeed or fail: And how you can make yours last.* New York, NY: Simon & Schuster, Inc.

Govindji, R., & Linley, P. A. (2007). Strengths use, self-concordance and well-being: Implications for strengths coaching and coaching psychologists. *International Coaching Psychology Review*, *2*, 143–153.

Grant, A. M., Campbell, E. M., Chen, G., Cottone, K., Lapedis, D., & Lee, K. (2007). Impact and the art of motivation maintenance: The effects of contact with beneficiaries on persistence behavior. *Organizational Behavior and Human Decision Processes*, *103*, 53–67.

Grant, A. M., & Parker, S. K. (2009). Redesigning work design theories: The rise of relational and proactive perspectives. *Academy of Management Annals*, *3*, 317–375.

Grant, H., & Dweck, C. (2003). Clarifying achievement goals and their impact. *Journal of Personality and Social Psychology*, *85(3)*, 541–553.

Hall, D. T. (2002). *Careers in and out of organizations.* Thousand Oaks, CA: Sage.

Hackman, J. R., Oldham, G., Janson, R., & Purdy, K. (1975). A new strategy for job enrichment. *California Management Review*, *17*, 57–71.

Harter, S. (2002). Authenticity. In C. R. Snyder and S. Lopez (Eds.), *Handbook of positive psychology* (pp. 382–394). New York, NY: Oxford University Press.

Harter, J., & Schmidt, F. (2002). *Employee engagement, satisfaction, and business-unit-level outcomes: A meta-analysis.* Gallup Technical Report. Lincoln, NE: Gallup, Inc.

Harter, J., Schmidt, F., & Hayes, T. (2002). Business-unit-level relationship between employee satisfaction, employee engagement, and business outcomes: A meta-analysis. *Journal of Applied Psychology*, *87*, 268–279.

Heaphy, E. D., & Dutton, J. E. (2008). Positive social interactions and the human body at work: Linking organizations and physiology. *Academy of Management Review, 33*, 137–162.

Heidegger, M. (1962). *Being and time* (J. MacQuarrie and E. Robinson, Trans.). London: SCM Press.

Hewlin, P. F. (2003). And the award for best actor goes to. . .: Facades of conformity in organizational settings. *Academy of Management Review, 28*, 633–656.

Hochschild, A. R. (1983). *The managed heart.* Berkeley, CA: University of California Press.

Hodges, T., & Clifton, D. (2004). Strengths-based development in practice. In P.A. Linley and S. Joseph (Eds.), *International handbook of positive psychology in practice: From research to application.* Hoboken, NJ: Wiley and Sons.

Ibarra, H. (2003). *Working identity: Unconventional strategies for reinventing your career.* Cambridge, MA: Harvard Business School Press.

Johnson, K. J., & Fredrickson, B. L. (2005). "We all look the same to me": Positive emotions eliminate the own-race bias in face recognition. *Psychological Science, 16*, 875–881.

Kahn, W. A. (2007). Meaningful connections: Positive relationships and attachments at work. In J. E. Dutton & B. Ragins (Eds.), *Exploring positive relationships at work: Building a theoretical and research foundation,* (p. 189–207). Mahwah, NJ: Lawrence Erlbaum.

King, L. A. (2001). The health benefits of writing about life goals. *Personality and Social Psychology Bulletin, 27*, 798–807.

Kumashiro, M., & Sedikides, C. (2005). Taking on board liability-focused information: Close positive relationships as a self-bolstering resource. *Psychological Science, 16*(9), 732–739.

Lawrence, P. R., & Nohria, N. (2002). *Driven: How human nature shapes our choices.* San Francisco, CA: Jossey Bass.

Liedtka, J. (2008). Strategy-making and the search for authenticity. *Journal of Business Ethics, 80*, 237–248.

Linley, P. A., Nielsen, K. M., Wood, A. M., Gillett, R., & Biswas-Diener, R. (2010). Using signature strengths in pursuit of goals: Effects on goal progress, need satisfaction, and well-being, and implications for coaching psychologists. *International Coaching Psychology Review, 5*(1), 8–17.

Lopez, F., & Rice, K. (2006). Preliminary development and validation of a measure of relationship authenticity. *Journal of Counseling Psychology, 53*(3), 362–371.

Losada, M., & Heaphy, E. (2004). The role of positivity and connectivity in the performance of business teams: A nonlinear dynamics model. *American Behavioral Scientist, 47*, 740–765.

Markus, H., & Wurf, E. (1987). The dynamic self-concept: A social psychological perspective. *Annual Review of Psychology, 38*, 299–337.

Maslow, A. (1954). *Motivation and personality.* New York, NY: Harper and Row.

Miller, J. B., & Stiver, I. P. (1997). *The Healing connection: How women form relationships in therapy and life.* Boston, MA: Beacon Press.

Milliken, F. J., Morrison, E. W., & Hewlin, P. F. (2003). An exploratory study of employee silence: Issues that employees don't communicate upward and why. *Journal of Management Studies, 40*, 1453–1476.

Nakamura, J., & Csikszentmihalyi, M. (2002). The concept of flow. In C. R. Snyder & S. J. Lopez (Eds.), *The handbook of positive psychology* (pp. 89–105). New York, NY: Oxford University Press.

Park, N., & Peterson, C. (2003). Virtues and organizations. In K. S. Cameron, J. E. Dutton, & R. E. Quinn (Eds.), *Positive organizational scholarship: Foundations of a new discipline* (pp. 33–47). San Francisco, CA: Berrett-Koehler.

Park, N., Peterson, C., & Seligman, M. (2004a). Strengths of character and well-being. *Journal of Social and Clinical Psychology, 23,* 603–619.

Park, N., Peterson, C., & Seligman, M. (2004b). Strengths of character and well-being: A closer look at hope and modesty. *Journal of Social and Clinical Psychology, 23,* 628–634.

Parker, S., & Axtell, C. (2001). Seeing another viewpoint: Antecedents and outcomes of employee perspective-taking. *Academy of Management Journal, 44*(6), 1085–1100.

Peterson, C., Park, N., & Seligman, M. (2005). Orientations to happiness and life satisfaction: The full life versus the empty life. *Journal of Happiness Studies, 6,* 25–41.

Peterson, C., & Park, N. (2006). Character strengths in organizations. *Journal of Organizational Behavior, 27,* 1149–1154.

Polzer, J. T., Milton, L. P., & Swann, W. B. (2002). Capitalizing on diversity: Interpersonal congruence in small work groups. *Administrative Science Quarterly, 47,* 296–324.

Porter, L. W., & Lawler, E. E. (1968). *Managerial attitudes and performance.* Homewood, IL: Richard D. Irwin, Inc.

Quinn, R.E. (2004). *Building the bridge as you walk on it: A guide for leading change.* San Francisco, CA: Jossey-Bass.

Rath, T. (2007). *Strengthsfinder 2.0.* New York, NY: Gallup Press.

Rath, T., & Clifton, D. (2004). *How full is your bucket? Positive strategies for work and life.* New York, NY: Gallup Press.

Roberts, L. M. (2007a). From proving to becoming: How positive relationships create a context for self-discovery and self-actualization. In Dutton, J. E., & Ragins, B. R. (2007). *Exploring positive relationships at work: Building a theoretical and research foundation* (pp. 29–46). New York, NY: Lawrence Erlbaum Associates.

Roberts, L. M. (2007b). Bringing your whole self to work: Lessons in authentic engagement from women leaders. In B. Kellerman & D. L. Rhode (Eds.), *Women and leadership: The state of play and strategies for change* (pp. 329–360). San Francisco, CA: Jossey-Bass.

Roberts, L. M., Cha, S. E., Hewlin, P. F., & Settles, I. H. (2009). Bringing the inside out: Enhancing authenticity and positive identity in organizations. In L. M. Roberts & J. E. Dutton (Eds.), *Exploring positive identities and organizations: Building a theoretical and research foundation* (pp. 149–169) New York, NY: Routledge.

Roberts, L. M., & Creary, S. (2011). Positive identity construction: Insights from classical and contemporary theoretical perspectives. In K. Cameron and G. Spreitzer (Eds.), *Oxford handbook of positive organizational scholarship* (pp. 70–83). New York, NY: Oxford University Press.

Roberts, L. M., Dutton, J. E., Spreitzer, G. M., Heaphy, E. D., & Quinn, R. E. (2005). Composing the reflected best-self portrait: Building pathways for becoming extraordinary in work organizations. *Academy of Management Review, 30,* 712–736.

Roberts, L. M., & Roberts, D. D. (2007). Testing the limits of antidiscrimination law: The business, legal, and ethical ramifications of cultural profiling at work. *Duke Journal of Gender Law & Policy, 14,* 369–405.

Roberts, L. M., Spreitzer, G., Dutton, J., Quinn, R., Heaphy, E., & Barker, B. (2005b). How to play to your strengths. *Harvard Business Review, 83*(1), 74–80.

Ryan, R., LaGuardia, J., & Rawsthorne, L. (2005). Self-complexity and the authenticity of self-aspects: Effects on well being and resilience to stressful events. *North American Journal of Psychology, 7,* 431–448.

Ryan, R. M., & Deci, E. L. (2001). On happiness and human potential: A review of research on hedonic and eudaimonic well-being. *Annual Review of Psychology, 52,* 141–166.

Ryff, C. (1989). Happiness is everything, or is it? Explorations on the meaning of psychological well-being. *Journal of Personality and Social Psychology, 57,* 1069–1081.

Ryff, C. D., & Singer, B. H. (2001). *Emotion, social relationships, and health.* New York, NY: Oxford University Press.

Seligman, M. E. P., Steen, T. A., Park, N., & Peterson, C. (2005). Positive psychology progress: Empirical validation of interventions. *American Psychologist, 60,* 410–421.

Settles, I. H. (2006). Use of an intersectional framework to understand Black women's racial and gender identities. *Sex Roles, 54,* 589–601.

Shamir, B., & Eilam, G. (2005). "What's your story?" A life-stories approach to authentic leadership development. *The Leadership Quarterly, 16,* 395–417.

Sheldon, K., & Lyubormirski, S. (2006). How to increase and sustain positive emotion: The effects of expressing gratitude and visualizing best possible selves. *The Journal of Positive Psychology, 1,* 73–82.

Spreitzer, G. (2006). Leadership development lessons from positive organizational studies. *Organizational Dynamics, 35,* 305–315.

Spreitzer, G. M., & Sonenshein, S. (2003). Positive deviance and extraordinary organizing. In K. Cameron, J. Dutton, & R. Quinn (Eds.), *Positive organizational scholarship* (pp. 207–224). San Francisco, CA: Berrett-Koehler.

Spreitzer, G., & Sonenshein, S. (2004). Toward the construct definition of positive deviance. *American Behavioral Scientist, 47,* 828–847.

Spreitzer, G., Stephens, J. P., & Sweetman, D. (2009). The Reflected Best Self field experiment with adolescent leaders: Exploring the psychological resources associated with feedback source and valence. *Journal of Positive Psychology, 4,* 331–348.

Spreitzer, G. M., Sutcliffe, K., Dutton, J. E., Sonenshein, S., & Grant, A. M. (2005). A socially embedded model of thriving at work. *Organization Science, 16,* 537–549.

Thoits, P. A. (1983). Multiple identities and psychological well-being: A reformulation and test of the social isolation hypotheses. *American Sociological Review, 48*(2), 174–187.

Vroom, V. H. (1964). *Work and motivation.* New York, NY: Wiley.

Waterman, A. S. (1993). Two conceptions of happiness: Contrasts of personal expressiveness (eudaimonia) and hedonic enjoyment. *Journal of Personality and Social Psychology, 64,* 678–691.

Wood, A. M., Linley, P. A., Maltby, J., & Hurling, R. (2010). *Use of positive psychological strengths leads to less stress and greater self-esteem, vitality, and positive affect over time: A three-wave longitudinal study and validation of the Strengths Use Scale.* Unpublished manuscript. Coventry, UK: Centre for Applied Positive Psychology.

Wrzesniewski, A. (2003). Finding positive meaning in work. In Cameron, K. S., Dutton, J. E., & Quinn, R. E. (Eds.). *Positive organizational scholarship: Foundations of a new discipline.* San Francisco, CA: Berrett-Koehler.

Wrzesniewski, A., McCauley, C. R., Rozin, P., & Schwartz, B. (1997). Jobs, careers, and callings: People's relations to their work. *Journal of Research in Personality, 31,* 21–33.

Wrzesniewski, A., & Dutton, J. E. (2001). Crafting a job: Revisioning employees as active crafters of their work. *Academy of Management Review, 26,* 179–201.

# CHAPTER 57

# ENCOURAGING EMPLOYEE HAPPINESS

THOMAS A. WRIGHT

Fordham University, USA

> The wide awake modern employer realizes quite clearly that the mental attitudes of his employees are of very great importance to the successful and profitable conduct of his business.
>
> (Rex B. Hersey, 1930, p. 290)

For Rex B. Hersey, one of the early leading lights of organizational research, the most important worker attitudes were those pertaining to emotional or psychological well-being (Hersey, 1932). As clearly evidenced by the introductory quote, Hersey considered these "mental attitudes" highly instrumental in the determination of the financial success [health] of an organization. In like manner, one of the principal investigators of the famous Hawthorne series of experiments on worker productivity and morale, plant superintendent of inspection G. A. Pennock (1930, p. 309), was also well aware of the importance of encouraging worker well-being to enhance an organization's overall health and betterment in noting "… that you can work much more efficiently in a contented frame of mind than you can when your mind is in a turmoil of worry, fear, or discontent."

Indeed, many of Hersey and Pennock's contemporaries (e.g., Kornhauser, 1933; Mayo, 1924; Putnam, 1930; Snow, 1923) were well aware of the prominent role worker happiness or psychological well-being (PWB) played on various individual efficiency *and* organizational health indicators. These early luminaries of management thought clearly understood that "human" resources were a viable, sustainable source of competitive advantage (Luthans, Luthans, & Luthans, 2004). Unfortunately, and fully 80 years after their work, relatively few of today's organizations actually practice this widely cited belief that such human resources as employee happiness really do count (Luthans & Youssef, 2004; Pfeffer, 1998).

Consistent with the theme of this book, the purpose of this chapter is to clearly demonstrate that an organization's human resources, in particular, the well-being of its employees, contributes significantly to the overall health of the organization. To that end, first a brief historical overview of the role of employee well-being in organizational research is introduced. Second, PWB is defined. Third, a review of the literature establishing relationships among employee well-being, job performance and employee retention is provided. Fourth, research linking PWB with employee cardiovascular health is introduced. Last, the chapter concludes with several promising directions for future research on encouraging employee well-being. Before tackling this important topic of employee well-being, it is appropriate to briefly explore what is meant by the term, organizational health.

## Organizational Health Defined

Historically, the typical definition of organizational health focused on organization-level parameters. For example, Miles (1965) considered an organization healthy if it was able to survive and successfully cope with threats to its existence over time. However, as noted by Tetrick and Quick (2003, p. 3), as a first consideration when examining the issue of organizational health, one must always ask the question in terms of "healthy for whom?" Unfortunately, personified by Miles' definition, a number of these early definitions tended to minimize, and at the extreme, neglect the "human" component in human resources. More recently, Cooper and Cartwright (1994) expanded this "survival of the fittest" definition to include the "human" component and defined a healthy organization as one that is not only financially successful, but also one that has a healthy workforce. In particular, Quick (1999) identified a number of factors contributing to a healthy organization, including having a high level of worker job satisfaction, achieving high productivity, maintaining high retention rates (low turnover) and having employees who demonstrate high levels of psychological and physiological health. Interestingly, as described next, this expanded view of what constitutes a healthy organization is consistent with the theoretical framework of a number of organizational research pioneers interested in better understanding issues surrounding employee health and well-being.

## Historical Overview of Well-Being in Organizational Research

Culminating with Roethlisberger and Dickson's (1939) *Management and the Worker* (written with the assistance of Harold A. Wright), the 1930s saw the burgeoning interest in a "happy/productive worker thesis" which contrasted research operationalizing happiness as well-being (Hersey, 1930) with happiness considered as job satisfaction (Hoppock, 1935; Wren, 1934; Roethlisberger & Dickson, 1939). On the well-being side, Hersey (1930; 1932) undertook a series of studies designed to investigate a possible employee well-being and productivity relationship. Incorporating rigorous, longitudinal field research designs, Hersey gathered a wide range of worker data on feelings of fatigue, level of cooperativeness, well-being, happiness, productivity and efficiency in an attempt to more fully understand the health and well-being of Depression-era employees. Unfortunately, the important work of Hersey and other early well-being researchers such as Anderson (1929) and Fisher and Hanna (1931) all but ceased with the Great Depression, and, with it, Roethlisberger and Dickson's (1939) landmark publication which championed the operationalization of "happiness" as job satisfaction.

In an attempt to better understand the "intangible" work factors that affect worker morale (i.e., satisfaction) and efficiency, Roethlisberger and Dickson (1939) undertook the formidable task of manually collating worker responses from 10,300 interviews taken during 1929 at the Operating Branch of the Western Electric Company. When completed, Roethlisberger and Dickson reported over 80,000 worker comments classified into 37 common topics. In particular, a number of comments, involving worker feelings on perceived advancement opportunities, forms of payment, and various issues surrounding supervision, proved to be of special interest. In fact, they formed the backdrop for the huge, developing interest immediately before, during and after World War II for studying various facets of worker morale.

Coding for whether the comment was favorably or unfavorably-toned, Roethlisberger and Dickson noted that workers generally felt unfavorable regarding their advancement opportunities, forms of payment, and how they were supervised. In addition, in one of the first attempts to distinguish level of worker morale by worker demographic characteristics, they found strong support that men were typically less satisfied than women on many of the 37 work-related topics. Roethlisberger and Dickson's (1939) work was consequential for many reasons, including the fact that for roughly the next 50 years, research investigating the happy/productive worker thesis focused on job satisfaction, not well-being, as the primary operationalization of employee happiness.

Wright and Cropanzano (2000) noted that in equating a happy employee with a satisfied employee, one is required to make at least two tacit assumptions. First, and by definition, job satisfaction is specific to one or more aspects of one's job. Job satisfaction does not explicitly measure aspects of one's life outside of work. Alternatively, when considering employee well-being, one is typically concerned with aspects of their life as a whole, both on and off the job. The second assumption involves the manner in which job satisfaction has been typically measured in applied research. While operationalized in a wide variety of ways, job satisfaction is typically considered to be an attitude (Weiss & Cropanzano, 1996). In sharp contrast to PWB, where commonly used indicators of job satisfaction typically measure both cognitive *and* affective components, PWB is primarily concerned with affective-based or emotional experiences. Considered together, PWB and job satisfaction are best considered as distinct constructs. Wright and his colleagues have provided empirical justification for this assumption (Wright & Cropanzano, 2000; Wright, Cropanzano, & Bonett, 2007).

After this 50-year well-being research hiatus, more recent research endeavors have consistently demonstrated that encouraging the PWB of an organization's employees has tangible benefits, probably even more so than their level of job satisfaction. These benefits not only foster the health and betterment of the employees themselves, but also the health and success of the organization. Incorporating a growing body of research, this chapter further extends the traditional view of happiness as job satisfaction and operationalizes happiness as PWB.

## Happiness Considered as Psychological Well-Being

Taking its conceptual roots from a long and distinguished list of scholarly ancestors, including Hippocrates, Galen, Kant, and Wundt, PWB is traditionally thought of in terms of the overall effectiveness of an individual's psychological functioning (Gechman & Wiener, 1975; Wright, 2005). In particular, using the circumplex model of emotion (described in the following paragraph) as the theoretical framework, PWB measures the hedonic or pleasantness dimension of individual feelings (Russell, 1980; Wright & Cropanzano, 2000).

The need to dimensionalize human feelings and emotions has long been recognized (Cropanzano & Wright, 2001). For example, Galen (AD 129—c.215) adopted a version of the four-humor theory (e.g., melancholic, choleric, sanguine, and phlegmatic) to describe various differences in human feelings and emotions (for a further discussion, see Wright, 2005). More recently, through the use of multidimensional scaling techniques, Russell and his colleagues (Russell, 1978, 1979, 1980; Russell, Weiss, & Mendelsohn, 1989) found that emotions can be organized in a roughly circular structure called a circumplex (Larsen & Diener, 1992; Russell et al., 1989; Wright & Bonett, 1997). As noted by Wright (2005), the circumplex structure has been shown to be quite robust and is generalizable to both adults and children across a variety of cultures.

The circumplex model makes two key assumptions about the nature of one's emotional balance (Larsen & Diener, 1992). First, human feelings share similarities as well as dissimilarities with other human feelings. Second, the circumplex model presupposes that the majority of emotions or feelings can be captured by two dimensions: activation and pleasantness. For example, the factor labeled as "hedonic tone" or "pleasantness-unpleasantness" is anchored by such adjective descriptors as "happy" and "joyous" on the high end and "sad" on the low end. My colleagues and I refer to this dimension as PWB (Cropanzano & Wright, 2001; Wright, 2005). Alternatively, PWB can be contrasted with other conceptualizations of employee feelings measuring the level of activation ("enthusiastic" and "excited") or "affect intensity" of emotional experience (Larsen & Diener, 1992; Wright, 2005). The most widely used of these activation-based measures, the Positive and Negative Affect Schedule (PANAS) scale, was developed by Watson and his colleagues (Watson, 1988; Watson, Clark, & Tellegen, 1988).

As I have noted previously (Wright, 2005; Wright & Cropanzano, 2007; Wright, 2010a), definitions of PWB incorporate several characteristics. First, PWB is a phenomenological or subjective experience (Cropanzano & Wright, 2001; Diener, 1994), meaning that someone is high/low in PWB to the degree that they believe themselves to be high/low in PWB. Second, PWB includes both the relative presence of positive emotions and the relative absence of negative emotions (for a further discussion of these characteristics, see Wright (2010b)). Third, PWB is best considered as a global judgment (Wright & Cropanzano, 2007). This means that PWB refers to one's life in the aggregate, that is, considered as a whole. Unlike job satisfaction, which is centered about the work context (Wright & Cropanzano, 2000), PWB is not aligned to any particular situation (Wright, 2005). Furthermore, PWB has consistently been shown to demonstrate temporal stability, though PWB is not so stable that it can't be influenced by a number of situational circumstances (Wright & Staw, 1999). For example, Cropanzano and Wright (1999) reported a 6-month test-retest correlation of

0.76 and a 5-year test–retest correlation of 0.60 for their measure of PWB. The fact that PWB has been shown to be responsive to various therapeutic interventions has relevance to human resource professionals interested in selection, training and development, and placement decisions (Seligman, 2002). Considered together, an individual exhibiting a high level of PWB indicates that the individual is experiencing a greater measure of positive as compared to negative feelings or emotions (Wright, 2010a).

Organizational researchers have long been aware of the extensive costs, in both human and financial terms, attributable to dysfunctional PWB (Quick, Quick, Nelson, & Hurrell, 1997). For instance, depression, loss of self-esteem, hypertension, alcoholism, and illicit drug consumption have all been associated with work-related dysfunctional PWB (Ivancevich & Matteson, 1980; Wright & Cropanzano, 2000). In turn, these variables have been related to decrements in a number of important work outcomes (Quick et al., 1997; Wright, 2010a, 2010b). Overviews of the role of PWB in the prediction of employee job performance, employee retention and cardiovascular health are provided next.

# Psychological Well-Being and Employee Job Performance

Over the last 20 years, organizational research has consistently established significant associations between various measures of employee well-being and employee job performance (Wright & Bonett, 1997; Wright, Bonett, & Sweeney, 1993; Wright & Cropanzano, 1998, 2000; Wright & Doherty, 1998; Wright & Staw, 1999). For example, Wright and Staw (1999, Study 1) established a significant correlation between well-being and job performance. Incorporating a 4-year design, with well-being measured at Times 1 and 2 and performance at Times 2, 3, and 4, bivariate correlations were established ranging from 0.25 to 0.52. Likewise, Wright and Hobfoll (2004) found that PWB was significantly correlated ($r = 0.37$, $p < 0.01$) with a composite measure of job performance. Similarly, Wright, Cropanzano, Denney and Moline (2002) established correlations of 0.37 between PWB (measured at Time 1) and job performance (measured at Time 1) and 0.45 between the same measure of PWB and job performance (measured at Time 2). As a final example, Wright, Cropanzano and Bonett (2007) found that PWB was significantly correlated ($r = 0.43$, $p < 0.01$) with a 2-item composite measure of performance. In addition to these consistent findings linking PWB with job performance, PWB also plays a significant role in the determination of who stays or voluntarily leaves their job.

# Psychological Well-Being and Employee Retention

As with job performance, the importance of employee well-being in the prediction of employee retention decisions has long been recognized in organizational research (Fisher & Hanna, 1931; Frost, 1920; Snow, 1923; Wright & Bonett, 2007). While employee turnover or withdrawal can certainly be functional from the organization's perspective, as when dissatisfied, poorly performing workers quit their job, the prevailing human resources approach is that high employee retention (or low turnover) is an indicant of organizational health (Quick, 1999).

Similar to the long-standing proposed relationship between job satisfaction and job performance (Houser, 1927; Kornhauser & Sharp, 1932), prevailing theory and research has long maintained the importance of job satisfaction in the retention process (Mobley, 1982). However, consistent with the rather modest findings regarding the proposed relationship between job satisfaction and job performance (e.g., Cherrington, Reitz, & Scott, 1971; Fisher, 1980), Hom and Griffeth (1995) reported meta-analytic findings demonstrating that, at best, job satisfaction typically accounts for less than 5% of employee withdrawal variance.

Alternatively, and consistent with its significant role in the prediction of employee performance, recent research has established that employee PWB is instrumental in the prediction of employee retention; for a further review, see Wright (2010a) and Wright and Bonett (2007). For example, Wright and Bonett (2007) found that every 1-point increase in reported PWB (measured on a 7-point scale) doubled the probability of the employee remaining on the job. Given that the average yearly salary for their employee sample was in excess of $100,000, and using Cascio's (2003) formula for determining cost, the potential cost of turnover in this sample was estimated to range from a minimum of $150,000 to $250,000 per employee. The benefits of employee PWB do not stop with employee performance and retention as PWB holds significant promise in the determination of cardiovascular health.

# Psychological Well-Being and Cardiovascular Health

According to the latest data from the American Heart Association (2010a), over 80 million Americans and countless other hundreds of millions worldwide are afflicted with one or more types of cardiovascular heart disease (CHD), with the majority suffering from high blood pressure. While high blood pressure has a number of sources, Wright (2010b) proposed that employees involved in stressful work have higher levels of blood pressure. This is unfortunate as the costs associated with CHD are quite consequential for both the employee and organization. More specifically, the American Heart Association recently estimated the direct and indirect 2010 costs of cardiovascular disease at over $500 billion (American Heart Association, 2010b). The problem is not specific to just the United States and is truly global in nature. It is estimated that 90% of the CHD burden resides in developing, Third World countries (Hecht & Hecht, 2005; Wright, 2010b).

Historically, cardiovascular health has typically been measured through the use of blood pressure indicators. Blood pressure readings are composed of two numbers, systolic blood pressure (SBP) and diastolic blood pressure (DBP). SBP measures the heart at work, meaning the amount of pressure during the heart's pumping phase or systole. Alternatively, DBP measures the heart during the resting phase between heartbeats or diastole (Saunders, 2001, p. 3; Wright, Cropanzano, Bonett, & Diamond, 2009). Traditionally, hypertension has been defined as having SBP in excess of 140 mmHg or DBP of 90 mmHg or more (i.e., 140/90). Blood pressure is measured as mmHg because the device used to measure blood pressure, a sphygmomanometer, uses a glass column filled with mercury (Hg) and calibrated in millimeters (Saunders, 2001, p. 3; Wright et al., 2009). Finally, the composite cardiovascular health measure, pulse product, is defined as the difference between SBP and DBP, multiplied by the pulse rate, and divided by 100 (Wright, 2010a).

Consider the following actual example: My pulse rate is currently 60. My SBP is 126 and my DBP is 78. My pulse product is $[60 \times (126 - 78)/100] = 28.8$. Pulse product and cardiovascular health efficiency tend to be negatively related. In other words, the lower the pulse product score the higher is one's cardiovascular efficiency. Preliminary research conducted by this author suggests that pulse product scores less than 40 are indicative of cardiovascular efficiency, although additional research is warranted, especially longitudinal in nature. In the present example, a score of 28.8 is considered by medical experts to be an excellent measure of cardiovascular efficiency, especially for someone over 50 years of age (Wright & Diamond, 2006).

At the individual level of analysis, the average heart attack translates to the loss of as much as 10–20 years from each victim's projected lifespan. As reported previously (Wright, 2010a; Wright & Diamond, 2006), this fact was graphically demonstrated to the author on a number of occasions in his role as both an academic researcher and management consultant. In a very tragic case, one of my research participants suffered a fatal heart attack while on the way to work and literally crashed his car into his workplace building. He was a man in his mid-forties, with a wife and teenage children. This individual knew firsthand about the benefits of being psychologically well. At the time of his tragic passing, he was an active participant in an ongoing research project investigating the role of PWB and psychological coping with cardiovascular health. On a number of occasions he had suggested to me that he could tell that his blood pressure would typically elevate when he was feeling psychologically distressed (low PWB). He was not alone in this appraisal as preliminary evidence indicates that PWB may play a significant role in employee cardiovascular health (Wright, Cropanzano, Bonett, & Diamond, 2009). To help better understand the potential role of PWB in cardiovascular health, a brief overview of the history of cardiovascular research in applied and organizational settings is now provided.

# Historical Overview of Cardiovascular Health

The earliest systematic application of blood pressure in behavioral research was conducted almost 100 years ago by Marsten (1917). Marsten's work focused on the role of SBP on deception. According to Marsten, examining an individual's blood pressure pattern was an excellent test to help determine whether that individual was attempting to deceive. In addition, this line of research was instrumental in providing a backdrop for subsequent work on the polygraph or lie-detector. Later work by Rackley (1930) provided support that blood pressure was related to a number of human emotions. Additionally, Elton Mayo (1924), one of the early pioneers of organizational research, recognized the significant role played by cardiovascular health in the determination of employee fatigue. Lovekin (1930) also contributed to establishing a cardiovascular health link to individual efficiency and organizational effectiveness. Interestingly, the obtained relationships among employee fatigue and the most widely used cardiovascular measures, pulse rate, SBP, and DBP, were less than robust in these early endeavors and were potentially contradictory in nature. In particular, while systolic and pulse rate typically increased, diastolic pressure often decreased with the increased workload (cf. Addis, 1922). Highly germane to the present discussion, Addis (1922) found that only the composite cardiovascular measure, pulse product, showed an increase proportionate with increased work.

Consistent with the findings of Addis (1922) and Lovekin (1930), Roethlisberger and Dickson (1939) proposed that composite cardiovascular measurements were capable of demonstrating accurate levels of actual worker physical energy expenditure. Unlike SBP and DBP considered individually, the fundamental purpose of composite cardiovascular measures is to assess the level of employee organic imbalance, or steady-state homeostasis. In turn, and based upon a definition of efficiency considered in terms of output per unit of energy, Roethlisberger and Dickson concluded that pulse product could be instrumental in the determination of efficient employee productivity. In particular, lower pulse product (at least within a particular range) translated to greater efficiency.

Remarkably, it would take another 70 years for organizational research to subsequently test the benefit of using pulse product as an indicator of employee cardiovascular health. Incorporating a sample of supervisory level management personnel, Wright, Cropanzano, Bonett, and Diamond (2009) examined the role of PWB in predicting employee cardiovascular health. More specifically, while neither DBP nor SBP were related to PWB, pulse product was negatively related ($r = -0.27$, $p < 0.01$) to PWB. That is, when PWB was high, pulse product was low (i.e., more efficient). In addition, PWB was related to pulse product even after controlling for such cardiovascular health risk factors as employee age, gender, weight, employee smoking behavior, and anxiety level. These results provide preliminary evidence that the more traditional approaches to measuring cardiovascular health, focusing narrowly on only systolic and diastolic blood pressure measurement, may lead to potentially misleading cardiovascular diagnoses.

Considered together, these findings demonstrate that PWB is related to employee job performance, retention and cardiovascular health. While impressive, when we consider ways to foster and encourage employee health, the extant body of well-being research is in need of further elaboration. I offer Fredrickson's (1998, 2001, 2003) broaden-and-build model of emotions as one approach well-suited to help in fostering and encouraging employee well-being.

# A Broadening-and-Building Approach to Encouraging Psychological Well-Being

According to Fredrickson's (2003) theory, such positive feelings as PWB have the necessary mechanisms to "broaden" an individual's momentary thought–action repertoires through expanding the obtainable array of potential thoughts and actions that readily come to mind (for a further discussion of the broaden-and-build approach, see Fredrickson & Branigan

(2001) and Wright (2010b)). More specifically, research has shown that relative to neutral states, positive feelings broaden or expand upon an individual's momentary thought–action repertoires. Alternatively, negative feelings have the opposite effect and narrow these mechanisms (Fredrickson & Losada, 2005). For example, research indicates that compared to those who are less well, psychologically well individuals tend to be more outgoing and extroverted, remember favorable events better, and are less likely to encode an ambiguous event as threatening (Wright, 2010b; Wright & Cropanzano, 2007).

This broadening of one's mindset is highly adaptive in assisting individuals to "build" reserves of physical, psychological, intellectual, and social resources (Wright & Hobfoll, 2004; Wright, 2005). As a consequence, this broadening and building process has a self-perpetuating effect on an individual's PWB resource supply. The end result is that individual's high on PWB are better able to foster and self-encourage their capacity to thrive, mentally flourish and psychologically grow (Fredrickson, 2001; Wright, 2010b). Furthermore, these individuals are typically more proactive and less prone to exhibit stress symptoms (Myers & Diener, 1995).

The broaden-and-build model suggests the potentially adaptive and interactive nature of positive PWB in encouraging individual and organizational health. More specifically, the adaptive or moderating nature of PWB is potentially more robust for those employees who are more psychologically well (Wright & Bonett, 2007; Wright et al., 2007). As a result, through the impetus provided by enhanced PWB, psychologically well employees are more easily able to "broaden-and-build" themselves and become more resilient, socially connected, be more satisfied, and derive more meaning from their work (Wrzesniewski & Dutton, 2001). In turn, these increased positive feelings result in higher productivity and efficiency, as manifested by increased job performance and retention rates (Wright & Bonett, 2007; Wright et al., 2007). Furthermore, these effects persist over time due, in part, to the differential manner in which psychologically well individuals recall events compared to those less psychologically well (Cropanzano & Wright, 2001).

# Future Research Directions

Although various forms of PWB (e.g., contented versus joyous) are similar constructs because they possess large amounts of pleasantness-based feelings, they are also different because they contain varying levels of activation (Wright, 2005). As noted previously (Wright, 2010a), the awareness and subsequent investigation of these types of distinctions can be highly beneficial in helping well-being researchers to better predict the role of PWB in employee-related behavior. Thus, the first avenue for further research involves positive scholars collectively working to develop a better understanding of the actual form and function of PWB.

A second direction for future research endeavors is to further examine the role of PWB in cardiovascular health. Wright et al. (2009) found the composite measure of cardiovascular health, pulse product, to be related to PWB while neither SBP nor DBP considered individually were related to PWB. Rigorous investigation must be undertaken to replicate the Wright et al. (2009) findings. More specifically, future work might consider focusing on the role of PWB as pulse product increases (becomes more inefficient) over time. For example, as an employee ages, SBP will typically rise while DBP will typically fall (Wright & Diamond, 2006).

This phenomenon is known as isolated systolic hypertension and is especially common in individuals over 50. This raises such interesting research questions as: What role does PWB play in helping to counteract this cardiovascular health aging process? If PWB does play a role in the process, does it differ as a function of the individual's specific pulse product reading? More generally, at what score (i.e., 40, 45, or 50) does pulse product become problematic to one's health?

A final suggestion for future research involves the examination of the possible role of character in employee PWB. Character can be defined as those interpenetrable and habitual qualities within individuals and applicable to organizations that both constrain and lead them to desire and pursue personal and societal good (Wright & Goodstein, 2007; Wright & Quick, 2011). The relevance of studying character is gaining in popularity in organizational research (Wright, 2010c; Wright & Huang, 2008; Wright & Quick, 2011). One reason for this popularity is that good character is considered by many to be a central and defining feature for individual health and well-being (Gavin, Quick, Cooper, & Quick, 2003; Wright & Huang, 2008). Character has also been suggested as encouraging long-term health and well-being at both the organizational and societal levels (Wright & Quick, 2011). For example, Wright and Quick (2011) identified such strengths of character as gratitude, humility, kindness, spirituality, zest, hope, and self-regulation as being beneficial in encouraging positive employee well-being. In addition, given that leadership is best considered in the context of emotional experience and social exchange (Ashkanasy & Dasborough, 2003), Wright and Quick (2011) suggested the possibility of a leader "well-being contagion" effect. That is, leaders who exhibit such strengths of character as humility, gratitude and kindness, may, through their actions, also foster the display of these strengths in their subordinates. Certainly, encouraging situations where character is related to well-being is a scenario that is beneficial to everyone.

While highly promising, the connection between well-being and character needs further examination. However, Wright and Quick's (2011) preliminary findings are consistent with the larger body of evidence suggesting possible linkages between PWB and such strengths of character as spirituality, forgiveness, zest, and hope (cf. Avey, Luthans, Smith, & Palmer, 2010; Peterson, Park, Hall, & Seligman, 2009; Peterson & Seligman, 2004). This is obviously an exciting time to be conducting research in employee PWB, with a number of promising opportunities for organizational scholars and practitioners alike.

# Summary Thoughts

In the present chapter, I have reviewed the literature examining relationships among PWB, job performance, employee retention, and cardiovascular health. The available data point to a common conclusion—employee PWB has significant benefit for both the employee and the employing organization. PWB has consistently been shown to be positively related to various measures of job performance. Field research has typically found significant correlations between PWB and job performance ratings in the 0.30–0.50 range, far surpassing the typical results obtained for job satisfaction and various measures of positive (PA) and negative affect (NA). This seems to be the case regardless of whether the criterion variables are objective indices or subjective ratings (Staw & Barsade, 1993; Staw, Sutton, & Pelled, 1994; Wright, 2005). The effect also holds in experimental, cross-sectional, and longitudinal studies, even after controlling for the effects of such possible confounding variables as age, gender, ethnicity, tenure, and educational level (Wright & Staw, 1999; Wright, Cropanzano, Denney, & Moline, 2002).

As with the relationship with job performance, PWB provides a value-added benefit in helping us to understand the employee decision to stay or withdraw from their organization. As a prime example of this value-added contribution, Wright and Bonett (2007) found that employees exhibiting high levels of PWB were not only better performers, they were also more likely to remain on the job. In light of these findings, Wright (2010a) noted that this knowledge affords organizations the opportunity to develop human resource strategies that enhance employee PWB and foster optimal levels of job performance and employee retention. Using this information, in Wright and Bonett's (2007) sample, the organization's human resources department was able to develop strategies designed to increase the accuracy of predicting employee retention by 60%. This substantial increase in predictive power promised potentially substantial cost savings for the department. Unfortunately, these tangible PWB benefits are not universally known to many of our academic and practitioner colleagues.

This fact was made quite evident to the author during a job interview a number of years ago. In attempting to discuss the benefits of considering employee PWB as a determinant of cardiovascular health with the interviewer, who happened to be the Department Head (my would-be future boss), I passionately stated that cost–benefit analysis aside, the study of PWB is a topic worthy of consideration on its own merit. Subsequently named the "health model" (Seligman & Csikszentmihalyi, 2000), this perspective has become a bedrock of the positive movements in both psychology and organizational behavior (Cameron, Dutton, & Quinn, 2003; Luthans, 2002; Seligman & Csikszentmihalyi, 2000; Wright, 2003). Less than prescient, my potential boss responded that he strongly disagreed with this health model assessment, further noting that the study of PWB and related other topics would only generate interest if it was considered from a cost–benefit perspective. It was made similarly clear that these types of topics would not garner job offers at highly regarded business schools (such as the one that he represented).

The interviewer's opinion is still held by too many of our colleagues in the organizational sciences. Given this state of affairs, I want to leave the reader with a final thought. The study of topics involving employee health and PWB clearly has a twofold value. Most certainly, PWB has a significant role in helping to determine the organization's bottom line: The significant role of PWB as a correlate of job performance, employee retention, and cardiovascular health clearly demonstrates this fact. In a narrow sense, my interviewer was correct. But as equally clearly shown in the work of a number of positive organizational scholars, the encouragement of employee PWB is an intrinsic good toward whose accomplishment we should all work (Macik-Frey, Quick, & Nelson, 2007). Oh, and by the way, the interviewer and I mutually agreed that I was not a good fit for their position . . . a decision which did much to "encourage" my PWB.

# References

Addis, T. (1922). Blood pressure and pulse rate reactions. *Archives of Internal Medicine*, 30, 246.
American Heart Association. (2010a). *Cardiovascular Diseases*. Retrieved September 1, 2010 from http://www.americanheart.org/downloadable/heart/126566515297ODS-3241%20heart strokeupdate_2010.

American Heart Association (2010b). Healthcare costs risk as risk factors remain widespread. Retrieved September 1, 2010 from http://newsroom.heart.org/pr/aha/909.aspx

Anderson, V. V. (1929). *Psychiatry in industry*. New York, NY: Harpers.

Ashkanasy, N. M., & Dasborough, M. T. (2003). Emotional awareness and emotional intelligence in leadership training. *The Journal of Education for Business, 79*, 18–22.

Avey, J. B., Luthans, F., Smith, R. M., & Palmer, N. F. (2010). Impact of positive psychological capital on employee well-being over time. *Journal of Occupational Health Psychology, 15*, 17–28.

Cameron, K. S., Dutton, J. E., & Quinn, R. E. (2003). *Positive organizational scholarship: Foundations of a new discipline*. San Francisco, CA: Berrett-Koehler.

Cascio, W. F. (2003). *Managing human resources: Productivity, quality of life, profits* (6th ed.). New York, NY: McGraw-Hill.

Cherrington, D. J., Reitz, H. J., & Scott, W. E. (1971). Effects of contingent and non-contingent reward on the relationship between satisfaction and task performance. *Journal of Applied Psychology, 55*, 531–536.

Cooper, C. L., & Cartwright, S. (1994). Healthy mind; Healthy organization—A proactive approach to occupational stress. *Human Relations, 47*, 455–471.

Cropanzano, R., & Wright, T. A. (1999). A five-year study of change in the relationship between well-being and job performance. *Consulting Psychology Journal: Practice and Theory, 51*, 252–265.

Cropanzano, R., & Wright, T. A. (2001). When a "happy" worker is really a "productive" worker: A review and further refinement of the happy-productive worker thesis. *Consulting Psychology Journal: Practice and Research, 53*, 182–199.

Diener, E. (1994). Assessing subjective well-being: Progress and opportunities. *Social Indicators Research, 31*, 103–157.

Fisher, C. D. (1980). On the dubious wisdom of expecting job satisfaction to correlate with performance. *Academy of Management Review, 5*, 607–612.

Fisher, V. E., & Hanna, J. V. (1931). *The dissatisfied worker*. New York, NY: Macmillan.

Fredrickson, B. L. (1998). What good are positive emotions? *Review of General Psychology, 2*, 300–319.

Fredrickson, B. L. (2001). The role of positive emotions in positive psychology: The broaden-and-build theory of positive emotions. *American Psychologist, 56*, 219–226.

Fredrickson, B. L. (2003). Positive emotions and upward spirals in organizations. In K. S. Cameron, J. E. Dutton, & R. E. Quinn (Eds.), *Positive organizational scholarship: Foundations of a new discipline* (pp. 163–175). San Francisco, CA: Berrett-Koehler.

Fredrickson, B. L., & Branigan, C. A. (2001). Positive emotions. In T. J. Mayne, & G. A. Bonnano (Eds.), *Emotion: Current issues and future directions* (pp. 123–151). New York, NY: Guilford Press.

Fredrickson, B. L., & Losada, M. F. (2005). Positive affect and the complex dynamics of human flourishing. *American Psychologist, 60*, 678–686.

Frost, E. (1920). What industry wants and does not want from the psychologist. *Journal of Applied Psychology, 4*, 18–24.

Gavin, J. H., Quick, J. C., Cooper, C. L., & Quick, J. D. (2003). A spirit of personal integrity: The role of character in executive health. *Organizational Dynamics, 32*, 165–179.

Gechman, A., & Wiener, Y. (1975). Job involvement and satisfaction as related to mental health and personal time devoted to work. *Journal of Applied Psychology, 60*, 521–523.

Hecht, B. K., & Hecht, F. (2005). Heart attack risks around the world. MedicineNet.com. Retrieved February 28, 2005 from http://www.medicinenet.com/scriptmain/art.asp?articlekey=38774.

Hersey, R. B. (1930). A monotonous job in an emotional crisis. *Personnel Journal, 9*, 290–296.
Hersey, R. B. (1932). Rate of production and emotional state. *Personnel Journal, 10*, 355–364.
Hom, P. W., & Griffeth, R. W. (1995). *Employee turnover*. Cincinnati, OH: South/Western.
Hoppock, R. (1935). *Job satisfaction*. New York, NY: Harper.
Houser, J. D. (1927). *What the employer thinks: Executives' attitudes toward employees*. Cambridge, MA: Harvard University Press.
Ivancevich, J. W., & Matteson, M. T. (1980). *Stress at work: A managerial perspective*. Glenview, IL: Scott, Foresman.
Kornhauser, A. (1933). The technique for measuring employee attitudes. *Personnel Journal, 9*, 99–107.
Kornhauser, A., & Sharp, A. (1932). Employee attitudes: Suggestions from a study in a factory. *Personnel Journal, 10*, 393–401.
Larsen, R. J., & Diener, E. (1992). Promises and problems with the circumplex model of emotion. *Review of Personality and Social Psychology, 13*, 25–59.
Lovekin, O. S. (1930). The quantitative measurement of human efficiency under factory conditions. *Journal of Industrial Hygiene, 12*, 99–120, 163–167.
Luthans, F. (2002). The need for and meaning of positive organizational behavior. *Journal of Organizational Behavior, 23*, 695–706.
Luthans, F., Luthans, K. W., & Luthans, B. C. (2004). Psychological capital management: Going beyond human and social capital. *Business Horizons, 47*, 45–50.
Luthans, F., & Youssef, C. M. (2004). Human, social, and now positive psychological capital management: Investing in people for competitive advantage. *Organizational Dynamics, 33*, 143–160.
Macik-Frey, M., Quick, J. C., & Nelson, D. L. (2007). Advances in occupational health: From a stressful beginning to a positive future. *Journal of Management, 33*, 809–840.
Marsten, W. H. (1917). Systolic blood pressure symptoms of deception. *Journal of Experimental Psychology, 2*, 117–163.
Mayo, E. (1924). Revery and industrial fatigue. *The Journal of Personnel Research, 3*, 273–281.
Miles, M. B. (1965). Planned change and organizational health: Figure and ground. In F. D. Carver & T. J. Sergiovanni (Eds.), *Organizations and human behavior: Focus on schools* (pp. 375–391). New York, NY: McGraw-Hill.
Mobley, W. H. (1982). *Employee turnover: Causes, consequences, and control*. Reading, MA: Addison-Wesley.
Myers, D. G., & Diener, E. (1995). Who is happy? *Psychological Science, 6*, 10–19.
Quick, J. C. (1999). Occupational health psychology: The convergence of health and clinical psychology with public health and preventive medicine in an organizational context. *Professional Psychology: Research and Practice, 30*, 123–128.
Quick, J. C., Quick, J. D., Nelson, D. L., & Hurrell, J. J. Jr. (1997). *Preventive stress management in organizations*. Washington, DC: American Psychological Association.
Pennock, G. A. (1930). Industrial research at Hawthorne: An experimental investigation of rest periods, working conditions and other conditions. *Personnel Journal, 8*, 296–313.
Peterson, C., Park, N., Hall, N., & Seligman, E. P. (2009). Zest and work. *Journal of Organizational Behavior, 30*, 161–172.
Peterson, C., & Seligman, M. E. P. (2004). *Character strengths and virtues: A handbook and classification*. New York, NY: Oxford University Press.
Pfeffer, J. (1998). *The human equation*. Cambridge, MA: Harvard Business School Press.
Putnam, M. L. (1930). Improving employee relations: A plan which uses data obtained from employees. *Personnel Journal, 8*, 314–325.

Rackley, L. E. (1930). The blood pressure and galvanic reflex as indicators of emotional states. *Journal of Applied Psychology*, 14, 497–504.

Roethlisberger, F. J., & Dickson, W. J. (1939). *Management and the worker*. Cambridge, MA: Harvard University Press.

Russell, J. A. (1978). Evidence of convergent validity of the dimensions of affect. *Journal of Personality and Social Psychology*, 36, 1152–1168.

Russell, J. A. (1979). Affective space is bipolar. *Journal of Personality and Social Psychology*, 37, 345–356.

Russell, J. A. (1980). A circumplex model of affect. *Journal of Personality and Social Psychology*, 39, 1161–1178.

Russell, J. A., Weiss, A., & Mendelsohn, G. A. (1989). The affect grid: A single-item scale of pleasure and arousal. *Journal of Personality and Social Psychology*, 57, 493–502.

Saunders, C. (2001). *Hypertension: Controlling the "silent killer."* Boston, MA: Harvard Health Publications.

Seligman, M. E. P. (2002). *Authentic happiness*. New York, NY: Free Press.

Seligman, M. E. P., & Csikszentmihalyi, M. (2000). Positive psychology: An introduction. *American Psychologist*, 55, 5–14.

Snow, A. J. (1923). Labor turnover and mental alertness test scores. *Journal of Applied Psychology*, 7, 285–290.

Staw, B. M., & Barsade, S. G. (1993). Affect and managerial performance: A test of the sadder-but-wiser vs. happier-and-smarter hypotheses. *Administrative Science Quarterly*, 38, 304–331.

Staw, B. M., Sutton, R. I., & Pelled, L. H. (1994). Employee positive emotion and favorable outcomes at the workplace. *Organization Science*, 5, 71–91.

Tetrick, L. E., & Quick, J. C. (2003). Prevention at work: Public health in occupational settings. In J. C. Quick & L. E. Tetrick (Eds.), *Handbook of occupational health psychology* (pp. 3–17). Washington, DC: American Psychological Association.

Watson, D. (1988). Intraindividual and interindividual analyses of positive and negative affect: Their relation to health complaints, perceived stress, and daily activities. *Journal of Personality and Social Psychology*, 54, 1020–1030.

Watson, D., Clark, L. A., & Tellegen, A. (1988). Development and validation of brief measures of positive and negative affect: The PANAS scales. *Journal of Personality and Social Psychology*, 54, 1063–1070.

Weiss, H. M., & Cropanzano, R. (1996). An affective events approach to job satisfaction. In B. M. Staw & L. L. Cummings (Eds.), *Research in organizational behavior* (Vol. 18, pp. 1–74). Greenwich, CT: JAI Press.

Wren, C. G. (1934). Vocational satisfaction of Stanford graduates. *Personnel Journal*, 13, 21–24.

Wright, T. A. (2003). Positive organizational behavior: An idea whose time has truly come. *Journal of Organizational Behavior*, 24, 437–442.

Wright, T. A. (2005). The role of "happiness" in organizational research: Past, present and future directions. In P. L. Perrewe & D. C. Ganster (Eds.), *Research in occupational stress and well-being* (Vol. 4, pp. 225–268). Amsterdam, the Netherlands: JAI Press.

Wright, T. A. (2010a). The role of psychological well-being in job performance, employee retention and cardiovascular health. *Organizational Dynamics*, 39, 13–23.

Wright, T. A. (2010b). More than meets the eye: The role of employee well-being in organizational research. In P. A. Linley, S. Harrington, & N. Page (Eds.), *Oxford handbook of positive psychology and work* (pp. 143–154). New York, NY: Oxford University Press.

Wright, T. A. (2010c). Character assessment in business ethics education. In D. G. Fisher & D. L. Swanson (Eds.), *Toward assessing business ethics education* (pp. 361–380). Charlotte, NC: Information Age Publishing.

Wright, T. A., & Bonett, D. G. (1997). The role of pleasantness and activation-based well-being in performance prediction. *Journal of Occupational Health Psychology, 2*, 212–219.

Wright, T. A., & Bonett, D. G. (2007). Job satisfaction and psychological well-being as nonadditive predictors of workplace turnover. *Journal of Management, 33*, 141–160.

Wright, T. A., Bonett, D. G., & Sweeney, D. A. (1993). Mental health and work performance: Results of a longitudinal study. *Journal of Occupational and Organizational Psychology, 66*, 277–284.

Wright, T. A., & Cropanzano, R. (1998). Emotional exhaustion as a predictor of job performance and turnover. *Journal of Applied Psychology, 83*, 486–493.

Wright, T. A., & Cropanzano, R. (2000). Psychological well-being and job satisfaction as predictors of job performance. *Journal of Occupational Health Psychology, 5*, 84–94.

Wright, T. A., & Cropanzano, R. (2007). The happy/productive worker thesis revisited. In J. Martocchio (Ed.), *Research in personnel and human resource management* (Vol. 26, pp. 269–313). Amsterdam, the Netherlands: Elsevier Ltd.

Wright, T. A., Cropanzano, R., & Bonett, D. G. (2007). The moderating role of employee positive well-being on the relation between job satisfaction and job performance. *Journal of Occupational Health Psychology, 12*, 93–104.

Wright, T. A., Cropanzano, R., Bonett, D. G., & Diamond, W. J. (2009). The role of employee psychological well-being in cardiovascular health: When the twain shall meet. *Journal of Organizational Behavior, 30*, 193–208.

Wright, T. A., Cropanzano, R., Denney, P. J., & Moline, G. L. (2002). When a happy worker is a productive worker: A preliminary examination of three models. *Canadian Journal of Behavioural Science, 34*, 146–150.

Wright, T. A., & Diamond, J. (2006). Getting the "pulse" of your employees: The use of cardiovascular research in better understanding behavior in organizations. *Journal of Organizational Behavior, 27*, 395–401.

Wright, T. A., & Doherty, E. M. (1998). Organizational behavior "rediscovers" the role of emotional well-being. *Journal of Organizational Behavior, 19*, 481–485.

Wright, T. A., & Hobfoll, S. E. (2004). Commitment, psychological well-being and job performance: An examination of Conservation of Resources (COR) theory and job burnout. *Journal of Business and Management, 9*, 389–406.

Wright, T. A., & Goodstein, J. (2007). Character is not "dead" in management research: A review of individual character and organizational-level virtue. *Journal of Management, 33*, 928–958.

Wright, T. A., Huang, C. -C. (2008). Character in organizational research: Past directions and future prospects. *Journal of Organizational Behavior, 29*, 981–987.

Wright, T. A., & Quick, J. C. (2011). The role of character in ethical leadership research. *Leadership Quarterly, 22*, 975–978.

Wright, T. A., & Staw, B. M. (1999). Affect and favorable work outcomes: Two longitudinal tests of the happy-productive worker thesis. *Journal of Organizational Behavior, 20*, 1–23.

Wrzesniewski, A., & Dutton, J. E. (2001). Crafting a job: Revisioning employees as active crafters of their work. *Academy of Management Review, 26*, 179–201.

# CHAPTER 58

# EXECUTIVE WELL-BEING

## JAMES CAMPBELL QUICK[1,2] AND JONATHAN D. QUICK[3]

[1]The University of Texas at Arlington, USA; [2]Lancaster University Management School, UK; [3]Management Sciences for Health, and Harvard Medical School, USA

EXECUTIVES and the management profession provide an important public service in a free economy. This public service is achieved through the products and services their organizations offer as well as through job and wealth creation. Executive well-being underpins the ability to produce these benefits. Therefore, building positive executive well-being has individual and collective value, while negative executive well-being is a threat to the executive, organization, family, and community. In this chapter, we will focus attention on the large majority of executives who make positive contributions to the public good. We will also discuss those few who do wrong, make negative headlines, and tarnish the management profession (Cohen, 2010; Goolsby, Mack, & Quick, 2010; Solomon, 1999).

Executive well-being may be positive or negative. While positive well-being seems intuitively clear and is associated with the accumulation of resource surpluses that benefit the executive and those with whom the executive works and lives (cf. Davidson et al., 2010), negative well-being is not as intuitively clear and may even sound contradictory. Davidson et al. (2010) define negative well-being in terms of stress, burnout, anxiety, depression, and negative mood. An executive example of negative well-being would be Patricia Dunn, former chairman of Hewlett-Packard (HP), who was notified on October 4, 2006 that four felony charges were being filed against her with the risk of 12 years in jail (Brady, 2010). As the following criminal process unfolded, Ms Dunn was diagnosed with advanced ovarian cancer. Ms Dunn fought both the criminal charges and the cancer. While the trial judge dropped the charges in 2007 in the interests of justice (Brady, 2010) and Ms Dunn lived 5 years beyond the 3-year life expectancy of her cancer, she ultimately passed away in late 2011 (Lublin, 2011).

To begin we will briefly define executive well-being. Next we will identify five pathways to positive well-being for executives through which they can build resource surpluses for personal and collective benefit. These are: strength of character, self-awareness, socialized power motivation, self-reliance, and diverse professional supports. We will then review the dark side of executive well-being by examining the threats and challenges to well-being. These include stress, burnout, social isolation, toxic effects of emotions, traumas, and tragedies. In addition, we consider the evidence and find that men and women executives do not have equal access on the pathways to positive well-being, nor do they have equal exposure to the threats and challenges. Understanding this asymmetry is critical for both men and women. We conclude the chapter by debunking two cultural myths. The first is the myth that executive women can "have it all." The second is the John Wayne myth that men can "go it alone." Finally, we close the chapter by offering six future directions for research in executive well-being.

## What is Executive Well-Being?

Executive well-being concerns happiness, health, and prosperity for the executive, the family, the organization, and the community. Executive well-being may be positive or negative (Davidson et al., 2010). Cameron (2007) notes that the positive and the negative are often intertwined such that neither is understood unless the opposite is simultaneously understood. This duality informed our review of the literature on executive well-being and led us to draw out the positive pathways and negative threats that contribute to executive well-being. The topic of well-being has been explored in a variety of philosophical and research literatures, including moral philosophy, psychology, organizational science, and public health. Here we provide a review of these literatures, and examine the definition of executive well-being.

Well-being as a concept is deeply anchored in moral philosophy, especially utilitarianism (Mill, 1910; *Stanford Encyclopedia of Philosophy*, 2008). While Adam Smith (1910) is best known for establishing political economics as a science, to his contemporaries he was a distinguished professor of moral philosophy. *The Theory of Moral Sentiments* (Smith, 1759) sets forth his moral philosophy, which hinges on three sets of passions: selfish, social, and unsocial. The selfish passions are the basis for individual interests, while the social passions are the basis for collective interests. He set forth his thinking about the moral sense, sympathy, the conscience as the basis for what is right and wrong, and propriety of action. For Smith (1759), self-interest and social interest were both important.

Well-being in this philosophical tradition focuses primarily on the individual; it is broad and wide, encompassing a whole life rather than some short-lived state of happiness, contentment, or health. Well-being in this context refers to what makes life good for the individual living that life; hence, positive well-being. In contrast, well-being in contemporary psychological literature is often defined in terms of the state of being happy, healthy, or prosperous. This state-based definition leads to the concept of subjective well-being, defined in terms of happiness, and thus leads to consideration of adaptation, goals, coping strategies, and dispositional influences (Diener, Suh, Lucas, & Smith, 1999). Overlapping with subjective well-being is psychological well-being (Wright & Cropanzano, 2004).

However, defining executive well-being only in terms of happiness is not appropriate given executives' central role in our collective well-being. Adam Smith's (1759) notions of both selfish and social passions elicit the contemporary concepts of individual interests and collective interests, the latter being the common good. To fully define executive well-being requires consideration of the greater good found in public health, occupational stress and well-being, and organizational well-being (Quick, Cooper, Nelson, Quick, & Gavin, 2003; Quick, Mack, Gavin, Cooper, & Quick, 2004; Quick & Quick, 2004; Rosenau, 1913; Wallace & Doebbeling, 1998). From these perspectives, the executive is viewed as an individual with the potential for positive impact on the family, the organization, and the community.

Executives are important organizational leaders uniquely positioned to impact individual and organizational health. The first two principles of preventive stress management capture the notion of the dynamics between the individual and the organization (J. D. Quick, Nelson, & Quick, 1998, p. 247; see also VandenBos, 2007).

> Principle 1: Individual and organizational health are interdependent.
> Principle 2: Leaders have a responsibility for individual and organizational health.

The focus here is on the "health" aspect of well-being. Further, the well-being of the individual is suggested to have an effect, either positive or negative, on other individuals throughout the system. This may be thought of as a contagion effect, with both positive and adverse consequences. Negative contagion might come from the toxic effects of emotions on other people at work (Frost, 2003), while positive contagion might result from ripples of zest (Peterson, Park, Hall, & Seligman, 2009) or vigor (Shirom, 2004).

Another source of information on executive health and well-being is the management and organizational literature (Danna & Griffin, 1999; Macik-Frey, Quick, & Nelson, 2007). Executive well-being is important because of its effects within the organization and the community beyond. Preventive interventions are the positive dimension of public health in organizational settings; they aim to enhance the positive or ameliorate the negative (cf. Elkind, 1931). The literature on occupational stress, for example, suggests that executives may be sources of positive stress at work (J. C. Quick, Mack, Gavin, Cooper, & Quick, 2004). On the other hand, good therapeutic treatment with one senior executive may serve as primary prevention for tens, hundreds, or even thousands of employees in organizations. While Moss' (1981) psychoanalytic work with Mobil executives may have been beneficial to the individuals receiving therapy, the intervention also had positive secondary effects on others with whom the executive worked and lived. In the next section we examine positive pathways to executive well-being, as well as threats that may detract from well-being.

# Pathways to Positive Well-Being

Donald Laird led one of the earliest inquiries into executive well-being at the Ford Motor Company in 1929 (Laird, 1929). Setting out to show how every executive could become his own psychologist, Laird focused on occupational skills and self-expression, management of fatigue and energy, personal development of the executive, and loyalty and morale. Since then, there has been a large body of empirical and clinical research on executives and executive well-being, which, as a whole, suggests that there are at least five pathways that can lead executives to states of positive well-being.

The five positive pathways we address in this section are: strength of character, self-awareness, socialized power motivation, self-reliance, and diverse professional supports. Each of these makes a unique positive contribution to the development and maintenance of an executive's well-being and resources.

## Strength of character

Strength of character is anchored in moral philosophy and more specifically within the virtue ethics tradition of Aristotle (310/1998, 2000). The character, or virtue-ethics tradition, was contemporarily interpreted by Solomon (1999) who examined ethics, goodness, and nobility within the American corporate system. He found American corporations rather philanthropic and comparatively virtuous, with some exceptions. More recently, Thompson, Grahek, Phillips, and Faye (2008) found that the "character to lead" was one of three cornerstones to excellence in executive performance. The other two cornerstones are "capacity to lead" and "commitment to lead." For Thompson and his colleagues, the term "character" encapsulates the integrity, ethics, and courage one needs to earn and maintain stakeholder trust, and to be accountable. The "Leadership Worth Following" executive performance model is the basis for both executive selection within an assessment center format and development done through executive coaching in a wide variety of settings (Thompson et al., 2008).

Goolsby, Mack, and Quick (2010) illustrate positive ethics and character in executives with case studies. For example, Dallas banking executive Joseph M. Grant, who acted as chairman and CEO of Texas American Bancshares in the 1980s, lost his bank and his financial worth in the Great Texas Banking Crash. Grant displayed strength of character in this crisis by fighting an uphill battle against the collapse of the Texas economy and the FDIC. This was exemplified in his refusal to abandon his key executive leadership position within the bank, despite the personal cost incurred through the ultimate failure of the bank. Rather than acting primarily out of self-interest, Grant demonstrated concern for the interests of his executive team, the bank's many stakeholders, and the community of Fort Worth, Texas.

Strength of character is the dimension of a person that provides fortitude and staying power in the face of great adversity. Grant's strength of character set the stage for his subsequent establishment of Texas Capital Bank, believed to be the largest start-up bank in US history, with initial capitalization of $80 million (Goolsby, Mack, & Quick, 2010). His integrity and courage were keys to the willingness of investors and colleagues to entrust him with significant wealth. Grant was later honored with a Horatio Alger Distinguished American Award at the US Supreme Court in 2010 for overcoming adversity. His strength of character was crucial to his ultimate success.

While strength of character is anchored in the tradition of moral philosophy, it is a subject of concern to Kets de Vries (2009a) in his in-depth clinical inquiry into executive and leader character. Rather than moralizing, his clinical inquiry offers insights into executives' character strengths that are the foundation for success and positive well-being. In the process of studying character strengths, Kets de Vries was also privy to the character flaws that lead in a very different direction. These flaws include being seduced by sex, money, and power as well as pathologic narcissism. Because character flaws often undercut success and lead to failure, the second positive pathway, self-awareness, becomes central to earning and maintaining positive well-being.

## Self-awareness

While executives often have rather low levels of self-awareness (Kets de Vries, 2009b), self-awareness can be a powerful pathway to well-being (Boyatzis & McKee, 2005). Clinical inquiry with executives and global leaders offers insight into the conflicts, confusions, and dilemmas that so often foil an executive's ability to achieve happiness and positive well-being (Kets de Vries, 2009b; Levinson, 1964/1985; Moss, 1981). Research by the Hay Group finds that without self-awareness, executives have a 96% probability of failing to exercise good self-management skills such as self-control. Self-awareness is therefore foundational to self-regulation in action and behavior. In addition, the Hay Group research finds that without self-awareness, executives have an 84% probability of failing to develop good social awareness skills, such as empathy. Hence, self-awareness is a crucial personal and interpersonal attribute, critical to executive well-being and function. Kets de Vries (2009b) shows how an executive's struggle with competing demands and inner conflicts can disturb psychological equilibrium and pursuit of happiness, and can lead to adverse effects on well-being.

However, the presence of self-awareness is no panacea. Self-awareness is foremost a guard against negative well-being. Self-awareness and personal insight do offer opportunities for positive action with resulting well-being. For example, by creating dissonance and exploring discrepancies between how an executive sees himself, how his family sees him, and how his leader sees him, Moss (1981) enabled executives to better understand their inner conflicts and tensions. Awareness of these conflicts and tensions opens positive pathways for actions leading to success, productive achievements, and happiness. Moss' creation of dissonance and discrepancy proves useful in surmounting or breaking through psychological defenses that are common to both executives and non-executives (Vaillant, 1977). As we will examine in a later section, the mature defenses, or adaptive mechanisms, have functional value in smoothing the way through life's threats and challenges.

## Socialized power motivation

In addition to conflicts and tensions, needs and motivation are powerful inner forces within executives. McClelland (1975) discovered that the best leaders and managers were those who had a high need for power accompanied by a relatively low need for affiliation. This inner need for power is differentiated from the need for achievement (i.e., doing things well) and need for affiliation (i.e., close, warm relationships). The need for power is concerned with exercising influence and making a difference.

Not all leaders and executives have the same motivation. McClelland and Burnham (2003) distinguished between those with a high need for personal achievement (imperial power), or self-aggrandizement, and those with a high need for interactive (socialized) power, or institutional advancement. The latter, socialized power motivation, is what makes for the best leaders and executives. This is consistent with Smith's (1759) emphasis on the social passions that balance the selfish passions. Thus, world-class executives who build positive well-being are those who are motivated to balance self-interest with the interests of others. Socialized leaders deliver top-quartile business results along with high morale because they work well with others (Burnham, 2002).

This distinguishing power-oriented characteristic is other-centered, versus self-centered, and may be consistent with the concept of altruism in Vaillant's (1977) Level IV adaptive ego mechanisms that facilitate positive well-being. Mature mechanisms include sublimation, altruism, suppression, anticipation, and humor. While the best executives have a power motivation to make an impact, influence others, change events, and make a difference, they channel this energy in socially desirable and constructive ways for the benefit of all concerned. The preoccupation with power and manipulation for personal gain alone is selfish, self-centered, and frequently self-defeating.

Imperial power motivation stands in contrast to socialized power motivation. The former leads to a preoccupation with personal power and self-serving interests. When unchecked, personal achievement and imperial power motivation become destructive to the interests of others, which include colleagues, family members, the organization, and the community. John Goolsby was able to check self-serving behavior as CEO of the Howard Hughes Corporation by putting in place ethics guidelines and standards that included enforcement mechanisms (Goolsby, Mack, & Quick, 2010). One example would be the annual certification that employees signed indicating their knowledge, understanding, and acceptance of the ethical standards of the company. Goolsby's rejection of imperial power motivation led to positive well-being for himself, his family, the company, and importantly for Howard Hughes' heirs.

## Self-reliance

J. C. Quick, Nelson, and Quick (1987) and Nelson, Quick, and Quick (1989) conducted in-depth biographical research aimed at understanding executives who maintained positive well-being, despite demands on their time and energy, and stressful circumstances.[1] While these men and women reported a variety of popular stress management techniques, including exercise, meditation, prayer, time management practices, and nutrition, none was consistent across all participants. Rather, the common denominator was their positive personal and professional relationships. These successful men and women were self-reliant, a paradoxical term referring to the capacity to work and act autonomously but also ask for support and guidance where needed.

Levinson (1996) saw the coming of this new age of self-reliance in which executives must turn to family and personal relationships as secure sources of support. Self-reliance means interdependent, not independent. The positive resources that accrue through secure interdependent relationships include emotional caring, informational guidance, evaluative feedback, instrumental support, and personal protection. Positive well-being results for executives when there is a surplus of these interpersonal resources at the executive's disposal (cf. Davidson et al., 2010). The self-reliant executive is neither reluctant to use nor anxious to draw on the support available within his or her interpersonal world. Self-reliance entails a reciprocal capacity to serve as a secure support for others in their times of need, trial, and tribulation. Self-reliance balances personal power and autonomy with positive interpersonal relationships and collaboration.

## Diverse professional supports

Related to self-reliance is the positive pathway of diverse professional supports. While self-reliance is the capacity to form and maintain healthy interpersonal relationships, this characteristic is complemented in an executive's environment by the presence of supportive networks. Two key supports are the executive's leadership team and the company's board of

---

[1] More recent, autobiographical research by Escobedo and Adolphs (2010) explores memories of moral events in considering the notion of becoming a better person. Their study examined both negative valence and positive valence associated with a person's recollections.

directors. The senior leadership team is best when composed of diverse expertise, talents, and perspectives. This is especially important in dynamic, changing environments. For example, the US and global health care environment is one of the most challenging and dynamic industries of our day (Management Sciences for Health, 2009). Change is a regular and endemic characteristic of this environment. Change ushers in continuing uncertainty and places constant pressure on executives and executive teams.

A leadership team that includes both optimistic and pessimistic points of view on the dynamic, changing environment affords the executive a richer set of information upon which to draw in decision making and action (Seligman, 1991). Thus, an executive team that balances these two contrasting psychological interpretative mechanisms can contribute to the team's fitness, functioning and well-being. The question an executive should ask is whether the team members' styles fit their function (Edwards, 1996). For example, optimism in executives responsible for finding new business might be very functional given the opportunities they seek and exploit. Alternatively, pessimism in chief financial officers may have value if that perspective cues them to keep a constant eye on averting or managing negative financial results. The executive who assembles a senior team based on diverse perspectives enriches the variance, diversity, and dialogue for good decision-making.

In addition to the executive's leadership team, a company's board of directors is another central support for executive well-being. For example, in restructuring the Howard Hughes Corporation, John Goolsby worked closely with Will Lummis as the chairman of the company's board of directors (Goolsby, Mack, & Quick, 2010). Creative tension and heartfelt communication between a chairman and a chief executive carries the positive potential for better decisions, better strategic planning, and more ethical outcomes for all concerned. This was exemplified in the Goolsby–Lummis relationship, with John Goolsby frequently seeking consultation and guidance from his chairman on complicated or controversial business decisions.

Merging the Chairman and CEO roles concentrates power inappropriately, while splitting these two key roles of Chairman and CEO serves to create more accountability. The Sarbanes-Oxley Act (SOX) of 2002 is a mandatory federal law that carries the potential for a positive impact on executive well-being through greater accountability. SOX is intended to create incentives for boards to be more engaged with executives for the well-being of the executive and the company. Diversity and heterogeneity among board members in functional expertise, gender, psychological interpretative mechanisms, and backgrounds may also add value.

As mentioned in the introduction, in addition to positive well-being there is the potential for negative well-being. Therefore, in addition to seeking strength through positive pathways, an executive must guard against the negative. For example, character flaws (versus strengths) contribute to executive failure and negative well-being. Hence, a slippery slope awaits the executive who misses the positive pathway. In addition, there are real threats and challenges to meet head on.

# Negative Well-Being: Threats and Challenges

The literature on executive health, happiness, prosperity, and well-being contains important cautionary information concerning real threats and challenges. Five prominent threats and challenges that lead to poor well-being are: stress, burnout, social isolation, toxic effects of emotions, traumas and tragedies. Each of these threats and challenges must be acknowledged and addressed in order to prevent the damage they inevitably cause. (Wright, Adkins, Nelson, & Quick, 2013).

## Stress

Levinson (1964/1985) identified executive stress as a prominent risk for work and mental health. He used his clinical, psychoanalytic model of inquiry to understand executive stress and mental or psychological problems. The role of inner conflicts and emotional tensions was central to his early concern with the fears, anger, and self-doubt that many executives experienced. Executives had difficulty talking about these powerful emotional forces with others in the organization. At the heart of executive stress for Levinson was the executive's ongoing quest for happiness and fulfillment of hopes, dreams, and aspirations that stood in contrast with the executive's current reality and circumstances. To maintain good mental health for effective performance and achievement, executives must be alert to these challenging inner forces.

Cooper and Marshall (1978) use a different theoretical and scientific approach to executive stress. They were concerned with the wide range of external, environmental sources of stress in complex industrial organizations. Their expanded model of sources of executive stress included: factors intrinsic to the job; career development; organizational structure and climate; interpersonal relations at work; and factors outside the organization, such as family demands that have spillover effects into the workplace. Their generalized model was circumscribed, but allowed for the possibility of changing the major causes of stress for individual professions to achieve a stress fingerprint for specific jobs and occupations. This stress model and its effects on executive well-being extends beyond physical sources of stress to identify a wide range of psychosocial demands. This makes their stress model much more appropriate for executives in a wide range of complex organizations.

The preventive stress management model of stress in organizations is applicable for a wide range of organizational members, especially executives (J. D. Quick, Nelson, & Quick, 1998). The unique contribution of this stress model is the prevention orientation that guards against harm to executive health and well-being. This strength-based model gives balanced attention to vulnerabilities within the executive, threats within the environment, and strength factors that guard and protect the executive. The explicit recognition of stress as a health risk factor leads directly to diagnostic assessments with individual executives and groups of executives that inform the range of prevention interventions, such as work restructuring, fitness regimes, and secure social support systems, that protect and defend the executive. While executive stress is a threat and a challenge, distress, loss, harm, or damage are not inevitable consequences.

## Burnout

In his work on the psychology of leadership, Levinson (2006) identified executive burnout as a major mental health concern. At the heart of the executive burnout problem was the executive's unremitted striving for achievement, recognition, advancement, and acquisition of a range of personal and social resources that ultimately led to energy depletion and emotional exhaustion. Levinson's (2006) initial recommendation for combating executive burnout was prevention. By engaging in practices that balanced the executive's effortful striving with other satisfying activities that allowed for energy recovery and rejuvenation, the leader was in a better position to stay fully yet appropriately engaged in productive work and personal life activities (Loehr & Schwartz, 2003). From 2001–2006, PepsiCo chairman Steve Reinemund used this full engagement model to prevent burnout and support energy management for PepsiCo executives. During the 2000s, senior leaders and executives in the American Orthopaedic Association became concerned with burnout as a prominent manifestation of professional stress (J. C. Quick et al., 2006). The resulting research found early signs of burnout and in addition found the family was a source of strength and renewal for these professional leaders (Saleh et al., 2007). Burnout symptoms included emotional exhaustion and cynicism, with some effects spilling over into the family environment (see Shirom (2011) for a detailed review of job-related burnout). This finding is consistent with the larger literature on the central role of social support systems as buffers against suffering and distress (House, Landis, & Umberson, 1988). House and his colleagues concluded that social isolation, or the absence of social supports, was a greater health risk than smoking. As we will see in the next section, social isolation is a significant threat to executive well-being.

## Social isolation

Social isolation is a challenge for those at the pinnacle of the organizational hierarchy. The isolation executives experience in top level positions is often referred to as the "loneliness of command" (Lynch, 2000; Nelson, Quick, & Quick, 1989; J. C. Quick & Quick, 2004). Loneliness of command as a problem of social isolation is often accompanied by distortions in the upward flow of information in the organizational hierarchy. Too often, feelings of insecurity or vulnerability on the part of followers mean that the closer you are to the top, the farther you are from the truth. Failures in upward communication have contributed to the Challenger and Columbia shuttle disasters, delayed investigation of the Madoff investment scandal, missteps in Iraq, and countless other failures in business and government (Bateman, 2008).

Senior executives benefit from combating social isolation and loneliness of command with a full range of 360-degree feedback. Executives may work to improve upward communication (Tourish, 2005) and rely on spouses and intimate family members to help them gauge the quality and reliability of information and feedback they receive (Levinson, 1996; Nelson, Quick, & Quick, 1989). The key to improving upward communication lies in creating an environment and culture that assures individuals they will not be punished for communicating bad news. When individuals observe and experience the organization's non-punitive responses, honesty and accuracy of upward communication increases.

Lynch (2000) suggests that heartfelt interpersonal communication is an important antidote for social isolation and problems associated with loneliness of command. This can be achieved through executive forums such as the Young Presidents' Organization (YPO), Vistage peer groups, or similar network opportunities in which executives form and maintain close interpersonal ties with those facing similar challenges and opportunities. The sharing of experience and information in a supportive and non-threatening context is a way to Lynch's heartfelt interpersonal communication.

## Toxic effects of emotions

Executives are in no way immune to the damage that the toxic effects of emotions like fear, anger, and rage (Frost, 2003) can have on well-being. Levinson (1964/1985) first drew attention to emotional tensions and inner conflicts with his examination of executive stress, realizing that unrecognized and mismanaged emotions can have harmful effects. Emotions, however, are not easily categorized as good or bad, positive or negative and the theory as well as research within this arena continues to mature (cf. Mayer, Salovey, & Caruso, 2004).

Balancing the open expression of emotion in the workplace with appropriate management and expression of that emotion is important to guarding against toxic effects that may unintentionally result. For example, in one IT company, a toxic e-mail from one vice president to another led to the receiving executive's dramatic, verbally abusive, and hostile confrontation with the vice president initiating the e-mail. Beyond the toxic effects between the two senior executives, there was a range of collateral damage for organizational witnesses to the overt event. The tension expressed with toxic effect was rooted in a work conflict between the two vice presidents. A healthier resolution to the conflict would have been achieved had the emotions and frustrations between the two been recognized, expressed, and resolved in a non-confrontational way.

Cameron (2007) has offered forgiveness as one antidote for the harm, damage, and negative fallout that accompany toxic effects of emotions at work. In the case of the two IT vice presidents, a diagnostic review of the incident with an executive coach led to a healing process of forgiveness that was accompanied by constructive, concrete behavioral changes on the part of both executives. Hence, a negative event was turned into an executive learning experience through which both vice presidents restored their relationship and moved forward, providing a constructive example for the entire company. While positive outcomes from negative events are not inevitable, they certainly are possible through deep interpersonal communication (J.C. Quick & Macik-Frey, 2004).

## Traumas and tragedies

Traumas and tragedies are negative life events that can adversely impact executive well-being. In the Grant Study, which followed a cohort of men over 35 years, Vaillant (1977) identified at least one personal or professional trauma or tragedy for each participant. However, these negative events never became the defining feature of the individual's life. Vaillant found that the adaptive mechanisms participants employed to cope with negative events were more important than the events themselves. These adaptive mechanisms defined the individual's psychological adjustment over time. Vaillant (1977, p. 80) classified these adaptive ego mechanisms from Level I (psychotic) to Level IV (mature). Level I adaptive ego mechanisms were associated with negative well-being, especially following trauma or tragedy. These psychotic defenses included denial of external reality, distortion, and delusional projection. Level IV adaptive ego mechanisms were associated with positive well-being even following trauma or tragedy. These mature mechanisms include sublimation, altruism, suppression, anticipation, and humor. When faced with trauma or tragedy, these mature adaptive mechanisms facilitate coping and subsequent adjustment to a new, changed reality.

To illustrate adaptive coping, we use a case example. Gerald Arpey was Executive Vice President for Operations for American Airlines on September 11, 2001 (J. C. Quick, Gavin,

Cooper, & Quick, 2008). Within an hour of his 7:15 am arrival at work that day, he learned that two American Airlines flights had been hijacked and flown into the World Trade Center and the Pentagon. By 10:50 am Central time, the remainder of American Airlines' fleet of domestic aircraft was accounted for and on the ground. Rather than allowing this national tragedy to define the airline, Mr Arpey's positive leadership in managing American Airline's response and all that followed set the stage for his subsequent advancement to president and CEO. Hence, the response and not the event became the defining features of the tragedy for him.

Katherine Graham faced a different set of circumstances when her husband Phil Graham, president and chief executive officer of *The Washington Post*, committed suicide. His sudden and unexpected death left her responsible for one of the largest and arguably most respected newspapers in America (J. D. Quick, Cooper, Gavin, & Quick, 2002). At the time of her husband's death, Katherine Graham was a full-time wife and mother. Her response to personal trauma led her to redefine herself professionally, as a prominent and respected news executive when she assumed the position that her late husband had held.

While the threats and challenges of stress, burnout, social isolation, toxic effects of emotions, and tragedy put executives at risk of poor well-being, the losses and harm are not irreversible. While there are clear advantages for executives who exploit the pathways to positive well-being, there are commensurate advantages for executives who guard against threats and challenges. A balanced approach that focuses on building strength while defending against vulnerability helps optimize executive well-being. We now turn to the asymmetric effects on men and women executives.

# Asymmetry Between Executive Men and Executive Women

Men and women executives may not yet have equal access to pathways for positive well-being or equal exposure to the risks of executive life. Hewlett (2002) reports a costly imbalance between the sexes, and some sobering facts about the professional lives of men and women. Her research shows significant differences between men and women who are high and ultra-high achievers, the latter certainly including successful executives. While 83% of ultra-high achieving men are married, only 57% of women are married. This statistic does not simply reflect the preferences of women executives: Hewlett has interviewed many who assumed they would eventually marry and have children. For these women, the absence of children became a regret. In the case of male high-achievers and executives, Hewlett (2002) found the percent of men who wanted and who actually had children was roughly the same. For men, there was neither the regret nor the disparity between desired and actual circumstances experienced by women.

Real-life cases, such as the experience of former Hewlett Packard Chairman and CEO Lew Platt, can inform the asymmetry. As a manager early in his career at HP, Platt did not understand the challenges his women colleagues discussed. All that changed in 1981, with the death of Platt's young wife, Susan. A general manager at the time, Platt struggled with the demands of his work combined with care for his two daughters, aged 9 and 11. He quickly recognized the reality of the struggles described by HP's women managers. His growing empathy for HP's women led him to be a corporate activist who helped transform HP policies (Abelson, 1999). Executive well-being must be discussed and considered differently for men and for women.

## Debunking Cultural Myths

We conclude with the desire to debunk two cultural myths that directly bear upon executive well-being. The first myth is that executive women can mirror men. Hewlett's (2002) data shatter this myth in a sobering fashion. The experience of the past few decades shows that women executives can succeed and make consequential, meaningful contributions to business. At the same time, they have faced serious challenges in simultaneously pursuing traditional roles as wives and mothers. Female executives are much less likely to have families than comparable male executives. While women can be wives, mothers, and executives—as shown by examples such as Xerox Chairman and CEO Ursula Burns and many of her women Fortune 500 peers (Branson, 2010)—and they must do so in their own individual ways.

The second myth is that real men can "go it alone." The data and evidence concerning executive men and positive well-being is rather convincing: healthy, secure relationships are instrumentally important to health and happiness. Positive well-being accrues through a network of strong relationships (House, Landis, & Umberson, 1988), providing a vital hedge against the threats and challenges that undermine success in work and personal life. More directly, a careful study of John Wayne's war and western film legacy reveals that he most often was a leader in a supportive team and rarely acted as a "lone ranger." Executive men benefit hugely from authentic interpersonal relationships (Lynch, 2000).

## Future Directions

To conclude, we identify six key questions for future research on executive well-being. These research questions support efforts to enhance positive well-being, guard against poor well-being, and address asymmetries in the experiences of men and women executives.

1. Character is an elusive yet important term, used in both academia and professional practice. How is character best defined and measured? Character is a topic that calls for deeper consideration and more thorough understanding in both theory and practice.
2. How does greater self-awareness lead to increased happiness? Empirical data and clinical observations suggest that poor self-awareness is a common problem for executives. Expanding the research on executive self-awareness and its relationship to executive well-being is a fruitful area for future research.
3. What motivation profiles help some executives rise to authority and power? Which of these profiles is associated with the greatest well-being? Executives may, or may not, be able to modify these profiles for greater success. This is fertile ground for inquiry.

4. How do different executive characteristics affect executive well-being? The characteristics we suggest examining include functional expertise, gender, race and ethnicity, religious orientation, and differences in thinking styles, psychological preferences, and emotional competencies.

5. What developmental experiences cultivate healthy strategies for coping with the threats and challenges of executive life? Managing poor well-being and the losses that accompany it has great value for the executive, work colleagues, family, and the organization. How effective are the commonly employed tools for achieving this, such as executive coaching, employee assistance programs, peer-to-peer executive groups, and others?

6. What are the policy pathways to redress the asymmetry in opportunities and challenges for men and women executives? Helping men and women achieve personal goals and aspirations while achieving success for the organization will have broad, collective benefits for executive well-being.

## Acknowledgments

The authors thank our editor Arran Caza, John Goolsby, and Sheri Schember Quick for comments on earlier drafts of this chapter. Jim thanks John and Judy Goolsby for the direction of an historic philanthropic gift that lead to the Goolsby Leadership Academy in 2003. Their generosity and continuing support have led to a host of positive impacts on students and faculty alike, at the University of Texas at Arlington and other institutions globally that have been inspired by Goolsby. Jim thanks Jacqualyn (Jackie) Fouse for her early and enthusiastic support in extending the Goolsbys' foundational gift to UT Arlington and its College of Business. She has been an inspiration to Goolsby Scholars and to faculty alike in an engaged, continuing way.

## References

Abelson, R. (1999, August 22). A push from the top shatters a glass ceiling. *New York Times*, p. 1.

Aristotle. (1998). *Nicomachean ethics* (D. Ross, Trans. Revised by J. L. Ackrill & J. O. Urmson). Oxford, UK: Oxford University Press.

Aristotle. (2000). *The Nicomachean ethics*. (R. Crisp, Trans.). Cambridge, UK: Cambridge University Press.

Bateman, T. (2008). Brief-but-powerful lessons from Katrina and Iraq. *Organizational Dynamics*, 37(4), 301–312.

Boyatzis, R., & McKee, A. (2005). *Resonant leadership*. Boston, MA: Harvard Business School Press.

Brady, D. (2010). Hard choices: Patricia Dunn. *Bloomberg Businessweek*, 17–23 May, 84.

Branson, D. M. (2010). *The last male bastion: Gender and the CEO suite in America's public companies*. New York, NY: Routledge.

Burnham, D. H. (2002). *Inside the mind of the world-class leader*. Boston, MA: Burnham Rosen Group.

Cameron, K. S. (2007). Forgiveness in organizations. In D. L. Nelson & C. L. Cooper (Eds.) *Positive organizational behavior* (pp. 129–142). Thousand Oaks, CA: Sage.

Cohen, W. (2010). *Drucker on leadership: New lessons from the father of modern management.* San Francisco, CA: Jossey-Bass.

Cooper, C. L. & Marshall, J. (1978). Sources of managerial and white collar stress. In C. L. Cooper & R. Payne (Eds.) *Stress at work* (pp. 81–105). Chichester, UK: John Wiley & Sons.

Danna, K., & Griffin, R. W. (1999). Health and well-being in the workplace: A review and synthesis of the literature. *Journal of Management, 25,* 357–384.

Davidson, O. B., Eden, D., Westman, M., Cohen-Charash, Y., Hammer, L. B., Kluger, A. N., … Spector, P. (2010). Sabbatical leave: Who gains and how much? *Journal of Applied Psychology, 95*(5), 953–964.

Diener, E., Suh, E. M., Lucas, E. R., & Smith, H. L. (1999). Subjective well-being: Three decades of progress. *Psychological Bulletin, 125,* 276–302.

Edwards, J. R. (1996). An examination of competing versions of the person-environment fit approach to stress. *Academy of Management Journal, 39,* 292–339.

Elkind, H. B. (Ed.). (1931). *Preventive management: Mental hygiene in industry.* New York, NY: B. C. Forbes.

Escobedo, J. R., & Adolphs, R. (2010). Becoming a better person: Temporal remoteness biases autobiographical memories for moral events. *Emotion, 10,* 511–518.

Frost, P.J. (2003). *Toxic emotions at work.* Cambridge, MA: Harvard Business School Press.

Goolsby, J. L., Mack, D. A., & Quick, J. C. (2010). Winning by staying in bounds: Good outcomes from positive ethics. *Organizational Dynamics, 39,* 248–257.

Hewlett, S. A. (2002). Executive women and the myth of having it all. *Harvard Business Review, 80,* 66–73.

House, J. S., Landis, K. R., & Umberson, D. (1988). Social relationships and health. *Science, 241,* 540–545.

Kets de Vries, M. (2009a). *Reflections on character and leadership.* Chichester, UK: John Wiley & Sons Ltd.

Kets de Vries, M. (2009b). *Sex, money, happiness and death: The quest for authenticity.* Hampshire, UK: Palgrave Macmillan.

Laird, D. (1929). *Psychology and profits.* New York, NY: B. C. Forbes Publishing Co.

Levinson, H. (2006). *Harry Levinson on the psychology of leadership.* Boston, MA: Harvard Business Review Book.

Levinson, H. (1996). A new age of self-reliance. *Harvard Business Review, July–August,* 162–173.

Levinson, H. (1964/1985). *Executive stress.* New York, NY: New American Library.

Loehr, J., & Schwartz, T. (2003). *The Power of full engagement.* New York, NY: Free Press.

Lublin, J. S. (2011). Former H-P Chairman Patricia Dunn has died. December 6, *The Wall Street Journal,* p. B3.

Lynch, J. J. (2000). *A cry unheard: The medical consequences of loneliness.* Baltimore, MD: Bancroft Press.

Macik-Frey, M., Quick, J. C., & Nelson, D. L. (2007). Advances in occupational health: From a stressful beginning to a positive future. *Journal of Management, 33,* 809–840.

Management Sciences for Health. (2009). *Annual Report.* Cambridge, MA: MSH.

Mayer, J. D., Salovey, P., & Caruso, D. R. (2004). Emotional intelligence: Theory, findings, and implications. *Psychological Inquiry, 15,* 197–215.

McClelland, D. C. (1975). *Power: The inner experience.* New York, NY: Irving.

McClelland, D. C., & Burnham, D. H. (2003). Power is the great motivator. *Harvard Business Review, January–February,* 1–10.

Mill, J. S. (1910). *Utilitarianism, liberty, and representative government.* London, UK: Dent.
Moss, L. (1981). *Management stress.* Reading, MA: Addison-Wesley.
Nelson, D. L., Quick, J. C., & Quick, J. D. (1989). Corporate warfare: Preventing combat stress and battle fatigue. *Organizational Dynamics, 18,* 65–79.
Park, N., Peterson, C., & Seligman, M. E. (2004). Strengths of character and well-being. *Journal of Social and Clinical Psychology, 23,* 603–619.
Peterson, C. & Seligman, M. E. P. (2004). *Character strengths and virtues.* Oxford, UK and New York, NY: American Psychological Association and Oxford University Press.
Peterson, C., Park, N., Hall, N., & Seligman, M. E. P. (2009). Zest and work. *Journal of Organizational Behavior, 30,* 161–172.
Quick, J. C., Cooper, C. L., Gavin, J. H., & Quick, J. D. (2008). *Managing executive health.* Cambridge, UK: Cambridge University Press.
Quick, J. C., Cooper, C. L., Nelson, D. L., Quick, J. D., & Gavin, J. H. (2003). Stress, health, and well-being at work. In J. Greenberg (Ed.), *Organizational behavior: The state of the science, Second Edition* (pp. 53–89). Mahwah, NJ: Lawrence Erlbaum Associates.
Quick, J. C., & Macik-Frey, M. (2004). Behind the mask: Coaching through deep interpersonal communication. *Consulting Psychology Journal, 56,* 67–74.
Quick, J. C., Mack, D. A., Gavin, J. H., Cooper, C. L., & Quick, J. D. (2004). Executives: Engines for positive stress. In P. L. Perrewé & D. C. Ganster (Eds.), *Research in Occupational Stress and Well-Being* (pp. 359–405). New York, NY: Elsevier Press.
Quick, J. C., Nelson, D. L., & Quick, J. D. (1987). Successful executives: How independent? *Academy of Management Executive, 1,* 139–145.
Quick, J. C. & Quick, J. D. (2004). Healthy, happy, productive work: A leadership challenge. *Organizational Dynamics, 33,* 329–337.
Quick, J. C., Saleh, K. J., Sime, W. E., Martin, W., Cooper, C. L., Quick, J. D., & Mont, M. A. (2006). Stress management skills for strong leadership: Is it worth dying for? *Journal of Bone & Joint Surgery, 88,* 271–225.
Quick. J. C., Wright, T. A., Adkins, J. A., Nelson, D. L., & Quick, J. D. (2013). *Preventive stress management in organizations, Second Edition.* Washington, DC: American Psychological Association.
Quick, J. D., Cooper, C. L. Gavin, J. H. & Quick, J. D. (2002). Executive health: Building self-reliance for challenging times. In Cooper, C. L. & Robertson, I. T. (Eds.), *International review of industrial and organizational psychology,* (pp. 187–216). West Sussex, UK: John Wiley & Sons, Inc.
Quick, J. D., Nelson, D. L., & Quick, J. C. (1998). The theory of preventive stress management in organizations. In C. L. Cooper (Ed.) *Theories of Organizational Stress,* (pp. 246–268). Oxford: Oxford University Press.
Rosenau, M. J. (1913). *Preventive medicine and hygiene.* New York, NY: D. Appleton & Co.
Saleh, K. J., Quick, J. C., Conaway, M., Sime, W. E., Martin, W., Hurwitz, S., & Einhorn, T. A. (2007). The prevalence and severity of burnout among academic orthopaedic departmental leaders. *Journal of Bone & Joint Surgery, 89,* 896–903.
Sarbanes-Oxley Act of 2002. (2002). Retrieved from http://www.soxlaw.com
Seligman, M. E. P. (1991). *Learned optimism.* San Francisco, CA: Barrett-Koehler Publishers.
Shirom, A. (2011). Job-related burnout: A review of major research foci and challenges. In J.C. Quick & L.E. Tetrick (Eds.), *Handbook of occupational health psychology, Second Edition* (pp. 223–242). Washington, DC: American Psychological Association.

Shirom, A. (2004). Feeling vigorous at work? The construct of vigor and the study of positive affect in organizations. In P. L. Perrewé & D. C. Ganster (Eds.), *Research in occupational stress and well being, Vol. 3: Emotional and physiological processes and positive intervention strategies*, (pp. 135–164). Oxford, UK: JAI Press/Elsevier.

Smith, A. (1759). *The theory of the moral sentiments*. Edinburgh, UK: A. Kincaid and J. Bell.

Smith, A. (1910). *An inquiry into the nature and causes of the wealth of nations*. Harvard Classics, Volume 10 (C. J. Bullock, Ed.). New York, NY: P.F. Collier & Son.

Solomon, R. C. (1999). *A Better Way to Think About Business*. New York, NY: Oxford University Press.

*Stanford encyclopedia of philosophy*. (2008). Palo Alto, CA: Stanford University.

Thompson, A. D., Grahek, M., Phillips, R. E., & Fay, C. L. (2008). In search of worthy leadership. *Consulting Psychology Journal: Practice and Research*, 60(4), 366–382.

Tourish, D. (2005). Critical upward communication: Ten commandments for improving strategy and decision making. *Long Range Planning*, 38, 485–503.

VandenBos, G. (Ed.). (2007). *APA dictionary of psychology*. Washington, DC: American Psychological Association.

Vaillant, G. E. (1977). *Adaptation to life*. Boston, MA: Little, Brown.

Wallace, R. B. & Doebbeling, B. N. (1998). *Maxcy-Rosenau-Last public health & preventive medicine, 14th edition*. Stamford, CN: Appleton & Lange.

Wright, T. A., & Cropanzano, R. (2004). The role of psychological well-being in job performance. *Organizational Dynamics*, 33, 338–351.

# SECTION VIII
# RELATIONSHIPS AND HAPPINESS

# CHAPTER 59

# INTRODUCTION TO RELATIONSHIPS AND HAPPINESS

## MELİKŞAH DEMİR

Northern Arizona University, USA

CLOSE relationships are central to people throughout their lives (Baumeister & Leary, 1995). Individuals spend a considerable amount of time with the members of their social networks—people who are relied on to support them in dealing with problems, whether mundane or significant, and with whom they share positive experiences. In posing the question "What makes people happy?" to a layperson or scholar, most would likely point to the importance of close relationships. Indeed, decades of theoretical and empirical work highlight that being in a close relationship, the number of close relationships one has, and the quality of relationship experiences in general, are robust and consistent correlates of happiness. Importantly, this statement can be generalized across cultures.

Since the seminal work of Watson (1930) and reviews by Wilson (1967) and Diener (1984), theory and research have explored the role of various types and dimensions of close relationships in happiness (e.g., Argyle, 2001; Diener & Biswas-Diener, 2008). Important advances include, first, the now well-established roles of attachment security, social support, and overall relationship quality in predicting happiness. These findings have been observed across samples, age groups, research methods, and cultures. Second, although close relationships are consistent correlates with happiness, research shows that the quality of social relationships is more important than the quantity—a pattern replicated across age and cultural groups. Third, the contribution of different types of close relationships (e.g., friendships and family relations) to happiness changes across the lifespan. This observation has been confirmed with various research methods. Fourth, relationship experiences with close others explain incremental variance in happiness relative to personality, which is a major predictor of happiness. This result too has been replicated with different research methods, and across age groups.

Given the progress made, current work in the area of close relationships and happiness has turned to more complex issues. For instance, in the adult attachment literature one relatively recent concern is with the long-term implications of security priming on relationship and individual well-being, and the processes responsible for these potential changes (Gillath, Selcuk, & Shaver, 2008). In the social support literature, researchers are trying to better understand the extent to which the social support-happiness link reflects the personalities of the recipients of support as well as the specific relationship between those who give support and those who receive it (Lakey, Chapter 62, this volume). Last, a current debate that spans the field pertains to the relative importance of close relationships to happiness. Recently, Lucas and his colleagues (Lucas & Dyrenforth, 2006; Lucas, Dyrenforth, & Diener, 2008) asserted that the role of relationship experiences has been overstated and that theories of happiness should be revised accordingly. These authors examined variables such as number of friends and marital status and suggested that shared method variance makes it difficult to confidently interpret the results.

As many of the chapters in this section suggest, there is evidence that counters Lucas and colleagues' claims about overstating the role of relationships in well-being. Nonetheless, this debate is an important one that is contributing to a closer examination of the methods used in research protocols, greater specificity regarding how the types and dimensions of relationship experiences (e.g., quality vs. quantity) influence happiness, and the study of variables that moderate the relationships–happiness link.

# Chapters in This Section

The contributors to this section are experts in their respective fields. Each chapter addresses the role of close relationships in happiness from a different perspective by providing an authoritative review and discussion of current theoretical and methodological issues. Each also makes suggestions of important directions for future research. These chapters will serve as a valuable resource for scholars investigating the associations of close relationships with happiness.

Saphire-Bernstein and Taylor's chapter on close relationships and happiness provides an historical overview of the research (Chapter 60). The authors conclude that marital quality is a stronger correlate of happiness than marital status, and that the impact of romantic relationships on happiness differs depending on the component of happiness assessed (i.e., life satisfaction vs. affect). They also explore gender differences in the relationship–happiness link.

Chapter 61 by Mikulincer and Shaver focuses on the relationship between different forms of adult attachment and happiness. Their review highlights that attachment-related differences influence not only the experience and expression of positive emotions in general but also the experience of these emotions in the context of close relationships. The authors provide evidence suggesting that the psychological benefits of experiencing positive emotions interact with attachment orientations. Finally, they highlight the role of security priming in happiness.

Chapter 62 on perceived social support and happiness by Lakey provides an in-depth review and addresses important theoretical and empirical issues. Lakey first describes the research indicating that perceived social support is robustly and consistently related to happiness. Next, he examines the extent to which this relationship reflects the personalities of support recipients and the unique relationships among providers and recipients of support.

Last, he considers the implications of current knowledge for future interventions and research.

Lastly in this section, Demir, Orthel, and Andelin (Chapter 63) focus on the relationships between various domains of friendship experiences and happiness, and the moderators and mediators of these. The authors suggest that friendship is a consistent correlate of happiness across age groups and cultures, and emphasize the stronger role of friendship quality relative to quantity. They highlight important theoretical and methodological issues and propose recommendations to advance our understanding.

## Future Directions

Although more is known about the role of different types of relationships in happiness compared to a few decades ago, marital relationships still receive more attention than other close relationships (e.g., friendships). This imbalance is understandable considering that intimate and marital relationships are viewed as the most central ones in the lives of individuals (Berscheid & Reis, 1998; Reis, Collins, & Berscheid, 2000). Yet, people also consider their relationships with different family members (e.g., siblings) and friends to be important and additional research is needed on these types of close relationships. It is also important to further investigate how the quality of different types of relationships might exert a "cumulative" impact on happiness (Demir, 2010; Saphire-Bernstein & Taylor, Chapter 60, this volume).

Close relationships are related to happiness. However, as highlighted in nearly every major review of the literature (e.g., Diener, Suh, Lucas, & Smith, 1999), the correlational nature of the majority of research impedes our understanding of the causal mechanisms underlying the association. Future research should employ alternative (e.g., longitudinal) designs to help further the field. Another direction for future research is the exploration of close relationships in happiness from an evolutionary perspective. For instance, it would be interesting to explore the implications of how solving different adaptive problems (e.g., reproductive success) across the lifespan impact the relationship–happiness link.

Last, an essential direction for future research pertains to addressing the issue of shared method variance. Lucas and his colleagues (Lucas & Dyrenforth, 2006; Lucas et al., 2008) appropriately noted that the overuse of self-report assessments presents a real obstacle to understanding the true importance of relationship experiences in happiness. As Saphire-Bernstein & Taylor, Chapter 60, this volume suggest, the task of future research is to measure relationship quality and happiness in ways that would avoid overlapping variance. This is an essential research endeavor, and its findings would significantly contribute to the advancement of the field.

In addition to these general directions for future research, there are specific questions requiring further attention from scholars. For instance, what are the roles of different attachment orientations in influencing responses to the positive life experiences and happiness of one's partner? Does relationship quality have different implications for different components of happiness? If yes, why?

Decades of theory and research leave no doubt that close relationships are important to happiness. Advanced questions and methods will enable us to further elaborate on the place of relationships in happiness. We are optimistic that many of these interesting issues will be addressed in the coming decade.

# References

Argyle, M. (2001). *The psychology of happiness* (2nd ed.). New York, NY: Routledge.

Baumeister, R. F., & Leary, M. R. (1995). The need to belong: Desire for interpersonal attachments as a fundamental human motivation. *Psychological Bulletin, 117*, 497–529.

Berscheid, E., & Reis, H. T. (1998). Attraction and close relationships. In D. T. Gilbert, S. T. Fiske, & G. Lindzey (Eds.), *The handbook of social psychology* (4th ed., pp. 13–281). Boston, MA: McGraw-Hill.

Demir, M. (2010). Close relationships and happiness among emerging adults. *Journal of Happiness Studies, 11*, 293–313.

Diener, E. (1984). Subjective well-being. *Psychological Bulletin, 95*, 542–575.

Diener, E., & Biswas-Diener, R. (2008). *Happiness: Unlocking the mysteries of psychological wealth*. Malden, MA: Blackwell Publishing.

Diener, E., Suh, E. M., Lucas, R. E., & Smith, H. L. (1999). Subjective well-being: Three decades of progress. *Psychological Bulletin, 125*, 276–302.

Gillath, O., Selcuk, E., & Shaver, P. R. (2008). Moving toward a secure attachment style: Can repeated security priming help? *Social and Personality Compass, 2*, 1651–1666.

Lucas, R. E., & Dyrenforth, P. S. (2006). Does the existence of social relationships matter for subjective well-being? In K. D. Vohs & E. J. Finkel (Eds.), *Self and relationships: Connecting intrapersonal and interpersonal processes* (pp. 254–273). New York, NY: Guilford.

Lucas, R. E., Dyrenforth, P. S., & Diener, E. (2008). Four myths about subjective well-being. *Social and Personality Psychology Compass, 2*, 2001–2015.

Reis, H. T., Collins, W. A., & Berscheid, E. (2000). The relationship context of human behavior and development. *Psychological Bulletin, 126*, 844–872.

Watson, G. B. (1930). Happiness among adult students of education. *Journal of Educational Psychology, 21*, 79–109.

Wilson, W. (1967). Correlates of avowed happiness. *Psychological Bulletin, 67*, 294–306.

# CHAPTER 60

# CLOSE RELATIONSHIPS AND HAPPINESS

SHIMON SAPHIRE-BERNSTEIN AND
SHELLEY E. TAYLOR

University of California, Los Angeles, USA

SOCIAL relationships have long been considered one of the strongest and most important predictors of happiness (Argyle, 2001; Campbell, Converse, & Rodgers, 1976; Myers, 2000). This assumption is in accord with the arguments of numerous scholars regarding the importance of group living and interpersonal relationships in shaping human evolution (e.g., Baumeister & Leary, 1995; Taylor et al., 2000). Empirical evidence that relationships are tied to happiness is plentiful. For example, support from family, friends, and especially from a significant other is tied to reports of greater subjective well-being (e.g., Walen, & Lachman, 2000; Gallagher, & Vella-Brodrick, 2008; Wan, Jaccard, & Ramey, 1996). Recently, however, critics have suggested that the status given to relationships in the field of happiness overstates their centrality and importance (e.g., Lucas & Dyrenforth, 2006; Lucas, Dyrenforth, & Diener, 2008). Although these critiques are themselves somewhat controversial, they underscore important gaps in the empirical record and force scholars to reconsider their assumptions about the strength of the association between social relationships and happiness.

We begin with issues of definitions and measurement. We then review empirical findings on the relative effects of relationship quantity and quality on happiness, or more specifically, subjective well-being. We especially profile the significant other relationship, which accounts for a substantial portion of the variance that relationships play in subjective well-being (SWB). Finally, we consider some less explored issues, such as the roles of gender, age, and culture in moderating the effects of relationships on happiness that may help to explicate some of the puzzlingly modest associations in the literature.

## SUBJECTIVE WELL-BEING: DEFINITION AND MEASUREMENT

In the relationships literature, happiness is most often studied as SWB (cf. Diener, 1984; Diener et al., 1999). SWB refers to the subjective perceptions people hold of: (1) the general hedonic tone of their day-to-day lives and (2) how well their lives are going overall (Diener, 1984). Researchers in this tradition most commonly subscribe to the tripartite model, which views SWB as being comprised of positive affect (PA), negative affect (NA), and life satisfaction (LS) (Andrews & Withey, 1976; Diener, 1984; Diener, Suh, Lucas, & Smith, 1999). In this review, we use the term happiness when addressing broad-based questions and perspectives, reserving the term SWB for references to specific theoretical and empirical work in the SWB tradition. Although a thorough discussion of the definitions of happiness is beyond the scope of this chapter (for recent reviews, see Miao, Koo & Oishi, Chapter 13, this volume; Schimmack, 2008), we adopt the tripartite model to highlight several key points: First, the model provides a useful framework for categorizing the results of studies utilizing a wide range of measures. For example, measures of mental health and depression are the most commonly used measures of SWB, yet such measures primarily capture NA; PA and LS are less frequently assessed (Reis, 2001). Second, the pattern of correlations observed between social relationships and happiness differs depending on which factor of SWB is assessed. For example, as will be seen, relationship quality is often more highly correlated with LS than with PA or NA, and so reviews that focus on affective correlates of relationships may overlook important effects on LS.

## Assessing Social Relationships

Early research on relationships and happiness investigated satisfaction with social life (Andrews & Withey, 1976; Campbell et al., 1976), but attention soon turned to quantitative measures, such as number of friends or confidants, social network size, degree of integration, and the frequency and amount of social activity (for a meta-analysis of early research, see Okun, Stock, Haring, & Witter, 1984). Reliable measures of marital relationships have existed for decades (e.g., Dyadic Adjustment Scale; Spanier, 1976), although they are infrequently employed in the study of SWB. Qualitative assessment of other relationships began to emerge during the 1980s as a surge of interest in social support led to the development of several well-validated measures that have continued to be widely used to the present day (for a comprehensive review of social support measurement, see Cohen, Underwood & Gottlieb, 2000). The National Study of Midlife Development in the United States (MIDUS) measures assess both the positive features of relationships (i.e. social support) and sources of relationship strain, such as conflict (Schuster, Kessler, & Aseltine, 1990). Intimacy and closeness, related constructs, have attracted a great deal of attention in the relationships literature in recent years (for a comprehensive review, see Mashek & Aron, 2004), but they have yet to be fully studied in relation to LS and SWB. Other measures, such as the Network of Relationships Inventory (NRI) (Furman & Buhrmester, 1985) assess the quantity and quality of a wide array of relationships. Social activity continues to be studied with more refined methods of measurement, such as experience sampling and the Day Reconstruction Method (Kahneman et al., 2004; Srivastava, Angelo, & Vallereux, 2008).

# Why should Relationships Matter for Happiness?

Although scholars frequently assume that relationships are important to happiness, the question of why this should be the case is less frequently addressed. Baumeister and Leary (1995) presented an influential articulation of the importance of relationships to human psychology, arguing that all humans have a fundamental "need to belong" that has been shaped by natural selection over the course of human evolution. They maintain that this need leads people to form relationships and resist their dissolution, with concomitant beneficial effects on adjustment and well-being. Other researchers have emphasized the importance of intimacy, defined as the perceived responsiveness of another to emotionally self-relevant disclosures that reflect key aspects of one's core psychological self (Reis, 2001). The primary functional argument for the importance of social relationships focuses on social support and its salutary effects on mental and physical health (for reviews, see Cohen et al., 2000; and Taylor, 2010).

# Are Relationships Important for Happiness?

Are relationships reliably related to happiness? If one considers objective, measureable aspects of an individual's relationships and social network, then the answer is yes, but modestly. Meta-analyses of the relation of objective social variables (such as number of relationships and number of friends) to SWB have obtained effect sizes in the small to moderate range (Lucas & Dyrenforth, 2006; Lucas et al., 2008). For example, a meta-analysis of the association between "social activity" and SWB found that the average effect on LS and happiness was $r = 0.16$ (Okun et al., 1984), and another meta-analysis found that the quantity of social activity had effects ranging from $r = 0.12$–$0.17$, depending on the specific dependent measure used (Pinquart & Sörensen, 2000). Cooper, Okamura, and Gurka (1992) assessed both the frequency of and satisfaction with social activities. Across several samples, they found that satisfaction with social activities was significantly correlated with PA ($r = 0.20$), NA ($r = -0.26$) and LS ($r = 0.38$), whereas the frequency of social activities was consistently related only to LS ($r = 0.19$). Note that these results indicate a stronger association of social activity with LS than with the affective components of SWB. Lucas and Dyrenforth (2006) analyzed data from the General Social Survey and found that the correlation between number of friends and happiness was only 0.13. From their analysis and the meta-analytic findings of Okun et al. (1984) and Pinquart and Sörensen (2000), Lucas and colleagues concluded that the impact of social relationships on happiness has been overstated, and that theories of SWB should be reconsidered accordingly (Lucas & Dyrenforth, 2006; Lucas et al., 2008). It should be noted, however, that Okun et al. (1984) included only studies published before 1980, and the Pinquart and Sörensen (2000) meta-analysis was conducted only on studies with elderly populations.

In sum, the effect of objective measures of social relationships on happiness may be modest, but the case is not closed. Effect sizes tend to be larger for subjective measures of the quality of social relationships, relative to objective measures. Wan and colleagues (1996) measured receipt of four types of support from four (for single mothers) or five (for married mothers and fathers) sources in a sample of parents (single fathers were not included due to low $n$). They were able to predict 35% of the variance in LS for married women and 15% of the variance in LS for married men, using all 20 support variables (including four measures of partner support). However, nearly all of the explained variance for married men was attributable to partner support, whereas the addition of the 16 other measures accounted for an additional 6.7% of the variance in married women's LS. Support from four sources (child's grandparents, relatives, friends, and coworkers) predicted a total of 9.6% of the variance in single mothers' LS. Demir (2010) measured quality and conflict (derived from the NRI) (Furman & Buhrmester, 1985) in relationships with mother, father, friends, and romantic partner (when relevant); these assessments accounted for 17% of the variance in a composite measure of happiness in single participants and 28% of the variance in happiness of participants in intimate relationships. Similar results were obtained by Walen and Lachman (2000), who used the MIDUS measures of social support and strain (Schuster et al., 1990) to assess the combined effects of family relationships, friendships, and intimate relationships on LS (27% variance explained), PA (16% variance explained), and NA (11% variance explained). These results are especially noteworthy, as they also demonstrate the need to distinguish among the three factors of SWB: the effects on LS are considerably larger than are the effects on PA and NA.

However, as Lucas and colleagues (2006; 2008) point out, such measures likely share common method variance with measures of SWB. This is especially true when similarly worded measures of relationships and SWB are used. For example, Alfonso, Allison, Rader and Gorman (1996) constructed an Extended Satisfaction With Life Scale that measured domain satisfactions by making only small modifications to the wording of satisfaction with life questions. Thus, it is not surprising that satisfaction with social life was highly correlated with LS ($r = 0.62$), as were satisfaction with family ($r = 0.41$) and romantic relationships ($r = 0.39$).

Despite such methodological concerns, it would be premature to draw strong conclusions about the strength of the correlation between relationships and happiness without consideration of additional issues. Chief among these are the diversity of relationships that characterize human social life and the possibility that factors such as gender and age may moderate the association of relationships with happiness.

# Intimate Relationships, Marriage, and Happiness

Although much of the extant literature on relationships and happiness has been devoted to global measures of overall relationship quality, the lion's share of the research has focused on the role of intimate and marital relationships. The mere fact of being married has been repeatedly linked to happiness, irrespective of the quality of the marital relationship (Dush & Amato, 2005; Haring-Hidore, Stock, Okun & Witter, 1985; Wan et al., 1996;

Williams, 2003). Indeed, marital status is frequently cited as one of the most well-established predictors of happiness (e.g., Argyle, 2001; Myers, 2000), although the size of the association between marital status and SWB is weak: In a meta-analysis, Haring-Hidore et al. (1985) found the average effect to be small ($d = 0.14$; $r = 0.07$).[1] As noted, critics have pointed to this and similar findings as evidence that reports of the importance of relationships to happiness have been exaggerated (Lucas & Dyrenforth, 2005).

Despite the weak overall effect size, two of Haring-Hidore et al.'s (1985) findings point to potentially important moderators of the relation of marriage to happiness. First, the average effect size for the relation of marital status to SWB was significantly larger for men ($d = 0.17$; $r = 0.085$) than it was for women ($d = 0.12$; $r = 0.06$), suggesting that gender may be an important factor to examine. In addition, effect size magnitude was significantly correlated with the age range of the samples ($r = -0.54$), such that being married was a stronger predictor of SWB in younger samples than it was in older samples (the possible roles of gender and age in moderating the link between relationships and happiness will be considered in more detail below). Unfortunately, the meta-analysis by Haring-Hidore et al. (1985) includes only studies published before 1980, and no authoritative meta-analysis on the marital status-SWB relation has appeared since that time.

## Changes in marital status and happiness

Some scholars have argued that analysis of the simple effect of marital status on happiness actually confounds the separate effects of being married relative to being a never-married single with the effect of being married relative to being divorced or widowed (Lucas & Dyrenforth, 2005). Indeed, research has found that the transition from singlehood to marriage is associated with a small increase in SWB (Haring-Hidore et al., 1985; Lucas, 2005; Williams, 2003). By contrast, the experience of divorce or the death of a spouse has a greater adverse effect than the positive effect of being married (Lucas, 2005). Other research has found a steady, linear relationship between various stages of relationship commitment (e.g., moving from singlehood to steady dating to marriage) and happiness (Dush & Amato, 2005).

## Marital quality and happiness

The literature on marital quality and happiness is large, but much of it has focused on how marital quality is related to depression, whereas the role of marital quality in PA and LS has not received as much attention. However, Dush and Amato (2005) compared the effects of marital status and "relationship happiness" (a composite of seven items) on multiple measures of happiness. They found that the correlation of marital status with a single-item global measure of "life happiness" was positive but modest (i.e. $r = 0.15$), whereas relationship happiness had a considerably stronger correlation with life happiness ($r = 0.42$). Similar results were obtained with measures of distress symptoms ($rs = -0.12$ and $-0.32$, respectively).

Proulx, Helms, and Buehler (2007) synthesized findings from 66 cross-sectional and 27 longitudinal studies of marital quality and happiness. They found an average effect of marital quality that was moderate in size for the cross-sectional studies ($r = 0.37$) and smaller but

---

[1] Effect size $d$ is reported when provided by the work cited, but the equivalent effect size $r$ is also provided in order to facilitate comparison with other effect sizes, which are for the most part reported as $r$.

significant in the longitudinal studies ($r = 0.25$). Both of these effects are considerably larger than the 0.07 average effect (in $r$) reported by Haring-Hidore et al. (1985) for marital status. In addition, the relation between marital quality and happiness was moderated by gender, such that the association was stronger for women than for men. Unfortunately, the Proulx et al. (2007) meta-analysis is limited by the scope of the literature search and the particular choice of happiness measures selected for inclusion; specifically, they included depression, anxiety, and symptoms of distress, but not LS, happiness, or PA.

## Marriage and happiness—a summary

The research affirms that there is an association between marital status and happiness, although it is not large. By contrast, the relation between marital quality and happiness is considerably stronger. Moreover, meta-analyses suggest that gender may moderate the effect of the marital relationship on happiness: Marital quality seems to be more closely associated with well-being for women than for men (Proulx et al., 2007). In the next section, we turn our attention to a consideration of such potential moderators of the link between relationships and happiness.

# Moderators of the Effect of Relationships on Happiness

Due to space limitations, our review of moderating variables is not comprehensive but rather serves to highlight a handful of moderators that have received substantial empirical attention: gender, age, and culture. Other potential moderators are also briefly considered.

## Gender

There are theoretical reasons to suggest that relationships may be more important to SWB for women than for men. Drawing on evolutionary theory, the tend-and-befriend model (Taylor, 2002; Taylor et al., 2000) hypothesizes that, because women were historically more involved in the care of dependent, immature offspring, they had greater needs to turn to their social groups in times of threat for joint protection of self and offspring than may have been true for men. As such, women may have developed more awareness of the quality of their social relationships, because of their greater needs to depend upon them.

Consistent with this perspective is a large literature in sociology and social psychology suggesting that relationships are more central to the activities and daily experience of women than men (see Taylor (2002) for a review). Relative to men, adult women maintain more same-sex close relationships, report more benefits from contacts with their female friends and relatives (although they are also more vulnerable to psychological stress resulting from stressful network events), and provide more frequent and more effective social support to others (Ptacek, Smith & Zana, 1992; Thoits, 1995). Moreover, studies in elderly populations have found that older married men rely almost entirely upon their wives for social support, whereas older women report receiving more social support in general and derive their support from a wider range of friends and family members (Antonucci & Akiyama, 1987; Gurung, Taylor & Seeman, 2003; Patrick, Cottrell & Barnes, 2001). Other research has found parallel differences throughout the life course (e.g., Umberson, Chen, House, Hopkins, & Slaten, 1996).

Whether gender differences in social support quality and structure translate into differences in the importance of these variables to happiness is unclear. In a study of older rural residents, Patrick and colleagues (2001) found that family support significantly predicted both PA and NA, over and above the effects of age, marital status, and education, in both men and women. When friend support was added in a subsequent step, only family support significantly predicted PA in men, whereas only the effect of friend support was significant in women (friend support did not significantly affect NA in either gender). However, this result should be interpreted with caution, as both family and friend support had positive effects on PA in both genders. In a similar vein, Antonucci and Akiyama (1987) used 15 measures of support quantity and quality to predict a single-item indicator of global happiness in older adults, accounting for 18% and 23% of the variance in men and women, respectively. With regard to marital quality, recall that the meta-analysis by Haring-Hidore and colleagues (1985) found that men's SWB was more affected by marital status than was women's SWB. Gender moderation of the association between marriage and happiness is found in other studies as well (e.g., Lucas, 2005; Umberson et al., 1996), although results are somewhat inconsistent, including some null findings (e.g., Williams, 2003).

Taken as a whole, the research suggests that the association between the quality of a person's relationships and happiness will differ by gender in a manner consistent with the tend-and-befriend model, specifically, that women's happiness will be more affected by relationship quality than is true for men. In a recent study, the quality of young adults' relationships (as indexed by the MIDUS measures) with their parents, siblings, close friends, and roommates was examined in relation to LS (Saphire-Bernstein, Taylor, Moore, Lam, & Seeman, 2010). For women, the quality of every one of the relationships was highly and significantly related to LS ($rs = 0.26$–$0.46$, mean $r = 0.33$, all $ps < 0.05$), whereas only the quality of close friendships were associated with LS for men ($r = 0.28$, $p < 0.05$; all other $rs = -0.02$ to $0.21$, $ps > 0.05$; mean $r = 0.14$). Gender differences in the magnitudes of these correlations were significant only in some cases, but the trend for a stronger correlation in women was present across all relationship types. The findings of this study, along with the meta-analysis by Proulx et al. (2007), support the assertion that relationships are more important determinants of happiness for women than is true for men.

# Age

Numerous scholars have speculated that the effect of relationships on happiness might be moderated by age. Ishii-Kuntz (1990) proposed that the relative influence of friends on happiness should decline in early adulthood and continue to remain low into early middle age, whereas family relationships should have a much greater influence on happiness during these years; by contrast, relationships with friends may predominate in the determination of happiness by late adulthood, where the influence of relationships with family members on happiness may be reduced. Ishii-Kuntz's rationale for these predictions is that people presumably concentrate on establishing themselves within their occupational and family contexts during early adulthood, whereas older adults may be more concerned with reciprocity in relationships, which is difficult to maintain with family members. Generally speaking, Ishii-Kuntz's (1990) empirical pattern supported these predictions.

## Culture

The effects of cultural variation on happiness has been an interest in the field for some time (for a review see Diener et al., 1999), but whether the presence and quality of relationships have different effects in different cultures has yet to be answered definitively. Kwan, Bond and Singelis (1997) measured the influence of "relationship harmony" and self-esteem on LS in college students from the USA and Hong Kong and found significant positive relations in both groups of about the same magnitude. Similar findings were reported by Kang, Shaver, Sue, Min, and Ying (2003). A cross-cultural study of SWB predictors in 42 countries found that the relationship between marital status and SWB was largely the same across cultures, although the association was moderated somewhat by national differences in individualism-collectivism (Diener, Gohm, Suh, & Oishi, 2000). Thus the available evidence suggests that culture may not strongly influence the association between relationships and happiness.

## Additional moderators of the relationships–happiness link

Other moderators of the association between relationships and happiness link merit consideration as well. The personality trait extraversion may moderate the effect of social relationships on happiness (e.g., Hotard, McFatter, McWhirter, & Stegall, 1989; Srivastava et al., 2008), and Demir (2008) recently found that identity formation moderated the association between relationship quality and SWB among emerging adults such that the correlation was stronger among those at more advanced levels of identity formation. Additional candidates for potential moderators include personal needs, values, goals, income and the successful resolution of developmental tasks.

# FUTURE DIRECTIONS IN THE STUDY OF RELATIONSHIPS AND HAPPINESS

This brief review highlights several important issues relevant to the future of research on relationships and happiness. First, the intuitive prediction that relationships are central to happiness is largely supported in the literature, although the effects are much stronger for quality of relationships than for objective features of relationships, such as number of friends or length of time married. Although shared method variance in the assessment of relationship quality and happiness is likely a contributor to these effects (cf. Lucas & Dyrenforth, 2006; Lucas et al., 2008), they also appear to represent a real contribution of relationship quality to happiness. For example, the robust gender differences in the association between quality of relationships and SWB cannot be explained by shared method variance.

Accordingly, the challenge for future researchers is to find ways to assess quality of relationships and SWB that avoid overlapping variance.

A second conclusion is that, on the whole, there is far more literature devoted to studying the association of the significant other relationship with happiness than to the association of other close relationships with happiness. This is an unfortunate gap, as family and friends are also likely to affect the degree to which people experience happiness. Researchers have recently begun to investigate the effect of friendship quality (Demir & Weitekamp, 2007) and the quality of the relationship with parents in both teens (Gohm, Oishi, Darlington, & Diener, 1998) and adults (Amato & Afifi, 2006) on SWB. However, additional research is needed, especially with regard to the relative and cumulative effects of the quality of different types of relationships on happiness.

Rather than simply documenting that the effects of relationships on happiness are positive, researchers should devote more attention to the parameters of relationships that make them important for happiness. For example, the robust finding in the social support literature that having a single confidante is more important to well-being than having a large number of social relationships should be a strong signal to researchers that there is much still to be learned about the pathways and mechanisms by which relationships affect happiness (see Taylor (2010) for a review).

The available literature makes clear that gender and age are likely to be important moderators of the impact of relationships on happiness. There is a robust gender difference, such that the quality of all relationships appears to matter more for women's happiness than is true for men (e.g., Proulx et al., 2007; Walen & Lachman, 2000; Wan et al., 1996). Although there is some evidence that this gender difference persists across the lifespan (e.g., Antonucci & Akiyama, 1987), changes in the patterns of relationships and their impact on happiness are likely to be found as a function of age as well.

Measurement issues plague the study of relationships and happiness. A disproportionate number of studies focus on how relationships are related to depression and psychological distress, yet PA and LS are also extremely important components of SWB (Diener, 1984; Reis, 2001; Schimmack, 2008), and measures of these constructs have received far less attention. Predictors of happiness may vary in the extent to which they predict these distinct subcomponents. For example, the LS component of SWB appears to be more strongly related to relationship quality than are the affective components of PA and NA (reviewed earlier). The exact reason for this differential relation is not known, as it is not predicted by current theories of SWB. According to the judgment model perspective (Kahneman, 1999), people are often unaware of the true sources of their momentary affective mood states but are likely to explicitly consider important facets of their life when providing retrospective evaluations of their lives as a whole. Thus it is possible that relationships do not have very strong effects on PA and NA but that they are nevertheless given priority in the conscious construction of LS judgments. Moreover, women may be more likely than men to draw on the quality of their existing relationships when considering their life as whole, which might account for the gender differences described previously (cf. Saphire-Bernstein et al., 2010). These issues provide potentially fruitful avenues of investigation for future research.

Direction of causality issues, best examined in longitudinal data, also merit consideration. To what extent does happiness lead people to construe their relationships as satisfying, and to what extent do satisfying relationships lead to happiness? This fundamental question has long been debated in the literature (reviewed in Diener et al., 1999), yet the issue remains far from settled (see Lyubomirsky, King & Diener, 2005). A related question concerns the effects of social networks on an individual's happiness. Fowler and Christakis (2009) recently presented evidence for the spread of happiness in social networks using longitudinal social network data. Future research on the role of network dynamics in the determination of happiness may reveal new and important effects on human happiness and well-being.

## Conclusion

Social relationships, especially intimate relationships, have measurable effects on happiness. Although the effects of objective relationship variables are relatively small, the role of relationship quality in happiness is considerably greater. When it comes to research on relationships and happiness, the outlook is bright and the questions are many. The task before us now is to answer them.

## Acknowledgments

Preparation of this article was supported by a grant from the National Science Foundation (SES-0525713).

## References

Alfonso, V. C., Allison, D. B., Rader, D. E., & Gorman, B. S. (1996). The extended satisfaction with life scale: Development and psychometric properties. *Social Indicators Research, 38,* 275–301.

Amato, P. J., & Afifi, T. D. (2006). Feeling caught between parents: Adult children's relations with parents and subjective well-being. *Journal of Marriage and Family, 68,* 222–235.

Andrews, F. M., & Withey, S. B. (1976). *Social indicators of well-being: Americans' perceptions of life quality.* New York, NY: Plenum.

Antonucci, T. C., & Akiyama, H. (1987). An examination of sex differences in social support among older men and women. *Sex Roles, 17,* 737–749.

Argyle, M. (2001). *The psychology of happiness* (2nd ed.). New York, NY: Routledge.

Baumeister, R. F., & Leary, M. R. (1995). The need to belong: Desire for interpersonal attachments as a fundamental human motivation. *Psychological Bulletin, 117,* 497–529.

Campbell, A., Converse, P. E., & Rodgers, W. L. (1976). *The quality of American life: Perceptions, evaluations, and satisfactions.* New York, NY: Russell Sage Foundation.

Cohen, S., Underwood, L. G., & Gottlieb, B. H. (Eds.). (2000). *Social support measurement and intervention: A guide for health and social scientists.* New York, NY: Oxford University Press.

Cooper, H., Okamura, L., & Gurka, V. (1992). Social activity and subjective well-being. *Personality and Individual Differences, 13,* 573–583.

Demir, M. (2008). Sweetheart, you really make me happy: Romantic relationship quality and personality as predictors of happiness among emerging adults. *Journal of Happiness Studies, 9,* 257–277.

Demir, M. (2010). Close relationships and happiness among emerging adults. *Journal of Happiness Studies, 11*, 293–313.

Demir, M., & Weitekamp, L. A. (2007). I am so happy 'cause today I found my friend: Friendship and personality as predictors of happiness. *Journal of Happiness Studies, 8*, 181–211.

Diener, E. (1984). Subjective well-being. *Psychological Bulletin, 95*, 542–575.

Diener, E., Gohm, C. L., Suh, E., & Oishi, S. (2000). Similarity of the relations between marital status and subjective well-being across cultures. *Journal of Cross-Cultural Psychology, 31*, 419–436.

Diener, E., Suh, E. M., Lucas, R. E., & Smith, H. L. (1999). Subjective well-being: Three decades of progress. *Psychological Bulletin, 125*, 276–302.

Dush, C. M. K., & Amato, P. R. (2005). Consequences of relationship status and quality for subjective well-being. *Journal of Social and Personal Relationships, 22*, 607–627.

Fowler, J. H., & Christakis, N. A. (2009). Dynamic spread of happiness in a large social network: Longitudinal analysis over 20 years in the Framingham heart study. *British Medical Journal, 338*, 23–36.

Furman, W. & Buhrmester, D. (1985). Children's perceptions of the personal relationships in their social networks. *Developmental Psychology, 21*, 1016–1024.

Gallagher, E. N., & Vella-Brodrick, D. A. (2008). Social support and emotional intelligence as predictors of subjective well-being. *Personality and Individual Differences, 44*, 1551–1561.

Gohm, C. L., Oishi, S., Darlington, J., & Diener, E. (1998). Culture, parental conflict, parental marital status, and the subjective well-being of young adults. *Journal of Marriage and Family, 60*, 319–334.

Gurung, R. A. R., Taylor, S. E., & Seeman, T. E. (2003). Accounting for changes in social support among married older adults: Insights from the MacArthur studies of successful aging. *Psychology and Aging, 18*, 487–496.

Haring-Hidore, M., Stock, W. A., Okun, M. A., & Witter, R. A. (1985). Marital status and subjective well-being: A research synthesis. *Journal of Marriage and Family, 4*, 947–953.

Hotard, S. R., McFatter, R. M., McWhirter, R. M., & Stegall, M. E. (1989). Interactive effects of extraversion, neuroticism, and social relationships on subjective well-being. *Journal of Personality and Social Psychology, 57*, 321–331.

Ishii-Kuntz, M. (1990). Social interaction and psychological well-being: Comparison across stages of adulthood. *International Journal of Aging and Human Development, 30*, 15–36.

Kahneman, D. (1999). Objective happiness. In D. Kahneman, E. Diener & N. Schwarz (Eds.), *Well-being: The foundations of hedonic psychology* (pp. 3–25). New York, NY: Russell Sage Foundation.

Kahneman, D., Krueger, A. B., Schkade, D., Schwarz, D., Schwarz, N., & Stone, A. A. (2004). A survey method for characterizing daily life experiences: The day reconstruction method. *Science, 306*, 1776–1780.

Kang, S.-M., Shaver, P. R., Sue, S., Min, K.-H., & Jing, H. (2003). Culture-specific patterns in the prediction of life satisfaction: Roles of emotion, relationship quality, and self-esteem. *Personality and Social Psychology Bulletin, 29*, 1596–1608.

Kwan, V. S. Y., Bond, M. H., & Singelis, T. M. (1997). Pancultural explanations for life satisfaction: Adding relationship harmony to self-esteem. *Journal of Personality and Social Psychology, 73*, 1038–1051.

Lucas, R. E. (2005). Time does not heal all wounds: A longitudinal study of reaction and adaptation to divorce. *Psychological Science, 16*, 945–950.

Lucas, R. E., & Dyrenforth, P. S. (2005). The myth of marital bliss? *Psychological Inquiry, 16*, 111–115.

Lucas, R. E., & Dyrenforth, P. S. (2006). Does the existence of social relationships matter for subjective well-being? In K. D. Vohs & E. J. Finkel (Eds.), *Self and relationships: Connecting intrapersonal and interpersonal processes* (pp. 254–273). New York, NY: Guilford.

Lucas, R. E., Dyrenforth, P. S., & Diener, E. (2008). Four myths about subjective well-being. *Social and Personality Psychology Compass, 2*, 2001–2015.

Lyubomirsky, S., King, L., & Diener, E. (2005). The benefits of frequent positive affect: Does happiness lead to success? *Psychological Bulletin, 131*, 803–855.

Mashek, D. J., & Aron, A. (Eds.). (2004). *Handbook of closeness and intimacy*. Mahwah, NJ: Erlbaum.

Myers, D. G. (2000). The funds, friends, and faith of happy people. *American Psychologist, 55*, 56–67.

Okun, M. A., Stock, W. A., Haring, M. J., & Witter, R. A. (1984). The social activity/subjective well-being relation: A quantitative synthesis. *Research on Aging, 6*, 45–65.

Patrick, J. H., Cottrell, L. E., & Barnes, K. A. (2001). Gender, emotional support, and well-being among the rural elderly. *Sex Roles, 45*, 15–29.

Pinquart, M., & Sörensen, S. (2000). Influences of socioeconomic status, social network, and competence on subjective well-being in later life: A meta-analysis. *Psychology and Aging, 15*, 187–224.

Proulx, C. M., Helms, H. M., & Buehler, C. (2007). Marital quality and personal well-being: A meta-analysis. *Journal of Marriage and Family, 69*, 576–593.

Ptacek, J. T., Smith, R. E., & Zanas, J. (1992). Gender, appraisal, and coping: A longitudinal analysis. *Journal of Personality, 60*, 747–770.

Reis, H. T. (2001). Relationship experiences and emotional well-being. In C. D. Ryff & B. H. Singer (Eds.), *Emotion, social relationships, and health* (pp. 57–86). New York, NY: Oxford University Press.

Saphire-Bernstein, S., Taylor, S. E., Moore, A. N., Lam, S., & Seeman, T. E. (2010). *Is relationship quality related to life satisfaction?* Manuscript under review.

Schimmack, U. (2008). The structure of subjective well-being. In M. Eid & R.J. Larsen (Eds.), *The science of subjective well-being* (pp. 97–123). New York, NY: Guilford.

Schuster, T. L., Kessler, R. C., & Aseltine, R. H. (1990). Supportive interactions, negative interactions, and depressed mood. *American Journal of Community Psychology, 18*, 423–438.

Spanier, G. B. (1976). Measuring dyadic adjustment: New scales for assessing the quality of marriage and similar dyads. *Journal of Marriage and Family, 38*, 15–28.

Srivastava, S., Angelo, K. M., & Vallereux, S. R. (2008). Extraversion and positive affect: A day reconstruction study of person-environment transactions. *Journal of Research in Personality, 42*, 1613–1618.

Taylor, S. E. (2002). *The tending instinct: How nurturing is essential to who we are and how we live*. New York, NY: Holt.

Taylor, S. E. (2010). Social support: A review. In H. S. Friedman (Ed.), *Oxford Handbook of Health Psychology*. New York, NY: Oxford University Press.

Taylor, S. E., Klein, L. C., Lewis, B. P., Gruenewald, T. L., Gurung, R. A. R., & Updegraff, J. A. (2000). Biobehavioral responses to stress in females: Tend-and-befriend, not fight-or-flight. *Psychological Review, 107*, 411–429.

Thoits, P. A. (1995). Stress, coping and social support processes: Where are we? What next? *Journal of Health and Social Behavior, (Extra Issue)*, 53–79.

Umberson, D., Chen, M. D., House, J. S., Hopkins, K., & Slaten, E. (1996). The effect of social relationships on psychological well-being: Are men and women really so different? *American Sociological Review, 61*, 837–857.

Walen, H. R., & Lachman, M. E. (2000). Social support and strain from partner, family, and friends: Costs and benefits for men and women in adulthood. *Journal of Social and Personal Relationships, 17*, 5–30.

Wan, C. K., Jaccard, J., & Ramey, S. L. (1996). The relationship between social support and life satisfaction as a function of family structure. *Journal of Marriage and Family, 58*, 502–513.

Williams, K. (2003). Has the future of marriage arrived? A contemporary examinations of gender, marriage, and psychological well-being. *Journal of Health and Social Behavior, 44*, 470–487.

CHAPTER 61

# ADULT ATTACHMENT AND HAPPINESS: INDIVIDUAL DIFFERENCES IN THE EXPERIENCE AND CONSEQUENCES OF POSITIVE EMOTIONS

MARIO MIKULINCER[1] AND PHILLIP R. SHAVER[2]

[1]School of Psychology, Interdisciplinary Center Herzliya, Israel;
[2]University of California, Davis, USA

"Happiness" is a rather thin hook on which to hang a discussion of attachment theory and research, because the theory concerns far more than a single emotion. Attachment theory was originally designed to explain why separation from or loss of a parent during childhood has such devastating effects on subsequent socioemotional development. In that sense it was part of what might, in retrospect, be called "negative psychology," to distinguish it from today's "positive psychology" (e.g., Seligman, 2002), although it was very positive in explaining the value of secure attachments.

In his campaign to explain the effects of poor or absent parenting, Bowlby (1969/1982), the creator of attachment theory, postulated an "attachment behavioral system"—an innate motivational system that causes a human infant to seek comfort or protection from an "older and wiser" person (*attachment figure*) when the infant is tired, in pain, frightened, or distressed. Achieving a sense of safety and security is, according to the theory, one of life's natural forms of what we might call happiness. But it could equally well be called love, security, gratitude, self-esteem, and any number of other labels for positive emotions.

In this chapter we briefly summarize attachment theory and explain its relevance to a variety of positive emotions. Our discussion is organized around relations between major patterns of attachment, on the one hand, and positive emotions, overall psychological well-being, positive emotions in the context of close relationships, emotional reactions to a relationship partner's happiness, and broaden-and-build consequences of positive emotions.

## Attachment Theory: Basic Concepts

According to attachment theory (Bowlby, 1973), interactions with attachment figures who are available and responsive in times of need facilitate the normal functioning of the attachment behavioral system and promote a stable sense of attachment security. When a person's attachment figures are not reliably available and supportive, however, proximity seeking fails to relieve distress, a sense of attachment security is not attained, and strategies of affect regulation other than proximity seeking (*secondary attachment strategies*, conceptualized in terms of two major dimensions, *anxiety* and *avoidance*) are adopted.

In studies of adolescents and adults, tests of these theoretical ideas have focused on a person's *attachment style*—the systematic pattern of relational expectations, emotions, and behaviors that results from internalization of a particular history of attachment experiences (Shaver & Mikulincer, 2002). Research, beginning with Ainsworth, Blehar, Waters, and Wall (1978) and continuing through recent studies by social and personality psychologists (reviewed by Mikulincer & Shaver, 2007a) indicates that attachment style can be measured in terms of two roughly orthogonal dimensions, attachment-related *anxiety* and *avoidance* (Brennan, Clark, & Shaver, 1998). The anxiety dimension reflects the degree to which a person worries that a partner will not be available in times of need. The avoidance dimension reflects the extent to which a person distrusts relationship partners' good will and strives to maintain behavioral independence and emotional distance. People who score low on both dimensions are said to be secure or to have a secure orientation to attachment. The two dimensions can be measured with reliable and valid self-report scales (e.g., the Experiences in Close Relationships Scale, or ECR; Brennan et al., 1998) and are associated in theoretically predictable ways with relationship quality and adjustment (see Mikulincer and Shaver (2007a) for a review).

In our model of attachment-system dynamics (Mikulincer & Shaver, 2007a), attachment anxiety involves what Cassidy and Kobak (1988) called *hyperactivating strategies*—intense, anxiety-driven efforts to attain closeness and safety. Hyperactivating strategies include attempts to elicit a partner's involvement and support through demanding, clinging, and controlling behaviors; overdependence on relationship partners as a source of security; and perception of oneself as relatively helpless and incompetent at regulating emotions (Mikulincer & Shaver, 2007a). Avoidant attachment is organized around *deactivating strategies* (Cassidy & Kobak, 1988)—defensive attempts to keep the attachment system down-regulated so as not to be further distressed by an attachment figure's frequent unavailability or disapproval of one's needs. Deactivating strategies involve denial of attachment needs and avoidance of emotional involvement, intimacy, or dependency in relationships. They also include the downplaying of threats and the suppression of distressing thoughts and feelings (Mikulincer & Shaver, 2007a).

Hyperactivating and deactivating strategies shape the quality of a person's emotional experiences, both negative and positive. Because the emphasis in the present volume is on happiness, we will mainly review research findings concerning attachment-related individual differences in the experience and consequences of positive emotions.

## Attachment Patterns and the Experience of Positive Emotions

By imparting a sense of safety and security, interactions with available and supportive attachment figures alleviate distress and evoke positive emotions such as relief, love, and gratitude. With repeated positive interactions, the sense of attachment security gradually becomes associated in a person's mind with memories of positive experiences and emotions. As a result, the evocation of mental representations of attachment security by either external or internal stimuli (e.g., the presence of a supportive other, visualizing the face of an attachment figure) automatically causes a person to feel more relaxed, relieved, loved, and happy. Because relatively secure individuals possess this kind of positivity-supporting memory network, they are generally able to maintain emotional balance and clear-headedness even in the face of threats or stressors (Mikulincer & Shaver, 2007a).

In contrast, interactions with unsupportive attachment figures in times of need interfere with the experience of positive emotions. In fact, people who score high on measures of anxious attachment may sometimes amplify their negative emotions in hopes of gaining an attachment figure's attention and support, and in so doing they are likely to view themselves as relatively vulnerable and weak. Avoidant individuals have learned to suppress or downplay emotions (Mikulincer & Orbach, 1995), whether positive or negative, because expressions of emotion are interpreted as invitations to closer relations with other people. In short, although anxious and avoidant strategies are guided by opposite relational goals (intensification versus inhibition of closeness and dependency), both can interfere with positive emotions.

In the following sections, we review research showing that both anxious and avoidant forms of attachment are associated with lower levels of well-being and less frequent or intense positive emotions. We also show how this reduction in positive emotion is manifested in close relationships and, specifically, in response to a partner's experiences and expressions of happiness.

### Attachment patterns and psychological well-being

Several studies have examined associations between attachment patterns and psychological well-being (see Mikulincer and Shaver (2007a) for a review). The findings consistently indicate that whereas attachment security is positively related to overall well-being, both forms of insecure attachment (anxious and avoidant) are inversely related to well-being. These results have been obtained in studies of both community samples and samples of people who were currently coping with unusually stressful events. They have also been obtained in cross-sectional, prospective, longitudinal, and cross-cultural studies (Shaver, Mikulincer, Alonso-Arbiol, & Lavy, 2010).

Some of the studies have compared the psychological well-being of people experiencing stress with that of people who were not under an unusual degree of stress, with the finding that attachment security promotes well-being even during times of stress (e.g., Berant, Mikulincer, & Florian, 2001). That is, stressful events mainly reduce the subjective well-being of insecure individuals, but do not affect people who are secure with respect to attachment. We believe this is the case partly because secure individuals' possess more effective emotion-regulation techniques and partly because they do not doubt their ability to cope, which eliminates a form of internal stress often added to stress imposed from outside. In this way, attachment security is similar to Bandura's (1997) well-known concept of self-efficacy.

## Attachment patterns and positive emotions

Using well-validated priming techniques, Mikulincer, Hirschberger, Nachmias, and Gillath (2001) provided experimental evidence for the hypothesized link between attachment security and positive emotions. They subliminally exposed participants to stimuli related to attachment security (e.g., the names of their security-enhancing attachment figures) or control stimuli (e.g., the names of mere acquaintances). The participants then rated how much they liked a series of Chinese ideographs (i.e., generally neutral stimuli). Security primes, compared with control primes, produced greater liking for the previously unfamiliar Chinese ideographs, suggesting that the security primes projected an aura of positive affect onto the previously neutral stimuli. This effect occurred even in experimentally induced threatening contexts, and it eliminated the otherwise negative effect of threat on liking for the Chinese ideographs.

Measures of attachment anxiety and avoidance have also been correlated with measures of positive affect (e.g., Gilbert et al., 2008; Shiota, Keltner, & John, 2006). For example, several studies have used the Positive and Negative Affect Schedule (PANAS), finding that attachment anxiety and avoidance are associated with lower positive affect scores (e.g., Barry, Lakey, & Orehek, 2007; Wearden, Lamberton, Crook, & Walsh, 2005). Similar associations have been observed in studies examining positive emotions during daily social interactions tracked over one or more weeks (e.g., Pierce & Lydon, 2001; Tidwell, Reis, & Shaver, 1996). In addition, Rom and Mikulincer (2003) found that attachment anxiety and avoidance were associated with fewer positive emotions during group interactions, and Gentzler and Kerns (2006) found that both anxiety and avoidance were associated with lower levels of recall of positive emotions for a positive event experienced during the previous month.

Attachment-related differences in the *experience* of positive emotions have also been noted in studies of the *expression* of positive emotions. For example, Sonnby-Borgstrom and Jonsson (2003) exposed people to pictures of happy and angry faces, assessed the activity of the participants' smile and frown muscles, and found that attachment-anxious individuals had more active "frown" muscles when viewing either happy or angry faces. Magai, Hunziker, Mesias, and Culver (2000) videotaped participants during an emotion-induction procedure and found that avoidant individuals expressed less joy (based on coded facial expressions). Similarly, Spangler and Zimmermann (1999) exposed participants to emotionally provocative film clips and found that avoidant individuals' smile muscles were less active during a comic film. Similar findings have been obtained with self-report measures of expressed positive emotions (e.g., Ducharme, Doyle, & Markiewicz, 2002) and of the bottling-up of positive emotions to conceal them from other people (Feeney, 1995).

In sum, research to date indicates that both dispositional and experimentally induced attachment security is associated with both explicit and implicit measures of positive emotions. This research also indicates that insecure attachment, either anxious or avoidant, tends to interfere with the elicitation, subjective experience, and expression of positive emotions.

## Attachment patterns and positive emotions in close relationships

Attachment researchers have also found that attachment insecurities interfere with the experience of positive emotions in close relationships. For example, Medway, Davis, Cafferty, Chappell, and O'Hearn (1995) found that attachment anxiety and avoidance were inversely associated with wives' expressions of positive emotions when reunited with their husbands following prolonged separations. In another study, Tucker and Anders (1998) videotaped dating couples while they discussed positive aspects of their relationship and found that more avoidant people smiled and laughed less during the conversation.

In two studies, we (Mikulincer, Shaver, & Slav, 2006) explored links between attachment insecurities and gratitude toward a relationship partner. In the first study, participants completed self-report measures of attachment anxiety and avoidance as well as dispositional gratitude, and recalled a specific incident in which they felt grateful to someone. They then rated the extent to which they experienced feelings of security, happiness, and love; narcissistic threats; generosity; a positive outlook on life; distrust of the partner's good will; a sense of inferiority and vulnerability; and feelings of obligation. Avoidant attachment was inversely associated with dispositional gratitude and with feelings of security, happiness/love, and generosity, and it was positively associated with narcissistic threats and distrust when feeling "grateful." Although attachment anxiety was not significantly associated with dispositional gratitude, it was positively related to feeling of security, happiness/love, and generosity, but also to narcissistic threats and feelings of inferiority and obligation. In other words, anxious attachment was associated with ambivalent experiences of gratitude. This is one of many examples of a point we mentioned at the outset of this chapter: Happiness is not a simple or isolated emotion; it often occurs in the context of a complex array of both positive and negative emotions.

In our second study, newlywed couples (both husbands and wives) completed a daily questionnaire each evening for 21 days. In the questionnaire they listed positive and negative behaviors exhibited by their partner on a given day (e.g., "My partner told me he/she loved me"; "I was concerned about some problem, and my partner provided me support and reassurance"; "My partner was inattentive and unresponsive to me"; "My partner criticized me") and rated the extent to which they felt grateful toward him or her that day. For both husbands and wives, avoidant but not anxious attachment predicted lower levels of daily gratitude. Moreover, less avoidant (i.e., more secure) husbands reported greater gratitude on days when they perceived more positive spousal behavior, whereas avoidant husbands reported relatively low levels of gratitude even on days when they noticed their wife's positive behavior. Overall, avoidant attachment was related to lower levels of gratitude even in contexts where gratitude would seem natural.

# Attachment patterns and emotional reactions to a partner's happiness

An important part of close relationships is sharing good feelings (Gottman, 1994), and we have learned that attachment insecurities interfere with this natural process. Here we will focus on ways in which attachment insecurities affect a person's reactions to: (1) *relationship-relevant partner happiness*—cases in which the partner's happiness results from one's own positive behavior (e.g., being available and supportive), and (2) *relationship-irrelevant partner happiness*—cases in which the partner's happiness results from attaining goals outside the relationship (e.g., career-related achievements).

## *Relationship-relevant partner happiness*

When a person's behavior benefits a partner—for example, by meeting the partner's needs and expectations—it can increase the partner's happiness, gratitude, and satisfaction with the relationship. In such cases, the benefactor is also likely to feel good, happy, and self-satisfied, and if he or she takes some credit for the partner's happiness, there is also likely to be a feeling of pride. In contrast, for relatively avoidant individuals, who do not place high priority on their partner's welfare (Mikulincer & Shaver, 2007a), a partner's happiness may not engender the avoidant individuals' own happiness. Similarly, for relatively anxious individuals, who tend to doubt their interpersonal efficacy and lovability (Mikulincer & Shaver, 2007a), engendering a partner's happiness may not result in unadulterated feelings of happiness and pride, because the anxious individuals may not take credit for the good outcome or expect that such good outcomes can be duplicated in the future.

In a study of these possibilities, we (Mikulincer & Shaver, 2005) asked participants to recall and describe (in writing) an episode in which they caused their partner to feel happy. We then asked them to rate the extent to which the recalled episode elicited pride, positive emotions, and distress-related emotions. It turned out that anxious individuals were likely to experience distress rather than happiness or pride in response to their partner's happiness, and avoidant individuals were less likely to express happiness in reaction to a happy partner.

## *Relationship-irrelevant partner happiness*

When one relationship partner feels good about attaining positive outcomes outside the relationship, the most common response in the other partner is what Clark, Fitness, and Brissette (2001) called "empathic happiness." This reaction includes a sense of closeness and common fate, along with joy and admiration for a partner's progress toward his or her goals. However, a partner's accomplishments may not arouse happiness in avoidant individuals, because their tendency to maintain emotional distance may inhibit identification with, and empathic feelings toward, their successful partner. Moreover, anxious individuals may not react with happiness, because they may worry that their successful partner will become interested in more attractive or successful partners, a worry related to anxious individuals' intense fear of separation and abandonment.

These ideas were tested in two studies by Sofer-Roth (2008). In the first study, participants were asked to recall a specific situation in which their partner told them about a personal achievement or a situation in which they expressed happiness because of a particular success, and then to rate the extent to which they felt happy, envious, jealous, or critical toward the partner. Avoidant attachment was negatively correlated with feelings of happiness and positively correlated with envy; attachment anxiety was positively correlated with criticism, jealousy, and envy.

In the second study, Sofer-Roth (2008) asked members of 55 newlywed couples to participate in a video-recorded laboratory interaction. After arriving at the laboratory, one partner (the *disclosing* partner) completed a battery of personality tests and received positive feedback about his or her abilities and skills. Following this positive feedback, the disclosing partner was reunited with the partner and the two were asked to wait together for 5 minutes. During this time, their interaction was video-recorded, and later, two judges independently rated: (1) the extent to which the disclosing partner expressed happiness about the positive feedback he or she received and (2) the extent to which the partner listened attentively to the disclosure and expressed happiness, admiration, boredom, criticism, or envy. After the disclosing partner's expression of happiness was statistically controlled, more avoidant participants were rated by objective judges as less expressive of happiness and admiration and more likely to appear bored. More anxious participants were rated as more envious.

Sofer-Roth (2008) also asked these couples to complete a daily diary questionnaire for 14 consecutive days. Each spouse independently indicated whether something good happened that day (outside the relationship) to his or her partner that caused the partner to feel good. Then, if such an event had occurred, they provided a brief description of it and rated their responses to the partner's good mood that day. More avoidant participants were less likely to feel happy in response to their partners' happiness, and more anxious participants were more likely to react with disapproval or criticism, fear, and envy.

Overall, research indicates that insecurely attached people are likely to experience negative rather than positive emotions in response to a partner's happiness. Although none of the reviewed studies assessed how these negative reactions affected a partner's happiness, we can speculate that such reactions undermine relationship capitalization ("the process of informing another person about the occurrence of a personal positive event and thereby deriving additional benefit from it"; Gable, Reis, Impett, & Asher, 2004, p. 228). In fact, Gable and Reis (2010) have reported that a partner's negative reaction to one's own positive experiences reduces happiness and relationship satisfaction.

# Attachment Patterns and the Psychological Consequences of Positive Emotions

According to the broaden-and-build theory of positive emotions (Fredrickson & Cohn, 2008), these emotions signal that all is going well and one can suspend vigilance and effort regarding potential dangers. This shift results in a more relaxed approach to processing information, which in turn encourages playful exploration, "loosening" of cognitive strategies, greater creativity, and the production of more novel and broad-ranging thoughts and actions. Over time, this broadening of thought and action, according to the theory, results in the amassing of resources that can sustain positive affect, good health, and longevity.

Indeed, research indicates that positive emotions produce wider visual search patterns, more creative problem solving, more inclusive mental categories, and more flexible goals and mindsets (as reviewed by Fredrickson & Cohn, 2008). The experience of positive emotions also predicts subsequent increases in psychological resilience, life satisfaction, and health (e.g., Lyubomirsky, King, & Diener, 2005).

We suspect that these psychological consequences of positive emotions are moderated by attachment orientations and are more likely to be found among people who score high on attachment security (i.e., low on anxiety and avoidance). We (Mikulincer & Shaver, 2007a) already know that such people are open to emotional experiences, relatively creative and exploration-oriented, and open to new information, whether positive or negative in nature (e.g., Mikulincer, 1997). They should find it easy and agreeable to loosen their cognitive strategies after experiencing positive emotions and to engage in carefree processing of information.

In contrast, attachment anxiety is likely to interfere with the broaden-and-build effects of positive emotions, because anxious hyperactivation intensifies the experience of negative emotions, interferes with the experience of positive emotions, and reduces cognitive openness and relaxed exploration (Mikulincer & Shaver, 2007a). As a result, anxious individuals may not react to positive emotions with broader and more creative thoughts and actions. Avoidant attachment may also interfere with the broaden-and-build effects of positive emotions. Although avoidant people defensively attempt to avoid or suppress negative emotions (Mikulincer & Shaver, 2003), the tendency to block emotions in general can interfere with positive emotions, thus limiting the opening and broadening effect of these emotions on cognitive processes. Moreover, avoidant individuals may not look favorably on relaxed cognitive exploration, because they prefer tight control, predictable order, and avoidance of ambiguous or novel stimuli (Mikulincer, 1997). This mindset may interfere with the broaden-and-build benefits of positive emotions.

These ideas received preliminary support in a series of three experiments by Mikulincer and Sheffi (2000). Participants were encouraged to have positive experiences (retrieving a happy memory or watching a brief comedy film) or to experience a neutral condition, and the openness of their semantic categories (e.g., furniture, vehicles) and their ability to solve problems creatively were assessed. As expected, people who scored relatively high on attachment security exhibited the usual broadening effect of positive emotions. Their mental categories became more inclusive and their performance on a creative problem-solving task improved following a positive mood induction. In contrast, no significant effect of the positive mood induction was found on the breadth of avoidant individuals' mental categories or on their creative problem solving, suggesting that their defenses interfered with potentially beneficial effects of the positive manipulation. Interestingly, anxiously attached participants reacted to positive inductions with *less* inclusive categorization and *reduced* creativity. For them, positive emotions may have aroused worries of the "crash" (disappointment) to follow. Only for secure individuals did positive affect have the broaden-and-build effects that Fredrickson and Cohn (2008) championed.

In an unpublished study, we built upon a diary study by Cohn, Fredrickson, Brown, Mikels, and Conway (2009) that examined links between positive emotions, resilience, and life satisfaction. We wanted to see whether attachment insecurities would moderate these links. We had 55 Israeli undergraduates come to a laboratory and complete the ECR (Brennan et al., 1998) and the Satisfaction with Life Scale (Diener, Emmons, Larsen, & Griffin, 1985). They then completed a questionnaire each evening for 21 days, rating on a

7-point scale (1 = *not at all* to 7 = *very much*) the extent to which they experienced ten positive emotions (e.g., joy, interest, love) and ten negative emotions (e.g., anger, fear, guilt) during the day. At the end of the 21-day period, the participants returned to the laboratory and completed the life satisfaction scale again.

Positive and negative emotion scores were calculated for each day and for all 21 days combined. Consistent with previous studies, attachment anxiety and avoidance were inversely related to the level of positive emotion experienced during the 21-day period, $rs$ of $-0.43$ and $-0.36$, $ps < 0.01$. Attachment anxiety was also positively associated with the level of negative emotion, $r(53) = 0.48$, $p < 0.01$. In addition, both attachment anxiety and avoidance were inversely associated with life satisfaction at Times 1 and 2, $rs > -0.30$, all $ps < 0.05$.

Replicating Cohn et al.'s (2009) findings, daily positive emotions across the 21-day period uniquely contributed to increases in life satisfaction between Time 1 and Time 2, $\beta = 0.24$, $p < 0.01$. The contribution of negative emotions was not significant, $\beta = -0.07$. Also as expected, the broadening-and-building effect of positive emotions on life satisfaction was qualified by significant interactions between daily positive emotions, on the one hand, and both attachment anxiety, $\beta = -.27$, $p < 0.01$, and avoidance, $\beta = -0.32$, $p < 0.01$, on the other. The experience of more positive emotions across the 21-day period was significantly associated with increased life satisfaction at Time 2 only when attachment anxiety and avoidance were relatively low ($-1$ standard deviation (SD)), $\beta$s of $0.51$ and $0.56$, $ps < 0.01$, but not when these insecurity scores were relatively high ($+1$ SD), $\beta$s of $-0.03$ and $-0.08$. These findings suggest that positive emotions have a broaden-and-build effect on people who score relatively high on attachment security, but they may not have much effect on people with insecure attachment histories.

# CAN INSECURITY-INDUCED BARRIERS TO LASTING HAPPINESS BE REMOVED?

We would be remiss, especially in a book about happiness, if we left readers suspended over a pit of insecure gloom. Because attachment theory and research have focused attention on early relationship determinants of fairly stable patterns of attachment security or insecurity, the research summarized here may seem to suggest that insecure individuals are doomed to a life without happiness, gratitude, or secure love. Fortunately, that is not the case. First of all, the predictability of security in adult couple relationships from infant–parent security decades earlier is fairly weak (Simpson, Collins, Tran, & Haydon, 2007). Instead of simple stability, there is an identifiable step-by-step path from infancy through childhood and adolescence to young adulthood, with both signs of continuity and considerable openness to change based on close relationship experiences at each stage. Moreover, even within adulthood, insecure individuals who have the benefit of a secure relationship partner, either in marriage or in psychotherapy, can become more secure (Shaver & Mikulincer, 2008).

We have conducted numerous studies (reviewed by Mikulincer & Shaver, 2007b) which show that subliminal and supraliminal security primes of different kinds (e.g., subliminal presentation of the names of people who were designated by participants as security-enhancing attachment figures; visualization of the faces of these figures) can boost the felt security levels of almost all individuals, regardless of attachment anxiety and avoidance scores, allowing them to experience more positive moods, reduce their intolerance of outgroup members, and become more compassionate and humane. It seems likely that longer-term priming interventions could create longer-term beneficial changes in felt security (Carnelley & Rowe, 2007; Gillath, Selcuk, & Shaver, 2008). Thus, we do not wish to suggest that happiness is beyond the reach of insecure individuals. We do suggest, however, that attachment insecurity can interfere with the experience, expression, and benefits of positive emotions, including happiness, if this insecurity is not ameliorated.

# Concluding Remarks

Recently, Lucas and his colleagues (Lucas & Dyrenforth, 2006; Lucas, Dyrenforth, & Diener, 2008) argued that the place of close relationships in theories of happiness has been overstated. Throughout this chapter we have shown, in contrast, that research inspired by attachment theory reveals strong links between a history of good relationships, the consequent development of a secure attachment pattern, and both happiness and a variety of other positive emotional states. Attachment patterns are systematically related to general psychological well-being, positive emotions in the context of close relationships, emotional reactions to a relationship partner's happiness, and the broaden-and-build consequences of positive emotions. Moreover, the effects of attachment patterns are consistent across samples and research methods and can be generalized across cultures (e.g., Shaver et al., 2010). We have also shown that recent studies have begun to show how insecurity can be ameliorated, opening the door to greater and more lasting happiness. Everything we have seen in our own multiyear program of research on attachment suggests that relationships and experiences in relationships are very important in determining the arousal, experience, expression, and consequences of happiness. Future studies should investigate the associations between attachment insecurities, experiences of happiness, reactions to a partner's happiness, and relationship capitalization.

# References

Ainsworth, M. D. S., Blehar, M. C., Waters, E., & Wall, S. (1978). *Patterns of attachment: Assessed in the strange situation and at home.* Hillsdale, NJ: Erlbaum.
Bandura, A. (1997). *Self-efficacy: The exercise of control.* New York, NY: Worth.
Barry, R. A., Lakey, B., & Orehek, E. (2007). Links among attachment dimensions, affect, the self, and perceived support for broadly generalized attachment styles and specific bonds. *Personality and Social Psychology Bulletin, 33,* 340–353.
Berant, E., Mikulincer, M., & Florian, V. (2001). The association of mothers' attachment style and their psychological reactions to the diagnosis of infant's congenital heart disease. *Journal of Social and Clinical Psychology, 20,* 208–232.
Bowlby, J. (1973). *Attachment and loss: Vol. 2. Separation: Anxiety and anger.* New York, NY: Basic Books.
Bowlby, J. (1982). *Attachment and loss: Vol. 1. Attachment* (2nd ed.). New York, NY: Basic Books. (Original work published 1969).

Brennan, K. A., Clark, C. L., & Shaver, P. R. (1998). Self-report measurement of adult romantic attachment: An integrative overview. In J. A. Simpson & W. S. Rholes (Eds.), *Attachment theory and close relationships* (pp. 46–76). New York, NY: Guilford Press.

Carnelley, K. B., & Rowe, A. C. (2007). Repeated priming of attachment security influences later views of self and relationships. *Personal Relationships, 14*, 307–320.

Cassidy, J., & Kobak, R. R. (1988). Avoidance and its relationship with other defensive processes. In J. Belsky & T. Nezworski (Eds.), *Clinical implications of attachment* (pp. 300–323). Hillsdale, NJ: Erlbaum.

Clark, M. S., Fitness, J., & Brissette, I. (2001). Understanding people's perceptions of relationships is crucial to understanding their emotional lives. In G. Fletcher & M. Clark (Eds.), *Blackwell handbook of social psychology: Interpersonal processes* (pp. 253–278). Oxford, UK: Blackwell Publishers.

Cohn, M. A., Fredrickson, B. L., Brown, S. L., Mikels, J. A., & Conway, A. M. (2009). Happiness unpacked: Positive emotions increase life satisfaction by building resilience. *Emotion, 9*, 361–368.

Diener, E., Emmons, R. A., Larson, R. J., & Griffin, S. (1985). The satisfaction with life scale: A measure of life satisfaction. *Journal of Personality Assessment, 49*, 1–5.

Ducharme, J., Doyle, A. B., & Markiewicz, D. (2002). Attachment security with mother and father: Associations with adolescents' reports of interpersonal behavior with parents and peers. *Journal of Social and Personal Relationships, 19*, 203–231.

Feeney, J. A. (1995). Adult attachment and emotional control. *Personal Relationships, 2*, 143–159.

Fredrickson, B. L., & Cohn, M. A. (2008). Positive emotions. In M. Lewis, J. Haviland, & L. F. Barrett (Eds.), *Handbook of emotions* (3rd ed., pp. 777–796). New York, NY: Guilford Press.

Gable, S. L., & Reis, H. T. (2010). Good news! Capitalizing on positive events in an interpersonal context. In M. P. Zanna (Ed.), *Advances in experimental social psychology*. New York, NY: Academic Press.

Gable, S. L., Reis, H. T., Impett, E., & Asher, E. R. (2004). What do you do when things go right? The intrapersonal and interpersonal benefits of sharing positive events. *Journal of Personality and Social Psychology, 87*, 228–245.

Gentzler, A. L., & Kerns, K. A. (2006). Adult attachment and memory of emotional reactions to negative and positive events. *Cognition and Emotion, 20*, 20–42.

Gilbert, P., McEwan, K., Mitra, R., Franks, L., Richter, A., & Rockliff, H. (2008). Feeling safe and content: A specific affect regulation system? Relationship to depression, anxiety, stress, and self-criticism. *The Journal of Positive Psychology, 3*, 182–191.

Gillath, O., Selcuk, E., & Shaver, P. R. (2008). Moving toward a secure attachment style: Can repeated security priming help? *Social and Personality Compass, 2*, 1651–1666.

Gottman, J. M. (1994). *What predicts divorce? The relationship between marital processes and marital outcomes*. Hillsdale, NJ: Erlbaum.

Lucas, R. E., & Dyrenforth, P. S. (2006). Does the existence of social relationships matter for subjective well-being? In K. D. Vohs & E. J. Finkel (Eds.), *Self and relationships: Connecting intrapersonal and interpersonal processes* (pp. 254–273). New York, NY: Guilford Press.

Lucas, R. E., Dyrenforth, P. S., & Diener, E. (2008). Four myths about subjective well-being. *Social and Personality Psychology Compass, 2*, 2001–2015.

Lyubomirsky, S., King, L. A., & Diener, E. (2005). The benefits of frequent positive affect. *Psychological Bulletin, 131*, 803–855.

Magai, C., Hunziker, J., Mesias, W., & Culver, L. (2000). Adult attachment styles and emotional biases. *International Journal of Behavioral Development, 24,* 301–309.

Medway, F. J., Davis, K. E., Cafferty, T. P., Chappell, K. D., & O'Hearn, R. E. (1995). Family disruption and adult attachment correlates of spouse and child reactions to separation and reunion due to Operation Desert Storm. *Journal of Social and Clinical Psychology, 14,* 97–118.

Mikulincer, M. (1997). Adult attachment style and information processing: Individual differences in curiosity and cognitive closure. *Journal of Personality and Social Psychology, 72,* 1217–1230.

Mikulincer, M., Hirschberger, G., Nachmias, O., & Gillath, O. (2001). The affective component of the secure base schema: Affective priming with representations of attachment security. *Journal of Personality and Social Psychology, 81,* 305–321.

Mikulincer, M., & Orbach, I. (1995). Attachment styles and repressive defensiveness: The accessibility and architecture of affective memories. *Journal of Personality and Social Psychology, 68,* 917–925.

Mikulincer, M., & Shaver, P. R. (2003). The attachment behavioral system in adulthood: Activation, psychodynamics, and interpersonal processes. In M. P. Zanna (Ed.), *Advances in experimental social psychology* (Vol. 35, pp. 53–152). New York, NY: Academic Press.

Mikulincer, M., & Shaver, P. R. (2005). Attachment theory and emotions in close relationships: Exploring the attachment-related dynamics of emotional reactions to relational events. *Personal Relationships, 12,* 149–168.

Mikulincer, M., & Shaver, P. R. (2007a). *Attachment in adulthood: Structure, dynamics, and change.* New York, NY: Guilford Press.

Mikulincer, M., & Shaver, P. R. (2007b). Boosting attachment security to promote mental health, prosocial values, and inter-group tolerance. *Psychological Inquiry, 18,* 139–156.

Mikulincer, M., Shaver, P. R., & Slav, K. (2006). Attachment, mental representations of others, and gratitude and forgiveness in romantic relationships. In M. Mikulincer & G. S. Goodman (Eds.), *Dynamics of romantic love: Attachment, caregiving, and sex* (pp. 190–215). New York, NY: Guilford Press.

Mikulincer, M., & Sheffi, E. (2000). Adult attachment style and cognitive reactions to positive affect: A test of mental categorization and creative problem solving. *Motivation and Emotion, 24,* 149–174.

Pierce, T., & Lydon, J. (2001). Global and specific relational models in the experience of social interactions. *Journal of Personality and Social Psychology, 80,* 613–631.

Rom, E., & Mikulincer, M. (2003). Attachment theory and group processes: The association between attachment style and group-related representations, goals, memories, and functioning. *Journal of Personality and Social Psychology, 84,* 1220–1235.

Seligman, M. E. P. (2002). *Authentic happiness: Using the new positive psychology to realize your potential for lasting fulfillment.* New York, NY: Free Press.

Shaver, P. R., & Mikulincer, M. (2008). Augmenting the sense of security in romantic, leader-follower, therapeutic, and group relationships: A relational model of psychological change. In J. P. Forgas & J. Fitness (Eds.), *Social relationships: Cognitive, affective, and motivational processes* (pp. 55–74). New York, NY: Psychology Press.

Shaver, P. R., Mikulincer, M., Alonso-Arbiol, I., & Lavy, S. (2010). Assessment of adult attachment across cultures: Conceptual and methodological considerations. In P. Erdman, K.-M. Ng, & S. Metzger (Eds.), *Attachment: Expanding the cultural connections* (pp. 89–108). New York, NY: Routledge/Taylor & Francis.

Shiota, M. N., Keltner, D., & John, O. P. (2006). Positive emotion dispositions differentially associated with big five personality and attachment style. *The Journal of Positive Psychology, 1*, 61–71.

Simpson, J. A., Collins, W. A., Tran, S., & Haydon, K. C. (2007). Attachment and the experience and expression of emotions in romantic relationships: A developmental perspective. *Journal of Personality and Social Psychology, 92*, 355–367.

Sofer-Roth, S. (2008). *Adult attachment and the nature of responses to a romantic partner's expression of personal happiness.* Unpublished PhD Dissertation. Bar-Ilan University, Ramat Gan, Israel.

Sonnby-Borgstrom, M., & Jonsson, P. (2003). Models-of-self and models-of-others as related to facial muscle reactions at different levels of cognitive control. *Scandinavian Journal of Psychology, 44*, 141–151.

Spangler, G., & Zimmermann, P. (1999). Attachment representation and emotion regulation in adolescents: A psychobiological perspective on internal working models. *Attachment and Human Development, 1*, 270–290.

Tidwell, M. C. O., Reis, H. T., & Shaver, P. R. (1996). Attachment, attractiveness, and social interaction: A diary study. *Journal of Personality and Social Psychology, 71*, 729–745.

Tucker, J. S., & Anders, S. L. (1998). Adult attachment style and nonverbal closeness in dating couples. *Journal of Nonverbal Behavior, 22*, 109–124.

Wearden, A. J., Lamberton, N., Crook, L., & Walsh, V. (2005). Adult attachment, alexithymia, and symptom reporting: An extension to the four category model of attachment. *Journal of Psychosomatic Research, 58*, 279–288.

# CHAPTER 62

# PERCEIVED SOCIAL SUPPORT AND HAPPINESS: THE ROLE OF PERSONALITY AND RELATIONAL PROCESSES

BRIAN LAKEY

Grand Valley State University, USA

A large literature indicates that people who perceive their family and friends as supportive have lower levels of psychological distress and disorder than those who doubt the supportiveness of their social networks. Given these findings, one might expect that support perceptions are also linked to happiness, and newly emerging research indicates that this is so. Yet, to what extent does the link between perceived support and happiness reflect the personality of support recipients and to what extent does the link reflect social influences? If social influences are important, to what extent does the link reflect the beneficial effects of objectively supportive providers? To what extent does the link reflect unique relationships between specific recipients and providers? As reviewed in this chapter, perceived support primarily reflects unique relationships but recipient personality also plays an important role. Surprisingly, the objectively supportive properties of providers appear to contribute relatively little to perceived support. This chapter reviews several theories that might explain perceived support's link to happiness when the link reflects unique relationships as well as when the link reflects trait-like characteristics of support recipients.

Perceived social support reflects people's subjective judgments about the availability of help from friends and family during times of need, as well as people's satisfaction with help received in the past (Lakey & Cohen, 2000). Perceived support is commonly operationalized using items such as those from Cutrona and Russell's (1987) widely-used *Social Provisions Scale*: "There are people I can depend on to help me if I really need it" and "I have close relationships that provide me with a sense of emotional security and well-being."

Perceived support is only moderately linked to measures of support actually received (i.e., enacted support) and is typically unrelated to measures of social integration, such as network size (Barrera, 1986; Bolger, Zuckerman, & Kessler, 2000; Lakey & Cohen, 2000).

## Perceived Support is Related to Emotional Well-Being and Happiness

Historically, research on perceived support has focused on explaining psychological distress and disorder, and this research consistently shows that people with high perceived support have lower levels of distress (Barrera, 1986; Cohen & Wills, 1985) and disorder (Lakey & Cronin, 2008; Ozer, Best, Lipsey, & Weiss, 2003) than do people with low support. Perceived support has also been consistently linked to happiness, defined as including positive evaluations of one's life (i.e., life satisfaction), high positive affect, and low negative affect (Diener, Suh, Lucas, & Smith, 1999). In contrast, enacted support and social integration are not generally associated with emotional well-being (Barrera, 1986; Bolger et al., 2000; Lakey & Cohen, 2000). The focus of the current chapter is on the links between perceived support and life satisfaction, as well as positive affect.

The link between perceived support and life satisfaction is typically in the $r = 0.20–0.40$ range. This has been observed across varied populations including college students (Diener & Fujita, 1995), community residents (Gallagher & Vella-Brodrick, 2008; Lawler-Row & Piferi, 2006), spinal cord injured patients (Hampton, 2003), patients with multiple sclerosis (Ryan, Rapport, Sherman, Hanks, Lisak, & Khan, 2007), geriatric rehabilitation patients (Wahl, Martin, Minnemann, & Marin, 2001) and caregivers of brain-injured patients (Ergh, Hanks, Rapport, & Coleman, 2003). The link has also been found across age groups including young adults (Diener & Fujita, 1995) and the elderly (Jones, Rapport, Hanks, Lichtenberg, & Telmet, 2003; Wahl et al., 2001), as well as in different countries such as Australia (Gallagher & Vella-Brodrick, 2008), Germany (Wahl et al., 2001), Pakistan (Suhail & Chaudhry, 2004), and the USA (Ergh et al., 2003; Jones et al., 2003; Lawler-Row & Piferi, 2006; Ryan et al., 2007). The link is robust across a range of measures such as Cutrona and Russell's (1987) *Social Provisions Scale* and Diener, Emmons, Larsen, & Griffin's (1985) *Satisfaction with Life Scale*. Importantly, a number of studies have found that the link remains significant even when other relevant variables (e.g., personality; illness severity) are controlled (Ergh et al., 2003; Gallagher & Vella-Brodrick, 2008; Hampton, 2003; Wahl et al., 2001).

Perceived support is also reliably linked to positive affect with correlations typically in the range of $r = 0.20–0.40$. As with life satisfaction, the link has been observed across a variety of populations including student (Diener & Fujita, 1995; Dunkley, Zuroff & Blankstein, 2003; Finch, 1998; Lakey, Tardiff, & Drew, 1994) and community samples in Australia (Gallagher & Vella-Brodrick, 2008), Canada (Nelson, 1990), England (Armitage & Harris, 2006), and the USA (Zautra, 1983), as well as among Asian American students (Lee, Su & Yoshida, 2005), Mexican-Americans (Holtzman & Gilbert, 1987), and community dwelling elderly (Jones et al., 2003; Robinson-Whelen, Tada, MacCallum, McGuire, & Kiecolt-Glaser, 2001). The link has also been observed in special populations such as young (16 years) Australian caregivers (Pakenham, Chiu, Bursnall, & Cannon, 2008) and adolescents in mental health treatment (McCaskill & Lakey, 2000). One exception is Curtis, Groarke, Coughlan, and Gsel (2004) who did not find the link in a sample of 52 Irish women with rheumatoid arthritis. As with life satisfaction, the link was observed with a number of different measures of perceived support, and several different measures of positive affect.

In conclusion, just as previous research has shown that perceived support is consistently linked to low psychological distress and low rates of psychological disorder, research also shows that people with high perceived support are happier than people with low perceived support. This conclusion might appear to contradict Lucas and Dyrenforth's (2006) view that the link between personal relationships and happiness has been overstated. However, it is important to note that these authors did not review the social support literature and instead focused on the presence or absence of personal relationships (e.g., marital status)—variables that are typically less strongly associated with emotional well-being than are measures of perceived support (Barrera, 1986; Bolger et al., 2000; Lakey & Cohen, 2000).

# The Role of Personality and Social Processes

Many social support researchers assume that the link between perceived support and happiness reflects social processes whereby interacting with specific support providers promotes happiness. However, the link also might reflect the trait-like personality characteristics of support recipients. That is, some people might be dispositionally happy and perceive others as supportive, regardless of their social interactions.

Unfortunately, the typical research design used in social support research cannot adequately distinguish between recipient personality and social processes. Consider the following questionnaire items: "It helps to turn to my romantic partner in times of need," and "I usually discuss my problems and concerns with my partner." Social support researchers would generally interpret responses to these items as reflecting the supportiveness of the respondents' partners, since these items are virtually identical to those on measures of perceived support. In contrast, attachment researchers would generally interpret responses to these items as reflecting the trait-like attachment styles of respondents. In fact, the items in question are from an adult romantic attachment measure (Fraley, Waller, & Brennan, 2000). Thus, the interpretation of whether responses to items reflect recipient personality or social processes appears to depend largely upon the theoretical preferences of the observers. This is not optimal, because if social support researchers want to study social influences and not recipient personality, it is essential to have methods that can clearly distinguish between the two.

Historically, investigators have attempted to isolate trait and social processes in social support in two ways. One approach has been to measure and control for recipient personality by using conventional personality measures. For example, an investigator might estimate the link between perceived support and happiness while controlling for participants' scores on measures of neuroticism or extroversion. Finding that the link between perceived support and happiness remains significant even when personality is controlled might lead to the conclusion that the link likely reflects social processes, because personality measures could not account for the link. Such an argument relies upon the assumption that personality measures reflect trait-like individual differences exclusively and this assumption is very likely wrong. Traditional personality measures also reflect social influences (Hendriks, 1996; Paulhus & Reynolds, 1995), and therefore by controlling for personality, one controls for trait and social influences, rather than trait influences alone.

A second approach has been to study social interaction. For example, an investigator might observe the support provided by one friend to another during a laboratory stressor. The investigator might observe that the providers who were rated as more supportive by observers actually provided more advice and that this advice forecasted recipients' problem solving performance in a subsequent task. The investigator might conclude that social processes have been isolated because social interaction was observed. However, one cannot rule out the possibility that recipients who elicited advice from their friends might have elicited advice from anyone, and that these recipients would have displayed good problem solving performance even if alone. In other words, even when social interactions are observed, one cannot rule out the possibility that social interactions reflect the trait-like personality characteristics of recipients.

An alternative approach to isolating trait and social processes is provided by generalizability (G) theory (Cronbach, Gleser, Nanda, & Rajaratnam, 1972) and the Social Relations Model (SRM; Kenny, 1994; Kenny, Kashy, & Cook, 2006). When recipients rate the same support providers, these methods can isolate recipient trait, provider, and relational influences. Recipient trait influences reflect the extent to which recipients differ in how supportive they see providers, averaged across providers. For example, on average, Andy sees providers as more supportive than does Mark. Provider influences reflect the extent to which recipients agree that providers differ in their supportiveness. For example, on average, recipients might agree that Kate is more supportive than Carol. Provider influences are identical to inter-rater agreement and thus reflect the extent to which supportiveness is an objective property of providers, insofar as inter-rater agreement is an appropriate index of objectivity. Relational influences reflect the extent to which recipients systematically disagree about the relative supportiveness of providers. For example, Mark might see Kate as more supportive than Carol and Andy might see Carol as more supportive than Kate. Relational influences reflect the extent to which supportiveness is a matter of personal taste, in the same way that art or music appreciation is a matter of taste. Although the definitions of recipient, provider, and relational influences are described in words here, their definitions within G/SRM approaches are quantitative. Quantitative definitions have a number of advantages, including defining influences so that they are unambiguously distinct (i.e., orthogonal) and permitting the estimation of their relative magnitudes.

The first estimates of the extent to which perceived support reflects recipient, provider, and relational influences were provided by Lakey, McCabe, Fisicaro, and Drew (1996). In Study 1, 43 Ph.D. students in clinical psychology rated four core faculty members on supportiveness. In Study 2, 51 sorority sisters rated five randomly-selected sisters. Correcting for measurement error and averaging across the two studies, 13% of the variance in perceived support reflected recipient trait influences, 15% reflected providers' objective supportiveness, and 72% reflected the unique relationships between specific recipients and providers.

Branje, van Aken, & van Lieshout (2002) studied 274 Dutch four-person families, in which each family member served in a specific family role (e.g., mother, father, offspring) and rated every other family member on supportiveness. Branje et al. (2002) divided relationship influences into 12 subcomponents (e.g., relational influences when mothers rated fathers or when older offspring rated younger offspring), provider influences into four subcomponents (e.g., when mothers were providers), and recipient influences into four subcomponents (e.g., when recipients were mothers). Combining the respective subcomponents, recipient influences accounted for 34% of the variance in perceived support, provider influences accounted for 3% and relational influences accounted for 59%. Thus, using a different type of sample and estimation procedure, Branje et al. (2002) substantially replicated Lakey et al. (1996) in showing that perceived support primarily reflected unique relationships as well as recipient traits to a lesser extent. The objectively supportive properties of providers accounted for surprisingly little variance. The same pattern of findings was reported in Lanz, Tagliabue, and Rosnati's study (2004) of Italian families and in Giblin and Lakey's (2010; Study 2) investigation of medical fellows rating fellowship faculty.

Weighing each study's estimates by the number of dyads in each study, and correcting for measurement error, Lakey (2010) estimated that relational influences account for 62% of the variance in perceived support, recipient trait influences 27%, and provider influences 7% (families accounted for 2%). Thus, when recipients rate a specific provider on an item such as "I usually discuss my problems and concerns with my partner" surprisingly little reflects the provider's objective supportiveness, nearly one-third reflects recipients' trait-like propensity to see others as supportive and nearly two-thirds reflects the unique relationship between specific recipients, and specific providers.

One limitation of the studies just described is that in evaluating fellow sorority members or immediate family members, recipients did not necessarily rate their most important support providers. Other studies have allowed recipients to rate their most important providers (Lakey & Scorboria, 2005), their mothers, fathers, and romantic partners (Barry, Lakey, & Orehek, 2007) or their mothers, fathers, and closest peers (Lakey, Orehek, Hain, & VanVleet, 2010). The disadvantage of these studies' designs was that because recipients rated different providers, it was not possible to separate provider and relational influences. Instead, provider and relational influences were combined into a single, social influences component. Across the 2500 dyads in the seven samples described by these studies, and after correcting for measurement error, 21% of the variance in perceived support reflected recipient influences and 79% reflected social influences.

## To what Extent does Happiness Reflect Trait and Social Processes?

Recent theory has conceptualized happiness as reflecting both a stable, trait-like set point, as well as fluctuations due to environmental influences (Diener et al., 1999; Headey & Wearing, 1989; Lyubomirsky & Sheldon, 2005). G and SRM analyses are ideal for isolating and studying these two types of influences. When recipients rate their happiness while in the presence of different providers, one can estimate the relative strength of trait and social influences on happiness. For example, in the same seven samples just described (Barry et al., 2007; Lakey et al. 2010; Lakey & Scoboria, 2005), recipients rated positive affect when with or thinking about important network members. Positive affect was more trait-like (44% of the variance) than was perceived support, but positive affect was also substantially socially influenced (56%). These averages were weighed by the number of dyads in each sample and corrected for measurement error.

Given that perceived support and positive affect are composed of both trait and social influences, to what extent does the often observed correlation between perceived support and positive affect reflect the trait-like characteristics of recipients as well as social influences? It is important to estimate correlations separately for both trait and social influences because the same two constructs can have different correlations depending upon which influence is analyzed. For example, Barry et al. (2007) found that attachment avoidance was unrelated to affect when the link reflected trait influences, but the two constructs were strongly linked when correlations reflected social influences. Similarly, Lakey et al. (2010) found that enacted support was linked to more negative affect when correlations reflected trait influences, but to less negative affect when correlations reflected social influences. In Barry et al. (2007), Lakey et al., (2010), and Lakey and Scoboria (2005), perceived support was linked to positive affect in every sample for both trait and social influences. The average correlations between perceived support and positive affect, corrected for measurement error and weighed by the number of dyads, were 0.53 and 0.62 for trait and social influences, respectively. Thus, that people with high perceived support are happier than people with low perceived support reflects both the trait-like predispositions of support recipients, as well as the effect of interacting with or thinking about important network members.

The studies just described are important because they are among the first to examine the link between perceived support and positive affect separately for both trait and social influences. Nonetheless, these studies have limitations. First, they asked recipients to estimate their typical positive affect when interacting with or thinking about different support providers. Recipients' judgments of typical affect might not correspond well to recipients' experiences when actually interacting with providers. Second, they confounded relational and provider influences in the same social influences component. It is important to verify that perceived support and positive affect are linked for relational influences specifically.

In two studies, (Neely et al., 2006; Veenstra et al., 2011) recipients had multiple conversations with the same providers, thus permitting estimation of both provider and relational influences. Recipients rated their own positive affect and providers' supportiveness immediately after each conversation. In both studies, perceived support and positive affect were significantly and strongly correlated for both trait ($\rho = 0.78$ and $0.50$) and relational influences ($\rho = 0.78$ and $0.77$). There were no significant provider influences.

To summarize, perceived support primarily reflects the unique relationships among specific recipients and providers, but also reflects the trait-like dispositions of recipients. Providers' objectively supportive properties play only a small role. Consistent with recent theory on happiness, a portion of happiness remains stable over time and across situations, whereas an equally large portion ebbs and flows depending upon with whom one is interacting. A specific recipient's perception of a specific provider's supportiveness is an excellent marker of the extent to which that provider will elicit high or low happiness in that recipient.

# Theoretical Perspectives on the Link Between Perceived Support and Happiness

## Stress and coping social support theory

The dominant theory in social support research is an extension of Lazarus and colleague's stress and coping theory (Lazarus and Folkman, 1984). According to this view (Cohen & Wills, 1985; Cutrona & Russell, 1990; Thoits, 1986), specific supportive actions provided by friends and family (i.e. enacted support), protect people from the ill effects of stressful life events (i.e., stress buffering) by promoting recipients' effective appraisal and coping. Perceived support reflects a history of having received effective enacted support.

Although stress and coping social support theory has generated a large research literature, the theory has some empirical limitations. First, although the direct link between perceived support and low distress is easily replicable, stress buffering effects are less so (Lakey & Cronin, 2008). Second, enacted support has not been consistently linked to low distress (Barrera, 1986; Bolger et al., 2000). Third, there is surprisingly little evidence that social support influences appraisal and coping (Lakey & Cohen, 2000). In addition to these empirical limitations, stress and coping social support theory's emphasis on stressful events might make it less applicable to happiness specifically as stressful events are primarily implicated in psychological distress and are often unrelated to positive affect (Headey & Wearing, 1989).

## Capitalization support

Gable and Reis (2010) have described an alternative approach to understanding social support and happiness that focuses on network members' responses to recipients' positive events (Gable & Reis, 2010). Capitalization support is hypothesized to promote well-being by enhancing positive affect and thought about both the positive event, as well as the relationship between the recipient and provider (Gable & Reis, 2010). Capitalization support appears to have good potential for explaining social support's link to happiness, because positive events are more closely linked to positive emotions than are negative events (Gable & Reis, 2010). Preliminary evidence for the role of capitalization support in happiness is promising. For example, capitalization support has been linked to greater positive affect, beyond the effects of the positive events themselves, as well as to greater relationship intimacy and satisfaction (Gable & Ries, 2010).

## Relational regulation theory

Another approach to understanding perceived support's link to happiness is relational regulation theory (RRT; Lakey & Orehek, 2011). RRT was derived inductively from two sets of findings: perceived support's link to emotional well-being does not appear to result primarily from stress and coping processes, and perceived support is primarily relational. RRT focuses on how people regulate their happiness through ordinary, yet affectively consequential conversation and shared activities. RRT hypothesizes that people vary substantially in the extent to which positive affect is elicited by specific other people, activities (e.g., work, sport), ideas (e.g., music, religion), things (e.g., cars, clothes) and animals (e.g., dog, cats). That is, positive affect is largely relational. A conversation or activity that makes one person happy makes another miserable. In conversation, recipients and providers talk about aspects of their lives that elicit uniquely favorable affect in both of them. In addition, recipients and providers share activities that elicit favorable affect in both of them. Thus, according to RRT, when a recipient rates a specific provider as supportive, this indicates that the provider is successful in helping regulate the recipient's affect through ordinary, yet affectively consequential conversation and shared activities.

Much of the evidence for RRT has already been reviewed in this chapter. Perceived social support is strongly relational as is the link between perceived support and positive affect. Other evidence is consistent with the theory. For example, RRT predicts that conversations will be most effective in regulating affect when people have similar patterns of affective responses to different aspects of their lives. Thus, perceived support should be linked to recipients' perceptions of their similarity to providers on attitudes, values, and activity preferences. In fact, perceived similarity is very strongly linked to perceived support specifically for relational influences (Neely et al., 2006).

# Trait Processes in the Link between Perceived Support and Happiness

## Genetic influences

Part of the reason why dispositionally happy people have high perceived support might be because perceived support and happiness are partly caused by the same genes. In fact, at least two studies provide evidence for genetic influences on perceived support. Kendler (1997) assessed over 2000 female twins in the USA on a range of perceived support measures and found strong effects for additive genetic and idiosyncratic environmental influences. Bergeman, Plomin, Pedersen, and McClearn (1991) studied over 400 Swedish twins and also found strong genetic and idiosyncratic environmental influences. Most interesting, Bergeman et al. (1991) found that part of the correlation between perceived support and life satisfaction reflected shared genetic influence.

## Information processing

Another reason why people with dispositionally high perceived support are dispositionally happy might be that such people are biased to interpret novel supportive actions and people as supportive (Lakey & Cassady, 1990). Studies testing interpretive biases ask participants to interpret standardized social support stimuli. Across a number of different investigative teams and types of samples, high perceived support people consistently interpreted standardized supportive stimuli more positively than did low perceived support participants (see Lakey (2010) for a review).

## Attachment processes

Several investigators have developed attachment theory models of social support (Collins, Guichard, Ford, & Feeney, 2004; Sarason, Pierce, & Sarason, 1990). In brief, attachment theory hypothesizes that interactions with primary caregivers in early childhood lead children to derive theories of themselves as deserving of care and other people as responsive. These theories become semi-permanent personality characteristics that exert life-long influences on close relationships. People with secure attachment styles develop more supportive relationships than people with insecure attachment styles, as a result of recipients' cognitive biases and social skills. For example, Anan and Barnett (1999) followed inner-city children over 2 years. Insecurely attached children showed more maladjustment, lower perceived support and negative interpretive biases at follow-up than did securely attached children. In adult romantic relationships, securely and insecurely attached romantic partners differed in expected ways in support seeking, support provision and support interpretation (Collins et al., 2004).

# IMPLICATIONS FOR INTERVENTION AND RESEARCH

The research reviewed in this chapter has a number of implications for research and intervention. One implication for research is that when studying social support and happiness, investigators should include perceived support measures given that perceived support is more strongly linked to emotional well-being than is enacted support or the presence of relationships. More importantly, unless G/SRM approaches are used, investigators should remember that perceived support reflects a blend of recipient traits as well as social influences and thus correlations between perceived support and happiness cannot be interpreted as reflecting social influences alone. Regarding interventions, it might be more effective to focus on the relational aspect of perceived support, as this aspect is the strongest determinant of perceived support and is linked strongly to happiness. Interventions designed to harness relational influences would be designed differently than interventions designed to harness recipient or provider influences (Lakey, 2010). Most social support interventions have been guided by the assumption that provider influences are strong. That is, objectively-supportive providers are made available to at-risk individuals. Yet, as described in this chapter, there is little in the way of objectively supportive providers. Perhaps it is not surprising that social support interventions following this rationale have not been especially effective (Hogan, Linden, & Najarian, 2002). Alternatively, relational interventions require matching specific providers with specific recipients such that unusually supportive relationships naturally emerge.

# SUMMARY AND CONCLUSIONS

People who perceive their family and friends as supportive are happier than people who doubt the supportiveness of their network members and this link reflects both the trait-like qualities of support recipients as well as the unique relationships between specific support providers and recipients. These findings fit with recent theory that describes happiness as composed of a portion that remains stable over time and across situations, as well as a portion that ebbs and flows depending upon social context. Recipients' perceptions of providers' supportiveness is an excellent marker of the extent to which a specific provider will elicit high or low happiness in a specific recipient. As defined in G/SRM approaches, trait and relational influences are independent and thus one needs separate theories to explain each. For example, genetic, information processing and attachment theory seem well-suited to explain the link between support and happiness when the link reflects trait influences. Stress and coping social support theory, capitalization support theory and relational regulation theory seem well-suited to explaining support's link to happiness when the link reflects relational influences.

## References

Anan, R. M., & Barnett, D. (1999). Perceived social support mediates between prior attachment and subsequent adjustment: A study of urban African American children. *Developmental Psychology, 35,* 1210–1222.

Armitage, C. J., & Harris, P. R. (2006). The influence of adult attachment on symptoms reporting: Testing a meditational model in a sample of the general population. *Psychology and Health, 21,* 351–366.

Barrera, M., Jr. (1986). Distinctions between social support concepts, measures and models. *American Journal of Community Psychology, 14,* 413–45.

Barry, R., Lakey, B., & Orehek, E. (2007). Links among attachment dimensions, affect and the self for broadly-generalized attachment styles and relationship-specific bonds. *Personality and Social Psychology Bulletin, 33,* 240–253.

Bergeman, C. S., Plomin, R., Pedersen, N. L., McClearn, G. E. (1991). Genetic mediation of the relationship between social support and psychological well-being. *Psychology and Aging, 6,* 640–646.

Bolger, N., Zuckerman, A., Kessler, R. C. (2000). Invisible support and adjustment to stress. *Journal of Personality and Social Psychology, 79,* 953–961.

Branje, S. J. T., van Aken, M. A. G., & van Lieshout, C. F. M. (2002). Relational support in families with adolescents. *Journal of Family Psychology, 16,* 351–362.

Cohen, S., & Wills, T. A. (1985). Stress, social support, and the buffering hypothesis. *Psychological Bulletin, 98,* 310–357.

Collins, N. L., Guichard, A. C., Ford, M. B., & Feeney, B. C. (2004). Working models of attachment: New developments and emerging themes. In S. W. Rholes & J. A. Simpson (Eds.), *Adult attachment: Theory, research, and clinical implications* (pp. 196–239). New York, NY: Guilford.

Cronbach, L. J., Gleser, G. C., Nanda, H., & Rajaratnam, N. (1972). *The dependability of behavioral measurements: Theory of generalizability for scores and profiles.* New York, NY: John Wiley & Sons.

Curtis, R., Groarke, A., Coughlan, R., & Gsel, A. (2004). The influence of disease severity, perceived stress, social support and coping in patients with chronic illness: a 1 year follow up. *Psychology, Health and Medicine, 9,* 456–475.

Cutrona, C. E., & Russell, D. W. (1987). The provisions of social relationships and adaptation to stress. *Advances in Personal Relationships, 1,* 37–67.

Cutrona, C. E., & Russell, D. W. (1990). Type of social support and specific stress: Toward a theory of optimal matching. In B. R. Sarason, I. G. Sarason, & G. R. Pierce (Eds.), *Social support: An interactional view* (pp. 319–366). New York: Wiley & Sons.

Diener, E., Emmons, R. A., Larsen, R. J., & Griffin, S. (1985). The satisfaction with life scale. *Journal of Personality Assessment, 49,* 71–75.

Diener, E., & Fujita, F. (1995). Resources, personal strivings, and subjective well-being: A nomothetic and idiographic approach. *Journal of Personality and Social Psychology, 68,* 926–935.

Diener, E., Suh, E. M., Lucas, R. E., & Smith, H. L. (1999). Subjective well-being: Three decades of progress. *Psychological Bulletin, 125,* 276–302.

Dunkley, D. M., Zuroff, D. C., & Blankstein, K. R. (2003). Self-critical perfectionism and daily affect: Dispositional and situational influences on stress and coping. *Journal of Personality and Social Psychology, 84,* 234–252.

Ergh, T. C., Hanks, R. A., Rapport, L. J., & Coleman, R. D. (2003). Social support moderates caregiver life satisfaction following traumatic brain injury. *Journal of Clinical and Experimental Neuropsychology, 25,* 1090–1101.

Finch, J. F. (1998). Social undermining, social satisfaction, and affect: A domain-specific lagged effects model. *Journal of Personality, 66,* 315–334.

Fraley, R. C., Waller, N. G., & Brennan, K. A. (2000). An item response theory analysis of self-report measures of adult attachment. *Journal of Personality & Social Psychology, 78,* 350–365.

Gable, S. L., & Reis, H. T. (2010). Good news! Capitalizing on positive events in an interpersonal context. In M. P. Zanna (Ed.), *Advances in experimental social psychology* (vol. 42, pp. 195–257). San Diego, CA: Elsevier Academic Press.

Gallagher, E. N., & Vella-Brodrick, D. A. (2008). Social support and emotional intelligence as predictors of subjective well-being. *Personality and Individual Differences, 44,* 1551–1561.

Giblin, F., & Lakey, B. (2010). Integrating mentoring and social support research within the context of stressful medical training. *Journal of Social and Clinical Psychology, 29,* 771–796.

Hampton, N. Z. (2003). Subject well-being among people with spinal cord injuries: The role of self-efficacy, perceived social support, and perceived health. *Rehabilitation Counseling Bulletin, 48,* 31–37.

Headey, B., & Wearing, A. (1989). Personality, life events, and subjective well-being: Toward a dynamic equilibrium model. *Journal of Personality and Social Psychology, 57,* 731–739.

Hendriks, A. A. J. (1996). The big five as tendencies in situations: A replication study. *Personality and Individual Differences, 21,* 527–535.

Hogan, B. E., Linden, W., & Najarian, B. (2002). Social support interventions. Do they work? *Clinical Psychology Review, 22,* 381–440.

Holtzman, E. H., & Gilbert, L. A. (1987). Social support networks for parenting and psychological well-being among dual-earner Mexican-American families. *Journal of Community Psychology, 15,* 176–186.

Jones, T. G., Rapport, L. J., Hanks, R. A., Lichtenberg, P. A., Telmet, K. (2003). Cognitive and psychosocial predictors of subjective well-being in urban older adults. *The Clinical Neuropsychologist, 17,* 3–19.

Kendler, K. S. (1997). Social support: A genetic-epidemiologic analysis. *American Journal of Psychiatry, 154,* 1398–1404.

Kenny, D. (1994). *Interpersonal perception: A social relations analysis.* New York, NY: Guilford Press.

Kenny, D. A., Kashy, D. A., & Cook, W. L. (2006). *Analysis of dyadic data.* New York, NY: Guilford.

Lakey, B. (2010). Social support: Basic research and new strategies for intervention. In J. E. Maddux & J. P. Tangney (Eds.), *Social Psychological Foundations of Clinical Psychology* (pp. 177–194). New York, NY: Guildford.

Lakey, B., & Cassady, P. B. (1990). Cognitive processes in perceived social support. *Journal of Personality and Social Psychology, 59*, 337–343.

Lakey, B., & Cohen, S. (2000). Social support theory and selecting measures of social support. In S. Cohen, L. U. Gordon & B. H. Gottlieb (Eds.) *Social support measurement and interventions: A guide for health and social scientists.* (pp. 29–52). New York, NY: Oxford University Press.

Lakey, B., & Cronin A. (2008). Low social support and major depression: research, theory and methodological issues. In K. S. Dobson & D. Dozois (Eds.), *Risk factors for depression.* (pp. 385–408). San Diego, CA: Academic Press.

Lakey, B., McCabe, K., Fisicaro, S., & Drew, J. (1996). Personal and environmental determinants of social support: Three generalizability studies. *Journal of Personality and Social Psychology, 70*, 1270–1280.

Lakey, B., & Orehek, E. (2011). Relational regulation theory: A new approach to explain the link between perceived support and mental health. *Psychological Review, 118*, 482–495.

Lakey, B., & Scoboria, A. (2005). Trait and social influences in the links among perceived social support, affect and self esteem. *Journal of Personality, 73*, 361–388.

Lakey, B., Tardiff, T., & Drew, J. B. (1994). Interpersonal stress: Assessment and relations to social support, personality and psychological distress. *Journal of Social and Clinical Psychology, 13*, 42–62.

Lanz, M., Tagliabue, S., & Rosnati, R. (2004). Il social relations model nello studio delle relazioni familiari. *Testing Psicometria Metodologia, 11*, 197–214.

Lawler-Row, K. A., & Piferi, R. L. (2006). The forgiving personality: Describing a life well lived? *Personality and Individual Differences, 41*, 1009–1020.

Lazarus, R. S., & Folkman, S. (1984). *Stress, appraisal and coping.* New York, NY: Springer.

Lee, R. M., Su, J., & Yoshida, E. (2005). Coping with intergenerational family conflict among Asian American college students. *Journal of Counseling Psychology, 52*, 389–399.

Lucas, R. E., & Dyrenforth, P. S. (2006). Does the existence of social relationships matter for subjective well-being? In K. D. Vohs & E. J. Finkel (Eds.), *Self and relationships: Connecting intrapersonal and interpersonal processes* (pp. 254–273). New York, NY: Guilford.

Lyubomirsky, S., Sheldon, K., & Schkade, D. (2005). Pursuing happiness: The architecture of sustainable change. *Review of General Psychology, 9*, 111–131.

McCaskill, J., & Lakey, B. (2000). Perceived support, social undermining and emotion: idiosyncratic and shared perspectives of adolescents and their families. *Personality and Social Psychology Bulletin, 26*, 820–832.

Neely, L. C., Lakey, B., Cohen, J. L., Barry, R., Orehek, E., Abeare, C. A., & Mayer, W. (2006). Trait and social processes in the link between social support and affect: An experimental laboratory investigation. *Journal of Personality, 74*, 1015–1046.

Nelson, G. (1990). Women's life strains, social support, coping and positive and negative affect: Cross-sectional and longitudinal tests of the two-factor theory of emotional well-being. *Journal of Community Psychology, 18*, 239–263.

Ozer, E. J., Best, S. R., Lipsey, T. L., & Weiss, D. S. (2003). Predictors of posttraumatic stress disorder and symptoms in adults: A meta-analysis. *Psychological Bulletin, 129*, 52–73.

Pakenham, K. I., Chiu, J. Bursnall, S., & Cannon, T. (2008). Relations between social support, appraisal and coping and both positive and negative outcomes in young carers. *Journal of Health Psychology, 12*, 89–102.

Paulhus, D. L., & Reynolds, S. (1995). Enhancing target variance in personality impressions: Highlighting the person in person perception. *Journal of Personality and Social Psychology*, 69, 1233–1242.

Robinson-Whelen, S., Tada, Y., MacCallum, R. C., McGuire, L., & Kiecolt-Glaser, J. K. (2001). Long-term caregiving: What happens when it ends? *Journal of Abnormal Psychology*, 110, 573–584.

Ryan, K. A., Rapport, L. J., Sherman, T. E., Hanks, R. A., Lisak, R., & Khan, O. (2007). Predictors of subjective well-being among individuals with multiple sclerosis. *The Clinical Neuropsychologist*, 21, 239–262.

Sarason, B. R., Pierce, G. R., & Sarason, I. G. (1990). Social support: The sense of acceptance and the role of relationships. In B. R. Sarason, I. G. Sarason, & G. R. Pierce (Eds.), *Social support: An interactional view* (pp. 97–128). New York: Wiley.

Suhail, K., & Chaudhry, H. R. (2004). Predictors of subjective well-being in an eastern Muslim culture. *Journal of Social and Clinical Psychology*, 23, 359–376.

Thoits, P. A. (1986). Social support as coping assistance. *Journal of Consulting and Clinical Psychology*, 54, 416–423.

Veenstra, A., Lakey, B., Cohen, J. L., Neely, L. C., Orehek, E., Barry, R., & Abeare, C. (2011). Forecasting the specific providers that recipients will perceive as unusually supportive. *Personal Relationships*, 18, 677–696.

Wahl, H., Martin, P., Minnemann, E., & Marin, S. (2001). Predictors of well-being and autonomy before and after geriatric rehabilitation. *Journal of Health Psychology*, 6, 339–354.

Watson, D., Clark, L. A., & Tellegen, A. (1988). Development and validation of brief measures of positive and negative affect: The PANAS scales. *Journal of Personality and Social Psychology*, 54, 1063–1070.

Zautra, A. J. (1983). Social resources and the quality of life. *American Journal of Community Psychology*, 11, 275–290.

CHAPTER 63

# FRIENDSHIP AND HAPPINESS

MELİKŞAH DEMİR, HALEY ORTHEL, AND
ADRIAN KEITH ANDELIN

Northern Arizona University, USA

FRIENDSHIP is a personal relationship that is cherished across the lifespan. A unique aspect of this precious bond pertains to its role in psychological well-being as has been specified in a number of theoretical arguments (e.g., Argyle, 2001; Baumeister & Leary, 1995; Myers, 1993). Decades of research have consistently documented that having friends, and friendship experiences like intimacy and friendship quality, are related to happiness. Notably, this relationship is not specific to one age or cultural group. Rather, friendship is a reliable correlate of happiness across age (e.g., Holder & Coleman, 2009; Hussong, 2000; Pinquart and Sörensen; 2000), ethnic (e.g., Taylor, Chatters, Hardison, & Riley, 2001) and cultural (e.g., Chan & Lee, 2006) groups.

In this chapter, we first focus on what is meant by friendship and happiness, and specify the domains of friendship studied in relation to happiness. We then review the theoretical arguments and empirical research pertaining to the role of friendship in happiness, and evaluate the importance of friendship experiences in happiness. Finally, we discuss directions for future research that would improve our understanding of the association between friendship and happiness.

## MEASUREMENT OF HAPPINESS AND FRIENDSHIP

### Assessing happiness

Happiness refers to the cognitive and affective evaluations of one's own life (Diener, Suh, Lucas, & Smith, 1999) and is defined in terms of global life satisfaction and the preponderance of positive affect (PA) over negative affect (NA). The cognitive component of happiness is typically measured with the Satisfaction with Life Scale (Diener, Emmons, Larsen & Griffin, 1985) and PA and NA are regularly assessed with The Positive and Negative Affect

Schedule (PANAS) (Watson, Clark, & Tellegen, 1988). Researchers have also relied on a variety of others measures, ranging from multiple item measures of overall happiness (e.g., Oxford Happiness Inventory) to single items of happiness, when investigating the association of friendship with happiness (e.g., Blieszner, 1995; Cheng & Furnham, 2002; Ellison, 1990; Gladow & Ray, 1986).

## Assessing friendship

Of the various empirical definitions of friendship, that suggested by Hays (1988) best captures the previous conceptualizations. According to Hays (1988, p. 395) friendship is a "voluntary interdependence between two persons over time, which is intended to facilitate the socio-emotional goals of the participants, and may involve varying types and degrees of companionship, intimacy, affection and mutual assistance." As the definition suggests, friendship is an affective and qualitative bond that involves the experience and satisfaction of several provisions. Theory and empirical work also suggest that friendship is a mixed blessing since it involves varying degrees of conflict (Berndt & McCandless, 2009; Demir & Weitekamp, 2007; Solano, 1986). Thus, friendship could be considered as having two major dimensions, overall quality (representing various provisions) and conflict.

An essential aspect of friendship is that individuals are likely to have several close friendships. This highlights the need to recognize the quantitative aspects of friendship as well. Recent research suggests that individuals have three to five close friends in general (Demir & Özdemir, 2010; Demir, Özdemir, & Weitekamp, 2007; Sheets & Lugar, 2005) and they can be differentiated in their degree of closeness (e.g., best, close and casual friendships) (Demir & Özdemir, 2010). However, simply assessing the number of friends one has, or the frequency of social interactions, does not provide insight into the quality of the friendship experience(s). The effects of friendship on happiness are best understood by distinguishing between friendship quality and quantity (Cantor, 1979; Demir & Weitekamp, 2007). Ideally, researchers should assess the number of friends one has *and* the overall quality of each of these friendships.

Studies investigating the association of friendship with happiness in several areas of research (e.g., gerontology) have assessed a range of variables. Specifically, research has focused on the number of friends, frequency of social activity, amount of time spent together, friendship satisfaction, and specific relationship provisions (e.g., support) or overall friendship quality. The quantitative aspects of friendship are typically assessed through self-reports of number of friends (e.g., Requena, 1995) and of the frequency of social contact with them (e.g., Ellison, 1990). As for the assessment of friendship satisfaction, researchers have typically used single-item self-report measures (e.g., Lyubomirsky, Tkach & DiMatteo, 2006). Investigators assessing friendship quality have either relied on scales developed for their studies to assess a specific provision of friendship (e.g., social support; Gladow & Ray, 1986) or have used measures of overall friendship quality that encompasses various theoretically identified provisions (e.g., Hussong, 2000). Well-established measures of overall friendship experiences that have been used frequently are the Network of Relationships Inventory (NRI) (Furman & Buhrmester, 1985) and the McGill Friendship Questionnaire-Friend's Functions (MFQ-FF) (Mendelson & Aboud, 1999).

# Do Friendship Experiences Matter for Happiness?

A belief commonly held by scholars and non-scholars alike, is that having friends and close relationship experiences plays an essential role in happiness. Indeed, this idea has been proposed and elaborated on since Aristotle (see Pangle, 2003). It is only more recently that researchers have begun to shed more light on the roles of friendship and friendship experiences in the promotion of happiness. For instance it has been noted that establishing and maintaining friendships contributes to happiness by fulfilling a fundamental human need for social interaction (Baumeister & Leary, 1995; Lyubomirsky, 2007). Other explanations have suggested that receiving support from a friend in times of need and the experience of intimacy in the friendship (e.g., self-disclosure) influence well-being (Diener & Biswas-Diener, 2008, Lyubomirsky, 2007; Reis, 2001; Taylor, 2010). Another view highlights the role of companionship and the pleasurable aspects of friendship (Argyle, 2001; Cooper, Okamura & Gurka, 1992; Demir & Weitekamp, 2007; Diener & Biswas-Diener, 2008). According to this perspective, spending time with friends and engaging in enjoyable activities might explain why friendship experiences contribute to individual happiness. Overall, the existing theoretical arguments elucidate why friendship experiences matter for happiness.

## Review of the empirical literature

It is important to highlight that research investigating the association of social relationships with happiness has mainly focused on romantic relationships and marriage (Berscheid & Reis, 1998; Saphire-Bernstein & Taylor, Chapter 60, this volume)—a point that is reflected in frequently cited reviews of the literature (Diener et al., 1999). Fortunately, this gap has begun to close. Here we provide a select review of studies that investigated the role of various friendship domains in happiness.

Several studies have shown that the number of friends one reports having and frequency of social interaction with friends are related to happiness. This association has been observed across age and ethnic groups (Berry & Hansen, 1996; Blieszner, 1995; Burt, 1987; Demir & Weitekamp, 2007; Ellison, 1990; Lee & Ishii-Kuntz, 1987; Mancini & Orthner, 1980; Taylor et al., 2001; Watson, Clark, McIntyre & Hamaker, 1992; Ying, 1995) as well as in different cultures (Chan & Lee, 2006; Requena, 1995). However, the strength of the association between the quantitative aspects of friendship and happiness has been small with correlations typically in the $r = 0.10-0.20$ range. This observation has been confirmed in recent meta-analyses (Lucas & Dyrenforth, 2006; Pinquart & Sörensen, 2000).

Compared with friendship quantity, research focusing on the role of friendship satisfaction and quality of friendships in happiness reports larger effect sizes. For instance, studies assessing satisfaction yield correlations in the $r = 0.20-0.50$ range (Cooper et al., 1992; Diener & Diener, 1995; Lyubomirsky et al., 2006; Rojas, 2006). Those assessing quality, either in relation to a single provision (e.g., support; Baldassare, Rosenfiled & Rook, 1984) or overall (Hussong, 2000), found moderate relationships to happiness (in the $r = 0.20-0.40$ range). This link has been observed in children (e.g., Holder & Coleman, 2009), adolescents (Cheng & Furnham,

2002; Demir & Urberg, 2004; Hussong, 2000), young and middle-aged adults (Demir et al., 2007; Demir & Weitekamp, 2007; Walen & Lachman, 2000) and the elderly (Baldassare et al., 1984; Gladow & Ray, 1986; see Pinquart & Sörensen, 2000). Importantly, the relationship between friendship quality and happiness is also reported across age groups and cultures (Camfield, Choudhury, & Devine, 2009; Chan & Lee, 2006; Demir et al., 2012; Lu, 1995, 1999).

As proposed earlier, since individuals are likely to have several friends and differentiate the degree of closeness between them, research should assess not only the number of friends one has, but also the overall quality of each of these relationships when investigating their role in happiness. Some recent studies that gathered relationship quality data for the participant's best and two next closest friends (Demir, 2007; Demir & Özdemir, 2010; Demir et al., 2007) found that the quality of each of these friendships (e.g., best friendship, first close friendship, second close friendship, etc.) was related to happiness to varying degrees. However, best friendship quality was more strongly associated with happiness than less close friends. In two of these studies (Demir, 2007; Demir et al., 2007) the role of friendship quality in happiness for less close friends varied as a function of best friendship quality. Specifically, a high level of first close relationship quality was related to higher levels of happiness only at a high level of best friendship quality; it did not make a difference to the individual's happiness when the best friendship was of a low quality. This interaction highlights the importance of best friendship experiences in happiness and suggests that the benefits associated with less close friendships are contingent on high quality experiences with one's best friend. As reviewed earlier, the literature indicates that the more friends an individual has, the happier he or she will be. However, in light of the findings just described, it is reasonable to suggest that it might not be the number of friends per se, but rather the degrees of friendship quality within one's network of closest friends that matters most to happiness.

Finally, a few studies have investigated the role of friendship conflict (including frequency, resolution, and management) in happiness. Some of these found a negative association with correlations in the −0.10 to −0.30 range (Berry, Willingham, & Thayer, 2000; Demir, 2010; Demir & Urberg, 2004; Demir & Weitekamp, 2007; Walen & Lachman, 2000) whereas others did not observe a link between the two constructs (Demir & Özdemir, 2010; Demir et al., 2007; Hussong, 2000). These conflicting findings highlight the need for more research on this topic.

Overall, the literature suggests that the role of friendship quality in happiness is stronger than that of friendship quantity. To date the only meta-analysis has focused on older adults, and this reported larger effect sizes for friendship quality relative to quantity, with life-satisfaction as the outcome (Pinquart & Sörensen, 2000). A comprehensive meta-analysis is needed to enable a better understanding of the relationships among friendship experiences and happiness. Ideally, this would investigate the roles of different friendship domains (i.e., number, satisfaction, quality, and conflict) in happiness, by taking various assessments of the constructs into account and exploring the potential moderators (e.g., age) of the friendship-happiness link.

## Importance of Friendship to Happiness

While the research indicates that friendship experiences (regardless of the domain assessed) are associated with happiness, their relative importance is unclear. Although Argyle (2001) suggested that social relationships are the "greatest single cause" of happiness, this perspective has recently been challenged. Following a review of the associations between happiness and number of friends and marital status, Lucas and his colleagues (Lucas & Dyrenforth, 2006; Lucas, Dyrenforth, & Diener, 2008) argued that the role of social relationships in happiness is overstated. Although Lucas et al. (2008) acknowledged that quality of social relationships could be more important than the quantity, they did not review any studies, but highlighted that issues such as shared method variance that could complicate the interpretation of results.

Is the role of friendship in happiness overstated? Even though no comprehensive meta-analysis is available, our understanding of the topic can be facilitated by taking the theoretical and empirical literature into account.

Many of the theoretical arguments focus on close relationships in general and rarely specifically highlight the importance of friendships to happiness. With the exception of Argyle's (2001) overreaching statement, several scholars proposed that social relationships are but one of the most commonly reported correlates with happiness (Baumeister & Leary, 1995; Berscheid & Reis, 1998; Diener et al., 1999; Myers, 2000; Reis, 2001). Argyle (2001), Edwards and Klemmack (1973) and Myers (1993) argued that friendship experiences are a major source of happiness when addressing the link between friendships and happiness. Empirical evidence is consistent with these propositions in that various domains of friendship experiences are consistently associated with happiness, with friendship quality (and satisfaction) being more strongly related than quantity.

Another way to consider the importance of friendship to happiness would be to examine its role relative to other major predictors. It is well-established that personality is one of the strongest predictors of happiness, accounting for as much as 50% of the variance (Diener et al., 1999). Could it be that the association between friendship and happiness is no longer significant once personality is taken into account? Evidence suggests that this is not the case: friendship experiences make an incremental contribution to happiness relative to the influence of personality (Demir, 2012; Demir & Weitekamp, 2007), a finding that has been replicated in different cultures (Doğan & Demir, 2009; Lu, 1999).

One issue in interpreting findings on the importance of friendship to happiness is that of shared method variance (Lucas et al., 2008). Both friendship experiences and happiness are typically assessed with self-report measures, and this practice probably inflates the associations obtained. Importantly however, the friendship–happiness relationship has been observed with other methods too including observational, experience sampling and longitudinal assessments (Berry & Hansen, 1996; Csikszentmihalyi & Hunter, 2003; Larson, 1990; Lu, 1999). In addition, self-reports of friendship quality (e.g., self-disclosure) are moderately correlated with observed behaviors (Grabill & Kerns, 2000), and observed social interactions are positively associated with happiness (Berry & Hansen, 1996). Although these studies lend support to the importance of friendship to happiness, further mixed-methods research is warranted.

Another related issue pertains to the fact that most of the research linking friendship to happiness is correlational. The assumption that friendship experiences lead to happiness is challenged by the possibility that being happy influences friendship experiences (e.g., Lyubomirsky, King, & Diener, 2005). For instance, in a longitudinal study among non-married elderly women, Adams (1988) reported that changes in well-being influenced number of friends rather than the other way around. Clearly, more research is needed before definitive conclusions about the directionality of the associations are drawn.

In sum, findings from different samples, cultures and research methods suggest that friendships are indeed important for happiness. Although it is unlikely that friendship is the greatest or only source of happiness, it is one of the most robust and frequent correlates with this outcome.

# Future Directions in the Study of Friendship

There are some important theoretical and methodological issues that need to be taken into account when investigating the relationship between friendship and happiness. In this section, we first describe some of these. We also suggest avenues for future research.

First, although there are well-established measures to assess friendship experiences, friendship is only one of the types of personal and social relationships that people have (McCarthy, 1989). It is important for researchers to clearly differentiate friendship from other close relationships, especially since individuals are likely to consider their relatives (e.g., siblings) and romantic partners as their friends (Demir & Weitekamp, 2007; Sheets & Lugar, 2005). Arguably, research results will be confounded if some participants identify those with whom they have familial or sexual relationships as friends, yet others do not.

Second, people have a range of definitions of friendship. These may be inconsistent with the literature or may overlap with other close relationships (e.g., siblings). Individuals report having fewer close friends than originally stated when presented with clearer definitions of friendship (Demir & Özdemir, 2010; Reisman, 1981). Thus, we recommend that researchers provide participants with an easy to understand definition that specifies the criteria against which to identify a friend (e.g., same sex, non-romantic partner, etc.). Assessing friendship without a clear articulation of the definition or without differentiation from other personal relationships weakens confidence in the conclusions from the results.

Third, it would be useful for research to examine the role of cross-sex friendships in happiness. To date, studies have overwhelmingly centered on same-sex friendships despite individuals establishing and maintaining cross-sex friendships across the lifespan (Monsour, 2002).

Fourth, while the relationship of friendship to happiness is well-established, less is known about the moderators and mediators of this association (Demir & Özdemir, 2010). Investigating when and how friendship influences happiness will further our understanding of the both constructs. For example, theory indicates that the role of relationship experiences in happiness might be more important for women than men (e.g., Turner, 1994). In the specific case of friendship, however, the results have not been consistent (Demir & Urberg, 2004; Hussong, 2000; Patrick, Cottrell, & Barnes, 2001). Moreover, cross-cultural research suggests that the associations of friendship satisfaction and quality with happiness are similar across gender (Demir et al., 2012; Diener & Diener, 1995). Further research is needed to investigate how gender might moderate the association between friendship and happiness.

Age too has been considered to be a potential moderator, with suggestions that the role of friendship in happiness might change across the lifespan (Hill, DelPriore, & Major, Chapter 65, this volume; Ishii-Kuntz, 1990; Pinquart & Sörensen, 2000). Friends are an important source of happiness among adolescents and single young adults, but their influence might decline once individuals are in a committed romantic relationship or are married, and are busy solving different adaptive problems, such as finding a job and establishing a family (Hill, DelPriore, & Major, Chapter 65, this volume). Thus, during early and middle adulthood, family relationships might have a greater influence on happiness; while in old age, friends may once again become a major source of happiness (Ishii-Kuntz, 1990). Research supports this pattern. For instance, Demir (2010) showed that for single, young adults, friendship quality strongly predicted happiness, but this was not true for young adults involved in a romantic relationship. Several studies also found that for married or cohabiting young or middle-aged adults, friendship experiences contributed less or not at all to well-being relative to relationship experiences with romantic partners and family members (e.g., Bertera, 2005; Walen & Lachman, 2000). Finally, in old age, interactions with friends have a stronger influence on happiness compared to those with family members (see Antonucci & Akiyama, 1995). A recent meta-analysis supported this by showing that in old age contact with friends (but not quality) was more strongly associated with happiness than contact with family members (Pinquart & Sörensen, 2000). In summary, evidence shows that friendship differentially affects happiness across the lifespan. More research is needed to investigate the correlates of this pattern and how it is impacted by the interaction of cross-cultural variables.

Another potential moderator of the friendship–happiness link could be the successful resolution of developmental tasks (Erikson, 1980). A few studies indicate that identity formation, a developmental task of late adolescence and young adulthood, influences the relationship between close relationship quality and happiness (Demir, 2008 (study 2); Demir, 2012). For instance, Demir (2012) found a stronger association between friendship quality and happiness in young adults with a better sense of who they are (i.e., displaying higher levels of identity formation) relative to those with low levels of identity formation ($rs = 0.39$ vs. 0.23). Further research on how progress toward or resolution of developmental tasks across the lifespan might moderate the friendship–happiness relationship would be valuable.

Last, while friendships are associated with happiness, little is known about the specific processes accounting for this link. Two recent studies with American samples addressed this limitation by investigating theoretically identified variables as potential mediators. Demir and Özdemir (2010) reported that satisfaction of basic psychological needs (e.g., autonomy, competence, and relatedness; Deci & Ryan, 2000) within the friendship, mediated the association between friendship quality and happiness. In another study, Demir et al. (2011) found that perceived mattering, defined as the "feeling that one is important to specific other(s)" (Marshall, 2001), accounted for the relationship between friendship and happiness. Importantly, the mediating roles of needs satisfaction and perceived mattering in these studies were obtained not only for the best friends but also for the next two closest friends of the individual, suggesting the generalizability of the models across friendships which differ in degree of closeness. It is the task of future research to identify other mediators so as to improve our understanding of the role of friendship in happiness.

# Conclusion

Decades of research have shown that friendship experiences, regardless of how they are assessed, are an essential, consistent, and robust correlate of happiness across the lifespan and across cultures. The evidence also indicates that friendship quality is more important than number. Given our current knowledge, it would be redundant to document the positive association between friendship and happiness unless different methods are used to assess friendship (e.g., observational studies) and relatively understudied ethnic and cultural populations are studied. Future research should also focus on theoretically specified variables that might explain when and how friendship is associated with happiness. This research has the potential to help us further understand the role of these two important variables—friendship and happiness—in our lives.

# REFERENCES

Adams, R. (1988). Which comes first: Poor psychological well-being or decreased friendship activity? *Activities, Adaptation, and Aging, 12,* 27–42.

Antonucci, T. C., & Akiyama, H. (1995). Convoys of social relations: Family and friendships within a life span context. In R. Blieszner & V. H. Bedford (Eds.), *Handbook of aging and the family* (pp. 355–372). Westport, CT: Greenwood Press.

Argyle, M. (2001). *The psychology of happiness* (2nd ed.). New York, NY: Routledge.

Baldassare, M., Rosenfield, S., & Rook, K. (1984). The types of social relations predicting elderly well-being. *Research on Aging, 6,* 549–559.

Baumeister, R. F., & Leary, M. R. (1995). The need to belong: Desire for interpersonal attachments as a fundamental human motivation. *Psychological Bulletin, 117,* 497–529.

Berndt, T. J., & McCandless, M. A. (2009). Methods for investigating children's relationshisp with friends. In K. H. Rubin, W. M. Bukowski, & B. Laursen (Eds.), *Handbook of peer interactions, relationships, and groups* (pp. 63–81). New York, NY: Guilford Press.

Berry, D. S., & Hansen, J. S. (1996). Positive affect, negative affect, and social interaction. *Journal of Personality and Social Psychology, 71,* 796–809.

Berry, D. S., Willingham, J. K., & Thayer, C. A. (2000). Affect and personality as predictors of conflict and closeness in young adults' friendships. *Journal of Research in Personality, 34,* 84–107.

Berscheid, E., & Reis, H. T. (1998). Attraction and close relationships. In D. T. Gilbert, S. T. Fiske, and G. Lindzey (Eds.), *The handbook of social psychology* (4th ed., pp. 13–281). Boston, MA: McGraw-Hill.

Bertera, E. M. (2005). Mental health in USA adults: The role of positive social support and social negativity in personal relationships. *Journal of Social and Personal Relationships, 22,* 3–48.

Blieszner, R. (1995). Friendship processes and well-being in the later years of life: Implications for interventions. *Journal of Geriatric Psychiatry, 28,* 165–182.

Burt, R. S. (1987). A note on strangers, friends, and happiness. *Social Networks, 9,* 311–331.

Camfield, L., Choudhury, K., & Devine, J. (2009). Well-being, happiness and why relationships matter: Evidence from Bangladesh. *Journal of Happiness Studies, 10,* 71–91.

Cantor, M. H. (1979). Neighbors and friends: An overlooked resource in the informal support system. *Research on Aging, 1,* 434–463.

Chan, Y. K., & Lee, R. P. L. (2006). Network size, social support and happiness in later life: A comparative study of Beijing and Hong Kong. *Journal of Happiness Studies, 7,* 87–112.

Cheng, H., & Furnham, A. (2002). Personality, peer relations and self-confidence as predictors of happiness and loneliness. *Journal of Adolescence, 25,* 327–339.

Cooper, H., Okamura, L., & Gurka, V. (1992). Social activity and subjective well-being. *Personality and Individual Differences, 13*, 573–583.

Csikszentmihalyi, M., & Hunter, J. (2003). Happiness in everyday life: The uses of experience sampling. *Journal of Happiness Studies, 4*, 185–199.

Deci, E. L., & Ryan, R. M. (2000). The "what" and "why" of goal pursuits: Human needs and the self-determination of behavior. *Psychological Inquiry, 11*, 227–268.

Demir, M. (2007). *Close friendships and happiness among young adults*. Unpublished PhD Dissertation. Wayne State University, Detroit, Michigan, USA.

Demir, M. (2008). Sweetheart, you really make me happy: Romantic relationship quality and personality as predictors of happiness among emerging adults. *Journal of Happiness Studies, 9*, 257–277.

Demir, M. (2010). Close relationships and happiness among emerging adults. *Journal of Happiness Studies, 11*, 293–313.

Demir, M. (2012). Friendship, identity and happiness. Manuscript under review.

Demir, M., Özdemir, M., & Weitekamp, L. A. (2007). Looking to happy tomorrow with friends: Best and close friendships as they predict happiness. *Journal of Happiness Studies, 8*, 243–271.

Demir, M., & Özdemir, M. (2010). Friendship, need satisfaction and happiness. *Journal of Happiness Studies, 11*, 243–259.

Demir, M., Özen, A., Achoui, M., Boholst, F. A., Cheng, C., et al. (2012). Friendship and happiness across cultures. Manuscript under review.

Demir, M., Özen, A., Doğan, A., Bilyk, N. A., Tyrell, F., & Nica, A.A. (2011). I matter to my friend, therefore I am happy: Friendship, mattering, and happiness. *Journal of Happiness Studies, 12*, 983–1005.

Demir, M., & Urberg, K. A. (2004). Friendship and adjustment among adolescents. *Journal of Experimental Child Psychology, 88*, 68–82.

Demir, M., & Weitekamp, L. A. (2007). I am so happy 'cause today I found my friend: Friendship and personality as predictors of happiness. *Journal of Happiness Studies, 8*, 181–211.

Diener, E., & Biswas-Diener, R. (2008). *Happiness: Unlocking the mysteries of psychological wealth*. Malden, MA: Blackwell Publishing.

Diener, E., & Diener, M. (1995). Cross-cultural correlates of life satisfaction and self-esteem. *Journal of Personality and Social Psychology, 68*, 653–663.

Diener, E., Emmons, R.A., Larsen, R.J., & Griffin, S. (1985). The satisfaction with life scale. *Journal of Personality Assessment, 49*, 71–75.

Diener, E., Suh, E. M., Lucas, R. E., & Smith, H. L. (1999). Subjective well-being: Three decades of progress. *Psychological Bulletin, 125*, 276–302.

Doğan, A., & Demir, M. (2009). The role of friendship and personality in predicting happiness among emerging adults in Turkey and the USA. Paper presented at the 4th Conference on Emerging Adulthood, Atlanta, GE, USA.

Edwards, J. N., & Klemmack, D. L. (1973). Correlates of life satisfaction: A reexamination. *Journal of Gerontology, 28*, 497–502.

Ellison, C. G., (1990). Family ties, friendships, and subjective well-being among Black Americans. *Journal of Marriage and the Family, 52*, 298–310.

Erikson, E. (1980). *Identity and the life-cycle*. New York, NY: Norton.

Furman, W., & Buhrmester, D. (1985). Children's perceptions of the personal relationships in their social networks. *Developmental Psychology, 21*, 1016–1024.

Gladow, N. W., & Ray, M. P. (1986). The impact of informal support systems on the well-being of low income single parents. *Family Relations: Journal of Applied Family and Child Studies, 35*, 113–123.

Grabill, C. M., & Kerns, K. A. (2000). Attachment style and intimacy in friendship. *Personal Relationships, 7,* 363–78.

Hays, R. B. (1988). Friendship. In S. W. Duck (Ed.) *Handbook of personal relationships: Theory, research, and interventions* (pp. 391–408). New York, NY: Wiley.

Hinde, R. A. (1997). *Relationships: A dialectical perspective.* East Sussex, UK: Psychology Press.

Holder, M. D., & Coleman, B. (2009). The contribution of social relationships to children's happiness. *Journal of Happiness Studies, 10,* 329–349.

Hussong, A. M. (2000). Perceived peer context and adolescent adjustment. *Journal of Research on Adolescence, 10,* 187–224.

Ishii-Kuntz, M. (1990). Social interaction and psychological well-being: Comparison across at age of adulthood. *International Journal of Aging and Human Development, 30,* 15–36.

Larson, R. (1990). The solitary side of life: An examination of the time people spend alone from childhood to old age. *Developmental Review, 10,* 155–183.

Lee, G. R., & Ishii-Kuntz, M. (1987). Social interaction, loneliness, and emotional well-being among the elderly. *Research on Aging, 9,* 459–482.

Lu, L. (1995). The relationship between subjective well-being and psychosocial variables in Taiwan. *Journal of Social Psychology, 135,* 351–357.

Lu, L. (1999). Personal and environmental causes of happiness. *Journal of Social Psychology, 139,* 79–90.

Lucas, R. E., & Dyrenforth, P. S. (2006). Does the existence of social relationships matter for subjective well-being? In E. J. Finkel & K. D. Vohs (Eds.), *Self and relationships: Connecting intrapersonal and interpersonal processes* (pp. 254–273). New York, NY: Guildford Press.

Lucas, R. E., Dyrenforth, P.S., & Diener, E. (2008). Four myths about subjective well-being. *Social and Personality Psychology Compass, 2,* 2001–2015.

Lyubomirsky, S. (2007). *The how of happiness: A new approach to getting the life you want.* New York, NY: Penguin.

Lyubomirsky, S., King, L., & Diener, E. (2005). The benefits of frequent positive affect: Does happiness lead to success? *Psychological Bulletin, 131,* 803–855.

Lyubomirsky, S., Tkach, C., & DiMatteo, M. R. (2006). What are the differences between happiness and self-esteem? *Social Indicators Research, 78,* 363–404.

Mancini, J. A., & Orthner, D. K. (1980). Situational influences on leisure satisfaction and morale in old age. *Journal of the American Geriatrics Society, 28,* 466–471.

Marshall, S. K. (2001). Do I matter? Construct validation of adolescents' perceived mattering to parents and friends. *Journal of Adolescence, 24,* 473–490.

McCarthy, B. (1989). Adult friendships. In G. Graham & H. Lafollette (Eds.), *Person to person* (pp. 32–45). Philadelphia, PA: Temple University Press.

Mendelson, M. J., & Aboud, F. E. (1999). Measuring friendship quality in late adolescents and young adults: McGill Friendship Questionnaires. *Canadian Journal of Behavioural Science, 31,* 130–132.

Monsour, M. (2002). *Women and men as friends. Relationships across the life span in the 21st Century.* Mahwah, NJ: Erlbaum.

Myers, D. G. (1993). *The pursuit of happiness.* New York, NY: William Morrow.

Myers, D. G. (2000). The funds, friends, and faith of happy people. *American Psychologist, 55,* 56–67.

Pangle, L. S. (2003). *Aristotle and the philosophy of friendship.* UK: Cambridge University Press.

Patrick, J. H., Cottrell, L. E., & Barnes, K. A. (2001). Gender, emotional support, and well-being among rural elderly. *Sex Roles, 45,* 15–29.

Pinquart, M., & Sörensen, S. (2000). Influences of socioeconomic status, social network, and competence on subjective well-being in later life. *Psychology and Aging, 15*, 187–224.

Reis, H. T. (2001). Relationship experiences and emotional well-being. In C. D. Ryff & B. H. Singer (Eds.), *Emotion, social relationships, and health* (pp. 57–86). New York, NY: Oxford University Press.

Reisman, J. M. (1981). Adult friendships. In S. Duck & R. Gilmour (Eds.), *Personal relationships 2: Developing personal relationships* (pp. 205–230). London, UK: Academic Press.

Requena, F. (1995). Friendship and subjective well-being in Spain. A cross-national comparison with the United States. *Social Indicators Research, 35*, 271–288.

Rojas, M. (2006). Life satisfaction and satisfaction in domains of life: Is it a simple relationship? *Journal of Happiness Studies, 7*, 467–497.

Solano, C. H. (1986). People without friends: Loneliness and its alternatives. In V. J. Derlega, & B. A. Winstead (Eds.), *Friendship and social interaction* (pp. 227–246). New York, NY: Springer-Verlag.

Sheets, V. L., & Lugar, R. (2005). Friendship and gender in Russia and the United States. *Sex Roles, 52*, 131–140.

Taylor, S. E. (2010). Social support: A review. In H. S. Friedman (Ed.), *Oxford handbook of health psychology* (pp. 189–214). New York, NY: Oxford University Press.

Taylor, R. J., Chatters, L. M., Hardison, C. B., & Riley, A. (2001). Informal social support networks and subjective well-being among African Americans. *Journal of Black Psychology, 27*, 439–463.

Turner, H. A. (1994). Gender and social support: Taking the bad with the good? *Sex Roles, 30*, 521–541.

Walen, H. R., & Lachman, M. E. (2000). Social support and strain from partner, family, and friends: Costs and benefits for men and women in adulthood. *Journal of Social and Personal Relationships, 17*, 5–30.

Watson, D., Clark, L. A., McIntyre, C. W., & Hamaker, S. (1992). Affect, personality, and social activity. *Journal of Personality and Social Psychology, 63*, 1011–1025.

Watson, D., Clark, L. E., & Tellegen, A. (1988). Development and validation of brief measures of positive and negative affect; The PANAS scales. *Journal of Personality and Social Psychology, 54*, 1063–1070.

Ying, Y. (1995). Cultural orientation and psychological well-being in Chinese Americans. *American Journal of Community Psychology, 23*, 893–911.

# SECTION IX

# DEVELOPMENT, STABILITY, AND CHANGE OF HAPPINESS

# CHAPTER 64

# INTRODUCTION TO DEVELOPMENT, STABILITY, AND CHANGE OF HAPPINESS

## KATE HEFFERON

University of East London, UK

How humans develop, maintain, and change their levels of happiness has been of interest to social and philosophical researchers for millennia. This section focuses on the research of happiness over time, reflecting on evolutionary perspectives, epidemiological research, and experimental findings in order to give readers insight to the current perspectives on the development, stability, and change of happiness.

In the opening chapter, "An Evolutionary Psychological Perspective on Happiness," Hill, DelPriore, and Major commence with a brief overview of the evolutionary barriers to happiness that exist in present-day life. They demonstrate how positive psychological concepts such as positive emotions, social relationships, and goal setting are linked to motivational reward systems, adaptation, and natural selection. The authors propose that an evolutionary perspective can provide positive psychology with a meta-theory to guide happiness research. Ultimately, this chapter sets up the section to challenge present day theories on the stability of happiness.

In his chapter "Set Point Theory May Now Need Replacing: Death of a Paradigm?" Bruce Headey contributes a unique review of analyses from an extensive longitudinal research data set that challenge the widely accepted "hedonic treadmill" theories. As a leading researcher in the area, Headey demonstrates evidence that over time, people can change their life satisfaction. Life goals, religious beliefs, and practices, as well as activity choices and personality types are proposed to change subjective well-being in either a negative or positive direction for the long term. Based on its critique of set point theory and the associated Easterlin paradox, the chapter calls for a new theory that better explains both changes in well-being and its stability over time.

Following from this, Sheldon, Boehm, and Lyubomirsky focus on correlational and experimental evidence that supports the importance of variety in sustaining happiness in their chapter, "Variety is the Spice of Happiness: The Hedonic Adaptation Prevention Model." The authors discuss the facts and findings on what hinders sustainable happiness, namely genetic predisposition, dynamic equilibrium, and the hedonic treadmill. Then they present evidence for sustainable happiness, exploring how variations in circumstances and activities can potentially bolster individuals to experience the upper end of their happiness "set range."

In the next chapter, "Promotion and Protection of Positive Mental Health: Towards Complete Mental Health in Human Development", Corey L. M. Keyes discusses the concept of mental health versus mental illness and tackles the societal implications of mental health promotion and protection policies. The dual continua model is used to demonstrate the importance of mental health (flourishing vs. languishing) on overall well-being. This chapter focuses primarily on data from the Midlife in the United States (MIDUS) study, contributing evidence of prevalence and the dynamic nature of mental health over a 20-year period.

One of the major reasons for changes in well being is through the experience of traumatic and devastating events. In their chapter, "Post-traumatic Growth: Eudaimonic Happiness in the Aftermath of Adversity," Joseph and Hefferon focus on the potential for eudaimonic happiness following tragic life events, a concept known as post-traumatic growth (PTG). Issues surrounding operationally defining growth, as well as predicting growth, are addressed and followed by a brief overview of the current models used to explain this phenomenon. Most importantly, this chapter suggests future directions for the area of PTG in terms of methodologies used, populations studied, and interventions facilitating the growth phenomenon. Overall, this chapter highlights that over the life course, negative experiences may happen that can actually enhance our perceptions of eudaimonic happiness and well being.

In the final chapter, "Creating a Stable Architectural Framework of Existence: Proposing a Model of Lifelong Meaning," Steger, Beeby, Garrett, and Kashdan delve further into the existential study of the self and meaning. From the biological aspects of the self to a thorough review of current definitions of meaning, the authors present a proposal for a new model of meaning through a lifespan perspective, presenting links between important landmarks in life and the benefits of having meaning.

In conclusion, current positive psychology research, focused on the facilitation of happiness, suggests that our happiness is not necessarily set in stone; there are experiences that can fundamentally shift our happiness trajectory. Furthermore, there are techniques, exercises, and changes to our daily life that we can make of our own accord to foster greater levels of happiness. This section challenges the concept of a happiness set point through the research undertaken by leading experts in the field of positive psychology, providing evidence that under some circumstances and through participation in certain activities, we can alter our happiness for the long term.

# CHAPTER 65

# AN EVOLUTIONARY PSYCHOLOGICAL PERSPECTIVE ON HAPPINESS

SARAH E. HILL, DANIELLE J. DELPRIORE, AND BRETT MAJOR

Texas Christian University, USA

When you ask people what they would most like out of life, the vast majority will report that they want to be happy. Yet, although most people report being happy most of the time (e.g., Biswas-Diener, Vitterso, Diener, 2005; Inglehart, 1990; Kesebir & Diener, 2008; Myers & Diener, 1995), for some, happiness is an elusive state. Why is the experience of happiness so easy for some to achieve yet so difficult for others? What are conditions under which we are expected to experience happiness compared to more aversive psychological states? There are a number of social, cognitive, cultural, and biological factors that play a role in addressing these complex questions. A growing body of research across subdisciplines in psychology has begun to uncover a number of key insights into the factors that can increase or decrease one's levels of overall happiness (e.g., Argyle, 2001; Diener, Gohm, Suh, & Oishi, 2000; Diener, Suh, Lucas, & Smith, 1999; Lyubomirksy, King, & Diener, 2005; Panksepp, 1998). For instance, one series of studies found that people are often instrumental in their own happiness. Individuals who intentionally engage in behaviors aimed at increasing their happiness report greater amounts of positive affect relative to those whose happiness is dependent on circumstances outside their immediate control (e.g., good weather) (Sheldon & Lyubomirksy, 2006a, 2006b). However, despite growing interest in this important area of research, surprisingly few researchers have begun to explore happiness from an evolutionary perspective (with a few notable exceptions, e.g., Buss, 2000a). Here we begin to redress this gap in the literature by providing an overview of evolutionary psychological research that is relevant to understanding this sought-after psychological state. First, we discuss some environmental cues and psychological states that can be detrimental to happiness. These include discrepancies between modern and ancestral environments and psychological mechanisms that have been shaped by selection to induce subjective distress. We will then address psychological features that have been selected to encourage people to feel happy and satisfied with their lives. Finally, we will close with some suggestions for how to harness our evolved psychologies to better promote positive affect and propose avenues for future research on happiness from an evolutionary perspective.

# BARRIERS TO HAPPINESS FROM AN EVOLUTIONARY PERSPECTIVE

Defining happiness in a way that satisfactorily captures the essence of this state is something that laypeople often find difficult; however, researchers have converged on an operational definition of this basic emotion that focuses on two key components believed to be central to its experience. The first of these components is subjective, addressing the balance of negative versus positive moods experienced by individuals on a day-to-day basis. The second is a more evaluative component that focuses on the amount of global satisfaction individuals express having with their lives (Diener et al., 1999; Kesebir & Diener, 2008). Although individual researchers vary somewhat in the degree to which their research emphasizes each component, almost all recognize that happiness includes both.

Researchers exploring happiness have successfully identified a number of key features of human social life that can add to—or detract from—its experience. Specifically, researchers have demonstrated links between happiness and factors such as health, wealth, and having quality social relationships with others (Corneau, 2009; Demir, 2008; Diener et al., 2000; North, Holahan, Moos, & Cronkite, 2008). With respect to relationship variables, for instance, researchers have found that marital quality and the quality of one's social and familial relationships are predictive of happiness (e.g., Chan & Lee, 2006; Corneau, 2009; North et al., 2008; Sedikides, 2005). Others have identified important individual differences in predispositions to experience happiness, many of which appear to have a substantial heritable component (Lykken & Tellegen, 1996; Tellegen et al., 1988). Taken together, these and similar findings indicate that happiness is dependent on factors both within and outside of one's immediate control.

What does an evolutionary psychological perspective have to offer in terms of better understanding this desirable affective state? From an evolutionary perspective, emotions—including those associated with happiness—are conceptualized as constituent parts of motivational systems that have been shaped by natural selection to produce behaviors that have increased fitness over evolutionary time (Cosmides & Tooby, 2000; Kenrick, Neuberg, Griskevicius, Becker, & Schaller, 2010). From this view, the subjective components of any given emotional state—including both positive and negative affect—are not viewed as being good or bad, per se. Instead, these states are considered in terms of their function as psychological carrots and sticks, selected for their ability to help guide our ancestors toward behaviors that facilitated acquisition of fitness-related goals (positive affect) and away from those behaviors that did not (negative affect). Accordingly, meeting such fitness-relevant goals in today's environment is expected to provide a happiness boost; conversely, any failure to meet these goals is expected to be met with the opposite.

The proposed function of positive and negative affect as being shaped by selection to play the psychological roles of carrot and stick implies three concerns that do not bode well for happiness being an achievable long-term state. First, because the psychological mechanisms from which our emotional states are derived were selected for in our evolutionary past, some of the environmental contingencies from which humans have historically derived their happiness (e.g., large close-knit social networks, direct benefits obtained from a day's work) are simply non-existent or exist in lesser supply than they did in the days of our ancestors, making the achievement of happiness more complicated than it may have been in the past. Secondly, because of the tremendous fitness costs associated with failing to meet such goals (e.g., death, failure to reproduce), some of the psychological states that facilitate successful survival and reproduction do not have the result of making us feel happy or satisfied with our lives (e.g., fears and phobias that protect individuals from poisonous snakes or spiders). Lastly, that positive affect plays an important role in motivating the pursuit of fitness-related goals means that happiness is likely a state to which one may become quickly acclimated. Accordingly, happiness may be difficult to sustain as an ambient resting state, as levels of happiness dissipate once one successfully confronts an adaptive problem. We will address each of these issues, closing with suggestions about how we may use knowledge of these potential pitfalls to better shape our lives in ways that promote long-term well-being.

# From Savannah to City: A Stone-Age Reward System in the Neon Now

The modern world is quite different from that in which ancestral humans spent the majority of their evolutionary history as hunter-gatherers, living in groups that likely consisted of between 50–200 individuals (Dunbar, 1993). Accordingly, humans have evolved as a highly social species whose well-being is dependent on having access to people with whom we have deep, meaningful relationships. Indeed, many studies find that happiness is inextricably linked with social support and having close relationships with others (e.g., Argyle, 1987; Corneau, 2009; Lewinsohn, Redner, & Seeley, 1991; Sarason, Sarason, & Pierce, 1990). However, in many ways our modern environment is arranged such that it is increasingly difficult to develop the close interpersonal bonds that characterized our evolutionary past (Nesse & Williams, 1994). For example, most people in the Western world live in small family units typically consisting of between one and four individuals. Rather than being part of a large, extended community of friends and allies, many of us live in large cities, surrounded by thousands of strangers. This way of life can create feelings of anonymity and detachment from one's community—feelings exacerbated by having to relocate or travel for employment purposes. These features of modern social life can pose challenges to an individual's ability to develop and maintain close social ties with kin and friendship networks, both of which are central to happiness (see, e.g., Argyle, 2001). Some evolutionary psychologists (e.g., Nesse, 2006) have suggested that this mismatch between our desire for interpersonal connection (Baumeister & Leary, 1995) and the decreased frequency of repeated interaction with others in modern life has implications for depression.

The activities in the modern environment also differ from those in which humans historically spent their waking hours. Today, much of our time awake is spent at places of employment. It is perhaps not surprising, then, that job satisfaction plays an important role in happiness (Argyle, 2001; Benin & Nienstedt, 1985; Davis & Smith, 2009; Warr & Clapperton, 2010). However, for many, deriving satisfaction from routine work tasks may be more difficult than it was for our ancestors. As hunter-gatherers, our ancestors necessarily had a close connection with the fruits of their labor. Food was gathered to feed one's family, and meat procured from cooperative hunting ventures was brought back to be shared with extended kin and social allies. People had an intimate connection with the work they performed because it had a direct impact on their survival. In contrast, many workers today spend long hours under fluorescent lighting, hunched over in front of computers in a manner that can be experienced as socially isolating and is often far-removed from the final product of their labor. This is not to say that we would prefer to revert back to the days of eating only what we kill. Most of us are perfectly content to spend our daylight hours indoors away from the "hostile forces of nature," a finding supported by reports that most people are satisfied with their jobs (Davis & Smith, 2009). However, long hours in the office coupled with a sense of disconnectedness from the impact of one's work can negatively influence happiness. Specifically, work-related stress and feeling that one's work is meaningless are associated with increased anxiety and depression (Maslach, Schaufeli, & Leiter, 2001), both of which are detrimental to well-being.

## Dissatisfied by Design: Adaptations that Cause Subjective Distress

An additional roadblock to human happiness is that we have an array of mechanisms that may have been specifically selected for based on their ability to make us feel miserable when contextually appropriate (e.g., Buss, 1989; Seligman, 1971). According to one evolutionary hypothesis, feelings of distress and discomfort are evolved psychological responses shaped by selection to signal strategic interference. Strategic interference theory (Buss, 1989) posits that many "negative" emotions—such as anger or jealousy—have been designed to signal that someone or something is impeding one's preferred behavioral strategy. Accordingly, these unpleasant psychological states function to: (1) focus an individual's attention on the source of strategic interference while temporarily screening out information that is less relevant to the adaptive problem being faced, (2) prompt storage of the relevant information in memory, (3) motivate action to reduce the strategic interference, and (4) motivate action to prevent future such interference.

The human mind likely contains numerous psychological adaptations that have been selected by the evolutionary process based on their ability to signal strategic interference. Examples include envy (Hill & Buss, 2006), anxiety (Marks & Nesse, 1994), depression (Nesse, 2005, 2006; Price & Sloman, 1987), fears and phobias (Marks, 1987), sexual jealousy (Buss, 1988; Buss, Larsen, Westen, & Semmelroth, 1992; Daly, Wilson, & Weghorst, 1982), low self-esteem (Hill & Buss, 2004; Kirkpatrick & Ellis, 2001, 2004), and anger and upset (Buss, 1989). Although distressing to the individual experiencing them, from an evolutionary perspective, such aversive emotional responses have been selected to aid in solving recurrent adaptive problems faced by our ancestors—such as loss of status, sexual coercion, the presence of environmental hazards (e.g., snakes and spiders), and sexual infidelity. Therefore, the experience of negative emotions—although subjectively unpleasant—enables recognition that there is an adaptive problem that needs to be addressed and subsequently motivates action to solve it.

## Psychological Features that Contribute to Well-Being

Happiness is hypothesized to serve as a psychological reward, an internal signaling device that tells us that an adaptive problem has been, or is in the process of being, solved successfully. The types of events and situations that are expected to have the greatest positive impact on happiness are those that are related to long-standing adaptive problems that humans have reliably faced throughout evolutionary time (e.g., securing high-quality food, achieving intimacy in personal relationships). Take, for instance, the concerns associated with producing and rearing children. Research indicates that children tend to fare better when they are raised by two investing parents compared to being raised by one (e.g., DeBell, 2008; Kenny & Schreiner, 2009; Schmeer, 2009). Accordingly, an evolutionary perspective would predict that having a loving spouse who is willing to invest in one's children should be related to increased happiness. Indeed, this appears to be true. Research demonstrates that single working mothers score lower on measures of happiness and life satisfaction—partially due to increased financial stress—than do their partnered counterparts (Bull & Mittelmark, 2009), and that women whose spouses invest more in the rearing of children are happier than those who do not. Promoting happiness is thus oftentimes merely a matter of exploiting knowledge of evolved desires and attempting to fulfill them (Buss, 2000a, 2000b). Not surprisingly, studies of private wishes and goals reveal that the motivations behind them are often intimately correlated with fitness (Buss, 2000a). Included among these are the desires for professional success and power, achieving intimacy in personal relationships, being more physically attractive, helping friends and relatives, securing personal safety and health, gaining access to high-quality food, and having personal and financial resources (King & Broyles, 1997; Petrie, White, Cameron, & Collins, 1999).

Taking steps to fulfill these desires and goals makes people feel happy (Sheldon & Hoon, 2007; Sheldon & Lyubomirsky, 2007; Tkach & Lyubomirsky, 2006), and the experience of positive affect serves as an internal reward and motivator, increasing the probability that the individual will continue working toward accomplishing his or her goals. In fact, current research suggests that the process of moving towards one's goals may actually be more important to happiness than the end-goal attainment. For instance, goal striving is associated with feelings of satisfaction and contentment, as long as adequate progress is being made toward the goals at hand (Carver, Lawrence, & Scheier, 1996; Csikszentmihalyi, 1990; Diener et al., 1999; Hsee & Abelson, 1991; Sheldon & Hoon, 2007; Sheldon & Lyubomirsky, 2007). Further, MacLeod, Coates, & Hetherton (2008) posit that not only is goal setting and planning linked to happiness, but that learning to set attainable goals is a strategy that can be utilized to boost well-being.

Additional support for the link between solving adaptive problems and happiness can be found in the many correlations between happiness and fitness indicators such as health, marital status, and access to financial resources. Researchers have found evidence of a strong link between happiness and self-perceived health (George & Landerman, 1984; Okun, Stock, Haring, & Witter, 1984), a domain that is highly relevant to survival and reproductive success. Also, individuals who have successfully solved the adaptive problem of securing a long-term mate appear to have greater happiness than their unmated counterparts. Specifically, happily married people report greater life satisfaction than those who have never been married or are divorced, separated, or widowed, even when variables such as age and income are controlled for (Glenn & Weaver, 1988; Gove, Hughes, & Style, 1983; Kamp Dush & Amato, 2005). This finding has been consistently demonstrated in national and regional surveys conducted in the USA (Gove & Shin, 1989) as well as in international studies (Bull & Mittlemark, 2009; Diener et al., 2000). Moreover, studies demonstrate that it is not only securing a long-term mate—but also the overall quality of the relationship experience—that matters for happiness. One might have secured a long-term mate while failing to enjoy high levels of happiness due to a lack of intimacy and trust in the relationship (Amato, 2007; Deci & Ryan, 2002; Demir, 2008; Kamp Dush & Amato, 2005; Keyes & Waterman, 2003; Seligman, 2002). In conclusion, most research is consistent with the view that solving the adaptive problem of securing a loving, trustworthy long-term mate seems to promote happiness (cf. DePaulo, 2006; DePaulo & Morris, 2005).

Research suggests that there is a relationship between happiness and the amount of financial resources available to individuals. For example, there is a strong positive association between the wealth of a nation and its inhabitants' average happiness and, although weaker, an association between wealth and happiness within nations, as well (Diener & Biswas-Diener, 2002; Diener, Sandvik, Seidlitz, & Diener, 1993). It is important to note, however, that those who overvalue material goods tend to be less happy overall, and that happiness in developed nations has not increased commensurate with higher levels of available wealth (Diener & Biswas-Diener, 2002; Diener & Oishi, 2000). Taken together, these findings suggest that having access to financial resources sufficient to solve important adaptive problems—such as securing access to food, clean water, and housing—has a significant impact on happiness. However, once these fitness-related goals are met, increased wealth does not correspond with increased happiness.

Another way that individuals can harness their evolved psychologies to promote happiness is through the use of modern technological advances to initiate, develop, and maintain interpersonal connections. There is compelling evidence for the relationship between happiness and having close friendships (e.g., Demir & Özdemir, 2010; Demir & Weitekamp, 2007), and technologies like cellular telephones, email, and airplanes enable us to strengthen our ties and free us from the barriers of physical distance. Moreover, dating and networking websites can also facilitate the development of new relationships, rendering geographical boundaries virtually obsolete. Twenty-first century humans have developed the capacity to stay in touch with even the most distant friends and relatives, and although using these technologies might not substitute for face-to-face contact, taking advantage of them may enhance the number and depth of relationships and social networks and, ultimately, promote happiness. Corneau (2009), for example, in a study of doctoral students, found that those with more face-to-face contact with the important people of their lives were happier than those with less face-to-face contact. In addition, those students who engaged in more total communication—whether face-to-face or through technologies like text and email—with those important to them were happier than those with less total communication. Similar results have been found with respect to the number of social contacts one has on Facebook (Ellison, Steinfield, & Lampe, 2007).

# Exploiting Our Evolved Psychologies to Promote Happiness

One of the major contributions of evolutionary psychology is its provision of a metatheory that can be used to guide researchers exploring questions about human psychology. Knowledge of the adaptive problems that humans have reliably solved over the course of evolutionary history has heuristic value from which one can derive predictions about the design of the mind, brain, and behavior. In particular, the application of evolutionary psychological principles to the study of happiness is likely to create new bodies of knowledge in this growing field of scientific interest.

One way that evolutionary psychologists might contribute to the scientific study of happiness is to empirically explore the relationship between the numerous domains of adaptive problems confronting humans over evolutionary history and the implications of these problems for happiness. Specifically, an evolutionary framework would predict a relatively strong, positive relationship between the importance of a given adaptive problem and its effect on well-being. That is, the more closely tied a domain's historical relevance is to reproductive success, the more individual successes (or failures) in that domain would be expected to increase (or decrease) happiness. We would predict, for instance, that a man's happiness would be more affected by his ability to acquire economic resources than his ability to bake the perfect soufflé (unless the latter ability had a bearing on the former).

Similarly, an evolutionary account of happiness would predict that the variables with the greatest impact on happiness will alter commensurate with the importance of solving different adaptive problems over the life course. For instance, scholars note that adaptive problems associated with mating are typically confronted and solved prior to problems associated with parenting or grandparenting (Buss, 1999, 2004). Thus, the ability to attract and gain sexual access to short-term mates might be more important to men in their twenties, whereas for men in their sixties, well-being might depend more on factors such as spousal health and the successes of one's children or grandchildren. Future research exploring the relationship between happiness and the relative importance of different adaptive problems over the life course may make a valuable contribution to the well-being literature.

Additional avenues of research informed by evolutionary theory include whether cultural attempts to attenuate some of the negative side effects of modern, urban living have been successful. Relocation due to jobs, schooling, and other social or economic factors is becoming more frequent than in the past. Studies exploring whether having ready access to email, cellular telephones, and cheap airfare impact both decisions to relocate and happiness would be of interest.

## Summary and Conclusions

Evolutionary psychology has provided important insights into a number of research domains within psychology, including the science of happiness. Discrepancies between current environments and those inhabited by our ancestors, psychological features that have evolved to cause distress, and the interaction between these factors can be detrimental to happiness. Evolutionary psychology also contributes to our understanding of variables that facilitate happiness and makes suggestions about ways we might use our evolved psychologies to enhance well-being. There is a paucity of research on happiness from an evolutionary perspective; nonetheless, early research from this perspective appears promising (Hill & Buss, 2006).

## References

Amato, P. (2007). Studying marriage and commitment with survey data. In S. L. Hofferth and L. M. Casper (Eds.), *Handbook of measurement issues in family research* (pp. 53–65). Mahwah, NJ: Lawrence Erlbaum Associates Publishers.

Argyle, M. (1987). *The psychology of happiness.* London, UK: Routledge.

Argyle, M. (2001). *The psychology of happiness* (2nd ed.). New York, NY: Routledge.

Baumeister, R. F., & Leary, M. R. (1995). The need to belong: Desire for interpersonal attachments as a fundamental human motivation. *Psychological Bulletin, 117,* 497–529.

Benin, M. H., & Nienstedt, B. C. (1985). Happiness in single- and dual-earner families: the effects of marital happiness, job satisfaction, and life cycle. *Journal of Marriage and Family, 47,* 975–984.

Biswas-Diener, R., Vitterso, J., & Diener, E. (2005). Most people are pretty happy, but there is cultural variation: The Inughuit, the Amish, and the Maasai. *Journal of Happiness Studies, 6*(3), 205–226.

Bull, T., & Mittelmark, M. (2009). Work life and mental wellbeing of single and non-single working mothers in Scandinavia. *Scandinavian Journal of Public Health, 37,* 562–568.

Buss, D. M. (1988). From vigilance to violence: Tactics of mate retention. *Ethology and Sociobiology, 9,* 291–317.

Buss, D. M. (1989). Conflict between the sexes: Strategic interference and the evocation of anger and upset. *Journal of Personality and Social Psychology, 56,* 735–747.

Buss, D. M. (1999). *Evolutionary psychology: The new science of the mind.* Boston, MA: Pearson Education, Inc.

Buss, D. M. (2004). *Evolutionary psychology: The new science of the mind* (2nd ed.). New York, NY: Pearson Education, Inc.

Buss, D. M. (2000a). The evolution of happiness. *American Psychologist, 55,* 15–23.

Buss, D. (2000b). *The dangerous passion: Why jealousy is as necessary as love and sex.* New York, NY: Free Press.

Buss, D. M., Larsen, R., Westen, D., & Semmelroth, J. (1992). Sex differences in jealousy: Evolution, physiology, and psychology. *Psychological Science, 3,* 251–255.

Carver, C. S., Lawrence, J. W., & Scheier, M. F. (1996). A control-process perspective on the origins of affect. In L. L. Martin & A. Tesser (Eds.), *Striving and feeling: Interactions among goals, affect, and regulation* (pp. 11–52). Mahwah, NJ: Erlbaum.

Chan, Y., & Lee, R. (2006). Network size, social support and happiness in later life: A comparative study of Beijing and Hong Kong. *Journal of Happiness Studies, 7*, 87–112.

Clark, W. A. V., Deurloo, M. C., & Dieleman, F. M. (1994). Tenure changes in the context of micro-level family and macro-level economic shifts. *Urban Studies, 31*, 137–154.

Corneau, A. (2009). Doctoral student social support and satisfaction with life. *Dissertation Abstracts International,* 69.

Cosmides, L., & Tooby, J. (2000). Evolutionary psychology and the emotions. In M. Lewis & J. M. Haviland-Jones (Eds.), *Handbook of emotions* (2nd ed., pp. 91–115.) New York, NY: Guilford.

Csikszentmihalyi, M. (1990). *Flow: The psychology of optimal experience.* New York, NY: Harper.

Daly, M., Wilson, M., & Weghorst, S. J. (1982). Male sexual jealousy. *Ethology and Sociobiology, 3*, 11–27.

Davis, J. A., & Smith, T. W. (2009). *General social surveys, 1972–2008: Cumulative codebook/ Principal Investigator, James A. Davis; Director and Co-Principal Investigator, Tom W. Smith; Co-Principal Investigator, Peter V. Marsden*. Chicago, IL: National Opinion Research Center.

DeBell, M. (2008). Children living without their fathers: Population estimates and indicators of educational well-being. *Social Indicators Research, 87*, 427–443.

Deci, E., & Ryan, R. (2002). *Handbook of self-determination research*. Rochester, NY: University of Rochester Press.

Demir, M. (2008). Sweetheart, you really make me happy: Romantic relationship quality and personality as predictors of happiness among emerging adults. *Journal of Happiness Studies, 9*, 257–277.

Demir, M., & Özdemir, M. (2010). Friendship, need satisfaction and happiness. *Journal of Happiness Studies, 11*, 243–259.

Demir, M., & Weitekamp, L. (2007). I am so happy 'cause today I found my friend: Friendship and personality as predictors of happiness. *Journal of Happiness Studies, 8*, 181–211.

DePaulo, B. (2006). *Singled out: How singles are stereotyped, stigmatized, and ignored, and still live happily ever after*. New York, NY: St Martin's Press.

DePaulo, B., & Morris, W. (2005). Singles in society and in science. *Psychological Inquiry, 16*, 57–83.

Dieleman, F., Clark, W. A. V., & Deurloo, M. C. (1995). Falling out of the homeowner market. *Housing Studies, 10*, 3–15.

Diener, E., & Biswas-Diener, R. (2002). Will money increase subjective well-being? *Social Indicators* Research, *57*, 119–169.

Diener, E., & Emmons, R. A. (1984). The independence of positive and negative affect. *Journal of Personality and Social Psychology, 47*, 1015–1117.

Diener, E., Gohm, C., Suh, E., & Oishi, S. (2000). Similarity of the relations between marital status and subjective well-being across cultures. *Journal of Cross-Cultural Psychology, 31*, 419–436.

Diener, E., & Oishi, S. (2000). Money and happiness: Income and subjective well-being across nations. In E. Diener and E. M. Suh (Eds.), *Culture and subjective well-being* (pp. 185–218). Cambridge, MA: The MIT Press.

Diener, E., Sandvik, E., Seidlitz, L., & Diener, M. (1993). The relationship between income and subjective well-being: Relative or absolute? *Social Indicators Research, 28*, 195–223.

Diener, E., Saptya, J. J., & Suh, E. M. (1998). Subjective well-being is essential to well-being. *Psychological Inquiry, 9*, 33–37.

Diener, E., Suh, E. M., Lucas, R. E., & Smith, H. L. (1999). Subjective well-being: Three decades of progress. *Psychological Bulletin, 125*, 276–302.

Dunbar, R. I. M. (1993). Coevolution of neocortical size, group size, and language in humans. *Behavioral and Brain Sciences, 16*, 681–735.

Ellison, N., Steinfield, C., & Lampe, C. (2007). The benefits of Facebook "friends": Social capital and college students' use of online social network sites. *Journal of Computer-Mediated Communication, 12*, 1143–1168.

George, L. K., & Landerman, R. (1984). Health and subjective well-being: A replicated secondary data analysis. *International Journal of Aging and Human Development, 19*, 133–156.

Glenn, N. D., & Weaver, C. N. (1988). The changing relationship of marital status to reported happiness. *Journal of Marriage and Family Relations, 50*, 317–324.

Gove, W. R., Hughes, M., & Style, C. B. (1983). Does marriage have positive effects on the psychological well-being of the individual? *Journal of Health and Social Behavior, 24*, 122–131.

Gove, W. R., & Shin, H. (1989). The psychological well-being of divorced and widowed men and women. *Journal of Family Issues, 11*, 4–35.

Hill, S. E., & Buss, D. M. (2004). The evolution of self-esteem. In M. H. Kernis (Ed.), *Self-esteem: Issues and answers* (pp. 328–333). New York, NY: Psychology Press.

Hill, S. E., & Buss, D. M. (2006). Envy and positional bias in the evolutionary psychology of management. *Managerial and Decision Economics, 27*, 131–143.

Hsee, C. K., & Abelson, R. P. (1991). Velocity relations: Satisfaction as a function of the first derivative of outcome over time. *Journal of Personality and Social Psychology, 60*, 341–347.

Inglehart, R. (1990). *Culture shift in advanced industrial society*. Princeton, NJ: Princeton University Press.

Kamp Dush, C., & Amato, P. (2005). Consequences of relationship status and quality for subjective well-being. *Journal of Social and Personal Relationships, 22*, 607–627.

Kenny, D. T., & Schreiner, I. (2009). Predictors of high-risk alcohol consumption in young offenders on community orders: Policy and treatment implications. *Psychology, Public Policy, and Law, 15*, 54–79.

Kenrick, D. T., Neuberg, S. L., Griskevicius, V., Becker, D. V., & Schaller, M. (2010). Goal driven cognition and functional behavior: The fundamental-motives framework. *Current Directions in Psychological Science, 19*, 63–67.

Kesebir, P., & Diener, E. (2008). In pursuit of happiness: Empirical answers to philosophical questions. *Perspectives on Psychological Science, 3*, 117–125.

Keyes, C., & Waterman, M. (2003). Dimensions of well-being and mental health in adulthood. In M. H. Bornstein, L. Davidson, C. L. M. Keyes, & K. A. Moore (Eds.), *Well-being: Positive development across the life course* (pp. 477–497). Mahwah, NJ: Lawrence Erlbaum Associates Publishers.

King, L. A., & Broyles, S. J. (1997). Wishes, gender, personality, and well-being. *Journal of Personality, 65*, 49–76.

Kirkpatrick, L. A., & Ellis, B. J. (2001). An evolutionary approach to self-esteem: Multiple domains and multiple functions. In M. Clark & G. Fletcher (Eds.), *The Blackwell handbook of social psychology, Vol. 2: Interpersonal processes* (pp. 411–436). Oxford, UK: Blackwell.

Kirkpatrick, L. A., & Ellis, B. J. (2004). An evolutionary approach to self-esteem research. In M. H. Kernis (Ed.), *Self-esteem: Issues and answers* (pp. 334–339). New York, NY: Psychology Press.

Lewinsohn, P. M., Redner, J. E., & Seeley, J. R. (1991). The relationship between life satisfaction and psychosocial variables: New perspectives. In F. Strack, M. Argyle, & N. Schwarz (Eds.), *Subjective well-being: An interdisciplinary perspective* (pp. 141–169). Oxford, UK: Pergamon Press.

Lykken, D., & Tellegen, A. (1996). Happiness is a stochastic phenomenon. *Psychological Science, 7*, 186–189.

Lyubomirsky, S., King, L., & Diener, E. (2005). The benefits of frequent positive affect: Does happiness lead to success? *Psychological Bulletin*, *131*, 803–855.

MacLeod, A., Coates, E., & Hetherton, J. (2008). Increasing well-being through teaching goal-setting and planning skills: Results of a brief intervention. *Journal of Happiness Studies*, *9*, 185–196.

Marks, I. M. (1987). *Fears, phobias, and rituals: Panic, anxiety, and their disorders*. New York, NY: Oxford University Press.

Marks, I. M., & Nesse, R. M. (1994). Fear and fitness: An evolutionary analysis of anxiety disorders. *Ethology and Sociobiology*, *15*, 247–261.

Maslach, C., Schaufeli, W. B., & Leiter, M. P. (2001). Job burnout. *Annual Review of Psychology*, *52*, 397–422.

Myers, D., & Diener, E. (1995). Who is happy? *Psychological Science*, *6*, 10–19.

Nesse, R. M. (1990). Evolutionary explanations of emotions. *Human Nature*, *1*, 261–289.

Nesse, R. M. (2005). Evolutionary psychology and mental health. In D. Buss (Ed.), *Handbook of evolutionary psychology* (pp. 903–937). Hoboken, N.J.: John Wiley and Sons.

Nesse, R. M. (2006). Evolutionary explanations for mood and mood disorders. In D. J. Stein, D. J. Kupfer, & A. F. Schatzberg (Eds.), *The American psychiatric publishing textbook of mood disorders* (pp. 159–175). Washington, D.C: American Psychiatric Publishing.

Nesse, R. M., & Williams, G. C. (1994). *Why we get sick*. New York, NY: New York Times Books.

North, R., Holahan, C., Moos, R., & Cronkite, R. (2008). Family support, family income, and happiness: A 10-year perspective. *Journal of Family Psychology*, *22*, 475–483.

Okun, M. A., Stock, W. A., Haring, M. J., & Witter, R. A. (1984). Health and subjective well-being: A meta-analysis. *International Journal of Aging and Human Development*, *19*, 111–132.

Panksepp, J. (1998). The quest for long-term happiness: To play or not to play. *Psychological Inquiry*, *9*, 56–66.

Petrie, K. J., White, G., Cameron, L. D., & Collins, J. P. (1999). Photographic memory, money and liposuction: survey of medical students' wish lists. *British Medical Journal*, *319*, 1593–1595.

Price, J. S., & Sloman, L. (1987). Depression as yielding behavior: An animal model based on Schjelderup-Ebb's pecking order. *Ethology and Sociobiology*, *8*, 85–98.

Sarason, B. R., Sarason, I. G., & Pierce, G. R. (1990). *Social support: An interactional view*. New York, NY: Wiley.

Schmeer, K. (2009). Father absence due to migration and child illness in rural Mexico. *Social Science and Medicine*, *69*, 1281–1286.

Sedikides, C. (2005). Close relationships – What's in it for us? *The Psychologist*, *18*, 490–493.

Seligman, M. E. (1971). Phobias and preparedness. *Behavioral Therapy*, *2*, 307–320.

Seligman, M. (2002). *Authentic happiness: Using the new positive psychology to realize your potential for lasting fulfillment*. New York, NY: Free Press.

Sheldon, K., & Hoon, T. (2007). The multiple determination of well-being: Independent effects of positive traits, needs, goals, selves, social supports, and cultural contexts. *Journal of Happiness Studies*, *8*, 565–592.

Sheldon, K., & Lyubomirsky, S. (2006a). Achieving sustainable gains in happiness: Change your actions, not your circumstances. *Journal of Happiness Studies*, *7*, 55–86.

Sheldon, K., & Lyubomirsky, S. (2006b). How to increase and sustain positive emotion: The effects of expressing gratitude and visualizing best possible selves. *The Journal of Positive Psychology*, *1*, 73–82.

Sheldon, K., & Lyubomirsky, S. (2007). Is it possible to become happier? (And if so, how?). *Social and Personality Psychology Compass, 1*, 129–145.

Tellegen, A., Lykken, D. T., Bouchard, T. J., Wilcox, K. J., Segal, N. L., & Rich, S. (1988). Personality similarity in twins reared apart and together. *Journal of Personality and Social Psychology, 54*, 1031–1039.

Tkach, C., & Lyubomirsky, S. (2006). How do people pursue happiness?: Relating personality, happiness-increasing strategies, and well-being. *Journal of Happiness Studies, 7*, 183–225.

Warr, P., & Clapperton, G. (2010). *The joy of work? Jobs, happiness, and you.* New York, NY: Routeledge.

# CHAPTER 66

# SET-POINT THEORY MAY NOW NEED REPLACING: DEATH OF A PARADIGM?

## BRUCE HEADEY

Melbourne Institute of Applied Economic & Social Research, Australia

Since its earliest days in the 1970s, empirical research on happiness, or subjective well-being (SWB), has been dominated by one scientific paradigm (Kuhn, 1962). That paradigm, initially labelled *adaptation theory*, then underwent numerous confusing name changes, and in its final incarnation is usually known as *set-point theory*. The main theme of the first part of this chapter is that the paradigm needs substantial revision and may need replacing. In the second part, I review some recent hypotheses and findings that may contribute to a new theory.

The central claim of set-point theory is that adults have stable levels of SWB. Of course they do not all have the same levels; some people are happier than others. According to the theory, stable differences are *set* by personality traits and other factors which are hereditary or determined early in life. It is recognized that major life events (e.g., getting married, being widowed) can cause fluctuations around the set-point, but the effects of events are supposed to be temporary. Individuals normally (so the theory holds) return to their previous set-point within a year or two (Brickman & Campbell, 1971; Clark, Diener, Georgellis, & Lucas, 2008; Lykken & Tellegen, 1996).

It is strange but true that until recently set-point theory had never been *directly* tested. The obvious way to test the theory is to interview a representative sample of adults for a decade or two. At each interview one would ask about levels of happiness or life satisfaction, and about recent life events (standard life events inventories exist for this purpose).[1] One would then find out whether happiness never changes, changes only temporarily due to life events, or can change more or less permanently due to life events *or* other factors.

---

[1] Most inventories in research use are based on the one developed by Holmes and Rahe (1967).

The German Socio-Economic Panel (SOEP) has run for 25 years and provides the first available dataset world-wide in which a large representative population sample has been repeatedly asked about their life satisfaction (Wagner, Frick, & Schupp, 2007). Detailed evidence will be provided later but essentially the German SOEP shows that while most people's levels of life satisfaction are stable or show just temporary fluctuations, there are substantial minorities who have recorded large and apparently permanent changes. Furthermore, these changes appear due, not to discrete life events, but to more or less conscious preferences, goals and choices.

In the rest of the chapter, we first trace the development of the set-point paradigm and seek to account for the fact that it has dominated the field for 40 years. Particular emphasis is placed on cracks in the theory—discordant evidence that has emerged in the last decade. Then we describe the German SOEP and summarize the key evidence that substantial minorities record long-term changes in SWB. Next we discuss lines of development which may point the way to a revised theory or perhaps a new paradigm. These developments are: (1) that preferences relating to life goals and religion affect SWB, as do (2) choices relating to social and community activity, and (3) that individuals who rate high on certain personality traits (high extraversion, high neuroticism, or both) may be more open to upward or downward changes in SWB than others.

# The Adaptation Theory/Set-point Theory Paradigm: Rise and Decline

T. S. Kuhn (1962), who coined the term "scientific paradigm," described how successful paradigms develop. They appear convincing because they take on board, not just evidence accounted for by an older theory or paradigm, but also account in a convincing and parsimonious way for new evidence which was discordant, or hard to reconcile with the old theory. The new paradigm continues to be given credence if it can successfully and cumulatively accommodate more layers of evidence and only comes under fire when new discordant data emerge *and* when a competing paradigm or at least competing lines of theory are offered.

Set-point theory did not really replace any previous paradigm. It was the first one to emerge when empirical research on SWB began in the late 1960s and early 1970s. Alternatively, one might perhaps claim that it replaced the "commonsense" view that happiness is subject to daily fluctuations, with the view that it is highly stable. In any event, from 1970 to 2000 the set-point paradigm appeared to account "successfully" for evidence about relationships between three sets of variables: stable person characteristics including personality traits; life events and measures of well-being (life satisfaction, positive affect); and ill-being (anxiety, depression, and stress).

Some researchers in the field of SWB may be surprised to read that something resembling set-point theory has been around for 40 years and has "dominated" their field. A reaction of this kind is understandable and is partly due to the propensity of social scientists to stick new labels on old bottles. What came to be called set-point theory in the mid-1990s (Lykken & Tellegen, 1996) is closely related to what was first termed the adaptation (or adaptation-level) theory of well-being in the early 1970s (Brickman & Campbell, 1971; Brickman,

Coates, & Janoff-Bulman, 1978). Brickman and Campbell observed that individuals soon reverted to their previous baseline (later called "set-point") level of happiness after experiencing what would usually be thought of as major life events. It was claimed that this was more or less true even of people who became paraplegics or who won a large amount of money in a lottery. In fact, the paraplegics did record a statistically significant fall in SWB, although the authors regarded it as "surprisingly small." The claim that "We are all on an hedonic treadmill" was the standard summary of this line of research. (Maybe the best label for the family of theories is "hedonic treadmill" theories.)

A few years after adaptation theory was proposed, Richard A. Easterlin (1974) suggested that it applied to the economics of well-being. The famous Easterlin paradox states that economic growth does not improve the human lot because people adapt completely to their improving fortunes. They make "social comparisons" with their neighbors, the Jones's, and if the Jones's are doing about as well as they are, they feel no happier than before. Aspirations are revised upwards and people expect an ever-increasing material standard of living.

It should be pointed out that Easterlin uses the concept of adaptation somewhat differently from Brickman and Campbell. The analogy employed by Brickman and Campbell was explicitly that of physical adaptation, such as getting accustomed to cold water after previously being immersed in warm water, and was based on the definition of "adaptation" in adaptation-level theory proposed by the psychophysicist Harry Helson (1964). In contrast, Easterlin describes adaptation as due to social comparison and rising expectations.

The Easterlin paradox has frequently been challenged but on each occasion Easterlin and colleagues have impressively countered the challenges. The most recent and radical challenge came from Stevenson and Wolfers (2008). They re-analyzed data from many countries and made the claim that, everywhere but in the USA, changes in real income have resulted in changes in happiness.[2] However, as Easterlin points out, their evidence is not compelling on a key point: it fails to show that changes in income can produce long-term changes in happiness, as opposed to temporary fluctuations (Easterlin, 2010).

Next, Costa and McCrae (1980) put forward a *personality theory of SWB*. They showed that individuals have differing SWB baselines or set-points partly due to differences in scores on the stable personality traits of extraversion (E) and neuroticism (N). Extraverts rated higher on SWB than introverts and relatively neurotic people rated lower than emotionally stable individuals.

In an extension of the personality theory of SWB, Headey and Wearing (1989, 1992) linked personality, life events, and SWB in what they termed *dynamic equilibrium theory*. Using data from an Australian panel study, they observed that history repeats itself in people's lives with the same life events tending to happen time and again to the same people. From this, it was inferred that events must be partly endogenous, and not as previously supposed exogenous. That is, the events that happen to a person must be partly driven by his or her stable characteristics. Other evidence supported this idea. For example, it was shown that extraverts tend to experience many positive events and that neurotic individuals experience many negative events (see also Magnus et al., 1993).[3] Further, extraverts magnify the impact

---

[2] The US exception, it is claimed, is due to rising income inequality which has left many households little or no better off, despite strong increases in real aggregate GDP (Stevenson and Wolfers, 2008).

[3] Magnus et al. (1993) replicated Headey and Wearing's (1989) results and confirmed that personality affects reports of relatively objective events (e.g., marriage, unemployment) and not just events which could be a matter of selective perception.

of positive events, extracting greater satisfaction from them than those low in extraversion (Lucas & Baird, 2004). Similarly, neurotic people suffer worse than others from the effects of adverse events (Larsen, 1992). People who rate high on both E and N experience many events of both kinds, and people who rate low on both E and N experience few events of either kind. The personality trait of openness to experience (O) is also implicated. People who rate high on O report many positive *and* many negative events, while people who rate low on O report few events of either kind (Headey & Wearing, 1989). However, O is not normally found to be directly related to SWB.

A non-obvious implication of Headey and Wearing's results is that, provided only a person's normal or predictable pattern of life events happens in any given period, SWB will not change. A person's SWB will change only when events occur which are abnormal for him or her. This pattern of results led Headey and Wearing to refer to "equilibrium levels" of well-being and ill-being (rather than "baselines" or "set-points") and to conceive of personality, life events, well-being, and ill-being as being in "dynamic equilibrium."

Some researchers have focused on the fact that the large majority of people in countries all over the world report levels of SWB above scale mid-points (i.e. more "satisfied" than "dissatisfied"). Multiple discrepancies theory (Michalos, 1985) and homeostatic theory (Cummins, 1995) seek to explain this outcome and describe the mechanisms which keep it in place.

In the mid-1990s Lykken and Tellegen (1996) crowned this line of development with their *set-point theory*. This was based on what appeared to be overwhelmingly convincing findings from the famous Minnesota twins study, indicating that heredity more generally, and not just the specific personality traits of E and N, was strongly related to SWB. In successive papers that used somewhat different approaches, they have claimed that genetic factors account for about 50% (Lykken & Tellegen, 1996) or even close to 100% (Lykken, 1999, 2000) of the variance in SWB. This last estimate plainly leads to the conclusion that SWB is more or less fixed for life and that neither individual efforts nor public policy can do much to enhance it.

# Easterlin's U-turn

Recently Easterlin, whose work had so strongly buttressed adaptation theory, has begun to question its accuracy. Making a distinction between economic and non-economic life domains, he is proposing that—with respect to the latter—the data do not in fact support an inevitable return to baseline (Easterlin, 2005, 2010). For example, in the domains of family life and health, he concludes that complete adaptation does not occur, although partial adaptation does. In the family domain, he notes Lucas, Clark, Georgellis, and Diener's (2003) research showing that some people who get married and stay married are happier in the long term. His strongest point relates to health. He cites a major North American survey, based on a national representative sample, which shows that people who become seriously disabled or have painful chronic conditions like rheumatoid arthritis have permanently lower levels of SWB than otherwise similar people who are not disabled (Mehnert, Kraus, Nadler, & Boyd, 1990). In the light of these data, Easterlin suggests that it is time for SWB researchers to stop relying on Brickman, Coates, and Janoff-Bulman's (1978) results on people with paraplegia.

Huppert (2005) has also contributed a review article that seriously questions set-point theory. Drawing on the classic mood research of Wessman and Ricks (1966; see also Davidson, 2002), she notes that, while this research is limited by being conducted in a laboratory setting, it does nonetheless indicate that people with relatively higher emotional reactivity may record changes in their set-points if exposed to either particularly favorable or adverse life events. She is also highly critical of Lykken's (2000) estimate that close to 100% of the variance in SWB could be due to genetic factors. A key finding of Lykken's from the Minnesota subset of identical (MZ) twins was that the scores of one twin at time 1 predicted the scores of his/her other twin 9 years later almost as well as it predicted his/her own score ($r = 0.54$ as compared to $r = 0.55$). Since 0.54/0.55 is nearly 100%, Lykken concluded that nearly all the variation in happiness set-points is due to differences in genetic make-up!

Huppert argues that this interpretation is highly questionable. If, instead of stressing the point about identical twins, one chose to emphasize the over-time correlations between scores of the same individuals—surely central to set-point theory—then one would conclude that scores at time 1 are only a moderately good predictor of scores nine years later ($r = 0.55$). Another key point, in Huppert's opinion, is that it is a mistake to assume that individuals with the same genes are nearly certain to experience the same levels of SWB.[4] The same genes can express themselves in different ways, depending on different life experiences, especially ones in early childhood.

The leading American researcher in the SWB field, Ed Diener, has taken a rather ambivalent view of recent developments in relation to set-point theory. He and his colleagues were quick to observe evidence of long-term change in life satisfaction in the German Panel (Diener, Lucas, & Scollon, 2006; Fujita & Diener, 2005). In subsequent articles they have sought to explain change by focussing on the effects of discrete life events (Clark et al., 2004, 2008). However, in their latest and most comprehensive assessment, they find that the only reasonably common event that causes long term change in set-points is long-term or repeated unemployment (Clark et al., 2008). Other events (including getting married or becoming a widow) appear, on average, to produce only temporary fluctuations in SWB. On this basis, they have reached the interim conclusion that set-point theory may not need major revision.

An alternative view of the current evidence is that long term changes in SWB—changes in set-points—are fairly common but are *not* mainly due to specific life events. We now turn to data from the German SOEP indicating what the scale of change might be, and also, what other explanations relating to preferences (including life goals, religion, and behavioral choices) might underpin this change.

# A Unique Dataset on Life Satisfaction: The German Socio-Economic Panel

The West German segment of the SOEP, which began in 1984 with 12,541 respondents, is the longest-running annual survey of life satisfaction. Everyone in the household aged 16 and

---

[4] While this point is noted by Lykken (2000) it has not been included in other investigators' commentaries on set-point theory.

above is interviewed. To ensure it maintains its representativeness those interviewees who leave a household to, for example, start their own family, continue to be interviewed along with this new household's members. The sample has also been augmented by the recruitment of new immigrant samples, a specific sample comprising those who are wealthy, and respondents who are associated with various government benefit recipient groups. While the main topics that are covered are family, income, and labour force dynamics, a question on life satisfaction has been included every year.

Life satisfaction is measured by a single item on a 0 ("totally dissatisfied") to 10 ("totally satisfied") scale. Although single-item measures do not optimally assess SWB, this question has reasonably adequate reliability and validity (Diener et al., 1999).

As will be discussed later in this chapter, individuals with certain personality traits are more likely to record changes in life satisfaction than others. However, the SOEP did not include measures of personality until 2005, when 3-item indices of the "Big Five" personality traits were included (Costa & McCrae, 1991). The five traits are neuroticism, extraversion, openness, agreeableness, and conscientiousness. Gerlitz and Schupp (2005) report that the brief scales included in SOEP are appropriate for survey purposes and replicate results for the well-validated longer scales.[5]

The SOEP also provides data relevant to a second line of SWB-related inquiry which hypothesizes links between life goals and SWB. Since 1990 goals have been measured intermittently in SOEP based on an a priori classification initially developed by Kluckhohn and Strodtbeck (1961) which covers:

- *Altruistic goals*: friendship, helping others, social and political activism.
- *Family life goals*: happy marriage, good relationships with children.
- *Success goals*: career success and material gains.

The SOEP questions on goals vary in different waves of the survey; here we use data from the 1990, 1995, and 2004 surveys in which the questions were nearly identical. In these three waves, either nine or ten items were included,[6] all questions were asked on a 1–4 scale (1—"very important" to 4—"not at all important"). In each wave, the items formed three distinct factors that replicated: a *success goals* factor, a *family goals* factor, and an *altruistic goals* factor (Headey, 2008b; Wagner, Frick, & Schupp, 2007).

## LIFE SATISFACTION SET-POINTS—HOW MANY CHANGE AND BY HOW MUCH?

Set-point is one of those concepts in social science that is widely used but rarely operationalized. Yet, understanding whether set-points can permanently change, and if they do, by how much, can only be resolved on the basis of clear definitions.

---

[5] In the current chapter personality is treated *as if* it is completely stable and is indexed by the first rather than the latest wave of SOEP. This assumption, however, is not completely accurate; personality can be modified by surgery, trauma, major life events, and, perhaps, by psychiatric counselling.

[6] Ten items were included in 1990 and 1995, and nine in 2004. The item dropped in 2004 related to the importance of having a wide circle of friends. It loaded on the altruism factor.

Table 66.1 Long-term change in life satisfaction set-points from 1984–1988 to 2004–2008[a]

| Change from 1984–88 (baseline) to ... | Change of 25 percentiles or more % | Change of 50 percentiles or more % |
| --- | --- | --- |
| 1989–93 | 23.8 | 4.8 |
| 1994–98 | 31.4 | 9.5 |
| 1999–03 | 37.6 | 11.8 |
| 2004–08 | 37.9 | 12.3 |

[a] Source: SOEP 1984–2008: a balanced sample of respondents who reported their life satisfaction every year (N = 1076). Results are weighted using a 1984–2008 longitudinal weight.

There are at least two reasonable approaches. One is to define a person's SWB set-point as the scale score s/he would be expected to obtain on the basis of her/his personality traits and other relatively stable individual characteristics. In practice, this approach is flawed because measured personality traits never account for more than about 20% of the variance in SWB (Headey, 2006, 2008a). A second approach, which is used here, is simply to average the SWB scores of individuals over a period of consecutive years (Fujita & Diener, 2005; Headey, 2006).[7] This is similar to the approach taken by economists when they want a proxy for "permanent income."

Table 66.1 shows percentages of the German panel sample who recorded "large" changes in life satisfaction in successive 5-year periods between 1984–1988 (the first 5 years of the survey) and 2004–2008 (the last 5 years available). The sample is restricted to individuals aged 25–64; precisely the mature age group whose personality traits and hence set-points are not supposed to change. Those under 25 are excluded because it is generally believed that their personality traits are still somewhat open to change (Roberts, Walton, & Viechtbauer, 2006). Individuals 65 and over are excluded because declining health could lower SWB (Gerstorf et al., 2010).

What might be considered a "large" change? The approach used in Table 66.1 is to show how many individuals recorded changes in life satisfaction large enough to move them up or down the distribution by 25 percentiles or more, and by 50 percentiles or more.

Set-point theory implies that individuals revert to their own set-points even over long periods. But what Table 66.1 shows is a cumulative pattern of change in which many people recorded large and long-term changes in their levels of life satisfaction. This is not compatible with set-point theory, as generally understood.

By 2004–2008 37.9% of the sample had increased or decreased life satisfaction by 25 percentiles or more, compared to their position in 1984–1988, and 12.3% had shifted by 50 percentiles or more. Although the change is cumulative, its rate is not constant. Rather it

---

[7] An objection to this approach is that one might not expect SWB to remain at or close to its set-point in periods when major life events occurred. This objection can be partly addressed by removing from the sample all individuals who experienced major events (e.g., marriage, unemployment, widowhood, etc.) during the periods under consideration. Headey did this using the SOEP data and found that the results presented in Table 66.1 were largely the same (Headey, 2010).

diminishes over time. These results are consistent with an interpretation that some stabilizing forces are present (e.g., personality traits), but that significant factors that produce change are also at work.

It should be mentioned that, although the German panel provides the longest record, results from similar British and Australian panels show patterns of change in SWB over shorter-time periods that parallel the German changes (Headey, 2006). A further point to note is that results in all three countries were virtually the same for men and women.

## LIFE GOALS AND RELIGION MATTER FOR HAPPINESS

In searching for factors that might influence these changes, one promising line of inquiry relates to the effects of life goals (life priorities), including religion, on SWB. It appears that life goal choices matter to happiness and life satisfaction (Headey, 2008b; Nickerson et al., 2003). If they do, it is a major blow to set-point theory. Clearly, it is contrary to the whole thrust of the theory, which emphasises genetic factors, to find that a person can improve his/her SWB by making conscious choices about life goals.

In approaching the issue of potential links between life goals and SWB, it is helpful to recall Easterlin's (2005) review of the literature on the family life and health domains. One inference he made was that people would be happier if they prioritized these domains above the economic domain. In thinking how to test this idea, it seems sensible to reformulate it in order to make it more general and more explanatory. Why might it be better for happiness to focus on some domains rather than others? Perhaps the key distinction lies between *zero sum* and *non-zero sum* domains of life. Zero sum domains are competitive—one person's gain is unavoidably another person's loss—whereas non-zero sum or positive sum domains are those in which "my gain can also promote your gain." Applying this distinction to the life goals measured in SOEP, it would appear that *altruistic goals* (friendship, social and political activism) and *family goals* could be regarded as non-zero sum, while *success goals* (career and material success) are predominantly zero sum.[8]

Table 66.2 shows how persistence in pursuit of life goals relates to changes in life satisfaction. The outcome variable is change in life satisfaction measured between 1990 (the first time the goals questions were asked) and 2008. Preliminary analyses indicated that what matters to life satisfaction is the consistent pursuit of goals rather than a focus on current priorities or transient changes (Headey, 2008b). So the predictor variable of interest is mean scores on goals/priorities for 1990, 1995, 2004, and 2008.

In undertaking the analyses, variables that might reasonably be thought of as antecedent to or coterminous with life goals, were controlled. In the first equation in Table 66.2 gender, age, and personality traits were controlled. It seems natural to treat these as antecedent to life goals. In the second equation marital status, education, income and health, which could

---

[8] These designations are admittedly imprecise. Some people might pursue career success and material goals non-competitively, and others might pursue family goals in a competitive zero sum manner.

Table 66.2 Impact of persistent pursuit of life goals on life satisfaction[a]

| Explanatory variables | Outcome variable: life satisfaction 2008 *minus* life satisfaction 1990 | |
|---|---|---|
| Altruistic goals (mean score: 1990; 1995; 2004; 2008) | 0.29*** | 0.31*** |
| Family goals (mean score: 1990; 1995; 2004; 2008) | 0.36*** | 0.22*** |
| Success goals (mean score: 1990; 1995; 2004; 2008) | 0.05[ns] | 0.02[ns] |
| Sample size | 1692 | 1692 |
| R-squared | 35.5% | 37.4% |

[a] OLS regressions (metric coefficients). The first equation includes controls for gender, age, age-squared, extraversion, neuroticism, internal locus, and a lagged (1990) dependent variable. The second equation includes additional controls for marital status, years of education, household disposable income and health disability.
***significant at 0.001; ns = not significant at 0.10.

partly be consequences of goals, were also controlled. Again, the analyses are confined to mature age adults (25–64).

The evidence indicates that persistently giving priority to non-zero sum life goals like altruistic and family goals is associated with gains in life satisfaction. Giving priority to success goals (zero sum goals) apparently has no bearing on life satisfaction.[9] There were no significant gender differences.

A final interesting point is that, for all countries for which data are available, average satisfaction levels are higher in non-zero sum domains (that relate to family, friendships, and community activities) than in zero sum domains (that relate to work, material living standards, and social status) (Andrews & Withey, 1976; Argyle, 2001; Campbell, Converse, & Rodgers, 1976; Diener et al., 1999; Headey, 2008b; Veenhoven, 1993). One explanation is that it is easier to experience satisfaction in domains where little or no competition with others is required.

Loosely related to the idea that non-zero sum life goals are beneficial for life satisfaction is the well known finding that religious people—whether identified by stated beliefs or by behaviors like church attendance—are more satisfied with life (for a recent review, see Myers, 2008). It is not clear if religious people act in a more non-zero sum way than others but their belief systems often emphasize altruism and the desirability of cooperative behavior.

Most research on the link between religion and life satisfaction has been cross-sectional and correlational and has been open to the possible objection that omitted variables (e.g., a stable family background which may be more common for children growing up in religious families)[10] could be responsible for the link. Recent research using the German panel indicates that the link is unlikely to be spurious. Individuals who become more religious over time show gains in life satisfaction, while those who become less religious record losses

---

[9] In cross-sectional analyses, the link between pursuit of success goals and life satisfaction was actually negative and significant (Headey, 2008b).

[10] This plausible suggestion made by Clark and Lelkes (2008).

(Headey et al., 2010). The finding holds even in fixed effects models in which all fixed background factors (e.g., stable family background) are controlled.

In sum, it appears that what economists broadly term "preferences"—more specifically, non-zero sum life goals and religion—can significantly affect life satisfaction.

## Social Networks and Participation

Next we consider the effects of some behavioral choices on SWB. As with life goals and religion, a demonstration that volitional behaviors affect SWB runs counter to set-point theory.

It has long been known that people with close friends and confidants are happier than people with inadequate intimate attachments (Argyle, 2001; Diener et al., 1999). It could be, however, that the ability to form close attachments is closely linked to more or less fixed personality traits, which implies that some individuals cannot readily "choose" to form attachments. More interesting, from a contra set-point perspective, is evidence that participation in ordinary social and political activities is associated with enhanced life satisfaction (Argyle, 2001). Further, it appears that individuals who are not "naturally" extraverted can be trained to act in a more extraverted manner, improving their communication skills and social networks (Argyle, 2001).

## Highly Extraverted and Highly Neurotic Individuals are More Prone to Long-term Change

Finally, we consider the possibility that people with certain personality traits may be more open to changes in SWB than others. This line of inquiry may seem odd in the sense that, in set-point theory, personality traits are thought of as the main factors stabilizing SWB. However, we have already noted previous research which shows that those higher in extraversion both experience more positive events than others and magnify the effects of these events, while those higher in neuroticism experience more adverse events and suffer worse short-term losses to SWB. Could it be that extraversion and neuroticism are also associated with *long-term change* in SWB? Specifically, we hypothesize that relatively extraverted individuals have a high "upside risk" of long-term gains in SWB, while those who rate high in neuroticism have a high "downside risk" of long term losses. The panel data enable us to test these hypotheses in a limited way. The sample is again confined to individuals aged 25–64 and the focus is on long-term changes in life satisfaction between 1984–1988 and 2004–2008 (Table 66.3).

The evidence indicates that relatively extraverted individuals were more likely than others to record gains in life satisfaction over this 25-year period. Stronger findings emerge for those who rate high in neuroticism: they were much more likely than others to record sharp losses in life satisfaction.

Table 66.3 Long-term change in life satisfaction: upside and downside risks[a]

| | Change in life satisfaction[b] | | |
|---|---|---|---|
| | All | Men | Women |
| Extraversion | 0.12*** | 0.13** | 0.11* |
| Neuroticism | −0.28*** | −0.33*** | −0.24*** |
| R-squared | 29.0% | 28.2% | 29.8% |
| Sample | 1593 | 784 | 809 |

Source: SOEP 1984–2008. Sample: balanced panel of respondents aged 25–64.
[a] OLS regressions (metric coefficients). The equations include controls for age, age-squared and a lagged dependent variable, Life Satisfaction$_{1984-88}$
[b] Life Satisfaction$_{2004-08}$ minus Life Satisfaction$_{1984-88}$.
***significant at 0.001; ** significant at 0.01; *significant at 0.05.

# Discussion

If set-point theory was a sinking tanker, its crew would have stopped trying to plug the leaks and would be abandoning ship. The theory was used to provide an integrated account of linkages among three sets of variables: stable person characteristics, life events, and measures of well-being and ill-being. But it was largely a theory of stability. Now that it is becoming clear that people can and do record substantial changes in SWB during their adult lifetimes, the theory cannot be satisfactorily defended. A new theory, and if possible a new paradigm, is needed to account for patterns of long-term change as well as stability.

In accounting for change, additional building blocks are required. It appears that discrete life events, previously regarded as the main factors implicated in long-term change, generally have only short-term effects. Two exceptions are the onset of a chronic health condition and long term or repeated unemployment. Both of these are linked to declines in SWB. Accounts of why SWB sometimes improves are noticeably lacking. Amusingly, the only event which has been shown usually to enhance SWB is elective cosmetic surgery (Frederick & Loewenstein, 1999; Wengle, 1986).

So if specific life events usually do not produce change in SWB, what does? In this chapter I suggest that some *preferences*, including life goals/priorities and religion, and behavioral *choices* can make a significant difference. Economists specialize in the study of consumer preferences and choices. Given the enormous increase in interest in the study of happiness (or "subjective utility") as a subfield of economics, it seems likely that economists will be able to identify a range of preferences and choices which affect SWB. Developments in "authentic happiness theory" are also promising. Most of the well-known proponents of authentic happiness theory have developed their ideas alongside set-point theory without explicitly challenging it. But their starting assumptions flatly contradict set-point theory. They view "authentic happiness" as depending, not just on satisfaction, but on *commitment* to worthwhile goals and *engagement* in "meaningful tasks" (Lyubomirsky, 2007; Seligman, 2002). So authentic happiness theorists, too, are strongly motivated to discover conscious preferences and choices that affect long-term SWB.

To conclude, these should be exciting times in SWB research. The field is opening up again. Set-point theory was of limited scope and stultifying in its implications. So we should probably stop strapping what Kuhn called "protective belts" onto the old theory. It is time to develop a new theory which can explain change as well as stability, and incorporate into that theory concepts and variables which the old paradigm ignored; concepts relating to life goals, preferences, and choices.

## Acknowledgments

I would like to thank Alex Wearing of the University of Melbourne for suggestions on which this paper is partly based. Data come mainly from the German Socio-Economic Panel (SOEP), which provides easily the longest time series on life satisfaction. Sincere thanks to the SOEP Director, Gert G. Wagner of the German Institute for Economic Research (DIW), and his colleagues.

## REFERENCES

Andrews, F. M., & Withey, S. B. (1976). *Social indicators of well-being*. New York, NY: Plenum.

Argyle, M. (2001). *The psychology of happiness*. New York, NY: Routledge.

Brickman, P. D., & Campbell, D. T. (1971). Hedonic relativism and planning the good society. In M. H. Appley (Ed.), *Adaptation level theory* (pp. 287–302). New York, NY: Academic Press.

Brickman, P. D., Coates, D., & Janoff-Bulmann, R. (1978). Lottery winners and accident victims: is happiness relative? *Journal of Personality and Social Psychology*, 36, 917–27.

Campbell, A., Converse, P. E., & Rodgers, W. R. (1976). *The quality of American life*. New York, NY: Sage.

Clark, A. E., Diener, E., Georgellis, Y., & Lucas, R. E. (2008). Lags and leads in life satisfaction: A test of the baseline hypothesis. *Economic Journal*, 118, 222–43.

Clark, A. E., Georgellis, Y., Lucas, R. E., & Diener, E. (2004). Unemployment alters the set point for life satisfaction. *Psychological Science*, 15, 8–13.

Clark, A. E., & Lelkes, O. (2008). *Deliver us from evil: religion as insurance*. Paris School of Economics Working Paper, Paris.

Costa, P. T., & McCrae, R. R. (1980). Influences of extraversion and neuroticism on subjective well-being. *Journal of Personality and Social Psychology*, 38, 668–78.

Costa, P. T., & McCrae, R. R. (1991). *NEO PI-R*. Odessa, FL: PAR.

Cummins, R. A. (1995). On the trail of the gold standard for life satisfaction. *Social Indicators Research*, 35, 179–200.

Davidson, R. J. (2002). Anxiety and affective style: role of prefrontal cortex and amygdala. *Biological Psychiatry*, 51, 68–80.

Diener, E., & Fujita, F. (1995). Resources, personal strivings and subjective well-being: a nomothetic and ideographic approach. *Journal of Personality and Social Psychology*, 68, 926–35.

Diener, E., Lucas, R. E., & Scollon, C. (2006). Beyond the hedonic treadmill: revising the adaptation theory of well-being. *Psychological Science*, 61, 305–14.

Diener, E., Suh, E. M., Lucas, R. E., & Smith, H. L. (1999). Subjective well-being: Three decades of progress. *Psychological Bulletin*, 25, 276–302.

Easterlin, R. A. (1974). Does economic growth improve the human lot? Some empirical evidence. In P. A. David & M. W. Reder (Eds.), *Nations and households in economic growth* (pp. 89–125). New York, NY: Academic Press.

Easterlin, R. A. (2005). Building a better theory of well-being. In L. Bruni and P. Porta (Eds.), *Economics and happiness: Framing the analysis* (pp. 29–64). Oxford: Oxford University Press.

Easterlin, R. A. (2010). *Happiness, growth and the life cycle.* New York, NY: Oxford University Press.

Frederick, S., & Loewenstein, G. (1999). Hedonic adaptation. In D. Kahneman, E. Diener, and N. Schwarz (Eds.), *Well-being: the foundations of hedonic psychology* (pp. 302–29). New York, NY: Russell Sage.

Fujita, F., & Diener, E. (2005). Life satisfaction set-point: Stability and change. *Journal of Personality and Social Psychology, 88,* 158–64.

Gerlitz, J. -Y. & Schupp, J. (2005). Zur Erhebung der Big-Five-basierten Persoenlichkeitsmerkmale im SOEP. Retrieved from http://www.diw.de/documents/publikationen/73/diw_01.c.43490.de/rn4.pdf

Gerstorf, D., Ram, N., Hidajat, M., Mayraz, G., Lindenberger, U., Schupp, J., & Wagner, G. G. (2010). Late-life decline in well-being across adulthood in Germany, the UK, and the US: something is seriously wrong at the end of life. *Psychology and Aging, 25,* 477–85.

Headey, B. W. (2006). Subjective well-being: revisions to dynamic equilibrium theory using national panel data and panel regression methods. *Social Indicators Research, 79,* 369–403.

Headey, B. W. (2008a). The set-point theory of well-being: negative results and consequent revisions. *Social Indicators Research, 85,* 389–403.

Headey, B. W. (2008b). Life goals matter to happiness: A revision of set-point theory. *Social Indicators Research, 86,* 213–31.

Headey, B. W., Schupp, J., Tucci, I., & Wagner, G. G. (2010). Authentic happiness theory supported by impact of happiness on life satisfaction: a longitudinal analysis with data for Germany. *Journal of Positive Psychology, 5,* 73–82.

Headey, B. W., & Wearing, A. J. (1989). Personality, life events and subjective well-being: towards a dynamic equilibrium model. *Journal of Personality and Social Psychology, 57,* 731–39.

Headey, B. W., & Wearing, A. J. (1992). *Understanding happiness: A theory of subjective well-being.* Melbourne, Australia: Longman Cheshire.

Helson, H. (1964). *Adaptation-Level theory: An experimental and systematic approach to behavior.* New York, NY: Harper and Row.

Holmes, T. H., & Rahe, R. H. (1967). The social readjustment rating scale. *Psychosomatic Medicine, 11,* 213–18.

Huppert, F. (2005). Positive mental health in individuals and populations. In F. Huppert, N. Baylis, & B. Keverne, *The science of well-being* (pp. 307–340). Oxford: Oxford University Press.

Kluckhohn, F. R., & Strodbeck, F. L. (1961). *Variations in value orientations.* Evanston, IL: Row, Peterson.

Kuhn, T. S. (1962). *The structure of scientific revolutions.* Chicago, IL: University of Chicago Press.

Larsen, R. J. (1992). Neuroticism and selective encoding and recall of symptoms: Evidence from a combined concurrent-retrospective study. *Journal of Personality and Social Psychology, 62,* 489–98.

Lucas, R. E., & Baird, B. M. (2004). Extraversion and emotional reactivity. *Journal of Personality and Social Psychology, 86,* 473–85.

Lucas, R. E., Clark, A. E., Georgellis, Y., & Diener, E. (2003). Re-examining adaptation and the set point model of happiness: Reactions to change in marital status. *Journal of Personality and Social Psychology, 84,* 527–39.

Lykken, D. (1999). *Happiness: What studies on twins show us about nature, nurture and the happiness set-point.* New York, NY: Golden Books.

Lykken, D. (2000). *Happiness: The nature and nurture of joy and contentment.* New York, NY: St Martin's Press.

Lykken, D., & Tellegen, A. (1996). Happiness is a stochastic phenomenon. *Psychological Science, 7,* 186–89.

Lyubomirsky, S. (2007). *The how of happiness.* New York, NY: Penguin.

Magnus, K., Diener, E., Fujita, F., & Pavot, W. (1993). Extraversion and neuroticism as predictors of objective life events: A longitudinal analysis. *Journal of Personality and Social Psychology, 65,* 1046–53.

Mehnert, T., Kraus, H. H., Nadler, R., & Boyd, M. (1990). Correlates of life satisfaction in those with a disabling condition. *Rehabilitation Psychology, 35,* 3–17.

Michalos, A. C. (1985). Multiple discrepancies theory. *Social Indicators Research, 16,* 347–413.

Myers, D. G. (2008). Religion and human flourishing. In M. Eid and R. J. Larsen (Eds.), *The science of subjective well-being* (pp. 323–46). New York, NY: Guilford Press.

Nickerson, C., Schwarz, N., Diener, E., & Kahneman, D. (2003). Zeroing in on the dark side of the American dream: A closer look at the negative consequences of the goal for financial success. *Psychological Science, 14,* 531–36.

Roberts, B. W., Walton, K., & Viechtbauer, W. (2006). Patterns of mean-level change in personality traits across the life course: A meta-analysis of longitudinal studies. *Psychological Bulletin, 132,* 3–27.

Scollon, C. N., & Diener, E. (2006). Love, work and changes in extraversion and neuroticism over time. *Journal of Personality and Social Psychology, 91,* 1152–65.

Seligman, M. E. P. (2002). *Authentic happiness: Using the new positive psychology to realise your potential for lasting fulfillment.* New York, NY: Free Press.

Stevenson, B., & Wolfers, J. (2008). Economic growth and subjective well-being: reassessing the Easterlin Paradox. *Brookings Papers on Economic Activity, Spring,* 1–102.

Veenhoven, R. (1993). *Happiness in nations, subjective appreciation of life in 56 nations, 1946-92.* Rotterdam, the Netherlands: Erasmus University Press.

Wagner, G. G., Frick, J. R., & Schupp, J. (2007). Enhancing the power of the German Socio-Economic Panel Study (SOEP)—evolution, scope and enhancements. *Schmoeller's Jahrbuch, 127,* 139–69.

Wengle, H. (1986). The psychology of cosmetic surgery: A critical overview of the literature 1960-1982. Part 1. *Annals of Plastic Surgery, 16,* 435–43.

Wessman, A. E., & Ricks, D. F. (1966). *Mood and personality.* New York, NY: Holt, Rinehart and Winston.

CHAPTER 67

# VARIETY IS THE SPICE OF HAPPINESS: THE HEDONIC ADAPTATION PREVENTION MODEL

KENNON M. SHELDON[1], JULIA BOEHM[2], AND SONJA LYUBOMIRSKY[3]

[1]University of Missouri, USA; [2]Harvard School of Public Health, USA; [3]University of California, Riverside, USA

By now, it has become a bromide that the US constitution and culture are built on the pursuit of happiness (Myers, 1992). According to this political philosophy, government should allow citizens to strive towards their own conception of happiness, and should assist them as much as possible to reach this goal. In return, citizens ought to make the most of the opportunity, ultimately contributing to the common good of all. The enduring appeal of this American ideal rests on the very plausible assumption that happiness is the fundamental objective of all human effort and activity, in all cultures, whether people are aware of it or not. By taking action, humans aim towards more positive conditions and feelings than they currently experience, or towards more positive future feelings than they might otherwise experience if they failed to act (Carver & Scheier, 1998). Accordingly, becoming happier is not only a hugely popular topic on the self-help shelves, it is increasingly becoming a stated policy goal of world governments, with the gross national happiness of the country (rather than its gross domestic product) as the primary quantity to be maximized (Stiglitz, Sen, & Fitoussi, 2009).

Given these developments, it is worth considering how, and how well, happiness can be increased. Extensive data support the idea that gross *national* happiness can be increased (or decreased) by factors such as national affluence (vs. poverty), peace (vs. war), democratic government (vs. tyrannical government), trust (vs. widespread corruption), and societal harmony (vs. ethnic conflict) (Diener, Diener, & Diener, 1995). Surprisingly, however, data supporting the idea that *individual* happiness can be permanently increased are rather weak. Indeed, there are reasons (discussed in the next section) to doubt that it is possible at all. Accordingly, our research during the last decade has been dedicated to understanding how much—and how—happiness can be maintained above an initial baseline. In other words, what (if anything) can people do in their lives to become happier?

In this chapter, we first discuss the two conceptual models that have guided our research on the possibility of sustained happiness increases at the individual level. Specifically, we will review the empirical support for our "sustainable happiness" model (SHM). Then, we will present and provide preliminary empirical support for our newer "hedonic adaptation prevention" (HAP) model. Finally, we will present two sets of new data, which will show that variety is not only the spice of life, but the spice of happiness as well.

# The Debatable Potentiality for Sustained Gains in Happiness

Several facts and findings give rise to skepticism about the feasibility of achieving sustainable gains in happiness. First, there is the growing consensus that subjective well-being (SWB) is strongly influenced by genetics, with a heritability of around 0.50 according to twin studies (Diener, Suh, Lucas, & Smith, 1999). This behavioral genetics research suggests that SWB may be characterized by a genetically-determined "set-point," a stable feature of temperament that appears to be immune to deliberate modification (Lykken & Tellegen, 1996; Tellegen et al., 1988). In other words, SWB may be the result of a homeostatic process that resists deviations away from a pre-programmed baseline (Cummins, 2003).

The empirical literature on longitudinal SWB is the source of a second and related reason for pessimism. In a 4-year panel study, Headey and Wearing (1989) found evidence for a "dynamic equilibrium" for well-being, such that, although people might shift up or down somewhat over time, in the long run they tend to end up where they began (see also Suh, Diener, & Fujita, 1996). Lucas, Clark, Georgellis, and Diener (2003) analyzed large-$N$ longitudinal data and found that, although positive events such as marriage afford a temporary boost in SWB, this boost is transient, typically fading within several years. These data also suggest that the happiness generated by positive life changes can never be more than a temporary "rush."

Yet a third reason for pessimism arises from literature suggesting that people have a powerful capacity to adapt to change—not just to sensory and perceptual changes, but to changes that have positive or negative emotional implications. Most famously, Brickman, Coates, and Janoff-Bulman's (1978) findings suggest that lottery winners may adapt to their newfound financial status, falling back to their prior emotional baseline over time. On the negative event side, Taylor, Lichtman, and Wood (1984) found evidence for complete adaptation to the adverse effects of breast cancer, 5 years after surgery. This general tendency to adapt to emotion-relevant change, such that one always winds up back where one started, has been termed "the hedonic treadmill" (Brickman & Campbell, 1971; Frederick & Loewenstein, 1999). The hedonic treadmill is without a doubt an adaptive feature of human nature, which helps people recover from the slings and arrows of negative experience. However, the hedonic treadmill is also a significant impediment to happiness seekers, because it implies that such seeking is doomed to failure in the end. Rather than try to become happier than they are, perhaps people should instead try to become content with what they have?

# The Sustainable Happiness Model

Our early work regarding these questions focused on the SHM (Lyubomirsky, Sheldon, & Schkade, 2005; Sheldon & Lyubomirsky, 2004, 2006), which divides the possible influences on SWB into three broad categories: genetics, circumstances, and activities (see Fig. 67.1). Genetics represents the "set-point," the temperamental and psychobiological characteristics with which one is born, which account for about 50% of the variance in SWB and will have a strong and lasting influence. Circumstances represent a person's demographic profile (gender, ethnicity, income, physical appearance, health status), as well as the influence of non-psychological variables such as a person's possessions, geographic location, and immediate surroundings. Circumstances account for about 10% of the variance in SWB, a surprisingly small figure that we believe is due to the essentially static nature of circumstances. The rest of the variance, according to the SHM, is accounted for by what people *do*—that is, the *intentional activities* that they undertake within their daily lives, for good or ill, and with varying degrees of pleasure and success. Of course, "activities" is a very broad category that can overlap with "circumstances," because many circumstances arise through activity, and because circumstances provide opportunities for differing kinds and amounts of activity. Still, the SHM focuses on the activities category as the best potential route for sustainably increasing one's SWB, because ongoing activities are dynamic and changeable, meaning that activity effects are best positioned to resist erosion by hedonic adaptation. One need not always do an activity at the same time of day, in the same place, in the same way, and with the same goals and purposes. Also, one can pursue an activity as an active process of exploration and discovery, continuously encountering pleasing new features and insights in the context of that activity. If being involved and engaged in life will not do it, then nothing will.

An emerging research literature has been building evidence for the SHM by examining the efficacy of various types and categories of activity for changing SWB. These include naturalistic longitudinal studies of personal goal pursuits (Sheldon & Cooper, 2008; Sheldon & Elliot, 1999; Sheldon & Kasser, 1998); longitudinal experimental studies of the effects of

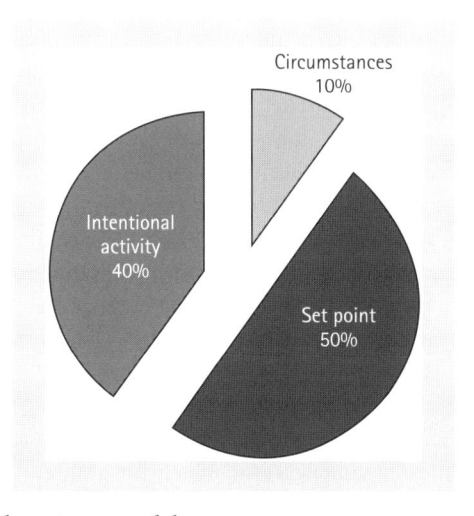

FIG. 67.1 Sustainable happiness model.

being asked to adopt new self-chosen life-activities (Sheldon & Lyubomirsky, 2007, 2009); and intervention studies of the effects of engaging in various happiness-relevant exercises such as expressing gratitude (Emmons & McCullough, 2003; Froh, Sefick, & Emmons, 2008; Lyubomirsky et al., 2005; Lyubomirsky, Dickerhoof, Boehm, & Sheldon, 2011; Seligman, Steen, Park, & Peterson, 2005), contemplating best possible selves (Burton & King, 2008; Lyubomirsky et al., 2009), committing acts of kindness (Dunn, Aknin, & Norton, 2008; Lyubomirsky et al., 2005; Otake, Shimai, Tanaka-Matsumi, Otsui, & Fredrickson, 2006), working on using personal strengths (Seligman et al., 2005), replaying one's happiest days (Lyubomirsky, Sousa, & Dickerhoof, 2006), and pausing to appreciate, savor, or be mindful of the good things in one's life (Fredrickson, Cohn, Coffey, Pek, & Finkel, 2008; Seligman et al., 2005). All of these activities have been shown to have the potential to boost mood or well-being and in many cases to maintain that increased level at a follow-up assessment period. In contrast, participants enjoined to engage in various control or comparison conditions (listing daily life events, making mere circumstantial changes, or pursuing materialistic or self-oriented goals) typically do not reap benefits, or reap benefits that are not as large or as long-lasting. A recent meta-analysis of 49 studies (total $N = 4235$) revealed that such positive interventions are indeed effective for enhancing well-being, with a medium-sized effect (mean $r = 0.29$; Sin & Lyubomirsky, 2009).

One instructive way to illustrate the propositions of the SHM, and to organize its findings thus far, is via a within-subject regression equation or growth curve model in which SWB at time $t$ is influenced by three major classes of factors: genetic/temperamental, circumstantial/demographic, and activity/motivational. The genetic set point defines the intercept or expected value, all other factors being equal. This factor's effects are theorized to be fixed and stable over time, and might be modeled with the trait measures of neuroticism, extraversion, or negative affectivity. Circumstances (positive or negative) have the potential to contribute positively or negatively to SWB at time $t$, but these effects are relatively small, and tend to erode over time (as shown by Sheldon & Lyubomirsky, 2009). Thus, one might include a "time elapsed since change" by change-type (activities vs. circumstances) interaction in the regression equation. New activities have a larger potential to continue contributing to SWB over time, because they can provide dynamically varying experiences that continue to elevate people's SWB over time (Sheldon & Lyubomirsky, 2007). In other words, a positive new activity, when kept fresh and interesting, can engender experiences that keep a person happier over a longer period than the person's genetics alone would indicate.

This within-subject regression approach well illustrates an important assumption of the SHM—that instead of a set "point" for SWB, people actually have a set "range." Thus, although a particular person may have limited potential for joy and ebullience and more of a tendency towards gloom and pessimism compared to others, that person might still at least achieve a chronic state of guarded contentment, which is better than chronic dejection and fear. Everyone has a characteristic range of possible SWB states, and thus the goal becomes to find ways to stay in the top end of one's own possible range (vs. regress back to one's own mean). The other terms in the model, beyond genetics, determine whether, and for how long, an individual can do this.

The foregoing material on "keeping things fresh and interesting" illustrates an important moderator of activity effects, according to the SHM—namely, *variety*. The happy newlyweds who settle down to domestic sameness and taken-for-grantedness, the proud new car owner who stops driving to fun places, and the formerly curious piano player who succumbs to the rote routines of practice and procedure will all return back to their initial baselines. Notably, the original SHM postulated that the longevity of activity effects on happiness likely depends on many other moderators besides variety, such as how diligently or successfully one performs the activity (Lyubomirsky et al., 2009; Sheldon & Lyubomirsky, 2006), how well the chosen activity fits one's personality and interests (Lyubomirsky, 2008), and whether the activity is intrinsic or extrinsic in content (Sheldon Gunz, Nichols, & Ferguson, 2010). However, it is fair to say that variety was construed in that model as the most important moderator of all, because of its crucial potential role in curtailing hedonic adaptation. Even so, this prediction has received little empirical attention to date. The primary purpose of this chapter is to redress this gap.

# THE HEDONIC ADAPTATION PREVENTION MODEL

First, however, we will discuss our newer HAP model, which grants a prominent role to variety and the processes by which variety can help to thwart hedonic adaptation. Fig. 67.2 depicts the entire HAP model, which is in essence a longitudinal expansion of the SHM.

The temporal model begins on the left, at Time 1 (T1), by positing that some kind of "positive change" has occurred in a person's life, resulting in an initial boost in mood or well-being. The model ends on the right at a Time 3 (or any subsequent) measurement of well-being, asking the question, "How can the initial boost be maintained at a later time?" The boxes and arrows in between the start and end points present our theorizing on how hedonic adaptation may be prevented, such that the initial boost is, in fact, maintained. We define "well-being" (WB) as global self-reports of happiness, satisfaction, and mood (as the measures are often interchangeable; Diener et al., 1999), and we define a "positive

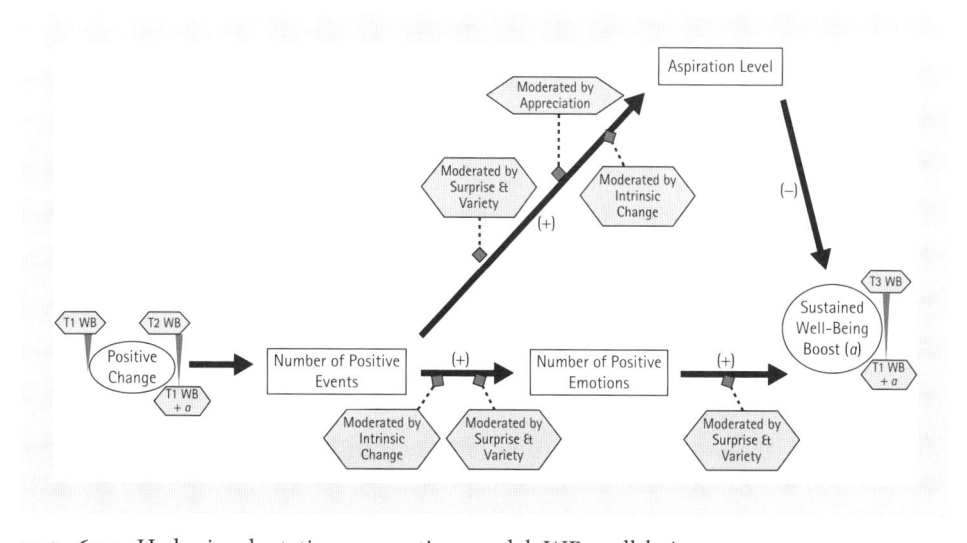

FIG. 67.2 Hedonic adaptation prevention model. WB, well-being.

change" as a noticeable and measurable alteration in one's life circumstances or one's life activities that has a measurable effect on well-being before and after the change. It is also worth noting that in principle the HAP model should apply to understanding adaptation to *negative* events, such that an initial blow (e.g., getting laid off) that reduces well-being and mood loses its negative impact over time. This application of the model, however, goes beyond the scope of this chapter (however, see Lyubomirsky (2011), for a detailed account of this extension). Still, we note that adaptation is often less complete to profoundly negative events (e.g., disability, divorce; Lucas, 2005, 2007; Lucas et al., 2003) than to seemingly equally profound positive events (e.g., marriage, receiving tenure). That is, more people go down and then stay down than those who go up and then stay up, suggesting that, in a sense, "bad is stronger than good" (Baumeister, Bratslavsky, Finkenauer, & Vohs, 2001). This makes our research agenda of finding ways to keep people in the upper end of their own set range even more difficult and challenging (Lyubomirsky, 2011).

The second step of the HAP model states that those undergoing a noticeable positive change at Time 1 will tend to experience a larger number of subsequent positive events compared to those who do not undergo a positive change. For example, a person who buys a beautiful work of art begins enjoying pleasurable experiences of looking at and savoring the art, and a person who starts playing in a band begins having pleasurable episodes of making music and sharing it with others. As these examples illustrate, the positive events deriving from positive changes can be actual life experiences and real-world outcomes resulting from one's actions in the new domain, or they can be internal "thought-events" in which one notices, appreciates, thinks about, or savors the original positive change. Doubtless, positive changes vary in both the quantity and quality of the positive events they produce, and the difference between different types of change has itself been a prominent topic for research inquiry (i.e., does gratitude generate longer-lasting happiness boosts than savoring?; do intrinsic or need-satisfying goals work better than extrinsic or non-satisfying goals?; e.g., Seligman et al., 2005; Sheldon & Lyubomirsky, 2009; Sheldon et al., 2010).

Moving to the next step, the HAP model specifies two major routes extending away from the positive events and toward final well-being. (We will ignore the many potential moderators in the model, returning to them later.) The "emotions" route (at the bottom) specifies that positive events produce positive emotional experiences, to varying degrees. In turn, the number of positive emotions impacts global judgments of well-being made at Time 3 or beyond. In this view, Time 3 happiness is higher (controlling for Time 1 and Time 2 happiness)—that is, the initial boost has been maintained—to the extent that there have been more discrete positive emotions experienced between Time 2 and Time 3. This lower route relies on a "bottom-up" conception of well-being (Diener, 1984), in which global happiness judgments are influenced by the number of salient positive experiences that come to mind as one makes the judgments. Someone who can recall many "warm glows" from recent experience will tend to rate him or herself as happier than someone who cannot recall many such experiences.

As a case in point, consider a couple who is nearing completion of an exciting renovation and addition to their home. Are they happier than they were 6 months ago, before construction began? Yes—the positive change (finally starting construction) produced many positive events, as each new facet of the house came into being, and as each subsequent set of engaging decisions arose. These events produced a quantity and variety of positive emotions (aesthetic pleasure, as their initial design choices came to life; closeness, as they collaborated on each new decision; pride, as they showed the evolving house to their friends). When they rate their happiness now, these memories, as well as the pleasure of living in the nearly finished product, elevate their reported happiness levels. However, if the couple had had fewer positive events (and perhaps more arguments!) due to conflicting aesthetic preferences, or had experienced fewer positive emotions (or more negative ones) due to the stress of living in a house under construction, then these facts would predict a less sustained boost at Time 3.

Note that hedonic adaptation processes could operate in this lower part of the model by reducing the number of positive events derived from the positive change (e.g., one no longer notices one's new car and forgets to take it for pleasurable drives) or by reducing the number of positive emotions derived from events (e.g., even while driving the car on a winding mountain road, one takes it for granted and no longer feels the same excitement and pride). Thus, the key to preventing adaptation and maintaining boosts, according to this part of the model, is to keep up the number of positive events and emotions. The car owner should make time in his schedule to drive and enjoy the car, perhaps taking it to automobile shows at which he and other owners of that model can meet and exchange ideas. In this way, adaptation to the car can be forestalled.

Now let us consider the top route in the model, the "aspirations" route. This part of the model explains the erosion of initial well-being gains in terms of cognitive processes that ensue from the initial positive change and its associated positive events. Thus, the upper route tackles hedonic adaptation at the level of judgmental processes and expectations. According to the model, the more positive events there are, the more one's expectations and aspirations regarding further positive events are increased (represented in the figure by the path from positive events to aspirations). In other words, when things are going well, one starts to take them for granted and starts assuming that they will always be there—perhaps even coming to feel entitled to the new positive situation, rather than appreciative of it. The new, more positive regime becomes the new status quo, making one susceptible to wanting (or craving) and expecting (or demanding) even more. Finally, the negatively-signed path from aspirations to Time 3 SWB indicates that the more one's aspirations and expectancies increase, the less the resulting Time 3 well-being. In other words, those who come to expect and feel that they deserve a greater quantity of positive events, and perhaps demand even more, derive less pleasure from those events, reducing their happiness. This process has been referred to as the "satisfaction treadmill" (Kahneman, 1999), and represents a top-down effect on well-being—one's standards and basis for judging one's global well-being have changed, resulting in a reduction in that estimate.

Returning to the "renovated house" example, suppose that the couple, now that they are ensconced in their redesigned house, begin to take for granted the spacious new bedroom and balcony, the vaulting 2-story entrance foyer, and the remodeled kitchen; in other words, they stop noticing or thinking about the positive changes, so that they fade into the background as they move on with their lives. Or worse, suppose they begin to look around at other houses in their new price category, recognizing desirable features in these houses they do not have, and feeling envy or greed as a result. Perhaps they begin to feel that their house does not match up well to this new level of standard, and begin aspiring to even further changes or an even better home. Such processes could undermine the initial happiness boost, working to return the couple to their initial baseline.

Notably, then, the HAP model recognizes the paradoxical effects of positive changes in life—that they can produce positive events that boost one's happiness, but at the same time, these events can change one's standards and expectations, working against one's happiness. Of course, neither pathway is certain or inevitable, and this is where the rest of the model comes in.

As can be seen in Fig. 67.2, we specify several moderators that are expected to affect the strength of various relations within the model. These moderators include the nature or content of the initial change (e.g., intrinsic vs. extrinsic, activity vs. circumstance, gratitude vs. neutral activity); the extent to which resultant positive events are surprising, novel, or unexpected; and the extent to which one continues to appreciate the original change, and recognize that it could easily "change back." Most important for this chapter's purposes, one of these key moderators is *variety*—the extent to which the positive events and positive emotions resulting from the change vary in their content, similarity, timing, and diversity. By definition, adaptation occurs only in response to constant or repeated stimuli, not to dynamically varying ones (Frederick & Loewenstein, 1999; see also Helson, 1964; Parducci, 1995). Variety, in both thoughts and behaviors, appears to be innately stimulating and rewarding (Berlyne, 1970; Pronin & E. Jacobs, 2008; Rolls, Rolls, Rowe, & Sweeney, 1981; see Ebstein et al., 1996; Suhara et al., 2001, for links to dopamine activity). Thus, variety appears as a moderator in three different places within the model (moderating the positive events to aspiration level link, the number of positive events to positive emotions link, and the number of positive emotions to sustained well-being link), endowing it with a special role for reducing hedonic adaptation and increasing the durability of happiness changes.

Despite its likely central relevance for understanding how to sustainably boost happiness, the construct of variety has received surprisingly little empirical attention in the literature. Thus, in the remainder of this chapter, we will describe the previously unpublished results from two longitudinal studies that support variety's important role in thwarting adaptation and thereby in prolonging well-being. These two studies—one correlational and one experimental—do not permit testing of the entire temporal sequence laid out in the HAP model, but they do permit testing of the key hypothesis that variety plays a moderating role in the process by which positive experiences bring about sustained well-being.

## STUDY 1: RATED VARIETY PREDICTS MAINTAINED WELL-BEING

For the first study, we recruited 134 introductory psychology students at the University of Missouri, USA, 38 men and 96 women (mostly Caucasian), who signed up online for a three-part investigation. Initially, participants attended small-group laboratory sessions in which they were told the following: "We are studying positive mood, and the factors that sustain it. We will assess your mood and happiness now and later in the semester, to see how they change." After completing the Positive and Negative Activation Scale (PANAS; Watson, Clark, & Tellegen, 1988), each participant was asked to attempt something "which might influence your mood." Seventy students were randomly assigned to identify a goal or activity change they could make in the next 2 weeks (i.e., "You might join a rewarding new group, club, or sports team, decide on a major or career direction which makes it clear how to focus your life, or take on some other important new project in your life"), and the remaining 64 were assigned to identify a circumstance they could change (i.e., "You might buy yourself something you need or want, arrange to get an on-campus parking permit, or drop a course that you were really going to have trouble with"). Research assistants examined each participant's listed change to make sure it fit the assigned category. Example activity changes listed included "Get involved in my sorority's rush committee," "Join an intramural basketball team," and "Introduce myself to all my professors"; example circumstance changes listed included "Get my old roommate to finish moving his stuff out," "Drop Physical Chemistry," and "Pay off my parking tickets."

After answering a filler questionnaire, participants completed the PANAS again, so we could examine the effects of the initial positive event (i.e., designating a positive change to make) on mood. Finally, approximately 2 weeks later, participants filled out an online survey in which they again were asked to complete the PANAS. Additionally, they were asked, "Did you actually make the change you said you would make? Please tell the truth – it is ok if you didn't (we expect that), we just need to know, for the purposes of our study." The data below concern only the 79 participants who responded "Yes" to this question. These students were asked to rate the variety of their change ("To what extent is the change something that *varies over time*, i.e., something that adds variety to your life?"), using a 1 (*not at all*) to 5 (*very much*) scale. Activity change participants reported slightly more variety in their change than circumstance change participants ($Ms$ = 3.10 vs. 2.74), but this finding did not reach significance, $t(77) = 1.54, p = 0.127$. Our results are collapsed across type of change (activity vs. circumstance), because this factor did not moderate the findings reported in this chapter; in other words, variety had the same effect in both conditions.

For each of the three time points, we computed a single "affect balance" score by subtracting negative affect from positive affect on the PANAS (Sheldon & Lyubomirsky, 2006). Preliminary full-sample analyses of these data indicated that affect balance increased between the beginning and the end of the first session (Time 1 to Time 2; $Ms$ = 1.42 vs. 1.71, $t(78) = 4.06, p < 0.01$), likely because participants were pleased to have made a commitment to a positive change. This fulfills the HAP model's assumption that there is an initial event that raises initial well-being. However, no difference emerged between Time 1 affect balance and Time 3 affect balance, 2 weeks later ($Ms$ = 1.42 and 1.51, $ns$), suggesting that the effects of making the initial change, if any, had on average dissipated by Time 3.

Thus the question becomes, which participants, if any, maintained their gains in well-being at Time 3? To address this question, we regressed Time 3 affect balance on Time 1 affect balance (so that positive change from Time 1 to Time 3 would be the focal quantity to be predicted) and also the rated variety of the change at Time 3. This analysis revealed a significant Time 1 affect balance effect (i.e., the test-retest coefficient; $\beta = 0.60, p < 0.01$). This coefficient is substantial but also indicates some variability or inconsistency between Time 1 and Time 3. In fact, as expected, rated variety significantly predicted this variability ($\beta = 0.19, p < 0.05$). This finding suggests that those who enacted their change (e.g., start walking to work) with greater variety (e.g., walking a different route to work every day this week) were more successful at maintaining their initial boost, consistent with a central proposition of the HAP model (although we did not have the data to examine which of the two routes in Fig. 67.2 were most affected).

At a second step of the equation, we entered Time 2 affect balance, and found a trend for the variety effect ($\beta =0.14, p = 0.10$), indicating that variety predicted enhanced affect balance controlling for both prior measures of well-being, a more rigorous standard implying that variety nearly predicted increased well-being after Time 2, when well-being was already elevated. At a third step of the equation, we controlled for which type of life change was made (activities or circumstances), finding neither a significant main effect nor a significant interaction with variety. Thus, in these data, the *variety* of the assigned change was a more robust predictor of maintained change than the exact *type* of change.

In sum, Study 1 supplied initial evidence that the degree of variety associated with a positive life change helps to maintain the longer-term effects of that change upon well-being. However, Study 1 was only correlational, and relied on participants' self-reports of variety rather than on a more objective means of varying how people experience a life change. To redress this shortcoming, for a second study, we collected experimental data with random assignment to further illuminate the role of variety.

## Study 2: Experimentally Assigned Variety Predicts Gains in Well-being

In the second study, 52 undergraduate students from an ethnically diverse campus of the University of California were invited to participate in a longitudinal investigation about "aspects of college students' lives over the course of a [school] quarter." Interested students attended an introductory laboratory session where they were asked to list numerous acts of kindness that they could feasibly perform in the future. Kind acts were described to participants as "acts that are not normally expected in your daily life (i.e., they are over and above what you typically do) and involve some sacrifice by you (e.g., in effort, energy, time, or money)."

After participants listed possible kind acts to do, they were instructed to perform the kind acts during the next 10 weeks. Participants logged in to an online diary to report what kind acts they had completed each week. Examples of such acts include "Taking out the trash in my [shared] apartment," "Letting a friend borrow a book for class," "Cooking dinner for my roommates" and "Letting several cars merge in front of me on the freeway." Importantly, some students were randomly told to repeat the same kind acts each week for the duration of the study (low variety condition), whereas other students were told to vary the acts that they performed and not repeat them (high variety condition). We hypothesized that those participants who practiced kind acts in new and different ways each week (i.e., the high variety condition) would derive more positive emotions from the activity and demonstrate enhanced well-being at the end of the 10-week intervention. By contrast, we hypothesized that those participants who practiced kind acts in routine, unvarying ways each week (i.e., the low variety condition) would derive less and less added positive emotions from the activity over time and thus demonstrate no change in well-being by the end of the 10-week intervention. In other words, people in the low variety condition were expected to adapt to practicing acts of kindness relatively quickly, whereas people in the high variety condition were expected to thwart adaptation by engaging in novel, changing activities.

We measured participants' happiness at baseline and immediately after the intervention period with the 4-item Subjective Happiness Scale (SHS; Lyubomirsky & Lepper, 1999). We then calculated change scores by subtracting baseline happiness from post-intervention happiness. Students in the high variety condition reported enhanced happiness following the intervention ($M$ = +0.03, SD = 0.75) relative to students in the low variety condition who actually reported diminished happiness following the intervention ($M$ = −0.78, SD = 1.16). These changes in well-being were significantly different for the high variety vs. low variety conditions, $t(50) = 3.00, p = 0.004$. This finding suggests that not only does implementing an intentional activity in new and unpredictable ways help bolster one's well-being, but that repeating an intentional activity without spontaneity and freshness may actually be detrimental to well-being. It is also worth noting that it may appear that high variety participants did not actually become happier, and that instead, low variety participants became unhappier. However, this pattern of results needs to be understood in the context of the typical temporal trend for students to become unhappier over the course of an academic quarter, as the workload increases and initial optimism gives way to less rosy realities. Seen this way, the high variety participants were able to avoid the typical decline in SWB shown by students as found in previous longitudinal intervention studies (e.g., Lyubomirsky et al., 2005).

In sum, our second study found that those randomly assigned to engage in more varied kindness activities derive higher maintained well-being at the end of the intervention, compared to those assigned to engage in less varied activities. This is consistent with the HAP model and also with a saying from first-century BC writer Publilius Syrus, who observed, "No pleasure endures unseasoned by variety." Notably, the main finding from this experimental study extends the correlational conclusions of Study 1, and further suggests that attending to variety in one's actions may be a powerful happiness enhancing strategy.

In conclusion, the two studies we have reported here provide the first support for an important feature of both the SHM and HAP models—the notion that varying how one does a "positive" activity may be crucial in determining whether that activity continues to have enhancing effects on peoples' well-being. Again, a key assumption of the HAP model is that an ongoing stream of fresh positive events and positive emotions are necessary to maintain a person in the upper end of his or her "set range." Hedonic adaptation is a powerful counterweight to this possibility, and in order to overcome it, one must continue to vary the positive experiences one has. We as researchers recognize this in our own lives; the thrill and satisfaction of conducting research is enhanced when we ask new questions, test new phenomena, and develop new theories. In this way, the potential "ho hum" of our work lives is forestalled, so that we can remain as excited about research as when we were graduate students. To return to the title of this chapter—variety is, indeed, the spice of happiness.

# References

Baumeister, R. F., Bratslavsky, E., Finkenauer, C., & Vohs, K. D. (2001). Bad is stronger than good. *Review of General Psychology*, 5, 323–370.

Berlyne, D. E. (1970). Novelty, complexity, and hedonic value. *Perception & Psychophysics*, 8, 279–286.

Brickman, P., & Campbell D. T. (1971). Hedonic relativism and planning the good society. In M. H. Appley (Ed.), *Adaptation-level theory* (pp. 287–302). New York, NY: Academic Press.

Brickman, P., Coates, D., & Janoff-Bulman, R. (1978). Lottery winners and accident victims: Is happiness relative? *Journal of Personality and Social Psychology*, 36, 917–927.

Burton, C. M., & King, L. A. (2008). Effects of (very) brief writing on health: The two-minute miracle. *British Journal of Health Psychology*, 13, 9–14.

Carver, C. S., & Scheier, M. F. (1998). *On the self-regulation of behavior*. New York, NY: Cambridge University Press.

Cummins, R. A. (2003). Normative life satisfaction: Measurement issues and a homeostatic model. *Social Indicators Research, 64,* 225–256.

Deutsch, F. M., & Lamberti, D. M. (1986). Does social approval increase helping? *Personality and Social Psychology Bulletin, 12,* 149–157.

Diener, E. (1984). Subjective well-being. *Psychological Bulletin, 95,* 542–575.

Diener, E., Diener, M., & Diener, C. (1995). Factors predicting the subjective well-being on nations. *Journal of Personality and Social Psychology, 69,* 851–864.

Diener, E., Suh, E. M., Lucas, R. E., & Smith, H. L. (1999). Subjective well-being: Three decades of progress. *Psychological Bulletin, 125,* 276–302.

Dunn, E. W., Aknin, L. B., & Norton, M. I. (2008). Spending money on others promotes happiness. *Science, 319,* 1687–1688.

Ebstein, R. P., Novick, O., Umansky, R., Priel, B. Osher, Y., Blaine, D., ... Belmaker, R. H. (1996). Dopamine D4 receptor (D4DR) exon III polymorphism associated with the human personality trait of novelty seeking. *Nature Genetics, 12,* 78–80.

Emmons, R. A., & McCullough, M. E. (2003). Counting blessings versus burdens: An experimental investigation of gratitude and subjective well-being in daily life. *Journal of Personality and Social Psychology, 84,* 377–389.

Emmons, R. A., & McCullough, M. E. (2004). *The psychology of gratitude.* New York, NY: Oxford University Press.

Frederick, S., & Loewenstein, G. (1999). Hedonic adaptation. In D. Kahneman, E. Diener, & N. Schwarz (Eds.), *Well-being: The foundations of hedonic psychology* (pp. 302–329). New York, NY: Russell Sage Foundation.

Fredrickson, B. L., Cohn, M. A., Coffey, K. A., Pek, J., & Finkel, S. M. (2008). Open hearts build lives: Positive emotions, induced through loving-kindness meditation, build consequential personal resources. *Journal of Personality and Social Psychology, 95,* 1045–1062.

Froh, J. J., Sefick, W. J., & Emmons, R. A. (2008). Counting blessings in early adolescents: An experimental study of gratitude and subjective well-being. *Journal of School Psychology, 46,* 213–233.

Headey, B., & Wearing, A. (1989). Personality, life events, and subjective well-being: Toward a dynamic equilibrium model. *Journal of Personality and Social Psychology, 57,* 731–739.

Helson, H. (1964). Current trends and issues in adaptation-level theory. *American Psychologist, 19,* 26–38.

Kahneman, D. (1999). Objective happiness. In D. Kahneman, E. Diener, & N. Schwarz (Eds.), *Well-being: The foundations of hedonic psychology* (pp. 3–25). New York, NY: Russell Sage Foundation.

Lucas, R. E. (2005). Time does not heal all wounds: A longitudinal study of reaction and adaptation to divorce. *Psychological Science, 16,* 945–950.

Lucas, R. E. (2007). Long-term disability has lasting effects on subjective well-being: Evidence from two nationally representative longitudinal studies. *Journal of Personality and Social Psychology, 92,* 717–730.

Lucas, R. E., Clark, A. E., Georgellis, Y., & Diener, E. (2003). Reexamining adaptation and the set point model of happiness: Reactions to changes in marital status. *Journal of Personality and Social Psychology, 84,* 527–539.

Lykken, D., & Tellegen, A. (1996). Happiness is a stochastic phenomenon. *Psychological Science, 7,* 186–189.

Lyubomirsky, S. (2008). *The how of happiness: A scientific approach to getting the life you want.* New York, NY: Penguin Press.

Lyubomirsky, S. (2011). Hedonic adaptation to positive and negative experiences. In S. Folkman (Ed.), *Oxford handbook of stress, health, and coping* (pp. 200–224). New York, NY: Oxford University Press.

Lyubomirsky, S., Dickerhoof, R., Boehm, J. K., & Sheldon, K. M. (2011). Becoming happier takes both a will and a proper way: An experimental longitudinal intervention to boost well-being. *Emotion, 11*, 391–402.

Lyubomirsky, S., & Lepper, H. (1999). A measure of subjective happiness: Preliminary reliability and construct validation. *Social Indicators Research, 46*, 137–155.

Lyubomirsky, S., Sheldon, K. M., & Schkade, D. (2005). Pursuing happiness: The architecture of sustainable change. *Review of General Psychology, 9*, 111–131.

Lyubomirsky, S., Sousa, L., Dickerhoof, R. (2006). The costs and benefits of writing, talking, and thinking about life's triumphs and defeats. *Journal of Personality and Social Psychology, 90*, 692–708.

Myers, D. G. (1992). *The pursuit of happiness.* New York, NY: William Morrow.

Otake, K., Shimai, S., Tanaka-Matsumi, J., Otsui, K., & Fredrickson, B. L. (2006). Happy people become happier through kindness: A counting kindnesses intervention. *Journal of Happiness Studies, 7*, 361–375.

Parducci, A. (1995). *Happiness, pleasure, and judgment: The contextual theory and its applications.* Mahwah, NJ: Erlbaum.

Pronin, E., & Jacobs, E. (2008). Thought speed, mood, and the experience of mental motion. *Perspectives on Psychological Science, 3*, 461–485.

Rolls, B. J., Rolls, E. T., Rowe, E. A., & Sweeney, K. (1981). Sensory specific satiety in man. *Physiology & Behavior, 27*, 137–142.

Seligman, M. E. P., Steen, T. A., Park, N., & Peterson, C. (2005). Positive psychology progress: Empirical validation of interventions. *American Psychologist, 60*, 410–421.

Sheldon, K. M., & Cooper, M. L. (2008). Goal striving and agentic and communal roles: Separate but functionally similar pathways to enhanced well-being. *Journal of Personality, 76*, 415–447.

Sheldon, K. M., & Elliot, A. J. (1999). Goal striving, need satisfaction, and longitudinal well-being: The self-concordance model. *Journal of Personality and Social Psychology, 76*, 482–497.

Sheldon, K. M., Gunz, A., Nichols, C., & Ferguson, Y. (2010). Extrinsic value orientation and affective forecasting: Overestimating the rewards, underestimating the costs. *Journal of Personality, 78*, 149–178.

Sheldon, K. M., & Kasser, T. (1998). Pursuing personal goals: Skills enable progress, but not all progress is beneficial. *Personality and Social Psychology Bulletin, 24*, 1319–1331.

Sheldon, K. M., & Lyubomirsky, S. (2009). Change your actions, not your circumstances: An experimental test of the Sustainable Happiness Model. In A. K. Dutt & B. Radcliff (Eds.), *Happiness, economics, and politics: Toward a multi-disciplinary approach* (pp. 324–342). Cheltenham, UK: Edward Elgar.

Sheldon, K. M., & Lyubomirsky, S. (2007). Is it possible to become happier? (And if so, how?) *Social and Personality Psychology Compass, 1*, 129–145.

Sheldon, K. M., & Lyubomirsky, S. (2004). Achieving sustainable new happiness: Prospects, practices, and prescriptions. In A. Linley & S. Joseph (Eds.), *Positive psychology in practice* (pp. 127–145). Hoboken, NJ: John Wiley & Sons.

Sheldon, K. M., & Lyubomirsky, S. (2006). Achieving sustainable gains in happiness: Change your actions, not your circumstances. *Journal of Happiness Studies, 7*, 55–86.

Sin, N. L., & Lyubomirsky, S. (2009). Enhancing well-being and alleviating depressive symptoms with positive psychology interventions: A practice-friendly meta-analysis. *Journal of Clinical Psychology: In Session, 65*, 467–487.

Stiglitz, J. E., Sen, A., & Fitoussi, J. (2009). *Report by the commission on the measurement of economic performance and social progress.* Retrieved from http://www.stiglitz-sen-fitoussi.fr/documents/rapport_anglais.pdf

Suh, E., Diener, E., & Fujita, F. (1996). Events and subjective well-being: Only recent events matter. *Journal of Personality and Social Psychology, 70*, 1091–1102.

Suhara, T. Yasuno, F., Sudo, Y., Yamamoto, M., Inoue, M., Okubo, Y., & Suzuki, K. (2001). Dopamine D2 receptors in the insular cortex and the personality trait of novelty seeking. *Neuroimage, 13*, 891–895.

Taylor, S. E., Lichtman, R. R., & Wood, J. V. (1984). Attributions, beliefs about control, and adjustment to breast cancer. *Journal of Personality and Social Psychology, 46*, 489–502.

Tellegen, A., Lykken, D. T., Bouchard, T. J., Wilcox, K. J., Segal, N. L., & Rich, S. (1988). Personality similarity in twins reared apart and together. *Journal of Personality and Social Psychology, 54*, 1031–1039.

Watson, D., Clark, L. A., & Tellegen, A. (1988). Development and validation of brief measures of positive and negative affect: The PANAS scales. *Journal of Personality and Social Psychology, 54*, 1063–1070.

CHAPTER 68

# PROMOTION AND PROTECTION OF POSITIVE MENTAL HEALTH: TOWARDS COMPLETE MENTAL HEALTH IN HUMAN DEVELOPMENT

COREY L. M. KEYES

Emory University, USA

MENTAL illness is serious, but it was not a public health priority until the last decade of the twentieth century, when the World Health Organization published the results of the first Global Burden of Disease study (Murray & Lopez, 1996). As is now well known, this study estimated the total contribution of 107 acute and chronic medical conditions and illnesses by including disability in the equation to calculate disability-adjusted life years (DALYs). The DALY reflects the total number of years in a population that were either lived with disability or abbreviated prematurely that are attributable to specific physical or mental conditions. Depression was the fourth leading cause of disease burden, accounting for 3.7% of DALYs in 1990, 4.4% in 2000, and projected to be 15% of DALYs by 2020 (Ustun, 1999; Ustun, Ayuso-Mateos, Chatterji, Mathers, & Murray, 2004).

The debate is no longer about whether mental illness is a serious public health issue. Rather, the new debate is what governments should do to reduce the number of cases of mental illness and those suffering from it. The de facto approach to mental illness and its burden has been treatment (Chisholm, Sanderson, Ayuso-Mateos, & Saxena, 2004) and risk-reduction prevention. But, evidence shows that the de facto approach has not reduced the prevalence or burden of mental disorder over the past several decades (Insel & Scolnick, 2006), nor has it prevented early age-of-onsets for mood, anxiety and substance abuse disorders (Kessler et al., 2005).

Mental health promotion seeks to elevate levels of positive mental health and protect against its loss (Davis, 2002; Keyes, 2007; Secker, 1998). Whereas treatment targets those with mental illness, and risk reduction prevention targets those vulnerable to mental illness, mental health promotion targets those with good mental health and those with less than optimal mental health—i.e., all members of a population. Mental health promotion is therefore amenable to a public health approach and is a complement rather than an alternative to treatment (Keyes, 2007).

Although it has important consequences for individual functioning and for society, mental illness represents only half of the developmental outcomes. It is also important to study developmental outcomes in mental health beyond psychopathology by including the study of positive mental health. Historically, good mental health has been viewed as the absence of mental disorder, despite conceptions that health in general is "something positive" (Sigerist, 1941) or well-being (World Health Organization, 1948), and not merely the absence of illness. Mental well-being—i.e., positive mental health—is now a focus of policy and science. The World Health Organization (2004) recently highlighted the need to promote good mental health, defined as "... a state of well–being in which the individual realizes his or her own abilities, can cope with the normal stresses of life, can work productively and fruitfully, and is able to make a contribution to his or her community" (p. 12).

Mental health has been operationalized under the rubric of subjective well-being (SWB), or individuals' evaluations of the quality of their lives. The nature of SWB has been divided into two streams of research. The first of these equates well-being with happiness or feeling good. The second approach to well-being focuses on human potential that, when cultivated, results in functioning well in life. These two streams of SWB research grew from two distinct philosophical viewpoints on happiness—one reflecting the hedonic tradition that championed positive emotions, and the other reflecting the eudaimonic tradition that championed striving toward excellence in functioning as an individual and a citizen.

As shown in Table 68.1, the hedonic tradition is reflected in research on *emotional* well-being, where scholars use measures of avowed satisfaction with life and positive affect (Bradburn, 1969; Diener, 1984; Gurin, Veroff, & Feld, 1960). The tradition of eudaimonia is reflected in research on *psychological* (Ryff, 1989) and *social* (Keyes, 1998) well-being. Here, scholars use multidimensional scales that ask individuals to evaluate how well they see themselves functioning in life as they strive to achieve secular standards of purpose, contribution, integration, autonomy, intimacy, acceptance, and mastery in life. When SWB is measured comprehensively, studies support the tripartite model consisting of emotional, psychological, and social well-being in US adults (Gallagher, Lopez, & Preacher, 2009), college students (Robitschek & Keyes, 2009), and adolescents (Keyes, 2005a).

# THE DUAL CONTINUA MODEL

Mental health promotion and protection (MHPP) is premised on the dual continua model—that mental health and mental illness belong to two separate but correlated dimensions in the population (Downie, Fyfe, & Tannahill, 1990; Health and Welfare Canada, 1988). Recent advances in the scientific measurement of positive mental health (Keyes, 2002) now permit scientific investigation of the long-standing hypothesis that mental health, like health in general, is a complete state.

### Table 68.1 Tripartite structure and specific dimensions reflecting positive mental health

Hedonia (i.e., emotional well-being)

- *Positive affect*: cheerful, interested in life, in good spirits, happy, calm and peaceful, full of life
- *Avowed quality of life:* mostly or highly satisfied with life overall or in domains of life
- Eudaimonia (Psychological and Social Well-Being)

Positive psychological functioning (i.e., psychological well-being)

- *Self-acceptance:* holds positive attitudes toward self, acknowledges, likes most parts of personality
- *Personal growth:* seeks challenge, has insight into own potential, feels a sense of continued development
- *Purpose in life:* finds own life has a direction and meaning
- *Environmental mastery:* exercises ability to select, manage, and mold personal environs to suit needs
- *Autonomy:* is guided by own, socially accepted, internal standards and values
- *Positive relations with others:* has, or can form, warm, trusting personal relationships

Positive social functioning (i.e., social well-being)

- *Social acceptance:* holds positive attitudes toward, acknowledges, and is accepting of human differences
- *Social growth (actualization):* believes people, groups, and society have potential to grow
- *Social contribution:* sees own daily activities as useful to and valued by society and others
- *Social coherence:* interest in society and social life, and finds them meaningful and somewhat intelligible
- *Social integration:* a sense of belonging to, and comfort and support from, a community

Findings from a series of papers based on the Midlife in the United States (MIDUS) study (Keyes, 2005b) as well as other populations using narrower measures of well-being (Greenspoon & Saklofske, 2001; Headey, Kelley, & Wearing, 1993; Huppert & Whittington, 2003; Masse et al., 1998; Suldo & Shaffer, 2008; Veit & Ware, 1983) support the two continuum model: one continuum indicating the presence and absence of positive mental health; the other indicating the presence and absence of mental illness symptoms. For example, the latent factors of mental illness and mental health correlated ($r = -0.53$) but only 28.1% of their variance is shared in the MIDUS data (Keyes, 2005b). Recently, this model has also been replicated in a random sample of US adolescents (ages 12–18 years) with data from the Panel Study of Income Dynamics Child Development Supplement (Keyes, 2009), in Dutch adults (Westerhof & Keyes, 2008, 2010) and in Setswana-speaking South-African adults (Keyes et al., 2008).

Based on the dual continua model shown in Fig. 68.1,[1] individuals can be categorized by their recent mental illness status and according to their level of mental health (languishing,

---

[1] Fig. 68.1 was commissioned by the Winnipeg Regional Health Authority's Mental Health Promotion Team and was created by the "That 2 Graphics" in Winnipeg, Manitoba Canada. Copyright of Fig. 68.1 remains with the author (Corey L. M. Keyes) and permission to reprint it should be directed to Corey L. M. Keyes.

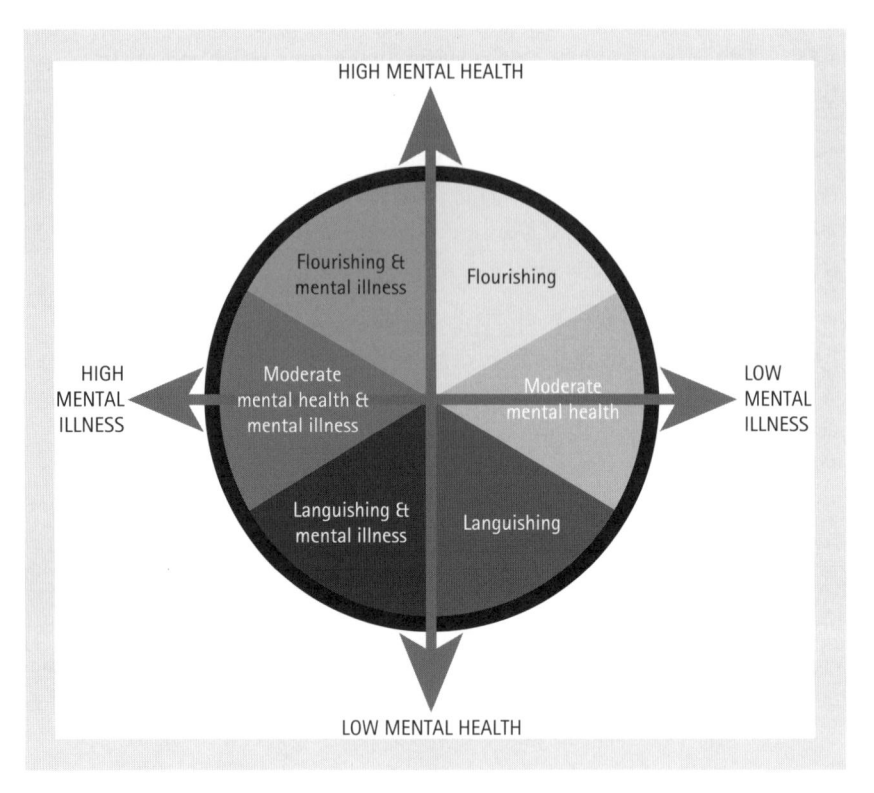

FIG. 68.1 The dual continua model. © 2010 CLM Keyes and the Winnipeg Regional Health Authority.

moderate, or flourishing). One implication of the dual continua model is that the absence of mental illness does not imply the presence of mental health. In the American adult population aged between 25 and 74, just over 75% were free of three common mental disorders during the past year (i.e., major depressive episode (MDE), panic disorder (PD), and generalized anxiety disorder (GAD)). However, while just over three-quarters were free of mental illness during the past year, only about 20% were flourishing. A second implication of the dual continua is that the presence of mental illness does not imply the absence of mental health. Of the 23% of adults with any mental illness, 14.5% had moderate, and 1.5% had flourishing mental health. Thus, almost 7 of every 10 adults with mental illness (MDE, PD, or GAD) had moderate or flourishing mental health (Keyes, 2002, 2005b, 2007). While the absence of mental illness does not mean the presence of mental health, the presence of mental illness does not imply the absence of some level of good mental health.

Another important implication of the dual continua model is that level of mental health should differentiate level of functioning among individuals free of, and those with, a mental illness. Put differently, anything less than flourishing mental health is associated with impaired functioning for those with a mental illness and individuals free of a mental illness. Findings consistently show that adults and adolescents who are diagnosed as anything less than flourishing mental health are functioning worse in terms of physical health outcomes, healthcare utilization, missed days of work, and psychosocial functioning (Keyes, 2002, 2005b, 2006, 2007, 2009). Across all outcomes to date, individuals who are flourishing function better (e.g., fewer missed days of work) than those with moderate mental health, who in turn function better than languishing individuals. This is true for individuals with a recent mental illness and for individuals free of a recent mental illness.

## Towards Promotion and Protection of Good Mental Health

Progress has been slow in bringing MHPP into the mainstream of policy debates about how to address the problem of mental illness. Admittedly, there has been a deficit of scientific evidence supporting the "promotion" and the "protection" axioms of MHPP. Central to the argument behind *promotion* is the hypothesis that gains in level of mental health should decrease the risk of mental illness over time. Central to the argument behind *protection* is the hypothesis that losses of mental health increase the risk of mental illness over time, and therefore efforts should be made to prevent, and to respond to, the loss of good mental health. Findings recently published (Keyes, Dhingra & Simoes, 2010) using the 10-year follow-up of the MIDUS national sample strongly supported the protection and promotion hypotheses.

In 1995 and in the 2005 follow-up of the MIDUS sample, adults completed the long form of the mental health continuum (MHC-LF; Keyes, 2002, 2005b) and the Composite International Diagnostic Interview Short Form (CIDI-SF; Kessler et al., 1998). Studies have shown that the CIDI-SF has excellent diagnostic sensitivity and diagnostic specificity as compared with diagnoses based on the full CIDI in the National Comorbidity Study (Kessler et al., 1999). During the telephone interview, the CIDI-SF was used to assess whether respondents exhibited symptoms indicative of MDE, GAD, and PD during the past 12 months.

## Prevalence and Stability

Does level of mental health remain stable over time, suggesting it may not be amenable to change? The prevalence of mental illness is about the same in 1995 (18.5%) as in 2005 (17.5%); approximately eight out of every ten adults were free of any mental illness in 1995 and in 2005. The prevalence of any mental illness and the absence of mental illness appear to be stable over time. However, of the 17.5% with any mental illness in 2005, just over half (52%) were "new cases" of mental illness insofar as these adults did not have any of the three mental disorders in 1995.

The prevalence of flourishing is 3.2% higher in 2005, up from 19.2% in 1995. The prevalence of moderate mental health is 3.7% lower in 2005, which is down from 64.1% in 1995. The prevalence of languishing is 0.5% higher in 2005, slightly up from 16.7% in 1995. Compared with mental illness, level of mental health—particularly moderate mental health and flourishing—appear slightly more dynamic at the level of the population. That is, there is a slight decline in moderate and slight increase in flourishing mental health at the level of the population. Like mental illness, mental health appears to be relatively stable at the level of population prevalence estimates.

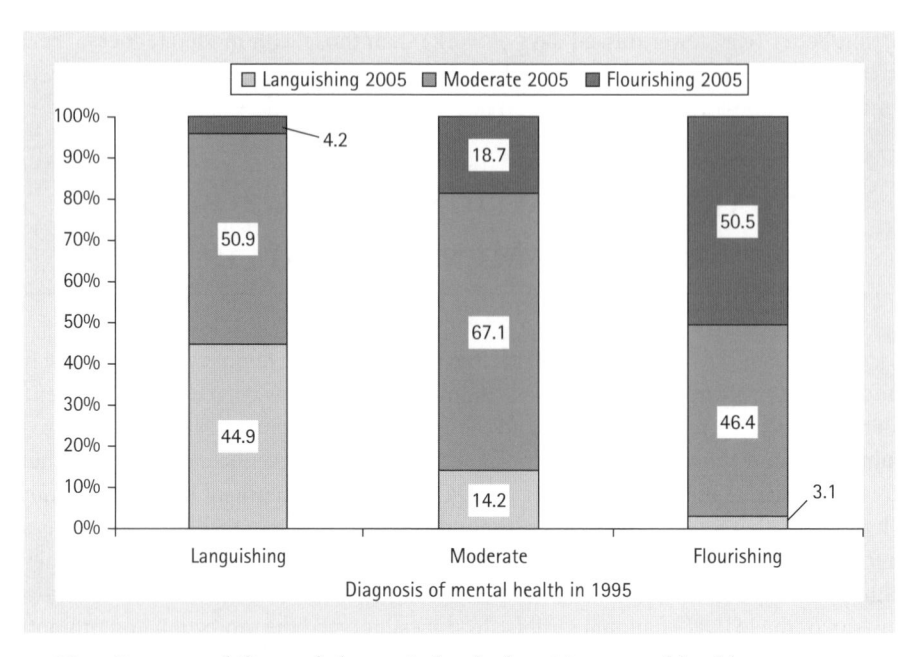

FIG. 68.2 Percent stability and change in level of positive mental health.

Fig. 68.2, however, reveals a more dramatic story of change in levels of mental health that is disguised by the apparent stability in population prevalence. Only 45% of those languishing in 1995 are languishing in 2005; 51% improved to moderate, and 4% improved to flourishing, mental health in 2005. Only half of those flourishing in 1995 are flourishing in 2005—46% declined to moderate, and 3% declined to languishing, mental health in 2005. Two-thirds of those with moderate mental health in 1995 had moderate mental health in 2005. Of those with moderate mental health in 1995, about 19% improved to flourishing, and 14% declined to languishing, mental health in 2005.

Although the percentage of change arising from moderate mental health appears small, recall that 64.1% of the sample had moderate mental health in 1995. Thus, it is almost entirely the 14% in declines from moderate mental health to languishing that counterbalance the 55% who improved from languishing to moderate and flourishing mental health that creates the apparent stable population prevalence of languishing in 1995 (16.7%) as in 2005 (17.2%). Similarly, it is almost entirely the 19% of improvement from moderate mental health to flourishing that counterbalances the 49.5% of decline from flourishing to moderate and languishing mental health that creates the apparent stable but slight rise in population prevalence of flourishing from 19.2% in 1995 to 22.4% in 2005.

# The Promotion and Protection Hypotheses

Fig. 68.3 presents the adjusted odds ratio (OR) of any mental illness in 2005 (i.e., whether respondents had either MDE, PD, or GAD) by change in positive mental health. The reference category consists of individuals who were flourishing in 1995 and 2005, or

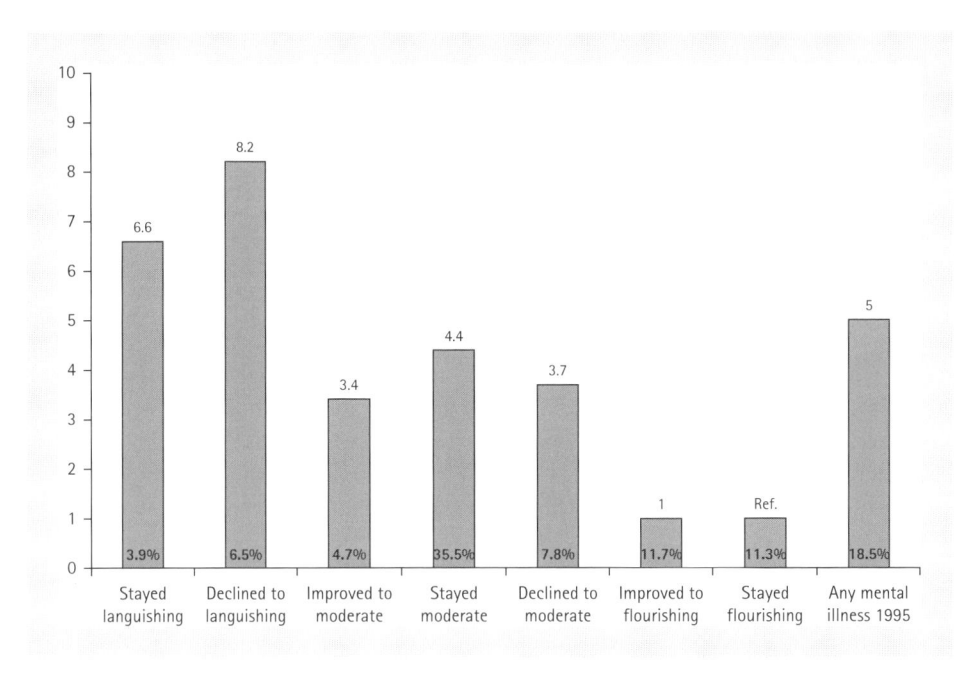

FIG. 68.3 Adjusted odds ratio of any 2005 mental illness (MDE, GAD, or PD) by change in positive mental health.

stayed flourishing. This model controlled for respondents' age, sex, race, education, marital status in 2005, employment status in 2005, and whether respondents had any of 25 physical health conditions in 1995. The adjusted odds ratio of any 2005 mental illness is at the top of each bar graph, and the proportion of individuals in that category of mental health change is recorded toward the bottom of each bar graph.

The findings strongly supported the protection hypothesis. Those who declined to moderate mental health were nearly 4 times (OR = 3.7) more likely to have a 2005 mental illness as those who stayed flourishing. Thus, the first loss of good mental health—from flourishing to moderate mental health—results in a rise in the risk of future mental illness. Adults whose mental health stayed at moderate were over 4 times (OR = 4.4) as likely to have a 2005 mental illness as those who stayed flourishing. Compared to those who stayed at moderate mental health, those who declined to languishing—almost all of whom had moderate mental health in 1995—represented an 86% increase in the odds ratio of a 2005 mental illness (i.e., 8.2 − 4.4 = 3.8 ÷ 4.4 = 0.864). Thus, protection against the loss of moderate mental health can mitigate the risk of future mental illness.

Findings also supported the promotion hypothesis. Individuals who stayed languishing were over 6 times (OR = 6.6), and those who improved to moderate mental health were over 3 times (OR = 3.4), as likely as those who stayed flourishing to have a 2005 mental illness. Compared to staying languishing, improving to moderate mental health cuts the risk of future mental illness by nearly half (i.e., 6.6 − 3.4 = 3.2 ÷ 6.6 = 0.484). Individuals who improved to flourishing—most of whom had moderate mental health in 1995—had no higher risk of future mental illness than those who stayed flourishing.

Individuals who had any of the three mental illnesses in 1995 were 5 times more likely than those who stayed flourishing to have one of the same mental illnesses in 2005. While past mental illness is a very good predictor of future mental illness, the findings in Keyes et al. (2010) illustrate that the absence of flourishing mental health results in nearly as high a risk, and sometimes higher, of future mental illness as those who started with one mental illness. Nearly half of the study sample was free of any mental illness in 1995 but had moderate mental health in 2005 (i.e., 7.8% declined + 35.5% stayed + 4.7% improved to moderate = 48% with moderate mental health in 2005) and were nearly as likely of having a mental illness in 2005 as the 18.5% who had a mental illness in 1995. Moreover, one in ten of the study sample was free of any mental illness in 1995 but had languishing mental health in 2005 (i.e., 3.9% stayed + 6.5% declined to languishing = 10.4%) and were more likely of having a mental illness in 2005 than the 18.5% who had a mental illness in 1995. In short, about six in every ten American adults (i.e., 48% with moderate + 10.4% with languishing mental health = 58.4%) who are otherwise free of MDE, GAD or PD have about as high or even higher risk of a future mental illness as individuals who had one of those mental disorders to start.

These analyses suggest that the loss of positive mental health may generate new cases of mental illness. Analysis of the same model reported in Fig. 68.3, after exclusion of adults with any 1995 mental illness, did not change findings of identified relationships between changes in mental health status and mental illness. For example, compared to those who stayed flourishing, individuals who either stayed languishing (OR = 7.5, p <0.001) or became languishing (OR = 7.0, p <0.001) had the highest risk of a new case of any 2005 mental illness. In turn, individuals who either stayed at moderate (OR = 3.8, p <0.009) or improved to moderate mental health (OR = 3.2) were over 3 times as likely as those who stayed flourishing to have a new case of any 2005 mental illness, although the latter was marginally significant at p = 0.076. Adults who declined from flourishing to moderate mental health were about 3 times (OR = 3.2, p <0.043) as likely as those who stayed flourishing to have a new case of any 2005 mental illness.

# Conclusion

The guiding ethos of medicine and public health are embodied in the myth of Asclepius, the Greek god of medicine and healing whose daughters gave rise to complementary conceptions of, and approaches to, health—Pathos requires Panacea and Salus requires Hygeia, where Panacea and Hygeia were daughters that respectively represented treatment of disease and promotion of health. The pathogenic approach is derived from the Greek word, *pathos*, meaning suffering and an emotion evoking a sympathetic response from those who have panaceas or treatments. The pathogenic approach views health as the absence of disease, illness, disability, and premature death. The salutogenic approach comes from the Latin word, *salus*, for health, which was considered a positive state. Here, health is monitored by the relative presence of positive states of human capacities and functioning (Strümpfer, 1995) that come from "hygienic" practices of health promotion and health maintenance.

A third and complementary conception of health derives from the word *hale*, which derives from the Old English word *hāl* and means whole or healthy. This, of course, is embodied in the World Health Organization's (1948) definition of health as a state of complete physical, mental, and social well-being and not merely the absence of disease or infirmity. This definition and conception of health is supported scientifically by the dual continuum model of mental health. This complete approach to mental healthcare simultaneously involves treatment (panaceas) and public MHPP; an approach that permits nations to deftly respond to illness, because more illness will have been avoided through the promotion and protection of good mental health.

Research supports the two fundamental axioms of MHPP for addressing the mental illness and mental health needs of the population. First, gains in mental health resulted in decreasing odds of mental illness over time, suggesting that promoting mental health could reduce the incidence and prevalence of mental illness. Second, losses of mental health resulted in increasing odds of mental illness over time, suggesting that protecting against loss of mental health could reduce the incidence and prevalence of mental illness. Third, mental health is dynamic over time, although the point prevalence estimates of any mental illness and level of mental health appear stable from 1995 to 2005. The reason for this apparent stability is that approximately half of the mental illness in 2005 represents new cases, while half of those flourishing in 2005 are new cases and over half of those languishing in 2005 are new cases.

Further, research suggests that governments should invest in MHPP to keep pace with—i.e., prevent—the rise of new cases of mental illness. While having had a mental illness in the past is a good predictor of future mental illness, our findings revealed that the absence of mental health is an equally good, and in some cases a better, predictor of future mental illness. Research suggests that as many as six in ten adults in the US population who are otherwise free of mental illness but have less than optimal mental health have as high, or higher, risk of a future mental illness compared with individuals who already have a mental illness. Failure to address the problem of the absence of positive mental health in populations means risking failure in attacking the problem of mental illness.

Ultimately, the research summarized here raises questions for: (1) national public mental health goals, and (2) creating effective techniques and interventions for MHPP. Government and public health officials can no longer blithely announce that they seek to promote the mental health of their population while investing only in treatment and risk reduction. The two continua model debunks this as a "wanting-doing gap" in public health policy, where policies pronounce national efforts to seek *health* but engage in activities directed primarily or solely toward *illness*. If you want better mental health, you must focus on positive mental health by promoting it and protecting against its loss. Governments cannot promote mental health by solely reducing mental illness, and no amount of wishful thinking will make this fact disappear. Nations can, of course, ignore the science supporting the two continua model, but this will serve only to sacrifice more lives to the recurrent, chronic, and incurable condition of mental illness. The alternative and complementary approach to treatment is public mental health promotion and protection.

# References

Bradburn, N. M. (1969). *The structure of psychological well-being*. Chicago, IL: Aldine.
Chisholm, D., Sanderson, K., Ayuso-Mateos, J. L., & Saxena, S. (2004). Reducing the global burden of depression: Population-level analysis of intervention cost-effectiveness in 14 world regions. *British Journal of Psychiatry, 184*, 393–403.

Davis, N. J. (2002). The promotion of mental health and the prevention of mental and behavioral disorders: Surely the time is right. *International Journal of Emergency Mental Health, 4,* 3–29.

Diener, E. (1984). Subjective well-being. *Psychological Bulletin, 95,* 542–575.

Downie, R. S., Fyfe, C., & Tannahill, A. (1990). *Health promotion: Models and values.* Oxford, UK: Oxford University Press.

Gallagher, M. W., Lopez, S. J., & Preacher, K. J. (2009). The hierarchical structure of well-being. *Journal of Personality, 77,* 1025–1049.

Greenspoon, P. J., & Saklofske, D. H. (2001). Toward an integration of subjective well-being and psychopathology. *Social Indicators Research, 54,* 81–108.

Gurin, G., Veroff, J., & Feld, S. (1960). *Americans view their mental health.* New York, NY: Basic Books.

Headey, B., Kelley, J., & Wearing, A. (1993). Dimensions of mental health: Life satisfaction, positive affect, anxiety, and depression. *Social Indicators Research, 29,* 63–82.

Health and Welfare Canada. (1988). *Mental health for Canadians: Striking a balance.* Ottawa, Canada: Supply and Services Canada.

Huppert, F. A., & Whittington, J. E. (2003). Evidence for the independence of positive and negative well-being: Implications for quality of life assessment. *British Journal of Health Psychology, 8,* 107–122.

Insel, T. R., & Scolnick, E. M. (2006). Cure therapeutics and strategic prevention: Raising the bar for mental health research. *Molecular Psychiatry, 11,* 11–17.

Kessler, R. C., Andrews, G., Mroczek, D., Ustun, B., & Wittchen, H–U. (1998). The world health organization composite international diagnostic interview short form (CIDI–SF). *International Journal of Methods in Psychiatric Research, 7,* 171–185.

Kessler, R. C., DuPont, R. L., Berglund, P., & Wittchen, H-U. (1999). Impairment in pure and comorbid generalized anxiety disorder and major depression at 12 months in two national surveys. *American Journal of Psychiatry, 156,* 1915–1923.

Kessler, R. C., Berglund, P., Demler, O., Jin, R., Merikangas, K. R., & Walters, E. E. (2005). Lifetime prevalence and age-of-onset distributions of DSM-IV disorders in the national comorbidity survey replication. *Archives of General Psychiatry, 62,* 593–602.

Keyes, C. L. M. (1998). Social well-being. *Social Psychology Quarterly, 61,* 121–140.

Keyes, C. L. M. (2002). The mental health continuum: From languishing to flourishing in life. *Journal of Health and Social Behavior, 43,* 207–222.

Keyes, C. L. M. (2005a). The subjective well-being of America's youth: Toward a comprehensive assessment. *Adolescent and Family Health, 4,* 3–11.

Keyes, C. L. M. (2005b). Mental illness and/or mental health? Investigating axioms of the complete state model of health. *Journal of Consulting and Clinical Psychology, 73,* 539–548.

Keyes, C. L. M. (2006). Mental health in adolescence: Is America's youth flourishing? *American Journal of Orthopsychiatry, 76,* 395–402.

Keyes, C. L. M. (2007). Promoting and protecting mental health as flourishing: A complementary strategy for improving national mental health. *American Psychologist, 62,* 95–108.

Keyes, C. L. M. (2009). The nature and importance of positive mental health in America's adolescents. In R. Gilman, E. S. Huebner, & M. J. Furlong (Eds.), *Handbook of positive psychology in schools* (pp. 9–23). New York, NY: Routledge.

Keyes, C. L. M., Dhingra, S. S., & Simoes, E. J. (2010). Change in level of positive mental health as a predictor of future risk of mental illness. *American Journal of Public Health, 100,* 2366–2371.

Keyes, C. L. M., Shmotkin, D., & Ryff, C. D. (2002). Optimizing well-being: The empirical encounter of two traditions. *Journal of Personality and Social Psychology, 82,* 1007–1022.

Keyes, C. L. M., Wissing, M., Potgieter, J. P., Temane, M., Kruger, A., & van Rooy, S. (2008). Evaluation of the Mental Health Continuum Short Form (MHC-SF) in Setswana speaking South Africans. *Clinical Psychology and Psychotherapy*, *15*, 181–192.

Masse, R., Poulin, C., Dassa, C., Lambert, J., Belair, S., & Battaglini, A. (1998). The structure of mental health higher-order confirmatory factor analyses of psychological distress and well-being measures. *Social Indicators Research*, *45*, 475–504.

Murray, C. J. L., & Lopez, A. D. (Eds.). (1996). *The global burden of disease: A comprehensive assessment of mortality and disability from diseases, injuries, and risk factors in 1990 and projected to 2020*. Cambridge, MA: Harvard School of Public Health.

Robitschek, C., & Keyes, C. L. M. (2009). The structure of Keyes' model of mental health and the role of personal growth initiative as a parsimonious predictor. *Journal of Counseling Psychology*, *56*, 321–329.

Ryff, C. D. (1989). Happiness is everything, or is it? Explorations on the meaning of psychological well–being. *Journal of Personality and Social Psychology*, *57*, 1069–1081.

Secker, J. (1998). Current conceptualizations of mental health and mental health promotion. *Health Education Research*, *13*, 57–66.

Sigerist, H. E. (1941). *Medicine and human welfare*. New Haven, CT: Yale University Press.

Strümpfer, D. J. W. (1995). The origins of health and strength: From 'salutogenesis' to 'fortigenesis'. *South African Journal of Psychology*, *25*, 81–89.

Suldo, S. M., & Shaffer, E. J. (2008). Looking beyond psychopathology: The dual-factor model of mental health in youth. *School Psychology Review*, *37*, 52–68.

US Public Health Service. (1999). *Mental health: A report of the Surgeon General*. Rockville, MD: Author.

Ustun, T. B. (1999). The global burden of mental disorders. *American Journal of Public Health*, *89*, 1315–1318.

Ustun, T. B., Ayuso-Mateos, J. L., Chatterji, S., Mathers, C. D., & Murray, C. J. L. (2004). Global burden of depressive disorders in the year 2000. *British Journal of Psychiatry*, *184*, 386–392.

Veit, C. T., & Ware, J. E. (1983). The structure of psychological distress and well-being in general populations. *Journal of Consulting and Clinical Psychology*, *51*, 730–742.

Westerhof, G. J., & Keyes, C. L. M. (2008). Mental health is more than the absence of mental illness. *Monthly Mental Health* (In Dutch, Summary in English), *63*, 808–820.

Westerhof, G. J., & Keyes, C. L. M. (2010). Mental illness and mental health: The two continua model across the lifespan. *Journal of Adult Development*, *17*, 110–119.

World Health Organization. (1948). World Health Organization constitution. In *Basic Documents*. Geneva: Author.

World Health Organization. (2004). *Promoting mental health: Concepts, emerging evidence, practice* (Summary report). Geneva: Author.

CHAPTER 69

# POST-TRAUMATIC GROWTH: EUDAIMONIC HAPPINESS IN THE AFTERMATH OF ADVERSITY

STEPHEN JOSEPH[1] AND KATE HEFFERON[2]

[1]Nottingham University, UK;
[2]University of East London, UK

In the two decades following the introduction of the diagnostic category of post-traumatic stress disorder (PTSD) in 1980, trauma became one of the most heavily researched topics in psychology. The majority of this research testified to the psychological problems experienced by survivors of various traumatic events—disasters, accidents, combat, and illnesses. But as evidence accumulated, what also became clear was that the majority of people who experience traumatic events do not develop severe and chronic problems. Moreover, qualitative clinical and research observations in the early 1990s began to document an unexpected finding: many survivors also reported positive changes in their lives. While this outcome was surprising, it was in fact consistent with many literatures, religions, and philosophies suggesting that exposure to adversity, extreme stress, and trauma can be beneficial. At first these observations went largely unnoticed in the trauma literature; it was thought that positive changes were rare occurrences reported by a minority. But with the growth of positive psychology in the late 1990s, research began focusing on the theme of positive post-traumatic outcomes. Over the past decade, hundreds of studies have found that positive changes are commonly reported. These have challenged us to rethink what we know about human adaptation following trauma.

Positive changes in the aftermath of adversity, is now a major field of research and clinical interest across the professions of counseling, psychology, and social work. Drawing from different perspectives and theoretical lineages, the experience of how traumatic events can serve as a springboard to psychological well-being has variously been conceptualized as adversarial growth; benefit-finding; flourishing; heightened existential awareness; perceived benefits; positive by-products; positive changes; positive meaning; self-renewal; stress-related growth; thriving; and transformational coping. The term, however, that has come to be most robustly used is post-traumatic growth, a phrase coined by two American researchers, Lawrence Calhoun and Richard Tedeschi. The aim of this chapter is to provide an overview of what we do and do not know about the science of post-traumatic growth, and also to help set the stage for future research.

## The Eudaimonic Aspect of Happiness

The relationship between post-traumatic growth and post-traumatic stress is frequently misunderstood. While it might be expected that those reporting growth should be free of distress, this is not always the case. Post-traumatic growth does not equate with an absence of distress. Furthermore, post-traumatic growth is not centered on the experience of positive emotional states. Rather, it refers to the eudaimonic aspects of happiness in which trauma can serve as a turning point out of which people derive or clarify their life meaning, values, purpose, and aspirations.

Within the empirical literature the more frequently researched hedonic aspects of happiness, such as the experience of positive emotional states, absence of negative emotional states, and satisfaction with life, are often described as *subjective* well-being. In contrast, the eudaimonic aspects of happiness are termed *psychological* well-being. Thus, while post-traumatic stress research has tended to focus on subjective well-being, post-traumatic growth focuses on psychological well-being. Seen this way, it is evident that these two conceptually distinct states can coexist and might interact over time, such that post-traumatic stress triggers post-traumatic growth, and post-traumatic growth reduces post-traumatic stress. Researchers are only just beginning to understand the interplay between post-traumatic stress and post-traumatic growth, and a holistic appreciation of psychological trauma must incorporate both of these literatures.

## Dimensions of Post-traumatic Growth

Post-traumatic growth is a wide-ranging term that describes the many different ways in which people talk about the positive changes in their lives following adversity. These can be grouped into three broad and related dimensions. First, relationships are enhanced. For example, people value their friends and family more, and feel increased compassion and kindness toward others. Second, people change their self-views in some way such as recognizing a sense of personal resilience, wisdom, and strength, perhaps coupled with a greater acceptance of their vulnerabilities and limitations. Third, there are alterations in life philosophy such as finding a fresh appreciation for each new day, a sense of what really matters in life, or experiencing a change in spiritual beliefs (Shaw, Joseph, & Linley, 2005).

## Operationalizing the Construct of Growth

Since the mid 1990s focus on post-traumatic growth, several psychometric tools have been developed to assess the construct. The first was the Changes in Outlook Questionnaire (CiOQ: Joseph, Williams, & Yule, 1993), a 26-item measure assessing both positive and negative changes in schema following adversity. This was followed by the 21-item Post-traumatic Growth Inventory (PTGI: Tedeschi & Calhoun, 1995, 1996), the 50-item Stress-Related Growth Scale (SRGS: Park, Cohen, & Murch, 1996), the 38-item Perceived Benefit Scales (PBS: McMillen & Fisher, 1998), and the 20-item Thriving Scale (TS: Abraído-Lanza, Guier, & Colón, 1998). Each offers an operational definition that reflects the particular theoretical and clinical perspectives of its authors, and empirical studies indicate that while they appear to be assessing a common core of positive changes, there are differences too (e.g., Joseph, Linley, Andrews, et al., 2005). The most widely used measure is the PTGI which indexes five domains: "(1) perceived changes in self (e.g., becoming stronger, more confident); (2) developing closer relationships with family, friends, neighbors, fellow trauma survivors and even strangers; (3) changing life philosophy/increased existential awareness; (4) changed priorities; and (5) enhanced spiritual beliefs" (Tedeschi & Calhoun, 1995, 1996). While this tool offers a useful descriptive perspective, its factorial structure has been debated with findings variously yielding single, three, and eight factor models (e.g., Joseph, Linley, & Harris, 2005; Linley, Andrews, & Joseph, 2007; Taku, Cann, Calhoun, & Tedeschi, 2008; see Joseph and Linley, 2008a for a review).

Factor analytic studies are of course limited by the questions constructed in their initial design. As research has expanded to include qualitative analysis, many aspects of participants' experiences have been found to be absent from current scales, suggesting that they do not adequately capture key elements of the growth process (Lechner, Stoelb, & Antoni, 2008; Manuel, 2007; Hefferon, Grealy, & Mutrie, 2008, 2009; Sabiston et al., 2008). Taking this forward, one avenue has been to integrate the construct of growth within the wider literature on psychological well-being and to seek convergence in these constructs, in recognition that growth following adversity is an exemplar of change in psychological well-being.

Recently, Regel and Joseph (2010) provide a new conceptualization (see Table 69.1) in which Ryff's six domains of psychological well-being (Ryff, 1989; Ryff & Singer, 1996): i.e., (1) self-acceptance, (2) autonomy, (3) purpose in life, (4) relationships, (5) sense of mastery, and (6) personal growth, are assessed in the context of psychological trauma. Work is underway to determine the structural properties of their associated measure, and how it relates to existing constructs of growth and well-being (see, Joseph, Maltby, Wood, Stockton, Hunt, and Regel, 2012). This may offer a fruitful new direction for research.

As researchers and clinicians in this field, there is no doubt in our minds that people can change following traumatic experiences in the ways described earlier. However, we are also aware that reports of growth that are assessed using questionnaires such as these, and which rely on retrospective accounts, are not always consistent with the changes that people actually make. This anomaly has plagued the field of growth and led to much misunderstanding.

The main critics of the field of post-traumatic growth tend to cite Festinger's Cognitive Dissonance Theory which states that a positive outlook or the rejection of negative thinking

### Table 69.1 Psychological Well-Being–Post-traumatic Changes Questionnaire (PWB-PTCQ)[a]

Think about how you feel about yourself at the present time. Please read each of the following statements and rate how you have changed as a result of the trauma.

5 = Much more so now
4 = A bit more so now
3 = I feel the same about this as before
2 = A bit less so now
1 = Much less so now

_____1. I like myself.
_____2. I have confidence in my opinions.
_____3. I have a sense of purpose in life.
_____4. I have strong and close relationships in my life.
_____5. I feel I am in control of my life.
_____6. I am open to new experiences that challenge me.
_____7. I accept who I am, with both my strengths and limitations.
_____8. I don't worry what other people think of me.
_____9. My life has meaning.
_____10. I am a compassionate and giving person.
_____11. I handle my responsibilities in life well.
_____12. I am always seeking to learn about myself.
_____13. I respect myself.
_____14. I know what is important to me and will stand my ground, even if others disagree.
_____15. I feel that my life is worthwhile and that I play a valuable role in things.
_____16. I am grateful to have people in my life who care for me.
_____17. I am able to cope with what life throws at me.
_____18. I am hopeful about my future and look forward to new possibilities.

Self-acceptance (statements 1, 7, & 13), autonomy (statements 2, 8, & 14), purpose in life (statements 3, 9, & 15), relationships (statements 4, 10, & 16), sense of mastery (statements 5, 11, & 17), and personal growth (statements 6, 12, & 18).

[a] Data from Joseph, S., Wood, A., Maltby, J., Stockton, H., Hunt, N., & Regel, S., Psychological Well-Being Posttraumatic Changes Questionnaire: Reliability and validity. *Psychological Trauma: Theory, Research, Policy and Practice.*

are actually detrimental, avoidance oriented tactics used by people to cope with traumatic events (Fromm, Andrykowski, & Hunt, 1996). From this perspective, any growth cited could simply be an attempt to reduce the dissonance created by the negative experiences of the trauma. Some psychologists have also questioned whether reporting post-traumatic growth is in fact a self-protective illusion—an attempt to gain a sense of control over circumstances by altering one's perceptions of them (Ford, Tennen, & Albert, 2008, p. 306;

Taylor & Brown, 1988). Responses to these types of criticism include Calhoun and Tedeschi's (2008) counter that despite research challenging the existence of growth, there are no measurement tools or agreed upon definitions for identifying illusions or distortions. In addition they hold that illusions of self-enhancement have only been found in a small number of participants and that the current quantitative measurements of growth do not correspond with social desirability measures. That is, people are not reporting growth just to "look good" in front of others. Last, it has been argued that obtaining objective, quantifiable evidence of growth is a less valid dependent variable than the "subjective sense that one has been bettered by their experience in some fundamental way" (Thornton, 2002, p. 162). From this perspective, how the person remembers the growth phenomena is more important than whether their memories are objectively correct or incorrect (Giorgi and Giorgi, 2003). We believe that while well-established illusory and self-protective psychological mechanisms likely color people's reports of their experiences, it is an over-simplification to use them to fully explain away post-traumatic growth.

## Predicting Growth

Reports of post-traumatic growth are common, with between 30–70% of people tending to cite some benefit following the adverse experience. Research has begun to explore the contexts in which growth can be predicted. For example, while an increased severity of disease is associated with growth, if the disease is perceived as too stressful, then anxiety will overwhelm the patient and inhibit the growth process (Lechner et al., 2008). In short, it would seem that the severity of trauma must be significant enough to affect the person, but not so overwhelming that growth is thwarted.

Research has also begun to document why some people and not others report benefits (Linley & Joseph, 2004). Although there is no distinct personality type that is associated with growth, characteristics of the individual and the social environment that enhance the likelihood of this occurring include: higher socioeconomic (Bower et al., 2005; Carpenter, 1999; Cordova, Chang et al., 2001) and educational status (Sears, Stanton, & Danoff-Burg, 2003); a younger age (Carpenter, 1999; Kurtz, Wyatt, & Kurtz, 1995); more time since diagnosis (Cordova, Cunningham, Carlson, & Andrykowski, 2001; Weiss, 2004b); optimism (Antoni et al., 2001); positive emotions (Linley & Joseph, 2004a); autonomous social support (Cadell, Regehr, & Hemsworth, 2003); problem focused coping (Urcuyo, Boyers, Carver, & Antoni, 2005); attendance at group based therapies (Cordova, 2008; Lechner et al., 2008); and post-traumatic event-related rumination (Calhoun, Cann, Tedeschi, & McMillan, 2000; Taku, Calhoun, Cann & Tedeschi, 2008; Taku, Cann, Tedeschi, & Calhoun, 2009).

Despite these interesting preliminary results a similar number of contrasting studies have documented non-significant associations between these factors and growth (Stanton, Bower, & Low, 2006). To date, the study designs have relied on relatively unsophisticated correlational analyses. However, based on the findings from the wider trauma literature it is likely that there are complex interactions between demographic, personality, coping, and social support variables. Thus there is a need for more sophisticated interactional research as well as longitudinal studies that test the capacity of proposed predictive factors to account for subsequent reports of growth.

# Theoretical Perspectives

Over the past 30 years, there have been a number of attempts to account for the experience of growth from adversity from a theoretical perspective (Aldwin, 1994; Hager, 1992; Miller & C'deBaca, 1994; O'Leary & Ickovics, 1995; O'Leary et al., 1998; Nerken, 1993; Schaefer & Moos, 1992). We will now review three of these explanations: shattered assumptions theory (Janoff-Bulman, 1992), the transformational model (Tedeschi & Calhoun, 2006), and the organismic valuing theory (Joseph & Linley, 2005).

## Shattered assumptions theory

While Janoff-Bulman's (1992) shattered assumptions theory was developed before the field of post-traumatic growth took root, it nonetheless provides a valuable perspective. Janoff-Bulman suggests that at the core of our inner world or personal narrative we hold fundamental assumptions about safety and security. Trauma occurs when these assumptions are tested and our sense of security is "shattered." Adjustment to trauma is defined as the process of rebuilding our assumptive world in light of the traumatic experience and thus acknowledging the trauma in a non-anxious way. Individuals need to make sense of and find value within their lives and the occurrence of trauma and tragedy creates an environment in which to do so. Although some researchers have criticized the theory as exaggerating the deleterious impact of trauma upon the self (Campbell, Brunell, & Foster, 2004; McMillen, 2004) the "shattering" of the former-self idea is a cornerstone of the two further explanations of post-traumatic growth described in this chapter.

## Transformational model

The transformational model (Tedeschi & Calhoun, 1995) proposes that post-traumatic growth results from excessive rumination (or cognitive processing) following a seismic event. In the wake of the event, the shattering of prior goals and beliefs leads to self-reflection as people try to make sense of what has happened. Although this can be distressing, this self-reflection process is indicative of mental activity that is directed at rebuilding the individual's beliefs, ideas, and values. The management of excessive rumination takes place in three stages: (1) the experience of automatic and intrusive thoughts; (2) the management of automatic and intrusive thoughts; and (3) deliberate rumination. Throughout these stages the person is also engaging in self-disclosure, attempting to reduce emotional distress, disengaging from previous goals, and changing schemas and narrative development. As a result of successful coping, the self-reflection that was initially automatic shifts towards a more constructive mental activity in which the person's narrative develops and which may involve a search for meaning and an ultimate perception of positive change. In addition, the person may achieve wisdom. The model recognizes that throughout the process distress can coexist alongside post-traumatic growth (Tedeschi & Calhoun, 2006).

## Organismic valuing theory

The organismic valuing theory stems from a person-centered approach (Rogers, 1959) and posits that all humans are intrinsically motivated towards growth (Joseph & Linley, 2005).

Drawing on shattered assumptions theory, it suggests that trauma challenges one's assumptive world and that people are intrinsically motivated to accommodate the new trauma-related information. The values and meaning that are attached to the accommodation process can be either negative or positive. Cognitive accommodation requires the person to re-experience and confront the meaning of their experience post trauma, resulting in post-traumatic alternating states of intrusion and denial.

Organismic valuing theory explicitly attempts to integrate research on growth with that on post-traumatic stress, with post-traumatic stress being regarded as a normal process, the end point of which can be growth. Rather than being inevitable, growth is viewed as easily thwarted by extrinsic factors leading to cognitive assimilation. As this overview indicates, the theory goes beyond the view of growth as an outcome only and also views it as a cognitive process.

Criticisms of these above models include that they lack robust theoretical foundations, (Ford et al., 2008), are too strongly focused on cognitive processing (Hobfoll et al., 2008; McMillen, 2004) and do not fully acknowledge the physical side (the body's role) in the growth process (Cozzolino, Staples, Meyers, & Samboceti, 2004; Hefferon et al., 2008, 2009; Lykins, Segerstrom, Averill, Evans, & Kemeny, 2007; Sabiston et al., 2007;). With the development of more sophisticated qualitative and quantitative research techniques it is likely that our understanding of post-traumatic growth, as well as its relationship to post-traumatic stress will continue to deepen.

## Does Growth Predict Outcome?

Growth theorists argue that positive changes are worthwhile clinical outcomes in their own right. However, researchers and clinicians from more traditional areas have expressed concerns about the utilitarian function of growth and have questioned whether it predicts other psychological, emotional and physical outcomes. In one of the most important studies to date, Frazier et al. (2001) found that early reports of positive changes that are sustained over time were associated with less distress at a 1-year follow-up. Other investigations have shown that people who report growth are less likely to experience problems of post-traumatic stress at 6 months (Linley, Joseph, & Goodfellow, 2008), and that those who report growth in the immediate aftermath of trauma have less psychological distress at 1–3 years post trauma (Tennen & Affleck, 2002). Generally, research suggests that reports of growth, particularly if they are sustained over time, predict better subsequent subjective well-being.

As much of the interest in growth originated from observations of people experiencing physical illnesses, a line of investigation has developed on the positive influence of growth on objective measures of physical recovery, general health and even mortality. The first of these was by Affleck, Tennen, Croog, and Levine (1987) who reported that heart attack patients who found benefits immediately after their first attack had reduced re-occurrence and morbidity statistics 8 years after the event. Subsequently, Epel, McEwen, and Ickovics (1998) documented that high levels of growth were related to lower cortisol levels in women exposed to laboratory stress, as did Cruess et al. (2000) who reported lower cortisol levels through an enhancement of benefit finding intervention among women with breast cancer. More recently, Dunigan, Carr, and Steel (2007) found that patients with hepatoma who scored high on growth survived, on average, up to 186 days longer than their lower scoring peers. This was argued to be due to higher peripheral blood leukocytes. Further, Bower et al. (1998) reported lower levels of mortality in HIV-positive men who experienced benefit finding after the recent AIDS-related death of someone close to them. Along similar lines, Milam (2004) found greater immune system functioning among HIV patients with higher levels of growth. In sum, not only do positive changes seem to lead to increases in subjective well-being, but also in physical well-being.

# New Research Directions

While the research described in earlier sections is encouraging and points to the clinical importance of work in this area, it would be premature to conclude that growth is inevitably associated with enhanced outcomes. In addition to the already described need for advances in psychometric scales, quantitative research, and theory, there are several developing areas of research that are likely to be informative. Those areas we discuss are not intended to be an exhaustive list but rather those we think it particularly worthwhile to draw attention to, and which inevitably reflect our own interests in qualitative health psychology and psychotherapeutic applications.

The first is qualitative research that enhances our understanding of growth beyond what existing self-report measures can tell us. This should be genuinely idiographic and able to capture people's experiences of change following adversity, without undue influence from existing research and conceptualization (Joseph et al., 2009). For this to happen, researchers will need to address the discrepancy between what is defined as "qualitative" (for a detailed review, see Hefferon et al. (2009) and what are "dressed up" quantitative interview schedules, (e.g., Elliot et al., 1999; Yardley, 2000), and begin to identify possible experiences of growth that are not recognized by the current tools (Manuel, 2007) particularly since it is becoming apparent that each trauma has unique domains of growth (Hefferon et al., 2009, 2010).

The second area is the relationship of growth with physical exercise. Within the UK, the promotion of exercise as an adjunct treatment for physical illness is increasing. Although exercise randomized controlled trial (RCT) interventions are new (with the first UK RCT having been conducted by Mutrie et al. in 2007), recent qualitative data supports the notion that participating in physical activity following physical trauma can facilitate the growth process (Hefferon et al., 2008; Sabiston et al., 2008). The physical movement, regaining of strength, developing a new identity as an athlete, acquiring a sense of mastery over the body and participation in "normal activity" are explanations provided by patients for why exercise enhanced their growth. There is a current need for longitudinal, quantitative data on the relationship between exercise and growth, and as we will consider, further investigation of exercise as a form of therapeutic intervention.

A third research direction emerging from sociological literature is the concept of illness diagnoses as a "teachable moment" or a "window of opportunity" that can be used by health programs and health practitioners to highlight possible lifestyle changes and promote responsibility for one's own health (Gritz et al., 2006; Humpel, Magee, & Jones, 2007). Research documents health behavior changes following trauma as including: taking self-responsibility;

monitoring one's health; listening to one's own body; improving health behaviors such as eating more nutritiously, partaking in greater levels of exercise, and reducing stress; undertaking routine health checks; vicarious health behaviors (friends and family members engaging in self examinations, diet change); ceasing risky behaviors (such as consuming drugs, alcohol and tobacco and having unprotected sex); and developing a new positive identification with one's body (for a full review, see Hefferon et al., 2009).

The fourth research area is to further understand the role of mortality salience (MS). Tedeschi and Calhoun (2006) suggest that post-traumatic growth research needs to focus more closely on growth in mortality salient environments. Mortality salience is a component of the widely accepted terror management theory (TMT). This theory suggests that there is an innate, biological need to survive and explores the management of the evolutionary driven cognitive realization of inevitable death (Pyszczynski, Greenberg, & Goldenberg, 2002). The mortality salience hypothesis suggests that when people are reminded of the inevitability of death, their world view defense strengthens and they seek to conform to the accepted beliefs and behaviors of their culture (Harmon-Jones et al., 1997). From this perspective, a traumatic and life threatening event, paired with the lifelong reminder of a person's close encounter with death (e.g., physical scars and deformity) creates a mortality salient environment.

The links between growth and mortality salience appear when researchers consider the existential, corporeal issues of trauma and examine the difference between the trauma type and the processes by which a person recovers and eventually grows. For example, a key issue with breast cancer is that the reminder of one's death (mortality salient environment) is always present in the form of lost hair, sickness, etc. during chemotherapy as well as scars and removed breasts post-treatment. These patients are never post-trauma and bear the ongoing reminder of their brush with death upon their physical self. Thus, it is argued that survivors of one-time occurrence traumas (e.g., natural disasters, sexual assault, and bereavement) rebuild their lives towards growth in a completely different way; the reminders of the event are not etched upon the body, and are not faced each and every time that body is viewed (Hefferon et al., 2009). Future research should continue to examine at least two questions that are pertinent to understanding mortality salience's role in growth: whether events that induce high mortality salience are associated with greater growth and whether reported growth differs across mortality salient environments (Tedeschi & Calhoun, 2006).

# Facilitating Post-traumatic Growth

Turning to psychotherapeutic applications, the facilitation of growth as a focus for therapeutic activity has also begun to receive attention. Tedeschi and Calhoun (2008) provide a step-by-step approach for working with patients in a clinical setting. Their primary advice for practitioners is to learn about the phenomenon themselves, and then "become the expert companion" on the patient's potential journey to growth. The main caveat here is that the practitioner must never push the growth concept as this may lead to increased pressure and anxiety as well as disappointment in the self if it is not experienced (otherwise known as the *tyranny of positive thinking*; Held, 1998). Therapists should be aware of the potential for positive change in their clients following stress and trauma. But it must also be recognized that adversity does not lead to positive change for everyone. Therefore, therapists need to be careful not to inadvertently imply that the person has in some way failed by not making more of their experience, or that there is anything inherently positive in the person's experience. Personal growth after trauma should be viewed as originating not from the event, but from within the person through the process of their struggle with the event and its aftermath.

Theoretical work such as that by Joseph (2004) and Joseph and Linley (2005) suggests that growth following adversity is a normal and natural process that people are innately motivated toward. Thus, the task of the therapist is not to supply people with the answers to their questions and tell them what meaning to find in their experience. People will do this for themselves. The task is to provide a safe and supportive opportunity for this to take place. Theirs is a person-centered approach that views the client as the "best expert" on themselves, and thus advises that what is important is not what the therapist *does* to the client, but rather what the therapist *provides*: a supportive social environment that is facilitated by a non-directive approach and which enables the client's intrinsic cognitive accommodation process. For traditional cognitive therapists this approach may be challenging and seem paradoxical, but as Murphy, Durkin, and Joseph (2011) explain, this is not to suggest that therapy be passive. On the contrary, non-directive therapy is dynamic, creative, and challenging for both client and therapist. A non-directive approach can and often does include all those elements of more directive manual based therapies, but it is in their application that they differ. Non-directive approaches respond to individual client needs and have the flexibility to incorporate techniques, such as homework tasks or the use of psychometric measures. Each technique however is suggested by the therapist in an attempt to understand and communicate their acceptance of the client rather than an attempt to reduce or treat symptoms or to force the client towards change and growth.

Support groups that are not specifically designed for the development of growth have also been found to facilitate benefit in trauma survivors (Hefferon et al., 2008; Lechner et al., 2008; Sabiston et al., 2008). For example, low-impact aerobics exercise classes are associated with positive physical and psychological outcomes (Biddle, 2000; Campbell et al. 2005; Courneya, 2000, 2002, 2003; Mutrie et al., 2007; Weert et al., 2005).

Hefferon et al. (2008) reported that one of the main benefits and potential facilitators of growth among breast cancer patients who participated in a 3-month exercise intervention during chemotherapy, was the fact that the interventions group was not focused in a negative, ruminative manner on their illness and grief, but rather on a healthy distraction within a non-stigmatized and non-pressurized environment. It is suggested that health practitioners and clinicians offer group therapies that center on a healthy form of distraction such as exercise. The most advantageous timeline for participation in these group-based therapies appears to be when patients are about to undergo their treatment (Cordova, 2008; Emslie et al., 2007; Sabiston et al., 2007; Stevinson & Fox, 2006).

# Conclusion

One of the most remarkable recent advances in our understanding of trauma is that in the aftermath of the struggle, it is common to find benefits. This perception of benefits may in turn be associated with higher levels of psychological functioning and improved health. This is not to overlook the personal devastation of psychological trauma, but to highlight that we must not overlook the fact that psychological trauma does not necessarily lead to a damaged life. Simply being aware of the possibility of benefits can offer hope to people. There is much research that is needed to further our understanding of the architecture of growth and its predictors, and there are emerging applications within the health and clinical domains to help foster this outcome.

## References

Abraído-Lanza, A. F., Guier, C., & Colón, R. M. (1998). Psychological thriving among Latinas with chronic illness. *Journal of Social Issues*, 54, 405–424.

Affleck, G., Tennen, H., Croog, S., & Levine, S. (1987). Causal attribution, perceived benefits, and morbidity after a heart attack: an 8-year study. *Journal of Consulting and Clinical Psychology*, 55(1), 29–35.

Bower, J. E., Kemeny, M. E., Taylor, S. E., & Fahey, J. L. (1998). Cognitive processing, discovery of meaning, CD4 decline, and AIDS-related mortality among bereaved HIV-seropositive men. *Journal of Consulting and Clinical Psychology*, 66(6), 979–986.

Cadell, S., Regehr, C., & Hemsworth, D. (2003). Factors contributing to posttraumatic growth: a proposed structural equation model. *American Journal of Orthopsychiatry*, 73(3), 279–287.

Calhoun, L. G., Cann, A., Tedeschi, R. G., & McMillan, J. (2000). A correlational test of the relationship between post-traumatic growth, religion, and cognitive processing. *Journal of Traumatic Stress*, 13, 521–527.

Calhoun, L. G., & Tedeschi, R. G. (2008). The paradox of struggling with trauma: Guidelines for practice and directions for research. In S. Joseph & A. Linley (Eds.), *Trauma, Recovery, and Growth: Positive Psychological Perspectives on Post-traumatic Stress* (pp. 325–337). Hoboken, NJ: Wiley.

Campbell, W. K., Brunell, A. B., & Foster, J. D. (2004). Sitting here in limbo: Ego shock and posttraumatic growth. *Psychological Inquiry*, 15(1), 22–26.

Carver, C. S. (1998). Resilience and thriving: Issues, models, and linkages. *Journal of Social Issues*, 54, 245–266.

Cordova, M. J., Cunningham, L. L., Carlson, C. R., & Andrykowski, M. A. (2001). Posttraumatic growth following breast cancer: a controlled comparison study. *Health Psychology*, 20(3), 176–185.

Cozzolino, P. J., Staples, A. D., Meyers, L. S., & Samboceti, J. (2004). Greed, death, and values: from terror management to transcendence management theory. *Personality & Social Psychology Bulletin*, 30(3), 278–292.

Cruess, D. G., Antoni, M. H., McGregor, B. A., Kilbourn, K. M., Boyers, A. E., Alferi, S. M., ... Kumar, M. (2000). Cognitive-behavioral stress management reduces serum cortisol by enhancing benefit finding among women being treated for early stage breast cancer. *Psychosomatic Medicine*, 62(3), 304–308.

Dunigan, J. T., Carr, B. I., & Steel, J. L. (2007). Post-traumatic growth, immunity and survival in patients with hepatoma. *Digestive Diseases and Sciences*, 52(9), 2452–2459.

Dunn, J., Lynch, B., Rinaldis, M., Pakenham, K. I., McPherson, L., Owen, N., ... Aitken, J. (2006). Dimensions of quality of life and psychosocial variables most salient to colorectal cancer patients. *Psycho-Oncology*, 15(1), 20–30.

Elliott, R., Fischer, C., & Rennie, D. (1999). Evolving guidelines for publication of qualitative research studies in psychology and related fields. *British Journal of Clinical Psychology*, *38*, 215–229.

Emslie, C., Whyte, F., Campbell, A., Mutrie, N., Lee, L., Ritchie, D. & Kearney, N. (2007). "I wouldn't have been interested in just sitting round a table talking about cancer"; exploring the experiences of women with breast cancer in a group exercise trial. *Health Education Research*, *22*, 827–838.

Epel, E. S., McEwen, B. S., & Ickovics, J. R. (1998). Embodying psychological thriving: Physical thriving in response to stress. *Journal of Social Issues*, *54*(2), 301–322.

Ford, J., Tennen, H., & Albert, D. (2008). A contrarian view of growth following adversity. In S. Joseph & A. Linley (Eds.), *Trauma, Recovery and Growth: Positive psychological perspectives on post-traumatic stress* (pp. 297–324). Hoboken, New Jersey: John Wiley & Sons.

Frazier, P., Conlon, A., & Glaser, T. (2001). Positive and negative life changes following sexual assault. *Journal of Consulting and Clinical Psychology*, *69*, 1048–1055.

Fromm, K., Andrykowski, M. A., & Hunt, J. (1996). Positive and negative psychosocial sequelae of bone marrow transplantation: implications for quality of life assessment. *Journal of Behavioral Medicine*, *19*(3), 221–240.

Giorgi, A., & Giorgi, B. (2003). Phenomenology. In J. A. Smith (Ed.), *Qualitative psychology: a practical guide to research methods* (pp. 25–50). London, UK: Sage Publications.

Hefferon, K., Grealy, M., & Mutrie, N. (2008). The perceived influence of an exercise class intervention on the process and outcomes of post-traumatic growth. *Journal of Mental Health and Physical Activity*, *1*, 32–39.

Hefferon, K., Grealy, M., & Mutrie, N. (2009). Post-traumatic growth and life threatening physical illness: a systematic review of the qualitative literature. *British Journal of Health Psychology*, (14), 2.

Hefferon, K., Grealy, M., & Mutrie, N. (2010). Transforming from cocoon to butterfly: the potential role of the body in the process of post-traumatic growth. *Journal of Humanistic Psychology*, *50*(2), 224–247.

Held, B. S. (2002). The tyranny of the positive attitude in America: Observation and speculation. *Journal of Clinical Psychology*, *58*(9), 965–991.

Held, B. S. (2004). The negative side of positive psychology. *Journal of Humanistic Psychology*, *44*(1), 9–46.

Hennessy, E., Stevinson, C., & Fox, K. (2005). Preliminary study of the lived experience of exercise for cancer survivors. *European Journal of Oncology Nursing*, *9*, 155–166.

Humpel, N., Magee, C., & Jones, S. C. (2007). The impact of a cancer diagnosis on the health behaviors of cancer survivors and their family and friends. *Supportive Care in Cancer*, *15*(6), 621–630.

Janoff-Bulman, R. (1992). *Shattered assumptions: Towards a new psychology of trauma*. New York, NY: Free Press.

Janoff-Bulman, R. (2004). Post-traumatic growth: Three explanatory models. *Psychological Inquiry*, *15*(1), 30–34.

Joseph, S. (2004). Client-centred therapy, post-traumatic stress disorder and post-traumatic growth. *Theory and practice. Psychology and Psychotherapy: Theory, Research, and Practice*, *77*, 101–120.

Joseph, S., Beer, C., Clarke, D., Forman, A., Pickersgill, M., Swift, J., & Tischler, V. (2009). Qualitative research into mental health: Reflections on epistemology. *Mental Health Review Journal*, *14*, 36–42.

Joseph, S., & Linley, A. (2005). Positive adjustment to threatening events: An organismic valuing theory of growth through adversity. *Review of General Psychology, 9*, 262–280.

Joseph, S. & Linley, P. A. (2008a). Psychological assessment of growth following adversity: A review. In S. Joseph, & P. A. Linley (Eds.), *Trauma, recovery, and growth: Positive psychological perspectives on post-traumatic stress* (pp. 21–38). Hoboken, NJ: John Wiley & Sons.

Joseph, S., & Linley, A. (2008b). Positive psychological perspectives on post-traumatic stress: an integrative psychological framework. In S. Joseph & A. Linley (Eds.), *Trauma, recovery and growth: Positive psychological perspectives on post-traumatic stress* (pp. 3–20). Hoboken, NJ: John Wiley & Sons.

Joseph, S., Linley, P. A., Andrews, L., Harris, G., Howle, B., Woodward, C., & Shevlin, M. (2005). Assessing positive and negative changes in the aftermath of adversity: Psychometric evaluation of the Changes in Outlook Questionnaire. *Psychological Assessment, 17*, 70–80.

Joseph, S., Linley, P. A., & Harris, G. (2005). Understanding positive change following trauma and adversity: Structural clarification. *Journal of Loss and Trauma, 10*, 83–96.

Joseph, S., Maltby, J., Wood, A. M., Stockton, H., Hunt, N., & Regel, S. (2012). The Psychological Well-Being–Post-Traumatic Changes Questionnaire (PWB-PTCQ): Reliability and Validity. *Psychological Trauma: Theory, Research, Practice, and Policy, 4*, 420–428.

Joseph, S., Williams, R., & Yule, W. (1993). Changes in outlook following disaster: the preliminary development of a measure to assess positive and negative responses. *Journal of Traumatic Stress, 6*, 271–279.

Kurtz, M. E., Wyatt, G., & Kurtz, J. C. (1995). Psychological and sexual well-being, philosophical/spiritual views, and health habits of long-term cancer survivors. *Health Care in Women International, 16*, 253–262.

Lechner, S., Stoelb, B., & Antoni, M. (2008). Group-based therapies for benefit finding in cancer. In S. Joseph & A. Linley (Eds.), *Trauma, recovery, and growth: Positive psychological perspectives on post-traumatic stress* (pp. 207–231). Hoboken, NJ: John Wiley & Sons.

Linley, P. A., Andrews, L., Joseph, S. (2007). Confirmatory factor analysis of the post-traumatic growth inventory. *Journal of Loss and Trauma, 12*, 321–332.

Linley, P. A., & Joseph, S. (2004). Positive change processes following trauma and adversity: A review of the empirical literature. *Journal of Traumatic Stress, 17*, 11–22.

Linley, P. A., Joseph, S., & Goodfellow, B. (2008). Positive changes in outlook following trauma and their relationship to subsequent post-traumatic stress, depression, and anxiety. *Journal of Social and Clinical Psychology, 27*, 877–891.

Lykins, E. L., Segerstrom, S. C., Averill, A. J., Evans, D. R., & Kemeny, M. E. (2007). Goal shifts following reminders of mortality: reconciling posttraumatic growth and terror management theory. *Personality & Social Psychology Bulletin, 33*, 1088–1099.

Manuel, J. C., Burwell, S. R., Crawford, S. L., Lawrence, R., Farmer, D., Hege, A., … Avis, N. (2007). Younger women's perceptions of coping with breast cancer. *Cancer Nursing, 30*, 85–94.

McMillen, J. C. (2004). Post-traumatic growth: What's it all about? *Psychological Inquiry, 15*, 48–52.

McMillen, J. C., & Fisher, R. H. (1998). The Perceived Benefits Scales: Measuring perceived positive life changes after negative events. *Social Work Research, 22*, 173–187.

Milam, J. (2004). Post-traumatic growth among HIV/AIDS patients. *Journal of Applied Social Psychology, 34*, 2353–2376.

Miller, W. R., & C'deBaca, J. (1994). Quantum change: Toward a psychology of transformation. In T. F. Heaherton & J. L. Weinberger (Eds.), *Can personality change?* (pp. 253–280). Washington, DC: American Psychological Association.

Murphy, D., Durkin, J., & Joseph, S. (2011). Growth in relationship: A post-medicalized vision for positive transformation. In N. Tehrani (Ed.), *Managing trauma in the workplace: Supporting workers and organisations* (pp. 267–282). Routledge: London.

Mutrie, N., Campbell, A. M., Whyte, F., McConnachie, A., Emslie, C., Lee, L., … Ritchie, D. (2007). Benefits of supervised group exercise programme for women being treated for early stage breast cancer: pragmatic randomised controlled trial. *British Medical Journal, 334*, 517–520B.

Nerken, I. R. (1993). Grief and the reflective self: towards a clearer model of loss resolution and growth. *Death Studies, 17*, 1–26.

O'Leary, V. (1998). Strength in the face of adversity: individual and social thriving—Thriving: broadening the paradigm beyond illness to health. *Journal of Social Issues, 5*, 425–445.

O'Leary, V., Alday, C. S., & Ickovics, J. (1998). Models of life change and post-traumatic growth. In R. G. Tedeschi, C. Park & L. G. Calhoun (Eds.), *Post-traumatic Growth*. Mahwah, NJ: Lawrence Erlbaum.

O'Leary, V., & Ickovics, J. (1995). Resilience and thriving in response to challenge: an opportunity for a paradigm shift in women's health. *Women's Health: Research on Gender, Behaviour and Policy, 1*, 121–142.

Park, C. L., Cohen, L. H., & Murch, R. L. (1996). Assessment and prediction of stress-related growth. *Journal of Personality, 64*, 71–105.

Regel, S., & Joseph, S. (2010). *Post-traumatic stress: The facts*. Oxford, UK: Oxford University Press.

Rogers, C. R. (1959). A theory of therapy, personality and interpersonal relationships. In S. Koch (Ed.), *Psychology: A study of science* (Vol. 3, pp. 184–256). New York, NY: McGraw-Hill.

Ryff, C. D. (1989). Happiness is everything, or is it? Explorations on the meaning of psychological well-being. *Journal of Personality and Social Psychology, 57*, 1069–1081.

Ryff, C. D., & Singer, B. H. (1996). Psychological well-being: Meaning, measurement, and implications for psychotherapy research. *Psychotherapy and Psychosomatics, 65*, 14–23.

Sabiston, C. M., McDonough, M. H., & Crocker, P. R. E. (2007). Psychosocial experiences of breast cancer survivors involved in a dragon boat program: Exploring links to positive psychological growth. *Journal of Sport & Exercise Psychology, 29*, 419–438.

Schaefer, J. A., & Moos, R. H. (1992). Life crisis and personal growth. In B. N. Carpenter (Ed.), *Personal coping: theory and application* (pp. 149–170). Westport, CT: Praeger.

Sears, S. R., Stanton, A. L., & Danoff-Burg, S. (2003). The yellow brick road and the emerald city: benefit finding, positive reappraisal coping and posttraumatic growth in women with early-stage breast cancer. *Health Psychology, 22*, 487–497.

Shaw, A., Joseph, S., & Linley, P. A. (2005). Religiosity, spirituality and post-traumatic growth: A systematic review. *Mental Health, Religion, and Culture, 8*, 1–11.

Stanton, A. L., Bower, J. E., & Low, C. A. (2006). Post-traumatic growth after cancer. In L. G. Calhoun & R. G. Tedeschi (Eds.), *Handbook of post-traumatic growth: Research and practice* (pp. 138–175). Mahwah, NJ: Lawrence Erlbaum Associates.

Stevinson, C., & Fox, K. R. (2006). Feasibility of an exercise rehabilitation programme for cancer patients. *European Journal of Cancer Care, 15*, 386–396.

Taku, K., Calhoun, L. G., Cann, A., & Tedeschi, R. G. (2008). The role of rumination in the coexistence of distress and post-traumatic growth among bereaved Japanese university students. *Death Studies, 32*, 428–444.

Taku, K., Cann, A., Tedeschi, R. G., & Calhoun, L. G. (2009). Intrusive versus deliberate rumination in post-traumatic growth across US and Japanese samples. *Anxiety, Stress, & Coping, 22*, 129–136.

Taylor, S., & Brown, J. (1988). Illusion and well-being: A social psychological perspective on mental health. *Psychological Bulletin, 103*, 193–210.

Taylor, S., & Brown, J. (1994). Positive illusions and well-being revisited: Separating fact from fiction. *Psychological Bulletin, 116*, 21–27.

Tedeschi, R. G., & Calhoun, L. G. (1995). *Trauma and transformation: Growing in the aftermath of suffering.* Thousand Oaks, CA: Sage publications.

Tedeschi, R. G., & Calhoun, L. G. (1996). The post-traumatic growth inventory: measuring the positive legacy of trauma. *Journal of Traumatic Stress, 9*, 455–471.

Tedeschi, R. G., & Calhoun, L. G. (2004). Post-traumatic growth: Conceptual foundations and empirical evidence. *Psychological Inquiry, 15*, 1–18.

Tedeschi, R. G., & Calhoun, L. G. (2006). Foundations of post-traumatic growth. In R. G. Tedeschi & L. G. Calhoun (Eds.), *Handbook of post-traumatic growth* (pp. 3–23). Mahwah, NJ: Lawrence Erlbaum Associates Inc.

Tennen, H., & Affleck, G. (2002). Benefit-finding and benefit-reminding. In C. R. Snyder & S. Lopez (Eds.), *Handbook of positive psychology* (pp. 584–596). New York, NY: Oxford University Press.

Thornton, A. A. (2002). Perceiving benefits in the cancer experience. *Journal of Clinical Psychology in Medical Settings, 9*, 153–165.

Urcuyo, K. R., Boyers, A. E., Carver, C. S., & Antoni, M. H. (2005). Finding benefit in breast cancer: Relations with personality, coping, and concurrent well-being. *Psychology & Health, 20*, 175–192.

Yardley, L. (2000). Dilemmas in qualitative health research. *Psychology and Health, 15*, 215–228.

# CHAPTER 70

# CREATING A STABLE ARCHITECTURAL FRAMEWORK OF EXISTENCE: PROPOSING A MODEL OF LIFELONG MEANING

MICHAEL F. STEGER[1,2], ANNA BEEBY[1], SAMANTHA GARRETT[1], AND TODD B. KASHDAN[3]

[1] Colorado State University, USA; [2] North-West University, South Africa;
[3] George Mason University, USA

In the children's book, *Parts* (Arnold, 2000), a little boy experiences Newton's second law of thermodynamics: entropy... things fall apart. For this boy, it starts with his hair, and in his imagining, he is seconds away from being completely bald. He envisions his skin unraveling like a mummy's linens, his arm detaching and being carried away by a thrown baseball, and the rest of his brain plopping from his nose presumably following something else grey and gooey he found in there. His hypochondria aside, it is one of the most amazing things about life that—unlike the most massive star, hardest granite, or most majestic glacier—for so much of our time here, we grow, build, come together, and sustain, rather than fall apart. But, inevitably, somewhere down the road for each of us, our bodies succumb to Newton's law of entropy, and, like the little boy in *Parts* we see ourselves fall to pieces. Even before then, we confront this central existential quandary. Anyone who's found their hair in the shower drain, watched their blood flow out of a cut, or picked off a desiccated scab has seen our body create, and lose, its parts. How long can we keep doing that? With all those cells being made and unmade, how much of us is still "us" after 10, 20, or 70 years? In the midst of all this biological churning—injury and enervation, insult and incubation—how do we retain the continuity of our experience? What connects our 80-year-old self to our 8-year-old self... so much smaller, so many experiences removed, so many biological changes distant?

In one of the most fascinating studies of the past 10 years, researchers from Sweden and California worked together to determine the birthdates of cells from several places throughout the human body (Spalding, Bhardwaj, Buchholz, Druid, & Frisén, 2005). The methodology is heady stuff, but essentially the researchers were able to use the stable decay rate of carbon 14 to extrapolate when a cell was "born" based on how much carbon 14 had been absorbed in the cell (accounting for the birth date of the person contributing the cell). To set the stage for the findings, it is important to recall that the pendulum has swung between the view that brain cells can only be lost and never generated and the view that neuroplasticity is a regular occurrence. Sure, brain tissue heals slowly, if at all, similar to heart and pancreatic tissue (Bergmann et al., 2009), but a number of lines of research have revealed neurogenesis in brain structures such as the hippocampus, and even the occipital lobe. As our hair, nails, and skin cells attest, many of the cells in our body have short lifespans. However, despite the enormous amount of time and money some people spend on these aforementioned cells, brain cells have a closer connection with who we are, and for this latter group of cells, the findings were striking. Stated simply, neuronal cells are as old as we are. Prior laboratory research suggests there is a fairly high level of plasticity and neurogenesis among the cells of the occipital lobe (Kaplan, 1981). For this reason, if there is a normative turnover in neuronal cells occurring, the signs should be most apparent in the occipital neurons. Instead, the cells that are translating the sensory image of this very page into the words you are reading at this moment have been with you as long as there has been a "you." It is interesting to think that although throat cells, intestinal cells, heart cells, and even bone cells get replaced (Bergmann et al., 2009; Spalding et al., 2005), our bodies preserve the cells in our brain. Throughout evolution, the human design has maintained an enormous supporting cast of glia, and allocated incredible proportions of our energy usage to keeping these brain cells alive. Perhaps this is just an accident, but at the very least, it suggests the possibility that it is evolutionarily adaptive for humans to maintain the cognitive continuity of our experience.

Regardless of the biological underpinnings that sustain a continuous experience of life, the theoretical construct that best captures this phenomenon is meaning in life. Meaning in life is, in essence, about what it is like, psychologically, to live a coherent life that links the present to the past, and projects our longings and aspirations into the future. Because meaning in life is a variable that theoretically embraces the span of our experience and weaves it into a seamless fabric, lifespan considerations are central to any understanding of what meaning in life scholarship is all about. In this chapter, we consider three ways of looking at meaning in life: experiencing meaning, seeking meaning, and the contents of the meaningful life. The principal aim of this chapter is to review what we know about how each of these dimensions plays out across the lifespan, and to offer a model of the factors that influence meaning along the way. First, we take a closer look at conceptual issues surrounding meaning in life, and the beneficial role meaning in life is thought to play in human flourishing.

To get a feel for how meaning in life might change and evolve across the life span, it is important to understand the conceptual building blocks of meaning. Meaning has been conceptualized in various ways in the literature (for a review see Steger, 2009), representing a range of related ideas. For example, meaning has been argued to include a sense of coherence and order to one's life (Reker, Peacock, & Wong, 1987; Reker & Wong, 1988; see also Antonovsky, 1987); the perceptions of connections and relationships among objects in the world (Baumeister, 1991; Heine, Proulx, & Vohs, 2006); developing and pursuing life goals (Battista & Almond, 1973; Frankl, 1963; Reker, 2000; Reker et al., 1987; see also Damon,

Menon, & Bronk, 2003; Ryff, 1989); and some sort of emotional feeling that one's life is significant and things are the way they are supposed to be (Battista & Almond, 1973; Crumbaugh & Maholick, 1964; Yalom, 1980). It is admirable that scholars have attempted to develop cognitive, behavioral, and affective elements of meaning in life. However, in our view, it makes little sense to try to argue that there is a special kind of emotion that only happens when meaning happens. That's somewhat like arguing that there's a special emotion of fixing a flat tire, recognizing a long-forgotten song on the radio, or flushing a slam dunk in an important basketball game. Meaning should make us feel joy, awe, elevation, contentment, serenity, or even an overwhelming flood of magnanimous interconnectedness, but there is no reason to insist that meaning is defined according to these concomitants. Instead, it may be more fruitful to look at the emotions that accompany (e.g., Steger, Frazier, Oishi, & Kaler, 2006) or perhaps influence (King, Hicks, Krull, & Del Gaiso, 2006) perceptions of meaning in life. The definition we favor is that meaning in life is "the extent to which people comprehend, make sense of, or see significance in their lives, accompanied by the degree to which they perceive themselves to have a purpose, mission, or over-arching aim in life" (Steger, 2009, p. 682). In this view, meaning boils down into *comprehension* of one's life, and having a lifelong *purpose*, where comprehension refers to people's higher-order mental models of life, and purpose refers to those aspirations people seek to achieve across their lifetimes (see also King et al., 2006; Park, 2010).

This definition highlights an unfortunate tendency that has emerged in writing about this area. It is all too common to see the terms "meaning in life" and "purpose in life" used synonymously. In dividing meaning into comprehension and purpose, it becomes clear that meaning in life cannot occur without having a purpose, and also that meaning encompasses both our sense of understanding, interpreting, and finding significant the experience of life, and the possession of a purpose. However, it is worth taking a moment to clarify the scope of that aspect of human endeavor captured by the term "purpose." Specifically, a purpose is thought to be a durable, sustainably organizing and generative, self-concordant life goal that confers important motivational advantages (Kashdan & McKnight, 2009). Meaning, thus, is built of a rich and accurate comprehension of the important features of the self and the world, which provides the foundation for generating powerful purposes (McKnight & Kashdan, 2009; Steger, 2009). Some have argued that purposes must include a desire to benefit some greater good (Damon, 2008; Damon et al., 2003), but, as with arguments that meaning must have its own emotions, this argument seems to include one potential kind of purpose with the definition of the overall construct. Nonetheless, this kind of self-transcendent goal may be a particularly beneficial kind of purpose to have, as has been argued several times (Frankl, 1988; Reker & Wong, 1988).

Theorists have suggested that the process of creating a sense of meaning begins in adolescence and continues throughout life (Fry, 1998). This literature has focused primarily on people's experience of meaning in life, what Steger and colleagues (e.g., Steger, 2006; Steger, Kashdan, Sullivan, & Lorentz, 2008) refer to as the presence of meaning. A second dimension of meaning in life refers to how much people are actively searching for meaning. Unlike the experience of meaning, the search for meaning appears to be unpleasant for the typical American adult with conventional interpretations suggesting that American adults seek meaning when they experience life as meaningless (Steger et al., 2008). In contrast, there is evidence that people from Asian cultures may experience the search for meaning as a positive part of their overall existential experience (Steger, Kawabata, Shimai, & Otake, 2008).

Just as people's developmental stages and challenges are thought to influence the experience of meaning in life, seeking meaning is thought to ebb and flow, with varying consequences across the lifespan (Steger, Oishi, & Kashdan, 2009).

A final dimension we consider here concerns the contents of meaning in life, or the sources from which people derive meaning. When people ask the question, "What makes life meaningful?" many times they are asking from what sources do people draw meaning. In general, a reading of the literature on sources of meaning supports high-quality relationships with other people as the most likely source of meaning for most people, although other sources are mentioned as well. Personal growth and actualization, health and well-being, existential or religious beliefs are usually listed by double-digit percentages of people, with other responses like service to others, materialistic comforts, or one's avocational activities appearing in a small minority of reports (e.g., Battista & Almond, 1973; Debats, 2000; DeVogler & Ebersole, 1980; O'Connor & Chamberlain, 1996; Prager, Savaka, & Bar-Tur, 2000).

While relationships are a hallmark of human experience across the lifespan, other potential sources of meaning might be expected to change with age and development. For example, the work people do has substantial implications for their experience of meaning in life (Steger & Dik, 2010; Steger et al., 2010), yet at the earliest and latest developmental stages, people usually do not work. As we consider how the experience of meaning in life might be influenced by developmentally-linked variables in the following section, we will also consider how the search for meaning and the sources of meaning also might be influenced by those factors.

## Model of Lifelong Meaning

The inspirational founder of meaning in life research, Viktor Frankl (1963) proposed that meaning comes from three primary areas: creative works, engaging with the world, and withstanding adversity with a noble attitude. These categories span such diverse factors as raising children and making a positive contribution to one's family, appreciating the beauty of a mountain vista or work of art, and confronting death with dignity. More recently, Baumeister (1991) proposed four "needs" for meaning: purpose, values, efficacy, and self-worth. These two influential ideas about what people need in order to judge their lives to be meaningful seem to share little overlap, although both models have implications for the development of meaning across the lifespan. Taking a step back, and thinking about our preferred definition of meaning in life, what researchers should be concerned with are those characteristics and experiences that foster the development of comprehension and purpose. Clearly, Baumeister's need of purpose maps onto purpose. In the model proposed by Steger (2009; 2012), there is a feedback loop between purpose and comprehension that facilitates increases in both comprehension (as a result of purpose-directed activity) and in purpose-directed energy (as a result of bringing purpose more in line with one's mental model of life, or comprehension). In this way, Baumeister's needs for self-worth, efficacy, and values can be seen as adding depth and precision to the comprehension side of meaning, with eventual benefits to be seen on the purpose side. Frankl's emphasis on creative acts speaks to the contributions people can make to the world around them, a notion that links up with Erikson's ideas about generativity to underscore the importance of having a lifelong concern with striving toward one's purpose. Engaging with the world and appreciating its beauty and blessings seems to be a critical part of deepening our understanding of the world around us and how we interact with it, which are core facets of comprehension. It is more difficult to determine whether nobly enduring suffering contributes more to comprehension or purpose. Meaning-making theory, which pertains directly to how people cope with adversity and suffering, discusses how tragic events can damage our certainty about both our mental models of life, and the goals we want to accomplish in our lifetimes (Park, 2010). It is probably best to conclude that how people respond to suffering has implications for either comprehension, purpose, or both, depending on personal and situational factors.

Thinking developmentally across the lifespan raises some new solutions to the enduring question of where meaning comes from in life. We propose a new hypothesis to anticipate the emergence and generation of meaning from childhood through the end of life. We propose that underlying the establishment of self-worth, efficacy, values, creativity, engagement, and noble suffering—and ultimately comprehension and purpose—are a set of mechanisms that accumulate and interact to cultivate and sustain meaning in life. We assume the development of sufficient cognitive capacities to accomplish the following tasks. Initially, children need to establish a sense of *identity*, accompanied by *connections with others*. In addition to providing the widespread benefits associated with positive self-views and a sense of belonging, identity and connectedness help people establish self schemas and social schemas. Children and adolescents then develop capacities for *establishing and pursuing goals*. However, having a purpose is substantially different from simply having any generic sort of goal (see Kashdan & McKnight, 2009; McKnight & Kashdan, 2009). Purposes are specified to be long-term in the extreme; engaging in such a pursuit requires the development of *positive future-oriented attitudes*. To this point, people have a clear sense of self, valued connections with other people in their lives, and are able to formulate goals based on who they are, and who they are around, and pursue them, elaborating them into lifelong passions. As these pieces come together—who we are, who is in our lives, what we are trying to accomplish, how that accomplishment-directed activity resonates into the future—they provide the raw materials out of which people build their highest-level schemas. We refer to these as *self-in-world views,* a play on the phrase worldviews, which usually refers to people's beliefs about the nature of the world (e.g., Janoff-Bulman, 1992; Koltko-Rivera, 2004; Leary & Tangney, 2003). Self-in-world views capture not only the nature of the world, but also position information about the self, important others, and what the self is trying to do in relation to others and the world. With the establishment of identity, connections with others, establishing and pursuing goals, positive future-oriented attitudes, and self-in-the-world views, comprehension and purpose are created, leading to meaning in life (see Fig. 70.1). In the next section, we briefly review some of the developmental literature relevant to these five hypothesized "meaning mechanisms." Following that, we will elaborate upon our hypothesis to derive predictions about how meaning may rise and fall across the lifespan.

# Identity

Erikson's (1968) prominent model of development posited a number of stages and tasks. Through childhood and adolescence, individuals are trying to establish their identities

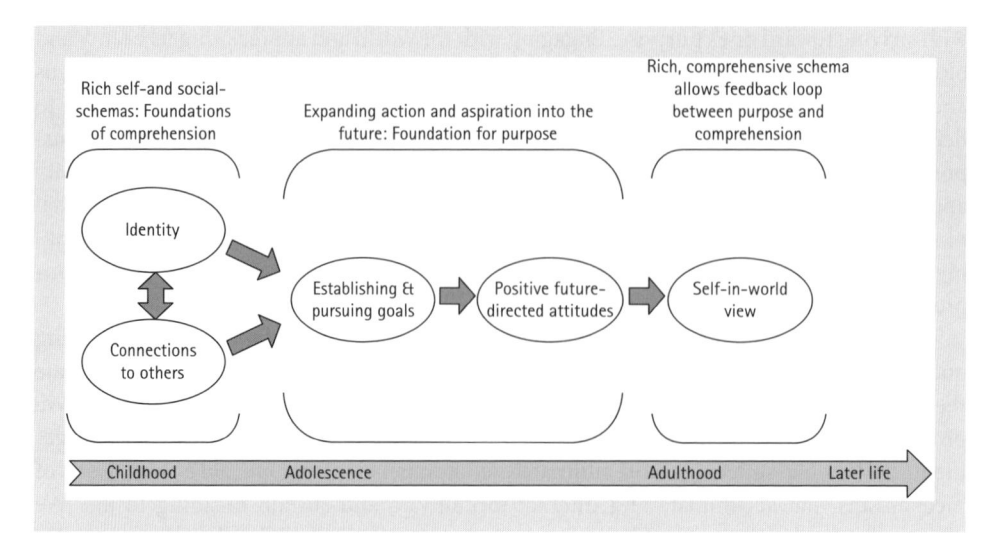

FIG. 70.1 The mechanisms of lifelong meaning hypothesis suggests that identity and connections to others build the schemas that provide the foundation for comprehension; that establishing and pursuing goals and developing positive future-directed attitudes propel action into the future and provide a foundation for purpose; and that the development of a rich comprehensive set of schemas of the self-in-the-world links purpose and comprehension, allowing for the deepening of both.

and self-concepts. Self-concepts provide more than personal understanding; they provide the central means by which people achieve a coherent comprehension of reality (Swann, Rentfrow, & Guinn, 2003). As identity develops, children and adolescents begin to forge links between themselves and abstract ideas, like beliefs (Damon, Menon, & Bronk, 2003). Identity development continues to be an important task into later stages, such as emerging adulthood (Arnett, 2000). This stage encompasses the college years and is marked by significant change and exploration. Arnett proposed that emerging adults feel free from many roles and expectations, and have not yet adopted the duties of adulthood. Because of this, exploration may reach its peak during this stage. Other lifespan approaches to meaning in life have also argued that people's emerging sense of identity is a critical component of personal meaning systems (Dittman-Kohli & Westerhof, 2000), and attaining meaning in life is most likely heavily reliant on attaining a sense of identity in both adolescence and emerging adulthood (Reker et al., 1987). We should expect the foundations for *experiencing* comprehension to be laid and built upon during these life stages. From Arnett's description, however, we might anticipate that this life stage is as much marked by exploring and *seeking* meaning in life as by heightened accrual of the presence of meaning. Emerging adults often enjoy a great deal of latitude and freedom, and they may regard the challenge of establishing enduring and valued identities as invigorating, as suggested by the epigraph to Arnett's article (2000, p. 469). Thus, identity should be regarded as a foundational support for meaning in life, and if identity comes to be degraded, questioned, or undermined at any life stage, life should seem less meaningful.

## Connecting with Others

Because of the unusually prolonged state of vulnerability that marks humans in their infancy, forming attachments to caregivers is literally necessary for survival for a long stretch of people's early years. Psychologically, this need for others appears to be sustained throughout the lifespan (Baumeister & Leary, 1995). As initial patterns for relating to others are solidified (e.g., attachment theory; Hazan & Shaver, 1987; Simpson, 1999), the challenge can be viewed as constituting a shift from maintaining nutritive connections to primary caregivers to establishing intimacy in the form of interpersonal relationships (Erikson, 1968; Reker et al., 1987). Friends, lovers, family members, close colleagues, and compatriots all help populate the world with people we know well enough to make them reassuringly predictable. In the best cases, they actually like us, and relationships serve not only as landmarks for developing an understanding of the world, but as avenues toward developing a positive identity. In addition, people we are close to model a variety of solutions for the problems we face in life, introducing us to new coping strategies, career options, musicians and artists, and perhaps purposes in life. In adolescence through young adulthood, these close relationships often take the form of romantic pairings, with many people venturing into creating a family in young adulthood. When these relationships are rewarding and positive, they appear to connect with a greater sense of meaning in life (e.g., Shek, 1995; Steger, Kashdan, & Oishi, 2009). Although the form and intent of relationships may vary across the lifespan—from biological sustenance to sexual and parental partnership—connecting with others directly impacts our comprehension of the world. In examples such as courtship, mentoring, or parenthood, these relationships may also provide varying degrees of purpose as well.

## Formulating and Pursuing Goals

Developing the ability to formulate and pursue appropriate goals is an essential part of living a satisfying and fulfilling life (Deci & Ryan, 2000). The cognitive capacities to set targets and strive for them emerge in childhood, and the ability to discern which goals are best for one's unique self can be seen among college students (e.g., Sheldon & Kasser, 1995). In many ways, college provides an excellent microcosm for understanding goal pursuit. College students have many goals (finding a romantic partner, getting a good job out of college), with highly variable timelines (30 minutes, 4 years), that often compete (staying at the party longer conflicts with studying for an important exam). Hopefully, this period of time is a good incubator for sufficient goal pursuit abilities because by young adulthood, people are not only investing heavily in romantic, parental, and familial relationships, but they are also immersed in a period of time in which careers and occupational trajectories are usually established. Balancing career demands with the activities necessary for healthy family relationships can be difficult (Halpern, 2005). Research on work-family conflict is beginning to reveal that such conflict can have negative effects on individuals' life satisfaction (Kossek & Ozeki, 1998), as well as meaning in life (Bonebright, Clay, & Ankenmann, 2000). This conflict is undoubtedly intensified among those raising children, adding additional stressors to parenthood. Parenting stress itself is associated with reduced well-being (e.g., Deater-Deckard, 1998). It is possible that at the very time young adults are cultivating lasting and intimate relationships they are also facing challenges integrating those relationships with emerging careers and growing responsibilities as parents. Succeeding at any of these activities requires the ability to formulate and pursue the right goals, as well as the ability to monitor progress, adopt new strategies, and disengage if necessary. Attempting to balance these important and competing challenges is an approach-approach conflict, and it is possible that at the same time these rich *sources* of meaning are enhancing the *experience* of meaning, that people are also confronting fundamental questions about meaning, sparking heightened meaning *seeking*.

## FUTURE-DIRECTED POSITIVE ATTITUDES

One of the ways in which people decide which goals they should expend energy pursuing is by considering whether that energy gets them closer to a desired future end-state. Purposes demand very long timeframes (e.g., Kashdan & McKnight, 2009), perhaps even the rest of one's life. To sacrifice anything in the present for the sake of a decades-removed outcome requires people to invest heavily in the future. Working parents must decide whether more time with the family is more important than more time at work; is moving to be closer to family better than moving for a better job? By middle-age adulthood, many of these "balancing" challenges faced by young adults are resolved. However, middle-age adults face their own developmental challenge to be productive and creative (Erikson, 1968; Reker et al., 1987). In essence, middle-aged adults continue to face goal pursuit challenges, but the timeframe they are thought to consider spans their remaining days. Often, people seek to build a lasting legacy and meaningful contribution through their careers. Even though disenchanted workers and unenthused workaholics report less meaning in life, work enjoyment is associated with more meaning (Bonebright et al., 2000). We would expect that to the extent that middle-age adults can achieve productive and satisfying careers, they should experience more meaning in life. Work autonomy and financial wealth often peak during middle-age adulthood. In addition, among those who have children, this is often a time when their children leave for college, affording middle-age adults the time to pursue dormant interests, to invest back into their primary romantic relationships and friendships, and to enjoy the vicarious and direct pleasures of watching their children accumulate achievements and begin their own families. Thus, middle-age adulthood could be a period of growth and rejuvenation of meaning for many, with earlier existential challenges surpassed, and later challenges like illness and mortality often decades away.

## SELF-IN-WORLD VIEW

As many others have noted, later life can be a period marked by loss; loss of relationships, physical health, and some of the roles that people have occupied for much of their lives (e.g., Fry, 2001; Wong, 2000). Older adults are especially vulnerable to the impact of stressful events in highly valued roles (Krause, 2004). Loss of physical functioning and independence also can detract from well-being in later life. Older adults who are frail or have persistent health problems report lower well-being than those who do not (Kirby, Coleman, & Daley, 2004). For many older adults, significant declines in physical health are accompanied by a move from community dwelling to institutional dwelling. Loss of loved ones and companions is ubiquitous and inevitable in later life; loss of a spouse is associated with a significant decline in well-being (Lund, Caserta, Dimond, & Shaffer, 1989). Older adults who lose partners struggle with attempts to create meaning from the loss as well as their own survival (Golsworthy & Coyle, 1999). Wong (1989, 2000) has argued that meaning in life may be the quality that prevents living from becoming unbearable in the face of physical decline, loss, and despair. In fact, there is evidence that existential factors like meaning in life, spirituality, and religion are more predictive of well-being than physical, social, or demographic factors (Fry, 2001). A central challenge for older adults is in preserving a perspective on their overarching place in the world around them that makes confronting the difficulty of later life manageable, and allows them to highlight the wisdom of their perspective. Ideally, well before these age-related losses are confronted, people have created a robust comprehension of their place in the world around them, and can draw on that wisdom (e.g., Baltes & Kunzmann, 2004; Baltes & Staudinger, 2000), even as their incentive to pursue grand, long-term goals is reduced. We would anticipate that generative self-in-world views are typically constructed on the way from young adulthood to middle-aged adulthood, and can serve as a resource in later life. With the advent of self-in-world views, we would hypothesize that the task of weaving meaning into life is complete.

## Extrapolating Levels of Meaning Across the Lifespan

In this chapter, we have attempted to develop a kind of "To Do" list for building meaning across the lifespan. At the same time, the model of lifelong meaning we propose generates further predictions concerning the experiencing, seeking, and sources dimensions of meaning. Few ideas have been offered to explain why some people judge their lives to be more meaningful than other people do. When this question does arise, the usual answer is that "high meaning" people have more sources of meaning (Reker, 2000), or have successfully resolved their search for meaning (Steger et al., 2009). Taking a cue from Baumeister (1991), the model we are hypothesizing predicts that as people establish an identity and connections with others, develop the capacity to formulate and pursue goals, and create positive future-directed attitudes and a robust self-in-world view, they satisfy, in a sense, their "needs" for meaning. These elements become fertile ground for the seeds of new sources of meaning to grow. According to our hypothesis, throughout much of the human lifespan, people should be expanding their repertoire of ways to draw meaning from the world as they age. Children can call upon emerging identities and connections with others (e.g., appreciating abilities, family, friends, and school affiliations), adolescents can call upon goal-directed activity (e.g., enjoying the pursuit of athletic or academic achievement), adults can call upon a positive vision of future purpose (e.g., building a career or raising children), and middle age adults can call upon a rich self-in-world view (e.g., developing wisdom, generativity, and a desire to leave a legacy). Thus, meaning should be higher among older people, at least up through middle age. As adults confront later life issues, they may see interpersonal connections disappear (though there is no reason to suspect that the remaining connections would be any less important), and have fewer goals that they pursue into an ever-shortening future. The challenge of later life development, then, is emphasizing identity and self-in-world views over striving to accomplish long-term goals. Fig. 70.2 displays our predictions about the course of meaning across the lifespan, breaking meaning out into comprehension, purpose, and seeking.

Empirical research generally supports these predictions, with numerous lines of research finding an upward trend toward a peak of meaning in middle age adulthood. From middle age adulthood into later life, results are somewhat mixed, with research using meaning in life measures that prioritized goal-related activity levels (more closely linked to purpose) indicating lower levels of meaning/purpose toward the end of life (see Pinquart, 2002) and research using meaning in life measures that prioritize perceptions of general meaningfulness and significance in one's life (more closely linked to comprehension) indicating a continued upward trajectory into later life (Steger, Oishi, & Kashdan, 2009). This same line of research also suggests an irregular downward trend for seeking meaning. One final observation that can be gleaned from Steger and colleagues' research is that, as predicted by developmental theories, the relation between seeking meaning and well-being is increasingly negative at later life stages. Thus, by considering the tasks and mechanisms people need to accrue in order to achieve meaningful lives, testable predictions can be made regarding what factors presage meaning, when they are established, and how they combine to predict the course of meaning across the lifespan.

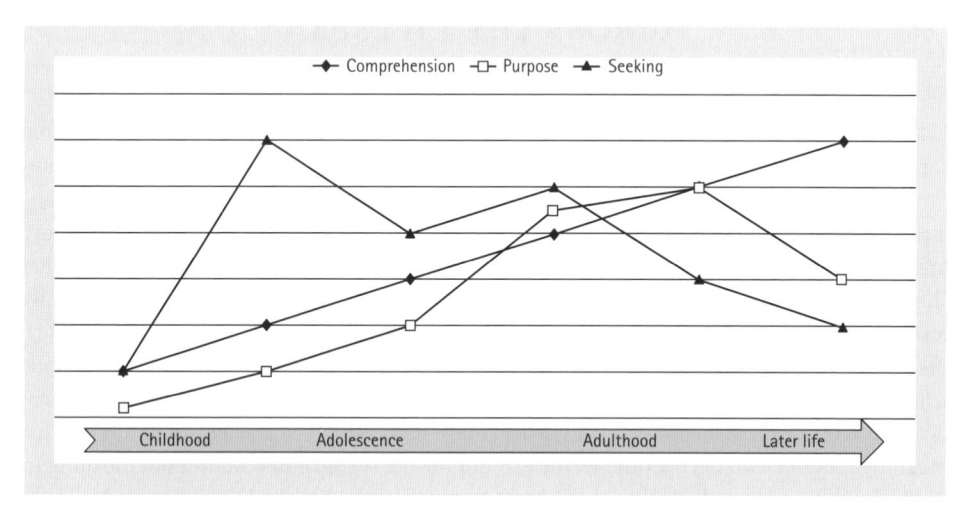

FIG. 70.2 Predictions from the mechanisms of lifelong meaning hypothesis for expected levels of comprehension, purpose, and seeking of meaning across the lifetime. This hypothesis predicts a steady increase in comprehension, a delayed but sharper peak of purpose by middle-age adulthood, and a general decline in seeking of meaning with normative spike in adolescence and during the years that present the greatest work–family conflict.

## Conclusion

Research on meaning in life seems to be accelerating in breadth and sophistication. For example, studies have been published recently linking low levels of meaning in life to foreshortened mortality (Boyle, Barnes, Buchman, & Bennett, 2009), and experimentally demonstrating the relevance of meaning and related factors to preferences for seeking novelty (Vess, Routledge, Landau, & Arndt, 2009), and the use of religion in medical decisions (Vess, Arndt, Cox, Routledge, & Goldenberg, 2009). Finding links between important landmarks in life is a core facet of meaning, and just as people face the challenge of collecting and connecting what is important in their lives, scholars who seek to understand happiness, well-being, and what makes life worth living face a challenge of synthesizing the various threads of meaning in life research while continuing to push the bounds of what we know. A lifespan perspective such as the one we present in this chapter offers new promise for this endeavor.

## References

Antonovsky, A. (1987). *Unraveling the mystery of health: How people manage stress and stay well*. San Francisco, CA: Jossey-Bass.

Arnett, J. J. (2000). Emerging adulthood: A theory of development from the late teens through the twenties. *American Psychologist, 55*, 469–480.

Arnold, T. (2000). *Parts*. New York, NY: Puffin.

Baltes, P. B., & Kunzmann, U. (2004). The two faces of wisdom: Wisdom as a general theory of knowledge and judgment about excellence in mind and virtue vs. wisdom as everyday realization in people and products. *Human Development, 47*, 290–299.

Baltes, P. B., & Staudinger, U. M. (2000). Wisdom: A metaheuristic (pragmatic) to orchestrate mind and virtue toward excellence. *American Psychologist, 55*, 122–136.

Battista, J., & Almond, R. (1973). The development of meaning in life. *Psychiatry, 36*, 409–427.

Baumeister, R. F. (1991). *Meanings of life*. New York, NY: Guilford.

Baumeister, R. F., & Leary, M. R. (1995). The need to belong: Desire for interpersonal attachments as a fundamental human motivation. *Psychological Bulletin, 117*, 497–529.

Bergmann, O., Bhardwaj, R. D., Bernard, S., Zdunek, S., Barnabé-Heider, F., Walsh, S., … Frisén, J. (2009). Evidence for cardiomyocyte renewal in humans. *Science, 324*(5923), 98–102.

Bonebright, C., Clay, D., & Ankenmann, R. (2000). The relationship of workaholism with work–life conflict, life satisfaction, and purpose in life. *Journal of Counseling Psychology, 47*(4), 469–477.

Boyle, P. A., Barnes, L. L., Buchman, A. S., & Bennet, D. A. (2009). Purpose in life is associated with mortality among community-dwelling older persons. *Psychosomatic Medicine, 71*, 574–579.

Crumbaugh, J. C. & Maholick, L. T. (1964). An experimental study in existentialism: The psychometric approach to Frankl's concept of noogenic neurosis. *Journal of Clinical Psychology, 20*, 200–207.

Damon, W. (2008). *The path to purpose: Helping our children find their calling in life*. New York, NY: Simon & Schuster.

Damon, W., Menon, J., & Bronk, K. C. (2003). The development of purpose during adolescence. *Applied Developmental Science, 7*, 119–128.

Deater-Deckard, K. (1998). Parenting stress and child adjustment: Some old hypotheses and new questions. *Clinical Psychology: Science and Practice*, 5(3), 314–332.

Debats, D. L. (2000). An inquiry into existential meaning: Theoretical, clinical, and phenomenal perspectives. In G. T. Reker & K. Chamberlain (Eds.), *Exploring existential meaning: Optimizing human development across the lifespan* (pp. 93–106). Thousand Oaks, CA: Sage Publications, Inc.

Deci, E., & Ryan, R. (2000). The 'what' and 'why' of goal pursuits: Human needs and the self-determination of behavior. *Psychological Inquiry*, 11(4), 227–268.

De Vogler, K. L., & Ebersole, P. (1980). Categorization of college students' meaning in life. *Psychological Reports*, 46, 387–390.

Dittman-Kohli, F., & Westerhof, G. J. (2000). The personal meaning system in a life-span perspective. In G. T. Reker & K. Chamberlian (Eds.), *Exploring existential meaning: Optimizing human development across the life span* (pp. 107–122). Thousand Oaks, CA: Sage Publications.

Erikson, E. H. (1968). *Identity: Youth and crisis*. New York, NY: Norton.

Frankl, V. E. (1988). *The will to meaning: foundations and applications of logotherapy* (expanded ed.). New York, NY: Penguin.

Frankl, V. E. (1963). *Man's search for meaning: An introduction to logotherapy*. New York, NY: Washington Square Press.

Fry, P. S. (1998). The development of personal meaning and wisdom in adolescence: A reexamination of moderating and consolidating factors and influences. In P. T. P. Wong & P. S. Fry (Eds.), *The human quest for meaning: A handbook of psychological research and clinical application* (pp. 91–110). Mahwah, NJ: Lawrence Erlbaum Associates, Publishers.

Fry, P. (2001). Predictors of health-related quality of life perspectives, self-esteem, and life satisfactions of older adults following spousal loss: An 18-month follow-up study of widows and widowers. *The Gerontologist*, 41(6), 787–798.

Golsworthy, R., & Coyle, A. (1999). Spiritual beliefs and the search for meaning among older adults following partner loss. *Mortality*, 4, 21–40.

Halpern, D. F. (2005). Psychology at the intersection of work and family: Recommendations for employers, working families, and policy makers. *American Psychologist*, 60, 367–409.

Hazan, C., & Shaver, P. R. (1987). Romantic love conceptualized as an attachment process. *Journal of Personality and Social Psychology*, 52, 511–24.

Heine, S., Proulx, T., & Vohs, K. (2006). The meaning maintenance model: On the coherence of social motivations. *Personality and Social Psychology Review*, 10(2), 88–110.

Janoff-Bulman, R. (1992). *Shattered assumptions: Towards a new psychology of trauma*. New York, NY: Free Press.

Kaplan, M. S. (1981). Neurogenesis in the 3-month-old rat visual cortex. *Journal of Comparative Neurolology*, 195, 323–338.

Kashdan, T. B., & McKnight, P. E. (2009). Origins of purpose in life: Refining our understanding of a life well lived. *Psychological Topics*, 18, 303–316.

King, L. A., Hicks, J. A., Krull, J. L., & Del Gaiso, A. K. (2006). Positive affect and the experience of meaning in life. *Journal of Personality and Social Psychology*, 90, 179–196.

Kirby, S. E., Colemen, P. G., & Daley, D. (2004). Spirituality and well-being in frail and nonfrail older adults. *Journal of Gerontology: Psychological Sciences*, 59B, P123–P129.

Koltko-Rivera, M. (2004). The psychology of worldviews. *Review of General Psychology*, 8(1), 3–58.

Kossek, E., & Ozeki, C. (1998). Work–family conflict, policies, and the job–life satisfaction relationship: A review and directions for organizational behavior–human resources research. *Journal of Applied Psychology*, 83(2), 139–149.

Krause, N. (2004). Stressors arising in highly valued roles, meaning in life, and the physical health status of older adults. *Journal of Gerontology: Psychological Sciences, 59B*, S287–S297.

Leary, M., & Tangney, J. (2003). The self as an organizing construct in the behavioral and social sciences. *Handbook of self and identity* (pp. 3–14). New York, NY: Guilford Press.

Lund, D., Caserta, M., Dimond, M., & Shaffer, S. (1989). Competencies, tasks of daily living, and adjustments to spousal bereavement in later life. *Older bereaved spouses: Research with practical applications* (pp. 135–152). Washington, DC: Hemisphere Publishing Corp.

McKnight, P. E., & Kashdan, T. B. (2009). Purpose in life as a system that creates and sustains health and well-being: An integrative, testable theory. *Review of General Psychology, 13*, 242–251.

O'Connor, K., & Chamberlain, K. (1996). Dimensions of life meaning: a qualitative investigation at mid-life. *British Journal of Psychology, 87*, 461–477.

Pinquart, M. (2002). Creating and maintaining purpose in life in old age: A meta-analysis. *Ageing International, 27*, 90–114.

Prager, E., Savaya, R. & Bar-Tur, L. (2000). The development of a culturally sensitive measure of sources of life meaning. In G. T. Reker, & K. Chamberlain, (Eds.), *Exploring existential meaning: Optimizing human development across the lifespan* (pp. 123–138). Thousand Oaks, CA: Sage Publications.

Reker, G. T. (2000). Theoretical perspectives, dimensions, and measurement of existential meaning. In G. T. Reker, & K. Chamberlain. (Eds.), *Exploring existential meaning: Optimizing human development across the life span* (pp. 107–122). Thousand Oaks, CA: Sage Publications.

Reker, G. T., Peacock., E. J., & Wong, P. T. P. (1987). Meaning and purpose in life and well-being: A life-span perspective. *Journal of Gerontology, 42*, 44–49.

Reker, G. T., & Wong, P. T. P. (1988). Aging as an individual process: Toward a theory of personal meaning. In J. E. Birren & V. L. Bengston (Eds.), *Emergent theories of aging* (pp. 214–246). New York, NY: Springer.

Ryff, C. D. (1989). Happiness is everything, or is it? Explorations on the meaning of psychological well-being. *Journal of Personality and Social Psychology, 57*, 1069–1081.

Shek, D. T. L. (1995). Adolescent mental health in different Chinese societies. *International Journal of Adolescent Medicine and Health, 8*, 117–155.

Sheldon, K., & Kasser, T. (1995). Coherence and congruence: Two aspects of personality integration. *Journal of Personality and Social Psychology, 68*(3), 531–543.

Simpson, J. A. (1999). Attachment theory in modern evolutionary perspective. In J. Cassidy & P. R. Shaver (Eds.), *Handbook of attachment: Theory, research and clinical applications* (pp. 115–140). New York, NY: Guilford Press.

Spalding, K. J., Bhardwaj, R. D., Buchholz, B. A., Druid, H., & Frisén, J. (2005). Retrospective birth dating of cells in humans. *Cell, 122*, 133–143.

Steger, M. F. (2009). Meaning in life. In C. R. Snyder & S. J. Lopez (Eds.), *Oxford handbook of positive psychology* (2nd ed.). New York, NY: Oxford University Press.

Steger, M. F. (2012). Experiencing meaning in life: Optimal functioning at the nexus of spirituality, psychopathology, and well-being. In P. T. P. Wong & P. S. Fry (Eds.), *The human quest for meaning* (2nd Ed.) pp. 165–184. New York: Routledge.

Steger, M. F., & Dik, B. J. (2010). Work as meaning. In P. A. Linley, S. Harrington, & N. Page, (Eds.), *Oxford handbook of positive psychology and work* (pp.131–142). Oxford, UK: Oxford University Press.

Steger, M. F., Frazier, P., Oishi, S., & Kaler, M. (2006). The meaning in life questionnaire: Assessing the presence of and search for meaning in life. *Journal of Counseling Psychology, 53*, 80–93.

Steger, M. F., Kashdan, T. B., & Oishi, S. (2008). Being good by doing good: Eudaimonic activity and daily well-being correlates, mediators, and temporal relations. *Journal of Research in Personality, 42,* 22–42.

Steger, M. F., Kashdan, T. B., Sullivan, B. A., & Lorentz, D. (2008). Understanding the search for meaning in life: Personality, cognitive style, and the dynamic between seeking and experiencing meaning. *Journal of Personality, 76,* 199–228.

Steger, M. F., Kawabata, Y., Shimai, S., & Otake, K. (2008). The meaningful life in Japan and the United States: Levels and correlates of meaning in life. *Journal of Research in Personality, 42,* 660–678.

Steger, M. F., Oishi, S., & Kashdan, T. B. (2009). Meaning in life across the life span: Levels and correlates of meaning in life from emerging adulthood to older adulthood. *Journal of Positive Psychology, 4,* 43–52.

Steger, M. F., Pickering, N., Adams, E., Burnett, J., Shin, J. Y., Dik, B. J., & Stauner, N. (2010). The quest for meaning: Religious affiliation differences in the correlates of religious quest and search for meaning in life. *Psychology of Religion and Spirituality* 2(4), 206–226.

Swann, W. B. Cr., Rentfrow, P. J., & Gunn, J. S. (2003). Self-verification: The search for coherence. In M. Leary & J. Tangney (Eds.), *Handbook of self and identity* (pp. 367–383). New York, NY: Guilford.

Vess, M., Routledge, C., Landau, M. J., & Arndt, J. (2009). The dynamics of death of meaning: The effects of death-relevant cognitions and personal need for structure on perceptions of meaning in life. *Journal of Personality and Social Psychology, 97,* 728–744.

Vess, M., Arndt, J., Cox, C. R., Routledge, C., & Goldenberg, J. L. (2009). The terror management of medical decisions: The effect of mortality salience and religious fundamentalism on support for faith-based medical intervention. *Journal of Personality and Social Psychology, 97,* 334–350.

Wong, P. T. P. (1989). Personal meaning and successful aging. *Canadian Psychology, 30,* 516–525.

Wong, P. T. P. (2000). Meaning in life and meaning in death in successful aging. In A. Tomer (Ed.), *Death attitudes and older adults: Theories, concepts, and* application (pp. 23–35). Philadelphia, PA: Taylor & Francis.

Yalom, I. D. (1980). *Existential psychotherapy.* New York, NY: Basic Books.

# SECTION X

# HAPPINESS INTERVENTIONS

# CHAPTER 71

# INTRODUCTION TO HAPPINESS INTERVENTIONS

## GORDON B. SPENCE[1] AND SUZY GREEN[2]

[1]University of Wollongong, Australia; [2]The Positivity Institute, Australia

> Happiness is as a butterfly which, when pursued, is always beyond our grasp, but which if you will sit down quietly, may alight upon you.
> (Nathaniel Hawthorne)

QUESTIONS about the quest for happiness continue to both fascinate and confuse. Few issues have received more attention across the history of human thought than those related to the cultivation and attainment of happiness (Tarnas, 2000). What is happiness? Should it be pursued directly? If so, how?

Yet despite two millennia of thought on the topic, the questions that consumed Socrates, Plato, and Aristotle are remarkably similar to those being debated today, and the opinions are just as diverse. One important difference however, is that the contemporary debate is being contributed to by a greater variety of people than would typically have participated in the lyceums of ancient Greece. Whilst the emergence of social media and greater global connectivity have facilitated this change, a paralleled increase in the reporting of positive psychological science in both the academic and popular media (Kristjansson, 2010) has greatly enabled interested laypeople to contribute to the dialogue.

These developments are both a blessing and a curse. They can be seen as a blessing in that they prompt individuals, groups, and entire communities to consider what makes them happy and to develop practical strategies to enhance their life experience (Seligman, Steen, Park, & Peterson, 2005). It seems likely that more people are currently contemplating such questions than at any other time in human history. These developments can also be viewed as a curse to the extent that the simplification of empirical work can lead to incomplete understanding about the contours of human happiness and well-being, and potentially to flawed attempts to translate research into effective practice (Spence, 2007). The result may be frustrated and futile attempts to cultivate happiness, which may have the paradoxical effect of making people unhappier.

## Moving (Carefully) Toward Happiness

A significant commercial market has developed in the areas of happiness and well-being (Flora, 2009) and, as experience within the related field of coaching attests, this brings its challenges. A primary issue is distinguishing between techniques and practices that are grounded in objective scientific evidence as opposed to pseudo-scientific believerism (Grant & Cavanagh, 2007). As a result these markets become difficult for consumers to navigate and bring a greater risk of harm (for a relevant discussion of the Human Potential Movement and its practices see Spence (2007) and Weigel (2002)).

In such circumstances the presence of a vibrant research community is critical because it can both advance knowledge in the field and help to safeguard the interests of the general public (Spence, Cavanagh, & Grant, 2006). Fortunately the scientific study of happiness is well established and much research has been done to guide our understanding of those strategies, practices, and methods that can reliably and lastingly enhance human happiness and well-being (e.g., Cohn & Fredrickson, 2010; Lyubomirsky, King, & Diener, 2005; Seligman et al., 2005).

Put simply, this section is about different ways people can be assisted to enhance the quality of their life experience. As psychologists we are most interested in interventions that impact upon various psychological processes and result in enhanced well-being. Whilst we think it important to declare our editorial bias (as it has strongly influenced the selection of chapters in this section), it is also important to acknowledge alternative approaches to the topic. In particular, we wish to draw attention to important work currently being conducted on matters that bear heavily upon the likelihood that individuals, groups and communities can experience happiness and well-being at all.

## The Pursuit of Happiness: A Broader View

As will become apparent in the following chapters, most psychologically-informed happiness interventions are designed for use with individuals and, to a lesser extent, for groups and organizations. However, a broader perspective can be taken in relation to the cultivation of happiness and well-being, and this is the primary concern of organizations that focus on issues such as the environment, social justice, global fair trade, and human rights. An example of this type of organization is the new economics foundation (nef), a charitable non-governmental organization based in the UK. For over 25 years nef has advocated for the cultivation of *real* economic well-being, which they argue can be created through economic, environmental and social practices that "put people and the planet first". What is notable about nef is their emphasis on effecting change at both macro and micro levels, and across a variety of program areas including social policy, climate change and energy, civic participation, public policy, and finance and business (nef, 2011; For a discussion of these issues also see Thompson, Marks, and Jackson (Chapter 38, this volume)).

At the macro level, nef attempts to influence how governments and organizations understand their social impact (through the publication of sustainability indicators, national well-being accounts, etc.), whilst also pursuing changes in the policies adopted by these bodies (e.g., the 21-hour working week policy framework). At the micro level, considerable effort is directed towards providing people with practical, low-cost (or no cost) tools that can be applied across all these program areas. Examples of such tools include guidelines for the coproduction of public services and time banking (social policy tools), the "Crowd Wise" method (a civic participation tool), and carbon ration books (a climate change tool).

We think the work of organizations like nef is worth acknowledging for at least two reasons. First, in stimulating societal-level change across a variety of arenas (i.e. political, social, environmental, economic, and psychological) they potentially create sociocultural conditions that are conducive to enhanced well-being and happiness at the individual and group levels. For example, time banks have been found to enhance social connections and foster greater cooperation at the local community level. Second, many of the practical recommendations and tools **nef** provides are designed to assist individuals, groups and communities to help themselves. For example, Crowd Wise provides people with a simple methodology for engaging in political and civic matters they might not otherwise feel capable of engaging. These tools are enabling as they give people options about how they direct the course of their lives, whilst also permitting choice, which is important for facilitating the satisfaction of basic psychological needs, such as autonomy (Deci & Ryan, 2000).

## Overview of the Section

As mentioned earlier, the chapters in this section focus primarily on the use of psychological approaches within several fields of interest. Whilst not all of the following authors would necessarily identify themselves as positive psychologists, all are oriented towards the same basic outcome: the enhancement of happiness and well-being.

The section can be roughly divided into four parts that address (1) specific happiness enhancing strategies and practices (Parks, Schueller, & Tasimi; Rashid), (2) alternative perspectives on change (Hayes; Spence & Grant), (3) the cultivation of happiness among older adults (Hsu & Langer) and, (4) treatment and recovery models for enduring mental illness (Fava & Ruini; Oades, Crowe, & Deane).

The section begins with "Increasing Happiness in the General Population: Empirically Supported Self-Help?" (Chapter 72). In this chapter, Parks, Schueller, and Tasimi explore increasing happiness in the general population through the use of techniques that have received an increasing amount of empirical support. After defining what constitutes a positive intervention, the authors use Seligman's (2002) conceptualization of happiness to review practices that build pleasure, engagement and meaning and argue that enough evidence now exists to claim a firm foundation for empirically supported self-help (ESS-H) interventions. Next, in Chapter 73, "Positive Psychology in Practice: Positive Psychotherapy," Rashid extends upon this work by locating many of the ESS-H practices within a 14-session positive psychotherapy (PPT) model. Whilst PPT also draws on Seligman's (2002) happiness framework, this chapter provides insights into how happiness enhancing practices can be structured into a coherent therapeutic model that is supported by relevant homework tasks.

In Chapter 74, "Happiness in Valued Living: Acceptance and Commitment Therapy as a Model for Change," Hayes introduces Acceptance and Commitment Therapy (ACT) and argues for its use as a model for guiding behavioral change. The ACT approach is an interesting one because it does not explicitly seek to cultivate happiness, but rather to improve life experience via greater experiential acceptance and a commitment to values-based living. While a brief summary of ACT research indicates that the model is indeed effective in enhancing traditional markers of happiness (e.g., life satisfaction), empirical work also indicates that psychological flexibility (which is a desired outcome in ACT) plays a mediating role in successful treatment outcomes. Spence and Grant continue the behavioral change theme in Chapter 75, "Coaching and Well-being: A Brief Review of Existing Evidence, Relevant Theory and Implications for Practitioners" with an exploration of goal-focused coaching. The chapter is divided into two parts. The first focuses on defining coaching, outlining the coaching process and reviewing evidence suggesting that coaching positively impacts a range of variables associated with subjective and psychological well-being. The second part considers the question of *why* coaching can be happiness enhancing and explores this through the lens of self-determination theory (Deci & Ryan, 1985). Whilst this is an interesting question in and of itself, developing better theoretical explanations of what occurs in coaching is sorely needed because coaching practice continues to remain relatively uninformed by relevant psychological theory (Spence & Oades, 2010).

The focus of the section then shifts to the cultivation of happiness and well-being in a specific population: older adults. In Chapter 76, "Mindfulness and Cultivating Well-being in Older Adults," Hsu and Langer argue that mindfulness is important to happiness in later life because it allows one to be liberated from mindsets that constrain choices, restrict possibilities, and prescribe what one should or must be like in old age. According to the authors, encouraging older adults to process information mindfully (by paying attention to novelty and context, whilst being situated in the present moment) has the important effect of displacing expectations that one will inevitably experience cognitive and physical decline and, instead, leads people to construct their world in ways that result in greater life engagement and satisfaction, and improved physical health.

The last two chapters focus on treatment and recovery models for enduring mental illness. In Chapter 77, "Well-being Therapy: Theoretical Background, Clinical Implications and Future Directions," Fava and Ruini outline a psychotherapeutic intervention, well-being therapy (WBT), which seeks to treat serious psychological distress (e.g., generalized anxiety disorder and major depression) by orienting individuals towards their episodes of well-being, identifying specific thoughts and beliefs that interrupt moments of well-being, and supporting people to pursue optimal experiences. The chapter includes a description of Ryff's (1989) six-dimensional model of psychological well-being, an outline of the structure of WBT, and a short review of validation studies conducted to date. In Chapter 78 of the section, "The Collaborative Recovery Model: Developing Positive Institutions to Facilitate Recovery in Enduring Mental Illness", Oades, Crowe and Deane present the Collaborative Recovery Model (CRM), a framework designed to guide a range interventions directed towards the consumers, carers, staff, and organizational systems involved in the provision of psychiatric services. After defining mental health recovery as "optimal functioning under adversity," the authors describe the guiding principles and components that underpin the model, briefly explain some tools that are central to the CRM, and provide three examples of how the model can facilitate recovery-focused service delivery at various levels of the mental health system.

In putting this section together, our aim has been to build a useful resource for practitioners and researchers interested in cultivating happiness and well-being. For practitioners, we hope the section will contain new insights into how happiness can be enhanced, along with an understanding of the evidence upon which these interventions are currently based. For researchers, we hope these chapters will provide new perspectives and stimulate interesting, testable research questions that can help to advance knowledge about the development of human happiness and well-being.

## References

Cohn, M. A., & Fredrickson, B. L. (2010). In search of durable positive psychology interventions: Predictors and consequences of long-term positive behavior change. *Journal of Positive Psychology, 5*(5), 355–366.

Deci, E. L., & Ryan, R. M. (1985). *Intrinsic motivation and self-determination in human behaviour.* New York, NY: Plenum Press.

Deci, E. L., & Ryan, R. M. (2000). The "what" and "why" of goal pursuits: Human needs and the self-determination of behaviour. *Psychological Inquiry, 11*(4), 227–268.

Flora, C. (2009). The pursuit of happiness. Retrieved January 19, 2011, from http://www.psychologytoday.com/articles/200812/the-pursuit-happiness

Grant, A. M., & Cavanagh, M. (2007). Evidence-based coaching: Flourishing or languishing? *Australian Psychologist, 42*(4), 239–254.

Kristjansson, K. (2010). Positive psychology, happiness, and virtue: The troublesome conceptual issues. *Review of General Psychology, 14*(4), 296–310.

Lyubomirsky, S., King, L., & Diener, E. (2005). The benefits of frequent positive affect: Does happiness lead to success? *Psychological Bulletin, 131*(6), 803–855.

nef. (2011). Programme areas. Retrieved January 19, 2011, from http://www.neweconomics.org/programmes

Ryff, C. D. (1989). Happiness is everything, or is it? Explorations on the meaning of psychological well-being. *Journal of Personality and Social Psychology, 57*(6), 1069–1081.

Seligman, M. E. P. (2002). *Authentic happiness.* New York, NY: Free Press.

Seligman, M. E. P., Steen, T. A., Park, N., & Peterson, C. (2005). Positive psychology progress: Empirical validation of interventions. *American Psychologist, 60*(5), 410–421.

Spence, G. B. (2007). Further development of evidence-based coaching: Lessons from the rise and fall of the human potential movement. *Australian Psychologist, 42*(2), 255–265.

Spence, G. B., Cavanagh, M. J., & Grant, A. M. (2006). Duty of care in an unregulated industry: Initial findings on the diversity and practices of Australian coaches. *International Coaching Psychology Review, 1*(1), 71–85.

Spence, G. B., & Oades, L. G. (2010). *Coaching with self-determination in mind: Using theory to inform coaching practice.* Unpublished manuscript.

Tarnas, R. (2000). *The passion of the western mind.* London, UK: Pimlico.

Weigel, R. G. (2002). The marathon encounter group—vision and reality: Exhuming the body for a last look. *Consulting Psychology Journal: Practice and Research, 54*(3), 186–198.

# CHAPTER 72

# INCREASING HAPPINESS IN THE GENERAL POPULATION: EMPIRICALLY SUPPORTED SELF-HELP?

ACACIA C. PARKS[1], STEPHEN M. SCHUELLER[2], AND ARBER TASIMI[3]

[1]Hiram College, USA; [2]University of California, San Francisco, USA ; [3]Yale University, USA

SELF-HELP is a burgeoning industry, and with good reason. Subthreshold depressive symptoms (often referred to as the "blues") are more than a nuisance; they are a serious public health issue. In addition to being at least as prevalent as major depressive disorder (MDD), subthreshold depressive symptoms lead to substantial functional impairment, and are a risk factor for the future development of MDD (Cuijpers & Smit, 2004; Flett, Vredenburg, & Krames, 1997; Judd, Akiskal, & Paulus, 1997). However, the existence of subthreshold depressive symptoms goes largely unaddressed by medicine and clinical psychology. For individuals whose lives are impaired by subthreshold depression, the dearth of other options often leads them to turn to self-help for relief.

Although there are several empirically-based self-help books that target depression (Burns, 1999; Lewinsohn, Muñoz, Youngren, & Zeiss, 1992) these typically draw from the literature on cognitive behavioral therapy (CBT; A. Beck, Rush, Shaw, & Emery, 1979; J. Beck, 1995). Problem-focused therapies such as CBT have reliably demonstrated efficacy as a treatment for MDD (DeRubeis et al., 2005), as have CBT-based self-help books (Cuijpers, 1997). However, it is not clear that a cognitive behavioral approach is ideal for populations with subclinical depressive symptoms. Whereas CBT for major depression often produces robust effect sizes in symptom reduction, an 8-week CBT-based program for individuals with subthreshold symptoms only led to small reductions in symptoms and prevention of future disorders (Seligman, Schulman, & Tryon, 2007).

A growing area of research and practice involves the promotion of mental well-being and happiness as a complement to previous approaches that primarily targeted the prevention and treatment of psychiatric disorders (National Research Council and Institute of Medicine, 2009). We believe that this is particularly appropriate for individuals with subthreshold depressive symptoms for three reasons.

First, it is theoretically plausible that increasing happiness will be effective against depression. Depression is characterized by a deficit in positive emotions (Forbes & Dahl, 2005; Seligman, Rashid, & Parks, 2006) and laboratory studies have demonstrated that positive emotions can both alleviate negative mood states and counteract the physical stress (e.g., cardiovascular reactivity) resulting from negative emotions (Fredrickson, Mancuso, Branigan, & Tugade, 2000). Indeed, interventions targeting happiness counteract existing depressive symptoms with moderate to large effect sizes (Seligman, Rashid, & Parks, 2006; Seligman, Steen, Park, & Peterson, 2005). As subthreshold depressive symptoms are a risk factor for MDD, reducing these may result in a decreased probability of future episodes of MDD (Seligman, Schulman, & Tryon, 2007). Thus, we have reason to believe that interventions targeting happiness are a reasonable approach to reducing depressive symptoms in non-clinical populations.

Second, there is preliminary evidence that happiness-focused approaches may be more acceptable to consumers than are problem-focused approaches, and as a result, may lead to better rates of adherence (Haidt, 2002; Seligman, Rashid, & Parks, 2006). Even if happiness-focused and problem-focused programs are equally efficacious when followed, if participants are more likely to participate in happiness-focused programs, they might be more *effective* than problem-focused programs if both are available for consumers. This is a particularly important consideration for non-clinical samples, where the need for change (and subsequent follow-through on treatment) is often less than for individuals with a mental disorder. So, in addition to being effective against depressive symptoms, happiness-focused interventions may have greater potential than problem-focused approaches for being used in the long-term.

Lastly, increasing happiness is an endeavor that is both worthwhile in its own right (see Lyubomirsky, King, & Diener, 2005), and practically feasible. It is on these two points that we will focus for the remainder of the chapter.

Self-help books and websites that target happiness—with a few recent exceptions (Emmons, 2007; Kashdan, 2009; Lyubomirsky, 2008; Seligman, 2002)—lack an empirical basis. Yet there remains a constant demand for self-help materials such as books or websites. Therefore, we argue that research-based materials must be more accessible to the public. Just as clinical psychology has sought to meet the demand for therapy with the empirically supported therapies movement (Chambless & Hollon, 1998), the goal of this chapter is to outline the beginnings of what will hopefully one day become a field that establishes techniques of empirically supported self-help (ESS-H) for increasing happiness.

In order to pursue such an enterprise, however, we must demonstrate that our efforts are based on a solid underlying science of happiness. To that end, we address two questions in this chapter: First, what is the theoretical basis of psychological interventions designed to increase happiness, and second, what positive interventions exist and what evidence supports their effectiveness? We conclude with some thoughts about what remains to be addressed in this line of research, suggesting some important future directions.

## Theoretical Framework: By What Means can Happiness be Increased?

Duckworth, Steen, and Seligman (2005) describe three paths by which happiness can be increased: pleasure, engagement, and meaning.

"Pleasure" deals with positive emotions such as joy, contentment, or gratitude. According to broaden-and-build theory (Frederickson, 2001), positive emotions broaden an individual's thought-action repertoire. In other words, positive emotional states expand the number of thoughts available to an individual, and subsequently, the number of actions they are willing to engage in, at a given moment. The broadening of an individual's momentary thought-action repertoire, in turn, results in increases in intellectual resources (faster learning performance; Bryan & Bryan, 1991), social resources (stronger social relationships; Lee, 1983), physical resources (cardiovascular recovery; Frederickson & Levenson, 1998), and psychological resources (resilience; Tugade & Fredrickson, 2004).

"Engagement" is marked by absorption, social engagement, and, in particular, flow. Flow refers to the state of complete absorption in a single activity that is challenging yet appropriate for one's level of skill (Csikszentmihalyi, 1975; Moneta & Csikszentmihalyi, 1996). When experiencing flow, an individual is living fully and optimally (Nakamura & Csikszentmihalyi, 2002). While many situations and activities can be conducive to flow, including hobbies, work, and social interactions, Seligman (2002) argued that one is most likely to experience flow when engaging in activities that make use of one's character strengths.

"Meaning" entails the connection to positive institutions, such as families, schools, communities, and societies (Peterson, 2006). Since meaning is created from a sense of belonging or attachment to something larger than oneself, such as a group (family, work) or spiritual purpose or being, it is posited that positive institutions will engender a meaningful life. Meaning in life provides clear goals and values for one to pursue and imbues actions with purpose (McKnight & Kashdan, 2009).

Peterson, Park, and Seligman (2005) provided initial empirical support for the idea that happiness is comprised of these three separate, but not mutually exclusive, components. In a sample of 845 adults who responded to online surveys, Peterson and his colleagues found that although the three domains of happiness are distinguishable—that is, each is independently predictive of life satisfaction—one can pursue all three simultaneously. Furthermore, individuals who reported pursuing all three were more satisfied than would be expected based on the predicted influence of each domain individually. In short, pleasure, engagement, and meaning each appear to contribute to life satisfaction on their own, but they also interact synergistically to produce even more life satisfaction when pursued in combination.

## Positive Interventions: Empirically Supported Techniques for Increasing Happiness

Positive interventions are cognitive or behavioral strategies that attempt to build well-being through psychological processes. According to recent meta-analyses (Sin & Lyubomirsky,

2009), positive interventions yield average increases in happiness ranging from small to moderate (r = 0.29) and decreases in depressive symptoms ranging from small to large (r = 0.31). In the following sections we provide an overview of existing techniques for increasing happiness divided into the three pathways defined by Seligman (2002). It should be noted, however, that this distinction is more theoretical than empirical and additional research is necessary to determine the extent to which the pleasure-engagement-meaning distinction is warranted.

# Building pleasure

Whilst there are several techniques that seek to cultivate, amplify, and prolong positive emotional experiences in the present, three approaches have proven to be particularly reliable for inducing positive emotion: savoring, loving-kindness meditation, and gratitude.

## Savoring

Savoring involves bringing conscious awareness to pleasurable momentary experiences, along with the attempt to make these experiences last (Peterson, 2006). Savoring is enabled by three preconditions: eliminating one's own concerns, attending to the present, and being aware of the positive aspects of the experience (Bryant & Veroff, 2007). In order to make savoring more likely, Bryant and Veroff (2007) recommend: (1) taking time out from everyday activity to savor, (2) becoming more open to experiences that could potentially be savored, and (3) attempting to narrow one's focus to the positive, pleasurable aspects of life. Peterson (2006) provides several specific techniques that can be used while savoring, including self-congratulation (focusing on the details of a personal victory and prolonging it), absorption (focusing completely on the experience), memory building (making efforts to remember positive experiences, such as taking photographs or keeping a journal), and sharpening perceptions (focusing on distinct aspects of an experience, such as paying attention to the temperature, texture, and taste components of a dessert).

Compared to other happiness-increasing activities, relatively few research studies have focused exclusively on savoring; instead, savoring generally appears as one of several techniques taught in a sequence. Savoring exercises typically involve taking a few moments, several times per day, to truly focus on and enjoy an experience such as taking a warm shower or sipping a warm cup of coffee (Seligman et al., 2006). Individuals who consistently savor are more optimistic, less depressed, and more satisfied with life (Bryant, 2003; Wood, Heimpel, & Michela, 2003). Recognizing the fleeting nature of the present moment can furthermore increase one's well-being (Kurtz, 2008).

## Loving-kindness meditation

In loving-kindness meditation (LKM), individuals practice directing their attention towards generating warm and tender feelings and extending those feelings towards others (Salzberg, 1995). In LKM, individuals are first directed to think of a person that they already hold positive and compassionate feelings towards. The meditative practice then guides participants to extend those feelings first towards themselves and then towards others radiating first to those closely connected to them and moving out towards all people. This can be accomplished through imagery (e.g., imagining oneself or the other smiling) or phrases (e.g., "I am warm," "I am safe"). Frederickson et al. (2008) have proposed LKM as a way of experimentally inducing positive emotion in a way that is more substantial and long-lasting than the short-term mood induction techniques typically used in the laboratory. After teaching LKM to 139 working adults, Frederickson and colleagues found that participants experienced increases in positive emotion over time. In line with broaden-and-build theory (Frederickson, 2001), these increases were associated with greater levels of social support and purpose in life, as well as decreased illness symptoms.

## *Gratitude*

Gratitude is the feeling that something good has happened to oneself combined with the acknowledgement that an outside source is responsible (Solomon, 1977). Given the substantial benefits of naturally-occurring gratitude (Emmons & McCullough, 2003), several techniques have been employed to teach gratitude to individuals. Emmons and McCullough (2003), for instance, studied gratitude journaling and its effect on well-being. Gratitude journaling refers to the practice of writing about the things, both big and small, that one is thankful for. Participants who completed weekly entries in a gratitude journal experienced higher levels of positive affect. Interestingly, gratitude also led to fewer physical symptoms, greater propensity to exercise, and higher sleep quality in participants. Lyubomirsky et al. (2005) experimented with different "doses" of gratitude and found that people benefited more when they made one weekly entry into a gratitude journal compared with more frequent entries. This study suggests that to be effective, an intervention must represent a substantial enough change in one's life to feel different to an individual.

Seligman et al. (2005) piloted two different gratitude exercises: "Three Good Things," in which the individual keeps a nightly journal of positive events and speculates as to their cause, and the "Gratitude Visit," in which the individual writes a letter to someone they wish to thank detailing their gratitude, and reads the letter out loud to the recipient. They compared these two exercises' effects on happiness and depressive symptoms with those of a placebo exercise and found that the Gratitude Visit resulted in large, immediate increases in self-reported happiness and decreases in self-reported depressive symptoms that did not last over time. In contrast, the Three Good Things exercise led to smaller, but more long-lasting increases that occurred one month after participants began using the exercise.

Grateful processing of events also promotes positive emotions and decreases negative emotions (Watkins, Woodward, Stone, & Kolts, 2003). Findings in studies with youth samples mirror those found in adult samples. For instance, in a study of middle school students, reflecting on what one is thankful for led to significant increases in gratitude, optimism, life satisfaction, and school satisfaction (Froh, Sefick, & Emmons, 2008). The benefits of this intervention on positive emotions, however, may be most pronounced with lower initial levels of positive affect (Froh, Kashdan, Ozimkowski, & Miller, 2008). This could be due to a ceiling effect limiting individuals high in positive affect from receiving additional benefits from this exercise. Another possibility is that individuals lower in positive affect were less grateful to begin with which would be consistent with the conclusion drawn by Lyubomirsky and colleagues (2005) that interventions need to be a significant enough shift from one's daily life to boost well-being.

Increasing gratitude through reflecting on good things throughout the day has gained considerable attention as a quick, simple, and easily disseminated positive intervention. In fact several Internet groups and web sites, such as Momentary.org, provide opportunities for individuals to journal about good things online and allow others to view one's journal. One study examined the use of an on-line application to promote connection across social network using the Three Good Things exercise (Munson, Lauterback, Newman, & Resnick, 2010). Although this study did not evaluate the impact of the application on user gratitude levels, it did assess the degree to which an internet application (which contained features such as automated reminders, privacy settings and a function that tracked how often users wrote about various topics) influenced the amount of gratitude expressed on-line. The results showed that people using the on-line gratitude application posted entries approximately twice as often as those who simply participated in an unstructured internet group (that was also focused on gratitude). Utilizing social networking sites in this way holds promise as a means of widely promoting and disseminating positive interventions.

## Building engagement

### Using signature strengths

Signature strengths are positive traits that an individual possesses, celebrates, and continually displays (Peterson, 2006). Peterson and Seligman (2004) identified 24 strengths, or positive traits, based on a list of criteria that requires strengths to be ubiquitous, morally valued, fulfilling, distinct, trait-like, and measurable, among other factors. These criteria were selected to identify strengths that are agreed-upon across cultures, and that can provide reasonable targets for study and intervention (Dahlsgaard, Seligman, & Peterson, 2005). These strengths are divided into six virtues (wisdom, courage, humanity, justice, temperance, and transcendence) and include such characteristics as creativity, honesty, leadership, forgiveness, kindness, and humor. To measure these characteristics Peterson and Seligman designed an online strengths assessment that provides instant feedback about an individual's top strengths. Since Seligman's (2002) theory posits that strengths are a logical path to achieving flow, it has been hypothesized that providing individuals with feedback on their strengths and encouraging them to use them more regularly should lead to enhanced engagement. Indeed, Seligman et al. (2005) found that asking people to utilize their "signature" strengths in a new way every day for a week resulted in decreased depressive symptoms and increased happiness (compared to a placebo exercise). These improvements were maintained at a 6-month follow-up.

### Engaging in social connections

Engagement and relationships often go hand in hand. Individuals often report that relationships are a primary source of engagement in their lives, and experiencing engagement with others is a predictor of relationship satisfaction (Duckworth, Steen, & Seligman, 2005). One exercise designed to build social engagement is active-constructive responding. Gable, Reis, Impett, and Asher (2004) proposed that individuals could respond to good news in either an active or passive and constructive or destructive manner. Table 72.1 provides an example of each style of responding to a hypothetical positive event (i.e. a job promotion). Couples that use more active-constructive responding, according to Gable, Gonzaga, and Strachman (2006), are more satisfied with their relationships and are less likely to break up 2 months later.

Table 72.1 Example of responding to good news of a job promotion

|         | Constructive | Destructive |
|---------|--------------|-------------|
| Active  | "That is great news! I am so happy for you! We should go out to dinner to celebrate the occasion!" | "Does this mean that you will have to put in extra hours? I'm assuming this promotion will be burdensome." |
| Passive | "Good for you." | "Do you know what the weather will be like tomorrow?" |

Although teaching individuals to respond more actively and constructively has not yet been tested in isolation, Seligman, Rashid and Parks (2006) included such an exercise as part of a 6-week Positive Psychotherapy program (see Rashid, Chapter 73, this volume). Specifically, their exercise asked participants to keep track of how they respond to good news, and to make an effort to respond actively and constructively when possible. Seligman and colleagues expected this exercise to result in increased life satisfaction, as the experimental data suggest that by responding actively and constructively, conversations are lengthened, partners become more engaged, and relationships are strengthened (Peterson, 2006).

Another technique for increasing social engagement are "acts of kindness," which consists of helping others (close friends or strangers) in ways that can range from relatively brief, simple acts (e.g., putting change in someone's parking meter or helping to fix someone's computer) to more time consuming acts (e.g., coordinating a fundraiser or spending the day helping a friend move house). Lyubomirsky, Sheldon, and Schkade (2005) asked participants to perform acts of kindness, either in a concentrated period of time once a week (e.g., five acts in 1 day) or spread out over the week (e.g., five acts in a week) for 6 weeks, and found that participants who did several acts of kindness at once reported higher levels of happiness and lower levels of negative affect and stress, whereas the group in which participants spread out their acts of kindness did not report any significant benefits as compared to the control group. In a further study, participants who varied the acts of kindness performed over an 8-week period received larger boosts in well-being compared to a group that repeated the same kind of acts each week (Tkach, 2006). Similar to reflecting on things one is grateful for, simply keeping track of kind acts seems to also produce psychological benefits (Otake et al., 2006).

## Flow and mastery

As the concept of engagement is closely tied to flow states, one would expect that interventions aimed at increasing flow would be an obvious way to increase engagement. Indeed, enhancing flow has been suggested as a possible intervention for increasing happiness as higher levels of engagement in life are correlated with higher levels of happiness (Schueller & Seligman, 2010). Unfortunately, no empirical investigations have directly tested an intervention aimed at increasing flow. However, as a key criterion for the experience of flow is a balance of challenge and skill, it is reasonable to conclude that feelings of mastery and competence are important to the cultivation of flow and that flow states may be induced through interventions that build these qualities. One class of intervention designed to do this, via increased engagement in rewarding activities, is *behavioral activation*. A recent meta-analysis of

20 studies and 1353 participants found that behavioral activation in both clinical and nonclinical samples led to reliable boosts in well-being compared to control conditions ($g = 0.52$; Mazzucchelli, Kane, & Rees, 2010).

## Building meaning

### Expressive writing

Writing has many different benefits for health, well-being, and emotional adjustment (Frattaroli, 2006; Smyth, 1998). The cognitive change theory of expressive writing posits that these benefits come from the creation of coherent and meaningful narratives of the event (Pennebaker & Seagal, 1999). Indeed, writing a narrative about an event induces analytic processing which might support the construction of meaning (Lyubomirsky, Sousa, & Dickerhoof, 2006). Humans show a tendency to explain ambiguous events and the meaning imbued can have powerful effects on emotions and behaviors (Abramson, Seligman, & Teasdale, 1978; Wilson & Gilbert, 2008).

When it comes to the positive aspects of life, writing and talking about one's goals can be particularly beneficial (Cheavens et al., 2006; Pham & Taylor, 1999; Rivkin & Taylor, 1999). Writing about life goals brings greater clarity and awareness to those goals, and in turn, having clear and valued goals is strongly related to positive psychological functioning (Emmons, 1986; King, 2001). Writing about life goals reduces goal conflict, which can result in reductions in risk for physical illness (Emmons & King, 1988; Pennebaker, 1998). Disclosive writing about goals has also been shown to improve self-regulation, which can lead to imagined goal success (Pham & Taylor, 1999; Rivkin & Taylor, 1999), and a greater sense of meaning about one's life purpose (King, 2001).

Sheldon and Lyubomirsky (2006) implemented an exercise that focuses on disclosive writing—"Best Possible Selves". Adapted from King (2001), this exercise required participants to visualize and write over a period of 4 weeks about their "ideal future life", in as much detail as possible. Participants experienced immediate reductions in negative affect and increases in positive affect. Moreover, they displayed more interest and higher degrees of motivation compared with the control group who merely wrote about life details (Sheldon & Lyubomirsky, 2006). This could be attributed to the fact that writing about one's possible selves can illuminate one's motivations, priorities, and values (Emmons, 1986; Omodei & Wearing, 1990). In bringing greater awareness to one's experiences and possible future the exercise seems to facilitate the process of meaning-making about one's life (Lyubomirsky, Sousa, & Dickerhoof, 2006).

### Reminiscing

Exercises that engage people in reminiscences about pleasant past memories (i.e. recalling positive experiences in great detail) seems to lead to a variety of emotional benefits, particularly among elderly individuals. Early research found that individuals who intentionally practiced reminiscence reported higher levels of positive affect (Fallot, 1980; Hedgepath & Hale, 1983). More recently, Cook (1998) and Bryant et al. (2005) reported similar results with a reminisce group that reported significant increases in life satisfaction compared to controls. In addition, Zauszniewski et al. (2004) reported that a 6-week group reminiscing intervention reduced negative emotion (depressive and anxiety symptoms) among elders in a retirement home. Interestingly, these effects seem to be especially potent when individuals use cognitive aids (such as vivid imagery) as opposed to physical reminders such as memorabilia or photographs (Cook, 1998).

In sum, there is a solid foundation for the science of sustainably increasing happiness and a variety of reliable methods and techniques have been developed for this purpose.

## Building Pleasure, Engagement, *and* Meaning: Positive Psychotherapy

Earlier, we discussed the findings that pleasure, engagement, and meaning are not mutually exclusive, that each pathway can independently lead to life satisfaction, and that these pathways interact synergistically with individuals who pursue all three reporting higher levels of life satisfaction than that expected by the independent contribution of each (Peterson, Park, & Seligman, 2005). While most of the studies discussed in this chapter have employed standalone exercises, this is practically rather than theoretically driven—in order to isolate the pattern of efficacy of each specific exercise. It is unlikely, however, that the use of standalone exercises is reflective of (or feasible in) everyday practice. Further, it is both possible and potentially more beneficial to target pleasure, engagement, *and* meaning, rather than focusing on any one route in particular.

Positive psychotherapy (PPT; Parks, 2012; Seligman, Rashid, & Parks, 2006) is an example of a more integrated positive intervention that addresses pleasure, engagement, and meaning. PPT contains exercises that are the same as, or similar to, many of the individually validated and empirically supported techniques already discussed. In both a pilot study and a replication, group PPT outperformed a no-intervention control group on measures of life satisfaction and depression in a sample of mild-to-moderately depressed undergraduates (Parks, 2012). Although research on PPT is still in its infancy, it shows promise as an integrated positive intervention that can be used with individuals with subthreshold depressive symptoms—a population for which there are few empirically-supported interventions.

## Concluding remarks

From increases in positive emotion and greater life satisfaction to decreases in depression, anxiety, and illness symptoms, positive interventions that build pleasure, engagement, and meaning exhibit both short-term and long-lasting effects on well-being. These techniques provide a solid foundation for the creation of ESS-H for increasing happiness—one in which techniques that have demonstrated efficacy in research can be woven together in book or web format and disseminated to the general public. However, there is much still to be done in the pursuit of a science of promoting happiness. Next, we discuss several future directions for research.

### Sustainability

Lyubomirsky, Sheldon, and Schkade (2005) argue that intentional activity is necessary in order to increase happiness, yet evidence suggests that initial boosts require continued effort to be sustained. Additional research is needed to assess patterns of use that participants display with each of these exercises—what percentage of people keep using each exercise naturally, and how can that percentage be maximized? To that end, it is worth considering how exercises can be modified and integrated into everyday life. Previous research has suggested that continued use is important, highlighting the need for activities that can be integrated into the daily practices of individuals who use them; at the same time, one must also find ways to keep activities novel in order to prevent hedonic adaptation (Lyubomirsky et al., 2005). Therefore, an important task for the future practice of these exercises is to find ways to address both objectives, promoting continued use while also providing room for variation.

The Gratitude Visit, for example, which provides large and immediate effects on happiness, is not designed, nor is it appropriate, for daily use. Furthermore, as described above, gratitude exercises are subject to becoming "stale" if practiced too frequently, so one must be careful when seeking to create a regular gratitude practice. However, there are ways to practice elements of this exercise on a more regular basis without rendering the practice vulnerable to hedonic adaptation. For example, an individual could make daily additions to a gratitude list—a compilation of all the things about a given person for which they are grateful—and then make monthly or yearly "gratitude reports" to that person. This modifies features of the Gratitude Visit—a powerful, one-time gratitude intervention—into a sustainable exercise that can be continuously practiced. Unlike the Gratitude Visit, which focuses on broad gratitude towards a person, and is thus very difficult to repeat, the "gratitude report" makes the content of the exercise variable (e.g., based on the ongoing behavior of a gratitude recipient chosen by the individual), which keeps the exercise "fresh," minimizing the potential for adaptation. At the same time, this new variation may retain the power of the original Gratitude Visit—which comes from the immediate and powerful effects of conveying gratitude to someone else in written form—by having the regular "gratitude report" experiences.

Technology also provides a powerful tool to increase the sustainability of these techniques. Indeed, research teams are currently utilizing mobile device applications for the monitoring and enhancement of happiness (e.g., Gilbert's www.trackyourhappiness.org or Signal Pattern's Live Happy mobile phone application based on Sonja Lyubomirsky's work). Furthermore, as previously mentioned, pilot studies have examined the feasibility and effectiveness of disseminating positive psychology exercises through popular social networking sites (Munson, Lauterbach, Newman, & Resnick, 2010). Technology provides a potentially powerful tool to increase the sustainability of these techniques.

## Person-activity fit

Taking personal preference or choice into consideration may maximize the benefits of these happiness strategies. Sheldon and Lyubomirsky (2006) propose the idea of "fit"; that is, assigning an exercise that is concordant with an individual's personality, values, interests, and goals. This idea could be accomplished by giving participants a list of strategies and later asking them which strategy they think would work best. For instance, an introvert assigned to complete the gratitude visit exercise may experience short-term benefits, but feel more comfortable with (and be more likely to continue) using exercises that align with personality-based preferences (e.g., Three Good Things). Schueller (2010) found that participants' self-reported preferences for an exercise predicted the number of days they engaged in the assigned exercise over a week period; thus, participant preference may well be an important consideration for practitioners using these techniques.

Along similar lines, an alternative model for accommodating individual differences in preference and responsiveness to specific exercises is the approach taken by Parks (2012). Each participant samples a variety of exercises, then in the time following the intervention, chooses one or two to continue practicing. In this way, participants are exposed to several techniques and have the opportunity to select what they continue to practice, but do so having tried each one rather than relying on their initial impressions of what may or may not be helpful for them.

In essence, flexibility is crucial for the success of happiness-increasing strategies. The more researchers can find ways to increase the flexibility of these strategies, the greater the likelihood that people will engage with them and benefit from them.

## Skepticism

Among the lay public, there exists a certain wariness of efforts to increase happiness as some kind of push to create an oblivious, unrealistic, or otherwise undesirable society (see Ehrenreich, 2009). A science of ESS-H can only thrive if it reaches the people for whom it is intended—and in order for it to have a broad audience, the suspicion and skepticism surrounding the idea of increasing happiness needs to be addressed.

An important first step in this direction is to place our primary goal of increasing happiness in a larger context that includes an important role for negative affective states and experiences. Despite scientific evidence that positive and negative affect are somewhat independent (Diener & Emmons, 1984), many members of the general public equate becoming happier with eliminating distress, and assume that the goal of positive psychology is to eradicate negative emotions altogether. However, it would be more accurate to say that we aim to shift the balance so that one's positive experiences outweigh one's negative experiences. Work by Fredrickson and colleagues suggest that a ratio of between 3:1 and 13:1 positive emotions to negative emotions is necessary in order to flourish psychologically (Fredrickson & Losada, 2005). Most notable about this finding is that there is an upper limit, above which positive emotion is not adaptive without sufficient negative emotion to anchor it. Thus, there is evidence that eliminating negative emotion is an undesirable outcome—if doing so *was* truly the goal of positive psychologists, the general public would be justified in being skeptical. Clearly acknowledging the importance of negative emotion may go a long way in allaying individuals' concerns about the enterprise of increasing happiness.

## FINAL THOUGHTS: IMPLICATIONS FOR PRACTICE

In this chapter, we have provided an overview of exercises that target each of three areas: pleasure, engagement, and meaning. As readers apply these exercises in practice with clients, we make the following suggestions:

- Try to address pleasure, engagement, *and* meaning, as it appears that maximal benefits occur when all three routes are pursued.

- Be flexible with which techniques are selected and how they are applied, taking into consideration client preference (to maximize adherence) and lifestyle (to maximize sustainability).
- Explore and address any misconceptions or skepticism that clients might have about the endeavor of increasing happiness, as such attitudes may interfere with progress.

Lastly, we recommend that practitioners think ahead towards making these techniques available to the general public in ways other than the standard one-to-one practitioner/patient model. Statistics demonstrate that this mode of dissemination has not been effective for getting empirically supported treatments to the general public—many individuals do not have access to therapy, and even if they do, many practicing therapists choose not to use such treatments (Hirschfeld et al., 1997; Stewart & Chambless, 2007). If empirically-based happiness-increasing interventions are to be widely disseminated to the general public, we must rely on some other means—it is for this reason that we believe ESS-H is the future of the dissemination of positive interventions.

# References

Abramson, L. Y., Seligman, M. E. P., Teasdale, J. D. (1978). Learned helplessness in humans: Critique and reformulation. *Journal of Abnormal Psychology*, 87, 49–74.

Beck, A. T., Rush, A. J., Shaw, B. F., & Emery, G. (1979). *Cognitive therapy of depression*. New York, NY: Guilford Press.

Beck, J. S. (1995). *Cognitive therapy: Basics and beyond*. New York, NY: Guilford Press.

Bryan, T., & Bryan, J. (1991). Positive mood and math performance. *Journal of Learning Disabilities*, 24, 490–494.

Bryant, F. B. (2003). Savoring Beliefs Inventory (SBI): A scale for measuring beliefs about savoring. *Journal of Mental Health*, 12, 175–196.

Bryant, F. B., Smart, C. M., & King, S. P. (2005). Using the past to enhance the present: Boosting happiness through positive reminiscence. *Journal of Happiness Studies*, 6, 227–260.

Bryant, F. B., & Veroff, J. (2007). *Savoring: A new model of positive experience*. Mahwah, NJ: Lawrence Erlbaum Associates.

Burns, D. D. (1999). *Feeling good: The new mood therapy* (2nd ed.). New York, NY: William Morrow.

Carson, J. W., Keefe, F. J., Lynch, T. R., Carson, K. M., Goli, V., Fras, A. M., & Thorp, S. R. (2005). Loving-kindness meditation for chronic low back pain: Results from a pilot trial. *Journal of Holistic Nursing*, 23, 287–304.

Chambless, D. L., & Hollon, S. D. (1998). Defining empirically supported therapies. *Journal of Consulting and Clinical Psychology*, 66, 7–18.

Cheavens, J. S., Feldman, D. B., Gum, A., Michael, S. T., & Snyder, C. R. (2006). Hope therapy in a community sample: A pilot investigation. *Social Indicators Research*, 77, 61–78.

Cook, E. A. (1998). Effects of reminiscence on life satisfaction of elderly female nursing home residents. *Health Care for Women International*, 19, 109–118.

Csikszentmihalyi, M. (1975). *Beyond boredom and anxiety*. San Francisco, CA: Jossey-Bass.

Cuijpers, P. (1997). Bibliotherapy in unipolar depression: A meta-analysis. *Journal of Behavior Therapy and Experimental Psychiatry*, 28, 139–147.

Cuijpers, P., & Smit, F. (2004). Subthreshold depression as a risk indicator for major depressive disorder: a systematic review of prospective studies. *Acta Psychiatrica Scandinavica*, 109, 325–331.

Dahlsgaard, K., Peterson, C., & Seligman, M. E. P. (2005). Shared virtue: The convergence of valued human strengths across culture and history. *Review of General Psychology, 9,* 203–213.

Davidson, R. J. (2000). Affective style, psychopathology, and resilience: Brain mechanisms and plasticity. *American Psychologist, 55,* 1196–1214.

DeRubeis, R.J., Hollon, S.D., Amsterdam, J.D., Shelton, R.C., Young, P.R., Salomon, R.M., ... Gallop, R. (2005). Cognitive therapy vs. medications in the treatment of moderate to severe depression. *Archives of General Psychiatry, 62,* 409–416.

Diener, E., & Emmons, R.A. (1984). The independence of positive and negative affect. *Journal of Personality and Social Psychology, 47,* 1105–1117.

Duckworth, A. L., Steen, T. A., & Seligman, M. E. P. (2005). Positive psychology in clinical practice. *Annual Review of Clinical Psychology, 1,* 629–651.

Ehrenreich, B. (2009). *Bright-sided: How the relentless promotion of positive thinking has undermined America.* New York, NY: Metropolitan Books.

Emmons, R. A. (1986). Personal strivings: An approach to personality and subjective well-being. *Journal of Personality and Social Psychology, 51,* 1058–1068.

Emmons, R. (2007). *Thanks: How the new science of gratitude can make you happier.* New York, NY: Houghton Mifflin Company.

Emmons, R. A., & King, L. A. (1988). Conflict among personal strivings: Immediate and long-term implications for psychological and physical well-being. *Journal of Personality and Social Psychology, 48,* 1040–1048.

Emmons, R. A., & McCullough, M. E. (2003). Counting blessings versus burdens: An experimental investigation of gratitude and subjective well-being in daily life. *Journal of Personality and Social Psychology, 84,* 377–389.

Fallot, R. D. (1980). The impact on mood of verbal reminiscing in later adulthood. *International Journal of Aging & Human Development, 10,* 385–400.

Flett, G.L., Vredenburg, K., & Krames, L. (1997). The continuity of depression in clinical and nonclinical samples. *Psychological Bulletin, 121,* 395–416.

Forbes, E. E., & Dahl, R. E. (2005). Neural systems of positive affect: Relevance to understanding child and adolescent depression? *Development and Psychopathology, 17,* 827–850.

Fordyce, M. W. (1977). Development of a program to increase personal happiness. *Journal of Counseling Psychology, 24,* 511–521.

Fordyce, M. W. (1983). A program to increase happiness: Further studies. *Journal of Counseling Psychology, 30,* 483–498.

Frattaroli, J. (2006). Experimental disclosure and its moderators: A meta-analysis. *Psychological Bulletin, 132,* 823–865.

Fredrickson, B. L. (2001). The role of positive emotions in positive psychology: The broaden-and-build theory of positive emotions. *American Psychologist, 56,* 218–226.

Frederickson, B. L., & Levenson, R. W. (1998). Positive emotions speed of recovery from the cardiovascular sequelae of negative emotions. *Cognition and Emotion, 12,* 191–220.

Fredrickson, B. L., & Losada, M. (2005). Positive affect and the complex dynamics of human flourishing. *American Psychologist, 60,* 678–686.

Fredrickson, B. L., Mancuso, R. A., Branigan, C., & Tugade, M. M. (2000). The undoing effect of positive emotions. *Motivation and Emotion, 24,* 237–258.

Fredrickson, B. L., Cohn, M. A., Coffey, K. A., Pek, J., & Finkel, S. (2008). Open hearts build lives: Positive emotions, induced through loving-kindness meditation, build consequential personal resources. *Journal of Personality and Social Psychology, 95,* 1045–1062.

Frijda, N. H., & Sundararajan, L. (2007). Emotion refinement: A theory inspired by Chinese poetics. *Perspectives of Psychological Science, 2*, 227–241.

Froh, J. J., Kashdan, T. B., Ozimkowski, K. M., & Miller, N. (2009). Who benefits the most from a gratitude intervention in children and adolescents? Examining positive affect as a moderator. *Journal of Positive Psychology, 4*, 408–422.

Froh, J. J., Sefick, W. J., & Emmons, R. A. (2008). Counting blessings in early adolescents: An experimental study of gratitude and subjective well-being. *Journal of School Psychology, 46*, 213–233.

Gable, S. L., Gonzaga, G. C., & Strachman, A. (2006). Will you be there for me when things go right? Supportive responses to positive event disclosures. *Journal of Personality and Social Psychology, 91*, 904–917.

Gable, S. L., Reis, H. T., Impett, E. A., & Asher, E. R. (2004). What do you do when things go right? The intrapersonal and interpersonal benefits of sharing positive events. *Journal of Personality and Social Psychology, 87*, 228–245.

Haidt, J. (2002). Elevation and the positive psychology of morality. In C. L. Keyes & J. Haidt (Eds.), *Flourishing* (pp. 275–290). Washington, DC: American Psychological Association.

Hedgepeth, B. E., & Hale, W. D. (1983). Effects of a positive reminiscing intervention on affect, expectancy, and performance. *Psychological Reports, 53*, 867–870.

Hirschfeld, R. M., Keller, M. B., Panico, S., Arons, B. S., Barlow, D., Davidoff, F., ... Wyatt, R. J. (1997). The National Depressive and Manic-Depressive Association consensus statement on the undertreatment of depression. *Journal of the American Medical Association, 277*, 333–340.

Johnson, D. P., Penn, D. L., Fredrickson, B. L., Meyer, P. S., Kring, A. M., & Brantley, M. (2009). Loving-kindness meditation to enhance recovery from negative symptoms of schizophrenia. *Journal of Clinical Psychology, 65*, 499–509.

Judd, L. L., Akiskal, H. S., & Paulus, M. P. (1997). The role and clinical significance of subsyndromal depressive symptoms (SDD) in unipolar major depressive disorder. *Journal of Affective Disorders, 45*, 5–18.

Kashdan, T. (2009). *Curious?: Discover the missing ingredient to a fulfilling life*. New York, NY: William Morrow.

King, L. A. (2001). The health benefits of writing about life goals. *Personality and Social Psychology Bulletin, 27*, 798–807.

Kurtz, J. L. (2008). Looking to the future to appreciate the present: The benefits of temporal scarcity. *Psychological Science, 19*, 1238–1241.

Lee, P. C. (1983). Play as a means for developing relationships. In R. A. Hinde (Ed.), *Primate social relationships* (pp. 82–89). Oxford, UK: Blackwell.

Lewinsohn, P. P., Muñoz, R., Youngren, M., & Zeiss, A. (1992). *Control your depression* (2nd ed.). New York, NY: Prentice Hall.

Lyubomirsky, S. (2008). *The how of happiness: A scientific approach to getting the life you want*. New York, NY: Penguin Press.

Lyubomirsky, S., King, L. A., & Diener, E. (2005). The benefits of frequent positive affect: Does happiness lead to success? *Psychological Bulletin, 131*, 803–855.

Lyubomirsky, S., Sheldon, K. M., Schkade, D. (2005). Pursuing happiness: The architecture of sustainable change. *Review of General Psychology, 9*, 111–131.

Lyubomirsky, S., Sousa, L., & Dickerhoof, R. (2006). The costs and benefits of writing, talking, and thinking about life's triumphs and defeats. *Journal of Personality and Social Psychology, 90*, 692–708.

Mazzycchelli, T. G., Kane, R. T., & Rees, C. S. (2010). Behavioral activation interventions for well-being: A meta-analysis. *Journal of Positive Psychology, 5*, 105–121.

McKnight, P. E., & Kashdan, T. B. (2009). Purpose in life as a system that creates and sustains health and well-being: An integrative testable theory. *Review of General Psychology, 13*, 242–251.

Moneta, G. B., & Csikszentmihalyi, M. (1996). The effect of perceived challenges and skills on the quality of subjective experience. *Journal of Personality, 64*, 275–310.

Munson, S., Lauterbach, D., Newman, M., & Resnick, P. (2010). Happier together: Integrating a wellness application into a social network site. In T. Ploug, P. F. V. Hasle, & H. Oinas-Kukkonen (Eds.), *Lecture notes in computer science* (Vol. 6137, pp. 27–39). Berlin Heidelberg: Springer-Verlag.

Nakamura, J., & Csikszentmihalyi, M. (2002). The concept of flow. In C. R. Snyder & S. J. Lopez (Eds.), *Handbook of Positive Psychology* (pp. 89–105).

National Research Council and Institute of Medicine. (2009). *Preventing mental, emotional, and behavioral disorders among young people: Progress and possibilities*. Washington, DC: National Academy Press.

Omodei, M. M., & Wearing, A. J. (1990). Need satisfaction and involvement in personal projects: Toward an integrative model of subjective well-being. *Journal of Personality and Social Psychology, 59*, 762–769.

Otake, K., Shimai, S., Tanaka-Matsumi, J., Otsui, K., & Fredrickson, B. L. (2006). Happy people become happier through kindness: A counting kindness intervention. *Journal of Happiness Studies, 7*, 361–375.

Parks, A. C. (2012). *A randomized trial of group positive psychotherapy for mild-moderate depressive symptoms in young adults*. Manuscript under review.

Pennebaker, J. W. (1998). Conflict and canned meat. *Psychological Inquiry, 9*, 219–220.

Pennebaker, J. W., & Segal, J. (1999). Forming a story: The health benefits of narrative. *Journal of Clinical Psychology, 55*, 1243–1254.

Peterson, C. (2006). *A primer in positive psychology*. New York, NY: Oxford University Press.

Peterson, C., Park, N., & Seligman, M. E. P. (2005). Orientations to happiness and life satisfaction: The full life versus the empty life. *Journal of Happiness Studies, 6*, 25–41.

Peterson, C., & Seligman, M. E. P. (2004). *Character Strengths and Virtues*. Oxford, UK: Oxford University Press.

Pham, L. B., & Taylor, S. E. (1999). From thought to action: Effects of process-versus outcome-based mental simulations on performance. *Personality and Social Psychology Bulletin, 25*, 250–260.

Rivkin, I. D., & Taylor, S. E. (1999). The effects of mental simulation on coping with controllable stressful events. *Personality and Social Psychology Bulletin, 25*, 1451–1462.

Ryan, R. M., & Deci, E. L. (2000). On happiness and human potentials: A review of research on hedonic and eudaimonic well-being. *Annual Review of Psychology, 52*, 141–166.

Schueller, S. M. (2010). Preferences for positive psychology exercises. *Journal of Positive Psychology, 5*, 192–203.

Schueller, S. M., & Seligman, M. E. P. (2010). Pursuit of pleasure, engagement, and meaning: Relationships to subjective and objective measures of well-being. *Journal of Positive Psychology, 5*, 253–263.

Seligman, M. E. P. (2002). *Authentic happiness*. New York, NY: Free Press.

Seligman, M. E. P., Rashid, T., & Parks, A. C. (2006). Positive psychotherapy. *American Psychologist, 61*, 774–788.

Seligman, M. E. P., Schulman, P., & Tryon, A. (2007). Group prevention of depression and anxiety symptoms. *Behaviour Research and Therapy*, 45, 1111–1126.

Seligman, M. E. P., Steen, T. A., Park, N., & Peterson, C. (2005). Positive psychology progress: Empirical validation of interventions. *American Psychologist*, 60, 410–421.

Salzberg, S. (1995). *Loving-kindness: The revolutionary art of happiness*. Boston, MA: Shambhala.

Sheldon, K. M., & Lyubomirsky, S. (2006). How to increase and sustain positive emotion: The effects of expressing gratitude and visualizing best possible selves. *The Journal of Positive Psychology*, 1, 73–82.

Sin, N. L., & Lyubomirsky, S. (2009). Enhancing well-being and alleviating depressive symptoms with positive psychology interventions: A practice-friendly meta-analysis. *Journal of Clinical Psychology: In Session*, 65, 467–487.

Smyth, J. M. (1998). Written emotional expression: Effect sizes, outcome types, and moderating variables. *Journal of Consulting and Clinical Psychology*, 66, 174–184.

Solomon, R. C. (1977). *The passions*. Garden City, NY: Anchor Books.

Stewart, R.E., & Chambless, D. L. (2007). Does psychotherapy research inform treatment decisions in private practice? *Journal of Clinical Psychology*, 63, 267–281.

Tkach, C. T. (2006). Unlocking the treasury of human kindness: Enduring improvements in mood, happiness, and self-evaluations. *Dissertation Abstracts International: Section B: The Sciences and Engineering*, 67, 603.

Tugade, M. M., & Fredrickson, B. L. (2004). Resilient individuals use positive emotions to bounce back from negative emotional experiences. *Journal of Personality and Social Psychology*, 86, 320–333.

Wallace, B. A., & Shapiro, S. L. (2006). Mental balance and well-being: Bridges between Buddhism and western psychology. *American Psychologist*, 61, 690–701.

Watkins, P. C., Woodward, K., Stone, T., & Kolts, R. D. (2003). Gratitude and happiness: The development of a measure of gratitude and its relationship with subjective well-being. *Social Behavior and Personality*, 31, 431–452.

Wilson, T. D., & Gilbert, D. T. (2008). Explaining away: A model of affective adaptation. *Perspectives on Psychological Science*, 3, 370–386.

Wood, J. V., Heimpel, S. A., & Michela, J. L. (2003). Savoring versus dampening: Self-esteem differences in regularity positive affect. *Journal of Personality and Social Psychology*, 85, 566–580.

Zauszniewski, J.A., Eggenschwiler, K., Preechawong, S., Chung, W., Airey, T.F., ... Roberts, B. L. (2004). Focused reflection reminiscence group for elders: Implementation and evaluation. *Journal of Applied Gerontology*, 23, 429–442.

CHAPTER 73

# POSITIVE PSYCHOLOGY IN PRACTICE: POSITIVE PSYCHOTHERAPY

## TAYYAB RASHID

University of Toronto Scarborough, Canada

"Doc, I want to be happy" is a desire often uttered by clients, yet rarely addressed in psychotherapy. Rather, psychotherapy does a good job of making clients less depressed and less anxious by uncovering childhood traumas, untwisting faulty thinking, or adjusting dysfunctional relationships. The positive aspects of human experience have traditionally not been the focus in psychotherapy. Positive psychotherapy (PPT) is empirically validated psychotherapy that directly builds positive emotions, character strengths, and meaning with the aims of undoing psychopathology and promoting happiness. This chapter suggests that psychotherapy presents opportunities for both accentuating the positive aspects of human experience and ameliorating the negatives. In it, the conceptual and theoretical underpinnings of PPT are discussed along with descriptions of how to conduct it, potential mechanisms of change, and a summary of pilot studies. Last, caveats, and future directions are offered.

## NEGATIVES IN PSYCHOTHERAPY

The human brain is oriented towards and more strongly responsive to experiences that might be labeled "negative" than to those that might be labeled "positive." This has had clear evolutionary value for human beings by helping to keep individuals and communities safe (e.g., by putting out fires and attacking trespassers) and meeting important needs (e.g., through competing for food, shelter, and mates). This negative attentional bias has been a critical factor in human success and, in the modern world it continues to be a dominant factor in the shaping of human experience (Cottrell & Neuberg, 2005; Ito, Larsen, Smith, & Cacioppo, 1998). For example, stories of evil arouse our curiosity more than accounts of virtue. Negative impressions and stereotypes are quicker to form and are more resistant to disconfirmation than positive ones (Baumeister, Bratslavsky, Finkenauer, & Vohs, 2001). Negative memories stay with us for days, months, or even years while positive memories tend to be transient (Fredrickson & Losada, 2005). Psychotherapy, through its traditional focus on illness and symptoms, has done well. It significantly outperforms placebos and may be more long-lasting than medications (Baldwin, Wampold, & Imel, 2007; Leykin & DeRubeis, 2009). However, psychotherapy has not necessarily enhanced happiness—at least not directly. Mainstream psychotherapy, for the most part, continues to operate on a deficit-oriented medical model in which psychotherapists assess and treat psychopathology. The medical model of psychotherapy has been widely criticized (Elkins, 2007) for offering only a narrow window of outcome that does not include psychological well-being and quality of life (Lampropoulos, 2001; Rapaport, Clary, Fayyad, & Endicott, 2005).

Historically, few interventions have explicitly attended to the positive resources that clients possess (e.g., Fordyce, 1983; Lichter, Haye, & Kammann, 1980). However, the recent surge in positive psychology has produced a number of empirically tested interventions that focus on positive attributes (e.g., Cheaven et al., 2006; Emmon & McCullough, 2003; Fredrickson, Cohn, Coffey, Pek, & Finkel, 2008; Govindji & Linley, 2007; Lyubomirsky, 2008; Steger, Kashdan & Oishi, 2008). Tested mostly with non-clinical samples, these interventions have tended to target single attributes rather than yielding a comprehensive psychotherapy similar to cognitive behavioral therapy or interpersonal therapy. While three comprehensive interventions have been designed and tested (Fava & Ruini, 2003; Fluckiger & Grosse Holtforth, 2008; Frisch, 2006) these are adjuncts to traditional deficit focused treatments. Hence, there is a dearth of clinically applicable psychotherapies that explicitly attend to both symptoms and strengths, whilst also utilizing strengths as an active treatment ingredient.

## Positive Psychotherapy

PPT is a therapeutic endeavor within positive psychology that aims to broaden the scope of traditional psychotherapy. Its central hypothesis is that building positive emotions, strengths, and meaning (in addition to treating symptoms) is efficacious in the treatment of psychopathology, and that this serves us best not when life is easy, but when life is difficult. During times of difficulty the negativity bias will often serve to amplify the unsavory aspects of individual life experience, effectively screening out the positive aspects. In essence, PPT seeks to balance attention by engaging clients in discussions about, say, an injustice done whilst also getting them to focus on recent acts of kindness. Similarly, along with insults, hubris, and hate, experiences of genuine praise, humility and harmony are also deliberately elicited. Pain associated with the trauma is empathetically attended to whilst also exploring the potential for growth. PPT assumes that the most potent resources needed to meet the challenges of life reside within the client and for psychologically distressed clients knowing about one's personal strengths and positive characteristics can be empowering and motivating. In short, PPT is a "build-what's-strong" supplement to the traditional "fix-what's-wrong" approach (Duckworth, Steen, & Seligman, 2005, p. 631).

PPT is based on three assumptions. First, much like Humanistic psychotherapies (Maslow, 1968; Rogers, 1959), PPT rests on the fundamental belief that psychopathology results when clients' inherent capacities for growth, fulfillment, and happiness are thwarted by sociocultural factors. Rather than happiness and psychopathology somehow residing inside the person, it is the interaction between the clients and their environment that engenders both happiness and psychopathology. Whenever people become "damaged" by these interactions, psychotherapy presents as a viable option for restoring these growth tendencies. The basic assumption is that it is not repairing weaknesses that makes clients stronger, but rather the enhancing of personal strengths and abilities (Govindji & Linley, 2007).

Second, positive emotions and strengths are authentic and as real as symptoms and disorders. These are not defenses, Pollyannaish illusions or clinical by-products of symptom relief that lie at the clinical peripheries without needing attention. PPT regards positive emotions and the strengths of clients as authentic and they are valued in their own right. The function of psychotherapy is not only to help clients to eliminate or manage symptoms but also to restore and nurture courage, kindness, modesty, perseverance, and emotional and social intelligence. Whilst the former may make life less painful, it is the latter that makes it fulfilling.

The final assumption is that effective therapeutic relationships can be formed through the discussion of positive personal characteristics and experiences (e.g., such as positive emotions, strengths and virtues, etc.). This opposes the traditional approach of many psychotherapies which aim to treat clients through deep analysis and discussions of their troubles. This portrayal of psychotherapy in the popular media tends to socialize clients to the belief that therapy exclusively entails talking about troubles, ventilating bottled-up emotions, and recovering self-esteem. It not only maintains an unhelpful stigma about mental health but also reinforces a belief in clients that they are somehow deeply flawed or damaged, with the only way "out" being several sessions of painful discussion about one's childhood traumas, dissatisfactions, unmet needs, etc. It is not that troubles are not worth discussing but this discussion is not the *sine qua non* of building a strong therapeutic relationship. Powerful therapeutic bonds can also be built by deeply discussing positive emotions and other positive experiences (Burton & King, 2004).

Explicitly focusing on positive emotions in therapy (such as hope), have been found to be effective (Cheaven et al., 2006; Luborsky, Cris-Cristoph, Alexander, Margolis, & Cohen, 1983). In addition, Fitzpatrick, Janzen, Chamodraka, & Park (2005) reported that engendering positive emotions, particularly in the early part of therapy, opens clients up to the therapeutic process, whilst Fitzpatrick and Stalikas (2008) emphasize that positive emotions are so integral to intrapersonal therapeutic change that they should be seriously considered as a common therapeutic factor. Finally, Brendtro and Shabazian (2004) have noted that children and families are more likely to become full participants in the therapeutic process when there is an explicit focus on strengths and other positive attributes. Clearly, when a therapist asks a client "What strengths do you bring to deal with your troubles?" it is likely to result in a very different discussion compared to the pathology-oriented question, "What weaknesses have contributed to your troubles?"

# Theoretical Foundations

PPT is primarily based on Seligman's (2002) conceptualization of happiness. Seligman decomposes the vague and fuzzy notion of "happiness" into three more scientifically measurable and manageable components or lives, the pleasant life, the engaged life, and the meaningful life.

## The pleasant life

This is the dimension of human experience endorsed by hedonic theories of happiness. It consists of experiencing positive emotions about the present, past, and future and learning skills to amplify the intensity and duration of these emotions. The positive emotions about the past include satisfaction, contentment, fulfillment, pride, and serenity. Positive emotions about the future include hope and optimism, faith, trust, and confidence. Positive emotions about the present include savoring and mindfulness.

Compared to negative emotions, positive emotions tend to be transitory, yet they play a key role in making thought processes more flexible, creative and efficient (Fredrickson, 2009). Research has also shown that positive emotions build resilience by "undoing" the effects of negative emotions (Fredrickson, Tugade, Waugh, & Larkin, 2003) and are robustly associated with longevity, marital satisfaction, friendship, income and resilience (for reviews see Fredrickson et al., 2008; Lyubomirsky, King, & Diener, 2005). In addition, Schwartz and colleagues (2002) have found that depressed clients seeking psychotherapy tend to experience a lower than 0.5 to 1 ratio of positive to negative emotion, whilst Fredrickson (2009) has reported findings that experiencing three positive emotions for every single negative emotion may be a threshold for flourishing. It appears, then, that lack of positive emotions and pleasure are not just symptoms of psychopathology but may partly cause it. Enhancing the pleasant life could be a goal of psychotherapy and it could be appealing for clients in a way that exploring the details of childhood traumas, arguing against catastrophic cognitions, or taking medication with potential adverse side-effects may not be.

## The engaged life

This dimension of happiness relates to the pursuit of engagement, involvement, and absorption in work, intimate relations, and leisure. The notion of engagement stems from Csikszentmihalyi's (1990) work on flow, which is the psychological state brought about by intense concentration and that typically results in temporal distortion (i.e. lost sense of time) for the performer. Provided one's skill levels are sufficient to meet the challenge of the task, individuals are likely to become deeply absorbed or "at one" with the experience.

Seligman (2002) proposes that one way to enhance engagement is to identify clients' salient character or "signature" strengths and then help them to find opportunities to use them more. Every client possesses signature strengths that are self-consciously owned and celebrated, and which feel authentic when used. In PPT, clients learn about undertaking intentional activities that use their signature strengths to create engagement. These activities are relatively more time-intensive and might include rock climbing, chess, basketball, dancing, creating or experiencing art, music, literature, spiritual activities, social interactions, and other creative pursuits like baking, gardening, playing with a child, and so on. Compared with sensory pleasures which fade quickly, these activities last longer, involve more thinking and interpretation, and do not habituate easily.

Engagement can be an important antidote to boredom, anxiety, and depression. Anhedonia, apathy, boredom, multitasking, and restlessness—hallmarks of many psychological disorders—are largely manifestations of disrupted attention (McCormick, Funderburk & Lee, 2005; Nakamura & Csikszentmihalyi, 2002). Intense engagement typically eliminates boredom and rumination because, in seeking to successfully complete a challenging task, attentional resources must be activated and directed towards the task at hand (leaving less attentional capacity for processing self-relevant, threat-related information). Additionally, a sense of accomplishment in the aftermath of engaged activity often leaves one reminiscing and basking, which are two forms of positive rumination (Feldman, Joormann & Johnson, 2008). Utilizing these features of engagement, therapeutic interventions have been successfully applied to undo symptoms (Grafanaki et al., 2007; Nakamura & Csikszentmihalyi, 2002).

## The meaningful life

The third dimension of Seligman's conceptualization is the pursuit of meaning. This consists of using signature strengths to belong to and serve something that is bigger than oneself. Victor Frankl (1963), a pioneer in the study of meaning, emphasized that happiness cannot be attained by desiring happiness. Rather, it must come as the unintended consequence of working for a goal greater than oneself. People who successfully pursue activities that connect them to such larger goals achieve a "meaningful life." There are a number of ways that this can be achieved: close interpersonal relationships, pursuing artistic, intellectual or scientific innovations, philosophical or religious contemplation, social or environmental activism, careers experienced as callings, and spirituality or other potentially solitary pursuits such as meditation (e.g., Stillman & Baumeister, 2009; Wrzesniewski, McCauley, Rozin, & Schwartz, 1997).

Regardless of the way in which a person establishes a meaningful life, doing so produces a sense of satisfaction and the belief that one has lived well (Ackerman, Zuroff, & Mosokowitz, 2000; Hicks & King, 2009). Meaning and purpose can motivate psychologically distressed clients to set and then steadily pursue goals. Therapy can be a useful venture to help clients define and set concrete goals, and clarify the overarching meaning associated with such goals, in ways that increase the likelihood of goal attainment (McNight & Kasdhan, 2009). There is also good evidence that having a sense of meaning and purpose helps individuals to recover or rebound quickly from adversity and buffers against feelings of hopelessness and uncontrollability (Graham, Lobel, Glass, & Lokshina, 2008; Lightsey, 2006). Furthermore, clients whose lives are imbued with meaning are more likely to persist rather than quit in the face of a difficult situation (McNight & Kasdhan, 2009). PPT asserts that a lack of meaning is not just a symptom, but a cause of depression and various psychological disorders. Through the meaningful life, PPT can help clients to forge connections to deal with psychological problems.

# THE FULL LIFE

The full life entails happiness and life satisfaction and is more than the sum of its components—pleasure, engagement, and meaning. These components are neither exclusive nor exhaustive. Peterson and colleagues (2005) found that pleasure, engagement, and meaning are empirically distinguishable routes to happiness but are not incompatible. As a result all can be pursued simultaneously, with each individually associated with life satisfaction. They also found that engagement and meaning were correlated more robustly with life satisfaction while pleasure was marginally correlated. These findings suggest that pleasure is not as strong a predictor of happiness and life satisfaction but that it is still relevant to happiness. Indeed, the pathological loss or pathological excess of pleasure is a devastating part of many affective disorders. Many psychologically distressed individuals try to quash their unhappiness by experiencing more and more pleasure. However, due to a genetically influenced set range, we cannot dramatically alter our ability to experience pleasure (Brickman and Campbell, 1971; Kahneman et al., 2006). In addition, we adapt quickly to pleasure. This does not make pleasure, especially sensory pleasure, a prime candidate for happiness. In contrast, we adapt slowly to activities which deeply engage us and are imbued with meaning. This is because during engaging experiences we are completely absorbed (e.g., an artist is immersed in his creation) and are required to continually adjust our relationship with the environment and with the challenge or task at hand. As we master the challenge in an activity, we strive for increasingly complex goals. Over time, a sense of meaning and purpose may evolve from this engagement, elevating engagement in artistic pursuits, for example, from being absorbing in the short term to being highly meaningful in the long term.

A full life entails pleasure, engagement, and meaning, through separate activities or through a single activity. In contrast, an empty life lacking these elements, particularly engagement and meaning, is partly causal of psychological problems.

# HOW DOES POSITIVE PSYCHOTHERAPY WORK?

As shown in Table 73.1, from the outset of PPT clients deeply explore their strengths and other positive attributes. The therapist initiates this in the first session by building a congenial and positive relationship with the client by encouraging them to introduce themselves through a real-life story that shows them at their best (Rashid & Ostermann, 2009). Clients are asked to identify their signature strengths by completing an online strengths measure: *Values In Action* (VIA; Peterson & Seligman, 2004). This provides the client and therapist with information that can be used to devise pathways towards purposeful, positive action (e.g., commitment to engagement enhancing activities; symptom related problem-solving) via the use of personal strengths. Clients are encouraged to develop their practical intelligence through the careful consideration of which signature strength is relevant to the problem, whether it conflicts with other strengths (e.g., should one be honest or kind?) and how to translate abstract signature strengths into concrete actions (Schwartz & Sharpe, 2006). Clients are then encouraged to write down grudges, bitter memories or resentments and

Table 73.1 An overview of the 14-session model of PPT

| Session and topic | | Description | Homework |
|---|---|---|---|
| 1 | Orientation to PPT. Lack of positive resources | The lack of positive resources like positive emotions, character strengths, and meaning is discussed in the context of perpetuating psychopathology. Ground rules, roles and responsibilities are discussed, along with the importance of completing homework. | Positive introduction: client writes one-page real life story which shows her/him at her/his best and which ends positively, not tragically. |
| 2 | Character strengths | Notion of engagement and flow is discussed. Character strengths are introduced. | Values in Action (VIA) Questionnaire: client completes on-line VIA. |
| 3 | Signature strengths and positive emotions | Signature strengths are discussed. The client and therapist collaborate to devise specific, measurable, and achievable goals targeting specific problems. The benefits of positive emotion are discussed. | Blessing journal: the client starts a journal to record three good things every night (big or small). |
| 4 | Good vs. bad memories | The role of bitter memories is discussed in terms of how they perpetuate psychological symptoms. The role of good memories is also highlighted. | Memories: the client writes about feelings of anger and bitterness and their impact in perpetuating distress. |
| 5 | Forgiveness | Forgiveness is introduced as a tool to transform anger and bitterness and to cultivate neutral or positive emotions. | Forgiveness Letter: the client describes a transgression, its related emotions and pledges to forgive the transgressor. Does not necessarily deliver the letter. |
| 6 | Gratitude | Gratitude is discussed as an enduring thankfulness. The roles of good and bad memories are discussed again, with an emphasis on gratitude. | Gratitude Letter: the client writes and delivers in person a gratitude letter to someone he/she never properly thanked. |
| 7 | Mid-therapy check | The forgiveness and gratitude assignments are followed up. Experiences related to the signature strengths and Blessing Journal activities discussed. Check in with client about any therapeutic gains. | Client completes the Forgiveness and Gratitude assignments. |
| 8 | Satisficing vs. maximizing | Concepts of satisficing (good enough) and maximizing are discussed. | Satisficing: client reviews ways to increase satisficing and devises personal action plan. |

| Session and topic | | Description | Homework |
|---|---|---|---|
| 9 | Hope and optimism | Optimism and hope are discussed in detail. The client is helped to think of times when important things were lost but other opportunities opened up. | One Door Closed, One Door Opened: client thinks of three doors that closed and then asks: What doors opened? |
| 10 | Positive communication | Discussion about active-constructive—a technique of positive communication. | Active-constructive responding: the client to look for active-constructive opportunities. |
| 11 | Signature strengths of others | The significance of recognizing and associating through character strengths of family members is discussed. | Family Strengths Tree: client asks family members to take the VIA. A family tree of strengths is drawn up and discussed at a gathering. |
| 12 | Savoring | Savoring is discussed, along with techniques and strategies to safeguard against adaptation. | Savoring Activity: client plans a savoring activity using specific techniques. |
| 13 | Gift of Time | The therapeutic benefits of helping others are discussed. | Gift of Time: client makes plans to give the gift of time doing something that also uses his/her signature strengths. |
| 14 | The Full Life | Full life is discussed as the integration of Pleasure, Engagement, and Meaning. Therapeutic gains and experiences are discussed and ways to sustain positive changes are devised. | |

then discuss in therapy the effects of holding onto them, whilst also considering the option of forgiveness. Research shows that personal written disclosures often ease the cognitive and emotional constrictions associated with painful memories and experiences (King & Miner, 2000; Pennebaker, 1997).

# The place of negative emotions in positive psychotherapy

It is not uncommon for exercises employed in PPT to generate negative and uncomfortable emotions. Despite what might be implied by the name, the focus of positive psychotherapy is not *exclusively* on the positive aspects of human experience. It would be naive to conceive of a life without negative experiences. As such, PPT does not deny negative emotions nor encourage clients to see the world through rose-colored glasses. Rather it aims to validate these experiences, whilst gently encouraging clients to explore their effects and seek out potential positives from their difficult and traumatic experiences. This is encouraged because research has shown that doing so tends to yield health benefits and promote psychological growth (Bonanno, 2004; Calhoun & Tedeschi, 2006). However, during these explorations it is important that the therapist not trivialize such experiences by, for instance, too quickly pointing out the positive opportunities that trauma, loss, or adversity may present for personal growth and development. Amidst the warmth, understanding, and goodwill created in PPT, a therapist who listens mindfully and can facilitate affective expression will be able to help the client explore and reflect upon these uncomfortable experiences in a way (and at a pace) that leads to positive outcomes. In so doing, clients can learn how to encounter negative experiences with a more positive mindset and reframe and label those experiences in ways that are helpful. By working diligently to articulate the positive aspects of a client's experience, the PPT therapist does not create a Pollyannaish or Panglossian epitome of happiness or a caricature of positive thinking. The therapist neither minimizes nor masks unavoidable negative events and experiences (such as abuse, neglect, and suffering) as positives. Such issues are dealt with in PPT using standard clinical protocols.

## The power of gratitude and savoring

PPT also explicitly focuses on cultivating positive emotions such as gratitude. Throughout the course of therapy clients are asked to write down three good things that happened to them, and why they happened, during the course of each day. This becomes an ongoing journal of blessings large and small. Most clients find this helpful not only in coping with negative experiences but also in cementing relationships through explicitly noticing (in a gratitude journal) the kind acts and gestures of friends and family. Thus, a new sense of appreciation develops for existing relationships. Clients are also asked to think of someone to whom they are grateful, but who they have never properly thanked. They compose a letter to them describing their gratitude and are asked to read the letter to that person by phone or in person. This exercise, when done in person, produces deeply touching positive emotions.

Clinical experience suggests most clients seek therapy as a means of managing the stressors associated with living in fast-paced, highly complex environments. PPT exercises such as satisficing versus maximizing (Schwartz et al., 2002) and savoring teach clients to deliberately slow down and enjoy experiences they would normally hurry through (e.g., eating a meal, taking a shower, or walking to work). When the experience is over, clients reflect and write down what they did, and how they felt differently compared to when they rushed through it. The last few exercises focus on close relationships because a meaningful life cannot be fostered without nurturing relationships, either with significant others, at work or within communities (Seligman, 2002; Stillman & Baumeister, 2009). Exercises that focus on the strengthening of interpersonal relationships include getting clients to explore the signature strengths of others, learning about active and constructive communication styles (Gable, Reis, Impett, & Asher, 2004), and participation in acts of generosity that involve devoting time to the concerns of others.

A potentially daunting task for a clinician practicing PPT is to ensure that what he or she purports to be "positive" is not perceived by clients as prescriptive. PPT has an empirical base that clearly documents the benefits of positive attributes. Just as medical research shows that eating vegetables and exercising are "good" for us, research also shows that adopting certain habits and behaviors are associated with happiness and well-being (Gable & Haidt, 2005). PPT exercises are custom-tailored to meet a client's immediate clinical needs (e.g., conflict with significant others, a romantic break-up, or career related issues) and the length of therapy and order of the exercises can be varied to suit each client's circumstances and the feasibility of completing the exercises.

# EVIDENCE

A small number of validation studies of PPT have been reported. Prior to the formal evaluation of PPT as an integrated treatment package, individual exercises were empirically validated (see Seligman, Steen, Park, & Peterson, 2005). In these studies, outcomes were evaluated using valid and reliable research measures such as the Beck Depression Inventory (BDI; Beck, Ward, Mendelson, Mock, & Erbaugh, 1961) and the Satisfaction with Life Scale (SWLS; Diener, Emmons, Larsen, & Griffin, 1985). More recently, the Positive Psychotherapy Inventory (PPTI) has been created to assess the specific active ingredients of the treatment, such as pleasure, engagement and meaning. Initial validation studies have shown this to be a valid and reliable measure (Guney, 2011; Seligman, Rashid & Parks, 2006).

The findings from initial PPT outcome studies have been encouraging. For example, Seligman, Rashid and Parks (2006) found that individual PPT with severely depressed clients led to more symptomatic improvement and longer remission from depressive disorder than both treatment-as-usual and treatment-as-usual plus antidepressant medication. PPT also measurably enhanced happiness as measured by the PPTI. Similarly, group PPT provided to mild to moderately depressed college students led to significantly fewer symptoms and increases in life satisfaction compared with the no-treatment control group. This improvement lasted for at least 1 year after treatment. PPT has also been found to increase the well-being of middle school children, with a large effect size (Rashid & Anjum, 2007). In addition, a controlled group intervention that used PPT exercises with community adults, enhanced happiness and life-satisfaction with medium effect sizes (Rashid & Anjum, 2009), whilst Akther (2009) recently used PPT exercises with adolescents experiencing addiction problems and found it effective in reducing substance use and in enhancing well-being.

Taken together, across samples and settings, the initial findings about the effectiveness of PPT are encouraging. However, more research is needed to evaluate PPT's effectiveness with a variety of psychological disorders, including comparisons with traditional symptom targeted treatments.

# MECHANISMS OF CHANGE

Psychologically disturbed individuals exaggerate the natural tendency to focus on and recall negative aspects of their experience (Nolen-Hoeksema, 2000). Several PPT exercises aim to reeducate attention, memory, and expectations away from the negative and catastrophic, and toward the positive and the hopeful. For example, keeping a gratitude journal can help to counteract the tendency to ruminate on the dissatisfying aspects of one's life (e.g., obstacles, disappointments) and orient clients towards events that enrich life and are vitalizing (e.g., caring acts, goal attainment). Similarly, the gratitude visit may shift a client's memory away from the unfavorable aspects of past relationships to savoring the good things about interactions with friends and family. This reeducation of attention, memory, and expectation is accomplished verbally as well as via journal writing. As noted previously, the cultivation of positive emotions helps individuals to flourish. The identification and use of signature strengths allows them to think more deeply about their positive qualities; this is likely to bolster self-confidence, enhance resilience and help clients to deal more effectively with psychological distress (Linley, Nielsen, Gillett, & Biswas-Diener, 2010).

Effective psychotherapy is a process that entails generating ideas and actions to solve problems. However, this cannot be done unless the therapist establishes a strong therapeutic alliance. When this occurs a focus on personal strengths is likely to be a more potent generator of change than a focus on personal weaknesses. For example, low mood and a loss of interest in previously enjoyed activities were hallmarks of one client in the individual PPT study. She spent much time ruminating on her problems. Through PPT, she discovered that an appreciation of beauty and curiosity were among her signature strengths and, with the help of her therapist, was able to design activities that tapped these strengths. After engaging in these activities, she reported a decrease in levels of unhelpful rumination.

In conducting PPT, some caveats are in order. First, PPT is not prescriptive. Rather, it is a descriptive approach based on converging scientific evidence indicating that certain benefits accrue when individuals attend to the positive aspects of their experience. Second, PPT is not a panacea and will not be appropriate for all clients in all situations. As such, clinical judgment is needed to determine the suitability of PPT for individual clients. Third, PPT therapists should not expect a linear progression of improvement because the motivation to change long-standing behavioral and emotional patterns fluctuates during the course of therapy. Finally, although pilot studies have reported promising findings, these should be viewed cautiously and will need to be replicated before any firm conclusions can be made about the efficacy of PPT, its generalizability or the role of possible mediating variables.

## Future Directions

After lagging behind deficit-oriented interventions, positive interventions are making promising advances. An issue of *Journal of Clinical Psychology: In Session* (issue May 65, 2009) focused exclusively on positive interventions for a variety of clinical disorders. A meta-analysis by Sin and Lyubomirsky (2009) of 51 positive interventions showed that these significantly enhance well-being and decrease depression. In a study that provides support for the theoretical foundation of PPT, Vella-Brodrick, Park and Peterson (2009) showed that pursuing pleasure, engagement and meaning leads to happiness. More recently, Meyer, Johnson, Parks, Iwanski, & Penn (2012) have empirically demonstrated that PPT improves psychological well-being, hope, savoring, psychological recovery, self-esteem, and helps in ameliorating psychiatric symptoms. Similarly, Govindji and Linley (2007) found that working on character strengths promotes well-being. The role of positive interventions to complement and supplement traditional clinical work is also being explored (e.g., Frisch, 2006; Karwoski, Garratt & llardi, 2006; Ruini & Fava, 2009). In addition to these empirical and clinical developments, a range of useful books on positive interventions and clinical practice has also begun to emerge (Conoley & Conoley, 2009; Frederickson, 2009; Joseph & Linley, 2006; Lyubomirsky, 2008; Magyar-Moe, 2009), as have a number of theoretical advances that incorporate strengths in clinical practices (e.g., Dick-Niderhauser, 2009; Lent, 2004; Smith, 2006; Wong, 2006). Taken together, this burgeoning body of work suggests that positive clinical interventions will be a significant therapeutic pillar that complements advances already made in psychotherapy.

With these promising developments, therapists practicing positive psychology need to keep in mind that humans quickly adapt to new circumstances. Creative, intentional and behavior-based positive interventions that correspond both to the values and strengths of clients need to be explored and designed with enough variety to ensure clients do not easily habituate to them. In addition, to justify the inclusion of PPT as a standalone treatment or as a supplement to mainstream clinical practice, more rigorous research is needed to determine whether a lack of positive emotions, engagement and meaning are causally linked to specific clinical disorders, and to vital outcomes in healthy living. Including positively oriented dependent variables may produce differential effects in treatment outcome research. Finally, longitudinal and prospective studies will help to clarify if PPT might be usefully employed as part of preventive strategies with at-risk populations.

## References

Ackerman, S., Zuroff, D. C., & Moskowitz, D. S. (2000). Generativity in midlife and young adults: Links to agency, communion, and subjective well-being. *International Journal of Aging & Human Development, 50*, 17–41.

Akther, M. (2009). *Applying positive psychology to alcohol-misusing adolescents: A pilot intervention*. Unpublished manuscript. University of East London.

Baldwin, S. A., Wampold, B. E., & Imel, Z. E. (2007). Untangling the alliance outcome correlation: Exploring the relative importance of therapist and patient variability in the alliance. *Journal of Consulting and Clinical Psychology, 75*, 842–852.

Baumeister, R. F., Bratslavsky, E., Finkenauer, C., & Vohs, K. D. (2001). Bad is stronger than good. *Review of General Psychology, 5*, 323–370.

Beck, A. T., Ward, C. H., Mendelson, M., Mock, J. E., & Erbaugh, J. K. (1961). An inventory for measuring depression. *Archives of General Psychiatry, 4*, 561–571.

Bonanno, G.A. (2004). Loss, trauma, and human resilience: Have we underestimated the human capacity to thrive after extremely aversive events? *American Psychologist, 59*, 20–28.

Brickman, P., & Campbell, D. T. (1971). Hedonic relativism and planning the good society. In M. H. Appley (Ed.), *Adaptation-level theory* (pp. 287–305). New York, NY: Academic Press.

Brendtro, L., & Shabazian, M. (2004). *Troubled children and youth, turning problems into opportunities*. Champaign, IL Research Press.

Burton, C.M., & King, L. A. (2004). The health benefits of writing about intensely positive experiences. *Journal of Research in Personality, 38*, 150–163.

Calhoun, L., & Tedeschi, R. (2006). *The handbook of posttraumatic growth: Research and practice*. Mahwah, NJ: Erlbaum.

Cheavens, J. S., Feldman, D. B., Gum, A., Michael, S. T, Snyder, C. R. (2006). Hope therapy in a community sample: A pilot investigation. *Social Indicators Research, 77*, 61–78.

Conoley, C. W., & Conoley, J. C. (2009). *Positive psychology and family therapy*. Hoboken, NJ: Wiley.

Cottrell C. A., Neuberg S. L. (2005). Different emotional reactions to different groups: a sociofunctional threat-based approach to "prejudice". *Journal of Personality and Social Psychology, 88*, 770–789.

Csikszentmihalyi, M. (1990). *Flow: The psychology of optimal experience.* New York, NY: HarperCollins.

Dick-Niederhauser, A. (2009). Therapeutic change and the experience of joy: Toward a theory of curative processes. *Journal of Psychotherapy Integration, 19*, 187–211.

Diener, E. Emmons, R. A., Larsen, R. J., & Griffin, S. (1985). The satisfaction with life scale. *Journal of Personality Assessment, 49*, 71–75.

Duckworth, A. L., Steen, T. A., & Seligman, M. E. P. (2005). Positive psychology in clinical practice. *Annual Review of Clinical Psychology, 1*, 629–651.

Elkins, D. N. (2007). The medical model in psychotherapy: Its limitations and failures. *Journal of Humanistic Psychology, 49*, 66–84.

Emmons, R. A., & McCullough, M. E. (2003). Counting blessings versus burdens: Experimental studies of gratitude and subjective well-being in daily life. *Journal of Personality and Social Psychology, 84*, 377–389.

Fava, G. A., & Ruini, C. (2003). Development and characteristics of a well-being enhancing psychotherapeutic strategy: Well-being therapy. *Journal of Behavior Therapy and Experimental Psychiatry, 34*, 45–63.

Feldman, G C., Joormann, J., & Johnson, S. L (2008). Responses to positive affect: A self-report measure of rumination and dampening. *Cognitive Therapy and Research, 32*, 507–525.

Fitzpatrick, M., & Stalikas, A. (2008). Positive emotions as generators of therapeutic change. *Journal of Psychotherapy Integration, 18*, 137–154.

Fitzpatrick, M. R., Janzen, J., Chamodraka, M., & Park, J. (2006). Client critical incidents in the process of early alliance development: A positive emotion-exploration spiral. *Psychotherapy Research, 16*, 486—498.

Fluckiger, C., Grosse Holtforth, M. (2008). Focusing the therapist's attention on the patient's strengths: a preliminary study to foster a mechanism of change in outpatient psychotherapy. *Journal of Clinical Psychology, 64*, 876–890.

Fordyce, M. W. (1983). A program to increase happiness: Further studies. *Journal of Consulting Psychology, 30*, 483–498.

Frankl, V. E. (1963). *Man's search for meaning: An introduction to logotherapy.* New York, NY: Washington Square Press.

Fredrickson, B. L. (2009). *Positivity: Discover the ratio that tips your life toward flourishing.* New York, NY: Crown.

Fredrickson, B. L., Cohn, M. A., Coffey, K. A., Pek, J., & Finkel, S. M. (2008). Open hearts build lives: Positive emotions, induced through loving-kindness meditation, build consequential personal resources. *Journal of Personality and Social Psychology, 95*, 1045–1062.

Fredrickson, B. L., Tugade, M. M., Waugh, C. E., & Larkin, G.R. (2003). What good are positive emotions in crises? A prospective study of resilience and emotions following the terrorist attacks on the United States on September 11th. *Journal of Personality and Social Psychology, 84*(2), 365–376.

Frisch, M. B. (2006). *Quality of life therapy: Applying a life satisfaction approach to positive psychology and cognitive therapy.* Hoboken, NJ: Wiley.

Gable, S. L., & Haidt, J. (2005). What (and why) is positive psychology? *Review of General Psychology, 9*, 103–110.

Gable, S. L, Reis, H. T., Impett, E. A., & Asher, E. R. (2004). What do you do when things go right? The intrapersonal and interpersonal benefits of sharing positive events. *Journal of Personality and Social Psychology, 87*, 228–245.

Govindji, R., & Linley, P. A. (2007). Strengths use, self-concordance and well-being: Implications for strengths coaching and coaching psychologists. *International Coaching Psychology Review*, 2, 143–153.

Graham, J. E., Lobel, M., Glass, P., & Lokshina, I. (2008). Effects of written constructive anger expression in chronic pain patients: Making meaning from pain. *Journal of Behavioral Medicine*, 31, 201–212.

Grafanaki, S., Brennan, M., Holmes, S., Tang, K., & Alvarez, S. (2007). "In search of flow" in counselling and psychotherapy: Identifying the necessary ingredients of peak moments of therapy interaction, person-centered and experiential psychotherapies. *International Journal of Person-Centred and Experiential Psychotherapies*, 6, 239–255.

Guney, S. (2011). The Positive Psychotherapy Inventory (PPTI): Reliability and validity study in Turkish population. *Social and Behavioral Sciences*, 29, 81–86.

Hicks, J. A., & King, L. A. (2009). Meaning in life as a subjective judgment and lived experience. *Social and Personality Psychology Compass*, 3/4, 638–658.

Hamilton, M. (1960). A rating scale for depression. *Journal of Neurology, Neurosurgery, and Psychiatry*, 23, 56–62.

Ito, T. A., Larsen, J. T., Smith, N. K., & Cacioppo, J. T. (1998). Negative information weighs more heavily on the brain: The negativity bias in evaluative categorizations. *Journal of Personality & Social Psychology*, 75, 887–900.

Joseph, S., & Linley, A. P. (2006). *Positive Therapy: A meta-theory for positive psychological practice*. New York, NY: Routledge.

Lopez S. J., Floyd R. K., Ulven J. C., Snyder C. R. (2000). Hope therapy: helping clients build a house of hope. In Snyder C.R, (ed.) *Handbook of hope: theory, measures and applications* (pp. 123–150). San Diego, CA: Academic Press.

Kahneman, D., Krueger, A. B., Schkade, D., Schwartz, N., & Stone, A. A. (2006). Would you be happier if you were richer? A focusing illusion. *Science*, 312, 1908–1910.

Karwoski, L., Garratt, G. M., Ilardi, S. S. (2006). On the integration of cognitive-behavioral therapy for depression and positive psychology. *Journal of Cognitive Psychotherapy*, 20, 159–170.

King, L., & Miner, K. (2000). Writing about the perceived benefits of traumatic events: Implications for physical health. *Personality and Social Psychology Bulletin*, 26, 220–230.

Lent, R. W. (2004). Towards a unifying theoretical and practical perspective on well-being and psychosocial adjustment. *Journal of Counselling Psychology*, 5, 482–509.

Leykin, Y., & DeRubeis R. J. (2009). Allegiance in psychotherapy outcome research: Separating association from bias. *Clinical Psychology: Science and Practice*, 16, 54–65.

Lichter, S. Haye, K., & Kammann, R. (1980). Increasing happiness through cognitive retraining. *New Zealand Psychologist*, 9, 57–64.

Lightsey, O. R. (2006). Resilience, meaning, and well-being. *The Counseling Psychologist*, 34, 96–107.

Linley, P. A., Nielsen, K. M., Gillett, R., & Biswas-Diener, R. (2010). Using signature strengths in pursuit of goals: Effects on goal progress, need satisfaction, and well-being, and implications for coaching psychologists. *International Coaching Psychology Review*, 5, 6–15.

Lampropoulos, G. K. (2001). Integrating psychopathology, positive psychology, and psychotherapy. *American Psychologist*, 56, 87–88.

Luborsky, L., Crits-Cristoph, P., Alexander, L., Margolis, M., & Cohen, M. (1983). Two helping alliance methods for predicting outcomes of psychotherapy, a counting signs vs. a global rating method. *Journal of Nervous and Mental Disease*, 171, 480–491.

Lyubomirsky, S. (2008). *The how of happiness*. London, UK: Sphere.

Lyubomirsky, S., King, L. A., & Diener, E. (2005). The benefits of frequent positive affect: Does happiness lead to success? *Psychological Bulletin*, *131*, 803–855.

Magyar-Moe, J. L. (2009). *Therapist's guide to positive psychological interventions*. New York, NY: Elsevier Academic Press.

Maslow, A. H. (1968). *Toward a psychology of being* (2nd ed.). New York, NY: Van Nostrand.

McCormick, B. P., Funderburk, J. A., & Lee, Y. (2005). Activity characteristics and emotional experience: Predicting boredom and anxiety in the daily life of community mental health clients. *Journal of Leisure Research*, *37*, 236–253.

McKnight, P. E., & Kashdan, T. B. (2009). Purpose in life as a system that creates and sustains health and well-being: An integrative, testable theory. *Review of General Psychology*, *13*, 242–251.

Meyer, P. S., Johnson, D. P., Parks, A. C., Iwanski, C., & Penn, D. L. (2012). Positive living: A pilot study of group positive psychotherapy for people with schizophrenia. *Journal of Positive Psychology*, *7*, 239–248.

Nakamura, J., & Csikszentmihalyi, M. (2002). The concept of flow. In C. R. Snyder & S. J. Lopez (Eds.), *Handbook of positive psychology* (pp. 89–105). New York, NY: Oxford University Press.

Nolen-Hoeksema, S. (2000). The role of rumination in depressive disorders and mixed anxiety/depressive symptoms. *Journal of Abnormal Psychology*, *109*, 504–511.

Pennebaker, J. W. (1997). Writing about emotional experiences as a therapeutic process. *Psychological Science*, *8*, 162–166.

Peterson, C., & Seligman, M. E. P. (2004). *Character strengths and virtues: A handbook and classification*. New York, NY: Oxford University Press and Washington, DC: American Psychological Association.

Peterson, C., Park, N., & Seligman, M. E. (2005). Orientations to happiness and life satisfaction: The full life versus the empty life. *Journal of Happiness Studies*, *6*, 25–41.

Radloff, L. S. (1977). The CES-D scale: A self-report depression scale for research in the general population. *Applied Psychological Measurement*, *1*, 385–401.

Rashid, T., & Anjum, A. (2009). Positive Intervention. Paper presented at the First International Positive Psychology Association's Conference, Philadelphia, PA.

Rashid, T., & Ostermann, R. F. O. (2009). Strength-based assessment in clinical practice. *Journal of Clinical Psychology: In Session*, *65*, 488–498.

Rashid, T., & Anjum. A (2007). Positive psychotherapy for children and adolescents. In J. R. Z. Abela & B. L. Hankin (Eds.), *Depression in children and adolescents: Causes, treatment and prevention*. New York, NY: Guilford Press.

Rapaport, M. H., Clary, C., Fayyad, R., & Endicott, J. (2005). Quality of life impairment in depressive and anxiety disorders. *American Journal of Psychiatry*, *162*, 1171–1178.

Rogers, C. R. (1959). A theory of therapy, personality and interpersonal relationships, as developed in the client-centered framework. In S. Koch (Ed.), *Psychology: A study of a science: Vol. 3. Foundations of the person and the social context* (pp. 184–256). New York, NY: McGraw-Hill.

Rozin, P., & Royzman, E. B. (2001). Negativity bias, negativity dominance, and contagion. *Personality and Social Psychology Review*, *5*, 296–320.

Ruini C., Fava G. A. (2009). Well-being therapy for generalized anxiety disorder. *Journal of Clinical Psychology*, *65*, 510–519.

Schwartz, B., Monterosso, J., Lyubomirsky, S., White, K., & Lehman, D. R. (2002). Maximizing versus satisficing: Happiness is a matter of choice. *Journal of Personality and Social Psychology*, *83*, 1178–1197.

Schwartz, B., & Sharpe, K. E. (2006). Practical wisdom: Aristotle meets positive psychology. *Journal of Happiness Studies, 7*, 377–395.

Schwartz, R. M., Reynolds, C. F., III, Thase, M. E., Frank, E., Fasiczka, A. L., & Haaga, D. A. F. (2002). Optimal and normal affect balance in psychotherapy of major depression: Evaluation of the balanced states of mind model. *Behavioural and Cognitive Psychotherapy, 30*, 439–450.

Seligman, M. E. P. (2002). *Authentic happiness: Using the new Positive Psychology to realize your potential for lasting fulfillment.* New York, NY: Free Press.

Seligman, M. E. P., Rashid, T., & Parks, A. C. (2006). Positive psychotherapy. *American Psychologist, 61*, 774–788.

Seligman, M. E. P., Steen, T. A., Park, N., & Peterson, C. (2005). Positive psychology progress: Empirical validation of interventions. *American Psychologist, 60*, 410–421.

Sin, N. L., & Lyubomirsky, S. (2009). Enhancing well-being and alleviating depressive symptoms with positive psychology interventions: A practice-friendly meta-analysis. *Journal of Clinical Psychology: In Session, 65*, 467–487.

Smith, E. J. (2006). The strength-based counseling model. *The Counseling Psychologist, 34*, 13–79.

Steger, M. F., Kashdan, T. B., & Oishi, S. (2008). Being good by doing good: Daily eudaimonic activity and well-being. *Journal of Research in Personality, 42*, 22–42.

Stillman, T. F., & Baumeister, R. F. (2009). Uncertainty, belongingness, and four needs for meaning. *Psychological Inquiry, 20*, 249–251.

Vella-Brodrick, D. A., Park, N., & Peterson, C. (2009). Three ways to be happy: Pleasure, engagement, and meaning: Findings from Australian and US samples. *Social Indicators Research, 90*, 165–179.

Wong, W.J. (2006). Strength-centered therapy: A social constructionist, virtue-based psychotherapy. *Psychotherapy, 43*, 133–146.

Wrzesniewski, A., McCauley, C., Rozin, P., & Schwartz, B. (1997). Jobs, careers, and callings: People's relations to their work. *Journal of Research in Personality, 31*, 21–33.

# CHAPTER 74

# HAPPINESS IN VALUED LIVING: ACCEPTANCE AND COMMITMENT THERAPY AS A MODEL FOR CHANGE

### LOUISE HAYES

Orygen Youth Health Research Centre, The University of Melbourne, Australia

> The amount of happiness that you have depends on the amount of freedom you have in your heart.
>
> (Thich Nhat Hanh)

ACCEPTANCE and Commitment Therapy (ACT) has an ultimate goal of helping individuals to develop behaviors that service their deepest values, thereby bringing joy and meaning into life (S. C. Hayes, Strosahl, & Wilson, 1999). From an ACT perspective, happiness along with other emotions is seen as a transient state that is sensitive to the fluctuations of daily living. The question "Am I happy?" is viewed as incidental to valuing questions such as, "What do I want my life to stand for?"

The purpose of this chapter is to review how Acceptance and Commitment Therapy (referred to as "ACT" not the individual letters "A-C-T") can contribute to improving the human condition. Happiness and suffering go hand in hand with this. First, I provide an overview of the social context in which ACT was developed and outline the core assumptions of ACT theory and therapy. I then review research outcomes for adults, and lastly consider ACT approaches with younger people.

# A Discontented Culture as the Context for ACT

In Westernized cultures we face a constant pull to seek happiness. Popular media, such as TV and magazines, prompt individuals to find happiness, to compare their level of happiness to that of others, and to implement remedies if they are less happy than expected. This obsession with happiness is growing rapidly. In 2008, approximately 4000 books were published on happiness compared to a mere 50 in 2000 (Flora, 2009).

Paradoxically, as a society, this search for happiness by attempting to eliminate suffering has not made us happier. Epidemiological evidence points to remarkably high rates of distress. Twelve-month prevalence estimates from the USA show that a staggering one in four people met criteria for a DSM-IV (*Diagnostic and Statistical Manual of Mental Disorders*, Fourth Edition) Axis I disorder (Kessler, Berglund, Demler, Jin, Merikangas, & Walters, 2005). Almost half these people were reported to have more than one disorder, and for over half, this disorder was moderate to severe. These data are based on diagnosed DSM-IV disorders only. If we add to this those problems that are not attributable to mental illness, then the full breadth of suffering becomes clearer. For example, in developed countries the leading causes of disease burden comes from lifestyle factors including alcohol and tobacco use, and obesity related illnesses (Ezzati, et al., 2002). Divorce, which was virtually non-existent 100 years ago, is now estimated to occur in 32% of marriages (Hewitt, Baxter, & Western, 2005). Workplace stress in the USA has been described as so commonplace that if you are *not* stressed there is a perception that you are not working hard enough (Peterson & Wilson, 2004). One can only conclude from these data that suffering is ubiquitous in Western society.

We have tended to respond to this distress by attempting to inoculate our children and young people from suffering. The assumption seems to be that if we can teach children to control "negative" emotions early in their life cycle, we will see lower rates of distress in adulthood. The results suggest that this strategy is not working. For example, a large sample epidemiological study ($N = 9863$) reported rates of depression of around 18% for school-based young people (Saluja et al., 2004), whilst a study of 26,000 university students in the USA indicated that suicidal thoughts were present for more than 50% of students, with 15% reporting serious consideration of suicide and 5% at least one suicide attempt (Drum, Brownson, Denmark, & Smith, 2009). School prevention programs are not reliably achieving long-term reductions in psychological distress (Merry et al., 2004).

This evidence for adults and young people indicates that unhappiness is not something that happens to "other people." We suffer. Additionally, often the happiness we envy in others is illusory. That is, we simply may not be able to see that they are also suffering.

The founders of ACT (S. C. Hayes et al., 1999) argue that Westernized assumptions that happiness is normal and distress is abnormal are indefensible. They contend that the medical model of disease (where the absence of disease represents physical health), has been generalized into a psychological science where the absence of distress equates to psychological well-being. They further argue that epidemiological data shows this to be a flawed assumption, one that has negatively impacted psychology's contribution to the understanding of human well-being.

ACT represents an alternative to the disease model. It considers language to be both central to understanding the Western pursuit of happiness and the source of universal suffering (S. C. Hayes et al., 1999). The central tenet of ACT is that only humans have language and only humans can suffer when no physical stimuli are present to cause distress. For example, whilst an animal will not be distressed if its needs for food, warmth, and shelter are met, humans can have an abundance of material wealth and be completely miserable. We use our language skills to predict the future, to worry about the past, and with regard to happiness, to compare ours to the happiness of others. These authors argue that we can understand language through a basic science of verbal behavior and that in doing so we can learn to use language without being trapped in it (S. C. Hayes et al., 1999).

ACT (S. C. Hayes et al., 1999) is one of a family of behavior therapies that includes dialectical behavior therapy (Linehan, 1993) and functional-analytic psychotherapy (Kohlenberg et al., 2005). As a therapeutic approach, ACT has mutual connections in the scientific laboratories of behavior analysts and is developing from both clinic and laboratory based work. It is grounded in a theory of verbal behavior called relational frame theory (RFT; S. C. Hayes, Barnes-Holmes, & Roche, 2001) and rests on clearly articulated philosophical assumptions of functional contextualism (FC). To understand ACT it is necessary to consider the theoretical and philosophical assumptions as well as the clinical model.

# Relational Frame Theory—A Theory of Verbal Behavior as the Foundation for ACT

RFT is the theory of human language and cognition upon which ACT was developed (S. C. Hayes, Barnes-Holmes, & Roche, 2001; S. C. Hayes, Strosahl, Bunting, Twohig, & Wilson, 2004). Whilst a detailed account of RFT is beyond the scope of this chapter (for a detailed discussion of RFT see Blackledge, 2003; S. C. Hayes, et al., 2001; Ramnerö & Törneke, 2008), an explanation of the basic concept of "relating" is helpful for linking the philosophy, theory, and therapy.

Whilst RFT has roots in Skinnerian operant conditioning and its core principles of reinforcement, punishment, and extinction, it builds upon it by adding the newly argued principle of verbal behavior—*arbitrarily applicable derived relational responding* (S. C. Hayes et al., 2001). To help clarify the meaning of the term, Table 74.1 outlines both a definition and a clinical example of how this verbal behavior can manifest itself in the school life of an adolescent (Sarah) with lowered mood and a history of being bullied.

Sarah's case shows how relational framing shapes subjective experience within the context of personal history through multiple exemplar training. Sarah made sense of her experience relationally, based on its contextual qualities, and transferred the stimulus function from her previous experiences of bullying to this new situation. The stimulus functions as a punishment because her social interactions are reduced. Two important caveats should be noted however. First, in any behavioral account, a functional assessment would be required, with behavior assessed contingently by considering antecedent, behavior and consequence. Second, her behavior would be considered arbitrary only if she has never

Table 74.1 Arbitrarily applicable derived relational responding: a definition and clinical example

| Term | Definition[a] | Example |
|---|---|---|
| | | Sarah reports to her therapist that when she walked past some kids at school today they stopped talking and she "knows" they think she is a "loser" and they do not like her |
| Arbitrarily applicable | Incoming stimuli are related to other stimuli through personal histories rather than any formal properties of the stimuli | Sarah's conclusions are *arbitrary* because there are no formal properties relating the ceased conversation to her conclusion. The notion is arbitrarily based on her verbal/social history |
| Derived | Humans use inference rather than direct experience | Sarah has *derived* from the ceased conversation that the kids do not like her |
| Relational responding | Humans relate stimuli in order to group the stream of incoming information from the environment into previously established relational networks | She has *related* their ceased conversation as equivalent to her previous experiences of bullying |

[a]Data from Bach and Moran (2008).

experienced a conversation stopping as she walked past (if she has, then her behavior is contingently controlled).

Findings from a rapidly expanding RFT research program are indicating that relational responding develops with language, is evident in early infancy (Lipkens, Hayes, & Hayes, 1993), and that children with delayed language abilities (as seen in autism) also display delayed relational responding. In addition, early intervention programs for children with developmental delays are showing that these basic language skills can be trained (Cairns, 2009) and that the cognitive components of some psychological disorders are also responsive to RFT training (Bach & Hayes, 2002).

# FUNCTIONAL CONTEXTUALISM— THE PHILOSOPHICAL FOUNDATION OF ACT

Functional contextualism (S. C. Hayes, 1993) is a philosophical worldview that is important to describe here because it is the psychological space in which ACT treatment occurs. It is perhaps easiest to understand FC by contrasting it with a mechanistic view, simply because the mechanistic view dominates our explanations of human functioning, particularly biological functioning. This does not imply that one worldview is superior to another.

From a mechanistic viewpoint, healthy functioning is seen when an individual reports happiness and satisfaction with life. At a clinical level one would look for an absence of pathological thinking and perhaps an affirmative answer to the question, "Are you happy?" In this worldview, cognitions are equated with the metaphor of a computer or machine and when a person is suffering there is a 'part' to be fixed in order to correct the problem. This mechanistic view is clearly evident in depression theories and treatments. For example, Beck postulated that schema were 'cognitive structures within the mind" (Beck, 1995, p. 166) and argued that depression occurs because people hold negative schemas of the self, world and future (Weersing & Brent, 2006). For Beck cognitions such as "I must win" are considered false beliefs, automatic thoughts, or defective schema (Persons, 2001) and should be replaced with new more rational ones such as "I would like to win" (Bach & Moran, 2008, p. 33). According to this view, thoughts are causes of feelings or behaviors, with irrational thoughts leading to negatively evaluated feelings and dysfunctional behavior. When thoughts are "corrected" it is presumed that feelings and behavior will also improve.

By way of contrast, in a functional contextualist worldview, suffering or unhappiness can be seen as either normal or problematic, depending on the context in which they occur. The act-in-context is the subject matter and therefore thoughts are not viewed as faulty, nor are they viewed as causes of behaviors or emotions (Ciarrochi, Robb, & Godsell, 2005). The target of change from this worldview is the *function* of thoughts—the thoughts themselves may or may not change. The underlying premise is one of pragmatism. There is no "right" solution, only solutions that will work for an individual (S. C. Hayes, Luoma, Bond, Masudam, & Lillis, 2004). Successful working is the goal and this is achieved when the individual attains valued living and achieves desired goals, which may or may not include feeling unhappy or having unhappy thoughts (Bach & Moran, 2008).

To summarize, from a theoretical and philosophical view, the assumption behind ACT is that wellness cannot be defined by an absence of suffering or unhappiness. Taking RFT as a theory of language, the goal is to use operant principles with a newly argued principle of verbal behavior (i.e. "relating") to effect more flexible verbal behavior. Additionally, ACT utilizes functional contextualism to help describe, predict, and influence behavior in the historical and situational context in which the individual interacts. With this understanding I will now focus on ACT as a psychological approach to change.

# The ACT Model for Creating Change in Human Behavior

ACT is a model for behavior change with six key processes. The aim of ACT is to increase psychological flexibility, which is: "the ability to contact the present moment more fully as a conscious human being, and to change or persist in behavior when doing so serves valued ends" (S. C. Hayes et al. 2006, p. 7). Notably, ACT does not aim to eliminate suffering or to eliminate negative cognitions.

The ACT model is most commonly depicted using two hexagons (see Figs 74.1 and 74.2). Fig. 74.1 depicts the model of psychological distress and its six core processes that contribute to psychological inflexibility. The model of psychological wellness is shown in Fig. 74.2 and depicts the six opposite processes that contribute to psychological flexibility.

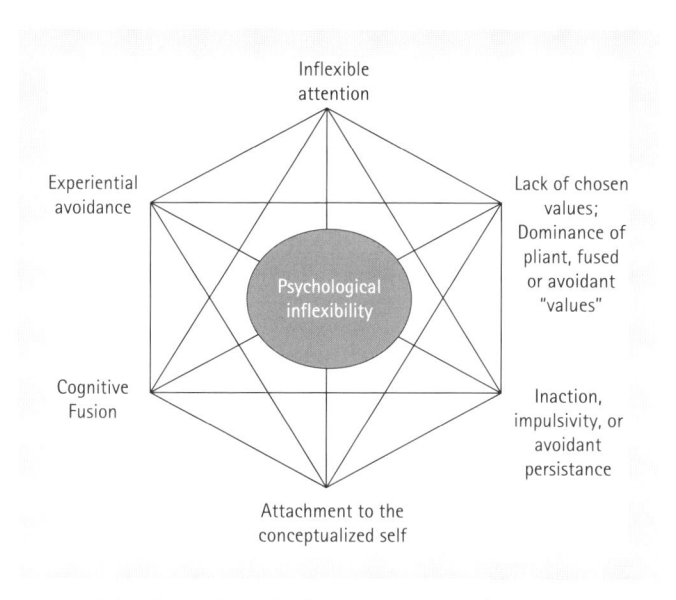

FIG. 74.1 ACT model of psychopathology. Reprinted from *Behaviour Research and Therapy*, 44 (1), Steven C. Hayes, Jason B. Luoma, Frank W. Bond, Akihiko Masuda, and Jason Lillis, Acceptance and Commitment Therapy: Model, processes and outcomes, pp. 1–25, Copyright (2006), with permission from Elsevier.

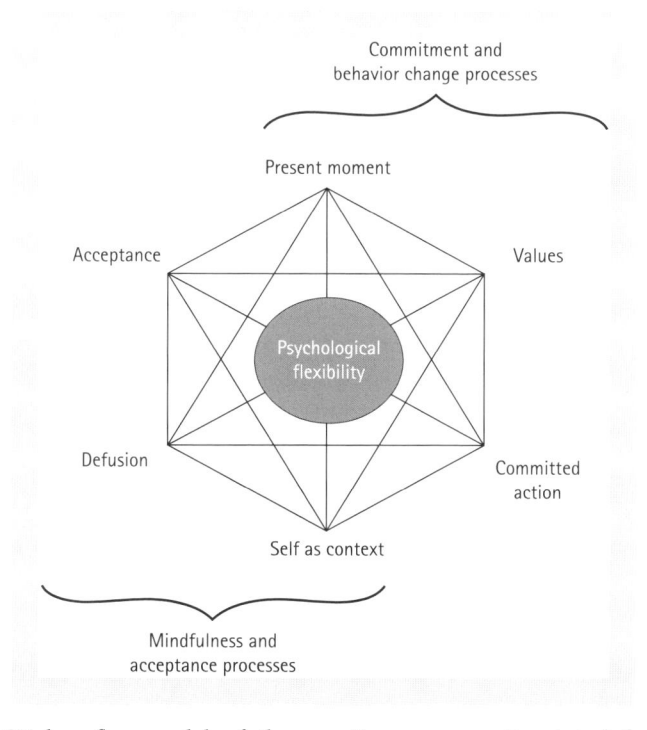

FIG. 74.2 ACT hexaflex model of therapeutic processes. Reprinted from *Behaviour Research and Therapy*, 44 (1), Steven C. Hayes, Jason B. Luoma, Frank W. Bond, Akihiko Masuda, and Jason Lillis, Acceptance and Commitment Therapy: Model, processes and outcomes, pp. 1–25, Copyright (2006), with permission from Elsevier.

Although each process will be described separately it should be noted that the six processes are overlapping rather than discrete. In practice, clinicians use experiential techniques to expand an individual's behavioral repertoire, ranging from metaphor, behavioral experiments, or physicalizing exercises. One strength of ACT is that the theory and model are clearly articulated. This is helpful because it allows therapists to create exercises (often spontaneously) in response to the behavioral change needs of clients. Fortunately, too many exercises and experiences have already been developed for use with a variety of client groups (Bach & Moran, 2008; Harris, 2007; S. C. Hayes & Smith, 2005; Strosahl & Robinson, 2008). As presented in Fig. 74.2, the ACT model begins with a functional assessment of the presenting problems.

## Avoidance versus acceptance

A wealth of empirical evidence shows that avoidance is a key factor in psychological problems (Foa, McNally, Steketee, & McCarthy, 1991; Zinbarg, Barlow, Brown, & Hertz, 1992). Avoidance is evident when an individual is unwilling to remain in contact with difficult private experiences or steps are taken to avoid the contexts in which they occur (S. C. Hayes et al., 1999). The ACT model proposes that acceptance is the alternative to avoidance. Component studies show that increased acceptance is associated with reductions in avoidance and improvements in quality of life (Eifert & Heffner, 2003; Levitt et al., 2004; Vowles et al., 2007). Clinically, acceptance is developed through willingness to have experiences. This involves exposure to difficult thoughts and feelings, including contrasting the paradoxical effects of pushing thoughts away with the experience of willingly accepting these difficult experiences and engaging in meaningful value driven behavior. Individuals are encouraged to take steps toward valued behavior even though distress may be present.

## Cognitive fusion versus cognitive defusion

Fusion occurs when thoughts become related to distressing stimuli. In ACT, thoughts and feelings are understood as being cumulative and contextually controlled, and therefore difficult to dismantle. Suppression of difficult thoughts has been shown to be ineffective, with greater suppression relating to higher dysfunction (Marcks & Woods, 2005, 2007). Thus, defusion techniques in ACT do not aim to stop difficult cognitions or override them with positive thinking. Rather an individual is encouraged to experience thoughts for what they are—symbols of one's history. Returning to the example of Sarah (see Table 74.1), the thought "I am a loser" is a thought that cannot be erased. She simply cannot have the experience of never having had that thought. Therefore, in certain contexts the thought "I am a loser" will arise. However, it is her behavioral response to her thought that causes the distress, not the thought as such. Defusion techniques aim to help clients notice that thoughts are symbols of history rather than descriptions of reality.

## Dominance of the conceptualized past or feared future versus contact with the present moment

ACT contrasts the suffering that arises when an individual spends more time thinking about the past or fearing the future (i.e. living in their heads), rather than living in the present moment. This is most evident with worrying and rumination. ACT helps individuals experience living in the present in a way that allows them to contrast it with the experience of worrying and ruminating about the past or future. To assist with this, a range of mindfulness techniques are used in ACT, with many adapted from other mindfulness-based interventions (for examples see, S. C. Hayes, 2004; Kabat-Zinn, 2005; Segal, Teasdale, & Williams, 2004). The direct experience of mindfulness becomes reinforcing and may elicit other behaviors that facilitate moving in valued directions.

## Self-as-content versus self-as-context

The processes entitled self-as-content versus self-as-context, can be confusing for people learning the ACT model. Self-as-content describes the conceptualized self, which is evident in the descriptors, labels, and images that an individual constructs (e.g., "I am right", or, "I am worthless"). In ACT when one is too attached to these conceptualizations they take on a regulatory role, reducing flexibility and inhibiting behavior (S. C. Hayes, Luoma, Bond, Masuda, & Lillis, 2006). ACT approaches this by using experiences that help an individual to gain perspective on this process and to experience their "self" as the context in which all thoughts and behaviors arise. In other words, their thoughts come and go, but they are not their thoughts. Mindfulness exercises are central here in creating an experience of this transcendent nature of the self. A common metaphor is the chessboard, where thoughts and other content are black and white chess pieces and the individual the unchanging chess board—able to hold all their experiences, thoughts and feelings (metaphor adapted from S. C. Hayes et al. (1999)).

## Lack of values clarity versus valued living

Values work is the heart of ACT. Values work is where clients find meaning and purpose— which the ACT sees as taking precedence over the transient emotion of happiness. Eliciting deep-seated values can provide the motivation needed for behavior change and build the willingness to experience unwanted thoughts and feelings that might accompany valued action. The model purports that lack of valued living, unclear values, and rigid verbal behavior ("I should do X …") are all evidence of psychological inflexibility (S. C. Hayes et al., 2006). These behaviors share a commonality in that they all pull the client away from behavior that is self-fulfilling. For example, an individual who shows excessive pliance would behave in socially expected ways in order to please the peer group, rather than behave in ways that are personally meaningful.

Experiential exercises are often used to make explicit how valued actions are the outcome of interest. The *Skiing Metaphor* is reproduced here as an example of how valued living can become overt:

> Suppose you go skiing. You take a lift to the top of a hill, and you are just about to ski down the hill when a man comes along and asks where you are going. "I'm going to the lodge at the bottom," you reply. He says, "I can help you with that," and promptly grabs you, throws you into a helicopter, flies you to the lodge, and disappears. So you look around kind of dazed, take a lift to the top of the hill, and you are just about to ski down it when that same man grabs you, throws you into the helicopter, and flies you to the lodge. You'd be upset, no? Skiing is not just the goal of getting to the lodge, because any number of activities can accomplish that for us. Skiing is how we are going to get there. You notice that getting to the lodge is

important because it allows us to do the process of skiing in a direction. If I tried to ski uphill instead of down, it wouldn't work. Valuing down over up is necessary in downhill skiing. There is a way to say this: outcome is the process through which process can become the outcome. We need goals, but we need to hold them lightly so that the real point of living and having goals can emerge (S. C. Hayes et al., 1999, p. 220)

## Inaction, impulsivity, or avoidant persistence versus committed action

ACT purports that individuals who are psychologically inflexible behave impulsively, have difficulty taking goal-directed action, and fail to keep commitments or avoid setting goals at all. In contrast, psychologically flexible individuals are able to take committed action that takes them in valued directions. Committed action includes standard behavioral techniques such as behavioral activation, skills training, and goal setting. The ACT therapist engages clients in values work as the driving force to commit to action. From there, basic behavioral interventions would be used, including small action changes, setting goals, and weekly homework.

# Research Investigating the ACT Model

Research testing the ACT model includes: (1) correlational studies that examine the processes in the model, (2) clinical treatment studies, and (3) outcome studies conducted in non-clinical settings (such as organizations, health and education contexts) where the focus is not on the treatment of mental illness (for a comprehensive review, see S. C. Hayes et al. (2006)). A short summary will now be presented.

In a meta-analysis of 32 studies with 6,628 participants, S. C. Hayes et al. (2006) found support for the underlying principles of ACT with adult samples. In this analysis psychological flexibility was associated with improved quality of life and life outcomes. Inflexibility has also been correlated with poorer mental health (Bond & Bunce, 2000, 2003; Donaldson-Feilder & Bond, 2004).

Outcome research with adults has shown that ACT is trans-diagnostic and can achieve positive long-term outcomes for depression, anxiety, psychosis, chronic pain, work stress, stigma, and burnout (S. C. Hayes et al., 2006; S. C. Hayes, Masuda, Bissett, Luoma, & Guerrero, 2004). In a review of 21 studies (S. C. Hayes et al., 2006) the weighted mean effect size was 0.66 at post-treatment ($N = 704$) and this was maintained at follow-up (ES = 0.66, $N = 519$). In addition, large post-treatment effect sizes (ES = 0.48, $N = 456$) have been reported for ACT in comparison to control groups with active well-specified treatments, effects that continued to improve through to follow-up (ES = 0.63, $N = 404$; S. C. Hayes et al., 2006).

With regard to outcome studies in non-clinical settings, ACT has been shown to improve well-being and general health in organizational contexts, where it is generally relabeled as Acceptance and Commitment Training, rather than therapy. The aim is to improve well-being, as evidenced by increased psychological flexibility. To test this effect in the workplace, Bond & Bunce (2000) used an experimental design and compared ACT with an alternative workplace intervention and a control group. They found that changes in workplace outcomes were mediated by increases in psychological flexibility, as seen by acceptance of undesirable thoughts and feelings (Bond & Bunce, 2000). Other studies have shown that counselors trained in ACT have reported lower rates of burnout (S. C. Hayes, Bissett, et al., 2004).

In health settings, ACT has also been shown to be an effective treatment. There is strong evidence for chronic pain treatment showing improvement in life satisfaction and less pain disability in adult and paediatric populations (Vowles & McCracken, 2010; Wicksell, Ahlqvist, Bring, Melin, & Olsson, 2008; Wicksell, Melin, Lekander, & Olsson, 2009; Wicksell, Melin, & Olsson, 2007). Positive findings have also been shown for management of chronic illness, including diabetes management (Gregg, Callaghan, Hayes, & Glenn-Lawson, 2007), epilepsy (Lundgren, Dahl, Yardi, & Melin, 2008), obesity and weight management (Forman, Butryn, Hoffman, & Herbert, 2009; S. C. Hayes et al., 1999), and cigarette smoking (Bricker, Mann, Marek, Liu, & Peterson, 2010).

Mediational analyses to test the process of change in ACT treatment work shows that ACT processes mediate the changes seen in therapy (Ciarrochi, Bilich, & Godsel, 2010). Many studies shave shown that post-test improvements in outcomes are mediated by psychological flexibility also measured at post-test. However, the strongest evidence of mediation is shown in studies where changes in flexibility precede changes in outcome. For example, using the Zettle and Hayes (1986) data on depression to test for mediation, S. C. Hayes et al. (2006) found that the believability of depressive thoughts taken mid-treatment were predictive of significantly different treatment outcomes for ACT when compared with CT.

## Changing Our Culture—Can ACT Help Future Generations?

Although it is a tall order, a task of psychology is to reduce suffering in future generations. It seems appropriate therefore to consider whether ACT might contribute meaningfully to this goal.

Adolescent studies are encouraging although more are needed. Empirical work on psychological inflexibility in adolescents (two samples, $N = 513$ and $N = 675$) has shown that inflexibility is positively correlated with clinical measures of anxiety, somatization, and behavior problems, and negatively correlated with quality of life, social skills and academic competence (Greco, Lambert, & Baer, 2008). With regard to treatment studies, Wicksell and colleagues trialed ACT on adolescents with chronic pain across two studies, a randomized controlled trial (RCT) (Wicksell et al., 2009) and an earlier pilot study (Wicksell et al., 2007) and found that ACT treatment resulted in significant improvements in functional ability, pain intensity, and pain-related discomfort. Finally, L. Hayes, Boyd, and Sewell (2011) also found positive results for ACT with adolescents in a randomized study comparing ACT to treatment as usual for depression in a psychiatric setting. With regard to intervention in schools, the one completed RCT, compared ACT to passive control with adolescents and showed significantly improved outcomes up to 2 years later on measures of stress and psychological flexibility (Livheim, 2004), and one study has also found ACT to be effective for group work with adolescents (L. Hayes, Rowse, & Turner, 2009). Although these results with young people are preliminary, future ACT research is likely to focus on prevention and early intervention for children and adolescents.

## Conclusion

Epidemiological data show that psychological distress is a significant problem in developed countries and that reducing the prevalence of distress at a population level is daunting. ACT may be a valuable approach for working with human suffering and unhappiness. ACT has philosophical foundations that emphasize the function of behaviors, and is based on a theory of verbal behavior that continues to be vigorously tested in laboratory studies. As a therapeutic and training model, ACT aims to develop psychological flexibility and encourage individuals to move in valued directions in life rather than wait until their unhappiness is resolved. Recent outcome and mediational studies suggest that psychological flexibility can be enhanced with ACT treatments and produce sustainable effects.

Perhaps the greatest strength of ACT comes from its comprehensive approach, where researchers and clinicians are working together across science and clinical applications. Although work on the model began more than 20 years ago, the past 10 years have seen an explosion in ACT and RFT work across the world with over 40 books published in nine languages and a wealth of empirical studies. This work is underpinned by a philosophical approach whereby human suffering is seen as part of the human condition. Developing greater psychological flexibility can help individuals to live with their difficult experiences as well as increase value-directed living. In this way, perhaps targeting our efforts toward helping people to increase meaning and value in their lives will result in wider societal changes. This demands that happiness is relegated to its rightful place, as an emotion that is pleasant but transient.

## Recommendations for Practitioners

- ACT is a comprehensive model of treatment that can be flexibly used where human suffering is evident. The model is transdiagnostic and useful in clinical and non-clinical settings.
- The breadth of research and treatment material for ACT is extensive. An online learning and research community can be found at the Association of Contextual Psychology website (http://www.contextualpsychology.org). This is a good place to explore the ACT literature, published books and articles, and practice materials.
- Many new practitioners find that ACT comes to life when they experience the model in ACT workshops. Written texts, used as the only means to learn ACT, may fall short in providing powerful behavioral experiences.
- ACT practitioners are encouraged to see how the model works in their own lives. The underlying assumption of the model is that we all suffer—practitioners and clients alike—and we can find greater meaning in life when we tune into our experience.

# References

Bach, P., & Hayes, S. C. (2002). The use of acceptance and commitment therapy to prevent the rehospitalisation of psychotic patients: A randomised controlled trial. *Journal of Consulting and Clinical Psychology, 70* (5), 1129–1139.

Bach, P. A., & Moran, D. J. (2008). *ACT in practice: Case conceptualizations in acceptance and commitment therapy*. Oakland, CA: New Harbinger.

Beck, J. S. (1995). *Cognitive therapy*. New York, NY: The Guilford Press.

Blackledge, J. T. (2003). An introduction to relational frame theory: Basics and applications. *The Behavior Analyst Today, 3*(4), 421–433.

Bond, F. W., & Bunce, D. (2000). Mediators of change in emotion-focused and problem-focused worksite stress management interventions. *Journal of Occupational Health Psychology, 5,* 156–163.

Bond, F. W., & Bunce, D. (2003). The role of acceptance and job control in mental-health, job satisfaction, and work performance. *Journal of Applied Psychology, 88*(6), 1057–1067.

Bricker, J. B., Mann, S. L., Marek, P. M., Liu, J., & Peterson, A. V. (2010). Telephone-delivered acceptance and commitment therapy for adult smoking cessation: A feasibility study. *Nicotine and Tobacco Research, 12*(4), 1–5.

Cairns, D. (2009). Raising a flexible, adaptive & empowered child: Applications of RFT in child development. 3rd Australian and New Zealand Conference on Acceptance and Commitment Therapy (ACT). Melbourne, 2009.

Ciarrochi, J., Bilich, L., & Godsel, C. (2010). Psychological flexibility as a mechanism of change in acceptance and commitment therapy. In R. Baer (Ed.), *Assessing mindfulness and acceptance: Illuminating the processes of change* (pp. 51–76). Oakland, CA: New Harbinger Publications, Inc.

Ciarrochi, J., Robb, H., & Godsell, C. (2005). Letting a little non-verbal air into the room: Insights from acceptance and commitment therapy Part 1: Philosophical and theoretical underpinnings. *Journal of Rational-Emotive and Cognitive Behavior Therapy, 23*(2), 79–106.

Donaldson-Feilder, E. J., & Bond, F. W. (2004). The relative importance of psychological acceptance and emotional intelligence to workplace well-being. *British Journal of Guidance and Counselling, 32*(2), 187–203.

Eifert, G. H., & Heffner, M. (2003). The effects of acceptance versus control contexts on avoidance of panic-related symptoms. *Journal of Behavior Therapy and Experimental Psychiatry, 34,* 293–312.

Ezzati, M., Lopez, A. D., Rodgers, A., Vander Hoorn, S., Murray, C. J. L., & Comparative Risk Assessment Collaborating Group. (2002). Selected major risk factors and global and regional burden of disease. *The Lancet, 360,* 1347–1360.

Flora, C. (2009, January). The pursuit of happiness. *Psychology Today*. Retrieved from http://psychologytoday.com/magazine/

Foa, E. B., McNally, R. J., Steketee, G. S., & McCarthy, P. R. (1991). A test of preparedness theory in anxiety-disordered patients using an avoidance paradigm. *Journal of Psychophysiology, 5*(2), 159–163.

Forman, E. M., Butryn, M. L., Hoffman, K. L., & Herbert, J. D. (2009). An open trial of an acceptance-based behavioral intervention for weight loss. *Cognitive and Behavioral Practice, 16*(2), 223–235.

Greco, L. A., Lambert, W., & Baer, R. A. (2008). Psychological inflexibility in childhood and adolescence: Development and evaluation of the Avoidance and Fusion Questionnaire for Youth. *Psychological Assessment, 20*(2), 93–102.

Gregg, J. A., Callaghan, G. M., Hayes, S. C., & Glenn-Lawson, J. L. (2007). Improving diabetes self-management through acceptance, mindfulness, and values: A randomized controlled trial. *Journal of Consulting and Clinical Psychology, 75*(2), 336–343.

Harris, R. (2007). *The happiness trap: Stop struggling and start living.* Wollombi, Australia: Exisle.

Hayes, L., Boyd, C., & Sewell, J. (2011). Acceptance and commitment therapy for the treatment of adolescent depression: A pilot study in a psychiatric outpatient setting. *Mindfulness, 2*(2), 86–94.

Hayes, L., Rowse, J., & Turner, S. (2009). *Acceptance and Commitment Therapy as depression treatment for adolescents.* Retrieved from http://www.beyondblue.org.au/index.aspx?link_id=6.713

Hayes, S. C. (1993). Analytic goals and the varieties of scientific contextualism. In S. C. Hayes, L. J. Hayes, H. W. Reese & T. R. Sarbin (Eds.), *Varieties of scientific contextualism* (pp. 11–27). Reno, NV: Context Press.

Hayes, S. C. (Ed.). (2004). *Acceptance and commitment therapy and the new behaviour therapies: Mindfulness, acceptance and relationship.* New York, NY: Guilford Press.

Hayes, S. C., Barnes-Holmes, D., & Roche, B. (Eds.). (2001). *Relational frame theory: A post skinnerian account of human language and cognition.* New York, NY: Kluwer Academic.

Hayes, S. C., Bissett, R., Roget, N., Padilla, M., Kohlenberg, B. S., & Fisher, G. (2004). The impact of acceptance and commitment training on stigmatizing attitudes and professional burnout of substance abuse counselors. *Behavior Therapy, 35*, 821–836.

Hayes, S. C., Luoma, J. B., Bond, F. W., Masuda, A., & Lillis, J. (2006). Acceptance and commitment therapy: Model, processes and outcomes. *Behaviour Research and Therapy, 44*(1), 1–25.

Hayes, S. C., Masuda, A., Bissett, R., Luoma, J., & Guerrero, L. F. (2004). DBT, FAP, and ACT: How empirically oriented are the new behavior therapy technologies? *Behavior Therapy, 35*, 35–54.

Hayes, S. C., & Smith, S. (2005). *Get out of your mind and into your life.* Oakland, CA: New Harbinger.

Hayes, S. C., Strosahl, K. D., Bunting, K., Twohig, M., & Wilson, K. G. (2004). What is acceptance and commitment therapy? In S. C. Hayes & K. D. Strosahl (Eds.), *Practical guide to acceptance and commitment therapy* (pp. 3–29). New York, NY: Springer Verlag.

Hayes, S. C., Strosahl, K. D., & Wilson, K. G. (1999). *Acceptance and commitment therapy: An experiential approach to behavior change.* New York, NY: The Guilford Press.

Hewitt, B., Baxter, J., & Western, M. (2005). Marriage breakdown in Australia. *Journal of Sociology, 41*(2), 163–183.

Kabat-Zinn, J. (2005). *Full catastrophe living: Using the wisdom of your body and mind to face stress, pain, and illness: Fifteenth anniversary edition.* New York, NY: Delta Trade Paperback/Bantam Dell.

Kessler, R. C., Berglund, P., Demler, O., Jin, R., Merikangas, K. R., Walters, E. E. (2005). Lifetime prevalence and age-of-onset distributions of *DSM-IV* disorders in the National Comorbidity Survey Replication. *Archives of General Psychiatry, 62*, 593–602.

Kohlenberg, R. J., Tsai, M., Garcia, R. F., Aguayo, L. V., Parra, A. F., & Virues-Ortega, J. (2005). Functional-analytic psychotherapy and acceptance and commitment therapy: Theory, applications and its relationships with traditional behavior analysis. *International Journal of Clinical and Health Psychology, 5*(2), 349–371.

Levitt, J. T., Brown, T. A., Orsillo, S. M., & Barlow, D. H. (2004). The effects of acceptance versus suppression of emotion on subjective and psychophysiological response to carbon dioxide challenge in patients with panic disorder. *Behavior Therapy*, 35, 747–766.

Linehan, M. M. (1993). *Cognitive-behavioral treatment of borderline personality disorder*. New York, NY: Guilford.

Lipkens, G., Hayes, S. C., & Hayes, L. J. (1993). Longitudinal study of derived stimulus relations in an infant. *Journal of Experimental Child Psychology*, 56, 201–239.

Livheim, F. (2004). *Acceptance and commitment therapy in schools to cope with stress and promote health: A randomized controlled trial*. Uppsala, Sweden: University of Uppsala.

Lundgren, T., Dahl, J., Yardi, N., & Melin, J. (2008). Acceptance and commitment therapy and yoga for drug refractory: A randomized controlled trial. *Epilepsy and Behavior*, 13(1), 102–108.

Marcks, B. A., & Woods, D. W. (2005). A comparison of thought expression to an acceptance-based technique in the management of personal intrusive thoughts: A controlled evaluation. *Behaviour Research and Therapy*, 43, 433–445.

Marcks, B. A., & Woods, D. W. (2007). Role of thought-related beliefs and coping strategies in the escalation of intrusive thoughts: An analog to obsessive-compulsive disorder. *Behaviour Research and Therapy*, 45, 2640–2651.

Merry, S., McDowell, H., Hetrick, S., Bir, J., & Muller, N. (2004). Psychological and/or educational interventions for the prevention of depression in children and adolescents. *The Cochrane Database of Systematic Reviews 2004, Issue 2*.

Persons, J. B. (2001). *Essential components of cognitive-behavioral therapy for depression*. Washington DC: American Psychological Association.

Peterson, M., & Wilson, J. F. (2004). Work stress in America. *International Journal of Stress Management*, 11(2), 91–113.

Ramnerö, J., & Törneke, N. (2008). *The ABCs of human behavior: Behavioral principles for the practicing clinician*. Oakland, CA: New Harbinger Publications, Inc.

Saluja, G., Iachan, R., Scheidt, P. C., Overpeck, M. D., Sun, W., & Giedd, J. N. (2004). Prevalence of and risk factors for depressive symptoms among young adolescents. *Archives of Pediatrics & Adolescent Medicine*, 158(8), 760–765.

Segal, A. V., Teasdale, J. D., & Williams, J. M. G. (2004). Mindfulness-based cognitive therapy: Theoretical rationale and empirical status. In S. C. Hayes, V. M. Follette & M. M. Linehan (Eds.), *Mindfulness and acceptance: Expanding the cognitive-behavioral tradition* (pp. 45–65). New York, NY: The Guilford Press.

Strosahl, K. D., & Robinson, P. J. (2008). *The mindfulness and acceptance workbook for depression: Using Acceptance and Commitment Therapy to move through depression and create a life worth living*. Oakland, CA: New Harbinger.

Vowles, K. E., & McCracken, L. M. (2010). Comparing the influence of psychological flexibility and traditional pain management coping strategies on chronic pain treatment outcomes. *Behaviour Research and Therapy*, 48(2), 141–146.

Vowles, K. E., McNeil, D. W., Gross, R. T., McDaniel, M. L., Mouse, A., Bates, M., ... McCall, C. (2007). Effects of pain acceptance and pain control strategies on physical impairment in individuals with chronic low back pain. *Behavior Therapy*, 38(4), 412–425.

Weersing, V. R., & Brent, D. A. (2006). Cognitive behavioral therapy for depression in youth. *Child and Adolescent Psychiatric Clinics of North America*, 15(4), 939–957.

Wicksell, R., Ahlqvist, J., Bring, A., Melin, L., & Olsson, G. L. (2008). Can exposure and acceptance strategies improve functioning and life satisfaction in people with chronic pain and whiplash-associated disorders (WAD)? A randomized controlled trial. *Cognitive Behaviour Therapy, 37*(3), 1–14.

Wicksell, R., Melin, L., Lekander, M., & Olsson, G. (2009). Evaluating the effectiveness of exposure and acceptance strategies to improve functioning and quality of life in longstanding pediatric pain: A randomized controlled trial. *Pain, 141*, 248–257.

Wicksell, R., Melin, L., & Olsson, G. (2007). Exposure and acceptance in the rehabilitation of adolescents with idiopathic chronic pain: A pilot study. *European Journal of Pain, 11*(3), 267–274.

Zettle, R. D., & Hayes, S. C. (1986). Dysfunctional control by client verbal behaviour: The context of reason giving. *The Analysis of Verbal Behavior, 4*, 30–38.

Zinbarg, R. E., Barlow, D. H., Brown, T. A., & Hertz, R. M. (1992). Cognitive-behavioral approaches to the nature and treatment of anxiety disorders. *Annual Review of Psychology, 43*, 235–267.

# CHAPTER 75

# COACHING AND WELL-BEING: A BRIEF REVIEW OF EXISTING EVIDENCE, RELEVANT THEORY, AND IMPLICATIONS FOR PRACTITIONERS

GORDON B. SPENCE[1] AND ANTHONY M. GRANT[2]

[1]University of Wollongong, Australia; [2]University of Sydney, Australia

This chapter is about coaching and its influence on human functioning and well-being. The chapter is presented in two sections. In the first section coaching is defined and accompanied by a brief description of its essential practices, along with a review of what is currently known empirically about its impact on human functioning and well-being. Having reviewed some evidence that supports the efficacy of coaching, the second section will focus on the important question: Why does coaching work? In proposing an answer to this question we will draw upon self-determination theory (SDT; Deci & Ryan, 1985), a metatheory of human functioning that we believe helps to theoretically ground the practice of coaching. We hope that this discussion will provide both a good general introduction to the field in its current state and stimulate an understanding of why coaching effectively contributes to well-being.

## What is Coaching?

Coaching is an action-oriented, collaborative process that seeks to facilitate goal attainment, self-directed learning, and/or enhance performance in the coachee's personal or professional

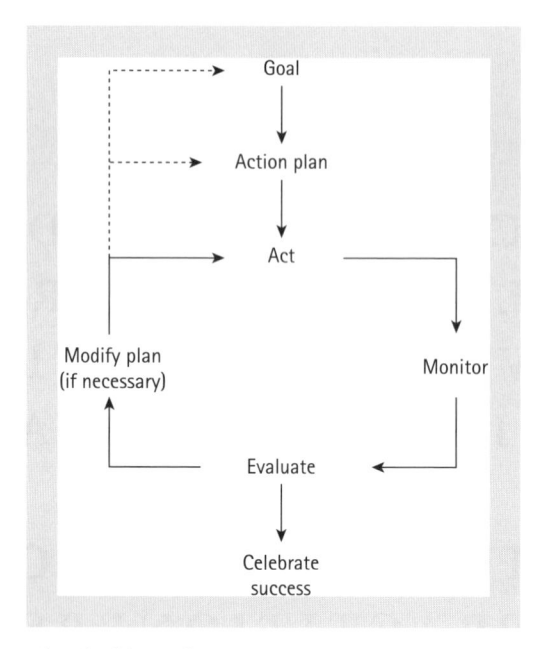

FIG. 75.1 Generic cycle of self-regulation.

life (Spence & Grant, 2007). The articulation of goals is central to the coaching process and these are generally set in a way that stretches an individual's current capacities or performance (Grant & Greene, 2001). In essence, the coaching process facilitates goal attainment by helping individuals to: (1) identify desired outcomes, (2) establish specific goals, (3) enhance motivation by identifying strengths and building self-efficacy, (4) identify resources and formulate action plans, (5) monitor and evaluate progress, and (6) modify action plans (where necessary). As shown in Fig. 75.1, this monitor–evaluate–modify process constitutes a cycle of self-regulated behavior that is key to creating intentional behavior change (Carver & Scheier, 1998). The role of the coach is to facilitate the coachee's movement through this self-regulatory cycle, by helping the coachee to develop specific action plans and then to monitor and to evaluate their progression toward those goals.

Much of a coach's skill lies in being able to accelerate goal attainment by helping individuals develop and implement solutions to the ongoing challenges faced during goal striving. Regardless of whether coaching occurs as brief, informal "on-the-fly" coaching (lasting, say, 10 minutes) or more lengthy, formal sessions (sometimes lasting up to 2 hours or more), considerable emphasis is placed on the coach to act as the facilitator (rather than the provider) of solutions. Increasingly this has led coaches to adopt the use of solution-focused and strengths-based techniques, which can assist coachees to tap into their personal strengths and resources (Berg & Szabo, 2005).

## Is coaching effective? What the research says

The first appearance of coaching in the peer-reviewed literature occurs in Gorby's (1937) report of senior staff coaching junior employees on how to reduce waste, and Bigelow's

(1938) article on how best to implement a sales coaching program. Despite its long history, the coaching literature is still relatively small, although it has grown significantly in recent years.

According to Grant (2010), in the 62 years between 1937 and 1999 only 93 papers on coaching were published, compared to 542 since 2000. However, of the 616 papers published since 1980, the vast majority have been opinion pieces, descriptive articles or theoretical discussions. Furthermore, of the 179 empirical papers published in this period, many are surveys (e.g., Coutu & Kauffman, 2009; Douglas & McCauley, 1999), descriptive studies about executive coaching (e.g., Bono, Purvanova, Towler, & Peterson, 2009), or research into the characteristics of coach training schools (e.g., Grant & O'Hara, 2006). As such, most of the extant empirical coaching literature comprises contextual or survey-based investigations, with little research focused on determining the efficacy of coaching as a methodology for creating purposeful positive change and enhancing well-being. Nevertheless, a brief overview of this literature follows and will be drawn from four areas: workplace/executive coaching; life coaching; health coaching and coaching within educational settings.

## Workplace and executive coaching

Although coaching is widely used in the workplace, only two randomized controlled studies of workplace coaching have been reported. In the first, Deviney (1994) examined the efficacy of supervisors acting as internal workplace coaches and found no changes in supervisors' feedback skills following a multiple-rater feedback intervention and coaching from their managers over a 9-week period. In the other study, Duijts, Kant, van den Brandt, and Swaen (2008) examined the effectiveness of coaching as a means of reducing work absence due to psychosocial health complaints. Whilst no decrease in absenteeism was observed, there was significantly lower burnout along with improvements in health, life satisfaction, and psychological well-being. These results suggest that coaching might enhance employee well-being.

There have been some quasi-experimental studies in the workplace using pre-test and post-test comparisons and non-randomized allocation to an intervention or control group. For example, Gyllensten and Palmer (2005) found that coaching was associated with lower levels of anxiety and workplace stress (compared with a control group), whilst Evers, Brouwers, and Tomic (2006) reported that executive coaching enhanced participants' self-efficacy and self-perceived ability to set personal goals. In addition, Barrett (2007) found that group coaching was effective for reducing burnout but not for improving productivity.

Finally, one study reported on the effectiveness of executive coaching (using a randomized controlled design). In this, participants received 360-degree feedback followed by four sessions of executive coaching. Coaching was found to reduce stress and depression, improve goal attainment, and increase resilience (Grant, Curtayne, & Burton, 2009).

## Life coaching

Given that commercial life coach training schools first emerged in the early 1990s, it is surprising that comparatively few outcome studies have been conducted on life coaching. In the first published study, Grant (2003a) used a within-subjects (pre–post) design to explore the efficacy of a group-based, solution-focused cognitive behavioral (SF-CB) life coaching program (n = 20). The results indicated that life coaching was associated with enhanced mental health, quality of life, and goal attainment. In a partial replication of this study, Green, Oades, and Grant (2006) tested the same SF-CB coaching program using a randomized controlled (pre–post) design and found that group life coaching was associated with increases in goal striving, well-being and hope, with some gains maintained at 30 weeks.

Extending this line of research, Spence and Grant (2007) compared the efficacy of individualized professional one-to-one coaching to peer coaching with an adult community sample (n = 63) over a 10-week period. The results indicated that coachees of professional coaches were more engaged in the coaching process and reported greater goal commitment and goal progression compared to peer coachees and controls. Whilst these participants also reported greater levels of environmental mastery, other facets of well-being did not change.

Finally, life coaching has also been found to be effective with young adults. Using a sample of 56 female high school students (mean age 16 years), Green, Grant, and Rynsaardt (2007) found that participation in SF-CB life coaching was associated with significant increases in levels of cognitive hardiness and hope, and significant decreases in depression.

## Health coaching

The use of coaching in health-related settings is steadily increasing and may prove a useful way of enhancing patient self-management and better utilization of healthcare resources (for a discussion see Kreitzer et al., 2008). Health coaching is a patient-centered process that consists of setting health-related goals, identifying obstacles to change, and mobilizing support and resources to enable change (Palmer, Tubbs, & Whybrow, 2003). It is typically a multifaceted intervention incorporating cognitive, behavioral and lifestyle change strategies, and includes the teaching of coping skills (Grey et al., 2009). A review of this literature reveals that health coaching is being used to address a variety of concerns in an array of settings. For example, Linden, Butterworth, and Prochaska (2010) provided chronically ill patients with telephone-based health coaching informed by motivational interviewing principles (Miller & Rollnick, 2002) and found that it increased their self-efficacy, lifestyle change scores and perceived health status.

In another study, Grey et al. (2009) explored the difference between general health education and coping skills-based health coaching with inner city youth at risk for type II diabetes. Results indicated that both groups showed some improvement in anthropometric measures, lipids, and depressive symptoms over 12 months, but students who received health coaching showed a greater improvement on indicators of metabolic risk than students who received education only. This confirmed earlier results reported by Spence, Cavanagh, and Grant (2008) who found that health goal attainment was greater when participants received coaching, compared to a directive, health education-only intervention.

Not all health coaching studies have reported such successes. Gorczynski, Morrow, and Irwin (2008) reported on the impact of coaching on physical activity participation, self-efficacy, social support, and perceived behavioral control among physically inactive youth. Whilst physical activity significantly increased for one participant, the other participants' activity levels remained unchanged. No significant changes were found across the other study variables. Similarly, an internet-based health coaching study conducted by Leveille et al. (2009) reported mixed findings. In investigating the efficacy of coaching aimed at enhancing communication between patients and their primary care physician, results showed that while coached patients received more information from their physicians there was no difference in the detection or management of screened conditions, symptom ratings, and quality of life between the coaching and non-coaching groups.

It appears that whilst life coaching and organizational coaching tend to be effective, health coaching is less so. This is perhaps unsurprising given that such behaviors tend to be anchored by decades of habit. Furthermore, it is difficult to determine whether the health coaching reported in the literature accurately reflects coaching (i.e., a client-centered process aimed at facilitating self-directed learning), or whether it is being utilized as an alternative way to deliver expert information.

Although health coaching for health-related behavior change may not be consistently effective, the use of workplace or executive coaching in health settings to change non-health-related behaviors has been more successful. For example, Taylor (1997) found that solution-focused coaching enhanced resilience in medical students, whilst Gattellari et al. (2005) reported that peer coaching by general practitioners improved the coachees' ability to make informed decisions about prostate-specific antigen screening. Also, Miller, Yahbe, Moyers, Martinez, and Pirritanol (2004) used a coaching program to help clinicians learn motivational interviewing skills and found that coaching with feedback was superior to training-only. Finally, Yu, Collins, Cavanagh, White, and Fairbrother (2008) found coaching was associated with significantly greater proactivity, core performance, goal-attainment, self-insight, motivation, positive affect and autonomy for 17 managers in a large teaching hospital.

## Coaching in educational settings

Whilst there is now a considerable amount of literature regarding coaching in educational settings much of it is student-focused and directed towards enhancing student learning, or overcoming literacy or learning difficulties (e.g., Merriman & Codding, 2008). We will not review this literature here, rather, we will focus on an emerging literature related to teacher-focused coaching (for a review see Denton & Hasbrouck, 2009). It should be noted that the term "coaching" in educational settings refers to a very broad range of applications, indicating technical or instructional coaching to increase the instructional skills of teachers (e.g., Brown, Reumann-Moore, Hugh, Du Plessis, & Christman, 2006) and reflective practice coaching, which is "a process in which teachers explore the thinking behind their practices" (Garmston, Linder, & Whitaker, 1993, p. 57).

Whilst little has been reported on the use of coaching to directly increase the well-being or happiness of students or teachers, it has been applied to facilitating professional development and enhancing leadership within educational settings. Much of this work has been conducted using peer coaching with both novice (Jenkins, Garn, & Jenkins, 2005; Suleyman, 2006) and experienced educators (Johnson, 2009). However, as in commercial organizations, some senior management in educational settings also engage in developmental coaching of subordinates (MacKenzie & Marnik, 2008). These coaching interventions can be relatively sophisticated with senior school leaders receiving coaching skills training within the context of a structured coaching program, and often incorporate ongoing supervision and impact evaluation (for an example see Simkins, Coldwell, Caillau, Finlayson, & Morgan, 2006). Globally, the use of professional coaches and consultants for leadership and professional development within educational settings has been increasing, with some studies yielding encouraging results (Allan, 2007; Contreras, 2009).

On the basis of the findings presented, coaching appears to be a promising methodology for facilitating goal attainment and enhancing well-being across a variety of domains. Whilst some of this evidence has been generated through the use of robust scientific methods, there is a pressing need for more research in each of the domains outlined; research that seeks to understand (1) the specific impact of coaching across domains, and (2) what processes coaching activates to generate these effects.

# How Does Coaching Impact Well-Being?

## Using self-determination theory to understand coaching efficacy

As outlined in the previous section, a growing body of empirical evidence indicates that coaching impacts an array of positive psychological characteristics, including various dimensions of subjective and psychological well-being (e.g., positive affect and environmental mastery). Whilst such findings are encouraging, there are two reasons that this work should be interpreted cautiously. First, the empirical coaching literature is still relatively small with few replications and considerable methodological variability. Second, most of the coaching research conducted to date has lacked firm theoretical foundations and occurred in the absence of clearly articulated, coherent research agendas. As a result, the evidence-base for coaching would best be described as disparate, largely atheoretical, and primarily comprised of "one-off" findings. Clearly, it is not yet a mature field of study.

These observations are not intended as criticisms of the field or those working within it. Rather, they are brief reflections on the current state of coaching research and serve as a reminder that maturation takes time and occurs via the steady accumulation of rigorous empirical work. Whilst we hope that dedicating the remainder of this chapter to SDT (Deci & Ryan, 1985) might provide a new perspective from which to formulate coaching research questions and so stimulate further empirical work, our primary aim is to introduce a well-researched theory of human motivation and goal-directed behavior that can both inform the practice of coaching and help to understand its beneficial effects.

## Coaching and well-being

What makes coaching an intervention that can influence well-being and happiness? Numerous explanations could be proposed to answer this question. One might be that coaching enhances well-being simply because it focuses on the subjective concerns of individuals and provides a helpful collaborator (i.e., the coach) to assist with resolving those concerns. According to this view, coaching would enhance well-being via the experience of being genuinely supported. A second explanation might be that coaching enhances well-being by providing coachees with rare opportunities to reflect on and (re)discover their personal strengths and capacities. From this perspective, well-being is enhanced through feelings of mastery that build over time. Alternatively, it could be argued that coaching enhances well-being by helping coachees to think deeply about their goals and encouraging them to use values and interests—rather than external inducements or introjects—as a basis for choosing commitments in life. According to this view, it is the developing sense of self-authorship and volition that would lead one to feel good.

Whilst these perspectives are intuitively appealing they provide only superficial explanations about how or why coaching might be expected to impact well-being. The potential value that SDT offers to coaches is that it can help to make sense of such "explanations" by providing a comprehensive account of human functioning and the processes that shape cognitive, emotional and behavioral self-regulation and development.

## Self-determination theory

As practitioners we have continually found SDT to be highly relevant, conceptually coherent, and, as we will argue, useful for understanding coaching practice at both macro and micro levels. At the macro level, SDT provides a metatheoretical account of growth tendencies, innate psychological needs, and environmental forces that shape human personality, behavioral self-regulation, and well-being (Ryan & Deci, 2000). Put more simply, the theory says much about what needs to happen if people are to "do well" and "feel good" throughout the course of their lives.

At the micro level, SDT can help practitioners to appreciate the importance of the client-coach relationship and understand that, through the process of *relating*, conditions can be created that are necessary for optimal growth and development. More specifically, the use of core micro-skills such as active listening, expressing empathy, exploring successes, identifying personal strengths, clarifying values, encouraging volitional acts and other supportive gestures help to enliven developmental processes that are central to (what is commonly referred to as) "human flourishing" (Keyes & Haidt, 2003).

### Some self-determination theory basics

According to Deci and Ryan (2000), "it is part of the adaptive design features of the human organism to engage in interesting activities, to exercise capacities, to pursue connectedness in social groups, and to integrate intrapsychic and interpersonal experiences into a relative unity" (p. 229). This statement conveys several ideas that we believe make SDT a relevant theoretical backdrop for coaching.

First, SDT adopts a positive view of human nature. Consistent with the basic tenets of humanistic psychology (Rogers, 1961), people are seen as possessing innate growth tendencies and, provided supportive socio-contextual conditions exist, will naturally seek out experiences that promote growth and development. Whilst SDT explicitly acknowledges that these innate tendencies exist, it also acknowledges the *organismic-dialectic* of human experience (Deci & Ryan, 1985). Simply put, a dialectic is the juxtaposition of conflicting forces or ideas. In SDT the dialectic of interest is the conflict that exists between the inherent growth orientation of humans and the disruptive power of various socio-contextual forces (e.g., excessive parental control, peer pressure and restrictive legislation) that act to thwart or stall these positive developmental tendencies (Ryan & Deci, 2000).

Second, SDT proposes that a person's level of functioning and well-being depends upon the satisfaction of three basic psychological needs: autonomy, competence and relatedness. According to the theory, people do well and feel at their best when the socio-cultural *conditions* of their lives (i.e., family relationships, friendships, workplace culture, political system, and cultural norms) support the innate needs of freely engaging in interesting activities (autonomy), producing valued outcomes via the use of their capacities (competence), *and* feeling closely and securely connected to significant others (relatedness).

Third, SDT conceptualizes the self *not* as a fixed, rigid core (i.e., "self-as-object") residing somewhere deep within the person. Rather, it is viewed as an active processor of experience, a dynamic psychic structure that continuously seeks to make meaning of the myriad internal and external events that comprise a person's life (i.e., "self-as-process") and integrate them into a coherent, unified sense of self. Specifically, Deci and Ryan (1985) argue that this processor works best when the conditions of a person's life support satisfaction of the needs for autonomy, relatedness and competence.

### Relevance to coaching

When an individual engages the services of a coach, they gain access to someone with the potential to facilitate basic need satisfaction via a relational process focused on the coachee's aspirations and salient concerns. In this way, the formation of a coaching relationship can represent a positive change in the sociocultural conditions of a coachee's life, provided that the relationship respects their core values and developing interests, acknowledges their capacities, and occurs against a backdrop of genuine caring, trust and honesty. From an SDT perspective, coaches who focus on the creation of these conditions help to create a platform for effective human action and the complex meaning-making process that represents the development of the self.

It should be noted that SDT is not a single theory. Rather, it is a set of four related mini-theories that have evolved over four decades (Deci & Ryan, 1985). Whilst each subtheory has its own specific focus (see Table 75.1), all address psychological processes that are interrelated and deemed to be important for psychological growth and development (for a comprehensive review see Deci & Ryan, 2000). As SDT views the satisfaction of basic needs as a prerequisite for human development and growth, attempts to understand coaching from this perspective are best focused on the extent to which coaching can satisfy needs for relatedness, competence and autonomy. The remainder of the chapter is focused on the ways that coaching might help to meet these needs.

## Coaching conversations: creating conditions for growth, development, and well-being

### Relatedness

Coaching is generally considered to be founded upon Rogerian, person-centered principles (Stober & Grant, 2006) that are reinforced through the use of core micro-skills such as active listening, empathy, unconditional positive regard and attentive and responsive body language. From an SDT perspective the use of such skills creates an atmosphere conducive

Table 75.1 SDT subtheories

| Subtheory | Scope |
|---|---|
| Basic needs theory | Ties optimal functioning and well-being to the joint satisfaction of 3 basic psychological needs: autonomy, competence, and relatedness. |
| Cognitive evaluation theory | Focuses on how intrinsic motivation (IM) is enhanced by social-cultural factors that lead people to feel effective (e.g., positive feedback) and is diminished by factors that constrain personal choice (e.g., threats) and lead people to *not* see themselves as the initiators of their own action |
| Organismic integration theory | Argues that extrinsically motivated behaviors can be regulated with differing levels of volition (i.e., external, introjected, identified, integrated) and proposes that these behaviors can, and usually do, become more self-endorsed over time (through internalization and integration processes) |
| Causality orientations theory | Describes three general motivational orientations; *autonomous orientation* (based on personal interests and self-endorsed values), *controlled orientation* (based on controls that govern how one should behave), and an *impersonal orientation* (based on the belief that one's efforts will be ineffectual) |

to satisfying the need for relatedness, through the establishment of good rapport and the development of a warm, trusting and caring relationship that is squarely focused on addressing the coachee's salient concerns. Importantly, whilst the coachee may have close relationships outside coaching, they may not have been consistently felt heard, understood, valued, and/or genuinely supported within these. If so, such conditions are unlikely to satisfy relatedness needs and impel people to seek connection with others by acting in accordance with their preferences, rather than one's own (such as when an adolescent disengages from pursuing a hobby because of parental disapproval or disinterest). In situations like this, coaching may help an inadequately supported person to feel safe enough to explore and consider more self-concordant forms of action.

## *Competence*

In keeping with the core assumptions of humanistic psychology (Maslow, 1954; Rogers, 1961), coaching assumes that people are essentially capable and possess potential that can emerge in the presence of supportive conditions (Grant, 2003b). A key strategy to uncover latent potential is the solution-focused approach (Berg & Szabo, 2005), which assumes people are highly capable and already enacting desirable, target behaviors. As such, coaching tends to orient people towards what they are doing well, what is working, as well as their personal strengths and ways in which those strengths might be put into daily use (Seligman, Steen, Park, & Peterson, 2005). Given this focus, coaches are generally striving to create conditions that will help clients develop feelings of competence. Various psychometric tools (e.g., strengths inventories) or more informal methods (e.g., achievement journals) can help to raise awareness of personal strengths and talents that may have been long forgotten, ignored or devalued, whilst also permitting the coachee to consider ways that these capacities might be better utilized within the context of their life.

*Autonomy*

Most coaching models and frameworks place the coachee at the centre of decision-making processes as a way of encouraging ownership of their development and growth (Grant, 2006). Whilst the coach will typically look to the coachee to provide impetus for any goals set throughout a coaching engagement, this principle is also applied within sessions. For example, the use of simple process models like GROW (Goal-Reality-Options-Wrap Up; Whitmore, 1996) encourage coachees to own their behavior change process by setting the agenda for each conversation. Oftentimes, however, clients can find the invitation to engage in the goal setting process uncomfortable. In our experience, this can occur because they are: (1) not clear on what they are striving for, (2) unfamiliar with being asked to take responsibility for their developmental agenda, or (3) fearful the process might not work (i.e., they might not attain their goals). Whatever the reason(s), when coaching is structured using models like GROW the implicit message is "you are free to choose what we work on and your choice will be respected and valued."

*Self-determination theory and case formulation*

Whilst psychotherapists and counselors have long used case formulations to understand client needs (Kuyken, Fothergill, Musa, & Chadwick, 2005), this practice appears less widely used in coaching (Corrie & Lane, 2010). SDT provides a practical perspective on human growth and development that makes it a useful lens through which to understand a coachee. Not surprisingly, an SDT-informed case formulation would begin with seeking to understand the degree to which the coachee has been able to satisfy their basic needs via their interactions with the world. For example, employees are often expected to direct energy and effort towards performance goals imposed by employers, and in this context it is not uncommon for them to feel controlled or coerced, with few options other than compliance. In such situations, a case formulation is likely to reveal a diminished sense of autonomy and indicate the potential usefulness of autonomy support strategies. This might include the coach assisting the coachee to try and understand what credible *rationale* might exist for such goals, genuinely *acknowledging* how the coachee might feel about the goals, and helping the coachee to make *choices* about how they engage in the goal striving process. Such strategies have been found to enhance autonomous need satisfaction in situations where personal choice is compromised (see Deci, Eghrari, Patrick, & Leone, 1994).

# The coaching process: supporting more self-determined living

The working alliance is key to the attainment of successful outcomes in coaching (Peltier, 2001). This is because the establishment of a warm, encouraging, affirming relationship has much to do with how much hope, courage, and resilience can be mustered to support goal striving and behavior change in the broader context of one's life. Consistent with the research on subjective vitality (see Ryan & Deci, 2008), it is expected that whenever a coaching relationship is supportive of basic psychological needs (as outlined earlier), a coachee is likely to feel a renewed sense of energy and a greater capacity to act in accordance with core aspects of the developing self.

Typically individuals come to coaching seeking help to attain personal and professional goals. Whilst for some these goals are clear and obvious, for many they are not, and a coach can help to resolve a variety of concerns such as not knowing what goals to set, struggling to strive towards goals set by others, and/or managing fluctuations in goal-related motivation. Fortunately, SDT has focused closely on goal striving processes (e.g., Sheldon & Elliot, 1998, 1999) and has yielded useful frameworks for helping individuals resolve such challenges.

## Goal ownership: a developmental trajectory

The developmental processes described in SDT are helpful for understanding how coaching might enhance well-being. According to the theory, whilst the organismic-dialectic makes most behavior extrinsically motivated (as opposed to intrinsically motivated) people adopt goals for a variety of reasons that can be plotted along a continuum of self-regulation varying from extrinsic regulation to intrinsic regulation (see Table 75.2). Furthermore, it argues that these motivational underpinnings greatly impact how much energy people direct towards goal striving and how much satisfaction is gained from their attainment. More specifically, SDT contends that externally regulated or controlled goals (those adopted primarily for money, praise, etc.) tend to be associated with feelings of pressure and tension and result in poorer continuity of effort. In contrast, more integrated or autonomous goals

Table 75.2 Varying levels of goal ownership associated with extrinsic motivation[a]

| Reason | Type | Motivation |
| --- | --- | --- |
| External | Controlled | Striving because somebody else wants you to or thinks you ought to, or because you'll get some kind of reward, praise, or approval for it. |
| Introjected | Controlled | Striving because you would feel ashamed, guilty, or anxious if you didn't. Rather than striving because someone else thinks you ought to, you feel this is a goal that you should strive for. |
| Identified | Autonomous | Striving because you really believe in the importance of the goal. Although this goal may once have been taught to you by others, now you endorse it freely and value it wholeheartedly. |
| Integrated | Autonomous | Striving because of the fun and enjoyment the goal provides you. While there may be good reasons to adopt the goal, the primary reason is simply your interest in the experience itself. |

[a]Adapted from The "What" and "Why" of Goal Pursuits: Human Needs and the Self-Determination of Behavior, Edward L. Deci, Richard M. Ryan, *Psychological Inquiry*, © Taylor & Francis, 2000, reprinted by permission of the publisher (Taylor & Francis Ltd, http://www.tandf.co.uk/journals).

(those aligned with one's values and interests) tend to be associated with feelings of congruence and greater long term effort (Sheldon & Elliot, 1998).

Most importantly, the theory proposes that people can (and do) move towards more autonomous action over time, via processes of internalization and integration (or assimilation) (Deci & Ryan, 1985). It further proposes that this developmental progression can be catalyzed by the presence of conditions that support the satisfaction of basic needs (as discussed earlier)—a proposition that has received considerable empirical support (e.g., Deci, et al., 1994; Sheldon & Elliot, 1999; Sheldon, Kasser, Smith, & Share, 2002).

## Implications for coaches

These findings have importance for coaches because they suggest it is possible to facilitate helpful shifts in goal motivation. This is particularly relevant when individuals are faced with the challenge of working towards goals that are not self-selected (as often occurs in organizational settings or health contexts) and over which they feel a diminished sense of ownership. In such situations a coach can potentially be helpful in one of two ways. First, they may be helpful by providing the person with the opportunity to reflect on the nature of the imposed goal and explore (positive and negative) implications of striving towards it. Having done so the coach can then encourage the coachee to make a choice about what s/he will do. In the event that s/he decides not to pursue such a goal, ongoing support may be required to manage the implications of that decision. If, on the other hand, s/he decides to pursue the goal and does so in a way that indicates a lack of subjective ownership (i.e., for external or introjected reasons), the coach may utilize an autonomy support strategy (e.g., the *rationale–acknowledgement–choice* framework) to help the coachee find ways of identifying with the goal and aligning it to their core values and developing interests. For example, Bob is prescribed an exercise program by his doctor and, with the help of his health coach, is able to develop ways of making the goal fun or more challenging (thereby increasing intrinsic motivation). In this case, a shift in the locus of causality would have occurred, away from external inducements (external motivation) and towards the person's values and developing interests (identified motivation). As indicated in Fig. 75.2, such a movement represents a shift towards core aspects of the person.

Second, a coach may help an individual to reframe the goal by exploring alternative perspectives and seeking to attach an alternative meaning to it. For example, Christine is told by her boss that she must raise the profile of her department and this goal is written into her performance agreement. Being an introvert this is not a goal she would have chosen for herself. However, rather than being stoic and enduring the discomfort associated with striving towards this goal (e.g., social networking and public presentations), an executive coach could help Christine to take a different perspective on the goal that results in her seeing that building the skills needed to attain this goal might be transferable to other areas of interest (e.g., organizing fundraisers for a charitable organization). If so, she would be in a position to *choose* what the goal would mean to her (an autonomous act) and more likely to be positively energized towards it (Ryan & Deci, 2008).

In summary, coaching can enhance more autonomous, self-determined living by helping individuals to make more conscious, intentional decisions about what goals they commit to (or not) in the context of their life or, in situations where there is little perceived choice, by choosing what these goals will mean to them.

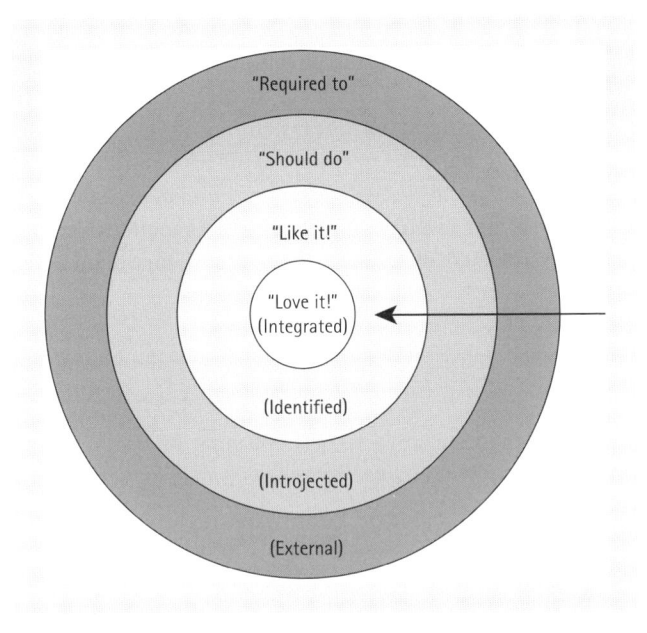

FIG. 75.2 Simple spatial representation of differing degrees of extrinsically motivated action.

## Recommendations for practitioners

As has already been stated, we believe that SDT is a relevant and practically useful theory for coaching. For those readers who are practicing coaches we offer the following suggestions:

- Consider using SDT for case formulations, either as the primary theoretical framework or as just one perspective for developing client understanding and possible interventions.
- Explore underlying goal motivation with your clients by referring to the different types of regulation described in Table 75.2 and graphically represented in Fig. 75.2.
- Seek out information about SDT across different domains of interest. The University of Rochester web site (http://www.psych.rochester.edu/SDT/) is a good place to start and is helpful because it organizes publications by a variety of research and application topics.
- As coaching is still not a mature field of study, care should be taken not to overstate what is known about it from the extant literature. Rather, if validation of one's practice is important (and cannot be gained from the existing knowledge base), the SDT literature may prove to be a useful resource to draw upon.

# Conclusion

In this chapter we have reviewed evidence from the peer-reviewed academic literature that is generally supportive of coaching as an intervention that enhances human functioning and well-being. We have also acknowledged that whilst this evidence-base is growing steadily, the field of coaching is still maturing and lacks empirical work that is firmly grounded in theory. There have been relatively few attempts to provide a detailed theoretical account of what happens in coaching, or to build our understanding about why coaching works in the way that it seems to. Through our brief overview of SDT and sketching out some implications for coaching, we hope this chapter will help practitioners to develop new or alternative perspectives on their work, and stimulate researchers to formulate their hypotheses against the backdrop of a well established, coherent, and relevant theory of human functioning and well-being.

# References

Allan, P. (2007). The benefits and impacts of a coaching and mentoring programme for teaching staff in a secondary school. *International Journal of Evidenced-Based Coaching and Mentoring*, 5(2), 12–21.

Barrett, P. T. (2007). The effects of group coaching on executive health and team effectiveness: A quasi-experimental field study. *Dissertation Abstracts International Section A*, 67, 26–40.

Berg, I. K., & Szabo, P. (2005). *Brief coaching for lasting solutions*. New York, NY: Norton.

Bigelow, B. (1938). Building an effective training program for field salesmen. *Personnel*, 14, 142–150.

Bono, J. E., Purvanova, R. K., Towler, A. J., & Peterson, D. B. (2009). A survey of executive coaching practices. *Personnel Psychology*, 62(2), 361–404.

Brown, D., Reumann-Moore, R., Hugh, R., Du Plessis, P., & Christman, J. B. (2006). *Promising inroads: Year one report of the Pennsylvania High School Coaching Initiative*. Pennsylvania, PA: Research For Action.

Carver, C. S., & Scheier, M. F. (1998). *On the self-regulation of behavior*. Cambridge, UK: Cambridge University Press.

Contreras, Y. M. (2009). A descriptive study: Coaching school leaders for 21st century schools: A new context for leadership development. *Dissertation Abstracts International Section A: Humanities and Social Sciences*, 69, 7-A, 25–38.

Corrie, S., & Lane, D. A. (2010). *Constructing stories, telling tales: A guide to formulation in applied psychology*. London, UK: Karnac.

Coutu, D., & Kauffman, C. (2009). *The realities of executive coaching: Harvard research report*. Cambridge, MA: Harvard Business Review.

Deci, E., Eghrari, H., Patrick, B. C., & Leone, D. R. (1994). Facilitating internalization: The self-determination theory perspective. *Journal of Personality*, 21(1), 119–142.

Deci, E. L., & Ryan, R. M. (1985). *Intrinsic motivation and self-determination in human behaviour*. New York, NY: Plenum Press.

Deci, E. L., & Ryan, R. M. (2000). The "what" and "why" of goal pursuits: Human needs and the self-determination of behaviour. *Psychological Inquiry*, 11(4), 227–268.

Denton, C. A., & Hasbrouck, J. (2009). A description of instructional coaching and its relationship to consultation. *Journal of Educational and Psychological Consultation*, 19(2), 150–175.

Deviney, D. E. (1994). The effects of coaching using mulitple rater feedback to change supervisor behavior. *Dissertation Abstracts International Section A*, 55, 114.

Douglas, C. A., & McCauley, C. D. (1999). Formal developmental relationships: A survey of organizational practices. *Human Development Quarterly*, 10(3), 203–220.

Duijts, S. F., Kant, I., van den Brandt, P. A., & Swaen, G. M. (2008). Effectiveness of a preventive coaching intervention for employees at risk for sickness absence due to psychosocial health complaints: Results of a randomized controlled trial. *Journal of Occupational & Environmental Medicine*, 50(7), 765–776.

Evers, W. J., Brouwers, A., & Tomic, W. (2006). A quasi-experimental study on management coaching effectiveness. *Consulting Psychology Journal: Practice & Research*, 58, 174–182.

Garmston, R., Linder, C., & Whitaker, J. (1993). Reflections on cognitive coaching. *Educational Leadership*, 51(2), 57–61.

Gattellari, M., Donnelly, N., Taylor, N., Meerkin, M., Hirst, G., & Ward, J. (2005). Does peer coaching increase GP capacity to promote informed decision making about FSA screening? A cluster randomised trial. *Family Practice*, 22, 253–265.

Gorby, C. B. (1937). Everyone gets a share of the profits. *Factory Management & Maintenance*, 95, 82–83.

Gorczynski, P., Morrow, D., & Irwin, J. D. (2008). The impact of co-active coaching on physically inactive 12 to 14 year olds in Ontario. *International Journal of Evidence Based Coaching and Mentoring*, 6(2), 13–26.

Grant, A. M. (2003a). The impact of life coaching on goal attainment, metacognition and mental health. *Social Behavior and Personality*, 31(3), 253–264.

Grant, A. M. (2003b). *Solution-focused coaching: Managing people in a complex world.* Harlow, UK: Pearson Education.

Grant, A. M. (2006). An integrative goal-focused approach to executive coaching. In D. R. Stober & A. M. Grant (Eds.), *Evidence based coaching handbook: Putting best practices to work for your clients* (pp. 153–192). Hoboken, NJ: Wiley & Sons.

Grant, A. M. (2010). *Workplace, executive and life coaching: An annotated bibliography from the behavioural science literature.* Unpublished paper: Coaching Psychology Unit, University of Sydney, Australia.

Grant, A. M., Curtayne, L., & Burton, G. (2009). Executive coaching enhances goal attainment, resilience and workplace well-being: A randomised controlled study. *Journal of Positive Psychology*, 4(5), 396–407.

Grant, A. M., & Greene, J. (2001). *Coach yourself: Make real change in your life.* London, UK: Momentum.

Grant, A. M., & O'Hara, B. (2006). The self-presentation of commercial Australian life coaching schools: Cause for concern? *International Coaching Psychology Review*, 1(2), 20–32.

Green, L. S., Grant, A. M., & Rynsaardt, J. (2007). Evidence-based life coaching for senior high school students: Building hardiness and hope. *International Coaching Psychology Review*, 2(1), 24–32.

Green, L. S., Oades, L. G., & Grant, A. M. (2006). Cognitive-behavioural, solution-focused life coaching: Enhancing goal striving, well-being and hope. *Journal of Positive Psychology*, 1(3), 142–149.

Grey, M., Jaser, S. S., Holl, M. G., Jefferson, V., Dziura, J., & Northrup, V. (2009). A multifaceted school-based intervention to reduce risk for type 2 diabetes in at-risk youth. *Preventive Medicine: An International Journal Devoted to Practice and Theory*, 49(2–3), 122–128.

Gyllensten, K., & Palmer, S. (2005). Can coaching reduce workplace stress: A quasi-experimental study. *International Journal of Evidence Based Coaching and Mentoring*, 3(2), 75–85.

Jenkins, J. M., Garn, A., & Jenkins, P. (2005). Preservice teacher observations in peer coaching. *Journal of Teaching in Physical Education*, 24(1), 2–23.

Johnson, N. W. (2009). *Peer coaching: A collegial support for bridging the research to practice gap.* Unpublished dissertation: University of Missouri–Columbia, MO.

Keyes, C. L. M., & Haidt, J. (Eds.). (2003). *Flourishing: Positive psychology and the life well-lived.* Washington, DC: American Psychological Association.

Kreitzer, M. J., Sierpina, V. S., Lawson, K., Kreitzer, M. J., Sierpina, V. S., & Lawson, K. (2008). Health coaching: innovative education and clinical programs emerging. *Explore: The Journal of Science & Healing, 4*(2), 154–155.

Kuyken, W., Fothergill, C. D., Musa, M., & Chadwick, P. (2005). The reliability and quality of cognitive case formulation. *Behaviour Research and Therapy, 43*, 1187–1201.

Leveille, S. G., Huang, A., Tsai, S. B., Allen, M., Weingart, S. N., & Iezzoni, L. I. (2009). Health coaching via an internet portal for primary care patients with chronic conditions: A randomized controlled trial. *Medical Care, 47*(1), 41–47.

Linden, A., Butterworth, S. W., & Prochaska, J. O. (2010). Motivational interviewing-based health coaching as a chronic care intervention. *Journal of Evaluation in Clinical Practice, 16*(1), 166–174.

MacKenzie, S. V., & Marnik, G. F. (2008). Rethinking leadership development: How school leaders learn in action. *Schools: Studies in Education, 5*(1/2), 183–204.

Maslow, A. H. (1954). *Motivation and personality.* New York, NY: Harper.

Merriman, D. E., & Codding, R. S. (2008). The effects of coaching on mathematics homework completion and accuracy of high school students with attention-deficit/hyperactivity disorder. *Journal of Behavioral Education, 17*(4), 339–355.

Miller, W. R., & Rollnick, S. (2002). *Motivational interviewing: Preparing people for change.* New York, NY: The Guilford Press.

Miller, W. R., Yahne, C. E., Moyers, T. B., Martinez, J., & Pirritano, M. (2004). A randomized trial of methods to help clinicians learn Motivational Interviewing. *Journal of Consulting & Clinical Psychology, 72*(6), 1050–1062.

Palmer, S., Tubbs, I., & Whybrow, A. (2003). Health coaching to facilitate the promotion of healthy behavior and achievment of health-related goals. *International Journal of Health Promotion & Education, 41*(3), 91–93.

Peltier, B. (2001). *The psychology of executive coaching.* New York, NY: Brunner-Routledge.

Rogers, C. R. (1961). *On becoming a person.* Boston, MA: Houghton Mifflin.

Ryan, R. M., & Deci, E. (2000). Self-determination theory and the facilitation of intrinsic motivation, social development, and well-being. *American Psychologist, 55*(1), 68–78.

Ryan, R. M., & Deci, E. L. (2008). From ego depletion to vitality: Theory and findings concerning the facilitation of energy available to the self. *Social and Personality Psychology Compass, 2*(2), 702–717.

Seligman, M. E. P., Steen, T. A., Park, N., & Peterson, C. (2005). Positive psychology progress: Empirical validation of interventions. *American Psychologist, 60*(5), 410–421.

Sheldon, K. M., & Elliot, A. J. (1998). Not all personal goals are personal: Comparing autonomous and controlled reasons for goals as predictors of effort and attainment. *Personality and Social Psychology Bulletin, 24*(5), 546–557.

Sheldon, K. M., & Elliot, A. J. (1999). Goal striving, need satisfaction, and longitudinal well-being: The self-concordance model. *Journal of Personality and Social Psychology, 76*(3), 482–497.

Sheldon, K. M., Kasser, T., Smith, K., & Share, T. (2002). Personal goals and psychological growth: Testing an intervention to enhance goal attainment and personality integration. *Journal of Personality, 70*(1), 5–31.

Simkins, T., Coldwell, M., Caillau, I., Finlayson, H., & Morgan, A. (2006). Coaching as an in-school leadership development strategy: experiences from leading from the middle. *Journal of In-service Education, 32*(3), 321–340.

Spence, G. B., Cavanagh, M. J., & Grant, A. M. (2008). The integration of mindfulness training and health coaching: an exploratory study. *Coaching: An International Journal of Theory, Research and Practice, 1*(2), 145–163.

Spence, G. B., & Grant, A. M. (2007). Professional and peer life coaching and the enhancement of goal striving and well-being: An exploratory study. *Journal of Positive Psychology, 2*(3), 185–194.

Stober, D. R., & Grant, A. M. (Eds.). (2006). *Evidence based coaching handbook: Putting best practices to work for your clients*. Hoboken, NJ: Wiley.

Suleyman, D. G. (2006). Impact of peer coaching on self-efficacy and instructional skills in TEFL teacher education. *System, 34*(2), 239–254.

Taylor, L. M. (1997). The relation between resilience, coaching, coping skills training, and perceived stress during a career-threatening milestone. *Dissertation Abstracts International Section B, 58*, 2738.

Whitmore, J. (1996). *Coaching for performance*. London, UK: Nicholas Brealey.

Yu, N., Collins, C. G., Cavanagh, M., White, K., & Fairbrother, G. (2008). Positive coaching with frontline managers: Enhancing their effectiveness and understanding why. *International Coaching Psychology Review, 3*(2), 110–122.

# CHAPTER 76

# MINDFULNESS AND CULTIVATING WELL-BEING IN OLDER ADULTS

## LAURA M. HSU[1] AND ELLEN J. LANGER[2]

[1]Merrimack College, USA; [2]Harvard University, USA

Our mindsets and predispositions shape our personal environments. In turn, our personal environments can shape us. In this chapter, it will be argued that the process of becoming more aware of our mindsets, particularly of the premature judgments we make about the world and other people, generates a quality of consciousness (i.e., mindfulness) that can lead to improvements in both physical and mental health. It will be further argued that the cultivation of mindful qualities is particularly important among older adults and can influence the degree to which one is able to live vibrantly and successfully towards the end of life.

Age perception is one category for which people tend to have premature cognitive commitments. Premature cognitive commitments result when we take in information about the world without questioning its validity, even though it would be to our advantage to do so. Numerous studies indicate that individuals have negative stereotypes about older adults as being forgetful, senile, feeble, and unattractive (cf. Nelson, 2002; Rodin & Langer, 1980). Research suggests that these stereotypes begin to develop around 6 years of age (Isaacs & Bearison, 1986) and persist into old age (Nosek, Banaji, & Greenwald, 2002). Because they are so pervasive, it can be difficult to disentangle the extent to which this period is necessarily a time of diminished capacities versus a function of our negative stereotypes or premature cognitive commitments.

Research shows that perceptions of old age are automatic, unconscious, and that they influence behaviors (Bargh, Chen, & Burrows, 1996; Levy & Langer, 1994). For example, Levy and Langer (1994) found that memory problems for older adults were related to the premature cognitive commitments people have about memory and aging. Age perception also influences behavior. In a study by Bargh and colleagues (1996), individuals who had been primed with negative stereotypes of old age walked more slowly to an elevator after leaving the experiment than did control participants.

While a number of studies illustrate how perceptions of old age can lead to impairments in cognitive functioning and physical behavior, research also shows that priming positive perceptions of aging can lead to improved cognitive functioning and positive health outcomes (e.g., Demakakos, Gjonca, & Nazroo, 2007; Siegel, Bradley, & Kasl, 2003). Although there has been a recent emphasis in research on positive aging (e.g., Cohen, 2005; Vaillant, 2002), deeply entrenched stereotypes still exist (Palmore, Branch, & Harris, 2005).

In this chapter, we will discuss how perceptions of old age are encoded mindlessly and how more mindful approaches are beneficial for both mental and physical health. For centuries, Cartesian mind–body dualism was accepted as a truism. However, numerous studies (e.g., Bargh et al., 1996; Langer, 1989; Langer & Rodin, 1976; Rodin & Langer, 1977) have demonstrated that the mind and body are inextricably linked, such that a change in mindset can induce a change in behavior and physiology.

We begin by explaining the difference between mindfulness and mindlessness. This distinction is then followed by five examples of how "mindless" cues in the environment can prime either negative or positive perceptions of age, with consequences for physical health. Next, we highlight the importance of perceived control and how our culturally embedded association between a loss of control and age is, in fact, largely illusory. We then describe how motivations of older adults are often misjudged based on assumptions about old age, and discuss how in our socially constructed world, people who struggle to adapt (e.g., older adults) are generally seen as being the "problem" (rather than the other way around). Finally, we show why evaluation—even positive evaluation—can be mindless and conclude with some implications and practical applications of the theory and research described. Our intention is for readers to adopt a more mindful approach to aging that involves an expanded view about old age and capabilities.

## Mindfulness and Mindlessness

Mindfulness is a state of mind that is flexible, open to novelty, and characterized by the active drawing of novel distinctions. When we are mindful, we become sensitive to context and perspective, and are situated in the present. We recognize the dynamic interactions between individuals and environments, and thus do not hold any perception of individuals and environments constant. Behavior may be guided, but not governed, by rules and routines.

In contrast, when we are mindless we are oblivious to context and perspective and become susceptible to the formation of premature cognitive commitments and rigid mindsets. Behavior is often governed by rule and routine. Mindlessness need not arise as a function of repeated experience or habit, but may come about from a single exposure to information.

We are susceptible to stereotypes about age because we mindlessly encode information about "others" perceived as personally irrelevant and rarely question it. We do not tend to look for counter-evidence or regard someone or something in new ways unless prompted to do so. The danger of seeing things in limited or stable terms is that we are likely to only notice information that fits with that view, making us prone to confirmation bias (Nickerson, 1998). As an example, if a grandfather plays catch with his teenage grandson and the next day has a sore arm, he may attribute his sore arm to his old age and not to the fact that he has not thrown a baseball for some time. It may not occur to him that his grandson's arm may be sore too. People frequently make attributions like this, unaware of the negative effects they may have. As a result of his sore arm, the grandfather may not play catch or do any other type of athletic activity that is considered as or more strenuous because it may be considered risky. If so, this relative inactivity over time may lead to negative consequences. Thus, the grandfather's beliefs about his abilities may lead to behaviors that continue to reinforce those beliefs and thus become self-confirming.

A more mindful approach would be to perceive oneself and others in multiple ways. Individuals would be seen as more than just a member of a particular group (i.e., elderly adults), but rather (for example) as a man with brown eyes, who likes baseball, wears hats, is social, and likes to laugh. Even if there is only limited information about another person, that person need not be thought of as one-dimensional.

In a study conducted by Djikic, Stapleton, and Langer (2008), participants were assigned to a control group which sorted photographs of old and young people, thus priming them for old age. After this activity, and once the experiment was supposedly finished, participants were timed for how slowly they walked to an elevator (as was reported by Bargh et al. (1996)). One experimental group sorted the photos into several groups. First, they were sorted based on age; then, they were sorted based on non-age-related categories like gender. A second experimental group generated their own non-age-related sorting categories, such as race or perceived beauty. The researchers examined whether the mindful act of re-categorizing would lead people to be immune to the "old age" prime because they would come to see the person in the photo as many things and not only old. The results show the experimental groups that did the mindful sorting did not demonstrate the stereotyped behavior of walking slowly to the elevator, while the control group replicated the Bargh et al. (1996) finding.

In addition to viewing others in multidimensional ways, it is important to mindfully view one's self. Individuals may internalize negative stereotypes and define themselves primarily in one way. Research shows that a multidimensional perspective, however, can buffer the effects of depression (Linville, 1987; Showers & Zeigler-Hill, 2007). If individuals see themselves in a single-minded way, any insult or contradiction to that self-concept places the entire self at risk. On the other hand, with a multidimensional view (e.g., older, career woman, mother, smart, funny, attractive, talented), in the case of a threat to one aspect of that self (through, for example, a negative stereotype of being older), the other aspects are still present and may be protective. When we see others and ourselves in a variety of social contexts and diverse roles we enhance our capacity to be mindful.

For many older adults, aging is associated with a narrowing of self-definition. Changes in ability, opportunity, or perspective may lead to comparisons with what one used to be able to do and to a focus on restrictions. If, however, differences are noted as differences rather than decrements, older adults may see themselves more positively. Broadening our understanding of identity-defining categories as well as the environmental and motivational influences that shape behavior, enables an emphasis on continuity across the lifespan, rather than loss.

## Malleability of Contexts

Can changes in mindset—specifically towards a younger mindset—result in physical changes that reflect a younger self? Langer (1989) explored this question in what has come to be referred to as the counterclockwise study. In the study, 75- and 80-year-old men were randomly assigned to one of two groups, both of which were taken to a week-long retreat. The first group (the experimental condition) was asked to *live as if* it was 20 years earlier, when they were age 55. They were told to conduct all conversations about the past in the present tense. The second group (the control condition) was instructed to *reflect on their lives* 20 years before when they were 55 years old, and to conduct conversations in the past tense.

Pre- and post-data were recorded for physical strength, perception, cognition, hearing, and visual thresholds, and self-report data of values and behavior were collected. In addition, photographs of the men in both groups were taken both prior to and after the experiment. In the experimental condition the researchers tried to "recreate" an atmosphere that would be reminiscent of events and experiences from 20 years before. They played popular music and television shows of that time. Participants were also asked to undertake tasks requiring them to reflect on the past, such as writing autobiographical sketches about their lives in 1959, with the experimental group using the present tense and the control group using the past tense. Participants in both groups were encouraged to be more independent and active by making their own meals and cleaning up after themselves.

At the end of the week, pre- and post-data from both groups were compared to see if there were any changes within and between groups. The results indicated that by the end of the week, both groups appeared younger by about 3 years as rated by independent judges who viewed "before" and "after" photographs. For both groups there were hearing, memory, and hand strength improvements, along with weight gain. That these changes were found in both groups illustrates how alterations in perception, and greater levels of independence and activity, can influence physiological measures even in a short period of time. There were also significant differences *between* the two groups. Compared with the control group, the men in the experimental condition had better joint flexibility, posture, and vision, as well as greater finger length due to diminished arthritis. On intelligence tests, 63% of the experimental group improved their scores compared to 44% of the control group.

The counterclockwise study illustrates that some declines in physical and mental health in later life may be a product of assumptions about how one is meant to age. Supposedly "irreversible" signs of aging were altered as a result of this psychological intervention. It should be noted that the men in this study, particularly those in the experimental group, had to exercise some degree of mindfulness in order to fully participate. While being at a retreat, socializing, and engaging in various activities might account for some of the changes observed for the control group, we believe the psychological change of mindset was responsible for the differences between the two groups. One group focused on "being" in the past and the second group on "reflecting" on the past. Arguably, motivational differences might be responsible for the pre–post test differences. However, these do not account for the men appearing younger by blind observers as well as for many of the other physiological changes.

Archival analyses by Hsu, Chung, and Langer (2010) illustrate how other, real-world contexts can prime old or young age and how such mindsets can result in either favorable or unfavorable health outcomes. The general hypothesis examined in these studies was that if individuals are in contexts that prime older age, they will age more quickly. The effects of age cues on health and longevity were investigated in five very different settings including women who went to a salon to get their hair cut and/or colored, individuals who wear uniforms at work, men who are balding, women who gave birth to their first child later in life, and individuals who married spouses a few years younger or older than them.

The results demonstrated that: (1) hair color and hair style are age-related cues—women who think they look younger after having their hair colored or cut have decreases in blood pressure. They also appear younger in photographs (in which their hair is cropped out) as assessed by independent raters. (2) Clothing is an age-related cue that is eliminated by the wearing of uniforms—individuals who wear work uniforms have lower morbidity than those who earn the same amount of money and do not wear work uniforms. (3) Men who bald prematurely see an older self and therefore age faster—prematurely bald men are at a higher risk of prostate cancer and coronary heart disease compared with men who do not prematurely bald.[1] (4) Women who bear their first child later in life are surrounded by younger age-related cues—older, first-time mothers have a longer life expectancy than women who bear their first child earlier in life, after controlling for level of education and total number of children. (5) Large spousal age differences result in age-incongruent cues—younger spouses live shorter lives and older spouses live longer lives than controls. These findings suggest that we have "social clocks" by which we believe there is a "right age" for certain behaviors and changes to take place (Helson & McCabe, 1994).

These results echo those studies of other cultures in which the elderly are venerated. They show that our idea of "old" may be a result of stereotypes that have limited relevance to actual potential. Levy and Langer (1994) tested whether cultural attitudes and stereotypes about old age might contribute to age-related memory loss. They sampled a group of young people and adults with normal hearing as well as young and elderly members of two communities—the mainland Chinese (whose elders are held in high esteem) and the deaf (who do not generally share the hearing world's negative views of old age). Each group was asked to list the first five words or descriptors that come to mind when thinking of someone old. As expected, the Chinese and the deaf were less likely to mention memory loss than the other groups. The hypothesis was that if negative views contribute to memory loss in old age, and mainland Chinese people and deaf Americans hold more positive views of aging than Americans who have their hearing, Chinese and deaf Americans should show less memory loss than elderly Americans. In memory tests, Levy and Langer (1994) found that while younger people from all the groups performed equally well, the older mainland Chinese and older deaf Americans tested better than older hearing Americans. If memory loss in old age was primarily determined by biology, older subjects would be expected to demonstrate similar memory skills across cultures. The results, however, indicate that age-related changes in health do not inevitably result in decline and are largely a function of our mindsets.

It appears that certain contexts cue age. If we are in these contexts, we could choose to attend to cues that best serve us, rather than being mindlessly susceptible to age-related stereotypes. Priming can result in positive changes, not just negative changes. For example, older adults (ages 61–85) primed with positive stereotypes of old age tended to choose life-prolonging interventions in a hypothetical medical situation, in contrast to older adults primed with negative stereotypes of old age who tended to refuse life-prolonging interventions (Levy, Ashman, & Dror, 1999/2000). This suggests that perceptions of old age can affect

---

[1] Whilst balding and prostate cancer share epidemiological and biological risk factors, the authors of the original study admit that the precise mechanisms leading to the development of balding and prostate cancer are largely unknown (Hawk, Breslow, & Graubard, 2000). Furthermore, other studies (cf. Kuper & Marmot, 2003; Levy, Hausdorff, Hencke, & Wei, 2000) have shown a link between perceived age and cardiovascular health after controlling for age and other known cardiovascular disease risk factors.

the decisions we make about our health, and that priming health and competence could reverse some of the debilities assumed to be hard-wired in humans.

While contexts serve as primes, it is important to recognize who actually controls the context. As situations can be viewed in many different ways, and situations influence behavior, individuals can choose the contexts that are likely to be most beneficial to them. For example, those who are in certain contexts or relationships (e.g., the younger spouse in a marriage) can be mindful of the potential power of negative cues. In this way, previously learned negative primes can be defused and cues that prime desired health behaviors can be created. Additionally, if one is truly mindful, factors like being the younger spouse or having gray hair would not matter because age would be regarded as a fluid category that is independent of context or social role. In fact, studies show that simply being more mindful has a significant positive impact on mental and physical well-being (Alexander, Langer, Newman, Chandler, & Davies, 1989; Burpee & Langer, 2005; Crum & Langer, 2007; Djikic et al., 2008; Langer, 1989, 1997, 2002, 2009; Langer, Djikic, Pirson, Madenci, & Donohue, 2010).

## The Socially Constructed World

Mindfulness entails sensitivity to context. As such, the physical world should not be seen as an accurate or stable reflection of how well one is adapted to their environment. The external world is socially constructed for younger people by younger people. Most objects were designed to meet the needs of designers and their concept of the "typical" person. For example, if an older person is having difficulty getting out of a car, this may be attributed to a weakening of leg muscles or the loss of a sense of balance. It is unlikely that an attribution would be made to the inadequacy of a car seat that does not swivel to allow the passenger to emerge straight ahead rather than sideways. While it may seem pointless to focus on the inadequacies of automobiles, consider how ridiculous it would be to conclude that a 25-year-old's difficulty in riding a tricycle is due to an enlargement of his limbs and a loss of flexibility.

Just as the external world might be enhanced for older adults, modifications made by older adults to the environment or to their way of doing things can lead to better functioning. Simple changes, such as building a shelf by one's entryway to put groceries down so that one no longer needs to bend down to pick them up, can have a meaningful impact on independence and well-being. Differences between being young and being older are differences, not decrements, and while aging means change, change does not necessitate decay. If older adults were viewed as more competent or the construction of the physical world was more mindfully considered, then there may not be a perception of necessary deterioration. However, the standard view that the world is stable is accepted mindlessly, rather than a mindful view that considers the changing needs and development of individuals.

## Perceived Control

Research demonstrates that actually exercising control in a given situation is less important than the belief—be it true or not—of the capacity to exercise control. Being given choice increases responsibility. When choice, and consequently, control, is taken away, one can feel powerless and depressed (Peterson, Maier, & Seligman, 1993). In visits to nursing homes, Langer and Rodin observed how little choice was given to residents (Langer & Rodin, 1976; Rodin & Langer, 1977). Many of the care systems that provide treatment for older adults can perpetuate feelings of dependence and loss of control. "Overhelping" can lead individuals to infer their own helplessness and incompetence and cause them to do poorly at a task they had previously been able to accomplish. In nursing homes, life is made as easy as possible for residents and this can be seen as positive. Without challenges, however, there is little room for a sense of mastery. Mastering something new fosters mindfulness and feels good, yet older adults are often denied this competence building.

Langer and her colleagues wanted to see whether giving more choice and responsibility to nursing home residents improved well-being. In one study (Langer & Rodin, 1976) a group of participant nursing home residents was encouraged to make more decisions for themselves. For example, they were allowed to choose where to receive visitors, and if and when to watch the movies that were shown at the home. Each also chose a houseplant to care for, decided where to place it in their room, as well as when and how much to water it. The researchers' intent was to make the nursing home residents more mindful, to help them engage with the world and live their lives more fully. Those in a second, control group were not instructed to make their own decisions; they were given houseplants but told that the nursing staff would care for them. A year and a half later, those in the experimental group showed pre–post test increases in cheerfulness, activity, and alertness and had half the number of deaths compared to the controls. Making choices resulted in mindfulness, which had positive consequences for health and well-being.

## Different Motivations at Different Ages

It would be helpful for observers to consider alternative explanations for others' behavior. We tend to make fundamental attribution errors in which we ascribe other peoples' behavior to their dispositions and our behavior to the situation (Ross, Amabile, & Steinmetz, 2005). If younger adults forget information, it may be brushed off as unimportant to begin with or just a momentary lapse in memory. When older adults forget information, however, it tends to be attributed to a stable factor—their age. Yet, it may be that the information a younger person cares about is different from what an older person cares about. To illustrate this point, Langer and her colleagues (Langer, Rodin, Beck, Weinman, & Spitzer, 1979) provided incentives to nursing home residents to increase their mindfulness. They divided the nursing home residents into an experimental group and two control groups. The experimental group was given chips that could be exchanged for gifts every time they found out and remembered information that the researchers had requested, such as when certain activities would take place and the nurses' names. As the residents wanted the gifts, the information they were asked to track now mattered to them. Residents in one control group were given chips as mementos, but not as motivation to earn future rewards. Residents in the second control group were neither given tasks to complete nor chips to have. After 3 weeks, the researchers found improvements in memory and concluded that when remembering mattered, memory improved. Several tests of cognitive ability were administered on the last day, including one asking residents to describe their roommates and another asking them to find novel uses for a familiar object. The experimental group was able to provide more detailed descriptions of their roommates and their rooms even though they were not asked to take note of these. They also outperformed the control groups in the "new use" portion of the study. Finally, the intervention resulted in an increase in longevity: at follow-up only 7% of the experimental group had passed away compared to more than four times this rate in the comparison groups.

Thus far, we have suggested that having positive views about aging can have positive mental and physical benefits. However, in the next section we will suggest that making evaluations about ourselves and others makes us vulnerable, and that being mindful is critical to sustaining happiness.

## The Mindlessness of Evaluation

When we are not locked into fixed evaluations, we have far more control over our well-being than we think. The prevalence of value judgments in our lives reveals little about the world and much about our minds. What is considered beautiful, unattractive, good, bad, virtuous, wicked, desirable, and undesirable are products of our mind. We may stay evaluative because positive evaluation helps us feel good in the short run. However, as soon as we agree to accept a positive evaluation as reason to feel good about ourselves, we open the door to the damaging consequences of perceived failure.

Langer, Janis, and Wolfer (1975) conducted an experimental investigation aimed at teaching people to be positive. They looked at the effects of a positive outlook on preoperative stress and found that patients became less stressed, took fewer pain relievers and sedatives, and were able to leave the hospital sooner than comparison groups. This example suggests a single-minded positive view can be more beneficial to health and well-being than a mindless negative view.

There are, however, problems inherent in teaching people to view things positively. First, the suggestion that things are positive implies that others are inherently negative; positive evaluations may inadvertently rob us of perceived control. Second, teaching people to be positive can lead evaluations to be tied to events, ideas, and people, and thus promote mindlessness. The mindful individual is able to recognize that each outcome has both positive and negative potential, and that choices can be made with respect to affective experience. Thus the person is able to reap the rewards both of a positive chosen outcome and of increased perceived control.

## Recommendations for Practice

Based on the theoretical and empirical work outlined in this chapter we now summarize some key recommendations for enhancing well-being in practice:

1. Identify qualities other than age that describe oneself and others (e.g., immediate circumstances, personality traits, gender, occupation).

2. Consider how context may influence thoughts about oneself and others (e.g., that gray hair acts as a prime for age-related stereotypes).
3. Think about how a certain age group can simultaneously be perceived as positive and negative. For example, older adults can be thought of as wise, experienced, and generous, or as dwelling on past solutions. Young people could be perceived as naïve, inexperienced, and self-absorbed or excited, engaged, and involved.
4. Increase choice-making—however small—as this fosters feelings of control and independence.
5. Consider alternative explanations or motives for others' actions. For example, an older adult might forget a name because they did not care to learn it in the first place.
6. Engage in cognitive training exercises. For example, Alexander et al. (1989) found that simple cognitive exercises, such as thinking of an object or topic in new and creative ways (e.g., suggesting unusual uses for common objects), improved cognitive function, mental health ratings, blood pressure, and ultimately, longevity in nursing home residents.

# Conclusion

Many of us have unwittingly been taught how to grow old by being exposed to mindsets that are more limiting than they need to be. While death is inevitable, we can certainly influence life before death. It is useful to recognize that our beliefs and much of the external world are social constructions, and that there are alternatives. In this chapter, we have suggested that mindfulness helps us to fight the negative effects of unconscious primes, to question the hidden decisions that rob us of choices, and to unpack and rebuild a socially constructed world that does not fit our own specifications. Rather than seeking to feel as we did when we were younger and treating old age as a time of inevitable cognitive and physical decline, the goal would be to engage in mindful living all the while we are alive. Being mindful means we are more engaged with our lives now, embracing the growth and experience we are gaining rather than holding on to memories of what we used to be able to do. It is a goal worth striving toward and one within our reach.

## References

Alexander, C. N., Langer, E. J., Newman, R. I., Chandler, H. M., & Davies, J. L. (1989). Transcendental meditation, mindfulness, and longevity: An experimental study with the elderly. *Journal of Personality and Social Psychology, 57*(6), 950–964.

Bargh, J.A., Chen, M., & Burrows, L. (1996). Automaticity of social behavior: Direct effects of trait construct and stereotype activation on action. *Journal of Personality and Social Psychology, 71*(2), 230–244.

Burpee, L. C., & Langer, E. J. (2005). Mindfulness and marital satisfaction. *Journal of Adult Development, 12*(1), 43–51.

Cohen, G. (2005). *The mature mind: The positive power of the aging brain.* New York, NY: Basic Books.

Crum, A. J., & Langer, E. J. (2007). Mindset matters: Exercise and the placebo effect. *Psychological Science, 18*(2), 165–171.

Demakakos, P., Gjonca, E., & Nazroo, J. (2007). Age identity, age perceptions, and health: Evidence from the English Longitudinal Study of Aging. *Annals of New York Academy of Sciences, 1114*, 279–287.

Djikic, M., Langer, E. J., & Stapleton, S. F. (2008). Reducing stereotyping through mindfulness: Decreasing effects of stereotype-activated behaviors. *Journal of Adult Development, 15*, 106–111.

Hawk, E., Breslow, R. A., & Graubard, B. I. (2000). Male pattern baldness and clinical prostate cancer in the epidemiologic follow-up of the first National Health and Nutrition Examination Survey. *Cancer Epidemiology, Biomarkers, and Prevention, 9*, 523–527.

Helson, R., & McCabe, L. (1994). The social clock project in middle age. In B. F. Turner & L. E. Troll (Eds.), *Women growing older: Psychological perspectives* (pp. 68–93). Thousand Oaks, CA: Sage.

Hsu, L. M., Chung, J., & Langer, E. J. (2010). The influence of age-related cues on health and longevity. *Perspectives on Psychological Science, 5*(6), 632–648.

Isaacs, L. W., & Bearison, D. J. (1986). The development of children's prejudice against the aged. *International Journal of Aging and Human Development, 23*, 175–194.

Kuper, H., & Marmot, M. (2003). Intimations of mortality: Perceived age of leaving middle age as a predictor of future health outcomes within the Whitehall II study. *Age and Ageing, 32*, 178–184.

Langer, E. (1989). *Mindfulness.* Reading, MA: Addison-Wesley.

Langer, E. (1997). *The power of mindful learning.* Reading, MA: Addison-Wesley.

Langer, E. J. (2009). *Counterclockwise.* New York, NY: Ballantine Books.

Langer, E., Djikic, M., Pirson, M., Madenci, A., & Donohue, R. (2010). Believing is seeing: Using mindlessness (mindfully) to improve visual acuity. *Psychological Science, 21*(5), 661–666.

Langer, E., Janis, I., & Wolfer, J. (1975). Reduction of psychological stress in surgical patients. *Journal of Experimental Social Psychology, 11*, 155–165.

Langer, E. & Rodin, J. (1976). The effects of enhanced personal responsibility for the aged: A field experiment in an institutional setting. *Journal of Personality and Social Psychology, 34*, 191–198.

Langer, E. J., Rodin, J., Beck, P., Weinman, C., & Spitzer, L. (1979). Environmental determinants of memory improvement in late adulthood. *Journal of Personality and Social Psychology, 37*, 2003–2013.

Levy, B. R., Ashman, O., & Dror I. (1999/2000). To be or not to be: The effects of aging stereotypes on the will to live. *Omega, 40*(3), 409–420.

Levy, B. R., Hausdorff, J., Hencke, R., & Wei, J. Y. (2000). Reducing cardiovascular stress with positive self-stereotypes of aging. *Journals of Gerontology: Psychological Sciences, 55*, 205–213.

Levy, B. R., & Langer, E. J. (1994). Memory advantage for deaf and Chinese elders: Aging free from negative premature cognitive commitments. *Journal of Personality and Social Psychology, 66*(6), 989–997.

Linville, P. W. (1987). Self-complexity as a cognitive buffer against stress-related depression and illness. *Journal of Personality and Social Psychology, 52*, 663–676.

Nelson, T. D. (2002). *Ageism: Stereotyping and prejudice against older persons.* Cambridge, MA: MIT Press.

Nickerson, R. S. (1998). Confirmation bias: A ubiquitous phenomenon in many guises. *Review of General Psychology, 2*(2), 175–220.

Nosek, B. A., Banaji, M. R., & Greenwald, A. G. (2002). Harvesting implicit group attitudes and beliefs from a demonstration website. *Group Dynamics, 6*, 101–115.

Palmore, E. B., Branch, L., & Harris, D. K. (Eds.) (2005). *Encyclopedia of ageism*. Binghamton, NY: Haworth Pastoral Press.

Peterson, C., Maier, S., & Seligman, M.E.P. (1993). *Learned helplessness: A theory for the age of personal control*. New York, NY: Oxford University Press.

Rodin, J. & Langer, E. (1977). Long-term effects of a control-relevant intervention among the institutionalized aged. *Journal of Personality and Social Psychology, 35*, 897–902.

Rodin, J. & Langer, E. (1980). Aging labels: the decline of control and the fall of self-esteem. *Journal of Social Issues, 36*, 12–29.

Ross, L. D., Amabile, T. M., & Steinmetz, J. L. (2005). Social roles, social control, and biases in social-perception processes. In D. L. Hamilton (Ed.), *Social cognition: Key readings* (pp. 324–332). New York, NY: Psychology Press.

Showers, C. J., & Zeigler-Hill, V. (2007). Compartmentalization and integration: The evaluative organization of contextualized selves. *Journal of Personality, 75*(6), 1181–1204.

Siegel, M., Bradley, E. H., & Kasl, S. V. (2003). Self-rated life expectancy as a predictor of mortality: Evidence from the HRS and AHEAD surveys. *Gerontology, 49*, 265–271.

Vaillant, G. E. (2002). *Aging well*. New York, NY: Little, Brown, and Company.

# CHAPTER 77

# WELL-BEING THERAPY: THEORETICAL BACKGROUND, CLINICAL IMPLICATIONS, AND FUTURE DIRECTIONS

GIOVANNI A. FAVA AND CHIARA RUINI

Department of Psychology, University of Bologna, Italy

The concepts of psychological well-being, quality of life, and optimal human functioning have long been neglected in the mental health professions. Historically, the main focus of research has been the development of psychotherapies that lead to symptom reduction, with psychological well-being viewed only as a by-product. This is likely due to the equating of psychological health with an absence of illness, rather than the presence of wellness (Ryff & Singer, 1996). There is increasing awareness that the concept of recovery in clinical psychiatry and psychology cannot simply be conflated with response to treatment or limited to the abatement of symptoms (Fava, Ruini, & Belaise, 2007; Oades, Crowe, & Deane, Chapter 78, this volume; Seligman, Rashid, & Parks, 2006; Sin & Lyubomirsky, 2009).

A growing body of literature highlights the existence of residual symptoms such as social and interpersonal maladjustments, irritability, anhedonia, and sleep disorders, even after apparently successful treatment of mood and anxiety disorders (Goldberg & Harrow, 2004; Judd et al., 2000; Paykel & Weissman, 1973; Papakostas et al., 2004). For example, remitted patients with mood and anxiety disorders have been found to have significantly lower levels of psychological well-being compared to healthy control subjects (Rafanelli et al., 2000). Most residual symptoms also occur in the prodromal phase of illness and may progress to become prodromes of relapse (Fava, Ruini, & Belaise, 2007). In recognition of this, psychotherapeutic treatments have been designed to specifically address residual symptomatology, with the finding that they improve the long-term outcomes of major depressive disorders (Fava, Ruini, & Rafanelli, 2005).

Clinicians working with patients with mood and anxiety disorders are often confronted with the unsatisfactory degree of remission that current therapeutic strategies yield and with the vexing problems of relapse and recurrence (Fava, Tomba, & Grandi, 2007). Ryff and Singer (1996) suggested that the absence of well-being creates conditions of vulnerability to possible future adversities, and that the route to enduring recovery lies not only in alleviating the negative, but also in engendering the positive. The need to advance intervention strategies and programs by including psychological well-being has become clear. In clinical populations with a high risk of relapse (such as major depression), increases in psychological well-being are likely to improve individual resilience and provide a buffer against life stresses. Interventions that target the positive may address aspects of functioning and health that are not typically part of conventional treatments (Fava, Tomba, & Grandi, 2007). In this chapter we will briefly introduce a positive psychotherapeutic approach, well-being therapy (WBT), a central proposition of which is that deficits in well-being are due to an inattention to positive experiences and a lack of capacity to sustain states of well-being when confronted with negative subjective experiences (e.g., negative automatic thoughts). The various phases of WBT will be described, followed by a brief review of WBT validation studies and a description of how WBT can be applied within different populations, particularly with young people.

# Well-Being Therapy: Theoretical Background

WBT was developed in response to the clinical need just outlined. It has been tested in controlled trials both as a single intervention (e.g., Fava, Rafanelli, Cazzaro, Conti, & Grandi, 1998a) and as a complement to cognitive behavioral therapy (CBT) (e.g., Fava, Ruini, Rafanelli, Finos, Conti, & Grandi, 2004; Fava, Ruini, Rafanelli, et al., 2005). Based on Ryff's (1989) six dimensions of psychological well-being (PWB; see Table 77.1), the goal of WBT is to facilitate a movement from impaired to optimal levels of well-being in each dimension (Fava, 1999; Fava & Ruini, 2003), improvements that have been reported by patients with affective disorders (Fava, Rafanelli, Cazzaro, et al., 1998a).

## Structure of well-being therapy

WBT is a short-term, 6–12-session treatment protocol, with 30–50-minute sessions typically conducted every week or fortnight. The WBT protocol emphasizes self-observation (Emmelkamp, 1974) and usually involves the use of a structured diary. It is directive, oriented towards current problems that hinder sustained PWB, and based on the growing awareness of the positive aspects of the self (Fava, 1999; Fava & Ruini, 2003). The initial treatment sessions focus on the development of skills and capacities that enable sustained attention to be directed towards positive daily experiences and emotions, with the later ones emphasizing the promotion of psychological well-being.

### *Initial sessions*

Early treatment sessions are primarily concerned with identifying episodes of well-being (no matter how short lived they are) and setting them in context. Through the use of

Table 77.1 Modification of the six dimensions of psychological well-being of Ryff's model (1989) for WBT

| Dimensions | Impaired level | Optimal level |
| --- | --- | --- |
| Environmental mastery | The subject experiences difficulties in managing everyday affairs; feels unable to change or improve surrounding context; is unaware of contextual opportunities; lacks sense of control over external world | The subject has a sense of mastery and competence in managing the environment; controls external activities; makes effective use of contextual opportunities; is able to create or choose contexts suitable to personal needs and values |
| Personal growth | The subject is experiencing a sense of personal stagnation; lacks a sense of improvement or expansion over time; feels bored and uninterested in life; feels unable to develop new attitudes or behaviors | The subject has a feeling of continued development; sees self as growing and expanding; is open to new experiences; has sense of realizing own potential; sees improvement in self and behavior over time |
| Purpose in life | The subject lacks a sense of meaning in life; has few goals or aims and lacks a sense of direction; does not see purpose in past life experiences; has no outlooks or beliefs that give life meaning | The subject has goals in life and a sense of directedness; feels there is meaning to the present and the past experiences in his/her life; holds beliefs that give life purpose; has aims and objectives for living |
| Autonomy | The subject is overly concerned with the expectations and evaluation of others; relies on judgment of others to make important decisions; conforms to social pressures to think or act in certain ways | The subject is self-determining and independent; is able to resist social pressures; regulates behavior from within; evaluates self by personal standards |
| Self-acceptance | The subject feels dissatisfied with self; is disappointed with what has occurred in the past; is troubled by certain personal qualities; wishes to be different from what he or she is | The subject has a positive attitude toward the self; accepts his/her good and bad qualities; feels positive about the past |
| Positive relations with others | The subject has few close, trusting relationships with others; finds it difficult to be open and is isolated and frustrated in interpersonal relationships; is not willing to make compromises to sustain important ties with others | The subject has warm and trusting relationships with others; is concerned about the welfare of others; is capable of strong empathy, affection, and intimacy; understands the give and take of human relationships |

a structured diary, patients are asked to report the circumstances surrounding their experiences of well-being, along with ratings on a 0–100 scale (with 0 indexing an absence of well-being and 100 the most well-being possible). Rather than being taught Ryff's (1989) PWB model, they are encouraged to use their own definitions. The purpose here is to enhance the capacity for self-observation.

While the use of Ryff's conceptual definitions are not made explicit to patients, the model can support WBT in several ways. For instance, pre- and post-therapy administrations of the 84-item Scales of Psychological Well-Being (Ryff, 1989) provide a useful index of the patient's psychological health as well as the effectiveness of the treatment. In addition, the six PWB dimensions can be progressively introduced to the patient as appropriate. For example, if the patient is struggling in these areas the therapist could explain that autonomy consists of having an internal locus of control, independence, and self-determination, or that personal growth involves being open to new experience and considering the self as expanding over time. Faulty thinking and alternative interpretations may then be discussed.

This early emphasis on identifying positive experiences is informed by the value of ameliorating hedonic deficits. Meehl (1975) described how those with low hedonic capacity should pay greater attention to the "hedonic book keeping" of their activities than would be necessary for people located midway or high on the hedonic capacity continuum. Meehl's observations have been confirmed in two controlled trials (Burton & King, 2004; Emmons & McCullough, 2003) in which attention to positive daily experiences resulted in improved levels of psychological well-being (Emmons & McCullough, 2003) or fewer health center visits for illness (Burton & King, 2004).

Patients are also encouraged to monitor the quality of their experience in everyday situations (e.g., work and leisure). Research shows that individuals preferentially invest their attention and psychic resources in activities associated with rewarding and challenging states of consciousness, and in particular, with optimal experience (Csikszentmihalyi & Csikszentmihalyi, 1988). Optimal experience is characterized by the perception of high environmental challenge and environmental mastery, deep concentration, involvement, enjoyment, clear goals, immediate feedback, and intrinsic motivation (Deci & Ryan, 1985). Given that cross-sectional studies have demonstrated that optimal experience can occur in any daily context (Delle Fave & Massimini, 2003; Massimini & Delle Fave, 2000), patients are asked to report their optimal experiences and identify the activities or situations that are associated with them.

Whilst this initial phase generally takes one to two sessions, this depends on the completion of the out-of-session homework. The identification of instances of well-being and of optimal experiences, and reporting them in the diary are indicators that the person is ready to move to the next phase, where the obstacles to sustained psychological well-being are targeted.

## Intermediate sessions

Once instances of well-being are properly recognized, the patient is encouraged to identify thoughts and beliefs that trigger an interruption of well-being. Whilst this surfacing of irrational, tension-evoking thoughts is similar to Rational–Emotive Therapy (Ellis & Becker, 1982) and Cognitive Therapy (Beck, Rush, Shaw, & Emery, 1979), the point of departure is that WBT focuses on what interrupts well-being, rather than what contributes to distress.

This phase is crucial, since it allows the therapist to differentiate which dimensions of PWB are impacted by irrational or automatic thoughts and which are not. The therapist may challenge these thoughts with questions, such as "What is the evidence for or against this idea?" or "Are you thinking in all-or nothing terms?" (Beck, Rush, Shaw, & Emery, 1979). The therapist may also reinforce and encourage activities that are likely to elicit well-being and optimal experiences by, for instance, assigning the task of undertaking a specific pleasurable activity for a certain duration each day. This reinforcement may also result in graded task assignments (Beck et al., 1979) with an emphasis on exposure to feared or challenging situations that the patient would normally avoid. The focus of this phase of well-being therapy is always on self-monitoring moments and feelings of well-being and graded task assignments. The therapist refrains from suggesting alternative interpretations, unless a satisfactory degree of self-observation (including identifying irrational or automatic thoughts) has been achieved. This intermediate phase may take place over two to three sessions, depending on the patient's motivation and ability, and it paves the way for specific well-being enhancing strategies. Identifying automatic thoughts in the diary indicates a readiness to move to the next phase, which is aimed at offering alternative interpretations to automatic thoughts.

## Final sessions

At this point the patient is typically able to identify experiences of well-being and the cognitions that interrupt them. The patient is also encouraged to pursue optimal experiences, even if this involves the risk of failure, or may be considered selfish by the patient. Monitoring episodes of well-being and their associated negative thoughts allows the therapist to detect specific impairments in well-being, which are interpreted and corrected according to Ryff's conceptual framework.

The techniques used in WBT to overcome impairments in PWB may include cognitive restructuring (i.e., modification of automatic or irrational thoughts), activity scheduling (e.g., mastery, pleasure, and graded exposure), assertiveness training (to improve autonomy), problem solving (to improve environmental mastery), and self-observation of positive experiences (Beck et al., 1979; Burton & King, 2004; Ellis & Becker, 1982; Emmons & McCullough, 2003; Pava, Fava, & Levenson, 1994). As often happens with CBT, simply becoming aware of problematic standards, beliefs, and assumptions can induce positive change. Oftentimes, however, modification requires more time and effort through, say, the use of a structured diary (Beck et al., 1979) It is only when insights about the impairment of well-being are translated into behavior change that significant improvements are possible. For instance, a patient who becomes aware of his or her impairments in autonomy (Ryff, 1989) may become more assertive and start speaking up more in social situations.

# Validation Studies

Several studies have assessed the clinical efficacy of WBT both as a standalone and complementary intervention. The findings are presented in the following sections.

## Residual phase of mood and anxiety disorders

The effectiveness of WBT in the residual phase of affective disorders was tested in a preliminary controlled investigation by Fava, Rafanelli, Cazzaro, et al. (1998a). Twenty patients with affective disorders (e.g., major depression, social phobia, obsessive–compulsive disorder) who had been successfully treated by behavioral (for the anxiety disorders) or pharmacological (for the mood disorders) methods, were randomly assigned to either WBT or CBT for residual symptoms. Both treatments were associated with significant reductions in residual symptoms (as measured by the Clinical Interview for Depression (CID); Paykel, 1985) and increases in PWB (Ryff, 1989). However, when the residual symptoms of the two groups were compared immediately after treatment, WBT had resulted in significantly greater reductions compared to CBT. WBT was also associated with a significant increase in PWB, particularly in the Personal Growth scale, when compared to CBT. While these preliminary results should be interpreted with caution, they do point to the feasibility of WBT for the residual stage of affective disorders.

### Treatment of generalized anxiety disorder

WBT has also been used to treat generalized anxiety disorder (GAD) (Fava, Ruini, Rafanelli, et al., 2005). Twenty patients diagnosed with GAD were randomly assigned either to eight sessions of CBT or to the sequential administration of four sessions of CBT followed by four sessions of WBT. Although both treatments were associated with reductions in anxiety, the CBT–WBT intervention resulted in significantly greater levels of symptom reduction and increases in PWB compared to CBT alone. A possible explanation for these findings is that when compared to the customary self-monitoring of episodes of distress in cognitive therapy (Beck & Emery, 1985), the monitoring of episodes of well-being facilitated by WBT may lead to a more comprehensive identification of automatic thoughts and more effective cognitive restructuring. These results indicate the potential advantages of adding WBT to the treatment of GAD and of the sequential use of treatment components for achieving more sustained recovery (also see Ruini and Fava (2009) for a case study of a young GAD patient successfully treated using the CBT–WBT protocol).

### Prevention of recurrent depression

One longitudinal study has assessed the integration of WBT into a CBT protocol for recurrent depression (Fava, Rafanelli, Grandi, Conti, & Belluardo, 1998b) with the aim of addressing both residual symptoms and lifestyle modifications. Forty patients with recurrent major depression who had been successfully treated with antidepressant medication were randomly assigned to either this integrated CBT and WBT protocol or to standard clinical management. In both groups, the antidepressant medications were gradually discontinued. The group that received the integrated CBT–WBT intervention had a significantly lower level of residual symptoms after drug discontinuation compared with the clinical management group. At a 2-year follow-up the CBT-WBT group had a significantly lower relapse rate (25%) than the clinical management group (80%), and at a 6-year follow-up (Fava et al., 2004) these rates were 40% for the former group and 90% for the latter. Further, even in the context of multiple relapses, those in the integrated CBT–WBT group had significantly fewer recurrences.

### Loss of clinical effect during drug treatment

The return of depressive symptoms during maintenance antidepressant treatment is a common and vexing clinical phenomenon (Baldessarini, Ghaemi, & Viguera, 2002; Bockting et al., 2008; Papakostas, Perlis, Seifert, & Fava, 2007). A number of pharmacological strategies have been suggested for addressing the loss of antidepressant efficacy, but with limited success (Chouinard & Chouinard, 2008; Schmidt et al., 2002). To examine whether an intervention that included WBT might improve the maintenance of medication effects, ten patients with recurrent depression who had relapsed while taking antidepressant drugs were randomly assigned either to a *dose increase* group or to a *same dose* group who also received the CBT–WBT protocol (Fava, Ruini, Rafanelli, & Grandi, 2002). Four of the five patients in the dose increase group responded to the larger dose, but all had relapsed while on that dose by 1-year follow-up. Four out of the five patients in the same dose plus CBT–WBT group responded, and only one had relapsed by the 1-year follow-up. These data suggest that combined CBT and WBT interventions may counteract decreases in long-term pharmacological efficacy in the treatment of depression. The mechanisms underlying the role of WBT in this outcome cannot be discerned from this study. Tolerance to antidepressant treatment has been associated with the activation of the hypothalamic–pituitary–adrenal (HPA) axis (Fava, 2003). Continued treatment with antidepressant drugs over the long term may induce changes in the serotoninergic receptors controlling the HPA axis and its activation may lead to a depressive relapse (Fava, 2003). Given preliminary evidence from a single case report that WBT induced a normalization of the HPA axis (Sonino & Fava, 2003) it may be through this mechanism that WBT restores and maintains remission with antidepressant drugs.

## Post-traumatic stress disorder

The treatment of post-traumatic stress disorder (PTSD) presents a major challenge from a psychotherapeutic perspective (Cottraux et al., 2008; Schnyder, 2005; Van Emmerik, Kamphuis, & Emmelkamp, 2008) and research aimed at ameliorating trauma-related psychiatric disorder is vital (Schnyder, 2005). While there are currently no controlled investigations on the use of WBT for treating PTSD, Belaise, Fava, and Marks (2005) reported two cases in which patients recovered from PTSD following WBT, even though their central trauma was discussed only in the initial history-taking session. These findings should be interpreted with caution since, for example, the patients may have remitted spontaneously. They are intriguing, however, because they suggest an alternative route for overcoming trauma and developing resilience. As such, further investigation is warranted.

# Future Directions

WBT has been recently modified and piloted with children and adolescents, both in clinical and educational settings.

## School interventions

Nowadays schools are viewed not only as the ideal setting for developing learning and educational processes, but also for building skills that promote resilience and psychological well-being (Caffo, Belaise, & Forresi, 2008). In the first pilot investigation (Ruini, Belaise, Brombin, Caffo, & Fava, 2006), 111 middle school students were randomly assigned to either a four-session CBT-based protocol or a four-session WBT-based equivalent. Classes were randomly selected and, as the main aim of the project was the promotion of psychological well-being, no specific problems or targets needed to be addressed. The students were assessed pre- and post-intervention using Ryff's PWB scales along with the Symptom Questionnaire (SQ; Kellner, 1987), which measures levels of anxiety, depression, hostility, and somatization. The results showed that there were comparable improvements in symptoms (particularly anxiety and somatization) and psychological well-being (particularly self-acceptance) across both the CBT- and WBT-based protocols (Ruini et al., 2006). This pilot investigation suggests that well-being enhancing strategies could play an important role in the prevention of psychological distress and the promotion of optimal functioning among children. However, since two of the four sessions shared common treatment ingredients (i.e. psychoeducation on emotions and cognitive restructuring), the specific contributions of each protocol could not be determined.

The specific effects of WBT and CBT approaches in schools have since been explored in another controlled investigation. This involved a longer intervention and adequate follow-up. In this study (Tomba et al., 2010), volunteer classes at junior high schools in Northern Italy (6th–8th grade) were randomly assigned to either a WBT-based protocol or a CBT-based anxiety management (AM) protocol (n = 162). The aim of this study was to test whether each strategy would differentially impact on its specific theoretically congruent target (i.e. well-being vs. distress). It was hypothesized that the WBT protocol would more effectively enhance well-being and optimal functioning whereas the AM protocol would more effectively reduce distress. Based on the experience gained from the pilot study just described (Ruini et al., 2006), the number of sessions was increased from four to six 2-hour sessions. The WBT protocol resulted in significant improvements in autonomy (PWB) and physiological anxiety, whereas the AM protocol ameliorated psychological distress (anxious symptoms). When the two interventions were compared using the covariance analyses for baseline measurements, the AM intervention produced a significant decrease in anxiety, whereas WBT resulted in significant improvements in interpersonal functioning. These effects were maintained at a 6-month follow-up, which suggests that it is possible to enduringly and positively impact on psychological well-being and distress using brief interventions in schools.

In light of the promising findings obtained with middle-school students, WBT interventions have been extended to high schools and applied with older students who are considered a more at risk population for mood and anxiety disorders (Clarke et al., 1995). In one study, Ruini et al. (2009) randomly assigned eight 9th grade classes and one 10th grade class to either a WBT-based protocol (five classes) or an attention-placebo protocol (four classes) that consisted of relaxation techniques, group discussion on common problems reported by students and conflict resolution. A total of 227 students participated.

The WBT-based protocol comprised six 2-hour sessions that were held once a week in the class and involved role-playing and group discussions. This intervention was more effective at promoting psychological well-being (particularly on the dimension of personal growth) and decreasing distress (i.e. symptoms of anxiety and somatization), compared with the attention placebo group. This corresponds with the findings of the intervention studies in middle schools (Ruini et al., 2006; Tomba et al., 2010), where the WBT approach yielded significant improvement in physical well-being and somatization. It suggests that school-based WBT could have important clinical implications in view of the high prevalence of somatic symptoms in children and adolescents (Ginsburg, Riddle, & Davies, 2006; Muris, Vermeer, & Horselenberg, 2008). In addition, whilst the decrease in anxiety was maintained for the WBT group at follow-up, the same was not true for improvements in the attention-placebo group. Promoting positive functioning and building individual strengths in young populations could result in more enduring effects than merely focusing on depressive or anxious symptoms.

## Child well-being therapy

Recently the standard WBT protocol has been modified and applied to a child population of patients with mood, anxiety and conduct disorders, with the aim of testing its impact on reducing symptoms, and improving skills and competencies (Albieri, Visani, Offidani, Ottolini, & Ruini, 2009). Four children with different DSM-IV diagnoses (i.e., oppositional-defiant disorder, attention-deficit hyperactivity disorder, major depressive disorder, and generalized anxiety disorder) were provided with this modified WBT protocol, without any form of accompanying pharmacological treatment. The WBT intervention consisted of seven 1-hour sessions conducted once a week and involving interactions between the child and the therapist using games and role-playing, a diary, and homework assignments. Although positive and negative emotions were discussed throughout the protocol, in the first four sessions negative emotions were emphasized, whereas in the last three sessions the focus was on enhancing psychological well-being. Two additional sessions on parental training were added to involve parents in the therapeutic process and to improve treatment adherence with their children. In all of the patients WBT was associated with a decrease in symptomatology (particularly anxiety and somatization) and an improvement in psychological well-being (particularly autonomy and interpersonal functioning) as measured by the PWB scales (Ryff, 1998) and direct teacher and parent observations. In two of the four patients, WBT was also associated with improvements in school performance.

WBT provides an innovative means of promoting PWB and optimal functioning in children (Caffo, Belaise, & Forresi, 2008) across different clinical presentations. These results are promising but further research using controlled designs is needed.

## Conclusions

WBT was originally developed as a strategy for promoting PWB in clinical populations where standard pharmacological or psychotherapeutic treatments were seen to be lacking. It was based on the assumption that impairments to well-being vary from one illness to another, from patient to patient, and even across episodes of the same illness in the same patient. This individualized approach characterizes the treatment protocol, which requires careful self-monitoring before any cognitive restructuring takes place. Unlike standard cognitive therapy, which is underpinned by specific assumptions (e.g., the cognitive triad in depression) (Beck et al., 1979), WBT evolves based on findings from self-observation in the diary. As a result of this process WBT may be used to address specific areas of concern in the course of treatment and in combination with other pharmacological and psychological approaches.

This flexibility provides realistic solutions to emerging evidence of the unsatisfactory degree of remission of single-line treatments and the need to address several areas of concern in interventions with patients who have mood and anxiety disorders (Fava, Tomba, & Grandi, 2007). While WBT might be unsuitable for acutely ill patients, such as those experiencing a major depressive episode in which negative thoughts are overwhelming, it appears well-matched to addressing psychological issues that other therapies have left unexplored. However, these conclusions are tentative and may be modified by additional research. Similarly, while clinical studies have thus far used individual WBT (with group WBT only being tested in educational settings) it is possible that a group format may offer a worthwhile avenue for clinical contexts.

Recommendations for practice:

1. WBT can be considered an effective psychotherapeutic strategy for improving PWB in clinical and educational settings.
2. WBT can be used sequentially after CBT or drug therapy to improve remission and relapse rates in mood and anxiety disorders.
3. While WBT has primarily been tested in patients in the residual phase of affective disorders, recent pilot studies indicate its use in addressing the loss of antidepressant efficacy in recurrent depression, PTSD, and psychological disorders in children.
4. A modified WBT protocol can be used in school settings with the aim of promoting PWB and preventing distress in children and adolescents.
5. New applications of WBT—in a group format with subclinical or normal populations—can be considered as strategies for mental health promotion.

# References

Albieri, E., Visani, D., Offidani, E., Ottolini, F., & Ruini, C. (2009). Well-being therapy in children with emotional and behavioral disturbances: A pilot investigation. *Psychotherapy and Psychosomatics, 78,* 387–390.

Baldessarini, R. J., Ghaemi, S. N., & Viguera, A. C. (2002). Tolerance in antidepressant treatment. *Psychotherapy and Psychosomatics, 71,* 177–179.

Beck, A. T., & Emery, G. (1985). *Anxiety disorder and phobia.* New York, NY: Basic Books.

Beck, A. T, Rush, A. J., Shaw, B. F., & Emery, G. (1979). *Cognitive therapy of depression.* New York, NY: Guilford Press.

Belaise, C., Fava, G. A., & Marks, I. M. (2005). Alternatives to debriefing and modifications to cognitive behavior therapy for posttraumatic stress disorder. *Psychotherapy and Psychosomatics, 74,* 212–217.

Bockting, C. L. H, ten Doesschate, M. C., Spijker, J., Spinhoven, P., Koeter, M. W. J., Schene, A. H., & the Delta Study Group (2008). Continuation and maintenance use of antidepressants in recurrent depression. *Psychotherapy and Psychosomatics, 77,* 17–26.

Burton, C. M., & King, L. A. (2004). The health benefits of writing about intensely positive experiences. *Journal of Research in Personality, 38,* 150–163.

Caffo, E., Belaise, C., & Forresi, B. (2008). Promotiong resilience and psychological well-being in vulnerable life stages. *Psychotherapy and Psychosomatics, 77,* 331–336.

Chouinard, G., & Chouinard, V. (2008). Atypical antipsychotics. *Psychotherapy and Psychosomatics, 77,* 69–77.

Clarke, G. N., Hawkins, W., Murphy, M., Sheeber, L. B., Lewinsohn, P. M., & Seeley, J. R. (1995). Targeted prevention of unipolar depressive disorder in an at-risk sample of high school adolescents: A randomized trial of a group cognitive intervention. *Journal of the American Academy of Child and Adolescent Psychiatry, 34*, 312–321.

Cottraux, J., Note, I., Yao, S. H., de Meg-Guillard, C., Bonasse, F., Djamoussian, D., … Chen, Y. (2008). Randomized controlled comparison of cognitive behavior therapy with Rogerian supportive therapy in chronic post-traumatic stress disorder. *Psychotherapy and Psychosomatics, 77*, 101–110.

Csikszentmihalyi, M., & Csikszentmihalyi, I. (Eds.). (1998). *Optimal experience. Psychological studies of flow in consciousness*. New York, NY: Cambridge University Press.

Deci, E. L., & Ryan R. M. (1985). *Intrinsic motivation and self-determination in human behavior*. New York, NY: Plenum Press.

Delle Fave, A., & Massimini, F. (2003). Optimal experience in work and leisure among teachers and physicians. *Leisure Studies, 22*, 323–342.

Ellis, A., & Becker, I. (1982). *A guide to personal happiness*. Hollywood, CA: Melvin Powers Wilshire Book Company.

Emmelkamp, P. M. G. (1974). Self-observation versus flooding in the treatment of agoraphobia. *Behaviour Research and Therapy, 12*, 229–237.

Emmons, R. A., & McCullough, M. E. (2003). Counting blessings versus burdens. *Journal of Personality and Social Psychology, 84*, 377–389.

Fava, G. A. (1999). Well-being therapy. *Psychotherapy and Psychosomatics, 68*, 171–178.

Fava, G. A. (2003). Can long-term treatment with antidepressant drugs worsen the course of depression? *Journal of Clinical Psychiatry, 64*, 123–133.

Fava, G. A., & Ruini, C. (2003). Development and characteristics of a well-being enhancing psychotherapeutic strategy: well-being therapy. *Journal of Behavior Therapy and Experimental Psychiatry, 34*, 45–63.

Fava, G. A., Rafanelli, C., Cazzaro, M., Conti S., & Grandi, S. (1998a). Well-being therapy. A novel psychotherapeutic approach for residual symptoms of affective disorders. *Psychological Medicine, 28*, 475–480.

Fava, G. A., Rafanelli, C., Grandi, S., Conti, S., & Belluardo, P. (1998b). Prevention of recurrent depression with cognitive behavioral therapy. *Archives of General Psychiatry, 55*, 816–820.

Fava, G. A., Ruini, C., & Belaise, C. (2007). The concept of recovery in major depression. *Psychological Medicine, 37*, 307–317.

Fava, G. A., Ruini, C., & Rafanelli, C. (2005). Sequential treatment of mood and anxiety disorders. *Journal of Clinical Psychiatry, 66*, 1392–1400.

Fava, G. A, Ruini, C., Rafanelli, C., Finos, L., Conti, S., & Grandi, S. (2004). Six year outcome of cognitive behavior therapy for prevention of recurrent depression. *American Journal of Psychiatry, 161*, 1872–1876.

Fava, G. A., Ruini, C., Rafanelli, C., Finos, L., Salmaso, L., Mangelli, L., & Sirigatti, S. (2005). Well-being therapy of generalized anxiety disorder. *Psychotherapy and Psychosomatics, 74*, 26–30.

Fava, G. A., Ruini, C., Rafanelli, C., & Grandi, S. (2002). Cognitive behavior approach to loss of clinical effect during long-term antidepressant treatment. *American Journal of Psychiatry, 159*, 2094–2095.

Fava, G. A., Tomba, E., & Grandi, S. (2007). The road to recovery from depression. *Psychotherapy and Psychosomatics, 76*, 260–265.

Ginsburg, G. S., Riddle, M. A., & Davies, M. (2006). Somatic symptoms in children and adolescents with anxiety disorders. *Journal of the American Academy of Child and Adolescent Psychiatry, 45*, 1179–1187.

Goldber, J. F., & Harrow, M. (2004). Consistency of remission and outcome in bipolar and unipolar mood disorders. *Journal of Affective Disorders, 81*, 123–131.

Judd, L. J., Paulus, M. J., Shettler, P. J., Akiskal, H. S., Endicott, J., Leon, A. C., … Keller, M. B. (2000). Does incomplete recovery from first lifetime major depressive episode herald a chronic course of illness? *American Journal of Psychiatry, 157*, 1501–1504.

Kellner, R. (1987). A symptom questionnaire. *Journal of Clinical Psychiatry, 48*, 269–274.

Massimini, F., & Delle Fave, A. (2000). Individual development in a bio-cultural perspective. *American Psychologist, 55*, 24–33.

Meehl, P. E. (1975). Hedonic capacity: some conjectures. *Bulletin of the Menninger Clinic, 39*, 295–307.

Muris, P., Vermeer, E., & Horselenberg, R. (2008). Cognitive development and the interpretation of anxiety-related physical symptoms in 4–13-year-old non-clinical children. *Journal of Behavior Therapy and Experimental Psychiatry, 39*, 73–86.

Papakostas, G. I., Petersen, T., Denninger, J. W., Tossani, E., Pava, J. A., Alpert J. E., … Fava, M. (2004). Psychosocial functioning during the treatment of major depressive disorder with fluoxetine. *Journal of Clinical Psychopharmacology, 24*, 507–511.

Papakostas, G. I., Perlis, R. H., Seifert, C., & Fava, M. (2007). Antidepressant dose reduction and the risk of relapse in major depressive disorder. *Psychotherapy and Psychosomatics, 76*, 266–270.

Pava, J. A., Fava, M., & Levenson, J. A. (1994). Integrating cognitive therapy and pharmacotherapy in the treatment and prophylaxis of depression. *Psychotherapy and Psychosomatics, 61*, 211–219.

Paykel, E. S. (1985). The clinical interview for depression. *Journal of Affective Disorders, 9*, 85–96.

Paykel, E. S. & Weissman, M. M. (1973). Social adjustment and depression. *Archives of General Psychiatry, 28*, 659–664.

Rafanelli, C., Park, S. K., Ruini, C., Ottolini, F., Cazzaro, M., & Fava, G. A. (2000). Rating well-being and distress. *Stress Medicine, 16*, 55–61.

Ruini, C., Belaise, C., Brombin, C., Caffo, E., & Fava, G. A. (2006). Well-being therapy in school settings: a pilot study. *Psychotherapy and Psychosomatics, 75*, 331–336.

Ruini, C., & Fava, G. A. (2009). Well-being therapy for generalized anxiety disorder. *Journal of Clinical Psychology, 65*, 510–519.

Ruini, C., Ottolini, F., Tomba, E., Belaise, C., Albieri, E., Visani, D., … Fava, G. A. (2009). School intervention for promoting psychological well-being in adolescence. *Journal of Behavior Therapy and Experimental Psychiatry, 40*, 522–532.

Ryan, R. M., & Deci, E. L. (2001). On happiness and human potential: a review of research on hedonic and eudaimonic well-being. *Annual Review of Psychology, 52*, 141–166.

Ryff, C. D. (1989). Happiness is everything, or is it? Explorations on the meaning of psychological well-being. *Journal of Personality and Social Psychology, 6*, 1069–1081.

Ryff, C. D., & Singer, B. (1996). Psychological well-being: meaning, measurement, and implications for psychotherapy research. *Psychotherapy and Psychosomatics, 65*, 14–23.

Ryff, C. D., & Singer, B. (2007). What to do about positive and negative items in studies of psychological well-being and ill-being? *Psychotherapy and Psychosomatics, 76*, 61–62.

Schmidt, M. E., Fava, M., Zhang, S., Gonzales, J., Raute, N.J., & Judge, R. (2002). Treatment approaches to major depressive disorder relapse. *Psychotherapy and Psychosomatics, 71*, 190–194.

Seligman, M. E., Rashid, T., & Parks, A.C. (2006). Positive psychotherapy. *American Psychologist, 61*, 774–88.

Schnyder, U. (2005). Why new psychotherapies for post-traumatic stress disorder? *Psychotherapy and Psychosomatics*, 74, 199–201.

Sin, N. L., & Lyubomirsky, S. (2009). Enhancing well-being and alleviating depressive symptoms with positive psychology interventions: a practice-friendly meta-analysis. *Journal of Clinical Psychology*, 65, 467–87.

Sonino, N., & Fava, G. A. (2003). Tolerance to antidepressant treatment may be overcome by ketoconazole. *Journal of Psychiatric Research*, 37, 171–173.

Tomba, E., Belaise, C., Ottolini, F., Ruini, C., Bravi, A., Albieri, E., ... Fava, G. A. (2010). Differential effects of well-being promoting and anxiety management strategies in a non clinical school setting. *Journal of Anxiety Disorders*, 24, 326–33.

Van Emmerik, A. A. P., Kamphuis, J. H., & Emmelkamp, P. M. G. (2008). Treating acute stress disorder and posttraumatic stress disorder with cognitive behavioral therapy and structured writing therapy. *Psychotherapy and Psychosomatics*, 77, 93–100.

# CHAPTER 78

# THE COLLABORATIVE RECOVERY MODEL: DEVELOPING POSITIVE INSTITUTIONS TO FACILITATE RECOVERY IN ENDURING MENTAL ILLNESS

LINDSAY G. OADES, TREVOR P. CROWE, AND FRANK P. DEANE

University of Wollongong, Australia

As this volume demonstrates, the science and practice of happiness continues to develop. One challenge before happiness researchers and practitioners, however, is the claim that they are engaged in a Pollyanna endeavor. What might this science and practice have to offer individuals at the "difficult end of the spectrum?" For example, how might happiness approaches assist those with severe and enduring mental illness as well as the systems and institutions that are charged with their care? This chapter describes an evolving effort in mental health services—the consumer recovery movement—which parallels the humanistic values of the professional and scientific movement of positive psychology.

Significant change is needed if mental health services are to become the type of organizations that can work with consumers to utilize personal strengths and draw upon the beneficial effects of positive emotions. In this chapter, the consumer view of recovery is described and then compared to positive psychology. The Collaborative Recovery Model (CRM) is presented as a way to assist mental health services to become more recovery oriented—based on consumer-driven definitions of recovery. We will argue that mental health service providers need to become positive institutions if they are truly to be considered recovery oriented. A variety of coaching tools used to implement the CRM are described and we provide an overview of three examples of the CRM in use across the mental health system. Future directions are then described and specific recommendations for practice are provided.

# Consumer-Defined Recovery in Mental Health

The movement towards recovery-oriented mental health service provision has emerged from growing consumer interest to define recovery in terms of personal experience, rather than mere symptom reduction. In many Western nations, this developing interest has helped to shape governmental health policy (Slade, Amering, & Oades, 2009). Rather than the traditional medical meaning of cure as the remission of symptoms, the term "recovery" is being used to describe the personal and transformational process of consumers living with mental illness (Andresen, Oades, & Caputi, 2003). This involves moving towards a preferred identity and a life of meaning—a framework where growth is possible—and challenging fatalistic diagnoses such as schizophrenia, whose prognoses suggest little room for the possibility of clinical healing or a meaningful life (Andresen et al., 2003). At an organizational level, mental health service providers (e.g., clinical mental health services, community organizations) have typically been symptom focused and done little to acknowledge the potential of consumers with mental disorders.

The consumer-defined recovery movement has generated much interest and debate (Corrigan, Giffort, Rashid, Leary, & Okeke, 1999; Slade, 2009). Slade, Amering, and Oades (2008) assert that whilst there has been a significant increase in the use of the term "recovery" in English-speaking mental health systems, the term lacks conceptual clarity. Consistent with the definition traditionally used in mental health services, these authors refer to "*clinical* recovery" as a sustained remission of symptoms. In contrast, "*personal* recovery" which emerged from patients who have lived with long-term illness emphasizes the individually-defined and lived experience. Andresen et al. (2003) refer to this type of recovery as the establishment of a fulfilling, meaningful life and a positive sense of identity founded on hopefulness and self-determination. Slade et al. (2008) report a consensus statement involving ten principles and descriptions of personal recovery as follows:

1. *Self-direction*—consumers lead, control, exercise choice over, and determine their own path of recovery.
2. *Individualized and person-centered*—there are multiple pathways to recovery based on the individual's unique needs, preferences, and experiences.
3. *Empowerment*—consumers have the authority to exercise choices and make decisions that impact on their lives and are educated and supported in doing so.
4. *Holistic*—recovery encompasses the varied aspects of an individual's life including mind, body, spirit, and community.
5. *Non-linear*—recovery is not a step-by-step process but one based on continual growth with occasional setbacks.

6. *Strengths-based*—recovery focuses on valuing and building on the strengths, resilience, coping abilities, inherent worth, and capabilities of the individual.
7. *Peer support*—the invaluable role of mutual support in recovery is recognized and promoted (i.e. consumers encouraging one another).
8. *Respect*—community, system, and societal acceptance and appreciation of consumers—including the protection of consumer rights and the elimination of discrimination and stigma—are crucial for achieving recovery.
9. *Responsibility*—consumers have responsibility for their own self-care and recovery journeys.
10. *Hope*—recovery provides the essential and motivating message that people can and do overcome the barriers and obstacles that confront them.

## Recovery and Positive Psychology

Resnick and Rosenheck (2006) highlighted the parallel themes and potential synergies between positive psychology and personal recovery with a primary focus on strengths. Other parallels include the emphasis on exploring phenomena other than illness. That is, recovery ideas that conceptualize the person's process of growth without using illness as the core framework. Positive psychology likewise does not use a negative starting point. In the same way that personal recovery research and practice may be informed by positive psychology principles, the discipline of positive organizational scholarship (POS: Cameron, Dutton, & Quinn, 2003) provides a useful way to address organizational challenges in developing recovery oriented mental health services (e.g., the need for optimistic staff members). Slade et al. (2008) report that an increased focus on recovery is being advocated as the guiding principle for mental health policy in many countries, including Australia, England, Ireland, and the USA. However, this momentum has not been matched by a clear conceptual framework or an agreed set of practices (Davidson, O'Connell, Tondora, Styron, & Kangas, 2006).

Furthermore, Slade (2010) asserts that the emerging evidence surrounding well-being makes it possible for health services to maintain a dual focus on the promotion of well-being and the treatment of illness. This is the context in which the CRM operates.

## The Collaborative Recovery Model as a Way to Implement Recovery Oriented Service Provision

The CRM was developed to facilitate recovery-oriented service provision via the use of a modular, systemic-level delivery framework. As discussed, it is informed by positive psychology and POS, which provide useful platforms upon which to build service reform and human growth. Oades, Crowe, and Nguyen (2009) report that the CRM was originally developed as a model to help practitioners use evidence-based skills with consumers in a manner consistent with the recovery movement (Deane, Crowe, King, Kavanagh, & Oades, 2006). The model includes assumptions and practices that champion human growth, hope (Salgado, Deane, Crowe, & Oades, 2010), meaning and self-determination—issues that have not been the mainstay in the history of psychiatric practice.

Table 78.1 illustrates the two guiding principles and four components of the model, detailing the knowledge, skills, and competencies required of practitioners and key related positive psychology constructs.

## Guiding principle 1: recovery as an individual process

As shown in Table 78.1, the first principle emphasizes the personal subjective ownership of the recovery process, including hopefulness and personal meaning. It covers issues related to personal identity, particularly the need to move beyond the illness and towards one's best possible self. Finally it encourages individuals to take responsibility for their own well-being (Andresen et al., 2003).

There are significant conceptual overlaps between Keyes's (2002) notion of flourishing and the idea of personal recovery as a journey that involves moving beyond illness (i.e. living a meaningful life despite experiencing symptoms of illness). Within the CRM, the *focus of recovery* concept is used to clarify the intervention or approach that is being utilized. For example, is the focus of a practitioner's team or unit mainly to remove or avoid symptoms, or is it to promote well-being? These are not fixed foci, and may change dependent on the illness.

Fig. 78.1 illustrates the Focus of Recovery concept which, similar to that of Keyes (2002), recognizes that a person can be working towards well-being even while still having symptoms. The top two quadrants represent the reduction and prevention of symptoms. The bottom left quadrant represents positive experiences, and the bottom right quadrant represents the use of positive traits (e.g., using strengths to generate positive experiences). These bottom quadrants, which correspond to approach motivation, are comparable to Ben-Shahar's (2007) equation in which happiness = present benefit (pleasure) + future benefit (meaning).

This recovery principle trains mental health practitioners to extend their thinking beyond the top quadrants, with one practical implication being the movement away from *avoidance* goal setting (the traditional province of medical care) and towards *approach* goal setting. While symptom management is important, consumers consistently state that it is only one part of their overall recovery process (Andresen et al., 2003). Furthermore, research also suggests that an avoidance focus is not optimal. For example, Elliot and Sheldon (1997) demonstrated that the pursuit of avoidance goals is related to: (1) less satisfaction with goal progress in general and more negative feelings about the progress towards personal goals; (2) decreased levels of self esteem, personal control and vitality; and (3) less life satisfaction and feelings of competence relating to goal pursuit.

Having a science of happiness to underpin the bottom two quadrants provides a fertile base to develop new practices and better equip mental health workforces to engage in well-being interventions. A financial analogy can also be used to assist practitioners and consumers to better understand the focus of recovery concept. The analogy, which draws on Frederickson's (2001) broaden-and-build theory, proposes that positive emotions

Table 78.1 Training and coaching competencies for the Collaborative Recovery Model

| Module | Knowledge domains | Protocol, skills, and attitudes | Competency | Key positive psychological constructs |
|---|---|---|---|---|
| Recovery as an individual process (Guiding principle 1) | Psychological recovery as a staged individual process involving: (1) hope, (2) meaning, (3) identity, (4) responsibility<br>The "system of recovery" concept<br>The "focus of recovery" concept | Protocol: self-identified stage of recovery<br>Attitude: a "growth mindset" – hopefulness towards consumers' ability to set, pursue and attain personally valued life goals | Employs the principle, in all interactions and across all protocols, that psychological recovery from mental illness is an individualized process | Flourishing<br>Resilience<br>Hope<br>Optimism<br>Well-being<br>Positive emotions<br>Meaning<br>Post-traumatic growth |
| Collaboration and autonomy support (Guiding principle 2) | Working alliance<br>Power and empowerment<br>Relationship rupture<br>Autonomy support<br>Barriers to collaboration<br>Working with relationship dynamics | Skill: develop and maintain a working alliance<br>Attitude: positive towards genuine collaboration | Employs the principle, in all interactions and across all protocols, of maximum collaboration and support of consumer autonomy | Autonomy<br>Self-determination<br>Coaching as applied positive psychology |
| Change enhancement (Component 1) | Stage of psychological recovery<br>Decisional balance<br>Motivational readiness and resistance<br>Psychological needs<br>Importance and confidence<br>Fixed versus growth mindset | Protocol: motivational interviewing, particularly decisional balance<br>Skill: use decisional balance techniques appropriate to assist consumer to clarify ambivalence regarding change<br>Attitude: to take partial responsibility for role in interactional aspects of motivation | Enhances consumer change by skillful use of motivational enhancement that is appropriate to the stage of recovery of the consumer | Intrinsic motivation<br>Growth mindset |

| Component | | | |
|---|---|---|---|
| Collaborative strengths and values (Component 2) | Values clarification<br>Values use<br>Strengths identification<br>Strengths use | Protocol: "Camera" values and strengths clarification method<br>Skill: assist a consumer to elicit personal values and strengths and assess how well they have been implemented recently<br>Attitude: to value reflective exercises notwithstanding current difficulties or symptoms | Assists consumers to clarify values and strengths and use them in the here and now | Values<br>Strengths |
| Collaborative life visioning and goal striving (Component 3) | Personal life vision<br>Valued directions<br>Goal identification, setting and striving<br>Meaning/manageability trade-off<br>Autonomous goals<br>Approach and avoidance goals<br>Proximal and distal goals | Protocol: "Compass" vision and goal striving method<br>Skill: elicit meaningful vision and manageable goals<br>Attitude: to be persistent in the face of obstacles | Persists flexibly and collaboratively with the components within the Compass to assist recovery by way of the development of an integrated meaningful life vision, valued directions, and manageable goals, which provide a broader purpose for actions | Best possible self<br>Autonomous goals<br>Approach goals<br>Self concordance |
| Collaborative action planning and monitoring (Component 4) | Health behavior change<br>Action planning<br>Homework<br>Self-efficacy<br>Monitoring<br>Self-management | Protocol: "MAP" action planning method<br>Skill: to assist with the development of comprehensive action plans<br>Attitude: to value "small actions" between the meetings of staff and consumers (between session activity) | Systematically and collaboratively assigns actions, and monitors progress toward action completion and goals, to enhance self-efficacy of consumer | Self-efficacy<br>Self-regulation<br>Self-responsibility |

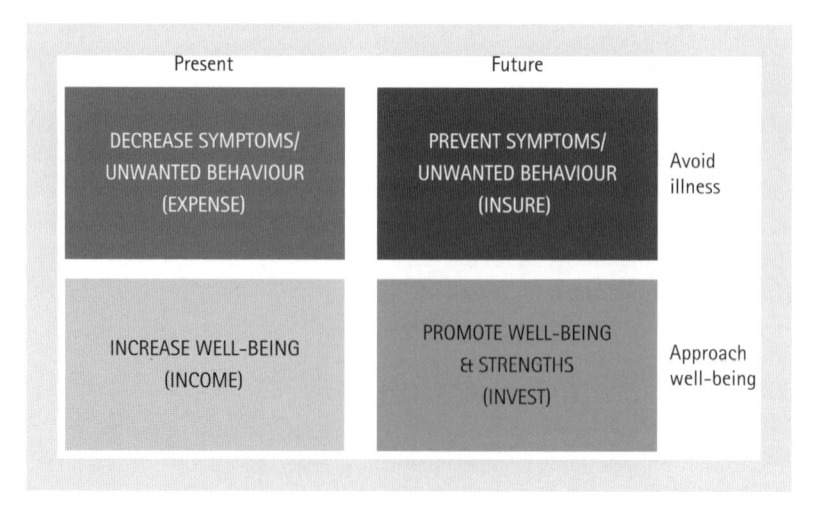

|  | Present | Future |  |
|---|---|---|---|
|  | DECREASE SYMPTOMS/ UNWANTED BEHAVIOUR (EXPENSE) | PREVENT SYMPTOMS/ UNWANTED BEHAVIOUR (INSURE) | Avoid illness |
|  | INCREASE WELL-BEING (INCOME) | PROMOTE WELL-BEING & STRENGTHS (INVEST) | Approach well-being |

FIG. 78.1 The focus of recovery concept.

(bottom left quadrant) help people to broaden their attention and commence building resources (bottom right quadrant). As the labeling in Fig. 78.1 shows, positive emotions can be understood as income, negative emotions/symptoms as expenses, relapse prevention as insurance against loss, and the development of strengths as investments. This analogy is helpful because it emphasizes the inter-relationship between the quadrants. For example, if one invests well (i.e. uses their strengths and values) they can generate more income (i.e. well-being). Hence, whilst the focus may be within a single area, the rewards are likely to be more widespread.

## Guiding principle 2: collaboration and autonomy support

This principle emphasizes important aspects of the working alliance in assisting human growth. As outlined in self-determination theory (Ryan & Deci, 2008), autonomy support underscores the importance of autonomy to well-being. This is particularly salient in mental health contexts due to the history of paternalism and control that has pervaded so many aspects of heath systems and patient care (Andresen et al., 2003).

There is substantial evidence that supports the link between the working alliance (i.e. the relationship between mental health worker and consumer) and recovery outcomes (Martin, Garske, & Davis, 2000). However, maintaining a strong working alliance often requires the mental health worker to manage interpersonal strains or alliance ruptures, reflect on his/her own reactions to the dynamics of the working relationship (e.g., increased frustration, desire to fix things or rescue the person, etc.), and maintain professional boundaries whilst striving to remain present with the person being supported. This is important as it encourages the worker to track and adjust her/his approach as required (e.g., rebuild trust, establish safety, confront, explore feelings, etc.), particularly in light of the sometimes subtle changes that can occur in the relationship. As the CRM is growth and future focused, it is conceptualized as a strengths-based coaching model, in which the relationships are coaching relationships rather than counseling relationships (Oades et al., 2009).

## CRM component 1: change enhancement

This component recognizes that many people (including consumers, carers, and practitioners) within the context of enduring mental illnesses, like schizophrenia, tend to believe that positive change is not possible. Change enhancement draws on skills from motivational interviewing, and directly challenges fixed mindsets (Dweck, 2006) regarding the potential for change. This component of the model also highlights the importance of intrinsic motivation and the personal meanings underpinning human change. It aims to shift both attitudes and beliefs about the potential for change.

## Component 2: collaborative strengths and values

The clarification and use of personal strengths and values is central to the model, and is the most popular component for consumers and practitioners alike. Whilst Rapp's (1998) strengths model is well known to mental health practitioners in a case management context, the CRM predominantly draws from contemporary research on character strengths, values and committed action (e.g., Hayes, 2004; Petersen & Seligman, 2004).

## Component 3: collaborative life visioning and goal striving

This third component assumes that despite adversity, a person is still capable of developing a vision for life. The vision involves articulating their best possible self and striving towards approach goals that are consistent with their personal values and utilize their strengths. Clarke, Oades, Crowe, and Deane (2006) describe the goal technology that has been used to operationalize the goal component of CRM. The Collaborative Goal Technology (CGT) uses a range of evidence-based practices in goal setting (e.g., goals being specific and time limited) to assist mental health practitioners and consumers to collaboratively develop goals. In a subsequent study, Clarke, Crowe, Oades, and Deane (2009) found that practitioners trained in CRM, which included the CGT, were more likely to apply these evidence-based principles. Additionally, Clarke, Oades, Crowe, Caputi, and Deane (2009) found that the goal attainment of people with enduring mental illness mediated the relationship between the distress caused by their symptoms and their perception of personal recovery. This finding suggests that goals are central to the recovery process and is consistent with the growth philosophy of the recovery movement. Positive psychology research continues to deepen our understanding of effective goal striving and its relationship to well-being (Brandtstadter, 2006).

## Component 4: collaborative action planning and monitoring

The fourth and final component of CRM is informed by research on the role of homework in cognitive behavioral therapies (Kazantzis, Deane, & Ronan, 2000). The term "action planning" is used in CRM because it does not carry the somewhat negative connotations of the word "homework," which often stem from unhappy school experiences. Meta-analyses have found that therapy outcomes are significantly better for those who receive and complete homework assignments (Kazantzis, Whittington, & Dattilio, 2010). Although this research has mostly focused on the treatment of depression and anxiety, there is increasing evidence of its importance in treating persistent and recurring mental illnesses such as schizophrenia (Deane, Glaser, Oades, & Kazantzis, 2005; Kelly & Deane, 2009). Working on agreed actions between meetings is thus an essential ingredient of CRM.

## THE COLLABORATIVE RECOVERY MODEL AS A COACHING MODEL

The CRM has been conceptualized as a strength-based person-centered coaching model (Oades et al., 2009). The Life Journey Enhancement Tools (LifeJET) (Oades & Crowe, 2008) have been designed to operationalize key components of the CRM delivered in a coaching style, where the relationship is more person-centered and focused on personal goals (rather than clinician-centered and focused on clinical goals). Based on the root metaphor of a journey (of recovery), the protocols are called the Camera, Compass, and MAP (an abbreviation for My Action Plan) (see Figs 78.2–78.4), and are designed to stimulate future-oriented and hope-inducing activities. The Camera, Compass, and MAP are modularized tools. Thus while it is preferable for them to be used in sequence they can be used alone.

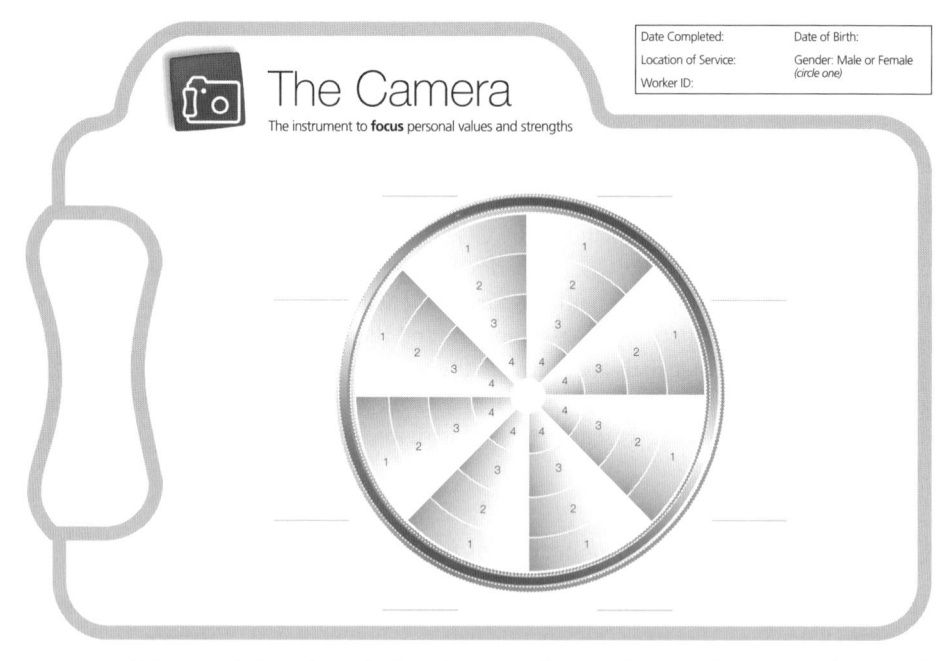

**FIG. 78.2** (Also see Color plate 7) The Camera values and strengths use coaching tool. Oades, L.G., Crowe, T.P. & Nguyen, M. (2009). Leadership coaching transforming mental health systems from the inside out: The Collaborative Recovery Model as person-centred strengths based coaching psychology. *International Coaching Psychology Review*, 4(1), 64–75. Reproduced with permission (© University of Wollongong).

FIG. 78.3 (Also see Color plate 8) The Compass valued direction and goal striving coaching tool. Oades, L.G., Crowe, T.P. & Nguyen, M. (2009). Leadership coaching transforming mental health systems from the inside out: The Collaborative Recovery Model as person-centred strengths based coaching psychology. *International Coaching Psychology Review*, 4(1), 64–75. Reproduced with permission (© University of Wollongong).

# The MAP

**My Action Plan:** The instrument to plan **what to do next**

| Valued Direction (from Compass) | Target goal (from Compass) | | |
|---|---|---|---|
| **Action name:** *Eg walking* | **Action Description:** What specific action is required to achieve the target level goal? *Eg Walking briskly on the oval next door three times a week in the morning* | | |
| **Date Set:** | How often | When | Where |
| **Social support** | **Resources** Who can give me practical help? With what? | **Information** Who can give me information when needed? What information? | **Emotional** Who can listen to and support me? |
| **Monitoring actions** | How will I monitor actions? *(eg diary, calendar recording what you have done)* | | |
| **Barriers** | What are my barriers? *(eg financial, time, motivation)* | | |
| **Solutions** | What are some solutions or backup plans? | | |
| **Confidence** (circle level of confidence) | Not at all confident    0 10 20 30 40 50 60 70 80 90 100    Very confident  Specific action listed above. Repeat if not over 70% confident. | | |
| **Review date:**  Make as soon as possible | **Review outcome:** | | |
| Date Completed: | Location of Service: | Worker ID: | Date of Birth: | Gender: Male or Female (circle one) |

FIG. 78.4 (Also see Color plate 9) The MAP action planning coaching tool. Oades, L.G., Crowe, T.P. & Nguyen, M. (2009). Leadership coaching transforming mental health systems from the inside out: The Collaborative Recovery Model as person-centred strengths based coaching psychology. *International Coaching Psychology Review*, 4(1), 64–75. Reproduced with permission (© University of Wollongong).

The Camera is used to help the individuals to identify valued life domains and strengths, examine the extent to which these have recently been pursued, and to focus their attention on areas of potential change.

The Compass evolved from the previously mentioned goal technology (Clarke et al., 2006). It is used to assist people to link their values with their goals, to quantify relative goal importance, and to identify different levels of potential attainment. The Compass enables ratings of successful goal pursuit as a function of importance and attainment. Goal attainment weighted by perceived importance can be calculated as a numeric index if desired.

Last, the MAP is an action-planning tool used to assist with homework setting for goal attainment tasks.

# The Collaborative Recovery Model as a Systemic Intervention

Unlike many discrete and individual positive psychological interventions (Magyar-Moe, 2009) the CRM (Oades et al., 2005), is a broad systemic framework guiding a range of interventions with consumers, carers, staff, and organizational systems. The systemic nature of the interventions is imperative given the ingrained culture and history of psychiatric service provision. As Park and Petersen (2003) assert, positive institutions enable people to use their positive traits such as strengths and values, which in turn yields positive experiences and positive emotions. In mental health services, organizations require change to enable staff and consumers to utilize strengths, to enable the possibility of the benefits of positive emotions. Without such comprehensive change, recovery oriented services are unlikely to succeed. The CRM has been developed to assist with recovery-oriented service provision for people with enduring mental illness, and is informed by the principles, evidence, and practices of positive psychology and POS (Cameron et al., 2003).

The relationship between mental health workers and the individual's wider support system is central to the recovery process. From a collaborative recovery perspective this system includes four parts nested in a broader community. The four interlinked parts are self as consumer, family carers, staff members and organizations (e.g., treatment services) in the community. Currently, there is research and practice being conducted using the LifeJET tools and CRM principles in all four parts of the mental health system. The extent to which that community encourages social inclusion (Lloyd & Deane, 2007) and non-stigmatizing attitudes can greatly support an individual's recovery (e.g., Quinn & Knifton, 2005). Similarly, mental health organizations that are attempting to deliver recovery-oriented treatment may also need to make wider "systems" changes to do so successfully.

The CRM is deliberately being developed as a systemic intervention rather than one restricted to solely focusing on individual interventions with clients. The guiding principles, components, and LifeJET protocol may be used for the self-development of individuals (self-coaching), used as part of a practitioner–client coaching relationship (practitioner coaching), used for carer recovery (carer coaching), and used at the organizational level, which may include practitioners coaching other practitioners (coaching) towards personal and professional development. This comprehensive systems intervention is seen as necessary to bring about the systemic and cultural transformation needed to generate recovery-oriented service provision.

There are opportunities for therapeutic activity at each of the four parts and in the wider community (e.g., interventions to increase understanding and acceptance of people with mental illness). Similarly, there are activities that can be promoted at the various intersections between the parts. For example, consumers or family members might be encouraged to take on advocacy roles within an organization to promote recovery. Examples of possible systemic interventions will now be provided.

## Example 1: a consumer-targeted intervention

The Flourish Program is targeted at consumers, and is more directly linked to well known positive psychology constructs (e.g., gratitude). This program packages many of the tools already described and is comprised of four components: (1) A handbook, consisting of eight learning modules (flourishing; using my strengths and values; mapping the journey of change; understanding change; living in the present; staying positive; building a success team; and reviewing my goals); (2) MP3 Audios complementing the handbook materials; (3) a consumer peer-led support group; and (4) telephone reminder calls (brief problem-solving coaching) (Oades et al., 2009). Each week participants are encouraged to complete one learning module, which involves reading the set topic's material, listening to audio resources, and completing set exercises. Semi-structured peer-facilitated group discussions are also conducted each fortnight.

## Example 2: a parallel staff-targeted intervention

One way of facilitating behavioral activation and enhancing empathy through experiencing first-hand resistance to change (i.e. empathic/behavioral resonance; Saunders, 2000), is to engage practitioners in activities that directly mirror those they are using with their clients. Morrissey and Tribe (2001) describe this type of parallel process as enabling the practitioner to have "the experience briefly of being like a client whom s/he does not actually resemble" (p. 104). The advantages of involving practitioners in professional or personal development coaching using the same LifeJET as they use with their clients include: (1) gaining direct personal guidance on the use of the protocols in a way that engages their own motivational resources and resistance tensions; (2) a likely personal benefit through the exploration of their values, goals, and so on; (3) an increased likelihood of converting desired life directions and goals into actions; and (4) since people favor practices from which they have experienced direct personal gains, a likely greater generalization of these into their routine clinical work.

## Example 3: an organization-wide targeted intervention

An example of a recent organization-wide implementation of the CRM is now provided. The organization is a large tertiary inpatient mental health facility in Ontario (Ontario Shores Centre for Mental Health Sciences). It services approximately 330 adolescent, adult, and elderly inpatient consumers and over 440 outpatient consumers with enduring mental illness, particularly schizophrenia spectrum disorders. The organization employs 1200 staff, with 700 clinical staff including nurses, occupational therapists, psychiatrists, psychologists, recreational therapists, service providers who have been patients, and social workers. The 500 non-clinical staff members include housekeeping, maintenance, and administration.

In November 2008, the organization embarked on a new initiative, "Rediscover and Recovery – the Shared Journey" (Malachowski, 2009). Consistent with the parallel process of growth described, the staff professional development training and coaching ("rediscovery") is being run directly alongside changes to the service delivery model which aims at becoming recovery focused. The facility's leadership committed to training all 1200 staff in the principles of the Collaborative Recovery Model including growth mindset, hope, and so on. The educational initiative was officially launched in January of 2009 and was implemented throughout the hospital over the next 18 months, bringing both consumers and clinical- and non-clinical-staff towards a common desired goal: a recovery-based organization. All clinical staff participated in a 5-day training module followed by ongoing workplace coaching. Recovery champions who were nominated by each unit received the training and coaching described in Table 78.1. They were trained first and acted as champions of change throughout the organization. These champions either assisted with further training, coached staff, or assisted with CRM-related questions on the respective wards. The training for all staff was completed in March 2010. The practice model for consumers mirrored that provided to staff, similar to Example 2 described earlier.

Broader organizational initiatives included changing policy documents to reflect the positive growth recovery language, including recovery-based metrics into balanced scorecard reporting, and altering electronic documentation to reflect the model. Staff incentives and recruitment are also currently being assessed for their congruence with the recovery and growth orientation. Consumer advocacy groups are also being supported to interpret and implement the program.

This intervention is being evaluated over an 18-month period with a repeated measures design, and an initial focus on staff outcomes, to be followed by consumer outcomes and satisfaction.

# Conclusion, Future Directions, and Recommendations

Within the English-speaking world, the call for recovery-oriented services is fast becoming mainstream policy. This growth-based philosophy of care can be greatly assisted by theory, research, and practice informed by positive psychology and POS. Future research needs to systematically examine the components within the CRM along with the interrelationships within the ecology of recovery. By definition a positive mental health organization should enable staff and consumers to use their strengths and values, which should in turn generate the opportunity for positive emotions. This is an exciting area for further research and practice examining the effects of CRM interventions on staff and consumer well-being.

Five key recommendations for practice are:

- Explicitly examine and discuss the possibility of change and the meaning of recovery with mental health consumers.
- Value the coaching working alliance as the springboard for change.
- Clarify strengths and values before commencing the goal setting and striving process with consumers.

- Explore ways that staff members can use Camera, Compass, and MAP tools in their personal lives, not only with consumers.
- Find opportunities to broaden the scope of CRM as a positive psychology intervention. That is, also focus on the team and organizational levels, and not solely at the one-on-one consumer level.

# References

Andresen, R., Caputi, P., & Oades, L. (2006). Stages of recovery instrument: Development of a measure of recovery from serious mental illness. *Australian and New Zealand Journal of Psychiatry, 40*, 972–980.

Andresen, R., Caputi, P., & Oades, L. G. (2010). Do clinical outcome measures assess consumer-defined recovery? *Psychiatry Research, 177*, 309–317.

Andresen, R., Oades, L. G., & Caputi, P. (2003). The experience of recovery from schizophrenia: Towards an empirically validated stage model. *Australian and New Zealand Journal of Psychiatry, 37*, 586–594.

Baumeister, R. F., Bratslavsky, E., Finkenauer, C., & Vohs, K. D. (2001). Bad is stronger than good. *Review of General Psychology, 5*, 323–370.

Baumeister, R. R., & Vohs, K. D. (2002). The pursuit of meaningfulness in life. In C. R. Snyder & S. J. Lopez (Eds.), *Handbook of Positive Psychology*, pp. 459–471. New York, NY: Oxford University Press.

Ben-Shahar, T. (2007). *Happier. Learn the secrets to daily joy and lasting fulfilment.* New York, NY: McGraw Hill.

Brandtstadter, J. (2006). Adaptive resources in later life: Tenacious goal pursuit and flexible goal adjustment. In I. S. Csikszentmihalyi (Ed.), *A life worth living: contributions to positive psychology* (pp. 143–164). New York, NY: Oxford University Press.

Cameron, K., Dutton, J. E., & Quinn, R. E. (Eds.). (2003). *Positive organizational scholarship: Foundations of a new discipline.* San Francisco, CA: Berrett-Koehler Publishers.

Cameron, K. S. (2008). *Positive leadership: strategies for extraordinary performance.* San Francisco, CA: Berrett-Koehler Publishers.

Clarke, S. P., Oades, L. G., Crowe, T. P., & Deane, F. P. (2006). Collaborative goal technology: Theory and practice. *Psychiatric Rehabilitation Journal, 30*, 129–136.

Clarke, S. P., Crowe, T. P., Oades, L. G., & Deane, F. P. (2009). Do goal setting interventions improve the quality of goals in mental health services? *Psychiatric Rehabilitation Journal, 32*(4), 292–299.

Clarke, S., Oades, L., Crowe, T., Caputi, P., & Deane, F. P. (2009). The role of symptom distress and goal attainment in assisting the psychological recovery in consumers with enduring mental illness. *Journal of Mental Health, 18*, 389–397.

Corrigan, P. W., Giffort, D., Rashid, F., Leary, M., & Okeke, I. (1999). Recovery as a psychological construct. *Community Mental Health Journal, 35*, 231–239.

Crowe, T. P., Deane, F. P., Oades, L. G., Caputi, P., & Morland, K. G. (2006). Effectiveness of a collaborative recovery training program in Australia in promoting positive views about recovery. *Psychiatric Services, 57*(10), 1497–1500.

Davidson, L., O'Connell, M., Tondora, J., Styron, T., & Kangas, K. (2006). The top 10 concerns about recovery encountered in mental health system transformation. *Psychiatric Services, 57*, 640–645.

Deane, F. P., Crowe, T., King, R., Kavanagh, D., & Oades, L. G. (2006). Challenges in implementing evidence-based practice into mental health services. *Australian Health Review, 30,* 305–309.

Deane, F. P., Glaser, N. M., Oades, L. G., & Kazantzis, N. (2005). Psychologists' use of homework assignments with clients who have schizophrenia. *Clinical Psychologist, 9,* 24–34.

Dweck, C. S. (2006). *Mindset: The new psychology of success.* New York, NY: Random House.

Elliot, A. J., & Sheldon, K. M. (1997). Avoidance achievement motivation: A personal goals analysis. *Journal of Personality and Social Psychology, 73,* 171–185.

Frederickson, B. L. (2001). The role of positive emotions in positive psychology: The broaden-and-build theory. *American Psychologist, 56,* 218–226.

Hayes, S. C. (2004). Acceptance and commitment therapy, relational frame theory, and the third wave of behavioural and cognitive therapies. *Behaviour Therapy, 35*(4), 639–665.

Kazantzis, N., Deane, F. P., & Ronan, K. (2000). Homework assignments in cognitive and behavioral therapy: A meta-analysis. *Clinical Psychology: Science & Practice, 7,* 189–202.

Kazantzis, N., Whittington, C., & Dattilio, F. (2010). Meta-analysis of homework effects in cognitive behavioural therapy: A replication and extension. *Clinical Psychology: Science & Practice, 17,* 144–156.

Kelly, P. J. & Deane, F. P. (2009). Does homework improve outcomes for individuals diagnosed with severe mental illness? *Australian and New Zealand Journal of Psychiatry, 43,* 968–975.

Keyes, C. L. M. (2002). The mental health continuum: From languishing to flourishing in life. *Journal of Health and Social Behavior, 43,* 207–222.

Linley, P. A., & Harrington, S. (2006). Strengths coaching: A potential-guided approach to coaching psychology. *International Coaching Psychology Review, 1*(1), 37–46.

Lloyd, C., & Deane, F. P. (2007). Community participation. In R. King, C. Lloyd, & T. Meehan (Eds.), (pp. 129–142). *Handbook of psychosocial rehabilitation.* Oxford, UK: Blackwell.

Magyar-Moe, J. L. (2009). *Therapist's guide to positive psychological interventions.* New York, NY: Elsevier.

Malachowski, C. K. (2009). Optimizing system and patient recovery. Rediscover and recovery: the shared journey project. *International Journal of Psychosocial Rehabilitation, 13*(2), 49–64.

Martin, D. J., Garske, J. P., & Davis, M. K. (2000). Relation of the therapeutic alliance with outcome and other variables: A meta-analytic review. *Journal of Consulting and Clinical Psychology, 68,* 438–450.

Morrissey, J., & Tribe, R. (2001). Parallel process in supervision. *Counselling Psychology Quarterly, 14*(2), 103–110.

Oades L. G., Andresen R., Crowe T. P., Malins G., Marshall S., & Turner A. (2008). *A handbook to flourish: A recovery-based self-development program.* Wollongong, Australia: Illawarra Institute for Mental Health, University of Wollongong.

Oades, L. G., Crowe, T. P., & Nguyen, M. (2009). Leadership coaching transforming mental health systems from the inside out: The Collaborative Recovery Model as person-centred strengths based coaching psychology. *International Coaching Psychology Review, 4*(1), 25–36.

Oades, L. G. & Crowe, T. P. (2008). *Life journey enhancement tools (Life JET).* Illawarra Institute for Mental Health, University of Wollongong.

Oades, L., Deane, F., Crowe, T., Lambert, W. G., Kavanagh, D., & Lloyd, C. (2005). Collaborative Recovery: an integrative model for working with individuals who experience chronic and recurring mental illness. *Australasian Psychiatry, 13,* 279–284.

Park, N., & Peterson, C. M. (2003). *Virtues and organizations*. In K. S. Cameron, J. E. Dutton, & R. E. Quinn (Eds.), *Positive organizational scholarship: Foundations of a new discipline*, pp. 33–47. San Francisco, CA: Berrett-Koehler.

Petersen, C., & Seligman, M. E. P. (2004). *Character strengths and virtues: A handbook and classification*. New York, NY: Oxford University Press.

Quinn, N., & Knifton, L. (2005). Promoting recovery and addressing stigma: Mental health awareness through community development in a low-income area. *International Journal of Mental Health Promotion, 7*, 37–44.

Rapp, C. A. (1998). *The strengths model: Case management with people suffering from severe and persistent mental illness*. New York, NY: Oxford University Press.

Resnick, S. G., & Rosenheck, R. A. (2006). Recovery and positive psychology: Parallel themes and potential synergies. *Psychiatric Services, 57*(1), 120–122.

Ryan, R. M., Huta, V., & Deci, E. L. (2008). Living well: A self determination theory perspective on eudaimonia. *Journal of Happiness Studies, 9*, 139–170.

Saunders, S. M. (2000). Examining the relationship between the therapeutic bond and the phases of treatment outcome. *Psychotherapy, 37*(3), 206–218.

Salgado, D., Deane, F. P., Crowe, T. P., & Oades, L. G. (2010). Hope and improvements in mental health service providers' recovery attitudes following training. *Journal of Mental Health, 19*, 243–248.

Seligman, M. E. P., & Csikszentmihalyi, M. (2000). Positive psychology: An introduction. *American Psychologist, 55*, 5–14.

Slade, M. (2009). *Personal recovery and mental illness: A guide for mental health professionals*. Cambridge, UK: Cambridge University Press.

Slade, M. (2010). Mental illness and well-being: The central importance of positive psychology and recovery approaches. *BMC Health Services Research, 10*, 26. Retrieved from http://www.biomedcentral.com/1472-6963/10/26.

Slade, M., Amering, M., & Oades, L. G. (2008). Recovery: an international perspective. *Epidemiologia e Psichiatria Sociale, 17*(2), 128–137.

# CHAPTER 79

# CONCLUSION: THE FUTURE OF HAPPINESS

## SUSAN A. DAVID[1,2], ILONA BONIWELL[3,4], AND AMANDA CONLEY AYERS[2]

[1]Harvard Medical School, USA; [2]Evidence Based Psychology, USA;
[3]The University of East London, UK; [4]Positran, Paris, France

Looking into the past, it is clear that our ancestors the world over were deeply concerned with happiness. In ancient Greece, Herodotus chronicled an arrogant king's illusions of happiness and his subsequent fall from grace (McMahon, Chapter 19). Meanwhile in China, philosophers including Confucius described how to attain happiness by living in harmony with "Heavenly patterns" (Ivanhoe, Chapter 20).

Indeed, in the early history of both Western and Eastern cultures, it was believed that a happy person was one favored by the gods. Eudaimonia, a prominent term in contemporary happiness research, originates from the notion of having at one's side a good daimon, "an emissary of the gods, a personal spirit who watches over each of us…" (McMahon, Chapter 19). Dangerously close in origin is the word demon, a fiend who threatens to move us toward languishing, a state identified as one of happiness's opposites (Pawelski, Chapter 25).

While it is clear that humanity's views of happiness have evolved over time, the age-old interest in attracting "daimons" and dispelling "demons" continues. In fact, the academic research community's interest in human well-being and flourishing has recently gained momentum. As described in the Introduction (Chapter 1), the production of this handbook follows from four major scientific developments, including the establishment of positive psychology, advances in the science of positive emotions, the emergence of positive organizational scholarship, and a world-wide reconsideration of gross domestic product as a sufficient measure of societal well-being.

Happiness is a topic that is universal, and at the same time deeply personal: it is important not only in scholarly discourse, but in our daily lives. Considering the breadth and depth of the topic, it would be presumptuous to predict the "future of happiness"; therefore we have titled this conclusion somewhat in jest. However, it never hurts to venture a guess, and this handbook allows us to make an educated one. We are confident that *The Oxford Handbook of Happiness* provides a state-of-the-art examination of happiness—one that spans both historical perspectives and scholarly disciplines. In this conclusion we have the opportunity to stand on the shoulders of the handbook's many contributors, and consider avenues of further exploration in terms of human well-being and flourishing.

# Exploring Meanings of "Happiness"

As described in the Introduction, the theoretical and research literature employs multiple definitions of happiness. It is no mistake that this volume contains an entire section devoted to "psychological definitions." Rather than narrowing the conversation or drawing firm conclusions about how to define happiness, the handbook's authors offer a wealth of expert views that help us consider nuances in understanding.

Hedonic and eudaimonic approaches to well-being are often described as fundamentally distinct. However, a theory like broaden-and-build described by Fredrickson and colleagues (Chapter 3) points to connections between *feeling* good and *developing* in a way that is optimal. Similarly, while pleasure-seeking does not necessarily lead to developmental flow experiences, it is clear that the sense of meaning and fulfillment derived from flow is enjoyable (Delle Fave, Chapter 5). Parks, Schueller, and Tasimi (Chapter 72) urge practitioners to "address pleasure, engagement, and meaning, as it appears that maximal benefits occur when all three routes are pursued" (p. 972). The work of these scholars and many others suggest that we may not be able to draw clear lines between pursuits of positive emotion (hedonia) and virtuous living (eudaimonia).

Subjective well-being (SWB) has been and continues to be an important conception of hedonic happiness. As described by Tov and Au (Chapter 35), it is a measure that has been used to compare happiness across nations; it is also the source of evidence for the oft-cited Easterlin paradox (Frey & Stutzer, Chapter 34). SWB authorities Pavot and Diener (Chapter 10) call for further exploration of similarities and differences between different well-being constructs, in particular Ryff's eudaimonic conception of psychological well-being (PWB). We agree that this is fertile ground for happiness scholars: such endeavors can bring clarity, as well as enhanced theory generation and testing.

# Interdisciplinary Collaboration

Happiness is not a simple construct, and the handbook's authors illustrate its multidimensional nature. For example, in his approach to examining life quality, Veenhoven (Chapter 12) deconstructs happiness into a fourfold matrix, composed of the intersections of outer and inner qualities with life chances and results. Each quadrant corresponds to particular aspects of life experience, such as the physical environment, bodily health, the social milieu, education, close relationships, job satisfaction, and mood.

A psychological orientation to happiness is important, but given its reach into a variety of life areas, it is clear that discourse cannot be restricted to psychology. Indeed, this handbook demonstrates that concern for human happiness permeates a wide range of contemporary disciplines, including spirituality, social policy, education, and business. While it is critical to deepen knowledge in each of these areas, it will also be valuable to pursue collaboration and understanding across disciplines. As referenced in the Introduction (Chapter 1) to the handbook, researchers and practitioners have the opportunity to expand beyond positive psychology to create a "positive social science." This handbook is a step forward in terms of establishing an integrated view of human well-being, and scholars will accomplish much by continuing in this direction.

## Addressing Gaps in Knowledge

A number of authors referred to their area of expertise as being in its "infancy." It is natural that gaps in available data will exist in any young research endeavor. Tov & Au (Chapter 35) highlight the disparity in well-being data from different parts of the world, as well as limitations in access to information from non-student samples. Cameron and Demir, in introducing their respective sections, call for longitudinal studies to elucidate causal mechanisms and provide information on relationships between time and well-being.

Indications of "incomplete" data illuminate significant opportunities for scholars who are adequately trained and who have the means to aid the collection process. As happiness research emerges from its infancy and finds its footing we can expect more robust data collection, methods, and study designs, leading to advancements in the field.

## Identifying Effective Interventions Across Domains

Early thinkers believed that human beings had some control over their happiness. Daoists followed the "Way" to a life of harmony (Ivanhoe, Chapter 20), and Aristotle promoted practicing goodness and virtue (McMahon, Chapter 19). In more recent history, however, psychologists tacitly adopted the "set-point theory," assuming that adults had stable levels of well-being. According to Headey (Chapter 66), there are many leaks in the "sinking tanker" of set-point theory. Adults can, and do, experience significant changes in happiness, and Headey posits that happiness is enhanced through life goals, preferences, and choices.

If we truly can augment our happiness, we must first identify effective approaches that achieve lasting results. Section X on "Happiness Interventions" includes scholarly accounts of methods including Acceptance and Commitment Therapy, coaching, and the Collaborative Recovery Model. However, descriptions of interventions are not restricted to this section of the handbook. Section IV, "Spiritual Approaches to Happiness," includes multiple accounts of traditions that have provided training to promote well-being and flourishing through the ages; this ancient wisdom continues to be available today. Section VI on "Positive Education" considers how we can intervene with young people to optimize their development. It includes descriptions of curricula oriented toward happiness and flourishing, as well as illustrative case studies.

As Parks, Schueller, and Tasimi (Chapter 72) attest, the demand for self-help materials continues, even as the effectiveness of most interventions remains unproven. The handbook shows that happiness is not only influenced through psychological intervention, but through a variety of avenues including spiritual practice, social policy, and the workplace. The implementation and empirical testing of happiness interventions is fertile territory for researchers and practitioners across domains.

## Conclusion

As James Pawelski warned in his introduction to Section III on "Philosophical Approaches to Happiness," we would be remiss to assume that the happiness of future generations will resemble our present experience. Aristotle and Confucius would surely be perplexed by the stresses and various threats to happiness we experience today in our globalized, digitized culture.

Still, their words and wisdom have found their way into this volume, and we do not find them irrelevant. We understand the fear of demons, and the allure of the daimon. While our descendants' understanding of happiness may be vastly different from what we know today, surely we are wedded by that common human thread of questing after happiness. *The Oxford Handbook of Happiness* offers the latest thinking and ideas for next steps in this ongoing journey.

# Contributor Index

Abenavoli, R. M.  609
Ahuvia, A.  482
Andelin, A. K.  860
Ashley, M.  579
Au, E. W. M.  448

Ballas, D.  465
Barker Caza, B.  693
Beeby, A.  941
Belliotti, R. A.  291
Boehm, J.  901
Boniwell, I.  1, 535, 1067
Brunwasser, S. M.  609

Cameron, K. S.  671, 676
Catalino, L. I.  17
Caza, A.  671, 676
Conley Ayers, A.  1, 1067
Conway, A. M.  17
Crowe, T. P.  1050
Crum, A. J.  73
Cummins, R. A.  185

David, S. A.  1, 1067
Deane, F. P.  1050
Delle Fave, A.  60
DelPriore, D. J.  875
Demir, M.  817, 860
Diener, E.  134
Dorling, D.  465

Fava, G. A.  1037
Ferssizidis, P.  101
Fox Eades, J. M.  579
Fredrickson, B. L.  17
Frey, B. S.  431

Garrett, S.  941
Gillham, J. E.  609

Gonzalez, R.  35
Grant, A. M.  1009
Green, S.  957
Griffin, D.  35

Haybron, D. M.  303
Hayes, L.  994
Headey, B.  887
Hefferon, K.  873, 926
Henry, J.  339, 411
Hernandez, K. M.  397
Hill, S. E.  875
Hsu, L. M.  1026
Huta, V.  201

Ivanhoe, P. J.  263
Izberk-Bilgin, E.  482

Jackson, T.  498
Jacobs Bao, K.  119
Joseph, S.  926

Kashdan, T. B.  101, 941
Keyes, C. L. M.  915
Koo, M.  174
Kwee, G. T. M.  357

Lakey, B.  847
Langer, E. J.  1026
Linkins, M.  609
Luthans, F.  751
Lyubomirsky, S.  119, 901

McGrath, H.  563
McInerney, L.  592
McMahon, D. M.  252
Mahoney, A.  397
Major, B.  875
Malinowski, P.  384

Marks, N. 498
Marquart, R. A. 101
Miao, F. F. 174
Mikulincer, M. 834
Morris, I. 644
Mulgan, G. 517
Myers, D. G. 88

Niemiec, C. P. 214
Noble, T. 563

Oades, L. G. 1050
Oishi, S. 174
Orthel, H. 860

Paragment, K. I. 397
Parker, S. K. 711
Parks, A. C. 962
Pavot, W. 134
Pawelski, J. O. 247, 326
Popovic, N. 551
Proctor, C. 579

Quick, J. C. 798
Quick, J. D. 798

Rashid, T. 978
Reivich, K. J. 609
Ricard, M. 344
Roberts, L. M. 767
Ruini, C. 1037
Ryan, R. M. 214

Salagame, K. K. K. 371
Salovey, P. 73
Saphire-Bernstein, S. 821
Schueller, S. M. 962
Searle, B. J. 711
Seligman, M. E. P. 609
Shaver, P. R. 834
Sheldon, K. M. 901
Spence, G. B. 957, 1009
Steger, M. F. 101, 941
Sternberg, R. J. 631
Stutzer, A. 431

Tasimi, A. 962
Taylor, S. E. 821
Thompson, S. 427, 498
Tiberius, V. 315
Tov, W. 448
Tugade, M. M. 17

van Deurzen, E. 279
Veenhoven, R. 161
Vitterso, J. 11, 155, 227

Warr, P. 733
White, J. 540
White, M. A. 657
Wright, T. A. 783
Wrzesniewski, A. 693

Youssef, C. M. 751

# Author Index

Abuhamdeh, S. 67
Albieri, E. 1045
Albrecht, G. A. 502
Amato, P. R. 825
Amering, M. 1051
Anderson, A. K. 19
Andrews, F. M. 233
Angerer, P. 717
Aristotle 156, 202, 254
Arnett, J. J. 946
Arora, R. 141
Augustine 255–6

Baarsma, B. E. 505
Bacon, Sir Francis 11
Ballas, D. 473–4
Barbano, M. F. 230
Barrington-Leigh, C. 49
Barsade, S. G. 682
Basu, S. 380
Baum, A. 502
Baumeister, R. F. 127, 823, 944
Bazerman, M. H. 54
Beauvoir, S. de. 287
Beck, P. 1032
Belaise, C. 1043
Belluardo, P. 1042
Bentham, J. 156
Billings, R. S. 723
Biswas-Diener, R. 330
Boehm, J. K. 50
Boethius 333–4
Bonanno, G. A. 103
Bonett, D. G. 785, 787, 788, 790
Bourland, S. L. 108
Bowlby, J. 834, 835
Brandstatter, E. 47
Branigan, C. 20
Branje, S. J. T. 850–1
Brickman, P. D. 889, 902

Brickson, S. L. 700
Brighouse, H. 648
Bright, D. 680
Brombin, C. 1043
Brown, S. L. 23
Bryant, F. B. 965
Buehler, C. 825–6
Buss, D. M. 878

Cador, M. 230
Caffo, E. 1043
Calarco, M. 681
Calhoun, L. G. 930, 931, 934
Cameron, K. S. 680–1
Campbell, A. 186–7
Campbell, D. T. 889
Camus, A. 286–7
Catalino, L. I. 23
Caza, A. 680
Cazzaro, M. 1041
Chen, S. T. 49
Christakis, N. A. 177
Chung, J. 1029
Clarke, S. P. 1057
Claxton, G. 647–8
Coffey, K. A. 23
Cohn, M. A. 23
Connor, L. 502
Conti, S. 1042
Conway, A. M. 23
Cooper, C. L. 805
Corneau, A. 880
Costa, P. T. 142, 889
Cropanzano, R. 785, 786, 787, 790
Crowe, T. P. 1057
Csikszentmihalyi, M. 60, 67, 204, 261, 523, 582, 683, 981–2

Dalal, A. K. 377
Daniels, K. 718

Daubman, K. A. 20
Davidson, R. J. 106
Deane, F. P. 1057
Deci, E. L. 1015
Delle Fave, A. 63, 65
Deviney, D. E. 1011
Diamond, W. J. 789, 790
Dickens, C. 644–5
Dickson, W. J. 785, 790
Diener, E. 127–8, 141, 232–3, 330, 891
Dodson, J. D. 65
Dorling, D. 473–4
Drew, J. 850
Duijts, S. F. 1011
Dush, C. M. K. 825
Dutton, J. E. 717

Easterlin, R. A. 141, 889, 890
EIU 509
Eliade, M. 401
Ellis, S. 672
Emmons, R. A. 966
Ericsson, K. A. 237

Fava, G. A. 1041, 1042, 1043
Faye, C. L. 801
Ferrer-i-Carbonell, A. 506
Finkel, S. M. 23
Fisicaro, S. 850
Fleming, I. 502
Fowler, J. H. 177
Frankl, V. E. 944, 982
Fredrickson, B. L. 20, 21, 23, 24, 230, 385, 966
Freeman, S. 502
Freud, S. 203
Frey, B. S. 436
Frijda, N. H. 231

Gable, S. L. 853
Gillath, O. 837
Gilovich, T. 53, 749
Glaser, J. 717
Goolsby, J. L. 801, 803, 804
Gorczynski, P. 1012
Gowdy, J. M. 506
Grahek, M. 801
Grandi, S. 1042, 1043
Grant, A. M. 717–18, 1011–12
Gray, J. A. 142

Grey, M. 1012
Griffin, D. 38, 43, 44, 52
Groot, W. 46
Gschneidinger, E. 43

Hackman, J. R. 714, 716
Haidt, J. 413
Harris, A. 49
Hayes, S. C. 995–6, 1002
Hays, R. B. 861
Headey, B. W. 889
Hefferon, K. 934, 935
Heidegger, M. 283–4
Helliwell, J. F. 49
Helms, H. M. 825–6
Hemenway, D. 53
Hernandez, K. M. 404
Herodotus 252–4
Hersey, R. B. 783–5
Hewlett, S. A. 808
Higginbotham, N. 502
Hirschberger, G. 837
Hirsh, J. B. 19
Holt, D. B. 485–6
Hornung, S. 717
Hsee, C. K. 53–4
Hsu, L. M. 1029
Huang, H. 49
Huismans, S. 94
Huppert, F. 891
Huta, V. 205–6, 208

Irwin, J. D. 1012
Isaacowitz, D. M. 20, 26
Isen, A. M. 20, 723
Ishii-Kuntz, M. 827

Jain, R. 379
Janis, I. 1033
Janoff-Bulman, R. 931
Jaspers, K. 287–8
Jex, S. M. 722
Johnson, K. J. 21
Johnson, S. 257–8
Joseph, S. 928

Kahneman, D. 55, 141
Kant, I. 1011
Karasek, R. A. J. 715

Kashdan, T. B.  105, 106
Kasser, T.  508
Kets de Vries, M.  801–2
Keyes, C. L. M.  331, 384, 917, 918, 919, 922
Kierkegaard, S.  280–1
Koestner, R.  506
Kraiger, K.  723
Krampe, R. T.  237
Krueger, A. B.  55

Laird, D.  800
Lakey, B.  850, 853
Langer, E. J.  1028–9, 1030, 1032, 1033
Leary, M. R.  823
Lekes, N.  506
Leonardelli, G. J.  28
Leutscher, T.  681
Leveille, S. G.  1012–13
Levinson, H.  805–6
Levy, B. R.  1030
Leyton, M.  231
Liberman, V.  50
Little, B.  236
Loewenstein, G. F.  54
Lucas, R. E.  127–8, 140–1
Luechinger, S.  438
Lykken, D.  890
Lyubomirsky, S.  50, 903, 968, 969

McCabe, K.  850
McCrae, R. R.  142, 889
McCullough, M. E.  98, 966
McGregor, I.  236
Mack, D. A.  801, 803, 804
Maddison, D.  502
Madey, S. F.  53, 741
Mahoney, A.  400, 402, 404
Marshall, J.  805
Marsten, W. H.  789
Maslow, A.  203
Massimini, F.  63, 65
Mayr, E.  155
Medvec, V. H.  53, 741
Meehl, P. E.  1040
Meier, S.  438
Merleau-Ponty, M.  286
Michalos, A. C.  186–7
Mikels, J. A.  23
Mikulincer, M.  835, 837, 838, 839, 841

Mill, J. S.  156, 232, 260–1
Misra, G.  377, 379
Mohan, K. K.  380
Mohan, Y.  380
Mooney, M.  98
Mora, C.  681
Morrow, D.  1012
Moss, L.  802
Muraven, M.  127
Murray-Swank, A.  404

Nachmias, O.  837
Nelson, D. L.  803
Nietzsche, F.  282, 295, 299, 300
Nowicki, G. P.  20
Nozick, R.  294, 321
Nussbaum, M. C.  319

Oades, L. G.  1051, 1057
Offidani, E.  1045
Oishi, S.  127–8
Oldham, G. R.  714, 716
Orehek, E.  853
Ottolini, F.  1045

Papa, A.  103
Parducci, A.  35
Pargament, K. I.  400, 402, 404
Park, N.  964
Parker, S. K.  717–18
Parks, A. C.  968
Pek, J.  23
Peterson, C.  964, 967
Phillips, R. E.  801
Pickett, K. E.  470, 471, 472
Prasad, V. S.  380
Pritchard, J.  473–4
Proulx, C. M.  825–6
Putnam, R.  94–5

Quick, J. C.  801, 803, 804
Quick, J. D.  803

Rafanelli, C.  1041, 1042, 1043
Rao, P. V. K.  380
Rashid, T.  968
Ray, G.  380
Regel, S.  928
Rehdanz, K.  502

Reis, H. T.  853
Roberts, Y.  649–50
Rodin, J.  1032
Roethlisberger, F. J.  785, 790
Ross, L. D.  50
Ross, Jr., W. T.  46
Rousseau, D. M.  717
Rousseau, J.-J.  258
Rowe, G.  19
Ruini, C.  1042, 1043, 1044, 1045
Russell, J. A.  786
Ryan, R. M.  205–6, 1015
Ryff, C. D.  204

Sartre, J.-P.  285–6
Schkade, D.  903, 968
Schmueli, D.  127
Schneider, B.  719, 720
Schopenhauer, A.  291–3
Schor, J. B.  485–6
Schwartz, S.  94
Schwarz, N.  37, 43, 45
Seligman, M. E. P.  1, 98, 205, 565, 665, 683, 964, 966, 967, 968, 981
Sen, A.  235, 321
Shaver, P. R.  835, 838, 839
Sheffi, E.  841
Sheldon, K. M.  903, 968, 969
Shinde, V. R.  379–80
Simonson, I.  46
Singh, J. K.  379
Slade, M.  1051
Slav, K.  838
Smith, A.  799
Smith, W.  502
Sofer-Roth, S.  839–40
Solnick, S. J.  53
Spector, P. E.  722
Spence, G. B.  1012
Spitzer, L.  1032
Staw, B. M.  682
Steger, M. F.  105, 944
Sternberg, R. J.  632
Strack, F.  37, 43, 45
Straume, L. V.  231
Stutzer, A.  436, 438
Suissa, J.  647
Swaen, G. M.  1011

Taylor, S. E.  826
Tedeschi, R. G.  930, 931, 934
Tellegen, A.  890
Tesch-Römer, C.  237
Thomas, B.  473–4
Thompson, A. D.  801
Tice, D. M.  127
Tocqueville, A. de.  260
Tomba, E.  1044
Tov, W.  141
Tugade, M. M.  24
Tversky, A.  36–8, 43, 44, 52

Vaillant, G. E.  807
van Aken, M. A. G.  850–1
van den Brandt, P. A.  1011
van den Brink, H. M.  46
van Lieshout, C. F. M.  850–1
van Praag, B. M. S.  505
Veroff, J.  965
Vickers, D.  473–4
Villacorta, M.  506
Viranjini, G.  380
Visani, D.  1045
Vittersø, J.  205, 231, 238

Wadhwa, B. S.  379
Wadlinger, H. A.  20, 26
Wan, C. K.  824
Warholm, V.  238
Warr, P. B.  712, 713, 734
Waterman, A. S.  204–5
Watson, B.  272
Wearing, A. J.  889
Weigel, M.  717
Weinmann, C.  1032
Welsch, H.  502
White, S. B.  54
Wilkinson, R. G.  470, 471, 472
Willoughby, B. L. B.  98
Wilson, D. S.  99
Withey, S. B.  233
Wolfer, J.  1033
Wright, T. A.  785, 786, 787, 788, 789, 790
Wrzesniewski, A.  717

Yerkes, R. M.  65
Yu, D. C. T.  193

Zhong, C. B.  28

# Subject Index

acceptance 419–20, 1000
acceptance and commitment therapy (ACT) 994–1004
accident victims 294
action planning 1057–8
action tendencies 18
activation 712
active-constructive responding 967–8
acts of kindness 968
acupuncture 416
adaptation 36, 42, 164, 178, 435, 436, 742–3, 807, 887, 888–9, 902
adaptive problem solving 879–80, 881
addiction 65
adjustment 168
adolescents
　acceptance and commitment therapy 1003
　depression 535–6
　prefrontal cortex development 27
advertising 486, 488
affect; *see also* emotions
　appreciations of life 167–8
　brain activation 2
　circumplex 712, 786
　endowment–contrast model 49–50
　mindfulness practice 392–3
　priming 723
　psychological capital 757–8
　in work 696–7
　work characteristic judgments 723–4
affective disorders, well-being therapy 1041–2
affective style 74
age; *see also* old age
　friendship and happiness association 865–6
　perception of 1026–8
　relationships and happiness 827–8
　subjective well-being 140, 176
air pollution 502
air travel 504–5

alcohol consumption 269, 273–4
alignment-related pathways 772–6
ambiguity 286, 287
amygdala 2
*ānanda* 374, 375
ancient Greeks 155–6, 174, 202, 216, 252–4, 332–3, 466–7
anomie 473–5
anticonsumerist movement 487
antidepressant efficacy, well-being therapy 1042–3
antidotes 353–4
antisocial activities 65
anxiety 19, 281
anxiety disorders 102–8, 1041–2
anxious attachment 835, 836
appraisal 722, 723, 756–7
appreciation 163, 167–8, 413–14
appreciative inquiry 587
approach 76, 102, 106–7, 109, 111–12
Aristippus 155, 202, 216
Aristotle 156, 202, 216, 254, 318–19, 466, 957
arousal 75
Arpey, Gerald 807–8
art of living 166, 168–9
*artha* 376, 379
arts policy 525
aspirations
　Daoism 272
　extrinsic and intrinsic 220–1
　income aspirations and happiness 435–6
assimilation effects 42–3
assimilation resistance 236–7
attachment 834–43
　basics of attachment theory 835
　positive emotions 836–42
　priming interventions 842–3
　psychological well-being 836–7
　social support 855
　style of attachment 835

attention
    functional well-being approach 237
    joint attention 21–2
    meditation 389, 390–1
    negative emotion-linked narrowing 19
    positive emotion-linked
        broadening 18–20, 21–2
attitudes
    to life 234
    meditation 389
    positive future-oriented 945, 948
attraction–selection–attrition
    framework 719–20
Australian Centre on Quality of Life
    (ACQOL) 189
authentic happiness theory 897
authenticity 283–4, 774–5
autonomy
    coaching 1018
    correlates of relative autonomy 219–20
    education 542–3
    eudaimonia 203–4
    good functioning 236
    healthcare 220
    need for 217–18
    in recovery 1056
    at work 220
avoidance 76, 102, 104, 1000
avoidant attachment 835, 836
avoidant persistence 1002
awareness 222
awareness-identity 378
awe 413


baby boomers 564
balance theory of wisdom 632–4
basic needs 541
behavior
    changing with acceptance and commitment
        therapy 998–1002
    indicator of happiness 192–3
behavioral activation 968–9
bereavement 24
Best Possible Selves exercise 969
Bhutan 2, 518
bicultural strategy 63–4
binary opposites 327, 328

biofeedback 597
biopsychosocial paradigm 427
biotope 163
bipolar spectrum disorders 111–12
blood pressure 788–9
board of directors 804
Bounce Back! 573–4
brain activity
    affective style 2
    meditation 391, 417
    social anxiety 106
brain development 27
brain plasticity 942
breast cancer 934, 935
broaden-and-build theory 18–25, 230, 385,
    840–1
    appraisal process 723
    embodied cognition 28
    neuroscience of 25–7
    positive emotions 27–8
    psychological capital 757
    psychological well-being 790–1
    social transmission 28
Buddhism 344–55, 357–68
    antidote use 353–4
    dependent origination 365
    *dukkha* 346
    ethics 354–5
    familiarization work 353
    *karma* 354, 365–6
    meditation 359, 363–5, 385–6, 389–90
    mind 348–9, 358–9
    negative emotions 349–51, 352–5
    pristine mindfulness meditation 363–5
    relational Buddhism 367–8
    *samsara* 344
    self 351–2, 360–1
    suffering 346–8
    *sukha* 81, 344
Buddhist psychology 360–3, 385
buffering 680, 683
burnout 715, 805–6


calling 405, 701–2, 773
Cantril ladder 55–6
capability 169
capitalization support 853

car use  504
cardiovascular health  788–90
career orientation  701–2
case formulation  1018
catastrophic thinking  107
causality, locus of  66
Celebrating Strengths framework  584–6
celebrity  547
cell birthdates  941–2
challenge–hindrance stressor
    framework  715–16
challenges  62, 65–6, 67–8
chances  161, 162–3
change enhancement  1057
Changes in Outlook Questionnaire  928
character strengths
    collaborative recovery model  1057
    depression reduction  111
    educating about  653, 662–3
    executive well-being  801
    organizational settings  755
charitable giving  95–7, 126
Check & Connect program  616–17
Chi-Tze  357–8
children
    depression  535–6
    measuring happiness of  192–3
    well-being therapy  1045
Chinese  263–77, 466
choice  894–5, 897
    choice–judgment discrepancy  51–4
    old age  1032
Christianity  254–6
chronic illness
    acceptance and commitment therapy  1003
    health coaching  1012–13
cigarette smoking  439
circumplex model  712, 786
climate change  502–3
clinical psychology  362
coaching  1009–22
    autonomy  1018
    case formulation  1018
    collaborative recovery model  1058–61
    competence  1017–18
    definition  1009–10
    educational settings  1013–14
    effectiveness  1010–14

executives  1011, 1013
    goal articulation and attainment  1010
    health coaching  1012–13
    life coaching  1011–12
    relatedness  1016–17
    self-determination theory  1014,
        1015–16, 1018
    supporting self-determined
        living  1018–20
    well-being and  1014–21
    in the workplace  1011, 1013
cognition
    appreciations of life  167
    embodied cognition  28–9
    positive emotion-linked broadening  20
    psychological capital  756–7
cognitive appraisal  756–7
cognitive balance  392
cognitive behavioral psychology  362
cognitive behavioral therapy  572, 962
cognitive defusion  1000
cognitive dissonance  928–9
cognitive flexibility  20
cognitive fusion  1000
cognitive impairment, happiness
    measurement  192–3
coherence  66
collaborative goal technology  1057
collaborative recovery model  1050–63
collectivist cultures  143, 178, 455, 485
committed action  1002
common method variance  824, 828, 864
community
    resource centers based in  64
    threat from consumer culture  486–7
community of enquiry  583
community service  623–4
comparisons  740–1
compassion  94, 414
competence  217, 1017–18
complete state model of mental health  331
computer games  600–1
conation  390, 758–9
confidence  753
conflict resolution  125–6
Confucianism  263–4, 265–6, 267, 269, 466
connectedness  945, 947
constitutional policy  433, 443

consumer culture theory 482, 485–7
   well-being in consumer societies 483–5, 487–8
consumer-defined recovery in mental health 1051–2
   consumer-targeted intervention 1062
contentment 293, 419–20
context
   acceptance and commitment therapy 995–6
   flow 61
   priming old age 1028–31
   at work 699–701
contingent models 36–7
contingent valuation method 441
continuum opposites 327, 328
contradictory opposites 327, 328
contraries 328
contrast
   adaptation as 42
   probability and 45
   range-frequency theory 35–6
   social comparison 47
   well-being 55–6
contrast–empathy model social comparison 47–9
control
   locus of 66, 564
   perceived control in old age 1031–2
coping 66, 125, 807–8
Coping with Stress Course 615
core affect 232
core self-evaluations 721, 723
core strengths 773–4
cortical-basal ganglia loops 27
counter-exampling 322
counterclockwise study 1029
creativity
   happiness 126
   positive emotions 20
   resilience 664
   success in workplace 123
   teaching wisdom 639
crime 526
critical thinking 639
Croesus 252–4
cultivation theory 488
cultural change, flow 63–4

cultural differences
   flow 62–4
   identity and consumerism 485
   income/subjective well-being link 141
   relationships/happiness link 828
   societal well-being 455
   subjective well-being 143–4, 178
cultural pursuits 525
cultural response bias 194

Daoism 263–4, 265, 266–7, 268, 269, 270–2, 273–4, 466
data cleaning 191
day reconstruction method 139, 176
deactivating strategies 835–6
defusion 1000
deliberate practice 237–8
delusion 294
demands, resources and 66
dependent origination 365
depression 109–11
   burden of 915
   children and adolescents 535–6
   cognitive behavioral therapy 962
   emotional reactivity 110
   happiness-focused interventions 963
   positive psychotherapy 987
   sub-threshold symptoms 962–3
   well-being therapy 1037, 1042
depressive disorders 109–12
deprivation 169–70
desecration 407
desire 292, 350
development
   flow 61
   meaning in life 945
   prefrontal cortex 27
   psychological capital 759–60
   spirituality 414–16
*dharma* 376, 378, 379, 380–1
diabetes control 124
diagnosis of illness 933–4
dialectic 1015
dialectical thinking 638
dialogical thinking 638
dialysis patients 307–8
differentiation 601

direct democracy  526
disability-adjusted life years (DALYs)  915
discrepancy theories  186–7
Dispositional Flow Scale  62
divorce  141, 407, 490, 825
dopaminergic system  26, 106, 230
downsizing  680
driving lessons  600
drug addiction  65
*duhkha*  81, 375
*dukkha*  346
Dunn, Patricia  798
dynamic equilibrium theory  743, 889–90, 902
dysdaimonia  331

Easterlin paradox  141, 428–9, 435, 889–91
ecology, *see* sustainable development
ecological fallacy  456
economic analysis of happiness  433–4
economic growth  176
economy  2–3, 509–10
education; *see also* teachers
   autonomy in  542–3
   basic needs provision  541
   biofeedback  597
   Bounce Back!  573–4
   Celebrating Strengths framework  584–6
   Check & Connect program  616–17
   classroom practice  579–89
   coaching role  1013–14
   cross-curricular approach  555–7
   differentiation techniques  601
   disengagement problems  616
   educating for happiness  645, 650–5
   emotional intelligence  596–8
   evidence-based teaching strategies  572
   feedback  601–2
   flourishing  648
   flow  582, 600–1
   Geelong Grammar School project  584, 657–67
   grit  649–50
   as happiness  645, 647–50
   happiness as an aim  646–7
   happiness lessons  551–61
   health-related  652–3
   high school positive psychology program  620–2
   history of well-being programs  593–4
   humor research  598–9
   indoctrination fears  559–60
   KidsMatter  573
   life-planning  547–8
   on meaning and purpose  654
   meaningful activities  583, 586
   meditation skills  598
   mindfulness in the classroom  582–3, 597–8
   Penn Resiliency Program  572, 584, 593, 617–20, 660–1, 663
   personal and social education  553–4
   personal development education  552–61
   Personal, Social, Health and Economic Education  593–4
   play  599–600
   policy development  522
   positive education  536, 568, 580, 657–67
   positive emotions  581–2, 595–6
   praise  601–2
   relationship management  545, 653
   religious perspective  542
   resilience  566–7, 612–24, 649–50
   SEAL  560, 572–3, 596
   self-esteem movement  565–6, 603, 665
   self-regulation  598
   social and emotional learning movement  567, 612–13
   storytelling  582, 584–5
   strengths-based approach  653, 662–3
   Strengths Gym  585, 587
   student well-being  568–74
   success link  546–7
   teaching for wisdom  634–40
   teaching positiveness  1033
   UK Resilience Programme  522, 594
   value issues  560
   well-being and  540–9
   well-being therapy  1043–5
   Wellington College happiness lessons  647, 650–4
   whole-school approach  554–5, 570, 584–6
   work aspect of  548–9
   worthwhile pursuits  541–9
   Zippy's Friends  593

efficacy 753
ego depletion 25, 127
egocentrism 345–6
egocentrism fallacy 635
electroencephalogram 106, 391
elevation 413
embodied cognition 28–9
emotional contagion 28, 720, 724–5
emotional happiness 186
emotional intelligence 73–84, 166
   education environments 596–8
   emotionally intelligent
      happiness 79–83
   facilitating function 76–8
   health effect 79
   social outcomes 78
   successful living 78–9
emotional state theories 303, 308–10
emotional well-being and perceived social
      support 848–9
emotions; *see also* affect; negative emotions;
      positive emotions
   action tendencies 18
   evolutionary perspective 876–7
   executive well-being 807
   facilitation role 76
   feelings and 229
   freeing 354
   functions 75–6, 229–31
   generalized anxiety disorder 108
   as messengers 75
   in mind 348–9
   motivation role 75–6
   reactivity in depression 110
   roller coaster metaphor 74
   transcendent 413–14
   weather metaphor 81
empathic happiness 839
empathy 47
employment contracts 697–8
enacted work design 718, 721–2
endorsement 310
endowment–contrast (E–C) model 35–56
   affective version 49–50
   choice–judgment discrepancy 54
   decomposition 39–44
   extensions 46–50
   generalization 44–5

   historical context 35–7
   methodological influences 36–7
   real-life applications 50–1
   well-being 55–6
energy conservation 505
engagement 309–10, 582–3, 621, 964, 967–9,
      981–2
   building 967–9
   definition 4
   at work 772–5
Enlightenment 256–9
environment
   concern for 506
   relationship development 877
   resilience promotion 610–11
   sustainable development 498–511, 526–7
   at work 700, 734–9
Epictetus 332–3
Epicurus 155, 332, 467
Eriksen flanker task 19
ethical-disengagement fallacy 635
ethics
   Buddhism 354–5
   as duties 679
   values and 633, 639
eudaimonia 201–11
   abstractness 208
   autonomy 203–4
   causes 207–8
   conceptions 201, 202–6
   defining 209–10
   definition 4
   factor analysis 206
   form of well-being 207
   life of meaning 205
   motives for activities 205–6
   opposite of 331
   outcomes 210
   personal expressiveness 204–5
   philosophical conceptions 202, 216,
      253–4, 263
   predictors 210–11
   psychological well-being 4, 204
   reflective equilibrium 318
   religious conceptions 202–3
   subjectivity 208
   subtlety 208
   theoretical conceptions 203

values 208-9
way of acting 206-7, 209-10
eudaimonic happiness 170-1, 676
eudaimonic well-being 81
evaluability model 53-4
evaluations 232-4
everyday democracy 526
evolutionary psychology 875-82
executive attention 19
executive coaching 1011, 1013
executive well-being 798-810
  burnout 805-6
  character strengths 801
  cultural myths 809
  definition 799-800
  emotions 807
  gender differences 808-9
  professional supports 803-4
  self-awareness 802
  self-reliance 803
  social isolation 806
  socialized power motivation 802-3
  stress 805
  toxic effects of emotions 807
  traumas and tragedies 807-8
exercise 525, 527, 933
existential opposites 329
existentialism 285-6
experience sampling method 62, 139
experience utility 51
experimental philosophy 323-4
expertise 237-8
expressive writing 969
external locus of control 564
external qualities of life 162
external regulation 219
extraversion 142, 828, 889-90, 896
extrinsic aspirations 220-1
extrinsic goals 489-90, 508
extrinsic motivation 218-19

Facebook 881
facial expression processing 106
factor analysis 191-2, 206
faith schools 542
fame 547
familiarization 353

family policy 521-2
fear 19
feedback 601-2, 776
feelings 228-32
fitness 163-4, 876-7
Flourish Program 1062
flourishing 3, 81, 384-6
  educational environments 648
  meditation 388
  mental illness 331
  positive emotions 23
flow 60-8, 204, 237, 309
  assessment 61-2
  contextual dimension 61
  cultural differences 62-4
  development 61
  developing countries, flow in 63, 64
  dimensions 60
  dynamic aspect 61
  engagement 968-9, 981-2
  features 60-1
  historical perspective 65-7
  learning environment 582, 600-1
  misuse of 64-5
  personality factors 67-8
  psychological structure 61
  role of 61
  technology use 68
  work-related 68, 523
Flow Questionnaire 61-2
Flow State Scale 62
flying 504-5
focus of recovery 1053
folk concepts 323-4
foolishness 634-5
foreign language teaching 640
forgiveness 94, 414, 807
freedom 285, 286
French women, well-being 55
friendship 860-7, 880-1, 896
fulfillment 582-3
full life 983
fully functioning 203
function well 235-8
functional contextualism 997-8
functional well-being 171-2, 228, 229, 231, 232, 236-7
fundamental attribution errors 1032

fusion 1000
future
　attitude orientated towards 945, 948
　expectations about 44–5
　fear of 1000–1

gambling 65
gamma oscillations 391
GDP 1–2, 451, 455
Geelong Grammar School project 584, 657–67
gender differences
　executive well-being 808–9
　friendship and happiness association 865
　relationships and happiness 826–7
　subjective well-being 140
generalizability theory 850
generalized anxiety disorder 107–8, 1042
genetic factors
　perceived social support 854
　subjective well-being 177, 890, 891, 902
Gentle Teaching 580–1
geography of happiness 465–78
German Socio-Economic Panel 888, 891–2
global processing 19
goals; see also life goals
　aspirations 220–1
　attainment 221–2
　　bipolar spectrum disorders 112
　　coaching 1010
　　subjective well-being 138
　intrinsic and extrinsic 489–90, 508
　job goals 721
　ownership 1019–20
　pursuit 221, 945, 947–8
　striving 879, 1057
good life 155–6, 161–72, 215–16, 218–22, 312
*Good Work Project* 523
goodness 93–7
Graham, Katherine 808
Grant, Joseph, M. 801
gratitude 94, 121–2, 413–14, 665, 966–7, 971, 986, 987–8
gratitude journal 966, 986
gray matter 27
green initiatives 527
green spaces 501

grit 649–50
GROW 1018
*guna* 379

habitability 162
habitat 163
happiness
　accurate-positive-self-appraisal 298–300
　aggregate indicators 442–3
　aim of education 646–7
　ancient Greek philosophy 252–4
　attachment 834–43
　behavioral indicators 192–3
　Buddhist view 81, 344–55
　Christianity's philosophy 254–6
　classroom practices 579–89
　close relationships 821–30; see also marriage
　construct 185–9
　creativity 126
　criteria of descriptive and normative adequacy 317
　cross-cultural equivalence of measurements 193–4
　early Chinese thought 263–77
　economic analysis 433–4
　educating for 645, 650–5
　education as 645, 647–50
　egocentrism 345–6
　emotional intelligence 79–83
　emotional state theories 303, 308–10
　endorsement 310
　engagement 309–10
　Enlightenment 256–9
　evolutionary psychological perspective 875–82
　friendship 860–7, 880–1, 896
　geography of 465–78
　health link 124–5, 126–7, 880
　illusion of 291–3
　importance of 311–13
　income level 123, 434–6
　Indian tradition 372–3
　job characteristics 734–9, 744–6
　lessons in 551–61
　life goal choices 894–5
　life satisfaction 303, 305–8

long-term psychological sense of  304
longevity  124
marriage  122–3, 824–6, 880
materialism  880
meaning of  170, 171, 185–6, 466–8, 676, 1068
measurement  120, 189–96, 310–11, 860–1
mental processes  739–44
multiple definitions  3–4
opposites of  326–35
organizational virtuousness  682–4
perceived social support  847–56
pleasure and  346
as positive emotions  330
positive self-appraisal  297–300
positive state of mind  293–6
prosocial behavior  126
psychological capital  756–9
psychological well-being  786–7
purely objective standards  296
purely subjective standards  297–8
relationship success  122–3, 125–6
religiousness  97–9, 895–6
rewards of  119–28
roller coaster of emotions  74
scientific study  11–12, 156
self-reports  120, 310–11
social relationships  122–3, 125–6
spending and saving money  488–9
standards  296–300
subjective well-being  186–9, 330
sustainable happiness model  903–5
unemployment  436–8
virtuousness link  682–4
wealth link  80, 880
well-being sense of happiness  304–5
work design  711–25
work success  123
yearning for  7–8
happy endings  46
*Hard Times* (Dickens)  644–5
hardiness  66
hatred  350–1
health
    autonomy in  220
    coaching  1012–13
    definition  4
    educating about  652–3

emotional intelligence  79
happiness link  124–5, 126–7, 880
meditation benefits  417–18
negative health  165
policy development  524
positive health  166
psychological well-being  788–9
self-perceived  880
subjective well-being link  144
heart attacks  789
hedonia  201
hedonic adaptation prevention model  905–8
Hedonic and Eudaimonic Motives for Activities scale  206
hedonic approach  3, 4, 216
hedonic happiness  581–2, 676, 981
hedonic treadmill  36, 82, 137, 178, 902
hedonic value  42
hedonic well-being  80–1
hedonism  542
    reflective equilibrium  318
heliotropism  683–4
helping behavior  126
heritability, *see* genetic factors
Hewlett Packard  808–9
high blood pressure  788–9
Hinduism/Sanātana Dharma  371–82, 416
    *ānanda*  374, 375
    *artha*  376, 379
    *dharma*  376, 378, 379, 380–1
    *duhkha*  375
    goals of life  376–7
    *guna*  379
    *kāma*  376, 379
    *moksha*  376, 379, 380
    *panchakosha*  377–8
    *paramapurushārtha*  378
    *preyas*  373–5
    *purushārtha*  376
    *shreyas*  373–5
    *sthitaprajna*  375
    *sukha*  375
    Upanishads  373–5, 377–8
history teaching  640
homeostasis  188–9
hope  752–3
household waste recycling  506
Howard Hughes Corporation  803, 804

humor 598–9
hunter-gatherers 878
hyperactivating strategies 835–6
hypertension 788–9
hypnotism 293–4

"I" 351
I-deals 717
identified regulation 219
identity
  awareness-identity 378
  consumerism 484–5
  meaning in life 945–6
  positive identity construction 769–71
  three aspects 351
  work and 696
illness diagnosis 933–4
immediate experience sampling measures 55
immigrants 64
immune function 124–5, 127
imperial power motivation 803
impulsivity 1002
inaction 1002
inclusion/exclusion model 45
income; *see also* wealth
  happiness 123, 434–6
  subjective well-being 141–2, 144, 176–7, 469, 470, 472–3, 491–2
  well-being 697–8
Indian psychology 379–80
individualist cultures 143, 178, 455, 485
individuation 203
indoctrination 559–60
inequality 11, 469–71, 472, 528
informant reports 139–40
information processing 854
integrated regulation 219
intentional action 365–6, 903–4
internal qualities of life 162
international cooperation programs 64
internet use 68, 880–1
interventions
  acceptance and commitment therapy 994–1004
  commercial market 958
  consumer-targeted 1062
  insecure attachment 842–3

intentional activities 904
mindfulness-based 361, 388, 392–3, 418, 1001
person-activity fit 971–2
positive interventions 964–70
positive psychotherapy 970, 978–89
post-traumatic growth 934–5
psychological capital training 759–60
rewards of happiness 121–2
self-help 963
social support 855
staff-targeted 1062
subjective well-being 178–9
systemic 1061–3
well-being therapy 1037–46
work-oriented 746
intrinsic aspirations 220–1
intrinsic goals 489–90, 508
intrinsic motivation 66–7, 218
intrinsically motivated orientation 67
introjected regulation 219
intuition pumps 321
invulnerability fallacy 635
item response theory 460
item weighting 190–1


job characteristics 714–15, 734–9, 744–6
job crafting 717, 773
job demands-control 715
job demands-resources 68, 715
job design 698
job enrichment 714, 772
job goals 721
job interviews 720
job orientation 701–2
job performance 787
job satisfaction 46–7, 523, 698–9, 784–5, 788, 878
joint attention 21–2
joy 266–74
judgment
  choice–judgment discrepancy 51–4
  contingent models 36–7


*kāma* 376, 379
*karma* 354, 365–6

KidsMatter 573
Kongzi 263, 264–9, 274–7

language 996
latent work design 718–21
laughter 598–9
leadership 792
leadership teams 803–4
learned optimism 572
learning difficulties 580–1
life-ability 162–3, 165–6
life coaching 1011–12
life goals
　choices and happiness 894–5
　Hinduism 376–7
　pursuit and attainment 220–2
Life Journey Enhancement Tools
　　(LifeJET) 1058
life of meaning 205
life philosophy 927
life-planning 547–8
life satisfaction 4, 135, 234, 303, 305–8, 441–2
　German Socio-Economic
　　Panel data 888, 891–2
　perceived social support 848
　positive emotions 23
　religious involvement 895–6
　set-points 892–4
life visioning 1057
limitations 287–8
literary examples 322–3
literature teaching 640
livability 162, 164–5
local environment and well-being 501–2
local processing 19
local well-being 473–5
locus of causality 66
locus of control 66, 564
loneliness 473–5
loneliness of command 806
longevity 124, 144
love of life 282
loving-kindness meditation 23, 122, 385, 965–6

*makarios* 255
"Making Listening Special" 580–1

marriage
　happiness 122–3, 824–6, 880
　sanctification 399–400, 401–2, 403
　subjective well-being 140–1, 176
mastery 968–9
mate attraction 880, 881
materialism 488–90, 507–9, 880
maternal positive affect 22
maturity 203
Mayer–Salovey model 596–7
meaning 583, 621, 941–51, 964, 982
　across the lifespan 949–50
　building 969–70
　in the classroom 583, 586
　comprehension 943, 944–5
　conceptualization 942–3
　connectedness 945, 947
　contents of 944
　definition 943
　development 945
　educating about 654
　elements 943
　experiencing 943
　goal pursuit 945, 947–8
　identity 945–6
　model of lifelong meaning 944–5
　optimal functioning 236
　positive future-oriented attitudes 945, 948
　purpose and 943, 944–5
　relationships 944, 947
　religion 98
　search for 300–1, 943–4
　self-in-world views 945, 948–9
　at work 699, 714
mechanistic view 997–8
media effects 488
medical model 332, 979
meditation
　affective balance 392
　attention 389, 390–1
　attitude 389
　brain activity 391, 417
　Buddhist tradition 359, 363–5, 385–6,
　　389–90
　calm abiding 387–8
　in the classroom 598
　definition 386–8
　flourishing 388

meditation (cont.)
　health benefits 417–18
　insight 387–8
　intention and 389
　loving-kindness 23, 122, 385, 965–6
　mental balance 390–3
　mindfulness-based 359, 363–5, 389–93
　neuroscience 389–90
　optimism 392
　psychological approaches 389–93
memory, endowment–contrast model 38
mental balance 390–3
mental flourishing 331
mental health
　complete state model 331
　consumer-defined recovery 1051–2
　dual continua model 916–19
　policy development 524
　positive mental health promotion and
　　protection 915–23
　stability of 919–20
　well-being 712–13
mental illness
　disability-adjusted life years 915
　dual continua model 916–19
　flourishing 331
mental processes 739–44
metaphysical comfort 265
MIDUS study 822, 917–19
Milestone School 580–1, 582
Millennium Ecosystem Assessment
　(MEA) 498
mind 348–9, 358–9
mindfulness 222, 388, 1027–8
　in the classroom 582–3, 597–8
　mental balance 390–3
　psychological approaches 389–93
mindfulness-based interventions 361, 388,
　392–3, 418, 1001
mindfulness meditation 359, 363–5, 389–93
mindlessness 1027
minorities 64
*moksha* 376, 379, 380
money and happiness 488–9; *see also*
　income; wealth
mood as information 38, 43–4
mood disorders, well-being therapy 1041–2
mood happiness 186

mood propensity 309
morally unworthy 293
mortality reduction 124
mortality salience 934
motivation
　age-related differences 1032–3
　emotions as motivators 75–6
　eudaimonia 205–6
　executive well-being 802–3
　extrinsic 218–19
　intrinsic 66–7, 218
multiple discrepancy theory 138
music 267–9

natural selection 876–7
　nature, sanctification of 406
Navajo 63–4
need fulfillment 138
negative emotions
　attention narrowing 19
　avoidance motivation 75–6
　in Buddhism 349–51, 352–5
　as facilitators 76
　generalized anxiety disorder 108
　messages relayed by 75
　positive psychotherapy 985–6
　strategic interference theory 878–9
　undoing by positive emotions 24–5
　value of 128, 229
　weak and substantive opposite of positive
　　emotions 330
　well-being 80
negative health 165
negotiation 125–6
neighborhood networks 526
neo-positivist research 482–3
neuroplasticity 942
neuropsychology 361–2
neuroscience
　broaden and build effects 25–7
　meditation 389–90
neuroticism 142, 721, 723, 889, 890, 896
new economics foundation 958–9
noble values 413
noise pollution 505
normative questions 316
North Karelia project 525

nuclear power stations 502
nucleus accumbens 27
nun study 124, 144

occupation, *see job headings*; work
occupational strain management
    programs 746
old age
  giving choices 1032
  meaning in life 948–9
  motivation 1032–3
  perceived control 1031–2
  policy development 524–5
  priming 1028–31
  socially constructed world 1031
  stereotyping 1026–8
Olympic medalists 53, 741
omnipotence fallacy 635
omniscience fallacy 635
optimal experience 60, 1040; *see also* flow
optimal functioning 235–8
optimism
  depression risk 108, 111
  meditation 392
  positive organizational behavior
      framework 753
  subjective well-being 177
orbitofrontal cortex 27
organismic-dialectic 1015
organismic valuing theory 931–2
organismic wellness 214–15
organizational health 784
organizations; *see also* work
  collaborative recovery model 1062
  definition of healthy organizations 784
  downsizing 680
  executive well-being 798–810
  history of well-being research 784–5
  positive organizational behavior 752–6
  positive organizational scholarship 2, 671
  psychological capital 751–62
  social capital 682–3
  virtuousness 676–86
outcomes
  eudaimonia 210
  positive psychotherapy 987
  post-traumatic growth 932–3

quality of life 161, 163
  subjective well-being 144, 179
own-race bias 21
Oxford Happiness Inventory 194–5


pain management 1003
*panchakosha* 377–8
*paramapurushārtha* 378
parents
  evolutionary perspective 879
  positive emotions and child
      development 22
  resilience program for 623
  sanctification of parenting 404–5
  work-family enrichment 703
Pareto optimality 52–3
PATHS program 615
Penn Resiliency Program 572, 584, 593,
    617–20, 660–1, 663
PepsiCo 806
Perceived Benefit Scales 928
perceived control in old age 1031–2
perceived social support 847–56
perceived work design 718, 722–4
"person" 351
person-activity fit 971–2
personal and social education 553–4
personal development education 552–61
personal expressiveness 204–5
personal growth 236–7
personal identity, *see* identity
personal recovery 1051–2
personal salience 743
Personal, Social, Health and Economic
    Education 593–4
Personal Synthesis Program 560
Personal Well-being Index (PWI) 196
personality
  flow 67–8
  perceived social support 849–51
  subjective well-being 136–7, 142–3,
      177, 889
  well-being 713
  worker happiness 744–5
perspective taking 775–6
philosophical method 315–24
physical body, sanctification of 406

physical exercise  525, 527, 933
picture processing  20
Platt, Lew  808–9
play  599–600
pleasant life  581–2, 621, 981
pleasure  964
  affect circumplex  712
  building  965–7
  feeling or evaluation  231–2
  happiness and  346
  Indian tradition  372–3
  role  230
  in Upanishads  373–5
pleasure principle  203
policy decisions
  age-related  524–5
  arts  525
  constitutional level  433, 443
  cultural pursuits  525
  education-related  522
  environmental sustainability  526–7
  family-related  521–2
  happiness research involvement  440–3
  health-related  524
  politico-economic process  433, 440–3
  redistribution  528
  safety  526
  social capital  526
  sports  525
  subjective well-being  428
  well-being  517–28
  work-related  522–4
pollution  502, 505
positional concerns  53
positional goods  547
Positive and Negative Affect Schedule (PANAS)  175, 330, 786, 837, 908–9
positive education  536, 568, 580, 657–67
positive emotions
  action tendencies  18
  approach motivation  76
  attachment patterns  836–42
  attention broadening  18–20, 21–2
  bereavement  24
  broaden-and-build theory  18–25, 230, 385, 840–1
  classification of distinct emotions  27–8
  cognitive flexibility  20
  coping skills  125
  creativity  20
  ego depletion  25
  embodied cognition  28–9
  as facilitators  76
  flourishing  23
  functions  230–1
  happiness as  330
  joint attention  21–2
  in learning environments  581–2, 595–6
  life satisfaction  23
  loving-kindness meditation  122
  messages relayed by  75
  parental  22
  perceived social support  848–9, 852
  pleasant life  981
  positive outcomes  80
  problem solving  20
  psychological capital  757
  psychopathology  101–13
  reflected best self  771
  resilience  23–5, 125
  social anxiety  105–6
  social cognition  21
  social transmission  28
  success  120
  therapeutic focus  980
  thought–outcome contingencies  25–6
  undoing negative emotions  24–5
  virtuousness  682
  weak and substantive opposite of negative emotions  330
  well-being  22–3, 80
positive health  166
positive identity construction  769–71
positive mental health promotion and protection  915–23
positive organizational behavior  752–6
positive organizational scholarship  2, 671
positive psychology  1–2, 568, 713
  high school program  620–2
  recovery and  1052
positive psychotherapy  970, 978–89
Positive Psychotherapy Inventory  987
positive self-appraisal  297–300
positive state of mind  293–6
positivity  331
post-traumatic growth  926–36

dimensions 927
facilitating 934–5
operationalizing the construct 928–30
outcome prediction 932–3
physical exercise 933
post-traumatic stress and 927
predicting 930
self-protective illusion 929–930
theoretical perspectives 931–2
Post-traumatic Growth Inventory 928
post-traumatic stress disorder 104, 927, 1043
power motivation 802–3
practical thinking 639
practice 237–8
praise 601–2
predicted utility 51
preference 896, 897
  happy endings 46
  reversals 36–7, 52
preference drift 46–7
prefrontal cortex 2, 27
prejudice 93–4
preventive stress management model 805
*preyas* 373–5
priming 723, 842–3, 1028–31
pristine mindfulness 363–5
proactive behaviors 717–18
probability, expectations about the future 45
problem solving 20, 619, 879–80, 881
Promoting Alternative Thinking Strategies (PATHS) program 615
promoting and protecting mental health 915–23
prosocial behavior 126
proxy data 191
psychic affirmation 310
psychic flourishing 310
psychic orientation 310
psychological capital (PsyCap) 751–62
  affective mechanism 757–8
  cognitive mechanism 756–7
  conative mechanism 758–9
  definition 754
  developing 759–60
  happiness and well-being 756–9

positive organizational behavior 752–6
  social mechanism 759
psychological empowerment 714
psychological needs 217
psychological selection 61
psychological well-being
  attachment patterns 836–7
  broaden-and-build approach 790–1
  cardiovascular health 788–9
  characteristics 786–7
  eudaimonic model 4, 204
  happiness as 786–7
  workers 783, 787–8, 792, 793
Psychological Well-being Scale 204
psychotherapy 979
  positive psychotherapy 970, 978–89
public goods 441–2
public policy, *see* policy decisions
public transport 504
pulse product 789, 790, 791–2
purpose 943, 944–5, 982
  educating about 654
  religiousness 98
  at work 696, 772–3
*puruṣārtha* 376

quality of life 4, 161–4

range-frequency theory 35–6
rational consumer hypothesis 438–40
reality principle 203
reconstructive analysis 317
recovery approach
  consumer-defined recovery 1051–2
  positive psychology 1052
  service provision 1052–8
recycling household waste 506
redistributive policies 528
reflected best self 767–77
reflective equilibrium 317–20
reflective thinking 636
Reinemund, Steve 806
relatedness 217, 1016–17
relational Buddhism 367–8
relational frame theory 996–7
relational interbeing 367–8

relational regulation theory 853–4
relational self 360
relationships; see also marriage
  affirmation 775–6
  age differences 827–8
  assessment 822
  attachment and positive emotions 838
  cultural differences 828
  educating about 545, 653
  emotional intelligence 78
  engaging in 967–8
  environmental barriers 877
  friendship 860–7, 880–1, 896
  gender differences 826–7
  good functioning 236
  importance of for happiness 823–4
  lessons in 653
  meaning in life 944, 947
  partner happiness 839–40
  post-traumatic growth 927
  psychological capital 759
  reflected best self 771
  resilience 611–12
  sanctification 403
  subjective well-being 144, 177
  success and happiness 122–3, 125–6
  at work 700
releasement 284
religion and religiousness; see also Buddhism; Hinduism/Sanātana Dharma
  benefits of beliefs 411–12
  charitable giving 95–7
  Christianity's philosophy of happiness 254–6
  education sector 542
  engaging in and well-being 88–99
  eudaimonic thought 202–3
  goodness 93–7
  happiness link 97–9, 895–6
  meaning and purpose 98
  prejudice 93–4
  self-control 98
  social support 98
  subjective well-being 142, 176
  terror management 99
  virtues 94
  volunteerism 94–5

reminiscences 969–70
resilience 610–12
  creativity 664
  education 566–7, 612–24, 649–50
  environments promoting 610–11
  parent program 623
  Penn Resiliency Program 572, 584, 593, 617–20, 660–1, 663
  positive emotions 23–5, 125
  positive organizational behavior framework 753
  relationships 611–12
  teacher program 622–3
  trauma response 103
  UK Resilience Programme 522, 594
resolution 284
resources, demands and 66
reward 26–7; see also success
Romanian orphanage children 22
rumination 931, 1001

safety policy 526
salutogenesis 66
samsara 344
Sanātana Dharma, see Hinduism/Sanātana Dharma
sanctification 397–408
  benefits 408
  defining 398–401
  marriage 399–400, 401–2, 403
  nature 406
  non-theistic 400–1
  parenting 404–5
  physical body 406
  sexuality 403–4
  strivings 402–3
  theistic 399–400
  threats to 407
  work 405–6
Sarbanes-Oxley Act (2002) 804
Sarkozy, Nicolas 3, 12, 519
satisfaction treadmill 907
satisfaction with life, see life satisfaction
Satisfaction with Life Scale 175, 195–6
saving money 489
savoring 965, 986
Scales of Psychological Well-being 195

scheme theory 236
schizophrenic-spectrum disorders 113
schools; *see also* education
    classroom practice 579–89
    policy development 522
    well-being therapy 1043–5
    whole-school approach 554–5,
        570, 584–6
science teaching 640
scientific knowledge 11
scientific paradigm 888
Seattle Social Development program 615
SEED skills 649
selection interviews 720
self 351–2
    Buddhist understanding 351–2, 360–1
    post-traumatic growth 927
    reflected best self 767–77
    well-being and sense of self 377–8
self-actualization 66, 166, 203
self-appraisal 297–300
self-awareness 802
self-content *vs* self-context 1001
self-control 98, 439
self-deception 285–6
self-determination theory 66–7, 236
    coaching efficacy 1014, 1015–16, 1018
    good life 218–22
    materialism 489
    meta-theoretical and theoretical
        underpinnings 217–18
self-efficacy 66, 68, 664–5, 742
self-esteem 177, 565–6, 603, 665
self-expansion 21
self-fulfillment 312
self-help 962–3
self-in-world views 945, 948–9
self-perceived health 880
self-realization 374
self-reflection 931
self-regulation
    anxiety disorders 102–3, 104, 105–6, 108
    in the classroom 598
self-reliance 803
sense of coherence 66
September 11 attacks 24, 93, 680, 807–8
set-point theory 136, 137, 188–9, 887, 888,
    890, 891, 892–4, 897, 902

sexual relationships
    sanctification 403–4
    social anxiety 106
shared method variance 824, 828, 864
shattered assumptions theory 931
shift work 699
shopping 483
*shreyas* 373–5
signature strengths 967, 981, 988
skills
    challenge and 62, 65–6, 67–8
    development 237–8
smoking behavior 439
Social and Emotional Aspects of Learning
    (SEAL) 560, 572–3, 596
social and emotional learning 567, 612–13
social anxiety disorder 104–7
social bonds, work-related 696
social capital 526, 682–3
social cognition 21
social comparison
    contrast–empathy model 47–9
    subjective well-being 138
Social Decision Making and Social Problem
    Solving Program 615
social dilemmas 503
social isolation 806
social networks 880–1, 896, 971
Social Relations Model 850
social relationships, *see* relationships
social support
    attachment theory 855
    capitalization support 853
    interventions 855
    perceived support and happiness 847–56
    psychological capital 759
    relational regulation theory 853–4
    religion 98
    stress and coping social support theory 853
    at work 700, 721–2, 759
social transmission 28
socialized power motivation 802–3
socially constructed world 1031
society
    cross-national comparisons of societal
        well-being 455
    livability and 165
    materialism-linked problems 490

solastalgia  502
soldiers, flow  65
Solon  252–4
spending money  488–9
spirit level hypothesis  470
spirituality  339; *see also* religion and religiousness
　route to well-being  420–1
　spiritual development  414–16
　spiritual experience  412
　spiritual practice  416–17
sports policy  525
spousal death  141, 825
Square of Opposition  327–8
stages on life's way  280–1
standard social science model  216
standards  296–300
stereotypes of old age  1026–8
*sthitaprajna*  375
Stoicism  155, 202, 332
storytelling  582, 584–5
strategic interference theory  878–9
Strath Haven Positive Psychology Curriculum  660
strengths; *see also* character strengths
　educating about  653, 662–3
　signature strengths  967, 981, 988
　at work  773–4
Strengths Gym  585, 587
stress
　demands and resources  66
　executives  805
stress and coping social support theory  853
Stress-Related Growth Scale  928
strivings  402–3
student well-being  568–74
subcontraries  328
Subjective Happiness Scale  175
subjective well-being  134–45, 171, 174–80
　affective component  3, 134–5, 449, 694
　age and  140, 176
　benefits of  144
　bottom-up versus top-down influences  136–7
　cognitive component  3–4, 135, 449, 694
　correlates  140–2
　cross-national comparisons  448–61
　cultural differences  143–4, 178

　definition  134–6, 694, 821–2
　demographic correlates  176
　discrepancy theories  186–7
　domain satisfaction  135
　dynamic equilibrium theory  743, 889–90, 902
　economic analysis  433–4
　economic growth  176
　four component model  135, 187
　gender differences  140
　genetic factors  177, 890, 891
　global measures  449–50
　goal attainment  138
　happiness as  330
　happiness as part of  186–9
　health link  144
　hedonic adaptation  178
　historical background  174–5
　homeostasis  188–9
　income level  141–2, 144, 176–7, 469, 470, 472–3, 491–2
　indirect assessment  139–40
　individual differences  177–8
　informant reports  139–40
　interventions  178–9
　life satisfaction  135
　local area characteristics  473
　longevity  144
　marital status  140–1, 176
　materialism  488–90
　measurement  138–40, 175–6, 189–96, 449–50, 465–60, 822
　multidimensional construct  3
　multiple measures  139
　narrow measures  450
　need fulfillment  138
　optimism  177
　outcomes  144, 179
　personality  136–7, 142–3, 177, 889
　policy development  428
　relationships  144, 177
　religiousness  142, 176
　self-esteem  177
　self-reports  139, 175
　set-point theory  136, 137, 188–9, 887, 888, 890, 891, 897, 902
　single item measures  138
　social comparison  138

stability over time 137
telic theories 138
theoretical approaches 136–8
tripartite theory 135, 187–8, 916
unemployment 437, 473
wealth link 176–7
working environment 144
substantive opposites 329
success 119–28
creativity 123, 126
education 546–7
emotional intelligence 78–9
physical health 124–5, 126–7
positive emotions 120
prosocial behavior 126
relationships 122–3, 125–6
at work 123
suffering 282, 346–8
sukha 81, 344, 375
support groups 935
survival 164
sustainable development 498–511, 526–7
sustainable happiness model 903–5
sustained attention 237
Swādhyāyee 379–80

tacit knowledge 633
Taoism, *see* Daoism
taxation 528
teachers
coaching 1013–14
danger of over-burdening 602
happiness of 586–7
resilience 622–3
role in teaching happiness 655
as role models of wisdom 639
technology 68, 880–1, 971
terror management 99, 934
therapeutic relationship 980
therapies, *see* interventions
thought experiments 321
thought–outcome contingencies 25–6
threat 19
Three Good Things 966, 967, 986
Thriving Scale 928
time 283
tobacco consumption 439

tragedies 807–8
tragedy of the commons 503
training
acceptance and commitment in the workplace 1002–3
psychological capital 759–60
transactional theory 722, 723
transcendent emotions 413–14
transformational model 931
translation equivalence 458–9
transport choice 504
trauma; *see also* post-traumatic growth; post-traumatic stress disorder
executive well-being 807–8
response to 103–4
shattered assumptions theory 931
tripartite model of subjective well-being 135, 187–8
trivial pursuits 295
true self 235
twin studies 143
tyranny of positive thinking 934

UK Resilience Programme 522, 594
unemployment 428, 436–8, 473, 522–3
United States of America, pursuit of happiness 259–60
unrealistic optimism fallacy 635
up-building 280–1
Upanishads 373–5, 377–8
upside-down people 272
utilitarianism 156
utility 51, 431–2, 439–40
utility of life 163, 166–7

valence 75
value(s)
acceptance and commitment therapy 1001–2
collaborative recovery model 1057
education environments 560
ethical 633, 639
eudaimonia 208–9
hedonic value 42
materialism 490
reflected best self 771
search for 300–1

variety 904–5, 908–11
virtual reality 294
virtue
　amplifying effects 682–3
　buffering effects 683
　defining virtuousness 676–7
　happiness link 682–4
　heliotropic effects 683–4
　interpersonal 413–14
　measurement 684
　moderators and mediators 685
　organizational 676–86
　positive emotions 682
　prediction 684–5
　religiousness 94
　well-being and 312–13
vision for life 1057
vitality 309, 768
　emotional intelligence 79
　reflected best self 768, 770–1, 776–7
　relational affirmation 776
　strength-based engagement 773–4, 777
vitamin model 735–9
volunteerism 94–5

wages and job satisfaction 46–7
water conservation 505
wealth; *see also* income
　fame and 547
　happiness link 80, 880
　inequality 11
　societal well-being 455
　subjective well-being 176–7
weather conditions 502–3
web activities 68, 880–1
well-being 3; *see also* functional well-being;
　　psychological well-being; subjective
　　well-being
　cardiovascular health 788–90
　coaching and 1014–21
　consumer culture theory 482, 485–7
　consumer society 483–5, 487–8
　contentment 419
　contrast 55–6
　contrast–empathy model 49
　defining 694
　education and 540–9

　endowment 55–6
　eudaimonia as a form of 207
　eudaimonic perspective 81
　executives 798–810
　experiential versus cognitive
　　influences 37
　hedonic perspective 80–1
　Hindu/Sanātana Dharma
　　perspective 371–82
　income level 697–8
　index of 56
　Indian tradition 372–3
　local environmental conditions 501–2
　local well-being 473–5
　materialism 507–8
　measurement 55, 379, 518–19
　mental health 712–13
　negative emotions 80
　personality traits 713
　positive emotions 22–3, 80
　psychological capital 756–9
　psychological route to 420–1
　public policy 517–28
　religious engagement 88–99
　self-control 439
　self-sense 377–8
　spiritual route to 420–1
　of students 568–74
　sustainable development 498–511
　variety 908–11
　virtue and 312–13
　work and 693–704
well-being therapy 1037–46
　affective disorders 1041–2
　for children 1045
　in schools 1043–5
　structure 1038–41
Wellington College 647, 650–4
whole-school approach 554–5, 570, 584–6
widowhood 141, 825
will to power 282, 300
windows 700
wine 269, 273–4
wisdom 631–41
　affirming relationships 775–6
　balance theory 632–4
　definition 631–2
　teaching for 634–40

work; *see also job headings*
　acceptance and commitment
　　training 1002–3
　affect in 696–7
　attributes of work 698–9
　authenticity 774–5
　autonomy 220
　coaching in the workplace 1011, 1013
　context 699–701
　core strengths 773–4
　in education 548–9
　employee retention 787–8
　employment contracts 697–8
　engagement 772–5
　environmental factors 700, 734–9
　family–work interface 703
　flow 68
　happiness and work design 711–25
　identity 696
　interventions 746
　meaningful nature 699, 714
　orientation 701–2
　person-centered approach to worker
　　happiness 739–44
　personal dispositions 744–5
　policy development 522–4
　proactive behaviors 717–18
　psychological well-being 783, 787–8,
　　792, 793
　purpose 696, 772–3
　reflected best self 767–77
　relational affirmation 775–6
　relationships 700
　sanctification of 405–6
　shift work 699
　social bonds 696
　social support 700, 721–2, 759
　subjective well-being 144
　success and happiness 123
　value creation 768–71, 773–4, 776–7
　well-being and 693–704
Work-related Flow Inventory
　(WOLF) 62
working alliance 1056
World Database of Happiness 450–4, 502
worry 107–8, 1001
writing 969

yoga 381

Zhuangzi 263, 264–6, 270–4, 275–7
Zippy's Friends 593